W9-ALM-397

DogFriendly.com's

LODGING GUIDE
for Travelers with Dogs

by
Tara Kain and Len Kain
DogFriendly.com, Inc.

PLEASE NOTE
Although the authors and publisher have tried to make the information as accurate as possible, they do not assume, and hereby disclaim, any liability for any loss or damage caused by errors, omissions, misleading information or potential travel problems caused by this book, even if such errors or omissions result from negligence, accident or any other cause.

CHECK AHEAD
We remind you, as always, to call ahead and confirm that the applicable establishment is still "dog-friendly" and that it will accommodate your pet.

DOGS OF ALL SIZES
If your dog is over 75-80 pounds, then please call the individual establishment to make sure that they allow your dog. Please be aware that establishments and local governments may also not allow particular breeds.

OTHER PARTIES DESCRIPTIONS
Some of the descriptions have been provided to us by our web site advertisers, paid researchers or other parties.

ISBN 13 - 978-0-9718742-8-2
ISBN 10 - 0-9718742-8-X

Printed in the United States of America

Cover Photographs taken by Len Kain, Tara Kain and Jodi Kain

Cover Photographs (top to bottom, left to right):
Sheraton Grand Sacramento Hotel
New York City Skyline
Long Beach Dog Zone
MacCallum House - Mendocino CA

TABLE OF CONTENTS

Introduction

DogFriendly.com's guides have helped over one million dog lovers plan vacations and trips with their dogs. Included in this book are over 8000 truly dog-friendly accommodations including nearly 2000 independent hotels, B&Bs and vacation rentals. The guide gives detailed pet policies, including how many dogs may be allowed per room, weight limits, fees and other useful information. In many cases, toll-free numbers and websites are given. Also very importantly, this dog-friendly lodging guide focuses on those places that allow dogs of all sizes and do not restrict dogs to smoking rooms only. Not included in this guide are places that allow, for example, only dogs up to ten pounds or require that your dog be carried or in a carrier while on the premises. Also, we do not think that places that require dog owners to stay in smoking rooms are dog-friendly and we do not include them. Accommodations in this book have been called by DogFriendly.com to verify pet policies although these policies do change often. There are also helpful road trip tips and airline pet policies. Thank you for selecting our pet travel guide and we hope you spend less time researching and more time actually going places with your dog. Enjoy your dog-friendly travels!

About Author Tara Kain

Tara Kain grew up with dogs and has always loved dogs. When she moved away from home, she discovered a whole new world through traveling. But whenever she traveled, the last thing she wanted was to leave her best friend behind. Tara often spent the whole time worrying about her pooch. So she began taking her dog. It was much tougher than she originally thought. Tara would spend several days researching and planning where her dog would be accepted and what else there was to do with her dog, aside from staying in a hotel room. Unfortunately, many places did not allow dogs, especially a large dog like her standard poodle. Many times when she found a supposedly "dog-friendly" hotel or motel, they would allow pets only in smoking rooms. In her opinion, because one travels with a dog should not limit them to a smoking room. So in June of 1998, she began to compile a list of dog-friendly places, notes and photos and began posting them on a web site called DogFriendly.com. This allowed her to easily keep track of the research and also help other dog lovers know about dog-friendly places. Today she still travels with her family, including the family dog. She is devoted to finding the best pet-friendly places and letting others know about them.

Tara has traveled over 150,000 miles across the United States and Canada with her dog. She serves as DogFriendly.com's President and editor-in-chief. She has written a number of magazine articles. Tara has been interviewed by numerous reporters about dog travel, dogs in the workplace and other issues concerning dogs in public places. DogFriendly.com and Tara have been featured in many articles over the years including in most major newspapers. She has appeared on CNN and CBS Television, did a live on-line forum for USA Today and has been a guest on many radio shows. Tara and her family reside in California, in the Sierra Nevada foothills near Sacramento.

About Author Len Kain

Len Kain began traveling with his dog when he was young. His family traveled with a camping trailer and brought along their standard poodle, Ricky. On trips, he found places and attractions that welcomed his best friend. When Len grew up and got his own dog, he continued the tradition of bringing his dog on trips with him. Len and his family have traveled over 150,000 miles across the country on road trips. Today he continues to travel and find fun and exciting dog-friendly places.

Currently, Len serves as DogFriendly.com's Vice President of Sales and Marketing. Len has been quoted numerous times in print, on radio and television about issues relating to traveling with dogs. Prior to joining DogFriendly.com Len served in various executive and management positions in several Silicon Valley and Internet Companies. Len holds a Bachelor of Engineering degree from Stevens Tech in New Jersey, a Master of Science degree from Stanford University and an MBA from the University of Phoenix. Len resides with his family in the Sierra Nevada foothills of California.

Your Comments and Feedback

We value and appreciate your feedback and comments. If you want to recommend a dog-friendly place or establishment, let us know. If you find a place that is no longer dog-friendly, allows small dogs only or allows dogs in smoking rooms only, please let us know. You can contact us using the following information.

Mailing Address and Contact Information:
DogFriendly.com, Inc.
6454 Pony Express Trail #33-233
Pollock Pines, CA 95726 USA
Toll free phone: 1-877-475-2275
email: email@ dogfriendly.com
http://www.dogfriendly.com

How To Use This Guide

General Guidelines

1. Please only travel with a well-behaved dog that is comfortable around other people and especially children. Dogs should also be potty trained and not bark excessively.

2. Always keep your dog leashed unless management specifically tells you otherwise.

3. Establishments listed in this book should allow well-behaved dogs of ALL sizes (at least up to 75 pounds) and in non-smoking rooms. If your dog is over 75-80 pounds, then please call the individual establishment to make sure they will allow your dog. We have listed some establishments which only allow dogs up to 50 pounds, but we try our best to make a note in the comments about the restrictions. All restaurants and attractions we list should allow dogs of all sizes.

4. Accommodations listed do not allow dogs to be left alone in the room unless specified by hotel management. If the establishment does not allow pets to be left alone, try hiring a local pet sitter to watch your dog in the room.

5. All restaurants listed as dog-friendly refer to outdoor seating only. While dogs are not permitted to sit in a chair at a restaurant's outdoor dining table, they should be allowed to sit or lay next to your table. We do not list outdoor restaurants that require your dog to be tied outside of a fenced area (with you at the dining table on one side and your dog on the other side of the fence). In our opinion, those are not truly dog-friendly restaurants. Restaurants listed may have seasonal outdoor seating.

6. Pet policies and management change often, especially within the lodging and restaurant industries. Please always call ahead to make sure an establishment still exists and is still dog-friendly.

7. After purchasing your book, please visit http://www.dogfriendly.com/updates for FREE book updates. We will do our best to let you know which places may no longer be dog-friendly.

Preparation for a Road Trip

A Month Before

If you don't already have one, get a pet identification tag for your dog. It should have your dog's name, your name and phone number. Consider using a cell phone number, a home number and, if possible, the number of where you will be staying.

Get a first aid kit for your dog. It comes in very handy if you need to remove any ticks. The kits are usually available at a pet store, a veterinary office or on the Internet.

If you do not already have a dog harness for riding the car, consider purchasing one for your dog's and your own safety. A loose dog in the car can fly into the windshield, out of the car, or into you and injure you or cause you to lose control of the car. Dog harnesses are usually sold at pet stores or on the Internet.

Make a trip to the vet if necessary for the following:

- A current rabies tag for your dog's collar. Also get paperwork with proof of the rabies vaccine.
- Dogs can possibly get heartworm from mosquitoes in the mountains, rural areas or on hikes. Research or talk to your vet and ask him or her if the area you are traveling to has a high risk of heartworm disease. The vet may suggest placing your dog on a monthly heartworm preventative medicine.
- Consider using some type of flea preventative for your dog, preferably a natural remedy. This is out of courtesy for the dog-friendly hotels plus for the comfort of your pooch.
- Make sure your dog is in good health.

Several Days Before

Make sure you have enough dog food for the duration of the trip.

If your dog is on any medication, remember to bring it along.

Some dog owners will also purchase bottled water for the trip, because some dogs can get sick from drinking water they are not used to. Talk to your vet for more information.

The Day Before

Do not forget to review DogFriendly.com's Etiquette for the Traveling Dog!

Road Trip Day

Remember to pack all of your dog's necessities: food, water, dog dishes, leash, snacks and goodies, several favorite toys, brush, towels for dirty paws, plastic bags for cleaning up after your dog, doggie first aid kit, possibly dog booties if you are venturing to an especially cold or hot region, and bring any medicine your dog might be taking.

Before you head out, put on that doggie seat belt harness.

On The Road

Keep it cool and well ventilated in the car for your dog.

Stop at least every 2-3 hours so your dog can relieve him or herself. Also offer him or her water during the stops.

Never leave your pet alone in a parked car - even in the shade with the window cracked open. According to the Los Angeles SPCA, on a hot day, a car can heat up to 160 degrees in minutes, potentially causing your pet (or child) heat stroke, brain damage, and even death.

If your dog needs medical attention during your trip, check the yellow pages phone book in the area and look under Veterinarians. If you do not see an emergency vet listed, call any local vet even   during the evening hours and they can usually inform you of the closest emergency vet.

Etiquette for the Traveling Dog

So you have found the perfect getaway spot that allows dogs, but maybe you have never traveled with your dog. Or maybe you are a seasoned dog traveler. But do you know all of your doggie etiquette? Basic courtesy rules, like your dog should be leashed unless a place specifically allows your dog to be leash-free. And do you ask for a paper bowl or cup for your thirsty pooch at an outdoor restaurant instead of letting him or her drink from your water glass?

There are many do's and don'ts when traveling with your best friend. We encourage all dog owners to follow a basic code of doggie etiquette, so places will continue to allow and welcome our best friends. Unfortunately all it takes is one bad experience for an establishment to stop allowing dogs. Let's all try to be on our best behavior to keep and, heck, even encourage new places to allow our pooches.

Everywhere...

- Well-Behaved Dogs. Only travel or go around town with a well-behaved dog that is friendly to people and especially children. If your dog is not comfortable around other people, you might consider taking your dog to obedience classes or hiring a professional trainer. Your well-behaved dog should also be potty trained and not bark excessively in a hotel or other lodging room. We believe that dogs should be kept on leash. If a dog is on leash, he or she is easier to bring under control. Also, many establishments require that dogs be on leash and many people around you will feel more comfortable as well. And last, please never leave your dog alone in a hotel or other lodging room unless you have the approval from the establishment's management.

- Leashed Dogs. Please always keep your dog leashed, unless management specifically states otherwise. Most establishments (including lodging, outdoor restaurants, attractions, parks, beaches, stores and festivals) require that your dog be on leash. Plus most cities and counties have an official leash law that requires pets to be leashed at all times when not on your property. Keeping your dog on leash will also prevent any unwanted contact with other people that are afraid of dogs, people that do not appreciate strange dogs coming up to them, and even other dog owners who have a leashed dog. Even when on leash, do not let your pooch visit with other people or dogs unless welcomed. Keeping dogs on leash will also protect them from running into traffic, running away, or getting injured by wildlife or other dogs. Even the most well-behaved and trained dogs can be startled by something, especially in a new environment.

- Be Considerate. Always clean up after your dog. Pet stores sell pooper scooper bags. You can also buy sandwich bags from your local grocery store. They work quite well and are cheap!

At Hotels or Other Types of Lodging...

- Unless it is obvious, ask the hotel clerk if dogs are allowed in the hotel lobby. Also, because of health codes, dogs are usually not allowed into a lobby area while it is being used for serving food like continental breakfast. Dogs may be allowed into the area once there is no food being served, but check with management first.

- Never leave your dog alone in the hotel room. The number one reason hotel management does not allow dogs is because some people leave them in the room alone. Some dogs, no matter how well-trained, can cause damage, bark continuously or scare the housekeepers. Unless the hotel management allows it, please make sure your dog is never left alone in the room. If you need to leave your dog in the room, consider hiring a local pet sitter.

- While you are in the room with your dog, place the Do Not Disturb sign on the door or keep the deadbolt locked. Many housekeepers have been surprised or scared by dogs when entering a room.

- In general, do not let your pet on the bed or chairs, especially if your dog sheds easily and might leave pet hair on the furniture. Some very pet-friendly accommodations will actually give you a sheet to lay over the bed so your pet can join you. If your pet cannot resist coming hopping onto the furniture with you, bring your own sheet.

- When your dog needs to go to the bathroom, take him or her away from the hotel rooms and the bushes located right next to the rooms. Try to find some dirt or bushes near the parking lot. Some hotels have a designated pet walk area.

At Outdoor Restaurants...

- Tie your dog to your chair, not the table (unless the table is secured to the ground). If your dog decides to get up and move away from the table, he or she will not take the entire table.

- If you want to give your dog some water, please ask the waiter/waitress to bring a paper cup or bowl of water for your dog. Do not use your own water glass. Many restaurants and even other guests frown upon this.

- Your pooch should lay or sit next to your table. At restaurants, dogs are not allowed to sit on the chairs or tables, or eat off the tables. This type of activity could make a restaurant owner or manager ban dogs. And do not let your pooch beg from other customers. Unfortunately, not everyone loves dogs!

- About Restaurant Laws regarding dogs at restaurants
State health codes in the United States prohibit all animals except for service animals inside indoor sections of restaurants. In recent years some health departments have begun banning dogs from some outdoor restaurant areas. It is complicated to determine where dogs are and are not allowed outdoors because most State laws are vague. They state something such as "Animals are not allowed on the premises of a food establishment". These laws also define animals to include "birds, vermin and insects" which are always present at outdoor restaurants. Various health departments have various interpretations of where the premises start and stop. Some allow dogs at outdoor areas where food is served, some allow dogs at outdoor areas only where you bring your own food to the table. Some will allow special pet-friendly areas or will allow dogs on the outside of the outer most tables. Any city or county can issue a variance to State law if it wants to allow dogs into outdoor (or indoor) restaurants. This can be done in two ways, directly by the local health department or through a vote of the local government. If a restaurant that you are visiting with your dog cites some curious requirement it is probably due to the health code. Please also understand that in all places the owner of a restaurant has the choice to not allow dogs with the exception of service dogs. Nationally, Austin, Dallas, Orlando and Alexandria forced law changes to allow dogs at outdoor restaurants when their health departments went too far in banning dogs from outdoor seats. Dogs are now allowed in outdoor areas in these cities through variances (or in Orlando's case) changing Florida state law. For up to date information, and more details, please see http://www.dogfriendly.com/dining . The laws are in a state of flux at the moment so please understand that they may change.

At Retail Stores...

- Keep a close eye on your dog and make sure he or she does not go to the bathroom in the store. Store owners that allow dogs inside assume that responsible dog owners will be entering their store. Before entering a dog-friendly store, visit your local pet store first. They are by far the most forgiving. If your dog does not go to the bathroom there, then you are off to a great start! If your dog does make a mistake in any store, clean it up. Ask the store clerk for paper towels or something similar so you can clean up any mess.

- In most states dogs are allowed in stores, shops and other private buildings with the exception of grocery stores and restaurants. The decision to allow dogs is the business owner's and you can always ask if you may bring your dog inside. Also in most states packaged foods (bottled sodas, waters, bags of cookies or boxes of snacks) does not cause a store to be classified as a grocery. Even pet stores do sell these items . In many states, drinks such as coffee, tea and water are also allowed. You can order food from a restaurant to a pet-friendly establishment (so long as the establishment is not also the restaurant with the kitchen) in most areas.

At Festivals and Outdoor Events...

Make sure your dog has relieved himself or herself before entering a festival or event area. The number one reason that most festival coordinators do not allow dogs is because some dogs go to the bathroom on a vendor's booth or in areas where people might sit.

Breed Specific Laws and the Effect of These Laws on Travel With Dogs

There has been a trend in cities, counties, states and provinces towards what is known as Breed-Specific Laws (BSL) in which a municipality bans or restricts the freedoms of dog owners with specific breeds of dogs. These laws vary from place to place and are effecting a greater number of dog owners every year. Most people may think that these laws effect only the "Pit Bull" but this is not always the case. Although the majority of dogs effected are pit-bulls other breeds of dogs as well as mixed breeds that include targeted breeds are also named in the various laws in North America. These laws range from registration requirements and leash or muzzle requirements to extreme laws in which the breed is banned from the municipality outright. Some places may even be permitted to confiscate a visitor's dog who unknowingly enters the region with a banned breed.

As of August 29, 2005 the province of Ontario, Canada (including Toronto, Niagara Falls, and Ottawa) passed a very broad breed-specific law banning Pit Bulls and "similar" dogs from the province. The law allows for confiscation of visiting dogs as well as dogs living in Ontario. It is extremely important that people visiting Ontario make sure that they are able to prove that their dog is not a Pit Bull with other documentation. Various cities throughout the U.S. and Canada have muzzle requirements for Pit Bulls and other restrictions on targeted breeds as well. Breed-specific laws do get repealed as well. In October, 2005 the city of Vancouver, BC removed its requirement that Pit Bulls be muzzled in public and now only requires dogs with a known history of aggressiveness to be muzzled.

The breed specific laws usually effect pit bull type dogs but are often vaguely written and may also effect mixed breed dogs that resemble the targeted breeds. These laws are always changing and can be passed by cities, counties and even states and provinces. We recommend that travelers with dogs check into whether they are effected by such laws. You may check www.DogFriendly.com/bsl for links to further information on BSL.

DogFriendly.com does not support breed-specific laws. Most people who take their dogs out in public are responsible and those that choose to train a dog to be viscous will simply choose another breed, causing other breeds to be banned or regulated in the future.

Customs Information for Traveling Between the United States and Canada

If you will be traveling between the United States and Canada, identification for Customs and Immigration is required. U.S. and Canadian citizens traveling across the border need the following:

People

- A passport is now required (or will shortly be required depending on your point of entry) to move between the U.S. and Canada. This is a new policy so be sure to have your passport with you. Children also need a passport of their own now.

Dogs

- Dogs must be free of evidence of diseases communicable to humans when possibly examined at the port of entry.

- Valid rabies vaccination certificate (including an expiration date usually up to 3 years from the actual vaccine date and a veterinarian's signature). If no expiration date is specified on the certificate, then the certificate is acceptable if the date of the vaccination is not more than 12 months before the date of arrival. The certificate must show that the dog had the rabies vaccine at least 30 days prior to entry.

- Young puppies must be confined at a place of the owner's choosing until they are three months old, then they must be vaccinated. They must remain in confinement for 30 days after the vaccination.

Chain Hotel Websites

Best Western	www.bestwestern.com
Candlewood Suites	www.ichotelsgroup.com
Clarion	www.choicehotels.com
Comfort Inn	www.choicehotels.com
Drury Inn	www.druryhotels.com
Hilton	www.hilton.com
Holiday Inn	www.ichotelsgroup.com
Howard Johnson	www.hojo.com
Kimpton Group	www.kimptonhotels.com
La Quinta	www.lq.com
Loews Hotels	www.loewshotels.com
Marriott	www.marriott.com
Motel 6	www.motel6.com
Novotel	www.novotel.com
Quality Inn	www.choicehotels.com
Red Roof Inn	www.redroof.com
Residence Inn	www.residenceinn.com
Sheraton	www.starwoodhotels.com
Sleep Inn	www.choicehotels.com
Staybridge Suites	www.ichotelsgroup.com
Studio 6	www.staystudio6.com
Super 8	www.super8.com
Towneplace Suites	www.towneplaceSuites.com
Westin	www.starwoodhotels.com

Traveling with a Dog By Air

Many airlines allow dogs to be transported with the traveling public. Small dogs, usually no more than 15 pounds and with shorter legs, may travel in a carrier in the cabin with you. They must usually be kept under the seat. Any larger dogs must travel in a kennel in the cargo hold. We do not recommend that dogs travel in the cargo hold of airplanes. Most airlines restrict cargo hold pet transportation during very hot and cold periods. Most require that you notify them when making reservations about the pet as they limit the number of pets allowed on each plane and the size of the carriers may vary depending on what type of plane is being used. There are no airlines that we are aware of today that will allow dogs larger than those that fit in a carrier under a seat to fly in the cabin. Service animals are allowed in the cabin and are harnessed during takeoff and landing. Below is a summary of the pet policies for airlines at the time of publication of this book.

Airline	Cabin – Small Dogs Allowed	Cargo – Dogs Allowed	Phone	Fees (US) (each way)	Web Link for More Information - May Change
Air Canada	No	Yes	888-247-2262 (US)	$105 US-Can $245 Overseas	No Dogs allowed on flights within Canada aircanada.com/en/travelinfo/airport/baggage/pets.html
Alaska Air / Horizon Air	Yes	Yes	800-252-7522	$75.00 Cabin $100 Cargo	alaskaair.com/www2/help/faqs/Pets.asp
America West/ US Airways	Yes	No	800-235-9292	$80.00	usairways.com/awa/content/traveltools/specialneeds/pets.aspx
American	Yes	Yes	800-433-7300	Cabin - $80 Cargo - $100	aa.com/content/travelInformation/specialAssistance/travelingWithPets.jhtml
Continental	Yes	Yes	Live animal desk - 800-575-3335 reserv 800-525-0280	$95 (Cabin), from $119 (Cargo)	continental.com/travel/policies/animals/default.asp
Delta	Yes	Yes	800-221-1212	Cabin - $75 Cargo - $150	delta.com/planning_reservations/special_travel_needs/pet_travel_information/pet_travel_options/index.jsp#Cargo
Frontier	Yes	Yes	800-432-1359	$100.00	frontierairlines.com/frontier/plan-book/travel-info-services/family-pets/traveling-with-pets.do
Independence	Yes	No	800-FLYFLYI	$35.00	flyi.com/tools/policies.aspx#traveling_pets
Jet Blue	Yes	No	800-538-2583	$75.00	jetblue.com/travelinfo/howToDetail.asp?topicId=%278%27
Northwest	Yes	Yes	800-225-2525	$80 Cabin $139+ Cargo	nwa.com/services/shipping/Cargo/products/ppet2.shtml
Southwest	No	No			
United	Yes	Yes	800-864-8331	Cabin - $85 Cargo - $100+	united.com/page/middlepage/0,6823,1047,00.html

* We do not recommend that dogs travel in the cargo hold of airplanes. Temperatures can range from freezing to sweltering and there can be delays on the runways, at the gates and elsewhere. These varying conditions can cause injury or even death to a pet.

Chapter 1

Top Dog-Friendly Destinations

Top Dog-Friendly Destinations - Please always call ahead to make sure that an establishment is still dog-friendly

What makes a dog-friendly city for visitors with dogs in tow?

- Is the city an appealing vacation spot and appealing for people traveling with dogs?

- Are there suitable pet-friendly hotels and lodging in the city?

- Can one get around the city easily? Does the public transportation system allow dogs?

- If you can't go on the public transportation, can you get around fairly easily by car?

- Are there attractions, such as boat and carriage rides, tours, tourist sites, and side trips that welcome your dog?

- Where can you eat wtih your pooch, other than in your hotel room? Are there outdoor cafes that welcome pets, or local dog-friendly parks where you can bring a picnic lunch?

- Can your dog visit any of the local beaches or parks? Are there any off-leash dog parks in town?

- Is the city supportive of the over twenty million people annually who travel with dogs? Does the city regulate or over-regulate what you can do with your dog? Has the city helped create more dog-friendly areas or has the city limited and restricted access to people with dogs, including travelers?

Here are DogFriendly.com's Top dog-friendly cities:

1. Boston, Massachusetts (see also Boston Area) - In Boston, you can see most of the best tourist sites without leaving your dog at home. Getting around Boston and the suburbs is easy as the Boston T (subway) allows leashed dogs of all sizes during non-rush hours. Follow the red arrows on the sidewalk along the 2 mile Freedom Trail, take one of a number of boat tours or whale watching tours that welcome pups. Visit one of the cities many parks including the Boston Common, Minute Man National Historical Park or the Arnold Arboretum. You can ride a horse and carriage ride together at the Faneuil Hall Marketplace. In Salem take a walking or trolley tour or visit the Salem Willows Amusement Park. For a weekend getaway near Boston you can take a dog-friendly ferry to Cape Cod, Martha's Vineyard or Nantucket or visit the dog-friendly beaches of Block Island.

2. Vancouver, British Columbia, Canada - Visit Historic Gastown, Granville Island and the Capilano Bridge and Park with your pooch. Many ferries allow leashed dogs of all sizes and the city's public transportation allows small dogs in carriers. The city has many outdoor restaurants and cafes and quite a few of the stores allow you to shop inside with your dog. When in Vancouver consider taking a dog-friendly trip to the Minter Gardens, Hell's Gate Airtram and to Victoria on Vancouver Island. While on Vancouver Island be sure to see the beautiful Butchart Gardens. There are numerous beaches and parks that welcome you and your dog. Vancouver boasts 7 off-leash dog beaches and over 20 off-leash dog parks giving your dog ample opportunity to run.

3. New York City - Stay in luxury at some of New York's most fashionable hotel addresses with your dog. The Regency, Soho Grand Hotel, Novotel and many W hotels all welcome dogs. If you want to stay outside of the city you can bring your dog on the Metro-North trains from Connecticut or the northern suburbs or on the Seastreak Ferry from New Jersey. There are also a number of Pet Taxi services in the city that you can call for transportation and some regular taxis will pick up dogs. Many of the famous stores and department stores in Manhattan will allow leashed dogs to accompany you. Take a walking tour of lower Manhattan, a carriage ride in Central Park, walk the Brooklyn Bridge or visit one of the 30 off-leash parks in the city. Or visit the William Secord Art Gallery on 76th Street. For canine swimming, check out the man-made swimming pond for dogs in Brooklyn's Prospect Park.

4. San Francisco, California - San Francisco is a great vacation site for a traveler with a dog. There are so many parks, off-leash areas and beaches. Try Baker Beach, Ocean Beach or Fort Funston. There are many off-leash dog areas sprinkled throughout the city. Visit Golden Gate Park, walk across the Golden Gate Bridge or shop in many dog-friendly stores in the Union Square area or throughout the city. Stay at a number of pet-friendly hotels including the Palace Hotel, the Four Seasons or the Hotel Palomar. San Francisco is a compact city and easy to walk around. Also, dogs are allowed on most of the public transportation, including the famous Cable Cars, Muni buses and trains. Small dogs are allowed on the regional BART trains that run to the East Bay. Every August the San Francisco Giants host their annual Dog Days of Summer baseball game where your dog is welcome to attend with you.

5. Austin, Texas - When visiting Austin you will have your choice of many fine dog-friendly hotels and motels. You can stay at the Hyatt Regency Lost Pines Resort or one of the many La Quinta Hotels, Red Roof Inns or other hotels throughout the city. You and your dog can take a walking tour of downtown, ride a horse and carriage or visit the Zilker Botanical Garden Austin has a large number of dog-friendly parks as well as ten off-leash dog areas. The most interesting tourist attraction in town may be the Congress Street Bat Colony. Around sunset from around March to November the bats all fly out looking for food. You may dine with your dog at many dog-friendly patio restaurants throughout the city.

Top Dog-Friendly Destinations - Please always call ahead to make sure that an establishment is still dog-friendly

6. Portland, Oregon - The Lucky Lab Brewing Company is a landmark establishment for dog owners. In addition to its two locations, a newcomer to the local dog scene is the Iron Mutt Coffee Company with an off-leash outdoor area to play in while coffee and food are enjoyed. Portland boosts over 20 off-leash dog parks, some of which are fenced; a city amusement park where leashed dogs are allowed; the Hoyt Arboretum and of course the Rose Gardens that the city is famous for. Also visit the Portland Saturday Market which is an open air market with artists, entertainment and all sorts of shops including pet items. Nearby Portland is excellent hiking in the Columbia River Gorge and throughout the Portland region.

7. Northern Virginia (see also Washington, DC) - During the summer months you may cruise the Potomac with your dog on the Potomac Riverboat Co. Canine Cruises. Visit the outdoor areas of historic Mount Vernon, the Iwo Jima Memorial, and the Theodore Roosevelt Memorial on Roosevelt Island. Hike the Mount Vernon Trail from Washington DC to Mount Vernon or visit over twenty off-leash dog parks with your dog. In historical Alexandria you can treat your dog to a carriage ride or attend the Doggie Happy Hour at the Old Town Holiday Inn Select during the summer months on Tuesdays and Thursdays. While in Northern Virginia you can visit the National Mall in Washington, where you and your dog can see all of the monuments from the outside and enjoy a visit to Georgetown and the C&O Canal.

8. Orlando, Florida - Orlando, long a popular people destination, has recently greatly improved it popularity with our four-legged friends. There are some fabulous pet-friendly resorts such as the Sheraton World Hotel and the Portofino Bay Hotel among many others. While there you can take a boat ride on the St. Johns River with your dog, shop in the dog-friendly Winter Park area and dine at Sam Snead's, the center of Florida doggy dining. It was here that former Florida Governor Jeb Bush signed Florida's doggy dining law. Fleet People's Park in Winter Park is an excellent off-leash dog park.

9. San Diego, California - San Diego is known for its beaches and, for dogs, it doesn't disappoint. There are two major off-leash beaches in San Diego and Coronado plus many other beaches that allow dogs on leash. With its warm, yet not too hot year-round weather, San Diego is perfect for those outdoor activities that shine during vacations with pups. There are many nice outdoor dog-friendly restaurants in San Diego, La Jolla and throughout the region. While in San Diego visit the very pet-friendly Otay Ranch Town Shopping Center with an off-leash dog park built into the shopping center.

10. Dallas / Fort-Worth - While in Dallas ride a carriage with your dog, take a walking tour or visit Pioneer Plaza. There are many fine hotels that are dog-friendly to fit all budgets. Fort Worth offers your dog Fort Woof, one of the countries nicest dog parks and a visit to the Stockyard Stations to watch the daily cattle drives. Dallas this year joined fellow Texas city Austin in officially allowing dogs in outdoor dining areas ending years of ambiguity on where you can eat in the city with your dog.

Honorable Mentions - While these five cities did not make our top ten this year they did make our honorable mentions as the five next best cities to vacation in with your pet.

- Chicago, IL

- Indianapolis, IN

- Philadelphia, PA

- Salt Lake City, UT

- Seattle, WA

Top Dog-Friendly Destinations - Please always call ahead to make sure that an establishment is still dog-friendly

Here are DogFriendly.com's Top dog-friendly Resort Locations:

1. Portland ME - This dog-friendly town has it all. Walking tours, cruises, beaches, parks and islands to visit. A number of off-leash dog parks. Nearby Boothbay is worth a visit.

2. Carmel / Monterey CA - Dog-Friendly Carmel City Beach, trails, shopping, outdoor restaurants and quaint lodging. Carmel and Monterey are easy areas to walk around.

3. Asheville / Blue Ridge NC - Walk the Asheville Urban Trail. Visit the grounds of the Biltmore Estate or shop at Biltmore Village. Drive the Blue Ridge Parkway.

4. Key West FL - Quaint B&B's, lots of outdoor dining. Charter a boat, walk the charming village streets.

5. Charlottesville VA - Visit Monticello and Red Hill Estates grounds, dog-friendly wineries, shop at the historic downtown mall. Visit dog-friendly Shenandoah park nearby.

6. Black Hills SD - You can see Mt. Rushmore from the pet area. A number of other attractions, hiking trails and parks. If you have kids visit the Flintstones Campground.

7. Lake Tahoe CA/NV - Visit the dog-friendly village and gondola at Squaw Valley. Rent a boat on the lake, swim at one of four beaches for dogs. Cross country skiing in Winter.

8. Cape May NJ - Visit Historic Cold Spring Village. Whale watch or charter boats. Visit wineries, parks, beaches and take the ferry to Lewes, DE.

9. Grand Canyon AZ - Dogs can walk along the rim and view the canyon with you. If you and your dog are up to hiking down the canyon try the Havasupai Reservation.

10. Hocking Hills OH - Dog-friendly accommodations and dog-friendly parks. Don't miss the caves and scenic hikes of Hocking Hills State Park. Rent a canoe or two.

Honorable Mentions - The following five places are also excellent vacation spots to visit with your dog -

- Bar Harbor/Acadia, ME

- Cape Cod, MA

- Pennsylvania Dutch Country, PA

- Mendocino, CA

- St Augustine, FL

Chapter 2

Dog-Friendly Lodging

United States

Alabama Listings

Best Western Abbeville Inn
1237 US Hwy 31 South
Abbeville, AL
334-585-5060 (800-780-7234)
Dogs are allowed for an additional
fee of $8 per night per pet. Multiple
dogs may be allowed.

Days Inn Andalusia
1604 Hwy 84 E Bypass
Andalusia, AL
334-427-0050 (800-329-7466)
Dogs up to 70 pounds are allowed.
There is a $10 per night pet fee per
pet. Reservations are recommended
due to limited rooms for pets. 2 dogs
may be allowed.

Best Western Athens Inn
1329 Hwy 72 East
Athens, AL
256-233-4030 (800-780-7234)
Dogs are allowed for an additional
fee of $10 per night per pet. Multiple
dogs may be allowed.

Days Inn Athens
1322 Hwy 72 East
Athens, AL
256-233-7500 (800-329-7466)
Dogs of all sizes are allowed. There
are no additional pet fees. 2 dogs
may be allowed.

Hampton Inn
1488 Thrasher Blvd
Athens, AL
256-232-0030
Dogs of all sizes are allowed. There
is a $25 per stay fee and a pet policy
to sign at check in. Multiple dogs
may be allowed.

Sleep Inn
1115 Audubon Lane
Athens, AL
256-232-4700 (877-424-6423)
Quiet dogs are allowed for an
additional fee of $10 per night per
pet. 2 dogs may be allowed.

Comfort Inn
2283 S College Street
Auburn, AL
334-821-6699 (877-424-6423)
Dogs up to 50 pounds are allowed
for an additional fee of $10 per night
per pet. Multiple dogs may be
allowed.

Best Western Hotel & Suites
5041 Academy Ln
Bessemer, AL
205-481-1950 (800-780-7234)
Dogs are allowed for an additional
one time fee of $15 per pet. Multiple
dogs may be allowed.

Days Inn Birmingham/Bessemer
1121 9th Avenue SW
Bessemer, AL
205-424-6078 (800-329-7466)
Dogs of all sizes are allowed. There
is a $6 per night pet fee per pet. 2
dogs may be allowed.

Motel 6 - Birmingham - Bessemer
1000 Shiloh Lane
Bessemer, AL
205-426-9646 (800-466-8356)
One well-behaved family pet per
room. Guest must notify front desk
upon arrival. Guest is liable for any
damages. In consideration of all
guests, pets must never be left
unattended in the guest rooms.

Candlewood Suites
600 Corporate Ridge Dr
Birmingham, AL
205-991-0272 (877-270-6405)
One dog up to 80 pounds or 2 dogs
totaling 80 pounds are allowed for
an additional $75 one time fee per
pet.

Days Inn Birmingham Airport
5101 Airport Hwy
Birmingham, AL
205-592-6110 (800-329-7466)
Dogs of all sizes are allowed. There
is a $25 one time per pet fee per
visit. 2 dogs may be allowed.

La Quinta Inn Birmingham
513 Cahaba Park Circle
Birmingham, AL
205-995-9990 (800-531-5900)
Dogs of all sizes are allowed. There
are no additional pet fees. Dogs
may not be left unattended, and
they must be leashed and cleaned
up after. Dogs are not allowed in
the food areas. Multiple dogs may
be allowed.

Microtel
251 Summit Pkwy
Birmingham, AL
205-945-5550
There is a pet waiver to sign.

Motel Birmingham Garden
Courtyards
7905 Crestwood Blvd
Birmingham, AL
205-956-4440
There is a $10 per day additional pet
fee.

Red Roof Inn - Birmingham
151 Vulcan Road
Birmingham, AL
205-942-9414 (800-RED-ROOF)
One well-behaved family pet per
room. Guest must notify front desk
upon arrival. Guest is liable for any
damages. In consideration of all
guests, pets must never be left
unattended in the guest rooms.

Residence Inn by Marriott
#3 Greenhill Parkway at U.S. H-280
Birmingham, AL
205-991-8686
Dogs of all sizes are allowed. There
is a $75 one time fee per stay.

Residence Inn by Marriott
50 State Farm Parkway
Birmingham, AL
205-943-0044
Dogs of all sizes are allowed. There
is a $75 one time fee per stay and a
pet policy to sign at check in.

Sheraton Birmingham Hotel
2101 Richard Arrington Jr. Blvd.
North
Birmingham, AL
205-324-5000 (888-625-5144)
Dogs up to 70 pounds are allowed.
There are no additional pet fees.
Dogs are not allowed to be left alone
in the room.

TownePlace Suites Birmingham
Homewood
500 Wildwood Circle
Birmingham, AL
205-943-0114
Dogs of all sizes are allowed. There
is a $75 one time pet fee per visit. 2
dogs may be allowed.

Days Inn Calera
11691 Hwy 25 and I-65
Calera, AL
205-668-0560 (800-329-7466)
Dogs of all sizes are allowed. There
is a $5 per night pet fee per pet. 2
dogs may be allowed.

Holiday Inn Express
357 Hwy 304
Calera, AL
205-668-3641 (877-270-6405)
hiexpress.com/caleraal
Dogs of all sizes are allowed for an
additional pet fee of $20 per night
per room. Multiple dogs may be
allowed.

Days Inn Camden
39 Camden Bypass
Camden, AL
334-682-4555 (800-329-7466)
Dogs up to 100 pounds are allowed.
There are no additional pet fees. 2
dogs may be allowed.

Comfort Inn
5917 H 157 NW
Cullman, AL
256-734-1240 (877-424-6423)
Dogs are allowed for an additional
pet fee of $20 per night per room.
Dogs must be crated when left alone
in the room. Multiple dogs may be
allowed.

Days Inn Cullman
1841 4th Street SW
Cullman, AL
256-739-3800 (800-329-7466)
Dogs of all sizes are allowed. There
is a $5 per night pet fee per pet. 2
dogs may be allowed.

Best Western River City Hotel
1305 Front Avenue SW
Decatur, AL
256-301-1388 (800-780-7234)
Dogs up to 10 pounds are allowed
for an additional one time fee of $25
per pet; the fee is $50 for dogs over
10 pounds. 2 dogs may be allowed.

Comfort Inn and Suites
2212 Danville Road SW
Decatur, AL
256-355-1999 (877-424-6423)
Quiet dogs are allowed for an
additional fee of $10 per night per
pet. Multiple dogs may be allowed.

Holiday Inn Hotel & Suites
1101 6th Ave, NE
Decatur, AL
256-355-3150 (877-270-6405)
Dogs of all sizes are allowed for an
additional pet fee of $20 per night
per room. Multiple dogs may be
allowed.

La Quinta Inn Decatur
918 Beltline Road SW
Decatur, AL
356-355-9977 (800-531-5900)
Dogs of all sizes are allowed. There
are no additional pet fees. Dogs
must be leashed, cleaned up after,
and crated when left alone in the
room. Multiple dogs may be allowed.

Bald Lake Lodge at Cheaha Resort
State Park
2141 Bunker Loop
Delta, AL

256-488-5115 (800-846-2654)
This lodge is located in a State Park
surrounded by a national forest that
displays spectacular scenery,
provides 6 hiking trails, and a variety
of activities and recreation. Dogs of
all sizes are allowed for a $10 per
night per pet additional fee for the
cabin or chalets. There is no
additional fee for dogs in the camp
area. Dogs may not be left
unattended unless crated, and they
must be leashed at all times, and
cleaned up after. Dogs are not
allowed on the beaches or in park
buildings. Dogs are allowed on the
trails. Known aggressive breeds are
not allowed at the lodge. Multiple
dogs may be allowed.

Comfort Inn
3593 Ross Clark Circle NW
Dothan, AL
334-793-9090 (877-424-6423)
Dogs up to 50 pounds are allowed
for an additional fee of $10 per night
per pet. Multiple dogs may be
allowed.

Days Inn Dothan
2841Ross Clark Circle
Dothan, AL
334-793-2550 (800-329-7466)
Dogs of all sizes are allowed. There
is a $5 per night pet fee per pet. 2
dogs may be allowed.

Holiday Inn Express
2195 Ross Clark Circle SE
Dothan, AL
334-794-8711 (877-270-6405)
Dogs of all sizes are allowed for an
additional $15 one time pet fee per
room. 2 dogs may be allowed.

Holiday Inn Express - Dothan West
3071 Ross Clark Circle
Dothan, AL
334-671-3700 (877-270-6405)
holiday-inn.com/dothan-westal
One dog of any size is allowed for
an additional pet fee of $10 per night
per room. Dogs may not be left
alone in the room.

Motel 6 - Dothan
2907 Ross Clark Circle Southwest
Dothan, AL
334-793-6013 (800-466-8356)
One well-behaved family pet per
room. Guest must notify front desk
upon arrival. Guest is liable for any
damages. In consideration of all
guests, pets must never be left
unattended in the guest rooms.

Quality Inn

3053 Ross Clark Circle
Dothan, AL
334-794-6601 (877-424-6423)
Dogs are allowed for an additional
one time pet fee of $25 per room.
Multiple dogs may be allowed.

Comfort Inn
615 Boll Weevil Circle
Enterprise, AL
334-393-2304 (877-424-6423)
Dogs are allowed for an additional
one time pet fee of $25 per room. 2
dogs may be allowed.

Comfort Suites
12 Paul Lee Parkway
Eufaula, AL
334-616-0114 (877-424-6423)
Dogs are allowed for an additional
one time pet fee of $25 per room.
Multiple dogs may be allowed.

Comfort Inn
83 Ted Bates Road
Evergreen, AL
251-578-4701 (877-424-6423)
Dogs are allowed for an additional
pet fee of $5 per night per pet.
Multiple dogs may be allowed.

Days Inn Evergreen
901 Liberty Hill Dr
Evergreen, AL
251-578-2100 (800-329-7466)
Dogs of all sizes are allowed. There
is a $10 per night pet fee per pet. 2
dogs may be allowed.

Holiday Inn Express
2682 South Mckenzie St
Foley, AL
251-943-9100 (877-270-6405)
Dogs up to 50 pounds are allowed
for an additional one time fee of $20
(plus tax) per pet. 2 dogs may be
allowed.

Adam's Outdoors Cherokee Camp
6110 Cherokee County Road #103
Fort Payne, AL
256-845-2988
Dogs of all sizes are allowed. There
are no additional pet fees. Multiple
dogs may be allowed.

Days Inn Birmingham/Fultondale
616 Decatur Hwy
Fultondale, AL
205-849-0111 (800-329-7466)
Dogs of all sizes are allowed. There
is a $6 per night pet fee per pet. 2
dogs may be allowed.

Comfort Suites
96 Walker Street
Gadsden, AL

256-538-5770 (877-424-6423)
Dogs are allowed for an additional one time pet fee of $15 per room. Multiple dogs may be allowed.

Motel 6 - Gadsden
1600 Rainbow Drive
Gadsden, AL
256-543-1105 (800-466-8356)
One well-behaved family pet per room. Guest must notify front desk upon arrival. Guest is liable for any damages. In consideration of all guests, pets must never be left unattended in the guest rooms.

Days Inn Guntersville
14040 Hwy 431 S
Guntersville, AL
256-582-3200 (800-329-7466)
Dogs of all sizes are allowed. There is a $25 one time pet fee per visit. 2 dogs may be allowed.

Holiday Inn
2140 Gunter Ave
Guntersville, AL
256-582-2220 (877-270-6405)
Dogs of all sizes are allowed for an additional one time pet fee of $15 per room. 2 dogs may be allowed.

Super 8 Guntersville Lake
14341 US Hwy 431 South
Guntersville, AL
256-582-8444 (800-800-8000)
Dogs up to 40 pounds are allowed. There is a $10 per night pet fee per pet. Smoking and non-smoking rooms are available for pet rooms. 2 dogs may be allowed.

Howard Johnson Express Inn
1957 Almon Street
Heflin, AL
256-463-2900 (800-446-4656)
Dogs of all sizes are welcome. There is a $5 one time pet fee.

Super 8 Homewood/Birmingham Area
140 Vulcan Rd
Homewood, AL
205-945-9888 (800-800-8000)
Dogs of all sizes are allowed. There is a $5 per night pet fee per pet. Smoking and non-smoking rooms are available for pet rooms. 2 dogs may be allowed.

Candlewood Suites
201 Exchange Place
Huntsville, AL
256-830-8222 (877-270-6405)
Dogs of all sizes are allowed for an additional pet fee of $75 per room for 1 to 6 days, and a fee of $150 for

over 6 days per room; dogs must be crated for housekeeping. 2 dogs may be allowed.

Guest House Suites
4020 Independence Dr
Huntsville, AL
256-837-8907
There is a $50 one time pet fee.

Hilton
401 Williams Avenue
Huntsville, AL
256-533-1400
Dogs up to 60 pounds are allowed for an additional one time pet fee of $25 per room. 2 dogs may be allowed.

Holiday Inn Express Hotel & Suites
3808 University Drive
Huntsville, AL
256-721-1000 (877-270-6405)
Dogs of all sizes are allowed for an additional $50 one time fee per room, and there is pet agreement to sign at check in. They ask a cell number be left if a pet is left alone in the room. 2 dogs may be allowed.

La Quinta Inn Huntsville Madison Square Mall
4890 University Drive Nw
Huntsville, AL
256-830-8999 (800-531-5900)
Dogs of all sizes are allowed. There are no additional pet fees. Please put the "Do Not Disturb" sign on the door when you are out and a dog is in the room uncrated. Dogs must be leashed at all times. Multiple dogs may be allowed.

La Quinta Inn Huntsville Research Park
4870 University Drive N.W.
Huntsville, AL
256-830-2070 (800-531-5900)
Dogs of all sizes are allowed. There are no additional pet fees. Dogs must be leashed and cleaned up after. Arrangements need to be made with housekeeping if more than one day's stay. 2 dogs may be allowed.

La Quinta Inn Huntsville Space Center
3141 University Dr. N.W.
Huntsville, AL
256-533-0756 (800-531-5900)
Dogs of all sizes are allowed. There are no additional pet fees. Dogs must be quiet, well behaved, leashed, and cleaned up after. Multiple dogs may be allowed.

Residence Inn by Marriott
6305 Residence Inn Road
Huntsville, AL
256-895-0444
Pets of all sizes are welcome. There is a $75 one time fee per stay.

Days Inn Leeds
1838 Ashville Rd
Leeds, AL
205-699-9833 (800-329-7466)
Dogs of all sizes are allowed. There is a $7 per night pet fee per pet. 2 dogs may be allowed.

Days Inn Huntsville Airport
102 Arlington Dr
Madison, AL
256-772-9550 (800-329-7466)
Dogs of all sizes are allowed. There is a $10 per night pet fee per pet. 2 dogs may be allowed.

Motel 6 - Huntsville - Madison
8995 Madison Boulevard, PO Box 6123
Madison, AL
256-772-7479 (800-466-8356)
One well-behaved family pet per room. Guest must notify front desk upon arrival. Guest is liable for any damages. In consideration of all guests, pets must never be left unattended in the guest rooms.

Best Western Battleship Inn
2701 Battleship Prkwy
Mobile, AL
251-432-2703 (800-780-7234)
Dogs are allowed for an additional one time pet fee of $25 per room. Multiple dogs may be allowed.

Days Inn Mobile/Tillmans
5480 Inn Drive
Mobile, AL
251-661-8181 (800-329-7466)
Dogs of all sizes are allowed. There is a $8 per night pet fee per pet. 2 dogs may be allowed.

Drury Inn
824 West I-65 Service Road South
Mobile, AL
251-344-7700 (800-378-7946)
Dogs of all sizes are permitted. Pets are not allowed in the breakfast area of the hotel. Pets are not to be left unattended, and each guest must assume liability for damage of property or other guest complaints. There is a limit of one pet per room.

La Quinta Inn Mobile
816 West I-65 Service Road South
Mobile, AL

251-343-4051 (800-531-5900)
Dogs of all sizes are allowed. There are no additional pet fees. Dogs must be leashed and cleaned up after. Please inform the front desk when leaving a dog alone in the room. Multiple dogs may be allowed.

Motel 6 - Mobile North
400 South Beltline Highway
Mobile, AL
251-343-8448 (800-466-8356)
One well-behaved family pet per room. Guest must notify front desk upon arrival. Guest is liable for any damages. In consideration of all guests, pets must never be left unattended in the guest rooms.

Motel 6 - Mobile West - Tillmans Corner
5488 Inn Road
Mobile, AL
251-660-1483 (800-466-8356)
One well-behaved family pet per room. Guest must notify front desk upon arrival. Guest is liable for any damages. In consideration of all guests, pets must never be left unattended in the guest rooms.

Red Roof Inn - Mobile North
33 I-65 Service Road
Mobile, AL
251-476-2004 (800-RED-ROOF)
One well-behaved family pet per room. Guest must notify front desk upon arrival. Guest is liable for any damages. In consideration of all guests, pets must never be left unattended in the guest rooms.

Red Roof Inn - Mobile South
5450 Cola Cola Road
Mobile, AL
251-666-1044 (800-RED-ROOF)
One well-behaved family pet per room. Guest must notify front desk upon arrival. Guest is liable for any damages. In consideration of all guests, pets must never be left unattended in the guest rooms.

Residence Inn by Marriott
950 W, I-65 Service Road South
Mobile, AL
251-304-0570
Pets of all sizes are welcome. There is a $75 one time fee per stay.

TownePlace Suites Mobile
1075 Montlimor Drive
Mobile, AL
251-345-9588
Dogs of all sizes are allowed. There is a $75 one time pet fee per visit. ₂ 2 dogs may be allowed.

Airport Inn (Days Inn)
1150 West South Blvd
Montgomery, AL
334-281-8000 (800-329-7466)
Dogs of all sizes are allowed. There is a $10 per night pet fee per pet. 2 dogs may be allowed.

Best Inns
5135 Carmichael
Montgomery, AL
334-270-9199
Dogs of all sizes are allowed. There are no additional pet fees. Multiple dogs may be allowed.

Best Western Monticello Inn
5837 Monticello Dr
Montgomery, AL
334-277-4442 (800-780-7234)
Dogs are allowed for an additional fee of $10 per night per pet. Multiple dogs may be allowed.

Days Inn Montgomery Midtown
2625 Zelda Rd
Montgomery, AL
334-269-9611 (800-329-7466)
Dogs of all sizes are allowed. There is a $5 per night pet fee per pet. 2 dogs may be allowed.

La Quinta Inn Montgomery
1280 East Blvd.
Montgomery, AL
334-271-1620 (800-531-5900)
Dogs of all sizes are allowed. There are no additional pet fees. Dogs must be leashed and cleaned up after. Crate or be with pet when the room is being serviced. Multiple dogs may be allowed.

Motel 6 - Montgomery
1051 Eastern Boulevard
Montgomery, AL
334-277-6748 (800-466-8356)
One well-behaved family pet per room. Guest must notify front desk upon arrival. Guest is liable for any damages. In consideration of all guests, pets must never be left unattended in the guest rooms.

Quality Inn and Suites Convention Center
2705 E S Boulevard
Montgomery, AL
334-288-2800 (877-424-6423)
Dogs are allowed for an additional fee of $10 per night per pet. Multiple dogs may be allowed.

Residence Inn by Marriott
1200 Himar Court
Montgomery, AL

334-270-3300
Pets of all sizes are welcome. There is a $75 one time fee per stay, and a pet policy to sign at check in. ₂

TownePlace Suites Montgomery
5047 Carmichael Drive
Montgomery, AL
334-396-5505
Dogs of all sizes are allowed. There is a $75 one time pet fee per visit. ₂ 2 dogs may be allowed.

Super 8 Moody
2451 Moody Parkway
Moody, AL
205-640-7091 (800-800-8000)
Dogs of all sizes are allowed. There is a $10 per night pet fee per pet. Smoking and non-smoking rooms are available for pet rooms. 2 dogs may be allowed.

Best Western Colonial Inn
293 Valley Road
Oneonta, AL
205-274-2200 (800-780-7234)
Dogs are allowed for an additional fee of $12 (plus tax) per night per pet. Multiple dogs may be allowed.

Motel 6 - Opelika
1015 Columbus Parkway
Opelika, AL
334-745-0988 (800-466-8356)
One well-behaved family pet per room. Guest must notify front desk upon arrival. Guest is liable for any damages. In consideration of all guests, pets must never be left unattended in the guest rooms.

Days Inn Anniston/Oxford
3 Recreation Dr
Oxford, AL
256-835-0300 (800-329-7466)
Dogs of all sizes are allowed. There is a $40 pet fee per stay. 2 dogs may be allowed.

Howard Johnson Express Inn
PO Box 3308
Oxford, AL
256-835-3988 (800-446-4656)
Dogs of all sizes are welcome. There are no additional pet fees.

Motel 6 - Anniston-Oxford/Talladega Spdwy
202 Grace Street
Oxford, AL
256-831-5463 (800-466-8356)
One well-behaved family pet per room. Guest must notify front desk upon arrival. Guest is liable for any damages. In consideration of all guests, pets must never be left

unattended in the guest rooms.

Quality Inn and Suites
858 H 231 S
Ozark, AL
334-774-7300 (877-424-6423)
Dogs are allowed for an additional one time fee of $25 per pet. Multiple dogs may be allowed.

Days Inn Shorter
450 Main St
Shorter, AL
334-727-6034 (800-329-7466)
Dogs of all sizes are allowed. There is a $10 per night pet fee per pet. 2 dogs may be allowed.

Holiday Inn Express
Hwy 231 at Hwy 29
Troy, AL
334-670-0012 (877-270-6405)
Dogs of all sizes are allowed for an additional $10 one time pet fee per room. 2 dogs may be allowed.

La Quinta Inn Tuscaloosa
4122 McFarland Blvd. E.
Tuscaloosa, AL
205-349-3270 (800-531-5900)
Dogs of all sizes are allowed. There are no additional pet fees. Dogs must be leashed and cleaned up after. Dogs may not be left unattended unless they will be quiet and well behaved. 2 dogs may be allowed.

Motel 6 - Tuscaloosa
4700 McFarland Boulevard East
Tuscaloosa, AL
205-759-4942 (800-466-8356)
One well-behaved family pet per room. Guest must notify front desk upon arrival. Guest is liable for any damages. In consideration of all guests, pets must never be left unattended in the guest rooms.

Alaska Listings

America's Best Suites
4110 Spenard Road
Anchorage, AK
907-243-3433 (800-237-8466)
Dogs of all sizes are allowed for a $100 fee, $50 of which is refundable for 1 dog, and a $150 fee, $50 of which is refundable for 2 dogs. Dogs must be declared at the time of reservations, and they must be well mannered, leashed, and cleaned up after. 2 dogs may be allowed.

Aurora Winds Resort Bed and Breakfast
7501 Upper O'Malley Rd
Anchorage, AK
907-346-2533
aurorawinds.com/
This B&B offers five rooms with private baths. They offer two acres of privacy. Pets must be leashed when outside of the room.

Long House Alaskan Hotel
4335 Wisconsin Street
Anchorage, AK
907-243-2133 (888-243-2133)
longhousehotel.com/
Rich in Alaskan character décor and able to accommodate the business or leisure traveler, this inn also sits across from Lake Hood and provides a large walk-in freezer for "catches". Dogs of all sizes are allowed for an additional fee of $10 per night per pet, and they have been known to keep doggy treats at the front desk. Dogs must be leashed and cleaned up after. 2 dogs may be allowed.

Merrill Field Inn
420 Sitka Street
Anchorage, AK
907-276-4547 (800-898-4547)
merrillfieldinn.com/
This inn is centrally located to a number of activities, shopping, and eateries, plus they also have an onsite restaurant specializing in American and Chinese cuisine. Dogs of all sizes are allowed for an additional fee of $7 per night per pet. Dogs must be leashed and cleaned up after. 2 dogs may be allowed.

Microtel Inn and Suites
5205 Northwood Drive
Anchorage, AK
907-245-5002 (800-898-4547)
microtelanchorage.com/
Specializing in clean, comfortable lodging, this airport inn can accommodate business or leisure travelers and they also sit central to numerous other attractions and activities. Dogs of all sizes are allowed for an additional fee of $10 per night per pet. Dogs must be leashed, cleaned up after, and kenneled when left alone in the room. 2 dogs may be allowed.

Millennium Alaskan Hotel
4800 Spenard Rd
Anchorage, AK
907-243-2300
This 248-room hotel is located on the eastern shore of Lake Spenard. There is a $50 refundable pet deposit.

Motel 6 - Anchorage - Midtown
5000 A Street
Anchorage, AK
907-677-8000 (800-466-8356)
One well-behaved family pet per room. Guest must notify front desk upon arrival. Guest is liable for any damages. In consideration of all guests, pets must never be left unattended in the guest rooms.

Parkwood Inn
4455 Juneau St
Anchorage, AK
907-563-3590
There is a $5 one time pet fee and a $50 refundable pet deposit if paying with cash.

Puffin Inn
4400 Spenard Road
Anchorage, AK
907-243-4044 (800-478-3346)
puffininn.net/
Offering many conveniences for the business or leisure traveler, they are also central to many other notable services and attractions. Dogs of all sizes are allowed for an additional fee of $3 per night per pet, unless the Pet Friendly Lodging package is purchased which includes a collapsible food/water bin, treats, a toy, sanitary bags, and a foldable dog food mat. Dogs must be leashed and cleaned up after. 2 dogs may be allowed.

Red Roof Inn - Anchorage
1104 E 5th Avenue
Anchorage, AK
907-274-1650 (800-RED-ROOF)
One well-behaved family pet per room. Guest must notify front desk upon arrival. Guest is liable for any damages. In consideration of all guests, pets must never be left unattended in the guest rooms.

Residence Inn by Marriott
1025 35th Ave.
Anchorage, AK
907-563-9844
Dogs of all sizes are allowed. There is an $85 one time fee per stay, plus $10 per night, and a pet policy to sign at check in.

Sourdough Visitors Lodge
801 E Erikson St
Anchorage, AK
907-279-4148 (800-777-3716)
There is a $100 refundable deposit

and a $50 one time pet fee.

Super 8 Anchorage
3501 Minnesota Dr
Anchorage, AK
907-276-8884 (800-800-8000)
Dogs of all sizes are allowed. There is a $25 returnable deposit required per room. Smoking and non-smoking rooms are available for pet rooms. 2 dogs may be allowed.

Long House Bethel Hotel
751 3rd Avenue
Bethel, AK
907-486-4300 (866-543-4613)
longhousebethelinn.com/
This guest house can accommodate large or small groups comfortably, and they make a good starting point for exploring the beauty of the area. Dogs of all sizes are allowed for an additional fee of $50 per pet per stay plus a $50 refundable deposit. Dogs must be leashed and cleaned up after. 2 dogs may be allowed.

Border City Motel & RV Park
Mile 1225 Alaska Hwy
Border City, AK
907-774-2205
There is one pet room in this hotel. There is a $50 additional refundable pet deposit.

Backwoods Lodge
At George Parks Hwy, Milepost 210
Cantwell, AK
907-768-2232
This motel's log building offers nine large comfortable rooms with satellite TVs, microwaves, refrigerators and barbecues. The property has a view of Mt. McKinley. They have hiking trails and a canoe which guests can use on a nearby small pond. Call ahead for reservations because they do tend to book up early, especially during the summer. The nice folks here give out pet blankets to put over the furniture if your dog is going to be on the bed or chairs. They are located about 30 miles from Denali National Park. Pets must be on leash when outside of the rooms and may not be left unattended in the room or in your car. Dogs under 70 pounds are allowed.

Alaska 7 Motel
Mile 270 Richardson Hwy
Delta Junction, AK
907-895-4848
Small to medium sized dogs are allowed in a few pet rooms in this motel.

Alaskan Steak House & Motel
265 Richardson Hwy
Delta Junction, AK
907-895-5175
wildak.net/~akstkhse/
Dogs of all sizes are allowed. There is a $50 one time additional pet fee.

Clearwater Lodge
7028 Remington Rd
Delta Junction, AK
907-895-5152
This is not actually a hotel but they have a number of camping cabins. Showers and bathrooms are in a separate building and you need to bring your own sleeping bags. There are no additional pet fees.

McKinley Chalet Resort
Milepost 238 George Parks H
Denali, AK
907-267-7234 (800-423-7846)
Nestled among tree on the shores of the Nenana River only a half mile from the Denali National Park, this resort sits close to a variety of recreational pursuits, and has on site a restaurant, a bar/lounge, and numerous amenities. They are open from mid-May to mid-September, weather permitting. Dogs of all sizes are allowed for no additional fee. Dogs must be leashed and cleaned up after. 2 dogs may be allowed.

McKinley Village Lodge
Mile 231 Alaska H3
Denali, AK
907-683-8900 (800-276-7234)
In addition to a number of amenities and close proximity to the Denali National Park, this lodge also has a full service restaurant, saloon, coffee stand, and a gift shop on site. Dogs of all sizes are allowed for no additional fee. Dogs must be leashed and cleaned up after. Multiple dogs may be allowed.

Best Western Fairbanks Inn
1521 S Cushman Street
Fairbanks, AK
907-456-6602 (800-780-7234)
Dogs up to 40 pounds are allowed for an additional pet fee of $10 per night per room. 2 dogs may be allowed.

Chena Hot Springs Resort
P.O. Box 73440
Fairbanks, AK
907-452-7867 (800-478-4681)
chenahotsprings.com/
This resort is a great place to view the Aurora Borealis due to it's location in the northern region and

it's distance from the city lights. They offer hotel rooms, cabins, RV parking and camping. There are lots of outdoor activities to do on this 440 acre resort. They are located approximately 60 miles east of Fairbanks. There is a $100 refundable deposit for pets.

Comfort Inn
1908 Chena Landings Loop
Fairbanks, AK
907-479-8080 (877-424-6423)
Dogs are allowed for an additional fee of $10 per night per pet. 2 dogs may be allowed.

Golden North Motel
4888 Old Airport Way
Fairbanks, AK
907-479-6201 (800-447-1910)
goldennorthmotel.com/
Dogs, but not cats, are allowed at this motel. There are no additional pet fees but a credit card is required for a refundable pet deposit.

Pike's Waterfront Lodge
1850 Hoselton Rd
Fairbanks, AK
907-456-4500 (877-774-2400)
pikeslodge.com/
Dogs of all sizes are allowed. There is a $10 additional pet fee.

Regency Fairbanks Hotel
95 10th Avenue
Fairbanks, AK
907-452-3200
One well behaved dog is allowed. There is a $100 pet deposit, $50 of which is refundable, and there is a pet policy to sign at check in.

Super 8 Fairbanks
1909 Airport Way
Fairbanks, AK
907-451-8888 (800-800-8000)
Dogs of all sizes are allowed. There is a $10 one time per pet fee per visit. Smoking and non-smoking rooms are available for pet rooms. 2 dogs may be allowed.

The New Caribou Hotel
Box 329
Glennallen, AK
907-822-3302 (800-478-3302)
alaskan.com/caribouhotel/
Rooms are in a log cabin style building. There is a $10 per day pet fee.

Bear Track Inn
255 Rink Creek Rd
Gustavus, AK
907-697-3017 (888-697-2284)

This log cabin style inn is located on 17 acres. They offer 14 rooms each with a private bath. They are open from January 1 to October 1. There is a $100 refundable pet deposit. The owners have a large dog. There are no roads leading to this inn, so you will need to take the ferry or plane from Juneau. Dogs must be crated on the boat or plane.

Glacier Bay Lodge and Tours
179 Bartlett Cove
Gustavus, AK
888-BAY-TOUR
Offering the only accommodations in the Glacier Bay National Park amid some of the most pristine wilderness and majestic scenery in the world, this rustic lodge offers modern amenities and a good starting point for a number of activities and recreation. Dogs of all sizes are allowed for no additional fee. Dogs must be under owner's control/care, leashed, and cleaned up after. Dogs are not allowed on public tours, at food service areas, or the gift shop. 2 dogs may be allowed.

Puffin's Bed and Breakfast
1/4 Mile Logging Rd
Gustavus, AK
907-697-2260 (800-478-2258)
puffintravel.com/P6.htm
This B&B is open May - September. They offer 5 cabins situated on 7 acres of land. There are no roads leading to this inn, so you will need to take the ferry or plane from Juneau. Dogs must be crated on the boat or plane.

Captain's Choice
108 2nd Avenue North
Haines, AK
907-766-3111 (800-478-2345)
capchoice.com/
Get panoramic views of the water from the Captain's Choice Motel. Dogs of all sizes are allowed. There is a $15 one time additional pet fee.

Eagle's Nest Motel
1069 Haines Hwy
Haines, AK
907-766-2891
Dogs of all sizes are allowed. There is a $10 one time additional pet fee.

Fort Seward Lodge
39 Mud Bay Rd
Haines, AK
907-766-2009 (877-617-3418)
ftsewardlodge.com/
Dogs of all sizes are allowed. There is a $10 per night pet fee and a $50 credit card pet deposit that will only

be charged if there is damage to the room. The hotel is closed in November and December each year.

Hotel Halsingland
13 Fort Seward Dr
Haines, AK
907-766-2000
hotelhalsingland.com
Dogs of all sizes are allowed. There is a $10 per night additional pet fee.

Thunderbird Motel
216 Dalton Street
Haines, AK
907-766-2131 (800-327-2556)
thunderbird-motel.com
Dogs of all sizes are allowed. There are no additional pet fees.

Best Western Bidarka Inn
575 Sterling Highway
Homer, AK
907-235-8148 (800-780-7234)
Dogs are allowed for an additional fee of $10 per night per pet. Multiple dogs may be allowed.

Heritage Hotel
147 E Pioneer Ave
Homer, AK
907-235-7787
There is a $10 per day pet fee. They usually place pets in smoking rooms but will give you a non-smoking room if requested.

Homer Seaside Cottages
58901 East End Road
Homer, AK
907-235-2716 (877-374-2716)
Only a block from the ocean and sandy beaches, this spacious cottage will sleep six and allow dogs for an additional fee of $5 per night per pet with a $15 minimum fee. Dogs may not be left unattended, and they must be leashed and cleaned up after at all times. 2 dogs may be allowed.

Jenny Lane Cottage
353 D Jenny Lane
Homer, AK
907-235-5434
akms.com/jennyln/
This cozy get-a-way is only a short walk to town and sits overlooking Kachemak Bay offering great views of area's landscapes, and it's variety of marine, bird, and wildlife. Dogs of all sizes are allowed (on approval) for an additional fee of $15 per night per room. Aggressive breed dogs are not allowed, and dogs must be quiet, well behaved,

leashed, and cleaned up after. 2 dogs may be allowed.

Lakewood Inn Bed and Breakfast
984 Ocean Dr #1
Homer, AK
907-235-6144
There is a $10 per day pet fee.

Otter Cove Resort
PO Box 2543
Homer, AK
907-235-7770 (800-426-6212)
ottercoveresort.com/
Accessed by water taxi or biplane, this lodging area offers a private beach and sets in a lush maritime forest with miles of scenic hiking trails. Dogs of all sizes are allowed for no additional fee, although having limited pet friendly facilities, they suggest calling ahead. Dogs must be quiet, well behaved, leashed, and cleaned up after at all times. Dogs are not allowed at the restaurant. 2 dogs may be allowed.

Extended Stay Deluxe
1800 Shell Simmons Drive
Juneau, AK
907-790-6435 (800-804-3724)
extendedstaydeluxe.com/
Dogs of all sizes are allowed for an additional fee of $25 per night per pet (maximum $75 each). Dogs must be well behaved, leashed, and cleaned up after. 2 dogs may be allowed.

Juneau Hotel
1250 W 9th Street
Juneau, AK
907-586-5666
juneauhotels.net/
Dogs up to 50 pounds or 18 inches high to the shoulder are allowed for an additional fee of a one time fee of $50 for a 1 to 3 day stay, and a $150 one time fee for over 3 days. Dogs must be declared at the time of reservation, and they must be quiet, leashed, and cleaned up after.

Prospector Hotel
375 Whittier Street
Juneau, AK
907-586-3737 (800-331-2711 (US & Hawaii))
prospectorhotel.com/
Business and leisure travelers will both enjoy the variety of amenities and recreational opportunities at this hotel. Dogs of all sizes are allowed for an additional $10 per night per pet. Dogs must be very friendly, well behaved, leashed, cleaned up after, and kenneled when left alone in the room. Dogs are not allowed in food

service areas. 2 dogs may be allowed.

Super 8
2295 Trout Street
Juneau, AK
907-789-4858 (800-800-8000)
super8.com/Super8/control/home
Dogs of all sizes are allowed for an additional one time pet fee of $25 per room. Dogs must be leashed and cleaned up after. 2 dogs may be allowed.

The Driftwood Lodge
435 Willoughby Ave
Juneau, AK
907-586-2280 (800-544-2239)
alaskan.com/driftwoodlodge/
There is a $5 per day pet fee.

Best Western Landing Hotel
3434 Tongass AVe
Ketchikan, AK
907-225-5166 (800-780-7234)
Dogs are allowed for an additional fee of $10 per night per pet. Multiple dogs may be allowed.

Black Bear Inn
5528 N Tongass H/H 7
Ketchikan, AK
907-225-4343
stayinalaska.com/
This premier waterfront inn offers elegant surroundings, great views, and many amenities. One dog is allowed in the Bunk House cabin for an additional pet fee of $10 per night. Dogs must be well behaved, leashed, and cleaned up after at all times. Dogs are not allowed on the furniture or beds, and if pets have a propensity to get on the furnishings, they request they be kenneled at night.

Super 8
2151 Sea Level Drive
Ketchikan, AK
907-225-9088 (800-800-8000)
super8.com/Super8/control/home
This waterside hotel will allow dogs of all sizes for an additional fee of $10 per room per stay. Dogs must be leashed and cleaned up after. 2 dogs may be allowed.

The Narrows Inn, Restaurant and Marina
4871 N Tongass H/H 7
Ketchikan, AK
907-247-2600 (888-686-2600)
narrowsinn.com/
This beautiful waterfront inn offer ocean front rooms, a restaurant and lounge, and numerous amenities.

Dogs of all sizes are allowed for an additional fee of $10 per night per pet. Dogs must be well mannered, leashed, and cleaned up after at all times. 2 dogs may be allowed.

Shelikof Lodge
211 Thorsheim Street
Kodiak, AK
907-486-4300
ptialaska.net/~kyle/index2.htm
This hotel offers a restaurant, lounge, and a number of amenities and services, as well as providing a good starting point for exploring the variety of activities and recreation in the area. One medium to large dog or 2 small dogs are allowed per room for no additional fee. Dogs are not allowed on the furniture and must be kenneled when left alone in the room. Dogs must be leashed and cleaned up after at all times.

A Cottage on the Bay
13710 Beach Drive
Lowell Point, AK
907-224-8237 (888-334-8237)
onthebayak.com/
This seasonal cottage sits on the shores of the scenic Resurrection Bay and offers a number of amenities, including freezer storage for any "catches" from the bay. Dogs of all sizes are allowed for no additional fee. Dogs must be well behaved, under owner's control/care, and cleaned up after at all times. Multiple dogs may be allowed.

Gold Miner's Hotel
918 S Colony Way
Palmer, AK
907-745-6160 (800-7ALASKA)
goldminershotel.com/
In addition to providing spacious accommodations, a restaurant, and a bar/lounge, they are also central to a variety of activities and recreational pursuits. Dogs of all sizes are allowed for a $50 to $100 refundable deposit with prior approval. Aggressive breed dogs are not allowed. Dogs must be quiet, well behaved, leashed, and cleaned up after at all times. 2 dogs may be allowed.

Paxson Inn and Lodge
Mile 185 Richardson H
Paxson, AK
907-822-3330
Sitting central to several fishing lakes and hiking trails, this inn also provides a restaurant and bar on site, and there is a camp area with hook-ups that allows dogs for no

additional fee. One dog is allowed per room at the lodge for an additional pet fee of $20 per night. Dogs must be leashed and cleaned up after.

Scandia House
110 N Nordic Drive
Petersburg, AK
907-772-4281 (800-722-5006)
scandiahousehotel.com/
Great views, convenient location, Jacuzzi rooms, and fresh muffins in the morning are some of the amenities offered here. Dogs of all sizes are allowed for an additional fee of $10 per night per pet. Dogs must be leashed and cleaned up after.

New Seward Hotel
217 5th Avenue
Seward, AK
907-224-8001 (800-655-8785)
hotelsewardalaska.com/
This premier hotel is only minutes from numerous sites of interest, recreational pursuits, food, and shopping. One dog of any sizes is allowed for an additional pet fee of $10 per night. Dogs must be well mannered, leashed, and cleaned up after.

Seward Cabins
31730 Bronze Avenue
Seward, AK
907-224-4891
sewardcabins.com/
Newly constructed with modern heated concrete cabins, these creek-side cabins offer year round recreational opportunities. Dogs of all sizes are allowed for no additional fee. Dogs must be under owner's control, leashed, and cleaned up after at all times. Multiple dogs may be allowed.

Super 8
404 Sawmill Creek Road
Sitka, AK
907-747-8804 (800-800-8000)
super8.com/Super8/control/home
Dogs of all sizes are allowed for an additional fee of $10 per night per pet. Dogs may not be left unattended in the room, and they must be leashed and cleaned up after. 2 dogs may be allowed.

Sgt Preston's Lodge
370 6th Ave
Skagway, AK
907-983-2521
Dogs of all sizes are allowed. There is a $15 one time additional pet fee. The entire hotel is non-smoking.

Westmark Inn Skagway
Third and Spring Streets
Skagway, AK
907-983-6000
westmarkhotels.com/skagway.php
This hotel only allows dogs in
smoking rooms only. There are no
additional pet fees.

Talkeetna Inn
25 Coffee Lane
Talkeetna, AK
907-733-7530 (888-582-4890)
talkeetna-bandb.com/index.html
This lakeside inn sits only a short
distance from the confluence of the
Talkeetna, Susitna and Chulitna
rivers, offering visitors spectacular
scenery, and a great starting point
for year round recreation. Dogs of all
sizes are allowed for no additional
fee; puppies are not allowed. Dogs
must be well behaved, leashed, and
cleaned up after at all times. 2 dogs
may be allowed.

Burnt Paw Cabins
Box 7
Tok, AK
907-883-4121
burntpawcabins.com
There is one pet-friendly cabin. Dogs
of all sizes are allowed. There is a
$25 refundable additional cash
deposit for pets.

Cleft on the Rock Bed and Breakfast
Mile 0.5 Sundog Trail
Tok, AK
907-883-4219
tokalaska.com/cleftroc.shtml
Pets are not allowed on the furniture.
The owner has a cat and your dog
needs to be ok around cats. There is
a $25 one time pet fee.

Showshoe Motel
Mile 1314 Alaska Hwy
Tok, AK
907-883-4511
alaska-snowshoemotel.com
Dogs of all sizes are allowed. There
is a $25 damage deposit required
that can be handled with a credit
card. Dogs must always be leashed
when outside of your room and they
may not be left unattended in the
room.

Westmark Tok Hotel
Alaska Hwy & Glenn Hwy
Tok, AK
907-883-5174
The hotel has a couple of pet rooms.
Dogs of all sizes are allowed. There
is no additional pet fee.

Young's Motel
Box 482
Tok, AK
907-883-4411
Dogs of all sizes are allowed. There
are no additional pet fees.

Tiekel River Lodge
Richardson Hwy, Mile 56
Valdez, AK
907-822-3259
There is a $10 per day pet fee. The
lodge is open from March through
September. There are no
designated smoking or non-
smoking rooms.

Totem Inn
144 E Egan Drive
Valdez, AK
907-835-4443
toteminn.com/
Only a few steps from the harbor,
this inn also offers cottages for rent,
an eatery open from 5 am to 11 pm
during the summer, and a gift shop
that carries hand made native art.
The cottages are non-smoking;
however rooms at the inn are
smoking-optional. Dogs of all sizes
are allowed for an additional fee of
$10 per night per pet. Dogs must be
well behaved, leashed, and cleaned
up after. Multiple dogs may be
allowed.

Best Western Lake Lucille Inn
1300 W Lake Lucille Drive
Wasilla, AK
907-373-1776 (800-780-7234)
Dogs are allowed for an additional
fee of $10 per night per pet. 2 dogs
may be allowed.

Stikine Inn
107 Front Street
Wrangell, AK
907-874-3388 (888-874-3388)
stikineinn.com/
Set in a lush environment rich in
marine, bird, and wild life as well as
natural and Native American
history, this ocean-side hotel offers
a great starting point for exploring
the area. Dogs of all sizes are
allowed for a refundable deposit of
$75 per room. Dogs must be
leashed, cleaned up after, and
crated when left alone in the room.
2 dogs may be allowed.

Arizona Listings

Best Western Baymont Inn & Suites
Benson, AZ
520-586-3646 (800-780-7234)
Dogs are allowed for an additional
fee of $10 per night per pet. 2 dogs
may be allowed.

Motel 6 - Benson
637 South Whetstone Commerce
Drive
Benson, AZ
520-586-0066 (800-466-8356)
One well-behaved family pet per
room. Guest must notify front desk
upon arrival. Guest is liable for any
damages. In consideration of all
guests, pets must never be left
unattended in the guest rooms.

Super 8 Benson
855 N Ocotillo Rd
Benson, AZ
520-586-1530 (800-800-8000)
Dogs of all sizes are allowed. There
is a $10 returnable deposit required
per room. Smoking and non-smoking
rooms are available for pet rooms. 2
dogs may be allowed.

Sleepy Dog Guest House
212A Opera Drive
Bisbee, AZ
520-432-3057
sleepydogguesthouse.com
There is a one bedroom and two
bedroom guest house overlooking
Bisbee. No credit cards, smoking
outside only. There are no additional
pet fees.

Days Inn Buckeye
25205 West Yuma Rd
Buckeye, AZ
623-386-5400 (800-329-7466)
Dogs of all sizes are allowed. There
is a $10 one time per pet fee per
visit. 2 dogs may be allowed.

Best Western Bullhead City Inn
1126 Hwy 95
Bullhead, AZ
928-754-3000 (800-780-7234)
Dogs are allowed for an additional
one time pet fee of $25 per room. 2
dogs may be allowed.

Comfort Inn
340 N Goswick Way
Camp Verde, AZ
928-567-9000 (877-424-6423)
Dogs up to 50 pounds are allowed
for an additional one time fee of $15
(plus tax) per pet. 2 dogs may be
allowed.

Days Inn Camp Verde
1640 W Finnie Flat Rd

Camp Verde, AZ
928-567-3700 (800-329-7466)
Dogs of all sizes are allowed. There is a $10 one time per pet fee per visit. Reservations are recommended due to limited rooms for pets. 2 dogs may be allowed.

Boulders Resort
34631 N Tom Darlington Rd
Carefree, AZ
480-488-9009
wyndham.com/Boulders/
There is a one-time $100 dog fee.

Carefree Resort and Villas
37220 Mule Train Road
Carefree, AZ
480-488-5300 (888-488-9034)
For a luxurious vacation getaway, a wedding, or a special business event, Carefree Resort wants your stay to be carefree. Backed by spectacular desert landscapes and mountain vistas, this full service resort and spa features spacious single and double guest rooms, luxury suites, casitas, and elegant condominiums in a private gated community. They are considered a premier golfing destination, and there is convenient access to 16 of Arizona's finest golf courses. They also offer such amenities as tennis courts/instruction, 3 pools, a clubhouse, fitness center, a grocery service, gourmet dining, room service, and a day spa and salon that offer a variety of massages and body treatments. Dogs of all sizes are allowed. There is a $50 one time fee per pet. Dogs must be quiet, leashed, cleaned up after, and the Do Not Disturb sign put on the door or a contact number left with the front desk if they are in the room alone. Multiple dogs may be allowed.

Days Inn Casa Grande
5300 N Sunland Gin Rd
Casa Grande, AZ
520-426-9240 (800-329-7466)
Dogs of all sizes are allowed. There is a $8 one time pet fee per visit. 2 dogs may be allowed.

Motel 6 - Casa Grande
4965 North Sunland Gin Road
Casa Grande, AZ
520-836-3323 (800-466-8356)
One well-behaved family pet per room. Guest must notify front desk upon arrival. Guest is liable for any damages. In consideration of all guests, pets must never be left unattended in the guest rooms.

Super 8 Casa Grande

2066 E Florence Blvd
Casa Grande, AZ
520-836-8800 (800-800-8000)
Dogs of all sizes are allowed. There is a $10 per night pet fee per pet. Smoking and non-smoking rooms are available for pet rooms. 2 dogs may be allowed.

Super 8 Catalina/Tucson Area
15691 N Oracle Rd
Catalina, AZ
520-818-9500 (800-800-8000)
Dogs of all sizes are allowed. There is a $5 per night pet fee per pet. Smoking and non-smoking rooms are available for pet rooms. 2 dogs may be allowed.

Comfort Inn Chandler
255 N. Kyrene Road
Chandler, AZ
480-705-8882 (877-424-6423)
tristarhotels.com/ci-chandler
This hotel offers a free full hot breakfast daily, wireless high speed internet access, a heated outdoor pool, cable TV with expanded HBO and laundry facilities. There are no additional pet fees.

Red Roof Inn - Phoenix Chandler
7400 West Boston Avenue
Chandler, AZ
480-857-4969 (800-RED-ROOF)
One well-behaved family pet per room. Guest must notify front desk upon arrival. Guest is liable for any damages. In consideration of all guests, pets must never be left unattended in the guest rooms.

Sheraton Wild Horse Pass Resort & Spa
5594 W. Wild Horse Pass Blvd.
Chandler, AZ
602-225-0100 (888-625-5144)
Dogs up to 80 pounds are allowed. Dogs are restricted to rooms on the first floor only. There are no additional pet fees. Dogs are not allowed to be left alone in the room.

Windmill Inn of Chandler
3535 W Chandler Blvd
Chandler, AZ
480-812-9600
There is no additional pet fee. There is a special pet section of the hotel.

Motel 6 - Douglas
111 16th Street
Douglas, AZ
520-364-2457 (800-466-8356)
One well-behaved family pet per room. Guest must notify front desk

upon arrival. Guest is liable for any damages. In consideration of all guests, pets must never be left unattended in the guest rooms.

Best Western Sunrise Inn
128 N Main St
Eager, AZ
928-333-2540 (800-780-7234)
Dogs are allowed for an additional one time fee of $10 per pet. Dogs may not be alone in the room. Multiple dogs may be allowed.

Red Roof Inn - Eloy
4015 West Outer Drive
Eloy, AZ
520-466-2522 (800-RED-ROOF)
One well-behaved family pet per room. Guest must notify front desk upon arrival. Guest is liable for any damages. In consideration of all guests, pets must never be left unattended in the guest rooms.

Best Western Kings House Motel
1560 East Route 66
Flagstaff, AZ
928-774-7186 (800-780-7234)
Dogs are allowed for an additional fee of $10 per night per pet. Multiple dogs may be allowed.

Best Western Pony Soldier Inn & Suites
3030 E Route 66
Flagstaff, AZ
928-526-2388 (800-780-7234)
Dogs are allowed for an additional one time fee of $15 per pet. Multiple dogs may be allowed.

Comfort Inn
2355 S Beulah Blvd
Flagstaff, AZ
928-774-2225 (877-424-6423)
Dogs are allowed for an additional fee of $10 per night per pet. Multiple dogs may be allowed.

Days Inn Flagstaff East
3601 E Lockett Rd
Flagstaff, AZ
928-527-1477 (800-329-7466)
Dogs of all sizes are allowed. There is a $10 one time per pet fee per visit. Reservations are recommended due to limited rooms for pets. 2 dogs may be allowed.

Days Inn Flagstaff Hwy 66
1000 West Rte 66
Flagstaff, AZ
928-774-5221 (800-329-7466)
Dogs of all sizes are allowed. There is a $10 per night pet fee per pet. Reservations are recommended due to

to limited rooms for pets. 2 dogs may be allowed.

Howard Johnson Inn
3300 E. Rt. 66
Flagstaff, AZ
800-437-7137 (800-446-4656)
Dogs of all sizes are welcome. There is a $7 one time pet fee.

La Quinta Inn & Suites Flagstaff
2015 South Beulah Blvd.
Flagstaff, AZ
928-556-8666 (800-531-5900)
Dogs of all sizes are allowed. Dogs must be well behaved, leashed, and cleaned up after. 2 dogs may be allowed.

Motel 6 - Flagstaff - Butler Ave
2010 East Butler Avenue
Flagstaff, AZ
928-774-1801 (800-466-8356)
One well-behaved family pet per room. Guest must notify front desk upon arrival. Guest is liable for any damages. In consideration of all guests, pets must never be left unattended in the guest rooms.

Motel 6 - Flagstaff East - Lucky lane
2440 East Lucky Lane
Flagstaff, AZ
928-774-8756 (800-466-8356)
One well-behaved family pet per room. Guest must notify front desk upon arrival. Guest is liable for any damages. In consideration of all guests, pets must never be left unattended in the guest rooms.

Motel 6 - Flagstaff West-Woodlands Village
2745 South Woodlands Village
Flagstaff, AZ
928-779-3757 (800-466-8356)
One well-behaved family pet per room. Guest must notify front desk upon arrival. Guest is liable for any damages. In consideration of all guests, pets must never be left unattended in the guest rooms.

Quality Inn
2500 E Lucky Lane
Flagstaff, AZ
928-226-7111 (877-424-6423)
Dogs are allowed for an additional pet fee of $10 per night per room. 2 dogs may be allowed.

Quality Inn
2000 S Milton Road
Flagstaff, AZ
928-774-8771 (877-424-6423)
Dogs are allowed for an additional pet fee of $10 per night per room. 2

dogs may be allowed.

Residence Inn by Marriott
3440 N. Country Club Drive
Flagstaff, AZ
928-526-5555
Dogs of all sizes are allowed. There is a $7.50 per night fee to a maximum of $75, and a pet policy to sign at check in.

Sleep Inn
2765 S Woodlands Village Blvd
Flagstaff, AZ
928-556-3000 (877-424-6423)
Dogs are allowed for an additional fee of $10 per night per pet. 2 dogs may be allowed.

Best Western Space Age Lodge
401 E Pima
Gila Bend, AZ
928-683-2273 (800-780-7234)
Dogs are allowed for no additional pet fee. 2 dogs may be allowed.

Comfort Inn at Round Mountain Park
1515 South Street
Globe, AZ
928-425-7575 (877-424-6423)
Dogs are allowed for an additional fee of $10 per night per pet. 2 dogs may be allowed.

Motel 6 - Globe
1699 East Ash Street
Globe, AZ
928-425-5741 (800-466-8356)
One well-behaved family pet per room. Guest must notify front desk upon arrival. Guest is liable for any damages. In consideration of all guests, pets must never be left unattended in the guest rooms.

Best Western Phoenix Goodyear Inn
55 N Litchfield Rd
Goodyear, AZ
623-932-3210 (800-780-7234)
Dogs are allowed for an additional fee of $10 per night per pet. Multiple dogs may be allowed.

Hampton Inn
2000 N Litchfield Road
Goodyear, AZ
623-536-1313
Dogs of all sizes are allowed. There are no additional pet fees, however there must be a credit card on file. Dogs are not allowed to be left alone in the room. Multiple dogs may be allowed.

Holiday Inn Express

1313 N. Litchfield Rd
Goodyear, AZ
623-535-1313 (877-270-6405)
Dogs of all sizes are allowed for no additional fee. Multiple dogs may be allowed.

Super 8 Goodyear/Phoenix Area
1710 N Dysart Rd
Goodyear, AZ
623-932-9622 (800-800-8000)
Dogs of all sizes are allowed. There is a $50 returnable deposit required per room. Reservations are recommended due to limited rooms for pets. Smoking and non-smoking rooms are available for pet rooms. 2 dogs may be allowed.

Red Feather Lodge
Highway 64
Grand Canyon, AZ
800-538-2345
redfeatherlodge.com
This motel is located just one mile south of the south entrance to the Grand Canyon National Park. Pets are welcome, but they must not be left unattended in the room. There is a $50 refundable pet deposit and a $10 pet fee per night per pet.

Big Ten Resort Cabins
45 Main Street
Greer, AZ
928-735-7578
bigtencabins.com
These are rustic Cabins located in the cozy town of Greer in the center of the White Mountains in AZ. They are located 13 Miles from Sunrise Ski Resort & many other outdoor activities. Some amenities include Satellite TV/VCR/DVD, fireplaces and bar-b-cues. Well behaved dogs are welcome for $15 each per night.

Best Western Sawmill Inn
1877 Hwy 260
Heber, AZ
928-535-5053 (800-780-7234)
Dogs are allowed for an additional fee of $10 per night per pet. 2 dogs may be allowed.

Best Western Adobe Inn
615 W Hopi Dr
Holbrook, AZ
928-524-3948 (800-780-7234)
Dogs are allowed for an additional one time pet fee of $6 per room. Multiple dogs may be allowed.

Best Western Arizonian Inn
2508 Navajo Blvd
Holbrook, AZ
928-524-2611 (800-780-7234)

Dogs are allowed for no additional pet fee with a credit card on file. Multiple dogs may be allowed.

Holiday Inn Express
1308 E Navajo Blvd
Holbrook, AZ
928-524-1466 (877-270-6405)
Dogs of all sizes are allowed for an additional $10 per night per pet for priority club members and $20 per night per pet if not a member. 2 dogs may be allowed.

Motel 6 - Holbrook
2514 Navajo Boulevard
Holbrook, AZ
928-524-6101 (800-466-8356)
One well-behaved family pet per room. Guest must notify front desk upon arrival. Guest is liable for any damages. In consideration of all guests, pets must never be left unattended in the guest rooms.

Best Western A Wayfarer's Inn and Suites
2815 E Andy Devine Avenue
Kingman, AZ
928-753-6271 (800-780-7234)
Dogs are allowed for an additional one time pet fee of $8 per room. 2 dogs may be allowed.

Best Western Kings Inn and Suites
2930 E Route 66
Kingman, AZ
928-753-6101 (800-780-7234)
Dogs are allowed for an additional one time pet fee of $8 per room. Multiple dogs may be allowed.

Days Inn
3381 E Andy Devine
Kingman, AZ
928-757-7337 (800-329-7466)
Dogs of all sizes are allowed. There is a $10 per night pet fee per pet. 2 dogs may be allowed.

Days Inn Kingman/West
3023 Andy Devine
Kingman, AZ
928-753-7500 (800-329-7466)
Dogs of all sizes are allowed. There is a $10 one time per pet fee per visit. 2 dogs may be allowed.

Mohave Inn
3016 E Andy Devine
Kingman, AZ
928-753-9555
Dogs of all sizes are allowed. There is a $5 per night per pet additional fee. Multiple dogs may be allowed.

Motel 6 - Kingman East

3351 East Andy Devine Avenue
Kingman, AZ
928-757-7151 (800-466-8356)
One well-behaved family pet per room. Guest must notify front desk upon arrival. Guest is liable for any damages. In consideration of all guests, pets must never be left unattended in the guest rooms.

Motel 6 - Kingman West
424 West Beale Street
Kingman, AZ
928-753-9222 (800-466-8356)
One well-behaved family pet per room. Guest must notify front desk upon arrival. Guest is liable for any damages. In consideration of all guests, pets must never be left unattended in the guest rooms.

Quality Inn
1400 E Andy Devine Avenue
Kingman, AZ
928-753-4747 (877-424-6423)
Dogs are allowed for an additional fee of $10 per night per pet. Multiple dogs may be allowed.

Super 8 Kingman
3401 E Andy Devine Ave
Kingman, AZ
928-757-4808 (800-800-8000)
Dogs of all sizes are allowed. There is a $10 one time per pet fee per visit. Smoking and non-smoking rooms are available for pet rooms. 2 dogs may be allowed.

Best Western Lake Place Inn
31 Wings Loop
Lake Havasu, AZ
928-855-2146 (800-780-7234)
Dogs are allowed for an additional fee of $7.50 per night per pet. Dogs may not be left alone in the room at any time. Multiple dogs may be allowed.

Motel 6 - Lake Havasu City
2176 Birch Square
Lake Havasu, AZ
928-855-5566 (800-466-8356)
One well-behaved family pet per room. Guest must notify front desk upon arrival. Guest is liable for any damages. In consideration of all guests, pets must never be left unattended in the guest rooms.

Hampton Inn
245 London Bridge Rd
Lake Havasu City, AZ
928-855-4071
Dogs of all sizes are allowed. There is a $25 per night per room fee, the rooms are on the 1st and 4th floors,

and dogs are not to be left alone in the room. Multiple dogs may be allowed.

Island Inn Hotel
1300 W McCulloch Blvd
Lake Havasu City, AZ
928-680-0606 (800-243-9955)
rentor.com/hotels/islanlin.htm
There is a $10 per day pet charge.

Motel 6 - Lake Havasu City Airport
111 London Bridge Road
Lake Havasu City, AZ
928-855-3200 (800-466-8356)
One well-behaved family pet per room. Guest must notify front desk upon arrival. Guest is liable for any damages. In consideration of all guests, pets must never be left unattended in the guest rooms.

The Wigwam Golf Resort & Spa
300 Wigwam Blvd.
Litchfield Park, AZ
623-935-3811
Dogs up to 80 pounds are allowed for no additional pet fees. Dogs must be crated when left alone in the room.

Motel 6 - Tucson North
4630 West Ina Road
Marana, AZ
520-744-9300 (800-466-8356)
One well-behaved family pet per room. Guest must notify front desk upon arrival. Guest is liable for any damages. In consideration of all guests, pets must never be left unattended in the guest rooms.

Arizona Golf Resort
425 S Power Road
Mesa, AZ
480-832-3202
azgolfresort.com/
There are no additional pet charges.

Best Western Mesa Inn
1625 E Main (Apache Trail)
Mesa, AZ
480-964-8000 (800-780-7234)
Dogs are allowed for an additional one time pet fee of $20 per room. Multiple dogs may be allowed.

Best Western Mezona Inn
250 West Main ST
Mesa, AZ
480-834-9233 (800-780-7234)
Dogs up to 50 pounds are allowed for an additional one time pet fee of $20 per room. 2 dogs may be allowed.

Best Western Superstition Springs

Inn
1342 S Power Road
Mesa, AZ
480-641-1164 (800-780-7234)
Dogs are allowed for an additional fee of $10 per night per pet. 2 dogs may be allowed.

Days Inn Mesa Country Club
333 West Juanita Ave
Mesa, AZ
480-844-8900 (800-329-7466)
Dogs of all sizes are allowed. There is a $10 one time per pet fee per visit. 2 dogs may be allowed.

Homestead Village
1920 W Isabella
Mesa, AZ
480-752-2266
There is a $75 one time pet fee.

Motel 6 - Phoenix Mesa - Country Club Dr
336 West Hampton Avenue
Mesa, AZ
480-844-8899 (800-466-8356)
One well-behaved family pet per room. Guest must notify front desk upon arrival. Guest is liable for any damages. In consideration of all guests, pets must never be left unattended in the guest rooms.

Motel 6 - Phoenix Mesa - Main St
630 West Main Street
Mesa, AZ
480-969-8111 (800-466-8356)
One well-behaved family pet per room. Guest must notify front desk upon arrival. Guest is liable for any damages. In consideration of all guests, pets must never be left unattended in the guest rooms.

Motel 6 - Phoenix Mesa - US 60
1511 South Country Club Drive
Mesa, AZ
480-834-0066 (800-466-8356)
One well-behaved family pet per room. Guest must notify front desk upon arrival. Guest is liable for any damages. In consideration of all guests, pets must never be left unattended in the guest rooms.

Residence Inn by Marriott
941 W. Grove Ave.
Mesa, AZ
480-610-0100
Dogs up to 100 pounds are welcome. There is a $75 one time fee, and a pet policy to sign at check in. 2 dogs may be allowed.

Sleep Inn
6347 E Southern Avenue

Mesa, AZ
480-807-7760 (877-424-6423)
Dogs up to 50 pounds are allowed for an additional pet fee per room of $25 for the 1st night and $10 for each additional night. 2 dogs may be allowed.

Holiday Inn Express Hotel & Suites Nogales
850 W. Shell Road
Nogales, AZ
520-281-0123 (877-270-6405)
Dogs of all sizes are allowed for an additional fee of $50 per night per pet. 2 dogs may be allowed.

Motel 6 - Nogales
141 W Mariposa Road
Nogales, AZ
520-281-2951 (800-466-8356)
One well-behaved family pet per room. Guest must notify front desk upon arrival. Guest is liable for any damages. In consideration of all guests, pets must never be left unattended in the guest rooms.

Best Western Arizonainn
716 Rimview Dr
Page, AZ
928-645-2466 (800-780-7234)
Dogs up to 60 pounds are allowed for an additional fee of $10 per night per pet. 2 dogs may be allowed.

Days Inn Lake Powell
961 N Hwy 89
Page, AZ
928-645-2800 (800-329-7466)
Dogs of all sizes are allowed. There is a $10 per night pet fee per pet. 2 dogs may be allowed.

Motel 6 - Page
P.O. Box 4450
Page, AZ
928-645-5888 (800-466-8356)
One well-behaved family pet per room. Guest must notify front desk upon arrival. Guest is liable for any damages. In consideration of all guests, pets must never be left unattended in the guest rooms.

Quality Inn at Lake Powell
287 N Lake Powell Blvd
Page, AZ
928-645-8851 (877-424-6423)
Dogs are allowed for no additional pet fee. 2 dogs may be allowed.

Wahweap Lodge and Marina
100 Lakeshore Drive
Page, AZ
928-645-2433
The lodge offers a fine dining

restaurant, gift shop, pool, lounge, and spectacular views of Lake Powell. Pets are allowed for an additional fee of $20 per night per room. Pets must be on a leash at all times when outside the room, and they are not to be left unattended or tied up outside on the patio or balcony. Dogs must be attended to or removed for housekeeping. If your pet is accustomed to being on the bed, they request you ask for a sheet to put over the bedspread. There is also a marina on site where they rent watercraft. Your pet may join you on a boat ride if you rent an 18' or 19' personal craft, as they are not allowed on the tour boats.

Hermosa Inn
5532 N Palo Cristi Rd
Paradise Valley, AZ
602-955-8614
hermosainn.com/home.asp
There is a $50 refundable pet deposit.

Best Western Parker Inn
1012 Geronimo Ave
Parker, AZ
928-669-6060 (800-780-7234)
Dogs are allowed for no additional pet fee. Multiple dogs may be allowed.

Motel 6 - Parker
604 California Avenue
Parker, AZ
928-669-2133 (800-466-8356)
One well-behaved family pet per room. Guest must notify front desk upon arrival. Guest is liable for any damages. In consideration of all guests, pets must never be left unattended in the guest rooms.

Best Western Payson Inn
801 N Beeline Hwy
Payson, AZ
928-474-3241 (800-780-7234)
Dogs are allowed for an additional pet fee of $25 per night per room. Multiple dogs may be allowed.

Motel 6 - Payson
101 West Phoenix Street
Payson, AZ
928-474-4526 (800-466-8356)
One well-behaved family pet per room. Guest must notify front desk upon arrival. Guest is liable for any damages. In consideration of all guests, pets must never be left unattended in the guest rooms.

Comfort Suites Peoria Sports Complex

8473 W Paradise Lane
Peoria, AZ
623-334-3993 (877-424-6423)
Dogs up to 50 pounds are allowed for an additional one time pet fee of $50 per room. 2 dogs may be allowed.

Holiday Inn Express Hotel & Suites
16771 N. 84th Avenue
Peoria, AZ
623-853-1313 (877-270-6405)
Dogs of all sizes are allowed for no additional fee. There is a pet agreement to sign at check in. 2 dogs may be allowed.

La Quinta Inn & Suites Phoenix West Peoria
16321 North 83rd Ave.
Peoria, AZ
623-487-1900 (800-531-5900)
Dogs of all sizes are allowed. There are no additional pet fees. Dogs must be leashed and cleaned up after. Multiple dogs may be allowed.

Best Western Bell Hotel
17211 N Black Canyon Hwy
Phoenix, AZ
602-993-8300 (800-780-7234)
Dogs are allowed for an additional fee of $10 per night per pet; the weekly rate is $30 per pet. Multiple dogs may be allowed.

Candlewood Suites
11411 North Black Canyon Highway
Phoenix, AZ
602-861-4900 (877-270-6405)
Dogs up to 80 pounds are allowed for an additional pet fee of $75 for up to 13 days and $150 for 14 days and over per room. 2 dogs may be allowed.

Clarion Hotel Phoenix Tech Center
5121 E La Puenta Avenue
Phoenix, AZ
480-893-3900 (877-424-6423)
Dogs are allowed for an additional one time pet fee of $25 per room. Multiple dogs may be allowed.

Comfort Inn
1711 W Bell Road
Phoenix, AZ
602-866-2089 (877-424-6423)
Dogs are allowed for an additional one time pet fee of $35 per room. 2 dogs may be allowed.

Comfort Inn
5050 N Black Canyon H
Phoenix, AZ
602-242-8011 (877-424-6423)
Dogs are allowed for an additional

one time pet fee of $35 per room. 2 dogs may be allowed.

Crowne Plaza
2532 W. Peoria Ave
Phoenix, AZ
602-943-2341 (877-270-6405)
Dogs of all sizes are allowed for an additional one time fee of $25 per pet, and they must be crated when left alone in the room. 2 dogs may be allowed.

Crowne Plaza
4300 E. Washington St
Phoenix, AZ
602-273-7778 (877-270-6405)
Dogs up to 50 pounds are allowed for an additional $50 one time fee per room. 2 dogs may be allowed.

Days Inn Phoenix Airport
3333 E Van Buren
Phoenix, AZ
602-244-8244 (800-329-7466)
Dogs of all sizes are allowed. There is a $20 one time per pet fee per visit. 2 dogs may be allowed.

Embassy Suites Hotel Phoenix - Biltmore
2630 E. Camelback
Phoenix, AZ
602-955-3992
Dogs up to 50 pounds are allowed. There is a $25 one time pet fee per visit. Dogs are not allowed to be left alone in the room.

Hilton
10 East Thomas Road
Phoenix, AZ
602-222-1111
Dogs up to 50 pounds are allowed for no additional pet fee with a credit card on file; there is a $50 refundable deposit if paying by cash. 2 dogs may be allowed.

Hilton
7677 North 16th Street
Phoenix, AZ
602-997-2626
Dogs up to 75 pounds are allowed for a $75 refundable deposit per pet. Multiple dogs may be allowed.

Hilton
11111 North 7th Street
Phoenix, AZ
602-866-7500
Dogs of all sizes are allowed. There is a $75 refundable deposit and a pet policy to sign at check in. 2 dogs may be allowed.

Holiday Inn - West

1500 N 51st Ave
Phoenix, AZ
602-484-9009 (877-270-6405)
Dogs of all sizes are allowed for an additional $25 one time fee per pet; dogs not may not be left alone in the room. 2 dogs may be allowed.

La Quinta Inn Phoenix Sky Harbor Airport North
4727 E Thomas Rd
Phoenix, AZ
602-956-6500 (800-531-5900)
Dogs of all sizes are allowed. There are no additional pet fees. Dogs must be leashed and cleaned up after. Please put the "Do Not Disturb" sign on the door if there is a dog alone in the room. Multiple dogs may be allowed.

La Quinta Inn Phoenix Thomas Road
2725 N. Black Canyon Hwy.
Phoenix, AZ
602-258-6271 (800-531-5900)
Dogs of all sizes are allowed. Dogs must be well behaved, leashed, and cleaned up after. Multiple dogs may be allowed.

Lexington Hotel at City Square
100 W Clarendon Ave
Phoenix, AZ
602-279-9811
There is a $100 refundable deposit required for dogs.

Motel 6 - Phoenix - Black Canyon
4130 North Black Canyon Highway
Phoenix, AZ
602-277-5501 (800-466-8356)
One well-behaved family pet per room. Guest must notify front desk upon arrival. Guest is liable for any damages. In consideration of all guests, pets must never be left unattended in the guest rooms.

Motel 6 - Phoenix - Sweetwater
2735 West Sweetwater Avenue
Phoenix, AZ
602-942-5030 (800-466-8356)
One well-behaved family pet per room. Guest must notify front desk upon arrival. Guest is liable for any damages. In consideration of all guests, pets must never be left unattended in the guest rooms.

Motel 6 - Phoenix Airport
214 South 24th Street
Phoenix, AZ
602-244-1155 (800-466-8356)
One well-behaved family pet per room. Guest must notify front desk upon arrival. Guest is liable for any damages. In consideration of all

guests, pets must never be left unattended in the guest rooms.

Motel 6 - Phoenix East
5315 East Van Buren Street
Phoenix, AZ
602-267-8555 (800-466-8356)
One well-behaved family pet per room. Guest must notify front desk upon arrival. Guest is liable for any damages. In consideration of all guests, pets must never be left unattended in the guest rooms.

Motel 6 - Phoenix North - Bell Rd
2330 West Bell Road
Phoenix, AZ
602-993-2353 (800-466-8356)
One well-behaved family pet per room. Guest must notify front desk upon arrival. Guest is liable for any damages. In consideration of all guests, pets must never be left unattended in the guest rooms.

Motel 6 - Phoenix Northern Avenue
8152 North Black Canyon Highway
Phoenix, AZ
602-995-7592 (800-466-8356)
One well-behaved family pet per room. Guest must notify front desk upon arrival. Guest is liable for any damages. In consideration of all guests, pets must never be left unattended in the guest rooms.

Motel 6 - Phoenix West
1530 North 52nd Drive
Phoenix, AZ
602-272-0220 (800-466-8356)
One well-behaved family pet per room. Guest must notify front desk upon arrival. Guest is liable for any damages. In consideration of all guests, pets must never be left unattended in the guest rooms.

Pointe Hilton Squaw Peak Resort
7677 N 16th Street
Phoenix, AZ
602-997-2626 (800-947-9784)
pointehilton.com/
Offering the best in luxury accommodations, this award-winning resort features a variety of fun activities and amenities for the business and leisure travelers. The amenities include 563 well appointed suites, 48,000 square feet of meeting space, 3 restaurants, a putting course, gaming courts, and a 9-acre waterpark. Dogs of all sizes are welcome. There is a refundable room deposit of $50 for small dogs, $75 for medium dogs, and $100 for large dogs. Dogs must be leashed and cleaned up after at all times, and they must be removed or crated for

housekeeping. 2 dogs may be allowed.

Pointe Hilton Tapatio Cliffs
11111 N 7th Street
Phoenix, AZ
602-866-7500 (800-947-9784)
pointehilton.com/
Nestled atop a desert mountain preserve with miles of scenic trails, this award winning resort features variety of fun activities and amenities for the business and leisure travelers, and is also home to the Lookout Mountain Golf Club. Some of the amenities include 547 elegantly appointed suites, 65,000 square feet of meeting space, 5 restaurants, a golf instruction academy, and a 3 1/2 acre water wonderland village. Dogs of all sizes are allowed for a $75 refundable deposit. Dogs must be leashed and cleaned up after at all times, and they must be removed or crated for housekeeping. 2 dogs may be allowed.

Red Roof Inn - Phoenix - Camelback
502 Camelback Road
Phoenix, AZ
602-264-9290 (800-RED-ROOF)
One well-behaved family pet per room. Guest must notify front desk upon arrival. Guest is liable for any damages. In consideration of all guests, pets must never be left unattended in the guest rooms.

Red Roof Inn - Phoenix Bell Road
17222 North Black Canyon Freeway
Phoenix, AZ
602-866-1049 (800-RED-ROOF)
One well-behaved family pet per room. Guest must notify front desk upon arrival. Guest is liable for any damages. In consideration of all guests, pets must never be left unattended in the guest rooms.

Red Roof Inn - Phoenix West
5215 West Willetta Street
Phoenix, AZ
602-233-8004 (800-RED-ROOF)
One Dog up to 80 pounds is allowed. There are no additional pet fees.

Residence Inn by Marriott
8242 N. Black Canyon Freeway
Phoenix, AZ
602-864-1900
Dogs of all sizes are welcome. There is a $75 one time fee, and a pet policy to sign at check in. 2 dogs may be allowed.

Residence Inn by Marriott
801 N. 44th Street
Phoenix, AZ
602-273-7221
Dogs up to medium size are welcome. There is a $75 per stay fee, and a pet policy to sign at check in. 2 dogs may be allowed.

Sheraton Crescent Hotel
2620 West Dunlop Avenue
Phoenix, AZ
602-943-8200 (888-625-5144)
Dogs up tp 60 pounds are allowed. There are no additional pet fees. Dogs are not allowed to be left alone in the room.

Sleep Inn Airport
2621 S 47th Place
Phoenix, AZ
480-967-7100 (877-424-6423)
Dogs up to 50 pounds are allowed for an additional one time pet fee of $25 per room. 2 dogs may be allowed.

Studio 6 - PHOENIX - DEER VALLEY
18405 North 27th Avenue
Phoenix, AZ
602-843-1151 (800-466-8356)
One well-behaved family pet per room. Guest must notify front desk upon arrival. Guest is liable for any damages. In consideration of all guests, pets must never be left unattended in the guest rooms.

Super 8 Phoenix/West I-10
1242 N 53rd Ave
Phoenix, AZ
602-415-0888 (800-800-8000)
Dogs of all sizes are allowed. There is a $15 per night pet fee per pet. Smoking and non-smoking rooms are available for pet rooms. 2 dogs may be allowed.

TownePlace Suites Phoenix Metrocenter Mall/I-17
9425 N Black Canyon Freeway
Phoenix, AZ
602-943-9510
Dogs of all sizes are allowed. There is a $75 one time pet fee per visit. 2 dogs may be allowed.

Best Western Inn of Pinetop
404 E White Mountain Boulevard
Pinetop, AZ
928-367-6667 (800-780-7234)
Dogs are allowed for an additional fee of $10 per night per pet. Multiple dogs may be allowed.

Buck Springs Resort
6126 Buck Springs Road
Pinetop, AZ
928-369-3554 (800-339-1909)
buckspringsresort.com/
Sitting on 20 acres of tall pines offering lots of hiking trails, this scenic resort features 20 one bedroom cottages and 4 three bedroom townhouses around a wonderful courtyard area with benches and a small raised pavilion. There are barbecues available, and all units have a covered front porch, cable TV, a wood burning stove, and are fully equipped with all the essentials, including the kitchen. Dogs of all sizes are allowed for an additional fee of $10 per night per pet, and they must be declared at the time of reservations. Dogs may only be left alone in the room if they will be well behaved and quiet, and they must be leashed and cleaned up after at all times. Multiple dogs may be allowed.

Holiday Inn Express
431E. White Mountain Blvd
Pinetop, AZ
928-367-6077 (877-270-6405)
Dogs of all sizes are allowed for an additional fee of $10 per night per pet. 2 dogs may be allowed.

Apple Creek Cottages
1001 White Spar
Prescott, AZ
928-445-7321 (888-455-8003)
applecreekcottages.com
These pet-friendly cottages are one, two or three bedrooms. Pets are allowed with a refundable $35.00 deposit.

Best Western Prescottonian
1317 E Gurley Street
Prescott, AZ
928-445-3096 (800-780-7234)
Dogs are allowed for an additional pet fee of $10 per night per room. Multiple dogs may be allowed.

Comfort Inn Ponderosa Pines
1290 White Spar Road
Prescott, AZ
928-778-5770 (877-424-6423)
Dogs up to 50 pounds are allowed for an additional fee of $10 per night per pet. 2 dogs may be allowed.

Lynx Creek Farm Bed and Breakfast
SR69 and Onyx Rd
Prescott, AZ
928-778-9573
There is an additional $10 per day pet fee. Pets may not be left in the room unattended.

Motel 6 - Prescott
1111 East Sheldon Street
Prescott, AZ
928-776-0160 (800-466-8356)
One well-behaved family pet per room. Guest must notify front desk upon arrival. Guest is liable for any damages. In consideration of all guests, pets must never be left unattended in the guest rooms.

Quality Inn and Suites Convention Center
4499 H 69
Prescott, AZ
928-777-0770 (877-424-6423)
Dogs are allowed for an additional pet fee per room of $40 for 1 or 2 days, and $10 for each additional day. 2 dogs may be allowed.

Super 8 Motel - Prescott
1105 E. Sheldon Street
Prescott, AZ
928-776-1282 (800-800-8000)
innworks.com/prescott
There is a $10 per stay additional pet fee. Up to three dogs are permitted in each room. The hotel allows a free 8 minute long distance call each night and offers a free continental breakfast. There is a pool and a laundry. On Sheldon St (BR 89), West of intersection of US 89 & AZ 69.

Days Inn Prescott
7875 E Hwy 69
Prescott Valley, AZ
928-772-8600 (800-329-7466)
Dogs of all sizes are allowed. There is a $50 returnable deposit required per room. 2 dogs may be allowed.

Motel 6 - Prescott Valley
8383 East US Route 69
Prescott Valley, AZ
928-772-2200 (800-466-8356)
One well-behaved family pet per room. Guest must notify front desk upon arrival. Guest is liable for any damages. In consideration of all guests, pets must never be left unattended in the guest rooms.

Super 8 Quartzsite
2050 Dome Rock Rd
Quartzsite, AZ
928-927-8080 (800-800-8000)
Dogs of all sizes are allowed. There is a $5 per night pet fee per pet. Smoking and non-smoking rooms are available for pet rooms. 2 dogs may be allowed.

Best Western Desert Inn

1391 Thatcher Blvd
Safford, AZ
928-428-0521 (800-780-7234)
Dogs up to 60 pounds are allowed for an additional fee of $6 per night per pet. Multiple dogs may be allowed.

Days Inn Safford
520 E Hwy 70
Safford, AZ
928-428-5000 (800-329-7466)
Dogs of all sizes are allowed. There is a $10 per night pet fee per pet. 2 dogs may be allowed.

Quality Inn and Suites
420 E H 70
Safford, AZ
928-428-3200 (877-424-6423)
Dogs are allowed for an additional fee of $20 per night per pet. Multiple dogs may be allowed.

3 Palms Resort Oasis Scottsdale
7707 E. McDowell Rd
Scottsdale, AZ
800-450-6013
scottsdale-resort-hotels.com
The hotel is located directly on El Dorado Park with miles of lakes and lawns. The hotel is near Old Town Scottsdale. Hotel provides rooms and suites, some with full kitchens.

Caleo Resort and Spa
4925 N Scottsdale Road
Scottsdale, AZ
480-945-7666 (800-528-7867)
caleoresort.com/
This boutique style luxury resort and spa creates a tropical ambiance with its lush garden courtyard, open-air architecture, and the Mediterranean-inspired lagoon and sandy beach pool surrounded by cabanas. Other features/amenities include a contemporary American bistro with indoor and outdoor dining, room service, and a hosted evening wine hour. Dogs of all sizes are allowed for no additional fee. Dogs must be well mannered, and leashed and cleaned up after at all times. 2 dogs may be allowed.

Camelback Inn-JW Marriott Resort & Spa
5402 E Lincoln Drive
Scottsdale, AZ
480-948-1700 (800-24-CAMEL (242-2635))
Dogs of all sizes are allowed. There are no additional pet fees. Dogs must be leashed, cleaned up after, and removed or crated for housekeeping. 2 dogs may be allowed.

Comfort Suites Old Town Scottsdale
3275 N Drinkwater Blvd
Scottsdale, AZ
480-946-1111 (877-424-6423)
Dogs are allowed for no additional pet fee. There may be 1 large or 2 small dogs per room. 2 dogs may be allowed.

Country Inns & Suites by Carlson
10801 N 89th Place
Scottsdale, AZ
480-314-1200
Dogs of all sizes are allowed. There is a $50 one time additional pet fee.

Firesky Resort and Spa
4925 North Scottsdale Rd
Scottsdale, AZ
480-945-7666
This Kimpton boutique hotel allows dogs of all sizes. It is located in the heart of Old Towne. There are no additional pet fees.

Hampton Inn
4415 N Civic Center Plaza
Scottsdale, AZ
480-942-9400
Dogs of all sizes are allowed. There is a $50 one time fee per stay. Multiple dogs may be allowed.

Homestead Village
3560 N Marshall Way
Scottsdale, AZ
480-994-0297
There is a $75 one time pet fee.

Hotel Indigo Scottsdale
4415 N. Civic Center Plaza
Scottsdale, AZ
480-941-9400
ScottsdaleHipHotel.com
This pet-friendly luxury hotel has no weight limit and no additional pet fees. Guest rooms have hardwood floors and there are a number of amenities, a lounge and a restaurant.

Inn at the Citadel
8700 E Pinnacle Peak Rd
Scottsdale, AZ
480-585-6133
This B&B is located in an adobe-like complex of stores and next to the foothills of Pinnacle Peak. There are no additional pet fees.

La Quinta Inn & Suites Phoenix Scottsdale
8888 E. Shea Blvd.
Scottsdale, AZ
480-614-5300 (800-531-5900)
Dogs of all sizes are allowed. There are no additional pet fees. Dogs may

not be left unattended, and they must be leashed and cleaned up after. Multiple dogs may be allowed.

Motel 6 - Scottsdale
6848 E Camelback Road
Scottsdale, AZ
480-946-2280 (800-466-8356)
One well-behaved family pet per room. Guest must notify front desk upon arrival. Guest is liable for any damages. In consideration of all guests, pets must never be left unattended in the guest rooms.

Residence Inn by Marriott
6040 N. Scottsdale Road
Scottsdale, AZ
480-948-8666
Dogs of any size are welcome. There is a $75 one time fee, and a pet policy to sign at check in. 2 dogs may be allowed.

Scottsdale Marriott at McDowell Mountains
16770 N Perimeter Drive
Scottsdale, AZ
480-502-3836 (800-288-6127)
Dogs up to 50 pounds are allowed. There is a $50 per night per room additional pet fee. Dogs may not be left alone in the room, and they must be leashed and cleaned up after. 2 dogs may be allowed.

Sleep Inn
16330 N Scottsdale Road
Scottsdale, AZ
480-998-9211 (877-424-6423)
Dogs up to 75 pounds are allowed for an additional fee of $10 per night per pet. Multiple dogs may be allowed.

The Inn at Pima
7330 N Pima Rd
Scottsdale, AZ
480-948-3800
There is a $10 per night additional pet fee. Dogs are not allowed in the lobby.

TownePlace Suites Scottsdale
10740 N 90th Street
Scottsdale, AZ
480-551-1100
Dogs of all sizes are allowed. There is a $75 one time pet fee per visit. 2 dogs may be allowed.

Best Western Inn of Sedona
1200 Hwy 89A
Sedona, AZ
928-282-3072 (800-780-7234)
Dogs are allowed for an additional pet fee of $20 per night per room.

Multiple dogs may be allowed.

El Portal - Sedona's Luxury Hacienda
95 Portal Lane
Sedona, AZ
928-203-9405 (800-313-0017)
elPortalsedona.com
There are five pet rooms at this 1910 adobe hacienda located in the center of Sedona. Pets are allowed for a $35 non-refundable cleaning fee.

Hilton
90 Ridge Trail Drive
Sedona, AZ
928-284-4040
Dogs up to 50 pounds are allowed for a $50 one time pet fee per room. 2 dogs may be allowed.

Kings Ransom Sedona Hotel
771 H 179
Sedona, AZ
928-282-7151 (800-846-6164)
kingsransomsedona.com/
Set on 8 scenic acres with superb views, this luxury boutique hotel also provides a great location for world class shopping, visiting art galleries, and numerous recreational activities. Some of the amenities include a 1-acre garden courtyard with a waterfall, a vast wilderness area behind the hotel for some great hiking adventures, an eatery, and all the rooms have a private balcony or patio. Dogs of all sizes are allowed for an additional fee of $15 per night per pet. Dogs must be well mannered, leashed and cleaned up after at all times, and they must be removed or crated for housekeeping. Directly adjacent to the property, the hotel created a Doggy Park complete with plastic bags and a receptacle for disposal. They ask that dogs are not walked in the courtyard, rather at the Doggy Park or on the trails behind the hotel.

Matterhorn Motor Lodge
230 Apple Ave
Sedona, AZ
928-282-7176
sedona.net/hotel/matterhorn/
This inn is located in the center of uptown Sedona.

Oak Creek Terrace Resort
4548 N. Hwy. 89A
Sedona, AZ
928-282-3562 (800-224-2229)
oakcreekterrace.com
Relax by the creek or in one of the Jacuzzi rooms. Dogs are welcome with a $35 non-refundable pet fee. Amenities include in-room fireplaces, barbecue and picnic areas, air

conditioning and cable TV.

Quail Ridge Resort
120 Canyon Circle Dr
Sedona, AZ
928-284-9327
quailridgeresort.com/
There is a $10 per day pet fee.

Sedona Rouge Hotel & Spa
2250 West Hwy 89A
Sedona, AZ
928-203-4111 (866-312-4111)
sedonarouge.com
Dogs up to 50 pounds are allowed at this chic hotel in West Sedona. There is a $100 refundable damage deposit and a $50 non-refundable cleaning fee. The hotel offers the Rouge & Pooch Package for each pet.

Sky Ranch Lodge
Airport Rd
Sedona, AZ
928-282-6400 (888-708-6400)
skyranchlodge.com/
There is a $10.00 per day pet fee, dogs up to 75 pounds ok.

The Views Inn Sedona
65 E Cortez Drive
Sedona, AZ
928-284-2487
A convenient location, clean, comfortable, and affordable, this inn also offers a pool, spa, and great views. Dogs of all sizes are allowed. There is a $10 per night per pet additional fee. Dogs must be leashed and cleaned up after. 2 dogs may be allowed.

Best Western Paint Pony Lodge
581 W Deuce of Clubs
Show Low, AZ
928-537-5773 (800-780-7234)
Dogs are allowed for an additional fee of $10 per night per pet. Multiple dogs may be allowed.

Days Inn Show Low
480 W Deuce of Clubs
Show Low, AZ
928-537-4356 (800-329-7466)
Dogs of all sizes are allowed. There is a $10 one time per pet fee per visit. 2 dogs may be allowed.

Motel 6 - Show Low
1941 East Duece of Clubs
Show Low, AZ
928-537-7694 (800-466-8356)
One well-behaved family pet per room. Guest must notify front desk upon arrival. Guest is liable for any damages. In consideration of all

guests, pets must never be left unattended in the guest rooms.

Sleep Inn
1751 W Deuce of Clubs
Show Low, AZ
928-532-7323 (877-424-6423)
Dogs are allowed for an additional fee of $15 (plus tax) per night per pet. 2 dogs may be allowed.

Best Western Mission Inn
3460 E Fry Blvd
Sierra Vista, AZ
520-458-8500 (800-780-7234)
Dogs are allowed for an additional fee of $10 per night per pet. Dogs may not be left alone in the room alone at any time. Multiple dogs may be allowed.

Candlewood Suites Sierra Vista
1904 S. Highway 92
Sierra Vista, AZ
520-439-8200 (877-270-6405)
Dogs up to 80 pounds are allowed for an additional $50 one time fee per pet. 2 dogs may be allowed.

Motel 6 - Sierra Vista - Fort Huachuca
1551 East Fry Boulevard
Sierra Vista, AZ
520-459-5035 (800-466-8356)
One well-behaved family pet per room. Guest must notify front desk upon arrival. Guest is liable for any damages. In consideration of all guests, pets must never be left unattended in the guest rooms.

Quality Inn
1631 S H 92
Sierra Vista, AZ
520-458-7900 (877-424-6423)
Dogs are allowed for an additional fee of $10 per night per pet. Multiple dogs may be allowed.

Super 8 Motel - Sierra Vista
100 Fab Avenue
Sierra Vista, AZ
520-459-5380 (800-800-8000)
innworks.com/sierravista
There is a $10 per stay additional pet fee. Up to three dogs are permitted in each room. The hotel allows a free 8 minute long distance call each night and offers a free continental breakfast. Children 12 and under are free.There is a pool and a laundry. I-10, Exit 302, straight on Buffalo Soldier Trail, 30 miles, through light to Fry Blvd.; Left 1 blk.

Hampton Inn

14783 W Grand Avenue
Surprise, AZ
623-537-9122
Dogs of all sizes are allowed. There is a $50 one time fee and a pet policy to sign at check in. They also request you kennel your pet when out. Multiple dogs may be allowed.

Quality Inn and Suites
16741 N Greasewood Street
Surprise, AZ
623-583-3500 (877-424-6423)
Dogs under 20 pounds are allowed for an additional fee of $10 per night per pet; the fee is $25 per night per pet for dogs over 20 pounds. 2 dogs may be allowed.

Comfort Inn and Suites
1031 E Apache Blvd
Tempe, AZ
480-966-7202 (877-424-6423)
Dogs are allowed for an additional one time pet fee of $25 per room. Multiple dogs may be allowed.

Country Inns & Suites by Carlson
1660 W Elliot Rd
Tempe, AZ
480-345-8585
Dogs of all sizes are allowed. There is a $55 additional pet fee every two nights. There is a $250 pet fee for stays over two weeks.

Hampton Inn
1429 N Scottsdale Road
Tempe, AZ
480-675-9799
Dogs of all sizes are allowed. There is a $50 per pet per stay fee and dogs are not to be left alone in the room. 2 dogs may be allowed.

Holiday Inn Express Hotel & Suites Tempe
1520 West Baseline Rd.
Tempe, AZ
480-831-9800 (877-270-6405)
Dogs of all sizes are allowed for an additional $10 per night per pet. A contact/cell number must be left if a pet is in the room alone. Multiple dogs may be allowed.

Motel 6 - Phoenix Tempe - Arizona State U
1612 North Scottsdale Road
Tempe, AZ
480-945-9506 (800-466-8356)
One well-behaved family pet per room. Guest must notify front desk upon arrival. Guest is liable for any damages. In consideration of all guests, pets must never be left unattended in the guest rooms.

Motel 6 - Phoenix Tempe - Broadway - ASU
513 West Broadway Road
Tempe, AZ
480-967-8696 (800-466-8356)
One well-behaved family pet per room. Guest must notify front desk upon arrival. Guest is liable for any damages. In consideration of all guests, pets must never be left unattended in the guest rooms.

Motel 6 - Phoenix Tempe - Priest Dr - ASU
1720 South Priest Drive
Tempe, AZ
480-968-4401 (800-466-8356)
All well-behaved dogs are welcome. There are no additional pet fees.

Red Roof Inn - Phoenix Airport
2135 West 15th Street
Tempe, AZ
480-449-3205 (800-RED-ROOF)
One well-behaved family pet per room. Guest must notify front desk upon arrival. Guest is liable for any damages. In consideration of all guests, pets must never be left unattended in the guest rooms.

Residence Inn by Marriott
5075 S. Priest Drive
Tempe, AZ
480-756-2122
Dogs of any size are welcome. There is a $75 one time fee, and a pet policy to sign at check in. 2 dogs may be allowed.

Sheraton Phoenix Airport Hotel Tempe
1600 South 52nd St.
Tempe, AZ
480-967-6600 (888-625-5144)
Dogs up to 75 pounds are allowed. There is a $75 one time refundable pet fee per visit. Dogs are not allowed to be left alone in the room.

Studio 6 - TEMPE
4909 South Wendler Drive
Tempe, AZ
602-414-4470 (800-466-8356)
All well-behaved dogs are welcome. There is a $10 per day pet fee up to a maximum of $50 per visit.

TownePlace Suites Tempe
5223 S Priest Drive
Tempe, AZ
480-345-7889
Dogs of all sizes are allowed. There is a $75 one time pet fee per visit. ₀ 2 dogs may be allowed.

Best Western Lookout Lodge
Hwy 80 W
Tombstone, AZ
520-457-2223 (800-780-7234)
Dogs are allowed for an additional fee of $20 per night per pet. 2 dogs may be allowed.

Trail Rider's Inn
13 N. 7th Street
Tombstone, AZ
520-457-3573 (800-574-0417)
trailridersinn.com
You and your pup can walk to the historic Tombstone district from this inn. They offer large, clean, quiet rooms and cable TV. There is a $5 per day pet fee.

Quality Inn Navajo Nation
Main Street & Moenave Road
Tuba City, AZ
928-283-4545 (877-424-6423)
Dogs up to 50 pounds are allowed for an additional fee of $10 per night per pet. 2 dogs may be allowed.

Best Western Executive Inn
Tucson, AZ
520-791-7551 (800-780-7234)
Dogs are allowed for a $20 one time fee plus an additional fee of $10 per night per pet. 2 dogs may be allowed.

Best Western InnSuites Hotel & Suites
6201 N Oracle Road
Tucson, AZ
520-297-8111 (800-780-7234)
Dogs are allowed for an additional fee one time fee of $50 per pet. 2 dogs may be allowed.

Best Western Las Brisas Hotel-Tucson Airport
7060 S Tucson Boulevard
Tucson, AZ
520-746-0271 (800-780-7234)
Dogs are allowed for an additional fee per pet of $30 for the 1st night and $15 for each additional night. Multiple dogs may be allowed.

Clarion Hotel Randolph Park
102 N Alvernon Way
Tucson, AZ
520-795-0330 (877-424-6423)
Dogs up to 50 pounds are allowed for an additional one time fee of $25 per pet. 2 dogs may be allowed.

Comfort Suites
6935 S Tucson Blvd
Tucson, AZ
520-295-4400 (877-424-6423)
Dogs up to 50 pounds are allowed

for an additional one time fee of $25 per pet. 2 dogs may be allowed.

Comfort Suites at Tucson Mall
515 W Automall Drive
Tucson, AZ
520-888-6676 (877-424-6423)
Dogs up to 50 pounds are allowed for an additional one time fee of $10 per pet. 2 dogs may be allowed.

Country Inns & Suites by Carlson
7411 N Oracle Rd
Tucson, AZ
520-575-9255
Dogs of all sizes are allowed. There is a $20 one time additional pet fee.

Doubletree
445 S Alvernon Way
Tucson, AZ
520-881-4200
Dogs up to 50 pounds are allowed. There is a $25 one time pet fee per room. 2 dogs may be allowed.

Hawthorn Suites Ltd
7007 E Tanque Verde Rd
Tucson, AZ
520-298-2300
There is a $25 pet fee per visit.

Holiday Inn Express
2548 E. Medina Rd.
Tucson, AZ
520-889-6600 (877-270-6405)
Dogs of all sizes are allowed for no additional fee; there is a pet agreement to sign at check in. 2 dogs may be allowed.

La Quinta Inn & Suites Tucson Airport
7001 South Tucson Blvd.
Tucson, AZ
520-573-3333 (800-531-5900)
Dogs of all sizes are allowed. There are no additional pet fees. Dogs must be leashed and cleaned up after. Multiple dogs may be allowed.

La Quinta Inn Tucson Downtown
750 West Starr Pass Blvd
Tucson, AZ
520-624-4455 (800-531-5900)
Dogs of all sizes are allowed. There are no additional pet fees; however, there is a pet waiver to sign at check in. Dogs may not be left unattended, and they must be leashed and cleaned up after. Multiple dogs may be allowed.

La Quinta Inn Tucson East
6404 E. Broadway
Tucson, AZ
520-747-1414 (800-531-5900)

Dogs of all sizes are allowed. There are no additional pet fees. Dogs must be leashed and cleaned up after. Multiple dogs may be allowed.

Lodge on the Desert
306 North Alvernon Way
Tucson, AZ
520-325-3366
lodgeonthedesert.com/
This lodge offers hacienda-style rooms and many have tile covered patios and fireplaces. Amenities include garden pathways, a pool and a restaurant with an outdoor patio where your pooch can join you. Room rates range from $79 to $269 depending on the season or type of room. Rates are subject to change. Pets are welcome for an additional $15 per day pet fee and a $50 refundable pet deposit. Well-behaved dogs of all sizes are welcome. All 35 rooms and suites are non-smoking and dogs are allowed in any of the rooms.

Loews Ventana Canyon Resort
7000 North Resort Drive
Tucson, AZ
520-299-2020
All well-behaved dogs of any size are welcome. This upscale hotel offers their "Loews Loves Pets" program which includes special pet treats, local dog walking routes, and a list of nearby pet-friendly places to visit. There are no pet fees.

Motel 6 - Tucson - 22nd Street
1222 South Freeway
Tucson, AZ
520-624-2516 (800-466-8356)
One well-behaved family pet per room. Guest must notify front desk upon arrival. Guest is liable for any damages. In consideration of all guests, pets must never be left unattended in the guest rooms.

Motel 6 - Tucson - Congress Street
960 S Freeway
Tucson, AZ
520-628-1339 (800-466-8356)
One well-behaved family pet per room. Guest must notify front desk upon arrival. Guest is liable for any damages. In consideration of all guests, pets must never be left unattended in the guest rooms.

Motel 6 - Tucson Airport
1031 East Benson Highway
Tucson, AZ
520-628-1264 (800-466-8356)
One well-behaved family pet per room. Guest must notify front desk upon arrival. Guest is liable for any

damages. In consideration of all guests, pets must never be left unattended in the guest rooms.

Quality Inn Airport
2803 E Valencia Road
Tucson, AZ
520-294-2500 (877-424-6423)
Dogs are allowed for an additional fee of $10 per night per pet. Multiple dogs may be allowed.

Red Roof Inn - Tucson North
4940 West Ina Road
Tucson, AZ
520-744-8199 (800-RED-ROOF)
One well-behaved guest must notify front desk upon arrival. Guest is liable for any damages. In consideration of all guests, pets must never be left unattended in the guest rooms.

Red Roof Inn - Tucson South
3700 East Irvington Road
Tucson, AZ
520-571-1400 (800-RED-ROOF)
One well-behaved family pet per room. Guest must notify front desk upon arrival. Guest is liable for any damages. In consideration of all guests, pets must never be left unattended in the guest rooms.

Residence Inn by Marriott
6477 E. Speedway Blvd
Tucson, AZ
520-721-0991
Dogs of all sizes are welcome. There is a $100 one time fee, and a pet policy to sign at check in. 2 dogs may be allowed.

Sheraton Tucson Hotel & Suites
5151 East Grant Rd.
Tucson, AZ
520-323-6262 (888-625-5144)
Dogs of all sizes are allowed. There are no additional pet fees. Dogs are not allowed to be left alone in the room.

Studio 6 - Tucson - Irvington Rd
4950 S Outlet Center Dr
Tucson, AZ
520-746-0030 (800-466-8356)
One well-behaved family pet per room. Guest must notify front desk upon arrival. Guest is liable for any damages. In consideration of all guests, pets must never be left unattended in the guest rooms.

Super 8 Tucson/Dwtn/University Area
1248 N Stone St
Tucson, AZ

520-622-6446 (800-800-8000)
Dogs of all sizes are allowed. There is a $8 per night pet fee per pet. Smoking and non-smoking rooms are available for pet rooms. 2 dogs may be allowed.

TownePlace Suites Tucson
405 W Rudasill Road
Tucson, AZ
520-292-9697
Dogs of all sizes are allowed. There is a $75 one time pet fee per visit. 2 dogs may be allowed.

Westward Look Resort
245 East Ina Road
Tucson, AZ
520-297-1151 (800-722-2500)
westwardlook.com
This resort comes highly recommended from one of our readers. They said it was the most pet-friendly resort around and they can't say enough good things about it. This former 1912 guest ranch, now a desert resort hideaway, is nestled in the foothills of Tucson's picturesque Santa Catalina Mountains. It offers guests a Southwestern experience on 80 desert acres. They have walking trails at the resort, tennis, swimming pools and much more. Special room rates can be as low as $69 during certain times and seasons. There is a $50 one time additional pet fee.

Windmill Suites
4250 N Campbell Avenue
Tucson, AZ
623-583-0133
Dogs of all sizes are allowed. There are no additional pet fees. Multiple dogs may be allowed.

Best Western Rancho Grande
293 E Wickenburg Way
Wickenburg, AZ
928-684-5445 (800-780-7234)
Dogs are allowed for an additional pet fee of $8 per night per room. Dogs may not be left alone in the room. Multiple dogs may be allowed.

Best Western Plaza Inn
1100 W Rex Allen Dr
Willcox, AZ
520-384-3556 (800-780-7234)
Dogs are allowed for an additional fee of $15 per night per pet. Multiple dogs may be allowed.

Days Inn Willcox
724 N Bisbee Ave
Willcox, AZ
520-384-4222 (800-329-7466)

Dogs of all sizes are allowed. There is a $5 per night pet fee per pet. 2 dogs may be allowed.

Motel 6 - Willcox
921 North Bisbee Avenue
Willcox, AZ
520-384-2201 (800-466-8356)
One well-behaved family pet per room. Guest must notify front desk upon arrival. Guest is liable for any damages. In consideration of all guests, pets must never be left unattended in the guest rooms.

Days Inn Williams
2488 W Rt 66
Williams, AZ
928-635-4051 (800-329-7466)
Dogs of all sizes are allowed. There is a $10 returnable deposit required per room. 2 dogs may be allowed.

Highlander Motel
533 W. Bill Williams Avenue
Williams, AZ
928-635-2541 (800-800-8288)
There is a $5/day pet charge. Room prices are in the $50 range. This motel is about 1 hour from the Grand Canyon.

Holiday Inn
950 N. Grand Canyon Blvd
Williams, AZ
928-635-4114 (877-270-6405)
Dogs of all sizes are allowed for no additional fee. Multiple dogs may be allowed.

Motel 6 - Williams East - Grand Canyon
710 West Bill Williams Avenue
Williams, AZ
928-635-4464 (800-466-8356)
One well-behaved family pet per room. Guest must notify front desk upon arrival. Guest is liable for any damages. In consideration of all guests, pets must never be left unattended in the guest rooms.

Motel 6 - Williams West - Grand Canyon
831 West Route 66
Williams, AZ
928-635-9000 (800-466-8356)
One well-behaved family pet per room. Guest must notify front desk upon arrival. Guest is liable for any damages. In consideration of all guests, pets must never be left unattended in the guest rooms.

Quality Inn Navajo Nation Capitol
48 W H 264
Window Rock, AZ

928-871-4108 (877-424-6423)
Dogs are allowed for no additional fee with a credit card on file; there is a $50 refundable deposit if paying by cash. Multiple dogs may be allowed.

Days Inn Winslow
2035 W Old Hwy Rt 66
Winslow, AZ
928-289-1010 (800-329-7466)
Dogs of all sizes are allowed. There is a $10 one time per pet fee per visit. 2 dogs may be allowed.

Econo Lodge
I40 & Exit 253 North Park Dr
Winslow, AZ
928-289-4687
There is a $5 per day additional pet fee.

La Posada
303 E 2nd Street
Winslow, AZ
928-289-4366
Dogs of all sizes are allowed. There is a $10 one time fee per room and a pet policy to sign at check in. Multiple dogs may be allowed.

Motel 6 - Winslow
520 Desmond Street
Winslow, AZ
928-289-9581 (800-466-8356)
One well-behaved family pet per room. Guest must notify front desk upon arrival. Guest is liable for any damages. In consideration of all guests, pets must never be left unattended in the guest rooms.

Motel 6 - Phoenix Sun City - Youngtown
11133 Grand Avenue
Youngtown, AZ
623-977-1318 (800-466-8356)
One well-behaved family pet per room. Guest must notify front desk upon arrival. Guest is liable for any damages. In consideration of all guests, pets must never be left unattended in the guest rooms.

Best Western Coronado Motor Hotel
233 4th Ave
Yuma, AZ
928-783-4453 (800-780-7234)
Dogs up to 50 pounds are allowed for no additional pet fee. Multiple dogs may be allowed.

Best Western InnSuites Hotel & Suites
1450 S Castle Dome Avenue
Yuma, AZ

928-783-8341 (800-780-7234)
Dogs are allowed for an additional one time pet fee of $50 per room. Multiple dogs may be allowed.

Comfort Inn
1691 S Riley Avenue
Yuma, AZ
928-782-1200 (877-424-6423)
Dogs are allowed for an additional pet fee of $10 per night per room. Multiple dogs may be allowed.

Motel 6 - Yuma - Oldtown
1640 South Arizona Avenue
Yuma, AZ
928-782-6561 (800-466-8356)
One well-behaved family pet per room. Guest must notify front desk upon arrival. Guest is liable for any damages. In consideration of all guests, pets must never be left unattended in the guest rooms.

Motel 6 - Yuma East
1445 East 16th Street
Yuma, AZ
928-782-9521 (800-466-8356)
One well-behaved family pet per room. Guest must notify front desk upon arrival. Guest is liable for any damages. In consideration of all guests, pets must never be left unattended in the guest rooms.

Quality Inn Airport
711 E 32nd Street
Yuma, AZ
928-726-4721 (877-424-6423)
Dogs are allowed for an additional one time pet fee of $25 per room. Multiple dogs may be allowed.

Shilo Inn- Conference Center & Resort Hotel
1550 S Castle Dome Road
Yuma, AZ
928-782-9511
Dogs of all sizes are allowed. There is a $10 per night per pet additional fee. Multiple dogs may be allowed.

Super 8 Yuma
1688 S Riley Ave
Yuma, AZ
928-782-2000 (800-800-8000)
Dogs of all sizes are allowed. There is a $10 per night pet fee per pet. Smoking and non-smoking rooms are available for pet rooms. 2 dogs may be allowed.

Arkansas Listings

Days Inn Alma
250 N US Hwy 71
Alma, AR
479-632-4595 (800-329-7466)
Dogs of all sizes are allowed. There is a $10 one time per pet fee per visit. Multiple dogs may be allowed.

Best Western Continental Inn
136 Valley St
Arkadelphia, AR
870-246-5592 (800-780-7234)
Dogs are allowed for an additional fee of $9 per night per pet. Multiple dogs may be allowed.

Comfort Inn
100 Crystal Palace
Arkadelphia, AR
870-246-3800 (877-424-6423)
Dogs are allowed for an additional fee of $35 per night per pet. Multiple dogs may be allowed.

Days Inn Arkadelphia
137 Valley St
Arkadelphia, AR
870-246-3031 (800-329-7466)
Dogs of all sizes are allowed. There is a $7 per night pet fee per pet. 2 dogs may be allowed.

Motel 6 - Arkadelphia
106 Crystal Palace Drive
Arkadelphia, AR
870-246-6333 (800-466-8356)
One well-behaved family pet per room. Guest must notify front desk upon arrival. Guest is liable for any damages. In consideration of all guests, pets must never be left unattended in the guest rooms.

Super 8 Arkadelphia/Caddo Valley Area
118 Valley
Arkadelphia, AR
870-246-8585 (800-800-8000)
Dogs up to 60 pounds are allowed. There is a $5 per night pet fee per pet. Smoking and non-smoking rooms are available for pet rooms. 2 dogs may be allowed.

Days Inn Beebe
100 Tammy Lane
Beebe, AR
501-882-2008 (800-329-7466)
Dogs of all sizes are allowed. There is a $10 per night pet fee per pet. 2 dogs may be allowed.

Best Western Inn
17036 Interstate 30
Benton, AR
501-778-9695 (800-780-7234)
Dogs are allowed for an additional fee of $6 per night per pet. Multiple dogs may be allowed.

Days Inn Benton
17701 I-30
Benton, AR
501-776-3200 (800-329-7466)
Dogs of all sizes are allowed. There is a $5 per night pet fee per pet. 2 dogs may be allowed.

La Quinta Inn & Suites Bentonville
1001 S.E. Walton
Bentonville, AR
479-271-7555 (800-531-5900)
Dogs of all sizes are allowed. There are no additional pet fees. Dogs may not be left unattended, and they must be leashed and cleaned up after. 2 dogs may be allowed.

TownePlace Suites Bentonville Rogers
3100 SE 14th Street
Bentonville, AR
479-621-0202
Dogs of all sizes are allowed. There is a $75 one time pet fee per visit. 2 dogs may be allowed.

Comfort Inn
1520 E Main Street
Blytheville, AR
870-763-7081 (877-424-6423)
Dogs are allowed for an additional one time pet fee of $15 per room. Multiple dogs may be allowed.

Days Inn Blytheville
102 Porter
Blytheville, AR
870-763-1241 (800-329-7466)
Dogs of all sizes are allowed. There is a $5 per night pet fee per pet. 2 dogs may be allowed.

Pear Tree Inn
239 North Service Road
Blytheville, AR
870-763-2300 (800-378-7946)
Dogs of all sizes are permitted. Pets are not allowed in the breakfast area of the hotel. Pets are not to be left unattended, and each guest must assume liability for damage of property or other guest complaints. There is a limit of one pet per room.

Days Inn Brinkley
2203 N Main St
Brinkley, AR
870-734-1052 (800-329-7466)
Dogs of all sizes are allowed. There is a $5 per night pet fee per pet. 2 dogs may be allowed.

Ivory Inn
I-40 and US Hwy 49N
Brinkley, AR
870-734-4680 (800-800-8000)
Dogs of all sizes are allowed. There is a $5 per night pet fee per pet. Smoking and non-smoking rooms are available for pet rooms. 2 dogs may be allowed.

Days Inn Cabot
1114 W Main St
Cabot, AR
501-843-0145 (800-329-7466)
Dogs of all sizes are allowed. There is a $5 per night pet fee per small pet and $10 per large pet. 2 dogs may be allowed.

Super 8 Cabot
15 Ryeland Drive
Cabot, AR
501-941-3748 (800-800-8000)
Dogs of all sizes are allowed. There is a $5 per night pet fee per pet. Smoking and non-smoking rooms are available for pet rooms. 2 dogs may be allowed.

Holiday Inn Express
1450 US Hwy 278 West
Camden, AR
870-836-8100 (877-270-6405)
Dogs of all sizes are allowed for no additional fee; dogs must be crated or removed for housekeeping. 2 dogs may be allowed.

Super 8 Camden
942 Adams Avenue South
Camden, AR
870-836-2535 (800-800-8000)
Dogs of all sizes are allowed. There is a $10 per night pet fee per pet. Smoking and non-smoking rooms are available for pet rooms. 2 dogs may be allowed.

Best Western Sherwood Motor Inn
I 40 and Exit 58
Clarksville, AR
479-754-7900 (800-780-7234)
Dogs are allowed for no additional pet fee. Multiple dogs may be allowed.

Candlewood Suites Conway
2360 Sanders St.
Conway, AR
501-329-8551 (877-270-6405)
Dogs of all sizes are allowed for an additional $75 one time fee per room. 2 dogs may be allowed.

Days Inn Conway
1002 E Oak St
Conway, AR
501-450-7575 (800-329-7466)
Dogs of all sizes are allowed. There is a $20 one time per pet fee per visit. 2 dogs may be allowed.

Howard Johnson Inn
I-40 & Hwy 65N
Conway, AR
501-329-2961 (800-446-4656)
House dogs up to 60 pounds are ok. There is a $10 one time pet fee.

Motel 6 - Conway
1105 US 65 North
Conway, AR
501-327-6623 (800-466-8356)
One well-behaved family pet per room. Guest must notify front desk upon arrival. Guest is liable for any damages. In consideration of all guests, pets must never be left unattended in the guest rooms.

Quality Inn
150 H 65N
Conway, AR
501-329-0300 (877-424-6423)
Dogs are allowed for an additional one time pet fee of $20 per room. Multiple dogs may be allowed.

Best Western King's Inn Conf Cntr
1920 Junction City Rd
El Dorado, AR
870-862-5191 (800-780-7234)
Dogs are allowed for a $50 refundable pet deposit. Multiple dogs may be allowed.

La Quinta Inn El Dorado
2303 Junction City Road
El Dorado, AR
870-863-6677 (800-531-5900)
Dogs of all sizes are allowed. There are no additional pet fees. There is a pet waiver to sign at check in. Dogs may not be left unattended, and they must be quiet, well behaved, leashed, and cleaned up after. Multiple dogs may be allowed.

Super 8 El Dorado
1925 Junction City Rd
El Dorado, AR
870-862-1000 (800-800-8000)
Dogs of all sizes are allowed. There is a $10 per night pet fee per pet. Smoking and non-smoking rooms are available for pet rooms. 2 dogs may be allowed.

Alpen-Dorf
6554 US 62

Eureka Springs, AR
479-253-9475 (800-771-9876)
There is a $5 per day pet fee.

Colonial Mansion Inn
154 Huntsville Rd
Eureka Springs, AR
479-253-7300 (800-638-2622)
There is a $2 per day pet fee.

Lazee Daze Log Cabin Resort
5432 Hwy 23S
Eureka Springs, AR
866-303-9578
innsite.com/inns/A000303.html
There is a $50 cash deposit required for pets. $30 of this will be refunded by mail if the room is clean. Well-behaved dogs only.

Motel 6 - Eureka Springs
3169 East Van Buren
Eureka Springs, AR
479-253-5600 (800-466-8356)
One well-behaved family pet per room. Guest must notify front desk upon arrival. Guest is liable for any damages. In consideration of all guests, pets must never be left unattended in the guest rooms.

Motel 6 - Fayetteville
2980 North College Avenue
Fayetteville, AR
479-443-4351 (800-466-8356)
One well-behaved family pet per room. Guest must notify front desk upon arrival. Guest is liable for any damages. In consideration of all guests, pets must never be left unattended in the guest rooms.

Red Roof Inn - Fayetteville, AR
1000 South Futrall Drive
Fayetteville, AR
479-442-3041 (800-RED-ROOF)
One well-behaved family pet per room. Guest must notify front desk upon arrival. Guest is liable for any damages. In consideration of all guests, pets must never be left unattended in the guest rooms.

Sleep Inn
728 Millsap Road
Fayetteville, AR
479-587-8700 (877-424-6423)
Dogs are allowed for an additional one time fee of $25 per pet. Multiple dogs may be allowed.

Best Western Colony Inn
2333 N Washington Ave
Forrest City, AR
870-633-0870 (800-780-7234)
Dogs are allowed for no additional pet fee. 2 dogs may be allowed.

Days Inn Forrest City
350 Barrow Hill Rd
Forrest City, AR
870-633-0777 (800-329-7466)
Dogs up to 90 pounds are allowed. There is a $5 per night pet fee per pet. 2 dogs may be allowed.

Holiday Inn
200 Holiday DR
Forrest City, AR
870-633-6300 (877-270-6405)
Dogs of all sizes are allowed for no additional fee. Multiple dogs may be allowed.

Baymont Inn & Suites Fort Smith
2123 Burnham Road
Fort Smith, AR
479-484-5770 (800-531-5900)
Dogs of all sizes are allowed. There are no additional pet fees. Dogs may not be left unattended for long periods, and they must be leashed, cleaned up after, and removed for housekeeping. Multiple dogs may be allowed.

Comfort Inn
2120 Burnham Road
Fort Smith, AR
479-484-0227 (877-424-6423)
Dogs are allowed for no additional pet fee. A contact must be left with the front desk is a pet is in the room alone. Multiple dogs may be allowed.

Days Inn Fort Smith
1021 Garrison Ave
Fort Smith, AR
479-783-0548 (800-329-7466)
Dogs of all sizes are allowed. There is a $5 per night pet fee per pet. 2 dogs may be allowed.

Holiday Inn
700 Rogers Ave
Fort Smith, AR
479-783-1000 (877-270-6405)
Dogs of all sizes are allowed for an additional $25 one time fee per pet. 2 dogs may be allowed.

Holiday Inn Express
6813 Phoenix Ave
Fort Smith, AR
479-452-7500 (877-270-6405)
Dogs up to 75 pounds are allowed for an additional fee of $10 per night pet. 2 dogs may be allowed.

Motel 6 - Ft Smith
6001 Rogers Avenue
Fort Smith, AR
479-484-0576 (800-466-8356)
One well-behaved family pet per

room. Guest must notify front desk upon arrival. Guest is liable for any damages. In consideration of all guests, pets must never be left unattended in the guest rooms.

Residence Inn by Marriott
3005 S. 74th
Fort Smith, AR
479-478-8300
Dogs up to 75 pounds are welcome. There is a $75 one time fee per pet, and a pet policy to sign at check in. 2 dogs may be allowed.

Comfort Inn
1210 H 62/65N
Harrison, AR
870-741-7676 (877-424-6423)
Dogs up to 50 pounds are allowed for an additional one time fee of $25 per pet. Multiple dogs may be allowed.

Holiday Inn Express Hotel & Suites Harrison
117 Hwy 43e
Harrison, AR
870-741-3636 (877-270-6405)
Dogs of all sizes are allowed for an additional fee of $25 for each 1 to 3 night stay per pet. Multiple dogs may be allowed.

Holiday Inn Express
2600 N Hervey
Hope, AR
870-722-6262 (877-270-6405)
Dogs of all sizes are allowed for no additional fee. Dogs may not be left alone in the room. Multiple dogs may be allowed.

Super 8 Hope
I-30 and Hwy 4
Hope, AR
870-777-8601 (800-800-8000)
Dogs of all sizes are allowed. There are no additional pet fees. Smoking and non-smoking rooms are available for pet rooms. 2 dogs may be allowed.

Historic Park Hotel
211 Fountain Street
Hot Springs, AR
501-624-5323
thehistoricparkhotel.com/r
Dogs of all sizes are allowed. There is a $15 one time fee per pet. Dogs are not allowed to be left alone in the room except for short periods. Multiple dogs may be allowed.

Howard Johnson Inn
400 West Grand Ave.
Hot Springs, AR

501-624-4441 (800-446-4656)
Well-behaved dogs of all sizes are allowed. There is a $10 per day additional pet fee per pet.

Days Inn North Little Rock/Jacksonville
1414 John Harden Dr
Jacksonville, AR
501-982-1543 (800-329-7466)
Dogs of all sizes are allowed. There is a $5 per night pet fee per pet. Reservations are recommended due to limited rooms for pets. 2 dogs may be allowed.

Comfort Inn and Suites
2911 Gilmore Drive
Jonesboro, AR
870-972-9000 (877-424-6423)
Dogs are allowed for an additional fee of $10 per night per pet. Multiple dogs may be allowed.

Holiday Inn Express Jonesboro
2407 Phillips Drive
Jonesboro, AR
870-932-5554 (877-270-6405)
Dogs up to about 35 pounds are allowed for no additional fee. 2 dogs may be allowed.

Motel 6 - Jonesboro
2300 South Caraway Road
Jonesboro, AR
870-932-1050 (800-466-8356)
One well-behaved family pet per room. Guest must notify front desk upon arrival. Guest is liable for any damages. In consideration of all guests, pets must never be left unattended in the guest rooms.

Super 8 Jonesboro
2500 S Caraway Rd
Jonesboro, AR
870-972-0849 (800-800-8000)
Dogs of all sizes are allowed. There is a $10 one time per pet fee per visit. Smoking and non-smoking rooms are available for pet rooms. 2 dogs may be allowed.

Gaston's White River Resort
1777 River Rd
Lakeview, AR
870-431-5202
gastons.com/
There are no pet fees. There are no designated smoking or non-smoking cottages.

Candlewood Suites West Little Rock
10520 West Markham
Little Rock, AR
501-975-3800 (877-270-6405)

One dog up to 60 pounds is allowed for an additional pet fee of $25 for up to 2 nights; $50 for 3 to 6 nights; $75 for 7 days, and $150 for 8 days or more.

Comfort Inn and Suites Airport
4301 E Roosevelt Road
Little Rock, AR
501-376-2466 (877-424-6423)
Dogs are allowed for an additional one time fee of $25 per pet. Multiple dogs may be allowed.

Days Inn Little Rock
3200 Bankhead Dr
Little Rock, AR
501-490-2010 (800-329-7466)
Dogs of all sizes are allowed. There is a $100 returnable deposit required per room. 2 dogs may be allowed.

Embassy Suites Hotel Little Rock
11301 Financial Centre Parkway
Little Rock, AR
501-312-9000
Dogs of all sizes are allowed. There is a $50 one time pet fee per visit. Dogs are not allowed to be left alone in the room.

La Quinta Inn Little Rock West
200 Shackleford Rd.
Little Rock, AR
501-224-0900 (800-531-5900)
Dogs of all sizes are allowed. There are no additional pet fees. Dogs may not be left unattended unless they will be quiet and well behaved, and they must be crated. Dogs must be leashed, cleaned up after, and removed for housekeeping. Multiple dogs may be allowed.

La Quinta Inn Little Rock at Rodney Parham Rd
1010 Breckenridge Drive
Little Rock, AR
501-225-7007 (800-531-5900)
Dogs of all sizes are allowed. There are no additional pet fees. Dogs must be crated or removed for housekeeping. Also, please put the "Do Not Disturb" sign on the door when you are out and a dog is in the room. Dogs must be leashed and cleaned up after. 2 dogs may be allowed.

La Quinta Inn North Little Rock - Landers Road
4100 E. McCain Blvd.
Little Rock, AR
501-758-8888 (800-531-5900)
Two large dogs or 3 small dogs are allowed. There are no additional pet fees. Dogs must be leashed and

cleaned up after.

Motel 6 - Little Rock South
7501 Interstate 30
Little Rock, AR
501-568-8888 (800-466-8356)
One well-behaved family pet per room. Guest must notify front desk upon arrival. Guest is liable for any damages. In consideration of all guests, pets must never be left unattended in the guest rooms.

Motel 6 - Little Rock West
10524 West Markham Street
Little Rock, AR
501-225-7366 (800-466-8356)
One well-behaved family pet per room. Guest must notify front desk upon arrival. Guest is liable for any damages. In consideration of all guests, pets must never be left unattended in the guest rooms.

Red Roof Inn - Little Rock
7900 Scott Hamilton Drive
Little Rock, AR
501-562-2694 (800-RED-ROOF)
One well-behaved family pet per room. Guest must notify front desk upon arrival. Guest is liable for any damages. In consideration of all guests, pets must never be left unattended in the guest rooms.

Residence Inn by Marriott
1401 S. Shackleford Road
Little Rock, AR
501-312-0200
Dogs of all sizes are welcome. There is a $75 one time fee, and a pet policy to sign at check in. Multiple dogs may be allowed.

Days Inn Lonoke
105 Dee Dee Lane
Lonoke, AR
501-676-5138 (800-329-7466)
Dogs of all sizes are allowed. There is a $5 per night pet fee per pet. Reservations are recommended due to limited rooms for pets. 2 dogs may be allowed.

Super 8 Lonoke
102 Dee Dee Lane
Lonoke, AR
501-676-6880 (800-800-8000)
Dogs of all sizes are allowed. There is a $10 per night pet fee per pet. Smoking and non-smoking rooms are available for pet rooms. 2 dogs may be allowed.

Best Western Coachman's Inn
420 East Main St
Magnolia, AR

870-234-6122 (800-780-7234)
Dogs are allowed for a $20 refundable deposit 2 dogs may be allowed.

Super 8 Malvern
3445 Oliver Lancaster Blvd
Malvern, AR
501-332-5755 (800-800-8000)
Dogs of all sizes are allowed. There is a $5 per night pet fee per pet. Smoking and non-smoking rooms are available for pet rooms. 2 dogs may be allowed.

Sunrise Point Resort
88 Sunrise Point Lane
Mountain Home, AR
870-491-5188 (888-887-7878)
norfork.com/sunrise
There is a $48 per week pet fee. All cabins are non-smoking.

Teal Point Resort
715 Teal Point Rd
Mountain Home, AR
870-492-5145
norfork.com/tealpoint/
There is a $35 per week pet fee. Dogs are allowed in some of the cabins. There are no designated smoking or non-smoking cabins.

Best Western Fiddlers Inn
601 Sylamore Ave
Mountain View, AR
870-269-2828 (800-780-7234)
Dogs are allowed for an additional fee of $7 per night per pet. There can be 1 large dog or 2 small dogs per room. 2 dogs may be allowed.

Country Inns & Suites by Carlson
901 Hwy 367 N
Newport, AR
870-523-5851
Dogs of all sizes are allowed. There are no additional pet fees.

Comfort Suites
14322 Frontier Drive
North Little Rock, AR
501-851-8444 (877-424-6423)
Dogs are allowed for an additional one time pet fee of $20 per room. 2 dogs may be allowed.

Howard Johnson Hotel
111 W. Pershing Blvd.
North Little Rock, AR
501-758-1440 (800-446-4656)
Dogs of all sizes are welcome. There is a $10 one time pet fee.

Motel 6 - Little Rock North
400 West 29th Street
North Little Rock, AR

501-758-5100 (800-466-8356)
One well-behaved family pet per room. Guest must notify front desk upon arrival. Guest is liable for any damages. In consideration of all guests, pets must never be left unattended in the guest rooms.

Red Roof Inn - North Little Rock
5711 Pritchard Drive
North Little Rock, AR
501-945-0080 (800-RED-ROOF)
One well-behaved family pet per room. Guest must notify front desk upon arrival. Guest is liable for any damages. In consideration of all guests, pets must never be left unattended in the guest rooms.

Residence Inn by Marriott
4110 Health Care Drive
North Little Rock, AR
501-945-7777
Dogs of all sizes are welcome. There is a $75 one time fee, and a pet policy to sign at check in. Multiple dogs may be allowed.

Black Oak Resort
8543 Oakland Road
Oakland, AR
870-431-8363
Dogs of all sizes are allowed. There is no fee for small dogs under 10 pounds, otherwise it is $8 per night per pet for the summer rates and $6 per night per pet are the winter rates. The dogs must be leashed when out. 2 dogs may be allowed.

Embassy Suites Hotel Northwest Arkansas
3303 Pinnacle Hills Parkway
Rogers, AR
479-254-8400
Dogs up to 50 pounds are allowed. There is a $75 one time pet fee per visit. Dogs are not allowed to be left alone in the room.

Residence Inn by Marriott
4611 W. Locust Street
Rogers, AR
479-636-5900
Dogs of all sizes are welcome. There is a $75 per pet one time fee, and a pet policy to sign at check in. Multiple dogs may be allowed.

Comfort Inn
3019 E Parkway Drive
Russellville, AR
479-967-7500 (877-424-6423)
Dogs are allowed for an additional fee of $10 (plus tax) per night per pet. Multiple dogs may be allowed.

Holiday Inn
2407 N. Arkansas
Russellville, AR
479-968-4300 (877-270-6405)
Dogs of all sizes are allowed for an additional $10 one time pet fee per room. Multiple dogs may be allowed.

Motel 6 - Russellville
215 West Birch Street
Russellville, AR
479-968-3666 (800-466-8356)
One well-behaved family pet per room. Guest must notify front desk upon arrival. Guest is liable for any damages. In consideration of all guests, pets must never be left unattended in the guest rooms.

Super 8 Russellville
2404 N Arkansas Ave
Russellville, AR
479-968-8898 (800-800-8000)
Dogs of all sizes are allowed. There is a $10 per night pet fee per pet. Smoking and non-smoking rooms are available for pet rooms. 2 dogs may be allowed.

Hampton Inn
3204 E Race Avenue
Searcy, AR
501-278-5546
Dogs of all sizes are allowed. There is a $25 per night per pet fee and a pet policy to sign at check in. Multiple dogs may be allowed.

Executive Inn
2005 S US 71B
Springdale, AR
479-756-6101 (800-544-6086)
There is a $10 one time pet fee.

Hampton Inn
1700 S 48th
Springdale, AR
479-756-3500
Dogs of all sizes are allowed. There are no additional pet fees, however a credit card will need to be on file, and there is a pet policy to sign at check in. Multiple dogs may be allowed.

Holiday Inn
1500 South 48th Street
Springdale, AR
479-751-8300 (877-270-6405)
Dogs of all sizes are allowed for an additional $25 one time pet fee per room. Multiple dogs may be allowed.

La Quinta Inn & Suites Springdale
1300 S. 48th Street
Springdale, AR
479-751-2626 (800-531-5900)
Dogs of all sizes are allowed. There

are no additional pet fees. Dogs may only be left in the room alone if they will be quiet and well behaved. Dogs must be leashed, cleaned up after, and crated or removed for housekeeping. Multiple dogs may be allowed.

Residence Inn by Marriott
1740 S 48th Street
Springdale, AR
479-872-9100
Dogs of all sizes are welcome. There is a $75 one time fee, and a pet policy to sign at check in. Multiple dogs may be allowed.

Best Western Duck Inn
704 W Michigan
Stuttgart, AR
870-673-2575 (800-780-7234)
Dogs are allowed for no additional fee with a credit card on file. Dogs must be crated when left alone in the room and for housekeeping. 2 dogs may be allowed.

Holiday Inn
5100 N. State Line Avenue
Texarkana, AR
870-774-3521 (877-270-6405)
Dogs totalling no more than 100 pounds are allowed per room for an additional one time pet fee of $50. Multiple dogs may be allowed.

La Quinta Inn Texarkana
5102 N State Line Road
Texarkana, AR
870-773-1000 (800-531-5900)
Dogs of all sizes are allowed. There are no additional pet fees. Dogs may only be left alone in the room if they will be quiet and well behaved. Dogs must be leashed, cleaned up after, and crated or removed for housekeeping. Multiple dogs may be allowed.

Quality Inn
5210 N Stateline Avenue
Texarkana, AR
870-772-0070 (877-424-6423)
Dogs under 40 pounds are allowed for an additional one time fee of $25 per pet; the fee is $35 per pet for dogs over 40 pounds. Multiple dogs may be allowed.

Super 8 Texarkana
325 E 51st Street
Texarkana, AR
870-774-8888 (800-800-8000)
Dogs of all sizes are allowed. There is a $15 one time per pet fee per visit. Smoking and non-smoking rooms are available for pet rooms. 2

dogs may be allowed.

Best Western Van Buren Inn
1903 N 6th Street
Van Buren, AR
479-474-8100 (800-780-7234)
Dogs are allowed for an additional fee of $25 per night per pet. Multiple dogs may be allowed.

Motel 6 - Van Buren
1716 Fayetteville Road
Van Buren, AR
479-474-8001 (800-466-8356)
One well-behaved family pet per room. Guest must notify front desk upon arrival. Guest is liable for any damages. In consideration of all guests, pets must never be left unattended in the guest rooms.

Motel 6 - West Memphis
2501 South Service Road
West Memphis, AR
870-735-0100 (800-466-8356)
One well-behaved family pet per room. Guest must notify front desk upon arrival. Guest is liable for any damages. In consideration of all guests, pets must never be left unattended in the guest rooms.

Red Roof Inn - West Memphis, AR
1401 North Ingram Boulevard
West Memphis, AR
870-735-7100 (800-RED-ROOF)
One well-behaved family pet per room. Guest must notify front desk upon arrival. Guest is liable for any damages. In consideration of all guests, pets must never be left unattended in the guest rooms.

Super 8 West Memphis
901 Martin Luther King Jr Drive
West Memphis, AR
870-735-8818 (800-800-8000)
Dogs of all sizes are allowed. There is a $25 returnable deposit required per room. Smoking and non-smoking rooms are available for pet rooms. 2 dogs may be allowed.

Days Inn Pine Bluff/White Hall
8006 Sheridan Rd
White Hall, AR
870-247-1339 (800-329-7466)
Dogs of all sizes are allowed. There is a $5 per night pet fee per pet. 2 dogs may be allowed.

California Listings

The Doors
North Hwy 1

Albion, CA
707-937-9200 (800-525-0049)
This vacation home rental is dog-friendly. There are no additional pet fees. Please call to make reservations.

Best Western Trailside Inn
343 N Main St
Alturas, CA
530-233-4111 (800-780-7234)
Dogs up to 50 pounds are allowed for an additional fee of $10 per night per pet. 2 dogs may be allowed.

Hacienda Motel
201 E 12th Street/H 299
Alturas, CA
530-233-3459
Dogs up to 50 pounds are allowed. There is an additional fee of $5 per night per pet. Dogs may not be left alone in the room at any time, and they must be well behaved, leashed, and cleaned up after. 2 dogs may be allowed.

Candlewood Suites Anaheim Resort
1733 South Anaheim Blvd
Anaheim, CA
714-808-9000 (877-270-6405)
One dog up to 80 pounds is allowed for an additional one time fee of $75.

Embassy Suites Hotel Anaheim - North near Disneyland
3100 E. Frontera
Anaheim, CA
714-632-1221
Dogs of all sizes are allowed. There is a $50 one time pet fee per visit. Dogs are not allowed to be left alone in the room.

Hilton
777 Convention Way
Anaheim, CA
714-750-4321
Dogs are allowed for no additional pet fee; there is a pet agreement to sign at check in. Dogs may not be left alone in the room at any time. Multiple dogs may be allowed.

Motel 6 - Anaheim - Fullerton East
1440 North State College Boulevard
Anaheim, CA
714-956-9690 (800-466-8356)
One well-behaved family pet per room. Guest must notify front desk upon arrival. Guest is liable for any damages. In consideration of all guests, pets must never be left unattended in the guest rooms.

Red Roof Inn - Anaheim Maingate
100 Disney Way

Anaheim, CA
714-520-9696 (800-RED-ROOF)
One well-behaved dog up to about 80 pounds is allowed. There are no additional pet fees.

Residence Inn by Marriott
1700 S Clementine Street
Anaheim, CA
714-533-3555
Dogs of all sizes are welcome. There is a $75 plus tax one time fee, and they request a credit card on file. Multiple dogs may be allowed.

Staybridge Suites
1855 South Manchester Avenue
Anaheim, CA
714-748-7700 (877-270-6405)
One dog of any size is allowed for an additional $100 one time fee per room.

Residence Inn by Marriott
125 S Festival Drive
Anaheim Hills, CA
714-974-8880
Dogs of all sizes are welcome. There is a $75 plus tax one time fee, and a pet policy to sign at check in. They also ask that you make arrangements for housekeeping. 2 dogs may be allowed.

AmeriHost Inn
2040 Factory Outlets Dr
Anderson, CA
530-365-6100
Dogs are allowed.

Best Western Knight's Inn
2688 Gateway Dr
Anderson, CA
530-365-2753 (800-780-7234)
Dogs are allowed for an additional fee of $15 per night per pet. 2 dogs may be allowed.

Best Western Cedar Inn and Suites
444 S Main St
Angels Camp, CA
209-736-4000 (800-780-7234)
Dogs are allowed for an additional fee of $15 per night per pet. Multiple dogs may be allowed.

Best Western Heritage Inn
3210 Delta Fair Boulevard
Antioch, CA
925-778-2000 (800-780-7234)
Dogs up to 30 pounds are allowed for an additional one time pet fee of $15 per room. 2 dogs may be allowed.

Apple Lane Inn B&B
6265 Soquel Drive
Aptos, CA
831-475-6868 (800-649-8988)
applelaneinn.com/
You and your well-behaved dog are allowed at this Victorian farmhouse built in the 1870s. It is situated on over 2 acres with fields, gardens, and apple orchards. There are also many farm animals such as horses, chickens, goats, ducks and geese. They have three double rooms and two suites with antique furniture. Each of the five rooms have private baths. Room stay includes a full breakfast, and afternoon and evening refreshments. Rates are $120 per night and up. There is a $25 charge for a dog, extra person or crib. No smoking is allowed indoors. This bed and breakfast is located on Soquel Drive, near Cabrillo Jr. College. From Hwy 17 south, exit Hwy 1 south towards Watsonville. Take the Park Avenue/New Brighton Beach exit. Turn left onto Park Ave. Turn right onto Soquel. It will be near Atherton Drive and before Cabrillo College.

Motel 6 - Los Angeles - Arcadia/Pasadena
225 Colorado Place
Arcadia, CA
626-446-2660 (800-466-8356)
One well-behaved family pet per room. Guest must notify front desk upon arrival. Guest is liable for any damages. In consideration of all guests, pets must never be left unattended in the guest rooms.

Residence Inn by Marriott
321 E Huntington Drive/Gateway
Arcadia, CA
626-446-6500
Pets of all sizes are allowed. There is a $75 one time fee, and a pet policy to sign at check in. Multiple dogs may be allowed.

Best Western Arcata Inn
4827 Valley West Blvd
Arcata, CA
707-826-0313 (800-780-7234)
Dogs are allowed for an additional one time pet fee of $20 per room. Multiple dogs may be allowed.

Comfort Inn
4701 Valley W Blvd
Arcata, CA
707-826-2827 (877-424-6423)
Dogs up to 75 pounds are allowed for an additional fee of $15 per night per pet. Multiple dogs may be allowed.

Motel 6 - Arcata - Humboldt University
4755 Valley West Boulevard
Arcata, CA
707-822-7061 (800-466-8356)
One well-behaved family pet per room. Guest must notify front desk upon arrival. Guest is liable for any damages. In consideration of all guests, pets must never be left unattended in the guest rooms.

Quality Inn
3535 Janes Road
Arcata, CA
707-822-0409 (877-424-6423)
Dogs are allowed for an additional fee of $10 per night per pet. Multiple dogs may be allowed.

Super 8 Arcata
4887 Valley W Blvd
Arcata, CA
707-822-8888 (800-800-8000)
Dogs of all sizes are allowed. There is a $5 per night pet fee per pet. Smoking and non-smoking rooms are available for pet rooms. 2 dogs may be allowed.

Ebbetts Pass Lodge
1173 Highway 4, Box 2591
Arnold, CA
209-795-1563
There is a $5 per day pet charge.

Motel 6 - Atascadero
9400 El Camino Real
Atascadero, CA
805-466-6701 (800-466-8356)
One well-behaved family pet per room. Guest must notify front desk upon arrival. Guest is liable for any damages. In consideration of all guests, pets must never be left unattended in the guest rooms.

Best Western Golden Key
13450 Lincoln Way
Auburn, CA
530-885-8611 (800-780-7234)
Dogs are allowed for an additional one time pet fee of $15 per room. Multiple dogs may be allowed.

Foothills Motel
13431 Bowman Road
Auburn, CA
530-885-8444 (800-292-5694)
This motel offers microwaves, refrigerators, HBO/cable TV, and a barbecue, gazebo and picnic area next to the pool. Dogs of all sizes are allowed for an additional $10 per night per pet, and there is a pet policy to sign. Dogs may not be left

alone in the room, and they must be leashed and cleaned up after. Multiple dogs may be allowed.

Motel 6 - Auburn
1819 Auburn Ravine Road
Auburn, CA
530-888-7829 (800-466-8356)
One well-behaved family pet per room. Guest must notify front desk upon arrival. Guest is liable for any damages. In consideration of all guests, pets must never be left unattended in the guest rooms.

Travelodge
13490 Lincoln Way
Auburn, CA
530-885-7025
There is a $10 per day pet fee.

Edgewater Beach Front Hotel
415 Crescent Avenue
Avalon, CA
310-510-0347 (1-866-INCATALINA)
This historic and scenic resort offers cable TV, VCR's, mini refrigerators, microwaves, electrical fire places, and close proximity to shopping, dining, and nightlife. Up to 2 dogs are allowed, however, 3 dogs are allowed if they are very small. There is an additional $50 one time pet fee per room. Dogs must be house trained, quiet, and well behaved. The resort can be seen from the ferry docking area, and is about a 10 minute walk.

Best Western Crystal Palace Inn & Suites
2620 Buck Owens Boulevard
Bakersfield, CA
661-327-9651 (800-780-7234)
Dogs up to 50 pounds are allowed for an additional fee of $10 per night per pet. Multiple dogs may be allowed.

Best Western Heritage Inn (Buttonwillow)
253 Trask St
Bakersfield, CA
661-764-6268 (800-780-7234)
Dogs are allowed for an additional fee of $10 per night per pet. Multiple dogs may be allowed.

Best Western Hill House
700 Truxton Ave
Bakersfield, CA
661-327-4064 (800-780-7234)
Dogs are allowed for an additional fee of $15 per night per pet. Multiple dogs may be allowed.

Days Hotel and Golf

4500 Buck Owens Blvd
Bakersfield, CA
661-324-5555
There is a $20 one time pet fee.

Doubletree
3100 Camino Del Rio Court
Bakersfield, CA
661-323-7111
Dogs of all sizes are allowed. There is a $15 one time pet fee per room. Multiple dogs may be allowed.

La Quinta Inn Bakersfield
3232 Riverside Dr.
Bakersfield, CA
661-325-7400 (800-531-5900)
Dogs of all sizes are allowed. There are no additional pet fees. Dogs must be housebroken, well behaved, leashed, and cleaned up after. Multiple dogs may be allowed.

Motel 6 - Bakersfield Convention Center
1350 Easton Drive
Bakersfield, CA
661-327-1686 (800-466-8356)
One well-behaved family pet per room. Guest must notify front desk upon arrival. Guest is liable for any damages. In consideration of all guests, pets must never be left unattended in the guest rooms.

Motel 6 - Bakersfield East
8223 East Brundage Lane
Bakersfield, CA
661-366-7231 (800-466-8356)
One well-behaved family pet per room. Guest must notify front desk upon arrival. Guest is liable for any damages. In consideration of all guests, pets must never be left unattended in the guest rooms.

Motel 6 - Bakersfield South
2727 White Lane
Bakersfield, CA
661-834-2828 (800-466-8356)
One well-behaved family pet per room. Guest must notify front desk upon arrival. Guest is liable for any damages. In consideration of all guests, pets must never be left unattended in the guest rooms.

Red Lion
2400 Camino Del Rio Court
Bakersfield, CA
661-327-0681
Dogs of all sizes are allowed. There is a $25 per pet fee for each three day stay and a pet policy to sign at check in. Multiple dogs may be allowed.

Residence Inn by Marriott
4241 Chester Lane
Bakersfield, CA
661-321-9800
Pets of all sizes are welcome. There
is a $75 one time fee, and a pet
policy to sign at check in. Multiple
dogs may be allowed.

Rio Bravo Resort
11200 Lake Ming Rd
Bakersfield, CA
661-872-5000
There is a $50 refundable pet
deposit.

Motel 6 - Los Angeles - Baldwin Park
14510 Garvey Avenue
Baldwin Park, CA
626-960-5011 (800-466-8356)
One well-behaved family pet per
room. Guest must notify front desk
upon arrival. Guest is liable for any
damages. In consideration of all
guests, pets must never be left
unattended in the guest rooms.

Travelodge
1700 W. Ramsey Street
Banning, CA
909-849-1000
A well-behaved large dog is allowed.
There is a $5 per day pet charge.

Best Western Desert Villa Inn
1984 E Main Street
Barstow, CA
760-256-1781 (800-780-7234)
Dogs are allowed for an additional
fee of $15 per night per pet. Multiple
dogs may be allowed.

Days Inn
1590 Coolwater Lane
Barstow, CA
760-256-1737 (800-329-7466)
There is a $10 per day pet fee.

Econo Lodge
1230 E. Main Street
Barstow, CA
760-256-2133
One large well-behaved dog is
permitted per room. There is a $5
per day pet fee.

Holiday Inn Express
1861 W. Main St.
Barstow, CA
760-256-1300 (877-270-6405)
holiday-inn.com
Dogs of all sizes are allowed for no
additional fee with a credit card on
file. If paying by cash, a $20
refundable deposit is required. 2
dogs may be allowed.

Holiday Inn Express Hotel and
Suites
2700 Lenwood Road
Barstow, CA
760-253-9200 (877-270-6405)
Dogs of all sizes are allowed for no
additional fee with a credit card on
file. If paying by cash, a $25
refundable deposit is required.
Multiple dogs may be allowed.

Motel 6 - Barstow
150 Yucca Avenue
Barstow, CA
760-256-1752 (800-466-8356)
One well-behaved family pet per
room. Guest must notify front desk
upon arrival. Guest is liable for any
damages. In consideration of all
guests, pets must never be left
unattended in the guest rooms.

Red Roof Inn - Barstow
2551 Commerce Parkway
Barstow, CA
760-253-2121 (800-RED-ROOF)
One well-behaved family pet per
room. Guest must notify front desk
upon arrival. Guest is liable for any
damages. In consideration of all
guests, pets must never be left
unattended in the guest rooms.

Super 8 Barstow
170 Coolwater Lane
Barstow, CA
760-256-8443 (800-800-8000)
Dogs of all sizes are allowed. There
is a $5 per night pet fee per pet.
Smoking and non-smoking rooms
are available for pet rooms. 2 dogs
may be allowed.

Best Western El Rancho Motor Inn
480 E 5th St
Beaumont, CA
951-845-2176 (800-780-7234)
Dogs are allowed for an additional
fee of $15 per night per pet for
small pets; the fee is $25 to $30 for
large dogs. Multiple dogs may be
allowed.

Houseboats.com
PO Box 1189
Bella Vista, CA
530-275-7950 (877-468-7326)
houseboats.com/2006
This houseboat rental company on
Lake Shasta welcomes pets on
many of their boats. Contact them
for reservations and further
information and terms.

Motel 6 - Los Angeles - Bellflower
17220 Downey Avenue
Bellflower, CA

562-531-3933 (800-466-8356)
One well-behaved family pet per
room. Guest must notify front desk
upon arrival. Guest is liable for any
damages. In consideration of all
guests, pets must never be left
unattended in the guest rooms.

Motel 6 - San Francisco - Belmont
1101 Shoreway Road
Belmont, CA
650-591-1471 (800-466-8356)
A well-behaved large dog is okay.
There are no additional pet fees for a
regular room. For a suite, there is a
$10 per day pet fee up to a maximum
of $50 per visit.

Best Western Heritage Inn
1955 East 2nd St
Benecia, CA
707-746-0401 (800-780-7234)
Quiet dogs are allowed for an
additional one time pet fee of $25 per
room. 2 dogs may be allowed.

Beau Sky Hotel
2520 Durant Ave
Berkeley, CA
510-540-7688
This small hotel offers personalized
service. Some rooms have
balconies. If your room doesn't, you
can sit at the chairs and tables in the
patio at the front of the hotel. Your
small, medium or large dog will feel
welcome here because they don't
discriminate against dog size. It is
located close to the UC Berkeley
campus and less than a block from
the popular Telegraph Ave (see
Attractions). There aren't too many
hotels in Berkeley, especially around
the campus. So if you are going, be
sure to book a room in advance. To
get there from Hwy 880 heading
north, take the Hwy 980 exit towards
Hwy 24/Walnut Creek. Then take the
Hwy 24 exit on the left towards
Berkeley/Walnut Creek. Exit at
Claremont Ave and turn left onto
Claremont Ave. Make a slight left
onto College Ave. Turn left onto
Haste St. Turn right onto Telegraph
Ave and then right onto Durant. The
hotel will be on the right. There are
no additional pet fees. All rooms are
non-smoking.

Golden Bear Motel
1620 San Pablo Ave
Berkeley, CA
510-525-6770
This motel has over 40 rooms. Eight
of the rooms have two-bedroom units
and there are four two-bedroom
cottages with kitchens. Parking is
free. To get there from Hwy 80

heading north, exit University Ave. Turn right onto University Ave, and then left on San Pablo Ave. The motel is on the left. There is a $10 per day additional pet fee.

Lake Oroville Bed and Breakfast
240 Sunday Drive
Berry Creek, CA
530-589-0700
lakeoroville.com/lakeoroville/
Dogs are welcome, but should be okay around other dogs. The owner has dogs and cats on the premises. There is a $10 per day pet fee. Children are also welcome.

The Tower-Beverly Hills Hotel
1224 S Beverwil Drive
Beverly Hills, CA
310-277-2800 (800-421-3212)
This 12 story, luxury hotel offers an upscale destination for business and leisure travelers with an outstanding location to numerous activities and recreation in the Los Angeles/Hollywood areas. Specializing in making you feel at home, they offer elegant accommodations, a heated pool, 24 hour room service, a complete business center, private balconies, an award winning restaurant with patio dining service, and more. Dogs of all sizes are allowed for no additional pet fee. Dogs must be well mannered, and leashed and cleaned up after at all times. Dogs may also join their owners at the outside dining tables. Multiple dogs may be allowed.

Bearhome
Call for info
Big Bear City, CA
619-889-2381
bigbearcabin.com/bearhome/
Dogs of all sizes are allowed for no additional fees at this vacation cabin at Big Bear Lake.

Access Big Bear Cabin Rentals
Call for Cabins
Big Bear Lake, CA
909-584-BEAR (800-817-3687)
inbigbear.com
These private cabins and vacation homes allow dogs. All have kitchens, TVs, barbecues and fireplaces.

Big Bear Cabins California
43630 Rainbow Lane
Big Bear Lake, CA
888-336-2891
bigbearcabinscalifornia.com
There is a $10 per day pet fee. Pets may not be left unattended in the cottages. According to a reader "4

cozy, clean and comfortable cottages on 40 acres adjoining BLM land. Very relaxed, run by nice people. Plenty of leash-free hiking right from your door."

Big Bear Cool Cabins
Book Online
Big Bear Lake, CA
909-866-7374 (800-550-8779)
bigbearcoolcabins.com
Big Bear Lake vacation rentals on or near the lake and ski slopes - all with fireplace, bbq, kitchen, and many with hot tubs, pool tables, docks, and more. Professional cleaning, fresh towels, and linens provided. No extra pet fee for responsible pet owners.

Big Bear Frontier Resort and Hotel
40472 Big Bear Blvd
Big Bear Lake, CA
800-420-4693
big-bear-cabins.com
The Big Bear Frontier is a group of cabins and motel rooms nestled in a beautiful mountain setting. The Big Bear Frontier is located on Big Bear Lake. It is located within easy walking distance of Big Bear Village. Amenities include pool, Jacuzzi, gym and more. There is a $15 per night pet fee. Pets may not be left unattended and must be kept on a leash when out of the room.

Big Bear Luxury Properties
Call to Arrange
Big Bear Lake, CA
909-866-4691 (888-866-4618)
bigbearlp.com
These vacation rentals in Big Bear vary from rustic cabins to lakefront homes. Contact them for a pet-friendly rental.

Eagle's Nest Lodge
41675 Big Bear Blvd.
Big Bear Lake, CA
909-866-6465 (888-866-6465)
bigbear.com/enbb/
There are 5 cabins and only 1 allows dogs, but it is a pretty nice cabin. It's called the Sierra Madre and includes a kitchen, fireplace and separate bedroom. You can order breakfast delivered to the room for an additional $10 per person.

Grey Squirrel Resort
39372 Big Bear Blvd
Big Bear Lake, CA
909-866-4335 (800-381-5569)
greysquirrel.com
This dog-friendly resort has cabins that accommodate from 1-2 people

up to 20 people. They have a heated pool, indoor spa, basketball and horseshoes. Some of the cabins have fireplaces and kitchens. All units have VCRs and microwaves. There is a $10 per day additional pet fee.

Holiday Inn
42200 Moonridge Rd
Big Bear Lake, CA
909-866-6666 (877-270-6405)
There is a $15 per day pet fee. Dogs may not be left alone in the room.

Majestic Moose Lodge
39328 Big Bear Blvd/H 18
Big Bear Lake, CA
909-866-9586 (877-585-5855)
majesticmooselodge.com
This getaway offers 20 unique cabins/rooms, and is nestled on 2 acres of lush park-like grounds among tall pine trees with plenty of indoor and outdoor recreational opportunities available. Some of the amenities include fireplaces and kitchens/kitchenettes, cable TV, VCRs, and large covered porches. Housebroken dogs of all sizes are allowed for an additional cash pet deposit of $100. Treats, a pet coverlet (to keep dog hair off the furniture), and waste bags are available at the front desk for their four-legged guests. There are several dog friendly hiking trails and eateries nearby. Dogs must be kenneled when left alone in the room, and they must be leashed and cleaned up after at all times. 2 dogs may be allowed.

Motel 6 - Big Bear
42899 Big Bear Boulevard
Big Bear Lake, CA
909-585-6666 (800-466-8356)
One well-behaved family pet per room. Guest must notify front desk upon arrival. Guest is liable for any damages. In consideration of all guests, pets must never be left unattended in the guest rooms.

Mountain Lodging Unlimited
41135 Big Bear Blvd
Big Bear Lake, CA
909-866-5500 (800-487-3168)
bigbearmtnlodging.com
Dogs are allowed in some of the vacation rentals, cabins, and motels. They will tell you which rentals allow dogs.

Mtn. Resort Adventure Hostel
PO Box 1951
Big Bear Lake, CA
909-866-8900

According to the people at the Hostel "Rent beds or private rooms in our cozy hostel overlooking Big Bear Lake. Fenced grass yard for dogs to play in. All dogs welcome as long as they are friendly with our dogs."

Pine Knot Guest Ranch
908 Pine Knot Ave.
Big Bear Lake, CA
909-866-3446 (800-866-3446)
pineknotguestranch.com
This dog-friendly guest ranch in Big Bear is in a wooded area. They have seven cabins and one guest room. There is an off-leash area for well-behaved and controlled dogs. The ranch has some llamas on the premises.

Robin Hood Resort
40797 Lakeview Drive
Big Bear Lake, CA
909-866-4643 (800-990-9956)
robinhoodresort.info/
This full service resort is located in a great little village across from Big Bear Lake that also offers a variety of entertainment, shops, dining, a small park, and a marina. Some of the amenities/features include an on-site restaurant with 3 dining rooms and outdoor dining, complimentary continental breakfast on the weekends, a banquet center, 2 taverns, in-room spas/fireplaces/kitchenettes, and wood-burning fireplaces. There are 2 pet-friendly rooms, and dogs of all sizes are allowed for no additional fee. Dogs must be quiet, well behaved, leashed, cleaned up after, and they may not be left alone in the room at any time. 2 dogs may be allowed.

Shore Acres Lodge
40090 Lakeview Drive
Big Bear Lake, CA
909-866-8200
bigbear.com/shorea/shorea.html
This resort has 11 cabins and is next to Big Bear Lake and has its own private boat dock. Other amenities include barbecues, volleyball, a children's playground, pool and spa.

Timber Haven Lodge
877 Tulip Lane
Big Bear Lake, CA
909-866-7207
Dogs are welcome in designated cabins. There is a $15 per dog per night pet fee. Ask about the pet policy when making reservations.

Timberline Lodge
39921 Big Bear Blvd.

Big Bear Lake, CA
909-866-4141
thetimberlinelodge.com/
The "Pets Welcome" sign at the main entrance will let you know your pup is more than welcome here. Some of the 13 cabins have fireplaces and full kitchens. There is also a playground for kids. There is a $10 per day additional pet fee per pet.

Wildwood Resort
40210 Big Bear Blvd.
Big Bear Lake, CA
909-878-2178 (888-294-5396)
wildwoodresort.com/
This cabin resort has about 15 cabins of various sizes. Most rooms have fireplaces and all cabins have private picnic benches and barbecues. There is also a pool & spa and if your pup is well-behaved, he or she can be tied to the rails on the inside of the pool area. It's a close drive to town and to some of the parks and attractions. Not too many restaurants within walking distance, but there is a local service that delivers food - check with the front desk. This is a nice place to relax and unwind. There is a $10 per day additional pet fee. There are no designed smoking or non-smoking cabins.

Big Pine Motel
370 S Main St
Big Pine, CA
760-938-2282
There is a $4 per day additional pet fee.

Bristlecone Motel
101 N. Main St.
Big Pine, CA
760-938-2067
According to one of our website readers "Neat,inexpensive rooms with kitchens or fridge and microwave. Barbecue and fish cleaning area. Easy day trip to the ancient Bristlecone Pine Forest, which is extremely dog friendly."

Big Sur Vacation Retreat
off Highway One
Big Sur, CA
831-624-5339 Ext 13
thawley.com/bigsur/
Rent this vacation rental by the week or longer. The home is situated on ten acres and at an elevation of 1,700 feet which is usually above the coastal fog and winds. Well-behaved dogs are welcome. No children under 10 years old allowed without the prior

consent of the owner. This rental is usually available between June and mid-October. Rates are about $2300 per week. The home is located about 45 minutes south of Carmel.

Best Western Bishop Holiday Spa Lodge
1025 N Main St (Hwy 395)
Bishop, CA
760-873-3543 (800-780-7234)
Dogs are allowed for an additional fee of $10 per night per pet. Multiple dogs may be allowed.

Bishop Village Motel
286 W Elm Street
Bishop, CA
888-668-5546
Dogs of all sizes are allowed. There is a $10 per night per pet additional pet fee. Multiple dogs may be allowed.

Comfort Inn
805 N Main Street
Bishop, CA
760-873-4284 (877-424-6423)
Dogs are allowed for an additional fee $5 per night per pet. Multiple dogs may be allowed.

Motel 6 - Bishop
1005 North Main Street
Bishop, CA
760-873-8426 (800-466-8356)
One well-behaved family pet per room. Guest must notify front desk upon arrival. Guest is liable for any damages. In consideration of all guests, pets must never be left unattended in the guest rooms.

Rodeway Inn
150 E Elm Street
Bishop, CA
760-873-3564
There is a $5 per day pet fee. Dogs are allowed in certain rooms only.

Vagabond Inn
1030 N Main Street
Bishop, CA
760-873-6351
There is a $5 per day pet fee.

Best Western Sahara Motel
825 W Hobson Way
Blythe, CA
760-922-7105 (800-780-7234)
Dogs are allowed for no additional pet fee. Dogs may not be left alone in the room. Multiple dogs may be allowed.

Comfort Suites Colorado River
545 E Hobson Way

Blythe, CA
760-922-9209 (877-424-6423)
Dogs are allowed for an additional fee of $15 per night per pet. Multiple dogs may be allowed.

Motel 6 - Blythe
500 West Donlon Street
Blythe, CA
760-922-6666 (800-466-8356)
One well-behaved family pet per room. Guest must notify front desk upon arrival. Guest is liable for any damages. In consideration of all guests, pets must never be left unattended in the guest rooms.

Best Western Bodega Coast Inn & Suites
Bodega Bay, CA
707-875-2217 (800-780-7234)
Dogs are allowed for an additional fee of $30 per night per pet. Multiple dogs may be allowed.

Bodega Bay and Beyond
575 Coastal H One
Bodega Bay, CA
707-875-3942
Dogs of all sizes are allowed. There is a a $50 per room per stay fee and a pet policy to sign at check in. Multiple dogs may be allowed.

Redwood Croft B&B
275 Northwest Drive
Bonny Doon, CA
831-458-1939
www2.cruzio.com/~cummings/ .
This bed and breakfast, located in the Santa Cruz Mountains, is set on a sunny hill amidst the redwood forest. It is the perfect country getaway, especially since they allow dogs. They are very dog-friendly. This B&B has two rooms each with a private bath and full amenities. The Garden Room has its own entrance, private deck with a secluded 7 foot Jacuzzi spa, full-size bed, woodburning stone fireplace and a loft with a queen futon. The West Room is sunny and spacious, has a California king bed and large bathroom with a double shower and roman tub. Room stay includes a lavish country breakfast. Room rates start at $165 per night. The dog-friendly Davenport Beach (see Parks) is only about 10-15 minutes away. Call the inn for directions or for a brochure.

Boonville Hotel
Highway 128
Boonville, CA
707-895-2210
This historic hotel was built in 1862.

Dogs and children are allowed in the Bungalow and the Studio rooms which are separate from the main building. Both of these rooms are in the creekside building with private entrances and yards. Room rates start at $225 per night and there is a $15 per day pet charge. Please note that their restaurant is closed on Tuesdays and Wednesdays. This hotel is in Anderson Valley, which is located 2 1/2 hours north of San Francisco.

Woodfin Suites
3100 E Imperial H
Brea, CA
714-579-3200
Dogs of all sizes are allowed. There is a $5 per night per pet fee and a pet policy to sign at check in. Multiple dogs may be allowed.

Walker River Lodge
100 Main Street
Bridgeport, CA
760-932-7021
Well behaved dogs of all sizes are allowed. There is a pet policy to sign at check in and there are no additional pet fees. Multiple dogs may be allowed.

Motel 6 - Buellton - Solvang Area
333 McMurray Road
Buellton, CA
805-688-7797 (800-466-8356)
One well-behaved family pet per room. Guest must notify front desk upon arrival. Guest is liable for any damages. In consideration of all guests, pets must never be left unattended in the guest rooms.

Rodeway Inn
630 Ave of Flags
Buellton, CA
805-688-0022
rodewayinn.com/
This motel (formerly Econo Lodge) is located about 4 miles from the village of Solvang. Amenities include cable TV and movies. Handicap accessible rooms are available. There is a $25 one time pet charge.

Santa Ynez Valley Marriott
555 McMurray Road
Buellton, CA
805-688-1000 (800-638-8882)
Dogs of all sizes are allowed. There is a $50 one time fee per pet. Dogs must be leashed, cleaned up after, and the Pet in Room sign put on the door and the front desk informed if they are in the room alone. The provide food and water bowls and a

designated pet walking area. Dogs are not allowed on the bed. 2 dogs may be allowed.

Motel 6 - Buena Park-Knotts/Disneyland
7051 Valley View Street
Buena Park, CA
714-522-1200 (800-466-8356)
One well-behaved family pet per room. Guest must notify front desk upon arrival. Guest is liable for any damages. In consideration of all guests, pets must never be left unattended in the guest rooms.

Quality Inn and Suites
7800 Crescent Avenue
Buena Park, CA
714-527-2201 (877-424-6423)
One dog is allowed for an a $75 refundable deposit plus $20 per night.

Red Roof Inn - Buena Park
7121 Beach Boulevard
Buena Park, CA
714-670-9000 (800-RED-ROOF)
One well-behaved family pet per room. Guest must notify front desk upon arrival. Guest is liable for any damages. In consideration of all guests, pets must never be left unattended in the guest rooms.

Hilton Burbank
2500 Hollywood Way
Burbank, CA
818-843-6000
Dogs are allowed for an additional one time pet fee of $50 per room; there is a pet agreement to sign at check in. This hotel is 100% non-smoking. 2 dogs may be allowed.

Holiday Inn
150 E Angeleno
Burbank, CA
818-841-4770 (877-270-6405)
Dogs of all sizes are allowed for an additional fee of $15 per night per pet. Multiple dogs may be allowed.

Safari Inn
1911 Olive Avenue
Burbank, CA
818-845-8586
Dogs of all sizes are allowed. There is a $25 one time fee per room per stay and a pet policy to sign at check in. If you are not paying with a credit card, then there would be a $200 cash refundable pet deposit. 2 dogs may be allowed.

Crowne Plaza Hotel San Francisco-Intl Airport

1177 Airport Blvd
Burlingame, CA
650-342-9200 (877-270-6405)
Dogs of all sizes are allowed for no additional fee; however, there is a $100 refunable pet deposit per room. 2 dogs may be allowed.

Doubletree
835 Airport Blvd
Burlingame, CA
650-344-5500
Dogs up to 50 pounds are allowed. There is a $20 one time fee per pet and a pet policy to sign at check in. 2 dogs may be allowed.

Embassy Suites Hotel San Francisco Airport/Burlingame
150 Anza Blvd.
Burlingame, CA
650-342-4600
Dogs of all sizes are allowed. There is a $50 one time fee per visit. Dogs are not allowed to be left alone in the room.

Red Roof Inn - San Francisco Airport
777 Airport Boulevard
Burlingame, CA
650-342-7772 (800-RED-ROOF)
One well-behaved dog is up to about 80 pounds is allowed. There are no additional pet fees.

San Francisco Airport Marriott
1800 Old Bayshore H
Burlingame, CA
650-692-9100 (800-228-9290)
Dogs of all sizes are allowed. There is a $75 one time additional pet fee per room. Dogs must be leashed, cleaned up after, removed or accompanied for housekeeping, and the Pet in Room sign put on the door if they are in the room alone. 2 dogs may be allowed.

Sheraton Gateway
600 Airport Blvd.
Burlingame, CA
650-340-8500 (888-625-5144)
Dogs up to 50 pounds are allowed for no additional pet fee; there is a pet agreement to sign at check in. Dogs are allowed on the 5th floor only, and they may not be left alone in the room.

Vagabond Inn
1640 Bayshore Highway
Burlingame, CA
650-692-4040 (800-522-1555)
vagabondinn.com
This motel overlooks the San Francisco Bay. It is located just south of the airport and about 16 miles

from downtown San Francisco. All rooms include coffee makers, cable television and air conditioning. Pets are an additional $10 per day.

Motel 6 - Bakersfield - Buttonwillow
20638 Tracy Avenue
Buttonwillow, CA
661-764-5153 (800-466-8356)
One well-behaved family pet per room. Guest must notify front desk upon arrival. Guest is liable for any damages. In consideration of all guests, pets must never be left unattended in the guest rooms.

Calistoga Ranch
580 Lommel Road
Calistoga, CA
707-254-2800
calistogaranch.com/
Nestled away in a private canyon, this 157 acre luxury resort is a great getaway with oak tree covered hills, a stream and private lake, and a private restaurant. Some of the amenities include natural spring-fed mineral pools, a heated outdoor pool, miles of hiking trails, 24 hour room service, a variety of indoor and outdoor spaces so visitors get to fully enjoy the surroundings, and much more. Dogs of all sizes are allowed for a $125 one time additional pet fee per room. Dogs must be well behaved, leashed, and cleaned up after. Multiple dogs may be allowed.

Hillcrest Country Inn
3225 Lake County Hwy
Calistoga, CA
707-942-6334
bnbweb.com/hillcrest
Hillcrest is a country home secluded on a hilltop with a view of vineyards and the Napa Valley. Rooms have fireplaces,balconies, some Jacuzzi tubs for 2 and HBO. There is swimming, hiking and fishing on 36 acres. Breakfast is served on weekends. There is an outdoor hot tub and a large cold water pool. Dogs of all sizes are allowed.

Meadowlark Inn
601 Petrified Forest Road
Calistoga, CA
707-942-5651 (800-942-5651)
meadowlarkinn.com/
On 20 scenic acres in the heart of wine country is this elegant Inn with gardens, hiking trails, meadows, forests, and horses grazing in pastures. Other features/amenities include a clothing optional mineral pool, hot tub, sauna, in-house massages, well appointed rooms,

and a full, gourmet breakfast. Dogs of all sizes are welcome for no additional fee. Dogs must be very well behaved, leashed, and cleaned up after at all times. 2 dogs may be allowed.

Pink Mansion Bed and Breakfast
1415 Foothill Blvd.
Calistoga, CA
707-942-0558
pinkmansion.com
This restored 1875 home offers modern amenities for wine country travelers. The Pink Mansion has been featured in The Wine Spectator, Best Places To Kiss and the New York Post. Dogs are allowed in one of their six rooms. Each room has a private bathroom. There is a $30 per day pet charge.

Motel 6 - Camarillo
1641 East Daily Drive
Camarillo, CA
805-388-3467 (800-466-8356)
One well-behaved family pet per room. Guest must notify front desk upon arrival. Guest is liable for any damages. In consideration of all guests, pets must never be left unattended in the guest rooms.

Cambria Pines Lodge
2905 Burton Drive
Cambria, CA
805-927-4200
This lodge is a 125 room retreat with accommodations ranging from rustic cabins to fireplace suites. It is nestled among 25 acres of Monterey Pines with forested paths and flower gardens. There is a $25 one time pet charge. Multiple dogs may be allowed.

Cambria Shores Inn
6276 Moonstone Beach Drive
Cambria, CA
805-927-8644 (800-433-9179)
cambriashores.com
Dogs are allowed for a $10.00 per night per dog fee. Pets must be leashed and never left alone. The inn offers local pet sitting services and provide treats for dogs. 2 dogs may be allowed.

Coastal Escapes Inc.
778 Main Street
Cambria, CA
805-927-3182 (800-578-2100)
calcoastvacationrentals.com/
There are a couple of hundred listings with this company and not all houses allow dogs. The properties are located in the picturesque communities of Cayucos and

Cambria, and offer an impressive diversity of accommodations from secluded forest settings to oceanfront headlands, and a variety of recreational opportunities nearby. Dogs of all sizes are allowed for one time cleaning fees of $75 to $125, depending on the property; the number of dogs allowed per house also depends on the property. Dogs must be house-trained, well behaved, leashed, and cleaned up after both inside and out.

Pine Lodge
2905 Burton Drive
Cambria, CA
805-927-4200
Dogs of all sizes are allowed. There is a $25 per night per pet fee and a pet policy to sign at check in. 2 dogs may be allowed.

The Big Red House
370- B Chelsea Lane
Cambria, CA
805-927-1390
thebigredhouse.com
The Big Red House is located 2 blocks from the beach. These vacation rentals have an ocean view from each room. There is a $200 refundable pet deposit.

Motel 6 - San Jose- Campbell
1240 Camden Avenue
Campbell, CA
408-371-8870 (800-466-8356)
One well-behaved family pet per room. Guest must notify front desk upon arrival. Guest is liable for any damages. In consideration of all guests, pets must never be left unattended in the guest rooms.

Residence Inn by Marriott
2761 S Bascom Avenue
Campbell, CA
408-559-1551
Dogs of all sizes are allowed. There is a $75 one time fee and a pet policy to sign at check in. . Multiple dogs may be allowed.

TownePlace Suites
700 E Campbell Avenue
Campbell, CA
408-370-4510 (800-257-3000)
This extended stay inn offers 95 well appointed suites, each with a full kitchen and living room area, is only minuets from numerous companies and popular attractions, and staff is available 24/7 to make the business or leisure traveler feel right at home. They also have a spa, barbecue area, and a large park and trails close by. Dogs of all sizes are

allowed for an additional one time pet fee of $75 per room, and there is a pet policy to sign at check in. Dogs may not be left alone in the rooms, and they must be leashed and cleaned up after at all times. 2 dogs may be allowed.

Motel 6 - Canoga Park
7132 De Soto Avenue
Canoga Park, CA
818-883-6666 (800-466-8356)
One well-behaved family pet per room. Guest must notify front desk upon arrival. Guest is liable for any damages. In consideration of all guests, pets must never be left unattended in the guest rooms.

Seaside Inn
34862 Pacific Coast Hwy.
Capistrano Beach, CA
949-496-1399 (800-25-BEACH)
seaside-inn.com
There is a $25 one time pet fee.

Capitola Inn
822 Bay Ave
Capitola, CA
831-462-3004
getawaylodging.com/capitolainn
This inn is located a few blocks from Capitola Village. They offer 56 rooms with either a private patio or balcony. There is a $20 per day pet charge.

Forest Avenue Guest House
Call to Arrange
Carlsbad, CA
760-803-3032
homepages.com/jeffpiro
This pet-friendly guest house sleeps 2 or more. The property is fenced and is about 1/2 acre in size. The 52 acre wooded Eucalyptus Forest next door has marked trails for walking your dog.

Inns of America
751 Raintree
Carlsbad, CA
760-931-1185
There is a $10 one time pet fee.

Motel 6 - Carlsbad Downtown
1006 Carlsbad Village Drive
Carlsbad, CA
760-434-7135 (800-466-8356)
One well-behaved family pet per room. Guest must notify front desk upon arrival. Guest is liable for any damages. In consideration of all guests, pets must never be left unattended in the guest rooms.

Motel 6 - Carlsbad South

750 Raintree Drive
Carlsbad, CA
760-431-0745 (800-466-8356)
One well-behaved pet is welcome. There are no additional pet fees, just let them know that you have a pet.

Quality Inn and Suites
751 Raintree Drive
Carlsbad, CA
760-931-1185 (877-424-6423)
Dogs up to 75 pounds are allowed for an additional fee of $10 per night per pet. 2 dogs may be allowed.

Ramada Carlsbad by the Sea
751 Macadamia Drive
Carlsbad, CA
760-438-2285 (800-644-9394)
ramadacarlsbad.com
This hotel has pet-friendly one bedroom suites. The hotel is 2 miles from Legoland. Up to 2 dogs per suite are allowed for a $25 per night pet fee.

Red Roof Inn - Carlsbad
6117 Paseo del Norte
Carlsbad, CA
760-438-1242 (800-RED-ROOF)
One well-behaved family pet per room. Guest must notify front desk upon arrival. Guest is liable for any damages. In consideration of all guests, pets must never be left unattended in the guest rooms.

Residence Inn by Marriott
2000 Faraday Avenue
Carlsbad, CA
760-431-9999
Pets of all sizes are allowed. There is a $75 one time fee, and a pet policy to sign at check in. Multiple dogs may be allowed.

West Inn and Suites
4970 Avenida Encinas
Carlsbad, CA
760-448-4500
westinnandsuites.com
Pets are allowed at this boutique hotel in Carlsbad for an additional pet fee of $75 per night.

West Inn and Suites
4970 Avenida Encinas
Carlsbad, CA
760-208-4929 (866-375-4705)
This boutique style, 4 star hotel offers the ultimate in luxury surroundings and recreational activities for both the business and leisure traveler. Some of the amenities include 2 fine dining restaurants, pool and Jacuzzi, a business center, library, and an on-

site pantry. They are also close to the beach and several attractions. Dogs of all sizes are allowed. There is a $75 per night per pet additional fee. Dogs may not be left alone in the room, and they must be leashed and cleaned up after. 2 dogs may be allowed.

Carmel Country Inn
Dolores Street & Third Avenue
Carmel, CA
831-625-3263 (800-215-6343)
carmelcountryinn.com
This dog-friendly bed and breakfast has 12 rooms and allows dogs in several of these rooms. It's close to many downtown outdoor dog-friendly restaurants (see Restaurants). A 20-25 minute walk will take you to the dog-friendly Carmel City Beach. There is a $20 per night per pet charge.

Casa De Carmel
Monte Verde & Ocean Ave
Carmel, CA
831-624-2429
There is an additional fee of $20 per day for 1 pet, and $30 a day for 2 pets.

Coachman's Inn
San Carlos St. & 7th
Carmel, CA
831-624-6421 (800-336-6421)
coachmansinn.com
Located in downtown, this motel allows dogs. It's close to many downtown outdoor dog-friendly restaurants (see Restaurants). A 20-25 minute walk will take you to the Carmel City beach which allows dogs. There is a $15 per day additional pet fee.

Cypress Inn
Lincoln & 7th
Carmel, CA
831-624-3871
cypress-inn.com
This hotel is located within walking distance to many dog-friendly outdoor restaurants in the quaint town of Carmel and walking distance to the Carmel City Beach. This is definitely a pet-friendly hotel. Here is an excerpt from the Cypress Inn's web page "Co-owned by actress and animal rights activist Doris Day, the Cypress Inn welcomes pets with open arms -- a policy which draws a high percentage of repeat guests. It's not unusual to see people strolling in and out of the lobby with dogs of all sizes. Upon arrival, animals are greeted with dog biscuits, and other pet pamperings." Room rates are

about $125 - $375 per night. If you have more than 2 people per room (including a child or baby), you will be required to stay in their deluxe room which runs approximately $375 per night. There is a $25 per day pet charge.

Happy Landing Inn
Monte Verde at 6th
Carmel, CA
831-624-7917 (800-297-6250)
carmelhappylanding.com
This dog-friendly B&B is located six blocks from the Carmel leash free beach and in the middle of Carmel-By-The-Sea. Pets of all sizes are allowed. There is a $20 per day pet fee for one pet and $30 per day for two pets. 2 dogs may be allowed.

Hofsas House Hotel
San Carlos Street
Carmel, CA
831-624-2745
There is a $15 per day additional pet fee. The hotel is located between 3rd Ave and 4th Ave in Carmel. Thanks to one of our readers for recommending this hotel.

Lincoln Green Inn
PO Box 2747
Carmel, CA
831-624-7738
vagabondshouseinn.com
These cottages are owned and booked through the dog-friendly Vagabond's House Inn in Carmel. One big difference between the two accommodations is that the Vagabond's House does not allow children, whereas the Lincoln Green does allow children. The Lincoln Green is located very close to a beach. All cottages are non-smoking and there is a $20 per day pet fee.

Sunset House
Camino Real and Ocean Ave
Carmel, CA
831-624-4884
sunset-carmel.com
There is a $20 one time pet fee. Thanks to one of our readers who writes "Great B&B, breakfast brought to your room every morning."

The Forest Lodge Cottages
Ocean Ave. and Torres St. (P.O. Box 1316)
Carmel, CA
831-624-7055
These cottages are surrounded by oak and pine trees among a large

garden area. They are conveniently located within walking distance to many dog-friendly restaurants and the dog-friendly Carmel City Beach. There is a $10 one time additional pet fee.

The Tradewinds at Carmel
Mission Street at 3rd Avenue
Carmel, CA
831-624-2776 (800-624-6665)
tradewindscarmel.com
This motel allows dogs in several of their rooms. They are a non-smoking inn. It's located about 3-4 blocks north of Ocean Ave and close to many outdoor dog-friendly restaurants in downtown Carmel. A 20-25 minute walk will take you to the dog-friendly Carmel City beach. There is a $25 per day pet charge.

Vagabond's House Inn B&B
P.O. Box 2747
Carmel, CA
831-624-7738 (800-262-1262)
vagabondshouseinn.com/
This dog-friendly bed and breakfast is located in downtown and has 11 rooms. It's close to many downtown outdoor dog-friendly restaurants. A 20-25 minute walk will take you to the dog-friendly Carmel City beach. Children 12 years and older are allowed at this B&B inn.

Wayside Inn
Mission St & 7th Ave.
Carmel, CA
831-624-5336 (800-433-4732)
ibts-waysideinn.com/
This motel allows dogs in several of their rooms and is close to many downtown outdoor dog-friendly restaurants. A 20-25 minute walk will take you to the dog-friendly Carmel City beach. Pets are welcome at no extra charge. Dogs up to about 75 pounds are allowed.

Carmel Valley Lodge
Carmel Valley Rd
Carmel Valley, CA
831-659-2261 (800-641-4646)
valleylodge.com
Your dog will feel welcome at this country retreat. Pet amenities include heart-shaped, organic homemade dog biscuits and a pawtographed picture of Lucky the Lodge Dog. Dogs must be on leash, but for your convenience, there are doggy-hitches at the front door of every unit that has a patio or deck and at the pool. There are 31 units which range from standard rooms to two bedroom cottages. A great community park is located across the street and several

restaurants with outdoor seating are within a 5 minute walk. Drive about 15 minutes from the lodge and you'll be in downtown Carmel or at one of the dog-friendly beaches. Dogs are an extra $10 per day and up to two dogs per room. There is no charge for children under 16. The lodge is located in Carmel Valley. From Carmel, head south on Hwy 1. Turn left on Carmel Valley Rd., drive about 11-12 miles and the lodge will be located at Ford Rd.

Forest Lodge Cottages
Corner of Ocean and Torres; P.O. Box 1316
Carmel by the Sea, CA
831-624-7023
Dogs of all sizes are allowed. There is a $100 one time pet fee and a pet policy to sign at check in. They request you exercise and relieve your pet off the grounds. 2 dogs may be allowed.

Holiday Inn Express Hotel and Suites
5606 Carpinteria Ave
Carpinteria, CA
805-566-9499 (877-270-6405)
Dogs of all sizes are allowed for an additional fee of $10 per night per pet. Multiple dogs may be allowed.

Motel 6 - Santa Barbara-Carpinteria North
4200 Via Real
Carpinteria, CA
805-684-6921 (800-466-8356)
One well-behaved family pet per room. Guest must notify front desk upon arrival. Guest is liable for any damages. In consideration of all guests, pets must never be left unattended in the guest rooms.

Motel 6 - Santa Barbara-Carpinteria South
5550 Carpinteria Avenue
Carpinteria, CA
805-684-8602 (800-466-8356)
One well-behaved family pet per room. Guest must notify front desk upon arrival. Guest is liable for any damages. In consideration of all guests, pets must never be left unattended in the guest rooms.

Holiday Inn Express
2532 Castro Valley Blvd
Castro Valley, CA
510-538-9501 (877-270-6405)
Dogs up to 75 pounds are allowed for an additional fee of $20 per night pet; the price may be adjusted lower for very small dogs. 2 dogs may be allowed.

Doral Desert Princess Resort
67967 Vista Chino
Cathedral City, CA
760-322-7000 (888-FUN-IN-PS (386-4677))
doralpalmsprings.com/
This 4-star golf resort offers elegance and comprehensive services for the business or leisure traveler. Some of the features include 27 holes of championship golf, 285 luxury guestrooms and suites, conference and banquet facilities, room service, pool/Jacuzzi/sauna, a gift shop, and golf and tennis shops. Dogs of all sizes are allowed for an additional $75 one time fee per pet. Dogs are placed in first floor rooms, and they may only be left alone in the room if they will be quiet and well behaved. Dogs must be leashed and cleaned up after at all times. Multiple dogs may be allowed.

Cayucos Beach Inn
333 South Ocean Avenue
Cayucos, CA
805-995-2828
There is a $10 one time pet fee. All rooms in the inn are non-smoking. Family pets are welcome. The inn even has a dog walk and dog wash area. Thanks to one of our readers for this recommendation. Multiple dogs may be allowed.

Cypress Tree Motel
125 S. Ocean Avenue
Cayucos, CA
805-995-3917
This pet-friendly 12-unit motel is located within walking distance to everything in town. Amenities include a garden area with lawn furniture and a barbecue. There is a $10 one time pet charge.

Dolphin Inn
399 S Ocean Ave
Cayucos, CA
805-995-3810
There is a $10 per day pet charge.

Shoreline Inn
1 North Ocean Avenue
Cayucos, CA
805-995-3681 (800-549-2244)
centralcoast.com/shorelineinn
This dog-friendly motel is located on the beach (dogs are not allowed on this State Beach). Dogs are allowed in the first floor rooms which have direct access to a patio area. There is a $10 per day charge for dogs.

Sunrise Motel & RV Park
54889 Highway 200 West
Cedarville, CA
530-279-2161
Located at the base of the dog-friendly Modoc National Forest, this motel offers all non-smoking rooms. There are no pet fees. If you are out during the day and cannot bring your pooch with you, they do have an outdoor kennel available for an extra $5.

Staybridge Suites
21902 Lassen St
Chatsworth, CA
818-773-0707 (877-270-6405)
Two dogs up to 25 pounds or one dog up to 50 pounds are allowed for an additional $150 one time pet fee for a 1-bedroom, and an additional $200 one time pet fee for a 2-bedroom. 2 dogs may be allowed.

Chico Oxford Suites
2035 Buisness Lane
Chico, CA
530-899-9090 (800-870-7848)
oxfordsuiteschico.com/
This hotel offers a variety of beautiful rooms, a full country breakfast buffet, an evening reception with two complimentary beverages and light hors d'ouevres. Also featured are a 24 hour gift/snack shop, business center, and an outdoor pool and Jacuzzi. Dogs up to about 75 pounds are allowed for an additional $35 one time pet fee per room. Dogs may only be left alone in the room if they will be quiet and well behaved, and a contact number is left with the front desk. Dogs must be leashed or crated, and cleaned up after. 2 dogs may be allowed.

Esplanade Bed & Breakfast
620 The Esplanade
Chico, CA
530-345-8084
now2000.com/esplanade/
Built in 1915, this Craftsman Bungalow has been completely restored. This B&B is located just steps from downtown Chico and Chico State University. Each room has a private bathroom and cable television. Enjoy their hearty breakfast served in the dining room or on the patio. Well-behaved dogs are allowed with a $20 refundable deposit. Children are also allowed.

Holiday Inn
685 Manzanita Ct
Chico, CA
530-345-2491 (877-270-6405)
Dogs of all sizes are allowed for an

additional one time pet fee of $30 per room. Multiple dogs may be allowed.

Motel 6 - Chico
665 Manzanita Court
Chico, CA
530-345-5500 (800-466-8356)
One well-behaved family pet per room. Guest must notify front desk upon arrival. Guest is liable for any damages. In consideration of all guests, pets must never be left unattended in the guest rooms.

Music Express Inn Bed and Breakfast
1091El Monte Avenue
Chico, CA
530-891-9833
now2000.com/musicexpress/
This B&B is located near the dog-friendly Bidwell Park, the third largest municipal park in the United States. The B&B offers nine rooms all with private baths, refrigerators and microwaves. All rooms are non-smoking. A well-behaved dog is allowed, but must be leashed when outside your room. Pets must be attended at all times. There are no pet fees. Children are also allowed.

Super 8 Chico
655 Manzanita Ct
Chico, CA
530-345-2533 (800-800-8000)
Dogs of all sizes are allowed. There is a $4 per night pet fee per pet. Dogs are not allowed to be left alone in the room. Smoking and non-smoking rooms are available for pet rooms. 2 dogs may be allowed.

Motel 6 - Chino - Los Angeles Area
12266 Central Avenue
Chino, CA
909-591-3877 (800-466-8356)
One well-behaved family pet per room. Guest must notify front desk upon arrival. Guest is liable for any damages. In consideration of all guests, pets must never be left unattended in the guest rooms.

Days Inn
Hwy 99 & Robertson Blvd
Chowchilla, CA
559-665-4821 (800-329-7466)
There is a $5 per day additional pet fee.

Motel 6 - San Diego - Chula Vista
745 E Street
Chula Vista, CA
619-422-4200 (800-466-8356)
One well-behaved family pet per room. Guest must notify front desk

upon arrival. Guest is liable for any damages. In consideration of all guests, pets must never be left unattended in the guest rooms.

Shinneyboo Creek Cabin Resort
11820 Eagle Lakes Road
Cisco, CA
530-587-5160
shinneyboocreek.com
These secluded cabins are located in the High Sierra, surrounded by the Tahoe National Forest. There is a $10 per pet per day additional pet fee. 2 dogs may be allowed.

Pacific Palms Resort and Conference Center
One Industry Hills Parkway
City of Industry, CA
626-810-4455 (800-524-4557)
pacificpalmsresort.com/main.htm
Sitting on 650 acres of meticulously landscaped grounds with 2 championship golf courses, 17 tennis courts, an Olympic-sized pool, miles of riding and hiking trails, and home to one of the most prestigious conference centers with cutting-edge technology in the US, this resort is a consummate retreat for the business or leisure traveler. Some of the amenities include 292 spacious well-appointed guestrooms and suites each with a balcony and many in-room amenities, and 2 outstanding restaurants and a lounge. Dogs of all sizes are allowed for an additional one time fee of $25 per pet. Dogs must be friendly and well behaved and removed or crated for housekeeping. Dogs must be kept on leash out of the room and cleaned up after at all times. 2 dogs may be allowed.

Best Western Big Country Inn
25020 West Dorris Ave
Coalinga, CA
559-935-0866 (800-780-7234)
Dogs are allowed for an additional fee of $10 per night per pet. Multiple dogs may be allowed.

Harris Ranch Inn and Restaurant
24505 W Dorris Avenue
Coalinga, CA
800-443-3322
Fine living and dining are combined for a great getaway here. Dogs of all sizes are allowed. There is a $20 one time additional pet fee per pet. Dogs may not be left alone in the room and they must be leashed and cleaned up after. Dogs are not allowed in the pool/spa or restaurant areas. Multiple dogs may

be allowed.

Motel 6 - Coalinga East
25008 West Dorris Avenue
Coalinga, CA
559-935-1536 (800-466-8356)
One well-behaved family pet per room. Guest must notify front desk upon arrival. Guest is liable for any damages. In consideration of all guests, pets must never be left unattended in the guest rooms.

Pleasant Valley Inn
25278 W Doris St
Coalinga, CA
559-935-2063
There is a $5 per day additional pet fee.

Becker's Bounty Lodge and Cottage
HCR #2 Box 4659
Coffee Creek, CA
530-266-3277
beckersbountylodging.com/
The lodge is a secluded mountain hideaway at the edge of the one-half million acre Trinity Alps Wilderness. Dogs are not allowed on the furniture. There is a $50 one time pet charge.

Blackberry Creek Garden Cottage
On SR-3
Coffee Creek, CA
530-266-3502
trinitycounty.com/blackbry.htm
There is a $15 per day additional pet fee. According to a reader "We just spent a week at this wonderful cottage, and it is a little piece of heaven for you and your dog. Nestled under the pines, cedars and redwoods the cottage has everything you need for the perfect vacation in the woods. Down the road is the greatest swimming hole in the Trinity River, and great hikes await you in every direction. Our dogs did not want to leave and neither did we. "

Andruss Motel
106964 Highway 395
Coleville, CA
530-495-2216
Dogs are allowed.

Golden Lotus Bed and Breakfast Inn
1006 Lotus Road
Coloma, CA
530-621-4562
This pre-Victorian B&B, located in the historic town of Coloma, is surrounded by herb gardens. Dogs are allowed in one of their rooms. Dogs must be well-behaved and owners must agree to pay for any

damages. There is a $20 per day additional pet fee.

Days Inn
2830 Iowa Ave
Colton, CA
909-788-9900 (800-329-7466)
A well-behaved large dog is okay. There is a $5 per day additional pet fee.

Columbia Gem Motel
22131 Parrotts Ferry Rd
Columbia, CA
209-532-4508
columbiagem.com/business/gem/
This dog-friendly motel offers gracious, country hospitality, comfort and privacy. The motel is set on a sunny park like acre beneath towering, majestic pines, cedars and sequoias, which provide a shady umbrella over their 6 cozy log cabins and 4 motel rooms. For a little extra, they can provide the perfect getaway with champagne on ice, flowers, wine, cheese, crackers, chocolates, or bubble bath waiting for you in your room. They can also arrange breakfast in bed or can help with any other ideas. The motel is located within walking distance (about 1 mile) from the popular dog-friendly Columbia State Historic Park. The Gold Mine Winery/Micro-Brewery is located about 1 block away from the motel. The winery has a nice outdoor covered patio and lawn area. They have free wine and beer tasting and they also make pizza from scratch, any way you like it. The management are of the belief that people who travel with their "best friends" are responsible pet owners and a pleasure to have as guests at The Gem. Dog owners are not penalized with an extra fee here. Instead, management has a simple, common sense pet regulation form they have each owner read and sign. Dogs are not to be left unattended in the rooms.

Holiday Inn
1050 Burnett Ave
Concord, CA
925-687-5500 (877-270-6405)
Dogs of all sizes are allowed for an additional fee of $10 per night per room. Multiple dogs may be allowed.

Best Western Inn-Corning
2165 Solano St
Corning, CA
530-824-2468 (800-780-7234)
Dogs are allowed for an additional fee of $10 per night per pet. Multiple dogs may be allowed.

Comfort Inn
910 H 99W
Corning, CA
530-824-5200 (877-424-6423)
Dogs are allowed for an additional one time fee of $10 per pet. Multiple dogs may be allowed.

Holiday Inn Express Hotel & Suites
3350 Sunrise Way
Corning, CA
530-824-6400 (877-270-6405)
Dogs of all sizes are allowed for an additional one time pet fee of $10 per room. 2 dogs may be allowed.

Motel 6 - Corona
200 North Lincoln Avenue
Corona, CA
951-735-6408 (800-466-8356)
One well-behaved family pet per room. Guest must notify front desk upon arrival. Guest is liable for any damages. In consideration of all guests, pets must never be left unattended in the guest rooms.

Coronado Bay Resort
4000 Coronado Bay Road
Coronado, CA
619-424-4000
Dogs of all sizes are allowed. There is a $25 one time fee per room and a pet policy to sign at check in. Multiple dogs may be allowed.

Coronado Island Marriott Resort
2000 Second Street
Coronado, CA
619-435-3000 (800-228-9290)
Dogs of all sizes are allowed. There is a $75 one time additional fee per pet. Dogs must be leashed, cleaned up after, and a contact number left with the front desk if they are alone in the room. Multiple dogs may be allowed.

Crown City Inn
520 Orange Ave
Coronado, CA
619-435-3116
crowncityinn.com/
This inn is located in beautiful Coronado which is across the harbor from downtown San Diego. Walk to several outdoor restaurants or to the Coronado Centennial Park. Room service is available. Pet charges are $8 per day for a designated pet room and $25 per day for a non-designated pet room. They have non-smoking rooms available. Pets must never be left unattended in the room.

Loews Coronado Bay Resort
4000 Coronado Bay Road
Coronado, CA
619-424-4000
All well-behaved dogs of any size are welcome. This upscale hotel offers their "Loews Loves Pets" program which includes special pet treats, local dog walking routes, and a list of nearby pet-friendly places to visit. There are no pet fees.

Holiday Inn
3131 S, Bristol Street
Costa Mesa, CA
714-557-3000 (877-270-6405)
Dogs of all sizes are allowed for an additional $50 one time pet fee per room. Multiple dogs may be allowed.

Motel 6 - Costa Mesa
1441 Gisler Avenue
Costa Mesa, CA
714-957-3063 (800-466-8356)
One well-behaved family pet per room. Guest must notify front desk upon arrival. Guest is liable for any damages. In consideration of all guests, pets must never be left unattended in the guest rooms.

Residence Inn by Marriott
881 W Baker Street
Costa Mesa, CA
714-241-8800
Dogs of all sizes are welcome. There is a $75 plus tax one time fee, and a pet policy to sign at check in. Multiple dogs may be allowed.

The Westin South Coast Plaza
686 Anton Blvd.
Costa Mesa, CA
714-540-2500 (888-625-5144)
Dogs up to 80 pounds are allowed. There are no additional pet fees.

Vagabond Inn
3205 Harbor Blvd
Costa Mesa, CA
714-557-8360
vagabondinn.com/
This motel offers a complimentary continental breakfast. The Bark Park dog park is located nearby. There is a $5 per day pet fee.

Yosemite Gold Country Motel
10407 Highway 49
Coulterville, CA
209-878-3400
yosemitegold.com/ygcm/
All rooms are completely furnished with a heater and air conditioner, color TV, telephones, bathroom with tub-shower and free coffee. Your dog is more than welcome here, but he or

she must stay on a leash when outside and should use their Doggie Park when going to the bathroom. Also, they require that you do not leave your dog outside unattended. This motel is located about hour from Yosemite Valley (40 min. to the main gate and 20 min. to the valley). There are no additional pet fees.

Town House Motel
444 US H 101S
Crescent City, CA
707-464-4176
Well behaved and friendly dogs are allowed. There is a $10 per night per pet fee and there is only 1 pet friendly room available. There are some breed restrictions. Multiple dogs may be allowed.

J & J Guest House
5515 Calumet Lane
Creston, CA
805-226-9558
Well behaved dogs of all sizes are allowed, but keep in mind it is a fairly small cabin of about 600 square fee. There are no additional pet fees. Multiple dogs may be allowed.

Tahoe Biltmore Lodge
#5 Hwy 28 (Hwy 28 and Stateline)
Crystal Bay, NV
775-831-0660 (800-BILTMORE (245-6673))
This inn offers 92 affordable, well appointed rooms and suites, and there are also some cottages available overlooking the lake. Amenities include room service, an outdoor spa and seasonal pool, a long list of entertainment and special events throughout the year, a nightclub, and 2 restaurants. Dogs of all sizes are allowed for a refundable deposit of $100 and an additional fee of $20 per night per pet. Dogs must be crated or removed for housekeeping, and crated when left alone in the room. Dogs must be leashed and cleaned up after at all times. Multiple dogs may be allowed.

Four Points by Sheraton Culver City
5990 Green Valley Circle
Culver City, CA
310-641-7740 (888-625-5144)
Dogs up to 50 pounds are allowed for an additional fee of $25 per night per pet. Dogs may not be left alone in the room.

Radisson Hotel Los Angeles Westside
6161 Centinela Avenue
Culver City, CA
310-649-1776

Dogs of all sizes are allowed. Dogs are allowed in first floor rooms only. These are all non-smoking rooms. There is a $50 one time pet fee, with a $100 refundable pet deposit.

Cypress Hotel
10050 S. DeAnza Blvd.
Cupertino, CA
408-253-8900
thecypresshotel.com/
Well-behaved dogs of all sizes are welcome at this pet-friendly hotel. The boutique hotel offers both rooms and suites. Hotel amenities include complimentary evening wine service, an a 24 hour on-site fitness room. There are no pet fees, just sign a pet liability form.

Woodfin Suite Hotel
5905 Corporate Ave
Cypress, CA
714-828-4000
All rooms are non-smoking. All well-behaved dogs are welcome. Every room is a suite with wetbars or full kitchens. Hotel amenities include a pool, exercise facility, complimentary video movies, and a complimentary hot breakfast buffet. There is a $5 per day pet fee and you will need to sign a pet waiver.

Doubletree
34402 Pacific Coast Highway
Dana Point, CA
949-661-1100
Dogs of all sizes are allowed. There is a $30 per night per room fee and a pet policy to sign at check in. Multiple dogs may be allowed.

Holiday Inn Express Hotel & Suites Dana Point-Harbor/Doheny Beach
34280 Pacific Coast Highway
Dana Point, CA
949-248-1000 (877-270-6405)
Dogs of all sizes are allowed for an additional $75 one time fee per room. 2 dogs may be allowed.

Best Western University Lodge
123 B Street
Davis, CA
530-756-7890 (800-780-7234)
Dogs are allowed for an additional fee of $10 per night per pet. Multiple dogs may be allowed.

Econo Lodge
221 D Street
Davis, CA
530-756-1040
Dogs are allowed.

Howard Johnson Hotel

4100 Chiles Road
Davis, CA
530-792-0800 (800-446-4656)
Dogs of all sizes are welcome. There is a $10 per day pet fee. They have one non-smoking pet room, but cannot guarantee it will be available.

Motel 6 - Davis - Sacramento Area
4835 Chiles Road
Davis, CA
530-753-3777 (800-466-8356)
One well-behaved family pet per room. Guest must notify front desk upon arrival. Guest is liable for any damages. In consideration of all guests, pets must never be left unattended in the guest rooms.

University Inn Bed and Breakfast
340 A Street
Davis, CA
530-756-8648
All rooms are non-smoking. There are no pet fees. Children are also allowed.

University Park Inn & Suites
1111 Richards Blvd.
Davis, CA
530-756-0910
stayanight.com/upi/upimain.htm
Located within walking distance of downtown Davis. They have one pet room available and there is a $10 per night pet charge.

Stovepipe Wells Village Motel
H 190
Death Valley, CA
760-786-2387
The Village Motel is a short distance from some of the most photographed sand dunes in the world. They offer such amenities as comfortable ground floor guest rooms, a Restaurant and Saloon, general store and gift shop, service station, private landing strip, and an on-site RV park. Dogs of all sizes are allowed for an additional $20 refundable deposit for the motel rooms; there is no fee or deposit for dogs in the RV park. Dogs may not be left unattended in motel rooms. Dogs must be leashed and cleaned up after. Dogs are allowed in public places only; they are not allowed on trails or in canyon areas. 2 dogs may be allowed.

Hilton
15575 Jimmy Durante Blvd
Del Mar, CA
858-792-5200
Dogs up to 60 pounds are allowed for a $150 refundable deposit plus a $50 one time pet fee per room.

Multiple dogs may be allowed.

Shilo Inn
2231 Girard Street
Delano, CA
661-725-7551
Your pet is welcome. Amenities include complimentary continental breakfast, in-room iron, ironing board & hair dryer, guest laundry, seasonal outdoor pool & spa. Conveniently located between Fresno & Bakersfield off Highway 99.

Hunter Mountain House
9379 Highway 79
Descanso, CA
619-659-0606
huntermountainhouse.com
This rustic stone home is located on 12 acres. As a historic gathering place for Native Americans for hundreds of years there are archeological sites and trails right at the property. There is a fenced yard and patio.

San Diego Backcountry Retreat
Call to Arrange
Descanso, CA
888-894-4626
haylapa.1888twigman.com
The Haylapa House is located on a small ranch east of San Diego. The Haylapa is one large open room. It has a full kitchen and bathroom. Outside, it has a fenced area for your dog and nearby hiking.

Best Western Inn Dixon
1345 Commercial Way
Dixon, CA
707-678-1400 (800-780-7234)
Dogs are allowed for an additional one time pet fee of $15 per room. Multiple dogs may be allowed.

The Topanga Treehouse
Call to Arrange
Dorrington, CA
415-488-0278
This two bedroom, two bath vacation rental is located on Highway 4 between Arnold and Bear Valley. It sleeps 4 people. Well behaved dogs are welcome with a $100 refundable security deposit. Dogs should be groomed and have flea control. Dog beds, dog bowls and treats are provided.

Embassy Suites Hotel Los Angeles - Downey
8425 Firestone Blvd.
Downey, CA
562-861-1900
Dogs of all sizes are allowed. There

is a $25 per night pet fee per pet. Dogs are not allowed to be left alone in the room.

Downieville Carriage House Inn
110 Commercial Street
Downieville, CA
530-289-3573
This 9 room inn is located in historic downtown Downieville and is open year round. Well-behaved dogs are allowed. Dogs should be able to get along well with other guests, as this is a house. There is a $15 per day pet fee.

Downieville Loft
208 Main Street
Downieville, CA
510-501-2516
This amazing retreat along the Yuba River offers many features and amenities, some of which include 2,700 feet of retreat space on 2 levels, 8 full-size skylights, all custom made furniture, a large well equipped kitchen with river views, 2 fireplaces and bathrooms, and excellent summer swimming and fishing just steps from the loft. Dogs of all sizes are welcome for an additional fee of $10 per night per pet. Dogs are not allowed on the furnishings, and they must be leashed and cleaned up after. Dogs may not be left alone in the loft. Multiple dogs may be allowed.

Durgan Flat Inn
121 River Street
Downieville, CA
530-289-3308
Dogs of all sizes are allowed. There are no additional pet fees with a credit card on file. There is a pet policy to sign at check in and they request you kennel your dog when out of the room. Multiple dogs may be allowed.

Old Well Motel
15947 State Highway 49
Drytown, CA
209-245-6467
This motel is located near the Shenandoah Valley. There is a $5 per day additional pet fee.

Best Western Country
3930 County Rd 89
Dunnigan, CA
530-724-3471 (800-780-7234)
Dogs are allowed for an additional one time pet fee of $20 per room. Multiple dogs may be allowed.

Dunsmuir Lodge

6604 Dunsmuir Avenue
Dunsmuir, CA
530-235-2884
dunsmuirlodge.net/
Located in a mountain setting on 4 landscaped acres with a beautiful meadow and great mountain views, this lodge offers country log home decor and all rooms open out to a central courtyard. Some of the amenities include a great location for many other recreational activities, barbecues, and if you like to fish, there is a place to clean and freeze your catch. Dogs of all sizes are allowed. There is no fee for 1 or 2 dogs; for a 3rd dog there is a $15 per night additional pet fee. Dogs may not be left alone in the rooms at any time, and there are designated areas to walk your pet. Dogs must be leashed, and they ask that pets are cleaned up after both inside and out. Multiple dogs may be allowed.

Railroad Park Resort
100 Railroad Park Road
Dunsmuir, CA
530-235-4440
rrpark.com/
Spend a night or more inside a restored antique railroad car at this unique resort. Dogs are allowed for an additional $10 per day. This resort also offers RV hookup spaces.

Four Seasons Hotel Silicon Valley
2050 University Ave.
East Palo Alto, CA
650-566-1200
Dogs of all sizes are allowed. There are no additional pet fees. Dogs are not allowed to be left alone in the room.

Motel 6 - San Diego - El Cajon
550 Montrose Court
El Cajon, CA
619-588-6100 (800-466-8356)
One well-behaved family pet per room. Guest must notify front desk upon arrival. Guest is liable for any damages. In consideration of all guests, pets must never be left unattended in the guest rooms.

Quality Inn Suites
1250 El Cajon Blvd
El Cajon, CA
619-588-8808 (877-424-6423)
Dogs are allowed for an additional one time pet fee of $10 per room. Multiple dogs may be allowed.

Thriftlodge
1220 W Main Street
El Cajon, CA
619-442-2576

Dogs of all sizes are allowed. There is a $10 per night per pet additional fee. 2 dogs may be allowed.

Motel 6 - El Centro
395 Smoketree Drive
El Centro, CA
760-353-6766 (800-466-8356)
One well-behaved family pet per room. Guest must notify front desk upon arrival. Guest is liable for any damages. In consideration of all guests, pets must never be left unattended in the guest rooms.

Motel 6 - Los Angeles - El Monte
3429 Peck Road
El Monte, CA
626-448-6660 (800-466-8356)
One well-behaved family pet per room. Guest must notify front desk upon arrival. Guest is liable for any damages. In consideration of all guests, pets must never be left unattended in the guest rooms.

Yosemite View Lodge
H 140
El Portal, CA
209-379-2681 (888-742-4371)
Just steps away from the entrance to the National Park, this lodge offers luxury accommodations and many extras. Some of the amenities include private balconies or patios, 1 indoor and 3 outdoor pools, 1 indoor and 5 outdoor spas, a cocktail lounge, gift shop, convenience store, restaurant, and a visitor and guide center. Dogs of all sizes are allowed for an additional fee of $10 per night per pet. Dogs must be leashed and cleaned up after at all times, and they may only be left alone in the room if they will be quiet, well behaved, and the Do Not Disturb sign is put on the door. Multiple dogs may be allowed.

Residence Inn by Marriott
2135 El Segundo Blvd
El Segundo, CA
310-333-0888
Dogs of all sizes are allowed. There is a $75 one time fee, and a pet policy to sign at check in. ₀ Multiple dogs may be allowed.

The Greenwood Pier Inn
5928 S H 1
Elk, CA
707-877-9997
Dogs of all sizes are allowed. There is a $15 per night per pet additional fee. Multiple dogs may be allowed.

The Griffin House Inn

5910 S H 1
Elk, CA
707-877-1820
griffinhouseinn.com/
Some of the amenities at this inn include a hearty breakfast delivered to your cottage door, wood burning stoves with firewood, private decks, and an on-site restaurant and pub. There is only one pet friendly cottage so be sure to declare your pet at the time of the reservation; this cottage also has a back yard. Dogs up to 75 pounds are allowed for an additional fee of $20 per pet per stay. Dogs must be leashed and cleaned up after at all times. The reservation number is 707-877-3422. 2 dogs may be allowed.

Best Western Encinitas Inn and Suites at Moonlight Beach
85 Encinitas Blvd
Encinitas, CA
760-942-7455 (800-780-7234)
Dogs are allowed for an additional one time pet fee of $50 per room. 2 dogs may be allowed.

Casa Leucadia
Call to Arrange
Encinitas, CA
760-633-4497
This large vacation rental in Encinitas can sleep up to 13 people. It consists of a main house and two separate suites. There is a nice yard and dogs are welcome.

Castle Creek Inn Resort
29850 Circle R Way
Escondido, CA
760-751-8800 (800-253-5341)

Comfort Inn
1290 W Valley Parkway
Escondido, CA
760-489-1010 (877-424-6423)
Dogs under 25 pounds are allowed for an additional one time fee of $15 per pet; the fee is $25 per pet for dogs over 25 pounds. 2 dogs may be allowed.

Motel 6 - Escondido
900 North Quince Street
Escondido, CA
760-745-9252 (800-466-8356)
One well-behaved family pet per room. Guest must notify front desk upon arrival. Guest is liable for any damages. In consideration of all guests, pets must never be left unattended in the guest rooms.

Palm Tree Lodge Motel
425 W Mission Avenue

Escondido, CA
760-745-7613
This hotel offers 38 guest rooms (some with kitchens or fireplaces), an outdoor pool and a restaurant on site. Dogs of all sizes are allowed. There is a $20 per night additional pet fee for one dog, and $30 per night for 2 dogs. Dogs may not be left alone in the rooms, and they must be well behaved, leashed, and cleaned up after. 2 dogs may be allowed.

Discovery Inn
2832 Broadway
Eureka, CA
707-441-8442
There is a $7 per day additional pet fee.

Motel 6 - Eureka
1934 Broadway Street
Eureka, CA
707-445-9631 (800-466-8356)
One well-behaved family pet per room. Guest must notify front desk upon arrival. Guest is liable for any damages. In consideration of all guests, pets must never be left unattended in the guest rooms.

The Eureka Inn
518 Seventh Street
Eureka, CA
707-442-6441 (800-862-4906)
eurekainn.com
This inn has been named a National Historical Place, and is a member of Historic Hotels of America. Dogs are allowed on the first floor and there is no pet fee. They have allowed well-behaved St. Bernards here before.

Extended Stay America
1019 Oliver Road
Fairfield, CA
707-438-0932
Dogs of all sizes are allowed. There is a $25 fee for the first night, and a $75 one time fee starting the 2nd night per room. Multiple dogs may be allowed.

Motel 6 - Fairfield North
1473 Holiday Lane
Fairfield, CA
707-425-4565 (800-466-8356)
One well-behaved family pet per room. Guest must notify front desk upon arrival. Guest is liable for any damages. In consideration of all guests, pets must never be left unattended in the guest rooms.

Quail Cove
P.O. Box 117

Fawnskin, CA
800-595-2683
quailcove.com/
This lodge offers rustic and cozy cabins in a quiet wooded surrounding on Big Bear Lake. They are located within walking distance to several restaurants, markets, marinas and some of the hiking trails and fishing spots. Pets are always welcome. There is a $10 per day pet charge. Never leave your pet unattended in the cabin.

Collingwood Inn
831 Main Street
Ferndale, CA
707-786-9219
Dogs of all sizes are allowed. There is a $25 per pet per stay fee and a pet policy to sign at check in. Multiple dogs may be allowed.

Best Western Apricot Inn
46290 W Panoche Rd
Firebaugh, CA
559-659-1444 (800-780-7234)
Dogs are allowed for an additional one time pet fee of $10 per room. Multiple dogs may be allowed.

Apple Tree Inn at Yosemite
1110 Highway 41
Fish Camp, CA
559-683-5111 (888-683-5111)
appletreeinn-yosemite.com/
This 54 unit inn is nestled among acres of trees. There is dog-friendly hiking right from the property on fire roads in the Sierra National Forest (on Jackson/Big Sandy Road which is also the road to the Yosemite Trails Pack Station). Pets must be leashed on the inn's property and in the forest. The next property over from the inn is the Tenaya Lodge which has several cafes with food to go. The inn is located two miles from the southern entrance to Yosemite National Park (about 45 minutes to Yosemite Valley). There is a $50 one time pet charge.

Narrow Gauge Inn
48571 Highway 41
Fish Camp, CA
559-683-7720
narrowgaugeinn.com/
This inn is located amidst pine trees in the Sierra Mountains. They are located about four miles from the southern entrance to Yosemite National Park (about 45 minutes to Yosemite Valley). There are some trails nearby in the dog-friendly Sierra National Forest near Bass Lake. All rooms are non-smoking. Dogs are allowed in the main level

rooms and there is a $25 one time per stay pet fee. Children are also welcome.

Tenaya Lodge
1122 Highway 41
Fish Camp, CA
888-514-2167
tenayalodge.com/
This classic resort with 244 guest rooms and suites has created an elegant retreat with all the modern services. The resort sits on 35 scenic acres only two miles from the south entrance of Yosemite National Park and offers many in-room amenities and a variety of dining choices. One dog up to 75 pounds is allowed per room. There is a $75 one time additional pet fee. Dogs may not be left unattended in the room, and they are not allowed in the shops and restaurants. Dogs must be leashed and cleaned up after at all times. They also offer a canine amenity package that includes treats, disposable mitts, a plush dog bed, water bowl, and a canine concierge fact sheet of fun areas to roam. With advanced booking they can also provide a dog walking/sitting service.

Lake Natoma Inn
702 Gold Lake Drive
Folsom, CA
916-351-1500
lakenatomainn.com/
This inn offers 120 guest rooms and 12 lakeview suites nestled in a wooded natural environment overlooking Lake Natoma. Enjoy over 20 miles of beautiful bike and dog-friendly walking trails along the American river. This inn is also located next to Historic Folsom. There is a $45 one time per stay pet fee and a $15 per day pet charge per pet.

Motel 6 - Fontana
10195 Sierra Avenue
Fontana, CA
909-823-8686 (800-466-8356)
One well-behaved family pet per room. Guest must notify front desk upon arrival. Guest is liable for any damages. In consideration of all guests, pets must never be left unattended in the guest rooms.

Beachcomber Motel
1111 N. Main Street
Fort Bragg, CA
707-964-2402 (800-400-SURF)
thebeachcombermotel.com/
This ocean front motel is next to a walking, jogging, and cycling trail

that stretches for miles along the coast. Many rooms have ocean views. They allow well-behaved dogs up to about 75-80 pounds. There is an additional $10 per day pet charge.

Cleone Gardens Inn
24600 N. Hwy 1
Fort Bragg, CA
707-964-2788 (800-400-2189)
cleonelodgeinn.com/
This park-like inn is on 5 acres. There are three pet rooms and an additional pet charge of $6 per day.

Delamere Seaside Cottages
16821 Ocean Drive
Fort Bragg, CA
707-964-3175
delamerecottages.com
These two small pet-friendly cottages are located on the Mendocino Coast and have nice ocean views. One cottage has two decks and the other has a gazebo. Your well-behaved dog is welcome.

Harbor View Seasonal Rental
Call to arrange.
Fort Bragg, CA
760-438-2563
Watch the boats go in and out of the harbor and listen to the sea lions and fog horns from this dog-friendly vacation rental. This 3,000 square foot house is entirely furnished. The main floor has a living room, dining room, kitchen, 2 bedrooms, 1 bathroom and a deck with a view of the harbor. The upstairs has a large master suite with a deck and a view of the bridge and ocean. The yard has redwood trees and even deer wandering through. This area is popular for year-round fishing. The rental is available throughout the year. Please call to inquire about rates and available dates.

Pine Beach Inn
16801 N H 1
Fort Bragg, CA
888-987-8388
pinebeachinn.com/index.html
Located on 11 lush, tranquil acres with its own private beach and cove, this scenic inn also features easy access to several other recreational activities, shopping, and dining. Some of the amenities include a large lawn with a gazebo, 2 championship tennis courts, and a restaurant (south of the border cuisine) and full bar. Dogs of all sizes are allowed for an additional $10 per night per pet. Dogs may not be left alone in the rooms, and they must be leashed and cleaned up after.

Multiple dogs may be allowed.

Quality Inn and Suites Tradewinds
400 S Main Street
Fort Bragg, CA
707-964-4761 (877-424-6423)
Dogs up to 80 pounds are allowed for an additional pet fee of $15 per night per room. 2 dogs may be allowed.

Shoreline Cottages
18725 N H 1
Fort Bragg, CA
707-964-2977
Adult dogs only are allowed, no puppies. There is a $10 per pet per stay pet fee. Multiple dogs may be allowed.

The Rendezvous Inn and Restaurant
647 North Main Street
Fort Bragg, CA
707-964-8142 (800-491-8142)
rendezvousinn.com/
A romantic and elegant destination, this beautifully crafted 1897 home offers charm, relaxation, beautiful gardens, a large sunny guest parlor, and an inviting ambiance. They can also tailor your stay with a food and wine pairing. Their award-winning restaurant offers French gourmet dining in a casual but elegant atmosphere, an extensive wine list, and seasonal outdoor dining where your four-legged companion may join you. Dogs of all sizes are welcome for no additional fee. Dogs must be leashed and cleaned up after. Multiple dogs may be allowed.

Residence Inn by Marriott
9930 Slater Avenue
Fountain Valley, CA
714-965-8000
Pets of all sizes are allowed. There is a $75 one time fee, and a pet policy to sign at check in. Multiple dogs may be allowed.

Best Western Garden Court Inn of Fremont
5400 Mowry Ave
Fremont, CA
510-792-4300 (800-780-7234)
Dogs are allowed for an additional fee of $15 per night per pet. Multiple dogs may be allowed.

La Quinta Inn & Suites Fremont
46200 Landing Pkwy.
Fremont, CA
510-445-0808 (800-531-5900)
Dogs of all sizes are allowed. There are no additional pet fees. Dogs must be quiet, well behaved, leashed

and cleaned up after. Multiple dogs may be allowed.

Motel 6 - Fremont North
34047 Fremont Boulevard
Fremont, CA
510-793-4848 (800-466-8356)
One well-behaved family pet per room. Guest must notify front desk upon arrival. Guest is liable for any damages. In consideration of all guests, pets must never be left unattended in the guest rooms.

Motel 6 - Fremont South
46101 Research Avenue
Fremont, CA
510-490-4528 (800-466-8356)
One well-behaved family pet per room. Guest must notify front desk upon arrival. Guest is liable for any damages. In consideration of all guests, pets must never be left unattended in the guest rooms.

Days Inn-Parkway
1101 N Parkway Dr
Fresno, CA
559-268-6211 (800-329-7466)
daysinn.com
This motel has a playground for the kids. They also have 2 two bedroom suites available. Room rates include a free breakfast. To get there from Hwy 99 south, take the Olive Ave exit. Turn right onto Olive Ave and then left onto North Parkway Drive. The motel will be on the right. There is a $5 per day additional pet fee.

Econo Lodge
445 N Parkway Dr
Fresno, CA
559-485-5019
A large well-behaved dog is okay. There is a $10 refundable pet deposit.

Holiday Inn Express and Suites
5046 N. Barcus Rd
Fresno, CA
559-277-5700 (877-270-6405)
Dogs up to 50 pounds are allowed for an additional $20 one time fee per room. 2 dogs may be allowed.

La Quinta Inn Fresno Yosemite
2926 Tulare
Fresno, CA
559-442-1110 (800-531-5900)
Dogs of all sizes are allowed. There are no additional pet fees, and there is a pet waiver to sign at check in. Dogs must be leashed and cleaned up after. Multiple dogs may be allowed.

Motel 6 - Fresno - Blackstone North
4245 North Blackstone Avenue
Fresno, CA
559-221-0800 (800-466-8356)
One well-behaved family pet per room. Guest must notify front desk upon arrival. Guest is liable for any damages. In consideration of all guests, pets must never be left unattended in the guest rooms.

Motel 6 - Fresno - Blackstone South
4080 North Blackstone Avenue
Fresno, CA
559-222-2431 (800-466-8356)
One well-behaved family pet per room. Guest must notify front desk upon arrival. Guest is liable for any damages. In consideration of all guests, pets must never be left unattended in the guest rooms.

Motel 6 - Fresno - SR 99
1240 North Crystal Avenue
Fresno, CA
559-237-0855 (800-466-8356)
One well-behaved family pet per room. Guest must notify front desk upon arrival. Guest is liable for any damages. In consideration of all guests, pets must never be left unattended in the guest rooms.

Quality Inn
4278 W Ashlan Avenue
Fresno, CA
559-275-2727 (877-424-6423)
Dogs are allowed for an additional one time pet fee of $30 per room 2 dogs may be allowed.

Red Roof Inn - Fresno - SR 99
5021 North Barcus Avenue
Fresno, CA
559-276-1910 (800-RED-ROOF)
One well-behaved family pet per room. Guest must notify front desk upon arrival. Guest is liable for any damages. In consideration of all guests, pets must never be left unattended in the guest rooms.

Residence Inn by Marriott
5322 N Diana Avenue
Fresno, CA
559-222-8900
Dogs of all sizes are allowed. There is a $75 plus tax one time fee, and a pet policy to sign at check in. 2 dogs may be allowed.

Super 8 Fresno/Highway 99
1087 N Parkway Dr
Fresno, CA
559-268-0741 (800-800-8000)
Dogs up to 60 pounds are allowed. There is a $10 per night pet fee per

pet. Smoking and non-smoking rooms are available for pet rooms. 2 dogs may be allowed.

TownePlace Suites Fresno
7127 N Fresno St
Fresno, CA
559-435-4600
Dogs of all sizes are allowed. There is a $75 one time pet fee per visit. 2 dogs may be allowed.

Travelodge
3093 N Parkway Dr
Fresno, CA
559-276-7745 (800-276-7745)
This motel shares a lobby with the Knights Inn. There is a $10 per day pet charge. To get there from Hwy 99 south, take the Shields Ave exit. Then turn right onto N Parkway Drive.

University Inn
2655 E Shaw Avenue
Fresno, CA
559-294-0224
A convenient location to numerous activities and recreation, this inn also offers a free continental breakfast, an outdoor pool and Jacuzzi, and an on-site restaurant. Dogs of all sizes are allowed for an additional pet deposit of $25 per room. Dogs may not be left alone in the rooms, and they must be leashed and cleaned up after. 2 dogs may be allowed.

Fullerton Marriott at California State University
2701 E Nutwood Avenue
Fullerton, CA
714-738-7800 (800-228-9290)
Dogs up to 50 pounds are allowed. There is a $100 refundable deposit plus a $20 per night per pet additional fee. Dogs must be well behaved, leashed, cleaned up after, removed or accompanied for housekeeping, and the Do Not Disturb sign put on the door if they are in the room alone. Multiple dogs may be allowed.

Anaheim Marriott Suites
12015 Harbor Blvd
Garden Grove, CA
714-750-1000 (800-228-9290)
Dogs of all sizes are allowed. There is a $15 per night per pet additional fee, and a pet policy to sign at check in. Dogs may not be left alone in the room, and they must be leashed and cleaned up after. Multiple dogs may be allowed.

Candlewood Suites

12901 Garden Grove Blvd
Garden Grove, CA
714-539-4200 (877-270-6405)
Dogs of all sizes are allowed for an additional pet fee of $75 per room for each 1 to 6 days. 2 dogs may be allowed.

Residence Inn by Marriott
11931 Harbor Blvd
Garden Grove, CA
714-591-4000
Dogs of all sizes are welcome. There is a $60 per pet per stay fee, and a pet policy to sign at check in. Multiple dogs may be allowed.

American River Bed and Breakfast Inn
Main and Orleans Streets
Georgetown, CA
530-333-4499
americanriverinn.com
They have certain pet rooms and you need to call in advance to make a reservation. All rooms are non-smoking. There is a refundable pet deposit.

Motel 6 - Gilroy
6110 Monterey Highway
Gilroy, CA
408-842-6061 (800-466-8356)
One well-behaved family pet per room. Guest must notify front desk upon arrival. Guest is liable for any damages. In consideration of all guests, pets must never be left unattended in the guest rooms.

Vagabond Inn
120 W. Colorado Street
Glendale, CA
818-240-1700
vagabondinn.com
This motel is located near Universal Studios. Amenities include a complimentary breakfast and during the week, a free USA Today newspaper. There is a $10 per day pet fee.

Motel 6 - Santa Barbara - Goleta
5897 Calle Real
Goleta, CA
805-964-3596 (800-466-8356)
One well-behaved family pet per room. Guest must notify front desk upon arrival. Guest is liable for any damages. In consideration of all guests, pets must never be left unattended in the guest rooms.

Econo Lodge
49713 Gorman Post Rd
Gorman, CA
661-248-6411

There is a $10 per day pet fee.

Gray Eagle Lodge
5000 Gold Lake Rd.
Graeagle, CA
800-635-8778 (800-635-8778)
grayeaglelodge.com/
Stay in a rustic cabin at this mountain getaway located in the Sierra Mountains, about 1.5 hours north of Truckee. There are many hiking trails within a short walk from the cabins. There are over 40 alpine lakes nearby. There is a $20 per pet, per day, fee with a maximum of 2 pets per cabin. Guests are expected to follow guidelines provided by the lodge and will sign a pet policy form upon arrival. Dogs up to 50 pounds are allowed.

Best Western Gold Country Inn
11972 Sutton Way
Grass Valley, CA
530-273-1393 (800-780-7234)
Dogs are allowed for an additional one time pet fee of $15 per room. Multiple dogs may be allowed.

Grass Valley Courtyard Suites
210 N Auburn Street
Grass Valley, CA
530-272-7696
gvcourtyardsuites.com/
This luxurious getaway offers a great location to several local points of interest, individually decorated guest rooms with fully equipped kitchens, fireplaces, a heated pool and spa, many in-room amenities, and an intimate lounge where guests may enjoy a continental breakfast or an evening of wine and hors d'oeuvres. Dogs of all sizes are welcome and receive their own canine cuddler to use during their stay. There is an additional $25 per pet per stay for dogs under 40 pounds, and an additional $50 per pet per stay for dogs over 40 pounds. Dogs may not be left alone in the room at any time, and they must be leashed and cleaned up after; they have provided a doggy station with a scooper and receptacles. 2 dogs may be allowed.

Swan Levine House Bed and Breakfast
328 South Church Street
Grass Valley, CA
916-272-1873
This renovated historic house was built in 1880. It was originally owned by a local merchant who made his fortune by selling mining equipment. He sold it to a doctor who converted the house into a hospital and it served as a community medical

center until 1968. There are four rooms, each with a private bath. They have one room available for guests who bring a large dog. Dogs are not to be left alone in the room. There is a $15 per day pet charge. They are also kid-friendly. They do have a cat that resides in the house.

Historic Groveland Hotel
18767 Main Street
Groveland, CA
209-962-4000 (800-273-3314.)
groveland.com/
Your dog or cat is welcome at this 1849 historic inn. Country Inns Magazine rated the Groveland Hotel as one of the Top 10 Inns in the United States. The inn is located 23 miles from Yosemite's main gate. Their restaurant can pack a gourmet picnic basket for your day trip to Yosemite. Make your reservations early as they book up quickly. This inn is located about an hour from Yosemite Valley. There is a $10 per day additional pet fee. All rooms are non-smoking.

Hotel Charlotte
18736 Main Street
Groveland, CA
209-962-6455
Dogs of all sizes are allowed. There is a $20 per night per pet fee and there is only 1 pet friendly room. 2 dogs may be allowed.

Sunset Inn
33569 Hardin Flat Rd.
Groveland, CA
209-962-4360
This inn offers three cabins near Yosemite National Park. The cabins are located on two acres and are surrounded by a dog-friendly National Forest at a 4500 foot elevation. All cabins are non-smoking and include kitchens and private bathrooms. Children are also welcome. The Sunset Inn is located just 2 miles from the west entrance to Yosemite, one mile from Highway 120. There is a $20 per day pet charge.

Yosemite Westgate Motel
7633 Hwy 120
Groveland, CA
209-962-5281 (800-253-9673)
This motel has one pet room available and it is a non-smoking room. There is a $10 per night pet fee. The motel is located about 40 minutes from Yosemite Valley.

Mar Vista Cottages
35101 S H 1

Gualala, CA
707-884-3522 (877-855-3522)
marvistamendocino.com/
This inn offers 12 housekeeping cottages with kitchens and an organic garden to harvest from. They will also stock the cottages with any essential needs if you call ahead. There are breathtaking ocean and coastal views with a short walk to the beach, 9 acres of scenic grounds, and hiking trails. Dogs of all sizes are welcome for an additional one time fee of $35 for one pet, and $50 if there are two pets. Dogs are allowed around the grounds, on the trails, and at the beach. Dogs must be at least 2 years old and completely housebroken; they are not permitted on the beds and furniture, and they may not be left alone in the cottage at any time. Dogs may be off lead only if they are under good voice control as there are other dogs and animals in residence. Dogs must be friendly, well behaved, and cleaned up after at all times. 2 dogs may be allowed.

Ocean View Properties
P.O. Box 1285
Gualala, CA
707-884-3538
oceanviewprop.com/
Ocean View Properties offers vacation home rentals on The Sea Ranch and Mendocino Coast. Some of their vacation homes are pet-friendly. They offer a wide variety of special vacation home rentals, located on the oceanfront, oceanside and hillside at The Sea Ranch. Each of the rental homes has a fully equipped kitchen, a fireplace or wood stove, blankets, pillows, and telephones. Most have hot tubs, televisions, VCR's, radios, CD/cassette players, and washer/dryers. Guests provide kindling, bed linens, and towels. With advance notice, linens can be rented and maid service can be hired. Please call and ask them which rentals are dog-friendly.

Sea Ranch Vacation Homes
P.O. Box 246
Gualala, CA
707-884-4235
searanchrentals.com/
Rent a vacation home for the weekend, week or longer along the coast or on a forested hillside. Some of their 50 homes allow well-behaved dogs.

Serenisea Vacation Homes

36100 Highway 1 S.
Gualala, CA
707-884-3836
serenisea.com
Serenisea maintains and manages a number of vacation homes and cottages in this community on the Mendocino coast. Some of them allow dogs of all sizes.

Surf Motel
39170 S. Highway 1
Gualala, CA
707-884-3571
gualala.com
There is a $10 per day pet charge.

Creekside Inn & Resort
16180 Neeley Rd
Guerneville, CA
707-869-3623
creeksideinn.com
Dogs are allowed in one of their cottages. During the summer it books up fast, so please make an early reservation. The inn will be able to help you find some pet-friendly hiking trails and beaches nearby.

Dawn Ranch Lodge
16467 Hwy. 116
Guerneville, CA
707-869-0656
dawnranch.com
This lodge is located minutes away from many wineries and has nearby access to the Russian River. There are a number of pet-friendly rooms equipped with doggie beds, water bowls and treats. There is a $50 one time non-refundable pet fee per room and up to two dogs are allowed. Dogs may dine on the outside patio at the restaurant.

Ferngrove Cottages
16650 H 116
Guerneville, CA
707-869-8105
This charming retreat offers cottages nestled among redwoods and colorful gardens. Some of the amenities include spa tubs, fireplaces and skylights, a delicious extended continental breakfast, pool and sun deck, a barbecue and picnic area, individual decks or patios, and it is only a short walk to the river/beaches and town. Dogs of all sizes are allowed. There is a $15 per night per pet additional fee. Dogs may not be left alone in the room, and they must be well behaved, leashed, and cleaned up after. Pit Bulls are not allowed. 2 dogs may be allowed.

River Village Resort and Spa

14880 River Road
Guerneville, CA
888-342-2624
rivervillageresort.com
This inn is located just minutes from
the Russian River. At this inn, dogs
are allowed in certain cottages and
there is a $10 per day pet fee.
Please do not walk pets on the lawn.
Children are also welcome.

Russian River Getaways
14075 Mill Street, P.O. Box 1673
Guerneville, CA
707-869-4560 (800-433-6673)
rrgetaways.com
This company offers about 40 dog-
friendly vacation homes in Russian
River wine country with leash free
beaches nearby. There are no pet
fees and no size limits for dogs.
There is a $75 refundable pet
deposit.

Motel 6 - Santa Nella - Los Banos
12733 South Highway 33
Gustine, CA
209-826-6644 (800-466-8356)
One well-behaved family pet per
room. Guest must notify front desk
upon arrival. Guest is liable for any
damages. In consideration of all
guests, pets must never be left
unattended in the guest rooms.

Motel 6 - Los Angeles - Hacienda
Heights
1154 South 7th Avenue
Hacienda Heights, CA
626-968-9462 (800-466-8356)
One well-behaved family pet per
room. Guest must notify front desk
upon arrival. Guest is liable for any
damages. In consideration of all
guests, pets must never be left
unattended in the guest rooms.

Comfort Inn
2930 N Cabrillo H
Half Moon Bay, CA
650-712-1999 (877-424-6423)
Dogs are allowed for an additional
pet fee of $10 per night per room. 2
dogs may be allowed.

Holiday Inn Express
230 S Cabrillo Hwy
Half Moon Bay, CA
650-726-3400 (877-270-6405)
holiday-inn.com
Dogs of all sizes are allowed for an
additional $10 per night per pet. 2
dogs may be allowed.

Motel 6 - Los Angeles - Harbor City
820 West Sepulveda Boulevard
Harbor City, CA

310-549-9560 (800-466-8356)
One well-behaved family pet per
room. Guest must notify front desk
upon arrival. Guest is liable for any
damages. In consideration of all
guests, pets must never be left
unattended in the guest rooms.

TownePlace Suites LAX/Mahattan
Beach
14400 Aviation Blvd
Hawthorne, CA
310-725-9696
Dogs of all sizes are allowed. There
is a $75 one time pet fee per visit. 2
dogs may be allowed.

Comfort Inn Cal State East Bay
24997 Mission Blvd
Hayward, CA
510-538-4466 (877-424-6423)
Dogs are allowed for an additional
fee of $15 per night per pet. 2 dogs
may be allowed.

Motel 6 - Hayward
30155 Industrial Parkway
Southwest
Hayward, CA
510-489-8333 (800-466-8356)
One well-behaved family pet per
room. Guest must notify front desk
upon arrival. Guest is liable for any
damages. In consideration of all
guests, pets must never be left
unattended in the guest rooms.

Vagabond Inn
20455 Hesperian Blvd.
Hayward, CA
510-785-5480
vagabondinn.com
This two story motel offers a heated
pool and spa. To get there from
Hwy 880 heading north, exit A
Street/San Lorenzo. Turn left onto A
Street. Then turn right onto
Hesperian Blvd. There is a $10 per
day additional pet fee per pet.

Baywood Gardens Inn
6952 Giovanetti Rd.
Healdsburg, CA
707-887-1400
A vacation rental located in a quiet
valley in Sonoma wine country.
Various size dog beds and dog
dishes are available.

Best Western Dry Creek Inn
198 Dry Creek Rd
Healdsburg, CA
707-433-0300 (800-780-7234)
Dogs are allowed for an additional
pet fee of $20 per night per room.
Multiple dogs may be allowed.

Duchamp Hotel
421 Foss Street
Healdsburg, CA
707-431-1300
duchamphotel.com
This hotel, located in Healdsburg,
allows dogs in two of their cottages.
Every cottage features a king bed,
oversized spa shower, private
terrace, fireplace, mini bar, and
more. Children over 16 years old are
allowed. The entire premises is non-
smoking. Dogs are not allowed in the
pool area and they request that you
take your dog away from the
cottages and hotel when they go to
the bathroom.

Best Western Inn of Hemet
2625 W Florida Avenue
Hemet, CA
951-925-6605 (800-780-7234)
Dogs are allowed for an additional
one time pet fee of $25 per room. 2
dogs may be allowed.

Motel 6 - Hemet
3885 West Florida Avenue
Hemet, CA
951-929-8900 (800-466-8356)
One well-behaved family pet per
room. Guest must notify front desk
upon arrival. Guest is liable for any
damages. In consideration of all
guests, pets must never be left
unattended in the guest rooms.

Days Suites
14865 Bear Valley Rd
Hesperia, CA
760-948-0600
There is a $7 per day pet fee.

Holiday Inn Express Hotel and Suites
9750 Keypoint Avenue
Hesperia, CA
760-244-7674 (877-270-6405)
Dogs of all sizes are allowed for an
additional $25 per night per pet.
Multiple dogs may be allowed.

Best Western Hollywood Hills Hotel
6141 Franklin Ave
Hollywood, CA
323-464-5181 (800-780-7234)
Dogs are allowed for an additional
fee of $25 per night per pet. 2 dogs
may be allowed.

Chateau Marmont Hotel
8221 Sunset Blvd
Hollywood, CA
323-656-1010
chateaumarmont.com/
Modeled after a royal residence in
France, grand eloquence awaits
guests to this castle on the hill. Some

of the features/amenities include a full service bar, gourmet dining either indoor or in a beautiful garden patio setting, many in room amenities, a heated outdoor pool, and personalized services. Dogs up to 100 pounds are allowed. There is a $100 one time additional pet fee per room and a pet policy to sign at check in. Dogs must be well behaved, leashed, cleaned up after, and the Do Not Disturb sign put on the door if they are in the room alone. 2 dogs may be allowed.

Motel 6 - Los Angeles - Hollywood
1738 North Whitley Avenue
Hollywood, CA
323-464-6006 (800-466-8356)
One well-behaved family pet per room. Guest must notify front desk upon arrival. Guest is liable for any damages. In consideration of all guests, pets must never be left unattended in the guest rooms.

Sorensen's Resort
14255 Highway 88
Hope Valley, CA
530-694-2203 (800-423-9949)
sorensensresort.com/
This secluded mountain resort is located in beautiful Hope Valley which is about 30 minutes south of South Lake Tahoe. Dogs are allowed in several of the cabins. The dog-friendly cabins sleep from two up to four people. Each cabin has a wood-burning stove (for heat) and kitchen. The Hope Valley Cross Country Ski Rentals are located on the premises (see Attractions). Hiking is available during the summer on the trails of the Toiyable National Forest. There are also several nearby lakes. Cabin rates start at $85 per night and go up to about $450 for a large bedroom cabin. There are no additional pet fees.

Ziegler's Trails End
1 Main St, P.O. Box 150
Hyampom, CA
530-628-4929 (800-566-5266)
zieglerstrailsend.com/
These cabins are on the South Fork of the Trinity River. This is in the middle of the dog-friendly Six Rivers National Forest.

Silver Pines Lodge
25955 Cedar St
Idyllwild, CA
909-659-4335
silverpinesidyllwild.com/
This lodge sits on 1 1/2 acres of wooded pine forest overlooking Strawberry Creek. The lodge is

approximately 2 blocks from the main village of Idyllwild where there are many eateries and shops. Each cabin is individually decorated and has its own unique features. Most rooms have fireplaces and about half have kitchens. Every room has its own refrigerator, bathroom, color cable TV and complimentary coffee. Dogs are welcome in all of the cabins, except the Foley Cabin. There is a $10 one time pet charge. They also ask that you please abide by the following pet rules. Never leave pets alone in the room. Pets should not go on the beds or furniture. Keep your dog leashed when on the property. Clean up after your pooch. Please wipe off your pets paws if it's snowy, rainy or muddy outside (they provide dog towels).

Stellar Summit Cabin
Call to arrange
Idyllwild, CA
626-482-6006
stellarsummitcabin.com
This secluded cabin is perched high on a hill in Idyllwild. There is a fenced deck, loft, Jacuzzi and views. There is a $15 pet fee per visit.

Tahquitz Inn
25840 Highway 243
Idyllwild, CA
909-659-4554 (877-659-4554)
tahquitzinn.com
This inn is located in the heart of Idyllwild and allows all well-behaved dogs. They offer one and two bedroom suites with a separate bedroom, kitchen and porches. The inn has also been a location for several Hollywood film shoots. All of their rooms accommodate dogs and there is a $10 per day pet charge.

The Fireside Inn
54540 N Circle Drive
Idyllwild, CA
877-797-FIRE (3473)
thefireside-inn.com/
Surrounded by the natural landscape of the San Jacinto Mountains, this comfortable inn offers 7 duplex cottages and a private cottage. Some of the amenities include wood-burning fireplaces in all cottages, outdoor seating, barbecue and picnic areas, and daily feeding of the birds and small animals of the area. Dogs of all sizes are allowed for an additional $20 one time pet fee per room. Dogs may not be left alone in the room at any time, and they must

be leashed and cleaned up after. 2 dogs may be allowed.

Independence Courthouse Motel
157 N Edwards Street
Independence, CA
760-878-2732
There is a $6 per day additional pet fee. All rooms are non-smoking.

Ray's Den Motel
405 N Edwards St
Independence, CA
760-878-2122
There is a $6 per day additional pet fee.

Wilder House Bed & Breakfast
325 Dusty Lane
Independence, CA
760-878-2119
wilderhouse.com

Best Western Date Tree Hotel
81-909 Indio Bvd
Indio, CA
760-347-3421 (800-780-7234)
Dogs are allowed for an additional fee of $10 per night per pet. Multiple dogs may be allowed.

Motel 6 - Indio - Palm Springs Area
82195 Indio Boulevard
Indio, CA
760-342-6311 (800-466-8356)
One well-behaved family pet per room. Guest must notify front desk upon arrival. Guest is liable for any damages. In consideration of all guests, pets must never be left unattended in the guest rooms.

Palm Shadow Inn
80-761 Highway 111
Indio, CA
760-347-3476
palmsshadowinn.com/
A well-behaved large dog is okay. Nestled among date palm groves, there are eighteen guest rooms which overlook nearly three acres of lawns, flowers and citrus trees. There is a $5 per day pet charge.

Royal Plaza Inn
82347 Hwy 111
Indio, CA
760-347-0911 (800-228-9559)
royalplazainn.com/
This motel offers a laundry room, whirlpool and room refrigerators. There is a $10 per day additional pet fee.

Rosemary Cottage
75 Balboa Ave
Inverness, CA

415-663-9338
rosemarybb.com/
Dogs are welcome at the Rosemary Cottage and The Ark Cottage. Families are also welcome. The Rosemary Cottage is a two room cottage with a deck and garden. It is adjacent to the Point Reyes National Seashore. The Ark Cottage is a two room cottage tucked in the forest a mile up the ridge from the village of Inverness. There is a $25 one time pet charge for one dog or a $35 one time pet charge for two dogs.

Candlewood Suites
16150 Sand Canyon Ave
Irvine, CA
949-788-0500 (877-270-6405)
Dogs up to 80 pounds are allowed for an additional $75 one time fee per pet for 1 to 6 days; 8 days or more is $150 per pet. 2 dogs may be allowed.

Hilton
18800 MacArthur Blvd
Irvine, CA
949-833-9999
Dogs up to 50 pounds are allowed for an additional one time fee of $50 per pet. Multiple dogs may be allowed.

Residence Inn by Marriott
2855 Main Street
Irvine, CA
949-261-2020
Dogs of all sizes are allowed. There is a $75 one time fee, and a pet policy to sign at check in. 2 dogs may be allowed.

Residence Inn by Marriott
10 Morgan
Irvine, CA
949-380-3000
Dogs of all sizes are allowed. There is a $75 plus tax one time fee, and a pet policy to sign at check in. Multiple dogs may be allowed.

Amador Motel
12408 Kennedy Flat Rd
Jackson, CA
209-223-0970
This motel has a large backyard, not completely enclosed, where you can walk your dog. They allow all well-behaved dogs. There are no additional pet fees.

Best Western Amador Inn
200 S Hwy 49
Jackson, CA
209-223-0211 (800-780-7234)
Dogs are allowed for an additional

fee of $10 per night per pet. Multiple dogs may be allowed.

Jackson Gold Lodge
850 N. State Hwy 49
Jackson, CA
209-223-0486
jacksongoldlodge.com/
This lodge has been dog-friendly for years. They allow dogs in the motel rooms and in the cottages. They have eight duplex cottages, each with a separate living room, kitchen, dining room, bedroom and patio. Amenities include a free continental breakfast. Dogs are an additional $10 per day. There are no designated smoking or non-smoking cottages.

National Hotel
18183 Main Street
Jamestown, CA
209-984-3446
Dogs up to 75 pounds are allowed. There is a $15 per night per pet additional fee. 2 dogs may be allowed.

Royal Hotel Bed and Breakfast
18239 Main Street
Jamestown, CA
209-984-5271
Dogs are not allowed in the hotel, but are allowed in one of the private cottages. This hotel is located in historic Jamestown, near Yosemite National Park. There is a $10 per day pet charge.

The National Hotel
18183 Main Street
Jamestown, CA
209-984-3446
national-hotel.com
Established in 1859, this is one of the oldest continuously operating hotels in California. Taking a day trip or going for a hike? Just ask for a picnic basket the day before and their chef will provide you with a meal to take with you and enjoy next to a cool Sierra Nevada stream or at one of the many picnic areas throughout the dog-friendly Stanislaus National Forest. There is a $10 per day pet charge. All rooms are non-smoking.

Jenner Inn
10400 H 1
Jenner, CA
707-865-2377
jennerinn.com/index.html
Located where the Russian River meets the Pacific Ocean, this unique resort features rooms, suites, and cottages set in historic

houses and cottages with something to fit everyone's budget. A full country breakfast is included, and cafe dining is also available. Dogs of all sizes are allowed for a $35 one time additional fee per pet. They have only four pet friendly rooms, and dogs may not be left alone in the room at any time. Dogs must be well behaved, leashed, and cleaned up after. Multiple dogs may be allowed.

Joshua Tree
6426 Valley View Street
Joshua Tree, CA
760-366-2212
Well behaved dogs of all sizes are allowed. There are no additional pet fees. Multiple dogs may be allowed.

Joshua Tree Highlands House
8178 Fleur Rd
Joshua Tree, CA
760-366-3636
joshuatreehighlandshouse.com
This company rents private homes and cabins about 3 minutes from the west entrance to Joshua Tree National Park. Each home is on about 5 acres.

Apple Tree Inn
4360 Highway 78
Julian, CA
800-410-8683
julianappletreeinn.com
This is a small country motel located near the historic gold mining town of Julian. Families are always welcome.There is a $10 per day pet charge and a $50 refundable pet deposit.

Pine Haven Cabin Rental
Call to Arrange.
Julian, CA
760-726-9888
pinehavencabin.com/
Enjoy this dog-friendly mountain getaway on 1.25 acres. The entire lot is securely fenced, offering your pet the freedom to run off-leash. The cabin has one bedroom plus a small loft upstairs, a bathroom with a tiled walk-in shower (no tub), and a fully equipped kitchen. The cabin sleeps 2 people and is off a small private lane, so you will have lots of privacy. No smoking allowed. For reservations call Teresa at 760-726-9888 or email to pinehavencabin@sbcglobal.net.

Big Rock Resort
Big Rock Road at Boulder Drive
June Lake, CA
760-648-7717
bigrockresort.net
Dogs of all sizes are allowed in some

of these one to three bedroom cabins right on June Lake. A maximum of one dog is allowed per cabin. There is a $15 per day additional pet fee. All cabins are non-smoking.

Double Eagle Resort and Spa
5587 Highway 158
June Lake, CA
760-648-7004
doubleeagle.com
This resort on 13 acres allows dogs of all sizes in some of the cabins. Dogs must be on leash on the premises at all times. All cabins are non smoking. There is a $15 per day additional pet fee up to a maximum of $60 for a stay.

June Lake Villager Inn
Boulder Dr & Knoll Ave
June Lake, CA
760-648-7712 (800-655-6545)
junelakevillager.com
Dogs of all sizes are allowed at this inn located in the village of June Lake. The inn has been here in business since the 1920s. Dogs of all sizes are allowed and there are no additional pet fees.

Edgewater Resort and RV Park
6420 Soda Bay Road
Kelseyville, CA
707-279-0208 (800-396-6224)
edgewaterresort.net/
This resort and RV park offers 61 campsites, 6 cabins, and a couple of houses. Some of the amenities include 600 feet of lakefront, a seasonal swimming pool, a 230 foot fishing pier, boat launch, clubhouse, picnic areas, and fire pits. Dogs of all sizes are allowed in the cabins and houses for an additional $10 per night per pet; the fee for RV and tent sites is $2.50 per night per pet. Dogs may not be left unattended outside at any time, may only be left alone in cabins if they are kenneled, and they must have proof of current shots. Dogs must be quiet, well behaved, be inside at night, and leashed and cleaned up after (there is a pet station with bags at the beach). They are not allowed in park buildings or the gated swimming pool area, but they are allowed at the beach. They have provided an "OK-9 Corral outside the general store with fresh water for your pet, and they offer a "pet tag" that says "Guest at Edgewater Resort" with an address and phone number of the resort for a $5 refundable deposit. 2 dogs may be allowed.

Birmingham Bed and Breakfast
8790 H 12
Kenwood, CA
707-833-6996 (800-819-1388)
birminghambb.com/
This beautiful 1915 inn is now a Historic Landmark and allows guests a visit to an elegant past; whether it's a stroll through the 2 acres of trees, berry patches, and gardens, or just resting on the big wrap around porch enjoying the amazing view. There is one pet friendly cottage that was built onto the original water tower, and is spacious with many features and amenities, including a fenced-in back yard. Dogs of all sizes are welcome for an additional fee of $10 per night per pet and a pet policy to sign at check in. Since there is a dog that lives on site, they ask that guests check in before removing pets from their car. Dogs may not be left alone in the cottage, and they must be friendly, well behaved, and leashed and cleaned up after at all times.

Falling Waters River Resort
15729 Sierra Way
Kernville, CA
760-376-2242
Two dogs of any size are welcome, but 3 dogs are allowed if they are all small. There is a $10 per night per pet fee and dogs may only be left unattended for short periods.

River View Lodge
2 Sirreta Street
Kernville, CA
760-376-6019
Dogs of all sizes are allowed. There is a $20 per night per room fee and a pet policy to sign at check in. Multiple dogs may be allowed.

Super 8 Kettleman City
33415 Powers Drive
Kettleman City, CA
559-386-9530 (800-800-8000)
Dogs of all sizes are allowed. There is a $10 one time per pet fee per visit. Smoking and non-smoking rooms are available for pet rooms. 2 dogs may be allowed.

Motel 6 - King City
3 Broadway Circle
King City, CA
831-385-5000 (800-466-8356)
One well-behaved family pet per room. Guest must notify front desk upon arrival. Guest is liable for any damages. In consideration of all guests, pets must never be left unattended in the guest rooms.

Motel Trees
15495 Highway 101 South
Klamath, CA
707-482-3152
This motel is located directly across Highway 101 from the dog-friendly Trees of Mystery attraction. The motel offers pet rooms and allows all well-behaved dogs. There is a $5 per pet per night fee. They have a AAA 2 diamond rating.

Kyburz Resort Motel
13666 Highway 50
Kyburz, CA
530-293-3382
kyburzresort.com
Nestled among the pines along 300 feet of the South Fork of the American River, this motel is located in the heart of the El Dorado National Forest. It is located about 30 minutes east of Placerville and about 15-20 minutes from Apple Hill. Well-behaved dogs are allowed and they must be leashed when outside your room. There is a $10 per day pet fee.

Andrea Villa Inn
2402 Torrey Pines Rd
La Jolla, CA
858-459-3311
andreavilla.com/
Nestled in the heart of beautiful La Jolla, this inn is conveniently located near cosmopolitan shopping and dining experiences. The beaches of La Jolla Shores are within easy walking distance. There is a $25 one time pet charge.

La Jolla Village Lodge
1141 Silverado Street
La Jolla, CA
858-551-2001
There is a $20 one time pet fee. Thanks to a reader for recommending this hotel.

La Valencia Hotel
1132 Prospect Street
La Jolla, CA
858-454-0771 (800-451-0772)
lavalencia.com/
This resort hotel blends European flair and old Southern California charm and hospitality with all the modern day amenities. Dogs up to 40 pounds are allowed for an additional one time pet fee of $75. Dogs must be quiet, well mannered, leashed, cleaned up after, and the Do Not Disturb sign put on the door if they are in the room alone. 2 dogs may be allowed.

Residence Inn by Marriott
8901 Gilman Drive
La Jolla, CA
858-587-1770
Dogs of all sizes are welcome, but only 2 large pets or 3 small pets are allowed per room. There is a $75 one time fee, and a pet policy to sign at check in.

San Diego Marriott La Jolla
4240 La Jolla Village Drive
La Jolla, CA
858-587-1414 (800-228-9290)
Dogs of all sizes are allowed. There is a $75 one time additional pet fee. Dogs must be leashed, cleaned up after, and a contact number left with the front desk if they are in the room alone. Multiple dogs may be allowed.

Motel 6 - San Diego - La Mesa
7621 Alvarado Road
La Mesa, CA
619-464-7151 (800-466-8356)
One well-behaved family pet per room. Guest must notify front desk upon arrival. Guest is liable for any damages. In consideration of all guests, pets must never be left unattended in the guest rooms.

La Quinta Inn & Suites Buena Park
3 Centerpointe Drive
La Palma, CA
714-670-1400 (800-531-5900)
Dogs of all sizes are allowed. There are no additional pet fees. Dogs must be quiet, well behaved, leashed and cleaned up after. Multiple dogs may be allowed.

La Porte Cabin Rentals
Main Street and Pike Road/P. O. Box 225
La Porte, CA
530-675-0850
laportecabins.com/index.html
This mountain retreat features clean, fully-equipped cabins and a bunkhouse; all with complete kitchens so just bring your own cuisine. There is satellite TV available, and the cabins have private porches. Dogs of all sizes are allowed for no additional fee. Dogs may only be left alone in the rooms if they will be quiet and well mannered, and they must be leashed and cleaned up after. Multiple dogs may be allowed.

Carriage House Bed and Breakfast
1322 Catalina Street
Laguna Beach, CA
949-494-8945 (888-335-8945)
carriagehouse.com
The Carriage House, a country style

bed & breakfast, was built in the early 1920's and is a designated landmark. They are located one mile south of downtown Laguna Beach in a quiet neighborhood. Well-mannered, flea protected, friendly dogs over 18 months old are allowed at an extra charge of $10 per pet per night. Please cover the beds with your own blanket, or ask for a sheet, if your dog sleeps on the bed. Towels are provided upon request for your pet. Never leave your pet unattended, unless they are "crated" and you'll need to leave a cell phone or number where you can be reached. Owners are responsible for any damages caused by pets. There is also a resident dog & cat on the property. Dogs must always be leashed in Laguna, even on the beach. There is a dog park for off-leash exercise in Laguna Canyon (closed on Wednesday's year round). During the summer, dogs are allowed on the beach from June 1-September 16 before 8 a.m. and after 6 p.m. only.

Casa Laguna Inn
2510 S. Coast Hwy
Laguna Beach, CA
949-494-2996 (800-233-0449)
casalaguna.com/
This Spanish-style bed and breakfast sits on a hillside with views of the ocean. It was voted Orange County's Best B&B four years in a row. The rooms are decorated with a blend of antique and contemporary furnishings. There are 15 guest rooms plus several guest suites and cottages. While in Laguna Beach, browse the variety of specialty shops or dine at one of the dog-friendly restaurants. Interested in a stroll on the beach? Main Beach (certain dog hours) is a short drive from the inn. There is a $25 per day additional pet fee.

Vacation Village
647 S Costal H
Laguna Beach, CA
949-494-8566
One dog up to 75 pounds is allowed. There is a $10 per night per pet additional fee.

Arrowhead Saddleback Inn
PO Box 1890
Lake Arrowhead, CA
800-858-3334 (800-358-8733)
lakeArrowhead.com/saddleback/
This historic inn was originally constructed in 1917 as the Raven Hotel. It is now totally restored and

a historical landmark. The inn is located at the entrance of the Lake Arrowhead Village. Dogs are allowed in some of the cottages. The cottages feature stone fireplaces, double whirlpool baths, heated towel racks and refrigerators. There is an $8 per day pet fee. Dog owners also need to sign a pet agreement.

Arrowhead Tree Top Lodge
27992 Rainbow Drive
Lake Arrowhead, CA
909-337-2311 (800-358-TREE)
lakeArrowhead.com/treetop/
This inn is nestled among the tall pines on four acres of heavily forested grounds. You and your pup can enjoy a stroll on their private nature trail or find a spot at Deep Creek to sit, relax and watch the squirrels and birds. Amenities include microwaves in each of the rustic alpine rooms. It is located within walking distance of the Lake Arrowhead Village. There is an $8 per day pet fee.

Gray Squirrel Inn
326 State Hwy 173
Lake Arrowhead, CA
909-336-3602 (888-719-3563)
graysquirrelinn.com/
This inn is near Lake Arrowhead and has ten guest rooms. Room amenities include mini-refrigerators and coffee makers. Dogs are welcome in some of the rooms. There are no additional pet fees.

Prophet's Paradise B&B
26845 Modoc Lane
Lake Arrowhead, CA
909-336-1969
This bed and breakfast has five stories which cascade down its alpine hillside. This provides guests with privacy and intimate decks. All rooms have private baths. Amenities include a gym, a pool room, ping-pong, and darts, a horseshoe pit and a nearby hiking trail. Room rates start at $100 per night and include a gourmet breakfast. Your well-behaved dog is welcome. The owners also have pets. There are no additional pet fees.

The Saddleback Inn
300 S. State Hwy 173
Lake Arrowhead, CA
800-858-3334
saddlebackinn.com
This pet-friendly inn, with rooms and cottages, overlooks Lake Arrowhead. There is a restaurant and bar on the premises.

Candlewood Suites
3 South Pointe Drive
Lake Forest, CA
949-598-9105 (877-270-6405)
Dogs of all sizes are allowed for an
additional $75 one time fee per pet.
Multiple dogs may be allowed.

Quails Inn Hotel
1025 La Bonita Drive
Lake San Marcos, CA
760-744-0120
There is a $10 per day pet fee. This
resort has a number of golf packages
available.

Sugarloaf Cottages Resort
19667 Lakeshore Drive
Lakehead, CA
800-953-4432
shastacabins.com/
These cottages are located near the
shore of Lake Shasta and have air
conditioning, heating, bathrooms,
linens and complete kitchens, but no
phones, televisions or maid service.
They charge a $5 per night pet fee
and allow only one pet per unit.

Tsasdi Resort Cabins
19990 Lakeshore Dr.
Lakehead, CA
530-238-2575
shastalakecabins.com/Cabins.html
All cabins have private baths, linens,
cable TV, air conditioning, heating,
outdoor barbecue and private decks,
most of which overlook Shasta Lake.
There is a $10 per day pet fee. In
order for them to continuing being
pet-friendly, they ask that all pets be
kept on a leash and not be left
unattended in the cabins or on the
decks. Please clean up after your
pets.

Best Western Antelope Valley Inn
44055 N Sierra Hwy
Lancaster, CA
661-948-4651 (800-780-7234)
Dogs are allowed for an additional
one time pet fee of $35 per room.
Multiple dogs may be allowed.

Motel 6 - Lancaster
43540 17th Street West
Lancaster, CA
661-948-0435 (800-466-8356)
One well-behaved family pet per
room. Guest must notify front desk
upon arrival. Guest is liable for any
damages. In consideration of all
guests, pets must never be left
unattended in the guest rooms.

Days Inn
14750 South Harlan Rd

Lathrop, CA
209-982-1959 (800-329-7466)
There is a $10 per day pet fee.

Inn at Lee Vining
45 2nd St
Lee Vining, CA
760-647-6300

Murphey's Hotel
51493 Hwy 395
Lee Vining, CA
760-647-6316
There is a $5 per day additional pet
fee. Dogs are not to be left alone in
rooms.

Motel 6 - Lemoore
1290 Sierra Circle
Lemoore, CA
559-925-6100 (800-466-8356)
One well-behaved family pet per
room. Guest must notify front desk
upon arrival. Guest is liable for any
damages. In consideration of all
guests, pets must never be left
unattended in the guest rooms.

Lewiston Valley RV Park
4789 Trinity Dam Blvd.
Lewiston, CA
530-778-3942
lewistonca.com/lewvally.htm
This RV park is on 8 acres and
offers 7 pull through sites and 2
back-in sites. The sites have 50
amp service. Amenities include a
seasonal heated pool. Within
walking distance is a family style
restaurant, gas station and mini-
mart. Well-behaved leashed dogs
are allowed. There is no pet fee.

Little River Inn
7901 N H 1
Littleriver, CA
707-937-5942
Dogs of all sizes are allowed. There
is a $25 plus tax fee per pet per
stay and a pet policy to sign at
check in. 2 dogs may be allowed.

S. S. Seafoam Lodge
6751 N H 1
Littleriver, CA
707-937-1827
seafoamlodge.com/
This lodge comprises a total of 8
separate buildings with 24 guest
accommodations and a conference
center. Located on 6 acres of
coastal gardens and pines, there
are spectacular ocean views and a
private cove and beach access.
Some of the amenities include a
Continental breakfast delivered to
your room, private baths and decks,

a hot tub, and conference facilities.
Dogs of all sizes are allowed for an
additional fee of $10 per night per
pet. Dogs may not be left alone in
the room at any time, and they must
be well mannered, leashed, and
cleaned up after. 2 dogs may be
allowed.

Motel 6 - Livermore
4673 Lassen Road
Livermore, CA
925-443-5300 (800-466-8356)
One well-behaved family pet per
room. Guest must notify front desk
upon arrival. Guest is liable for any
damages. In consideration of all
guests, pets must never be left
unattended in the guest rooms.

Residence Inn by Marriott
1000 Airway Blvd
Livermore, CA
925-373-7252
Dogs of all sizes are allowed. There
is a $75 plus tax one time fee, and a
pet policy to sign at check in. Please
remove pet or kennel for
housekeeping. Multiple dogs may be
allowed.

Super 8 Lompoc
1020 E Ocean Ave
Lompac, CA
805-735-6444 (800-800-8000)
Dogs of all sizes are allowed. There
is a $10 one time per pet fee per
visit. Smoking and non-smoking
rooms are available for pet rooms. 2
dogs may be allowed.

Days Inn - Vandenberg Village
3955 Apollo Way
Lompoc, CA
805-733-5000 (800-329-7466)
There is a $250 refundable deposit
and a $20 one time pet fee. Dogs
may not be left alone in the rooms.

Motel 6 - Lompoc
1521 North H Street
Lompoc, CA
805-735-7631 (800-466-8356)
One well-behaved family pet per
room. Guest must notify front desk
upon arrival. Guest is liable for any
damages. In consideration of all
guests, pets must never be left
unattended in the guest rooms.

Quality Inn and Suites
1621 N H Street
Lompoc, CA
805-735-8555 (877-424-6423)
Dogs are allowed for an additional
one time fee of $25 per pet. 2 dogs
may be allowed.

California Listings - Please always call ahead to make sure an establishment is still dog-friendly.

Alabama Hills Inn
1920 South Main
Lone Pine, CA
760-876-8700 (800-800-6468)
ca-biz.com/alabamahillsinn/
There is a $5 per day pet fee. There is a large grass area near the hotel to walk your dog. The area around the hotel is where many Western films have been made.

Best Western Frontier Motel
1008 S Main St
Lone Pine, CA
760-876-5571 (800-780-7234)
Dogs are allowed for no additional pet fee. 2 dogs may be allowed.

Guesthouse International Hotel
5325 E Pacific Coast Highway
Long Beach, CA
562-597-1341
guesthouselb.com/
Located by several other attractions and recreational activities, this hotel offers a courtesy shuttle service to the attractions within a 5 mile radius. Some of the features/amenities include 142 spacious, stylish rooms with conveniences for leisure and business travelers, gardens, a complimentary continental breakfast, and a heated, tropically landscaped pool complete with cascading waterfall. Dogs of all sizes are allowed for an additional $10 per night per pet. Dogs may only be left for short periods, and they must be crated and a contact number left with the front desk. Dogs must be leashed and cleaned up after at all times. Multiple dogs may be allowed.

Hilton
701 West Ocean Blvd
Long Beach, CA
562-983-3400
Quiet, well behaved dogs are allowed for no additional pet fee with a credit card on file. There is a $100 refundable deposit if paying by cash. 2 dogs may be allowed.

Long Beach Marriott
4700 Airport Plaza Drive
Long Beach, CA
562-425-5210 (800-228-9290)
Dogs of all sizes are allowed. There is a $75 refundable deposit per room. Dogs must be quiet, well behaved, leashed, cleaned up after, and a contact number left with the front desk if they are in the room alone. 2 dogs may be allowed.

Motel 6 - Long Beach - International

City
1121 East Pacific Coast Highway
Long Beach, CA
562-591-3321 (800-466-8356)
One well-behaved family pet per room. Guest must notify front desk upon arrival. Guest is liable for any damages. In consideration of all guests, pets must never be left unattended in the guest rooms.

Motel 6 - Los Angeles - Long Beach
5665 East 7th Street
Long Beach, CA
562-597-1311 (800-466-8356)
One well-behaved family pet per room. Guest must notify front desk upon arrival. Guest is liable for any damages. In consideration of all guests, pets must never be left unattended in the guest rooms.

Residence Inn by Marriott
4111 E Willow Street
Long Beach, CA
562-595-0909
Dogs of all sizes are allowed. There is a $75 one time fee, and a pet policy to sign at check in. Multiple dogs may be allowed.

Residence Inn by Marriott
4931 Katella Avenue
Los Alamitos, CA
714-484-5700
Dogs up to 75 pounds are allowed. There is a $75 one time fee, and a pet policy to sign at check in. 2 dogs may be allowed.

Residence Inn by Marriott
4460 El Camino Real
Los Altos, CA
650-559-7890
Dogs of all sizes are allowed. There is a $75 one time fee per pet, and a pet policy to sign at check in. Multiple dogs may be allowed.

Beverly Hills Plaza Hotel
10300 Wilshire Blvd
Los Angeles, CA
310-275-5575 (800-800-1234)
This unique all-suite hotel offers luxury accommodations with a modern European decor and an elegant atmosphere to please the business or leisure traveler. Offering a convenient location to several attractions, they also feature the Le Petit Cafe/Bar, many in-room amenities, a heated outdoor pool with cabanas and a Jacuzzi, private balconies, room service, a 24 hour gift shop and front desk, and a concierge staff. Dogs up to 60 pounds are allowed. There is a $500 refundable deposit

plus a $200 one time additional pet fee per pet and a pet policy to sign at check in. Dogs may only be left alone in the room if they will be quiet and well behaved. Dogs must be leashed and cleaned up after at all times. 2 dogs may be allowed.

Beverly Laurel Hotel
8018 Beverly Blvd
Los Angeles, CA
323-651-2441
There is a $25 per day pet fee. Up to two pets per room are allowed. Thanks to one of our readers who wrote "Our large German Shepherd was welcome."

Hilton
5711 West Century Blvd
Los Angeles, CA
310-410-4000
Dogs up to 50 pounds are allowed for an additional fee of $25 per night per pet. Multiple dogs may be allowed.

Hotel Sofitel
8555 Beverly Blvd
Los Angeles, CA
310-278-5444
sofitel.com
This upscale hotel is located next to West Hollywood and Beverly Hills. You and your dog will feel most welcome at this hotel. Since parking is limited in this area, your car will be valet parked. They open the car doors not only for you, but for your dog too. You can feel comfortable registering at the front desk with your pup at your side and then taking the elevator to the room that awaits you. There is a restaurant at this hotel that has outdoor dining where your dog is also welcome. Room rates run about $150-250 per night, but your dog will be treated first class.

La Quinta Inn & Suites LAX
5249 West Century Blvd
Los Angeles, CA
310-645-2200 (800-531-5900)
Dogs of all sizes are allowed. There are no additional pet fees, but they request to meet your pet, and to know that you have a pet so as to inform housekeeping. Dogs must be leashed and cleaned up after. Multiple dogs may be allowed.

Le Meridien Hotel
465 South La Cienega Blvd.
Los Angeles, CA
310-247-0400
Dogs up to 50 pounds are allowed. This luxury class hotel is located in one of the most prestigious areas in

Los Angeles. They welcome both business and leisure travelers, as well as your dog of any size. Room rates at this first class hotel start at the low $300s per night. They sometimes offer special weekend rates. There is an additional $100 pet fee for the first night and an additional $25 for each additional day.

Los Angeles Airport Marriott
5855 W Century Blvd
Los Angeles, CA
310-641-5700 (800-228-9290)
Dogs of all sizes are allowed. There are no additional pet fees. Dogs must be quiet, leashed, cleaned up after, and a contact number left with the front desk if they are in the room alone. Multiple dogs may be allowed.

Residence Inn by Marriott
1177 S Beverly Drive
Los Angeles, CA
310-277-4427
Pets of all sizes are welcome. There is an $80 N/R cleaning fee plus $10 per night for one pet; $15 per night for two pets, and an additional $5 per night for each pet thereafter. There is also a pet policy to sign at check in. Multiple dogs may be allowed.

Travelodge Hotel at LAX
5547 W. Century Blvd.
Los Angeles, CA
310-649-4000
travelodge.com
This inn offers free parking, a feature not found with many of the L.A./West Hollywood hotels. They welcome pets here at this 2 story inn which has interior/exterior corridors, a gift shop and heated pool. It is located about one mile east of the Los Angeles Airport. There is a $10 per day additional pet fee per pet.

Vagabond Inn
3101 S. Figueroa St.
Los Angeles, CA
213-746-1531 (800-522-1555)
vagabondinn.com
This motel is located just 2 blocks from the University of Southern California (USC) and 2 miles from the LA Convention Center. It features an outdoor swimming pool, cable television, air conditioning and many more amenities. There is a $10 per day pet fee.

W Los Angeles Westwood
930 Hilgard Avenue
Los Angeles, CA
310-208-8765
Dogs up to 80 pounds are allowed.

There is a $100 one time per stay pet fee and a $25 per night additional pet fee.

Days Inn
2169 East Pacheco Blvd
Los Banos, CA
209-826-9690 (800-329-7466)
There is a $5 per day pet fee.

Sunstar Inn
839 W. Pacheco Blvd
Los Banos, CA
209-826-3805
There is a $10 per day additional pet fee.

Days Inn
14684 Aloma St
Lost Hills, CA
661-797-2371 (800-329-7466)

Motel 6 - Lost Hills
14685 Warren Street
Lost Hills, CA
661-797-2346 (800-466-8356)
One well-behaved family pet per room. Guest must notify front desk upon arrival. Guest is liable for any damages. In consideration of all guests, pets must never be left unattended in the guest rooms.

Days Inn
25327 Ave 16
Madera, CA
559-674-8817 (800-329-7466)
There is a $5 per day pet fee.

Madera Valley Inn
317 North G St
Madera, CA
559-664-0100
Dogs are allowed for an additional one time pet fee of $15 per room. Multiple dogs may be allowed.

Motel 6 - Madera
22683 Avenue 18 1/2
Madera, CA
559-675-8697 (800-466-8356)
One well-behaved family pet per room. Guest must notify front desk upon arrival. Guest is liable for any damages. In consideration of all guests, pets must never be left unattended in the guest rooms.

Convict Lake Resort
HCR - 79, Box 204
Mammoth Lakes, CA
760-934-3800 (800-992-2260)
convictlakeresort.com/
Since 1929, this scenic resort area has been a popular get-a-way offering a wide range of services, amenities, land and water

recreational opportunities, and a full line-up of planned activities throughout the year. Their on site restaurant features a French country cuisine with an extensive wine list, and indoor and outdoor dining service (weather permitting) where your pet may join you at the outside tables. Some of the resort amenities include a spacious full-service cocktail lounge, barbecues, fully equipped kitchens, TV with HBO, a multi-functional general store, boat rentals, and a campground (no pet fee). Well mannered dogs of all sizes are allowed for an additional $20 per pet per stay. Dogs must be on no more than a 6 foot leash, and cleaned up after at all times. Multiple dogs may be allowed.

Crystal Crag Lodge
P.O. Box 88
Mammoth Lakes, CA
760-934-2436
This lodge offers cabins at 9,000 feet elevation on beautiful Lake Mary in the dog-friendly Inyo National Forest. Lake Mary is known as one of the best fishing spots in the Eastern Sierra, regularly producing trophy size trout. You will find a number of other lakes, most of the best hiking trailheads, Lake Mary Store, and some of the best scenery that the Eastern Sierra has to offer within walking distance of your cabin. The cabins, all non-smoking, have full kitchens and baths. Most cabins have living rooms with fireplaces. The lodge also offers 14-foot aluminum boats with or without a motor. Dogs are allowed on the boats as well. Please note that the lodge is only open during the summer season, from about late May to early October. Dogs are allowed for an additional $8 per day charge. Pets must never be left unattended in the cabins.

Edelweiss Lodge
1872 Old Mammoth Road
Mammoth Lakes, CA
760-934-2445 (877-2Edelweiss)
Edelweiss-Lodge.com
Cabins on a 1 acre wooded site near hiking trails, lakes and streams. Dogs of all sizes are allowed. There is a $15 per day pet fee. All rooms are non-smoking. Multiple dogs may be allowed.

Mammoth Creek Inn
663 Old Mammoth Road
Mammoth Lakes, CA
760-934-6162
There is a $25 per day per pet fee.

Well-behaved pets are welcome. Just make sure you mention you will be bringing a pet as they have specific "pet-friendly" rooms. Pets may not be left alone in the rooms unless they are trained to stay in a crate. This inn is located within walking distance to grocery and boutique shopping, restaurants, cross country skiing, snowshoe area and Mammoth's biking and running path. Amenities include in room high speed Internet access, limited in room dining, indoor dry sauna, hot tub, and a game, movie and book library.

Motel 6 - Mammoth Lakes
3372 Main Street
Mammoth Lakes, CA
760-934-6660 (800-466-8356)
One well-behaved family pet per room. Guest must notify front desk upon arrival. Guest is liable for any damages. In consideration of all guests, pets must never be left unattended in the guest rooms.

Shilo Inn
2963 Main Street
Mammoth Lakes, CA
760-934-4500 (800-222-2244)
Your dog is welcome here. Each room in this motel is a mini-suite complete with microwaves, refrigerators and more. This motel is located across the street from the Visitors Center which has trails that border up to the Shady Rest Park where there are many hiking trails. If you are there in the winter, try some cross-country skiing with your pup. The cross country ski rental store is very close to this motel (see Attractions.) There is a $10 per day additional pet fee per pet.

Sierra Lodge
3540 Main Street
Mammoth Lakes, CA
760-934-8881
There is a $10 per night pet fee. Amenities include continental breakfast and kitchenettes in the rooms. All rooms are non-smoking.

Swiss Chalet
3776 Viewpoint Road
Mammoth Lakes, CA
760-934-2403
This inn offers a few pet rooms. All rooms are non-smoking. Dogs must be one year or older and only one pet per room. Pets cannot be left unattended in the room. There is a $5 per day pet fee.

Tamarack Lodge

P.O. Box 69/Lake Mary Road
Mammoth Lakes, CA
760-934-2442 (800-MAMMOTH (626-6684))
tamaracklodge.com/
This historic lodge has been in operation since 1924 with their cabins and lodge rooms ranging from simple and rustic to deluxe accommodations. On site is the Lakefront Restaurant specializing in blending classic French cuisine with regional influences of the eastern Sierra. There is outdoor dining service when weather permits, and your pooch is allowed to join you on the outer deck. Watercraft rentals, fishing, easy to strenuous hiking trails, and other recreational pursuits are available throughout the summer. Their cabins have private bathrooms, porches, and telephones. Dogs are allowed in the summer and in the cabins only. There is an additional fee of $30 per night per pet. Dogs must be well behaved, under owner's control at all times, and be leashed and cleaned up after. 2 dogs may be allowed.

Villa De Los Pinos #3
3252 Chateau Rd
Mammoth Lakes, CA
760-722-5369
mammoth-lakes-condo.com
This is a year-round vacation rental townhouse-style condominium in Mammoth Lakes. The amenities include two downstairs bedrooms, two bathrooms, a large living room, dining room, and kitchen. The condo is fronted by a large deck overlooking the development courtyard (where dogs are allowed off-leash), swimming pool, and Jacuzzi building. All dogs are welcome. The $25 per visit pet fee helps with the cleaning.

Best Western Executive Inn & Suites
1415 E Yosemite Avenue
Manteca, CA
209-825-1415 (800-780-7234)
Dogs up to 50 pounds are allowed for an additional one time pet fee of $30 per room. There may be 2 small or one large dog per room. 2 dogs may be allowed.

Motel 6 - Monterey - Marina
100 Reservation Road
Marina, CA
831-384-1000 (800-466-8356)
One well-behaved family pet per room. Guest must notify front desk upon arrival. Guest is liable for any

damages. In consideration of all guests, pets must never be left unattended in the guest rooms.

Indian Peak Ranch MountainTop Hideaway
Call to arrange
Mariposa, CA
209-966-5259
indianpeakranch.com
This mountaintop vacation rental is located on 122 acres. To make reservations or for more information see www.indianpeakranch.com or call.

The Mariposa Lodge
5052 Hwy 140
Mariposa, CA
209-966-3607 (800-341-8000)
mariposalodge.com
Thanks to one of our readers for recommending this hotel. Here is what they said about it: "We stayed here after a clogged 4 hour drive from San Jose, CA. Mia at the front desk was courteous and friendly -- not what you always get when you are traveling with a 90 lb dog (black lab). The room was large, new and very nice. Lovely pool and Jacuzzi. A little sitting area under a patch of trees with benches. It was very warm and Mia recommended a restaurant where we could sit outside and take our dog. Castillos on 5th Street. Our extra nice waitress brought him water and us an excellent Mexican dinner. Couldn't have been nicer. All in all Mariposa and the hotel was an A+ experience." If you take Highway 140, this motel is located about 50 minutes from Yosemite Valley (45 min. to the main gate and about 10 min. to the valley). Pets are an additional $10 per pet per night.

Best Western Yosemite Way Station Motel
4999 State Highway 140
Mariposa (Yosemite), CA
209-966-7545 (800-780-7234)
Dogs are allowed for an additional fee of $10 per night per pet. Multiple dogs may be allowed.

Century House Inn
433 Lawndale Court
McCloud, CA
530-964-2206
mccloudcenturyhouse.com/
Gracefully resting along the southern slope of Mount Shasta among green lawns and tall pines in the town's historic district, this retreat features elegant, individually decorated rooms, and many have porches or decks. Dogs of all sizes are allowed,

but they must be declared at time of reservation prior to arrival. There is no fee for 1 pet; for 2 dogs or more there is an additional fee of $10 per night per pet. Dogs must be leashed and cleaned up after at all times, and be removed or crated for housekeeping. Multiple dogs may be allowed.

Stoney Brook Inn
309 W Colombero Road
McCloud, CA
800-369-6118
There are only 2 pet friendly suites available; 1 dog is allowed in one, and in the other, 2 pets are allowed. There is a $17 one time additional fee per pet. 2 dogs may be allowed.

Abigail's Bed & Breakfast
Heart Of the Historical Village
Mendocino, CA
800-962-0934
whitegateinn.com/abigails.php
Pets are welcome in both Abigail's Bed & Breakfast and the Whitegate Inn cottage. They are not allowed in the main house. The cottage has 4 bedrooms and 3 baths. Stroll with your dog in beautiful Mendocino and nearby state parks.

Blackberry Inn
44951 Larkin Road
Mendocino, CA
707-937-5281 (800-950-7806)
blackberryinn.biz/
Located at one of California's most beautiful locations overlooking the Mendocino Bay, this country inn offers ocean views, finely appointed rooms with fresh cut flowers daily from their garden, and a Continental breakfast. There are 2 pet-friendly rooms available, and dogs must be friendly as there are other animals (wild and domestic) on the property. Dogs are allowed for an additional fee of $10 per night per pet. Dogs may not be left alone in the rooms or in cars on the property at any time, and they must be leashed and cleaned up after. Multiple dogs may be allowed.

Coastal Getaways
10501 Ford Street POB1355
Mendocino, CA
707-937-9200 (800-525-0049)
coastgetaways.com
Coastal Getaways has over 5 vacation homes that allow dogs. Most of the homes have ocean front views and one is located in the quaint village of Mendocino. The rates range from $140 to $250 and up per night. They also have weekly rates. For more information, please call 800-525-0049.

Inn at Schoolhouse Creek
7051 N. Highway 1
Mendocino, CA
707-937-5525
schoolhousecreek.com
With 8+ acres of ocean view gardens, meadows, forest, hiking trails and a secluded beach cove you and your pets will truly feel like you've gotten away from it all. To help your pets get in the vacation mood they will be welcomed with their own pet basket that includes a bed, towel, blanket and a treat. At the end of your day, relax in the ocean view hot tub.

Little River Inn
7901 Highway One
Mendocino, CA
707-937-5942
littleriverinn.com
This coastal resort has oceanview rooms, some with fireplaces and Jacuzzis. There are gardens to walk through and breakfast and dinner are available in the restaurant. Pets are $25 per night, per pet.

MacCallum House
45020 Albion Street
Mendocino, CA
707-937-0289
maccallumhouse.com
Pets of all varieties are welcomed at the MacCallum House Inn, located in the heart of the Mendocino Village. Pets are allowed in the cottages and Barn and are provided with blankets and sheets. The original Victorian mansion, built in 1882 by William H. Kelley, was a wedding gift to his daughter, Daisy MacCallum, and is a historic landmark. Rooms include a full breakfast and a complimentary wine hour is served in the Grey Whale Bar featuring wines from throughout the California wine country. Children are also welcome.

Mendocino Seaside Cottages
10940 Lansing St
Mendocino, CA
707-485-0239
romancebythesea.com/
Accommodations have Jacuzzi spas, wet bars,& fireplaces. It is located within easy walking distance of Mendocino.

Pacific Mist Inn and Cabins
6051 Highway One
Mendocino, CA
707-937-1543 (800-955-6478)
pacificmistinn.com
These cabins and inn allow dogs. The cabins have kitchenettes and there is a spa.

Stanford Inn by the Sea and Spa
44850 Comptche Ukiah Rd and Highway One
Mendocino, CA
707-937-5615
stanfordinn.com
This resort is specially designed to accommodate travelers with pets. The inn is rustic and elegant. Amenities include feather beds, wood burning fireplaces, antiques, sofas, televisions with VCRs and DVDs. The resort offers complimentary breakfast featuring a choice from organic selections of omelets, waffles, burritos, and more. A large pool, sauna and Jacuzzi are protected from the fog by a solarium. Massage in the Forest provides massage and body work and yoga. The Inn's Catch A Canoe & Bicycles, too! offers kayaking and canoeing on Big River Estuary as well as mountain biking and. Special canoes are set-up to provide secure footing for your dog as well as a bowl of fresh water (Big River is tidal and for eight miles and therefore salty). The Ravens vegetarian/vegan restaurant serves organic cuisine. Well behaved pets may join you at breakfast or dinner in a dining area created especially for them. Feed and water dishes, covers to protect bedding and furniture, sleeping beds and treats are provided in the rooms. There is a $25 pet fee per stay.

Sweetwater Spa & Inn
44840 Main Street
Mendocino, CA
707-937-4076 (800-300-4140)
sweetwaterspa.com/
Sweetwater Spa & Inn offers a unique variety of accommodations, including cabin and vacation home rentals. They give dog treats at check-in as well as sheets for the guests to cover furniture and towels for wet paws in the rainy season. Some of the rentals are located in the village of Mendocino. The other rentals are located around the Mendocino area. There is a two night minimum on weekends and three night minimum on most holidays. All units are non-smoking. Your well-behaved dog is welcome. Room rates start at the low $100s and up. There is a $15 per day additional pet fee.

The Blair House Inn

45110 Little Lake Street
Mendocino, CA
707-937-1800 (800-699-9296)
blairhouse.com/
Although built in 1888, this home has been called a "Victorian Treasure", and it still offers luxury surroundings, beautifully appointed rooms, gardens and ocean vistas. Room rates include breakfast and a complimentary bottle of wine. They have one pet-friendly cottage, and dogs of all sizes are allowed for an additional fee of $10 per night per pet. Dogs may not be left alone in the cottage at any time, and they must be well mannered, leashed, and cleaned up after. 2 dogs may be allowed.

Motel 6 - Merced North
1410 V Street
Merced, CA
209-384-2181 (800-466-8356)
One well-behaved family pet per room. Guest must notify front desk upon arrival. Guest is liable for any damages. In consideration of all guests, pets must never be left unattended in the guest rooms.

Quality Inn
1213 V Street
Merced, CA
209-723-3711 (877-424-6423)
Dogs are allowed for no additional pet fee. 2 dogs may be allowed.

Travelodge
1260 Yosemite Park Way
Merced, CA
209-722-6225
There is a $10 per day additional pet fee.

Vagabond Inn
1215 R Street
Merced, CA
209-722-2737

Child's Meadow Resort
41500 Highway 36E
Mill Creek, CA
530-595-3383
Dogs are allowed in this all season resort. Located between the towns of Susanville and Red Bluff, this quiet resort is on 18 acres of picturesque meadows and streams at the end of the Shasta/Cascade Mountain Range. The resort is just 9 miles from the southwest entrance to Lassen Volcanic National Park. RV hookups are available at the resort. There is no pet charge for the campground but there may be a pet fee for the cabins or motel.

Holiday Inn Express Mill Valley-Sausalito
160 Shoreline Highway
Mill Valley, CA
415-332-5700 (877-270-6405)
Dogs of all sizes are allowed for an additional $75 one time fee per room. 2 dogs may be allowed.

Clarion Hotel San Francisco Airport
401 E Millbrae Avenue
Millbrae, CA
650-692-6363 (877-424-6423)
One dog is allowed for an additional one time pet fee of $50.

Best Western Brookside Inn
400 Valley Way
Milpitas, CA
408-263-5566 (800-780-7234)
Dogs up to 50 pounds are allowed for an additional fee of $10 per night per pet. 2 dogs may be allowed.

Embassy Suites Hotel Milpitas - Silicon Valley
901 E. Calaveras Boulevard
Milpitas, CA
408-942-0400
Dogs of all sizes are allowed. There is a $50 one time pet fee per visit. Dogs are not allowed to be left alone in the room. 2 dogs may be allowed.

Residence Inn by Marriott
1501 California Circle
Milpitas, CA
408-941-9222
Dogs of all sizes are allowed. There is a $75 one time fee, and a pet policy to sign at check in. 2 dogs may be allowed.

Sheraton San Jose Hotel
1801 Barber Lane
Milpitas, CA
408-943-0600 (888-625-5144)
Dogs of all sizes are allowed. You must sign a pet policy. Dogs are not to be left alone in the rooms.

TownePlace Suites Milpitas Silicon Valley
1428 Falcon Drive
Milpitas, CA
408-719-1959
Dogs of all sizes are allowed. There is a $75 one time pet fee per visit. . 2 dogs may be allowed.

Miranda Gardens Resort
6766 Avenue of the Giants
Miranda, CA
707-943-3011
mirandagardens.com/

The cottages are surrounded by flowering gardens and surrounded by ancient redwoods. From this resort, you can take day trips to the Avenue of the Giants or the Lost Coast. All cottages are non-smoking. Children are welcome and the resort has a children's play area. Pets are allowed in certain cabins and there is a $50 one time pet charge.

Motel 6 - Modesto
1920 West Orangeburg Avenue
Modesto, CA
209-522-7271 (800-466-8356)
One well-behaved family pet per room. Guest must notify front desk upon arrival. Guest is liable for any damages. In consideration of all guests, pets must never be left unattended in the guest rooms.

Red Lion
1612 Sisk Road
Modesto, CA
209-521-1612
Dogs of all sizes are allowed. There is a $50 per pet per stay fee and a pet policy to sign at check in. Multiple dogs may be allowed.

Vagabond Inn
2025 W Orangeburg Ave
Modesto, CA
209-577-8008
A well-behaved large dog is okay.

Best Western Desert Winds
16200 Sierra Hwy
Mojave, CA
661-824-3601 (800-780-7234)
Dogs up to 50 pounds are allowed for an additional fee of $10 per night per pet. 2 dogs may be allowed.

Econo Lodge
2145 SR 58
Mojave, CA
661-824-2463
There is a $5 per day pet fee.

Motel 6 - Mojave
16958 State Route 58
Mojave, CA
661-824-4571 (800-466-8356)
One well-behaved family pet per room. Guest must notify front desk upon arrival. Guest is liable for any damages. In consideration of all guests, pets must never be left unattended in the guest rooms.

Grandma's House Bed and Breakfast
20280 River Blvd
Monte Rio, CA
707-865-1865
This dog-friendly bed and breakfast

inn is located on the Russian River. The inn offers three rooms, all with private bathrooms. Each room also includes a private phone line, TV and VCR, refrigerator, microwave, and more. One of the rooms is handicapped accessible. Clean, well-behaved dogs may accompany their owners, with advance notice, for $10 per dog per day. There is a $75 damage and cleaning deposit, refundable (if not needed) at departure. Owners are expected to clean up behind their dog on the grounds. Pooper-scooper bags are available for this purpose. Dogs must not be left unattended in the room for long periods. Owners are responsible for not letting their dog disturb other guests and making sure their dog is not destructive to the property.

San Ysidro Ranch
900 San Ysidro Lane
Montecito, CA
805-969-5046
Dogs of all sizes are allowed. There is a $100 one time fee per pet. Multiple dogs may be allowed.

Bay Park Hotel
1425 Munras Avenue
Monterey, CA
831-649-1020
Dogs of all sizes are allowed. There is a $20 per room per stay additional pet fee. Dogs are not allowed to be left alone in the room. Multiple dogs may be allowed.

Best Western The Beach Resort
2600 Sand Dunes Dr
Monterey, CA
831-394-3321 (800-780-7234)
Dogs are allowed for an additional pet fee of $25 per night per room for non-ocean view rooms; the fee is $50 per night per room for ocean view rooms. Multiple dogs may be allowed.

Best Western Victorian Inn
487 Foam St
Monterey, CA
831-373-8000 (800-780-7234)
Dogs are allowed for an additional pet fee of $30 per night per room. 2 dogs may be allowed.

El Adobe Inn
936 Munras Ave.
Monterey, CA
831-372-5409
This inn is located on Munras Ave. about 1/2 mile east of Hwy 1. There is a $10 per day additional pet fee.

Hyatt Regency Monterey
1 Old Golf Course Road
Monterey, CA
831-372-1234
The warm colors and fireplaces throughout this resort offer a relaxed atmosphere for the business or leisure traveler. Amenities include spacious guestrooms, room service, pools, a golf course, tennis courts, massage therapy, dining and entertainment, an award winning sports bar, and a 24 hour fully automated business center. Dogs of all sizes are allowed. There is a $50 one time additional pet fee per room. Dogs must be crated when left alone in the room, and they must be leashed and cleaned up after. 2 dogs may be allowed.

Monterey Fireside Lodge
1131 10th Street
Monterey, CA
831-373-4172 (800-722-2624)
montereyfireside.com/
All 24 rooms have gas fireplaces. There is an additional $20/day pet charge.

Motel 6 - Monterey
2124 North Fremont Street
Monterey, CA
831-646-8585 (800-466-8356)
One well-behaved family pet per room. Guest must notify front desk upon arrival. Guest is liable for any damages. In consideration of all guests, pets must never be left unattended in the guest rooms.

Comfort Inn
23330 Sunnymead Blvd
Moreno Valley, CA
951-242-0699 (877-424-6423)
Dogs up to 50 pounds are allowed for an additional fee of $10 per night per pet. 2 dogs may be allowed.

Econo Lodge
24412 Sunnymead Blvd
Moreno Valley, CA
909-247-6699
There is a $50 refundable pet deposit and a $5 per day pet fee.

Residence Inn by Marriott
18620 Madrone Parkway
Morgan Hill, CA
408-782-8311
Dogs up to 100 pounds are allowed. There is a $75 one time fee and a pet policy to sign at check in. 2 dogs may be allowed.

Bayfront Inn
1150 Embarcadero
Morro Bay, CA
805-772-5607
bayfront-inn.com
There is a $10 per day pet charge.

Best Western El Rancho
2460 Main St
Morro Bay, CA
805-772-2212 (800-780-7234)
One dog is allowed for a $15 one time pet fee per room; a second dog is an additional $10 one time pet fee. Pets must be declared at the time of reservations. 2 dogs may be allowed.

Days Inn
1095 Main Street
Morro Bay, CA
805-772-2711 (800-329-7466)
There is an $11 per day pet fee.

Motel 6 - Morro Bay
298 Atascadero Road
Morro Bay, CA
805-772-5641 (800-466-8356)
All well behaved dogs are welcome. There are no additional pet fees.

Pleasant Inn Motel
235 Harbor Street
Morro Bay, CA
805-772-8521
pleasantinnmotel.com/
This motel, family owned and operated, is just one block east of the beautiful Morro Bay waterfront and one block west of old downtown. All rooms are non-smoking. Dogs and cats are welcome for an extra $5 per day.

Best Western Tree House Motor Inn
111 Morgan Way
Mount Shasta, CA
530-926-3101 (800-780-7234)
Dogs up to 40 pounds are allowed for an additional fee of $10 per night per pet. 2 dogs may be allowed.

Dream Inn Bed and Breakfast
326 Chestnut Street
Mount Shasta, CA
530-926-1536
home.att.net/~dreaminn
Dogs (and children) are welcome at this bed and breakfast inn. The Victorian home, built in 1904 and completely restored, is located at 3,500 ft. in downtown Mount Shasta. Lying at the base of 14,162 ft. Mount Shasta, they are surrounded by National Forest. The inn offers 4 bedrooms with shared bathrooms. The owners also have a dog on the premises. There are no pet fees.

Econo Lodge
908 S. Mt. Shasta Blvd.
Mount Shasta, CA
530-926-3145
econolodge.com
There is an additional $5 per day pet charge. There is a limit of one dog per room.

Mount Shasta Ranch Bed and Breakfast
1008 W. A. Barr Rd.
Mount Shasta, CA
530-926-3870
stayinshasta.com
Dogs are allowed at this ranch style house bed and breakfast built in 1923. This B&B offers 12 bedrooms including a cottage. Five of the rooms have private bathrooms. There is a $10 one time per stay, per pet fee. Children are also welcome.

Mountain Air Lodge
1121 S Mount Shasta Blvd
Mount Shasta, CA
530-926-3411
There is an additional $7 per day pet charge.

Swiss Holiday Lodge
2400 S. Mt. Shasta Blvd.
Mount Shasta, CA
530-926-3446
There is an additional $5 per day pet charge.

Residence Inn by Marriott
1854 El Camino West
Mountain View, CA
650-940-1300
Dogs of all sizes are allowed. There is a $75 one time fee per pet, and a pet policy to sign at check in. They also request a credit card to be on file. Multiple dogs may be allowed.

Tropicana Lodge
1720 El Camino Real
Mountain View, CA
650-961-0220
Pets may not be left alone in the rooms.

Beazley House Bed & Breakfast Inn
1910 First Street
Napa, CA
707-257-1649
beazleyhouse.com
This Bed and Breakfast is located in a residential area in historic downtown Napa. There is a $25 per day per dog charge, with a maximum of 2 dogs.

Napa River Inn

500 Main Street
Napa, CA
707-251-8500
napariverinn.com/
This beautiful inn sits on 2.5 picturesque acres along the Napa River, is on the National Registry of Historic Places, and offer top amenities to visitors and their pets. They participate in a pet VIP program which gives your pooch their own in-house care package too. It includes a blanket, feeding mat with stainless steel bowls, a Cab-Bone-Nay dog biscuit made with real wine, and a supply of doggy clean up bags. Small to medium sized dogs are welcome for an additional $25 per night per pet. Dogs must be well mannered, leashed, and cleaned up after. Dogs may only be left alone in the room if they will be quiet and they are in a kennel. Multiple dogs may be allowed.

Napa Valley Country Cottage
Mt Veeder Rd
Napa, CA
707-226-6621
napavalleycasa.com
This one bedroom country cottage is located on 12 acres in the heart of Napa Valley wine country. The house has a full kitchen, Living room with Satelite TV,CD player, and a stereo. The property has walking paths, a seasonal creek, and gardens in a wooded setting. The property is fenced and has electric gates. They accept any well behaved pets. Pets are not to be left unattended.

The Chablis Inn
3360 Solono Ave
Napa, CA
707-257-1944 (800-443-3490)
chablisinn.com
There is a 150 pound limit for dogs. There is a $10 per day additional pet fee. All rooms are non-smoking.

The Inn On First
1938 First Street
Napa, CA
707-253-1331 (866-253-1331)
theinnonfirst.com
This circa 1900 B&B is located in downtown Napa. There is a $25 per day per dog pet fee. Up to two dogs are allowed per room. Your dog will receive a dog basket upon arrival.

The Napa Inn Bed and Breakfast
1137 Warren Street
Napa, CA
707-257-1444

napainn.com
Located on a quiet street in historic, downtown Napa, this inn is within an easy walking distance of shops and restaurants. Dogs are allowed in one room, the garden cottage. This private cottage is decorated in French Provincial prints. It has a queen size bed, sofa, fireplace, French doors overlooking a private flower garden, skylight, wet bar with refrigerator and microwave, and an outdoor spa. It sleeps up to four people. There is a $20 per day pet charge.

Days Inn and Suites
1215 Hospitality Lane
Needles, CA
760-326-5836 (800-329-7466)

Econo Lodge
1910 N. Needles Hwy
Needles, CA
760-326-3881
There is a $5 per day pet fee.

Motel 6 - Needles
1420 J Street
Needles, CA
760-326-3399 (800-466-8356)
One well-behaved family pet per room. Guest must notify front desk upon arrival. Guest is liable for any damages. In consideration of all guests, pets must never be left unattended in the guest rooms.

Travelers Inn
1195 3rd Street Hill
Needles, CA
760-326-4900

The Outside Inn
575 E. Broad Street
Nevada City, CA
530-265-2233
outsideinn.com/
This inn is located in a quiet residential neighborhood two blocks from downtown Nevada City. This completely renovated 1940's era motor court features never smoked in rooms under tall pines. Children and pets are welcome. There is a $10 per night pet charge.

Motel 6 - Newark
5600 Cedar Court
Newark, CA
510-791-5900 (800-466-8356)
One well-behaved family pet per room. Guest must notify front desk upon arrival. Guest is liable for any damages. In consideration of all guests, pets must never be left unattended in the guest rooms.

Residence Inn by Marriott
35466 Dumbarton Court
Newark, CA
510-739-6000
Dogs of all sizes are allowed. There is a $75 one time fee, and a pet policy to sign at check in. Multiple dogs may be allowed.

Woodfin Suite Hotel
39150 Cedar Blvd.
Newark, CA
510-795-1200
All well-behaved dogs are welcome. Every room is a suite with a full kitchen. Hotel amenities include free video movies and a complimentary hot breakfast buffet. There is a $50 one time per stay pet fee.

Motel 6 - Thousand Oaks South
1516 Newbury Rd
Newbury Park, CA
805-499-0711 (800-466-8356)
One well-behaved family pet per room. Guest must notify front desk upon arrival. Guest is liable for any damages. In consideration of all guests, pets must never be left unattended in the guest rooms.

Best Western Newport Beach Inn
6208 W Coast Highway
Newport, CA
949-642-8252 (800-780-7234)
Dogs up to 50 pounds are allowed for an additional one time pet fee of $50 per room. 2 dogs may be allowed.

Motel 6 - Sacramento - North Highlands
4600 Watt Avenue
North Highlands, CA
916-973-8637 (800-466-8356)
One well-behaved family pet per room. Guest must notify front desk upon arrival. Guest is liable for any damages. In consideration of all guests, pets must never be left unattended in the guest rooms.

Motel 6 - Los Angeles - Van Nuys/Sepulveda
15711 Roscoe Boulevard
North Hills, CA
818-894-9341 (800-466-8356)
One well-behaved family pet per room. Guest must notify front desk upon arrival. Guest is liable for any damages. In consideration of all guests, pets must never be left unattended in the guest rooms.

Agate Bay Realty Lake Tahoe
Call to Arrange

North Lake Tahoe, CA
530-546-4256 (800-550-6740)
agatebay.com
These vacation rentals are located in North Tahoe. Many of the homes are dog-friendly, and some offer lake views or easy access to beaches.

Enchanted Vacation Properties
Call to Arrange
North Lake Tahoe, CA
530-546-2066
enchantedvacationproperties.com
These vacation rentals are located on the north side of Lake Tahoe. Dogs of all sizes are welcome. Pet amenities include dog beds, dog bowls and treats, dog toys and a doggie guest book. There are no pet fees.

Motel 6 - Palm Springs North
63950 20th Avenue
North Palm Springs, CA
760-251-1425 (800-466-8356)
One well-behaved family pet per room. Guest must notify front desk upon arrival. Guest is liable for any damages. In consideration of all guests, pets must never be left unattended in the guest rooms.

Motel 6 - Los Angeles - Norwalk
10646 Rosecrans Avenue
Norwalk, CA
562-864-2567 (800-466-8356)
One well-behaved family pet per room. Guest must notify front desk upon arrival. Guest is liable for any damages. In consideration of all guests, pets must never be left unattended in the guest rooms.

Inn Marin
250 Entrada Drive
Novato, CA
415-883-5952 (800-652-6565)
innmarin.com/
Inn Marin invites both business and leisure travelers. Nestled in a beautiful resort setting and richly restored, this inn welcomes your best friend. Amenities include a large outdoor heated pool and spa, garden patio area with barbecue, exercise facility, guest laundry facility and a continental breakfast. Rooms include data ports, voice mail and two line speaker phone, iron and ironing board, and handicapped rooms/facilities are available. They are located just off Highway 101, perfect for the business or tourist traveler. There is a $20 one time pet fee. You are required to bring a crate if you plan to leave your dog alone in the room.

Oakridge Inn
780 Ventura Avenue
Oak View, CA
805-649-4018
oakridgeinn.com/
This great getaway offers 33 spacious, clean, nicely appointed rooms. Some of the features/amenities include a heated pool and spa, complimentary continental breakfast, and a convenient location to several other attractions and activities. Dogs up to 50 pounds are allowed for an additional pet fee of $15 per night per pet. They may require an additional pet deposit for very hairy dogs. Dogs must be quiet, leashed, cleaned up after, and they may not be left alone in the room at any time. Multiple dogs may be allowed.

A Bed of Roses
43547 Whispering Pines Drive
Oakhurst, CA
559-642-6975 (877-624-7673)
abedofrosesbandb.com/
Individually, beautifully decorated rooms with private baths, a freshly prepared hearty breakfast, 24 hour cookie jar and snacks, an outdoor swimming pool and hot tub with lighted waterfalls, a petting zoo, and spectacular views are just a few of the features of this inn. Rooms with Jacuzzi tubs, skylights, private outdoor decks, and wood burning stoves, are also available. Although pet rooms are limited, dogs of all sizes are welcome for an additional fee of $20 per night per pet, and advanced reservations are required with a valid credit card. Reservations may be made toll free at 877-624-7673. A throw blanket, extra towels, a comfortable sleeping pad, water bowl, and treats are provided for canine guests. Dogs must be leashed or crated when in common areas, and be cleaned up after at all times. Dogs are not allowed on the furniture in the room or the common use areas, and they are not allowed in the dining room. 2 dogs may be allowed.

Pine Rose Inn Bed and Breakfast
41703 Road 222
Oakhurst, CA
559-642-2800 (866-642-2800)
pineroseinn.com/
The inn is located 13 miles from the south gate of Yosemite National Park, 2 miles from Bass Lake and surrounded by the Sierra National Forest. The entire inn is non-smoking, except for outside. There is

a $10 per day pet charge. Dogs and other pets are welcome.

La Quinta Inn Oakland Airport/Coliseum
8465 Enterprise Way
Oakland, CA
510-632-8900 (800-531-5900)
Dogs of all sizes are allowed. There are no additional pet fees. Dogs must be leashed and cleaned up after. Multiple dogs may be allowed.

Motel 6 - Oakland - Embarcadero
1801 Embarcadero
Oakland, CA
510-436-0103 (800-466-8356)
One well-behaved family pet per room. Guest must notify front desk upon arrival. Guest is liable for any damages. In consideration of all guests, pets must never be left unattended in the guest rooms.

Motel 6 - Oakland Airport
8480 Edes Avenue
Oakland, CA
510-638-1180 (800-466-8356)
One well-behaved family pet per room. Guest must notify front desk upon arrival. Guest is liable for any damages. In consideration of all guests, pets must never be left unattended in the guest rooms.

Quality Inn
8471 Enterprise Way
Oakland, CA
510-562-4888 (877-424-6423)
Dogs are allowed for an additional fee of $10 per night per pet. 2 dogs may be allowed.

Inn at Occidental
3657 Church Street
Occidental, CA
707-874-1047 (800-522-6324)
innatoccidental.com/
Set among towering redwoods, this completely restored Victorian inn offers world class comfort and elegance in a country setting. Some of the amenities/features include a welcoming veranda, antiques, a complimentary Sonoma-harvest gourmet breakfast, an afternoon hors d'oeuvre and wine reception, private baths, fireplaces, and spa tubs. They offer a spacious cottage for guests with pets. Dogs of all sizes are allowed for an additional $25 per night per pet. Dogs must be kenneled when left unattended in the cottage, and they must be well behaved, leashed, and cleaned up after. Dogs are not allowed on the furnishings. 2 dogs may be allowed.

Occidental Hotel
3610 Bohemian Hwy
Occidental, CA
707-874-3623
There is an $8.70 per day pet fee for each pet. Dogs must be on leash and may not be left alone in the rooms.

Best Western Marty's Valley Inn
3240 E Mission Avenue
Oceanside, CA
760-757-7700 (800-780-7234)
Dogs up to 50 pounds are allowed for an additional fee of $10 per night per pet. 2 dogs may be allowed.

La Quinta Inn San Diego - Oceanside
937 N. Coast Highway
Oceanside, CA
760-450-0730 (800-531-5900)
Dogs of all sizes are allowed. There are no additional pet fees. Dogs may not be left unattended, and they must be leashed and cleaned up after. Multiple dogs may be allowed.

Motel 6 - Oceanside
3708 Plaza Drive
Oceanside, CA
760-941-1011 (800-466-8356)
One well-behaved family pet per room. Guest must notify front desk upon arrival. Guest is liable for any damages. In consideration of all guests, pets must never be left unattended in the guest rooms.

Motel 6 - Oceanside Downtown
909 North Coast Highway
Oceanside, CA
760-721-1543 (800-466-8356)
One well-behaved family pet per room. Guest must notify front desk upon arrival. Guest is liable for any damages. In consideration of all guests, pets must never be left unattended in the guest rooms.

Best Western Casa Ojai
1302 E Ojai Ave
Ojai, CA
805-646-8175 (800-780-7234)
Dogs are allowed for an additional one time fee of $25 per pet. Multiple dogs may be allowed.

Lavender Inn
210 E Matilija Street
Ojai, CA
805-646-6635
lavenderinn.com/
This tranquil retreat offers 7 rooms and an attached cottage, each with

its own unique décor of bold colors and detail, and it is conveniently located to several other attractions and activities. The private gardens and fountains are breathtaking complete with tall oaks, mountain views, and a wonderful variety of lavenders. A separate building on the property houses an intimate day spa that offer a variety of massages. One dog up to 50 pounds is allowed for an additional one time fee of $25. They may accept a slightly larger dog in the cottage only. Dogs must be quiet, well behaved, leashed and cleaned up after.

Ojai Valley Inn and Spa
905 Country Club Road
Ojai, CA
805-646-2420
ojairesort.com/
This award-winning historic resort is elegance inside and out with 220 tree-shaded acres that include luxury accommodations, a premier championship golf course, a comprehensive 31,000 square foot spa village, and a first-of-its-kind artist cottage where local artists inspire and help guests to create in a variety of media. In addition to several amenities, they also offer in room dining, handcrafted picnics, a cocktail lounge, and several dining options featuring California Central Coast cuisine prepared with locally harvested, seasonal foods and herbs. Dogs of all sizes are allowed but they must be acknowledged at the time of reservations. There is a $50 per night additional pet fee per room for the first 3 nights for a total of no more than $150. Dogs must be quiet, leashed, cleaned up after, and crated when left alone in the room. 2 dogs may be allowed.

Ranch Motel
2051 S Highway 395
Olancha, CA
760-764-2387
Dogs are allowed.

Bear Valley Inn
88 Bear Valley Road
Olema, CA
415-663-1777
bearvinn.com/contact/index.html
Offering a step into an elegant past, this nicely appointed historic 1910 inn offers a great location for other local attractions and recreational activities, including hundreds of miles of multi-use trails. Dogs are welcome in the cottage but not the main house. The cottage has a nice deck and offers a full kitchen supplied with

homemade granola, fresh fruit and yogurt, and coffee and organic teas. There is an additional pet fee of $20 per room per stay. Dogs must be well mannered, leashed, cleaned up after, and crated when left alone in the cottage. 2 dogs may be allowed.

Olema Inn
10,000 Sir Francis Drake Blvd
Olema, CA
415-663-9559
theolemainn.com/index.html
Only moments from beautiful coastline, this restored inn offers elegant rooms, exceptional fine dining from a mostly organic menu, a splendid outdoor patio, lush gardens, and more. Dogs of all sizes are allowed for no additional fee. Dogs must be well mannered, leashed, and cleaned up after. Multiple dogs may be allowed.

Country Inns & Suites by Carlson
231 North Vineyard Avenue
Ontario, CA
909-937-6000
Dogs of all sizes are allowed. There is a $50 one time additional pet fee. Some rooms have full kitchens and wireless high-speed Internet access. There is an outdoor pool and a fitness center.

La Quinta Inn & Suites Ontario Airport
3555 Inland Empire Blvd
Ontario, CA
909-476-1112 (800-531-5900)
Dogs of all sizes are allowed. There are no additional pet fees, but a credit card must be on file. Dogs must be crated if left alone in the room, and be leashed and cleaned up after. Multiple dogs may be allowed.

Motel 6 - Ontario Airport
1560 East 4th Street
Ontario, CA
909-984-2424 (800-466-8356)
One well-behaved family pet per room. Guest must notify front desk upon arrival. Guest is liable for any damages. In consideration of all guests, pets must never be left unattended in the guest rooms.

Red Roof Inn - Ontario Airport
1818 East Holt Boulevard
Ontario, CA
909-988-8466 (800-RED-ROOF)
One well-behaved family pet per room. Guest must notify front desk upon arrival. Guest is liable for any damages. In consideration of all guests, pets must never be left

unattended in the guest rooms.

Residence Inn by Marriott
2025 Convention Center Way
Ontario, CA
909-937-6788
Dogs of all sizes are allowed. There is a $75 one time fee, and a pet policy to sign in check in. Multiple dogs may be allowed.

Motel 6 - Anaheim Stadium - Orange
2920 West Chapman Avenue
Orange, CA
714-634-2441 (800-466-8356)
One well-behaved dog up to about 80 pounds is allowed. There are no additional pet fees.

Days Inn
1745 Feather River Blvd
Oroville, CA
530-533-3297 (800-329-7466)
One large dog per room is okay. There is a $7 per day pet fee.

Motel 6 - Oroville
505 Montgomery Street
Oroville, CA
530-532-9400 (800-466-8356)
One well-behaved family pet per room. Guest must notify front desk upon arrival. Guest is liable for any damages. In consideration of all guests, pets must never be left unattended in the guest rooms.

Travelodge
580 Oroville Dam Blvd
Oroville, CA
530-533-7070
There is a $40 refundable pet deposit.

Casa Sirena Hotel and Resort
3605 Peninsula Rd
Oxnard, CA
805-985-6311
There is a $50 one time pet fee. There is an on-site tennis court and an exercise room. Some rooms have views of the Channel Islands Harbor.

Residence Inn by Marriott
2101 W Vineyard Avenue
Oxnard, CA
805-278-2200
Dogs of all sizes are allowed. There is a $75 one time fee, and a pet policy to sign at check in. Multiple dogs may be allowed.

Vagabond Inn
1245 N. Oxnard Blvd.
Oxnard, CA

805-983-0251
vagabondinn.com
Amenities at this motel include a free continental breakfast and weekday newspaper. They also have an on-site coffee shop, which might be helpful in getting food to go for the room. Pets are an additional $5 per day.

Andril Fireplace Cottages
569 Asilomar Blvd
Pacific Grove, CA
831-375-0994
There is an additional fee of $14 per day for a pet. Well-behaved dogs are allowed.

Lighthouse Lodge and Suites
1249 Lighthouse Ave
Pacific Grove, CA
831-655-2111

Best Western Las Brisas Hotel
222 S Indian Canyon Drive
Palm, CA
760-325-4372 (800-780-7234)
Dogs are allowed for an additional pet fee per room of $35 for the 1st night, and $15 for each additional night. Dogs may not be left alone in the room. 2 dogs may be allowed.

Best Western Palm Desert Resort
74695 Highway 111
Palm Desert, CA
760-340-4441 (800-780-7234)
Dogs are allowed for an additional pet fee of $10 per night per room. Multiple dogs may be allowed.

Comfort Suites
39-585 Washington Street
Palm Desert, CA
760-360-3337 (877-424-6423)
Dogs up to 50 pounds are allowed for an additional one time pet fee of $20 per room. Dogs may not be left alone in the room. Multiple dogs may be allowed.

Motel 6 - Palm Desert - Palm Springs Area
78100 Varner Road
Palm Desert, CA
760-345-0550 (800-466-8356)
One well-behaved family pet per room. Guest must notify front desk upon arrival. Guest is liable for any damages. In consideration of all guests, pets must never be left unattended in the guest rooms.

Residence Inn by Marriott
38305 Cook Street
Palm Desert, CA
760-776-0050

Dogs of all sizes are allowed. There is a $75 one time fee, and a pet policy to sign at check in. Multiple dogs may be allowed.

The Inn at Deep Canyon
74470 Abronia Trail
Palm Desert, CA
760-346-8061 (800-253-0004)
inn-adc.com/
This hotel features a palm garden, pool and fully-equipped kitchenettes. They have pet-friendly rooms available. There is a $10 per day additional pet fee.

7 Springs Resort and Hotel Palm Springs
950 N. Indian Canyon Dr.
Palm Springs, CA
800-355-3578
palm-springs-hotels.cc
7 Springs Inn and Suites offers a variety of accommodations in the heart of Palm Springs. Enjoy fully furnished suites with Kitchens, free daily Continental Breakfast, Heated Pool, Jacuzzi, barbecue area, Remote control T.V., direct dial telephones, free parking. Close to area shopping, restaurants, casinos, golf, tennis, and Indian canyons. Pets are welcome for a $15 per night fee. Pets cannot be left unattended and must be kept on a leash when out of the room.

Casa Cody Country Inn
175 S. Cahuilla Rd.
Palm Springs, CA
760-320-9346
casacody.com
This is a quaint romantic historic inn that was founded in the 1920s. The founder, Harriet Cody, was a cousin of Buffalo Bill. The inn is nestled against the mountains and has adobe buildings. The rooms have fireplaces, kitchens and private patios. There is a $10 per day pet charge.

Hilton
400 E Tahquitz Canyon Way
Palm Springs, CA
760-320-6868
Dogs are allowed for a $100 refundable deposit plus $25 per night per pet. Dogs may not be left alone in the room at any time. Multiple dogs may be allowed.

La Serena Villas
339 South Belardo Road
Palm Springs, CA
760-325-3216
These dog-friendly villas cater to those who prefer a relaxing,

secluded hideaway in Palm Springs. Built in the 1930's, the villas are nestled in the foothills of the San Jacinto Mountains. Palm Springs Village is within walking distance. Your pet is welcome. There is a $10 per day pet charge. Pets must be on leash and please pick up after your dog.

Motel 6 - Palm Springs Downtown
660 South Palm Canyon Drive
Palm Springs, CA
760-327-4200 (800-466-8356)
One well-behaved family pet per room. Guest must notify front desk upon arrival. Guest is liable for any damages. In consideration of all guests, pets must never be left unattended in the guest rooms.

Motel 6 - Palm Springs East-E Palm Canyon
595 East Palm Canyon Drive
Palm Springs, CA
760-325-6129 (800-466-8356)
One well-behaved family pet per room. Guest must notify front desk upon arrival. Guest is liable for any damages. In consideration of all guests, pets must never be left unattended in the guest rooms.

Orchid Tree Inn
261 South Belardo Road
Palm Springs, CA
760-325-2791
This inn has two pet rooms. Dogs must be attended at all times and leashed when outside the room. There is a $250 refundable pet deposit.

Palm Springs Hotels Caliente Tropics Resort
411 E. Palm Canyon Drive
Palm Springs, CA
800-658-5975
calientetropics.com
Well-behaved dogs up to 60 pounds are allowed. Leashed pets are allowed in the lawn and pool areas. Pets may not be left alone in the rooms. There is no smoking indoors at the Caliente Tropics Resort.

Palm Springs Riviera Resort
1600 North Indian Canyon Drive
Palm Springs, CA
760-327-8311
This 24 acre full service resort with 476 guest rooms allows well-behaved dogs of all sizes. Each room features oversized beds, individually controlled central air conditioning and heating units, small refrigerators, irons and ironing boards and multi-line phones with

dataports. Amenities at the resort include an 18-hole putting course, nine tennis courts, a volleyball and basketball court and a workout room. They are located one mile from Palm Canyon Drive. There is a $20 per day pet fee and a $200 refundable pet deposit.

Quality Inn
1269 E Palm Canyon Drive
Palm Springs, CA
760-323-2775 (877-424-6423)
Dogs are allowed for no additional pet fee. 2 dogs may be allowed.

San Marino Hotel
225 West Baristo Road
Palm Springs, CA
800-676-1214
sanmarinohotel.com/
The hotel, a favorite of writers and artists, is the closest lodging to the Palm Springs historic shopping area. Dogs are allowed, but not in the poolside rooms. There is a $10 per day pet charge.

Super 8 Lodge - Palm Springs
1900 N. Palm Canyon Drive
Palm Springs, CA
760-322-3757 (800-800-8000)
innworks.com/palmsprings
There is a $10 per stay additional pet fee. Up to three dogs are permitted in each room. The hotel allows a free 8 minute long distance call each night and offers a free continental breakfast. There is a pool and a laundry. Off I-10, from West take Hwy 111 (N. Palm Canyon Drive); from East take Indian Avenue. The hotel is next to Billy Reed's restaurant.

Vacation Palm Springs
1401 N Palm Canyon Drive, Suite 201
Palm Springs, CA
760-778-7832
Dogs of all sizes are allowed. There is a $60 per room per stay fee and a pet policy to sign at check in. Multiple dogs may be allowed.

Motel 6 - Palmdale
407 West Palmdale Boulevard
Palmdale, CA
661-272-0660 (800-466-8356)
One well-behaved family pet per room. Guest must notify front desk upon arrival. Guest is liable for any damages. In consideration of all guests, pets must never be left unattended in the guest rooms.

Super 8 Palmdale

200 W Palmdale Blvd
Palmdale, CA
661-273-8000 (800-800-8000)
Dogs of all sizes are allowed. There is a $10 per night pet fee per pet. Smoking and non-smoking rooms are available for pet rooms. 2 dogs may be allowed.

Motel 6 - Palo Alto
4301 El Camino Real
Palo Alto, CA
650-949-0833 (800-466-8356)
One well-behaved family pet per room. Guest must notify front desk upon arrival. Guest is liable for any damages. In consideration of all guests, pets must never be left unattended in the guest rooms.

Sheraton Palo Alto Hotel
625 El Camino Real
Palo Alto, CA
650-328-2800 (888-625-5144)
Dogs of all sizes are allowed. You must sign a pet policy. Dogs are not allowed to be left alone in the room.

The Westin Palo Alto
675 El Camino Real
Palo Alto, CA
650-321-4422 (888-625-5144)
Dogs up to 80 pounds are allowed. There are no additional pet fees. Dogs are not allowed to be left alone in the room.

Panamint Springs Resort
Highway 190
Panamint Springs, CA
775-482-7680
deathvalley.com/
There is a $5 per day additional pet fee. The resort is located on Highway 190, 48 miles east of Lone Pine and 31 miles west of Stovepipe Wells.

Comfort Inn Central
5475 Clark Road
Paradise, CA
530-876-0191 (877-424-6423)
Dogs are allowed for an additional fee of $10 (plus tax) per night per pet. Multiple dogs may be allowed.

Ponderosa Gardens Motel
7010 The Skyway
Paradise, CA
530-872-9094
True to its name, this motel features a garden like setting, a pool and Jacuzzi, gift shop, picnic grounds, and a continental breakfast. Dogs of all sizes are allowed for an additional fee of $6 per night per pet. Dogs may not be left alone in the room at any time, and they must be leashed and

cleaned up after. Multiple dogs may be allowed.

Hilton
168 South Los Robles Avenue
Pasadena, CA
626-577-1000
Dogs up to 50 pounds are allowed for an additional one time pet fee of $50 per room. Multiple dogs may be allowed.

Motel 6 - Paso Robles
1134 Black Oak Drive
Paso Robles, CA
805-239-9090 (800-466-8356)
One well-behaved family pet per room. Guest must notify front desk upon arrival. Guest is liable for any damages. In consideration of all guests, pets must never be left unattended in the guest rooms.

Best Western Villa Del Lago Inn
2959 Speno Drive
Patterson, CA
209-892-5300 (800-780-7234)
Pets allowed with Restrictions

The Lodge at Pebble Beach
1700 17 Mile Drive
Pebble Beach, CA
831-624-3811 (800-654-9300)
With a long list of accolades to its name, this elegant inn offers attentive hospitality, world-class luxury suites with a fireplace, and a patio or balcony-each offering stunning views, 4 championship golf courses, and great hiking trails. Dogs up to 25 pounds are allowed. There are no additional pet fees. Dogs may not be left unattended in the rooms, and they must be leashed and cleaned up after at all times. Dogs are allowed on the trails; they are not allowed on the golf courses. 2 dogs may be allowed.

Best Western Petaluma Inn
200 S McDowell Boulevard
Petaluma, CA
707-763-0994 (800-780-7234)
Dogs are allowed for an additional one time pet fee of $10 per room. 2 dogs may be allowed.

Motel 6 - Petaluma
1368 North McDowell Boulevard
Petaluma, CA
707-765-0333 (800-466-8356)
One well-behaved family pet per room. Guest must notify front desk upon arrival. Guest is liable for any damages. In consideration of all guests, pets must never be left

unattended in the guest rooms.

Quality Inn
5100 Montero Way
Petaluma, CA
707-664-1155 (877-424-6423)
Dogs up to 50 pounds are allowed for an additional pet fee of $15 per night per room. 2 dogs may be allowed.

Sheraton Sonoma County - Petaluma
745 Baywood Dr.
Petaluma, CA
707-283-2888 (888-625-5144)
Dogs of all sizes are allowed. Pet rooms are available on the first floor only. You must sign a pet policy when checking in with a dog. Dogs are not allowed to be left alone in the room. 2 dogs may be allowed.

Anderson Valley Inn
8480 H 128
Philo, CA
707-895-3325
Dogs only, and of all sizes are allowed. There is a $25 one time fee for 1 dog and a 2nd dog would be an additional $10 one time fee. No pit bulls are allowed, and dogs must be on a leash at all times. Dogs may not be left alone at any time. 2 dogs may be allowed.

Highland Ranch
18941 Philo Greenwood Rd.
Philo, CA
707-895-3600
highlandranch.com/home.html
This 125 year old ranch house sits along the mountainside among majestic trees with 8 individually decorated cabins nestled around it. At this country resort you can take in a wide variety of land and water recreation and activities, a massage, a yoga class, trek a hundred miles of multi-use trails, or take part in a myriad of other events. They also feature good home-cooked meals served family-style in the main house. Dogs of all sizes are welcome for no additional fee. They are greeted with treats, and some towels and blankets that they'll need after a day of enjoying country life. Dogs must be well mannered, leashed, and cleaned up after. Multiple dogs may be allowed.

Days Inn - Pico Rivera
6540 S. Rosemead Blvd
Pico Rivera, CA
562-942-1003 (800-329-7466)
There is a $15 per day pet fee.

Motel 6 - Pinole
1501 Fitzgerald Drive
Pinole, CA
510-222-8174 (800-466-8356)
One well-behaved family pet per room. Guest must notify front desk upon arrival. Guest is liable for any damages. In consideration of all guests, pets must never be left unattended in the guest rooms.

Pioneer Town Motel
5040 Curtis Road
Pioneertown, CA
760-365-4879
All of this rustic motel's 20 rooms are decorated with the authentic charm of an era past, but updated with Satellite TV, HBO, a kitchen area, microwave, a refrigerator, and shaded seating areas where you can enjoy the views. Because the town was built also as a movie set to be a complete old west town, many Western stars and movie greats of the past have slept in these rooms while shooting films here. Dogs of all sizes are allowed. There is a $10 per night per pet additional fee. Dogs may not be left alone in the rooms, and they must be leashed and cleaned up after. 2 dogs may be allowed.

Cottage Inn by the Sea
2351 Price Street
Pismo Beach, CA
805-773-4617
Dogs of all sizes are allowed. There is a $10 per night per pet fee and a pet policy to sign at check in. Multiple dogs may be allowed.

Motel 6 - Pismo Beach
860 4th Street
Pismo Beach, CA
805-773-2665 (800-466-8356)
One well-behaved family pet per room. Guest must notify front desk upon arrival. Guest is liable for any damages. In consideration of all guests, pets must never be left unattended in the guest rooms.

Oxford Suites
651 Five Cities Drive
Pismo Beach, CA
805-773-3773 (800-982-SUITE)
oxfordsuites.com
This motel is located within a short drive of the dog-friendly Pismo State Beach. Amenities include a year-round pool & spa, complimentary full breakfast buffet, an evening reception with beverages & light hor d'oeuvres. Room amenities for the guest suites include a work table,

sofa, microwave oven, refrigerator, TV/VCR, and wheelchair accessibility. There is a $10 per day pet charge. Dogs must never be left unattended in the room, even if they are in a crate.

Sea Gypsy Motel
1020 Cypress Street
Pismo Beach, CA
805-773-1801
seagypsymotel.com/
This motel is located on the beach and they allow dogs of any size. There is a $15 per day pet charge.

Motel 6 - Pittsburg
2101 Loveridge Road
Pittsburg, CA
925-427-1600 (800-466-8356)
One well-behaved family pet per room. Guest must notify front desk upon arrival. Guest is liable for any damages. In consideration of all guests, pets must never be left unattended in the guest rooms.

Residence Inn by Marriott
700 W Kimberly Ave
Placentia, CA
714-996-0555
Dogs of all sizes are welcome. There is a $75 one time fee, and a pet policy to sign at check in. 2 dogs may be allowed.

Best Western Placerville Inn
6850 Greenleaf Dr
Placerville, CA
530-622-9100 (800-780-7234)
Dogs are allowed for an additional fee of $25 per night per pet. Multiple dogs may be allowed.

Fleming Jones Homestead B&B
3170 Newtown Road
Placerville, CA
530-344-0943
robinsnestranch.com
This historic homestead is a B&B at a working miniature horse ranch. It is located 5 minutes from Placerville and near the Apple Hill farms that are open to the public each fall. Well-behaved dogs are welcome in the Woodshed and Bunkhouse rooms of the B&B. There is a $10 per day per dog. Dogs may not be left unattended and guests are responsible for any damages caused by their pets.

Residence Inn by Marriott
700 Ellinwood Way
Pleasant Hill, CA
925-689-1010
Dogs of all sizes are welcome.

There is a $100 one time fee, and a pet policy to sign at check in. Multiple dogs may be allowed.

Best Western Pleasanton Inn
5375 Owens Ct
Pleasanton, CA
925-463-1300 (800-780-7234)
Dogs are allowed for an additional fee of $20 per night per pet. 2 dogs may be allowed.

Motel 6 - Pleasanton
5102 Hopyard Road
Pleasanton, CA
925-463-2626 (800-466-8356)
One well-behaved family pet per room. Guest must notify front desk upon arrival. Guest is liable for any damages. In consideration of all guests, pets must never be left unattended in the guest rooms.

Residence Inn by Marriott
11920 Dublin Canyon Road
Pleasanton, CA
925-227-0500
Pets of all sizes are allowed. There is a $75 one time fee, and a pet policy to sign at check in. Multiple dogs may be allowed.

Point Reyes Station Inn Bed and Breakfast
11591 Highway One, Box 824
Point Reyes Station, CA
415-663-9372
pointreyesstationinn.com/
They offer private, romantic rooms with thirteen foot vaulted ceilings, whirlpool baths, fireplaces and views of rolling hills. This inn is located at the gateway of the Point Reyes National Seashore. Well-behaved dogs are welcome and there is no extra pet charge. Children are also welcome.

Tree House Bed and Breakfast Inn
73 Drake Summit, P.O. Box 1075
Point Reyes Station, CA
415-663-8720
treehousebnb.com/
This inn offers a secluded and peaceful getaway in West Marin. It is located on the tip of Inverness Ridge with a view of Point Reyes Station. The Point Reyes National Seashore is nearby. All three rooms have a private bathroom. Pets and children are always welcome. Smoking is allowed outdoors. There are no pet fees.

Motel 6 - Los Angeles - Pomona
2470 South Garey Avenue
Pomona, CA

909-591-1871 (800-466-8356)
One well-behaved family pet per room. Guest must notify front desk upon arrival. Guest is liable for any damages. In consideration of all guests, pets must never be left unattended in the guest rooms.

Sheraton Suites Fairplex
601 West McKinley Ave.
Pomona, CA
909-622-2220 (888-625-5144)
Dogs of all sizes are allowed. Pet rooms are available on the second floor only. You must sign a pet policy when checking in with a dog. Dogs are not allowed to be left alone in the room.

Shilo Inn
3200 Temple Ave
Pomona, CA
909-598-0073 (800-222-2244)
shiloinns.com
Amenities include a complimentary breakfast buffet, outdoor pool & spa, guest laundry, fitness center and fresh fruit, popcorn & coffee. Rooms include microwaves, refrigerators, hair dryers, iron/ironing boards and more. There is a $10 per day additional pet fee.

Motel 6 - Porterville
935 West Morton Avenue
Porterville, CA
559-781-7600 (800-466-8356)
One well-behaved family pet per room. Guest must notify front desk upon arrival. Guest is liable for any damages. In consideration of all guests, pets must never be left unattended in the guest rooms.

Bucks Lake Lodge
23685 Bucks Lake
Quincy, CA
530-283-2262
There is a $10 per day additional pet fee. Dogs are allowed in the cabins, but not the motel section. The cabins are not designated as smoking or non-smoking. Thanks to one of our readers for this recommendation.

Best Western Heritage Inn
11269 Point East Dr
Rancho Cordova, CA
916-635-4040 (800-780-7234)
Dogs up to 60 pounds are allowed for an additional one time fee of $25 per pet. 2 dogs may be allowed.

Inns of America
12249 Folsom Blvd
Rancho Cordova, CA
916-351-1213 (800-826-0778)

innsofamerica.com/sac12.htm
This motel offers a complimentary continental breakfast. To get there from Sacramento, take Hwy 50 and exit Hazel Ave. Turn right onto Hazel. Then turn right onto Folsom Blvd. The hotel will be on the right. There is a $5 per day additional pet fee.

Motel 6 - Sacramento - Rancho Cordova East
10694 Olson Drive
Rancho Cordova, CA
916-635-8784 (800-466-8356)
One well-behaved family pet per room. Guest must notify front desk upon arrival. Guest is liable for any damages. In consideration of all guests, pets must never be left unattended in the guest rooms.

Residence Inn by Marriott
2779 Prospect Park Drive
Rancho Cordova, CA
916-851-1550
Pets of all sizes are allowed. There is a $75 one time fee, and a pet policy to sign at check in. 2 dogs may be allowed.

TownePlace Suites Ontario Airport
9645 Milliken Avenue
Rancho Cucamonga, CA
714-256-2070
Dogs of all sizes are allowed. There is a $75 one time pet fee per visit. . 2 dogs may be allowed.

Motel 6 - Palm Springs - Rancho Mirage
69570 SR 111
Rancho Mirage, CA
760-324-8475 (800-466-8356)
One well-behaved family pet per room. Guest must notify front desk upon arrival. Guest is liable for any damages. In consideration of all guests, pets must never be left unattended in the guest rooms.

Rancho Las Palmas Marriott Resort and Spa
41000 Bob Hope Drive
Rancho Mirage, CA
760-568-2727 (800-458-8786)
Dogs of all sizes are allowed. There is a $75 one time additional pet fee per room. Dogs must be leashed, cleaned up after, removed or accompanied for housekeeping, and the Do Not Disturb sign put on the door if they are in the room alone. 2 dogs may be allowed.

Best Western Antelope Inn
203 Antelope Boulevard

Red Bluff, CA
530-527-8882 (800-780-7234)
Dogs are allowed for an additional fee of $7 per night per pet. Multiple dogs may be allowed.

Comfort Inn
90 Sale Lane
Red Bluff, CA
530-529-7060 (877-424-6423)
Dogs are allowed for an additional fee of $15 per night per room. 2 dogs may be allowed.

Motel 6 - Red Bluff
20 Williams Avenue
Red Bluff, CA
530-527-9200 (800-466-8356)
One well-behaved family pet per room. Guest must notify front desk upon arrival. Guest is liable for any damages. In consideration of all guests, pets must never be left unattended in the guest rooms.

Sportsman's Lodge
768 Antelope Blvd
Red Bluff, CA
530-527-2888
rbsportsmanlodge.com/
Some of the amenities at this lodge include refrigerators in all the rooms and a swimming pool. Dogs of all sizes are allowed. There is a $7 additional fee per pet for a small to medium dog; the fee may be higher for larger or heavily-haired dogs. Dogs may not be left unattended in the rooms at any time, and they must be well behaved, leashed, and cleaned up after. 2 dogs may be allowed.

Travelodge
38 Antelope Blvd
Red Bluff, CA
530-527-6020
There is a $6 per day pet fee.

Bridge Bay Resort
10300 Bridge Bay Road
Redding, CA
530-275-3021 (800-752-9669)
This is a complete resort that offers a full-service marina with tackle and bait, small boats and houseboat rentals, dining, a lounge, gift shop, convenience store, banquet rooms, a pool, and lakeside accommodations. Dogs of all sizes are welcome for an additional fee of $10 per night per pet, plus a $50 deposit if paying by cash. There is no additional pet fee for the dogs on the boats. Dogs may be left alone in the rooms for a short time if they are house-trained and they will be quiet and well behaved. Dogs must be leashed and cleaned

up after at all times. Multiple dogs may be allowed.

Fawndale Lodge and RV Resort
15215 Fawndale Road
Redding, CA
800-338-0941
members.aol.com/fawnresort/
Nestled in the pines, this lodge offers acres of lawn, a pool and easy access to many recreational activities. All rooms are non-smoking. There is a $1 per day pet charge.

Holiday Inn Redding
1900 Hilltop Drive
Redding, CA
530-221-7500 (877-270-6405)
Quiet dogs of all sizes are allowed for an additional $10 per night per pet. Multiple dogs may be allowed.

La Quinta Inn Redding
2180 Hilltop Drive
Redding, CA
530-221-8200 (800-531-5900)
Dogs of all sizes are allowed. There are no additional pet fees. Dogs may not be left unattended at any time, and they must be leashed and cleaned up after. Multiple dogs may be allowed.

Motel 6 - Redding Central
1640 Hilltop Drive
Redding, CA
530-221-1800 (800-466-8356)
One well-behaved family pet per room. Guest must notify front desk upon arrival. Guest is liable for any damages. In consideration of all guests, pets must never be left unattended in the guest rooms.

Motel 6 - Redding North
1250 Twin View Boulevard
Redding, CA
530-246-4470 (800-466-8356)
One well-behaved family pet per room. Guest must notify front desk upon arrival. Guest is liable for any damages. In consideration of all guests, pets must never be left unattended in the guest rooms.

Motel 6 - Redding South
2385 Bechelli Lane
Redding, CA
530-221-0562 (800-466-8356)
One well-behaved family pet per room. Guest must notify front desk upon arrival. Guest is liable for any damages. In consideration of all guests, pets must never be left unattended in the guest rooms.

Ponderosa Inn
2220 Pine St
Redding, CA
530-241-6300 (800-626-1900)
Dogs are allowed for an additional pet fee of $10 for the 1st night and $5 for each additional night; add $5 to each night for a 2nd dog. 2 dogs may be allowed.

Quality Inn
2059 Hilltop Drive
Redding, CA
530-221-6530 (877-424-6423)
Dogs are allowed for an additional one time pet fee of $15 per room. 2 dogs may be allowed.

River Inn
1835 Park Marina Drive
Redding, CA
530-241-9500 (800-995-4341)
redding-online.com/riverinn.htm
This inn is adjacent to the Sacramento River and has a private grass area next to their lake. There is a $6 per day pet charge. Thanks to one of our readers for recommending this inn.

Shasta Lodge
1245 Pine Street
Redding, CA
530-243-6133
There is a $20 refundable pet deposit. There is also a $5 per day pet fee.

Dean Creek Resort Motel
4112 Redwood Drive
Redway, CA
707-923-2555 (877-923-2555)
Located along the Eel River in Giant Redwood country, and only three miles from the famous "Avenue of the Giants", this resort offers a long list of amenities and recreation. Pets are allowed for an additional fee of $6 per night per pet for the motel. There is an RV park on site where dogs are an additional $1.50 per night per pet. Dogs may not be left unattended at any time, either in the motel or in the RV park. Dogs are allowed on the trails and on the beach. Dogs must be leashed and cleaned up after. Please check with the resort for breed restrictions. 2 dogs may be allowed.

Hotel Sofitel
223 Twin Dolphin Dr
Redwood City, CA
650-598-9000
sofitel.com
This nice 8 story dog-friendly hotel is located off Hwy 101 and Marine World Parkway. There is a $25 one

time pet fee.

Best Western Empire Inn
475 W Valley Blvd
Rialto, CA
909-877-0690 (800-780-7234)
Dogs are allowed for an additional fee of $15 per night per pet. Multiple dogs may be allowed.

Motel 6 - Ridgecrest
535 South China Lake Boulevard
Ridgecrest, CA
760-375-6866 (800-466-8356)
One well-behaved family pet per room. Guest must notify front desk upon arrival. Guest is liable for any damages. In consideration of all guests, pets must never be left unattended in the guest rooms.

La Quinta Inn Ripon
1524 Colony Road
Ripon, CA
209-599-8999 (800-531-5900)
Dogs of all sizes are allowed. There are no additional pet fees. Dogs must be leashed and cleaned up after. Multiple dogs may be allowed.

Motel 6 - Riverside East
1260 University Avenue
Riverside, CA
951-784-2131 (800-466-8356)
One well-behaved family pet per room. Guest must notify front desk upon arrival. Guest is liable for any damages. In consideration of all guests, pets must never be left unattended in the guest rooms.

Motel 6 - Riverside South
3663 La Sierra Avenue
Riverside, CA
951-351-0764 (800-466-8356)
One well-behaved family pet per room. Guest must notify front desk upon arrival. Guest is liable for any damages. In consideration of all guests, pets must never be left unattended in the guest rooms.

Doubletree
One Doubletree Drive
Rohnert Park, CA
707-584-5466
There is a fee of $15 per night per pet if the dogs are under 50 pounds, and you can have up to three dogs. The fee is $25 per night per pet if the dogs are over 50 pounds, and you can have up to two dogs.

Motel 6 - Rohnert Park
6145 Commerce Boulevard
Rohnert Park, CA
707-585-8888 (800-466-8356)

One well-behaved family pet per room. Guest must notify front desk upon arrival. Guest is liable for any damages. In consideration of all guests, pets must never be left unattended in the guest rooms.

Best Western Inn
6500 Redwood Drive
Rohnert Parl, CA
707-584-7435 (800-780-7234)
Dogs up to 50 pounds are allowed for an additional one time pet fee of $10 per room. Multiple dogs may be allowed.

Motel 6 - Los Angeles - Rosemead
1001 South San Gabriel Boulevard
Rosemead, CA
626-572-6076 (800-466-8356)
One well-behaved family pet per room. Guest must notify front desk upon arrival. Guest is liable for any damages. In consideration of all guests, pets must never be left unattended in the guest rooms.

Oxford Suites
130 N Sunrise Ave
Roseville, CA
916-784-2222 (800-882-SUITE)
This inn features a health club, self-service laundry, heated pool and spa, and video rentals. Each room has a separate living area, 2 phones, 2 TVs, a microwave, refrigerator and more. To get there from Hwy 80, exit Douglas Blvd. and head east. Then turn left on N Sunrise Ave. There is a $15 one time pet fee.

Residence Inn by Marriott
1930 Taylor Road
Roseville, CA
916-772-5500
Dogs of all sizes are allowed. There is a $75 one time fee, and a pet policy to sign at check in. Multiple dogs may be allowed.

Motel 6 - Los Angeles - Rowland Heights
18970 East Labin Court
Rowland Heights, CA
626-964-5333 (800-466-8356)
One well-behaved family pet per room. Guest must notify front desk upon arrival. Guest is liable for any damages. In consideration of all guests, pets must never be left unattended in the guest rooms.

Motel 6 - Riverside West
6830 Valley Way
Rubidoux, CA
951-681-6666 (800-466-8356)
One well-behaved family pet per

room. Guest must notify front desk upon arrival. Guest is liable for any damages. In consideration of all guests, pets must never be left unattended in the guest rooms.

Best Western Sandman Motel
236 Jibboom Street
Sacramento, CA
916-443-6515 (800-780-7234)
Dogs are allowed for an additional one time fee of $25 per pet. Multiple dogs may be allowed.

Canterbury Inn Hotel
1900 Canterbury Rd
Sacramento, CA
916-927-0927
This inn is located about a 5-10 minute drive from Old Sacramento. Guest laundry services are available. To get there from Hwy 160, take the Leisure Lane ramp towards Canterbury Rd. Turn right onto Canterbury Rd. There is a $5 per day additional pet fee.

Clarion Hotel Mansion Inn
700 16th Street
Sacramento, CA
916-444-8000 (877-424-6423)
Dogs are allowed for an additional one time fee of $50 per pet. Multiple dogs may be allowed.

Doubletree
2001 Point West Way
Sacramento, CA
916-929-8855
Well behaved dogs up to 50 pounds are allowed. There is a $50 one time fee per room and a pet policy to sign at check in. Multiple dogs may be allowed.

Holiday Inn Express
728 16 Street
Sacramento, CA
916-444-4436 (877-270-6405)
Dogs are allowed for an additional $50 one time pet fee per room. 2 dogs may be allowed.

Inn At Parkside
2116 6th Street
Sacramento, CA
916-658-1818 (800-995-7275)
innatparkside.com
This pet-friendly Sacramento B&B is located in downtown Sacramento within walking distance of the State Capitol and Old Town.

La Quinta Inn Sacramento Downtown
200 Jibboom St.
Sacramento, CA

916-448-8100 (800-531-5900)
Dogs of all sizes are allowed. There are no additional pet fees. Dogs must be leashed and cleaned up after. Multiple dogs may be allowed.

Motel 6 - Sacamento South
7407 Elsie Avenue
Sacramento, CA
916-689-6555 (800-466-8356)
One well-behaved family pet per room. Guest must notify front desk upon arrival. Guest is liable for any damages. In consideration of all guests, pets must never be left unattended in the guest rooms.

Motel 6 - Sacramento Central
7850 College Town Drive
Sacramento, CA
916-383-8110 (800-466-8356)
One well-behaved family pet per room. Guest must notify front desk upon arrival. Guest is liable for any damages. In consideration of all guests, pets must never be left unattended in the guest rooms.

Motel 6 - Sacramento Downtown
1415 30th Street
Sacramento, CA
916-457-0777 (800-466-8356)
One well-behaved family pet per room. Guest must notify front desk upon arrival. Guest is liable for any damages. In consideration of all guests, pets must never be left unattended in the guest rooms.

Motel 6 - Sacramento North
5110 Interstate Avenue
Sacramento, CA
916-331-8100 (800-466-8356)
One well-behaved family pet per room. Guest must notify front desk upon arrival. Guest is liable for any damages. In consideration of all guests, pets must never be left unattended in the guest rooms.

Motel 6 - Sacramento Southwest
7780 Stockton Boulevard
Sacramento, CA
916-689-9141 (800-466-8356)
One well-behaved family pet per room. Guest must notify front desk upon arrival. Guest is liable for any damages. In consideration of all guests, pets must never be left unattended in the guest rooms.

Motel 6 - Sacramento-Old Sacramento North
227 Jibboom Street
Sacramento, CA
916-441-0733 (800-466-8356)
One well-behaved family pet per

room. Guest must notify front desk upon arrival. Guest is liable for any damages. In consideration of all guests, pets must never be left unattended in the guest rooms.

Red Lion
1401 Arden Way
Sacramento, CA
916-922-8041
Dogs of all sizes are allowed. There is a $25 per room per stay fee and a pet policy to sign at check in. Multiple dogs may be allowed.

Red Roof Inn - Sacramento
3796 Northgate Boulevard
Sacramento, CA
916-927-7117 (800-RED-ROOF)
One well-behaved family pet per room. Guest must notify front desk upon arrival. Guest is liable for any damages. In consideration of all guests, pets must never be left unattended in the guest rooms.

Residence Inn by Marriott
2410 W El Camino Avenue
Sacramento, CA
916-649-1300
Dogs of all sizes are allowed. There is a $75 one time fee, and a pet policy to sign at check in. Multiple dogs may be allowed.

Residence Inn by Marriott
1530 Howe Avenue
Sacramento, CA
916-920-9111
Pets of all sizes are allowed. There is a $75 one time fee, and a pet policy to sign at check in. Please do not leave the pet unattended or kennel for housekeeping. Multiple dogs may be allowed.

Sheraton Grand Sacramento Hotel
1230 J St. (13th & J St)
Sacramento, CA
916-447-1700 (888-625-5144)
The dog-friendly Sheraton Grand Sacramento Hotel is located directly across the street from the Capitol Park and within easy walking distance of Downtown Plaza and Old Sacramento. Dogs are allowed for a $100 refundable pet deposit. Dogs are allowed on the 6th floor only, and they may not be left alone in the room. 2 dogs may be allowed.

Motel 6 - Salinas North - Monterey Area
140 Kern Street
Salinas, CA
831-753-1711 (800-466-8356)
One well-behaved family pet per

room. Guest must notify front desk upon arrival. Guest is liable for any damages. In consideration of all guests, pets must never be left unattended in the guest rooms.

Motel 6 - Salinas South - Monterey Area
1257 De La Torre Boulevard
Salinas, CA
831-757-3077 (800-466-8356)
One well-behaved family pet per room. Guest must notify front desk upon arrival. Guest is liable for any damages. In consideration of all guests, pets must never be left unattended in the guest rooms.

Residence Inn by Marriott
17215 El Rancho Way
Salinas, CA
831-775-0410
Pets of all sizes are allowed. There is a $75 one time fee, and a pet policy to sign at check in. 2 dogs may be allowed.

Best Western Hospitality Lane
294 E Hospitality Ln
San Bernadino, CA
909-381-1681 (800-780-7234)
Dogs up to 50 pounds are allowed for an additional fee of $10 per night per pet. 2 dogs may be allowed.

Hilton
285 E Hospitality Lane
San Bernardino, CA
909-889-0133
Dogs up to 75 pounds are allowed for a $100 refundable deposit plus a $50 one time pet fee per room. 2 dogs may be allowed.

Motel 6 - San Bernardino North
1960 Ostrems Way
San Bernardino, CA
909-887-8191 (800-466-8356)
One well-behaved family pet per room. Guest must notify front desk upon arrival. Guest is liable for any damages. In consideration of all guests, pets must never be left unattended in the guest rooms.

Motel 6 - San Bernardino South
111 West Redlands Boulevard
San Bernardino, CA
909-825-6666 (800-466-8356)
One well-behaved family pet per room. Guest must notify front desk upon arrival. Guest is liable for any damages. In consideration of all guests, pets must never be left unattended in the guest rooms.

Staybridge Suites

1350 Huntington Avenue
San Bruno, CA
650-588-0770 (877-270-6405)
Dogs of all sizes are allowed for an additional $150 one time pet fee per room. Multiple dogs may be allowed.

Best Western Casablanca Inn
1601 N El Camino Real
San Clemente, CA
949-361-1644 (800-780-7234)
Dogs are allowed for an additional pet fee of $25 per night per room. Dogs must be declared at the time of reservations. 2 dogs may be allowed.

Holiday Inn
111 S. Ave. De Estrella
San Clemente, CA
949-361-3000 (877-270-6405)
Dogs of all sizes are allowed for an additional fee of $20 per night per pet. Multiple dogs may be allowed.

Best Western Lamplighter Inn and Suites
6474 El Cajon Blvd
San Diego, CA
619-582-3088 (800-780-7234)
Dogs up to 50 pounds are allowed for an additional fee of $15 per night per pet. Multiple dogs may be allowed.

Best Western Mission Bay
2575 Clairemont Drive
San Diego, CA
619-275-5700 (800-780-7234)
Dogs are allowed for an additional pet fee of $20 per night per room. Multiple dogs may be allowed.

Doubletree
7450 Hazard Center Drive
San Diego, CA
619-297-5466
Dogs of all sizes are allowed. There is a $50 one time pet fee per room. Multiple dogs may be allowed.

Four Points by Sheraton San Diego
8110 Aero Drive
San Diego, CA
858-277-8888 (888-625-5144)
Dogs are allowed for a $100 deposit; $25 is non-refundable. Dogs may not be left alone in the room.

Harborview Inn and Suites
550 W Grape Street
San Diego, CA
619-233-7799
This 3 story hotel is only minutes from a variety of attractions and recreational opportunities. Some of the amenities include a free continental breakfast, room service,

and accommodations for both the business and leisure traveler. Dogs of all sizes are welcome for a $10 per night per pet additional fee. Dogs may not be left unattended in the room at any time, and they must be quiet, leashed, and cleaned up after. Multiple dogs may be allowed.

Holiday Inn on the Bay
1355 N Harbor Dr
San Diego, CA
619-232-3861 (877-270-6405)
basshotels.com/holiday-inn
Dogs up to 60 pounds are allowed for an additional $25 per pet per stay with a $75 refundable deposit and a pet agreement to sign at check in. 2 dogs may be allowed.

Homestead Suites
7444 Mission Valley Rd
San Diego, CA
619-299-2292
There is a $75 one time pet fee per visit.

Hotel Solamar
453 6th Avenue
San Diego, CA
619-531-8740 (877-230-0300)
hotelsolamar.com/
This hip luxury boutique hotel features a vibrant décor, a great location to the area's best shopping, dinning, and entertainment, and a full list of amenities for the business or leisure traveler. They feature elegantly appointed rooms, an evening wine hour, 24 hour room service from the adjacent J6Restaurant and J6Bar, a pool and spa, and several in-room amenities. Dogs of all sizes are welcome for no additional pet fee. Dogs must be friendly, quiet, leashed and cleaned up after, and the Dog in Room sign put on the door if they are in the room alone. 2 dogs may be allowed.

La Quinta Inn San Diego Rancho Penasquitos
10185 Paseo Montril
San Diego, CA
858-484-8800 (800-531-5900)
Dogs up to 60 pounds are allowed. There are no additional pet fees, but a credit card must be on file. Dogs must be crated when left alone in the room or place the Do Not Disturb sign on the door. Dogs must be leashed and cleaned up after. 2 dogs may be allowed.

Motel 6 - San Diego - Hotel Circle
2424 Hotel Circle North
San Diego, CA
619-296-1612 (800-466-8356)

One well-behaved family pet per room. Guest must notify front desk upon arrival. Guest is liable for any damages. In consideration of all guests, pets must never be left unattended in the guest rooms.

Motel 6 - San Diego Airport/Harbor
2353 Pacific Highway
San Diego, CA
619-232-8931 (800-466-8356)
One well-behaved family pet per room. Guest must notify front desk upon arrival. Guest is liable for any damages. In consideration of all guests, pets must never be left unattended in the guest rooms.

Motel 6 - San Diego Downtown
1546 2nd Avenue
San Diego, CA
619-236-9292 (800-466-8356)
One well-behaved family pet per room. Guest must notify front desk upon arrival. Guest is liable for any damages. In consideration of all guests, pets must never be left unattended in the guest rooms.

Motel 6 - San Diego North
5592 Clairemont Mesa Boulevard
San Diego, CA
858-268-9758 (800-466-8356)
One well-behaved family pet per room. Guest must notify front desk upon arrival. Guest is liable for any damages. In consideration of all guests, pets must never be left unattended in the guest rooms.

Ocean Villa Inn
5142 West Point Loma Blvd
San Diego, CA
619-224-3481 (800-759-0012)
oceanvillainn.com
Ocean Villa Inn is in the Ocean Beach district near the Dog Beach. They allow pets in all of their downstairs rooms with a $100.00 refundable deposit and a one time per stay fee of $25.00.

Old Town Inn
4444 Pacific H
San Diego, CA
619-260-8024 (800-643-3025)
oldtown-inn.com/oldtown.htm
This scenic inn offers deluxe and economy units, a complimentary continental breakfast, heated swimming pool, close proximity to several attractions and recreational opportunities, and beautiful well-kept grounds. Dogs up to 50 pounds are allowed for an additional fee of $10 per night per pet. Dogs may not be left alone in the room, and they must be leashed

and cleaned up after. 2 dogs may be allowed.

Pacific Beach Home
812 Law Street
San Diego, CA
858-366-2586
This vacation rental in the Pacific Beach neighborhood of San Diego allows up to two dogs. Dogs up to 60 pounds are allowed. There is a $10 per night additional pet fee and a $150 additional refundable deposit for guests with pets.

Pacific Inn Hotel & Suites
1655 Pacific Hwy
San Diego, CA
619-232-6391
There is a $20 per day per pet additional pet fee.

Premier Inn
2484 Hotel Circle Place
San Diego, CA
619-291-8252
premierinns.com
There is no pet fee.

Premier Inn
3333 Channel Way
San Diego, CA
619-223-9500
premierinns.com
There is no pet fee.

Red Lion
2270 Hotel Circle N
San Diego, CA
619-297-1101
Dogs up to 75 pounds are allowed. There is a $75 refundable pet deposit. 2 dogs may be allowed.

Residence Inn by Marriott
5400 Kearny Mesa Road
San Diego, CA
858-278-2100
Pets of all sizes are welcome. There is a $75 one time fee, and a pet policy to sign at check in. 2 dogs may be allowed.

Residence Inn by Marriott
1865 Hotel Circle S
San Diego, CA
619-881-3600
Dogs of all sizes are allowed. There is a $75 one time fee, and a pet policy to sign at check in. Multiple dogs may be allowed.

Residence Inn by Marriott
11002 Rancho Carmel Drive
San Diego, CA
858-673-1900
Dogs of all sizes are allowed. There

is a $75 one time fee, and a pet policy to sign at check in. Multiple dogs may be allowed.

Residence Inn by Marriott
12011 Scripps Highland Drive
San Diego, CA
858-635-5724
Dogs of all sizes are allowed. There is a $75 one time fee and a pet policy to sign at check in. Multiple dogs may be allowed.

Residence Inn by Marriott
5995 Pacific Mesa Court
San Diego, CA
858-552-9100
Dogs of all sizes are allowed. There is a $75 one time fee and a pet policy to sign at check in. Multiple dogs may be allowed.

Sheraton San Diego Hotel and Marina
1380 Harbor Island Drive
San Diego, CA
619-291-2900 (888-625-5144)
Dogs up to 80 pounds are allowed. There are no additional pet fees.

Sheraton Suites San Diego
701 A. Street
San Diego, CA
619-696-9800 (888-625-5144)
Dogs up to 80 pounds are allowed. There are no additional pet fees.

Staybridge Suites
6639 Mira Mesa Blvd
San Diego, CA
858-453-5343 (877-270-6405)
Dogs up to 50 pounds are allowed for an additional $75 one time pet fee per room. 2 dogs may be allowed.

Staybridge Suites
11855 Ave of Industry
San Diego, CA
858-487-0900 (877-270-6405)
Dogs up to 80 pounds are allowed for an additional $75 one time fee per room. 2 dogs may be allowed.

Staybridge Suites
6639 Mira Mesa Blvd
San Diego, CA
858-453-5354 (877-270-6405)
Dogs of all sizes are allowed. There is a $75 one time fee per room and a pet policy to sign at check in. Multiple dogs may be allowed.

Staybridge Suites
1110 A Street
San Diego, CA
619-795-4000 (877-270-6405)
One dog of any size is allowed.

There is a $75 one time fee and a pet policy to sign at check in.

The Hohe's Beach House
4905 Dixie Drive
San Diego, CA
858-273-0324
The Hohe House is a non-smoking 2 bedroom/2 bath, Ocean View, vacation rental in the Pacific Beach neighborhood. The Hohe House sleeps 6 and is fully furnished with all linens provided. There is a 4 night minimum during the low season, $200 nightly, (Mid-Sept to Mid-June), and rates vary for low to high season, from $1275 to $1875 weekly. A $350 refundable, security deposit is required to reserve a week's stay. There is a $10 per night pet fee. Well-behaved dogs over 18 months and under 80 pounds are welcome.

Vagabond Inn-Point Loma
1325 Scott St.
San Diego, CA
619-224-3371 (800-522-1555)
vagabondinn.com
This motel is located less than five miles from downtown San Diego and Sea World. It is close to the popular Dog Beach in Ocean Beach. The motel features an outdoor swimming pool, family unit rooms, cable television and more hotel amenities. Dogs up to about 70-75 pounds are allowed and there is an additional $10 per day pet fee.

W San Diego
421 West B. Street
San Diego, CA
619-231-8220
Dogs up to 80 pounds are allowed. There is a $100 one time per stay pet fee and a $25 per night pet charge.

Motel 6 - Los Angeles - San Dimas
502 West Arrow Highway
San Dimas, CA
909-592-5631 (800-466-8356)
One well-behaved family pet per room. Guest must notify front desk upon arrival. Guest is liable for any damages. In consideration of all guests, pets must never be left unattended in the guest rooms.

Red Roof Inn - San Dimas
204 North Village Court
San Dimas, CA
909-599-2362 (800-RED-ROOF)
One well-behaved family pet per room. Guest must notify front desk upon arrival. Guest is liable for any damages. In consideration of all

guests, pets must never be left unattended in the guest rooms.

Argonaut Hotel Fisherman's Wharf
495 Jefferson Street
San Francisco, CA
415-563-0800 (866-415-0704)
argonauthotel.com
This Kimpton boutique hotel allows dogs of all sizes. The hotel is an entirely non-smoking hotel and is located near Fisherman's Wharf. There are no additional pet fees.

Best Western Tuscan Inn Fisherman Wharf
425 Northpoint St
San Francisco, CA
415-561-1100 (800-780-7234)
Well behaved dogs are allowed for no additional pet fee. 2 dogs may be allowed.

Campton Place Hotel
340 Stockton Street
San Francisco, CA
415-781-5555
camptonplace.com
This dog-friendly hotel holds many awards including "Top 100 Hotels in the World" by Conde Nast Traveler. Room rates are approximately $230 to $345 a night. There is a $35 per day additional pet fee.

Casa Francisquita
Call or Email to Arrange
San Francisco, CA
415-431-9907
casafrancisquita.com/
This lower level flat between the Noe Valley and Castro neighborhoods accommodates two adults and children or pets. Dogs of all sizes are welcome and there is no additional pet fee.

Crowne Plaza - Union Square
480 Sutter Street
San Francisco, CA
415-398-8900 (877-270-6405)
Dogs up to 50 pounds are allowed for no additional fee; however, there is a $100 refundable pet deposit per room. 2 dogs may be allowed.

Days Inn - Lombard St
2358 Lombard Street
San Francisco, CA
415-922-2010 (800-329-7466)
There is a $10 per day pet fee. A well-behaved large dog is okay. Dogs may not be left alone in the rooms and you are responsible for any damage to the room by your pet.

Four Seasons Hotel San Francisco

757 Market St.
San Francisco, CA
415-633-3000
Dogs are allowed for no additional pet fee. Dogs may not be left alone in the room. Pet sitting services are available.

Halcyon Hotel
649 Jones Street
San Francisco, CA
415-929-8033
Dogs of all sizes are allowed. There is a $50 refundable pet deposit. Multiple dogs may be allowed.

Harbor Court Hotel
165 Steuart Street
San Francisco, CA
415-882-1300
harborcourthotel.com/
Well-behaved dogs of all sizes are welcome at this pet-friendly hotel. Amenities include a complimentary evening wine reception, and an adjacent fitness room. There are no pet fees, just sign a pet liability form. 2 dogs may be allowed.

Holiday Inn San Francisco-Fishermans Wharf
1300 Columbus Avenue
San Francisco, CA
415-771-9000 (877-270-6405)
Dogs of all sizes are allowed for no additional fee. 2 dogs may be allowed.

Hotel Beresford Arms
701 Post Street
San Francisco, CA
415-673-2600 (800-533-6533)
beresford.com/arms/default.htm
Although listed on the National Register of Historic Places, this hotel offers guests many modern conveniences and luxuries, including a great location to several nearby attractions. Amenities/features include well appointed rooms and suites, Jacuzzi bathtubs, complimentary morning coffee/tea and pastries, and a complimentary afternoon tea and wine social. One dog is allowed per room; there is no additional pet fee. Dogs may not be left alone in the room, and they must be leashed and cleaned up after at all times.

Hotel Diva
440 Geary Street
San Francisco, CA
800-553-1900
hoteldiva.com/
At the hub of Union Square, this ultra modern hotel offers exceptional personalized service for the leisure or business traveler, and a convenient location for a wide variety of shopping, entertainment, and dining opportunities. One dog up to 70 pounds is allowed for an additional one time pet fee of $75. This is a Personality Hotel property and one of four local hotels that offer the "Every Doggie is a Diva Package" with prices starting at $189 per night. This deluxe package includes the overnight accommodations (so no additional $75 fee), a bottle of water, a designer pet bowl, a personalized dog tag, a plush sheep skin throw, a 1 hour VIP dog walking tour highlighting favored parks and fire hydrants (Monday through Friday-noon to 1pm), and an amenity box with treats, biscuits, 2 flavors of dog food, and a red paw print bandana. Dogs must be leashed, cleaned up after, and crated if left alone in the room.

Hotel Metropolis
25 Mason Street
San Francisco, CA
800-553-9100
hotelmetropolis.com/
This 1930, 105 room hotel will indulge your senses with a bit of paradise featuring rich fabrics, bright colors, custom furnishings, and each floor of this 10 story hotel gives reflection to the elements of earth, wind, fire, or water. They feature many in room amenities, exceptional personalized service for the leisure or business traveler, and a convenient location for a wide variety of shopping, entertainment, and dining opportunities. One dog up to 70 pounds is allowed for an additional one time pet fee of $75. This is a Personality Hotel property and one of four local hotels that offer the "Every Doggie is a Diva Package" with prices starting at $189 per night. This deluxe package includes the overnight accommodations (so no additional $75 fee), a bottle of water, a designer pet bowl, a personalized dog tag, a plush sheep skin throw, a 1 hour VIP dog walking tour highlighting favored parks and fire hydrants (Monday through Friday-noon to 1pm), and an amenity box with treats, biscuits, 2 flavors of dog food, and a red paw print bandana. Dogs must be leashed, cleaned up after, and crated if left alone in the room.

Hotel Monaco
501 Geary Street

San Francisco, CA
415-292-0100 (866-622-5284)
monaco-sf.com
This Kimpton boutique hotel allows dogs of all sizes. There are no additional pet fees.

Hotel Palomar
12 Fourth Street
San Francisco, CA
415-348-1111
hotelpalomar.com/
Well-behaved dogs of all sizes are welcome at this pet-friendly hotel. The boutique hotel offers both rooms and suites. Hotel amenities include room service, an on-site 24 hour fitness room and complimentary high speed Internet access. There are no pet fees, just sign a pet liability form. Pets cannot be left alone in the room.

Hotel Triton
342 Grant Avenue
San Francisco, CA
415-394-0500
hoteltriton.com
Well-behaved dogs of all sizes are welcome at this pet-friendly hotel. The boutique hotel offers both rooms and suites. Hotel amenities include a complimentary evening wine reception, room service, and a 24 hour on-site fitness room. There are no pet fees, just sign a pet liability form.

Hotel Union Square
114 Powell Street
San Francisco, CA
800-553-1900
hotelunionsquare.com/
Known as the city's original boutique-style hotel, and graced with a great location in Union Square right on the cable car line, this striking 1913 hotel offers 131 stylish guest rooms with full private baths, a 1930's Art Deco lobby, beautiful jewel toned décor, and many in-room amenities. One dog up to 70 pounds is allowed for an additional one time pet fee of $75. This is a Personality Hotel property and one of four local hotels that offer the "Every Doggie is a Diva Package" with prices starting at $189 per night. This deluxe package includes the overnight accommodations (so no additional $75 fee), a bottle of water, a designer pet bowl, a personalized dog tag, a plush sheep skin throw, a 1 hour VIP dog walking tour highlighting favored parks and fire hydrants (Monday through Friday-noon to 1pm), and an amenity box with treats, biscuits, 2 flavors of dog

food, and a red paw print bandana. Dogs must be leashed, cleaned up after, and crated if left alone in the room.

Kensington Park Hotel
450 Post Street
San Francisco, CA
800-553-9100
kensingtonparkhotel.com/
This stylish hotel offers luxury, modern day conveniences, 92 richly detailed-finely appointed rooms, exceptional personalized service for the leisure or business traveler, and a convenient location for a wide variety of shopping, entertainment, and dining opportunities. They are also home to the Farallon Restaurant; an attraction in and of itself. One dog up to 70 pounds is allowed for an additional one time pet fee of $75. This is a Personality Hotel property and one of four local hotels that offer the "Every Doggie is a Diva Package" with prices starting at $189 per night. This deluxe package includes the overnight accommodations (so no additional $75 fee), a bottle of water, a designer pet bowl, a personalized dog tag, a plush sheep skin throw, a 1 hour VIP dog walking tour highlighting favored parks and fire hydrants (Monday through Friday-noon to 1pm), and an amenity box with treats, biscuits, 2 flavors of dog food, and a red paw print bandana. Dogs must be leashed, cleaned up after, and crated if left alone in the room.

Marina Motel - on Lombard Street
2576 Lombard St.
San Francisco, CA
415-921-9406 (800-346-6118)
marinamotel.com/
All friendly dogs are welcome regardless of size. Walk to the Golden Gate Bridge along Crissy Field beach five blocks away. Miles of hiking trails in the historical Presidio Park are nearby. All rooms have refrigerators, coffee makers, irons and hair dryers. There is no pet fee for stays of one week or longer otherwise there is a $10/night pet fee. Dogs may not be left unattended in the room at any time. There is free garage parking for overnight guests of the hotel.

Monticello Inn
127 Ellis Street
San Francisco, CA
415-392-8800
monticelloinn.com
Well-behaved dogs of all sizes are

welcome at this pet-friendly hotel. The boutique hotel offers both rooms and suites. Hotel amenities include complimentary evening wine service, evening room service, hotel library with magazines, newspapers and books, and a Borders Books and Music room service. There are no pet fees, just sign a pet liability form.

Palace Hotel
2 New Montgomery Street
San Francisco, CA
415-512-1111
There is a $75 one time pet fee. This is a Sheraton Hotel.

Prescott Hotel
545 Post Street
San Francisco, CA
415-563-0303
prescotthotel.com/
Well-behaved dogs of all sizes are allowed at this pet-friendly hotel. The luxury boutique hotel is located in Union Square and offers both rooms and suites. Hotel amenities include room service and an on-site 24 hour fitness room. There are no pet fees, just sign a pet liability form.

San Francisco Lofts
1501 Mariposa, Suite 328
San Francisco, CA
415-810-3322
Dogs of all sizes are allowed. There is a pet policy to sign at check in and there are no additional pet fees. 2 dogs may be allowed.

San Francisco Marriott Fisherman's Wharf
1250 Columbus Avenue
San Francisco, CA
415-775-7555 (800-228-9290)
Dogs of all sizes are allowed. There is a $100 one time additional pet fee per room. Dogs may be left for short periods alone in the room only if they will be quiet and a contact number is left with the front desk. Dogs must be leashed and cleaned up after. 2 dogs may be allowed.

Serrano Hotel
405 Taylor Street
San Francisco, CA
415-885-2500
serranohotel.com
Well-behaved dogs of all sizes are welcome at this pet-friendly hotel. The luxury boutique hotel offers both rooms and suites. Hotel amenities include an evening hospitality hour, and a 24 hour on-site fitness room. There are no pet

fees, just sign a pet liability form. Multiple dogs may be allowed.

Sheraton Fisherman's Wharf Hotel
2500 Mason St.
San Francisco, CA
415-362-5500 (888-625-5144)
Dogs up to 80 pounds are allowed. Only 5 rooms are available in the hotel for dogs. You must sign a pet policy. Dogs are not allowed to be left alone in the room.

Sir Francis Drake Hotel
450 Powell St
San Francisco, CA
415-392-7755 (800-795-7129)
sirfrancisdrake.com
This Kimpton boutique hotel allows dogs of all sizes. There are no additional pet fees.

The Inn San Francisco
943 S Van Ness Avenue
San Francisco, CA
415-641-0188
Well behaved, friendly, dogs of all sizes are allowed. There are no additional pet fees. Dogs may not be left alone at any time and they are not allowed in the gardens. Multiple dogs may be allowed.

The Laurel Inn
444 Presidio Ave.
San Francisco, CA
415-567-8467
thelaurelinn.com/
This pet-friendly hotel is a boutique hotel in San Francisco's atmospheric Pacific Heights neighborhood. This newly renovated hotel includes a classic 1960's modern architectural design. Amenities include a complimentary continental breakfast served daily in the lobby, free indoor parking, laundry and valet service, room service from Dine-One-One and more.

The Palace Hotel
2 New Montgomery St.
San Francisco, CA
415-512-1111
Dogs up to 80 pounds are allowed. There is a $100 nonrefundable pet fee per visit. Dogs are restricted to 1st and 2nd floor rooms only. Dogs are not allowed to be left alone in the room.

The W San Francisco
181 3rd St.
San Francisco, CA
415-777-5300
Dogs of all sizes are allowed. There is a $100 nonrefundable one time pet

fee per visit. Dogs are allowed in the living room of the hotel cafe and there is a special menu available at the cafe. Dogs are not allowed to be left alone in the room.

Clarion Hotel San Jose Airport
1355 N 4th Street
San Jose, CA
408-453-5340 (877-424-6423)
Dogs are allowed for an additional fee of $10 per night per pet. Multiple dogs may be allowed.

Crowne Plaza Hotel San Jose-Downtown
282 Almaden Blvd
San Jose, CA
408-998-0400 (877-270-6405)
Two small dogs or 1 dog up to 50 pounds is allowed for an additional $50 one time fee per pet. 2 dogs may be allowed.

Fairmont Hotel
170 S Market Street
San Jose, CA
408-998-1900
fairmont.com/sanjose/
This luxury hotel offers 731 beautifully appointed guest rooms and 74 suites, and being set in the high-tech Silicon Valley, they are fully equipped for the business traveler. Vacationers can enjoy the historic grandeur of the inn and its close proximity to several recreational activities. Some of the features include several dining options, a lounge, pool and spa, and many in room amenities. Dogs of all sizes are allowed for an additional one time fee of $75 per pet. Dogs may not be left alone in the room at any time, and they must be leashed and cleaned up after. 2 dogs may be allowed.

Hilton
300 Almaden Blvd
San Jose, CA
408-287-2100
Dogs are allowed for no additional pet fee; there is a pet agreement to sign at check in. Multiple dogs may be allowed.

Holiday Inn San Jose
1740 North First Street
San Jose, CA
408-793-3300 (877-270-6405)
Dogs of all sizes are allowed for an additional $50 per night per pet. Multiple dogs may be allowed.

Homewood Suites
10 W Trimble Rd

San Jose, CA
408-428-9900
homewoodsuites.com
This inn is located in north San Jose, near Milpitas. The inn offers kitchens in each room. There are about half a dozen restaurants next door in a strip mall, many of which have outdoor seating. They require a $275 deposit, and $200 is refundable. The $75 fee is a one time pet charge.

Howard Johnson Express Inn
1215 South 1st St.
San Jose, CA
408-280-5300 (800-446-4656)
Well-behaved dogs of all sizes are allowed. There is a $5 per day additional pet fee.

Motel 6 - San Jose Airport
2081 North 1st Street
San Jose, CA
408-436-8180 (800-466-8356)
One well-behaved family pet per room. Guest must notify front desk upon arrival. Guest is liable for any damages. In consideration of all guests, pets must never be left unattended in the guest rooms.

Motel 6 - San Jose South
2560 Fontaine Road
San Jose, CA
408-270-3131 (800-466-8356)
One well-behaved family pet per room. Guest must notify front desk upon arrival. Guest is liable for any damages. In consideration of all guests, pets must never be left unattended in the guest rooms.

Residence Inn by Marriott
6111 San Ignacio Avenue
San Jose, CA
408-226-7676
Dogs of all sizes are allowed. There is a $75 one time fee and a pet policy to sign at check in. Multiple dogs may be allowed.

Staybridge Suites
1602 Crane Court
San Jose, CA
408-436-1600 (877-270-6405)
Dogs of all sizes are allowed for a $200 one time fee per pet. Multiple dogs may be allowed.

San Juan Inn
410 The Alameda #156
San Juan Bautista, CA
831-623-4380
Located near the center of Monterey Peninsula, you'll enjoy excellent nearby hiking trails at this

inn. One dog of any size is allowed. There is a $10 per night additional pet fee. Dogs may not be left alone in the room, and they must be leashed and cleaned up after.

Best Western Capistrano Inn
27174 Ortega Highway
San Juan Capistrano, CA
949-493-5661 (800-780-7234)
Dogs up to 50 pounds are allowed for an additional one time fee of $25 per pet. 2 dogs may be allowed.

Best Western Royal Oak Hotel
214 Madonna Road
San Luis Obispo, CA
805-544-4410 (800-780-7234)
royaloakhotel.com
There is a $15 pet fee for each 5 days at the hotel.

Holiday Inn Express
1800 Monterey Street
San Luis Obispo, CA
805-544-8600 (877-270-6405)
Dogs of all sizes are allowed for an additional $30 one time pet fee per room. Multiple dogs may be allowed.

Motel 6 - San Luis Obispo North
1433 Calle Joaquin
San Luis Obispo, CA
805-549-9595 (800-466-8356)
One well-behaved family pet per room. Guest must notify front desk upon arrival. Guest is liable for any damages. In consideration of all guests, pets must never be left unattended in the guest rooms.

Motel 6 - San Luis Obispo South
1625 Calle Joaquin
San Luis Obispo, CA
805-541-6992 (800-466-8356)
One well-behaved family pet per room. Guest must notify front desk upon arrival. Guest is liable for any damages. In consideration of all guests, pets must never be left unattended in the guest rooms.

Sands Suites & Motel
1930 Monterey Street
San Luis Obispo, CA
805-544-0500 (800-441-4657)
sandssuites.com/
This motel is close to Cal Poly. Amenities include a heated pool and spa, free continental breakfast, self serve laundry facilities and wheelchair accessibility. There is a $10 one time pet fee.

Vagabond Inn
210 Madonna Rd.
San Luis Obispo, CA

805-544-4710 (800-522-1555)
vagabondinn.com
This motel is located near Cal Poly.
Amenities include a heated pool and
whirlpool, complimentary continental
breakfast, dry cleaning/laundry
service and more. There is a $5 per
day pet charge.

Residence Inn by Marriott
2000 Winward Way
San Mateo, CA
650-574-4700
Pets of all sizes are allowed. There is
a $75 plus tax one time fee per pet
and a pet policy to sign at check in.
Multiple dogs may be allowed.

Residence Inn by Marriott
1071 Market Place
San Ramon, CA
925-277-9292
Dogs of all sizes are allowed. There
is a $75 one time fee and a pet
policy to sign at check in. Multiple
dogs may be allowed.

San Ramon Marriott
2600 Bishop Drive
San Ramon, CA
925-867-9200 (800-228-9290)
Dogs of all sizes are allowed. There
can be up to 2 large or 3 small to
medium dogs per room. There is a
$75 one time additional pet fee per
room. Dogs may not be left alone in
the room at any time, and they must
be leashed and cleaned up after.

Best Western Cavalier Oceanfront
Resort
9415 Hearst Dr
San Simeon, CA
805-927-4688 (800-780-7234)
Dogs are allowed for no additional
pet fee. 2 dogs may be allowed.

Motel 6 - San Simeon - Hearst
Castle Area
9070 Castillo Drive
San Simeon, CA
805-927-8691 (800-466-8356)
One well-behaved family pet per
room. Guest must notify front desk
upon arrival. Guest is liable for any
damages. In consideration of all
guests, pets must never be left
unattended in the guest rooms.

Silver Surf Motel
9390 Castillo Drive
San Simeon, CA
805-927-4661 (800-621-3999)
silversurfmotel.com/
This coastal motel is situated around
a courtyard in a park like setting.
There are beautiful flower gardens,

majestic pine trees, and scenic
ocean views. Some rooms offer
private balconies, fireplaces or
ocean views. Amenities include an
indoor pool & spa, and guest
laundry facility. There is a $10 per
day pet charge.

Motel 6 - San Ysidro - San Diego
160 East Calle Primera
San Ysidro, CA
619-690-6663 (800-466-8356)
One well-behaved family pet per
room. Guest must notify front desk
upon arrival. Guest is liable for any
damages. In consideration of all
guests, pets must never be left
unattended in the guest rooms.

Candlewood Suites
2600 S. Red Hill Avenue
Santa Ana, CA
949-250-0404 (877-270-6405)
Dogs up to 80 pounds are allowed
for an additonal pet fee of $75 per
room for each 1 to 6 days. 2 dogs
may be allowed.

La Quinta Inn Santa Ana
2721 Hotel Terrace
Santa Ana, CA
714-540-1111 (800-531-5900)
Dogs up to 75 pounds are allowed.
There are no additional pet fees.
Dogs must be leashed, cleaned up
after, and removed for
housekeeping. 2 dogs may be
allowed.

Motel 6 - Santa Ana
1623 East 1st Street
Santa Ana, CA
714-558-0500 (800-466-8356)
One well-behaved family pet per
room. Guest must notify front desk
upon arrival. Guest is liable for any
damages. In consideration of all
guests, pets must never be left
unattended in the guest rooms.

Red Roof Inn - Irvine - Orange
County Airport
1717 East Dyer Road
Santa Ana, CA
949-261-1515 (800-RED-ROOF)
One well-behaved family pet per
room. Guest must notify front desk
upon arrival. Guest is liable for any
damages. In consideration of all
guests, pets must never be left
unattended in the guest rooms.

Red Roof Inn - Santa Ana
2600 North Main Street
Santa Ana, CA
714-542-0311 (800-RED-ROOF)
One well-behaved family pet per

room. Guest must notify front desk
upon arrival. Guest is liable for any
damages. In consideration of all
guests, pets must never be left
unattended in the guest rooms.

Best Western Beachside Inn
336 W Cabrillo Blvd
Santa Barbara, CA
805-965-6556 (800-780-7234)
Dogs are allowed for an additional
fee of $20 per night per pet. 2 dogs
may be allowed.

Casa Del Mar Hotel
18 Bath Street
Santa Barbara, CA
805-963-4418 (800-433-3097)
casadelmar.com
This popular Mediterranean-style inn
is within walking distance of several
restaurants, shops and parks.
Amenities include a relaxing
courtyard Jacuzzi and sun deck
surrounded by lush gardens year
round. All rooms are non-smoking
and equipped with a writing desk and
chair or table, telephone, color TV
with remote control, and private
bathroom. There is a 2 or 3 night
minimum stay on the weekends. Pets
are welcome. They allow up to two
pets per room and there is a $15 per
pet per night charge. Pets must
never be left alone or unattended,
especially in the rooms. Children
under 12 are free and there is no
charge for a crib. State Street, a
popular shopping area, is within
walking distance.

Fess Parkers Doubletree Resort
633 E Cabrillo Blvd
Santa Barbara, CA
805-564-4333
Dogs of all sizes are allowed. There
are no additional pet fees. Multiple
dogs may be allowed.

Four Seasons Resort
1260 Channel Dr.
Santa Barbara, CA
805-969-2261
Dogs up to 50 pounds are allowed
for no additional pet fee. Dogs may
not be left alone in the room. Pet
sitting services are available.

Montecito Del Mar
316 W Montecito St
Santa Barbara, CA
805-962-2006
There is a $10 per day pet fee. Dogs
up to 50 pounds are permitted.

Motel 6 - Santa Barbara - Beach
443 Corona Del Mar

Santa Barbara, CA
805-564-1392 (800-466-8356)
One well-behaved family pet per room. Guest must notify front desk upon arrival. Guest is liable for any damages. In consideration of all guests, pets must never be left unattended in the guest rooms.

Motel 6 - Santa Barbara - State Street
3505 State Street
Santa Barbara, CA
805-687-5400 (800-466-8356)
One well-behaved family pet per room. Guest must notify front desk upon arrival. Guest is liable for any damages. In consideration of all guests, pets must never be left unattended in the guest rooms.

San Ysidro Ranch
900 San Ysidro Lane
Santa Barbara, CA
805-969-5046
sanysidroranch.com
This is an especially dog-friendly upscale resort located in Santa Barbara. They offer many dog amenities including a Privileged Pet Program doggie turn down and several miles of trails and exercise areas. Pet Massage Service is available. Choose from the Slow & Gentle Massage or the Authentic Reiki massage for your dog. Dogs are allowed in the freestanding cottages and prices start around $600 and up per night. There is a $100 per pet non-refundable cleaning fee.

Secret Garden Inn and Cottages
1908 Bath street
Santa Barbara, CA
805-687-2300 (800-676-1622)
secretgarden.com
Dogs are allowed in six of the cottages. There is a $50 refundable pet deposit. Dogs are not allowed in the main house.

Candlewood Suites
481 El Camino Road
Santa Clara, CA
403-241-9305 (877-270-6405)
One dog up to 80 pounds is allowed for an additional pet fee of $75 for a 1 to 6 day stay, and $150 for 7 or more days.

Guesthouse Inn & Suites
2930 El Camino Real
Santa Clara, CA
408-241-3010
All rooms have microwaves and refrigerators. There is a $10 per day additional pet fee.

Madison Street Inn
1390 Madison Street
Santa Clara, CA
408-249-5541
madisonstreetinn.com/
This attractive inn sits on one third acre of lush greens and gardens and features a pool and spa, fine dining, a house with a parlor and six guest rooms. Dogs of all sizes are allowed for a $75 refundable pet deposit. Dogs must be quiet, well mannered, and leashed and cleaned up after. 2 dogs may be allowed.

Motel 6 - Santa Clara
3208 El Camino Real
Santa Clara, CA
408-241-0200 (800-466-8356)
One well-behaved family pet per room. Guest must notify front desk upon arrival. Guest is liable for any damages. In consideration of all guests, pets must never be left unattended in the guest rooms.

Santa Clara Marriott
2700 Mission College Blvd
Santa Clara, CA
408-988-1500 (800-228-9290)
Dogs of all sizes are allowed. There is a $100 refundable pet deposit per room. Dogs must be leashed, cleaned up after, and either crated or the Do Not Disturb sign put on the door, and the front desk informed if they are in the room alone. Multiple dogs may be allowed.

Vagabond Inns
3580 El Camino Real
Santa Clara, CA
408-241-0771
Dogs of all sizes are allowed. There is a $10 per night per pet additional fee. Multiple dogs may be allowed.

Residence Inn by Marriott
25320 The Old Road
Santa Clarita, CA
661-290-2800
Dogs of all sizes are allowed. There is a $75 one time fee per pet plus $10 per night per pet and a pet policy to sign at check in. Multiple dogs may be allowed.

Buck's Beach Bungalow
341 35th Avenue
Santa Cruz, CA
831-476-0170
Dogs of all sizes are allowed. There is a pet policy to sign at check in and there are no additional pet fees.

Multiple dogs may be allowed.

Casa Del Barco
108 7th Avenue
Santa Cruz, CA
650-491-0036
Dogs only are allowed here and in all sizes. There is a $500 refundable deposit per stay and a pet policy to sign at check in. Multiple dogs may be allowed.

Continental Inn
414 Ocean Street
Santa Cruz, CA
831-429-1221 (800-343-6941)
continentalinnsantacruz.com/
Elegant, yet affordable, this inn is only minutes from several other local attractions. Some of the amenities include a complimentary continental breakfast and morning paper, an outdoor heated pool and spa, and several in-room extras. Dogs of all sizes are allowed for an additional $10 per night per pet. Dogs may not be left alone in the room, and they must be leashed and cleaned up after. Multiple dogs may be allowed.

Edgewater Beach Motel
525 Second Street
Santa Cruz, CA
831-423-0440 (888-809-6767)
edgewaterbeachmotel.com/
This motel has ocean views, beach views, and 17 uniquely designed suites (for one to eight people). Some of the rooms have ocean views, microwaves, refrigerators. A couple of the rooms have fireplaces, private lawns and full kitchens. Non-smoking rooms are available. While dogs are not allowed on the Boardwalk or on the nearby beach, they are allowed on the West Cliff Drive Walkway. Walk to the waterfront, then go north (away from the Boardwalk) along the sidewalk on the street closest to the ocean. It will become a walkway that is used by walkers, joggers and bicyclists. If you walk about 1 1/2 - 2 miles, you'll reach several dog beaches (see Parks). To get to the motel, take Hwy 17 south. Take the Hwy 1 North exit. Then take the Ocean St exit on the left towards the beaches. Head towards the beach on Ocean St and then turn right on San Lorenzo Blvd. Turn left on Riverside Ave and then right on 2nd St. The motel will be on the left. Ample parking is available in their parking lot. There is a $20 one time additional pet fee.

Guesthouse International
330 Ocean Street

Santa Cruz, CA
831-425-3722
There is a $10 per day pet fee.

Redtail Ranch by the Sea
Call to Arrange.
Santa Cruz, CA
831-429-1322
redtailranch.com/
This 3 bedroom, 1 1/2 bath ranch house is located on a 72 acre horse ranch, the Redtail Ranch. The house features a 180 degree ocean view of the Monterey Bay and views of the coastal hills. The house sleeps 1 to 8 people and comes with a complete full kitchen. The home is located about a 5 minute drive to local beaches, a 1 hour drive to Monterey, Carmel and Big Sur, and a 1 1/2 hour scenic coastal drive to San Francisco. The rental is available year-round for nightly, weekly, and extended vacation rentals.

Motel 6 - Los Angeles - Santa Fe Springs
13412 Excelsior Drive
Santa Fe Springs, CA
562-921-0596 (800-466-8356)
One well-behaved family pet per room. Guest must notify front desk upon arrival. Guest is liable for any damages. In consideration of all guests, pets must never be left unattended in the guest rooms.

Best Western Big America
1725 North Broadway
Santa Maria, CA
805-922-5200 (800-780-7234)
Dogs are allowed for no additional pet fee. Multiple dogs may be allowed.

Holiday Inn Hotel & Suites
2100 North Broadway
Santa Maria, CA
805-928-6000 (877-270-6405)
Dogs of all sizes are allowed for an additional fee of $25 per night per pet. Multiple dogs may be allowed.

Motel 6 - Santa Maria
2040 North Preisker Lane
Santa Maria, CA
805-928-8111 (800-466-8356)
One well-behaved family pet per room. Guest must notify front desk upon arrival. Guest is liable for any damages. In consideration of all guests, pets must never be left unattended in the guest rooms.

LeMerigot Hotel-A JWMarriott Beach Hotel and Spa
1740 Ocean Avenue

Santa Monica, CA
310-395-9700
This hotel has a "Pet Friendly Accommodations Program", and dogs of all sizes are welcome. They offer a unique assortment of boutique amenities, a sitting service, and special food fare for your pet. There is a $150 refundable deposit plus a $35 one time additional fee per pet. Dogs must be leashed, cleaned up after, and the Do Not Disturb sign put on the door if they are in the room alone. Multiple dogs may be allowed.

Loews Santa Monica Beach Hotel
1700 Ocean Avenue
Santa Monica, CA
310-458-6700
All well-behaved dogs of any size are welcome. This upscale hotel offers their "Loews Loves Pets" program which includes special pet treats, local dog walking routes, and a list of nearby pet-friendly places to visit. There are no pet fees.

Sheraton Delfina Santa Monica Hotel
530 West Pico Blvd.
Santa Monica, CA
310-399-9344 (888-625-5144)
Dogs of all sizes are allowed. There is a $50 additional pet fee. Pet rooms are limited to ground floor cabanas. You must sign a pet policy when checking in with a dog. Dogs are not allowed to be left alone in the room. 2 dogs may be allowed.

The Fairmont Miramar Hotel Santa Monica
101 Wilshire Blvd
Santa Monica, CA
310-576-7777 (800-257-7544)
fairmont.com/santamonica/
Nestled atop the scenic bluffs of Santa Monica beach, this hotel features historic elegance with all the modern-day conveniences and services. Some of the features/amenities include 302 stylish guest rooms, 32 secluded garden bungalows, casual elegant indoor and outdoor dining, and 24 hour room service. There can be up to 3 dogs in one room if they are all small, otherwise there are only 2 dogs allowed per room. There is a $25 per night per pet additional fee, and a pet policy to sign at check in. Dogs may not be left alone in the room at any time, and they must be leashed and cleaned up after.

Viceroy Hotel

1819 Ocean Avenue
Santa Monica, CA
310-260-7500
Well behaved dogs of all sizes are allowed. There is a $175 refundable deposit and a pet policy to sign at check in. Multiple dogs may be allowed.

Holiday Inn Express
28976 W. Plaza Drive
Santa Nella, CA
209-826-8282 (877-270-6405)
Dogs of all sizes are allowed for an additional $8 one time pet fee per room. Multiple dogs may be allowed.

Best Western Garden Inn - Santa Rosa
1500 Santa Rosa Avenue
Santa Rosa, CA
707-546-4031 (800-780-7234)
thegardeninn.com
Dogs up to 50 pounds are allowed at this hotel in the heart of the Sonoma Valley wine region. A maximum of two dogs per room are allowed with a $15 per night pet fee.

Comfort Inn
2632 Cleveland Avenue
Santa Rosa, CA
707-542-5544 (877-424-6423)
Quiet dogs are allowed for a $30 refundable deposit plus an additional fee $15 per night per room. 2 dogs may be allowed.

Days Inn
3345 Santa Rosa Ave
Santa Rosa, CA
707-568-1011 (800-329-7466)
There is a $10 per day additional pet fee.

Holiday Inn Express
870 Hopper Ave
Santa Rosa, CA
707-545-9000 (877-270-6405)
Dogs up to 60 pounds are allowed for an additional $20 one time pet fee per room. 2 dogs may be allowed.

Los Robles Lodge
1985 Cleveland Ave
Santa Rosa, CA
707-545-6330 (800-255-6330)
bluejaylodge.com/page7.html
Dogs are allowed, but not in the poolside rooms or executive suites. There is a $10 per day pet charge.

Motel 6 - Santa Rosa North
3145 Cleveland Avenue
Santa Rosa, CA
707-525-9010 (800-466-8356)
One well-behaved family pet per

room. Guest must notify front desk upon arrival. Guest is liable for any damages. In consideration of all guests, pets must never be left unattended in the guest rooms.

Motel 6 - Santa Rosa South
2760 Cleveland Avenue
Santa Rosa, CA
707-546-1500 (800-466-8356)
One well-behaved family pet per room. Guest must notify front desk upon arrival. Guest is liable for any damages. In consideration of all guests, pets must never be left unattended in the guest rooms.

Santa Rosa Motor Inn
1800 Santa Rosa Ave
Santa Rosa, CA
707-523-3480
There is a $10 per day pet fee and a refundable pet deposit.

The Days Inn
3345 Santa Rosa Avenue
Santa Rosa, CA
707-545-6330 (800-329-7466)
daysinn.com/DaysInn/control/home
This inn offers a complimentary breakfast and swimming pool in addition to other amenities. Dogs of all sizes are allowed for a $25 per night per pet additional fee. Dogs must be quiet and removed or crated for housekeeping. Dogs must be leashed and cleaned up after. 2 dogs may be allowed.

Best Western
6020 Scott's Valley Drive
Scotts Valley, CA
831-438-6666 (800-780-7234)
Dogs of all sizes are allowed. There can be one large dog or 2 small dogs per room. There is a $100 refundable pet deposit per room. Dogs must be leashed, cleaned up after, and the front desk informed if they are in the room alone.

Hilton
6001 La Madrona Drive
Scotts Valley, CA
831-440-1000
Dogs are allowed for an additional fee of $25 per night per pet. Multiple dogs may be allowed.

Sea Ranch Lodge
60 Sea Walk Drive
Sea Ranch, CA
707-785-2371 (800-SEA-RANCH (732-7262))
searanchlodge.com/
Shinning with a natural rustic elegance along a dramatic ocean

side location, this award-winning 20 room lodge is an idyllic retreat for special events, and the business or leisure traveler. Some the features/amenities include miles of scenic hiking trails, a full breakfast, exquisite wining and dining with the freshest ingredients available and ocean views, and Concierge Services. Friendly dogs of all sizes are allowed for an additional one time fee of $50 per pet. Dogs must be leashed and cleaned up after at all times, and pet rooms are located on the 1st floor only. Canine guests receive a welcome package that includes a welcome note with suggestions for activities, a cookie, bottled water, a cushy bed, a furniture cover, food/water bowls, and a place mat. 2 dogs may be allowed.

The Cliffs Resort
2757 Shell Beach Road
Shell Beach, CA
805-773-5000 (800-826-7827)
cliffsresort.com/hotel/
With a multi-million dollar renovation and a visually stunning location, this award winning resort features a private oceanfront cliff setting with access to the beach, indoor or outdoor dining and many in room amenities. Dogs are welcome on the 1st floor only, and there is a $50 one time additional pet fee per room. Normally one dog is allowed per room, but they may allow 2 dogs if they are 10 pounds or under. Canine guests are greeted with an amenity kit that includes a comfy bed, a clip ID tag, a treat, water, and food and water bowls. Dogs may be left alone in the room only if they will be quiet and well behaved, and they must be removed or crated for housekeeping. Dogs must be leashed and cleaned up after at all times.

Best Western Carriage Inn
5525 Sepulveda Boulevard
Sherman, CA
818-787-2300 (800-780-7234)
Dogs are allowed for no additional fee with a credit card on file. Multiple dogs may be allowed.

Motel 6 - Simi Valley
2566 North Erringer Road
Simi Valley, CA
805-526-3533 (800-466-8356)
One well-behaved family pet per room. Guest must notify front desk upon arrival. Guest is liable for any damages. In consideration of all

guests, pets must never be left unattended in the guest rooms.

Royal Copenhagen Inn
1579 Mission Drive
Solvang, CA
800-624-6604
This inn is located in the heart of the Solvang village. Walk to dog-friendly restaurants, stores and parks. Well-behaved dogs are allowed. There is no pet fee.

Wine Valley Inn
1554 Copenhagen Drive
Solvang, CA
805-688-2111
winevalleyinn.com/
A luxurious blend of old world ambiance and modern day comforts, this chateau-style retreat offers accommodations for all tastes and budgets. Set among beautifully landscaped courtyards complete with koi ponds, a stone fireplace, and private gardens are individually decorated guest rooms, cottages, and a grand suite, all with many in-room amenities. Dogs of all sizes are allowed for a $100 refundable deposit plus an additional pet fee of $25 per night per pet. Dogs may not be left alone in the room at any time, and they must be leashed and cleaned up after at all times. Multiple dogs may be allowed.

Best Western Sonoma Valley Inn
550 2nd St W
Sonoma, CA
707-938-9200 (800-780-7234)
Dogs are allowed for an additional pet fee of $25 per night per room. Multiple dogs may be allowed.

Renaissance Lodge at Sonoma
1325 Broadway
Sonoma, CA
707-935-6600
Dogs of all sizes are allowed. There is a $75 one time fee per room and a pet policy to sign at check in. Multiple dogs may be allowed.

Best Western Sonora Oaks
19551 Hess Avenue
Sonora, CA
209-533-4400 (800-780-7234)
One dog is allowed for an additional pet fee of $25 per night.

Pesce's Garden
862 Shaws Flat Road
Sonora, CA
209-532-2678 (866-957-3723)
pescesgarden.com
This vacation rental 3/4 mile from

downtown Sonora is a 4 bedroom - 4 bath historical house that was once a boarding house for the Faxon Mine. Dogs of all sizes are allowed for a $10 per day per pet fee. Depending on availability at some times you can rent only one room with private bath. Please mention that you are bringing your dog when making reservations.

Sonora Aladdin Motor Inn
14260 Mono Way (Hwy 108)
Sonora, CA
209-533-4971
aladdininn.com
This motel's rooms offer Southwest decor with king or queen sized beds, table & chairs, refrigerators, coffee makers, climate control, cable TV & HBO, and direct dial phones with free local & credit card calls. They also feature a guest laundry. Dogs are welcome with a $5 one time charge. The motel is about an hour and a half from Yosemite.

Blue Spruce Inn Bed and Breakfast
2815 Main Street
Soquel, CA
831-464-1137
bluespruce.com
A well-behaved dog is allowed in the Secret Garden Room. This room offers a private enclosed garden that includes an outdoor hot tub for two, a small sitting area with gas fireplace and comfortable reading chairs, private bathroom and more. There is a $25 one time pet charge. Please abide by the following pet rules. If your dog will be allowed on the furniture, please cover it first with a sheet. If you take your pooch to the dog beach, please rinse him or her off in the outside hot and cold shower before entering the room. This bed and breakfast does offer a VIP (Very Important Pets) program for your pooch. This includes a dog bone, water bowl and poop bags upon arrival.

3 Peaks Resort and Beach Club - South Lake Tahoe Hotel
931 Park Avenue
South Lake Tahoe, CA
800-957-5088
lake-tahoe-california-hotels.com
The 3 Peaks Resort and Beach Club is a family resort near the center of South Lake Tahoe. All pets are welcome for a $15 per night fee. Pets cannot be left unattended and must be kept on a leash when out of the room.

7 Seas Inn
4145 Manzanita Ave

South Lake Tahoe, CA
530-544-7031 (800-800-SEAS)
sevenseastahoe.com
This motel is located one block from the casinos and near Heavenly Ski Resort. There is a 2000 Square foot dog run and pet sitting is available.

Alder Inn
1072 Ski Run Blvd
South Lake Tahoe, CA
530-544-4485 (800-544-0056)
alderinntahoe.com
Minutes from Heavenly Valley Ski Resort and the casinos. All rooms have a small refrigerator and microwave. There is a $10.00 per night pet fee.

Buckingham Properties Lake Tahoe
Call to Arrange
South Lake Tahoe, CA
530-542-1114 (800-503-0051)
BuckinghamTahoeRentals.com
This company offers elegant and unique vacation rentals which allow dogs. Their properties range from deluxe cabins to luxurious lakefront homes. The homes are located on the south shore from Glenbrook in Nevada to Camp Richardson in California.

Colony Inn at South Lake Tahoe
3794 Montreal Road
South Lake Tahoe, CA
530-544-6481
gototahoe.com/rooms/colony.html
The Colony Inn at South Lake Tahoe is located just 1.5 blocks from Harrah's and the other casinos and just down the street from Heavenly Ski Resort. Want to experience the beautiful outdoors? The Colony Inn's backyard is National Forest Land, featuring dog-friendly hiking, mountain biking, and peace and quiet. There is a $25 refundable pet deposit, and pets cannot be left unattended in the rooms.

Fireside Lodge
515 Emerald Bay Rd.
South Lake Tahoe, CA
530-544-5515 (800-My-Cabin)
tahoefiresidelodge.com/
This inn offers log cabin style suites. The rooms have a unique "Country Mountain" theme decor with crafted fireplaces, and custom woodwork. Each room offers a microwave, refrigerator and coffee-maker, private bath w/shower, cable TV and VCR with numerous free videos available in their Gathering Room. Full kitchen units are available as well as private 1 to 4

bedroom cabins, off the property. There is a $20 per day pet charge.

Hollys Place
1201 Rufus Allen Blvd.
South Lake Tahoe, CA
530-544-7040 (800-745-7041)
hollysplace.com
This resort and retreat has 5 cabins on 2.5 fenced acres near South Lake Tahoe. There is a pet fee of $15 per night per dog. Multiple dogs may be allowed.

Inn at Heavenly B&B
1261 Ski Run Boulevard
South Lake Tahoe, CA
530-544-4244 (800-692-2246)
innatheavenly.com/
You and your dog are welcome at this log-cabin style bed and breakfast lodge. The property is all dog-friendly and dogs are allowed everywhere but their Gathering Room. They offer 14 individual rooms each with a private bath and shower. Room conveniences include refrigerators, microwaves and VCRs. Some rooms have a fireplace. Three to four bedroom cabins are also available. The lodge is located on a 2-acre wooded park complete with picnic areas, barbecues and log swings. Continental breakfast is served and snacks are available throughout the day. One large dog is allowed per room and pet charges apply. Room rates range from the low to mid $100s per night. Call for cabin prices. The owners have friendly dogs on the premises. The lodge is located in South Lake Tahoe. There is a $20 per day pet fee per pet.

Motel 6 - South Lake Tahoe
2375 Lake Tahoe Boulevard
South Lake Tahoe, CA
530-542-1400 (800-466-8356)
One well-behaved family pet per room. Guest must notify front desk upon arrival. Guest is liable for any damages. In consideration of all guests, pets must never be left unattended in the guest rooms.

Spruce Grove Cabins and Suites
3599 Spruce Ave
South Lake Tahoe, CA
530-544-6481
Spruce Grove Cabins puts you amidst a mountain resort off of Ski Run Blvd. Well behaved dogs of all sizes are allowed. There is a $10 per night fee for one dog any size; each pet thereafter is an additional $5 per night per pet fee. There is a pet policy to sign at check in. There is also a large fenced area for a safe

place to off-leash your pet. Multiple dogs may be allowed.

Stonehenge Vacation Properties
Call to Arrange.
South Lake Tahoe, CA
800-822-1460 (800-822-1460)
tahoestonehenge.com/
This vacation rental company offers several elegant and unique dog-friendly vacation homes located around South Lake Tahoe.

Tahoe Keys Resort
599 Tahoe Keys Blvd
South Lake Tahoe, CA
530-544-5397 (800-698-2463)
petslovetahoe.com
They feature approximately 50 pet friendly cabins, condos and homes in South Lake Tahoe. All dogs receive treats upon check-in. A $25.00 pet fee is taken per reservation. There is also a $100.00 refundable security deposit upon check in.

Tahoe Tropicana
4132 Cedar Avenue
South Lake Tahoe, CA
530-541-3911
Dogs of all sizes are allowed. There is a $5 per night per pet additional fee Sunday through Thursday, and $10 per night per pet additional fee Friday and Saturday nights. Multiple dogs may be allowed.

TahoeWoods Lodging
See Website or Call
South Lake Tahoe, CA
415-444-0777
These three vacation homes in South Lake Tahoe feature at least 5 bedrooms and access to the Tahoe National Forest.

The Nash Cabin
3595 Betty Ray
South Lake Tahoe, CA
415-759-6583
Dogs of all sizes are allowed. There are no additional pet fees. Multiple dogs may be allowed.

Embassy Suites Hotel San Francisco Airport South
250 Gateway boulevard
South San Francisco, CA
650-589-3400
Dogs of all sizes are allowed. There is a $50 one time pet fee per visit. Dogs are not allowed to be left alone in the room.

Howard Johnson Express Inn
222 South Airport Blvd.
South San Francisco, CA

650-589-9055 (800-446-4656)
Dogs of all sizes are welcome. There is a $10 per day pet fee.

La Quinta Inn San Francisco Airport
20 Airport Blvd.
South San Francisco, CA
650-583-2223 (800-531-5900)
Dogs of all sizes are allowed. There are no additional pet fees. Dogs must be leashed and cleaned up after. Be sure to inform the front desk you have a pet, and put the Do Not Disturb sign on the door if the dog is alone in the room. Multiple dogs may be allowed.

Motel 6 - San Francisco Airport
111 Mitchell Avenue
South San Francisco, CA
650-877-0770 (800-466-8356)
One well-behaved family pet per room. Guest must notify front desk upon arrival. Guest is liable for any damages. In consideration of all guests, pets must never be left unattended in the guest rooms.

Vagabond Inn
222 S. Airport Blvd
South San Francisco, CA
650-589-9055
Amenities include microwaves and refrigerators in some rooms. There is a $10 per day pet charge. This inn was formerly a Howard Johnson Inn.

El Bonita Motel
195 Main Street
St Helena, CA
707-963-3216 (800-541-3284)
elbonita.com/
Amenities at this motel include a continental breakfast, pool, whirlpool, sauna, and over two acres of peaceful gardens. Room amenities include microwaves, refrigerators, and more. Room rates start at about $130 per night and up. There is a $5 per day pet charge.

Harvest Inn
One Main Street
St Helena, CA
707-963-9463 (800-950-8466)
harvestinn.com/
This inn is nestled among 8-acres of award winning landscape. Most guest rooms feature wet bars, unique brick fireplaces and private terraces. Amenities include two outdoor heated pools and whirlpool spas and jogging and bike trails bordering the grounds. Dogs are allowed in the standard rooms. There is a $75 one time pet charge.

Motel 6 - Stanton
7450 Katella Avenue
Stanton, CA
714-891-0717 (800-466-8356)
One well-behaved family pet per room. Guest must notify front desk upon arrival. Guest is liable for any damages. In consideration of all guests, pets must never be left unattended in the guest rooms.

Beach Front Retreat
90 Calle Del Ribera
Stinson Beach, CA
415-383-7870
beachtime.org
This vacation home rental offers 3 bedrooms, 2 baths, a fireplace and a beach deck with barbecue. You can view the ocean from the balcony located next to the master bedroom. There is an additional $50 one time per stay pet charge

Comfort Inn
2654 W March Lane
Stockton, CA
209-478-4300 (877-424-6423)
Dogs up to 50 pounds are allowed for an additional one time pet fee of $15 per room. 2 dogs may be allowed.

La Quinta Inn Stockton
2710 W. March Ln.
Stockton, CA
209-952-7800 (800-531-5900)
Dogs of all sizes are allowed. There are no additional pet fees. Dogs must be leashed and cleaned up after. The Do Not Disturb sign must be placed on the door if there is a pet alone in the room. Multiple dogs may be allowed.

Motel 6 - Stockton - Charter Way West
817 Navy Drive
Stockton, CA
209-946-0923 (800-466-8356)
One well-behaved family pet per room. Guest must notify front desk upon arrival. Guest is liable for any damages. In consideration of all guests, pets must never be left unattended in the guest rooms.

Motel 6 - Stockton - I-5 Southeast
1625 French Camp Turnpike Road
Stockton, CA
209-467-3600 (800-466-8356)
One well-behaved family pet per room. Guest must notify front desk upon arrival. Guest is liable for any damages. In consideration of all guests, pets must never be left

unattended in the guest rooms.

Motel 6 - Stockton North
6717 Plymouth Road
Stockton, CA
209-951-8120 (800-466-8356)
One well-behaved family pet per
room. Guest must notify front desk
upon arrival. Guest is liable for any
damages. In consideration of all
guests, pets must never be left
unattended in the guest rooms.

Residence Inn by Marriott
March Lane and Brookside
Stockton, CA
209-472-9800
Pets of all sizes are allowed. There is
a $70 per pet per stay fee and a pet
policy to sign at check in. Multiple
dogs may be allowed.

Travelodge
1707 Fremont St
Stockton, CA
209-466-7777
There is a $25 refundable pet
deposit.

Motel 6 - Sunnyvale North
775 North Mathilda Avenue
Sunnyvale, CA
408-736-4595 (800-466-8356)
One well-behaved family pet per
room. Guest must notify front desk
upon arrival. Guest is liable for any
damages. In consideration of all
guests, pets must never be left
unattended in the guest rooms.

Motel 6 - Sunnyvale South
806 Ahwanee Avenue
Sunnyvale, CA
408-720-1222 (800-466-8356)
One well-behaved family pet per
room. Guest must notify front desk
upon arrival. Guest is liable for any
damages. In consideration of all
guests, pets must never be left
unattended in the guest rooms.

Residence Inn by Marriott
750 Lakeway
Sunnyvale, CA
408-720-1000
Dogs of all sizes are allowed. There
is a $75 one time fee and a pet
policy to sign at check in. Multiple
dogs may be allowed.

Residence Inn by Marriott
1080 Stewart Drive
Sunnyvale, CA
408-720-8893
Dogs of all sizes are allowed. There
is a $75 one time fee and a pet
policy to sign at check in. Multiple

dogs may be allowed.

Sheraton Sunnyvale Hotel
1100 North Mathilda Ave.
Sunnyvale, CA
408-745-6000 (888-625-5144)
Dogs up to 80 pounds are allowed.
You must sign pet policy. Dogs are
not allowed to be left alone in the
room.

Staybridge Suites
900 Hamlin Court
Sunnyvale, CA
408-745-1515 (877-270-6405)
Dogs of all sizes are allowed for an
additional $75 one time pet fee per
room. 2 dogs may be allowed.

The Maple Tree Inn
711 El Camino Real
Sunnyvale, CA
408-720-9700 (800-423-0243)
mapletreeinn.com
Located in the heart of Silicon
Valley, this pet friendly hotel
features a fitness room and
complimentary high-speed Internet
access. The hotel allows dogs of all
sizes. There is a $10 per night pet
fee per pet.

TownePlace Suites Sunnyvale
Mountain View
606 S Bernardo Avenue
Sunnyvale, CA
408-733-4200
Dogs of all sizes are allowed. There
is a $75 one time pet fee per visit. .
2 dogs may be allowed.

Woodfin Suite Hotel
635 E. El Camino Real
Sunnyvale, CA
408-738-1700
All well-behaved dogs are welcome.
All rooms are suites with full
kitchens. Hotel amenities include a
heated pool. There is a $5 per day
pet fee.

Budget Host Frontier Inn
2685 Main St
Susanville, CA
530-257-4141

River Inn
1710 Main St
Susanville, CA
530-257-6051
There is an $11 per day additional
pet fee. One large dog per room is
allowed.

Motel 6 - Los Angeles - Sylmar
12775 Encinitas Avenue
Sylmar, CA

818-362-9491 (800-466-8356)
One well-behaved family pet per
room. Guest must notify front desk
upon arrival. Guest is liable for any
damages. In consideration of all
guests, pets must never be left
unattended in the guest rooms.

Percy's Place
Email or call to arrange
Tahoe City, CA
510-898-2962
percysplace.com
Percy's Place is a 3-bedroom, 2-bath
home just outside Tahoe City. The
rental is a short walk to a US Forest
Service trail. Dogs of all sizes are
allowed. Please email
percy@percysplace.com to make
reservations.

Tahoe Lake And Mountain Properties
P.O. Box 8258
Tahoe City, CA
530-386-1622
tahoelamp.com
This vacation rental company on the
west side of the lake provides pet-
friendly vacation rentals. There are
no additional pet fees and dogs of all
sizes are welcome. Dogs may not be
left alone in the rentals.

Tahoe Moon Properties
P.O. Box 7521
Tahoe City, CA
530-581-2771 (866-581-2771)
tahoemoonproperties.com
They have over 15 beautiful homes
that allow well-behaved dogs. All of
the houses are close to Tahoe City
or ski areas. Bath and bed linens are
provided. There are a few dog rules;
no dogs on the furniture, dogs are
not to be left alone in the house, you
must clean up after your dog and pet
owners are responsible for any
damages. Rates start at $150 per
night with a 2 night minimum. There
is a $30 per dog charge.

Holiday House
7276 North Lake Blvd
Tahoe Vista, CA
530-546-2369 (800-294-6378)
tahoeholidayhouse.com
This lodge in North Tahoe welcomes
you and your dog. The hotel is
located 1 mile west of the Hwy
267/Hwy 28 intersection near
restaurants and activities.

Rustic Cottages
7449 N Lake Blvd
Tahoe Vista, CA
530-546-3523
Dogs of all sizes are allowed. There
is a $15 per night per pet fee and

dogs may not be left unattended. They request to clean up after your pet, keep it leashed, and they are not allowed on the furniture. Multiple dogs may be allowed.

Waters of Tahoe Vacation Properties
PO Box 312
Tahoe Vista, CA
530-546-8904 (800-215-8904)
watersoftahoe.com
These vacation homes are near the Tahoe National Forest and the lake. They provide pet amenities such as a dog basket with treats, toys, an extra leash, dog bowls and other miscellaneous goodies.

Norfolk Woods Inn
6941 West Lake Blvd.
Tahoma, CA
530-525-5000
norfolkwoods.com/
This inn only allows dogs in the cabins ... but your pup won't mind. They have wonderful cozy cottages with kitchens. They only have 4 cabins, so call ahead. Also note that the entire premises is smoke free. Located directly in front of this inn is the Tahoe bike trail where you and your pup can walk or run for several miles. The trail is mostly paved except for a small dirt path section. The inn is located approx. 8-9 miles south of Tahoe City on Hwy 89. There is a $10 per day additional pet fee per pet.

Tahoma Lodge
7018 West Lake Blvd
Tahoma, CA
530-525-7721
Dogs only are allowed and up to 75 pounds. There is a $10 per night per pet fee, and they ask you kennel your dog when out. There are some breed restrictions. 2 dogs may be allowed.

Tahoma Meadows Bed and Breakfast
6821 W. Lake Blvd.
Tahoma, CA
530-525-1553
tahomameadows.com/
A well-behaved dog is allowed only if you let them know in advance that you are bringing your dog. Pets are allowed in one of their cabins, the Mountain Hideaway (previously known as Dogwood). There is an extra $25 one time pet charge per stay, plus a security deposit.

Best Western Mountain Inn
418 W Tehachapi Blvd
Tehachapi, CA

661-822-5591 (800-780-7234)
Dogs are allowed for no additional pet fee. Multiple dogs may be allowed.

Travelodge
500 Steuber Rd
Tehachapi, CA
661-823-8000
There is a $7 per day pet fee.

Comfort Inn-Wine Country
27338 Jefferson Avenue
Temecula, CA
951-296-3788 (877-424-6423)
Dogs are allowed for an additional fee per pet of $20 for the 1st night and $10 for each night after. 2 dogs may be allowed.

Motel 6 - Temecula - Rancho California
41900 Moreno Drive
Temecula, CA
951-676-7199 (800-466-8356)
One well-behaved family pet per room. Guest must notify front desk upon arrival. Guest is liable for any damages. In consideration of all guests, pets must never be left unattended in the guest rooms.

Thousand Oaks Inn
75 W. Thousand Oaks Blvd.
Thousand Oaks, CA
805-497-3701
This motel allows both dogs and cats. They have a $75 non-refundable pet deposit.

Red Roof Inn - Palm Springs - Thousand Palms
72215 Varner Road
Thousand Palms, CA
760-343-1381 (800-RED-ROOF)
One well-behaved family pet per room. Guest must notify front desk upon arrival. Guest is liable for any damages. In consideration of all guests, pets must never be left unattended in the guest rooms.

Buckeye Tree Lodge
46,000 Sierra Drive/H 198
Three Rivers, CA
559-561-5900
buckeyetree.com/
This lodge sits in the Kaweah River Canyon along the banks of the Kaweah River. The beautiful grounds offer a grassy lawn, a picnic area on the river surrounded by Sycamore trees, an outdoor pool, and miles of multi-use trails to explore. Dogs of all sizes are allowed for an additional fee of $8 per night per pet. Dogs may not be

left alone in the rooms at any time, and they must be well behaved, leashed, and cleaned up after. Multiple dogs may be allowed.

Sequoia Village Inn
45971 Sierra Drive/H 198
Three Rivers, CA
559-561-3652
sequoiavillageinn.com/
Neighboring the Sequoia National Park, this inn features spectacular mountain and river scenery, 1.3 acres of native oak trees, grasses, an abundance of wildflowers, and 8 private chalet and/or cottages. Some of the amenities include a seasonal swimming pool and spa, satellite TV, kitchens with basic needs/utilities, and beautiful hand-crafted accommodations. Dogs of all sizes are allowed for an additional fee of $8 per night per pet. Dogs may not be left alone in the rooms at any time, and they must be well behaved, leashed, and cleaned up after. Multiple dogs may be allowed.

Holiday Inn
19800 S Vermont Ave
Torrance, CA
310-781-9100 (877-270-6405)
Dogs up to 80 pounds are allowed for no additional fee with a credit card on file, otherwise a $50 refundable cash deposit is required. 2 dogs may be allowed.

Residence Inn by Marriott
3701 Torrance Blvd
Torrance, CA
310-543-4566
Well behaved dogs of all sizes are allowed. There is a $75 one time fee, and a pet policy to sign at check in. 2 dogs may be allowed.

Staybridge Suites
19901 Prairie Avenue
Torrance, CA
310-371-8525 (877-270-6405)
Dogs of all sizes are allowed for an additional $150 per stay for a 1 bedroom, and a $250 per stay in a 2 bedroom. 2 dogs may be allowed.

Motel 6 - Tracy
3810 North Tracy Boulevard
Tracy, CA
209-836-4900 (800-466-8356)
One well-behaved family pet per room. Guest must notify front desk upon arrival. Guest is liable for any damages. In consideration of all guests, pets must never be left unattended in the guest rooms.

Beautiful Tahoe Donner Home -
Sleeps 12!
Visit Website to Book
Truckee, CA
408-354-5779
dogfriendlyrentalsllc.com
This non-smoking vacation rental is
located across the street from the
Tahoe National Forest in Truckee.
The pet-friendly house sleeps up to
12 people and guests have access to
the recreation facilities available in
the community.

Best Western Town & Country Lodge
1051 N Blackstone Street
Tulare, CA
559-688-7537 (800-780-7234)
Dogs are allowed for an additional
one time pet fee of $20 per room.
Multiple dogs may be allowed.

Days Inn
1183 N Blackstone St
Tulare, CA
559-686-0985 (800-329-7466)
There is a $5 per day pet fee.

Howard Johnson Express Inn
1050 E Rankin Ave
Tulare, CA
559-688-6671 (800-446-4656)
There is a $6 per day pet fee.

Motel 6 - Tulare
1111 North Blackstone Drive
Tulare, CA
559-686-1611 (800-466-8356)
One well-behaved family pet per
room. Guest must notify front desk
upon arrival. Guest is liable for any
damages. In consideration of all
guests, pets must never be left
unattended in the guest rooms.

Best Western Orchard Inn
5025 N Golden State Boulevard
Turlock, CA
209-667-2827 (800-780-7234)
Dogs are allowed for an additional
one time fee of $25 per pet. Multiple
dogs may be allowed.

Motel 6 - Turlock
250 South Walnut Avenue
Turlock, CA
209-667-4100 (800-466-8356)
One well-behaved family pet per
room. Guest must notify front desk
upon arrival. Guest is liable for any
damages. In consideration of all
guests, pets must never be left
unattended in the guest rooms.

29 Palms Inn
73950 Inn Avenue
Twentynine Palms, CA

760-367-3505
29palmsinn.com/
A natural high mountain desert
oasis, this wonderful retreat is
located on 30 acres of natural
preserve and offers a variety of
well- appointed accommodations
and amenities. They also have a
great garden to supply their
seasonally influenced restaurant
with fresh new tastes of the
seasons, and there is dining inside
or at the poolside tables. Dogs of all
sizes are allowed for an additional
one time fee of $35 per pet. Dogs
may only be left alone if they will be
well behaved, and they must be
leashed and cleaned up after.
Multiple dogs may be allowed.

Circle C Lodge
6340 El Rey Avenue
Twentynine Palms, CA
760-367-7615 (800-545-9696)
circleclodge.com/
The lush private oasis setting of this
12 room lodge offers a wonderful
contrast to the spectacular views it
provides of the Mojave Desert.
Some of the amenities include a
continental breakfast, fully equipped
kitchenettes with private baths, a
garden courtyard with barbecue,
heated pool, and spa, and it is a
great starting point for several other
local attractions. There is only 1 pet
room available here, so
reservations well in advance are
suggested. Dogs of all sizes are
allowed for an additional fee of $15
per night per pet. Dogs may not be
left alone in the room at any time,
and they must be leashed and
cleaned up after at all times. 2 dogs
may be allowed.

Harmony Hotel
71161 29 Palms H/H 62
Twentynine Palms, CA
760-367-3351
harmonymotel.com/
Known as the perfect location for
both artistic inspiration and dramatic
visual beauty, this motel offers
close proximity to several other
attractions and recreational
pursuits, an outdoor pool and spa,
art from those inspired here, and
several amenities for a comfortable
stay. Dogs of all sizes are allowed
for an additional fee of $15 per night
per pet with a credit card on file.
Dogs must be tick and flea free,
housetrained, and friendly. Dogs
may not be left alone in the room,
and they must be leashed and
cleaned up after at all times. 2 dogs
may be allowed.

Motel 6 - Twentynine Palms
72562 Twentynine Palms Highway
Twentynine Palms, CA
760-367-2833 (800-466-8356)
One well-behaved family pet per
room. Guest must notify front desk
upon arrival. Guest is liable for any
damages. In consideration of all
guests, pets must never be left
unattended in the guest rooms.

Days Inn
950 North State St
Ukiah, CA
707-462-7584 (800-329-7466)
There is a $10 per day per pet fee.

Motel 6 - Ukiah
1208 South State Street
Ukiah, CA
707-468-5404 (800-466-8356)
One well-behaved family pet per
room. Guest must notify front desk
upon arrival. Guest is liable for any
damages. In consideration of all
guests, pets must never be left
unattended in the guest rooms.

Crowne Plaza
32083 Alvarado-Niles Road
Union City, CA
510-489-2200 (877-270-6405)
Dogs of all sizes are allowed for an
additional fee of $60 per night per
pet, and when paying by cash
instead of a credit card there is a
$200 refundable deposit. Multiple
dogs may be allowed.

Sheraton Universal Hotel
333 Universal Hollywood Drive
Universal City, CA
818-980-1212 (888-625-5144)
Dogs up to 70 pounds are allowed at
this luxury hotel near Universal
Studios. There are no additional pet
fees. Pet Sitting can be arranged by
the hotel.

Best Western Heritage Inn
1420 E Monte Vista Ave
Vacaville, CA
707-448-8453 (800-780-7234)
Dogs up to 60 pounds are allowed
for no additional pet fee. 2 dogs may
be allowed.

Motel 6 - Vacaville
107 Lawrence Drive
Vacaville, CA
707-447-5550 (800-466-8356)
One well-behaved family pet per
room. Guest must notify front desk
upon arrival. Guest is liable for any
damages. In consideration of all
guests, pets must never be left

unattended in the guest rooms.

Residence Inn by Marriott
360 Orange Drive
Vacaville, CA
707-469-0300
Pets of all sizes are allowed. There is a $75 one time fee per pet and a pet policy to sign at check in. Multiple dogs may be allowed.

Best Western Inn at Marine World
1596 Fairgrounds Dr
Vallejo, CA
707-554-9655 (800-780-7234)
Dogs are allowed for an additional one time fee of $35 per pet. 2 dogs may be allowed.

Motel 6 - Vallejo - Maritime North
597 Sandy Beach Road
Vallejo, CA
707-552-2912 (800-466-8356)
One well-behaved family pet per room. Guest must notify front desk upon arrival. Guest is liable for any damages. In consideration of all guests, pets must never be left unattended in the guest rooms.

Motel 6 - Vallejo - Six Flags East
458 Fairgrounds Drive
Vallejo, CA
707-642-7781 (800-466-8356)
One well-behaved family pet per room. Guest must notify front desk upon arrival. Guest is liable for any damages. In consideration of all guests, pets must never be left unattended in the guest rooms.

Motel 6 - Vallejo - Six Flags West
1455 Marine World Parkway
Vallejo, CA
707-643-7611 (800-466-8356)
One well-behaved family pet per room. Guest must notify front desk upon arrival. Guest is liable for any damages. In consideration of all guests, pets must never be left unattended in the guest rooms.

Quality Inn
44 Admiral Callaghan Lane
Vallejo, CA
707-643-1061 (877-424-6423)
Dogs are allowed for an additional fee of $15 per night per pet. 2 dogs may be allowed.

Crowne Plaza Hotel - Ventura Beach
450 E Harbor Blvd
Ventura, CA
805-648-2100 (877-270-6405)
Dogs of all sizes are allowed for an additional $50 one time pet fee per room. 2 dogs may be allowed.

La Quinta Inn Ventura
5818 Valentine Rd.
Ventura, CA
805-658-6200 (800-531-5900)
Dogs of all sizes are allowed. There are no additional pet fees. Dogs must be leashed and cleaned up after. Dogs must be crated or attended to for housekeeping. Multiple dogs may be allowed.

Motel 6 - Ventura Beach
2145 East Harbor Boulevard
Ventura, CA
805-643-5100 (800-466-8356)
One well-behaved family pet per room. Guest must notify front desk upon arrival. Guest is liable for any damages. In consideration of all guests, pets must never be left unattended in the guest rooms.

Motel 6 - Ventura South
3075 Johnson Drive
Ventura, CA
805-650-0080 (800-466-8356)
One well-behaved family pet per room. Guest must notify front desk upon arrival. Guest is liable for any damages. In consideration of all guests, pets must never be left unattended in the guest rooms.

Vagabond Inn
756 E. Thompson Blvd.
Ventura, CA
805-648-5371
vagabondinn.com
Amenities at this motel include a free continental breakfast, weekday newspaper, and heated Jacuzzi. They also have an on-site coffee shop, which might be helpful in getting food to go for the room. There is a $10 per day pet fee. Dogs are allowed in a few of the non-smoking rooms.

Howard Johnson Express Inn
16868 Stoddard Wells Rd.
Victorville, CA
760-243-7700 (800-446-4656)
Dogs of all sizes are welcome. There is a $10 per day pet fee per pet.

Motel 6 - Victorville
16901 Stoddard Wells Road
Victorville, CA
760-243-0666 (800-466-8356)
One well-behaved family pet per room. Guest must notify front desk upon arrival. Guest is liable for any damages. In consideration of all guests, pets must never be left unattended in the guest rooms.

Red Roof Inn - Victorville
13409 Mariposa Road
Victorville, CA
760-241-1577 (800-RED-ROOF)
One well-behaved family pet per room. Guest must notify front desk upon arrival. Guest is liable for any damages. In consideration of all guests, pets must never be left unattended in the guest rooms.

Holiday Inn
9000 W. Airport Drive
Visalia, CA
559-651-5000 (877-270-6405)
Dogs of all sizes are allowed for an additional $25 per night per pet. Multiple dogs may be allowed.

La Quinta Inn San Diego Vista
630 Sycamore Ave.
Vista, CA
760-727-8180 (800-531-5900)
Dogs of all sizes are allowed. There are no additional pet fees. Dogs may not be left unattended, and they must be leashed and cleaned up after. Multiple dogs may be allowed.

The St. George Hotel
16104 Main Street
Volcano, CA
209-296-4458
stgeorgehotel.com/
A well-behaved large dog is allowed in one of the bungalow rooms. The non-smoking pet-friendly room has hardwood floors, a queen bed, a private bath and garden views. Upon arrival, your pooch will receive treats and an extra blanket. There is a $20 per day pet charge.

Motel 6 - Walnut Creek
2389 North Main Street
Walnut Creek, CA
925-935-4010 (800-466-8356)
One well-behaved family pet per room. Guest must notify front desk upon arrival. Guest is liable for any damages. In consideration of all guests, pets must never be left unattended in the guest rooms.

Best Western Rose Garden Inn
740 Freedom Blvd
Watsonville, CA
831-724-3367 (800-780-7234)
Dogs are allowed for an additional fee of $15 per night per pet. 2 dogs may be allowed.

Comfort Inn
112 Airport Blvd
Watsonville, CA
831-728-2300 (877-424-6423)

Dogs up to 15 pounds are allowed for an additional fee per pet of $35 for each 1 to 3 nights stay; the fee is $50 for each 1 to 3 nights for dogs over 15 pounds. 2 dogs may be allowed.

Motel 6 - Watsonville - Monterey Area
125 Silver Leaf Drive
Watsonville, CA
831-728-4144 (800-466-8356)
One well-behaved family pet per room. Guest must notify front desk upon arrival. Guest is liable for any damages. In consideration of all guests, pets must never be left unattended in the guest rooms.

Red Roof Inn - Watsonville
1620 West Beach Street
Watsonville, CA
831-740-4520 (800-RED-ROOF)
One well-behaved family pet per room. Guest must notify front desk upon arrival. Guest is liable for any damages. In consideration of all guests, pets must never be left unattended in the guest rooms.

Comfort Inn Central
1844 Shastina Drive
Weed, CA
530-938-1982 (877-424-6423)
Dogs are allowed for an additional fee of $10 (plus tax) per night per pet. Multiple dogs may be allowed.

Lake Shastina Golf Resort
5925 Country Club Drive
Weed, CA
530-938-3201
lakeshastinagolfresort.net/
Dogs are allowed in some of the condos at this 18 hole golf course resort. There is a $25 one time pet charge.

Motel 6 - Weed - Mount Shasta
466 North Weed Boulevard
Weed, CA
530-938-4101 (800-466-8356)
One well-behaved family pet per room. Guest must notify front desk upon arrival. Guest is liable for any damages. In consideration of all guests, pets must never be left unattended in the guest rooms.

Le Montrose Suites
900 Hammond Street
West Hollywood, CA
310-855-1115 (800- 776-0666)
lemontrose.com/
A multi-million dollar renovation transformed this hotel into an elegant, stylish urban retreat with many conveniences for the business or leisure traveler. Some of the features include personalized services, several in-room amenities, a business center, and a beautiful outdoor pool and sunning area. Dogs up to 50 pounds are allowed for an additional $100 one time pet fee per room. Dogs may only be left alone in the room if they will be quiet, well behaved, and a contact number is left with the front desk. They also request that the sliding glass door is closed if a pet is in the room alone. Dogs must be leashed and cleaned up after at all times. Dogs are not allowed in food service areas or on the roof. Multiple dogs may be allowed.

Motel 6 - Sacramento West
1254 Halyard Drive
West Sacramento, CA
916-372-3624 (800-466-8356)
One well-behaved family pet per room. Guest must notify front desk upon arrival. Guest is liable for any damages. In consideration of all guests, pets must never be left unattended in the guest rooms.

Days Inn
7144 McCracken Rd
Westley, CA
209-894-5500 (800-329-7466)
There is a $10 per day additional pet fee.

Econo Lodge
7100 McCracken Rd
Westley, CA
209-894-3900
There is a $10 per day pet fee.

Super 8 Westley/Modesto Area
7115 McCracken Road
Westley, CA
209-894-3888 (800-800-8000)
Dogs of all sizes are allowed. There is a $10 per night pet fee per pet. Smoking and non-smoking rooms are available for pet rooms. 2 dogs may be allowed.

Motel 6 - Westminster North
13100 Goldenwest Street
Westminster, CA
714-895-0042 (800-466-8356)
One well-behaved family pet per room. Guest must notify front desk upon arrival. Guest is liable for any damages. In consideration of all guests, pets must never be left unattended in the guest rooms.

Motel 6 - Westminster South - Long Beach
6266 Westminster Avenue
Westminster, CA
714-891-5366 (800-466-8356)
One well-behaved family pet per room. Guest must notify front desk upon arrival. Guest is liable for any damages. In consideration of all guests, pets must never be left unattended in the guest rooms.

Howard Creek Ranch Inn B&B
40501 N. Highway 1
Westport, CA
707-964-6725
howardcreekranch.com/
Howard Creek Ranch is a historic, 40 acre ocean front farm located about 5-6 hours north of San Francisco. Accommodations include cabins, suites and rooms. It is bordered by miles of beach and mountains. They offer award winning gardens, fireplaces or wood stoves, farm animals, a hot tub, and a sauna. Dog-friendly beaches nearby include Westport Union Landing State Beach in Westport, MacKerricher State Park 3-4 miles north of Fort Bragg and the 60 mile Sinkyone Wilderness Area (Lost Coast). Outdoor restaurants nearby are Jenny's Giant Burgers and Sea Pal (in Fort Bragg). Room rates are $80 and up (includes a full hearty ranch breakfast). There is a $10 plus tax per day pet charge. Certain dog rules apply: don't leave your dog alone in the room, dogs must be supervised and attended at all times, bring towels to clean up your pooch if he/she gets dirty from outside, clean up after your dog, and if your dog will be on the bed, please use a sheet to cover the quilt (sheets can be provided). The inn is located 3 miles north of Westport.

Motel 6 - Los Angeles - Whittier
8221 South Pioneer Boulevard
Whittier, CA
562-692-9101 (800-466-8356)
One well-behaved family pet per room. Guest must notify front desk upon arrival. Guest is liable for any damages. In consideration of all guests, pets must never be left unattended in the guest rooms.

Comfort Inn
400 C Street
Williams, CA
530-473-2381 (877-424-6423)
Dogs are allowed for an additional fee of $10 per night per pet. 2 dogs may be allowed.

Holiday Inn Express Hotel and Suites
374 Ruggieri Way
Williams, CA

530-473-5120 (877-270-6405)
Dogs of all sizes are allowed for an additional $25 one time fee per room. Multiple dogs may be allowed.

Motel 6 - Williams
455 4th Street
Williams, CA
530-473-5337 (800-466-8356)
One well-behaved family pet per room. Guest must notify front desk upon arrival. Guest is liable for any damages. In consideration of all guests, pets must never be left unattended in the guest rooms.

Best Western Golden Pheasant Inn
249 N Humboldt Ave
Willows, CA
530-934-4603 (800-780-7234)
Dogs are allowed for an additional fee of $10 per night per pet. Multiple dogs may be allowed.

Days Inn
475 N Humboldt Ave
Willows, CA
530-934-4444 (800-329-7466)
There is a $5 per day additional pet fee.

Motel 6 - Willows
452 Humboldt Avenue
Willows, CA
530-934-7026 (800-466-8356)
One well-behaved family pet per room. Guest must notify front desk upon arrival. Guest is liable for any damages. In consideration of all guests, pets must never be left unattended in the guest rooms.

Wickyup Bed and Breakfast Cottage
22702 Avenue 344
Woodlake, CA
559-564-8898
wickyup.com/
Dogs are allowed in the Calico Room Cottage. It offers bunk beds, a half-bath, and a discrete, enclosed outdoor shower. The cottage is located in the garden and has a private entrance.

Holiday Inn Express
2070 Freeway Drive
Woodland, CA
530-662-7750 (877-270-6405)
Dogs of all sizes are allowed for an additional $20 one time fee per pet. Multiple dogs may be allowed.

Motel 6 - Woodland - Sacramento Area
1564 East Main Street
Woodland, CA
530-666-6777 (800-466-8356)

One well-behaved family pet per room. Guest must notify front desk upon arrival. Guest is liable for any damages. In consideration of all guests, pets must never be left unattended in the guest rooms.

Sacramento - Days Inn
1524 East Main Street
Woodland, CA
530-666-3800 (800-329-7466)
There is a $10 per day pet fee.

Warner Center Marriott
21850 Oxnard Street
Woodland Hills, CA
818-887-4800
warnercentermarriott.com
You and your dog are welcome at this Marriott hotel in the heart of the west San Fernando Valley. The hotel is located just off Highway 101 near Topanga Plaza and the Promenade Mall. There is a one time non-refundable $50 pet fee.

The Other Place and the Long Valley Ranch
P.O. Box 49
Yorkville, CA
707-894-5322
Dogs of all sizes are allowed. There is no additional pet fee for 2 pets. If there are more than 2 pets the fee is $25 per night per pet Multiple dogs may be allowed.

The Redwoods In Yosemite
PO Box 2085; Wawona Station
Yosemite National Park, CA
209-375-6666 (888-225-6666)
redwoodsinyosemite.com
Dog-friendly vacation rentals inside Yosemite National Park offer year-round vacation rentals that range in size from one to six bedrooms. Some of the rentals allow pets, but not all, so please specify your need for a pet unit when you make your reservation. There is a $10/night pet fee (per pet). Please abide by Yosemite's pet regulations, which require that pets be leashed at all times and are not permitted on many Park trails (a couple of exceptions are paved paths in the Valley Floor and a couple of short trails in the south Yosemite area). The rentals are located approximately 10 minutes inside the southern entrance of Yosemite National Park and offer 120 privately owned vacation rentals.

Vintage Inn
6541 Washington St.
Yountville, CA
707-944-1112 (800-351-1133)

vintageinn.com
This inn is located in the small town of Yountville and is located within walking distance of several dog-friendly restaurants. Amenities at this pet-friendly inn include a continental champagne breakfast, afternoon tea, coffee & cookies, a heated pool, two tennis courts, and award winning gardens. Room amenities include a wood burning fireplace in every room, refrigerator with a chilled welcome bottle of wine, terry robes, nightly turn down service, hair dryer, in room iron & ironing board and more. If you need to leave your room, but can't take your pooch with you, the concierge can arrange for a dog sitter. They also have a list of nearby dog-friendly outdoor restaurants. Room rates start at about $200 per night and up. There is a $30 one time pet charge.

Yountville Inn
6462 Washington Street
Yountville, CA
707-944-5600
Dogs of all sizes are allowed. There is a $100 one time fee per room and a pet policy to sign at check in. Multiple dogs may be allowed.

Best Western Miner's Inn
122 E Miner St
Yreka, CA
530-842-4355 (800-780-7234)
Dogs are allowed for an additional fee of $5 per night per pet for dogs under 20 pounds, and $10 per night per pet for dogs over 20 pounds. Multiple dogs may be allowed.

Comfort Inn
1804 E Fort Jones Road
Yreka, CA
530-842-1612 (877-424-6423)
Dogs up to 50 pounds are allowed for a $50 refundable deposit plus an additional fee of $10 per night per pet. 2 dogs may be allowed.

Motel 6 - Yreka
1785 South Main Street
Yreka, CA
530-842-4111 (800-466-8356)
One well-behaved family pet per room. Guest must notify front desk upon arrival. Guest is liable for any damages. In consideration of all guests, pets must never be left unattended in the guest rooms.

Relax Inn
1210 S Main Street
Yreka, CA
530-842-2791
Dogs of all sizes are allowed. There

is a $5 per night per pet additional fee. Multiple dogs may be allowed.

Days Inn
700 N Palora Ave
Yuba City, CA
530-674-1711 (800-329-7466)
There is a $7 per day pet fee.

Motel 6 - Yuba City
965 Gray Avenue
Yuba City, CA
530-790-7066 (800-466-8356)
One well-behaved family pet per room. Guest must notify front desk upon arrival. Guest is liable for any damages. In consideration of all guests, pets must never be left unattended in the guest rooms.

Super 8 Yucca Val/Joshua Tree Nat Pk Area
57096 29 Palm Hwy
Yucca Valley, CA
760-228-1773 (800-800-8000)
Dogs of all sizes are allowed. There is a $20 returnable deposit required per room. Smoking and non-smoking rooms are available for pet rooms. 2 dogs may be allowed.

Zephyr Cove Resort
460 Highway 50
Zephyr Cove, NV
775-588-6644
tahoedixie2.com/Resort.html
Thanks to one of our readers for recommending this resort. Dogs are allowed in the cabins but not in the lodge or cabin number one. That still leaves a nice selection of cabins to choose from. There is a $10 per day pet fee. This resort is located near South Lake Tahoe on the Nevada side. Dogs are allowed on the beaches at the northern side of the resort about a two block walk from the cabins.

Colorado Listings

Best Western Alamosa Inn
2005 Main Street
Alamosa, CO
719-589-2567 (800-780-7234)
Dogs are allowed for an additional one time fee of $15 per pet. Multiple dogs may be allowed.

Harmel's Ranch Resort & Spa
6748 County Road 742
Almont, CO
970-641-1740 (800-235-3402)
harmels.com

Harmels is a dude ranch that allows you to bring your leashed dog with you. They have a three night minimum in their 37 cabins. The Ranch borders on the Gunnison National Forest which allows leashed dogs on its hiking trails. There is a $10 per night pet fee. The ranch also features barbecues, hayrides and horseback riding and has some nearby swimming holes for dogs.

Hotel Aspen
110 W. Main Street
Aspen, CO
970-925-3441 (800-527-7369)
hotelaspen.com
This dog-friendly hotel is located right on Main Street in Aspen. Rooms are large and beautifully appointed and they come equipped with a wet bar, small refrigerator, coffee maker, microwave, iron, ironing board, hairdryer, humidifier, VCR, and air conditioning. Most rooms open onto terraces or balconies and some have private Jacuzzis. They have a $20 per night charge for pets.

Hotel Jerome
330 E Main Street/H 82
Aspen, CO
970-920-1000 (800-331-7213)
This luxury hotel has been in service for more than a hundred years in the magnificent setting of the Rocky Mountains. Amenities include elegant accommodations, world class cuisine with 2 fine dining restaurants and outdoor dining in summer, 2 taverns, heated outdoor pool/Jacuzzi, underground parking, and much more. Dogs of all sizes are allowed. There is a $75 one time additional pet fee per pet. Dogs must be leashed and cleaned up after at all times. Multiple dogs may be allowed.

The Sky Hotel
709 East Durant Avenue
Aspen, CO
970-925-6760
Well-behaved dogs of all kinds and sizes are welcome at this pet-friendly hotel. The luxury boutique hotel offers both rooms and suites. Hotel amenities include a heated outdoor pool, and a fitness room. There are no pet fees, just sign a pet waiver.

The St. Regis Hotel
315 East Dean Street
Aspen, CO
970-920-3300 (800-325-3535)

destinationaspen.com/stregis/
There is a one time $50 pet charge. The hotel can also arrange a dog sitter or dog walker if you need to leave the room and cannot take your dog.

La Quinta Inn Denver Aurora
1011 S. Abilene St.
Aurora, CO
303-337-0206 (800-531-5900)
Dogs of all sizes are allowed. There are no additional pet fees. Dogs must be crated when left alone in the room, and they must be leashed and cleaned up after. 2 dogs may be allowed.

Motel 6 - Denver East - Aurora
14031 East Iliff Avenue
Aurora, CO
303-873-0286 (800-466-8356)
One well-behaved family pet per room. Guest must notify front desk upon arrival. Guest is liable for any damages. In consideration of all guests, pets must never be left unattended in the guest rooms.

Sleep Inn Denver International Airport
15900 E 40th Avenue
Aurora, CO
303-373-1616 (877-424-6423)
Depending on the size of the pet, dogs are allowed for an additional $10 to $15 per night per pet. 2 dogs may be allowed.

Comfort Inn Beaver Creek
0161 W Beaver Creek Blvd
Avon, CO
970-949-5511 (877-424-6423)
Dogs up to 60 pounds are allowed for an additional one time pet fee per room. 2 dogs may be allowed.

Glen Isle Resort
Highway 285 (near milepost marker 221)
Bailey, CO
303-838-5461
Dogs are welcome in the cabins (no designated smoking or non-smoking cabins). All cabins contain fully equipped kitchens, private baths, easy chairs, bedding and linens, fireplaces (wood provided) and gas heat. Resort amenities include a children's playground, games and game room and a library. The resort is within walking distance of the Pike National Forest and the Platte River. There you will find hours of dog-friendly hiking trails. There is a $5 per day pet charge. The resort is located 45 miles southwest of Denver.

Boulder Outlook Motel and Suites
800 28th Street
Boulder, CO
303-443-3322 (800-542-0304)
This luxury hotel offers a wide variety of amenities and services, some of which include a chlorine-free heated indoor pool, a hot tub, a bouldering wall for climbing, an Adventure guide onsite to book outdoor activities, complimentary continental breakfast, restaurants, a bar, concierge level service, and a lot more. They welcome dogs and have a fully fenced in dog run complete with disposal amenities located adjacent to the designated pet rooms. They will also arrange for dog walking services or a vet if needed. Dogs of all sizes are allowed. There is a $10 per night per pet additional fee. Dogs may be left alone in the room only if they will be quiet, and they must be leashed and cleaned up after. Multiple dogs may be allowed.

Foot of the Mountain Motel
200 Arapahoe Ave.
Boulder, CO
303-442-5688
Pets are welcome at this log cabin motel. There is an additional $5 per day pet charge. There are no designated smoking or non-smoking cabins.

Holiday Inn Express
4777 North Broadway
Boulder, CO
303-442-6600 (877-270-6405)
Dogs of all sizes are allowed for an additional per room pet fee of $20 for the 1st night, and $40 for 2 nights or more 2 dogs may be allowed.

Homewood Suites
4950 Baseline Rd.
Boulder, CO
303-499-9922
There is a one time $50 pet charge.

New West Inn
970 28th Street
Boulder, CO
303-443-7800 (800-800-8000)
Dogs of all sizes are allowed. There is a $50 returnable deposit required per room. There is a $5 per night pet fee per pet. Reservations are recommended due to limited rooms for pets. 2 dogs may be allowed.

Quality Inn and Suites
2020 Arapahoe Ave
Boulder, CO
303-449-7550 (877-424-6423)

Dogs up to 65 pounds are allowed for a $100 refundable deposit plus an additional fee of $15 per night per pet. 2 dogs may be allowed.

Residence Inn by Marriott
3030 Center Green Drive
Boulder, CO
303-449-5545
Dogs of all sizes are allowed. There is a $50 to $75 fee per pet depending on the length of stay and a pet policy to sign at check in. Multiple dogs may be allowed.

Breckenridge Wayside Inn
165 Tiger Rd.
Breckenridge, CO
970-453-5540 (800-927-7669)
toski.com/wayside/
Clean, comfortable motel rooms which are centrally located in Summit County, just 5 minutes to Breckenridge. Thanks to one of our readers who writes "Low-key, no-frills motel. A few miles from the heart of town but right on the main highway." Amenities include a free continental breakfast and free Hot Spiced Cider with cheese & crackers. Dogs are allowed at the motel, but not allowed in lodge area because they have three dogs of their own. There is a $20 refundable pet deposit.

Great Divide Lodge
550 Village Road
Breckenridge, CO
970-547-5550 (888-906-5698)
This full-service, slopeside hotel features 208 spacious, luxury guestrooms rich with amenities, 24 hour guest service, indoor and outdoor pools and hot tubs, a large sun deck, in room dining, a restaurant and lounge, expansive mountain views, and heated underground parking. Although pet friendly rooms are limited, dogs up to 45 pounds are allowed for an additional fee of $30 per night per pet, plus a $150 refundable deposit, with advance reservations. Dogs must be well behaved, leashed, and cleaned up after. 2 dogs may be allowed.

TownePlace Suites Boulder Broomfield
480 Flatiron Blvd
Broomfield, CO
303-466-2200
Dogs of all sizes are allowed. There is a $75 one time pet fee per visit. 2 dogs may be allowed.

Best Western Vista Inn

733 US Highway 24 N
Buena Vista, CO
719-395-8009 (800-780-7234)
Dogs are allowed for an additional fee of $10 per night per pet. 2 dogs may be allowed.

Comfort Inn
282 S Lincoln
Burlington, CO
719-346-7676 (877-424-6423)
Dogs are allowed for a $50 refundable deposit plus an additional pet fee of $10 per night per room. 2 dogs may be allowed.

Best Western Royal Gorge
1925 Fremont Drive
Canon City, CO
719-275-3377 (800-780-7234)
Dogs up to 50 pounds are allowed for an additional one time pet fee of $50 per room. The fee may be slightly higher for heavy shedding dogs. 2 dogs may be allowed.

Comfort Inn
282 S Lincoln
Canon City, CO
719-275-8676 (877-424-6423)
Dogs are allowed for no additional pet fee. 2 dogs may be allowed.

Comfort Inn
311 Royal Gorge Blvd/H50
Canon City, CO
719-276-6900 (877-424-6423)
Dogs are allowed for an additional fee of $10 per night per pet. Multiple dogs may be allowed.

Holiday Inn Express
110 Latigo Lane
Canon City, CO
719-275-2400 (877-270-6405)
Dogs of all sizes are allowed for an additional fee of $15 per night per pet. 2 dogs may be allowed.

Quality Inn & Suites
3075 E H 50
Canyon City, CO
719-275-8676 (877-424-6423)
Dogs of all sizes are allowed. There are no additional pet fees. Multiple dogs may be allowed.

Comfort Inn and Suites
920 Cowen Drive
Carbondale, CO
970-963-8880 (877-424-6423)
Dogs are allowed for an additional fee of $25 per night per pet. Multiple dogs may be allowed.

Best Western Inn & Suites of Castle Rock

595 Genoa Way
Castle Rock, CO
303-814-8800 (800-780-7234)
Dogs up to 50 pounds are allowed for an additional fee of $15 (plus tax) per night per pet. 2 dogs may be allowed.

Comfort Suites
4755 Castleton Way
Castle Rock, CO
303-814-9999 (877-424-6423)
Dogs are allowed for an additional pet fee of $10 per night per room. Multiple dogs may be allowed.

Days Inn and Suites Castle Rock
4691 Castleton Way
Castle Rock, CO
303-814-5825 (800-329-7466)
Dogs of all sizes are allowed. There is a $10 per night pet fee per pet. 2 dogs may be allowed.

Hampton Inn
4830 Castleton Way
Castle Rock, CO
303-660-9800
Dogs of all sizes are allowed. There is a $25 one time fee. Dogs are not to be left alone in the room, and they will not accept Bit Pulls. Multiple dogs may be allowed.

Holiday Inn Express
884 Park Street
Castle Rock, CO
303-660-9733 (877-270-6405)
Dogs of all sizes are allowed for an additional fee of $10 per night per pet. Dogs must be friendly and well groomed. Multiple dogs may be allowed.

Super 8 Castle Rock
1020 Park St
Castle Rock, CO
303-688-0800 (800-800-8000)
Dogs of all sizes are allowed. There are no additional pet fees. Dogs are not allowed to be left alone in the room. Smoking and non-smoking rooms are available for pet rooms. 2 dogs may be allowed.

Howard Johnson Express Inn
530 So. Grand Mesa Drive
Cedaredge, CO
970-856-7824 (800-446-4656)
Dogs of all sizes are welcome. There is a $10 per day pet fee per pet.

Candlewood Suites
6780 South Galena St
Centennial, CO
303-792-5393 (877-270-6405)
Dogs of all sizes are allowed for an

additional per room pet fee of $75 for a 1 to 6 nights stay, and $125 for 7 nights or more. 2 dogs may be allowed.

Embassy Suites Hotel Denver Tech Center
10250 E. Costilla Avenue
Centennial, CO
303-792-0433
Dogs of all sizes are allowed. There is a $75 one time pet fee per visit. Dogs are not allowed to be left alone in the room. 2 dogs may be allowed.

Steamboat Lake Marina Camper Cabins
P. O. Box 867/H 62
Clark, CO
970-879-7019
Located in the scenic Steamboat Lake State Park at 8,100 feet on a beautiful 1,100 acre lake, this marina is now offering rental cabins for year round campers. Nestled in the pines and of log construction, the cabins each have a small refrigerator/freezer, coffee maker, some with table and chairs, and all have electric heat and fire pits. There is a convenience store at the marina, coin operated showers, flush toilets, and running water close to sites. Boat rentals are also available, and your dog is allowed to join you. Dogs of all sizes are allowed in the cabins. There is a $5 per night per pet additional fee. Dogs must be leashed and cleaned up after, and under owner's control at all times. A park pass is also required in addition to cabin fees. 2 dogs may be allowed.

Best Western Grande River Inn & Suites
3228 I-70 Business Loop
Clifton, CO
970-434-3400 (800-780-7234)
Dogs are allowed for an additional fee of $20 per night per pet. 2 dogs may be allowed.

Best Western The Academy Hotel
8110 N Academy Boulevard
Colorado Springs, CO
719-598-5770 (800-780-7234)
Dogs up to 50 pounds are allowed for an additional fee of $10 per night per pet. 2 dogs may be allowed.

Candlewood Suites
6450 North Academy Blvd
Colorado Springs, CO
719-533-0011 (877-270-6405)
Dogs of all sizes are allowed for an additional $75 one time fee per

room. 2 dogs may be allowed.

Clarion Hotel
314 W Bijou Street
Colorado Springs, CO
719-471-8680 (877-424-6423)
Dogs are allowed for an additional fee of $10 per night per pet. Multiple dogs may be allowed.

Comfort Inn North
6450 Corporate Center Drive
Colorado Springs, CO
719-262-9000 (877-424-6423)
Dogs are allowed for an additional fee of $10 per night per pet. Multiple dogs may be allowed.

Days Inn Colorado Springs
8350 Razorback Rd
Colorado Springs, CO
719-266-1314 (800-329-7466)
Dogs of all sizes are allowed. There is a $10 per night pet fee per pet. 2 dogs may be allowed.

Days Inn Colorado Springs
2850 S Circle Dr
Colorado Springs, CO
719-527-0800 (800-329-7466)
Dogs of all sizes are allowed. There is a $25 one time per pet fee per visit. 2 dogs may be allowed.

Econo Lodge Inn and Suites World Arena
1623 South Nevada
Colorado Springs, CO
719-632-6651
choicehotels.com/hotel/co725
This hotel has a large wooded park on site. They also have a staff veterinarian. There is no size restrictions for dogs. There is a playground for children on site. Pets and their owners may select either smoking or non smoking rooms. There is a $20 refundable pet deposit. Pets must be crated if left in rooms and are not allowed to stay if they engage in persistent or periodic barking. Pets must be leashed while on the hotel property outside of the guest room.

La Quinta Inn & Suites Colorado Springs South AP
2750 Geyser Dr.
Colorado Springs, CO
719-527-4788 (800-531-5900)
Dogs up to 80 pounds are allowed. There are no additional pet fees. Leave a cell number with the front desk if your dog is alone in the room, and make arrangements with housekeeping if staying more than one day. Dogs may not be left

unattended, and they must be leashed and cleaned up after. Multiple dogs may be allowed.

La Quinta Inn Colorado Springs Garden of the Gods
4385 Sinton Rd.
Colorado Springs, CO
719-528-5060 (800-531-5900)
Dogs of all sizes are allowed. There are no additional pet fees. Dogs may not be left unattended, and they must be leashed and cleaned up after. Multiple dogs may be allowed.

Motel 6 - Colorado Springs
3228 N Chestnut Street
Colorado Springs, CO
719-520-5400 (800-466-8356)
One well-behaved family pet per room. Guest must notify front desk upon arrival. Guest is liable for any damages. In consideration of all guests, pets must never be left unattended in the guest rooms.

Radisson Inn & Suites Colorado Springs Airport
1645 N. Newport Road
Colorado Springs, CO
719-597-7000
Up to 2 dogs per room are allowed. Each dog must be not larger than 50 pounds. There is a $100 refundable pet deposit and a $25 non-refundable one time pet fee per visit.

Radisson Inn Colorado Springs North
8110 North Academy Blvd
Colorado Springs, CO
719-598-5770
Dogs of any size are allowed. Pets are welcome but need to stay in first floor rooms. There is a $50 refundable pet deposit.

Red Roof Inn - Colorado Springs
8280 Highway 83
Colorado Springs, CO
719-598-6700 (800-RED-ROOF)
One well-behaved family pet per room. Guest must notify front desk upon arrival. Guest is liable for any damages. In consideration of all guests, pets must never be left unattended in the guest rooms.

Residence Inn by Marriott
3880 N Academy Blvd
Colorado Springs, CO
719-574-0370
Dogs of all sizes are allowed. There is a $75 one time fee and a pet policy to sign at check in. Multiple dogs may be allowed.

Residence Inn by Marriott

2765 Geyser Drive
Colorado Springs, CO
719-576-0101
Dogs of all sizes are allowed. There is a $75 one time fee and a pet policy to sign at check in. Multiple dogs may be allowed.

Sheraton Colorado Springs Hotel
2886 South Circle Dr.
Colorado Springs, CO
719-576-5900 (888-625-5144)
Dogs up to 60 pounds are allowed for a $50 refundable deposit per pet. Dogs may not be left alone in the room.

Staybridge Suites
7130 Commerce Center Dr
Colorado Springs, CO
719-590-7829 (877-270-6405)
Dogs of all sizes are allowed for an additional $150 one time pet fee per room. Multiple dogs may be allowed.

Super 8 Colorado Spring/Hwy 24
605 Peterson Rd
Colorado Springs, CO
719-597-4100 (800-800-8000)
Dogs of all sizes are allowed. There is a $10 per night pet fee per pet. Smoking and non-smoking rooms are available for pet rooms. 2 dogs may be allowed.

TownePlace Suites Colorado Springs
4760 Centennial Blvd
Colorado Springs, CO
719-594-4447
Dogs of all sizes are allowed. There is a $20 per night pet fee per pet or there is a $75 one time pet fee per visit. 2 dogs may be allowed.

Anasazi Motor Inn
640 S. Broadway
Cortez, CO
970-565-3773 (800-972-6232)
There is a $50 refundable pet deposit.

Best Western Turquoise Inn & Suites
535 E Main Street
Cortez, CO
970-565-3778 (800-780-7234)
Dogs are allowed for an additional one time pet fee of $15 per room. Multiple dogs may be allowed.

Days Inn Cortez
430 N State Hwy 145
Cortez, CO
970-565-8577 (800-329-7466)
Dogs of all sizes are allowed. There

is a $10 per night pet fee per pet. Pet must be kept in kennel when left alone. 2 dogs may be allowed.

Holiday Inn Express
2121 East Main
Cortez, CO
970-565-6000 (877-270-6405)
One dog of any size is allowed for no additional pet fee with a credit card on file.

Best Western Deer Park Inn & Suites
262 Commerce Street (Hwy 13)
Craig, CO
970-824-9282 (800-780-7234)
Dogs are allowed for a $100 refundable deposit plus an additional one time pet fee of $10 per room. 2 dogs may be allowed.

Holiday Inn Hotel and Suites
300 Colorado Hwy 13
Craig, CO
970-824-4000 (877-270-6405)
Dogs of all sizes are allowed for no additional fee. 2 dogs may be allowed.

Super 8 Craig
200 Hwy 13 South
Craig, CO
970-824-3471 (800-800-8000)
Dogs of all sizes are allowed. There is a $4 per night pet fee per pet. Smoking and non-smoking rooms are available for pet rooms. 2 dogs may be allowed.

The Ruby of Crested Butte
624 Gothic Avenue
Crested Butte, CO
970-349-1338
Dogs of all sizes are allowed. There is a pet policy to sign at check in and there are no additional fees. 2 dogs may be allowed.

Best Western Sundance
903 Main Street
Delta, CO
970-874-9781 (800-780-7234)
Dogs are allowed for an additional fee of $10 per night per pet. Dogs may not be left alone in the room alone. Multiple dogs may be allowed.

Comfort Inn
180 Gunnison River Drive
Delta, CO
970-874-1000 (877-424-6423)
Quiet dogs are allowed for an additional fee of $10 per night per pet. Multiple dogs may be allowed.

Cameron Motel
4500 E Evans

Denver, CO
303-757-2100
Dogs of all sizes are allowed. There is a $5 per night per pet additional fee. Dogs must be well behaved, leashed, and cleaned up after. Multiple dogs may be allowed.

Comfort Inn
401 E 58th Avenue
Denver, CO
303-297-1717 (877-424-6423)
Dogs up to 50 pounds are allowed for an additional fee of $10 per night per pet. 2 dogs may be allowed.

Comfort Inn Downtown
401 17th Street
Denver, CO
303-296-0400 (877-424-6423)
Dogs are allowed for an additional one time fee of $50 per pet. 2 dogs may be allowed.

Days Inn Central Denver
620 Federal Blvd
Denver, CO
303-571-1715 (800-329-7466)
Dogs of all sizes are allowed. There is a $50 returnable deposit required per room. There is a $25 one time pet fee per visit. 2 dogs may be allowed.

Denver East Drury Inn
4380 Peoria Street
Denver, CO
303-373-1983 (800-378-7946)
Dogs of all sizes are permitted. Pets are not allowed in the breakfast area of the hotel. Pets are not to be left unattended, and each guest must assume liability for damage of property or other guest complaints. There is a limit of one pet per room.

Doubletree
3203 Quebec Street
Denver, CO
303-321-3333
Dogs of all sizes are allowed. There is a $20 one time fee per pet. No pit bulls are allowed per Denver law. 2 dogs may be allowed.

Embassy Suites Hotel Denver - Aurora
4444 N. Havana
Denver, CO
303-375-0400
Dogs of all sizes are allowed. There are no additional pet fees. Dogs are not allowed to be left alone in the room.

Embassy Suites Hotel Denver - Southeast (Hampden Ave.)

7525 East Hampden Ave.
Denver, CO
303-696-6644
Dogs of all sizes are allowed. There is a $50 one time pet fee per visit. Dogs are not allowed to be left alone in the room.

Four Points by Sheraton Denver South East
6363 East Hampden Ave.
Denver, CO
303-758-7000 (888-625-5144)
Dogs of all sizes are allowed. There are no additional pet fees. Dogs are not allowed to be left alone in the room.

Guest House Inn
3737 Quebec St.
Denver, CO
303-388-6161 (800-2-RAMADA)
There is a $100 refundable pet deposit.

Hampton Inn
5001 S Ulster Street
Denver, CO
303-894-9900
Well behaved dogs of all sizes are allowed. There are no additional pet fees, and a pet policy to sign at check-in. Multiple dogs may be allowed.

Holiday Inn
4849 Bannock Street
Denver, CO
303-292-9500 (877-270-6405)
Dogs of all sizes are allowed for an additional $50 one time pet fee per room. 2 dogs may be allowed.

Hotel Monaco Denver
1717 Champa Street at 17th
Denver, CO
303-296-1717
monaco-denver.com/
Well-behaved dogs of all sizes are welcome at this pet-friendly hotel. The luxury boutique hotel offers both rooms and suites. Hotel amenities include complimentary evening wine service, a 24 hour on-site fitness room, and a gift shop. There are no pet fees, just sign a pet liability form.

Hotel Teatro
1100 Fourteenth Street
Denver, CO
303-228-1100
hotelteatro.com/
Dogs are allowed at this luxury boutique hotel. There is no extra pet charge.

Inn at Cherry Creek
233 Clayton Street
Denver, CO
303-377-8577
innatcherrycreek.com/
Located in the heart of the Cherry Creek North shopping and restaurant district, this unique hotel features 35 cozy quest rooms and 2 corporate residences with an outdoor roof-top terrace that is perfect for open air parties. There are many in-room amenities, and a full service restaurant/bar that puts focus on a fresh seasonally influenced menu. Dogs of all sizes are allowed for an additional pet fee of $10 per night per room. Dogs may only be left alone in the room if they will be quiet and well behaved. Dogs must be leashed and cleaned up after at all times. Multiple dogs may be allowed.

JW Marriott Denver at Cherry Creek
150 Clayton Lane
Denver, CO
303-316-2700 (800-228-9290)
Dogs of all sizes are welcome with treats and special attention. There is a pet registration form to fill out, and they provide bedding, personalized bowls, and a pet walking service. There are no additional fees. Dogs must be quiet, well behaved, leashed, cleaned up after, and a contact number left with the front desk if they are in the room alone. Multiple dogs may be allowed.

La Quinta Inn Denver Central
3500 Park Ave. West
Denver, CO
303-458-1222 (800-531-5900)
Dogs of all sizes are allowed. There are no additional pet fees. Dogs must be crated with the "Do Not Disturb" sign on the door when left alone in the room, and crated or removed for housekeeping. Dogs must be leashed and cleaned up after. Multiple dogs may be allowed.

La Quinta Inn Denver Cherry Creek
1975 S. Colorado Blvd.
Denver, CO
303-758-8886 (800-531-5900)
Dogs of all sizes are allowed. There are no additional pet fees. Dogs may not be left unattended, and they must be leashed and cleaned up after. Multiple dogs may be allowed.

Loews Denver Hotel
4150 East Mississippi Ave.
Denver, CO
303-782-9300
All well-behaved dogs of any size are welcome. This upscale hotel offers

their "Loews Loves Pets" program which includes special pet treats, local dog walking routes, and a list of nearby pet-friendly places to visit. There are no pet fees.

Marriott TownePlace Suites - Downtown
685 Speer Blvd
Denver, CO
303-722-2322 (800-257-3000)
towneplacesuites.com/dencb
Marriott TownePlace Suites is an all suite hotel designed for the extended stay traveler. All studio, one, and two-bedroom suites offer full kitchens and weekly housekeeping. Pets are welcome for a non-refundable fee of $20 a day up to $200.00. On-site amenities include a guest laundry, business center, fitness room and free parking.

Motel 6 - Denver
3050 West 49th Avenue
Denver, CO
303-455-8888 (800-466-8356)
One well-behaved family pet per room. Guest must notify front desk upon arrival. Guest is liable for any damages. In consideration of all guests, pets must never be left unattended in the guest rooms.

Motel 6 - Denver - Airport
12020 East 39th Avenue
Denver, CO
303-371-1980 (800-466-8356)
One well-behaved family pet per room. Guest must notify front desk upon arrival. Guest is liable for any damages. In consideration of all guests, pets must never be left unattended in the guest rooms.

Oxford Hotel
1600 17th St
Denver, CO
303-628-5400 (800-228-5838)
theoxfordhotel.com
This hotel is located in Denver's trendy LoDo District. Please mention that you are bringing a pet when making reservations.

Red Lion
4040 Quebec Street
Denver, CO
303-321-6666
Dogs of all sizes are allowed. There is a $25 one time fee per pet. Multiple dogs may be allowed.

Red Roof Inn - Denver Airport
6890 Tower Road
Denver, CO
303-371-5300 (800-RED-ROOF)

One well-behaved family pet per room. Guest must notify front desk upon arrival. Guest is liable for any damages. In consideration of all guests, pets must never be left unattended in the guest rooms.

Residence Inn by Marriott
2777 Zuni Street
Denver, CO
303-458-5318
Dogs of all sizes are allowed. There is a $75 one time fee and a pet policy to sign at check in. Multiple dogs may be allowed.

Staybridge Suites
4200 East Virginia Avenue
Denver, CO
303-321-5757 (877-270-6405)
Dogs of all sizes are allowed for an additional pet fee of $20 per night per room for up to 4 nights; 5 nights or more is $150, and there is a pet agreement to sign. Dogs must be crated when alone in the room. 2 dogs may be allowed.

Super 8 Denver/I-25 and 58th Ave
5888 N Broadway
Denver, CO
303-296-3100 (800-800-8000)
Dogs up to 60 pounds are allowed. There is a $25 one time per pet fee per visit. Smoking and non-smoking rooms are available for pet rooms. 2 dogs may be allowed.

The Curtis Hotel
1405 Curtis Street
Denver, CO
800-525-6651
There is a $50 refundable pet deposit.

The Timbers
4411 Peoria Street
Denver, CO
303-373-1444
Dogs of all sizes are allowed. There is a $25 per stay per room fee and a pet policy to sign at check in. 2 dogs may be allowed.

The Westin Tabor Center
1672 Lawrence St.
Denver, CO
303-572-9100 (888-625-5144)
Dogs up to 50 pounds are allowed. There are no additional pet fees. Dogs are not allowed to be left alone in the room.

TownePlace Suites Denver Downtown
685 Speer Blvd
Denver, CO

303-722-2322
Dogs of all sizes are allowed. There is a $20 per night pet fee per pet. 2 dogs may be allowed.

TownePlace Suites Denver Southeast
3699 S Monaco Parkway
Denver, CO
303-759-9393
Dogs of all sizes are allowed. There is a $25 per night pet fee per pet. . 2 dogs may be allowed.

Best Western Ptarmigan Lodge
652 Lake Dillon Drive
Dillon, CO
970-468-2341 (800-780-7234)
Dogs are allowed for an additional one time fee of $15 per pet. Multiple dogs may be allowed.

Super 8 Dillon/Breckenridge Area
808 Little Beaver Trail
Dillon, CO
970-468-8888 (800-800-8000)
Dogs up to 60 pounds are allowed. There is a $15 one time per pet fee per visit. Smoking and non-smoking rooms are available for pet rooms. 2 dogs may be allowed.

Comfort Inn
2930 N Main Avenue
Durango, CO
970-259-5373 (877-424-6423)
Dogs are allowed for an additional fee of $10 per night per pet. Multiple dogs may be allowed.

Days Inn Durango
1700 County Rd 203
Durango, CO
970-259-1430 (800-329-7466)
Dogs of all sizes are allowed. There are no additional pet fees. Multiple dogs may be allowed.

Doubletree
501 Camino Del Rio
Durango, CO
970-259-6580
Dogs up to 50 pounds are allowed. There is a $15 per night per room pet fee. 2 dogs may be allowed.

Holiday Inn
800 Camino Del Rio
Durango, CO
970-247-5393 (877-270-6405)
Dogs of all sizes are allowed for an additional fee of $10 per night per pet. 2 dogs may be allowed.

Quality Inn and Suites
455 S Camino Del Rio
Durango, CO

970-259-7900 (877-424-6423)
Dogs are allowed for an additional fee of $10 (plus tax) per night per pet. Multiple dogs may be allowed.

Rochester Hotel
726 E. Second Ave.
Durango, CO
970-385-1920 (800-664-1920)
rochesterhotel.com/
This beautifully renovated hotel offers fifteen spacious rooms with high ceilings, king or queen beds, and private baths, and is decorated in an Old West motif. This hotel, located in downtown Durango, was designated as "The Flagship Hotel of Colorado" by Conde' Nast Traveler. They are very pet-friendly and offer two pet rooms, with a $20 per day pet charge.

Best Western Eagle Lodge
200 Loren Ln
Eagle, CO
970-328-6316 (800-780-7234)
Dogs are allowed for an additional fee of $10 per night per pet. 2 dogs may be allowed.

Holiday Inn Express
I-70 Exit 147 & Pond Rd
Eagle, CO
970-328-8088 (877-270-6405)
Dogs of all sizes are allowed for an additional one time pet fee of $40 per room. 2 dogs may be allowed.

Denver Tech Center Drury Inn & Suites
9445 East Dry Creek Road
Englewood, CO
303-694-3400 (800-378-7946)
Dogs of all sizes are permitted. Pets are not allowed in the breakfast area of the hotel. Pets are not to be left unattended, and each guest must assume liability for damage of property or other guest complaints. There is a limit of one pet per room.

Hampton Inn
9231 E Arapahoe Road
Englewood, CO
303-792-9999
Dogs of all sizes are allowed. There is a $10 per night per pet fee and a pet policy to sign at check in. Multiple dogs may be allowed.

Holiday Inn Express Hotel and Suites
7380 South Clinton St
Englewood, CO
303-662-0777 (877-270-6405)
Dogs of all sizes are allowed for an additional pet fee of $50 per night per room. 2 dogs may be allowed.

Residence Inn by Marriott
8322 S Valley Highway
Englewood, CO
720-895-0200
Dogs of all sizes are allowed. There is a $75 one time fee and a pet policy to sign at check in. Multiple dogs may be allowed.

Residence Inn by Marriott
6565 S Yosemite
Englewood, CO
303-740-7177
Dogs of all sizes are allowed. There is a $75 one time fee per pet and a pet policy to sign at check in. Multiple dogs may be allowed.

Sheraton Denver Technical Center Hotel
7007 South Clinton St.
Englewood, CO
303-799-6200 (888-625-5144)
Dogs up to 80 pounds are allowed for no additional pet fee. Dogs may not be left alone in the room.

TownePlace Suites Denver Tech Center
7877 S Chester Street
Englewood, CO
720-875-1113
Dogs of all sizes are allowed. There is a $25 per night ($200 max) pet fee per pet. 2 dogs may be allowed.

Holiday Inn
101 South St. Vrain Avenue
Estes Park, CO
970-586-2332 (877-270-6405)
Dogs of all sizes are allowed for an additional one time pet fee of $30 per room. Multiple dogs may be allowed.

Motel 6 - Greeley - Evans
3015 8th Avenue
Evans, CO
970-351-6481 (800-466-8356)
One well-behaved family pet per room. Guest must notify front desk upon arrival. Guest is liable for any damages. In consideration of all guests, pets must never be left unattended in the guest rooms.

Sleep Inn
3025 8th Avenue
Evans, CO
970-356-2180 (877-424-6423)
One or 2 dogs are allowed for an additional one time pet fee of $15 per room; the fee is $25 for 3 to 4 dogs. Multiple dogs may be allowed.

Best Western Kiva Inn
1638 E Mulberry Street
Fort Collins, CO
970-484-2444 (800-780-7234)
Dogs are allowed for an additional fee of $10 per night per pet. Dogs may not be left alone in the room at any time. Multiple dogs may be allowed.

Best Western University Inn
914 S College Avenue
Fort Collins, CO
970-484-1984 (800-780-7234)
Dogs are allowed for an additional pet fee of $15 per night per room. Dogs may not be left alone in the room. Multiple dogs may be allowed.

Comfort Suites
1415 Oakridge Drive
Fort Collins, CO
970-206-4597 (877-424-6423)
Dogs are allowed for an additional pet fee of $15 per night per room. Multiple dogs may be allowed.

Days Inn Fort Collins
3625 E Mulberry St
Fort Collins, CO
970-221-5490 (800-329-7466)
Dogs of all sizes are allowed. There is a $5 per night pet fee per pet. 2 dogs may be allowed.

Fort Collins Marriott
350 E Horsetooth Road
Fort Collins, CO
970-226-5200 (800-228-9290)
Well behaved dogs of all sizes are allowed. There is a $10 per room per stay additional pet fee. Dogs must be quiet, housebroken, leashed, cleaned up after, and a contact number left with the front desk if they are in the room alone. Multiple dogs may be allowed.

Hampton Inn
1620 Oakridge Drive
Fort Collins, CO
970-229-5927
Well behaved dogs up to 50 pounds are allowed. There is a $25 per pet per stay fee and a pet policy to sign at check in. Dogs may not be left in the room unattended. Multiple dogs may be allowed.

Hilton
425 W Prospect Road
Fort Collins, CO
970-482-2626
Quiet, well behaved dogs are allowed for an additional one time pet fee of $25 per room. Multiple dogs may be allowed.

Holiday Inn Express Hotel & Suites
Ft. Collins
1426 Oakridge Drive
Fort Collins, CO
970-225-2200 (877-270-6405)
Dogs of all sizes are allowed for an additional one time pet fee of $30 per room. Multiple dogs may be allowed.

Motel 6 - Fort Collins
3900 East Mulberry
Fort Collins, CO
970-482-6466 (800-466-8356)
One well-behaved family pet per room. Guest must notify front desk upon arrival. Guest is liable for any damages. In consideration of all guests, pets must never be left unattended in the guest rooms.

Quality Inn and Suites
4001 S Mason Street
Fort Collins, CO
970-282-9047 (877-424-6423)
Dogs are allowed for an additional one time fee of $25 per pet 2 dogs may be allowed.

Residence Inn by Marriott
1127 Oakridge Drive
Fort Collins, CO
970-223-5700
Dogs of all sizes are allowed. There is a $75 one time fee and a pet policy to sign at check in. Multiple dogs may be allowed.

Sleep Inn
3808 Mulberry Street
Fort Collins, CO
970-484-5515 (877-424-6423)
Dogs are allowed for an additional one time pet fee of $10 per room. 2 dogs may be allowed.

Sundance Trail Guest Ranch
17931 Red Feather Lakes Rd
Fort Collins, CO
970-224-1222 (800-357-4930)
sundancetrail.com
This is a summer family Dude Ranch. During Fall, Winter and Spring this is a Country Lodge with horse back riding. There are no additional pet fees and the entire ranch is non-smoking.

Motel 6 - Fort Lupton
65 South Grand Avenue
Fort Lupton, CO
303-857-1800 (800-466-8356)
One well-behaved family pet per room. Guest must notify front desk upon arrival. Guest is liable for any damages. In consideration of all guests, pets must never be left

unattended in the guest rooms.

Best Western Park Terrace Inn & Memories Restaurant
725 Main Street
Fort Morgan, CO
970-867-8256 (800-780-7234)
One dog is allowed for a pet fee of $10 per night; a 2nd dog is an additional $5 per night, and a credit card must be on file. 2 dogs may be allowed.

Holiday Inn
1129 N. Summit Blvd
Frisco, CO
970-668-5000 (877-270-6405)
Dogs of all sizes are allowed for an additional one time pet fee of $20 per room. Multiple dogs may be allowed.

Hotel Frisco
308 Main Street
Frisco, CO
970-668-5009 (800-262-1002)
Dogs are welcome at this classic Rocky Mountain lodge which is located on Frisco's historic Main Street. The hotel offers two dog-friendly rooms with access to the back porch and to the doggie run. Enjoy hiking and swimming with your dog right from the hotel's front door! Dog amenities include dog beds and treats. Dog sitting and walking services are also available. There is a $10 per day pet fee.

Woods Inn
Second Ave and Granite St
Frisco, CO
970-668-2255
woodsinn.biz
The Woods Inn is located in the heart of Colorado ski country. They offer a range of accommodations, from full condo-style suites to single bunks. Breckenridge is just minutes away and Vail is not far. There is a $15 one time per stay pet charge.

Comfort Inn
400 Jurassic Avenue
Fruita, CO
970-858-1333 (877-424-6423)
Quiet dogs are allowed for no additional pet fee with a credit card on file. Multiple dogs may be allowed.

La Quinta Inn & Suites Fruita
570 Raptor Road
Fruita, CO
970-858-8850 (800-531-5900)
Dogs of all sizes are allowed. There are no additional pet fees. Dogs

must be crated when left alone in the room, and they may not be left unattended at all between the hours or 8 pm and 9 am. Dogs must be kept leashed. Multiple dogs may be allowed.

Hotel Colorado
526 Pine Street
Glenwood Springs, CO
970-945-6511 (800-544-3998)
This elegant hotel offers a superior setting and a great location near a wide variety of recreational opportunities. Dogs of all sizes are allowed. There is a $15 per night per pet additional fee. Dogs must be declared at check in, and they prefer that dogs are not left alone in the room because the hotel is also registered as a "haunted hotel". If it is necessary for a short time, a Do Not Disturb sign can be put on the door. If there is a chance they may become uncomfortable and/or bark, they request you leave a contact number at the front desk, and they must be crated unless they will be relaxed and quiet. Dogs must be well behaved, leashed, and cleaned up after. Multiple dogs may be allowed.

Quality Inn and Suites on the River
2650 Gilstrap Court
Glenwood Springs, CO
970-945-5995 (877-424-6423)
Dogs are allowed for an additional pet fee of $10 per night per room. Dogs may not be left alone in the room. Multiple dogs may be allowed.

Red Mountain Inn
51637 H 6/24
Glenwood Springs, CO
970-945-6353 (800-748-2565)
Dogs of all sizes are allowed. There is a $10 per night per pet additional fee. Dogs may only be left alone in the room if they will be well behaved and quiet, and the Do Not Disturb sign is put on the door. Dogs must be leashed and cleaned up after. 2 dogs may be allowed.

Candlewood Suites
895 Tabor Street
Golden, CO
303-232-7171 (877-270-6405)
Dogs up to 80 pounds are allowed for an additional $75 one time fee per pet. 2 dogs may be allowed.

Clarion Collection The Golden Hotel
800 11th Street
Golden, CO
303-279-0100 (877-424-6423)
Dogs are allowed for a $100 refundable deposit plus an additional

pet fee of $15 per night per room. 2 dogs may be allowed.

Comfort Suites
11909 W 6th Avenue
Golden, CO
303-231-9929 (877-424-6423)
Dogs are allowed for no additional pet fee. Multiple dogs may be allowed.

Denver Marriott West
1717 Denver West, Marriott Blvd
Golden, CO
303-279-9100 (800-228-9290)
Dogs of all sizes are allowed. There is a $50 one time additional pet fee per room. Dogs must be leashed, cleaned up after, and the Do Not Disturb sign put on the door if they are in the room alone. Multiple dogs may be allowed.

La Quinta Inn Denver Golden
3301 Youngfield Service Rd.
Golden, CO
303-279-5565 (800-531-5900)
Dogs of all sizes are allowed. There are no additional pet fees. Dogs may only be left unattended in the room if they will be quiet and well behaved. Multiple dogs may be allowed.

Quality Suites at Evergreen Parkway
29300 H 40
Golden, CO
303-526-2000
Dogs are allowed for a $50 refundable pet deposit. Multiple dogs may be allowed.

Best Western Sandman Motel
708 Horizon Drive
Grand Junction, CO
970-243-4150 (800-780-7234)
One dog is allowed for an additional one time pet fee of $25.

Holiday Inn
755 Horizon Drive
Grand Junction, CO
970-243-6790 (877-270-6405)
Dogs of all sizes are allowed for no additional pet fee. Dogs may not be left alone in the room at any time. 2 dogs may be allowed.

La Quinta Inn & Suites Grand Junction
2761 Crossroads Blvd.
Grand Junction, CO
970-241-2929 (800-531-5900)
Dogs of all sizes are allowed. There are no additional pet fees. Dogs may not be left unattended, and they must be leashed and cleaned up after. Dogs must be crated or removed for

housekeeping. Multiple dogs may be allowed.

Motel 6 - Grand Junction
776 Horizon Drive
Grand Junction, CO
970-243-2628 (800-466-8356)
One well-behaved family pet per room. Guest must notify front desk upon arrival. Guest is liable for any damages. In consideration of all guests, pets must never be left unattended in the guest rooms.

Quality Inn
733 Horizon Drive
Grand Junction, CO
970-245-7200 (877-424-6423)
Dogs are allowed for an additional one time pet fee of $10 per room. 2 dogs may be allowed.

Super 8 Grand Junction
728 Horizon Dr
Grand Junction, CO
970-248-8080 (800-800-8000)
Dogs of all sizes are allowed. There is a $10 per night pet fee per pet. Smoking and non-smoking rooms are available for pet rooms. 2 dogs may be allowed.

Mountain Lakes Lodge
10480 H 34
Grand Lake, CO
970-627-8448
Dogs of all sizes are allowed. There is a $10 per night per pet fee and a pet policy to sign at check in. They also provide a care package for your dog. 2 dogs may be allowed.

La Quinta Inn & Suites Denver Englewood/Tech Ctr
9009 E. Arapahoe Road
Greenwood Village, CO
303-799-4555 (800-531-5900)
Dogs of all sizes are allowed. There are no additional pet fees. Dogs must be leashed, cleaned up after, removed for housekeeping, and the front desk notified if there is a pet in the room alone. 2 dogs may be allowed.

Motel 6 - Denver South - South Tech Center
9201 East Arapahoe Road
Greenwood Village, CO
303-790-8220 (800-466-8356)
One well-behaved family pet per room. Guest must notify front desk upon arrival. Guest is liable for any damages. In consideration of all guests, pets must never be left unattended in the guest rooms.

Sleep Inn Denver Tech Center
9257 E Costilla Avenue
Greenwood Village, CO
303-662-9950 (877-424-6423)
Dogs are allowed for an additional one time fee of $25 per pet. 2 dogs may be allowed.

Gunnison Lodging Company
412 E. Tomichi Ave
Gunnison, CO
970-641-0700 (866-641-0700)
gunnisonlodging.com
Your dog is welcome at the Gunnison Inn and the Cottages within easy walking distance to many amenities and parks.

Residence Inn by Marriott
93 W Centennial Blvd
Highlands Ranch, CO
303-683-5500
Dogs of all sizes are allowed. There is a $75 one time fee and a pet policy to sign at check in. Multiple dogs may be allowed.

Holiday Inn Express
27994 US Hwy 50 Frontage Road
La Junta, CO
719-384-2900 (877-270-6405)
Dogs of all sizes are allowed for an additional pet fee of $15 per night per room. 2 dogs may be allowed.

Bearadise Cabins & RV Park
404 S Oak Street
LaVeta, CO
719-742-6221
Dogs of all sizes are allowed. There are no additional pet fees. Multiple dogs may be allowed.

La Quinta Inn & Suites Denver Southwest Lakewood
7190 West Hampden Ave.
Lakewood, CO
303-969-9700 (800-531-5900)
Dogs of most sizes are allowed; no extra large dogs. There are no additional pet fees. Dogs may only be left unattended in the room if they will be very quiet and well behaved, and leave the "Do Not Disturb" sign on the door. Dogs must be leashed. 2 dogs may be allowed.

Motel 6 - Denver - Lakewood
480 Wadsworth Boulevard
Lakewood, CO
303-232-4924 (800-466-8356)
One well-behaved family pet per room. Guest must notify front desk upon arrival. Guest is liable for any damages. In consideration of all guests, pets must never be left unattended in the guest rooms.

Quality Suites Southwest
7260 W Jefferson
Lakewood, CO
303-988-8600
Dogs up to 60 pounds are allowed for no additional pet fee. 2 dogs may be allowed.

Residence Inn by Marriott
7050 W Hampden Avenue
Lakewood, CO
303-985-7676
Dogs of all sizes are allowed. Up to 2 dogs and one cat can be in the studios, and up to 3 dogs in the 2 bedroom suites. There is a $75 one time fee and a pet policy to sign at check in. .

Sheraton Denver West Hotel
360 Union Blvd.
Lakewood, CO
303-987-2000 (888-625-5144)
Dogs are allowed for no additional pet fee. Dogs are restricted to rooms on the 4th floor only, and they may only be left alone in the room for very short periods. 2 dogs may be allowed.

Super 8 Lakewood/Denver Area
7240 W Jefferson Ave
Lakewood, CO
303-989-4600 (800-800-8000)
Dogs of all sizes are allowed. There is a $10 per night pet fee per pet. Smoking and non-smoking rooms are available for pet rooms. 2 dogs may be allowed.

Best Western Denver Southwest
3440 S Vance Street
Lakewood (Denver), CO
303-989-5500 (800-780-7234)
Dogs are allowed for no additional pet fee. Multiple dogs may be allowed.

Best Western Cow Palace Inn
1301 N Main Street
Lamar, CO
719-336-7753 (800-780-7234)
Dogs are allowed for no additional pet fee. Multiple dogs may be allowed.

Super 8 Lamar
1202 N Main
Lamar, CO
719-336-3427 (800-800-8000)
Dogs of all sizes are allowed. There are no additional pet fees. Smoking and non-smoking rooms are available for pet rooms. 2 dogs may be allowed.

Best Western Bent's Fort Inn
E US 50
Las Animas, CO
719-456-0011 (800-780-7234)
Dogs are allowed for an additional fee of $10 per night per pet. Multiple dogs may be allowed.

Best Western Limon Inn
925 T Avenue Junction I-70 & Highway 24
Limon, CO
719-775-0277 (800-780-7234)
Dogs are allowed for an additional fee of $20 per night per pet. Multiple dogs may be allowed.

Holiday Inn Express Hotel & Suites Littleton
12683 West Indore Place
Littleton, CO
720-981-1000 (877-270-6405)
Dogs of all sizes are allowed for no additional pet fee. A contact number must be left with the front desk if a pet is in the room alone. Multiple dogs may be allowed.

TownePlace Suites Denver Southwest/Littleton
10902 W Toller Drive
Littleton, CO
303-972-0555
Dogs of all sizes are allowed. There is a $10 one time pet fee per visit. . 2 dogs may be allowed.

Staybridge Suites
7820 Park Meadows Dr
Lone Tree, CO
303-649-1010 (877-270-6405)
Dogs of all sizes are allowed for an additional pet fee of $20 per night per room to a total of no more than $100 per stay. 2 dogs may be allowed.

Holiday Inn Express Hotel & Suites Longmont
1355 Dry Creek Drive
Longmont, CO
303-684-0404 (877-270-6405)
Dogs of all sizes are allowed for an additional one time pet fee of $30 per room. 2 dogs may be allowed.

Residence Inn by Marriott
1450 Dry Creek Drive
Longmont, CO
303-702-9933
Dogs of all sizes are allowed. There is a $50 one time fee for up to 6 nights, and a $100 one time fee after 6 days. 2 dogs may be allowed.

Super 8 Longmont/Del Camino

Area
10805 Turner Blvd
Longmont, CO
303-772-0888 (800-800-8000)
Dogs of all sizes are allowed. There are no additional pet fees. Dogs are not allowed to be left alone in the room. Smoking and non-smoking rooms are available for pet rooms. 2 dogs may be allowed.

Super 8 Longmont/Twin Peaks Area
2446 N Main St
Longmont, CO
303-772-8106 (800-800-8000)
Dogs of all sizes are allowed. There is a $5-7 per night pet fee per pet depending on size. Smoking and non-smoking rooms are available for pet rooms. 2 dogs may be allowed.

Comfort Inn
1196 Dillon Road
Louisville, CO
303-604-0181 (877-424-6423)
Dogs are allowed for an additional pet fee of $10 per night per room. 2 dogs may be allowed.

La Quinta Inn & Suites Denver Louisville Boulder
902 Dillon Rd.
Louisville, CO
303-664-0100 (800-531-5900)
Dogs of all sizes are allowed. There are no additional pet fees. There is a pet waiver to sign at check in, and a cell number needs to be left with the front desk if your pet is left alone in the room. Also, place the "Do Not Disturb" sign on the door so housekeeping does not enter. There is a specified pet area where dogs are to be taken, and they must be leashed and cleaned up after. Multiple dogs may be allowed.

Quality Inn and Suites
960 W Dillon Road
Louisville, CO
303-327-1215 (877-424-6423)
Dogs are allowed for an additional pet fee of $15 per night per room. 2 dogs may be allowed.

Residence Inn by Marriott
845 Coal Creek Circle
Louisville, CO
303-665-2661
Dogs of all sizes are allowed There is a $75 one time fee, and a pet policy to sign at check in. Multiple dogs may be allowed.

Best Western Crossroads Inn & Conference Center
5542 E US Highway 34

Loveland, CO
970-667-7810 (800-780-7234)
Dogs are allowed for an additional fee of $15 per night per pet for 1 to 6 days; the weekly fee is $30 per week per pet. Multiple dogs may be allowed.

Far View Lodge
Mesa Verde National Park
Mancos, CO
970-529-4421
Far View Lodge sits on a high shoulder of the Mesa Verde, offering panoramic vistas into three states. There is a $50 refundable pet deposit. Pets are allowed in some of the standard rooms.

Morefield Lodge and Campground
34879 H 160
Mancos, CO
800-449-2288
Dogs of all sizes are allowed. There is a $25 per night per pet additional fee. Dogs may not be left unattended, and they must be leashed and cleaned up after. There is an RV and campground on site where dogs are allowed at no extra fee. Dogs may not be on the trails or in the camp buildings. Multiple dogs may be allowed.

Best Western Red Arrow
1702 E Main Street
Montrose, CO
970-249-9641 (800-780-7234)
Dogs up to 60 pounds are allowed for an additional fee of $10 per night per pet. 2 dogs may be allowed.

Black Canyon Motel
1605 E. Main Street
Montrose, CO
970-249-3495 (800-348-3495)
innfinders.com/blackcyn/
There is a $5 per day additional pet fee.

Holiday Inn Express Hotel & Suites
1391 South Townsend Ave
Montrose, CO
970-240-1800 (877-270-6405)
Dogs of all sizes are allowed for no additional pet fee. 2 dogs may be allowed.

Quality Inn and Suites
2751 Commercial Way
Montrose, CO
970-249-1011 (877-424-6423)
Dogs are allowed for an additional fee of $10 per night per pet. Multiple dogs may be allowed.

San Juan Inn

1480 Highway 550 South
Montrose, CO
970-249-6644
There is a $12 per day pet charge.

Best Western Lodge at Nederland
55 Lakeview Drive
Nederland, CO
303-258-9463 (800-780-7234)
Dogs are allowed for an additional fee of $10 per night per pet. Multiple dogs may be allowed.

Comfort Inn
191 5th Avenue
Ouray, CO
970-325-7203 (877-424-6423)
Dogs are allowed for an additional fee of $10 per night per pet. Multiple dogs may be allowed.

Rivers Edge Motel
110 7th Avenue
Ouray, CO
970-325-4621
There is a $10 per day pet charge.

Fireside Inn
1600 E Hwy 160
Pagosa Springs, CO
970-264-9204 (888-264-9204)
They offer modern one and two bedroom cabins (built in 1996) with fireplaces, hot tubs, kitchens and more. The cabins are located on seven acres on the San Juan River. Dogs and horses are welcome. There is a $7.50 per day additional pet fee.

High Country Lodge
3821 E Hwy 160
Pagosa Springs, CO
970-264-4181 (800-862-3707)
Dogs are allowed in the cabins. There is a $15 one time pet charge. All cabins are non-smoking.

Holiday Inn Express Hotel and Suites
221 Grand Valley Way
Parachute, CO
970-285-2330 (877-270-6405)
Dogs up to 50 pounds are allowed for an additional one time pet fee of $25 per room. 2 dogs may be allowed.

Holiday Inn Select
19308 Cottonwood Drive
Parker, CO
303-248-2147 (877-270-6405)
Dogs of all sizes are allowed. There is an additional one time pet fee of $75 per room if the pet is kept crated; the fee is $150 per room if the pet is uncrated in the room. 2

dogs may be allowed.

Best Western Eagleridge Inn & Suites
4727 N Elizabeth Street
Pueblo, CO
719-543-4644 (800-780-7234)
Dogs are allowed for an additional pet fee of $15 per night per room. Multiple dogs may be allowed.

Hampton Inn
4703 North Freeway
Pueblo, CO
719-544-4700
Dogs up to 50 pounds are allowed. There is a $15 per room per stay fee. Multiple dogs may be allowed.

Motel 6 - Pueblo - Highway 50
960 Highway 50 West
Pueblo, CO
719-543-8900 (800-466-8356)
One well-behaved family pet per room. Guest must notify front desk upon arrival. Guest is liable for any damages. In consideration of all guests, pets must never be left unattended in the guest rooms.

Motel 6 - Pueblo I-25
4103 North Elizabeth Street
Pueblo, CO
719-543-6221 (800-466-8356)
One well-behaved family pet per room. Guest must notify front desk upon arrival. Guest is liable for any damages. In consideration of all guests, pets must never be left unattended in the guest rooms.

Sundance Trail Guest Ranch
17931 Red Feather Lakes Road
Red Feather Lakes, CO
970-224-1222
Dogs of all sizes are allowed. There are no additional pet fees. Multiple dogs may be allowed.

River's Edge
15184 Highway 133
Redstone, CO
970-963-8368
Dogs of all sizes are allowed, however there can only be a maximum of 2 large or 3 small dogs to a room. There are no additional pet fees.

Buckskin Inn
101 Ray Avenue
Rifle, CO
970-625-1741 (877-282-5754)
buckskininn.com/
Amenities include Satellite TV, multiple HBO, microwaves, refrigerators, and free local calls.

There is no charge for a pet, but please let staff know when reserving a room. Pets cannot be left unattended in the rooms. Multiple dogs may be allowed.

Super 8 Salida
525 W Rainbow
Salida, CO
719-539-6689 (800-800-8000)
Dogs of all sizes are allowed. There are no additional pet fees. Smoking and non-smoking rooms are available for pet rooms. 2 dogs may be allowed.

Woodland Motel
903 W 1st Street
Salida, CO
719-539-4980
One large dog or up to 3 small dogs are allowed per room. There are no additional pet fees.

Days Inn Summit County
580 Silverthorne Lane
Silverthorne, CO
970-468-8661 (800-329-7466)
Dogs of all sizes are allowed. There is a $10 per night pet fee per pet. 2 dogs may be allowed.

Quality Inn and Suites
530 Silverthorne Lane
Silverthorne, CO
970-513-1222 (877-424-6423)
Dogs are allowed for an additional fee of $10 per night per pet. Multiple dogs may be allowed.

Canyon View Motel
661 Greene Street
Silverton, CO
970-387-5400
Every room really does have a canyon view here. Dogs of all sizes are welcomed with complimentary biscuits, and there are no additional pet fees. Dogs may not be left alone in the room, and they must be leashed and cleaned up after. Multiple dogs may be allowed.

The Wyman Hotel & Inn
1371 Greene Street
Silverton, CO
970-387-5372 (800-609-7845)
This hotel and inn, the recipient of several accolades for food and service and listed on the National Register of Historic Places, offer the ambiance of a bed and breakfast, and personal service for any special occasion. They feature a full gourmet breakfast each morning, and a 3-course candlelight diner each evening. Dogs of all sizes are

allowed. There is a $25 one time additional pet fee per pet, and a pet policy to sign at check in. Dogs may not be left alone in the room, and they must be leashed and cleaned up after. 2 dogs may be allowed.

Alpiner Lodge
424 Lincoln Ave.
Steamboat Springs, CO
970-879-1430 (800-538-7519)
toski.com/sli/2s.html
There is an $15 one time pet fee.

Comfort Inn
1055 Walton Creek Road
Steamboat Springs, CO
970-879-6669 (877-424-6423)
Dogs are allowed for no additional pet fee. 2 dogs may be allowed.

Holiday Inn
3190 S. Lincoln Ave
Steamboat Springs, CO
970-879-2250 (877-270-6405)
basshotels.com/holiday-inn
Dogs of all sizes are allowed for an additional fee of $10 per night per pet. Multiple dogs may be allowed.

La Quinta Inn Steamboat Springs
3155 Ingles Lane
Steamboat Springs, CO
970-871-1219 (800-531-5900)
Dogs of all sizes are allowed. There is a $10 per night per stay additional fee. Dogs may not be left unattended unless they will be quiet, well behaved, and a contact number left with the front desk. Dogs must be leashed and cleaned up after. Multiple dogs may be allowed.

Rabbit Ears Motel
201 Lincoln Avenue /H 40
Steamboat Springs, CO
970-879-1150
This motel is located across from the famous Steamboat Health and Recreation Association and their natural hot spring pools as well as several other worthy local attractions. Some of the amenities offered are a free full continental breakfast, discounted Hot Springs Pool passes, and a large gathering room. Dogs of all sizes are allowed. There is a $12 one time additional pet fee per room. Dogs may not be left alone in the room, and they must be leashed and cleaned up after. 2 dogs may be allowed.

Sheraton Steamboat Resort & Conference Center
2200 Village Inn Court

Steamboat Springs, CO
970-879-2220 (888-625-5144)
Dogs up to 80 pounds are allowed for an additional one time pet fee of $35 per room. Dogs may not be left alone in the room.

Best Western Golden Prairie Inn
700 Colorado Avenue
Stratton, CO
719-348-5311 (800-780-7234)
Dogs are allowed for an additional fee of $10 per night per pet. Multiple dogs may be allowed.

Hotel Columbia Telluride
300 W. San Juan Ave.
Telluride, CO
970-728-0660 (800-201-9505)
columbiatelluride.com/
This full service resort hotel welcomes your best friend. They are located just two blocks from the downtown shops and restaurants. There is a $15 per day pet charge. All rooms are non-smoking.

Mountain Lodge Telluride
457 Mountain Village Blvd.
Telluride, CO
866-368-6867
mountainlodgetelluride.com
This rustic pet-friendly lodge is located in Telluride's Mountain Village Resort community with views of the San Juan Mountains. There are 125 dog-friendly rooms in the lodge. There is a $25 per day pet fee up to a maximum of $100 per stay. The lodge offers pet beds, bowls and treats to their dog visitors and have pet pick-up stations around the property.

Wyndham Peaks Resort
136 Country Club Drive
Telluride, CO
970-728-6800 (800-789-2220)
thepeaksresort.com/
There is a $50 per day pet charge.

Motel 6 - Denver - Thorton
6 West 83rd Place
Thornton, CO
303-429-1550 (800-466-8356)
One well-behaved family pet per room. Guest must notify front desk upon arrival. Guest is liable for any damages. In consideration of all guests, pets must never be left unattended in the guest rooms.

Sleep Inn
12101 N Grant Street
Thornton, CO
303-280-9818 (877-424-6423)
Dogs up to 70 pounds are allowed

for an additional fee of $5 per night per pet. 2 dogs may be allowed.

Quality Inn
3125 Toupal Drive
Trinidad, CO
719-846-4491 (877-424-6423)
Dogs up to 50 pounds are allowed for an additional one time pet fee of $15 per room. 2 dogs may be allowed.

Super 8 Trinidad
1924 Freedom Rd
Trinidad, CO
719-846-8280 (800-800-8000)
Dogs of all sizes are allowed. There is a $11.09 one time per pet fee per visit. Smoking and non-smoking rooms are available for pet rooms. 2 dogs may be allowed.

Antlers at Vail
680 W. Lionshead Place
Vail, CO
970-476-2471 (800-843-8245)
antlersvail.com/
This hotel and condo complex is definitely dog-friendly. They have had large doggie guests like a 250 pound mastiff. They have several pet rooms and there is a $15 per day pet charge. There are no designated smoking or non-smoking units.

Holiday Inn
2211 N Frontage Road
Vail, CO
866-317-2739 (877-270-6405)
Dogs up to 50 pounds are allowed for an additional fee of $25 per night per room. 2 dogs may be allowed.

Lifthouse Condominiums
555 E Lionshead Circle
Vail, CO
970-476-2340 (800-654-0635)
lifthousevail.com/index.cfm
Looking out upon Vail's ski runs, the Lifthouse has a great location for many other activities, and offer several in-house amenities. Dogs of all sizes are allowed for an additional fee of $25 per night per pet. Dogs must be crated or removed for housekeeping, and they must be leashed and cleaned up after at all times. 2 dogs may be allowed.

Best Western Rambler
457 US Highway 85 87
Walsenburg, CO
719-738-1121 (800-780-7234)
Dogs up to 50 pounds are allowed for an additional fee of $10 per night per pet. 2 dogs may be allowed.

Jack's Cabin
30 County Road 388
Wentmore, CO
719-784-3160
Dogs of all sizes are allowed. There are no additional pet fees and they request you kennel your pet when out. Also do not let your pets out alone at night. 2 dogs may be allowed.

Residence Inn by Marriott
5010 W 88th Place
Westminister, CO
303-427-9500
Dogs of all sizes are allowed. There is a $75 one time fee and a pet policy to sign at check in. Multiple dogs may be allowed.

Doubletree
8773 Yates Drive
Westminster, CO
303-427-4000
Well behaved pets are allowed. There can be 3 small dogs or 2 large dogs per room, and no extra large dogs are allowed. Dogs are not allowed to be left in the room, except for short periods for meals in the hotel. There are no additional pet fees and they request to keep your dogs out of the public and food areas.

La Quinta Inn & Suites Westminster Promenade
10179 Church Ranch Way
Westminster, CO
303-438-5800 (800-531-5900)
Dogs of all sizes are allowed. There are no additional pet fees. Dogs must be leashed and cleaned up after. Multiple dogs may be allowed.

La Quinta Inn Denver Northglenn
345 West 120th Ave.
Westminster, CO
303-252-9800 (800-531-5900)
Dogs of all sizes are allowed. There are no additional pet fees. Dogs must be crated when left alone in the room. Dogs must be leashed and cleaned up after. Multiple dogs may be allowed.

La Quinta Inn Denver Westminster Mall
8701 Turnpike Dr.
Westminster, CO
303-425-9099 (800-531-5900)
One large dog or 2 small to medium dogs are allowed. There are no additional pet fees. Dogs must be leashed.

The Westin Westminster
10600 Westminster Blvd.
Westminster, CO
303-410-5000 (888-625-5144)
Dogs of all sizes are allowed. There are no additional pet fees. Dogs are not allowed to be left alone in the room.

Motel 6 - Denver (West)
9920 West 49th Avenue
Wheat Ridge, CO
303-424-0658 (800-466-8356)
One well-behaved family pet per room. Guest must notify front desk upon arrival. Guest is liable for any damages. In consideration of all guests, pets must never be left unattended in the guest rooms.

Motel 6 - Denver West - Wheat Ridge S
10300 South I-70 Frontage Road
Wheat Ridge, CO
303-467-3172 (800-466-8356)
One well-behaved family pet per room. Guest must notify front desk upon arrival. Guest is liable for any damages. In consideration of all guests, pets must never be left unattended in the guest rooms.

Best Western Alpenglo Lodge
78665 US Highway 40
Winter PARK, CO
970-726-8088 (800-780-7234)
Dogs are allowed for an additional one time pet fee of $10 per room. Multiple dogs may be allowed.

Beaver Village Lodge
79303 H 40
Winter Park, CO
970-726-5741
Dogs of all sizes are allowed. There are no additional pet fees. Multiple dogs may be allowed.

Connecticut Listings

Residence Inn by Marriott
55 Simsbury Road
Avon, CT
800-331-3131
Dogs of all sizes are allowed. There is a $25 per day fee up to a total of $250 for the month and a pet policy to sign at check in. Multiple dogs may be allowed.

Microtel Inn and Suites
80 Benedict Road

Bethel, CT
203-748-8318
Dogs of all sizes are allowed. There is a $100 refundable deposit plus $10 per night per pet and a pet policy to sign at check in. Multiple dogs may be allowed.

Motel 6 - NEW HAVEN - BRANFORD
320 E Main Street
Branford, CT
203-483-5828 (800-466-8356)
One well-behaved family pet per room. Guest must notify front desk upon arrival. Guest is liable for any damages. In consideration of all guests, pets must never be left unattended in the guest rooms.

Holiday Inn
1070 Main Street
Bridgeport, CT
203-334-1234 (877-270-6405)
Dogs up to 80 pounds are allowed for an additional fee of $10 per night per pet plus a $50 refundable deposit per room. 2 dogs may be allowed.

Twin Tree Inn
1030 Federal Rd
Brookfield, CT
203-775-0220
There is a $10.00 one time pet fee.

Holiday Inn
80 Newtown Rd
Danbury, CT
203-792-4000 (877-270-6405)
Dogs of all sizes are allowed for an additional fee of $15 per night per pet. Multiple dogs may be allowed.

Quality Inn and Suites
78 Federal Road
Danbury, CT
203-743-6701 (877-424-6423)
Dogs are allowed for an additional fee of $20 per night per pet. 2 dogs may be allowed.

Residence Inn by Marriott
22 Segar Street
Danbury, CT
203-797-1256
Dogs of all sizes are allowed. There is a $75 one time fee and a pet policy to sign at check in. They also request to please not leave your pet unattended. 2 dogs may be allowed.

Sheraton Danbury Hotel
18 Old Ridgebury Road
Danbury, CT
203-794-0600 (888-625-5144)
Dogs up to 80 pounds are allowed. There are no additional pet fees.

Dogs are not allowed to be left alone in the room.

Holiday Inn Express & Suites Killingly
16 Tracy Road
Dayville, CT
860-779-3200 (877-270-6405)
Dogs of all sizes are allowed for an additional $10 per night per pet. Multiple dogs may be allowed.

Holiday Inn
363 Roberts St
East Hartford, CT
860-528-9611 (877-270-6405)
Dogs of all sizes are allowed for an additional one time pet fee of $35 per room. 2 dogs may be allowed.

Sheraton Hartford Hotel
100 East River Drive
East Hartford, CT
860-528-9703 (888-625-5144)
Dogs of all sizes are allowed. There are no additional pet fees. Dogs are not allowed to be left alone in the room. 2 dogs may be allowed.

Motel 6 - HARTFORD - ENFIELD
11 Hazard Avenue
Enfield, CT
860-741-3685 (800-466-8356)
One well-behaved family pet per room. Guest must notify front desk upon arrival. Guest is liable for any damages. In consideration of all guests, pets must never be left unattended in the guest rooms.

Red Roof Inn - Enfield, CT
5 Hazard Avenue
Enfield, CT
860-741-2571 (800-RED-ROOF)
One well-behaved family pet per room. Guest must notify front desk upon arrival. Guest is liable for any damages. In consideration of all guests, pets must never be left unattended in the guest rooms.

Best Western Black Rock Inn
100 Kings Highway Cutoff
Fairfield, CT
203-659-2200 (800-780-7234)
Dogs are allowed for an additional fee of $20 per night per pet. Multiple dogs may be allowed.

Delmar Greenwich Harbor Hotel
500 Steamboat Road
Greenwich, CT
203-661-9800 (866-335-2627)
thedelamar.com/index2.html
This luxury waterfront inn has mooring on its own private dock (yachts up to 160'), sits near a

cornucopia of eateries and shops, offers indoor or outdoor dining, and most of the room have spacious balconies that overlook the harbor. Dogs up to 45 pounds are allowed for an additional fee of $25 per night per pet. Dogs get their own special welcome package; some items included are a cushy doggie bed, personalized ID tag, a bottle of Figi water, and a food and water bowl. Dogs must be quiet, well mannered, leashed, and cleaned up after. 2 dogs may be allowed.

Homespun Farm Bed and Breakfast
306 Preston Road/H 164
Griswold, CT
860-376-5178 (888-889-6673)
homespunfarm.com/
This colonial farmhouse inn is listed on the National Register of Historic Places as well as being a certified National Wildlife Federation Backyard Wildlife Habitat. Dogs of all sizes are allowed for an additional pet fee of $15 per night per room, and they only allow one guest with a pet to stay at a time. Dogs must be leashed, cleaned up after, and securely crated and the front desk informed when they are alone in the room. Please use a mat under their water/food dishes or feed pets outside, wipe dogs off before entering if they are wet (towel provided), and place your own throw on any furniture pets may want to be on. Dogs must be declared at the time of registration, and be quiet and friendly as there are other pets in residence. Multiple dogs may be allowed.

Days Inn Hartford Dwtn
207 Brainard Rd
Hartford, CT
860-247-3297 (800-329-7466)
Dogs of all sizes are allowed. There is a $5 per night pet fee per pet. 2 dogs may be allowed.

Holiday Inn Express Hartford - Downtown
440 Asylum Street
Hartford, CT
860-246-9900 (877-270-6405)
Dogs of all sizes are allowed for an additional one time pet fee of $50 per room. Multiple dogs may be allowed.

Motel 6 - Hartford Downtown
100 Weston Street
Hartford, CT
860-724-0222 (800-466-8356)
One well-behaved family pet per room. Guest must notify front desk upon arrival. Guest is liable for any

damages. In consideration of all guests, pets must never be left unattended in the guest rooms.

Residence Inn by Marriott
942 Main Street
Hartford, CT
860-524-5550
Dogs of all sizes are welcome. There is a $75 one time fee and a pet policy to sign at check in. Multiple dogs may be allowed.

Copper Beach Inn
46 Main Street
Ivoryton, CT
860-767-0330 (888-809-2056)
copperbeechinn.com/
This 1890 inn rests in a beautiful garden setting, has been the recipient of several awards for the inn itself, for their 4-diamond restaurant, and for their 5,000+ bottle wine cellar. Dogs of all sizes are welcome on the 1st floor of the Carriage House for an additional fee of $35 per night for 1 dog, and there is an additional fee of $10 per night if there is a 2nd dog. Dogs must be leashed, cleaned up after, and may only be left alone in the room if they are crated and will be quiet and well behaved. 2 dogs may be allowed.

Interlaken Inn
74 Interlaken Road
Lakeville, CT
860-435-9878
interlakeninn.com/
Charming resort with lakes to swim in, trails to walk and a PUPS amenity package. In the heart of the cultural Berkshires! The hotel offers 30 open acres, a great property with lake frontage to frolic on and off-leash play areas too! There are miles of pet-friendly walking and hiking trails nearby. There is a $15 per day pet fee.

Abbey's Lantern Hill Inn
780 Lantern Hill Road
Ledyard, CT
860-572-0483
abbeyslanternhill.com/
Nestled among the trees and rolling countryside, this contemporary inn features fireplaces, Jacuzzis, 6 outer decks, and it is also close to other activities, recreation, and a couple of casinos. Dogs of all sizes are allowed in the private bungalow. There is no fee for one dog. There is an additional $15 one time fee for a second dog. Dogs must be leashed, cleaned up after, and may only be left alone in the room if they will be quiet and well behaved. 2 dogs may

be allowed.

Litchfield Hills B&B
548 Bantam Road/H 202
Litchfield, CT
860-567-2057
litchfieldhillsbnb.com/
This 1735 colonial inn is surrounded by untouched woodlands, beautiful gardens, stone patios and pathways, and they are located within a short distance to many other attractions, activities, and recreation. Dogs of all sizes are allowed for no additional pet fee. Dogs must be quiet, well behaved, leashed, and cleaned up after. 2 dogs may be allowed.

Clarion Suites Inn
191 Spencer Street
Manchester, CT
860-643-5811 (877-424-6423)
Dogs are allowed for an additional fee of $20 per night per pet. 2 dogs may be allowed.

Residence Inn by Marriott
201 Hale Road
Manchester, CT
860-432-4242
Well behaved dogs of all sizes are welcome. There is a $75 one time fee and a pet policy to sign at check in. Multiple dogs may be allowed.

Candlewood Suites
1511 East Main Street
Meriden, CT
203-379-5048
One dog up to 80 pounds is allowed for an additional pet fee of $75 for 1 to 6 days, and $150 for 7+ days per room.

Residence Inn by Marriott
390 Bee Street
Meriden, CT
203-634-7770
Dogs of all sizes are allowed. There is a $75 one time fee and a pet policy to sign at check in. Multiple dogs may be allowed.

Red Roof Inn - Milford
10 Rowe Avenue
Milford, CT
203-877-6060 (800-RED-ROOF)
One well-behaved family pet per room. Guest must notify front desk upon arrival. Guest is liable for any damages. In consideration of all guests, pets must never be left unattended in the guest rooms.

Residence Inn by Marriott
62 Rowe Ave

Milford, CT
203-283-2100
Dogs of all sizes are allowed. There is a $75 one time fee and a pet policy to sign . Multiple dogs may be allowed.

Days Inn Hartford
1845 Meridian Waterbury Turnpike
Milldale, CT
860-621-9181 (800-329-7466)
Dogs of all sizes are allowed. There is a $10 per night pet fee per pet. Reservations are recommended due to limited rooms for pets. 2 dogs may be allowed.

Econo Lodge
251 Greenmanville Avenue
Mystic, CT
860-536-9666 (877-424-6423)
choicehotels.com/
Only 5 miles from the airport and central to many other attractions, this hotel, formally the Old Mystic Motor Lodge, welcomes dogs of all sizes for an additional fee of $10 per night per pet. Dogs must be leashed and cleaned up after at all times. Multiple dogs may be allowed.

Harbour Inne & Cottage
15 Edgemont Street
Mystic, CT
860-572-9253
harbourinne-cottage.com/
The Harbour Inne & Cottage B&B is an easy walk to all the shops, restaurants and sights of downtown Mystic. The inn has a social area with a fireplace and piano. The four bedrooms each have a private bath, kitchen privileges, cable television and are air conditioned. Pets are welcome for $10 per night.

Residence Inn by Marriott
40 Whitehall Avenue
Mystic, CT
860-536-5150
Dogs of all sizes are allowed. There is a $75 one time fee and a pet policy to sign at check in. Multiple dogs may be allowed.

Premiere Hotel and Suites
3 Long Wharf Drive
New Haven, CT
203-777-5337
newhavensuites.com
Pets of all sizes are allowed. There is a $75 one time fee and a pet policy to sign at check in. Multiple dogs may be allowed.

Red Roof Inn - New London
707 Colman Street

New London, CT
860-444-0001 (800-RED-ROOF)
One well-behaved family pet per room. Guest must notify front desk upon arrival. Guest is liable for any damages. In consideration of all guests, pets must never be left unattended in the guest rooms.

Motel 6 - NEW LONDON - NIANTIC
269 Flanders Road
Niantic, CT
860-739-6991 (800-466-8356)
One well-behaved family pet per room. Guest must notify front desk upon arrival. Guest is liable for any damages. In consideration of all guests, pets must never be left unattended in the guest rooms.

High Acres
222 NW Corner Road
North Stonington, CT
860-887-4355 (888-680-7829 (STAY))
highacresbb.com/
This 150 acre, groomed hilltop 18th century estate is a delight of green meadows, wildflowers, gardens, woodlands, and country charm, with horses in the fields, numerous hiking trails, and many other activities and recreation only a few minutes away. They have 1 pet friendly room, and dogs of all sizes are allowed for no additional fee. Dogs must be quiet, well behaved, cleaned up after, and they must have their own bedding as they are not allowed on the furnishings. Dogs may be off lead on the estate only if they are under firm voice control. 2 dogs may be allowed.

Old Lyme Inn
85 Lyme Street
Old Lyme, CT
860-434-2600 (800-434-5352)
oldlymeinn.com/
This small, but elegant inn is just minutes from the beach and two large outlet malls. Dogs of all sizes are allowed for a $50 refundable deposit per stay. Dogs may not be left alone in the room, and they must be leashed and cleaned up after at all times. 2 dogs may be allowed.

King's Inn
5 Heritage Rd
Putnam, CT
860-928-7961

Residence Inn by Marriott
1001 Bridgeport Avenue
Shelton, CT
203-926-9000
Pets of all sizes are allowed. There is

a $75 one time fee per pet and a pet policy to sign at check in. Multiple dogs may be allowed.

Iron Horse Inn
969 Hopmeadow St
Simsbury, CT
860-658-2216 (800245-9938)

Howard Johnson Express Inn
462 Queen Street
Southington, CT
860-621-0181 (800-446-4656)
Dogs of all sizes are welcome. There is a $10 per day pet fee.

Motel 6 - HARTFORD - SOUTHINGTON
625 Queen Street
Southington, CT
860-621-7351 (800-466-8356)
One well-behaved family pet per room. Guest must notify front desk upon arrival. Guest is liable for any damages. In consideration of all guests, pets must never be left unattended in the guest rooms.

Residence Inn by Marriott
778 West Street
Southington, CT
860-621-4440
Pets of all sizes are allowed. There is a $75 one time fee per pet for a minimum of 5 nights stay and a pet policy to sign at check in. Multiple dogs may be allowed.

Sheraton Stamford Hotel
2701 Summer Street
Stamford, CT
203-359-1300 (888-625-5144)
Dogs up to 50 pounds are allowed. There are no additional pet fees. Dogs are not allowed to be left alone in the room.

Stamford Marriott Hotel and Spa
Two Stamford Forum
Stamford, CT
203-357-9555 (800-732-9689)
Dogs of all sizes are allowed. There is a $20 per night per room additional pet fee. Dogs must be quiet, leashed, cleaned up after, and the Dog in Room sign put on the door and a contact number left with the front desk if they are in the room alone. Multiple dogs may be allowed.

Howard Johnson Express Inn
451 Hartford Turnpike
Vernon, CT
860-875-0781 (800-446-4656)
Dogs of all sizes are welcome. There is a $10 per day pet fee per

pet.

Quality Inn Conference Center
51 Hartford Turnpike/H 83
Vernon, CT
860-646-5700 (877-424-6423)
Dogs are allowed for an additional fee of $25 per night per pet. 2 dogs may be allowed.

Beach Plum Inn
1935 Boston Post Rd
Westbrook, CT
860-399-9345
There are no additional pet fees. Dogs are allowed in the cabins.

Motel 6 - HARTFORD - WETHERSFIELD
1341 Silas Deane Highway
Wethersfield, CT
860-563-5900 (800-466-8356)
One well-behaved family pet per room. Guest must notify front desk upon arrival. Guest is liable for any damages. In consideration of all guests, pets must never be left unattended in the guest rooms.

Residence Inn by Marriott
100 Dunfey Lane
Windsor, CT
860-688-7474
Dogs of all sizes are allowed. There is a $75 one time fee and a pet policy to sign at check in. 2 dogs may be allowed.

Candlewood Suites Windsor Locks
149 Ella Grasso Turnpike
Windsor Locks, CT
860-623-2000 (877-270-6405)
Dogs of all sizes are allowed for an additional pet fee of $75 for 1 to 6 nights, and $150 for 7+ nights per room. 2 dogs may be allowed.

Homewood Suites
65 Ella Grasso Turnpike
Windsor Locks, CT
860-627-8463
There is a $150 one time pet charge and guests need to sign a pet policy.

Motel 6 - HARTFORD - WINDSOR LOCKS
3 National Drive
Windsor Locks, CT
860-292-6200 (800-466-8356)
One well-behaved family pet per room. Guest must notify front desk upon arrival. Guest is liable for any damages. In consideration of all guests, pets must never be left unattended in the guest rooms.

Sheraton Bradley Airport Hotel

1 Bradley International Airport
Windsor Locks, CT
860-627-5311 (888-625-5144)
Dogs of all sizes are allowed. There
are no additional pet fees. Dogs are
not allowed to be left alone in the
room.

Elias Child House
50 Perrin Road
Woodstock, CT
860-974-9836 (877-974-9836)
eliaschildhouse.com/
Rich in colonial craftsmanship, this
inn sits on 47 acres of woodlands
and pastures with an in-ground pool,
walking trails, great shopping
opportunities close by, and they even
offer hearth cooking demonstrations;
there are 2 walk-in cooking hearths.
Dogs of all sizes are allowed for an
additional fee of $20 per night per
pet. Dogs must go with the owners
when they leave the premises, but
can be crated in the room if they are
on the property. Dogs must be well
mannered, leashed, cleaned up
after, and be friendly to other animals
as there is another dog there who
likes to greet the canine visitors. 2
dogs may be allowed.

D.C. Listings

Crowne Plaza
14th and K Street NW
Washington, DC
202-682-0111 (877-270-6405)
One dog up to 50 pounds or 2 dogs
totalling no more than a combined
weight of 50 pounds is allowed for a
$250 refundable pet deposit per
room. 2 dogs may be allowed.

Hilton
1919 Connecticut Avenue NW
Washington, DC
202-483-3000
Dogs are allowed for no additional
pet fee. 2 dogs may be allowed.

Hotel George
15 E Street, NW
Washington, DC
202-347-4200
hotelgeorge.com
This Kimpton boutique hotel allows
dogs of all sizes. There are no
additional pet fees.

Hotel Harrington
436 11th Street NW
Washington, DC
202-628-8140

Dogs of all sizes are allowed. There
are no additional pet fees. Dogs are
not allowed to be left unattended.
Multiple dogs may be allowed.

Hotel Helix
1430 Rhode Island Ave
Washington, DC
202-462-9001
hotelhelix.com/
Well-behaved dogs of all sizes are
welcome at this hotel. The boutique
hotel offers both rooms and suites.
Amenities include room service,
and a 24 hour on-site exercise
room. There are no pet fees.

Hotel Madera
1310 New Hampshire Ave
Washington, DC
202-296-7600
hotelmadera.com/
Well-behaved dogs of all sizes are
welcome at this boutique hotel.
Amenities include an evening wine
hour, and room service. There are
no pet fees.

Hotel Monaco
700 F Street NW
Washington, DC
202-628-7177
monaco-dc.com/
Well-behaved dogs of all sizes are
welcome. There is no pet fee.

Hotel Palomar
2121 P Street NW
Washington, DC
202-448-1800 (877-866-3070)
hotelpalomar-dc.com/
This Kimpton boutique hotel allows
dogs of all sizes. There are no
additional pet fees.

Hotel Rouge
1315 16th Street NW
Washington, DC
202-232-8000
rougehotel.com/
Well-behaved dogs of all sizes are
welcome at this luxury boutique
hotel. Amenities include
complimentary high speed Internet
access in the rooms, 24 hour room
service, and a 24 hour on-site
fitness room. There are no pet fees.

Hotel Washington
515 15th St NW
Washington, DC
202-638-5900
hotelwashington.com/
There are no additional pet fees.

L'Enfant Plaza Hotel
480 L'Enfant Plaza, SW

Washington, DC
202-484-1000
This centrally located hotel in
Washington, DC is near the
Smithsonian, the National Mall and
all of the major attractions. Rooms
and suites are available. Pets are
welcome to accompany guests at the
hotel.

Marriott Wardman Park Hotel
2660 Woodley Road NW
Washington, DC
202-328-2000 (800-228-9290)
Dogs up to 50 pounds are allowed.
There is a $50 one time additional
pet fee. Dogs must be well behaved,
leashed, cleaned up after, and the
Do Not Disturb sign put on the door
and the front desk notified if they are
in the room alone.

Motel 6 - Washington
6711 Georgia Avenue
Washington, DC
202-722-1600 (800-466-8356)
One well-behaved family pet per
room. Guest must notify front desk
upon arrival. Guest is liable for any
damages. In consideration of all
guests, pets must never be left
unattended in the guest rooms.

Park Hyatt Washington
1201 24th St NW
Washington, DC
202-789-1234
There are no additional pet fees.

Red Roof Inn - Washington, DC -
Downtown
500 H Street Northwest
Washington, DC
202-289-5959 (800-RED-ROOF)
One well-behaved family pet per
room. Guest must notify front desk
upon arrival. Guest is liable for any
damages. In consideration of all
guests, pets must never be left
unattended in the guest rooms.

Residence Inn by Marriott
333 E Street SW
Washington, DC
282-484-8280
Dogs of all sizes are allowed. There
is a $200 one time fee plus $10 per
night per room and a pet policy to
sign at check in. Multiple dogs may
be allowed.

Residence Inn by Marriott
2120 P Street NW
Washington, DC
202-466-6800
Dogs of all sizes are allowed. There
is a $75 one time fee and a pet

policy to sign at check in. Multiple dogs may be allowed.

Residence Inn by Marriott
1199 Vermont Avenue NW
Washington, DC
202-898-1100
Dogs of all sizes are allowed. There is a $150 one time fee plus $8 per night per room and a pet policy to sign at check in. Multiple dogs may be allowed.

Sofitel Lafayette Square
806 15th Street N.W.
Washington, DC
202-730-8441
sofitel.com
There are no additional pet fees.

The Fairmont, Washington DC
2401 M Street NW
Washington, DC
202-429-2400 (800-257-7544)
fairmont.com/washington/
This elegant hotel surrounds visitors inside and out with the luxurious colors of nature, and the 415 spacious, beautifully appointed guestrooms offer features for the business or leisure traveler. They offer ?Gold Floor? accommodations, a garden courtyard, gift shop, restaurants and lounge, in room dining, an indoor pool and spa, and numerous in room amenities. Dogs of all sizes are welcome for no additional fee; there is a pet policy to sign at check in. Dogs may not be left alone in the room at any time, and they must be cleaned up after. They also feature the ?Very Important Dog? program where your pet is greeted with healthy treats, water, and a placemat. Guests with pets also receive 5% of their room rate donated to the Animal Rescue League, walking maps, a list of pet-friendly restaurants, cafes and stores, and a special ?Paw? sign for the room. Multiple dogs may be allowed.

The Jefferson Hotel
1200 16th St. NW
Washington, DC
202-347-2200
Well-behaved dogs of any size are welcome. There is a $25 per day additional pet fee.

The Madison, A Loews Hotel
1177 Fifteenth St. NW
Washington, DC
202-862-1600
All well-behaved dogs of any size are welcome. This upscale hotel offers their "Loews Loves Pets" program

which includes special pet treats, local dog walking routes, and a list of nearby pet-friendly places to visit. There are no pet fees.

The Williard - Washington
1401 Pennsylvania Avenue NW
Washington, DC
202-628-9100
One dog up to 40 pounds is allowed for an additional one time pet fee of $100.

Topaz Hotel
1733 N Street NW
Washington, DC
202-393-3000 (800-775-1202)
topazhotel.com
This Kimpton boutique hotel allows dogs of all sizes. There are no additional pet fees.

Delaware Listings

Bethany Beach House
Off Central Avenue
Bethany Beach, DE
443-621-6649
quietresortbeachhouse.com/
This spacious home puts visitors within minutes of over a dozen golf courses, the beach, the boardwalk, and a number of eateries, attractions, and recreation. Dogs of all sizes are welcome for a refundable deposit of $75 per pet, and there is also a large fenced yard for them to enjoy. A visit to their website shows a number of pets who have enjoyed their visits here. The city enforces a leash and pooper-scooper law, and dogs are not allowed on the beach or boardwalk from May 15th to September 30th. At all other times dogs must be leashed and cleaned up after. Multiple dogs may be allowed.

Lagoon Front/#125307
217 Belle Road
Bethany Beach, DE
954-782-8277
This vacation house sits facing the lagoon for great crabbing right off the deck, is just 3 blocks from the beach, is large enough to accommodate family reunions and group retreats, and is also close to many other interests and activities. Dogs of all sizes are allowed for no additional pet fee, and they must be housetrained and cleaned up after at all times. Dogs are allowed on

the lower level of the house and on the fenced-in back deck only. Dogs are allowed on the beach on no more than a 6 foot leash, and are not to be walked where people are sunbathing. 2 dogs may be allowed.

Waterfront Retreat/#125305
104 Petherton Drive
Bethany Beach, DE
954-782-8277
Facing the canal just one block from the beach, this retreat is large enough to accommodate family reunions and group retreats, and it is quite close to innumerable shops, restaurants, activities, and recreational pursuits. Dogs of all sizes are allowed for no additional pet fee, and they must be housetrained and cleaned up after at all times. Dogs are allowed on the lower level of the house and on the fenced-in back deck only. Dogs are allowed on the beach on no more than a 6 foot leash, and are not to be walked where people are sunbathing. 2 dogs may be allowed.

Holiday Inn Select
630 Naamans Rd
Claymont, DE
302-792-2700 (877-270-6405)
Dogs of all sizes are allowed for an additional one time pet fee of $50 per pet. Multiple dogs may be allowed.

Atlantic Oceanside Hotel
1700 Coastal H
Dewey Beach, DE
302-227-8811 (800-422-0481)
atlanticoceanside.com/
Dogs of all sizes are allowed for an additional fee of $5 per night per pet, and a credit card must be on file. Dogs are not allowed in the motel rooms from Memorial Day through Labor Day; however, they are allowed at their Suites property year round. Pets may only be left alone in rooms for a short time if they will be quiet and well behaved. Dogs must be leashed, cleaned up after, and removed for housekeeping. Multiple dogs may be allowed.

Ocean Block #47227
given at time of reservations
Dewey Beach, DE
302-542-3570
vrbo.com/47227
This duplex vacation rental is only a few steps from the Atlantic Ocean and great bay views, sleeps up to 12 people, is only a short distance from town, and offers a fenced in dog run. Dogs of all sizes are allowed for a one time additional pet fee of $200.

Dogs must be housebroken, leashed, and cleaned up after. 2 dogs may be allowed.

Sea-Esta Motel I
2306 Hwy 1
Dewey Beach, DE
302-227-7666
seaesta.com/
There is a $6.00 charge per pet per night. There are no designated smoking or non-smoking rooms.

Comfort Inn
222 S DuPont H
Dover, DE
302-674-3300 (877-424-6423)
Dogs are allowed for an additional one time pet fee of $35 per room. 2 dogs may be allowed.

Red Roof Inn - Dover, DE
652 N DuPont Hwy
Dover, DE
302-730-8009 (800-RED-ROOF)
One well-behaved family pet per room. Guest must notify front desk upon arrival. Guest is liable for any damages. In consideration of all guests, pets must never be left unattended in the guest rooms.

Sheraton Dover Hotel
1570 North DuPont Highway
Dover, DE
302-678-8500 (888-625-5144)
Dogs of all sizes are allowed. There is a $50 one time nonrefundable pet fee per visit. Dogs are not allowed to be left alone in the room.

Comfort Inn and Suites
507 N Dupont H
Georgetown, DE
302-854-9400 (877-424-6423)
Dogs are allowed for an additional one time pet fee of $15 per room. 2 dogs may be allowed.

Lazy L at Willow Creek - A B&B Resort
16061 Willow Creek Road
Lewes, DE
302-644-7220
lazyl.net
Located on 8 secluded acres overlooking a marsh and creek, the Lazy L offers creature comforts for pets and pet owners. They offer 5 large rooms with Queen sized beds, a swimming pool, hot tub, pool table, guest kitchen and a barbecue. The dogs have a fenced in 1 acre run area, are allowed to sleep in the guest rooms and stay by themselves while you shop or go to dinner.

Sleep Inn
1595 H One
Lewes, DE
302-645-6464 (877-424-6423)
One dog is allowed for an additional pet fee of $25 per night.

The King's Inn
151 Kings H
Lewes, DE
302-645-6438
kingsinnlewes.com/
Large rooms with high ceilings and adorned with stained glass, this 1888 home also features many modern amenities. Dogs of all sizes are allowed for an additional fee of $5 per night per pet. Dogs must be quiet, leashed or crated when out of the room, and cleaned up after at all times. Multiple dogs may be allowed.

Motel 6 - Wilmington
1200 West Avenue/South Highway 9
New Castle, DE
302-571-1200 (800-466-8356)
One well-behaved family pet per room. Guest must notify front desk upon arrival. Guest is liable for any damages. In consideration of all guests, pets must never be left unattended in the guest rooms.

Quality Inn Skyways
147 N Dupont H
New Castle, DE
302-328-6666 (877-424-6423)
Dogs are allowed for an additional fee of $10 per night per pet. Multiple dogs may be allowed.

Rodeway Inn
111 S Dupont Hwy
New Castle, DE
302-328-6246
There is a $10 per day pet fee.

Days Inn Newark
900 Churchmans Rd
Newark, DE
302-368-2400 (800-329-7466)
Dogs of all sizes are allowed. There is a $10 per night pet fee per pet. 2 dogs may be allowed.

Howard Johnson Inn
1119 South College Avenue
Newark, DE
302-368-8521 (800-446-4656)
Dogs of all sizes are welcome. There is a $10 per day pet fee.

Quality Inn University
1120 S College Avenue
Newark, DE

302-368-8715 (877-424-6423)
Dogs are allowed for an additional fee of $10 per night per pet. 2 dogs may be allowed.

Red Roof Inn - Wilmington, DE
415 Stanton Christiana Road
Newark, DE
302-292-2870 (800-RED-ROOF)
One well-behaved family pet per room. Guest must notify front desk upon arrival. Guest is liable for any damages. In consideration of all guests, pets must never be left unattended in the guest rooms.

Residence Inn by Marriott
240 Chapman Road
Newark, DE
302-453-9200
Pets of all sizes are allowed. There is a $50 per day fee up to a total of $200 per room and a pet policy to sign at check in. Multiple dogs may be allowed.

Staybridge Suites Wilmington-Newark
270 Chapman Road
Newark, DE
302-366-8097 (877-270-6405)
Dogs of all sizes are allowed for an additional $10 per night per pet. Multiple dogs may be allowed.

American Hotel
329 Z Airport Road
Rehoboth, DE
302-226-0700
Dogs of all sizes are allowed. There is a $20 per night per pet fee and a pet policy to sign at check in. Multiple dogs may be allowed.

Sea Esta Motel III
1409 DE 1
Rehoboth Beach, DE
302-227-4343 (800-436-6591)
seaesta.com/
There is a $6 per day additional pet fee.

The Homestead at Rehoboth
35060 Warrington Road
Rehoboth Beach, DE
302-226-7625
homesteadatrehoboth.com/
This charming country inn sits on 2 acres by the ocean and is only a short walk to the beach and the boardwalk; they are also a short distance from tax-free shopping. Dogs of all sizes are welcome, but if they are over 80 pounds, prior arrangements must be made. There is an additional fee of $15 per night per pet. Dogs must be cleaned up

after inside and out; clean-up bags and a towel (if wet or sandy from the beach) are provided. They ask that you cover the bed if your pet will be on it, and they may only be left for short periods alone in the room. Dogs may be off lead if they respond well to voice command. 2 dogs may be allowed.

Best Western Brandywine Valley Inn
1807 Concord Pike
Wilmington, DE
302-656-9436 (800-780-7234)
Dogs are allowed for an additional one time pet fee of $25 per room. Multiple dogs may be allowed.

Days Inn Wilmington
5209 Concord Pike
Wilmington, DE
302-478-0300 (800-329-7466)
Dogs of all sizes are allowed. There is a $10 per night pet fee per pet. 2 dogs may be allowed.

Sheraton Suites Wilmington
422 Delaware Ave.
Wilmington, DE
302-654-8300 (888-625-5144)
Dogs up to 80 pounds are allowed. There are no additional pet fees. Dogs are not allowed to be left alone in the room.

Florida Listings

Candlewood Suites
644 Raymond Avenue
Altamonte Springs, FL
407-767-5757 (877-270-6405)
A dog up to 50 pounds is allowed for an additional one time pet fee of $75 for 1 to 6 days, and $150 for 7or more days.

Embassy Suites Hotel Orlando - North
225 Shorecrest Drive
Altamonte Springs, FL
407-834-2400
Dogs of all sizes are allowed. There is a $20 per night pet fee per pet. Dogs are not allowed to be left alone in the room. Multiple dogs may be allowed.

Amelia Island Oceanfront Condo
1323 Beach Walker Road
Amelia Island, FL
904-642-5563
ameliaislandcondo.blogspot.com
This pet-friendly condo with 1500 square feet is located on the ocean

and a few miles from Fernandina Beach.

Florida House Inn
22 South 3rd Street
Amelia Island, FL
800-258-3301 (800-258-3301)
floridahouseinn.com/
Built in 1857, this registered historic inn/bed and breakfast is located in the heart of the Fernandina Beach Historic District. This dog-friendly inn offers nine comfortable bedrooms and two suites, all with private baths. Six rooms have working fireplaces, two have old fashioned claw-footed tubs and two have large Jacuzzi tubs. All accommodations are air-conditioned and offer access to their spacious porches, perfect for rocking and relaxing. They are located near the Victorian seaport village. Walk through the 30 block historic district. Browse a variety of quaint stores, antique shops and restaurants along Centre Street, the main thoroughfare. There is a $15 per day pet fee. Dogs must be on a flea program.

Rancho Inn
240 Hwy 98
Apalachicola, FL
850-653-9435
There is a $6 per day pet charge.

The Gibson Inn
Market St and Avenue C
Apalachicola, FL
850-653-2191
gibsoninn.com/
Restored in 1983, this historic country inn overlooks the water and St. George Island. Rooms are furnished in period, with four-poster beds, ceiling fans, antique armoires, brass and porcelain bathroom fixtures, and claw-foot tubs. There is a $5.30 per day pet charge.

Howard Johnson Express Inn
1317 S. Orange Blossom Trail
Apopka, FL
407-886-1010 (800-446-4656)
Dogs of all sizes are welcome. There is a $10 per day pet fee. The hotel has two pet rooms, one smoking and one non-smoking.

Best Western Arcadia Inn
504 South Brevard Ave
Arcadia, FL
863-494-4884 (800-780-7234)
Dogs are allowed for an additional pet fee of $15 per night per room. 2 dogs may be allowed.

Residence Inn by Marriott
19900 W. Country Club Drive
Aventura, FL
786-528-1001
Well behaved dogs of all sizes are allowed. There is a $75 one time fee per pet and a pet policy to sign at check in. 2 dogs may be allowed.

Residence Inn by Marriott
525 NW 77th Street
Boca Raton, FL
561-994-3222
Pets of all sizes are allowed. There is a $75 one time fee and a pet policy to sign at check in. Multiple dogs may be allowed.

TownePlace Suites Boca Raton
5110 NW 8th Avenue
Boca Raton, FL
561-994-7232
Dogs of all sizes are allowed. There is a $75 one time pet fee per visit. 2 dogs may be allowed.

Hyatt Regency Coconut Point Resort & Spa
5001 Coconut Road
Bonita Springs, FL
239-444-1234
Stay at this pet-friendly resort along the south Florida western Gulf Coast. The resort is situated on 26 acres and has a championship golf course, tennis course and numerous swimming pools, bars and restaurants. Dogs up to 50 pounds are welcome to accompany you. There is a $100 reservation fee for pets and a $50 per day additional pet fee. You must provide proof of your dogs rabies, distemper and parvo vaccinations.

Howard Johnson Express Inn
6511 14th St. W (US 41)
Bradenton, FL
941-756-8399 (800-446-4656)
Dogs of all sizes are welcome. There is a $5 per day pet fee for pets under 20 pounds, $10 per day pet fee for pets over 20 pounds.

Motel 6 - Bradenton
660 67th Street Circle E
Bradenton, FL
941-747-6005 (800-466-8356)
One well-behaved family pet per room. Guest must notify front desk upon arrival. Guest is liable for any damages. In consideration of all guests, pets must never be left unattended in the guest rooms.

La Quinta Inn & Suites Tampa Bay

Brandon
310 Grand Regency Blvd.
Brandon, FL
813-643-0574 (800-531-5900)
Dogs of all sizes are allowed. There are no additional pet fees. There is a pet policy to sign at check in. Dogs must be housetrained, and a cell number left with the front desk if the dog is in the room alone. Please put the Do Not Disturb sign on the door. Dogs must be leashed and cleaned up after. Multiple dogs may be allowed.

Best Western Brooksville I-75
30307 Cortez Blvd
Brooksville, FL
352-796-9481 (800-780-7234)
Dogs are allowed for an additional one time fee of $25 per pet. 2 dogs may be allowed.

Days Inn Brooksville
6320 Windmere Rd
Brooksville, FL
352-796-9486 (800-329-7466)
Dogs of all sizes are allowed. There is a $10 one time per pet fee per visit. 2 dogs may be allowed.

Bayview B&B
PO Box 35, 12251 Shoreview Dr
Cape Coral, FL
941-283-7510
webbwiz.com/bayviewbb
The bed and breakfast has one room that allows pets. There is a $100 refundable pet deposit.

Quality Hotel Nautilus
1538 Cape Coral Parkway
Cape Coral, FL
239-542-2121
Dogs up to 50 pounds are allowed for an additional pet fee of $16.65 per night per room. 2 dogs may be allowed.

Vacation Rentals on Beach
Cape San Blas, FL
770-569-9215
TheCapeEscape.com
These six vacation rentals are located on a dog-friendly white sandy beach. The vacation rentals are in the gated Barrier Dunes with access to pools, tennis courts and fishing ponds.

Super 8 Chipley
1700 Main Street
Chipley, FL
850-638-8530 (800-800-8000)
Dogs of all sizes are allowed. There is a $5 per night pet fee per pet. Dogs are not allowed to be left alone

in the room. Reservations are recommended due to limited rooms for pets. Smoking and non-smoking rooms are available for pet rooms. 2 dogs may be allowed.

Candlewood Suites
13231 49th Street North
Clearwater, FL
727-573-3344 (877-270-6405)
Dogs up to 80 pounds are allowed for an additional one time fee of $75 per pet; for dogs over 80 pounds the fee is $150 per pet. 2 dogs may be allowed.

Residence Inn by Marriott
5050 Ulmerton Road
Clearwater, FL
727-573-4444
Dogs of all sizes are allowed. There is a $75 one time fee per pet and a pet policy to sign at check in. Multiple dogs may be allowed.

Super 8 Clearwater/St Pete Airport
13260 34th Street
Clearwater, FL
727-572-8881 (800-800-8000)
Dogs of all sizes are allowed. There is a $10 per night pet fee per pet. Reservations are recommended due to limited rooms for pets. Smoking and non-smoking rooms are available for pet rooms. 2 dogs may be allowed.

TownePlace Suites St Petersburg Clearwater
13200 49th Street North
Clearwater, FL
727-299-9229
Dogs of all sizes are allowed. There is a $75 one time pet fee per visit. 2 dogs may be allowed.

Sea Spray Inn
331 Coronado Drive
Clearwater Beach, FL
727-442-0432
clearwaterbeach.com/seaspray/
Sea Spray Inn is just a one minute walk to the Gulf of Mexico. There are 6 rooms, 4 with full kitchens, 2 rooms have refrigerators. There are microwaves in rooms, cable TV and a swimming pool.

Howard Johnson Inn & Even Par Pub
20329 US Hwy 27
Clermont, FL
352-429-9033 (800-446-4656)
Dogs of all sizes are welcome. There is a $25 per visit pet fee.

Secluded Sunsets

10616 South Phillips Road
Clermont, FL
352-429-0512 (866-839-2180)
secludedsunsets.com
This is a pet friendly duplex on Pine Island Lake. It has a two bedroom unit sleeping up to 6 adults and 3 pets and a one bedroom unit sleeping up to 4 adults and 2 pets overlooking a central Florida spring fed lake. Pet fees are $5 per pet per night. Amenities include a Hot tub, 4 person paddle boat, 2 person canoe, gas and charcoal grills, fire pit area for evening campfires, swimming, fishing, satellite TV and fully furnished kitchens.

Best Western Cocoa Inn
4225 West King St
Cocoa, FL
321-632-1065 (800-780-7234)
Dogs up to 80 pounds are allowed for an additional fee of $10 per night per pet. 2 dogs may be allowed.

Holiday Inn
1300 N. Atlantic Ave
Cocoa Beach, FL
321-783-2271 (877-270-6405)
Dogs up to 50 pounds are allowed for an additional fee of $10 per night per pet with a $50 deposit; $25 is refundable. 2 dogs may be allowed.

La Quinta Inn Cocoa Beach
1275 N. Atlantic Avenue
Cocoa Beach, FL
321-783-2252 (800-531-5900)
Dogs of all sizes are allowed. There are no additional pet fees. There is a pet waiver to sign at check in. Dogs must be leashed and cleaned up after. Dogs may not be left unattended unless they will be quiet and well behaved. Multiple dogs may be allowed.

Motel 6 - Cocoa Beach
3701 North Atlantic Avenue
Cocoa Beach, FL
321-783-3103 (800-466-8356)
All well-behaved dogs are welcome, just let the hotel know that you have a pet.

Quality Suites
3655 N Atlantic Avenue
Cocoa Beach, FL
321-783-6868
A dog up to 50 pounds is allowed for a $100 refundable pet deposit.

South Beach Inn
1701 South Atlantic Ave
Cocoa Beach, FL
321-784-3333 (800-546-6835)

southbeachinn.com
There is a $15 per day pet fee. There are no designated smoking or non-smoking rooms.

Surf Studio Beach Resort
1801 S. Atlantic Ave.
Cocoa Beach, FL
321-783-7100
There is a $25 per day pet charge. There are no designated smoking or non-smoking rooms, but they keep the rooms very clean.

Residence Inn by Marriott
2835 Tigertail Avenue
Coconut Grove, FL
305-285-9303
Dogs of all sizes are allowed. There is a $75 one time fee and a pet policy to sign at check in. Multiple dogs may be allowed.

La Quinta Inn Ft. Lauderdale Coral Springs
3701 University Dr.
Coral Springs, FL
954-753-9000 (800-531-5900)
Dogs of all sizes are allowed. There are no additional pet fees. Dogs may not be left unattended unless they will be quiet and well behaved. Dogs must be leashed and cleaned up after. 2 dogs may be allowed.

Studio 6 - Ft Lauderdale - Coral Springs
5645 University Drive
Coral Springs, FL
954-796-0011 (800-466-8356)
One well-behaved family pet per room. Guest must notify front desk upon arrival. Guest is liable for any damages. In consideration of all guests, pets must never be left unattended in the guest rooms.

Wellesley Inn Coral Springs
3100 N. University Drive
Coral Springs, FL
954-344-2200 (800-531-5900)
Dogs of all sizes are allowed. There are no additional pet fees. Dogs must be leashed and cleaned up after. Multiple dogs may be allowed.

Days Inn Crestview
4255 S Ferdon Blvd
Crestview, FL
850-682-8842 (800-329-7466)
Dogs of all sizes are allowed. There is a $10 per night pet fee per pet. 2 dogs may be allowed.

Super 8 Crestview
3925 S Ferdon blvd
Crestview, FL

850-682-9649 (800-800-8000)
Dogs of all sizes are allowed. There is a $5 per night pet fee per pet. Smoking and non-smoking rooms are available for pet rooms. 2 dogs may be allowed.

Best Western Crystal River Resort
614 NW Hwy 19
Crystal River, FL
352-795-3171 (800-780-7234)
Dogs are allowed for an additional fee of $3 per night per pet. Dogs may not be left alone in the room. Multiple dogs may be allowed.

Days Inn Crystal River
2380 NW Hwy 19
Crystal River, FL
352-795-2111 (800-329-7466)
Dogs of all sizes are allowed. There is a $10 per night pet fee per pet. 2 dogs may be allowed.

Motel 6 - Dania Beach
825 E Dania Beach Boulevard
Dania, FL
954-921-5505 (800-466-8356)
One well-behaved family pet per room. Guest must notify front desk upon arrival. Guest is liable for any damages. In consideration of all guests, pets must never be left unattended in the guest rooms.

Sheraton Fort Lauderdale Airport Hotel
1825 Griffin Rd.
Dania, FL
954-920-3500 (888-625-5144)
Dogs up to 75 pounds are allowed for no additional fees; there is a pet agreement to sign at check in. Dogs may not be left alone in the room.

Best Western Maingate South
2425 Frontage Road
Davenport, FL
863-424-2596 (800-780-7234)
Dogs are allowed for no additional pet fee. 2 dogs may be allowed.

Hampton Inn
44117 H 27
Davenport, FL
863-420-9898
Dogs of all sizes are allowed. There is a $25 per day per room fee and a pet policy to sign at check in. Multiple dogs may be allowed.

La Quinta Inn Daytona Beach
2725 International Speedway
Daytona Beach, FL
386-255-7412 (800-531-5900)
Dogs of all sizes are allowed. There are no additional pet fees. Dogs

must be leashed and cleaned up after. Multiple dogs may be allowed.

Quality Inn Ocean Palms
2323 S Atlantic Avenue
Daytona Beach, FL
386-255-0476 (877-424-6423)
Dogs are allowed for an additional pet fee of $10 per night per room. Multiple dogs may be allowed.

Super 8 Daytona Beach/Speedway Area
2992 W International Speedway Blvd
Daytona Beach, FL
386-253-0643 (800-800-8000)
Dogs of all sizes are allowed. There is a $10 per night pet fee per pet. Reservations are recommended due to limited rooms for pets. Smoking and non-smoking rooms are available for pet rooms. 2 dogs may be allowed.

Sand Castle Motel
3619 S Atlantic Avenue
Daytona Beach Shores, FL
386-767-3182
There is only one dog friendly room and dogs of all sizes are allowed. There is a $15 per room additional pet fee. 2 dogs may be allowed.

Days Inn De Funiak Springs
472 Hugh Adams Rd
De Funiak Springs, FL
850-892-6115 (800-329-7466)
Dogs of all sizes are allowed. There is a $10 per night pet fee per pet. 2 dogs may be allowed.

Comfort Inn
50 S Ocean Drive
Deerfield Beach, FL
954-428-0650 (877-424-6423)
Dogs are allowed for an additional one time fee per pet of $25 for dogs 25 pounds or under; the fee is $40 per pet for dogs over 25 pounds. 2 dogs may be allowed.

Comfort Suites
1040 Newport Center Drive
Deerfield Beach, FL
954-570-8887 (877-424-6423)
Dogs are allowed for an additional fee of $10 per night per pet. Multiple dogs may be allowed.

La Quinta Inn Ft. Lauderdale Deerfield Beach
351 W Hillsboro Blvd.
Deerfield Beach, FL
954-421-1004 (800-531-5900)
Dogs of all sizes are allowed. There are no additional pet fees. Dogs must be leashed and cleaned up

after. Dogs must be attended to or crated for housekeeping. Multiple dogs may be allowed.

Super 8 Defuniak Springs
402 Hugh Adams Rd
Defuniak Springs, FL
850-892-1333 (800-800-8000)
Dogs of all sizes are allowed. There is a $10 per night pet fee per small pet and $25 per large pet. Smoking and non-smoking rooms are available for pet rooms. 2 dogs may be allowed.

Holiday Inn
350 International Speedway Blvd
Deland, FL
386-738-5200 (877-270-6405)
Dogs up to about 65 pounds are allowed for an additional one time pet fee of $25 per room. Dogs must be crated or removed for housekeeping. 2 dogs may be allowed.

Howard Johnson Express Inn
2801 E. New York Ave.
Deland, FL
386-736-3440 (800-446-4656)
Dogs of all sizes are welcome. There is a $10 per day pet fee.

Residence Inn by Marriott
1111 E Atlantic Avenue
Delray Beach, FL
561-276-7441
Pets of all sizes are allowed. There is a $75 one time fee and a pet policy to sign at check in. Multiple dogs may be allowed.

Days Inn Destin
1029 Hwy 98 E
Destin, FL
850-837-2599 (800-329-7466)
Dogs of all sizes are allowed. There is a $20 per night pet fee per pet. 2 dogs may be allowed.

Motel 6 - Destin
405 Highway 98 E #A
Destin, FL
850-837-0007 (800-466-8356)
One well-behaved family pet per room. Guest must notify front desk upon arrival. Guest is liable for any damages. In consideration of all guests, pets must never be left unattended in the guest rooms.

Comfort Inn
2625 H 207
Elkton, FL
904-829-3435 (877-424-6423)
Dogs are allowed for an additional pet fee of $10 per night per room.

Multiple dogs may be allowed.

Shoney's Inn-Bradenton
4915 17th Street East
Ellenton, FL
941-729-0600
There is a $10 one time pet charge.

Topaz Motel
1224 S Oceanshore Blvd
Flagler Beach, FL
386-439-3301
Dogs only, and of all sizes are allowed. There is a $10 per stay per room additional pet fee. Multiple dogs may be allowed.

Whale Watch Motel
2448 S Oceanshore Blvd
Flagler Beach, FL
386-439-2545
There is a $10 per day pet fee. They have a few non-smoking pet rooms.

Candlewood Suites Ft. Lauderdale Air/ Seaport
1120 W. State Road 84
Fort Lauderdale, FL
954-522-8822 (877-270-6405)
Dogs up to 80 pounds are allowed for an additional one time pet fee of $75 per room; it's a one time fee of $150 for dogs over 80 pounds. 2 dogs may be allowed.

Embassy Suites Hotel Ft. Lauderdale 17th Street
1100 Southeast 17th Street
Fort Lauderdale, FL
954-527-2700
Dogs of all sizes are allowed. There are no additional pet fees. Dogs are not allowed to be left alone in the room.

Hampton Inn
2301 SW 12th Avenue
Fort Lauderdale, FL
954-524-9900
Dogs of all sizes are allowed. There is a an additional $50 per stay per room. Multiple dogs may be allowed.

La Quinta Inn Ft. Lauderdale Cypress Creek I-95
999 West Cypress Creek Rd.
Fort Lauderdale, FL
954-491-7666 (800-531-5900)
Dogs of all sizes are allowed. There are no additional pet fees. Dogs must be leashed and cleaned up after. Dogs must be attended to or crated for housekeeping. Multiple dogs may be allowed.

La Quinta Inn Ft. Lauderdale Tamarac East
3800 W. Commercial Boulevard
Fort Lauderdale, FL
954-485-7900 (800-531-5900)
Dogs of all sizes are allowed. There are no additional pet fees. Dogs may not be left unattended, and they must be leashed and cleaned up after. 2 dogs may be allowed.

Motel 6 - Ft Lauderdale
1801 SR 84
Fort Lauderdale, FL
954-760-7999 (800-466-8356)
One well-behaved family pet per room. Guest must notify front desk upon arrival. Guest is liable for any damages. In consideration of all guests, pets must never be left unattended in the guest rooms.

Sheraton Yankee Clipper Hotel
1140 Seabreeze Blvd.
Fort Lauderdale, FL
954-524-5551 (888-625-5144)
Dogs up to 70 pounds are allowed for no additional pet fee. Dogs may not be left alone in the room.

TownePlace Suites Fort Lauderdale West
3100 Prospect Rd
Fort Lauderdale, FL
954-484-2214
Dogs of all sizes are allowed. There is a $75 one time pet fee per visit. 2 dogs may be allowed.

Best Western Springs Resort
18051 South Tamiami Trail Hwy 41
Fort Myers, FL
239-267-7900 (800-780-7234)
One dog is allowed for a pet fee of $15 per night; a 2nd dog is an additional $5 per night. 2 dogs may be allowed.

Country Inns & Suites by Carlson
13901 Shell Point Plaza
Fort Myers, FL
239-454-9292
Dogs of all sizes are allowed. There is a $10 per day additional pet fee up to a maximum of $50 per stay.

Econolodge N
13301 N Cleveland
Fort Myers, FL
239-995-0571
Dogs of all sizes are allowed. There is a $5.35 per night per pet fee and a pet policy to sign at check in. Multiple dogs may be allowed.

Holiday Inn Fort Myers Downtown Historic

2431 Cleveland Ave.
Fort Myers, FL
239-332-3232 (877-270-6405)
Dogs of all sizes are allowed for an additional one time pet fee of $75 per room. 2 dogs may be allowed.

Howard Johnson Express Inn
13000 North Cleveland Ave.
Fort Myers, FL
239-656-4000 (800-446-4656)
Dogs of all sizes are welcome. There is a $10 per day pet fee per pet.

Howard Johnson Inn
4811 Cleveland Ave.
Fort Myers, FL
239-936-3229 (800-446-4656)
Dogs of all sizes are welcome. There is a $25 pet fee every 3 days.

La Quinta Inn Fort Myers
4850 S. Cleveland Ave.
Fort Myers, FL
239-275-3300 (800-531-5900)
One dog of any size is allowed. There are no additional pet fees. Dogs may not be left unattended, and they must be leashed and cleaned up after.

Motel 6 - Ft Myers
3350 Marinatown Lane
Fort Myers, FL
239-656-5544 (800-466-8356)
One well-behaved family pet per room. Guest must notify front desk upon arrival. Guest is liable for any damages. In consideration of all guests, pets must never be left unattended in the guest rooms.

Residence Inn by Marriott
2960 Colonial Blvd
Fort Myers, FL
239-936-0110
Pets of all sizes are allowed. There is a $75 one time fee and a pet policy to sign at check in. Multiple dogs may be allowed.

Motel 6 - Ft Pierce
2500 Peters Road
Fort Pierce, FL
772-461-9937 (800-466-8356)
One well-behaved family pet per room. Guest must notify front desk upon arrival. Guest is liable for any damages. In consideration of all guests, pets must never be left unattended in the guest rooms.

Royal Inn
222 Hernando Street
Fort Pierce, FL
561-464-0405
royalinnbeach.com

There are no additional pet fees. Pets must be well-behaved. The hotel has limited pet rooms. Please call ahead to reserve a pet room.

Fairway Inn
203 Miracle Strip Pkwy.
Fort Walton Beach, FL
850-244-8663
There is a $25 one time pet fee.

Rodeway Inn
314 Miracle Strip Parkway
Fort Walton Beach, FL
850-243-6162
Dogs of all sizes are allowed. There is a $10 plus tax per night per pet additional fee. Multiple dogs may be allowed.

Best Western Gateway Grand
4200 NW 97th Blvd
Gainesville, FL
352-331-3336 (800-780-7234)
Dogs are allowed for an additional pet fee of $20 per night per room. Multiple dogs may be allowed.

Comfort Inn
2435 SW 13th Street
Gainesville, FL
352-373-6500 (877-424-6423)
Dogs are allowed for an additional fee of $10 per night per pet. Multiple dogs may be allowed.

Days Inn Gainesville/I-75
7516 Newberry Rd
Gainesville, FL
352-332-3033 (800-329-7466)
Dogs of all sizes are allowed. There is a $7 per night pet fee per pet. 2 dogs may be allowed.

La Quinta Inn Gainesville
920 N.W. 69th Terrace
Gainesville, FL
352-332-6466 (800-531-5900)
Dogs of all sizes are allowed. There are no additional pet fees. Dogs must be leashed and cleaned up after. Dogs must be crated or removed for housekeeping. Multiple dogs may be allowed.

Magnolia Plantation Bed and Breakfast
305 SE 7th Street
Gainesville, FL
352-375-6653 (800-201-2379)
magnoliabnb.com
The Magnolia Plantation has 6 private historic cottages located within walking distance of downtown Gainesville. It is surrounded by 1.5 acres of lush gardens. They have no pet fees or weight restrictions,

and only require that pets be kept on a leash while wandering around the property. Pets are not permitted in the main house but are allowed in one of the six cottages.

Motel 6 - Gainesville - Univ. of Florida
4000 SW 40th Boulevard
Gainesville, FL
352-373-1604 (800-466-8356)
One well-behaved family pet per room. Guest must notify front desk upon arrival. Guest is liable for any damages. In consideration of all guests, pets must never be left unattended in the guest rooms.

Red Roof Inn - Gainesville, FL
3500 SW 42nd Street
Gainesville, FL
352-336-3311 (800-RED-ROOF)
One well-behaved family pet per room. Guest must notify front desk upon arrival. Guest is liable for any damages. In consideration of all guests, pets must never be left unattended in the guest rooms.

Hibiscus Coffee Guest House
85 Defuniak St
Grayton Beach, FL
850-231-2733
hibiscusflorida.com
There are no additional pet fees. There is one room available for pets.

Howard Johnson Inn
33224 US Hwy. 27 South
Haines City, FL
863-422-8621 (800-446-4656)
Dogs of all sizes are welcome. There is a $10 pet fee for the first night and $5 for the second night.

Howard Johnson Hotel
7707 NW 103 St.
Hialeah Gardens, FL
305-521-1000 (800-446-4656)
There is a $100 one time additional pet fee.

Days Inn Fort Lauderdale/Airport South
2601 N 29th Ave
Hollywood, FL
954-923-7300 (800-329-7466)
Dogs of all sizes are allowed. There is a $10 per night pet fee per pet. Reservations are recommended due to limited rooms for pets. 2 dogs may be allowed.

Sun Cruz Inn
340 Desoto St.
Hollywood, FL
954-925-7272

suncruzinn.com
This 17 unite motel and apartment building has studios and efficiencies. Pet walking is available for a fee. There is a deposit and other pet fees. Call the hotel for more information.

Hollywood - Ft. Lauderdale Oceanfront Rental
South Ocean Drive
Hollywood Beach, FL
786-208-7004
This two bedroom, two bathroom condo near the beach allows dogs up to 80 pounds.

Park Inn Homosassa Springs
4076 S Suncoast Blvd
Homosassa, FL
352-628-4311
Dogs of all sizes are allowed. There is a $15 per day additional pet fee.

Barrett Beach Bungalows
19646 Gulf Blvd
Indian Shores, FL
727-455-2832
barrettbeachbungalows.com
Beachfront bungalows plus a cottage in the heart of picturesque Indian Shores. One, two and three bedroom bungalows and a pool. Any number and size of pets welcome. Private dog runs with each bungalow. Enjoy sunsets, volleyball and barbecues in your own backyard.

Vacation Shores
19742 Gulf Blvd
Indian Shores, FL
727-593-7164 (866-714-2588)
vacationshores.com
This beachfront vacation rental property has six units. There is a $100 pet fee for each pet.

Candlewood Suites
4990 Belfort Road
Jacksonville, FL
904-296-7785 (877-270-6405)
Dogs of all sizes are allowed for an additional pet fee of $75 for 1 to 14 nights, and $150 for 15 or more nights per room. Multiple dogs may be allowed.

Hampton Inn
1170 Airport Entrance Road
Jacksonville, FL
904-741-4980
Well behaved dogs of all sizes are allowed. There are no additional pet fees. Multiple dogs may be allowed.

Homewood Suites
8737 Baymeadows Rd

Jacksonville, FL
904-733-9299 (800-555-0807)
There is a $75 one time pet fee.

La Quinta Inn Jacksonville Airport North
812 Dunn Ave.
Jacksonville, FL
904-751-6960 (800-531-5900)
Dogs of all sizes are allowed. There are no additional pet fees. Dogs are not allowed to go through the lobby during food service hours. Dogs may only be left unattended if they are crated and will be quiet. Dogs must be leashed and cleaned up after. Multiple dogs may be allowed.

La Quinta Inn Jacksonville Baymeadows
8255 Dix Ellis Trail
Jacksonville, FL
904-731-9940 (800-531-5900)
Dogs of all sizes are allowed. There are no additional pet fees. Dogs must be leashed and cleaned up after. Multiple dogs may be allowed.

La Quinta Inn Jacksonville Orange Park
8555 Blanding Blvd
Jacksonville, FL
904-778-9539 (800-531-5900)
Dogs of all sizes are allowed. There are no additional pet fees. Dogs must be leashed and cleaned up after, and removed or crated for housekeeping. Multiple dogs may be allowed.

Motel 6 - Jacksonville - Orange Park
6107 Youngerman Circle
Jacksonville, FL
904-777-6100 (800-466-8356)
One well-behaved family pet per room. Guest must notify front desk upon arrival. Guest is liable for any damages. In consideration of all guests, pets must never be left unattended in the guest rooms.

Motel 6 - Jacksonville Airport
10885 Harts Road
Jacksonville, FL
904-757-8600 (800-466-8356)
One well-behaved family pet per room. Guest must notify front desk upon arrival. Guest is liable for any damages. In consideration of all guests, pets must never be left unattended in the guest rooms.

Motel 6 - Jacksonville Southeast
8285 Dix Ellis Trail
Jacksonville, FL
904-731-8400 (800-466-8356)

One well-behaved family pet per room. Guest must notify front desk upon arrival. Guest is liable for any damages. In consideration of all guests, pets must never be left unattended in the guest rooms.

Ramada Inn
3130 Hartley Road
Jacksonville, FL
904-268-8080
Dogs of all sizes are allowed. There is a $100 refundable deposit plus a $50 one time fee per pet and a pet policy to sign at check in. 2 dogs may be allowed.

Red Roof Inn - Jacksonville - Orange Park
6099 Youngerman Circle
Jacksonville, FL
904-777-1000 (800-RED-ROOF)
One well-behaved family pet per room. Guest must notify front desk upon arrival. Guest is liable for any damages. In consideration of all guests, pets must never be left unattended in the guest rooms.

Red Roof Inn - Jacksonville - Southpoint
6969 Lenoir Avenue East
Jacksonville, FL
904-296-1006 (800-RED-ROOF)
One well-behaved family pet per room. Guest must notify front desk upon arrival. Guest is liable for any damages. In consideration of all guests, pets must never be left unattended in the guest rooms.

Red Roof Inn - Jacksonville Airport
14701 Airport Entrance Road
Jacksonville, FL
904-741-4488 (800-RED-ROOF)
One well-behaved family pet per room. Guest must notify front desk upon arrival. Guest is liable for any damages. In consideration of all guests, pets must never be left unattended in the guest rooms.

Residence Inn by Marriott
1310 Airport Road
Jacksonville, FL
904-741-6550
Dogs of all sizes are allowed. There is a $75 one time fee and a pet policy to sign at check in. Multiple dogs may be allowed.

Residence Inn by Marriott
8365 Dix Ellis Trail
Jacksonville, FL
904-733-8088
Dogs of all sizes are allowed. There is a $75 one time fee and a pet

policy to sign at check in. Nearby is Dogwood Park, a 25 acre doggy play area complete with an array of treats and toys, and special digging, running and playing areas. Multiple dogs may be allowed.

Residence Inn by Marriott
10551 Deerwood Park Blvd
Jacksonville, FL
904-996-8900
Dogs of all sizes are allowed. There is a $75 one time fee and a pet policy to sign at check in. Multiple dogs may be allowed.

Studio 6 - Jacksonville -
Baymeadows
8765 Baymeadows Road
Jacksonville, FL
904-731-7317 (800-466-8356)
One well-behaved family pet per room. Guest must notify front desk upon arrival. Guest is liable for any damages. In consideration of all guests, pets must never be left unattended in the guest rooms.

Days Inn Jasper
8182 SR 6 West
Jasper, FL
386-792-1987 (800-329-7466)
Dogs of all sizes are allowed. There is a $10 per night pet fee per pet. 2 dogs may be allowed.

Holiday Inn Express-North Palm Beach
13950 US Hwy 1
Juno Beach, FL
561-622-4366 (877-270-6405)
Dogs of all sizes are allowed for an additional pet fee of $10 per night per room in the Standard Building, and $20 per night per room for the Executive Building. Multiple dogs may be allowed.

Ambrosia House Tropical Lodging
622 Fleming Street
Key West, FL
305-296-9838 (800-535-9838)
ambrosiakeywest.com/
This inn, located on almost two private acres, offers a variety of rooms, suites, town houses and a cottage, all with private baths. The inn is located in the heart of historic Old Town. There is a one time non-refundable pet fee of $25. There is no weight limit or limit to the number of pets.

At Home In Key West, Inc.
905 Truman Avenue
Key West, FL
305-296-7975 (888-459-9378)

athomekeywest.com
Rent a pet-friendly condo or cottage in Key West. Call for prices and availability.

Atlantic Shores (adults only)
510 South Street
Key West, FL
305-296-2491
Dogs of all sizes are allowed. There is a $10 one time additional pet fee per room. Multiple dogs may be allowed.

Avalon
1317 Duval Street
Key West, FL
305-294-8233
One dog of any size is allowed. There is a pet policy to sign at check in and there are no additional fees.

Chelsea House
707 Truman Avenue
Key West, FL
305-296-2211 (800-845-8859)
There is a $15 per day pet charge.

Courtney's Place
720 Whitmarsh Lane
Key West, FL
305-294-3480 (800-869-4639)
keywest.com/courtney.html
This inn has historic guest cottages. There are no designated smoking or non-smoking cottages.

Douglas House and Cuban Club Suites
419 Amelia St
Key West, FL
305-294-5269 (800-833-0372)
cubanclub.com
Small dogs are welcome at the Douglas House. Large dogs are welcome at the Cuban Club Suites. There is a $10 per day pet fee. There are no designated smoking or non-smoking rooms.

Francis Street Bottle Inn
535 Francis Street
Key West, FL
305-294-8530 (800-294-8530)
bottleinn.com/aboutus.htm
Dogs are allowed, including well-behaved large dogs. There is a $25 one time pet fee.

Key West Vacation Rentals
1075 Duval Street
Key West, FL
800-797-8787
vacationrentalskeywest.com
Special doggy treats upon check-in. Pets welcome in suites, cottages,

condos and homes. Amenities include 4 pools and most suites offer private Jacuzzis. Specializing in weddings, honeymoons, and romantic escapes. There is a $10 per pet per night charge. Dogs of all sizes and breeds are welcome.

Key West's Center Court - Bed and Breakfast and Cottages
1075 Duval Street
Key West, FL
800-797-8787
centercourtkw.com/
Special doggy treats upon check-in. Pets welcome in suites, cottages, condos and homes. Amenities include 4 pools and most suites offer private Jacuzzis. Specializing in weddings, honeymoons, and romantic escapes. There is a $10 per pet per night charge. Dogs of all sizes and breeds are welcome. Multiple dogs may be allowed.

Key West's Travelers Palm - Inn and Cottages
915 Center Street
Key West, FL
800-294-9560
travelerspalm.com/
Special dog treats upon check-in. Dogs are welcome in the suites and cottages. Amenities include premier Old Town locations and 3 heated pools. Dogs of all sizes and breeds are welcome.

Pelican Landing Resort and Marina
915 Eisenhower Drive
Key West, FL
305-296-9976
keywestpelican.com
Waterfront condos each with 2 bedrooms and 2 baths. A boat slip comes with each condo. The Subtropic Dive Center is located next door. There is a heated swimming pool and all well-behaved dogs and cats are welcome.

Seascape Tropical Inn
420 Olivia St
Key West, FL
305-296-7776 (800-765-6438)
seascapetropicalinn.com
Pets are allowed in all of the cottages and two rooms in the main guesthouse. There is a $25 one time pet fee. All rooms are non-smoking. Children are allowed in the cottages. The owner has two dogs on the premises.

Sheraton Suites Key West
2001 S. Roosevelt Blvd.
Key West, FL
305-292-9800 (888-625-5144)

Dogs of all sizes are allowed. There are no additional pet fees. Dogs are not allowed to be left alone in the room.

Sunrise Suites Resorts
3685 Seaside Drive
Key West, FL
305-296-6661
Dogs of all sizes are allowed. There is a $30 per night per room fee if the dog is small without much hair; it is $30 per night per pet if the dog is large or has a lot of hair. 2 dogs may be allowed.

Whispers
409 William St
Key West, FL
305-294-5969 (800-856-7444)
whispersbb.com
Dogs are allowed, but no puppies please. There is a $25 one time pet fee. Children over 10 years old are allowed.

Best Western Maingate East Hotel & Suites
4018 W Vine Street
Kissimmee, FL
407-870-2000 (800-780-7234)
Dogs are allowed for an additional pet fee per room of $75 for each 1 to 7 days. 2 dogs may be allowed.

Caribbean Villas Privately Owned Condo near Disney
Call to Arrange
Kissimmee, FL
407-973-8924
myfloridacondorental.com
This privately-owned condominium vacation rental is 2 bedroom 2 bath. It's located in Caribbean Villas in Kissimmee, Florida. There is no additional pet fee.

Days Suites Orlando/Maingate East
5820 W Irlo Bronson Hwy
Kissimmee, FL
407-396-7900 (800-DAYS-INN)
Dogs of all sizes are allowed. There is a $10 per night pet fee per pet. Reservations are recommended due to limited rooms for pets. 2 dogs may be allowed.

Homewood Suites Orlando-Disney Resort
3100 Parkway Blvd.
Kissimmee, FL
407-396-2229 (800-225-5466)
There is a $250 pet deposit and $200 of the deposit is refundable. ($50 pet charge)

Howard Johnson Hotel

8660 W. Irlo Bronson Memorial Hwy
Kissimmee, FL
407-396-4500 (800-446-4656)
Dogs up to 50 pounds are allowed. There is a $25 per week pet fee.

La Quinta Inn & Suites
Orlando/Maingate
3484 Polynesian Isle Blvd
Kissimmee, FL
407-997-1700 (800-531-5900)
Dogs of all sizes are allowed. There are no additional pet fees. Dogs must be leashed and cleaned up after. A call number must be left with the front desk, and the Do Not Disturb sign placed on the door if there is a pet inside alone. Make arrangements with housekeeping if you need your room serviced. 2 dogs may be allowed.

Larson's Family Inn
6075 West U.S. Hwy. 192
Kissimmee, FL
407-396-6100
There is a $150 refundable pet deposit and a $10 per day pet charge. Dogs up to 50 pounds are allowed.

Motel 6 - Orlando-Kissimmee Main Gate East
5731 W Irlo Bronson Highway
Kissimmee, FL
407-396-6333 (800-466-8356)
One well-behaved family pet per room. Guest must notify front desk upon arrival. Guest is liable for any damages. In consideration of all guests, pets must never be left unattended in the guest rooms.

Motel 6 - Orlando-Kissimmee Main Gate West
7455 W Irlo Bronson Highway
Kissimmee, FL
407-396-6422 (800-466-8356)
One well-behaved family pet per room. Guest must notify front desk upon arrival. Guest is liable for any damages. In consideration of all guests, pets must never be left unattended in the guest rooms.

Park Inn & Suites Maingate East
6075 W Irlo Bronson Hwy
Kissimmee, FL
407-396-6100
Dogs of all sizes are allowed. There is a $10 per day additional pet fee and a $150 refundable pet deposit.

Radisson Resort Worldgate
3011 Maingate Lane
Kissimmee, FL
407-396-1400

Dogs up to 50 pounds are allowed. There is a $75 one time additional pet fee.

Red Roof Inn - Kissimmee
4970 Kyngs Heath Road
Kissimmee, FL
407-396-0065 (800-RED-ROOF)
One well-behaved family pet per room. Guest must notify front desk upon arrival. Guest is liable for any damages. In consideration of all guests, pets must never be left unattended in the guest rooms.

Sun N Fun Vacation Homes
Bear Path
Kissimmee, FL
407-932-4079 (800-874-3660)
sunnfunusa.com/page2/index.html
These vacation Homes are located just 5 minutes to Disney and very close to other area attractions. All homes have private screened pools and fenced yards. Most homes welcome well-behaved pets and their families. There is a pet fee of $30 per pet, per week plus a $300 security deposit, which is refundable assuming there is no damage.

The Idyll Mouse One
8092 Roaring Creek
Kissimmee, FL
603-524-4000
theidyllmouse.com/one/index.html
2 Vacation Home Rentals near Disney World. Each house has many luxuries. One house is a 7 bedroom, four bath. The other is a 4 bedroom, 3 bath.

Comfort Inn
8442 Palm Parkway
Lake Buena Vista, FL
407-996-7300 (877-424-6423)
Dogs up to 50 pounds are allowed for an additional fee of $10 per night per pet. 2 dogs may be allowed.

Best Western Inn
3598 US Hwy 90 West
Lake City, FL
386-752-3801 (800-780-7234)
Dogs are allowed for an additional fee of $10 (plus tax) per night per pet. There may be one average sized dog or 2 very small dogs per room. 2 dogs may be allowed.

Days Inn Lake City
3430 North US Hwy 441
Lake City, FL
386-758-4224 (800-329-7466)
Dogs of all sizes are allowed. There is a $10 per night pet fee per pet. 2 dogs may be allowed.

Motel 6 - Lake City
3835 US 90
Lake City, FL
386-755-4664 (800-466-8356)
One well-behaved family pet per room. Guest must notify front desk upon arrival. Guest is liable for any damages. In consideration of all guests, pets must never be left unattended in the guest rooms.

Super 8 Lake City
I-75 and Hwy 47
Lake City, FL
386-752-6450 (800-800-8000)
Dogs of all sizes are allowed. There is a $5 per night pet fee per pet under 10 pounds and $10 per pet over 10 pounds. Reservations are recommended due to limited rooms for pets. Smoking and non-smoking rooms are available for pet rooms. 2 dogs may be allowed.

Candlewood Suites
1130 Greenwood Blvd
Lake Mary, FL
407-585-3000 (877-270-6405)
Dogs up to 60 pounds are allowed for an additional fee of $12 per night per pet for 1 to 14 days; it is $150 one time fee for 15 or more days per pet. 2 dogs may be allowed.

La Quinta Inn & Suites Orlando Lake Mary
1060 Greenwood Blvd.
Lake Mary, FL
407-805-9901 (800-531-5900)
Dogs of all sizes are allowed. There are no additional pet fees. Dogs must be leashed and cleaned up after. A cell number must be left with the front desk and the Do Not Disturb sign on the door, if pets are in the room alone. Multiple dogs may be allowed.

Super 8 Lake Wales
541 W Central Ave
Lake Wales, FL
863-676-7925 (800-800-8000)
Dogs of all sizes are allowed. There are no additional pet fees. Smoking and non-smoking rooms are available for pet rooms. 2 dogs may be allowed.

La Quinta Inn & Suites Lakeland
1024 Crevasse St.
Lakeland, FL
863-859-2866 (800-531-5900)
Dogs of all sizes are allowed. There are no additional pet fees. Dogs must be leashed and cleaned up after. Dogs may not be left

unattended unless they will be quiet and well behaved. Multiple dogs may be allowed.

Motel 6 - Lakeland
3120 US 98 North
Lakeland, FL
863-682-0643 (800-466-8356)
One well-behaved family pet per room. Guest must notify front desk upon arrival. Guest is liable for any damages. In consideration of all guests, pets must never be left unattended in the guest rooms.

Residence Inn by Marriott
3701 Harden Blvd
Lakeland, FL
863-680-2323
Dogs of all sizes are allowed. There is a $75 one time fee and a pet policy to sign at check in. Multiple dogs may be allowed.

Motel 6 - Lantana
1310 W Lantana Road
Lantana, FL
561-585-5833 (800-466-8356)
One well-behaved family pet per room. Guest must notify front desk upon arrival. Guest is liable for any damages. In consideration of all guests, pets must never be left unattended in the guest rooms.

Super 8 Leesburg
1392 N Blvd West
Leesburg, FL
352-787-6363 (800-800-8000)
Dogs of all sizes are allowed. There is a $10 per night pet fee per pet. Smoking and non-smoking rooms are available for pet rooms. 2 dogs may be allowed.

Days inn MacClenny
1499 S 6th St
MacClenny, FL
904-259-5100 (800-DAYS-INN)
Dogs of all sizes are allowed. There is a $10 per night pet fee per pet. Reservations are recommended due to limited rooms for pets. 2 dogs may be allowed.

Changing Tides Cottages
225 Boca Ciega Dr
Madeira Beach, FL
727-397-7706
changingtidescottages.com
These one and two bedroom cottages are located near Boca Ciega Bay. They are fully equipped. There are no cleaning fees but there is a pet fee of $5 per day or $25 per week.

Island Paradise Cottages & Apartments of Madeira Beach
13215 2nd Street East
Madeira Beach, FL
727-395-9751
islandparadise.com
Some of these vacation rentals allow dogs with prior approvals. Call them to make reservations.

Snug Harbor Inn Waterfront Bed and Breakfast
13655 Gulf Blvd
Madeira Beach, FL
727-395-9256 (866-395-9256)
snugharborflorida.com
This bed and breakfast offers a location on the waterfront, continental breakfast, and a boat slip. Pets are welcome with prior approval.

Best Western Marianna Inn
2086 Highway 71
Marianna, FL
850-526-5666 (800-780-7234)
Dogs up to 50 pounds are allowed for an additional fee of $10 per night per pet. 2 dogs may be allowed.

Quality Inn
2175 H 71S
Marianna, FL
850-526-5600 (877-424-6423)
Dogs are allowed for an additional pet fee of $7 per night per room for smoking rooms, and $12 per night per room for non-smoking rooms. Multiple dogs may be allowed.

Crane Creek Inn
909 E Melbourne Ave
Melbourne, FL
321-768-6416
cranecreekinn.com
The Inn is at 909 and 907 E. Melbourne Ave. There are no additional pet fees. Children are not allowed at the inn.

Hilton
200 Rialto Place
Melbourne, FL
321-768-0200
Dogs up to 70 pounds are allowed for no additional pet fee with a credit card on file; there is a $50 refundable deposit required if paying cash. 2 dogs may be allowed.

La Quinta Inn & Suites Melbourne
7200 George T. Edwards Drive
Melbourne, FL
321-242-9400 (800-531-5900)
Dogs of all sizes are allowed. There are no additional pet fees. Dogs must be leashed and cleaned up

after. Multiple dogs may be allowed.

Beach Bungalow
Call to Arrange
Melbourne Beach, FL
321-984-1330
1stbeach.com
The Beach Bungalow is 3 large, luxurious 2 bedroom oceanfront villas with private gardens in a small beach town. Dogs of any size are allowed with a $50 cleaning fee. The private gardens are entirely fenced and the floors are tile and hardwood.

Hampton Inn
2500 Brickell Avenue
Miami, FL
305-854-2070
Well behaved dogs of all sizes are allowed. There are no additional pet fees. Multiple dogs may be allowed.

Homestead Village-Miami Airport
8720 NW 33rd Street
Miami, FL
305-436-1811 (888-782-9473)
There is a $75 one time pet charge.

La Quinta Inn & Suites Miami Airport West
8730 NW 27th St.
Miami, FL
305-436-0830 (800-531-5900)
One large dog (over 50 pounds) or two medium to small dogs are allowed. There are no additional pet fees. Dogs must be leashed and cleaned up after.

Quality Inn South at the Falls
14501 S Dixie H (H1)
Miami, FL
305-251-2000 (877-424-6423)
Dogs are allowed for an additional pet fee of $10 per night per room. 2 dogs may be allowed.

Red Roof Inn - Miami Airport
3401 Northwest LeJeune Road
Miami, FL
305-871-4221 (800-RED-ROOF)
One well-behaved family pet per room. Guest must notify front desk upon arrival. Guest is liable for any damages. In consideration of all guests, pets must never be left unattended in the guest rooms.

Residence Inn by Marriott
1212 NW 82nd Avenue
Miami, FL
305-591-2211
Dogs of all sizes are allowed. There is a $75 one time fee and a pet policy to sign at check in. Multiple dogs may be allowed.

Staybridge Suites
3265 NW 87th Avenue
Miami, FL
305-500-9100 (877-270-6405)
Dogs of all sizes are allowed for an additional one time pet fee of $125 per pet. 2 dogs may be allowed.

TownePlace Suites Miami Airport West/Doral Area
10505 NW 36th Street
Miami, FL
305-718-4144
Dogs of all sizes are allowed. There is a $75 one time pet fee per visit. 2 dogs may be allowed.

TownePlace Suites Miami Lakes/Miramar Area
8079 NW 154 Street
Miami, FL
305-512-9191
Dogs of all sizes are allowed. There is a $75 one time pet fee per visit. 2 dogs may be allowed.

Wellesley Inn Miami Lakes
7925 NW 154th Street
Miami, FL
305-821-8274 (800-531-5900)
Dogs of all sizes are allowed. There is a $10 per night per room additional pet fee. Dogs must be leashed, cleaned up after, and crated when left alone in the room. Multiple dogs may be allowed.

Brigham Gardens Guesthouse
1411 Collins Avenue
Miami Beach, FL
305-531-1331
brighamgardens.com
This guesthouse offers hotel Rooms, Studios and one Bedroom Apartments. Pets are welcome for a nightly fee of $6.00.

Hotel Leon
841 Collins Avenue
Miami Beach, FL
305-673-3767
hotelleon.com/
This hotel is a stone's throw from the beach and in the heart of the Art Deco District of Miami Beach.

Hotel Ocean
1230 Ocean Drive
Miami Beach, FL
800-783-1725
hotelocean.com
Pets are welcome in this Miami Beach boutique hotel. They have created a special package that includes a bed, treats, and walking service for only $19.95 per pet per

day. The regular pet fee is $15.00 per pet per day.

Loews Miami Beach Hotel
1601 Collins Avenue
Miami Beach, FL
305-604-1601
All well-behaved dogs of any size are welcome. This upscale hotel offers their "Loews Loves Pets" program which includes special pet treats, local dog walking routes, and a list of nearby pet-friendly places to visit. While pets are not allowed in the pool, they are welcome to join you at the side of the pool or at the pool bar. There are no pet fees.

South Beach Marriott
161 Ocean Drive
Miami Beach, FL
305-536-7700 (800-228-9290)
Dogs up to 100 pounds are allowed. There is a $150 one time additional pet fee per room. Dogs must be leashed, cleaned up after, and the Do Not Disturb sign put on the door if they are in the room alone. 2 dogs may be allowed.

Red Roof Inn - Pensacola East - Milton
2672 Avalon Boulevard
Milton, FL
850-995-6100 (800-RED-ROOF)
One well-behaved family pet per room. Guest must notify front desk upon arrival. Guest is liable for any damages. In consideration of all guests, pets must never be left unattended in the guest rooms.

Residence Inn by Marriott
14700 SW 29th Street
Miramar, FL
954-450-2717
Pets of all sizes are welcome. There is a $75 one time fee and a pet policy to sign at check in. 2 dogs may be allowed.

La Quinta Inn Naples Airport
185 Bedzel Circle
Naples, FL
239-352-8400 (800-531-5900)
Dogs of all sizes are allowed. There are no additional pet fees. Dogs may not be left unattended in the rooms except for a short time, and they must be well behaved and kept on leash. Multiple dogs may be allowed.

Red Roof Inn - Naples
1925 Davis Boulevard
Naples, FL
239-774-3117 (800-RED-ROOF)
One well-behaved family pet per

room. Guest must notify front desk upon arrival. Guest is liable for any damages. In consideration of all guests, pets must never be left unattended in the guest rooms.

Residence Inn by Marriott
4075 Tamiami Trail N
Naples, FL
239-659-1300
Dogs of all sizes are allowed. There is a $75 one time fee and a pet policy to sign at check in. Please kennel your pet if you are out of the room. 2 dogs may be allowed.

Staybridge Suites
4805 Tamiami Trail North
Naples, FL
239-643-8002 (877-270-6405)
Dogs of all sizes are allowed for an additional one time pet fee of $150 per room. 2 dogs may be allowed.

EastWind Villas
New Smyrna Beach, FL
386-428-1387
newsmyrnabeachvillas.com
Five pet-friendly vacation rentals are available near the beach . High Speed Internet access is available in the rentals. There are no weight restrictions for dogs and each vacation rental allows up to two pets. Dogs must be on a flea program.

Comfort Inn
101 H 85N
Niceville, FL
850-678-8077 (877-424-6423)
Dogs of all sizes are allowed. There is a $10 per night per pet fee and a pet policy to sign at check in. Multiple dogs may be allowed.

Red Roof Inn - Ft Lauderdale
4800 Powerline Road
Oakland Park, FL
954-776-6333 (800-RED-ROOF)
One well-behaved family pet per room. Guest must notify front desk upon arrival. Guest is liable for any damages. In consideration of all guests, pets must never be left unattended in the guest rooms.

Comfort Inn
4040 W Silver Springs Blvd
Ocala, FL
352-629-8850 (877-424-6423)
Dogs are allowed for an additional fee per night per pet of $5 for dogs up to 10 pounds; $10 for 11 to 20 pounds, and $20 for 21 to 50 pound dogs. 2 dogs may be allowed.

Days Inn

3811 NW Bonnie Heath Rd
Ocala, FL
352-629-7041 (800-329-7466)
Dogs of all sizes are allowed. There is a $5 per night pet fee per pet. 2 dogs may be allowed.

Days Inn Ocala
3620 W Silver Springs Blvd
Ocala, FL
352-629-0091 (800-329-7466)
Dogs of all sizes are allowed. There is a $10 per night pet fee per pet. 2 dogs may be allowed.

Hilton
3600 Southwest 36th Avenue
Ocala, FL
352-854-1400
Dogs are allowed for an additional one time pet fee of $50 per room. They have a treat package for each of their canine guests. 2 dogs may be allowed.

Howard Johnson Inn
3951 NW Blitchton Rd.
Ocala, FL
352-629-7021 (800-446-4656)
Dogs of all sizes are welcome. There is a $20 per day pet fee.

La Quinta Inn & Suites Ocala
3530 S.W. 36th Ave.
Ocala, FL
352-861-1137 (800-531-5900)
Dogs of all sizes are allowed. There are no additional pet fees. Dogs must be leashed, cleaned up after, and removed or attend to the pet for housekeeping. Dogs must be leashed and cleaned up after. Multiple dogs may be allowed.

Red Roof Inn - Ocala
120 NW 40th Avenue
Ocala, FL
352-732-4590 (800-RED-ROOF)
One well-behaved family pet per room. Guest must notify front desk upon arrival. Guest is liable for any damages. In consideration of all guests, pets must never be left unattended in the guest rooms.

Red Roof Inn - Orlando West
11241 Colonial Drive
Ocoee, FL
407-347-0140 (800-RED-ROOF)
One well-behaved family pet per room. Guest must notify front desk upon arrival. Guest is liable for any damages. In consideration of all guests, pets must never be left unattended in the guest rooms.

Comfort Inn

445 S Volusia Avenue
Orange City, FL
386-775-7444 (877-424-6423)
Dogs are allowed for an additional fee of $10 per night per pet. Multiple dogs may be allowed.

Comfort Inn
341 Park Avenue
Orange Park, FL
904-644-4444 (877-424-6423)
Dogs are allowed for an additional fee of $30 per pet for each 1 to 3 days stay. Multiple dogs may be allowed.

Celebration World Resort
7503 Atlantis Way
Orlando, FL
407-997-7421
Dogs up to 40 pounds are allowed as long as they have proof of up to date shots. There is a $50 one time pet fee per room. 2 dogs may be allowed.

Comfort Suites Universal South
9350 Turkey Lake Road
Orlando, FL
407-351-5050 (877-424-6423)
Dogs up to 50 pounds are allowed for an additional one time pet fee of $49 per room. 2 dogs may be allowed.

Country Inns & Suites by Carlson
5440 Forbes Place
Orlando, FL
407-856-8896
Dogs up to 75 pounds are allowed. There is a $150 one time pet fee.

Days Inn Orlando North
2500 W 33rd St
Orlando, FL
407-841-3731 (800-329-7466)
Dogs of all sizes are allowed. There is a $10 per night pet fee per pet. 2 dogs may be allowed.

Hard Rock Hotel
5800 Universal Blvd
Orlando, FL
407-503-2000 (800-BEASTAR (232-7827))
This full service resort has many extras such as a 12,000 square foot pool with a sand beach, an underwater sound system, interactive fountains, and a water slide, a variety of planned activities and recreation, and express access and transportation to the Universal Orlando Theme Park. Dogs of all sizes are welcome for an additional one time pet fee of $25 per room. Guests must have a health certificate

for each pet obtained within 10 days prior to arrival. Dogs must be quiet, well behaved, leashed, cleaned up after, and removed for housekeeping. Dogs must be walked in designated areas only, and they are not allowed in pool/lounge, or restaurant areas. Dogs are not allowed in Club rooms. 2 dogs may be allowed.

Holiday Inn Express Lake Buena Vista
8686 Palm Pkwy.
Orlando, FL
407-239-8400 (877-270-6405)
Dogs of all sizes are allowed for an additional one time fee of $50 per pet. 2 dogs may be allowed.

Holiday Inn Hotel & Suites Main Gate Universal Studios
5905 Kirkman Road
Orlando, FL
407-351-3333 (877-270-6405)
Quiet dogs of all sizes are allowed for an additional one time pet fee of $50 per room. Multiple dogs may be allowed.

La Quinta Inn & Suites Orlando Airport North
7160 N. Frontage Rd.
Orlando, FL
407-240-5000 (800-531-5900)
Dogs of all sizes are allowed. There are no additional pet fees. Dogs may not be left unattended, and they must be leashed and cleaned up after. Dogs must be removed or crated for housekeeping. Multiple dogs may be allowed.

La Quinta Inn & Suites Orlando Convention Center
8504 Universal Blvd.
Orlando, FL
407-345-1365 (800-531-5900)
Dogs of all sizes are allowed. There are no additional pet fees. Dogs must be leashed and cleaned up after. Dogs must be crated if left alone in the room. Multiple dogs may be allowed.

La Quinta Inn & Suites Orlando UCF
11805 Research Pkwy.
Orlando, FL
407-737-6075 (800-531-5900)
Dogs of all sizes are allowed. There are no additional pet fees. Dogs must be leashed and cleaned up after. A call number must be left at the front desk, and the Do Not Disturb sign left on the door, if there is a pet alone inside. 2 dogs may be allowed.

La Quinta Inn Orlando Airport West
7931 Daetwyler Dr.
Orlando, FL
407-857-9215 (800-531-5900)
Dogs of all sizes are allowed. There are no additional pet fees. Dogs must be leashed and cleaned up after. Dogs may not be left unattended unless they will be quiet and well behaved. Multiple dogs may be allowed.

La Quinta Inn Orlando International Dr
8300 Jamaican Court
Orlando, FL
407-351-1660 (800-531-5900)
Dogs of all sizes are allowed. There are no additional pet fees. Dogs must be leashed and cleaned up after. Dogs must be well behaved, and the Do Not Disturb must be on the door if there is a pet alone inside. Multiple dogs may be allowed.

La Quinta Inn Orlando South
2051 Consulate Drive
Orlando, FL
407-240-0500 (800-531-5900)
Dogs of all sizes are allowed. There are no additional pet fees. Dogs may not be left unattended, and they must be leashed and cleaned up after. Multiple dogs may be allowed.

Motel 6 - Orlando - International Drive
5909 American Way
Orlando, FL
407-351-6500 (800-466-8356)
One well-behaved family pet per room. Guest must notify front desk upon arrival. Guest is liable for any damages. In consideration of all guests, pets must never be left unattended in the guest rooms.

Motel 6 - Orlando - Winter Park
5300 Adanson Road
Orlando, FL
407-647-1444 (800-466-8356)
One well-behaved family pet per room. Guest must notify front desk upon arrival. Guest is liable for any damages. In consideration of all guests, pets must never be left unattended in the guest rooms.

Portofino Bay Hotel
5601 Universal Blvd
Orlando, FL
407-503-1000 (800-BEASTAR (232-7827))
Built to resemble an Italian Riviera

seaside village, this beautiful bay hotel features 3 themed swimming pools, special privileges to the areas best golf courses, and express access and transportation to the Universal Orlando Theme Park. Dogs of all sizes are welcome for an additional one time pet fee of $25 per room. Guests must have a health certificate for each pet obtained within 10 days prior to arrival. Dogs must be quiet, well behaved, leashed and cleaned up after, and removed for housekeeping. Dogs must be walked in designated areas only, and they are not allowed in pool/lounge, or restaurant areas. Dogs are not allowed in Club rooms. 2 dogs may be allowed.

Quality Inn Plaza
9000 International Drive
Orlando, FL
407-996-8585 (877-424-6423)
Dogs up to 50 pounds are allowed for an additional fee of $10 per night per pet. Multiple dogs may be allowed.

Red Roof Inn - Orlando Convention Center
9922 Hawaiian Court
Orlando, FL
407-352-1507 (800-RED-ROOF)
One well-behaved family pet per room. Guest must notify front desk upon arrival. Guest is liable for any damages. In consideration of all guests, pets must never be left unattended in the guest rooms.

Residence Inn SeaWorld
11000 Westwood Blvd.
Orlando, FL
407-313-3600 (800-331-3131)
residenceinnseaworld.com/
There is a $150 one time pet fee.

Residence Inn by Marriott
11651 University Blvd
Orlando, FL
407-513-9000
Well behaved dogs of all sizes are allowed. There is a $25 plus tax per night fee up to 5 nights, not to exceed $125 per stay. There is a pet policy to sign at check in and they ask that you do not leave your pet unattended unless you leave a number where you can be reached or a cell number. Multiple dogs may be allowed.

Residence Inn by Marriott
11450 Marbella Palm Court
Orlando, FL
407-465-0075
Dogs of all sizes are allowed. There

is a $75 one time fee and a pet policy to sign at check in. Multiple dogs may be allowed.

Royal Pacific Resort
6300 Hollywood Way
Orlando, FL
407-503-3000 (800-BEASTAR (232-7827))
Nestled in a lush lagoon setting, this full service family resort features such extras as authentic luaus with entertainment, a large pool with a sandy beach and interactive water play area, and express access and transportation to the Universal Orlando Theme Park. Dogs of all sizes are welcome for an additional one time pet fee of $25 per room. Guests must have a health certificate for each pet obtained within 10 days prior to arrival. Dogs must be quiet, well behaved, leashed and cleaned up after, and removed for housekeeping. Dogs must be walked in designated areas only, and they are not allowed in pool/lounge, or restaurant areas. Dogs are not allowed in Club rooms. Multiple dogs may be allowed.

The Safari Hotel & Suites Lake Buena Vista
12205 S. Apopka Vineland Road
Orlando, FL
407-239-0444
Dogs up to 80 pounds are allowed. There are no additional pet fees. Dogs are not allowed to be left alone in the room.

TownePlace Suites Orlando East/UCF
11801 High Tech Avenue
Orlando, FL
407-243-6100
Dogs of all sizes are allowed. There is a $75 one time pet fee per visit. 2 dogs may be allowed.

Travelodge Orlando Centroplex
409 N. Magnolia Ave.
Orlando, FL
407-423-1671 (800-578-7878)
There is a $10 per day pet charge. Dogs up to 50 pounds are allowed.

Days Inn Daytona/Ormond Beach
1608 N US Hwy 1
Ormond Beach, FL
386-672-7341 (800-329-7466)
Dogs of all sizes are allowed. There is a $5 per night pet fee per pet. 2 dogs may be allowed.

Motel 6 - Palm Bay
1170 Malabar Road SE

Palm Bay, FL
321-951-8222 (800-466-8356)
One well-behaved family pet per room. Guest must notify front desk upon arrival. Guest is liable for any damages. In consideration of all guests, pets must never be left unattended in the guest rooms.

Heart of Palm Beach
160 Royal Palm Way
Palm Beach, FL
561-655-5600
There is a $100 non-refundable pet fee. Pet owners must sign a pet waiver.

Plaza Inn
215 Brazilian Avenue
Palm Beach, FL
561-832-8666 (800-233-2632)
plazainnpalmbeach.com/
This pet friendly hotel has accommodated dogs up to 100 pounds. This inn, located on the Island of Palm Beach, is a historic 50 room hotel which has been fully renovated with warm textures of lace, polished wood, antiques and quality reproductions. Take a look at their website for pictures of this elegant inn. There are no pet fees.

The Chesterfield Hotel
363 Cocoanut Row
Palm Beach, FL
561-659-5800
You are allowed to have 2 to 3 pets up to 40 to 50 pounds, and it will depend on the size of the room. There is a $75 one time fee per room and a pet policy to sign at check in.

Best Western Palm Harbor Hotel
37611 US Highway 19 N
Palm Harbor, FL
727-942-0358 (800-780-7234)
Dogs are allowed for an additional fee of $10 per night per pet. Multiple dogs may be allowed.

Red Roof Inn - Clearwater - Palm Harbor
32000 US 19 North
Palm Harbor, FL
727-786-2529 (800-RED-ROOF)
One well-behaved family pet per room. Guest must notify front desk upon arrival. Guest is liable for any damages. In consideration of all guests, pets must never be left unattended in the guest rooms.

La Quinta Inn & Suites Panama City
1030 East 23rd Street
Panama City, FL

850-914-0022 (800-531-5900)
Dogs of all sizes are allowed. There are no additional pet fees. Dogs must be quiet, well behaved, leashed and cleaned up after. A call number must be left at the front desk, and the Do Not Disturb sign left on the door, if there is a pet alone inside. Multiple dogs may be allowed.

Comfort Inn
3 New Warrington Road
Pensacola, FL
850-455-3233 (877-424-6423)
Dogs under 50 pounds are allowed for an additional one time pet fee of $25 per room. The fee is $25 per pet per night for dogs over 50 pounds. 2 dogs may be allowed.

Days Inn Pensacola/Historic Downtown
710 N Palafox St
Pensacola, FL
850-438-4922 (800-329-7466)
Dogs of all sizes are allowed. There is a $10 per night pet fee per pet. 2 dogs may be allowed.

La Quinta Inn Pensacola
7750 North Davis Hwy.
Pensacola, FL
850-474-0411 (800-531-5900)
Dogs up to 50 pounds are allowed. There are no additional pet fees. Dogs must be leashed and cleaned up after. Multiple dogs may be allowed.

Motel 6 - Pensacola East
7226 Plantation Road
Pensacola, FL
850-474-1060 (800-466-8356)
One well-behaved family pet per room. Guest must notify front desk upon arrival. Guest is liable for any damages. In consideration of all guests, pets must never be left unattended in the guest rooms.

Motel 6 - Pensacola North
7827 N Davis Highway
Pensacola, FL
850-476-5386 (800-466-8356)
One well-behaved family pet per room. Guest must notify front desk upon arrival. Guest is liable for any damages. In consideration of all guests, pets must never be left unattended in the guest rooms.

Quality Inn
6550 Pensacola Blvd
Pensacola, FL
850-477-0711 (877-424-6423)
Dogs of all sizes are allowed. There is a $25 one time fee if the dog is

under 40 pounds, and there is a $50 one time fee if the dog is over 40 pounds. Multiple dogs may be allowed.

Red Roof Inn - Pensacola University Mall
7340 Plantation Road
Pensacola, FL
850-476-7960 (800-RED-ROOF)
One well-behaved family pet per room. Guest must notify front desk upon arrival. Guest is liable for any damages. In consideration of all guests, pets must never be left unattended in the guest rooms.

Super 8 Pensacola/Davis Hwy
7220 Plantation Rd
Pensacola, FL
850-476-8038 (800-800-8000)
Dogs of all sizes are allowed. There is a $20 per night pet fee per pet. Smoking and non-smoking rooms are available for pet rooms. 2 dogs may be allowed.

Howard Johnson
9359 US Hwy 19 N
Pinellas Park, FL
727-577-3838 (800-446-4656)
Dogs of all sizes are allowed. There is a $10 per night pet fee per pet. 2 dogs may be allowed.

La Quinta Inn Tampa Bay Pinellas Park Clearwater
7500 Hwy 19 North
Pinellas Park, FL
727-545-5611 (800-531-5900)
Dogs of all sizes are allowed. There are no additional pet fees. Dogs must be leashed and cleaned up after. Dogs must be healthy; tick and flea free, and be removed for housekeeping. 2 dogs may be allowed.

Days Inn Plant City
301 S Frontage Rd
Plant City, FL
813-752-0570 (800-329-7466)
Dogs of all sizes are allowed. There is a $20 per first night and $15 for each additional night pet fee per pet. 2 dogs may be allowed.

Best Western Plantation - Sawgrass
1711 N University Drive
Plantation, FL
954-556-8200 (800-780-7234)
Dogs up to 60 pounds are allowed for an additional fee per pet of $25 for each 1 to 7 days. 2 dogs may be allowed.

Holiday Inn

1711 N. University Dr
Plantation, FL
954-472-5600 (877-270-6405)
Dogs of all sizes are allowed for an additional one time pet fee of $25 per room. 2 dogs may be allowed.

Staybridge Suites
410 North Pine Island Rd
Plantation, FL
954-577-9696 (877-270-6405)
Dogs of all sizes are allowed for an additional one time pet fee of $100 per room. 2 dogs may be allowed.

Days Inn Pompano Beach
1411 NW 31st Ave
Pompano Beach, FL
954-972-3700 (800-329-7466)
Dogs up to 60 pounds are allowed. There is a $25 per night pet fee per pet. Reservations are recommended due to limited rooms for pets. 2 dogs may be allowed.

Motel 6 - Pompano Beach
1201 NW 31st Avenue
Pompano Beach, FL
954-977-8011 (800-466-8356)
One well-behaved family pet per room. Guest must notify front desk upon arrival. Guest is liable for any damages. In consideration of all guests, pets must never be left unattended in the guest rooms.

Sawgrass Marriott Resort, Spa, and Villas
1000 PGA TOUR Blvd
Ponte Vedra Beach, FL
904-285-7777 (800-457-GOLF (4653))
Dogs of all sizes are allowed at the villas, which are 1 bedroom. There is a $25 per night per pet additional fee or $75 per pet by the week. Dogs must be quiet, leashed, cleaned up after, and a contact number left with the front desk if they are in the room alone. Dogs must be removed or accompanied for housekeeping. Multiple dogs may be allowed.

Comfort Inn
11810 H 19
Port Richey, FL
727-863-3336 (877-424-6423)
Dogs are allowed for an additional fee of $10 per night per pet. Multiple dogs may be allowed.

Holiday Inn - Port St. Lucie
10120 S. Federal Highway
Port St Lucie, FL
772-337-2200 (877-270-6405)
Dogs of all sizes are allowed for an

additional pet fee of $50 for each 1 to 7 days per room. 2 dogs may be allowed.

Motel 6 - Punta Gorda
9300 Knights Drive
Punta Gorda, FL
941-639-9585 (800-466-8356)
One well-behaved family pet per room. Guest must notify front desk upon arrival. Guest is liable for any damages. In consideration of all guests, pets must never be left unattended in the guest rooms.

Days Inn Sanford
4650 West SR 46
Sanford, FL
407-323-6500 (800-329-7466)
Dogs of all sizes are allowed. There is a $10 per night pet fee per pet. 2 dogs may be allowed.

Rose Cottage Inn & Tea Room
1301 S Park Ave
Sanford, FL
407-323-9448
rosecottageinn.com
There is a $10 per day additional dog fee. Dogs are not allowed on the furniture.

Super 8 Sanford
4750 SR 46 West
Sanford, FL
407-323-3445 (800-800-8000)
Dogs of all sizes are allowed. There is a $10 returnable deposit required per room. Smoking and non-smoking rooms are available for pet rooms. 2 dogs may be allowed.

Signal Inn
1811 Olde Middle Gulf Drive
Sanibel, FL
800-992-4690
signalinn.com
Signal Inn, situated in a quiet, peaceful and casual atmosphere on the Gulf, consists of 19 furnished elevated beach houses. The pet fee (per pet) is $80 per week or $55 for 3 nights. Only particular units allow pets so please inquire about pets when contacting the inn.

Tropical Winds Motel & Cottages
4819 Tradewinds Drive
Sanibel Island, FL
239-472-1765
Dogs of all sizes are allowed. There is a $15 per night per pet additional fee. Puppies are not allowed to be left alone in the room, and adult dogs for short periods. Multiple dogs may be allowed.

Florida Listings - Please always call ahead to make sure an establishment is still dog-friendly.

Calais Motel Apartments
1735 Stickney Point Road
Sarasota, FL
941-921-5797 (800-822-5247)
thecalais.com/
There is a $15 per day pet charge
and there are no designated smoking
or non-smoking rooms.

Coquina On the Beach Resort
1008 Ben Franklin Drive
Sarasota, FL
941-388-2141 (800-833-2141)
coquinaonthebeach.com/
There is a $30 one time pet charge.
There are no designated smoking or
non-smoking rooms.

Quality Inn and Suites
4800 N Tamiami Trail
Sarasota, FL
941-355-7091 (877-424-6423)
Dogs are allowed for an additional
fee of $20 per night per pet. Multiple
dogs may be allowed.

Residence Inn by Marriott
1040 University Parkway
Sarasota, FL
941-358-1468
Pets of all sizes are allowed. There is
a $75 one time fee and a pet policy
to sign at check in. Multiple dogs
may be allowed.

Siesta Holiday House
1011-1015 Cresent Street
Sarasota/Siesta Key, FL
941-312-9882
Dogs of all sizes are allowed. There
is a $100 refundable deposit. Small
non-hairy dogs are free, otherwise
there is a maximum fee of $25 per
room per stay. The fee also depends
on the breed, how much hair and
how large the dog is. 2 dogs may be
allowed.

Quality Inn and Suites Conference
Center
6525 H 27 N
Sebring, FL
863-385-4500 (877-424-6423)
Dogs are allowed for an additional
fee of $20 per night per pet. Multiple
dogs may be allowed.

Dog-Friendly Fenced Vacation Home
near Tampa/Disney.
1 mile East of I-75, 1/4 mile off of I-4
Seffner, FL
866-980-1234
This pet-friendly vacation rental sits
on one fenced acre near I-75 and I-4.

Turtle Beach Resort
9049 Midnight Pass Road

Siesta Key, FL
941-349-4554
turtlebeachresort.com/
This resort was featured in the
Florida Living Magazine as one of
the best romantic escapes in
Florida. There is a pet charge
added, which is about 10% of the
daily room rate.

Banana Bay Club
8254 Midnight Pass Road
Siesta Key,Sarasota, FL
941-346-0113
Dogs of all sizes are allowed. There
is a $25 one time additional pet fee
per room. Multiple dogs may be
allowed.

Days Inn Ocala/East
5001 E Silver Springs Blvd
Silver Springs, FL
352-236-2891 (800-329-7466)
Dogs of all sizes are allowed. There
is a $10 per night pet fee per pet. 2
dogs may be allowed.

Best Western St Augustine I-95
2445 SR 16
St Augustine, FL
904-829-1999 (800-780-7234)
Dogs are allowed for an additional
pet fee of $10 per night per room. 2
dogs may be allowed.

Days Inn St Augustine/Outlet
Center Mall
2560 SR 16
St Augustine, FL
904-824-4341 (800-329-7466)
Dogs of all sizes are allowed. There
is a $10 per night pet fee per pet. 2
dogs may be allowed.

Howard Johnson Express Inn
137 San Marco Ave.
St Augustine, FL
904-824-6181 (800-446-4656)
Dogs of all sizes are welcome.
There is a $10 per day pet fee.

Inn at Camachee Harbor
201 Yacht Club Dr.
St Augustine, FL
904-825-0003 (800-688-5379)
camacheeinn.com
Fourteen of the nineteen rooms at
this inn are pet friendly. The inn is
located at the Camachee Harbor
only about five minutes from historic
St Augustine. You will need to get
special permission from
management to leave a pet alone in
the room.

Ocean Blue Motel
10 Vilano Road

St Augustine, FL
904-829-5939
Dogs of all sizes are allowed. There
is a $10 per night per pet additional
fee, and a credit card needs to be on
file. Multiple dogs may be allowed.

Holiday Inn - St Augustine Beach
860 A1A Beach Blvd
St Augustine Beach, FL
904-471-2555 (877-270-6405)
Dogs up to 60 pounds are allowed
for an additional fee of $20 per night
per pet. 2 dogs may be allowed.

An Angel's Dream
2008 E Pelican Court
St George Island, FL
850-927-3520
Dogs of all sizes are allowed. There
are no additional pet fees. Multiple
dogs may be allowed.

Collins Vacation Rentals
60 E Gulf Beach Drive
St George Island, FL
850-927-2900
Dogs of all sizes are allowed. There
is a pet policy to sign at check in and
there are no additonal pet fees.
Multiple dogs may be allowed.

Don Cesar Beach Resort
3400 Gulf Blvd
St Pete Beach, FL
866-728-2206
Dogs of all sizes are allowed. There
is a $25 one time fee per pet and a
pet policy to sign at check in. They
also require a health certificate for
your pet validated within the past 10
days. Multiple dogs may be allowed.

TradeWinds Island Grand
5500 Gulf Blvd
St Pete Beach, FL
727-363-2380
This 4 diamond resort offers water
sports, paddleboats, water trykes,
WiFi connections and business
center computers. There are five
restaurants on site, five swimming
pools, two whirlpools, concierge
service and a kids activity center. Up
to 2 pets are allowed per room up to
80 pounds each. There is a $30 per
pet per day additional pet fee.

La Quinta Inn Tampa Bay St.
Petersburg
4999 34th Street North
St Petersburg, FL
727-527-8421 (800-531-5900)
Dogs of all sizes are allowed. There
are no additional pet fees. Dogs
must be leashed and cleaned up
after, and they request that you use

the dog walk area. Dogs may not be left unattended unless they will be quiet and well behaved. They do not allow aggressive breeds. Multiple dogs may be allowed.

Valley Forge Motel
6825 Central Avenue
St Petersburg, FL
727-345-0135
There is a $5 per day pet charge or a fee of $25 per week for a pet.

Best Western Motor Inn
1290 North Temple Avenue
Starke, FL
904-964-6744 (800-780-7234)
Dogs are allowed for an additional fee of $11.10 per night per pet. Multiple dogs may be allowed.

Days Inn Starke
1101 N Temple
Starke, FL
904-964-7600 (800-329-7466)
Dogs of all sizes are allowed. There is a $10 per night pet fee per pet. 2 dogs may be allowed.

Pirates Cove Resort and Marina
4307 S.E. Bayview Street
Stuart, FL
772-287-2500
There are no additional pet fees. Pets must be well-behaved. The hotel has limited pet rooms. Please call ahead to reserve a pet room.

La Quinta Inn Sunrise/Sawgrass Mills
13651 N.W. 2nd Street
Sunrise, FL
954-846-1200 (800-531-5900)
Dogs may not be left unattended, and they must be leashed and cleaned up after. Dogs must be well behaved and housebroken. Dogs may not be left unattended, and they must be leashed and cleaned up after. Multiple dogs may be allowed.

Wellesley Inn Sunrise at Sawgrass Mills
13600 Northwest 2nd Street
Sunrise, FL
954-845-9929 (800-531-5900)
A dog up to 60 pounds is allowed. There is a $10 per night additional pet fee. Dogs may not be left unattended, and they must be leashed and cleaned up after.

Best Western Pride Inn and Suites
2016 Apalachee Pkwy
Tallahassee, FL
850-656-6312 (800-780-7234)
Dogs are allowed for an additional

fee of $10 per night per pet. Multiple dogs may be allowed.

Doubletree
101 S Adams Street
Tallahassee, FL
850-224-5000
Dogs of all sizes are allowed. There is a $200 one time fee per pet and a pet policy to sign at check in. Multiple dogs may be allowed.

Econo Lodge
2681 N. Monroe St.
Tallahassee, FL
850-385-6155 (800-55-ECONO)
There is a $10 per day pet fee.

Holiday Inn Tallahassee-Capitol-East
1355 Apalachee Parkway
Tallahassee, FL
850-877-3171 (877-270-6405)
Dogs up to 90 pounds are allowed for an additional one time pet fee of $35 per room. 2 dogs may be allowed.

La Quinta Inn Tallahassee North
2905 North Monroe
Tallahassee, FL
850-385-7172 (800-531-5900)
Dogs of all sizes are allowed. There are no additional pet fees. Dogs must be leashed and cleaned up after. Dogs may not be left unattended unless they will be quiet and well behaved. Multiple dogs may be allowed.

La Quinta Inn Tallahassee South
2850 Apalachee Pkwy.
Tallahassee, FL
850-878-5099 (800-531-5900)
Dogs of all sizes are allowed. There are no additional pet fees. Dogs must be leashed and cleaned up after. Dogs may not be left unattended unless they will be quiet and well behaved, and they need to be attended to or removed for housekeeping. Multiple dogs may be allowed.

Motel 6 - Tallahassee - Downtown
1027 Apalachee Parkway
Tallahassee, FL
850-877-6171 (800-466-8356)
One well-behaved family pet per room. Guest must notify front desk upon arrival. Guest is liable for any damages. In consideration of all guests, pets must never be left unattended in the guest rooms.

Motel 6 - Tallahassee North
1481 Timberlane Road

Tallahassee, FL
850-668-2600 (800-466-8356)
One well-behaved family pet per room. Guest must notify front desk upon arrival. Guest is liable for any damages. In consideration of all guests, pets must never be left unattended in the guest rooms.

Motel 6 - Tallahassee West
2738 N Monroe Street
Tallahassee, FL
850-386-7878 (800-466-8356)
One well-behaved family pet per room. Guest must notify front desk upon arrival. Guest is liable for any damages. In consideration of all guests, pets must never be left unattended in the guest rooms.

Red Roof Inn - Tallahassee
2930 Hospitality Street
Tallahassee, FL
850-385-7884 (800-RED-ROOF)
One well-behaved family pet per room. Guest must notify front desk upon arrival. Guest is liable for any damages. In consideration of all guests, pets must never be left unattended in the guest rooms.

Residence Inn by Marriott
1880 Raymond Diehl Road
Tallahassee, FL
850-442-0093
Pets of all sizes are allowed. There is a $75 one time fee and a pet policy to sign at check in. Multiple dogs may be allowed.

Staybridge Suites Tallahassee I-10 East
1600 Summit Dr.
Tallahassee, FL
850-219-7000 (877-270-6405)
Dogs of all sizes are allowed for an additional pet fee of $50 per room for 1 to 5 nights, and each night thereafter is $10 per night per room. 2 dogs may be allowed.

TownePlace Suites Tallahassee North/Capital Circle
1876 Capital Circle NE
Tallahassee, FL
850-219-0122
Dogs of all sizes are allowed. There is a $75 one time pet fee per visit. 2 dogs may be allowed.

Wellesley Inn Fort Lauderdale-Tamarac
5070 North State Road 7
Tamarac, FL
954-484-6909 (800-531-5900)
Dogs of all sizes are allowed. There are no additional pet fees. Dogs

must be leashed and cleaned up after. Multiple dogs may be allowed.

Best Western Brandon Hotel and Conf Cntr
9331 Adamo Dr
Tampa, FL
813-621-5555 (800-780-7234)
One dog up to 50 pounds is allowed for an additional one time $25 pet fee.

Best Western Tampa
734 S Dale Mabry Highway
Tampa, FL
813-490-2378 (800-780-7234)
Dogs are allowed for an additional fee of $10 per night per pet. Multiple dogs may be allowed.

Comfort Inn Airport at RJ Stadium
4732 N Dale Mabry
Tampa, FL
813-874-6700 (877-424-6423)
Dogs are allowed for an additional one time pet fee of $25 per room. Multiple dogs may be allowed.

Hampton Inn
5628 W Waters Avenue
Tampa, FL
813-901-5900
Dogs of all sizes are allowed. There is a $10 per night pet fee. Multiple dogs may be allowed.

Holiday Inn Express Hotel & Suites Tampa-Fairgrounds-Casino
8610 Elm Fair Boulevard
Tampa, FL
813-490-1000 (877-270-6405)
Dogs of all sizes are allowed for an additional fee of $10 per night per pet. Multiple dogs may be allowed.

Holiday Inn Express Hotel and Suites
8310 Galbraith Road
Tampa, FL
813-910-7171 (877-270-6405)
Dogs of all sizes are allowed for an additional pet fee of $50 for each 1 to 7 days stay. Multiple dogs may be allowed.

La Quinta Inn & Suites USF (Near Busch Gardens)
3701 East Fowler Ave.
Tampa, FL
813-910-7500 (800-531-5900)
Dogs of all sizes are allowed. There are no additional pet fees. Dogs may be alone in the room if they will be quiet, well behaved, a contact number is left with the front desk, and the Do Not Disturb sign is left on the door. Dogs must be leashed and cleaned up after. Multiple dogs may

be allowed.

La Quinta Inn Tampa Brandon West
602 S. Falkenburg Road
Tampa, FL
813-684-4007 (800-531-5900)
Dogs of all sizes are allowed. There are no additional pet fees. Dogs may not be left unattended at any time, and they must be quiet, well behaved, leashed, and cleaned up after. Multiple dogs may be allowed.

La Quinta Inn Tampa East-Fairgrounds
4811 U.S. Highway 301 N.
Tampa, FL
813-626-0885 (800-531-5900)
Dogs of all sizes are allowed. There are no additional pet fees. There is a pet waiver to sign at check in. Dogs may not be left unattended, and they must be leashed and cleaned up after. Multiple dogs may be allowed.

Motel 6 - Tampa Downtown
333 E Fowler Avenue
Tampa, FL
813-932-4948 (800-466-8356)
One well-behaved family pet per room. Guest must notify front desk upon arrival. Guest is liable for any damages. In consideration of all guests, pets must never be left unattended in the guest rooms.

Motel 6 - Tampa East - Fairgrounds
6510 US 301
Tampa, FL
813-628-0888 (800-466-8356)
One well-behaved family pet per room. Guest must notify front desk upon arrival. Guest is liable for any damages. In consideration of all guests, pets must never be left unattended in the guest rooms.

Red Roof Inn - Tampa Brandon
10121 Horace Avenue
Tampa, FL
813-681-8484 (800-RED-ROOF)
One well-behaved family pet per room. Guest must notify front desk upon arrival. Guest is liable for any damages. In consideration of all guests, pets must never be left unattended in the guest rooms.

Red Roof Inn - Tampa Busch
2307 East Busch Boulevard
Tampa, FL
813-932-0073 (800-RED-ROOF)
One well-behaved family pet per room. Guest must notify front desk upon arrival. Guest is liable for any damages. In consideration of all

guests, pets must never be left unattended in the guest rooms.

Red Roof Inn - Tampa Fairgrounds
5001 North US 301
Tampa, FL
813-623-5245 (800-RED-ROOF)
One well-behaved family pet per room. Guest must notify front desk upon arrival. Guest is liable for any damages. In consideration of all guests, pets must never be left unattended in the guest rooms.

Residence Inn by Marriott
101 E. Tyler Street
Tampa, FL
813-221-4224
Pets of all sizes are allowed. There is a $75 one time fee and a pet policy to sign at check in. Multiple dogs may be allowed.

Residence Inn by Marriott
4312 Boy Scout Blvd
Tampa, FL
813-877-7988
Pets of all sizes are allowed. There is a $75 one time fee and a pet policy to sign at check in. Multiple dogs may be allowed.

Sheraton Riverwalk Hotel
200 North Ashley Dr.
Tampa, FL
813-223-2222 (888-625-5144)
Dogs up to 80 pounds are allowed. There are no additional pet fees. Dogs are not allowed to be left alone in the room.

Sheraton Suites Tampa Airport
4400 West Cypress St.
Tampa, FL
813-873-8675 (888-625-5144)
Dogs up to 50 pounds are allowed. There are no additional pet fees. Dogs are not allowed to be left alone in the room.

TownePlace Suites Tampa North/I-75 Fletcher
6800 Woodstork Rd
Tampa, FL
813-975-9777
Dogs of all sizes are allowed. There is a $75 one time pet fee per visit. 2 dogs may be allowed.

Residence Inn by Marriott
13420 North Telecom Parkway
Temple Terrace, FL
813-972-4400
Pets of all sizes are allowed. There is a $75 one time fee and a pet policy to sign at check in. Multiple dogs may be allowed.

Comfort Inn
3655 Cheney H
Titusville, FL
321-269-7110 (877-424-6423)
Dogs are allowed for an additional fee of $10 per night per pet. 2 dogs may be allowed.

Days Inn Space Coast/Titusville
3755 Cheney Hwy
Titusville, FL
321-269-4480 (800-329-7466)
Dogs of all sizes are allowed. There is a $10 per night pet fee per pet. Reservations are recommended due to limited rooms for pets. 2 dogs may be allowed.

Hampton Inn
4760 Helen Hauser Blvd
Titusville, FL
321-383-9191
Dogs of all sizes are allowed. There is a $25 one time fee per pet. Multiple dogs may be allowed.

Riverside Inn
1829 Riverside Drive
Titusville, FL
321-267-7900
This inn was formerly the Howard Johnson Lodge. There is a $5 per day additional pet fee.

A Whisper of Treasure Island
279 104th Avenue
Treasure Island, FL
727-363-0800 (888-987-2673)
whispersresort.com
Watch the dolphins swim by from this resort on the Gulf of Mexico. One dog of any size or two smaller dogs are allowed in guestrooms. There is a $75 per week pet fee per dog.

Lorelei Resort Motel
10273 Gulf Blvd
Treasure Island, FL
727-360-4351
Dogs of all sizes are allowed. There is no additional fee for up to 2 pets. If you have more than 2 pets the fee is $10 per night per pet. Multiple dogs may be allowed.

Days Inn Venice
1710 S Tamiami Trail
Venice, FL
941-493-4558 (800-329-7466)
Dogs of all sizes are allowed. There is a $15 one time small pet or $30 large per pet fee per visit. 2 dogs may be allowed.

Holiday Inn Venice-Sarasota Area
455 US Highway 41 Bypass North
Venice, FL
941-485-5411 (877-270-6405)
Dogs of all sizes are allowed for an additional one time pet fee of $30 per room. Multiple dogs may be allowed.

Motel 6 - Venice
281 US 41 Bypass North
Venice, FL
941-485-8255 (800-466-8356)
One well-behaved family pet per room. Guest must notify front desk upon arrival. Guest is liable for any damages. In consideration of all guests, pets must never be left unattended in the guest rooms.

Howard Johnson Inn
4431 West New Haven Ave.
West Melbourne, FL
321-768-8439 (800-446-4656)
Dogs up to 50 pounds are allowed. There is a $20 one time per day pet fee.

Days Inn West Palm Beach North
2300 45th St
West Palm Beach, FL
561-689-0450 (800-329-7466)
Dogs of all sizes are allowed. There is a $10 per night pet fee per pet. 2 dogs may be allowed.

Hibiscus House Bed & Breakfast
501 30th Street
West Palm Beach, FL
561-863-5633 (800-203-4927)
hibiscushouse.com/
This bed and breakfast was ranked by the Miami Herald as one of the ten best in Florida. The owner has a dog, and there are no pet charges. Large dogs usually stay in the cottage.

La Quinta Inn & Suites West Palm Beach
1910 Palm Beach Lakes Boulevard
West Palm Beach, FL
561-689-8540 (800-531-5900)
Dogs of all sizes are allowed. There are no additional pet fees. Dogs must be leashed, cleaned up after, and a contact number left with the front desk if there is a pet in the room alone. Multiple dogs may be allowed.

La Quinta Inn West Palm Beach
5981 Okeechobee Blvd
West Palm Beach, FL
561-697-3388 (800-531-5900)
Dogs of all sizes are allowed. There are no additional pet fees. Dogs must be leashed and cleaned up after. Dogs must be crated if left alone in the room. Multiple dogs may be allowed.

Radisson Suite Inn Palm Beach Airport
1808 South Australian Avenue
West Palm Beach, FL
561-689-6888
Dogs of all sizes are allowed. There is a $75 one time pet fee.

Red Roof Inn - West Palm Beach
2421 Metrocentre Boulevard East
West Palm Beach, FL
561-697-7710 (800-RED-ROOF)
One well-behaved family pet per room. Guest must notify front desk upon arrival. Guest is liable for any damages. In consideration of all guests, pets must never be left unattended in the guest rooms.

Residence Inn by Marriott
2461 Metrocentre Blvd
West Palm Beach, FL
561-687-4747
Pets of all sizes are allowed. There is a $75 one time fee per pet and a pet policy to sign at check in. Multiple dogs may be allowed.

Residence Inn by Marriott
2605 Weston Road
Weston, FL
954-659-8585
Dogs of all sizes are allowed. There is a $75 one time fee and a pet policy to sign at check in. Multiple dogs may be allowed.

TownePlace Suites Fort Lauderdale Weston
1545 Three Village Rd
Weston, FL
954-659-2234
Dogs of all sizes are allowed. There is a $75 one time pet fee per visit. 2 dogs may be allowed.

Days Inn Wildwood
551 E SR 44
Wildwood, FL
352-748-7766 (800-329-7466)
Dogs of all sizes are allowed. There is a $10 per night pet fee per pet. 2 dogs may be allowed.

Georgia Listings

Red Roof Inn - Atlanta Acworth
5320 Cherokee Street
Acworth, GA
770-974-5400 (800-RED-ROOF)

One well-behaved family pet per room. Guest must notify front desk upon arrival. Guest is liable for any damages. In consideration of all guests, pets must never be left unattended in the guest rooms.

Super 8 Acworth
4970 Cowan Rd
Acworth, GA
770-966-9700 (800-800-8000)
Dogs of all sizes are allowed. There is a $8 per night pet fee per pet. Smoking and non-smoking rooms are available for pet rooms. 2 dogs may be allowed.

Comfort Inn
107 Princeton Blvd
Adairsville, GA
770-773-2886 (877-424-6423)
Dogs are allowed for an additional fee of $10 per night per pet. Multiple dogs may be allowed.

Days Inn Adel
1200 W 4th St
Adel, GA
229-896-4574 (800-329-7466)
Dogs of all sizes are allowed. There is a $5 per night pet fee per pet. 2 dogs may be allowed.

Hampton Inn
1500 W Fourth Street
Adel, GA
229-896-3099
Dogs of all sizes are allowed on the 3rd floor rooms. There is a $10 per night per pet fee. Multiple dogs may be allowed.

Super 8 Adel/I-75
1103 W 4th Street
Adel, GA
229-896-2244 (800-800-8000)
Dogs of all sizes are allowed. There is a $5 per night pet fee per pet. Smoking and non-smoking rooms are available for pet rooms. 2 dogs may be allowed.

Best Western Albany Mall Inn & Suites
2729 Pointe North Boulevard
Albany, GA
229-446-2001 (800-780-7234)
Dogs are allowed for an additional fee of $10 per night per pet. Multiple dogs may be allowed.

Holiday Inn - Albany Mall
2701 Dawson Rd
Albany, GA
229-883-8100 (877-270-6405)
Dogs of all sizes are allowed for an additional one time pet fee of $25 per

room. 2 dogs may be allowed.

Knights Inn
1201 Schley Avenue
Albany, GA
229-888-9600 (800-843-5644)
There is a $10 one time pet charge.

Motel 6 - Albany
201 South Thornton Drive
Albany, GA
229-439-0078 (800-466-8356)
One well-behaved family pet per room. Guest must notify front desk upon arrival. Guest is liable for any damages. In consideration of all guests, pets must never be left unattended in the guest rooms.

La Quinta Inn & Suites Atlanta Alpharetta
1350 North Point Dr.
Alpharetta, GA
770-754-7800 (800-531-5900)
Dogs of all sizes are allowed. There are no additional pet fees. Dogs must be leashed and cleaned up after, and removed or crated for housekeeping. Multiple dogs may be allowed.

Residence Inn by Marriott
1325 North Point Drive
Alpharetta, GA
770-587-1151
Pets of all sizes are allowed. There is a $75 one time fee and a pet policy to sign at check in. Multiple dogs may be allowed.

Residence Inn by Marriott
5465 Windward Parkway West
Alpharetta, GA
770-664-0664
Pets of all sizes are allowed. There is a $75 one time fee and a pet policy to sign at check in. Multiple dogs may be allowed.

TownePlace Suites Atlanta Alpharetta
7925 Westside Parkway
Alpharetta, GA
770-664-1300
Dogs of all sizes are allowed. There is a $75 one time pet fee per visit. 2 dogs may be allowed.

Holiday Inn Express
1607 Hwy 280 East
Americus, GA
229-928-5400 (877-270-6405)
Dogs of all sizes are allowed for an additional one time pet fee of $15 per room. 2 dogs may be allowed.

Days Inn Ashburn

823 E Washington Ave
Ashburn, GA
229-567-3346 (800-329-7466)
Dogs of all sizes are allowed. There is a $5 per night pet fee per pet. 2 dogs may be allowed.

Comfort Suites
255 North Avenue
Athens, GA
706-995-4000 (877-424-6423)
Dogs up to 60 pounds are allowed for an additional fee of $25 per night per pet. Multiple dogs may be allowed.

Airport Drury Inn & Suites
1270 Virginia Avenue
Atlanta, GA
404-761-4900 (800-378-7946)
Dogs of all sizes are permitted. Pets are not allowed in the breakfast area of the hotel. Pets are not to be left unattended, and each guest must assume liability for damage of property or other guest complaints. There is a limit of one pet per room.

Best Western Granada Suite Hotel - Midtown
1302 W Peachtree Street NW
Atlanta, GA
404-876-6100 (800-780-7234)
Dogs are allowed for an additional pet fee per room of $50 for each 1 to 7 days. 2 dogs may be allowed.

Doubletree
3400 Norman Berry Drive
Atlanta, GA
404-763-1600
Dogs up to 50 pounds are allowed. There is a $50 one time fee per pet. 2 dogs may be allowed.

Hawthorn Suites
1500 Parkwood Circle
Atlanta, GA
770-952-9595
There is a $100 one time pet fee and there is a 2 dog limit per room. There is also a $50 refundable pet deposit.

Hilton
255 Courtland Street NE
Atlanta, GA
404-767-9000
Dogs are allowed for no additional pet fee. 2 dogs may be allowed.

Holiday Inn - Airport North
1380 Virginia Ave
Atlanta, GA
404-762-8411 (877-270-6405)
Dogs of all sizes are allowed for an additional one time pet fee of $50 per room. 2 dogs may be allowed.

Holiday Inn Atlanta Northeast
Doraville
2001 Clearview Ave.
Atlanta, GA
770-455-3700 (877-270-6405)
Dogs of all sizes are allowed for an additional pet fee of $25 per night per room. Multiple dogs may be allowed.

Holiday Inn Select-Atlanta Perimeter
4386 Chamblee-Dunwoody Rd.
Atlanta, GA
770-457-6363 (877-270-6405)
Dogs of all sizes are allowed for an additional one time fee of $75 per room. Multiple dogs may be allowed.

Hotel Indigo
683 Peachtree St NE
Atlanta, GA
404-874-9200 (800-HOLIDAY)
Dogs of all sizes are allowed for no additional fee. Multiple dogs may be allowed.

La Quinta Inn & Suites Atlanta Perimeter Medical
6260 Peachtree Dunwoody
Atlanta, GA
770-350-6177 (800-531-5900)
Dogs of all sizes are allowed. There are no additional pet fees. Dogs must be well behaved, leashed, and cleaned up after. Dogs must be crated if left unattended in the room. Multiple dogs may be allowed.

Laurel Hill
1992 McLendon Avenue
Atlanta, GA
404-377-3217
Well behaved and friendly dogs of all sizes are allowed. There is a $25 one time fee per room and pets must be leashed and kept out of the food areas. Multiple dogs may be allowed.

Motel 6 - Atlanta Northeast
2820 Chamblee - Tucker Road
Atlanta, GA
770-458-6626 (800-466-8356)
One well-behaved family pet per room. Guest must notify front desk upon arrival. Guest is liable for any damages. In consideration of all guests, pets must never be left unattended in the guest rooms.

Red Roof Inn - Atlanta Airport North
1200 Virginia Avenue
Atlanta, GA
404-209-1800 (800-RED-ROOF)
One well-behaved family pet per room. Guest must notify front desk upon arrival. Guest is liable for any

damages. In consideration of all guests, pets must never be left unattended in the guest rooms.

Red Roof Inn - Atlanta Druid Hills
1960 North Druid Hills Road
Atlanta, GA
404-321-1653 (800-RED-ROOF)
One well-behaved family pet per room. Guest must notify front desk upon arrival. Guest is liable for any damages. In consideration of all guests, pets must never be left unattended in the guest rooms.

Residence Inn by Marriott
2960 Piedmont Road NE
Atlanta, GA
404-239-0677
Pets of all sizes are allowed. There is a $75 one time fee per pet and a pet policy to sign at check in. Multiple dogs may be allowed.

Residence Inn by Marriott
2220 Lake Blvd
Atlanta, GA
404-467-1660
Pets up to 70 pounds are allowed. There is a $75 one time fee and a pet policy to sign at check in. 2 dogs may be allowed.

Residence Inn by Marriott
1041 W Peachtree Street
Atlanta, GA
404-872-8885
Pets of all sizes are allowed. There is a $75 one time fee and a pet policy to sign at check in. 2 dogs may be allowed.

Residence Inn by Marriott
1365 Peachtree Street
Atlanta, GA
404-745-1000
Pets up to 75 pounds are allowed. There is a $75 one time fee and a pet policy to sign at check in. 2 dogs may be allowed.

Residence Inn by Marriott
6096 Barfield Road
Atlanta, GA
404-252-5066
Pets of all sizes are allowed. There is a $75 one time fee per pet and a pet policy to sign at check in. Multiple dogs may be allowed.

Residence Inn by Marriott
1901 Savoy Drive
Atlanta, GA
770-455-4446
Pets of all sizes are allowed. There is a $75 one time fee and a pet policy to sign at check in. Multiple

dogs may be allowed.

Sheraton Atlanta Hotel
165 Courtland Street at International Blvd.
Atlanta, GA
404-659-6500 (888-625-5144)
Dogs up to 80 pounds are allowed. There are no additional pet fees. Dogs are not allowed to be left alone in the room.

Sheraton Buckhead Hotel Atlanta
3405 Lenox Road NE
Atlanta, GA
404-261-9250 (888-625-5144)
Dogs up to 80 pounds are allowed. There are no additional pet fees. Dogs are not allowed to be left alone in the room.

Sheraton Gateway Hotel Atlanta Airport
1900 Sullivan Road
Atlanta, GA
770-997-1100 (888-625-5144)
Dogs up to 80 pounds are allowed for no additional pet fee. There is a pet agreement to sign at check in, and dogs may not be left alone in the room.

Staybridge Suites - Atlanta Buckhead
540 Pharr Road NE
Atlanta, GA
404-842-0800 (877-270-6405)
Dogs of all sizes are allowed for an additional one time fee of $150 per pet. 2 dogs may be allowed.

Staybridge Suites - Perimeter
4601 Ridgeview Rd
Atlanta, GA
678-320-0111 (877-270-6405)
Dogs of all sizes are allowed for an additional one time pet fee of $150 per room. 2 dogs may be allowed.

The Westin Atlanta Airport
4736 Best Road
Atlanta, GA
404-762-7676 (888-625-5144)
Dogs of all sizes are allowed. There are no additional pet fees. Dogs are not allowed to be left alone in the room.

The Westin Atlanta Perimeter North
7 Concourse Pkwy
Atlanta, GA
770-395-3900 (888-625-5144)
Dogs of all sizes are allowed for a $25 refundable deposit, and there is a pet agreement to sign at check in. Dogs may not be left alone in the room.

TownePlace Suites Atlanta Northlake
3300 Northlake Parkway
Atlanta, GA
770-938-0408
Dogs of all sizes are allowed. There is a $75 one time pet fee per visit. 2 dogs may be allowed.

Comfort Inn Medical Center Area
1455 Walton Way
Augusta, GA
706-722-2224 (877-424-6423)
Dogs are allowed for an additional one time pet fee of $25 per room. 2 dogs may be allowed.

Country Inns & Suites Riverwalk
Three Ninth Street
Augusta, GA
706-774-1400
Dogs up to 50 pounds are allowed. There are no additional pet fees.

Holiday Inn
2155 Gordon Hwy
Augusta, GA
706-737-2300 (877-270-6405)
Dogs of all sizes are allowed for an additional pet fee of $35 per room for each 1 to 7 days stay. Multiple dogs may be allowed.

La Quinta Inn Augusta
3020 Washington Rd.
Augusta, GA
706-733-2660 (800-531-5900)
Dogs of all sizes are allowed. There are no additional pet fees. Dogs must be crated if left alone in the room, be leashed at all times, and cleaned up after. Multiple dogs may be allowed.

Red Roof Inn - Augusta
4328 Frontage Road
Augusta, GA
706-228-3031 (800-RED-ROOF)
One well-behaved family pet per room. Guest must notify front desk upon arrival. Guest is liable for any damages. In consideration of all guests, pets must never be left unattended in the guest rooms.

The Partridge Inn
2110 Walton Way
Augusta, GA
706-737-8888 (800-476-6888)
Designated a Historic Hotel of America, this has been a full service hotel for business and leisure travelers for more than a hundred years. They have added a full complement of state of the art renovations to blend its rich past with all the modern comforts and amenities you would expect of a luxury retreat. Some of the amenities/features include the award winning Verandah Grill and the Bamboo Room and Piano Bar with live music, large meeting rooms, event planners/caterers for conferences or social affairs, a great Sunday brunch, richly furnished rooms/studios/suites, a secluded courtyard pool, room service, and more than a ¼ mile of verandahs and balconies. Dogs of all sizes are allowed. There is a $25 one time fee for one dog, and a second dog would be an additional $10 one time fee. Dogs may not be left alone in the room at any time, and they must be leashed and cleaned up after. 2 dogs may be allowed.

A Toccoa Riverfront Cabin Vacation
Call to Arrange.
Blairsville, GA
478-862-9733
toccoa-riverfront-cabin.com
A North Georgia mountain cabin on the Toccoa River. Located near Blue Ridge/Blairsville/Dahlonega. Very private. Sleeps 6. Central heat/AC, fireplace, satellite TV, barbecue grill, swings, screened porch, catfish pond and river fishing year-round. Fenced acreage and barn for horses. Pets are welcome.

My Mountain Cabin Rentals
P.O. Box 388
Blue Ridge, GA
800-844-4939
1MyMountain.com
These are rental cabins in the beautiful Blue Ridge area of North Georgia. Pets are allowed in most of the cabins for a $10 per night fee per pet and a $150 refundable damage deposit. Please notify the management that you are bringing a pet when making reservations.

Avenair Mtn Cabin Rentals North Georgia
1862 Old Highway 76
Blue Ridge, GA
706-632-0318 (800-MTN-CABINS)
avenairmtncabins.com
These cabin rentals are located in Georgia's Blue Ridge Mountains about 1 1/2 hours from Atlanta. Many, but not all, of the cabins are pet-friendly.

Black Bear Cabin Rentals
21 High Park Drive Ste 7
Blue Ridge, GA
706-632-4794 (888-902-2246)
blackbearcabinrentals.com
Black Bear Cabin Rentals are available with mountain views, water access and forests all around. Pets are allowed with a pet fee.

Tica Cabin Rentals Inc.
699 East Main Street
Blue Ridge, GA
706-632-4448 (800-871-8422)
ticacabins.com
There are a number of pet-friendly vacation rentals some with excellent views and various amenities. From one to five bedrooms are available. Call for more information or to reserve the cabins.

Best Western Braselton Inn
303 Zion Church Rd
Braselton, GA
706-654-3081 (800-780-7234)
Dogs are allowed for an additional fee of $10 per night per pet. 2 dogs may be allowed.

Holiday Inn Express
2069 Highway 211
Braselton, GA
770-867-8100 (877-270-6405)
Dogs of all sizes are allowed for an additional one time pet fee of $20 per room. Multiple dogs may be allowed.

Days Inn Bremen
35 Price Creek Rd
Bremen, GA
770-537-4646 (800-329-7466)
Dogs of all sizes are allowed. There is a $5 per night pet fee per pet. 2 dogs may be allowed.

Embassy Suites Hotel
500 Mall Blvd
Brunswick, GA
912-264-6100 (800-EMBASSY)
embassysuites.com/es/brunswick
Located 2 miles off I-95, the Embassy Suites offers complementary full breakfast and an evening reception. Dogs up to 100 pounds are allowed with a $15 per day pet fee.

La Quinta Inn & Suites Brunswick
165 Warren Mason Blvd
Brunswick, GA
912-265-7725 (800-531-5900)
A dog up to 60 pounds is allowed. There are no additional pet fees. Dogs may not be left unattended, and they must be leashed at all times, and cleaned up after. 2 dogs may be allowed.

Motel 6 - Brunswick
403 Butler Drive
Brunswick, GA

912-264-8582 (800-466-8356)
One well-behaved family pet per room. Guest must notify front desk upon arrival. Guest is liable for any damages. In consideration of all guests, pets must never be left unattended in the guest rooms.

Red Roof Inn - Brunswick I-95
25 Tourist Drive
Brunswick, GA
912-264-4720 (800-RED-ROOF)
One well-behaved family pet per room. Guest must notify front desk upon arrival. Guest is liable for any damages. In consideration of all guests, pets must never be left unattended in the guest rooms.

Super 8 Brunswick/St Simons Island Area
5280 New Jesup Hwy
Brunswick, GA
912-264-8800 (800-800-8000)
Dogs of all sizes are allowed. There is a $10 per night pet fee per pet. Smoking and non-smoking rooms are available for pet rooms. 2 dogs may be allowed.

Best Western Inn and Suites
101 Dunbar Rd
Byron, GA
478-956-3056 (800-780-7234)
Dogs are allowed for an additional fee of $10 per night per pet. Multiple dogs may be allowed.

Quality Inn
915 H 53E
Cahoun, GA
706-629-9501 (877-424-6423)
Dogs are allowed for an additional fee of $8 to $10 depending on length of stay and size of pet. 2 dogs may be allowed.

Days Inn Cairo
35 US Hwy 84 E
Cairo, GA
229-377-4400 (800-329-7466)
Dogs of all sizes are allowed. There is a $10 per night pet fee per pet. 2 dogs may be allowed.

Days Inn Calhoun
1220 Redbud Rd
Calhoun, GA
706-629-8877 (800-329-7466)
Dogs of all sizes are allowed. There is a $5 per night pet fee per pet. 2 dogs may be allowed.

Super 8 Calhoun/Dalton Area
1446 US Hwy 41 North
Calhoun, GA
706-602-1400 (800-800-8000)

Dogs of all sizes are allowed. There is a $5 per night pet fee per pet. Smoking and non-smoking rooms are available for pet rooms. 2 dogs may be allowed.

Crossroads Hotel
1202 S. Park Street
Carrollton, GA
770-832-2611
There is a $25 one time pet fee.

Days Inn Carrollton
180 Centennial Rd
Carrollton, GA
770-214-0037 (800-329-7466)
Dogs of all sizes are allowed. There is a $6 per night pet fee per pet. 2 dogs may be allowed.

Quality Inn and Suites
160 Centennial Drive
Carrollton, GA
770-832-2611 (877-424-6423)
Dogs are allowed for an additional fee of $20 per night per pet. Multiple dogs may be allowed.

Days Inn Cartersville
5618 Hwy 20 SE
Cartersville, GA
770-382-1824 (800-329-7466)
Dogs of all sizes are allowed. There is a $10 per night pet fee per pet. 2 dogs may be allowed.

Holiday Inn
I-75 and US 411, Exit 293
Cartersville, GA
770-386-0830 (877-270-6405)
Dogs up to 50 pounds are allowed for an additional $10 per night per pet. 2 dogs may be allowed.

Howard Johnson Express Inn
25 Carson Loop NW
Cartersville, GA
770-386-0700 (800-446-4656)
Dogs of all sizes are welcome. There is a $5 per day pet fee.

Motel 6 - Cartersville
5657 Highway 20
Cartersville, GA
770-386-1449 (800-466-8356)
One well-behaved family pet per room. Guest must notify front desk upon arrival. Guest is liable for any damages. In consideration of all guests, pets must never be left unattended in the guest rooms.

Quality Inn
235 S Dixie Avenue
Cartersville, GA
770-386-0510 (877-424-6423)
One dog is allowed for an additional

pet fee of $5.60 per night.

Super 8 Cartersville
41 SR 20 Spur SE
Cartersville, GA
770-382-8881 (800-800-8000)
Dogs of all sizes are allowed. There is a $5 per night pet fee per pet. Smoking and non-smoking rooms are available for pet rooms. 2 dogs may be allowed.

Days Inn Atlanta Airport
4505 Best Road
College Park, GA
404-767-1224 (800-329-7466)
Dogs of all sizes are allowed. There is a $10 per night pet fee per pet. 2 dogs may be allowed.

Days inn Atlanta West
4979 Old National Hwy
College Park, GA
404-669-8616 (800-DAYS-INN)
Dogs of all sizes are allowed. There is a $20 one time per pet fee per visit. 2 dogs may be allowed.

Holiday Inn Express Atlanta Airport-College Park
4601 Best Road
College Park, GA
404-761-6500 (877-270-6405)
Dogs up to 50 pounds are allowed for an additional one time fee of $50 per pet. 2 dogs may be allowed.

Howard Johnson Express Inn
2480 Old National Pkwy.
College Park, GA
404-766-0000 (800-446-4656)
Dogs of all sizes are welcome. There is a $10 per day pet fee.

Motel 6 - Atlanta Airport South
2471 Old National Parkway
College Park, GA
404-761-9701 (800-466-8356)
One well-behaved family pet per room. Guest must notify front desk upon arrival. Guest is liable for any damages. In consideration of all guests, pets must never be left unattended in the guest rooms.

Holiday Inn Columbus-North I-185
2800 Manchester Expressway
Columbus, GA
706-324-0231 (877-270-6405)
Dogs of all sizes are allowed for an additional one time fee of $25 per pet. Multiple dogs may be allowed.

La Quinta Inn Columbus
3201 Macon Rd, Suite 200
Columbus, GA
706-568-1740 (800-531-5900)

Dogs of all sizes are allowed. There are no additional pet fees. Dogs must be crated if left alone in the room, be leashed, and cleaned up after. Multiple dogs may be allowed.

La Quinta Inn Columbus State University
2919 Warm Springs Road
Columbus, GA
706-323-4344 (800-531-5900)
Dogs of all sizes are allowed. There are no additional pet fees. There is a pet waiver to sign at check in, and they request dogs be taken to the designated pet area to due their business. Dogs may not be left unattended, and they must be leashed and cleaned up after. Multiple dogs may be allowed.

Motel 6 - Columbus
3050 Victory Drive
Columbus, GA
706-687-7214 (800-466-8356)
One well-behaved family pet per room. Guest must notify front desk upon arrival. Guest is liable for any damages. In consideration of all guests, pets must never be left unattended in the guest rooms.

Residence Inn by Marriott
2670 Adams Farm Road
Columbus, GA
706-494-0050
Dogs of all sizes are allowed. There is a $75 one time fee and a pet policy to sign at check in. Multiple dogs may be allowed.

Admiral Benbow Inn
30747 Hwy 441 S.
Commerce, GA
706-335-5183
There is a $15 one time pet fee per pet per visit.

Comfort Inn
165 Eisenhower Drive
Commerce, GA
706-335-9001 (877-424-6423)
Dogs are allowed for an additional fee of $10 per night per pet. Multiple dogs may be allowed.

Howard Johnson Inn
148 Eisenhower Drive
Commerce, GA
706-335-5581 (800-446-4656)
Dogs of all sizes are welcome. There is a $10 one time pet fee.

Red Roof Inn - Commerce
157 Eisenhower Drive
Commerce, GA
706-335-3640 (800-RED-ROOF)

One well-behaved family pet per room. Guest must notify front desk upon arrival. Guest is liable for any damages. In consideration of all guests, pets must never be left unattended in the guest rooms.

Super 8 Commerce
152 Eisenhower Dr
Commerce, GA
706-336-8008 (800-800-8000)
Dogs of all sizes are allowed. There is a $10 per night pet fee per pet. Smoking and non-smoking rooms are available for pet rooms. 2 dogs may be allowed.

Hampton Inn
1340 Dogwood Drive
Conyers, GA
770-483-8838
Dogs of all sizes are allowed. There is a $25 one time fee and a pet policy to sign at check in. Multiple dogs may be allowed.

La Quinta Inn & Suites Atlanta Conyers
1184 Dogwood Dr.
Conyers, GA
770-918-0092 (800-531-5900)
Dogs of all sizes are allowed. There are no additional pet fees. Dogs may not be left unattended, and they must be well behaved, leashed, and cleaned up after. Multiple dogs may be allowed.

Best Western Colonial Inn
1706 East 16th Avenue
Cordele, GA
229-273-5420 (800-780-7234)
Dogs are allowed for an additional one time fee of $10 per pet. 2 dogs may be allowed.

Super 8 Cordele
1618 E 16th Ave
Cordele, GA
229-273-2456 (800-800-8000)
Dogs of all sizes are allowed. There are no additional pet fees. Smoking and non-smoking rooms are available for pet rooms. 2 dogs may be allowed.

Comfort Inn
2965 J Warren Road
Cornelia, GA
706-778-9573 (877-424-6423)
Dogs up to 50 pounds are allowed for an additional one time pet fee of $50 per room. 2 dogs may be allowed.

Bend of the River Cabins and Chalets

319 Horseshoe Lane
Dahlonega, GA
706-219-2040
Dogs of all sizes are allowed. There is a $10 per night per pet additional fee. Dogs are not allowed on the beds and must be kept leashed when out. 2 dogs may be allowed.

Hidden River Cabin
1104 Horseshoe Bend Rd.
Dahlonega, GA
770-518-9942
georgiacabins.tripod.com
Cabin with fenced yards. There is a $50 weekly pet fee.

Motel 6 - Dalton
2200 Chattanooga Road
Dalton, GA
706-278-5522 (800-466-8356)
One well-behaved family pet per room. Guest must notify front desk upon arrival. Guest is liable for any damages. In consideration of all guests, pets must never be left unattended in the guest rooms.

Comfort Inn
703 Frontage Road
Darien, GA
912-437-4200 (877-424-6423)
Dogs are allowed for an additional fee of $10 per night per pet. Multiple dogs may be allowed.

Super 8 Darien/I-95
Highway 251 & I 95
Darien, GA
912-437-6660 (800-800-8000)
Dogs of all sizes are allowed. There is a $10 per night pet fee per pet. Smoking and non-smoking rooms are available for pet rooms. 2 dogs may be allowed.

Best Western Dawson Village Inn
76 North Georgia Ave
Dawsonville, GA
706-216-4410 (800-780-7234)
Dogs are allowed for an additional fee of $10 per night per pet. 2 dogs may be allowed.

Comfort Inn
127 Beartooth Parkway
Dawsonville, GA
706-216-1900 (877-424-6423)
Dogs up to 60 pounds are allowed for an additional fee of $15 per night per pet. Multiple dogs may be allowed.

Days Inn Decatur
4300 Snapfinger Woods Drive
Decatur, GA
770-981-5670 (800-329-7466)

Dogs up to 60 pounds are allowed. There is a $25 one time per pet fee per visit. 2 dogs may be allowed.

Best Western Executive Inn and Suites
2121 Hwy 441 South
Dublin, GA
478-275-2650 (800-780-7234)
Dogs are allowed for an additional one time fee of $15 for 1 pet; $25 for 2 pets, and $40 for 3 pets. Multiple dogs may be allowed.

Candlewood Suites - Atlanta
3665 Shackleford Road
Duluth, GA
678-380-0414 (877-270-6405)
Dogs of all sizes are allowed for an additional pet fee of $75 for 1 to 6 days, and $150 for 7 days or more. 2 dogs may be allowed.

Days Inn Atlanta/Duluth
1920 Pleasant Hill Rd
Duluth, GA
770-476-8700 (800-329-7466)
Dogs of all sizes are allowed. There is a $10 per night pet fee per pet. 2 dogs may be allowed.

Hampton Inn
1725 Pineland Road
Duluth, GA
770-931-9800
Dogs of all sizes are allowed. There is a $75 one time fee per pet and a pet policy to sign at check in. Multiple dogs may be allowed.

Holiday Inn - Gwinnett Center
6310 Sugarloaf Parkway
Duluth, GA
770-476-2022 (877-270-6405)
Dogs of all sizes are allowed for an additional one time fee of $25 per pet. Multiple dogs may be allowed.

Holiday Inn Express Atlanta-Gwinnett Mall
3670 Shackleford Rd.
Duluth, GA
770-935-7171 (877-270-6405)
Dogs of all sizes are allowed; however there is only 1 large dog or 2 small dogs permitted per room. There is a $50 one time fee per pet. 2 dogs may be allowed.

Studio 6 - Atlanta Gwinnett Place
3525 Breckinridge Boulevard
Duluth, GA
770-931-3113 (800-466-8356)
One well-behaved family pet per room. Guest must notify front desk upon arrival. Guest is liable for any damages. In consideration of all

guests, pets must never be left unattended in the guest rooms.

Serenity Cabin Rentals
Call to Arrange
Ellijay, GA
706-889-0163 (800-MTN-MEMS)
myserenitycabins.com
Pets are welcome at a number of these rental cabins. There is a $10 per pet per night additional pet fee.

Sliding Rock Cabins
177 Mossy Rock Lane
Ellijay, GA
706-636-5895
slidingrockcabins.com
Located midway between Ellijay and Blue Ridge, Sliding Rock Cabins offers beautifully decorated full log and rustic style cabins with large hot tubs. Pets always stay free and Sliding Rock Cabins provides a large bed for them along with food and water bowls, all natural treats, toys, and towels for the water loving dogs.

Relax Inn (Days Inn)
1201 S 2nd St
Folkston, GA
912-496-2514 (800-329-7466)
Dogs of all sizes are allowed. There is a $4 per night pet fee per pet. 2 dogs may be allowed.

Super 8 Forest Park/Stadium/Atlanta Area
410 Old Dixie Way
Forest Park, GA
404-363-8811 (800-800-8000)
Dogs of all sizes are allowed. There is a $7 per night pet fee per pet. Smoking and non-smoking rooms are available for pet rooms. 2 dogs may be allowed.

Best Western Hilltop Inn
951 Highway 42 North
Forsyth, GA
478-994-9260 (800-780-7234)
One dog is allowed for an additional per night fee of $15 for 1 or 2 nights; 3 or more nights is $30 per night. Add an additional $5 per night for a 2nd dog. Dogs may not be left alone in the room. 2 dogs may be allowed.

Comfort Inn
333 Harold G Clark Parkway
Forsyth, GA
478-994-3400 (877-424-6423)
Dogs are allowed for an additional fee of $10 per night per pet. Multiple dogs may be allowed.

Days Inn Forsyth
343 N Lee St
Forsyth, GA
478-994-2900 (800-329-7466)
Dogs up to 60 pounds are allowed. There is a $10 per night pet fee per pet. 2 dogs may be allowed.

Hampton Inn
520 Holiday Circle
Forsyth, GA
478-994-9697
Dogs of all sizes are allowed, however there can only be one large or 2 to 3 medium to small dogs per room. There are no additional pet fees.

Holiday Inn
480 Holiday Circle
Forsyth, GA
478-994-5691 (877-270-6405)
Dogs of all sizes are allowed for an additional one time pet fee of $10 per room. Multiple dogs may be allowed.

Holiday Inn Express Forsyth
520 Holiday Circle
Forsyth, GA
478-994-9697 (877-270-6405)
Dogs of all sizes are allowed for an additional one time pet fee of $10 per room. Multiple dogs may be allowed.

Motel 6 - Gainesville
1585 Monroe Drive
Gainesville, GA
770-532-7531 (800-466-8356)
One well-behaved family pet per room. Guest must notify front desk upon arrival. Guest is liable for any damages. In consideration of all guests, pets must never be left unattended in the guest rooms.

Motel 6 - Grovetown - Augusta
459 Park West Drive
Grovetown, GA
706-651-8300 (800-466-8356)
One well-behaved family pet per room. Guest must notify front desk upon arrival. Guest is liable for any damages. In consideration of all guests, pets must never be left unattended in the guest rooms.

Residence Inn by Marriott
3401 International Blvd
Hapeville, GA
404-761-0511
Pets of all sizes are allowed. There is a $100 one time fee and a pet policy to sign at check in. Multiple dogs may be allowed.

Best Western Lake Hartwell Inn & Suites

1357 E Franklin Street
Hartwell, GA
706-376-4700 (800-780-7234)
Dogs under 25 pounds are allowed for an additional one time pet fee per room; the fee is $40 for dogs over 25 pounds. 2 dogs may be allowed.

Georgia Mountain Rentals
8817 N. Main St.
Helen, GA
709-878-8400 (877-883-8400)
georgiamtnrentals.com
This vacation rental company offers log cabins, condos and chalets in the Georgia mountains in and around Helen. Each property has different amenities and many allow pets.

Days Inn Hinesville
738 Oglethorpe
Hinesville, GA
912-368-4146 (800-329-7466)
Dogs of all sizes are allowed. There is a $15 one time per pet fee per visit. 2 dogs may be allowed.

Garden Inn and Suites
1630 Bass Cross Rd
Hogansville, GA
706-637-5400 (800-DAYS-INN)
Dogs of all sizes are allowed. There is a $10 per night pet fee per pet. 2 dogs may be allowed.

Buccaneer Beach Resort
85 S. Beachview Dr.
Jekyll Island, GA
912-635-2261
There is a pet fee of $10 per day.

Jekyll Oceanfront Resort
975 North Benchview Drive
Jekyll Island, GA
912-635-2531 (800-431-5190)
jekyllinn.com/
This 15 acre resort is the largest oceanfront resort hotel in Jekyll Island. The resort is also home to the largest public golf course in Georgia. Amenities include an outdoor pool, playground and more. All guest rooms are non-smoking and have either one king bed or two double beds. Rollaway beds, cribs, microwaves and refrigerators are also available for a minimal fee. Or you can stay in one of the Villas, which are two-level townhouses that come with a separate bedroom, kitchen, dining area, living room, bathrooms, and private patio. There is a $25 per night per pet charge plus tax. Dogs up to 50 pounds are allowed.

Oceanside Inn and Suites

711 Beachview Dr.
Jekyll Island, GA
912-635-2211 (800-228-5150)
This beachfront motel's amenities include a playground and room service. There is a $10 per day pet charge.

Quality Inn and Suites
700 N Beachview Drive
Jekyll Island, GA
912-635-2202 (877-424-6423)
Dogs up to 50 pounds are allowed for an additional fee of $10 per night per pet. 2 dogs may be allowed.

Best Western Kennesaw Inn
3375 Busbee Dr
Kennesaw, GA
770-424-7666 (800-780-7234)
Dogs are allowed for an additional fee of $10 per night per pet. Multiple dogs may be allowed.

La Quinta Inn Kennesaw
2625 George Busbee Parkway NW
Kennesaw, GA
770-426-0045 (800-531-5900)
Dogs of all sizes are allowed. There are no additional pet fees. There is a pet waiver to sign at check in. Dogs must be leashed and cleaned up after. Multiple dogs may be allowed.

Red Roof Inn - Atlanta Town Center Mall
520 Roberts Court Northwest
Kennesaw, GA
770-429-0323 (800-RED-ROOF)
One well-behaved family pet per room. Guest must notify front desk upon arrival. Guest is liable for any damages. In consideration of all guests, pets must never be left unattended in the guest rooms.

Residence Inn by Marriott
3443 Busbee Drive NW
Kennesaw, GA
770-218-1018
Pets of all sizes are allowed. There is a $75 one time fee and a pet policy to sign at check in. Multiple dogs may be allowed.

TownePlace Suites Atlanta Kennesaw
1074 Cobb Place Blvd NW
Kennesaw, GA
770-794-8282
Dogs of all sizes are allowed. There is a $75 one time pet fee per visit. 2 dogs may be allowed.

Best Western Kings Bay Inn
1353 Hwy 40 East

Kingsland, GA
912-729-7666 (800-780-7234)
Dogs are allowed for an additional fee of $9 per night per pet. Multiple dogs may be allowed.

Comfort Inn
111 Edenfield Road
Kingsland, GA
912-729-6979 (877-424-6423)
Dogs are allowed for an additional fee of $10 per night per pet. Multiple dogs may be allowed.

Super 8 Kingsland/Kings Bay Area
120 Edenfield Dr
Kingsland, GA
912-729-6888 (800-800-8000)
Dogs of all sizes are allowed. There is a $5 per night pet fee per pet. Smoking and non-smoking rooms are available for pet rooms. 2 dogs may be allowed.

Days Inn LaGrange
2606 Whitesville Rd
LaGrange, GA
706-882-8881 (800-329-7466)
Dogs of all sizes are allowed. There is a $10 per night pet fee per pet. 2 dogs may be allowed.

Days Inn Lafayette
2209 North Main Street
Lafayette, GA
706-639-9362 (800-329-7466)
Dogs of all sizes are allowed. There is a $5 per night pet fee per small pet and $10 per large pet. 2 dogs may be allowed.

Days Inn Valdosta/Lake Park
4913 Timber Dr
Lake Park, GA
229-559-0229 (800-329-7466)
Dogs of all sizes are allowed. There is a $4 per night pet fee per pet. 2 dogs may be allowed.

Best Western Regency Inn & Suites
13705 Jones Street
Lavonia, GA
706-356-4000 (800-780-7234)
Dogs are allowed for an additional one time fee of $15 per pet. 2 dogs may be allowed.

Super 8 Lavonia
14227 Jones St
Lavonia, GA
706-356-8848 (800-800-8000)
Dogs up to 60 pounds are allowed. There is a $10 per night pet fee per pet or $25 per visit per pet. Reservations are recommended due to limited rooms for pets. Smoking and non-smoking rooms are

available for pet rooms. 2 dogs may be allowed.

Days Inn Lawrenceville
731 Duluth Hwy
Lawrenceville, GA
770-995-7782 (800-329-7466)
Dogs of all sizes are allowed. There is a $20 per night pet fee per pet. 2 dogs may be allowed.

Motel 6 - Atlanta - Lithia Springs
920 Bob Arnold Boulevard
Lithia Springs, GA
678-945-0606 (800-466-8356)
One well-behaved family pet per room. Guest must notify front desk upon arrival. Guest is liable for any damages. In consideration of all guests, pets must never be left unattended in the guest rooms.

Motel 6 - Atlanta East - Panola Road
2859 Panola Road
Lithonia, GA
770-981-6411 (800-466-8356)
One well-behaved family pet per room. Guest must notify front desk upon arrival. Guest is liable for any damages. In consideration of all guests, pets must never be left unattended in the guest rooms.

Red Roof Inn - Locust Grove, GA
4832 Bill Gardner Parkway
Locust Grove, GA
678-583-0004 (800-RED-ROOF)
One well-behaved family pet per room. Guest must notify front desk upon arrival. Guest is liable for any damages. In consideration of all guests, pets must never be left unattended in the guest rooms.

Best Western Riverside Inn
2400 Riverside Drive
Macon, GA
478-743-6311 (800-780-7234)
Dogs up to 10 pounds are allowed for an additional pet fee of $10 per night; the fee is $25 per night for dogs over 10 pounds. 2 dogs may be allowed.

Comfort Inn and Suites
3935 Arkwright Road
Macon, GA
478-757-8688 (877-424-6423)
Dogs up to 10 pounds are allowed for an additional pet fee of $15 per night per room; the fee is $20 per night per room for dogs over 10 pounds. Multiple dogs may be allowed.

La Quinta Inn & Suites Macon
3944 River Place Dr.

Macon, GA
478-475-0206 (800-531-5900)
Housetrained dogs of all sizes are allowed. There are no additional pet fees. A contact number must be left with the front desk if your pet is in the room alone. Dogs must be leashed, cleaned up after, and crated or removed for housekeeping. Multiple dogs may be allowed.

Motel 6 - Macon
4991 Harrison Road
Macon, GA
478-474-2870 (800-466-8356)
One well-behaved family pet per room. Guest must notify front desk upon arrival. Guest is liable for any damages. In consideration of all guests, pets must never be left unattended in the guest rooms.

Red Roof Inn - Macon
3950 River Place Drive
Macon, GA
478-477-7477 (800-RED-ROOF)
One well-behaved family pet per room. Guest must notify front desk upon arrival. Guest is liable for any damages. In consideration of all guests, pets must never be left unattended in the guest rooms.

Residence Inn by Marriott
3900 Sheraton Drive
Macon, GA
478-475-4280
Pets of all sizes are allowed. There is a $75 one time fee and a pet policy to sign at check in. Multiple dogs may be allowed.

Sleep Inn
140 Plantation Inn Drive
Macon, GA
478-476-8111 (877-424-6423)
Dogs up to 20 pounds are allowed for an additional fee of $10 per night per pet; the fee is $20 to $25 per night per pet for dogs over 20 pounds. 2 dogs may be allowed.

Days Inn Madison
2001 Eatonton Hwy
Madison, GA
706-342-1839 (800-329-7466)
Dogs of all sizes are allowed. There is a $10 per night pet fee per pet. 2 dogs may be allowed.

Red Roof Inn - Madison
2080 Eatonton Road
Madison, GA
706-342-3433 (800-RED-ROOF)
One well-behaved family pet per room. Guest must notify front desk

upon arrival. Guest is liable for any damages. In consideration of all guests, pets must never be left unattended in the guest rooms.

Super 8 Madison
2091 Eatonton Rd
Madison, GA
706-342-7800 (800-800-8000)
Dogs of all sizes are allowed. There is a $10 per night pet fee per pet. Smoking and non-smoking rooms are available for pet rooms. 2 dogs may be allowed.

Days Inn Manchester
2546 Roosevelt Hwy
Manchester, GA
706-846-1247 (800-329-7466)
Dogs of all sizes are allowed. There is a $10 per night pet fee per pet. 2 dogs may be allowed.

Comfort Inn
2100 Northwest Parkway
Marietta, GA
770-952-3000 (877-424-6423)
Dogs up to 50 pounds are allowed for an additional one time pet fee of $25 per room. 2 dogs may be allowed.

Crowne Plaza Hotel Atlanta-Marietta
1775 Parkway Place Se
Marietta, GA
770-428-4400 (877-270-6405)
Dogs of all sizes are allowed for an additional one time pet fee of $75 per room. Multiple dogs may be allowed.

Days Inn Atlanta/Marietta
753 N Marietta Parkway
Marietta, GA
678-797-0233 (800-329-7466)
Dogs of all sizes are allowed. There is a $15 one time per pet fee per visit. 2 dogs may be allowed.

La Quinta Inn Atlanta Marietta
2170 Delk Rd.
Marietta, GA
770-951-0026 (800-531-5900)
Dogs of all sizes are allowed. There are no additional pet fees. Dogs must be leashed and cleaned up after. Multiple dogs may be allowed.

Motel 6 - Atlanta Northwest - Marietta
2360 Delk Road
Marietta, GA
770-952-8161 (800-466-8356)
One well-behaved family pet per room. Guest must notify front desk upon arrival. Guest is liable for any damages. In consideration of all guests, pets must never be left

unattended in the guest rooms.

Studio 6 - Atlanta - Marietta
2360 Delk Road
Marietta, GA
770-952-2395 (800-466-8356)
One well-behaved family pet per
room. Guest must notify front desk
upon arrival. Guest is liable for any
damages. In consideration of all
guests, pets must never be left
unattended in the guest rooms.

Comfort Inn
80 H 81W
McDonough, GA
770-954-9110 (877-424-6423)
Dogs are allowed for an additional
fee of $10 per night per pet. 2 dogs
may be allowed.

Days Inn Atlanta/McDonough
744 Highway 155 S
McDonough, GA
770-957-5261 (800-329-7466)
Dogs of all sizes are allowed. There
is a $7 per night pet fee per pet. 2
dogs may be allowed.

Quality Inn and Suites
930 H 155 S
McDonough, GA
770-957-5291 (877-424-6423)
Dogs are allowed for an additional
fee of $10 per night per pet. Multiple
dogs may be allowed.

Super 8 McDonough
1170 Hampton Rd
McDonough, GA
770-957-2458 (800-800-8000)
Dogs of all sizes are allowed. There
is a $5 per night pet fee per pet.
Smoking and non-smoking rooms
are available for pet rooms. 2 dogs
may be allowed.

Days Inn Milledgeville
2551 N Columbia St
Milledgeville, GA
478-453-8471 (800-329-7466)
Dogs of all sizes are allowed. There
is a $10 per night pet fee per pet. 2
dogs may be allowed.

Holiday Inn Express Hotel & Suites
1839 North Columbia Street
Milledgeville, GA
478-454-9000 (877-270-6405)
Dogs of all sizes are allowed for an
additional one time fee of $25 per
pet. Multiple dogs may be allowed.

Traveler's Rest
318 N Dody Street
Montezuma, GA
478-472-0085

Well behaved dogs of all sizes are
allowed. There is a pet policy to
sign at check in and there are no
additional pet fees. Multiple dogs
may be allowed.

Best Western Southlake Inn
6437 Jonesboro Rd
Morrow, GA
770-961-6300 (800-780-7234)
Dogs are allowed for an additional
fee of $10 per night per pet. Multiple
dogs may be allowed.

Quality Inn and Suites Southlake
6597 Joneboro Road
Morrow, GA
770-960-1957 (877-424-6423)
Dogs are allowed for an additional
fee of $10 per night per pet. 2 dogs
may be allowed.

Red Roof Inn - Atlanta South
1348 Southlake Plaza Drive
Morrow, GA
770-968-1483 (800-RED-ROOF)
One well-behaved family pet per
room. Guest must notify front desk
upon arrival. Guest is liable for any
damages. In consideration of all
guests, pets must never be left
unattended in the guest rooms.

Sleep Inn
2185 Mt Zion Parkway
Morrow, GA
770-472-9800 (877-424-6423)
Dogs are allowed for an additional
fee of $10 per night per pet. Multiple
dogs may be allowed.

South Drury Inn & Suites
6520 S. Lee Street
Morrow, GA
770-960-0500 (800-378-7946)
Dogs of all sizes are permitted. Pets
are not allowed in the breakfast
area of the hotel. Pets are not to be
left unattended, and each guest
must assume liability for damage of
property or other guest complaints.
There is a limit of one pet per room.

La Quinta Inn Newnan
600 Bullsboro Drive
Newnan, GA
770-502-8430 (800-531-5900)
Dogs of all sizes are allowed. There
are no additional pet fees. There is
a pet waiver to sign at check in.
Dogs are not allowed in dining
areas, and they may not be left
unattended in the room. Dogs must
be leashed and cleaned up after.
Multiple dogs may be allowed.

Motel 6 - Newnan

40 Parkway North
Newnan, GA
770-251-4580 (800-466-8356)
One well-behaved family pet per
room. Guest must notify front desk
upon arrival. Guest is liable for any
damages. In consideration of all
guests, pets must never be left
unattended in the guest rooms.

Super 8 Newnan
1455 Hwy 29 South
Newnan, GA
770-683-0089 (800-800-8000)
Dogs of all sizes are allowed. There
is a $10 per night pet fee per pet.
Smoking and non-smoking rooms
are available for pet rooms. 2 dogs
may be allowed.

Best Western Diplomat Inn
6187 Dawson Boulevard
Norcross, GA
770-448-8686 (800-780-7234)
Dogs are allowed for no additional
pet fee with a credit card on file;
there is a $50 refundable deposit if
paying cash. Multiple dogs may be
allowed.

Days Inn Atlanta NE
5990 Western Hills Dr
Norcross, GA
770-368-0218 (800-329-7466)
Dogs of all sizes are allowed. There
is a $10 per night pet fee per pet. 2
dogs may be allowed.

La Quinta Inn Norcross
5945 Oakbrook Parkway
Norcross, GA
770-368-9400 (800-531-5900)
Dogs of all sizes are allowed. There
is a $10 refundable deposit per
room. There is a pet waiver to sign at
check in. Dogs may not be left
unattended, and they must be quiet,
well behaved, leashed, and cleaned
up after. Multiple dogs may be
allowed.

Motel 6 - Atlanta Northeast -
Norcross
6015 Oakbrook Parkway
Norcross, GA
770-446-2311 (800-466-8356)
One well-behaved family pet per
room. Guest must notify front desk
upon arrival. Guest is liable for any
damages. In consideration of all
guests, pets must never be left
unattended in the guest rooms.

Northeast Drury Inn & Suites
5655 Jimmy Carter Blvd
Norcross, GA
770-729-0060 (800-378-7946)

Dogs of all sizes are permitted. Pets are not allowed in the breakfast area of the hotel. Pets are not to be left unattended, and each guest must assume liability for damage of property or other guest complaints. There is a limit of one pet per room.

Red Roof Inn - Atlanta - Peachtree Industrial Boulevard
5395 Peachtree Industrial Boulevard
Norcross, GA
770-446-2882 (800-RED-ROOF)
One well-behaved family pet per room. Guest must notify front desk upon arrival. Guest is liable for any damages. In consideration of all guests, pets must never be left unattended in the guest rooms.

Red Roof Inn - Atlanta Indian Trail
5171 Brook Hollow Parkway
Norcross, GA
770-448-8944 (800-RED-ROOF)
One well-behaved family pet per room. Guest must notify front desk upon arrival. Guest is liable for any damages. In consideration of all guests, pets must never be left unattended in the guest rooms.

Residence Inn by Marriott
5500 Triangle Drive
Norcross, GA
770-447-1714
Pets are allowed to the total of 75 pounds. There is a $75 one time fee per pet and a pet policy to sign at check in.

TownePlace Suites Atlanta Norcross/Peachtree Corners
6640 Bay Circle
Norcross, GA
770-447-8446
Dogs of all sizes are allowed. There is a $75 one time pet fee per visit. 2 dogs may be allowed.

Country Inns & Suites by Carlson
4535 Oakwood Road
Oakwood, GA
770-535-8080
Dogs of all sizes are allowed. There is a $10 per day additional pet fee.

Holiday Inn Hotel & Suites - Peachtree City
203 Newgate Rd
Peachtree City, GA
770-487-4646 (877-270-6405)
Dogs of all sizes are allowed for an additional $20 per night per pet. Multiple dogs may be allowed.

Days Inn Perry
201 Lect Dr

Perry, GA
478-987-8777 (800-329-7466)
Dogs of all sizes are allowed. There is a $10 per night pet fee per pet. There is a $20 per night pet fee per pet for dog shows. 2 dogs may be allowed.

New Perry Hotel & Motel
800 Main Street
Perry, GA
478-987-1000
Dogs of all sizes are allowed. There is a $10 per night per pet fee if the pet is under 45 pounds, and there is a $15 per night per pet fee if the dog is over 45 pounds. There is a pet policy to sign at check in. Multiple dogs may be allowed.

Quality Inn
1504 Sam Nunn Blvd
Perry, GA
478-987-1345 (877-424-6423)
Dogs are allowed for an additional pet fee of $10 per night per room. Multiple dogs may be allowed.

Super 8 Perry
102 Plaza Drive
Perry, GA
478-987-0999 (800-800-8000)
Dogs of all sizes are allowed. There is a $10 per night pet fee per pet. Smoking and non-smoking rooms are available for pet rooms. 2 dogs may be allowed.

Econo Lodge
500 E. US 80
Pooler, GA
912-748-4124 (888-econo-50)
econolodge-savannah.com
There is a $10 additional fee. Pets are allowed in the pet rooms on the ground floor. The hotel offers free cable w/HBO, a continental breakfast, free local calls, an outdoor pool, and in-room coffee. The hotel is located 11 miles from downtown Savannah near Interstate 95.

Quality Inn
301 Govenor Treutlen Drive
Pooler, GA
912-748-6464 (877-424-6423)
Dogs up to 50 pounds are allowed for an additional fee of $15 per night per pet. 2 dogs may be allowed.

Red Roof Inn - Savannah Airport
20 Mill Creek Circle
Pooler, GA
912-748-0370 (800-RED-ROOF)
One well-behaved family pet per room. Guest must notify front desk

upon arrival. Guest is liable for any damages. In consideration of all guests, pets must never be left unattended in the guest rooms.

Days Inn Richland
46 Nicholson St
Richland, GA
229-887-9000 (800-329-7466)
Dogs of all sizes are allowed. There is a $5 per night pet fee per pet. 2 dogs may be allowed.

Days Inn Savannah/Richmond Hill
3926 HIGHWAY 17
Richmond Hill, GA
912-756-3371 (800-329-7466)
Dogs of all sizes are allowed. There is a $5 per night pet fee per pet. 2 dogs may be allowed.

Motel 6 - Savannah - Richmond Hill
4071 US 17
Richmond Hill, GA
912-756-3543 (800-466-8356)
One well-behaved family pet per room. Guest must notify front desk upon arrival. Guest is liable for any damages. In consideration of all guests, pets must never be left unattended in the guest rooms.

Days Inn Rincon
582 Columbia Ave
Rincon, GA
912-826-6966 (800-329-7466)
Dogs of all sizes are allowed. There is a $10 per night pet fee per pet. 2 dogs may be allowed.

Days Inn Rockmart
105 GTM Parkway
Rockmart, GA
770-684-9955 (800-329-7466)
Dogs of all sizes are allowed. There is a $5 per night pet fee per pet. 2 dogs may be allowed.

Howard Johnson Express Inn
1610 Martha Berry Blvd.
Rome, GA
706-291-1994 (800-446-4656)
Dogs of all sizes are welcome. There is a $5 per day pet fee.

Studio 6 - Atlanta Roswell
9955 Old Dogwood Road
Roswell, GA
770-992-9449 (800-466-8356)
One well-behaved family pet per room. Guest must notify front desk upon arrival. Guest is liable for any damages. In consideration of all guests, pets must never be left unattended in the guest rooms.

Clarion Inn and Suites

16 Gateway Blvd
Savannah, GA
912-920-3200 (877-424-6423)
Dogs are allowed for an additional
fee of $35 per night per pet. Multiple
dogs may be allowed.

Holiday Inn
7100 Abercorn St
Savannah, GA
912-352-7100 (877-270-6405)
Dogs of all sizes are allowed: There
is an additional one time fee of $25
per pet for dogs 25 pounds and
under, and $35 per pet for dogs over
25 pounds. 2 dogs may be allowed.

Joan's on Jones Bed and Breakfast
17 West Jones Street
Savannah, GA
912-234-3863 (800-407-3863)
bbonline.com/ga/savannah/joans/
This bed and breakfast has one pet
suite. There is a $50 one time pet
charge.

La Quinta Inn Savannah I-95
6 Gateway Blvd. South
Savannah, GA
912-925-9505 (800-531-5900)
Dogs of all sizes are allowed. There
are no additional pet fees. Dogs
must be well behaved, leashed, and
cleaned up after. Multiple dogs may
be allowed.

La Quinta Inn Savannah Midtown
6805 Abercorn St.
Savannah, GA
912-355-3004 (800-531-5900)
Dogs of all sizes are allowed. There
are no additional pet fees; however,
a credit card must be on file. Dogs
must be leashed and cleaned up
after. A contact number must be left
with the front desk if the pet is in the
room alone. Multiple dogs may be
allowed.

La Quinta Inn Savannah Southside
8484 Abercorn Street
Savannah, GA
912-927-7660 (800-531-5900)
Dogs of all sizes are allowed. There
are no additional pet fees. Dogs may
only be left in the room alone if they
will be quiet, well behaved, and you
have informed the front desk. Dogs
must be kept leashed. Multiple dogs
may be allowed.

Quality Inn
3 Gateway Blvd
Savannah, GA
912-925-2770 (877-424-6423)
Dogs up to 50 pounds are allowed
for an additional fee of $10 per night

per pet. 2 dogs may be allowed.

Red Roof Inn - Savannah
405 Al Henderson Boulevard
Savannah, GA
912-920-3535 (800-RED-ROOF)
One well-behaved family pet per
room. Guest must notify front desk
upon arrival. Guest is liable for any
damages. In consideration of all
guests, pets must never be left
unattended in the guest rooms.

Residence Inn by Marriott
5710 White Bluff Road
Savannah, GA
912-356-3266
Dogs of all sizes are allowed. There
is a $75 one time fee and a pet
policy to sign at check in. 2 dogs
may be allowed.

Southern Chic Guesthouse
418 East Charlton Street
Savannah, GA
678-859-0674
southern-chic.com
Located in historic district of
Savannah, Georgia. There are no
additional pet fees.

Staybridge Suites Savannah Airport
One Clyde E. Martin Dr.
Savannah, GA
912-965-1551 (877-270-6405)
Dogs of all sizes are allowed for an
additional one time pet fee per room
of $25 for the 1st night; $50 for 2 or
3 nights, and $150 for 4 or more
nights. 2 dogs may be allowed.

Staybridge Suites Savannah
Historic District
301 East Bay Street
Savannah, GA
912-721-9000 (877-270-6405)
Dogs of all sizes are allowed for an
additional one time pet fee of $75
per room. 2 dogs may be allowed.

The Manor House Bed & Breakfast
201 West Liberty Street
Savannah, GA
912-233-9597 (800-462-3595)
There are no pet fees. There are no
designated smoking or non-
smoking rooms.

TownePlace Suites Savannah
Midtown
11309 Abercom Street
Savannah, GA
912-920-9080
Dogs of all sizes are allowed. There
is a $75 one time pet fee per visit. .
2 dogs may be allowed.

Holiday Inn Express Atlanta/Smyrna-
Cobb Galleria
2855 Spring Hill Parkway
Smyrna, GA
770-435-4990 (877-270-6405)
Dogs of all sizes are allowed for an
additional one time pet fee of $25 per
room. Multiple dogs may be allowed.

Red Roof Inn - Atlanta North Windy
Hill
2200 Corporate Plaza
Smyrna, GA
770-952-6966 (800-RED-ROOF)
One well-behaved family pet per
room. Guest must notify front desk
upon arrival. Guest is liable for any
damages. In consideration of all
guests, pets must never be left
unattended in the guest rooms.

Residence Inn by Marriott
2771 Cumberland Blvd
Smyrna, GA
770-433-8877
Pets of all sizes are allowed. There is
a $75 one time fee and a pet policy
to sign at check in. Multiple dogs
may be allowed.

Beachview House
537 Beachview Drive
St Simons Island, GA
603-524-4000
beachviewhouse.com/
This historic 1892 House on
Cumberland Island offers a fully
fenced in yard, 3 bedrooms, 4 baths
and sleeps up to 9. Pets welcome
with prior approval.

Best Western University Inn
1 Jameson Ave
Statesboro, GA
912-681-7900 (800-780-7234)
Dogs are allowed for an additional
fee of $20 per night per pet. Multiple
dogs may be allowed.

Motel 6 - Atlanta South - Stockbridge
7233 Davidson Parkway
Stockbridge, GA
770-389-1142 (800-466-8356)
One well-behaved family pet per
room. Guest must notify front desk
upon arrival. Guest is liable for any
damages. In consideration of all
guests, pets must never be left
unattended in the guest rooms.

Red Roof Inn - Atlanta Southeast
637 SR 138 West
Stockbridge, GA
678-782-4100 (800-RED-ROOF)
One well-behaved family pet per
room. Guest must notify front desk
upon arrival. Guest is liable for any

damages. In consideration of all guests, pets must never be left unattended in the guest rooms.

Best Western Gwinnett Inn
77 Gwinco Boulevard
Suwanee, GA
770-271-5559 (800-780-7234)
Dogs up to 20 pounds are allowed for an additional pet fee of $15 per night per room; the fee is $20 per night per pet for dogs over 20 pounds. 2 dogs may be allowed.

Comfort Inn
2945 H 317
Suwanee, GA
770-945-1608 (877-424-6423)
Dogs are allowed for an additional one time pet fee of $25 per room. 2 dogs may be allowed.

Motel 6 - Suwanee
3103 Lawrenceville Suwanee Road
Suwanee, GA
770-945-8372 (800-466-8356)
One well-behaved family pet per room. Guest must notify front desk upon arrival. Guest is liable for any damages. In consideration of all guests, pets must never be left unattended in the guest rooms.

Red Roof Inn - Atlanta Suwanee
77 Gwinco Boulevard
Suwanee, GA
770-271-5559 (800-RED-ROOF)
One well-behaved family pet per room. Guest must notify front desk upon arrival. Guest is liable for any damages. In consideration of all guests, pets must never be left unattended in the guest rooms.

Best Western Bradford Inn
688 S Main Street
Swainsboro, GA
478-237-2400 (800-780-7234)
Dogs are allowed for an additional fee of $10 per night per pet. Multiple dogs may be allowed.

Best Western Thomaston Inn
1207 Hwy 19 N
Thomaston, GA
706-648-2900 (800-780-7234)
Dogs are allowed for an additional fee of $5 to $10 per night per pet depending on the pet's size. 2 dogs may be allowed.

Comfort Inn
14866 H 19S
Thomasville, GA
229-228-5555 (877-424-6423)
Dogs are allowed for a $30 refundable deposit. Multiple dogs

may be allowed.

Days Inn Thomasville
15375 US 19 S
Thomasville, GA
229-226-6025 (800-329-7466)
Dogs of all sizes are allowed. There is a $10 per night pet fee per pet. Reservations are recommended due to limited rooms for pets. 2 dogs may be allowed.

Best Western White Columns Inn
1890 Washington
Thomson, GA
706-595-8000 (800-780-7234)
Dogs are allowed for an additional fee of $10 per night per pet. Multiple dogs may be allowed.

Days Inn Thomson
2658 Cobbham Rd
Thomson, GA
706-595-2262 (800-329-7466)
Dogs of all sizes are allowed. There is a $10 per night pet fee per pet. 2 dogs may be allowed.

Days Inn Tifton
1199 Hwy 82 W
Tifton, GA
229-382-8505 (800-329-7466)
Dogs of all sizes are allowed. There is a $6 per night pet fee per pet. 2 dogs may be allowed.

Hampton Inn
720 H 319S
Tifton, GA   *ok @ Cracker Barrell
229-382-8800
Well behaved dogs of all sizes are allowed. There are no additional pet fees. Multiple dogs may be allowed.

Holiday Inn
I-75 & US 82W
Tifton, GA
229-382-6687 (877-270-6405)
Dogs of all sizes are allowed for no additional fee. Multiple dogs may be allowed.

Motel 6 - Tifton
579 Old Omega Road
Tifton, GA
229-388-8777 (800-466-8356)
One well-behaved family pet per room. Guest must notify front desk upon arrival. Guest is liable for any damages. In consideration of all guests, pets must never be left unattended in the guest rooms.

Super 8 Tifton
I-75 and W 2nd Street
Tifton, GA
229-382-9500 (800-800-8000)

Dogs of all sizes are allowed. There is a $5 per night pet fee per pet. Smoking and non-smoking rooms are available for pet rooms. 2 dogs may be allowed.

Days Inn Townsend
RR 4 Box 3130M
Townsend, GA
912-832-4411 (800-329-7466)
Dogs of all sizes are allowed. There is a $10 per night pet fee per pet. 2 dogs may be allowed.

Motel 6 - Stone Mountain
1819 Mountain Industrial Boulevard
Tucker, GA
770-496-1317 (800-466-8356)
One well-behaved family pet per room. Guest must notify front desk upon arrival. Guest is liable for any damages. In consideration of all guests, pets must never be left unattended in the guest rooms.

Red Roof Inn - Atlanta Tucker Northeast
2810 Lawrenceville Highway
Tucker, GA
770-496-1311 (800-RED-ROOF)
One well-behaved family pet per room. Guest must notify front desk upon arrival. Guest is liable for any damages. In consideration of all guests, pets must never be left unattended in the guest rooms.

Studio 6 - Atlanta Northlake
1795 Crescent Centre Boulevard
Tucker, GA
770-934-4040 (800-466-8356)
One well-behaved family pet per room. Guest must notify front desk upon arrival. Guest is liable for any damages. In consideration of all guests, pets must never be left unattended in the guest rooms.

Motel 6 - Atlanta Airport - Union City
3860 Flatshoals Road
Union City, GA
770-969-0110 (800-466-8356)
One well-behaved family pet per room. Guest must notify front desk upon arrival. Guest is liable for any damages. In consideration of all guests, pets must never be left unattended in the guest rooms.

Red Roof Inn - Atlanta Union City
6710 Shannon Parkway
Union City, GA
770-306-7750 (800-RED-ROOF)
One well-behaved family pet per room. Guest must notify front desk upon arrival. Guest is liable for any damages. In consideration of all

guests, pets must never be left unattended in the guest rooms.

Best Western King of the Road
1403 N Saint Augustine Road
Valdosta, GA
229-244-7600 (800-780-7234)
Dogs up to 50 pounds are allowed for an additional pet fee of $10 per night per room. 2 dogs may be allowed.

Days Inn Valdosta Conference Cntr
1827 West Hill Ave
Valdosta, GA
229-249-8800 (800-329-7466)
Dogs of all sizes are allowed. There is a $5 per night pet fee per pet. 2 dogs may be allowed.

Howard Johnson Express Inn
1330 St. Augustine Rd.
Valdosta, GA
229-249-8900 (800-446-4656)
Dogs up to 65 pounds are allowed. There is a $5 per day pet fee.

La Quinta Inn & Suites Valdosta
1800 Clubhouse Drive
Valdosta, GA
229-247-7755 (800-531-5900)
Dogs of all sizes are allowed. There are no additional pet fees. Dogs must be quiet, well behaved, leashed and cleaned up after. Dogs may not be left unattended in the room for long periods, and they are not allowed in the lobby or pool area. Multiple dogs may be allowed.

Motel 6 - Valdosta - University
2003 West Hill Avenue
Valdosta, GA
229-333-0047 (800-466-8356)
One well-behaved family pet per room. Guest must notify front desk upon arrival. Guest is liable for any damages. In consideration of all guests, pets must never be left unattended in the guest rooms.

Quality Inn South
1902 W Hill Avenue
Valdosta, GA
229-244-4520 (877-424-6423)
Dogs up to 50 pounds are allowed for an additional fee of $8 per night per pet. 2 dogs may be allowed.

Super 8 Valdosta/Conf Center Area
1825 W Hill Ave
Valdosta, GA
229-249-8000 (800-800-8000)
Dogs of all sizes are allowed. There is a $5 per night pet fee per pet. Smoking and non-smoking rooms are available for pet rooms. 2 dogs

may be allowed.

Days Inn Vidalia
1503 Lyons Hwy 280 East
Vidalia, GA
912-537-9251 (800-329-7466)
Dogs of all sizes are allowed. There is a $5 per night pet fee per pet. 2 dogs may be allowed.

Holiday Inn Express
2619 E First Street
Vidalia, GA
912-537-9000 (877-270-6405)
Dogs of all sizes are allowed for no additional fee, and they must be crated when left alone in the room. 2 dogs may be allowed.

Best Western White House Inn
2526 White House Parkway
Warm Springs, GA
706-655-2750 (800-780-7234)
Dogs are allowed for an additional fee of $15 per night per pet. Multiple dogs may be allowed.

Comfort Inn and Suites
95 S H 247
Warner Robins, GA
478-922-7555 (877-424-6423)
Dogs are allowed for an additional one time pet fee of $25 per room. 2 dogs may be allowed.

Holiday Inn
1725 Memorial Drive
Waycross, GA
912-283-4490 (877-270-6405)
Dogs of all sizes are allowed for an additional one time fee of $15 per room. Multiple dogs may be allowed.

Hawaii Listings

Hawaii, as a rabies free territory, has strict requirements for dogs entering the state from the rest of the U.S. and other countries. There is a 120 day quarantine for pets unless they meet a strict set of criteria. In general, this includes microchipping and vaccinating for rabies and may take up to 6 months to prepare for a trip. If everything is done properly it is now possible to take your dog with you out of the airport on your date of arrival in Hawaii. For more information see Hawaii on the following page: http://www.dogfriendly.com/server/travel/info/customs/travelcustoms.shtml#hawaii

Haiku Private Home Rental
Call to Arrange.
Haiku, HI
808-575-9610
This 3 bedroom, 3 bathroom house rental is on 4 acres of landscaped grounds. Well-behaved dogs are allowed.

North Shore Vacation Rental
Call to Arrange.
Haiku, HI
307-733-3903
This 3 bedroom, 2 bathroom vacation home allows well-behaved dogs.

Bjornen's Mac Nut Farm and Vacation Rental
805 Kauhi Ula Road
Hilo, HI
808-969-7753
This large room with a king bed, a kitchenette and a private entrance is located on a 25 acre fenced property within 1 1/2 miles of Hilo. It also has a swimming pool and hot tub. Rates are $100 per day with a two day minimum. Well behaved dogs are allowed. Owners may be willing to pet-sit for you. Dogs must be up to date on their vaccines and be flea and tick free. You can also contact them via email at e.bjornen@hawaiiantel.net.

Hilo Seaside Retreat Rentals
Call to Arrange.
Hilo, HI
808-961-6178
hilo-inns.com
This private home offers two private suites available for rent. The rentals are located about 10 minutes from the Hilo Airport. Well-behaved dogs are allowed.

Hilo Vacation Rental
Call to Arrange.
Hilo, HI
707-865-1200
This 3 bedroom, 2 bathroom vacation home rental allows well-behaved dogs.

Ka Waile'a
Call to Arrange.
Hilo, HI
808-933-1451
halau-o-kahiwahiwa.com
This studio cabin rental is located about 15 miles north of Hilo. Well-behaved dogs are allowed.

The Kahala Hotel and Resort
5000 Kahala Avenue
Honolulu, HI

808-739-8888 (800-367-2525)
kahalaresort.com/
Located on a secluded beach only minuets from all that Waikiki has to offer, this luxury resort also provides a long list of amenities and on-site activities. One dog up to 40 pounds is allowed for an additional $150 one time pet fee. There is a pet agreement to sign at check in, and dogs must be up to date on all vaccinations.

W Honolulu - Diamond Head
2885 Kalakaua Avenue
Honolulu, HI
808-922-1700
In addition to a wide range of amenities and on-site activities, this beautiful luxury resort offers a great starting point for exploring many local sites of interest and activities. Dogs up to 50 pounds are allowed for an additional one time pet fee of $100 per room. 2 dogs may be allowed.

Paradise Cottage Vacation Rental
Call to Arrange.
Kaihua, HI
808-254-3332
This private cottage rental sleeps six people, and has air-conditioning. Well-behaved dogs are allowed for an extra charge.

Kailua Beach Vacation Home
Call to Arrange.
Kailua, HI
808-230-2176
This 5 bedroom, 2 bathroom vacation home allows well-behaved dogs. It is located about 30 minutes from the Honolulu Airport.

Kailua Vacation Home
Call to Arrange.
Kailua, HI
808-263-0039
This 3 bedroom, 2 bathroom house is located within a short drive to the town of Kailua, and just a few miles to the ocean. Dogs are allowed.

Garden Island Inn
3445 Wilcox Road
Kalapaki Beach - Lihue, HI
808-245-7227 (800 648 0154)
gardenislandinn.com/
Located in the heart of the city's harbor area, this lush garden retreat offers numerous activities and recreational opportunities, and a great location for exploring the island. One dog is allowed for no additional pet fee.

Makaleha Mountain Retreat

Call to Arrange.
Kapaa, HI
808-822-5131
This vacation rental home has 2 bedroom and 1 bathroom, plus a studio. Well-behaved dogs are allowed.

The Westin Maui Resort and Spa
2365 Kaanapali Parkway
Lahaina, HI
808-667-2525 (888-625-5144)
An elegant getaway, this resort sits along white sandy beaches and offers guests a long list of amenities and recreational opportunities. Dogs up to 40 pounds are allowed for no additional pet fee with advance registration; they must be current on shots, and they may not be left alone in the room at any time. Dogs are allowed on the beach here on leash. 2 dogs may be allowed.

Coco's Kauai B&B Rental
Call to Arrange.
Makaweli, HI
808-338-0722
cocoskauai.com
This 2 bedroom, 1 bathroom vacation rental allows well-behaved dogs. The rental is about five minutes from historic Waimea.

Vacation Rental on Princeville Golf Course
Call to Arrange.
Princeville, HI
415-584-1134
This 3 bedroom, 3.5 bathroom home on the golf course allows well-behaved dogs.

Hale Kukui Cottage Rentals
Call to Arrange.
Waipio, HI
808-775-7130
They offer one to three bedroom cottages, all with private baths. Well-behaved dogs are allowed.

Idaho Listings

High Country Inn
4232 Old Ahsahka Grade
Ahsahka, ID
208-476-7570
thehighcountryinn.com/
Set in a lovely meadow surrounded by ponderosa pines, this mountain retreat offers several amenities; some of which include a great hiking trail, a home cooked

breakfast (and dinner on request), a large beer and wine selection, special treats from the kitchen, and a hot tub. Pets of all sizes are allowed for an additional $25 per pet per stay. Dogs must be well-trained, have their own bed and/or crate, be cleaned up after at all times, and friendly as there is another dog and other pets in residence. Dogs are not allowed on the beds or furniture, and they must be crated if they are shedders. Dogs may not be left alone in the room, so there is an outdoor kennel available for guests free of charge. 2 dogs may be allowed.

Suoer 8 Ashton
1370 Highway 20N
Ashton, ID
208-652-3699 (800-800-8000)
Dogs of all sizes are allowed. There is a $10 per night pet fee per pet. Smoking and non-smoking rooms are available for pet rooms. 2 dogs may be allowed.

Best Western Blackfoot Inn
750 Jensen Grove Dr
Blackfoot, ID
208-785-4144 (800-780-7234)
Dogs are allowed for no additional pet fee. Multiple dogs may be allowed.

Super 8 Blackfoot
1279 Parkway Dr
Blackfoot, ID
208-785-9333 (800-800-8000)
Dogs of all sizes are allowed. There is a $10 one time pet fee per visit. Smoking and non-smoking rooms are available for pet rooms. 2 dogs may be allowed.

Doubletree
475 W Parkcenter Blvd
Boise, ID
208-345-2002
Dogs of all sizes are allowed. There is a $10 per night per pet fee. Multiple dogs may be allowed.

Doubletree
2900 Chinden Blvd
Boise, ID
208-343-1871
One dog up to 50 pounds is allowed. There is a $25 one time fee and a pet policy to sign at check in.

Econo Lodge
4060 W. Fairview Ave.
Boise, ID
208-344-4030 (800-553-2666)
Dogs up to 70 pounds allowed.

There is a $10 per day pet fee.

Holiday Inn - Airport
3300 Vista Ave
Boise, ID
208-344-8365 (877-270-6405)
Dogs of all sizes are allowed for an additional one time pet fee of $25 per room. Multiple dogs may be allowed.

Motel 6 - Boise - Airport
2323 Airport Way
Boise, ID
208-344-3506 (800-466-8356)
One well-behaved family pet per room. Guest must notify front desk upon arrival. Guest is liable for any damages. In consideration of all guests, pets must never be left unattended in the guest rooms.

Red Lion
1800 Fairview Avenue
Boise, ID
208-344-7691
Dogs of all sizes are allowed. There is a pet policy to sign at check in and there are no additional fees. Multiple dogs may be allowed.

Residence Inn by Marriott
1401 Lusk (Capitol & University)
Boise, ID
208-344-1200
Pets of all sizes are allowed. There is a $75 one time fee and a pet policy to sign at check in. Multiple dogs may be allowed.

Rodeway Inn
1115 N Curtis Road
Boise, ID
208-376-2700
Dogs of all sizes are allowed. There is a $10 per night per pet fee and a pet policy to sign at check in. Multiple dogs may be allowed.

Super 8 Boise
2773 Elder St
Boise, ID
208-344-8871 (800-800-8000)
Dogs of all sizes are allowed. There is a $25 returnable deposit required per room. Reservations are recommended due to limited rooms for pets. Smoking and non-smoking rooms are available for pet rooms. Multiple dogs may be allowed.

Best Western Caldwell Inn and Suites
908 Specht Ave
Caldwell, ID
208-454-7225 (800-780-7234)
Dogs are allowed for an additional fee of $5 per night per pet. Multiple

dogs may be allowed.

La Quinta Inn Caldwell
901 Specht Ave
Caldwell, ID
208-454-2222 (800-531-5900)
Dogs of all sizes are allowed. There are no additional pet fees. Dogs must be quiet, well behaved, leashed, and they request dogs be taken to the dog run out back. Multiple dogs may be allowed.

Best Inn & Suites
280 W. Appleway
Coeur D'Alene, ID
208-765-5500
There are no pet fees. This was formerly the Comfort Inn

Best Western Coeur D'Alene Inn
414 W Appleway
Coeur D'Alene, ID
208-765-3200 (800-780-7234)
Dogs are allowed for an additional pet fee of $25 per night per room. Multiple dogs may be allowed.

Days Inn Coeur D'Alene
2200 Northwest Blvd
Coeur D'Alene, ID
208-667-8668 (800-329-7466)
Dogs of all sizes are allowed. There is a $10 per night pet fee per pet. 2 dogs may be allowed.

La Quinta Inn & Suites Coeur D Alene East
2209 E Sherman Ave
Coeur D'Alene, ID
208-667-6777 (800-531-5900)
Dogs of all sizes are allowed. There are no additional pet fees. Please leash and clean up after your pet. Multiple dogs may be allowed.

La Quinta Inn Coeur D Alene Appleway
280 W Appleway
Coeur D'Alene, ID
208-765-5500 (800-531-5900)
Dogs of all sizes are allowed. There are no additional pet fees. Please leash and clean up after your pet. Multiple dogs may be allowed.

Shilo Inn
702 W. Appleway
Coeur D'Alene, ID
208-664-2300 (800-222-2244)
There is a $25 per stay pet charge for up to two pets.

Dog Bark Park Inn
2421 H 95
Cottonwood, ID
208-962-3647

dogbarkparkinn.com/index.htm
Definitely a unique traveling experience! The inn is built into the shape of a 30 foot tall Beagle and its 12 foot tall "puppy". They offer a 2nd floor private deck with sleeping accommodations for four, a cozy reading nook in the dog's nose, and an extended continental breakfast. The owners' obvious love of dogs shows in the folk-art style wooden canine carvings (over 60 different breeds) that are offered in their gift store. Carvings from real or still life (like pictures), and tours of the studio where they are made are also available. They are open seasonally and at times close when business may take them away, so call ahead. Dogs of all sizes are welcome for an additional $10 per night per pet. Dogs may not be left alone in the room at any time, or on the beds, and they must be well behaved, leashed and cleaned up after. 2 dogs may be allowed.

Pine Motel Guest House
105 S MainH33
Driggs, ID
208-354-2774 (800-354-2778)
This guest house is surrounded by an acre of tree covered lawn, and a big country breakfast is an option they also offer. One large dog or 2 small dogs are allowed per room. There is a $10 per night per pet additional fee. Dogs may only be left alone in the room if they will be quiet and well behaved. Dogs must be leashed and cleaned up after.

Woods River Inn
601 Main Street/H 75
Hailey, ID
208-578-0600 (877-542-0600)
woodriverinn.com/
Located in the Sun Valley area of Idaho, this motel offers oversized, well-appointed guest rooms, and conveniences for both the vacation or business traveler. Some of the amenities include Jacuzzi, fireplace, and full kitchen suites, an indoor heated pool and hot tub, and a complimentary expanded Continental breakfast. Dogs of all sizes are welcome. There is a $25 one time additional pet fee per room, and a damage waiver to sign at check in. Dogs must be quiet, well behaved, leashed, and cleaned up after. Dogs may not be left alone in the room at any time. 2 dogs may be allowed.

Holiday Inn Express Hotel & Suites Hayden-Coeur D'Alene North
151 W. Orchard St.

Hayden, ID
208-772-7900 (877-270-6405)
Dogs of all sizes are allowed for an additional $10 per night per pet. Dogs may not be left alone in the room. 2 dogs may be allowed.

Super 8 Heyburn/Burley Area
336 South 600 West
Heyburn, ID
208-678-7000 (800-800-8000)
Dogs of all sizes are allowed. There is a $5 per night pet fee per pet. Reservations are recommended due to limited rooms for pets. Smoking and non-smoking rooms are available for pet rooms. 2 dogs may be allowed.

Best Western Driftwood Inn
575 River Pkwy
Idaho Falls, ID
208-523-2242 (800-780-7234)
Dogs are allowed for an additional fee of $10 per night per pet. Multiple dogs may be allowed.

Comfort Inn
195 S Colorado Avenue
Idaho Falls, ID
208-528-2804 (877-424-6423)
Dogs are allowed for an additional one time pet fee of $10 per room. 2 dogs may be allowed.

Motel 6 - Idaho Falls
1448 W Broadway
Idaho Falls, ID
208-522-0112 (800-466-8356)
One well-behaved family pet per room. Guest must notify front desk upon arrival. Guest is liable for any damages. In consideration of all guests, pets must never be left unattended in the guest rooms.

Shilo Conference Hotel
780 Lindsay Blvd
Idaho Falls, ID
208-523-0088 (800-222-2244)
There are no additional pet fees.

Best Western Sawtooth Inn and Suites
2653 South Lincoln
Jerome, ID
208-324-9200 (800-780-7234)
Two dogs are allowed for a $100 refundable deposit; there is an additional $100 refundable deposit for 3 dogs. Multiple dogs may be allowed.

Morning Star Lodge
602 Bunker Avenue
Kellogg, ID
208-783-1111 (866-344-2675)

This premier condominium lodge sits in the heart of the Silver Mountain Resort's new Gondola Village just steps from shopping, dinning, and a variety of recreational activities. Some of the amenities include fully furnished kitchenettes, a large community room with a big-screen TV, and rooftop hot tubs. Dogs are allowed for an additional $30 one time fee per pet. Dogs may only be left alone in the room if they will be quiet, well behaved, checked on regularly, and a contact number is left with the front desk. Dogs must be leashed and cleaned up after at all times. Dogs are also allowed on the 3.1 mile long gondola to the top of the mountain during the summer season. 2 dogs may be allowed.

Silverhorn Motor Lodge
699 W Cameron Avenue
Kellogg, ID
208-783-1151
silverhornmotorinn.com/
This motor lodge is just 6 blocks from Gondola Village, and a 3.1 mile long gondola (the longest single stage people carrier in the world) to the top of the mountain and spectacular views. In the summer, your pet may join you on this journey. The lodge offers an in-house restaurant, the largest hot tub in town, and spacious rooms with private baths. Dogs of all sizes are allowed for no additional fee. Dogs may not be left alone in the room unless you are somewhere in the lodge where they can reach you, and then only if they will be quiet and well mannered. Dogs must be leashed and cleaned up after at all times. Multiple dogs may be allowed.

Super 8 Kellogg
601 Bunker Ave
Kellogg, ID
208-783-1234 (800-800-8000)
Dogs of all sizes are allowed. There are no additional pet fees. Dogs are not allowed to be left alone in the room. Smoking and non-smoking rooms are available for pet rooms. 2 dogs may be allowed.

Best Western Tyrolean Lodge
260 Cottonwood
Ketchum, ID
208-726-5336 (800-780-7234)
Dogs are allowed for an additional fee of $10 per night per pet. 2 dogs may be allowed.

Comfort Inn

2128 8th Avenue
Lewiston, ID
208-798-8090 (877-424-6423)
Dogs are allowed for an additional fee of $10 per night per pet. Multiple dogs may be allowed.

Guest House Inn and Suites
1325 Main Street
Lewiston, ID
208-746-1393
This inn is located only 1 block from the Snake River and the Clearwater Rivers, and some of the amenities they offer include a complimentary continental breakfast, a cocktail lounge, seasonal outdoor pool, and a hot tub. Dogs of all sizes are welcome for an additional fee of $10 per night per pet. Dogs may not be left alone in the room at any time, and they must be leashed and cleaned up after. 2 dogs may be allowed.

Holiday Inn Express Lewiston
2425 Nez Perce Drive
Lewiston, ID
208-750-1600 (877-270-6405)
Dogs of all sizes are allowed for an additional one time pet fee of $10 per room. Multiple dogs may be allowed.

Red Lion
621 21st Street
Lewiston, ID
208-799-1000
Dogs of all sizes are allowed. There is a $10 per night pet fee and a pet policy to sign at check in. All pet rooms are located on the first floor. Multiple dogs may be allowed.

Super 8 Lewiston
3120 North South Hwy
Lewiston, ID
208-743-8808 (800-800-8000)
Dogs of all sizes are allowed. There is a $5 per night pet fee per pet. Reservations are recommended due to limited rooms for pets. Smoking and non-smoking rooms are available for pet rooms. 2 dogs may be allowed.

Brundage Inn
1005 W Lake Street/H 55
McCall, ID
208-634-2344 (800-643-2009)
This inn is an enchanting family style lodge only a few blocks from Payette Lake, and is also a perfect launching spot for bikers, hikers, and skiers. Some of the amenities include TV/VCRs with cable, kitchens, family suites, some rooms with fireplaces, outside barbecue grills and tables, and all rooms include a microwave

and refrigerator. Two small dogs (10 pounds or under each) or one dog of average size is welcome for a $20 per night per pet additional fee. Dogs must be well mannered, leashed, and cleaned up after at all times. Dogs are not allowed on the furniture or beds. 2 dogs may be allowed.

The Western Mountain Lodge
415 Third St
McCall, ID
208-634-6300
Dogs are allowed for an additional fee of $10 per night per pet. Multiple dogs may be allowed.

Candlewood Suites Meridian
1855 S. Silverstone Way
Meridian, ID
208-888-5121 (877-270-6405)
Dogs up to 80 pounds are allowed for an additional pet fee of $12.50 per night. Dogs must be crated when left alone in the room. 2 dogs may be allowed.

Motel 6 - Meridian
1047 South Progress Avenue
Meridian, ID
208-888-1212 (800-466-8356)
One well-behaved family pet per room. Guest must notify front desk upon arrival. Guest is liable for any damages. In consideration of all guests, pets must never be left unattended in the guest rooms.

Hillcrest Motel
706 North Main Street
Moscow, ID
208-882-7579 (800-368-6564)
There is a $5 per day pet charge.

La Quinta Inn Moscow-Pullman
185 Warbonnet Drive
Moscow, ID
208-882-5365 (800-531-5900)
Dogs of all sizes are allowed. There are no additional pet fees. Dogs may not be left unattended at any time, and they must be leashed and cleaned up after. Multiple dogs may be allowed.

Palouse Inn
101 Baker Street
Moscow, ID
208-882-5511
Dogs of all sizes are allowed. They have 4 pet friendly rooms; 2 of which are non-smoking. There is a $7 per night per room additional pet fee. Multiple dogs may be allowed.

Super 8 Moscow
175 Peterson Dr

Moscow, ID
208-883-1503 (800-800-8000)
Dogs up to 80 pounds are allowed. There is a $10 per night pet fee per pet. Smoking and non-smoking rooms are available for pet rooms. 2 dogs may be allowed.

Best Western Foothills Motor Inn
1080 Hwy 20
Mountain Home, ID
208-587-8477 (800-780-7234)
Dogs up to 50 pounds are allowed for an additional fee of $10 per night per pet. Multiple dogs may be allowed.

Hampton Inn
5750 Franklin Road
Nampa, ID
208-442-0036
Dogs up to 50 pounds are allowed. There is a $20 one time fee per room and a pet policy to sign at check in. Dogs are not allowed to be left alone in the room. Multiple dogs may be allowed.

Elkin's Resort on Priest Lake
404 Elkins Road
Nordman, ID
208-443-2432
elkinsresort.com/
There is a $15 per day pet charge and there are no designated smoking or non-smoking cabins.

Helgeson Place Hotel Suites
125 Johnson Avenue
Orofino, ID
208-476-5729 (800-404-5729)
helgesonhotel.com/
This hotel is situated right on the Lewis and Clark trail, and they offer a great location for activities and recreation and serve a continental breakfast. Dogs of all sizes are allowed for an additional $15 per night per pet. Dogs must be quiet, well behaved, leashed, and cleaned up after. Multiple dogs may be allowed.

Best Western CottonTree Inn
1415 Bench Road
Pocatello, ID
208-237-7650 (800-780-7234)
Dogs are allowed for no additional pet fee with a credit card on file. Multiple dogs may be allowed.

Cavanaughs Pocatello Hotel
1555 Pocatello Creek Road
Pocatello, ID
208-233-2200 (800-325-4000)
There are no additional pet fees.

Comfort Inn
1333 Bench Road
Pocatello, ID
208-237-8155 (877-424-6423)
Dogs are allowed for an additional fee of $10 per night per pet. Multiple dogs may be allowed.

Holiday Inn
1399 Bench Rd
Pocatello, ID
208-237-1400 (877-270-6405)
Dogs of all sizes are allowed for an additional pet fee of $10 per night per room. Pets are not allowed on the furniture or beds. Multiple dogs may be allowed.

Motel 6 - Pocatello - Chubbuck
291 West Burnside Avenue
Pocatello, ID
208-237-7880 (800-466-8356)
One well-behaved family pet per room. Guest must notify front desk upon arrival. Guest is liable for any damages. In consideration of all guests, pets must never be left unattended in the guest rooms.

Red Lion
1555 Pocatello Creek Road
Pocatello, ID
208-233-2200
Dogs of all sizes are allowed. There are no additional pet fees. Multiple dogs may be allowed.

Super 8 Pocatello
1330 Bench Rd
Pocatello, ID
208-234-0888 (800-800-8000)
Dogs of all sizes are allowed. There is a $2 per night pet fee per pet in smoking rooms. There is a $10 per night pet fee per pet in non-smoking rooms. 2 dogs may be allowed.

Motel 6 - Sandpoint
477255 Highway 95 North
Ponderay, ID
208-263-5383 (800-466-8356)
One well-behaved family pet per room. Guest must notify front desk upon arrival. Guest is liable for any damages. In consideration of all guests, pets must never be left unattended in the guest rooms.

Comfort Inn
3105 E Seltice Way
Post Falls, ID
208-773-8900 (877-424-6423)
Dogs are allowed for an additional one time pet fee of $20 per room. 2 dogs may be allowed.

Howard Johnson Express Inn

West 3647 5th Ave.
Post Falls, ID
208-773-4541 (800-446-4656)
Dogs of all sizes are welcome. There is a $5 per day pet fee.

Sleep Inn
157 S Pleasantview Road
Post Falls, ID
208-777-9391 (877-424-6423)
Dogs are allowed for an additional one time fee of $20 per room. There may be up to 2 medium sized dogs or up to 3 small dogs per room. Multiple dogs may be allowed.

Sleep Inn
100 Pleasant View Road
Post Falls, ID
208-777-9394 (877-424-6423)
Dogs of all sizes are allowed. There is a $20 one time fee per room and a pet policy to sign at check in. 2 dogs may be allowed.

Hill's Resort
4777 W. Lakeshore Rd.
Priest Lake, ID
208-443-2551
hillsresort.com/
There is a $150 per week pet charge. Dogs are also allowed on the beaches.

Comfort Inn
885 W Main Street
Rexburg, ID
208-359-1311 (877-424-6423)
Dogs are allowed for no additional fee. Dogs may not be left alone in the room. Multiple dogs may be allowed.

Days Inn Rexburg
271 South 2nd West
Rexburg, ID
208-356-9222 (800-329-7466)
Dogs of all sizes are allowed. There are no additional pet fees. Pet must be kept in kennel when left alone. Reservations are recommended due to limited rooms for pets. 2 dogs may be allowed.

Salmon River Motel
1203 S H 95
Riggins, ID
208-628-3231
salmonrivermotel.com/
This motel is situated in a deep canyon at the confluence of the Salmon River and the Little Salmon Rivers, and fishing is a favorite pastime. Amenities include clean, spacious rooms, cable TV, and a convenient location for hunters, hikers, and sightseers. Dogs up to 50

pounds are allowed for no additional fee with a credit card on file. Dogs are not allowed on the beds or furnishings, and they must be leashed and cleaned up after at all times. 2 dogs may be allowed.

Syringa Lodge
13 Gott Lane
Salmon, ID
208-756-4424 (877-580-6482)
syringalodge.com/
Made of large spruce logs, this beautiful lodge is located on a bluff which offers great views of the river and mountains. Some of the features/amenities include a home-cooked breakfast served in the dining room or on the sun porch, six porches, a great room with an ornate fireplace, and private baths. One dog is allowed per room for an additional $10 one time fee. Dogs must be quiet, well mannered, and leashed and cleaned up after at all times.

Best Western Edgewater Resort
56 Bridge Street
Sandpoint, ID
208-263-3194 (800-780-7234)
Dogs are allowed for an additional fee of $10 per night per pet. Dogs may not be left alone in the room. Multiple dogs may be allowed.

Super 8 Sandpoint
476841 Hwy 95 North
Sandpoint, ID
208-263-2210 (800-800-8000)
Dogs of all sizes are allowed. There is a $5 per night pet fee per pet. Smoking and non-smoking rooms are available for pet rooms. 2 dogs may be allowed.

Mountain Village Resort
P. O. Box 150/ @ H 75/21
Stanley, ID
208-774-3661 (800-843-5475)
mountainvillage.com/
This 61 room lodge offers a warm, inviting decor, a natural hot springs for guests, and satellite television. Dogs of all sizes are allowed for an additional fee of $8 per night per pet. Dogs must be well behaved, leashed, cleaned up after, and the Do Not Disturb sign put on the door if they are in the room alone. Multiple dogs may be allowed.

Comfort Inn
1893 Canyon Springs Road
Twin Falls, ID
208-734-7494 (877-424-6423)
Dogs are allowed for an additional

fee of $20 per night per pet. Multiple dogs may be allowed.

Motel 6 - Twin Falls
1472 Blue Lake Boulevard North
Twin Falls, ID
208-734-3993 (800-466-8356)
One well-behaved family pet per room. Guest must notify front desk upon arrival. Guest is liable for any damages. In consideration of all guests, pets must never be left unattended in the guest rooms.

Red Lion
1357 Blue Lakes Blvd N
Twin Falls, ID
208-734-5000
Dogs up to 80 pounds are allowed. There is a $50 refundable deposit per room and a pet policy to sign at check in. 2 dogs may be allowed.

Hells Canyon Jet Boat Trips and Lodging
1 mile S of White Bird on Old H 95
White Bird, ID
800-469-8757
Dogs of all sizes are allowed. There are no additional pet fees. There is one pet-friendly room available, and dogs may not be left unattended in the room at any time. Dogs must be leashed and cleaned up after.

Coeur d' Alene Casino Resort Hotel
27068 S H 95
Worley, ID
800-523-2464
cdacasino.com/
This luxury gaming resort offers over 200 finely appointed rooms, over 100,000 square feet of gaming space, several eateries, a heated swimming pool and Jacuzzi, top-name entertainment, and they have a world class golf course adjacent to the hotel. Dogs of all sizes are allowed for an additional $15 per night per pet. Dogs must be well mannered, leashed, and cleaned up after. Multiple dogs may be allowed.

Illinois Listings

Super 8 Altamont
3091 E Mill Drive
Altamont, IL
618-483-6300 (800-800-8000)
Dogs of all sizes are allowed. There is a $10 per night pet fee per pet. Smoking and non-smoking rooms are available for pet rooms. 2 dogs may be allowed.

Budget Inn
1900 Homer M Adams Pkwy
Alton, IL
618-463-0800 (800-DAYS-INN)
Dogs of all sizes are allowed. There is a $20 per night pet fee per pet. 2 dogs may be allowed.

Comfort Inn
11 Crossroads Court
Alton, IL
618-465-9999 (877-424-6423)
Dogs are allowed for no additional pet fee. 2 dogs may be allowed.

Holiday Inn
3800 Homer Adams Parkway
Alton, IL
618-462-1220 (877-270-6405)
Dogs of all sizes are allowed for an additional one time pet fee of $25 per room. Dogs may not be left alone in the room. Multiple dogs may be allowed.

Super 8 Alton
1800 Homer Adams Parkway
Alton, IL
618-465-8885 (800-800-8000)
Dogs up to 100 pounds are allowed. There is a $50 returnable deposit required per room. Smoking and non-smoking rooms are available for pet rooms. 2 dogs may be allowed.

Best Western Regency Inn
350 N Highway 173
Antioch, IL
847-395-3606 (800-780-7234)
Dogs are allowed for a $50 refundable deposit plus an additional pet fee of $15 per night per room. 2 dogs may be allowed.

Comfort Inn
610 E Springfield
Arcola, IL
217-268-4000 (877-424-6423)
Dogs are allowed for an additional fee of $7 per night per pet. Multiple dogs may be allowed.

La Quinta Inn Chicago Arlington Heights
1415 W. Dundee Rd.
Arlington Heights, IL
847-253-8777 (800-531-5900)
Dogs of all sizes are allowed. There are no additional pet fees. Dogs must be leashed and cleaned up after. Dogs must be crated or removed for housekeeping. Multiple dogs may be allowed.

Motel 6 - Chicago N Central-Arlington Hgt

441 West Algonquin Road
Arlington Heights, IL
847-806-1230 (800-466-8356)
One well-behaved family pet per room. Guest must notify front desk upon arrival. Guest is liable for any damages. In consideration of all guests, pets must never be left unattended in the guest rooms.

Red Roof Inn - Chicago-Arlington Heights
22 West Algonquin Road
Arlington Heights, IL
847-228-6650 (800-RED-ROOF)
One well-behaved family pet per room. Guest must notify front desk upon arrival. Guest is liable for any damages. In consideration of all guests, pets must never be left unattended in the guest rooms.

Sheraton Chicago Northwest
3400 West Euclid Ave.
Arlington Heights, IL
847-394-2000 (888-625-5144)
Dogs up to 70 pounds are allowed for no additional pet fee with a credit card on file. Dogs may not be left alone in the room.

Motel 6 - Chicago Southwest - Aurora
2380 North Farnsworth Avenue
Aurora, IL
630-851-3600 (800-466-8356)
One well-behaved family pet per room. Guest must notify front desk upon arrival. Guest is liable for any damages. In consideration of all guests, pets must never be left unattended in the guest rooms.

Staybridge Suites
4320 Meridian Parkway
Aurora, IL
630-978-2222 (877-270-6405)
Dogs of all sizes are allowed for an additional one time fee of $75 per room, and pets must be declared at the time of reservations. 2 dogs may be allowed.

La Quinta Inn & Suites Chicago North Shore
2000 Lakeside Drive
Bannockburn, IL
847-317-7300 (800-531-5900)
Dogs of all sizes are allowed. There are no additional pet fees. Dogs may not be left unattended unless they will be quiet, well behaved, and a contact number is left with the front desk. Dogs must be leashed and cleaned up after. Multiple dogs may be allowed.

Days Inn Benton
711 W Main
Benton, IL
618-439-3183 (800-329-7466)
Dogs of all sizes are allowed. There is a $10 per night pet fee per pet. 2 dogs may be allowed.

Days Inn Bloomington
1707 W Market St
Bloomington, IL
309-829-6292 (800-329-7466)
Dogs of all sizes are allowed. There is a $10 per night pet fee per pet. 2 dogs may be allowed.

La Quinta Inn Bolingbrook
225 W. South Frontage Road
Bolingbrook, IL
630-226-0000 (800-531-5900)
Dogs of all sizes are allowed. There are no additional pet fees. Dogs must be crated, and the front desk notified, when left alone in the room, and they must be leashed and cleaned up after. Multiple dogs may be allowed.

Motel 6 - Kankakee - Bourbonnais
1311 Illinois SR 50 North
Bourbonnais, IL
815-933-2300 (800-466-8356)
One well-behaved family pet per room. Guest must notify front desk upon arrival. Guest is liable for any damages. In consideration of all guests, pets must never be left unattended in the guest rooms.

Days Inn Cairo
RR 1 Box 10
Cairo, IL
618-734-0215 (800-329-7466)
Dogs of all sizes are allowed. There are no additional pet fees. Pet must be kept in kennel when left alone. 2 dogs may be allowed.

Holiday Inn Express Calumet Park
12800 S. Ashland Ave
Calumet Park, IL
708-389-2600 (877-270-6405)
Dogs of all sizes are allowed for an additional one time fee of $25 per pet. Multiple dogs may be allowed.

Motel 6 - Carbondale
700 East Main Street
Carbondale, IL
618-457-5566 (800-466-8356)
One well-behaved family pet per room. Guest must notify front desk upon arrival. Guest is liable for any damages. In consideration of all guests, pets must never be left unattended in the guest rooms.

Super 8 Carbondale
1180 E Main
Carbondale, IL
618-457-8822 (800-800-8000)
Dogs of all sizes are allowed. There are no additional pet fees. Smoking and non-smoking rooms are available for pet rooms. 2 dogs may be allowed.

Best Western Carlinville Inn
I-55 & IL Route 108
Carlinville, IL
217-324-2100 (800-780-7234)
One dog up to 50 pounds is allowed for an additional pet fee of $10 per night per room.

Super 8 Carlyle Lake
1371 William Rd
Carlyle, IL
618-594-8888 (800-800-8000)
Dogs of all sizes are allowed. There is a $10 returnable deposit required per room. Pet must be kept in kennel when left alone. Reservations are recommended due to limited rooms for pets. Smoking and non-smoking rooms are available for pet rooms. 2 dogs may be allowed.

Comfort Inn
933 H 49
Casey, IL
217-932-2212 (877-424-6423)
Dogs are allowed for an additional fee of $10 per night per pet. Multiple dogs may be allowed.

Motel 6 - St Louis East-Caseyville
2431 Old Country Inn Road
Caseyville, IL
618-397-8867 (800-466-8356)
One well-behaved family pet per room. Guest must notify front desk upon arrival. Guest is liable for any damages. In consideration of all guests, pets must never be left unattended in the guest rooms.

Drury Inn & Suites
905 W. Anthony Drive
Champaign, IL
217-398-0030 (800-378-7946)
Dogs of all sizes are permitted. Pets are not allowed in the breakfast area of the hotel. Pets are not to be left unattended, and each guest must assume liability for damage of property or other guest complaints. There is a limit of one pet per room.

Red Roof Inn - Champaign
212 West Anthony Drive
Champaign, IL
217-352-0101 (800-RED-ROOF)
One well-behaved family pet per

room. Guest must notify front desk upon arrival. Guest is liable for any damages. In consideration of all guests, pets must never be left unattended in the guest rooms.

Super 8 Champaign
202 Marketview Dr
Champaign, IL
217-359-2388 (800-800-8000)
Dogs of all sizes are allowed. There is a $7 per night pet fee per pet. Only non-smoking rooms are used for pets. 2 dogs may be allowed.

Super 8 St Charles
1520 E Main St
Charles, IL
630-377-8388 (800-800-8000)
Dogs of all sizes are allowed. There is a $50 returnable deposit required per room. There is a $10 per night pet fee per pet. Smoking and non-smoking rooms are available for pet rooms. 2 dogs may be allowed.

Claridge Hotel
1244 North Dearborn Parkway
Chicago, IL
312-787-4980 (800-245-1258)
claridgehotel.com/
There is a $25 refundable pet deposit.

Hilton
720 S Michigan Avenue
Chicago, IL
312-922-4400
Dogs up to 85 pounds are allowed for no additional pet fee with a credit card on file (required), and there is a pet agreement to sign. 2 dogs may be allowed.

Hilton
O'Hare International Airport, P.O. Box 6641
Chicago, IL
773-686-8000
2 dogs may be allowed.

Hilton
17 E Monroe Street
Chicago, IL
312-726-7500
Dogs are allowed for no additional fee; there is a pet agreement to sign at check in. 2 dogs may be allowed.

Hotel Allegro
171 West Randolph Street
Chicago, IL
312-236-0123
allegrochicago.com/
Well-behaved dogs of all sizes are welcome at this pet-friendly hotel. The luxury boutique hotel offers

both rooms and suites. Hotel amenities include complimentary evening wine served in the living room, a gift shop, and an on-site fitness center. There are no pet fees.

Hotel Burnham
1 West Washington
Chicago, IL
312-782-1111
burnhamhotel.com
Dogs of all kinds and sizes are welcome at this pet-friendly hotel. The luxury boutique hotel offers both rooms and suites. Hotel amenities include a fully equipped fitness room, and complimentary evening wine in the lobby. There are no pet fees, just sign a pet liability form.

Hotel Monaco Chicago
225 North Wabash
Chicago, IL
312-960-8500
monaco-chicago.com/
Well-behaved dogs of all sizes are welcome at this pet-friendly hotel. The luxury boutique hotel offers both rooms and suites. Hotel amenities include complimentary evening wine service, 24 hour room service, and an on-site fitness room. There are no pet fees, just sign a pet liability form.

House of Blues Hotel
333 North Dearborn
Chicago, IL
312-245-0333
All well-behaved dogs of any size are welcome at this downtown hotel. There are no pet fees. Dogs are not allowed in the Bar or Restaurant.

Howard Johnson Inn
720 N. LaSalle Street
Chicago, IL
312-664-8100 (800-446-4656)

Red Roof Inn - Chicago Downtown
162 East Ontario Street
Chicago, IL
312-787-3580 (800-RED-ROOF)
One well-behaved family pet per room. Guest must notify front desk upon arrival. Guest is liable for any damages. In consideration of all guests, pets must never be left unattended in the guest rooms.

Residence Inn by Marriott
201 E Walton
Chicago, IL
312-943-9800
Pets of all sizes are allowed. There is a $75 one time fee per pet and a pet policy to sign at check in. 2 dogs may be allowed.

Sheraton Chicago Hotel and Towers
301 E. North Water St.
Chicago, IL
312-464-1000 (888-625-5144)
Dog up to 75 pounds are allowed for no additional pet fee. A credit card must be on file and there is a pet agreement to sign. Dogs may not be left alone in the room.

The James Chicago
55 East Ontario
Chicago, IL
877-526-3755
lenoxsuites.com/index.php
This very dog-friendly luxury boutique hotel rolls out the red carpet for your dog. There is a $75 fee for a dog. The hotel provides in-room bowls and snacks for your dog and has additional options for massages or room service bones from the hotel's steakhouse.

W Chicago City Center
172 West Adams St.
Chicago, IL
312-332-1200
Dogs up to 60 pounds are allowed for a $100 one time fee plus an additional $25 per night per room. Dogs may not be left alone in the room.

W Chicago Lakeshore
644 N. Lakeshore Dr.
Chicago, IL
312-943-9200
Dogs up to 80 pounds are allowed for a $100 one time fee plus an additional $25 per night per room. Dogs may not be left alone in the room.

Super 8 Chiillicothe
615 S Fourth Street
Chillicothe, IL
309-274-2568 (800-800-8000)
Dogs of all sizes are allowed. There is a $50 returnable deposit required per room. Smoking and non-smoking rooms are available for pet rooms. 2 dogs may be allowed.

Collinsville Drury Inn
602 N. Bluff
Collinsville, IL
618-345-7700 (800-378-7946)
Dogs of all sizes are permitted. Pets are not allowed in the breakfast area of the hotel. Pets are not to be left unattended, and each guest must assume liability for damage of property or other guest complaints. There is a limit of one pet per room.

Holiday Inn
1000 Eastport Plaza Dr
Collinsville, IL
618-345-2800 (877-270-6405)
Dogs of all sizes are allowed for an additional one time pet fee of $25 per room. Multiple dogs may be allowed.

Motel 6 - St Louis East - Collinsville
295-A North Bluff Road
Collinsville, IL
618-345-2100 (800-466-8356)
One well-behaved family pet per room. Guest must notify front desk upon arrival. Guest is liable for any damages. In consideration of all guests, pets must never be left unattended in the guest rooms.

Hampton Inn
13330 S Cicero Avenue
Crestwood, IL
708-597-3330
Dogs of all sizes are allowed. There are no additional pet fees. Multiple dogs may be allowed.

Super 8 Crystal Lake
577 Crystal Point Dr
Crystal Lake, IL
815-788-8888 (800-800-8000)
Dogs up to 80 pounds are allowed. There is a $10 per night pet fee per pet. Smoking and non-smoking rooms are available for pet rooms. 2 dogs may be allowed.

Comfort Inn
383 Lynch Drive
Danville, IL
217-443-8004 (877-424-6423)
Dogs are allowed for no additional pet fee. Multiple dogs may be allowed.

Sleep Inn
361 Lynch Drive
Danville, IL
217-442-6600 (877-424-6423)
Dogs are allowed for an additional fee of $10 per night per pet. Dogs may not be left alone in the room. Multiple dogs may be allowed.

Baymont Inn Decatur
5100 Hickory Point Frontage RD
Decatur, IL
217-875-5800 (800-531-5900)
Dogs of all sizes are allowed. There are no additional pet fees. Dogs may not be left unattended, and they must be quiet and kept leashed. Multiple dogs may be allowed.

Residence Inn by Marriott

530 Lake Cook Road
Deerfield, IL
847-940-4644
Pets up to 75 pounds are allowed. There is a $15 per night per pet fee for up to five nights for a maximum total of $75 per pet and a pet policy to sign at check in. 2 dogs may be allowed.

Days Inn O'Hare
2175 E Touhy Ave
Des Plaines, IL
847-635-1300 (800-329-7466)
Dogs of all sizes are allowed. There is a $30 one time per pet fee per visit. 2 dogs may be allowed.

Comfort Inn
136 Plaza Drive
Dixon, IL
815-284-0500 (877-424-6423)
Dogs up to 50 pounds are allowed for an additional fee of $10 per night per pet. 2 dogs may be allowed.

Quality Inn and Suites
154 Plaza Drive
Dixon, IL
815-288-2001 (877-424-6423)
Dogs up to 50 pounds are allowed for an additional fee of $10 per night per pet. 2 dogs may be allowed.

Red Roof Inn - Chicago - Downers Grove
1113 Butterfield Road
Downers Grove, IL
630-963-4205 (800-RED-ROOF)
One well-behaved family pet per room. Guest must notify front desk upon arrival. Guest is liable for any damages. In consideration of all guests, pets must never be left unattended in the guest rooms.

Super 8 Dwight
14 E Northbrook Dr
Dwight, IL
815-584-1888 (800-800-8000)
Dogs of all sizes are allowed. There is a $5.48 per night pet fee per pet. Reservations are recommended due to limited rooms for pets. Smoking and non-smoking rooms are available for pet rooms. 2 dogs may be allowed.

Motel 6 - Peoria - East
104 West Camp Street
East Peoria, IL
309-699-7281 (800-466-8356)
One well-behaved family pet per room. Guest must notify front desk upon arrival. Guest is liable for any damages. In consideration of all guests, pets must never be left

unattended in the guest rooms.

Days Inn Effingham
1412 W Fayette Ave
Effingham, IL
217-342-9271 (800-329-7466)
Dogs of all sizes are allowed. There is a $5 per night pet fee per pet. 2 dogs may be allowed.

Holiday Inn Express
1103 Avenue of Mid America
Effingham, IL
217-540-1111 (877-270-6405)
Dogs of all sizes are allowed for an additional one time pet fee of $20 per room. Multiple dogs may be allowed.

Howard Johnson Express Inn
1606 W Fayette Ave.
Effingham, IL
217-342-4667 (800-446-4656)
Dogs of all sizes are welcome. There is a $5 per day pet fee per pet.

Super 8 Effingham
1400 Thelma Keller Ave
Effingham, IL
217-342-6888 (800-800-8000)
Dogs of all sizes are allowed. There are no additional pet fees. Smoking and non-smoking rooms are available for pet rooms. 2 dogs may be allowed.

Days Inn El Paso
630 W Main St
El Paso, IL
309-527-7070 (800-329-7466)
Dogs of all sizes are allowed. There is a $5 per night pet fee per pet. 2 dogs may be allowed.

Quality Inn
500 Tollgate Road
Elgin, IL
847-608-7300 (877-424-6423)
One dog is allowed for an additional pet fee of $10 per night.

Rim Rock's Dogwood Cabins
Karbers Ridge/Pounds Hollow blacktop
Elizabethtown, IL
618-264-6036
rimrocksdogwoodcabins.com/
Surrounded by The Shawnee National Forest, these new rustic cabins offer modern comforts (like screened porches, showers, and supplied kitchens), close proximity to a wide variety of land and water recreation, and some fantastic scenery. Dogs of all sizes are allowed for no additional fee. Dogs may not be left unattended, and they must be leashed and cleaned up

after. 2 dogs may be allowed.

Motel 6 - Chicago - Elk Grove
1601 Oakton Street
Elk Grove Village, IL
847-981-9766 (800-466-8356)
One well-behaved family pet per room. Guest must notify front desk upon arrival. Guest is liable for any damages. In consideration of all guests, pets must never be left unattended in the guest rooms.

Sheraton Suites Elk Grove Village
121 Northwest Point Blvd.
Elk Grove Village, IL
847-290-1600 (888-625-5144)
Dogs up to 75 pounds are allowed for no additional pet fee with a credit card on file. Dogs may not be left alone in the room.

Comfort Suites
100 Ludwig Drive
Fairview Heights, IL
618-394-0202 (877-424-6423)
Dogs up to 50 pounds are allowed for an additional fee of $10 per night per pet. Multiple dogs may be allowed.

Fairview Heights Drury Inn & Suites
12 Ludwig Drive
Fairview Heights, IL
618-398-8530 (800-378-7946)
Dogs of all sizes are permitted. Pets are not allowed in the breakfast area of the hotel. Pets are not to be left unattended, and each guest must assume liability for damage of property or other guest complaints. There is a limit of one pet per room.

Super 8 Fairview Heights IL/St Louis MO Area
45 Ludwig Drive
Fairview Heights, IL
618-398-8338 (800-800-8000)
Dogs of all sizes are allowed. There are no additional pet fees. Smoking and non-smoking rooms are available for pet rooms. 2 dogs may be allowed.

Best Western Lorson Inn
201 Gary Hagen Dr
Flora, IL
618-662-3054 (800-780-7234)
Dogs are allowed for a $25 refundable deposit. Dogs may not be left alone in the room. Multiple dogs may be allowed.

Cloran Mansion
1237 Franklin Street
Galena, IL
815-777-0583 (866-234-0583)

cloranmansion.com/
Sitting on 1½ acres of landscaped lawns and gardens, this 1880 Italianate Victorian mansion provides guests a venue for a romantic getaway, plus they offer a number of in-house amenities, a pond with 2 waterfalls, and a beautiful cottage that is pet friendly; dogs are not allowed in the mansion. Breakfast is still served in the main house for cottage guests. Dogs are allowed for a one time pet fee of $25. Dogs must be well behaved, leashed or crated, and cleaned up after. 2 dogs may be allowed.

Eagle Ridge Inn and Resort
444 Eagle Ridge Drive
Galena, IL
815-777-2444 (800-240-1681)
eagleridgeresortonline.com/
Thousands of lush acres, landscaped grounds, gardens, spectacular views, world class golfing and dining, a full service spa, a variety of recreation, venues for any occasion, and more are to be found at this resort. Dogs of all sizes are allowed for an additional one time fee of $75, and complimentary home-baked doggie "cookies" greet pets upon arrival. Dogs under 20 pounds are welcome in the standard rooms; over 20 pounds are allowed in the villas only. Dogs must be well behaved, leashed or crated, and cleaned up after at all times. Dogs must be crated when left alone if housekeeping still needs to service the room.

Galena Rentals
95 Heatherdowns Lane
Galena, IL
773-631-5253
Located near the General Golf Course and the Shenandoah Riding Center, this 2 bedroom, 2 bathroom home offers a number of amenities and access to the owner's club and outdoor pool. Dogs of all sizes are allowed for no additional fee. Dogs may not be left unattended, and they must be leashed and cleaned up after. 2 dogs may be allowed.

Goldmoor Inn and Gardens
9001 Sand Hill Road
Galena, IL
815-777-3925 (800-255-3925)
goldmoor.com/Inn
Located only 6 miles from town, this beautiful estate offers a variety of accommodations, amenities, services, and lush landscaped grounds and gardens. Dogs of all sizes are allowed for no additional

fee in the cabins. Dogs must be well behaved, leashed, cleaned up after, and crated when left alone in the room. 2 dogs may be allowed.

Tierra Linda
826 South Rocky Hill Road
Galena, IL
815-777-1234
beautifulearth.com/
Lush greenery, a wooden suspension bridge, a pond, beach, waterfalls, a forest, and more can be enjoyed on the 11 acres at this turn-of-the-century farmhouse turned bed and breakfast. Dogs of all sizes are allowed for an additional fee of $20 per night per pet. Dogs may not be left unattended on the property without prior arrangements; doggy sitting can be arranged for $10 for the 1st 2 hours plus $5 per half hour thereafter with specials for those staying more than 3 days. Male dogs must be neutered, and all dogs must be vaccinated, well behaved, and friendly towards other dogs and people. Dogs must be quiet, and be cleaned up after at all times. Dogs are not allowed on the bed without a clean cover blanket. 2 dogs may be allowed.

Comfort Inn
907 W Carl Sandburg Drive
Galesburg, IL
309-344-5445 (877-424-6423)
Dogs are allowed for an additional one time pet fee of $20 per room. Multiple dogs may be allowed.

Holiday Inn Express Galesburg
2285 Washington Street
Galesburg, IL
309-343-7100 (877-270-6405)
Dogs of all sizes are allowed for an additional one time pet fee of $25 per room. 2 dogs may be allowed.

Super 8 Galesburg Dwtn
260 W Main St
Galesburg, IL
309-342-5174 (800-800-8000)
Dogs of all sizes are allowed. There is a $7 per night pet fee per pet. Smoking and non-smoking rooms are available for pet rooms. 2 dogs may be allowed.

Motel 6 - Chicago North - Glenview
1535 Milwaukee Avenue
Glenview, IL
847-390-7200 (800-466-8356)
One well-behaved dog is allowed per room. There are no additional pet fees.

Staybridge Suites
2600 Lehigh Avenue
Glenview, IL
847-657-0002 (877-270-6405)
Dogs of all sizes are allowed for an additional pet fee of $50 for 1 to 5 nights, plus $10 per night per room thereafter to a maximum pet fee of $300, and there is a pet agreement to sign at check-in. Multiple dogs may be allowed.

Super 8 Grayville
2060 County Rd 2450 North
Grayville, IL
618-375-7288 (800-800-8000)
Dogs of all sizes are allowed. There is a $10 per night pet fee per pet. Smoking and non-smoking rooms are available for pet rooms. 2 dogs may be allowed.

Comfort Suites
5430 Grand Avenue
Gurnee, IL
847-782-0890 (877-424-6423)
Dogs are allowed for an additional one time fee of $50 per pet. 2 dogs may be allowed.

La Quinta Inn Chicago/Gurnee
5688 N. Ridge Road
Gurnee, IL
847-662-7600 (800-531-5900)
Dogs up to 100 pounds are allowed. There are no additional pet fees. Dogs may not be left unattended, and they must be well behaved, leashed, and cleaned up after. They are not allowed in the pool area. 2 dogs may be allowed.

Holiday Inn Express Highland
20 Central Blvd
Highland, IL
618-651-1100 (877-270-6405)
Dogs of all sizes are allowed for an additional fee of $20 per night per pet. 2 dogs may be allowed.

Candlewood Suites
2875 Greenspoint Parkway
Hoffman Estates, IL
847-490-1686 (877-270-6405)
Dogs up to 80 pounds are allowed for an additional pet fee per room of $75 for 1 to 6 nights, and $150 for 7or more nights. 2 dogs may be allowed.

La Quinta Inn Chicago Hoffman Estates
2280 Barrington Rd.
Hoffman Estates, IL
847-882-3312 (800-531-5900)
Dogs of all sizes are allowed. There are no additional pet fees. Dogs

must be leashed and cleaned up after. Dogs must be removed or crated for housekeeping. Multiple dogs may be allowed.

Red Roof Inn - Chicago- Hoffman Estates
2500 Hassell Road
Hoffman Estates, IL
847-885-7877 (800-RED-ROOF)
One well-behaved family pet per room. Guest must notify front desk upon arrival. Guest is liable for any damages. In consideration of all guests, pets must never be left unattended in the guest rooms.

Super 8 Jacksonville
1003 W Morton Ave
Jacksonville, IL
217-479-0303 (800-800-8000)
Dogs of all sizes are allowed. There is a $10 per night pet fee per pet. Smoking and non-smoking rooms are available for pet rooms. 2 dogs may be allowed.

Motel 6 - Chicago Joliet - I-55
3551 Mall Loop Drive
Joliet, IL
815-439-1332 (800-466-8356)
One well-behaved family pet per room. Guest must notify front desk upon arrival. Guest is liable for any damages. In consideration of all guests, pets must never be left unattended in the guest rooms.

Motel 6 - Joliet - I-80
1850 McDonough Road
Joliet, IL
815-729-2800 (800-466-8356)
One well-behaved family pet per room. Guest must notify front desk upon arrival. Guest is liable for any damages. In consideration of all guests, pets must never be left unattended in the guest rooms.

Red Roof Inn - Joliet
1750 McDonough Street
Joliet, IL
815-741-2304 (800-RED-ROOF)
One well-behaved family pet per room. Guest must notify front desk upon arrival. Guest is liable for any damages. In consideration of all guests, pets must never be left unattended in the guest rooms.

Red Roof Inn - Chicago- Lansing
2450 173rd Street
Lansing, IL
708-895-9570 (800-RED-ROOF)
One well-behaved family pet per room. Guest must notify front desk upon arrival. Guest is liable for any

damages. In consideration of all guests, pets must never be left unattended in the guest rooms.

Candlewood Suites
1100 N. US Highway 45
Libertyville, IL
847-247-9900 (877-270-6405)
Dogs of all sizes are allowed for an additional one time pet fee per room of $25 for 1 to 6 days; 7 or more days is a fee of $150. Multiple dogs may be allowed.

Days Inn Libertyville
1809 N Milwaukee Ave
Libertyville, IL
847-816-8006 (800-329-7466)
Dogs of all sizes are allowed. There is a $5 per night pet fee per pet. 2 dogs may be allowed.

Staybridge Suites
100 Barclay Blvd
Lincolnshire, IL
847-821-0002 (877-270-6405)
Dogs of all sizes are allowed for an additional pet fee per room of $50 for 1 to 7days, plus $5 for each day thereafter. Multiple dogs may be allowed.

Comfort Inn
1010 E Columbian N Blvd
Litchfield, IL
217-324-9260 (877-424-6423)
A dog up to 75 pounds is allowed for an additional pet fee of $15 per night.

Holiday Inn Express Litchfield
1405 W. Hudson Drive
Litchfield, IL
217-324-4556 (877-270-6405)
Dogs of all sizes are allowed for no additional fee. Multiple dogs may be allowed.

Residence Inn by Marriott
2001 S. Highland Avenue
Lombard, IL
630-629-7800
Pets of all sizes are welcome, however, only 3 medium to small pets or 2 large pets per room are allowed. There is a $75 one time fee and a pet policy to sign at check in.

TownePlace Suites Chicago Lombard
455 E 22nd Street
Lombard, IL
630-932-4400
Dogs of all sizes are allowed. There is a $75 one time pet fee per visit. 2 dogs may be allowed.

Super 8 Macomb

313 University Drive
Macomb, IL
309-836-8888 (800-800-8000)
Dogs of all sizes are allowed. There is a $10 per night pet fee per pet. Smoking and non-smoking rooms are available for pet rooms. 2 dogs may be allowed.

Days Inn Marion
1802 Bittle Place
Marion, IL
618-997-1351 (800-329-7466)
Dogs of all sizes are allowed. There is a $5 per night pet fee per pet. 2 dogs may be allowed.

Drury Inn
2706 W. DeYoung
Marion, IL
618-997-9600 (800-378-7946)
Dogs of all sizes are permitted. Pets are not allowed in the breakfast area of the hotel. Pets are not to be left unattended, and each guest must assume liability for damage of property or other guest complaints. There is a limit of one pet per room.

Motel 6 - Marion
1008 Halfway Road
Marion, IL
618-993-2631 (800-466-8356)
One well-behaved family pet per room. Guest must notify front desk upon arrival. Guest is liable for any damages. In consideration of all guests, pets must never be left unattended in the guest rooms.

OldSquat Inn
14160 Liberty School Road
Marion, IL
618-982-2916
Well behaved dogs of most sizes are allowed; they can't take extra large dogs. There is a $10 per night per pet additional fee. Multiple dogs may be allowed.

Red Carpet Inn & Suites
8101 Express Dr, Rte 8, Box 348-1
Marion, IL
618-993-3222
There is a $5 per day additional pet fee. Dogs may not be left alone in the rooms.

Super 8 Marion
2601 W De Young
Marion, IL
618-993-5577 (800-800-8000)
Dogs of all sizes are allowed. There are no additional pet fees. Smoking and non-smoking rooms are available for pet rooms. 2 dogs may be allowed.

La Quinta Inn Chicago/Matteson
5210 W. Southwick Drive
Matteson, IL
708-503-0999 (800-531-5900)
Dogs of all sizes are allowed. There are no additional pet fees. There is a pet waiver to sign at check in, and dogs must be leashed and cleaned up after. Multiple dogs may be allowed.

Comfort Inn
1307 Kailash Drive
Mendota, IL
815-538-3355 (877-424-6423)
Dogs are allowed for no additional pet fee. Dogs must be quiet and they may not be left alone in the room. 2 dogs may be allowed.

Comfort Inn
2118 E 5th Street
Metropolis, IL
618-524-7227 (877-424-6423)
Dogs are allowed for an additional fee of $10 per night per pet. 2 dogs may be allowed.

Day Plaza Inn
1415 E 5th Street/H 45
Metropolis, IL
618-524-9341 (800-329-7466)
daysinn.com
Dogs of all sizes are allowed for an additional fee of $7 per night per pet. Dogs must be leashed when out of the room, and cleaned up after at all times. 2 dogs may be allowed.

Holiday Inn Express
2179 East 5th Street
Metropolis, IL
618-524-8899 (877-270-6405)
Dogs up to 35 pounds are allowed for an additional fee of $10 per night per pet; the fee is $20 per night per pet for dogs over 35 pounds. 2 dogs may be allowed.

Motel 6 - Minonk
1312 North Carolyn Drive
Minonk, IL
309-432-3663 (800-466-8356)
One well-behaved family pet per room. Guest must notify front desk upon arrival. Guest is liable for any damages. In consideration of all guests, pets must never be left unattended in the guest rooms.

Super 8 Mokena/Frankfort/I-80
9485 W 191st Street
Mokena, IL
708-479-7808 (800-800-8000)
Dogs of all sizes are allowed. There is a $10 per night pet fee per pet.

Smoking and non-smoking rooms are available for pet rooms. 2 dogs may be allowed.

Comfort Inn
2600 52nd Street
Moline, IL
309-762-7000 (877-424-6423)
Dogs up to 50 pounds are allowed for an additional fee of $10 per night per pet. 2 dogs may be allowed.

Holiday Inn Express - Airport
6910 27th Street
Moline, IL
309-762-8300 (877-270-6405)
Dogs of all sizes are allowed for an additional fee of $25 per night per pet. Multiple dogs may be allowed.

La Quinta Inn Moline Airport
5450 27th St.
Moline, IL
309-762-9008 (800-531-5900)
Dogs of all sizes are allowed. There are no additional pet fees. Dogs must be quiet, leashed, and cleaned up after. A cell number must be left with the front desk if your dog is alone in the room. Multiple dogs may be allowed.

Motel 6 - Moline - Quad Cities
2359 69th Avenue
Moline, IL
309-764-8711 (800-466-8356)
One well-behaved family pet per room. Guest must notify front desk upon arrival. Guest is liable for any damages. In consideration of all guests, pets must never be left unattended in the guest rooms.

Quality Inn and Suites
6920 27th Street
Moline, IL
309-762-1711 (877-424-6423)
Dogs are allowed for no additional pet fee. Dogs must be quiet and they may not be left alone in the room. 2 dogs may be allowed.

Days Inn Monee
80 Hampton Rd
Morris, IL
815-942-9000 (800-329-7466)
Dogs of all sizes are allowed. There are no additional pet fees. 2 dogs may be allowed.

Best Western Ashland House & Conference Center
201 E Ashland Street
Morton, IL
309-263-5116 (800-780-7234)
Dogs are allowed for an additional one time pet fee of $15 per room.

Multiple dogs may be allowed.

Drury Inn
145 N 44th Street
Mount Vernon, IL
618-244-4550 (800-378-7946)
Dogs of all sizes are permitted. Pets are not allowed in the breakfast area of the hotel. Pets are not to be left unattended, and each guest must assume liability for damage of property or other guest complaints. There is a limit of one pet per room.

Holiday Inn
222 Potomac Blvd
Mount Vernon, IL
618-244-7100 (877-270-6405)
Dogs of all sizes are allowed for an additional one time fee $10 per pet. 2 dogs may be allowed.

Motel 6 - Mt Vernon
333 South 44th Street
Mount Vernon, IL
618-244-2383 (800-466-8356)
One well-behaved family pet per room. Guest must notify front desk upon arrival. Guest is liable for any damages. In consideration of all guests, pets must never be left unattended in the guest rooms.

Super 8 Mt Vernon
401 S 44th Street
Mount Vernon, IL
618-242-8800 (800-800-8000)
Dogs of all sizes are allowed. There are no additional pet fees. Smoking and non-smoking rooms are available for pet rooms. 2 dogs may be allowed.

Thrifty Inn
100 North 44th Street
Mount Vernon, IL
618-244-7750 (800-378-7946)
Dogs of all sizes are permitted. Pets are not allowed in the breakfast area of the hotel. Pets are not to be left unattended, and each guest must assume liability for damage of property or other guest complaints. There is a limit of one pet per room.

Crowne Plaza
510 E Rt 83
Mundelein, IL
847-949-5100 (877-270-6405)
Dogs of all sizes are allowed for no additional fee with a credit card on file, and there is a pet agreement to sign at check in. Multiple dogs may be allowed.

America's Best Value Inn
128 E Walnut St

Murphysboro, IL
618-687-2244
Dogs of all sizes are allowed. There are no additional pet fees. Smoking and non-smoking rooms are available for pet rooms. 2 dogs may be allowed.

Best Western Naperville Inn
1617 N Naperville Road
Naperville, IL
630-505-0200 (800-780-7234)
Dogs are allowed for an additional fee of $10 per night per pet. Multiple dogs may be allowed.

Red Roof Inn - Chicago- Naperville
1698 West Diehl Road
Naperville, IL
630-369-2500 (800-RED-ROOF)
One well-behaved family pet per room. Guest must notify front desk upon arrival. Guest is liable for any damages. In consideration of all guests, pets must never be left unattended in the guest rooms.

Best Western University Inn
6 Traders Circle
Normal, IL
309-454-4070 (800-780-7234)
Dogs are allowed for an additional pet fee of $10 per night per room. Multiple dogs may be allowed.

Candlewood Suites Bloomington-Normal
203 Susan Drive
Normal, IL
309-862-4100 (877-270-6405)
Dogs of all sizes are allowed for an additional one time pet fee of $75 per room. Multiple dogs may be allowed.

Comfort Suites
3108 Greenbriar Drive
Normal, IL
309-452-8588 (877-424-6423)
Dogs are allowed for an additional fee of $20 per night per room. Multiple dogs may be allowed.

Motel 6 - Normal - Bloomington Area
1600 North Main Street
Normal, IL
309-452-0422 (800-466-8356)
One well-behaved family pet per room. Guest must notify front desk upon arrival. Guest is liable for any damages. In consideration of all guests, pets must never be left unattended in the guest rooms.

Red Roof Inn - Chicago-Northbrook
340 Waukegan Road
Northbrook, IL
847-205-1755 (800-RED-ROOF)

One well-behaved family pet per room. Guest must notify front desk upon arrival. Guest is liable for any damages. In consideration of all guests, pets must never be left unattended in the guest rooms.

Comfort Inn
1100 Eastgate Drive
OFallon, IL
618-624-6060 (877-424-6423)
Dogs are allowed for a $50 refundable deposit per pet. Multiple dogs may be allowed.

Howard Johnson Express Inn
116 Regency Park
OFallon, IL
618-628-1200 (800-446-4656)
Well-behaved dogs of all sizes are allowed. There is a $10 per day additional pet fee.

Quality Inn
1409 W H 50
OFallon, IL
618-628-8895 (877-424-6423)
Dogs up to 50 pounds are allowed for an additional pet fee of $10 for the 1st night and $5 for each additional night per room Multiple dogs may be allowed.

Residence Inn by Marriott
790 Jorie Blvd
Oak Brook, IL
630-571-1200
Pets up to 100 pounds are allowed. There is a $75 one time fee and a pet policy to sign at check in. 2 dogs may be allowed.

Staybridge Suites
200 Royce Blvd
Oakbrook Terrace, IL
630-953-9393 (877-270-6405)
Dogs of all sizes are allowed for an additional one time pet fee of $75 per room. Multiple dogs may be allowed.

Candlewood Suites Ofallon, Il - St. Louis Area
1332 Park Plaza Drive
Ofallon, IL
618-622-9555 (877-270-6405)
Two dogs up to 80 pounds are allowed for an additional one time fee of $75 per room; a 3rd dog is an additional $75 fee. Multiple dogs may be allowed.

Super 8 Okawville
812 N Henhouse Rd
Okawville, IL
618-243-6525 (800-800-8000)
Dogs of all sizes are allowed. There is a $5 per night pet fee per pet.

Smoking and non-smoking rooms are available for pet rooms. 2 dogs may be allowed.

Hotel Indigo Chicago - Schaumburg North
920 E. Northwest Hwy.
Palatine, IL
847-359-6900
Dogs up to 80 pounds are allowed for an additional pet fee of $25 per room. 2 dogs may be allowed.

Motel 6 - Chicago Northwest - Palatine
1450 East Dundee Road
Palatine, IL
847-359-0046 (800-466-8356)
One well-behaved family pet per room. Guest must notify front desk upon arrival. Guest is liable for any damages. In consideration of all guests, pets must never be left unattended in the guest rooms.

Comfort Suites
1812 W War Memorial Drive
Peoria, IL
309-688-3800 (877-424-6423)
Dogs are allowed for an additional one time fee of $25 (plus tax) per room. 2 dogs may be allowed.

Hotel Pere Marquette
501 Main Street
Peoria, IL
309-637-6500 (800-447-1676)
hotelperemarquette.com/
There is a $100 refundable pet deposit.

Jameson Inn and Suites
4112 N Brandywine
Peoria, IL
309-685-2556 (800-JAMESON (526-3766))
This inn offers a number of amenities including a swimming pool. Dogs are allowed for an additional one time fee of $15 per pet. Dogs must be leashed and cleaned up after at all times. 2 dogs may be allowed.

Mark Twain Hotel
225 NE Adams Street
Peoria, IL
309-676-3600 (866-325-6351)
marktwainhotel.com/
Warmly and richly decorated, this 110 room hotel has undergone extensive renovations?turning it from ordinary to extra-ordinary with many comforts and amenities; there is also a restaurant and cyber-cafe on site. Dogs of all sizes are allowed for a $50 refundable

deposit per pet. Dogs must be leashed, cleaned up after, and crated when left alone in the room. 2 dogs may be allowed.

Red Roof Inn - Peoria
1822 West War Memorial Drive
Peoria, IL
309-685-3911 (800-RED-ROOF)
One well-behaved family pet per room. Guest must notify front desk upon arrival. Guest is liable for any damages. In consideration of all guests, pets must never be left unattended in the guest rooms.

Residence Inn by Marriott
2000 W War Memorial Drive
Peoria, IL
309-681-9000
Pets of all sizes are allowed. There is a $75 one time fee and a pet policy to sign at check in. Multiple dogs may be allowed.

Super 8 Peoria
1816 W War Memorial Dr
Peoria, IL
309-688-8074 (800-800-8000)
Dogs of all sizes are allowed. There is a $50 returnable deposit required per room. Smoking and non-smoking rooms are available for pet rooms. 2 dogs may be allowed.

La Quinta Inn Peru
4389 Venture Drive
Peru, IL
815-224-9000 (800-531-5900)
Dogs of all sizes are allowed. There are no additional pet fees. There is a pet waiver to sign at check in. Dogs may not be left unattended in the room unless they will be very quiet and well behaved. Dogs must be leashed and cleaned up after. 2 dogs may be allowed.

Comfort Inn
1821 W Reynolds Street (H116W)
Pontiac, IL
815-842-2777 (877-424-6423)
Dogs are allowed for an additional fee of $10 per night per pet. 2 dogs may be allowed.

Super 8 Pontiac
601 S Deerfield Rd
Pontiac, IL
815-844-6888 (800-800-8000)
Dogs of all sizes are allowed. There is a $5 per night pet fee per pet. Smoking and non-smoking rooms are available for pet rooms. 2 dogs may be allowed.

Three Roses Bed and Breakfast

209 E. Howard Street/H 116
Pontiac, IL
815-844-3404
threerosesbedandbreakfast.com/
Victorian décor creates a warm,
romantic ambiance for guests, and in
addition to personalized breakfasts,
they also offer an optional extensive
dinner menu. Housebroken dogs of
all sizes are allowed for no additional
fee. Dogs must be leashed when not
in the house, and cleaned up after at
all times. 2 dogs may be allowed.

Super 8 Pontoon Beach IL/St Louis
MO Area
4141 Timberlake Dr
Pontoon Beach, IL
618-931-8808 (800-800-8000)
Dogs of all sizes are allowed. There
is a $20 per night pet fee per pet.
Reservations are recommended due
to limited rooms for pets. Smoking
and non-smoking rooms are
available for pet rooms.

Days Inn Princeton
2238 N Main St
Princeton, IL
815-875-3371 (800-329-7466)
Dogs up to 60 pounds are allowed.
There is a $6 per night pet fee per
pet. 2 dogs may be allowed.

Comfort Inn
4122 Broadway
Quincy, IL
217-228-2700 (877-424-6423)
Dogs are allowed for an additional
fee of $10 per night per pet. 2 dogs
may be allowed.

Days Inn Quincy Riverside
200 Maine St
Quincy, IL
217-223-6610 (800-329-7466)
Dogs of all sizes are allowed. There
is a $10 one time per pet fee per
visit. 2 dogs may be allowed.

Super 8 Quincy
224 N 36th
Quincy, IL
217-228-8808 (800-800-8000)
Dogs of all sizes are allowed. There
are no additional pet fees. Smoking
and non-smoking rooms are
available for pet rooms. 2 dogs may
be allowed.

Best Western Heritage Inn
420 South Murray Rd
Rantoul, IL
217-892-9292 (800-780-7234)
Dogs up to 50 pounds are allowed
for an additional fee of $5 per night
per pet. 2 dogs may be allowed.

Days Inn Rantoul
801 W Champaign
Rantoul, IL
217-893-0700 (800-329-7466)
Dogs of all sizes are allowed. There
is a $10 one time per pet fee per
visit. 2 dogs may be allowed.

Best Western Robinson Inn
1500 W Main Street
Robinson, IL
618-544-8448 (800-780-7234)
Dogs are allowed for an additional
pet fee of $5 per night per room.
Multiple dogs may be allowed.

Comfort Inn and Suites
1133 N 7th Street
Rochelle, IL
815-562-5551 (877-424-6423)
Dogs are allowed for an additional
fee of $15 per night per pet. Multiple
dogs may be allowed.

Four Points by Sheraton Rock
Island
226 17th St.
Rock Island, IL
309-794-1212 (888-625-5144)
Dogs of all sizes are allowed for an
additional one time pet fee of $30
per room. Dogs may not be left
alone in the room.

Motel 6 - Rockford
7712 Potawatomi Trail
Rockford, IL
815-397-8000 (800-466-8356)
One well-behaved family pet per
room. Guest must notify front desk
upon arrival. Guest is liable for any
damages. In consideration of all
guests, pets must never be left
unattended in the guest rooms.

Quality Suites
7401 Walton Street
Rockford, IL
815-227-1300
Dogs are allowed for an additional
pet fee of $25 per night per room. 2
dogs may be allowed.

Red Roof Inn - Rockford
7434 East State Street
Rockford, IL
815-398-9750 (800-RED-ROOF)
One well-behaved family pet per
room. Guest must notify front desk
upon arrival. Guest is liable for any
damages. In consideration of all
guests, pets must never be left
unattended in the guest rooms.

Residence Inn by Marriott
7542 Colosseum Drive

Rockford, IL
815-227-0013
Dogs up to 65 pounds are allowed.
There is a $75 one time fee and a
pet policy to sign at check in. 2 dogs
may be allowed.

Holiday Inn Rolling Mdws-
Schaumburg Area
3405 Algonquin
Rolling Meadows, IL
847-259-5000 (877-270-6405)
Dogs up to 25 pounds are allowed
for an additional one time pet fee of
$50 per room. 2 dogs may be
allowed.

Motel 6 - Chicago NW - Rolling
Meadows
1800 Winnetka Circle
Rolling Meadows, IL
847-818-8088 (800-466-8356)
One well-behaved family pet per
room. Guest must notify front desk
upon arrival. Guest is liable for any
damages. In consideration of all
guests, pets must never be left
unattended in the guest rooms.

Comfort Inn
1235 Lake View Drive
Romeoville, IL
630-226-1900 (877-424-6423)
There is one pet friendly room, and
dogs up to 50 pounds are allowed for
an additional one time fee of $15 per
pet. 2 dogs may be allowed.

Doubletree
5460 N River Road
Rosemont, IL
847-292-9100
Dogs up to 100 pounds are allowed.
There is a $250 refundable deposit
per pet. 2 dogs may be allowed.

Embassy Suites Hotel Chicago -
O'Hare Rosemont
5500 North River Road
Rosemont, IL
847-678-4000
Sitting central to numerous activities,
recreation, and sites of interest, this
upscale all-suite hotel offers many
amenities, eateries, and a tavern on
site. Dogs of all sizes are allowed for
an additional fee of a $100
deposit?$75 is refundable. Dogs
must be quiet, leashed or crated,
cleaned up after, and crated when in
the room alone.

Residence Inn by Marriott
7101 Chestnut Street
Rosemont, IL
847-375-9000
Dogs of all sizes are welcome. There

is a $75 one time fee and a pet policy to sign at check in. Multiple dogs may be allowed.

Sheraton Gateway Suites Chicago O'Hare
6501 North Mannheim Road
Rosemont, IL
847-699-6300 (888-625-5144)
Offering luxury accommodations, this hotel also has a restaurant, lounge, and bakery café, and they sit central to many of the city's services, recreational pursuits, and sites of interest. Dogs of all sizes are allowed for no additional fee. Dogs must be quiet, leashed or crated, and cleaned up after at all times. 2 dogs may be allowed.

The Westin O'Hare
6100 North River Road
Rosemont, IL
847-698-6000 (888-625-5144)
westinohare.com
Offering luxury accommodations, this hotel has a restaurant, lounge, and bakery café, and they also sit central to many of the city's services, recreational pursuits, and sites of interest. Dogs of all sizes are allowed for no additional fee. Dogs must be quiet, leashed or crated, and cleaned up after at all times. 2 dogs may be allowed.

Super 8 Salem
118 Woods Lane
Salem, IL
618-548-5882 (800-800-8000)
Dogs of all sizes are allowed. There are no additional pet fees. Smoking and non-smoking rooms are available for pet rooms. 2 dogs may be allowed.

The Oscar Swan Country Inn
3315 Elizabeth-Scales Road
Scales Mound, IL
815-541-0653
oscarswangalena.com/
Located on 30 acres of green rolling hills, this full restored inn offers a good venue for business or leisure travelers with indoor and outdoor meeting spaces and catering services. Dogs of all sizes are allowed for no additional fee. Dogs must be well behaved, leashed, and cleaned up after. 2 dogs may be allowed.

Candlewood Suites
1200 East Bank Drive
Schaumburg, IL
847-517-7644 (877-270-6405)
Dogs of all sizes are allowed for an additional pet fee of $75 for 1 to 14

nights, and $150 for 15 or more nights per room. 2 dogs may be allowed.

Chicago - Schaumburg Drury Inn
600 N. Martingale
Schaumburg, IL
847-517-7737 (800-378-7946)
Dogs of all sizes are permitted. Pets are not allowed in the breakfast area of the hotel. Pets are not to be left unattended, and each guest must assume liability for damage of property or other guest complaints. There is a limit of one pet per room.

Hawthorn Suites Schaumburg
1251 E. American Lane
Schaumburg, IL
847-706-9007 (800-527-1133)
hawthornschaumburg.com
The hotel has 135 Suites. Studio, One and Two-bedroom Suites are available. They offer all guests a complimentary hot breakfast buffet daily, evening reception Monday thru Thursday, and Dinner on Wednesday evenings. They have an indoor pool and fitness center, and passes to both Lifetime Fitness and Bally Total Fitness for guests to use. They offer full kitchens in each guestroom, high speed internet access, and a daily paper. Pets are welcome. There is a one time fee of $50-$100.00 depending on the size of the dog.

La Quinta Inn Chicago Schaumburg
1730 E. Higgins Rd.
Schaumburg, IL
847-517-8484 (800-531-5900)
Dogs of all sizes are allowed. There are no additional pet fees. Dogs may not be left unattended, and they must be leashed and cleaned up after. Dogs are not allowed in the lobby. Multiple dogs may be allowed.

Residence Inn by Marriott
1610 Mc Connor Parkway
Schaumburg, IL
847-517-9200
Pets of all sizes are allowed. There is a $75 one time fee and a pet policy to sign at check in. Multiple dogs may be allowed.

Staybridge Suites
901 East Woodfield Office Court
Schaumburg, IL
847-619-6677 (877-270-6405)
Dogs of all sizes are allowed: There is an additional one time pet fee per room of $150 for pets in a 1 bedroom, and an an additional one time pet fee of $200 for a 2

bedrooom. 2 dogs may be allowed.

Candlewood Suites - O'Hare
4021 North Manheim Road
Schiller Park, IL
847-671-4663 (877-270-6405)
Dogs of all sizes are allowed for an additional one time pet fee per room of $75 for 1 to 6 nights, and of $150 for 7nights or more. Multiple dogs may be allowed.

Comfort Suites O'Hare Airport
4200 N River Road
Schiller Park, IL
847-233-9000 (877-424-6423)
Dogs are allowed for a $50 refundable deposit plus an additional one time fee of $50 per pet. 2 dogs may be allowed.

Days Inn Sheffield
16733 Hwy 40
Sheffield, IL
815-454-2361 (800-329-7466)
Dogs of all sizes are allowed. There is a $11 per night pet fee per pet. 2 dogs may be allowed.

Motel 6 - Chicago South- South Holland
17301 South Halsted Street
South Holland, IL
708-331-1621 (800-466-8356)
One well-behaved family pet per room. Guest must notify front desk upon arrival. Guest is liable for any damages. In consideration of all guests, pets must never be left unattended in the guest rooms.

Comfort Inn
200 Comfort Drive
South Jacksonville, IL
217-245-8372 (877-424-6423)
Dogs are allowed for an additional pet fee of $15 per night per room. Dogs must be crated when left alone in the room and be removed for housekeeping. 2 dogs may be allowed.

Drury Inn & Suites
3180 S. Dirksen Parkway
Springfield, IL
217-529-3900 (800-378-7946)
Dogs of all sizes are permitted. Pets are not allowed in the breakfast area of the hotel. Pets are not to be left unattended, and each guest must assume liability for damage of property or other guest complaints. There is a limit of one pet per room.

Holiday Inn Express Hotel & Suites Springfield
3050 S. Dirksen Pkwy

Springfield, IL
217-529-7771 (877-270-6405)
Dogs up to 50 pounds are allowed for an additional one time pet fee of $20 per room. 2 dogs may be allowed.

Howard Johnson Inn
1701 David Jones Parkway
Springfield, IL
217-541-8762 (800-446-4656)
Well-behaved dogs of all sizes are allowed. There is no additional pet fee. A pet deposit may be required if paying with cash.

Motel 6 - Springfield
6011 South 6th Street Road
Springfield, IL
217-529-1633 (800-466-8356)
One well-behaved family pet per room. Guest must notify front desk upon arrival. Guest is liable for any damages. In consideration of all guests, pets must never be left unattended in the guest rooms.

Pear Tree Inn by Drury Hotel
3190 S Dirksen Parkway
Springfield, IL
217-529-9100 (800-DRURYINN (378-7946))
Dogs of all sizes are allowed for an additional one time pet fee of $25 per stay. Dogs must be leashed and cleaned up after. 2 dogs may be allowed.

Red Roof Inn - Springfield,Il
3200 Singer Avenue
Springfield, IL
217-753-4302 (800-RED-ROOF)
One well-behaved family pet per room. Guest must notify front desk upon arrival. Guest is liable for any damages. In consideration of all guests, pets must never be left unattended in the guest rooms.

Signature Inn
3090 Stevenson Drive
Springfield, IL
217-529-6611 (800-JAMESON (526-3766))
This inn offers a number of amenities including an indoor swimming pool. Dogs are allowed for an additional fee of $10 per night per pet. Dogs may not be left alone in the room, and they must be leashed and cleaned up after at all times. Dogs are not allowed in food service areas. 2 dogs may be allowed.

Sleep Inn
3470 Freedom Drive
Springfield, IL

217-787-6200 (877-424-6423)
Dogs are allowed for an additional one time pet fee of $25 per room. Multiple dogs may be allowed.

Staybridge Springs
4231 Schooner Drive
Springfield, IL
217-793-6700 (877-270-6405)
Dogs up to 50 pounds are allowed for an additional one time pet fee of $75 per room. Multiple dogs may be allowed.

Best Western Inn of St. Charles
1635 E Main Street
St Charles, IL
630-584-4550 (800-780-7234)
Dogs are allowed for an additional fee of $10 per night per pet, and there is a pet agreement to sign at check in. Multiple dogs may be allowed.

La Quinta Inn Chicago/Tinley Park
7255 W. 183rd Street
Tinley Park, IL
708-633-1200 (800-531-5900)
Dogs of all sizes are allowed. There are no additional fees. If pets are left in the room, please hang the "Do Not Disturb" sign. Dogs must be removed from the room for housekeeping, be leashed, and cleaned up after. Multiple dogs may be allowed.

Red Roof Inn - Troy
2030 Formosa Road
Troy, IL
618-667-2222 (800-RED-ROOF)
One well-behaved family pet per room. Guest must notify front desk upon arrival. Guest is liable for any damages. In consideration of all guests, pets must never be left unattended in the guest rooms.

Super 8 Troy
910 Edwardsville Rd
Troy, IL
618-667-8888 (800-800-8000)
Dogs of all sizes are allowed. There is a $10 per night pet fee per pet. Smoking and non-smoking rooms are available for pet rooms. 2 dogs may be allowed.

Sleep Inn
1908 N Lincoln Avenue
Urbana, IL
217-367-6000 (877-424-6423)
Dogs are allowed for an additional fee of $5 per night per pet. Multiple dogs may be allowed.

Days Inn Vandalia

1920 Kennedy Blvd
Vandalia, IL
618-283-4400 (800-329-7466)
Dogs of all sizes are allowed. There is a $10 returnable deposit required per room. 2 dogs may be allowed.

Motel 6 - Chicago West - Villa Park
10 West Roosevelt Road
Villa Park, IL
630-941-9100 (800-466-8356)
One well-behaved family pet per room. Guest must notify front desk upon arrival. Guest is liable for any damages. In consideration of all guests, pets must never be left unattended in the guest rooms.

Candlewood Suites
27 W 300 Warrenville Road
Warrenville, IL
630-836-1650 (877-270-6405)
Dogs up to 50 pounds are allowed for an additional pet fee per room of $50 for 1 to 6 nights, and of $150 for 7 nights or more. 2 dogs may be allowed.

Residence Inn by Marriott
28500 Bella Vista Parkway
Warrenville, IL
630-393-3444
Pets of all sizes are allowed. There is a $75 one time fee and a pet policy to sign at check in. Multiple dogs may be allowed.

Super 8 Washington/Peoria Area
1884 Washington Rd
Washington, IL
309-444-8881 (800-800-8000)
Dogs of all sizes are allowed. There is a $8 per night pet fee per pet. Reservations are recommended due to limited rooms for pets. Smoking and non-smoking rooms are available for pet rooms. 2 dogs may be allowed.

Candlewood Suites
1151 South Waukegan Road
Waukegan, IL
847-578-5250 (877-270-6405)
A dog up to 80 pounds is allowed for an additional pet fee of $75 for 1 to 6 days, and a fee of $150 for 7 or more days.

Residence Inn by Marriott
1440 S White Oak Drive
Waukegan, IL
847-689-9240
Pets of all sizes are allowed. There is a $75 one time fee and a pet policy to sign at check in. Multiple dogs may be allowed.

Super 8 Wenona
I39 and IL 17 Exit 35
Wenona, IL
815-853-4371 (800-800-8000)
Dogs of all sizes are allowed. There
is a $5 per night pet fee per pet.
Reservations are recommended due
to limited rooms for pets. Smoking
and non-smoking rooms are
available for pet rooms. 2 dogs may
be allowed.

TownePlace Suites Chicago West
Dundee/Elgin
2185 Marriot Drive
West Dundee, IL
847-608-6320
Dogs of all sizes are allowed. There
is a $75 one time pet fee per visit. 2
dogs may be allowed.

Candlewood Suites
8000 Capital Drive
Wheeling, IL
847-520-1684 (877-270-6405)
Dogs of all sizes are allowed for an
additional one time fee per pet of $75
for 1 to 7 nights, and a fee of $150
for 8 days or more. 2 dogs may be
allowed.

Red Roof Inn - Chicago -
Willowbrook
7535 Robert Kingery Highway
Willowbrook, IL
630-323-8811 (800-RED-ROOF)
One well-behaved family pet per
room. Guest must notify front desk
upon arrival. Guest is liable for any
damages. In consideration of all
guests, pets must never be left
unattended in the guest rooms.

Super 8 Woodstock
1220 Davis Rd
Woodstock, IL
815-337-6808 (800-800-8000)
Dogs of all sizes are allowed. There
is a $5 per night pet fee per pet
under 40 pounds and $10 per pet
over 40 pounds. Smoking and non-
smoking rooms are available for pet
rooms. 2 dogs may be allowed.

Indiana Listings

Days Inn Anderson
5901 Scatterfield Rd
Anderson, IN
765-649-0451 (800-329-7466)
Dogs of all sizes are allowed. There
is a $10 per night pet fee per pet.
Reservations are recommended due
to limited rooms for pets. 2 dogs may

be allowed.

Motel 6 - Anderson
5810 Scatterfield Road
Anderson, IN
765-642-9023 (800-466-8356)
One well-behaved family pet per
room. Guest must notify front desk
upon arrival. Guest is liable for any
damages. In consideration of all
guests, pets must never be left
unattended in the guest rooms.

La Quinta Inn & Conference Center
Auburn
306 Touring Drive
Auburn, IN
260-920-1900 (800-531-5900)
Dogs of all sizes are allowed. There
are no additional pet fees, however
no discounts/coupons can be
applied to the room. There is a pet
waiver to sign at check in. Dogs
must be leashed and cleaned up
after. Multiple dogs may be allowed.

Super 8 Avon/Raceway
Pk/Indianapolis Area
8229 E US 36
Avon, IN
317-272-8789 (800-800-8000)
Dogs of all sizes are allowed. There
is a $15 one time per pet fee per
visit. Smoking and non-smoking
rooms are available for pet rooms. 2
dogs may be allowed.

Super 8 Bedford
501 Bell Back Rd
Bedford, IN
812-275-8881 (800-800-8000)
Dogs of all sizes are allowed. There
is a $10 per night pet fee per pet.
Smoking and non-smoking rooms
are available for pet rooms. 2 dogs
may be allowed.

Days Inn Bloomington
200 Matlock Rd
Bloomington, IN
812-336-0905 (800-329-7466)
Dogs of all sizes are allowed. There
is a $10 per night pet fee per pet. 2
dogs may be allowed.

Hampton Inn
2100 N Walnut
Bloomington, IN
812-334-2100
Dogs of all sizes are allowed. There
are no additional pet fees. 2 dogs
may be allowed.

Motel 6 - Bloomington - Indiana
University
1800 North Walnut Street
Bloomington, IN

812-332-0820 (800-466-8356)
One well-behaved family pet per
room. Guest must notify front desk
upon arrival. Guest is liable for any
damages. In consideration of all
guests, pets must never be left
unattended in the guest rooms.

TownePlace Suites Bloomington
105 S Franklin Road
Bloomington, IN
812-334-1234
Dogs of all sizes are allowed. There
is a $75 one time pet fee per visit. 2
dogs may be allowed.

Best Western Green Tree Inn
(Louisville KY area)
1425 Broadway
Clarksville, IN
812-288-9281 (800-780-7234)
Dogs up to 50 pounds are allowed
for no additional pet fee. Dogs must
be crated when left alone in the
room. 2 dogs may be allowed.

Holiday Inn
505 Marriott Drive
Clarksville, IN
812-283-4411 (877-270-6405)
Dogs of all sizes are allowed for an
additional one time pet fee of $35 per
room. Multiple dogs may be allowed.

Motel 6 - Cloverdale
924 North Main Street
Cloverdale, IN
765-795-3000 (800-466-8356)
One well-behaved family pet per
room. Guest must notify front desk
upon arrival. Guest is liable for any
damages. In consideration of all
guests, pets must never be left
unattended in the guest rooms.

Super 8 Columbia City
351 W Plaza Dr
Columbia City, IN
260-244-2655 (800-800-8000)
Dogs of all sizes are allowed. There
is a $50 returnable deposit required
per room. Smoking and non-smoking
rooms are available for pet rooms. 2
dogs may be allowed.

Holiday Inn
2480 Jonathon Moore Pike
Columbus, IN
812-372-1541 (877-270-6405)
Dogs of all sizes are allowed for an
additional one time pet fee of $25 per
room, and dogs must be crated when
left alone in the room. Multiple dogs
may be allowed.

Capitol Inn
St Rd 135 & I-64, PO Box 773

Corydon, IN
812-738-4192
There is a $10 per day additional pet fee.

Super 8 Corydon
168 Pacer Dr
Corydon, IN
812-738-8887 (800-800-8000)
Dogs of all sizes are allowed. There are no additional pet fees. Smoking and non-smoking rooms are available for pet rooms. 2 dogs may be allowed.

Comfort Inn
2991 N Gandhi Street
Crawfordsville, IN
765-361-0665 (877-424-6423)
Dogs are allowed for an additional fee of $10 per night per pet. Multiple dogs may be allowed.

Motel 6 - Dale
1334 North Washington Street
Dale, IN
812-937-2294 (800-466-8356)
One well-behaved family pet per room. Guest must notify front desk upon arrival. Guest is liable for any damages. In consideration of all guests, pets must never be left unattended in the guest rooms.

Comfort Inn
1302 S 13th Street
Decatur, IN
260-724-8888 (877-424-6423)
Dogs are allowed for an additional pet fee of $5 per night per room. 2 dogs may be allowed.

Days Inn Decatur
1033 N 13th St
Decatur, IN
260-728-2196 (800-329-7466)
Dogs up to 60 pounds are allowed. There are no additional pet fees. 2 dogs may be allowed.

Ohio River Cabins
13445 N H 66
Derby, IN
812-836-2289
Dogs of all sizes are allowed. There is a $15 per night per pet additional fee. Multiple dogs may be allowed.

Candlewood Suites Elkhart
300 North Pointe Blvd.
Elkhart, IN
574-262-8600 (877-270-6405)
Dogs of all sizes are allowed for an additional pet fee per room of $25 for the 1st night, and $10 per night per room thereafter. 2 dogs may be allowed.

Red Roof Inn - Elkhart
2902 Cassopolis Street
Elkhart, IN
574-262-3691 (800-RED-ROOF)
One well-behaved family pet per room. Guest must notify front desk upon arrival. Guest is liable for any damages. In consideration of all guests, pets must never be left unattended in the guest rooms.

Super 8 Elkhart
345 Windsor Ave
Elkhart, IN
574-264-4457 (800-800-8000)
Dogs of all sizes are allowed. There is a $2 per night pet fee per pet. Smoking and non-smoking rooms are available for pet rooms. 2 dogs may be allowed.

Best Western Gateway Inn and Suites
324 Rusher Creek Rd
Evansville, IN
812-868-8000 (800-780-7234)
Dogs are allowed for an additional one time fee of $15 per pet. Multiple dogs may be allowed.

Comfort Inn
19622 Elpers Road
Evansville, IN
812-867-1600 (877-424-6423)
Dogs are allowed for an additional fee of $10 per night per pet. There may be 1 large or 2 small dogs per room. 2 dogs may be allowed.

Comfort Inn East
8331 E Walnut Street
Evansville, IN
812-476-3600 (877-424-6423)
Dogs are allowed for an additional pet fee of $10 per night per room. 2 dogs may be allowed.

Days Inn Evansville East
4819 Tecumseh Lane
Evansville, IN
812-473-7944 (800-329-7466)
Dogs of all sizes are allowed. There is a $5 per night pet fee per pet. 2 dogs may be allowed.

Motel 6 - Evansville
4321 US 41 North
Evansville, IN
812-424-6431 (800-466-8356)
One well-behaved family pet per room. Guest must notify front desk upon arrival. Guest is liable for any damages. In consideration of all guests, pets must never be left unattended in the guest rooms.

North Drury Inn
3901 US 41 North
Evansville, IN
812-423-5818 (800-378-7946)
Dogs of all sizes are permitted. Pets are not allowed in the breakfast area of the hotel. Pets are not to be left unattended, and each guest must assume liability for damage of property or other guest complaints. There is a limit of one pet per room.

Residence Inn by Marriott
8283 E Walnut
Evansville, IN
812-471-7191
Pets of all sizes are allowed. There is a $75 one time fee and a pet policy to sign at check in. 2 dogs may be allowed.

Ramada Inn
9791 North by Northeast Blvd
Fishers, IN
317-558-4100
Dogs of all sizes are allowed. There is a pet policy to sign at check in and there are no additional pet fees. Multiple dogs may be allowed.

Staybridge Suites
9780 Crosspoint Blvd
Fishers, IN
317-577-9500 (877-270-6405)
Dogs of all sizes are allowed for an additional one time fee of $95 per pet. 2 dogs may be allowed.

Studio 6 - Indianapolis - Fishers
8250 North By Northeast Boulevard
Fishers, IN
317-913-1920 (800-466-8356)
One well-behaved family pet per room. Guest must notify front desk upon arrival. Guest is liable for any damages. In consideration of all guests, pets must never be left unattended in the guest rooms.

Best Western Luxbury Inn Fort Wayne
5501 Coventry Ln
Fort Wayne, IN
260-436-0242 (800-780-7234)
Dogs are allowed for an additional fee of $15 per night per pet. Multiple dogs may be allowed.

Candlewood Suites Fort Wayne - Nw
5251 Distribution Drive
Fort Wayne, IN
260-484-1400 (877-270-6405)
Dogs of all sizes are allowed for an additional fee of $12 per night per pet. Multiple dogs may be allowed.

Comfort Suites

5775 Coventry Lane
Fort Wayne, IN
260-436-4300 (877-424-6423)
Dogs are allowed for an additional
one time pet fee of $50 per room 2
dogs may be allowed.

Fort Wayne Marriott
305 E Washington Center Road
Fort Wayne, IN
260-484-0411 (800-228-9290)
Dogs of all sizes are allowed. There
is a $75 one time additional pet fee
per room. Dogs may not be left alone
in the room, and they must be
leashed and cleaned up after.
Multiple dogs may be allowed.

Motel 6 - Ft Wayne
3003 West Coliseum Boulevard
Fort Wayne, IN
260-482-3972 (800-466-8356)
One well-behaved family pet per
room. Guest must notify front desk
upon arrival. Guest is liable for any
damages. In consideration of all
guests, pets must never be left
unattended in the guest rooms.

Quality Hotel
3330 W Coliseum Blvd
Fort Wayne, IN
260-484-7711
Dogs are allowed for an additional
one time pet fee of $75 per room
Multiple dogs may be allowed.

Red Roof Inn - Ft Wayne
2920 Goshen Road
Fort Wayne, IN
260-484-8641 (800-RED-ROOF)
One well-behaved family pet per
room. Guest must notify front desk
upon arrival. Guest is liable for any
damages. In consideration of all
guests, pets must never be left
unattended in the guest rooms.

Residence Inn by Marriott
4919 Lima Road
Fort Wayne, IN
260-484-4700
Pets of all sizes are allowed. There is
a $75 one time fee and a pet policy
to sign at check in. Multiple dogs
may be allowed.

Residence Inn by Marriott
7811 W Jefferson Blvd
Fort Wayne, IN
260-432-8000
Dogs of all sizes are allowed. There
is a $75 one time fee and a pet
policy to sign at check in. Multiple
dogs may be allowed.

Hotel 7

2180 E King St
Franklin, IN
317-736-8000
Dogs of all sizes are allowed. There
is a $10 per night pet fee per pet.
Pet must be kept in kennel when
left alone. 2 dogs may be allowed.

Motel 6 - Louisville - Georgetown
1079 North Luther Road
Georgetown, IN
812-923-0441 (800-466-8356)
One well-behaved family pet per
room. Guest must notify front desk
upon arrival. Guest is liable for any
damages. In consideration of all
guests, pets must never be left
unattended in the guest rooms.

Best Western Inn
900 Lincolnway E
Goshen, IN
574-533-0408 (800-780-7234)
Dogs are allowed for no additional
pet fee. Dogs must be crated when
left alone in the room, and they
must be removed or crated for
housekeeping. 2 dogs may be
allowed.

Quality Inn and Suites
2270 N State Street
Greenfield, IN
317-462-7112 (877-424-6423)
Dogs are allowed for an additional
fee of $10 per night per pet. 2 dogs
may be allowed.

Holiday Inn Express
915 Ann Blvd
Greensburg, IN
812-663-5500 (877-270-6405)
Dogs of all sizes are allowed for no
additional fee. 2 dogs may be
allowed.

Red Roof Inn - Greenwood, IN
110 Sheek Road
Greenwood, IN
317-887-1515 (800-RED-ROOF)
One well-behaved family pet per
room. Guest must notify front desk
upon arrival. Guest is liable for any
damages. In consideration of all
guests, pets must never be left
unattended in the guest rooms.

Motel 6 - Hammond - Chicago Area
3840 179th Street
Hammond, IN
219-845-0330 (800-466-8356)
One well-behaved family pet per
room. Guest must notify front desk
upon arrival. Guest is liable for any
damages. In consideration of all
guests, pets must never be left
unattended in the guest rooms.

Super 8 Howe
7333 N State Rte 9
Howe, IN
260-562-2828 (800-800-8000)
Dogs of all sizes are allowed. There
are no additional pet fees. Smoking
and non-smoking rooms are
available for pet rooms. 2 dogs may
be allowed.

Days Inn Huntington
2996 W Park Dr
Huntington, IN
260-359-8989 (800-329-7466)
Dogs up to 60 pounds are allowed.
There is a $7 per night pet fee per
pet. 2 dogs may be allowed.

Candlewood Suites
8111 Bash Street
Indianapolis, IN
317-595-9292 (877-270-6405)
Dogs of all sizes are allowed for an
additional one time pet fee per room
of $25 for 1 to 6 nights; the fee is
$75 for 7 or more nights. Multiple
dogs may be allowed.

Candlewood Suites Indianapolis
Airport
5250 W. Bradbury Street
Indianapolis, IN
317-241-9595 (877-270-6405)
Dogs of all sizes are allowed for an
additional one time pet fee per room
of $25 for 1 to 6 nights; the fee is
$75 for 7 or more nights. Multiple
dogs may be allowed.

Candlewood Suites Indianapolis City
Centre
1152 N White River Pkwy, West
Drive
Indianapolis, IN
317-536-7700 (877-270-6405)
Dogs up to 80 pounds are allowed
for an additional fee of $5 per night
per pet. 2 dogs may be allowed.

Comfort Suites-Fishers
9760 Crosspoint Blvd
Indianapolis, IN
317-578-1200 (877-424-6423)
Dogs of all sizes are allowed. There
is a $10 per night per room additional
pet fee. Multiple dogs may be
allowed.

Days Inn Castleton
8275 Craig St
Indianapolis, IN
317-841-9700 (800-329-7466)
Dogs of all sizes are allowed. There
is a $5 per night pet fee per pet. 2
dogs may be allowed.

Days Inn Indianapolis
2150 N Post Road
Indianapolis, IN
317-899-2100 (800-329-7466)
Dogs of all sizes are allowed. There is a $5 per night pet fee per pet. 2 dogs may be allowed.

Days Inn Indianapolis
3401 South Keystone Ave
Indianapolis, IN
317-788-0500 (800-329-7466)
Dogs of all sizes are allowed. There is a $5 per night pet fee per pet. 2 dogs may be allowed.

Days Inn Indianapolis East
7314 E 21st Street
Indianapolis, IN
317-359-5500 (800-329-7466)
Dogs of all sizes are allowed. There is a $5 per night pet fee per pet. 2 dogs may be allowed.

Drury Inn
9320 N. Michigan Road
Indianapolis, IN
317-876-9777 (800-378-7946)
Dogs of all sizes are permitted. Pets are not allowed in the breakfast area of the hotel. Pets are not to be left unattended, and each guest must assume liability for damage of property or other guest complaints. There is a limit of one pet per room.

Holiday Inn
6990 E. 21st St
Indianapolis, IN
317-359-5341 (877-270-6405)
Dogs up to 50 pounds are allowed for an additional one time fee of $25 per pet. 2 dogs may be allowed.

La Quinta Inn Indianapolis East
7304 East 21st Street
Indianapolis, IN
317-359-1021 (800-531-5900)
Dogs of all sizes are allowed. There are no additional pet fees. Dogs may not be left unattended, and they must be leashed and cleaned up after. Multiple dogs may be allowed.

La Quinta Inn Indianapolis East - Post Drive
2349 Post Drive
Indianapolis, IN
317-897-2300 (800-531-5900)
Dogs of all sizes are allowed. There are no additional pet fees. Dogs may only be left alone in the room if they will be quiet and well behaved. Also, please put the "Do Not Disturb" sign on the door when you are out and a dog is in the room. Dogs must be kept leashed. Multiple dogs may be

allowed.

La Quinta Inn Indianapolis North at Pyramids
3880 W. 92nd St
Indianapolis, IN
317-872-3100 (800-531-5900)
Dogs of all sizes are allowed. There is a $10 one time pet fee. Dogs may not be left unattended unless they will be quiet and well behaved. Dogs must be crated or removed for housekeeping. 2 dogs may be allowed.

Motel 6 - Indianapolis - Airport
5241 West Bradbury Avenue
Indianapolis, IN
317-248-1231 (800-466-8356)
One well-behaved family pet per room. Guest must notify front desk upon arrival. Guest is liable for any damages. In consideration of all guests, pets must never be left unattended in the guest rooms.

Motel 6 - Indianapolis - Keystone/I-465
9402 Haver Way
Indianapolis, IN
317-848-2423 (800-466-8356)
One well-behaved family pet per room. Guest must notify front desk upon arrival. Guest is liable for any damages. In consideration of all guests, pets must never be left unattended in the guest rooms.

Motel 6 - Indianapolis East
2851 North Shadeland Avenue
Indianapolis, IN
317-546-5864 (800-466-8356)
One well-behaved family pet per room. Guest must notify front desk upon arrival. Guest is liable for any damages. In consideration of all guests, pets must never be left unattended in the guest rooms.

Motel 6 - Indianapolis South
5151 Elmwood Avenue
Indianapolis, IN
317-783-5555 (800-466-8356)
One well-behaved family pet per room. Guest must notify front desk upon arrival. Guest is liable for any damages. In consideration of all guests, pets must never be left unattended in the guest rooms.

Quality Inn and Suites
4345 Southport Crossing Way
Indianapolis, IN
317-859-8888 (877-424-6423)
Dogs are allowed for an additional fee of $10 per night per pet. Multiple dogs may be allowed.

Quality Inn and Suites Airport
2631 S Lynhurst Drive
Indianapolis, IN
317-381-1000 (877-424-6423)
Dogs are allowed for an additional one time fee of $10 per pet. 2 dogs may be allowed.

Red Roof Inn - Indianapolis North
9520 Valparaiso Court
Indianapolis, IN
317-872-3030 (800-RED-ROOF)
One well-behaved family pet per room. Guest must notify front desk upon arrival. Guest is liable for any damages. In consideration of all guests, pets must never be left unattended in the guest rooms.

Red Roof Inn - Indianapolis Northeast
8325 Bash Road
Indianapolis, IN
317-577-0455 (800-RED-ROOF)
One well-behaved family pet per room. Guest must notify front desk upon arrival. Guest is liable for any damages. In consideration of all guests, pets must never be left unattended in the guest rooms.

Red Roof Inn - Indianapolis South
5221 Victory Drive
Indianapolis, IN
317-788-9551 (800-RED-ROOF)
One well-behaved family pet per room. Guest must notify front desk upon arrival. Guest is liable for any damages. In consideration of all guests, pets must never be left unattended in the guest rooms.

Red Roof Inn - Indianapolis Speedway
6415 Debonair Lane
Indianapolis, IN
317-293-6881 (800-RED-ROOF)
One well-behaved family pet per room. Guest must notify front desk upon arrival. Guest is liable for any damages. In consideration of all guests, pets must never be left unattended in the guest rooms.

Residence Inn by Marriot
3553 Founders Road
Indianapolis, IN
317-872-0462
Pets of all sizes are allowed, however there can only be 1 large or 2 small pets in the standard rooms, and up to 3 pets in the Penthouse suite. There is a $75 one time fee and a pet policy to sign at check in.

Residence Inn by Marriott

Indiana Listings - Please always call ahead to make sure an establishment is still dog-friendly.

9765 Crosspoint Blvd
Indianapolis, IN
317-842-1111
Pets of all sizes are welcome. There is a $75 one time fee and a pet policy to sign at check in. Multiple dogs may be allowed.

Residence Inn by Marriott
6220 Digital Way
Indianapolis, IN
317-275-6000
Pets up to 75 pounds are allowed. There is a $75 one time fee and a pet policy to sign at check in. 2 dogs may be allowed.

Sheraton Indianapolis Hotel & Suites
8787 Keyston Crossing
Indianapolis, IN
317-846-2700 (888-625-5144)
Dogs up to 80 pounds are allowed. There are no additional pet fees. Dogs are not allowed to be left alone in the room.

Staybridge Suites
9780 Crosspoint Blvd
Indianapolis, IN
317-577-9500 (877-270-6405)
Dogs of all sizes are allowed for an additional one time fee of $95 per pet. 2 dogs may be allowed.

Super 8 Indianapolis/Airport/NW
2602 N High School Road
Indianapolis, IN
317-291-8800 (800-800-8000)
Dogs of all sizes are allowed. There is a $5.60 per night pet fee per pet. Smoking and non-smoking rooms are available for pet rooms. 2 dogs may be allowed.

Super 8 Indianapolis/Airport/South
4502 S Harding St
Indianapolis, IN
317-788-4774 (800-800-8000)
Dogs of all sizes are allowed. There is a $5 per night pet fee per pet. Smoking and non-smoking rooms are available for pet rooms. 2 dogs may be allowed.

Super 8 Indianapolis/East
8850 E 21st Street
Indianapolis, IN
317-895-5402 (800-800-8000)
Dogs of all sizes are allowed. There is a $6 per night pet fee per pet. Smoking and non-smoking rooms are available for pet rooms. 2 dogs may be allowed.

TownePlace Suites Indianapolis Keystone
8468 Union Chapel Rd

Indianapolis, IN
317-255-3700
Dogs of all sizes are allowed. There is a $75 one time pet fee per visit. 2 dogs may be allowed.

TownePlace Suites Indianapolis Park
5802 W 71st Street
Indianapolis, IN
317-290-8900
Dogs of all sizes are allowed. There is a $75 one time pet fee per visit. 2 dogs may be allowed.

Days Inn Jasper
272 Brucke Strasse
Jasper, IN
812-482-6000 (800-329-7466)
Dogs of all sizes are allowed. There is a $10 per night pet fee per pet. 2 dogs may be allowed.

Days Inn Louisville/Jeffersonville
350 Eastern Blvd
Jeffersonville, IN
812-288-9331 (800-329-7466)
Dogs of all sizes are allowed. There is a $10 per night pet fee per pet. 2 dogs may be allowed.

Motel 6 - Louisville N-Jeffersonville
2016 Old US 31 East
Jeffersonville, IN
812-283-7703 (800-466-8356)
One well-behaved family pet per room. Guest must notify front desk upon arrival. Guest is liable for any damages. In consideration of all guests, pets must never be left unattended in the guest rooms.

TownePlace Suites Louisville North
703 North Shore Drive
Jeffersonville, IN
812-280-8200
Dogs of all sizes are allowed. There is a $10 one time per pet fee per visit. 2 dogs may be allowed.

Comfort Inn
522 Essex Drive
Kokomo, IN
765-452-5050 (877-424-6423)
Dogs are allowed for an additional one time pet fee of $15 per room. 2 dogs may be allowed.

Hampton Inn
2920 S Reed Road
Kokomo, IN
765-455-2900
Dogs of all sizes are allowed. There are no additional pet fees. Multiple dogs may be allowed.

Motel 6 - Kokomo

2808 South Reed Road
Kokomo, IN
765-457-8211 (800-466-8356)
One well-behaved family pet per room. Guest must notify front desk upon arrival. Guest is liable for any damages. In consideration of all guests, pets must never be left unattended in the guest rooms.

Comfort Suites
31 Frontage Road
Lafayette, IN
765-447-0016 (877-424-6423)
Dogs are allowed for an additional fee of $10 per night per pet. Multiple dogs may be allowed.

Days Inn Lafayette
151 Frontage Rd
Lafayette, IN
765-446-8558 (800-329-7466)
Dogs of all sizes are allowed. There are no additional pet fees. 2 dogs may be allowed.

Holiday Inn Express
201 Frontage Rd
Lafayette, IN
765-449-4808 (877-270-6405)
Dogs of all sizes are allowed for no additional fee. Multiple dogs may be allowed.

Red Roof Inn - Lafayette
4201 SR 26 East
Lafayette, IN
765-448-4671 (800-RED-ROOF)
One well-behaved family pet per room. Guest must notify front desk upon arrival. Guest is liable for any damages. In consideration of all guests, pets must never be left unattended in the guest rooms.

TownePlace Suites Lafayette
163 Frontage Road
Lafayette, IN
765-446-8668
Dogs of all sizes are allowed. There is a $75 one time pet fee per visit. 2 dogs may be allowed.

Quality Inn and Suites at the Casinos
1000 Eads Parkway
Lawrenceburg, IN
812-539-4770 (877-424-6423)
Dogs are allowed for an additional fee of $10 per night per pet. Multiple dogs may be allowed.

Comfort Inn
210 Sam Ralston Road
Lebanon, IN
765-482-4800 (877-424-6423)
Dogs up to 50 pounds are allowed for an additional fee of $10 per night

161

per pet. 2 dogs may be allowed.

Holiday Inn Express
335 N. Mt Zion Rd
Lebanon, IN
765-483-4100 (877-270-6405)
Dogs of all sizes are allowed for no
additional fee. 2 dogs may be
allowed.

Quality Inn and Suites
505 S H 39
Lebanon, IN
765-482-0500 (877-424-6423)
Dogs are allowed for an additional
fee of $10 per night per pet. Multiple
dogs may be allowed.

Super 8 Markle
610 Annette Drive
Markle, IN
260-758-8888 (800-800-8000)
Dogs up to 80 pounds are allowed.
There is a $7 per night pet fee per
pet. Smoking and non-smoking
rooms are available for pet rooms. 2
dogs may be allowed.

Best Western Martinsville Inn
50 Bill's Boulevard
Martinsville, IN
765-342-1842 (800-780-7234)
Dogs are allowed for an additional
fee of $5 per night per pet. Multiple
dogs may be allowed.

La Quinta Inn Merrillville
8210 Louisiana St.
Merrillville, IN
219-738-2870 (800-531-5900)
Dogs of all sizes are allowed. There
are no additional pet fees. Dogs
must be leashed and cleaned up
after. Multiple dogs may be allowed.

Motel 6 - Merrillville
8290 Louisiana Street
Merrillville, IN
219-738-2701 (800-466-8356)
One well-behaved family pet per
room. Guest must notify front desk
upon arrival. Guest is liable for any
damages. In consideration of all
guests, pets must never be left
unattended in the guest rooms.

Red Roof Inn - Merrillville
8290 Georgia Street
Merrillville, IN
219-738-2430 (800-RED-ROOF)
One well-behaved family pet per
room. Guest must notify front desk
upon arrival. Guest is liable for any
damages. In consideration of all
guests, pets must never be left
unattended in the guest rooms.

Residence Inn by Marriott
8018 Delaware Place
Merrillville, IN
219-791-9000
Dogs of all sizes are allowed. There
is a $75 one time fee and a pet
policy to sign at check in. Multiple
dogs may be allowed.

Super 8 Merrillville/Gary Area
8300 Louisiana St
Merrillville, IN
219-736-8383 (800-800-8000)
Dogs of all sizes are allowed. There
are no additional pet fees. Smoking
and non-smoking rooms are
available for pet rooms. 2 dogs may
be allowed.

Red Roof Inn - Michigan City
110 West Kieffer Road
Michigan City, IN
219-874-5251 (800-RED-ROOF)
One well-behaved family pet per
room. Guest must notify front desk
upon arrival. Guest is liable for any
damages. In consideration of all
guests, pets must never be left
unattended in the guest rooms.

Red Roof Inn - Mishawaka - Notre
Dame
1325 East University Drive Court
Mishawaka, IN
574-271-4800 (800-RED-ROOF)
One well-behaved family pet per
room. Guest must notify front desk
upon arrival. Guest is liable for any
damages. In consideration of all
guests, pets must never be left
unattended in the guest rooms.

Days Inn Muncie
3509 N Everbrook Lane
Muncie, IN
765-288-2311 (800-329-7466)
Dogs of all sizes are allowed. There
is a $10 one time per pet fee per
visit. 2 dogs may be allowed.

Super 8 Muncie
3601 W Fox Ridge Lane
Muncie, IN
765-286-4333 (800-800-8000)
Dogs of all sizes are allowed. There
is a $10 per night pet fee per pet.
Smoking and non-smoking rooms
are available for pet rooms. 2 dogs
may be allowed.

Budget Inn
5243 South SR 3
New Castle, IN
765-987-8205 (800-800-8000)
Dogs of all sizes are allowed. There
is a $5 per night pet fee per pet.
Smoking and non-smoking rooms

are available for pet rooms. 2 dogs
may be allowed.

Quality Inn and Suites
16025 Prosperity Drive
Noblesville, IN
317-770-6772 (877-424-6423)
Dogs up to 25 pounds are allowed
for an additional fee of $10 per night
per pet; the fee is $20 per night per
pet for dogs over 25 pounds. 2 dogs
may be allowed.

Days Inn Indianapolis Plainfield
2245 Hadley Rd
Plainfield, IN
317-839-5000 (800-329-7466)
Dogs of all sizes are allowed. There
is a $10 per night pet fee per pet. 2
dogs may be allowed.

Days Inn Plymouth
2229 N Michigan St
Plymouth, IN
574-935-4276 (800-329-7466)
Dogs of all sizes are allowed. There
is a $10 per night pet fee per pet. 2
dogs may be allowed.

Comfort Inn
2300 Willowcreek Road
Portage, IN
219-763-7177 (877-424-6423)
Dogs are allowed for an additional
one time fee of $20 per pet. Multiple
dogs may be allowed.

Super 8 Portage
6118 Melton Rd
Portage, IN
219-762-8857 (800-800-8000)
Dogs of all sizes are allowed. There
are no additional pet fees. Smoking
and non-smoking rooms are
available for pet rooms. 2 dogs may
be allowed.

Days Inn Princeton
2110 W Broadway
Princeton, IN
812-386-1200 (800-329-7466)
Dogs of all sizes are allowed. There
is a $10 per night pet fee per pet. 2
dogs may be allowed.

Holiday Inn Express
4788 Nesbitt Drive
Rensselaer, IN
866-866-7560 (877-270-6405)
Dogs of all sizes are allowed for an
additional one time fee of $15 per
pet. 2 dogs may be allowed.

Days Inn Richmond
5775 National Rd East
Richmond, IN
765-966-4900 (800-329-7466)

Dogs of all sizes are allowed. There is a $10 per night pet fee per pet. 2 dogs may be allowed.

Holiday Inn
5501 National Rd E
Richmond, IN
765-966-7511 (877-270-6405)
Dogs of all sizes are allowed for an additional one time fee of $20 per room. 2 dogs may be allowed.

Lee's Inn
6030 National Rd. E.
Richmond, IN
765-966-6559

Motel 6 - Richmond
419 Commerce Drive
Richmond, IN
765-966-6682 (800-466-8356)
One well-behaved family pet per room. Guest must notify front desk upon arrival. Guest is liable for any damages. In consideration of all guests, pets must never be left unattended in the guest rooms.

Super 8 Richmond
2525 Chester Blvd
Richmond, IN
765-962-7576 (800-800-8000)
Dogs of all sizes are allowed. There is a $5 per night pet fee per pet. Smoking and non-smoking rooms are available for pet rooms. 2 dogs may be allowed.

Super 8 Scottsburg
1522 W McClain Ave
Scottsburg, IN
812-752-2122 (800-800-8000)
Dogs of all sizes are allowed. There is a $10 per night pet fee per pet. Smoking and non-smoking rooms are available for pet rooms. 2 dogs may be allowed.

Days Inn Seymour
302 S Commerce Dr
Seymour, IN
812-522-3678 (800-329-7466)
Dogs of all sizes are allowed. There is a $5 per night pet fee per pet. 2 dogs may be allowed.

Motel 6 - Seymour North
365 Tanger Boulevard
Seymour, IN
812-524-7443 (800-466-8356)
One well-behaved family pet per room. Guest must notify front desk upon arrival. Guest is liable for any damages. In consideration of all guests, pets must never be left unattended in the guest rooms.

Super 8 Seymour
401 Outlet Blvd
Seymour, IN
812-524-2000 (800-800-8000)
Dogs of all sizes are allowed. There is a $5 per night pet fee per pet. Dogs are not allowed to be left alone in the room. Smoking and non-smoking rooms are available for pet rooms. 2 dogs may be allowed.

Comfort Inn
36 W Rampart Road
Shelbyville, IN
317-398-8044 (877-424-6423)
Dogs up to 60 pounds are allowed. There is a $10 per night per room additional pet fee. 2 dogs may be allowed.

Super 8 Shipshewana
740 S Van Buren
Shipshewana, IN
260-768-4004 (800-800-8000)
Dogs up to 60 pounds are allowed. There is a $8 per night pet fee per pet. Smoking and non-smoking rooms are available for pet rooms. 2 dogs may be allowed.

Comfort Suites
52939 H 933 N
South Bend, IN
574-272-1500 (877-424-6423)
Dogs are allowed for an additional one time pet fee of $20 per room. Multiple dogs may be allowed.

Motel 6 - South Bend
52624 US 31 North
South Bend, IN
574-272-7072 (800-466-8356)
One well-behaved family pet per room. Guest must notify front desk upon arrival. Guest is liable for any damages. In consideration of all guests, pets must never be left unattended in the guest rooms.

Quality Inn University
515 N Dixieway
South Bend, IN
574-272-6600 (877-424-6423)
Dogs are allowed for no additional fee with a credit card on file. Multiple dogs may be allowed.

Residence Inn by Marriott
716 N Niles Avenue
South Bend, IN
574-289-5555
Pets of all sizes are allowed. There is a $75 one time fee and a pet policy to sign at check in. Multiple dogs may be allowed.

Sleep Inn
4134 Lincolnway West
South Bend, IN
574-232-3200 (877-424-6423)
choicehotels.com/hotel/in264
This hotel located near Notre Dame and Century Center welcomes up to 2 dogs of 50 pounds or less.

Motel 6 - Indianapolis West - Speedway
6330 Debonair Lane
Speedway, IN
317-293-3220 (800-466-8356)
One well-behaved family pet per room. Guest must notify front desk upon arrival. Guest is liable for any damages. In consideration of all guests, pets must never be left unattended in the guest rooms.

Red Roof Inn - Taylorsville
10330 North US 31
Taylorsville, IN
812-526-9747 (800-RED-ROOF)
One well-behaved family pet per room. Guest must notify front desk upon arrival. Guest is liable for any damages. In consideration of all guests, pets must never be left unattended in the guest rooms.

Holiday Inn Express Hotel & Suites
310 Orchard Hill Drive
Tell City, IN
812-547-0800 (877-270-6405)
Dogs of all sizes are allowed for an additional one time fee of $10 per night per pet. 2 dogs may be allowed.

Drury Inn
3040 South US Hwy 41
Terre Haute, IN
812-238-1206 (800-378-7946)
Dogs of all sizes are permitted. Pets are not allowed in the breakfast area of the hotel. Pets are not to be left unattended, and each guest must assume liability for damage of property or other guest complaints. There is a limit of one pet per room.

Holiday Inn
3300 US 41 S.
Terre Haute, IN
812-232-6081 (877-270-6405)
Dogs of all sizes are allowed for an additional one time pet fee of $15 per room. 2 dogs may be allowed.

Pear Tree Inn
3050 South US Hwy 41
Terre Haute, IN
812-234-4268 (800-378-7946)
Dogs of all sizes are permitted. Pets are not allowed in the breakfast area

of the hotel. Pets are not to be left unattended, and each guest must assume liability for damage of property or other guest complaints. There is a limit of one pet per room.

Best Western Valparaiso Inn
760 Morthland Drive
Valparaiso, IN
219-464-8555 (800-780-7234)
Dogs are allowed for an additional fee of $15 per night per pet. 2 dogs may be allowed.

Quality Inn
600 Old Wheatland Road
Vincennes, IN
812-886-9900 (877-424-6423)
Dogs are allowed for no additional pet fee. 2 dogs may be allowed.

Days Inn Warsaw
2575 E Center St
Warsaw, IN
574-267-3344 (800-329-7466)
Dogs of all sizes are allowed. There is a $10 per night pet fee per pet. 2 dogs may be allowed.

Ramada Plaza Hotel
2519 E Center Street
Warsaw, IN
574-269-2323
Dogs of all sizes are allowed. There are no additional pet fees. Multiple dogs may be allowed.

Iowa Listings

Super 8 Adair
111 5th St
Adair, IA
641-742-5251 (800-800-8000)
Dogs of all sizes are allowed. There is a $20 returnable deposit required per room. Smoking and non-smoking rooms are available for pet rooms. 2 dogs may be allowed.

Howard Johnson Express Inn
2701 Adventureland Drive
Altoona, IA
515-967-4886 (800-446-4656)
Dogs of all sizes are welcome. There is a $6 per day pet fee per pet.

Motel 6 - Des Moines East - Altoona
3225 Adventureland Drive
Altoona, IA
515-967-5252 (800-466-8356)
One well-behaved family pet per room. Guest must notify front desk upon arrival. Guest is liable for any

damages. In consideration of all guests, pets must never be left unattended in the guest rooms.

Holiday Inn
I-80 Exit 225
Amana, IA
319-668-1175 (877-270-6405)
amanaholidayinn.com/info.htm
Dogs of all sizes are allowed for an additional one time pet fee of $15 per room. Multiple dogs may be allowed.

Best Western Garden Inn & Suites
Ames, IA
515-296-2500 (800-780-7234)
One dog is allowed for no additional pet fee; there is fee of $10 per night per pet for each additional dog. Multiple dogs may be allowed.

Super 8 Anamosa
100 Grant Wood Dr
Anamosa, IA
319-462-3888 (800-800-8000)
Dogs of all sizes are allowed. There is a $10.50 one time per pet fee per visit. Smoking and non-smoking rooms are available for pet rooms. 2 dogs may be allowed.

Days Inn Ankeny
105 NE Delaware
Ankeny, IA
515-965-1995 (800-329-7466)
Dogs of all sizes are allowed. There is a $5 per night pet fee per pet. 2 dogs may be allowed.

Motel 6 - Avoca
211 West Marty Drive
Avoca, IA
712-343-6507 (800-466-8356)
One well-behaved family pet per room. Guest must notify front desk upon arrival. Guest is liable for any damages. In consideration of all guests, pets must never be left unattended in the guest rooms.

Jumer's Castle Lodge
I-74 at Spruce Hills Drive
Bettendorf, IA
319-359-7141 (800-285-8637)
jumers.com/documents/betwel.htm
There is a $25 refundable pet deposit.

Super 8 Boone/Ames Area
1715 S Story St
Boone, IA
515-432-8890 (800-800-8000)
Dogs of all sizes are allowed. There is a $50 returnable deposit required per room. Smoking and non-smoking rooms are available for pet

rooms. 2 dogs may be allowed.

Sleep Inn
4130 H 21
Brooklyn, IA
319-685-4500 (877-424-6423)
Dogs up to 50 pounds are allowed for a $15 to $25 refundable deposit plus an additional fee of $10 per night per pet. 2 dogs may be allowed.

Best Western Pzazz Fun City
3001 Winegard Drive
Burlington, IA
319-753-2223 (800-780-7234)
Dogs are allowed for no additional pet fee; there is a pet agreement to sign at check in. 2 dogs may be allowed.

Quality Inn
3051 Kirkwood
Burlington, IA
319-753-0000 (877-424-6423)
Dogs are allowed for an additional fee of $10 per night per pet. 2 dogs may be allowed.

Super 8 Burlington
3001 Kirkwood
Burlington, IA
319-752-9806 (800-800-8000)
Dogs of all sizes are allowed. There is a $10 one time per pet fee per visit. Dogs are not allowed to be left alone in the room. Smoking and non-smoking rooms are available for pet rooms. 2 dogs may be allowed.

Super 8 Carter LakeEppley/Omaha Area
3000 Airport Dr
Carter Lake, IA
712-247-5588 (800-800-8000)
Dogs of all sizes are allowed. There is a $10 one time per pet fee per visit. Smoking and non-smoking rooms are available for pet rooms. 2 dogs may be allowed.

Best Western Cooper's Mill Hotel
100 F Avenue NW
Cedar, IA
319-366-5323 (800-780-7234)
Dogs are allowed for an additional pet fee of $5 per night per room. Multiple dogs may be allowed.

Comfort Inn South
390 33rd Avenue
Cedar Rapids, IA
319-363-7934 (877-424-6423)
Dogs are allowed for an additional one time pet fee of $10 per room. Multiple dogs may be allowed.

Motel 6 - Cedar Rapids
3325 Southgate Court SW
Cedar Rapids, IA
319-366-7523 (800-466-8356)
One well-behaved family pet per
room. Guest must notify front desk
upon arrival. Guest is liable for any
damages. In consideration of all
guests, pets must never be left
unattended in the guest rooms.

Residence Inn by Marriott
1900 Dodge Road NE
Cedar Rapids, IA
319-395-0111
Pets of all sizes are allowed. There is
a $75 one time fee and a pet policy
to sign at check in. Multiple dogs
may be allowed.

Sleep Inn and Suites
1416 S Grand Avenue
Charles City, IA
641-257-6700 (877-424-6423)
Dogs up to 100 pounds are allowed
for an additional pet fee of $10 per
night per room. 2 dogs may be
allowed.

Super 8 Charles City
1411 S Grand Ave
Charles City, IA
641-228-2888 (800-800-8000)
Dogs of all sizes are allowed. There
is a $10 per night pet fee per pet.
Smoking and non-smoking rooms
are available for pet rooms. 2 dogs
may be allowed.

Super 8 Cherokee
1400 N Second St
Cherokee, IA
712-225-4278 (800-800-8000)
Dogs of all sizes are allowed. There
are no additional pet fees. Smoking
and non-smoking rooms are
available for pet rooms. 2 dogs may
be allowed.

Super 8 Clear Lake
2809 4th Ave S
Clear Lake, IA
641-357-7521 (800-800-8000)
Dogs of all sizes are allowed. There
is a $10 returnable deposit required
per room. Dogs are not allowed to be
left alone in the room. Smoking and
non-smoking rooms are available for
pet rooms. 2 dogs may be allowed.

Best Western Frontier Motor Inn
2300 Lincolnway
Clinton, IA
563-242-7112 (800-780-7234)
Dogs are allowed for an additional
fee of $10 per night per pet. The fee
may be slightly lower for very small

pets. Multiple dogs may be allowed.

Country Inns & Suites by Carlson
2224 Lincoln Way
Clinton, IA
563-244-9922
Dogs of all sizes are allowed. There
is a $10 per day additional pet fee.

Motel 6 - Clinton
1522 Lincoln Way
Clinton, IA
563-243-8841 (800-466-8356)
One well-behaved family pet per
room. Guest must notify front desk
upon arrival. Guest is liable for any
damages. In consideration of all
guests, pets must never be left
unattended in the guest rooms.

Super 8 Clinton
1711 Lincolnway
Clinton, IA
563-242-8870 (800-800-8000)
Dogs of all sizes are allowed. There
is a $10.50 one time per pet fee per
visit. Smoking and non-smoking
rooms are available for pet rooms. 2
dogs may be allowed.

Chase Suite Hotel by Woodfin
11 428 Forest Ave.
Clive, IA
515-223-7700
All well-behaved dogs are welcome.
Every room is a suite with a full
kitchen. Hotel amenities include a
pool, exercise facility, and a
complimentary breakfast buffet.
There is a $5 per day pet fee and a
$50 refundable pet deposit.

Comfort Inn
1402 N Walnut Street
Colfax, IA
515-674-4455 (877-424-6423)
Dogs are allowed for an additional
pet fee of $12.50 (plus tax) per
night per room. 2 dogs may be
allowed.

Days Inn Coralville
205 2nd St (Hwy 6)
Coralville, IA
319-354-4400 (800-329-7466)
Dogs of all sizes are allowed. There
is a $10 per night pet fee per pet.
Reservations are recommended
due to limited rooms for pets. 2
dogs may be allowed.

Holiday Inn Coralville
1220 First Avenue
Coralville, IA
319-351-5049 (877-270-6405)
Dogs of all sizes are allowed for an
additional one time pet fee of $20

per room. 2 dogs may be allowed.

Motel 6 - Iowa City
810 1st Avenue
Coralville, IA
319-354-0030 (800-466-8356)
One well-behaved family pet per
room. Guest must notify front desk
upon arrival. Guest is liable for any
damages. In consideration of all
guests, pets must never be left
unattended in the guest rooms.

Days Inn Council Bluffs
3619 9th Ave
Council Bluffs, IA
712-323-2200 (800-329-7466)
Dogs of all sizes are allowed. There
is a $10 per night pet fee per pet. 2
dogs may be allowed.

Days Inn Lake Manawa
3208 South 7th Street
Council Bluffs, IA
712-366-9699 (800-329-7466)
Dogs of all sizes are allowed. There
is a $10 one time per pet fee per
visit. Reservations are recommended
due to limited rooms for pets. 2 dogs
may be allowed.

Motel 6 - Council Bluffs
3032 South Expressway Street
Council Bluffs, IA
712-366-2405 (800-466-8356)
One well-behaved family pet per
room. Guest must notify front desk
upon arrival. Guest is liable for any
damages. In consideration of all
guests, pets must never be left
unattended in the guest rooms.

Quality Inn and Suites
3537 W Broadway
Council Bluffs, IA
712-328-3171 (877-424-6423)
Dogs are allowed for an additional
fee of $10 per night per pet. Pit Bulls
are not allowed. Multiple dogs may
be allowed.

Super 8 Council Bluffs IA/Omaha NE
Area
2712 S 24th Street
Council Bluffs, IA
712-322-2888 (800-800-8000)
Dogs of all sizes are allowed. There
are no additional pet fees. Smoking
and non-smoking rooms are
available for pet rooms. 2 dogs may
be allowed.

Baymont Inn & Suites Davenport
400 Jason Way Court
Davenport, IA
563-386-1600 (800-531-5900)
Dogs of all sizes are allowed. There

are no additional pet fees. Dogs may only be left alone in the room if they will be quiet and well behaved. Dogs must be leashed and cleaned up after, and they are not allowed in the pool or breakfast area. Multiple dogs may be allowed.

Best Western SteepleGate Inn
100 West 76th St
Davenport, IA
563-386-6900 (800-780-7234)
Dogs are allowed for an additional fee of $10 per night per pet. Multiple dogs may be allowed.

Country Inns & Suites by Carlson
140 East 55th Street
Davenport, IA
563-388-6444
Dogs up to 75 pounds are allowed. There is a $25 one time additional pet fee. If a non-smoking room is desired, please specifically request one. The hotel has complimentary high-speed Internet access.

Days Inn Davenport East
3202 E Kimberly Rd
Davenport, IA
563-359-7165 (800-329-7466)
Dogs of all sizes are allowed. There is a $25 one time per pet fee per visit. 2 dogs may be allowed.

La Quinta Inn Davenport
3330 E. Kimberly Rd
Davenport, IA
563-359-3921 (800-531-5900)
Dogs of all sizes are allowed. There are no additional pet fees. There is a pet waiver to sign at check in. Dogs must be leashed and cleaned up after. Multiple dogs may be allowed.

Motel 6 - Davenport
6111 North Brady Street
Davenport, IA
563-391-8997 (800-466-8356)
One well-behaved family pet per room. Guest must notify front desk upon arrival. Guest is liable for any damages. In consideration of all guests, pets must never be left unattended in the guest rooms.

Residence Inn by Marriott
120 E 55th Street
Davenport, IA
563-391-8877
Dogs of all sizes are allowed. There is a $75 one time fee and a pet policy to sign at check in. Multiple dogs may be allowed.

Staybridge Suites Davenport
4729 Progress Drive

Davenport, IA
563-359-7829 (877-270-6405)
Dogs of all sizes are allowed for an additional one time fee of $50 per pet. Multiple dogs may be allowed.

Super 8 Decorah
810 Highway 9 E
Decorah, IA
563-382-8771 (800-800-8000)
Dogs of all sizes are allowed. There are no additional pet fees. Smoking and non-smoking rooms are available for pet rooms. 2 dogs may be allowed.

Days Inn Denison
315 Chamberlin Dr
Denison, IA
712-263-2500 (800-329-7466)
Dogs of all sizes are allowed. There is a $5.60 per night pet fee per pet. 2 dogs may be allowed.

Super 8 Denison
502 Boyer Valley Rd
Denison, IA
712-263-5081 (800-800-8000)
Dogs of all sizes are allowed. There is a $5 per night pet fee per pet. Smoking and non-smoking rooms are available for pet rooms. 2 dogs may be allowed.

Best Western Des Moines Airport Hotel
1810 Army Post Road
Des Moines, IA
515-287-6464 (800-780-7234)
Dogs up to 60 pounds are allowed for an additional pet fee of $25 per night per room. 2 dogs may be allowed.

Comfort Inn
5231 Fleur Drive
Des Moines, IA
515-287-3434 (877-424-6423)
Dogs are allowed for an additional one time pet fee of $10 per room. Multiple dogs may be allowed.

Days Inn West/Urbandale
10841 Douglas Ave
Des Moines, IA
515-278-2811 (800-329-7466)
Dogs of all sizes are allowed. There is a $10 per night pet fee per pet. 2 dogs may be allowed.

Hotel Fort Des Moines
1000 Walnut Street
Des Moines, IA
515-243-1161 (800-532-1466)
hotelfortdm.com/
This dog-friendly hotel is on the National Register of Historic Places.

La Quinta Inn Des Moines/West-Clive
1390 N.W. 118th Street
Des Moines, IA
515-221-9200 (800-531-5900)
Dogs of all sizes are allowed. There are no additional pet fees. Dogs may not be left unattended, and they must be leashed and cleaned up after. Multiple dogs may be allowed.

Motel 6 - Des Moines North
4940 NE 14th Street
Des Moines, IA
515-266-5456 (800-466-8356)
One well-behaved family pet per room. Guest must notify front desk upon arrival. Guest is liable for any damages. In consideration of all guests, pets must never be left unattended in the guest rooms.

Motel 6 - Des Moines South - Airport
4817 Fleur Drive
Des Moines, IA
515-287-6364 (800-466-8356)
One well-behaved family pet per room. Guest must notify front desk upon arrival. Guest is liable for any damages. In consideration of all guests, pets must never be left unattended in the guest rooms.

Red Roof Inn - Des Moines
4950 NE 14th Street
Des Moines, IA
515-266-6800 (800-RED-ROOF)
One well-behaved family pet per room. Guest must notify front desk upon arrival. Guest is liable for any damages. In consideration of all guests, pets must never be left unattended in the guest rooms.

Mainstay Suites
1275 Associates Drive
Dubuque, IA
563-557-7829
Dogs are allowed for an additional one time pet fee of $20 per room. Multiple dogs may be allowed.

Comfort Inn
4055 McDonald Drive
Dubuque, IA
563-556-3006 (877-424-6423)
Dogs are allowed for an additional one time pet fee of $10 per room. Multiple dogs may be allowed.

Days Inn Dubuque
1111 Dodge St
Dubuque, IA
563-583-3297 (800-329-7466)
Dogs of all sizes are allowed. There is a $5 per night pet fee per pet. 2

dogs may be allowed.

Comfort Inn
527 16th Avenue SE
Dyersville, IA
563-875-7700 (877-424-6423)
Dogs are allowed for an additional one time pet fee of $12.50 per room. Multiple dogs may be allowed.

Super 8 Dyersville
925 15th Ave SE
Dyersville, IA
563-875-8885 (800-800-8000)
Dogs of all sizes are allowed. There is a $10 per night pet fee per pet. Smoking and non-smoking rooms are available for pet rooms. 2 dogs may be allowed.

Quality Inn and Suites
1000 E Iowa Street
Eldridge, IA
563-285-4600 (877-424-6423)
Dogs are allowed for an additional one time pet fee of $12.50 per room. There must be a credit card on file, and dogs must be crated when left alone in the room. 2 dogs may be allowed.

Sleep Inn and Suites
2008 Central Avenue/H 9
Estherville, IA
712-362-5522 (877-424-6423)
Dogs are allowed for an additional one time fee of $20 (plus tax) per pet. 2 dogs may be allowed.

Super 8 Estherville
1919 Central Ave
Estherville, IA
712-362-2400 (800-800-8000)
Dogs of all sizes are allowed. There is a $4 per night pet fee per pet. Smoking and non-smoking rooms are available for pet rooms. 2 dogs may be allowed.

Best Western Fairfield Inn
2200 W Burlington
Fairfield, IA
641-472-2200 (800-780-7234)
Dogs are allowed for an additional one time pet fee of $25 per room. Multiple dogs may be allowed.

Super 8 Forest City
1215 Hwy 69 South
Forest City, IA
641-585-1300 (800-800-8000)
Dogs of all sizes are allowed. There is a $5 per night pet fee per pet. Smoking and non-smoking rooms are available for pet rooms. 2 dogs may be allowed.

Comfort Inn and Suites
6169 Reve Court
Fort Madison, IA
319-372-6800 (877-424-6423)
Dogs are allowed for an additional pet fee of $10 per night per room. Multiple dogs may be allowed.

Quality Inn and Suites Highlander Conference Center
2525 N Dodge Street
Iowa City, IA
319-354-2000 (877-424-6423)
Dogs are allowed for an additional one time fee of $10 per pet. 2 dogs may be allowed.

Sheraton Iowa City Hotel
210 S. Dubuque St.
Iowa City, IA
319-337-4058 (888-625-5144)
Dogs up to 80 pounds are allowed. There are no additional pet fees. Dogs are not allowed to be left alone in the room.

Inn At Merle Hay
5055 Merle Hay Rd
Johnston, IA
515-270-1111
There is a $30 refundable deposit and a $10 one time pet charge.

Super 8 Keokuk
3511 Main St
Keokuk, IA
319-524-3888 (800-800-8000)
Dogs of all sizes are allowed. There is a $10 per night pet fee per pet. Pet must be kept in kennel when left alone. Smoking and non-smoking rooms are available for pet rooms. 2 dogs may be allowed.

Comfort Inn and Suites Riverview
902 Mississippi View Court
Le Claire, IA
563-289-4747 (877-424-6423)
Dogs are allowed for no additional pet fee with a credit card on file; there is a $25 refundable deposit if paying cash. Multiple dogs may be allowed.

Holiday Inn Express Le Claire Riverfront-Davenport
1201 Canal Shore Drive
Le Claire, IA
563-289-9978 (877-270-6405)
Dogs of all sizes are allowed for an additional pet fee of $12 per night per room. 2 dogs may be allowed.

Super 8 Le Mars
1201 Hawkeye Ave SW
Le Mars, IA
712-546-8800 (800-800-8000)

Dogs of all sizes are allowed. There is a $10 per night pet fee per pet. Reservations are recommended due to limited rooms for pets. Smoking and non-smoking rooms are available for pet rooms. 2 dogs may be allowed.

Best Western Regency Inn
3303 South Center St
Marshalltown, IA
641-752-6321 (800-780-7234)
Dogs are allowed for no additional pet fee. 2 dogs may be allowed.

Comfort Inn
2613 S Center Street/H 14
Marshalltown, IA
641-752-6000 (877-424-6423)
Dogs are allowed for an additional pet fee of $10 per night per room. 2 dogs may be allowed.

Super 8 Marshalltown
18 E Berle Rd
Marshalltown, IA
641-753-8181 (800-800-8000)
Dogs of all sizes are allowed. There is a $10 per night pet fee per pet. Smoking and non-smoking rooms are available for pet rooms. 2 dogs may be allowed.

Days Inn Mason City
2301 4th St SW
Mason City, IA
641-424-0210 (800-329-7466)
Dogs of all sizes are allowed. There is a $10 one time per pet fee per visit. 2 dogs may be allowed.

Holiday Inn
2101 4th St, SW
Mason City, IA
641-423-1640 (877-270-6405)
Dogs of all sizes are allowed for an additional one time pet fee of $15 per room. Multiple dogs may be allowed.

Days Inn Missouri Valley
1967 Hwy 30
Missouri Valley, IA
712-642-4003 (800-329-7466)
Dogs of all sizes are allowed. There is a $5 per night pet fee per pet. 2 dogs may be allowed.

Ramada Limited
1200 East Baker St.
Mount Pleasant, IA
319-385-0571
innovativehotels.com
The hotel offers King and Queen Rooms, 18 Suites, hot and cold Breakfast, an Indoor Pool and Hot Tubs. There is plenty of open space to walk your pet. The pet fee is a one

time $8.00 charge.

Super 8 Mt Pleasant
1000 N Grand Ave
Mount Pleasant, IA
319-385-8888 (800-800-8000)
Dogs of all sizes are allowed. There
is a $10 per night pet fee per pet.
Smoking and non-smoking rooms
are available for pet rooms. 2 dogs
may be allowed.

Sleep Inn and Suites
310 Virgil Avenue
Mount Vernon, IA
319-895-0055 (877-424-6423)
Dogs are allowed for an additional
one time fee of $12.50 per pet.
Multiple dogs may be allowed.

Comfort Inn
115 Cleveland Street
Muscatine, IA
563-263-1500 (877-424-6423)
Dogs are allowed for an additional
fee of $10 per night per pet. 2 dogs
may be allowed.

Holiday Inn
2915 N. Hwy 61
Muscatine, IA
563-264-5550 (877-270-6405)
Dogs up to 50 pounds are allowed
for an additional one time pet fee of
$10 per room. 2 dogs may be
allowed.

Days Inn Newton
1605 W 19th St South
Newton, IA
641-792-2330 (800-329-7466)
Dogs of all sizes are allowed. There
is a $10 per night pet fee per pet. 2
dogs may be allowed.

Super 8 Oelwein
210 10th Street SE
Oelwein, IA
319-283-2888 (800-800-8000)
Dogs of all sizes are allowed. There
is a $10 per night pet fee per pet.
Smoking and non-smoking rooms
are available for pet rooms. 2 dogs
may be allowed.

Super 8 Onawa
22868 Filbert Ave
Onawa, IA
712-423-2101 (800-800-8000)
Dogs of all sizes are allowed. There
is a $5 per night pet fee per pet.
Smoking and non-smoking rooms
are available for pet rooms. 2 dogs
may be allowed.

Terribles Lakeside Casino Resort
777 Casino Drive

Osceola, IA
641-342-9511 (877-477-5253)
Dogs of all sizes are allowed. There
are no additional pet fees. Dogs
may not be left unattended in the
rooms unless they are crated, and
they must be quiet, well behaved,
leashed, and cleaned up after.
There is an RV camping area on
site where dogs are also allowed. 2
dogs may be allowed.

Comfort Inn and Suites
910 W 16th
Pella, IA
641-621-1421 (877-424-6423)
Dogs up to 50 pounds are allowed
for an additional fee of $10 per night
per pet. 2 dogs may be allowed.

Sleep Inn and Suites
5850 Morning Star Court
Pleasant Hill, IA
515-299-9922 (877-424-6423)
Dogs up to 50 pounds are allowed
for an additional fee of $13 per night
per pet. 2 dogs may be allowed.

Clarion Hotel and Conference
Center
707 Fourth Street
Sioux City, IA
712-277-4101 (877-424-6423)
Dogs are allowed for an additional
one time pet fee of $20 per room. 2
dogs may be allowed.

Comfort Inn
4202 S Lakeport Street
Sioux City, IA
712-274-1300 (877-424-6423)
Dogs are allowed for an additional
one time pet fee of $10 per room.
Dogs may not be left alone in the
room at any time. Multiple dogs may
be allowed.

Motel 6 - Sioux City
6166 Harbor Drive
Sioux City, IA
712-277-3131 (800-466-8356)
One well-behaved family pet per
room. Guest must notify front desk
upon arrival. Guest is liable for any
damages. In consideration of all
guests, pets must never be left
unattended in the guest rooms.

Quality Inn Hotel & Conference
Center
1401 Zenith Drive
Sioux City, IA
712-277-3211 (877-424-6423)
Dogs of all sizes are allowed. There
are no additional pet fees. Multiple
dogs may be allowed.

Super 8 Spirit Lake
2203 Circle Drive W
Spirit Lake, IA
712-336-4901 (800-800-8000)
Dogs of all sizes are allowed. There
are no additional pet fees. Smoking
and non-smoking rooms are
available for pet rooms. 2 dogs may
be allowed.

Comfort Inn
425 Timberland Drive
Story City, IA
515-733-6363 (877-424-6423)
Dogs are allowed for an additional
pet fee of $12.50 per night per room.
2 dogs may be allowed.

Super 8 Stuart
203 SE 7th St
Stuart, IA
515-523-2888 (800-800-8000)
Dogs of all sizes are allowed. There
is a $25 returnable deposit required
per room. Smoking and non-smoking
rooms are available for pet rooms. 2
dogs may be allowed.

Days Inn Toledo
403 Hwy 30 West
Toledo, IA
641-484-5678 (800-329-7466)
Dogs of all sizes are allowed. There
is a $10 per night pet fee per pet.
Reservations are recommended due
to limited rooms for pets. 2 dogs may
be allowed.

Super 8 Toledo/Tama Area
207 W Highway 30
Toledo, IA
641-484-5888 (800-800-8000)
Dogs of all sizes are allowed. There
is a $25 returnable deposit required
per room. Smoking and non-smoking
rooms are available for pet rooms. 2
dogs may be allowed.

Sleep Inn
11211 Hickman Road
Urbandale, IA
515-270-2424 (877-424-6423)
Dogs are allowed for an additional
fee of $10 per night per pet. Multiple
dogs may be allowed.

Days Inn Walcott
2889 N Plainview Dr
Walcott, IA
563-284-6600 (800-329-7466)
Dogs of all sizes are allowed. There
is a $10 per night pet fee per pet. 2
dogs may be allowed.

Super 8 Walnut
2109 Antique City Dr
Walnut, IA

712-784-2221 (800-800-8000)
Dogs of all sizes are allowed. There is a $10 per night pet fee per pet. Smoking and non-smoking rooms are available for pet rooms. 2 dogs may be allowed.

Holiday Inn Express
2141 Laporte Rd
Waterloo, IA
319-233-9191 (877-270-6405)
Dogs of all sizes are allowed for an additional $10 per night per pet. Multiple dogs may be allowed.

Motel 6 - Waterloo
2343 Logan Avenue
Waterloo, IA
319-236-3238 (800-466-8356)
One well-behaved family pet per room. Guest must notify front desk upon arrival. Guest is liable for any damages. In consideration of all guests, pets must never be left unattended in the guest rooms.

Quality Inn and Suites
226 W 5th Street
Waterloo, IA
319-235-0301 (877-424-6423)
Dogs are allowed for an additional fee of $10 per night per pet. Multiple dogs may be allowed.

Motel 6 - Des Moines West
7655 Office Plaza Drive North
West Des Moines, IA
515-267-8885 (800-466-8356)
One well-behaved family pet per room. Guest must notify front desk upon arrival. Guest is liable for any damages. In consideration of all guests, pets must never be left unattended in the guest rooms.

Sheraton West Des Moines Hotel
1800 50th St.
West Des Moines, IA
515-223-1800 (888-625-5144)
A dog up to 50 pounds is allowed for an additional one time pet fee of $75. Dogs may not be left alone in the room.

Staybridge Suites West Des Moines
6905 Lake Dr.
West Des Moines, IA
515-223-0000 (877-270-6405)
Dogs of all sizes are allowed for no additional fee. Multiple dogs may be allowed.

West Des Moines Marriott
1250 Jordan Creek Parkway
West Des Moines, IA
515-267-1500 (800-228-9290)
Dogs of all sizes are allowed. There

is a $75 one time fee per room. Dogs must be quiet, well behaved, leashed, cleaned up after, and a contact number left with the front desk if they are in the room alone. 2 dogs may be allowed.

Best Western Norseman Inn
I 35 and Exit 144
Williams, IA
515-854-2281 (800-780-7234)
Well behaved dogs are allowed for no additional pet fee. Dogs are not allowed on the furniture or bed, and they may not be left alone in the room at any time. Dogs must be well groomed, and heavy shedders are not allowed. 2 dogs may be allowed.

Kansas Listings

Days Inn Abilene
1709 N Buckeye Ave
Abilene, KS
785-263-2800 (800-329-7466)
Dogs of all sizes are allowed. There is a $10 per night pet fee per pet. 2 dogs may be allowed.

Holiday Inn Express Hotel & Suites
110 East Lafayette St
Abilene, KS
785-263-4049 (877-270-6405)
Dogs of all sizes are allowed for an additional one time fee per pet of $10 for each 1 to 6 days stay. 2 dogs may be allowed.

Super 8 Abilene
2207 N Buckeye
Abilene, KS
785-263-4545 (800-800-8000)
Dogs of all sizes are allowed. There is a $10 per night pet fee per pet. There is a $50 returnable deposit required per room. Smoking and non-smoking rooms are available for pet rooms. 2 dogs may be allowed.

Best Western Atrium Gardens
3232 N Summit Street
Arkansas City, KS
620-442-7700 (800-780-7234)
Dogs are allowed for an additional fee of $10 per night per pet. Multiple dogs may be allowed.

The Inn on Oak Street
1003 L Street
Atchison, KS
913-367-1515
Well behaved dogs are allowed for

no additional pet fees. 2 dogs may be allowed.

Comfort Inn
2225 S Range Avenue
Colby, KS
785-462-3833 (877-424-6423)
Dogs are allowed for an additional fee of $5 per night per pet. Multiple dogs may be allowed.

Days Inn Colby
I-70 and Hwy 25
Colby, KS
785-462-8691 (800-329-7466)
Dogs of all sizes are allowed. There is a $5 per night pet fee per pet. Reservations are recommended due to limited rooms for pets. 2 dogs may be allowed.

Holiday Inn Express Hotel & Suites
645 West Willow
Colby, KS
785-462-8787 (877-270-6405)
Dogs of all sizes are allowed for an additional pet fee of $10 per night per room. Multiple dogs may be allowed.

Motel 6 - Colby
1985 South Range Avenue
Colby, KS
785-462-8201 (800-466-8356)
One well-behaved family pet per room. Guest must notify front desk upon arrival. Guest is liable for any damages. In consideration of all guests, pets must never be left unattended in the guest rooms.

Quality Inn
1950 S Range Avenue
Colby, KS
785-462-3933 (877-424-6423)
Dogs up to 50 pounds are allowed for an additional fee of $5 per night per pet. 2 dogs may be allowed.

The Cottage House Hotel
25 North Neosho
Council Grove, KS
620-767-6828 (800-727-7903)
cottagehousehotel.com/
This wonderfully restored Victorian Prairie home gives visitors a sense of the old west with a touch of luxury. Dogs are allowed for an additional fee of $15 per night per pet. Multiple dogs may be allowed.

Best Western Country Inn & Suites
506 N 14th Avenue
Dodge City, KS
620-225-7378 (800-780-7234)
Dogs are allowed for an additional fee of $25 per night per pet. Dogs

must be crated when left alone in the room. 2 dogs may be allowed.

Boot Hill Bed and Breakfast
603 W Spruce
Dodge City, KS
620-225-0111
boothilldodgecity.com/
Relive a bit of the old west at this great old house at the top of Boot Hill. Dogs are allowed for no additional pet fee, but they must be declared at the time of reservations at all times. Dogs must be quiet and well mannered. 2 dogs may be allowed.

Holiday Inn Express
2320 W. Wyatt Earp
Dodge City, KS
620-227-5000 (877-270-6405)
Dogs of all sizes are allowed for an additional one time pet fee of $25 per room. Multiple dogs may be allowed.

Nendels Inn and Suites
2523 E Wyatt Earp Blvd
Dodge City, KS
316-225-3000

Super 8 Dodge City
1708 W Wyatt Earp Blvd
Dodge City, KS
620-225-3924 (800-800-8000)
Dogs of all sizes are allowed. There are no additional pet fees. Smoking and non-smoking rooms are available for pet rooms. 2 dogs may be allowed.

Kuhrt Prairie Castle Guest House and Lodge
2735 Road 75
Edson, KS
785-899-5306
kuhrtranch.com/
Noted as a bird-lovers paradise, this beautiful estate retreat sits along the south fork of the Beaver River in a lush green setting. Although dogs are not allowed in the Castle rooms, they are allowed in the lodge for no additional pet fees. 2 dogs may be allowed.

Days Inn Elizabethtown
2010 N Mulberry
Elizabethtown, KS
270-769-5522 (800-329-7466)
Dogs of all sizes are allowed. There is a $10 one time per pet fee per visit. 2 dogs may be allowed.

Best Western Garden Prairie Inn
1400 N Hwy 156
Ellsworth, KS
785-472-3116 (800-780-7234)

Dogs are allowed for no additional pet fee.

Americas Best Value Inn
2913 W. Highway 50
Emporia, KS
620-342-7567 (800-800-8000)
innworks.com/emporia
There is a $10 per stay additional pet fee. Up to three dogs are permitted in each room. The hotel allows a free 8 minute long distance call each night and offers a free continental breakfast. KS Turnpike, Exit 127 or 127B. I-35, Exit 128 (Industrial Rd). South to US 50, Right 1 block.

Best Western Hospitality House
3021 W Hwy 50
Emporia, KS
620-342-7587 (800-780-7234)
Dogs are allowed for no additional pet fee.

Candlewood Suites Emporia
2602 Candlewood Drive
Emporia, KS
620-343-7756 (877-270-6405)
Dogs up to 50 pounds are allowed for an additional one time pet fee of $50 per room. 2 dogs may be allowed.

Comfort Inn
2836 W 18th Avenue
Emporia, KS
620-342-9700 (877-424-6423)
Dogs are allowed for an additional one time pet fee of $15 per room. 2 dogs may be allowed.

Days Inn Emporia
3032 W Hwy 50
Emporia, KS
620-342-1787 (800-329-7466)
Dogs of all sizes are allowed. There are no additional pet fees. 2 dogs may be allowed.

Motel 6 - Emporia
2630 West 18th Avenue
Emporia, KS
620-343-1240 (800-466-8356)
One well-behaved family pet per room. Guest must notify front desk upon arrival. Guest is liable for any damages. In consideration of all guests, pets must never be left unattended in the guest rooms.

First Interstate Inn
2222 S Main St
Fort Scott, KS
316-223-5330
There is a $5 per day pet fee.

Best Western Red Baron Hotel
US Hwy 50 E Side @ Hwy 83
Garden City, KS
620-275-4164 (800-780-7234)
Dogs are allowed for no additional pet fee.

Best Western Wheat Lands Hotel and Conf Cntr
1311 E Fulton
Garden City, KS
620-276-2387 (800-780-7234)
Dogs are allowed for no additional pet fee.

Days Inn Garden City
1818 Commanche
Garden City, KS
620-275-5095 (800-329-7466)
Dogs of all sizes are allowed. There are no additional pet fees. 2 dogs may be allowed.

Holiday Inn Express Hotel & Suites
2502 E. Kansas Ave
Garden City, KS
620-275-5900 (877-270-6405)
Dogs of all sizes are allowed for an additional one time pet fee of $25 per room. 2 dogs may be allowed.

Super 8 Garden City
2808 N Taylor
Garden City, KS
620-275-9625 (800-800-8000)
Dogs of all sizes are allowed. There is a $5 per night pet fee per small pet and $10 per large pet. Smoking and non-smoking rooms are available for pet rooms. 2 dogs may be allowed.

Super 8 Gardner
2001 E Santa Fe
Gardner, KS
913-856-8887 (800-800-8000)
Dogs of all sizes are allowed. There is a $10 per night pet fee per pet. Smoking and non-smoking rooms are available for pet rooms. 2 dogs may be allowed.

Super 8 Goodland
2520 South Hwy 27
Goodland, KS
785-890-7566 (800-800-8000)
Dogs of all sizes are allowed. There is a $20 returnable deposit required per room. There is a $5 per night pet fee per pet. Smoking and non-smoking rooms are available for pet rooms. 2 dogs may be allowed.

Best Western Angus Inn
2920 10th St
Great Bend, KS
620-792-3541 (800-780-7234)
Dogs are allowed for an additional

fee of $5 per night per pet. 2 dogs may be allowed.

Days Inn Great Bend
4701 10th Street
Great Bend, KS
620-792-8235 (800-329-7466)
Dogs of all sizes are allowed. There is a $5 per night pet fee per pet. 2 dogs may be allowed.

Super 8 Motel - Great Bend
3500 Tenth Street
Great Bend, KS
620-793-8486 (800-800-8000)
innworks.com/greatbend
There is a $10 per stay additional pet fee. Up to three dogs are permitted in each room. The hotel allows a free 8 minute long distance call each night and offers a free continental breakfast. There is a pool and a laundry. US 56, West of US 281 btwn Lincoln & Harrison, near Wal-Mart.

Best Western Vagabond Motel
2524 Vine St
Hays, KS
785-625-2511 (800-780-7234)
Dogs are allowed for no additional pet fee. Dogs may not be left alone in the room. 2 dogs may be allowed.

Days Inn Hays
3205 Vine
Hays, KS
785-628-8261 (800-329-7466)
Dogs of all sizes are allowed. There is a $7 per night pet fee per pet. Reservations are recommended due to limited rooms for pets. 2 dogs may be allowed.

Hampton Inn
3801 Vine Street
Hays, KS
785-625-8103
Dogs of all sizes are allowed. There are no additional pet fees. Multiple dogs may be allowed.

Holiday Inn
3603 Vine St
Hays, KS
785-625-7371 (877-270-6405)
Dogs of all sizes are allowed for an additional one time pet fee of $20 per room. Multiple dogs may be allowed.

Motel 6 - Hays
3404 Vine Street
Hays, KS
785-625-4282 (800-466-8356)
One well-behaved family pet per room. Guest must notify front desk upon arrival. Guest is liable for any

damages. In consideration of all guests, pets must never be left unattended in the guest rooms.

Red Roof Inn - Holton
Holton, KS
785-364-3172 (800-RED-ROOF)
One well-behaved family pet per room. Guest must notify front desk upon arrival. Guest is liable for any damages. In consideration of all guests, pets must never be left unattended in the guest rooms.

Americas Best Value Inn
1315 E. 11th Avenue
Hutchinson, KS
620-662-6394 (800-800-8000)
innworks.com/hutchinson
There is a $10 per stay additional pet fee. Up to three dogs are permitted in each room. The hotel allows a free 8 minute long distance call each night and offers a free continental breakfast. There is a pool and a laundry. KS 61 & E 11th Avenue.

Holiday Inn Express Hotel and Suites
1601 Super Plaza Ave
Hutchinson, KS
620-669-5200 (877-270-6405)
Dogs of all sizes are allowed for no additional fee. 2 dogs may be allowed.

Best Western Inn
1315 N State St
Iola, KS
620-365-5161 (800-780-7234)
Dogs are allowed for an additional pet fee of $5 per night per room. 2 dogs may be allowed.

Log Cabin Retreat
250 Xavier Road
Jamestown, KS
620-241-2981 (800-324-8052)
retreatlogcabin.com/
Located on 10 pastoral acres overlooking Sportsman Lake and the Jamestown Wildlife Refuge, this retreat will allow dogs for no additional pet fees with advance reservations. Dogs must be house trained and well mannered. 2 dogs may be allowed.

Best Western JC Inn
NW quad I-70 and E Chestnut St
Junction City, KS
785-210-1212 (800-780-7234)
Dogs are allowed for an additional pet fee of $10 per night per room. Multiple dogs may be allowed.

Days Inn Junction City
1024 S Washington
Junction City, KS
785-762-2727 (800-329-7466)
Dogs of all sizes are allowed. There are no additional pet fees. 2 dogs may be allowed.

Holiday Inn Express
120 East Street
Junction City, KS
785-762-4200 (877-270-6405)
Dogs of all sizes are allowed for an additional fee of $5 per night per pet, plus a $50 refundable deposit. 2 dogs may be allowed.

Motel 6 - Junction City
1931 Lacy Drive
Junction City, KS
785-762-2215 (800-466-8356)
One well-behaved family pet per room. Guest must notify front desk upon arrival. Guest is liable for any damages. In consideration of all guests, pets must never be left unattended in the guest rooms.

Best Western Inn and Conf Cntr
501 Southeast Blvd
Kansas City, KS
913-677-3060 (800-780-7234)
Dogs are allowed for no additional pet fee. Dogs may not be left alone in the room. Multiple dogs may be allowed.

Windy Heights Inn
607 Country Heights Road
Lakin, KS
620-355-7699
windyheightsbandb.com/
This inn offers a variety of indoor and outdoor activities for guests. Well mannered dogs are allowed for no additional pet fees. 2 dogs may be allowed.

Best Western Townsman Motel
123 E 14th
Larned, KS
620-285-3114 (800-780-7234)
Dogs under 30 pounds are allowed for no additional pet fee. The fee is $10 per night per pet for dogs over 30 pounds. 2 dogs may be allowed.

Best Western Lawrence
2309 Iowa Street
Lawrence, KS
785-843-9100 (800-780-7234)
Dogs are allowed for an additional pet fee of $7.50 per night per room. 2 dogs may be allowed.

Golden Rule Motel
515 McDonald Drive

Kansas Listings - Please always call ahead to make sure an establishment is still dog-friendly.

Lawrence, KS
785-842-5721 (800-800-8000)
innworks.com/lawrence
There is a $10 per stay additional pet fee. Up to three dogs are permitted in each room. The hotel allows a free 8 minute long distance call each night and offers a free continental breakfast. There is a pool and a laundry. I-70 (KS Turnpike), Exit 202, South 1 mile.

Holiday Inn
200 McDonald Drive
Lawrence, KS
785-841-7077 (877-270-6405)
Dogs of all sizes are allowed for an additional one time pet fee of $25 per room. Multiple dogs may be allowed.

Quality Inn
801 Iowa Street
Lawrence, KS
785-842-5100 (877-424-6423)
Dogs are allowed for an additional fee of $10 per night per pet. 2 dogs may be allowed.

Motel 6 - Kansas City Southwest - Lenexa
9725 Lenexa Drive
Lenexa, KS
913-541-8558 (800-466-8356)
One well-behaved family pet per room. Guest must notify front desk upon arrival. Guest is liable for any damages. In consideration of all guests, pets must never be left unattended in the guest rooms.

Gateway Inn
720 E H 74
Liberal, KS
620-624-0242
Dogs are allowed for an additional fee of $10 per night per pet. 2 dogs may be allowed.

Holiday Inn Manhattan At The Campus
1641 Anderson Avenue
Manhattan, KS
785-539-7531 (877-270-6405)
Dogs of all sizes are allowed for an additional fee of $25 per night per pet. Multiple dogs may be allowed.

Motel 6 - Manhattan
510 Tuttle Creek Boulevard
Manhattan, KS
785-537-1022 (800-466-8356)
One well-behaved family pet per room. Guest must notify front desk upon arrival. Guest is liable for any damages. In consideration of all guests, pets must never be left unattended in the guest rooms.

Best Value Inn - McPherson
2110 E. Kansas
McPherson, KS
620-241-8881 (800-800-8000)
innworks.com/mcpherson
There is a $10 per stay additional pet fee. Up to three dogs are permitted in each room. The hotel allows a free 8 minute long distance call each night and offers a free continental breakfast. There is a pool and a laundry. I-135, Exit 60, on US 56 (Kansas Ave Frontage Road) near Wal-Mart & KFC.

Best Western Holiday Manor
2211 E Kansas Avenue
McPherson, KS
620-241-5343 (800-780-7234)
Dogs are allowed for an additional fee of $10 per night per pet. 2 dogs may be allowed.

Best Value Inn - Newton
1620 E. 2nd Street
Newton, KS
316-283-7611 (800-800-8000)
innworks.com/newton
There is a $10 per stay additional pet fee. Up to three dogs are permitted in each room. The hotel allows a free 8 minute long distance call each night and offers a free continental breakfast. There is a pool and a laundry. I-135, Exit 31, East 1-1/2 blocks to Spencer, Left on Spencer.

Best Western Red Coach Inn
1301 E 1st
Newton, KS
316-283-9120 (800-780-7234)
Dogs are allowed for no additional pet fee. Dogs may not be left alone in the room. Multiple dogs may be allowed.

Days Inn Newton
105 Manchester
Newton, KS
316-283-3330 (800-329-7466)
Dogs of all sizes are allowed for an additional fee. There is a $10 one time per pet fee per visit. 2 dogs may be allowed.

Econo Lodge of Olathe
209 E. Flaming Road
Olathe, KS
913-829-1312
Well behaved dogs of all sizes are allowed. There is a $5 to $10 per night per pet additional fee depending on the size of the dog.

Holiday Inn

101 W 151st Street
Olathe, KS
913-829-4000 (877-270-6405)
Dogs of all sizes are allowed for an additional pet fee per room of $30 for each 1 to 5 days stay. Multiple dogs may be allowed.

Sleep Inn
20662 W 151st Street
Olathe, KS
913-390-9500 (877-424-6423)
Dogs are allowed for an additional fee of $11.35 per night per pet. Multiple dogs may be allowed.

Candlewood Suites
11001 Oakmont
Overland Park, KS
913-469-5557 (877-270-6405)
Dogs up to 70 pounds are allowed for an additional one time pet fee of $75 per room for 1 to 7 nights; the fee is $150 for 8 or more days. 2 dogs may be allowed.

Chase Suite Hotel
6300 W 110th Street
Overland Park, KS
913-491-3333
woodfinsuitehotels.com/
Dogs are allowed for an additional fee of $10 per night per pet. Multiple dogs may be allowed.

Comfort Inn and Suites
7200 W 107th Street
Overland Park, KS
913-648-7858 (877-424-6423)
Dogs are allowed for an additional fee of $10 per night per pet. Dogs may not be left alone in the room. Multiple dogs may be allowed.

Holiday Inn
7240 Shawnee Mission Pkwy
Overland Park, KS
913-262-3010 (877-270-6405)
Dogs of all sizes are allowed for an additional one time pet fee of $75 per room. 2 dogs may be allowed.

Red Roof Inn - Kansas City Overland Park
6800 West 108th Street
Overland Park, KS
913-341-0100 (800-RED-ROOF)
One well-behaved family pet per room. Guest must notify front desk upon arrival. Guest is liable for any damages. In consideration of all guests, pets must never be left unattended in the guest rooms.

Residence Inn by Marriott
12010 Blue Valley Parkway
Overland Park, KS

913-491-4444
Pets of all sizes are allowed. There is a $75 one time fee and a pet policy to sign at check in. Multiple dogs may be allowed.

Sheraton Overland Park Hotel at the Convention Center
6100 College Blvd.
Overland Park, KS
913-234-2100 (888-625-5144)
Dogs up to 80 pounds are allowed. There are no additional pet fees. Dogs are not allowed to be left alone in the room.

Super 8 Overland Park/S Kansas City Area
10750 Barkley
Overland Park, KS
913-341-4440 (800-800-8000)
Dogs of all sizes are allowed. There is a $25 one time per pet fee per visit. Only non-smoking rooms are used for pets. 2 dogs may be allowed.

Best Western Parsons Inn
101 Main Street
Parsons, KS
620-423-0303 (800-780-7234)
Dogs are allowed for an additional fee of $5 per night per pet. 2 dogs may be allowed.

Days Inn Pratt
1901 E First St
Pratt, KS
620-672-9465 (800-329-7466)
Dogs of all sizes are allowed. There is a $3 per night pet fee per pet. 2 dogs may be allowed.

Hillcrest Inn
1336 E First
Pratt, KS
620-672-6407 (800-336-2779)
Dogs are allowed for an additional fee of $6 per night per pet. Multiple dogs may be allowed.

Days Inn Russell
1225 S Fossil St
Russell, KS
785-483-6660 (800-329-7466)
Dogs of all sizes are allowed. There is a $5 per night pet fee per pet. 2 dogs may be allowed.

Best Western Heart of America Inn
632 Westport Blvd
Salina, KS
785-827-9315 (800-780-7234)
Dogs are allowed for no additional pet fee. Multiple dogs may be allowed.

Best Western Mid-American Inn
1846 N 9th St
Salina, KS
785-827-0356 (800-780-7234)
Dogs are allowed for no additional pet fee with a credit card on file. There is a $50 refundable deposit if paying cash. Multiple dogs may be allowed.

Holiday Inn
1616 W Crawford
Salina, KS
785-823-1739 (877-270-6405)
Dogs of all sizes are allowed for an additional one time fee of $25 per pet. Multiple dogs may be allowed.

Holiday Inn Express Hotel & Suites
201 East Diamond Drive
Salina, KS
785-827-9000 (877-270-6405)
Dogs of all sizes are allowed for additional one time fee of $10 per pet. Multiple dogs may be allowed.

Hunters Leigh
4109 E North Street
Salina, KS
785-823-6750 (800-889-6750)
huntersleighbandb.com/
This grand country English Manor estate features a tranquil setting along the scenic Smoky Hill River. Well mannered dogs are allowed for no additional fee. 2 dogs may be allowed.

Motel 6 - Salina
635 West Diamond Drive
Salina, KS
785-827-8397 (800-466-8356)
One well-behaved family pet per room. Guest must notify front desk upon arrival. Guest is liable for any damages. In consideration of all guests, pets must never be left unattended in the guest rooms.

Super 8 Salina/I-135
1640 W Crawford
Salina, KS
785-823-9215 (800-800-8000)
Dogs of all sizes are allowed. There is a $10 per night pet fee per pet. Smoking and non-smoking rooms are available for pet rooms. 2 dogs may be allowed.

Best Western Candlelight Inn
2831 SW Fairlawn Rd
Topeka, KS
785-272-9550 (800-780-7234)
Dogs are allowed for an additional fee of $8 per night per pet. Multiple dogs may be allowed.

Best Western Topeka Inn and Suites
700 SW Fairlawn St
Topeka, KS
785-228-2223 (800-780-7234)
Quiet dogs are allowed for an additional one time fee of $8 per pet. Multiple dogs may be allowed.

Candlewood Suites
914 South West Henderson
Topeka, KS
785-271-7822 (877-270-6405)
Dogs up to 50 pounds are allowed for an additional one time fee per room of $75 for a 1 to 6 nights stay; the fee is $150 for 7 or more days. 2 dogs may be allowed.

Comfort Inn
1518 SW Wanamaker Road
Topeka, KS
785-273-5365 (877-424-6423)
Dogs are allowed for an additional pet fee of $10 per night per room. 2 dogs may be allowed.

Days Inn Topeka
1510 S W Wanamaker Rd
Topeka, KS
785-272-8538 (800-329-7466)
Dogs of all sizes are allowed. There is a $5 per night pet fee per pet. 2 dogs may be allowed.

Motel 6 - Topeka Northwest
709 Fairlawn Road
Topeka, KS
785-272-8283 (800-466-8356)
One well-behaved family pet per room. Guest must notify front desk upon arrival. Guest is liable for any damages. In consideration of all guests, pets must never be left unattended in the guest rooms.

Motel 6 - Topeka West
1224 Wanamaker Road SW
Topeka, KS
785-273-9888 (800-466-8356)
One well-behaved family pet per room. Guest must notify front desk upon arrival. Guest is liable for any damages. In consideration of all guests, pets must never be left unattended in the guest rooms.

Quality Inn
1240 S W Wanamaker Road
Topeka, KS
785-273-6969 (877-424-6423)
Dogs are allowed for an additional fee of $5 per night per pet. Multiple dogs may be allowed.

Residence Inn by Marriott
1620 SW Westport Drive
Topeka, KS

785-271-8903
Pets of all sizes are allowed. There is a $75 one time fee and a pet policy to sign in at check in. Multiple dogs may be allowed.

Butterfield Trail Bunkhouse
RR 2 Box 86, 23033 T Road
WaKeeney, KS
785-743-2322
butterfieldtrailbunkhouse.com/
This is a popular destination for nature or history fans and fishing/hunting enthusiast. Dogs are allowed for an additional pet fee of $10 per night per room. Dogs are not allowed on the furnishings or the bed. Multiple dogs may be allowed.

Best Western Wakeeney Inn & Suites
525 S 1st Street
Wakeeney, KS
785-743-2700 (800-780-7234)
Dogs are allowed for no additional pet fee for up to 2 dogs; there is an additional fee of $10 per night per pet for more than 2 dogs. Multiple dogs may be allowed.

Simmer Motel
1215 W H 24
Wamego, KS
785-456-2304
Dogs of all sizes are allowed. There is a $5 one time per pet additional fee. Multiple dogs may be allowed.

Super 8 Wamego
1300 Lilac Lane
Wamego, KS
785-458-8888 (800-800-8000)
Dogs of all sizes are allowed. There is a $5 per night pet fee per pet. Smoking and non-smoking rooms are available for pet rooms. 2 dogs may be allowed.

Best Western Wichita North/Park City
915 E 53rd St North
Wichita, KS
316-832-9387 (800-780-7234)
Dogs are allowed for an additional one time pet fee of $20 per room. 2 dogs may be allowed.

Candlewood Suites
570 South Julia
Wichita, KS
316-942-0400 (877-270-6405)
Dogs up to 80 pounds are allowed for an additional one time pet fee per room of $75 for a 1 to 6 nights stay; the fee is $150 for 7 or more nights. Multiple dogs may be allowed.

Candlewood Suites
3141 N. Webb Road
Wichita, KS
316-634-6070 (877-270-6405)
Dogs of all sizes are allowed for an additional one time pet fee per room of $75 for 1 to 6 nights; the fee is $150 for 7 or more nights. Multiple dogs may be allowed.

Comfort Inn East
9525 E Corporate Hills
Wichita, KS
316-686-2844 (877-424-6423)
Dogs are allowed for an additional one time pet fee of $10 (plus tax) per room. Multiple dogs may be allowed.

Comfort Inn South
4849 S Laura
Wichita, KS
316-522-1800 (877-424-6423)
Dogs are allowed for an additional one time pet fee of $10 per room. 2 dogs may be allowed.

Hampton Inn
9449 E Corporate Hills
Wichita, KS
316-686-3576
Dogs of all sizes are allowed. There are no additional pet fees. Multiple dogs may be allowed.

Holiday Inn Express
4848 S. Laura Street
Wichita, KS
316-529-4848 (877-270-6405)
Dogs of all sizes are allowed for an additional one time pet fee of $25 per room. Multiple dogs may be allowed.

Holiday Inn Hotel & Suites Wichita Dwtn-Convention Center
221 East Kellogg
Wichita, KS
316-269-2090 (877-270-6405)
Dogs up to 50 pounds are allowed for no additional fee with a credit card on file. 2 dogs may be allowed.

Motel 6 - Wichita
465 South Webb Road
Wichita, KS
316-684-6363 (800-466-8356)
One well-behaved family pet per room. Guest must notify front desk upon arrival. Guest is liable for any damages. In consideration of all guests, pets must never be left unattended in the guest rooms.

Motel 6 - Wichita Airport
5736 West Kellogg Drive
Wichita, KS

316-945-8440 (800-466-8356)
One well-behaved family pet per room. Guest must notify front desk upon arrival. Guest is liable for any damages. In consideration of all guests, pets must never be left unattended in the guest rooms.

Residence Inn by Marriott
411 S Webb Road
Wichita, KS
316-686-7331
Pets of all sizes are allowed. There is a $75 one time fee and a pet policy to sign at check in. Multiple dogs may be allowed.

TownePlace Suites Wichita East
9444 E 29th Street North
Wichita, KS
316-631-3773
Dogs of all sizes are allowed. There is a $75 one time pet fee per visit. 2 dogs may be allowed.

Kentucky Listings

Best Western River Cities
31 Russell Plaza Dr
Ashland, KY
606-326-0357 (800-780-7234)
Dogs are allowed for an additional pet fee of $5 per night per room. Dogs may not be left alone in the room. 2 dogs may be allowed.

Days Inn Ashland
12700 SR 180
Ashland, KY
606-928-3600 (800-329-7466)
Dogs of all sizes are allowed. There is a $10 per night pet fee per pet. 2 dogs may be allowed.

Holiday Inn Express Hotel & Suites Ashland
13131 Slone Court
Ashland, KY
606-929-1720 (877-270-6405)
Dogs of all sizes are allowed for an additional one time pet fee of $25 per room. Multiple dogs may be allowed.

Best Western General Nelson
411 W Stephen Foster Ave
Bardstown, KY
502-348-3977 (800-780-7234)
Dogs are allowed for an additional one time fee of $10.60 per pet. 2 dogs may be allowed.

Days Inn Bardstown
1875 New Haven Dr

Bardstown, KY
502-348-9253 (800-329-7466)
Dogs of all sizes are allowed. There is a $10 one time per pet fee per visit. Pet must be kept in kennel when left alone. 2 dogs may be allowed.

Hampton Inn
985 Chambers Blvd
Bardstown, KY
502-349-0100
Well behaved dogs of all sizes are allowed. There are no additional pet fees. Dogs are not allowed to be left alone in the room. Multiple dogs may be allowed.

Days Inn Beaver Dam
1750 US Hwy 231
Beaver Dam, KY
270-274-0851 (800-329-7466)
Dogs of all sizes are allowed. There is a $10 per night pet fee per pet. 2 dogs may be allowed.

Holiday Inn Express Hotel & Suites
173 Carroll Rd
Benton, KY
270-527-5300 (877-270-6405)
Dogs of all sizes are allowed for an additional pet fee of $10 per night per room. Multiple dogs may be allowed.

Boone Tavern Hotel
100 Main Street
Berea, KY
606-986-9358 (800-366-9358)
4berea.com/tavern/
This hotel is one of the registered Historic Hotels of America. It is owned by Berea College and is staffed by students.

Days Inn Berea
1029 Cooper Dr
Berea, KY
859-986-7373 (800-329-7466)
Dogs of all sizes are allowed. There is a $5 per night pet fee per pet. 2 dogs may be allowed.

Super 8 Berea
196 Prince Royal Dr
Berea, KY
859-986-8426 (800-800-8000)
Dogs of all sizes are allowed. There is a $5.50 per night pet fee per pet. Smoking and non-smoking rooms are available for pet rooms. 2 dogs may be allowed.

Drury Inn
3250 Scottsville Road
Bowling Green, KY
270-842-7100 (800-378-7946)

Dogs of all sizes are permitted. Pets are not allowed in the breakfast area of the hotel. Pets are not to be left unattended, and each guest must assume liability for damage of property or other guest complaints. There is a limit of one pet per room.

Holiday Inn
1021 Wilkinson Trace
Bowling Green, KY
270-745-0088 (877-270-6405)
Dogs up to 75 pounds are allowed for an additional one time pet fee of $50 per room. 2 dogs may be allowed.

Motel 6 - Bowling Green
3139 Scottsville Road
Bowling Green, KY
270-843-0140 (800-466-8356)
One well-behaved family pet per room. Guest must notify front desk upon arrival. Guest is liable for any damages. In consideration of all guests, pets must never be left unattended in the guest rooms.

Quality Inn
1919 Mel Browning Street
Bowling Green, KY
270-846-4588 (877-424-6423)
Dogs are allowed for an additional fee of $10 per night per pet. Multiple dogs may be allowed.

Red Roof Inn - Bowling Green, KY
3140 Scottsville Road
Bowling Green, KY
270-781-6550 (800-RED-ROOF)
One well-behaved family pet per room. Guest must notify front desk upon arrival. Guest is liable for any damages. In consideration of all guests, pets must never be left unattended in the guest rooms.

Comfort Inn
149 Willabrook Drive
Brooks, KY
502-957-6900 (877-424-6423)
Dogs up to 50 pounds are allowed for an additional pet fee of $10 per night per room. 2 dogs may be allowed.

Holiday Inn Express
153 Broadbent Blvd
Cadiz, KY
270-522-3700 (877-270-6405)
Dogs of all sizes are allowed for an additional one time pet fee of $20 per room. Multiple dogs may be allowed.

Super 8 Cadiz
154 Hospitality Lane

Cadiz, KY
270-522-7007 (800-800-8000)
Dogs of all sizes are allowed. There is a $5 per night pet fee per pet. Smoking and non-smoking rooms are available for pet rooms.

Holiday Inn Express
102 Plantation Drive
Campbellsville, KY
270-465-2727 (877-270-6405)
Dogs of all sizes are allowed for an additional fee of $10 per night per pet. Multiple dogs may be allowed.

Super 8 Carrollton
130 Slumber Lane
Carrollton, KY
502-732-0252 (800-800-8000)
Dogs of all sizes are allowed. There is a $10 per night pet fee per pet. Smoking and non-smoking rooms are available for pet rooms. 2 dogs may be allowed.

Best Western Executive Inn
10 Slumber Lane
Carrollton, KY
502-732-8444 (800-780-7234)
Dogs are allowed for an additional fee of $10 per night per pet. Multiple dogs may be allowed.

Best Western Corbin Inn
2630 Cumberland Falls Rd
Corbin, KY
606-528-2100 (800-780-7234)
Dogs are allowed for an additional fee of $10 per night per pet. Multiple dogs may be allowed.

Days Inn Corbin
1860 Cumberland Falls Rd
Corbin, KY
606-528-8150 (800-329-7466)
Dogs up to 60 pounds are allowed. There is a $10 per night pet fee per pet. 2 dogs may be allowed.

Holiday Inn Express
96 Daniel Dr
Danville, KY
859-236-8600 (877-270-6405)
Dogs of all sizes are allowed for an additional one time pet fee of $10 per room. Dogs may not be left alone in the room. Multiple dogs may be allowed.

Super 8 Danville
3663 Hwy 150/127 Bypass
Danville, KY
859-236-8881 (800-800-8000)
Dogs of all sizes are allowed. There is a $5 per night pet fee per pet. Smoking and non-smoking rooms are available for pet rooms. 2 dogs

may be allowed.

Holiday Inn Express
1050 Fashion Ridge Rd
Dry Ridge, KY
859-824-7121 (877-270-6405)
Dogs of all sizes are allowed for an additional fee of $10 per night per pet. 2 dogs may be allowed.

Eddy Creek Marina Resort
7612 H 93S
Eddyville, KY
270-388-2271
Dogs of all sizes are allowed. There is a $100 refundable pet deposit. Dogs must be leashed and cleaned up after. This lodge is seasonal, as is the RV park also on site. The RV park allows pets for no additional fee or deposit. Dogs are allowed on the trails. Multiple dogs may be allowed.

Best Western Atrium Gardens
1043 Executive Drive
Elizabethtown, KY
270-769-3030 (800-780-7234)
Dogs are allowed for an additional one time fee of $25 per pet. Multiple dogs may be allowed.

Comfort Inn
2009 N Mulberry Street
Elizabethtown, KY
270-765-4166 (877-424-6423)
Dogs up to 75 pounds are allowed for an additional fee of $10 per night per pet. 2 dogs may be allowed.

Kentucky Cardinal Inn
642 E Dixie Ave
Elizabethtown, KY
270-765-6139
Dogs are allowed for an additional one time pet fee of $25 per room. 2 dogs may be allowed.

Motel 6 - Elizabethtown
1042 North Mulberry Street
Elizabethtown, KY
270-769-3102 (800-466-8356)
One well-behaved family pet per room. Guest must notify front desk upon arrival. Guest is liable for any damages. In consideration of all guests, pets must never be left unattended in the guest rooms.

Residence Inn by Marriott
2811 Circleport Drive
Erlanger, KY
859-282-7400
Dogs of all sizes are allowed. There is a $100 one time fee and a pet policy to sign at check in. 2 dogs may be allowed.

Best Western Inn Florence
7821 Commerce Dr
Florence, KY
859-525-0090 (800-780-7234)
Dogs are allowed for an additional fee of $15 per night per pet.

La Quinta Inn & Suites Cincinnati Airport/Florence
350 Meijer Drive
Florence, KY
859-282-8212 (800-531-5900)
Dogs of all sizes are allowed. There are no additional pet fees. Dogs may only be left alone in the room if they will be quiet and well behaved. Dogs must be leashed and cleaned up after. Multiple dogs may be allowed.

Motel 6 - Cincinnati South - Florence
7937 Dream Street
Florence, KY
859-283-0909 (800-466-8356)
One well-behaved family pet per room. Guest must notify front desk upon arrival. Guest is liable for any damages. In consideration of all guests, pets must never be left unattended in the guest rooms.

Quality Inn and Suites
7915 H 42
Florence, KY
859-371-4700 (877-424-6423)
Dogs are allowed for an additional fee of $10 per night per pet. There may be 1 large or 2 small dogs per room. 2 dogs may be allowed.

Red Roof Inn - Cincinnati Airport - Florence, KY
7454 Turfway Rd
Florence, KY
859-647-2700 (800-RED-ROOF)
One well-behaved family pet per room. Guest must notify front desk upon arrival. Guest is liable for any damages. In consideration of all guests, pets must never be left unattended in the guest rooms.

Super 8 Florence KY/Cincinnati OH Area
7928 Dream St
Florence, KY
859-283-1228 (800-800-8000)
Dogs of all sizes are allowed. There is a $5 per night pet fee per pet. Smoking and non-smoking rooms are available for pet rooms. 2 dogs may be allowed.

Super 8 Fort Mitchell KY/Cincinnati OH Area

2350 Royal Drive
Fort Mitchell, KY
859-341-2090 (800-800-8000)
Dogs of all sizes are allowed. There is a $7 per night pet fee per pet. Smoking and non-smoking rooms are available for pet rooms. 2 dogs may be allowed.

Americas Best Value Inn
1225 U.S. Highway 127 S.
Frankfort, KY
502-875-3220 (800-800-8000)
innworks.com/frankfort
There is a $10 per stay additional pet fee. Up to three dogs are allowed in each room. The hotel allows a free 8 minute long distance call each night and offers a free continental breakfast. Children 12 and under are free. There is a pool and a laundry. I-64, Exit 53B to US 127. 1 mile North.

Days Inn Franklin
103 Trotter Lane
Franklin, KY
270-598-0163 (800-329-7466)
Dogs of all sizes are allowed. There is a $5 per night pet fee per pet. 2 dogs may be allowed.

Super 8 Franklin
2805 Scottsville Rd
Franklin, KY
270-586-8885 (800-800-8000)
Dogs of all sizes are allowed. There is a $5 per night pet fee per pet. Smoking and non-smoking rooms are available for pet rooms. 2 dogs may be allowed.

Days Inn Georgetown North
385 Cherry Blossom Way
Georgetown, KY
502-863-5000 (800-329-7466)
Dogs of all sizes are allowed. There is a $5 per night pet fee per pet. 2 dogs may be allowed.

Hotel Ivy
250 Outlet Center Drive
Georgetown, KY
502-867-1648
Dogs of all sizes are allowed. There is a $25 per night pet fee per pet. Smoking and non-smoking rooms are available for pets. 2 dogs may be allowed.

Motel 6 - Lexington North - Georgetown
401 Cherry Blossom Way
Georgetown, KY
502-863-1166 (800-466-8356)
One well-behaved family pet per room. Guest must notify front desk upon arrival. Guest is liable for any

damages. In consideration of all guests, pets must never be left unattended in the guest rooms.

Best Western Kentucky-Barkley Lakes Inn
720 Complex Dr
Grand Rivers, KY
270-928-2700 (800-780-7234)
Dogs are allowed for an additional fee of $10 per night per pet. 2 dogs may be allowed.

Super 8 Hazard
125 Village Lane
Hazard, KY
606-436-8888 (800-800-8000)
Dogs of all sizes are allowed. There is a $10 per night pet fee per pet. Smoking and non-smoking rooms are available for pet rooms. 2 dogs may be allowed.

Holiday Inn
2910 Ft. Campbell Blvd
Hopkinsville, KY
270-886-4413 (877-270-6405)
Dogs of all sizes are allowed for an additional one time pet fee of $25 per room. Multiple dogs may be allowed.

Days Inn Kuttawa
139 Days Inn Dr
Kuttawa, KY
270-388-5420 (800-329-7466)
Dogs of all sizes are allowed. There is a $10 one time per pet fee per visit. 2 dogs may be allowed.

Comfort Suites
1500 E Crystal Drive
La Grange, KY
502-225-4125 (877-424-6423)
Dogs are allowed for an additional fee of $10 per night per pet. Multiple dogs may be allowed.

Best Western Hancock Inn
9040 US Highway 60 West
Lewisport, KY
270-295-3234 (800-780-7234)
Dogs are allowed for a $50 pet deposit; $35 is refundable. Multiple dogs may be allowed.

Days Inn Lexington
1987 North Broadway
Lexington, KY
859-299-1202 (800-329-7466)
Dogs of all sizes are allowed. There is a $10 per night pet fee per pet. 2 dogs may be allowed.

Days Inn Lexington South
5575 Athens-Boonesboro Rd
Lexington, KY
859-263-3100 (800-329-7466)

Dogs of all sizes are allowed. There is a $5 per night pet fee per pet. 2 dogs may be allowed.

Four Points by Sheraton Lexington
1538 Stanton Way
Lexington, KY
859-259-1311 (888-625-5144)
Dogs of all sizes are allowed. There is a $100 nonrefundable one time pet fee per visit. Dogs are not allowed to be left alone in the room.

Hampton Inn
2251 Elkhorn Road
Lexington, KY
859-299-2613
Well behaved dogs of all sizes are allowed. There are no additional pet fees. If you leave your dog in the room you must leave a cell number, and dogs may not be in food areas. Multiple dogs may be allowed.

Holiday Inn
5532 Athens-Boonesboro Rd
Lexington, KY
859-263-5241 (877-270-6405)
Dogs of all sizes are allowed for an additional one time pet fee of $25 per room. 2 dogs may be allowed.

Holiday Inn Express Hotel & Suites
Lexington-Downtown/University
1000 Export Street
Lexington, KY
859-389-6800 (877-270-6405)
Dogs of all sizes are allowed for an additional one time fee of $25 per pet. 2 dogs may be allowed.

Motel 6 - Lexington East
2260 Elkhorn Road
Lexington, KY
859-293-1431 (800-466-8356)
One well-behaved family pet per room. Guest must notify front desk upon arrival. Guest is liable for any damages. In consideration of all guests, pets must never be left unattended in the guest rooms.

Red Roof Inn - Lexington
1980 Haggard Court
Lexington, KY
859-293-2626 (800-RED-ROOF)
One well-behaved family pet per room. Guest must notify front desk upon arrival. Guest is liable for any damages. In consideration of all guests, pets must never be left unattended in the guest rooms.

Red Roof Inn - Lexington South
2651 Wilhite Drive
Lexington, KY
859-277-9400 (800-RED-ROOF)

One well-behaved family pet per room. Guest must notify front desk upon arrival. Guest is liable for any damages. In consideration of all guests, pets must never be left unattended in the guest rooms.

Red Roof Inn - Lexington Southeast
100 Canebrake Drive
Lexington, KY
859-543-1877 (800-RED-ROOF)
One well-behaved family pet per room. Guest must notify front desk upon arrival. Guest is liable for any damages. In consideration of all guests, pets must never be left unattended in the guest rooms.

Residence Inn by Marriott
1080 Newtown Pike
Lexington, KY
859-231-6191
Pets of all sizes are allowed. There is a $75 one time fee and a pet policy to sign at check in. Multiple dogs may be allowed.

Residence Inn by Marriott
2688 Pink Pigeon Parkway
Lexington, KY
859-263-9979
Pets of all sizes are allowed. There is a $75 one time fee and a pet policy to sign at check in. Multiple dogs may be allowed.

Sleep Inn
1920 Plaudit Place
Lexington, KY
859-543-8400 (877-424-6423)
Dogs are allowed for an additional one time pet fee of $15 per room. Multiple dogs may be allowed.

Super 8 Lexington/Dwtn
925 Newtown Pike
Lexington, KY
859-231-6300 (800-800-8000)
Dogs of all sizes are allowed. There is a $5 per night pet fee per pet. Smoking and non-smoking rooms are available for pet rooms. 2 dogs may be allowed.

Super 8 Lexington/Winchester Road
2351 Buena Vista Rd
Lexington, KY
859-299-6241 (800-800-8000)
Dogs of all sizes are allowed. There is a $10 per night pet fee per pet. Smoking and non-smoking rooms are available for pet rooms. 2 dogs may be allowed.

Budget Host Westgate Inn
254 W Daniel Boone Parkway
London, KY

606-878-7330
There are no additional pet fees.

Days Inn London
2035 W 192 Bypass
London, KY
606-864-7331 (800-329-7466)
Dogs of all sizes are allowed. There is a $5.50 per night pet fee per pet. 2 dogs may be allowed.

Holiday Inn Express Hotel & Suites
506 Minton Drive
London, KY
606-862-0077 (877-270-6405)
Dogs of all sizes are allowed for an additional one time fee of $15 per pet. Multiple dogs may be allowed.

Red Roof Inn - London I-75
110 Melcon Lane
London, KY
606-862-8844 (800-RED-ROOF)
One well-behaved family pet per room. Guest must notify front desk upon arrival. Guest is liable for any damages. In consideration of all guests, pets must never be left unattended in the guest rooms.

Super 8 London
285 W Highway 80
London, KY
606-878-9800 (800-800-8000)
Dogs of all sizes are allowed. There is a $5.50 per night pet fee per pet. Smoking and non-smoking rooms are available for pet rooms. 2 dogs may be allowed.

Aleksander House Bed and Breakfast
1213 South First Street
Louisville, KY
502-637-4985 (866-637-4985)
aleksanderhouse.com/
Stay at an 1882 Victorian bed and breakfast located in historic Old Louisville. Near downtown and Churchill Downs. There is a fenced in yard. Well-behaved dogs of all sizes are permitted. Dogs must be quiet and friendly and recently bathed. There is a $20 pet fee.

Best Western Airport East/Expo Center
1921 Bishop Ln
Louisville, KY
502-456-4411 (800-780-7234)
Dogs are allowed for an additional one time pet fee of $25 per room. 2 dogs may be allowed.

Best Western Brownsboro Inn/Louisville East
4805 Brownsboro Road

Louisville, KY
502-893-2551 (800-780-7234)
Dogs are allowed for an additional one time fee of $25 per pet. 2 dogs may be allowed.

Breckinridge Inn
2800 Breckinridge Lane
Louisville, KY
502-456-5050
There is a $50 one time pet charge.

Candlewood Suites
1367 Gardiner Lane
Louisville, KY
502-357-3577 (877-270-6405)
Dogs of all sizes are allowed for an additional one time pet fee of $75 per room, and there is a pet agreement to sign at check-in. 2 dogs may be allowed.

Candlewood Suites
11762 Commonwealth Drive
Louisville, KY
502-261-0085 (877-270-6405)
Dogs up to 85 pounds are allowed for an additional pet fee per room of $75 for 1 to 15 days; the fee is $150 for 16 nights or more. 2 dogs may be allowed.

Clarion Hotel and Conference Center
9700 Bluegrass Parkway
Louisville, KY
502-491-4830 (877-424-6423)
Dogs are allowed for an additional one time pet fee of $75 per room. Multiple dogs may be allowed.

Days Inn Louisville Airport
9340 Blairwood Rd
Louisville, KY
502-425-8010 (800-329-7466)
Dogs up to 60 pounds are allowed. There is a $15 one time per pet fee per visit. 2 dogs may be allowed.

Drury Inn & Suites
9501 Blairwood Road
Louisville, KY
502-326-4170 (800-378-7946)
Dogs of all sizes are permitted. Pets are not allowed in the breakfast area of the hotel. Pets are not to be left unattended, and each guest must assume liability for damage of property or other guest complaints. There is a limit of one pet per room.

Hilton
500 Fourth Avenue
Louisville, KY
502-585-3200
Dogs are allowed for a $50 refundable pet deposit. Multiple

dogs may be allowed.

Holiday Inn
1325 S. Hurstbourne Pkwy
Louisville, KY
502-426-2600 (877-270-6405)
Dogs of all sizes are allowed for an additional one time pet fee of $39 per room. Multiple dogs may be allowed.

Holiday Inn - Airport
2715 Fern Valley Rd
Louisville, KY
502-964-3311 (877-270-6405)
Dogs of all sizes are allowed for an additional one time pet fee of $35 per room. Multiple dogs may be allowed.

Holiday Inn Express Louisville-I-265 East
3711 Chamberlain Lane
Louisville, KY
502-814-0004 (877-270-6405)
Dogs up to 50 pounds are allowed for an additional fee of $30 per night per pet. 2 dogs may be allowed.

La Quinta Inn & Suites Louisville
4125 Preston Highway
Louisville, KY
502-368-0007 (800-531-5900)
Dogs up to 60 pounds are allowed. There are no additional pet fees. There is a pet waiver to sign at check in. Dogs are not to use the front entrance; they are to be brought in the side doors. Dogs must be leashed and cleaned up after. Multiple dogs may be allowed.

Motel 6 - Louisville Airport
3200 Kemmons Drive
Louisville, KY
502-473-0000 (800-466-8356)
One well-behaved family pet per room. Guest must notify front desk upon arrival. Guest is liable for any damages. In consideration of all guests, pets must never be left unattended in the guest rooms.

Quality Inn and Suites
3255 Bardstown Road
Louisville, KY
502-454-0451 (877-424-6423)
Dogs are allowed for an additional fee of $10 per night per pet. 2 dogs may be allowed.

Red Roof Inn - Louisville Airport
4704 Preston Highway
Louisville, KY
502-968-0151 (800-RED-ROOF)
One well-behaved family pet per room. Guest must notify front desk upon arrival. Guest is liable for any damages. In consideration of all

guests, pets must never be left unattended in the guest rooms.

Red Roof Inn - Louisville East
9330 Blairwood Road
Louisville, KY
502-426-7621 (800-RED-ROOF)
One well-behaved family pet per room. Guest must notify front desk upon arrival. Guest is liable for any damages. In consideration of all guests, pets must never be left unattended in the guest rooms.

Red Roof Inn - Louisville SE - Fairgrounds
3322 Red Roof Place
Louisville, KY
502-456-2993 (800-RED-ROOF)
One well-behaved family pet per room. Guest must notify front desk upon arrival. Guest is liable for any damages. In consideration of all guests, pets must never be left unattended in the guest rooms.

Residence Inn by Marriott
700 Phillips Lane
Louisville, KY
502-363-8800
Dogs of all sizes are allowed. There is a $75 one time fee and a pet policy to sign at check in. They also request you kennel your pet when out. Multiple dogs may be allowed.

Residence Inn by Marriott
120 N Hurstbourne Parkway
Louisville, KY
502-425-1821
Dogs of all sizes are allowed. There is a $75 one time fee and a pet policy to sign at check in. Multiple dogs may be allowed.

Residence Inn by Marriott
3500 Springhurst Commons Drive
Louisville, KY
502-412-1311
Dogs of all sizes are allowed. There is a $75 one time fee and a pet policy to sign at check in. Multiple dogs may be allowed.

Sleep Inn
3330 Preston H, Gate 6
Louisville, KY
502-368-9597 (877-424-6423)
Dogs are allowed for an additional fee of $10 per night per pet. Dogs must be crated when left alone in the room. Multiple dogs may be allowed.

Staybridge Suites
11711 Gateworth Way
Louisville, KY
502-244-9511 (877-270-6405)

One dog up to 50 pounds is allowed for an additional pet fee of $150 to $175 depending on the room.

Super 8 Louisville/Airport
4800 Preston Hwy
Louisville, KY
502-968-0088 (800-800-8000)
Dogs of all sizes are allowed. There is a $10 one time per pet fee per visit. Smoking and non-smoking rooms are available for pet rooms. 2 dogs may be allowed.

Travelodge
9340 Blairwood Rd.
Louisville, KY
502-425-8010 (800-578-7878)
There is a $15 one time pet charge.

Days Inn Madisonville
1900 Lantaff Blvd
Madisonville, KY
270-821-8620 (800-329-7466)
Dogs of all sizes are allowed. There is a $10 per night pet fee per pet. 2 dogs may be allowed.

Days Inn Mayfield
1101 W Housman St
Mayfield, KY
270-247-3700 (800-329-7466)
Dogs of all sizes are allowed. There is a $10 per night pet fee per pet. 2 dogs may be allowed.

Super 8 Maysville
550 Tucker Dr
Maysville, KY
606-759-8888 (800-800-8000)
Dogs of all sizes are allowed. There is a $5 per night pet fee per pet. Dogs are not allowed to be left alone in the room. Smoking and non-smoking rooms are available for pet rooms. 2 dogs may be allowed.

Comfort Inn and Suites
2650 H 801N
Morehead, KY
606-780-7378 (877-424-6423)
Dogs are allowed for an additional fee of $10 per night per pet. Multiple dogs may be allowed.

Holiday Inn Express
110 Toms Drive
Morehead, KY
606-784-5796 (877-270-6405)
Dogs of all sizes are allowed for an additional one time fee of $10 per pet. Multiple dogs may be allowed.

Motel 6 - Morgantown
1460 South Main Street
Morgantown, KY

270-526-9481 (800-466-8356)
One well-behaved family pet per room. Guest must notify front desk upon arrival. Guest is liable for any damages. In consideration of all guests, pets must never be left unattended in the guest rooms.

Best Western Pennyrile Inn
Pennyrile Pkwy Exit 37
Morton's Gap, KY
270-258-5201 (800-780-7234)
Dogs are allowed for an additional fee of $7 per night per pet. 2 dogs may be allowed.

Days Inn Mt Sterling
705 Maysville Rd
Mount Sterling, KY
859-498-4680 (800-329-7466)
Dogs of all sizes are allowed. There is a $5 per night pet fee per pet. 2 dogs may be allowed.

Best Western University Inn
1507 N 12th St
Murray, KY
270-753-5353 (800-780-7234)
Well behaved dogs are allowed for an additional one time pet fee of $10 per room. Dogs must be removed or crated for housekeeping. Multiple dogs may be allowed.

Days Inn Murray
517 S 12th St
Murray, KY
270-753-6706 (800-329-7466)
Dogs of all sizes are allowed. There is a $10 per night pet fee per pet. 2 dogs may be allowed.

Murray Plaza Court
502 S. 12th Street
Murray, KY
270-753-2682
There are no pet fees.

Days Inn Owensboro
3720 New Hartford Rd
Owensboro, KY
270-684-9621 (800-329-7466)
Dogs of all sizes are allowed. There is a $5 per night pet fee per pet. 2 dogs may be allowed.

Motel 6 - Owensboro
4585 Frederica Street
Owensboro, KY
270-686-8606 (800-466-8356)
One well-behaved family pet per room. Guest must notify front desk upon arrival. Guest is liable for any damages. In consideration of all guests, pets must never be left unattended in the guest rooms.

Sleep Inn
51 Bon Harbor Hills
Owensboro, KY
270-691-6200 (877-424-6423)
Dogs up to 60 pounds are allowed
for an additional fee of $10 per night
per pet. 2 dogs may be allowed.

America's Best Value Inn
5125 Old Cairo Rd
Paducah, KY
270-575-9605
Dogs of all sizes are allowed. There
is a $5 per night pet fee per small pet
and $10 per large pet. Pet must be
kept in kennel when left alone.
Smoking and non-smoking rooms
are available for pet rooms. 2 dogs
may be allowed.

Drury Inn
3975 Hinkleville Road
Paducah, KY
270-443-3313 (800-378-7946)
Dogs of all sizes are permitted. Pets
are not allowed in the breakfast area
of the hotel. Pets are not to be left
unattended, and each guest must
assume liability for damage of
property or other guest complaints.
There is a limit of one pet per room.

Drury Suites
2930 James-Sanders Blvd
Paducah, KY
270-441-0024 (800-378-7946)
Dogs of all sizes are permitted. Pets
are not allowed in the breakfast area
of the hotel. Pets are not to be left
unattended, and each guest must
assume liability for damage of
property or other guest complaints.
There is a limit of one pet per room.

Hampton Inn
5006 Hinkleville
Paducah, KY
270-442-4500
Dogs of all sizes are allowed. There
are no additional pet fees. Dogs are
not allowed to be left alone in the
room. Multiple dogs may be allowed.

Motel 6 - Paducah
5120 Hinkleville Road
Paducah, KY
270-443-3672 (800-466-8356)
One well-behaved family pet per
room. Guest must notify front desk
upon arrival. Guest is liable for any
damages. In consideration of all
guests, pets must never be left
unattended in the guest rooms.

Pear Tree Inn
5002 Hinkleville Road
Paducah, KY

270-444-7200 (800-378-7946)
Dogs of all sizes are permitted. Pets
are not allowed in the breakfast
area of the hotel. Pets are not to be
left unattended, and each guest
must assume liability for damage of
property or other guest complaints.
There is a limit of one pet per room.

Travel Inn
1380 S. Irvin Cobb Dr.
Paducah, KY
270-443-8751 (800-228-5151)
There are no additional pet fees.

Travelodge
5001 Hinkleville Rd
Paducah, KY
270-442-3334 (800-800-8000)
Dogs of all sizes are allowed. There
is a $10 per night pet fee per pet.
Smoking and non-smoking rooms
are available for pet rooms. 2 dogs
may be allowed.

Super 8 Prestonsburg
80 Shoppers Pth
Prestonsburg, KY
606-886-3355 (800-800-8000)
Dogs of all sizes are allowed. There
is a $20 one time pet fee per first
night and a $5 per additional night
pet fee. Smoking and non-smoking
rooms are available for pet rooms. 2
dogs may be allowed.

Comfort Suites
2007 Colby Taylor Drive
Richmond, KY
859-624-0770 (877-424-6423)
Dogs are allowed for an additional
fee of $10 per night per pet. Multiple
dogs may be allowed.

Holiday Inn Express Hotel & Suites
1990 Colby Taylor Drive
Richmond, KY
859-624-4055 (877-270-6405)
Dogs of all sizes are allowed for an
additional one time fee of $25 per
pet. Multiple dogs may be allowed.

La Quinta Inn Richmond
1751 Lexington Rd.
Richmond, KY
859-623-9121 (800-531-5900)
Dogs of all sizes are allowed. There
are no additional pet fees. Dogs
must be leashed and cleaned up
after. Multiple dogs may be allowed.

Red Roof Inn - Lexington -
Richmond
111 Bahama Ct
Richmond, KY
859-625-0084 (800-RED-ROOF)
One well-behaved family pet per

room. Guest must notify front desk
upon arrival. Guest is liable for any
damages. In consideration of all
guests, pets must never be left
unattended in the guest rooms.

Best Western Shelbyville Lodge
115 Isaac Shelby Dr
Shelbyville, KY
502-633-4400 (800-780-7234)
Dogs are allowed for an additional
fee of $10 per night per pet. Multiple
dogs may be allowed.

Holiday Inn Hotel & Suites
110 Club House Drive
Shelbyville, KY
502-647-0109 (877-270-6405)
Dogs of all sizes are allowed for an
additional one time pet fee of $20 per
room. Multiple dogs may be allowed.

Motel 6 - Louisville South -
Sheperdsville
144 Paroquet Springs Drive
Shepherdsville, KY
502-543-4400 (800-466-8356)
One well-behaved family pet per
room. Guest must notify front desk
upon arrival. Guest is liable for any
damages. In consideration of all
guests, pets must never be left
unattended in the guest rooms.

Comfort Inn
82 Jolin Drive
Somerset, KY
606-677-1500 (877-424-6423)
Dogs are allowed for an additional
fee of $10 per night per pet. 2 dogs
may be allowed.

Days Inn Somerset
125 North Highway 27
Somerset, KY
606-678-2052 (800-329-7466)
Dogs of all sizes are allowed. There
is a $10 one time per pet fee per
visit. If pet is very large the fee is $20
per pet per visit. 2 dogs may be
allowed.

Rose Hill Inn Bed & Breakfast
233 Rose Hill
Versailles, KY
859-873-5957 (800-307-0460)
rosehillinn.com/
Dogs are welcome in the cottage and
the apartment at this bed &
breakfast. The owners also have
dogs which reside on the premise.
There is a $15 one time pet charge.

Ivy Lodge
11177 Frontage Rd
Walton, KY
859-485-2200

Cumberland Inn.
Williamsburg, Ky Exit 11 on east of I 75

Dogs up to 60 pounds are allowed. There is a $25 returnable deposit required per room. There is a $10 one time per pet fee per visit. 2 dogs may be allowed.

Super 8 Williamsburg
30 W Hwy 92
Williamsburg, KY
606-549-3450 (800-800-8000)
Dogs of all sizes are allowed. There is a $10 one time per pet fee per visit. Smoking and non-smoking rooms are available for pet rooms. 2 dogs may be allowed.

Best Western Country Squire
1307 West Lexington Ave
Winchester, KY
859-744-7210 (800-780-7234)
Dogs are allowed for an additional fee of $10 (plus tax) per night per pet. Multiple dogs may be allowed.

Quality Inn and Suites
960 Interstate Drive
Winchester, KY
859-737-3990 (877-424-6423)
Dogs are allowed for an additional fee per pet of $10 for 1 to 2 days, and $20 for 3 or 4 days. 2 dogs may be allowed.

Louisiana Listings

Clarion Hotel
2716 N MacArthur Drive
Alexandria, LA
318-487-4261 (877-424-6423)
Dogs up to 60 pounds are allowed for an additional pet fee of $15 per night per room. 2 dogs may be allowed.

Holiday Inn Downtown
701 4th Street
Alexandria, LA
318-442-9000 (877-270-6405)
Dogs of all sizes are allowed for an additional one time pet fee of $50 per room. Multiple dogs may be allowed.

La Quinta Inn & Suites Alexandria
6116 West Calhoun Dr.
Alexandria, LA
318-442-3700 (800-531-5900)
Dogs of all sizes are allowed. There are no additional pet fees. Dogs must be leashed and cleaned up after. The Do Not Disturb sign must be on the door if a pet is in the room alone. Multiple dogs may be allowed.

Motel 6 - Alexandria
546 MacArthur Drive
Alexandria, LA
318-445-2336 (800-466-8356)
One well-behaved family pet per room. Guest must notify front desk upon arrival. Guest is liable for any damages. In consideration of all guests, pets must never be left unattended in the guest rooms.

Super 8 Alexandria/MacArthur Dr
700 MacArthur Dr
Alexandria, LA
318-445-6541 (800-800-8000)
Dogs of all sizes are allowed. There is a $20 one time per pet fee per visit. Smoking and non-smoking rooms are available for pet rooms. 2 dogs may be allowed.

Chase Suite Hotel by Woodfin
5522 Corporate Blvd
Baton Rouge, LA
225-927-5630
All well-behaved dogs are welcome. Every room is a suite and hotel amenities include a video rental library. There is a $5 per day pet fee.

La Quinta Inn Baton Rouge
2333 S. Acadian Thruway
Baton Rouge, LA
225-924-9600 (800-531-5900)
Dogs of all sizes are allowed. There are no additional pet fees. Dogs must be leashed and cleaned up after. The Do Not Disturb sign must be on the door if a pet is in the room alone. Multiple dogs may be allowed.

Motel 6 - Baton Rouge East
9901 Gwen Adele Avenue
Baton Rouge, LA
225-924-2130 (800-466-8356)
One well-behaved family pet per room. Guest must notify front desk upon arrival. Guest is liable for any damages. In consideration of all guests, pets must never be left unattended in the guest rooms.

Motel 6 - Baton Rouge Southeast
10445 Reiger Road
Baton Rouge, LA
225-291-4912 (800-466-8356)
One well-behaved family pet per room. Guest must notify front desk upon arrival. Guest is liable for any damages. In consideration of all guests, pets must never be left unattended in the guest rooms.

Red Roof Inn - Baton Rouge
11314 Boardwalk Drive

Baton Rouge, LA
225-275-6600 (800-RED-ROOF)
One well-behaved family pet per room. Guest must notify front desk upon arrival. Guest is liable for any damages. In consideration of all guests, pets must never be left unattended in the guest rooms.

Residence Inn by Marriott
10333 N Mall Drive
Baton Rouge, LA
225-293-8700
Dogs of all sizes are allowed. There is a $75 one time pet fee and a pet policy to sign at check in. Multiple dogs may be allowed.

Sheraton Baton Rouge Convention Center Hotel
102 France St.
Baton Rouge, LA
225-242-2600 (888-625-5144)
Dogs of all sizes are allowed. There are no additional pet fees. Dogs are not allowed to be left alone in the room

TownePlace Suites Baton Rouge South
8735 Summa Avenue
Baton Rouge, LA
225-819-2112
Dogs of all sizes are allowed. There is a $75 one time pet fee per visit. 2 dogs may be allowed.

University Inn & Conference Center
2445 S. Acadian Thruway
Baton Rouge, LA
225-236-4000 (888-368-7578)
Dogs up to 100 pounds are allowed. There is a $25 per night per pet additional fee. Dogs must be well behaved, leashed, and cleaned up after. They may be left alone in the room, but if there is a chance they could bark, they request you leave a contact number at the front desk. There is an outdoor pet lawn area for daily walks, and doggie treats, too. 2 dogs may be allowed.

Days Inn Bossier City
200 John Wesley Blvd
Bossier City, LA
318-742-9200 (800-329-7466)
Dogs of all sizes are allowed. There is a $5 per night pet fee per pet. 2 dogs may be allowed.

Motel 6 - Shreveport
210 John Wesley Boulevard
Bossier City, LA
318-742-3472 (800-466-8356)
One well-behaved family pet per room. Guest must notify front desk

upon arrival. Guest is liable for any damages. In consideration of all guests, pets must never be left unattended in the guest rooms.

Residence Inn by Marriott
1001 Gould Drive
Bossier City, LA
318-747-6220
Dogs of all sizes are allowed. There is a $75 one time fee and a pet policy to sign at check in. Multiple dogs may be allowed.

Best Western Of Breaux Bridge
2088-B Rees St
Breaux Bridge, LA
337-332-1114 (800-780-7234)
Well behaved dogs up to 30 pounds are allowed for an additional fee of $10 per night per pet, and a credit card must be on file. 2 dogs may be allowed.

Holiday Inn Express
2942 H Grand Point Hwy
Breaux Bridge, LA
337-667-8913 (877-270-6405)
Dogs of all sizes are allowed for an additional one time pet fee of $25 per room. Multiple dogs may be allowed.

The Castle Inn
1415 Prytania Street
Creole Gardens, LA
504-897-0540
Dogs of all sizes are allowed. There is a $100 refundable pet deposit. Multiple dogs may be allowed.

La Quinta Inn Crowley
9565 Egan Highway
Crowley, LA
337-783-6500 (800-531-5900)
Dogs of all sizes are allowed. There are no additional pet fees. There is a pet waiver to sign at check in. Dogs must be leashed, cleaned up after, and crated if left in the room alone. Multiple dogs may be allowed.

Best Western Delhi Inn
135 Snider Rd
Delhi, LA
318-878-5126 (800-780-7234)
Dogs are allowed for an additional fee of $10 per night per pet. Multiple dogs may be allowed.

Best Western Hammond Inn and Suites
107 Duo Drive
Hammond, LA
985-419-2001 (800-780-7234)
Dogs are allowed for an additional one time pet fee of $10 per room. Multiple dogs may be allowed.

Best Western University Inn
46053 North Puma Drive
Hammond, LA
985-345-0003 (800-780-7234)
Dogs are allowed for an additional fee of $10 (plus tax) per night per pet. Multiple dogs may be allowed.

TownePlace Suites New Orleans Metairie
5424 Citrus Blvd
Harahan, LA
504-818-2400
Dogs of all sizes are allowed. There is a $75 one time pet fee per visit. 2 dogs may be allowed.

La Quinta Inn New Orleans Airport
2610 Williams Blvd.
Kenner, LA
504-466-1401 (800-531-5900)
Dogs of all sizes are allowed. There are no additional pet fees. Dogs must be crated when left alone in the room, and they may not be left in the room for long periods. Dogs must be quiet, well behaved, leashed, and cleaned up after. Multiple dogs may be allowed.

Motel 6 - New Orleans - Airport
2830 Loyola Drive
Kenner, LA
504-466-9666 (800-466-8356)
One well-behaved family pet per room. Guest must notify front desk upon arrival. Guest is liable for any damages. In consideration of all guests, pets must never be left unattended in the guest rooms.

Best Western La Place Inn
4289 Main Street
La Palce, LA
985-651-4000 (800-780-7234)
Dogs are allowed for an additional one time pet fee of $25 per room. Multiple dogs may be allowed.

Best Western Posada Ana Inn-Lafayette
126 Alcide Dominique
Lafayette, LA
337-289-9907 (800-780-7234)
Dogs are allowed for no additional pet fee. Multiple dogs may be allowed.

Comfort Inn
1421 SE Evangeline Thruway
Lafayette, LA
337-232-9000 (877-424-6423)
Dogs are allowed for a $50 refundable deposit. Dogs must be crated when left alone in the room. 2 dogs may be allowed.

Days Inn Lafayette
1620 N University
Lafayette, LA
337-237-8880 (800-329-7466)
Dogs of all sizes are allowed. There is a $10 one time per pet fee per visit. 2 dogs may be allowed.

Holiday Inn Lafayette-Us167
2032 Ne Evangeline Thruway
Lafayette, LA
337-233-6815 (877-270-6405)
Dogs of all sizes are allowed for an additional one time fee of $30 per pet. Multiple dogs may be allowed.

La Quinta Inn & Suites Lafayette
1015 West Pinhook Road
Lafayette, LA
337-291-1088 (800-531-5900)
Dogs up to 60 pounds are allowed. There are no additional pet fees. Dogs must be leashed and cleaned up after. No aggressive breeds are allowed. Multiple dogs may be allowed.

La Quinta Inn Lafayette
2100 NE Evangeline Thruway
Lafayette, LA
337-233-5610 (800-531-5900)
Dogs up to 100 pounds are allowed. There are no additional pet fees. Dogs must be leashed and cleaned up after. 2 dogs may be allowed.

Motel 6 - Lafayette
2724 NE Evangeline Thruway
Lafayette, LA
337-233-2055 (800-466-8356)
One well-behaved family pet per room. Guest must notify front desk upon arrival. Guest is liable for any damages. In consideration of all guests, pets must never be left unattended in the guest rooms.

Quality Inn
2216 NE Evangeline Thruway
Lafayette, LA
337-234-0383 (877-424-6423)
Dogs up to 60 pounds are allowed for an additional fee of $25 per night per pet for dogs under 25 pounds, and the fee is $40 per night per pet for dogs over 25 pounds. 2 dogs may be allowed.

Red Roof Inn - Lafayette, LA
1718 North University Avenue
Lafayette, LA
337-233-3339 (800-RED-ROOF)
One well-behaved family pet per room. Guest must notify front desk upon arrival. Guest is liable for any damages. In consideration of all

guests, pets must never be left unattended in the guest rooms.

Howard Johnson Express Inn
103 Nibor Lane
Lafayette/Scott, LA
337-593-0849 (800-446-4656)
Dogs of all sizes are welcome. There is a $25 refundable pet deposit.

Best Suites of America
401 Lakeshore Drive
Lake Charles, LA
337-439-2444
There are no additional pet fees.

Days Inn Lake Charles
1010 Martin Luther King Hwy
Lake Charles, LA
337-433-1711 (800-329-7466)
Dogs of all sizes are allowed. There is a $10 per night pet fee per pet. 2 dogs may be allowed.

La Quinta Inn Lake Charles
1320 MLK Hwy 171 N
Lake Charles, LA
337-436-5998 (800-531-5900)
Dogs of all sizes are allowed. There are no additional pet fees. There is a pet waiver to sign at check in. Dogs may not be left unattended, and they must be leashed and cleaned up after. Multiple dogs may be allowed.

La Quinta Inn New Orleans Causeway
3100 I-10 Service Rd.
Metairie, LA
504-835-8511 (800-531-5900)
Dogs of all sizes are allowed. There are no additional pet fees. Dogs must be leashed and cleaned up after. Dogs must be removed for housekeeping. Multiple dogs may be allowed.

La Quinta Inn New Orleans Veterans
5900 Veterans Memorial Blvd
Metairie, LA
504-456-0003 (800-531-5900)
Dogs of all sizes are allowed. There are no additional pet fees. Dogs must be well behaved, leashed, and cleaned up after. Multiple dogs may be allowed.

Best Western Minden Inn
1411 Sibley Rd
Minden, LA
318-377-1001 (800-780-7234)
Dogs are allowed for an additional fee of $10 per night per pet. Multiple dogs may be allowed.

Motel 6 - Monroe
1501 Martin L King Drive

Monroe, LA
318-322-5430 (800-466-8356)
One well-behaved family pet per room. Guest must notify front desk upon arrival. Guest is liable for any damages. In consideration of all guests, pets must never be left unattended in the guest rooms.

Days Inn Morgan City
7408 Hwy 182 East
Morgan City, LA
985-384-5750 (800-329-7466)
Dogs of all sizes are allowed. There is a $25 one time per pet fee per visit. 2 dogs may be allowed.

Holiday Inn
520 Roderick Street
Morgan City, LA
985-385-2200 (877-270-6405)
Dogs of all sizes are allowed for an additional one time pet fee of $50 per room. 2 dogs may be allowed.

Super 8 Natchitoches
5821 Hwy 1 Bypass
Natchitoches, LA
318-352-1700 (800-800-8000)
Dogs of all sizes are allowed. There is a $10 per night pet fee per pet in smoking rooms. There is a $25 per night pet fee per pet in non-smoking rooms. 2 dogs may be allowed.

Holiday Inn
2915 Highway 14
New Iberia, LA
337-367-1201 (877-270-6405)
Dogs up to 50 pounds are allowed for an additional one time pet fee of $25 per room. 2 dogs may be allowed.

Best Western Patio Downtown Motel
2820 Tulane Avenue
New Orleans, LA
504-822-0200 (800-780-7234)
Centrally located, The Best Western Patio is located just minutes from destinations such as The French Quarter, Harrah's Casino, The Riverwalk and the historic Garden District. There is a $35.00 pet fee per stay.

Best Western St. Christopher Hotel
114 Magazine Street
New Orleans, LA
504-648-0444 (800-780-7234)
Dogs up to 50 pounds are allowed for an additional one time fee of $50 per pet. Multiple dogs may be allowed.

Chimes Bed and Breakfast

Constantinople St & Coliseum St
New Orleans, LA
504-899-2621 (800-729-4640)
Dogs that stay here need to like children and cats. Please clean up after your pet. Pets are not to be left alone in the room.

Clarion Collection Garden District Hotel
2203 St Charles Avenue
New Orleans, LA
504-566-1200 (877-424-6423)
Dogs of all sizes are allowed. There is a $50 one time additional fee per pet. Multiple dogs may be allowed.

Drury Inn & Suites
820 Poydras Street
New Orleans, LA
504-529-7800 (800-378-7946)
Dogs of all sizes are permitted. Pets are not allowed in the breakfast area of the hotel. Pets are not to be left unattended, and each guest must assume liability for damage of property or other guest complaints. There is a limit of one pet per room.

French Quarter Courtyard
1101 N Rampart
New Orleans, LA
504-522-7333 (800-290-4233)
neworleans.com/fqch/main.html
There is a $25 one time pet fee.

Holiday Inn
124 Royal Street
New Orleans, LA
504-529-7211 (877-270-6405)
Dogs of all sizes are allowed for an additional one time fee of $75 per pet plus a $75 refundable deposit. 2 dogs may be allowed.

La Quinta Inn New Orleans Bullard
12001 I-10 Service Rd.
New Orleans, LA
504-246-3003 (800-531-5900)
Dogs of all sizes are allowed. There are no additional pet fees. Dogs must be leashed and cleaned up after. Dogs must be crated if left alone in the room, and they may not be left for long periods. Multiple dogs may be allowed.

La Quinta Inn New Orleans Crowder
8400 I-10 Service Rd.
New Orleans, LA
504-246-5800 (800-531-5900)

Lions Inn
2517 Chartres Street
New Orleans, LA
504-945-2339
Well behaved dogs of most sizes are

allowed; they can't accept extra large dogs. There is an additional $10 per stay. Multiple dogs may be allowed.

Loews Hotel
300 Poydras Street
New Orleans, LA
504-595-3300
Dogs of all sizes are allowed. There are no additional pet fees. Multiple dogs may be allowed.

Motel 6 - New Orleans
12330 I-10 Service Road
New Orleans, LA
504-240-2862 (800-466-8356)
One well-behaved family pet per room. Guest must notify front desk upon arrival. Guest is liable for any damages. In consideration of all guests, pets must never be left unattended in the guest rooms.

Pontchartrain Hotel
2031 St. Charles Avenue
New Orleans, LA
504-524-0581
pontchartrainhotel.com
Located in the historic Garden District of New Orleans, The Pontchartrain Hotel has been open to guests since the 1920's. There are 118 rooms and suites, each individually designed. There is a $50 non-refundable pet fee, $10 each additional pet over 2 pets.

Residence Inn by Marriott
345 St. Joseph
New Orleans, LA
504-522-1300
Dogs of all sizes are allowed. There is a $75 one time fee and a pet policy to sign at check in. Multiple dogs may be allowed.

Sheraton New Orleans Hotel
500 Canal St.
New Orleans, LA
504-525-2500 (888-625-5144)
Dogs up to 80 pounds are allowed. There are no additional pet fees. Dogs are not allowed to be left alone in the room.

Studio 6 - New Orleans
12330 I-10 Service Road
New Orleans, LA
504-240-9778 (800-466-8356)
One well-behaved family pet per room. Guest must notify front desk upon arrival. Guest is liable for any damages. In consideration of all guests, pets must never be left unattended in the guest rooms.

Windsor Court Hotel

300 Gravier Street
New Orleans, LA
504-523-6000 (800-403-4945)
Dogs up to 100 pounds are allowed. There is a $150 one time fee per pet and a pet policy to sign at check in. 2 dogs may be allowed.

Best Western of Opelousas
5791 I-49 S Service Road
Opelousas, LA
337-942-6250 (800-780-7234)
One dog is allowed for an additional pet fee of $10 per night.

Motel 6 - Baton Rouge - Port Allen
2800 I-10 Frontage Road
Port Allen, LA
225-343-5945 (800-466-8356)
One well-behaved family pet per room. Guest must notify front desk upon arrival. Guest is liable for any damages. In consideration of all guests, pets must never be left unattended in the guest rooms.

Super 8 Port Allen/W Baton Rouge Area
821 Lobdell Hwy
Port Allen, LA
225-381-9134 (800-800-8000)
Dogs of all sizes are allowed. There is a $20 one time pet fee per visit. Smoking and non-smoking rooms are available for pet rooms. 2 dogs may be allowed.

Holiday Inn Express Shreveport-Airport
5105 Westwood Park Drive
Shreveport, LA
318-631-2000 (877-270-6405)
Dogs of all sizes are allowed for an additional one time pet fee of $50 per room. Multiple dogs may be allowed.

La Quinta Inn & Suites Shreveport Airport
6700 Financial Circle
Shreveport, LA
318-671-1100 (800-531-5900)
Dogs up to 100 pounds are allowed. There are no additional pet fees. Dogs must be leashed, cleaned up after, and a contact number must be left with the front desk if there is a pet in the room alone. Multiple dogs may be allowed.

Red Roof Inn - Shreveport
7296 Greenwood Road
Shreveport, LA
318-938-5342 (800-RED-ROOF)
One well-behaved family pet per room. Guest must notify front desk upon arrival. Guest is liable for any

damages. In consideration of all guests, pets must never be left unattended in the guest rooms.

Motel 6 - New Orleans - Slidell
136 Taos Street
Slidell, LA
985-649-7925 (800-466-8356)
One well-behaved family pet per room. Guest must notify front desk upon arrival. Guest is liable for any damages. In consideration of all guests, pets must never be left unattended in the guest rooms.

Days Inn Sulphur
2654 Hwy 108
Sulphur, LA
337-312-0108 (800-329-7466)
Dogs of all sizes are allowed. There is a $10 per night pet fee per pet. 2 dogs may be allowed.

La Quinta Inn Sulphur
2600 South Ruth
Sulphur, LA
337-527-8303 (800-531-5900)
Dogs of all sizes are allowed. There are no additional pet fees. Dogs must be quiet, leashed, and cleaned up after. Multiple dogs may be allowed.

Holiday Inn Express Hotel and Suites
603 Constitution Drive
West Monroe, LA
318-807-6000 (877-270-6405)
Quiet dogs of all sizes are allowed for an additional one time pet fee of $25 per room. Multiple dogs may be allowed.

Quality Inn and Suites
503 Constitution Drive
West Monroe, LA
318-387-2711 (877-424-6423)
Dogs are allowed for an additional one time pet fee of $25 per room. Multiple dogs may be allowed.

Red Roof Inn - West Monroe
102 Constitution Drive
West Monroe, LA
318-388-2420 (800-RED-ROOF)
One well-behaved family pet per room. Guest must notify front desk upon arrival. Guest is liable for any damages. In consideration of all guests, pets must never be left unattended in the guest rooms.

Best Western Winnfield
700 West Court St
Winnfield, LA
318-628-3993 (800-780-7234)
Dogs are allowed for an additional fee of $10 per night per pet. 2 dogs

may be allowed.

Maine Listings

Oceanside Meadows Inn
Prospect Harbor Road
Acadia Schoodic, ME
207-963-5557
oceaninn.com/
In addition to being a working inn since 1860, it is also a 200 acre preserve of numerous, carefully maintained habitats and eco-systems, and home to the Oceanside Meadows Institute for the Arts and Sciences' located in a restored barn between the inn's two guest buildings where they have a variety of events, classes, and musical performances. There are also gardens, a private beach, hiking trails, and many local recreational pursuits. Dogs of all sizes are allowed for an additional fee of $8 per night per pet. There is only one party with a pet allowed at a time in each of the two buildings. Dogs may not be left unattended at any time, and they must be very well behaved, leashed, and cleaned up after. 2 dogs may be allowed.

Arundel Meadows Inn
1024 Portland Road
Arundel, ME
207-985-3770
arundelmeadowsinn.com
From the months of April through December, this 1800's farm house (renovated in the 1990's) offers it's ambiance to guests and their four-legged companions. Dogs of all sizes are welcome for no additional pet fee, unless extra cleaning is required. Dogs must be well behaved, leashed, and cleaned up after. 2 dogs may be allowed.

Augusta Hotel and Suites
390 Western Avenue
Augusta, ME
207-622-6371
There are no pet fees unless you stay more than one week. Then there is a $20 one time pet fee.

Best Western Senator Inn and Spa
284 Western Ave @Turnpike 95
Augusta, ME
207-622-5804 (800-780-7234)
Dogs are allowed for an additional fee of $9 per night per pet. Multiple dogs may be allowed.

Comfort Inn Civic Center

281 Civic Center Drive
Augusta, ME
207-623-1000 (877-424-6423)
Dogs are allowed for no additional pet fee, but a credit card must be on file. Multiple dogs may be allowed.

Holiday Inn
110 Community Drive
Augusta, ME
207-622-4751 (877-270-6405)
Dogs of all sizes are allowed for no additional fee, and they may not be left alone in the room. Multiple dogs may be allowed.

Motel 6 - AUGUSTA
18 Edison Drive
Augusta, ME
207-622-0000 (800-466-8356)
One well-behaved family pet per room. Guest must notify front desk upon arrival. Guest is liable for any damages. In consideration of all guests, pets must never be left unattended in the guest rooms.

Best Western White House Inn
155 Littlefield Ave
Bangor, ME
207-862-3737 (800-780-7234)
Dogs are allowed for no additional pet fee with a credit card on file. Multiple dogs may be allowed.

Comfort Inn
750 Hogan Road
Bangor, ME
207-942-7899 (877-424-6423)
Dogs are allowed for an additional one time pet fee of $10 per room. Multiple dogs may be allowed.

Days Inn Bangor Airport
250 Odlin Rd
Bangor, ME
207-942-8272 (800-329-7466)
Dogs of all sizes are allowed. There is a $6 per night pet fee per pet. 2 dogs may be allowed.

Motel 6 - Bangor
1100 Hammond Street
Bangor, ME
207-947-6921 (800-466-8356)
One well-behaved family pet per room. Guest must notify front desk upon arrival. Guest is liable for any damages. In consideration of all guests, pets must never be left unattended in the guest rooms.

The Phenix Inn
20 Broad Street
Bangor, ME
207-947-0411

maineguide.com/bangor/phenixinn/
Pets are welcome in the first floor rooms. They have two non-smoking pet rooms. There is a $5 per day additional pet fee.

Acadia Acres
205 Knox Road
Bar Harbor, ME
207-288-5055
acadiaacres.net/
There are now 2 pet friendly, fully equipped homes available here; the Knox House in Bar Harbor that offers its own 150+ yard golf practice area, with 6 acres of open fields for your pup to run, and the Jordan Point House on 23 acres in Lamoine that overlooks the Bar Harbor Golf Course and the water. This house also has a 20' x 50' foot fenced shaded yard with a doggy door so pups can be comfortable inside or out if the owners are away. Dogs of all sizes are allowed for an additional fee of $25 per dog. Dogs must be house trained, well behaved, and cleaned up after inside and out. The phone listed is the daytime number; for calls after 4 pm (to 9 pm) EST the number is 207-288-4065. 2 dogs may be allowed.

Balance Rock Inn
21 Albert Meadow
Bar Harbor, ME
207-288-2610 (800-753-0494)
The oceanfront inn is within walking distance of many restaurants and shops in downtown Bar Harbor. Choose from fourteen individually decorated rooms at the inn, many of which offer an ocean view and private balcony. They also offer a heated outdoor pool and fitness room. Room rates for this inn average $200 to $300 per night but can start at $95 and go up to almost $600 per night. There is also a $30 per day pet fee.

Days Inn Frenchman's Bay
120 Eden St
Bar Harbor, ME
207-288-3321 (800-329-7466)
Dogs of all sizes are allowed. There are no additional pet fees. 2 dogs may be allowed.

Gale's Gardens Guesthouses
Daylily Lane
Bar Harbor, ME
207-733-8811
galesgardensguesthouse.com
There are two vacation rentals available that can be rented separately or together. The dog-friendly properties are located one

mile from the Acadia National Park Entrance and four miles to the center of Bar Harbor.

Hanscom's Motel and Cottages
273 H 3
Bar Harbor, ME
207-288-3744
hanscomsmotel.com/
This vintage motor court is only a 5 minute walk to a private rocky beach, sits among giant oaks, white pines, and landscaped grounds/gardens, has shady picnic areas with barbecues, and an outdoor heated pool with a roomy sundeck. Dogs of all sizes are allowed for an additional fee of $8 per night per pet. Dogs may be left alone only for short periods and only if they will be quiet and well behaved. Dogs must be leashed and cleaned up after at all times. 2 dogs may be allowed.

Hutchins Mountain View Cottages
286 H 3
Bar Harbor, ME
207-288-4833 (800-775-4833)
hutchinscottages.com/
Trees and grazing fields grace this 20 acre country retreat that is only a mile from the Acadia National Park's visitor center. Dogs of all sizes are welcome for no additional pet fee. Dogs must be quiet, well behaved, leashed, and cleaned up after in common areas. 2 dogs may be allowed.

Rose Eden Cottages
864 State Highway 3
Bar Harbor, ME
207-288-3038
roseeden.com
This small cottage complex offers ten non-smoking cottages and some of them have kitchenettes. They are located just 4 miles to the entrance of Acadia National Park and about 10 minutes from downtown Bar Harbor. Harbor Point Beach, which allows leashed dogs, is located within walking distance. Room rates range from about $40 to $80 per night depending on the season and size of the cottage. One dog is allowed per cottage and there is a $10 per day pet charge.

Summertime Cottages
1 Bloomfield Road
Bar Harbor, ME
207-288-2893
summertimebarharbor.com/
Secluded by giant pine tress and about a block from the ocean, these vacation rentals offer a great starting point for several activities and

recreation; 150 miles of hiking trails, 56 miles of carriage roads, and proximity to the tallest summit on the Eastern seaboard where the US gets its first light of sun each day. Dogs of all sizes are welcome for no additional fee; Rottweilers and Pit Bulls are not allowed. Dogs must be well mannered, leashed, and cleaned up after. Multiple dogs may be allowed.

The Ledgelawn Inn
66 Mount Desert Street
Bar Harbor, ME
207-288-4596 (800-274-5334)
This bed and breakfast inn has a $25 per night pet charge. The B&B is totally non-smoking and there are 8 pet rooms, each with separate entrances.

Town and Country Cottage
230 H 3
Bar Harbor, ME
207-288-3439
townandcountrycottage.com/
Although only minutes from several other attractions and activities, this nicely appointed cottage features a large furnished deck with a barbecue grill, and a sizable lawn with a woodland meadow beyond. Dogs of all sizes are welcome for no additional pet fee. Dogs must be quiet, leashed, cleaned up after, and crated when left alone in the room. Dogs may only be left alone in the room for a short time and then only if they will be well behaved. 2 dogs may be allowed.

Fairhaven Inn
118 North Bath Rd.
Bath, ME
207-443-4391 (888-443-4391)
mainecoast.com/fairhaveninn
This B&B with 8 guest rooms overlooks the Kennebec River. Your dog is welcome to join you for your vacation here.

The Inn at Bath
969 Washington Street
Bath, ME
207-443-4294 (800-423-0964)
innatbath.com/
This well appointed 1800's Greek revival home sits among the trees within easy walking distance to town, and they are also close to two ocean beaches and numerous recreational opportunities. Dogs of all sizes are allowed for an additional fee of $15 per night per pet. Dogs must be quiet, leashed, and cleaned up after. Dogs may not be left alone in the room at any

time. 2 dogs may be allowed.

Comfort Inn Ocean's Edge
159 Searsport Avenue/H 1
Belfast, ME
207-338-2090 (877-424-6423)
Dogs are allowed for an additional pet fee of $10 per night per room, and they must be declared at the time of reservations. 2 dogs may be allowed.

Day Lily Cottage
Call to Arrange
Belfast, ME
207-342-5444
landworkswaterfront.com
This vacation rental is a newly remodeled 1920 stone bungalow nestled in lovely country gardens. The cottage sits 20 feet from stairs leading to the beach. There are three bedrooms, two baths and can sleep 6. Pets welcome with $125.00 non-refundable one time fee. No Smoking. Can be rented with Tranquility Cottage next door to sleep 12.

Bethel Inn and Country Club
7 Broad Street
Bethel, ME
207-824-2175
bethelinn.com
This country resort allows dogs in some of their rooms. Pets are welcome in some of guest buildings and luxury townhouses, but not in the Chapman Building or the main inn. All well-behaved dogs of any size are allowed in non-smoking rooms and there is a one to two dogs per room limit. There is a $10 per day pet fee. During the winter, dogs are also allowed on a special 2km cross-country skijoring trail.

Sudbury Inn
151 Main Street
Bethel, ME
207-824-2174
Dogs of all sizes are allowed. There are no additional pet fees. Multiple dogs may be allowed.

The Inn at the Rostay
186 Mayville Road
Bethel, ME
888-754-0072
Dogs of all sizes are allowed. There is a $10 one time fee per room for small pets and a $10 per pet fee for large pets. They are not allowed on the beds and dogs are not allowed to be left alone in the room. There is a pet policy to sign at check in. 2 dogs may be allowed.

Calais Motor Inn
293 Main Street
Calais, ME
207-454-7111
There is a $10 per day pet charge.

International Motel
276 Main Street
Calais, ME
207-454-7515
Dogs are allowed in the older building only and not in the motel office. There are no additional pet fees.

Blue Harbor House
67 Elm Street
Camden, ME
207-236-3196 (800-248-3196)
blueharborhouse.com/
Dogs are allowed in one of the suites in the Carriage House at this Village Inn. There are no additional pet fees.

Camden Harbour Inn
83 Bayview Street
Camden, ME
207-236-4200 (800-236-4266)
4chi.com/
The Camden Harbour Inn, built in 1874, overlooks the historic and picturesque Camden harbor. Be sure to ask for their "Pooch Package" which includes dog cookies upon arrival, pet bowls for food and water, cushioned dog bed or bedspread cover, a basket of treats and towels for muddy paws. Thanks to one of our readers who writes "Great hotel and home to a beautiful elderly yellow labrador named Bo. Great lobster restaurant at the marina which on our visit had 7 dogs with owners... beautiful place." There is a $20 one time pet fee.

Camden Riverhouse Hotel & Inns
11 Tannery Lane
Camden, ME
207-236-0500 (800-755-7483)
camdenmaine.com
This downtown hotel allows your dog of any size for $15 per night additional pet fee. Dogs may not be left unattended in the room.

Fisherman's Cottage
113 Bayview Street
Camden, ME
207-342-5444
landworkswaterfront.com
100-year-old fisherman cottage in a deluxe neighborhood. Ocean view from the master bedroom, living room, and kitchen. An easy walk to Camden, easy access to beach and beautiful walking and biking roads. Stone terrace across front of house for ocean harbor viewing. Available year-round. Three bedrooms, two baths, linens provided, telephone, television, cable, VCR, washer/dryer, ocean view. Sleeps six. Pets welcome with non-refundable deposit of $125.00. No Smoking. $1,800 per week.

Lord Camden Inn
24 Main Street
Camden, ME
207-236-4325 (800-336-4325)
lordcamdeninn.com
The Lord Camden Inn is located in the heart of downtown Camden. Many rooms boast ocean views, full balconies and kitchenettes. Dogs are welcome and pampered at the Lord Camden Inn with doggy biscuits and a list of activities and day care options awaiting your arrival in your room. Two well-behaved dogs are allowed per room (no size restrictions), and dogs are not to be left unattended. There is an additional $20 per pet per night fee. The hotel is open year round.

Inn By The Sea
40 Bowery Beach Road
Cape Elizabeth, ME
207-799-3134 (800-888-4287)
innbythesea.com/
Thanks to one of our readers for these comments: "This hotel is an amazing place for dog lovers. It's a four star hotel that treats your puppy like any other hotel guest. There are two suites (bedroom, kitchen, living room) that are specifically appointed for dogs. Water dishes, biscuits, towels for paws, and outside hoses are provided. There are four nearby state parks and the hotel itself borders a feral area which my dog spent hours on end exploring. There's even a fenced-in kennel area, complete with a dog house, if you want to leave your pet for an hour and go for dinner. Wonderful place, they love dogs, great recreation, beautiful rooms, great hotel restaurant - truly a superb experience." This hotel also offers dog walking service with 24-hour notification. They even have a special pet menu with items like gourmet chuck burgers, grilled range chicken, NY sirloin strip steak with potatoes and vegetables, and for dessert, vanilla ice cream or doggie bon bons. If you are there during Thanksgiving, Christmas or the Fourth of July, they offer a special pet holiday menu. The hotel asks that all pets be kept on a leash when not in their suite and that pets are not left alone in the suite. When making a reservation, they do require that you tell them you are bringing your pet. There are no pet fees. All rooms are non-smoking. Multiple dogs may be allowed.

Castine Harbor Lodge
147 Perkins Street
Castine, ME
207-326-4335
castinemaine.com/
This 1893 waterfront hotel features 250 feet of ocean-facing porches overlooking the bay, clay tennis courts, one of the country's oldest 9-hole golf courses, a steak and seafood restaurant and bar, and access to several historic walking trails. Dogs of all sizes are allowed for an additional fee of $10 per night per pet. Dogs may not be left alone in the room at any time, and they must be very well behaved, always kept leashed, and cleaned up after. 2 dogs may be allowed.

The Pilgrim's Inn
20 Main Street
Deer Isle, ME
207-348-6615 (888-778-7505)
pilgrimsinn.com/
This 1793 restored historic inn overlooks the picturesque Northwest Harbor, features a tavern restaurant, a large mill pond, and offers 3 cottages that are pet friendly. Dogs of all sizes are welcome, but there can only be 1 large or 2 small to medium dogs per room. Dogs may only be left alone in the room while dining on the property, and they must be leashed and cleaned up after at all times.

Milliken House
29 Washington Street
Eastport, ME
207-853-2955
Well behaved dogs of all sizes are allowed. There are no additional pet fees. Multiple dogs may be allowed.

Sheepscot River Inn
306 Eddy Road
Edgecomb, ME
207-882-6343
Dogs of all sizes are allowed. There is a $10 per night per room fee and a pet policy to sign at check in. Multiple dogs may be allowed.

Holiday Inn
215 High Street
Ellsworth, ME

207-667-9341 (877-270-6405)
Dogs of all sizes are allowed for an additional pet fee of $20 per night for 1 pet; $30 per night for 2 pets, and $40 per night for 3 dogs. Multiple dogs may be allowed.

Best Western Freeport Inn
31 US Rt 1
Freeport, ME
207-865-3106 (800-780-7234)
Dogs are allowed for no additional pet fee. Multiple dogs may be allowed.

Harraseeket Inn
162 Main Street
Freeport, ME
207-865-9377 (800-342-6423)
harraseeketinn.com/
Whether it's for the perfect vacation package, a shopping adventure (over 170 shops only 2 blocks away), or a romantic getaway, this inn also offers amenities like a live Jazz brunch on Sundays, award winning dining, and an indoor pool. Dogs of all sizes are allowed for an additional fee of $25 per night per pet, and advance notification is required. For their canine guests they place a doggy bed, a small can of dog food, water and food dishes, 4 small clean-up duty bags, and a small treat in the room. Dogs must be kept leashed when out of the room and they must be cleaned up after at all times. Dogs are not to be left alone in the room for more than 2 hours and only then if they will be quiet and well mannered. Dogs must be removed for housekeeping, and they are not allowed in the main building. 2 dogs may be allowed.

The Main Idyll Motor Court
1411 H 1
Freeport, ME
207-865-4201
maineidyll.com/
This motor court features 20 cottages set among a grove of trees with play and barbecue/picnic areas, hiking trails, and they also provide a doggie comfort station. Dogs of all sizes are allowed for an additional $4 per night per pet. Dogs must be leased and cleaned up after. They may only be left for a short time alone in the room, and then only if they will be quiet and well behaved. 2 dogs may be allowed.

The Crocker House
967 Point Road
Hancock, ME
207-422-6808 (877-715-6017)
crockerhouse.com/

Built in 1884 (restored 1986), this seasonally operating inn sits only 300 feet from the water, offers 11 uniquely differing rooms, a restaurant and full bar, and they are within easy walking distance to several activities and attractions. Dogs of all sizes are welcome for no additional pet fee. Dogs must be under owner's control at all times and be cleaned up after.

Crocker House Country Inn
967 Point Road
Hancock Point, ME
207-422-6806
Dogs of all sizes are allowed. There are no additional pet fees. 2 dogs may be allowed.

Captain Jefferds Inn
5 Pearl Street
Kennebunkport, ME
207-967-2311 (800-839-6844)
captainjefferdsinn.com/
This historic inn has a $20 per day pet charge. They ask that you please never leave your dog alone in the room.

Lodge At Turbat's Creek
Turbats Creek Rd at Ocean Avenue
Kennebunkport, ME
207-967-8700
There are no additional pet fees.

The Colony Hotel
140 Ocean Avenue
Kennebunkport, ME
207-967-3331
Dogs of all sizes are allowed. There is a $25 per night per pet additional fee. Multiple dogs may be allowed.

The Yachtsman Lodge and Marina
Ocean Avenue
Kennebunkport, ME
207-967-2511
yachtsmanlodge.com/
Sitting right on the waterfront with all the rooms having its own patio overlooking the river, has inspired the redesign of the rooms to reflect those of a luxury yacht. This seasonal inn also provides a great starting point to several local attractions. Dogs of all sizes are allowed for an additional fee of $25 per night per pet, and they must be declared at the time of registration as pet friendly rooms are limited. Dogs may be left alone only for short periods and only if they will be quiet, well behaved, and a contact number is left with the front desk. Dogs must be leashed and cleaned up after at all times. 2 dogs may be allowed.

Enchanted Nights
29 Wentworth Street
Kittery, ME
207-439-1489
Dogs of all sizes are allowed. There are no additional pet fees. Dogs are not allowed to be left unattended. Multiple dogs may be allowed.

Motel 6 - Lewiston
516 Pleasant Street
Lewiston, ME
207-782-6558 (800-466-8356)
One well-behaved family pet per room. Guest must notify front desk upon arrival. Guest is liable for any damages. In consideration of all guests, pets must never be left unattended in the guest rooms.

Pine Grove Cottages
2076 Atlantic H
Lincolnville, ME
207-236-2929 (800-530-5265)
pinegrovemaine.com/
Offering 9 well-equipped cottages on 3 pine treed acres, all with private decks and barbecues, this seasonal retreat is also close to several other attractions, eateries, shops, and recreation. Dogs of all sizes are welcome for no additional pet fee. Dogs may be left alone only for short periods and only if they will be quiet, well behaved, and crated. Please keep dogs off the furniture, and they must be leashed and cleaned up after at all times. They also invite your pooch in when you register for some water and a cookie, and if ok with the pet owner they would like to take a photo of the pet to go with all the other doggy guest photos. 2 dogs may be allowed.

Gateway Inn
Route 157
Medway, ME
207-746-3193
Dogs of all sizes are allowed. There are no additional pet fees. Multiple dogs may be allowed.

Best Western Black Bear Inn and Conf Cntr
4 Godfrey Dr
Orono, ME
207-866-7120 (800-780-7234)
Quiet dogs are allowed for an additional fee of $3 per night per pet. Multiple dogs may be allowed.

Embassy Suites Hotel Portland
1050 Westbrook Street
Portland, ME
207-775-2200

Dogs of all sizes are allowed. There are no additional pet fees. Dogs are not allowed to be left alone in the room. Multiple dogs may be allowed.

Holiday Inn
81 Riverside St
Portland, ME
207-774-5601 (877-270-6405)
Dogs of all sizes are allowed for an additional one time pet fee of $35 per room. 2 dogs may be allowed.

Howard Johnson Plaza Hotel
155 Riverside
Portland, ME
207-774-5861 (800-446-4656)
Dogs of all sizes are welcome. There is a $50 refundable pet deposit.

Motel 6 - Portland
One Riverside Street
Portland, ME
207-775-0111 (800-466-8356)
One well-behaved family pet per room. Guest must notify front desk upon arrival. Guest is liable for any damages. In consideration of all guests, pets must never be left unattended in the guest rooms.

The Inn at St John
939 Congress Street
Portland, ME
207-773-6481 (800-636-9127)
innatstjohn.com/index.php
This 1897 inn, originally built to accommodate train travelers, now offers free pick up for plane, train, or bus travelers, and it has been fully restored in European style with 3 levels of lodging offered. Dogs of all sizes are allowed for an additional fee of $10 per night per pet. Dogs may not be left alone in the room at any time, and they have a list of pet sitters if the need arises. Dogs must be well mannered, leashed, and cleaned up after. 2 dogs may be allowed.

Old Granite Inn
546 Main Street
Rockland, ME
207-594-9036
Well behaved pets of all sizes are allowed. There are no additional pet fees. Dogs are not allowed to be left alone in the room, and they must be very good around cats. 2 dogs may be allowed.

Linnel Motel
986 Prospect Avenue
Rumford, ME
207-364-4511 (800-446-9038)
Dogs of all sizes are allowed. There

is a $5 per night per room additional pet fee and dogs may not be left unattended. Leash at all times when on the grounds. Multiple dogs may be allowed.

Hampton Inn
48 Industrial Park Road
Saco, ME
207-282- 7222
Dogs of all sizes are allowed. There are no additional pet fees, and there is a pet policy to sign at check in. Pet rooms are on the 3rd floor and dogs are not allowed in any of the food areas. Multiple dogs may be allowed.

Super 8 Sanford/Kennebunkport Area
1892 Main St
Sanford, ME
207-324-8823 (800-800-8000)
Dogs of all sizes are allowed. There is a $15 per night pet fee per pet. Smoking and non-smoking rooms are available for pet rooms. 2 dogs may be allowed.

Residence Inn by Marriott
800 Roundwood Drive
Scarborough, ME
207-883-0400
Dogs of all sizes are allowed. There is a $75 one time fee and a pet policy to sign at check in. Multiple dogs may be allowed.

TownePlace Suites Portland Scarborough
700 Roundwood Drive
Scarborough, ME
207-883-6800
Dogs of all sizes are allowed. There is a $75 one time pet fee per visit. 2 dogs may be allowed.

Best Western Merry Manor Inn
700 Main St
South Portland, ME
207-774-6151 (800-780-7234)
Dogs are allowed for no additional pet fee. Multiple dogs may be allowed.

Comfort Inn Airport
90 Maine Mall Road
South Portland, ME
207-775-0409 (877-424-6423)
Dogs are allowed for an additional one time pet fee of $25 per room. Multiple dogs may be allowed.

Holiday Inn Express Hotel & Suites
South Portland
303 Sable Oaks Drive
South Portland, ME

207-775-3900 (877-270-6405)
Dogs of all sizes are allowed for an additional one time fee of $20 per pet. Multiple dogs may be allowed.

Howard Johnson Hotel
675 Main St.
South Portland, ME
207-775-5343 (800-446-4656)
Dogs of all sizes are welcome. There are no additional pet fees.

Portland Marriott at Sable Oaks
200 Sable Oaks Drive
South Portland, ME
207-871-8000 (800-228-9290)
Dogs of all sizes are allowed. There is a $35 one time fee per pet. Dogs must be leashed, cleaned up after, crated or removed for housekeeping, and the Do Not Disturb sign is put on the door if they are in the room alone. Multiple dogs may be allowed.

Sheraton South Portland Hotel
363 Maines Mall Rd.
South Portland, ME
207-775-6161 (888-625-5144)
Dogs up to 80 pounds are allowed. There are no additional pet fees. Dogs are not allowed to be left alone in the room.

The Willard Beach House
14 Myrtle Avenue
South Portland, ME
207-799-9824
vacationinmaine.net/
Both of their pet friendly rentals, the Willard Beach House condo and the Carriage House with its private back yard, offer views of the ocean and Willard Beach, which has an oceanside walkway connecting a lighthouse and a fort. Dogs of all sizes are welcome for no additional pet fee. Dogs must be leashed and cleaned up after. 2 dogs may be allowed.

Flander's Bay Cabins
22 Harbor View Drive
Sullivan, ME
207-422-6408
Dogs of all sizes are allowed. There is a $35 one time fee if the dogs are under 30 pounds and there is a $35 per pet fee if they are over the 30 pounds. Dogs are not allowed to be left alone in the cabins. Multiple dogs may be allowed.

Harbor Watch Motel
Swans Island, ME
207-526-4563
To get to this motel on Swans Island,

take the ferry from Bass Harbor in Southwest Harbor to Swans Island. Leashed dogs and cars are allowed on the Maine State Ferries. Dogs are allowed for an additional $10 per day pet fee. Rooms rates range from about $60 to $80 per night.

The East Wind Inn
21 Mechanic Street
Tenants Harbor, ME
207-372-6366 (800-241-VIEW (8439))
eastwindinn.com/
This seasonal Historic Inn sits at the water's edge and has 23 spacious guest rooms, a wrap-around porch for watching all the harbor activity, and a central location to numerous other activities and recreation. One dog of any size is allowed for an additional fee of $15 per night. Dogs may not be left alone in the room at any time, and they must be leashed and cleaned up after.

Holiday Inn
375 Main Street
Waterville, ME
207-873-0111 (877-270-6405)
Dogs of all sizes are allowed for no additional fee, and they may not be left alone in the room. Multiple dogs may be allowed.

Maryland Listings

Four Points Hotels by Sheraton
980 Hospitality Way
Aberdeen, MD
410-273-6300 (888-625-5144)
fourpointsaberdeen.com/
There are no additional pet fees.

Red Roof Inn - Aberdeen
988 Hospitality Way
Aberdeen, MD
410-273-7800 (800-RED-ROOF)
One well-behaved family pet per room. Guest must notify front desk upon arrival. Guest is liable for any damages. In consideration of all guests, pets must never be left unattended in the guest rooms.

Homestead Hotel
120 Admiral Chochrane Drive
Annapolis, MD
410-571-6600
This extended stay hotel suggests one pet is allowed per room; however they may allow additional pets. There is an additional pet fee of $25 per day to a maximum of $75.

Dogs must be quiet, well mannered, leashed, and cleaned up after at all times.

Loews Annapolis Hotel
126 West Street
Annapolis, MD
410-263-7777
All well-behaved dogs of any size are welcome. This upscale hotel offers their "Loews Loves Pets" program which includes special pet treats, local dog walking routes, and a list of nearby pet-friendly places to visit. There are no pet fees.

Sheraton Annapolis Hotel
173 Jennifer Rd.
Annapolis, MD
410-266-3131 (888-625-5144)
Dogs up to 80 pounds are allowed. There are no additional pet fees. Dogs are not allowed to be left alone in the room.

TownePlace Suites Baltimore Fort Meade
120 National Business Pkwy
Annapolis Junction, MD
301-498-7477
Dogs of all sizes are allowed. There is a $75 one time pet fee per visit. . 2 dogs may be allowed.

Brookshire Suites
120 E. Lombard Street
Baltimore, MD
410-625-1300
All well-behaved dogs are welcome at this suites hotel. There are no pet fees.

Four Points by Sheraton BWI Airport
7032 Elm Rd.
Baltimore, MD
410-859-3300 (888-625-5144)
Dogs of all sizes are allowed. There is a $25 per night pet fee per pet. Dogs are not allowed to be left alone in the room.

Motel 6 - Baltimore West
1654 Whitehead Court
Baltimore, MD
410-265-7660 (800-466-8356)
One well-behaved family pet per room. Guest must notify front desk upon arrival. Guest is liable for any damages. In consideration of all guests, pets must never be left unattended in the guest rooms.

Pier 5 Hotel
711 Eastern Avenue
Baltimore, MD
410-539-2000

The entire hotel offers a smoke free environment. All well-behaved dogs are welcome and there are no pet fees.

Residence Inn by Marriott
4980 Mercantile Road
Baltimore, MD
410-933-9554
Dogs of all sizes are allowed. There is a $75 one time fee and a pet policy to sign at check in. Multiple dogs may be allowed.

Residence Inn by Marriott
7335 Wisconsin Avenue
Baltimore, MD
301-718-0200
Dogs of all sizes are allowed. There is a $200 non-refundable cleaning fee plus $10 per night per pet and a pet policy to sign at check in. Multiple dogs may be allowed.

Sheraton Baltimore City Center Hotel (formally Wyndham)
101 W Fayette Street
Baltimore, MD
410-752-1100 (888-625-5144)
Dogs up to 80 pounds are allowed for no additional fee. There is a pet waiver to sign at check in. Dogs must be well mannered, leashed or crated, and cleaned up after. Multiple dogs may be allowed.

Sheraton Baltimore North Hotel
903 Dulaney Valley Blvd.
Baltimore, MD
410-321-7400 (888-625-5144)
Dogs of all sizes are allowed. There are no additional pet fees. Dogs are not allowed to be left alone in the room.

Sheraton Inner Harbor Hotel
300 South Charles St.
Baltimore, MD
410-962-8300 (888-625-5144)
Dogs up to 50 pounds are allowed. There are no additional pet fees. Dogs are not allowed to be left alone in the room.

The Admiral Fell Inn
888 South Broadway
Baltimore, MD
410-522-7377
All well-behaved dogs are welcome and there no pet fees.

Tremont Park Hotel
8 East Pleasant Street
Baltimore, MD
410-576-1200 (800-TREMONT)
Dogs may stay in four of the one bedroom suites in this hotel. They'll

provide bowls for food and water, a treat and a Pampered Pet Placement. There is a $10 pet service fee that will be donated to the American Humane Society if there is no damage.

Sheraton College Park Hotel
4095 Powder Mill Rd.
Beltsville, MD
301-937-4422 (888-625-5144)
Dogs of all sizes are allowed. There are no additional pet fees. Dogs are not allowed to be left alone in the room.

TownePlace Suites Bowie Town Center
3700 Town Center Blvd
Bowie, MD
301-292-8045
Dogs of all sizes are allowed. There is a $75 one time pet fee per visit. 2 dogs may be allowed.

Hyatt Regency Chesapeake Bay Golf Resort, Spa and Marina.
100 Heron Blvd
Cambridge, MD
410-901-1234 (888) 591 1234)
This beautiful bay shore hotel has many features and amenities for the business or leisure traveler with a full service business center, a championship golf course and a 150 slip marina. Dogs up to 70 pounds are welcome for an additional fee of $50 per night per pet, and reservations must be made at least 7 days in advance or more as there are only 9 pet-friendly rooms available. Current shot records must be provided upon arrival, and dogs must be under owner?s control, leashed, and cleaned up after at all times. 2 dogs may be allowed.

Days Inn Camp Springs/Andrews AFB
5001 Mercedes Blvd
Camp Springs, MD
301-423-2323 (800-329-7466)
Dogs of all sizes are allowed. There is a $10 per night pet fee per pet. 2 dogs may be allowed.

Motel 6 - Washington, DC SE - Camp Springs
5701 Allentown Road
Camp Springs, MD
301-702-1061 (800-466-8356)
One well-behaved family pet per room. Guest must notify front desk upon arrival. Guest is liable for any damages. In consideration of all guests, pets must never be left unattended in the guest rooms.

Motel 6 - Washington, DC - Capitol Heights
75 Hampton Park Boulevard
Capitol Heights, MD
301-499-0800 (800-466-8356)
One well-behaved family pet per room. Guest must notify front desk upon arrival. Guest is liable for any damages. In consideration of all guests, pets must never be left unattended in the guest rooms.

Brampton Inn
25227 Chestertown Road
Chestertown, MD
410-778-1860 (866-305-1860)
bramptoninn.com/
Stately and romantic, this historical estate sits on 20 wooded and landscaped acres just a short distance from river. Dogs of all sizes are allowed in one of the cottages for an additional $30 per night. Dogs must be leashed and cleaned up after. 2 dogs may be allowed.

Chase Suite Hotel by Woodfin
10710 Beaver Dam Road
Cockeysville, MD
410-584-7370
All well-behaved dogs are welcome. All rooms are suites with a full kitchen. Hotel amenities include a complimentary breakfast buffet. There is a $5 per day pet fee.

Sheraton Columbia Hotel
10207 Wincopin Circle
Columbia, MD
410-730-3900 (888-625-5144)
Dogs up to 50 pounds are allowed. There are no additional pet fees. Dogs are not allowed to be left alone in the room.

Staybridge Suites
8844 Columbia 100 Pkwy
Columbia, MD
410-964-9494 (877-270-6405)
Dogs of all sizes are allowed for an additional one time pet fee of $75 per room. 2 dogs may be allowed.

Holiday Inn
100 S. George St
Cumberland, MD
301-724-8800 (877-270-6405)
Dogs of all sizes are allowed for an additional one time pet fee of $10 per room. Multiple dogs may be allowed.

Railey Mountain Lake Vacations
5 Vacation Way
Deep Creek Lake, MD

301-387-2124 (800-846-RENT (7368))
deepcreek.com/
Offering a variety of property options and amenities in numerous recreational areas, this agency has about 125 pet friendly vacation rentals available in the Deep Creek Lake area. Dogs of all sizes are allowed for an additional fee of $45 for the 1st two days and $12 each night after, or $84 for the weekly rate per pet (the standard fee for any rental). Pets are not allowed in non-pet homes, and they must be pre-registered and paid for prior to arrival. Pets must be under owner's control/care at all times. 2 dogs may be allowed.

Days Inn Easton
7018 Ocean Eastyway
Easton, MD
410-822-4600 (800-329-7466)
Dogs of all sizes are allowed. There is a $13.08 per night pet fee per pet. 2 dogs may be allowed.

Tidewater Inn
101 E Dover Street
Easton, MD
410-822-1300 (800.237.8775)
tidewaterinn.com/
This inn also offers a restaurant and lounge (dogs not allowed). Dogs of all sizes are allowed for an additional $25 per pet per stay. Dogs must be quiet, well behaved, leashed, and cleaned up after. 2 dogs may be allowed.

Best Western Invitation Inn
1709 Edgewood Rd
Edgewood, MD
410-679-9700 (800-780-7234)
Dogs are allowed for an additional one time pet fee of $15 per room. 2 dogs may be allowed.

Knights Inn
262 Belle Hill Rd
Elkton, MD
410-392-6680
There is a $10 per day pet fee.

Motel 6 - Elkton
223 Belle Hill Road
Elkton, MD
410-392-5020 (800-466-8356)
One well-behaved family pet per room. Guest must notify front desk upon arrival. Guest is liable for any damages. In consideration of all guests, pets must never be left unattended in the guest rooms.

Residence Inn by Marriott

4950 Beaver Run
Ellicott City, MD
410-997-7200
Dogs of all sizes are allowed. There is a $75 one time fee and a pet policy to sign at check in. Multiple dogs may be allowed.

Turf Valley Resort
2700 Turf Valley Road
Ellicott City, MD
410-465-1500 (888-833-8873)
turfvalleyresort.com
Turf Valley Resort has over 1000 acres of land with golf, spas, meeting rooms, a children's playground, a driving range and more. Pets are allowed for a $150 one time additional pet fee.

Comfort Inn
7300 Executive Way
Frederick, MD
301-668-7272 (877-424-6423)
Dogs are allowed for an additional one time pet fee of $10 per room. Multiple dogs may be allowed.

Holiday Inn - Frederick
999 W Patrick St
Frederick, MD
301-662-5141 (877-270-6405)
Dogs of all sizes are allowed for no additional fee. Multiple dogs may be allowed.

Holiday Inn - Holidome
5400 Holiday Dr
Frederick, MD
301-694-7500 (877-270-6405)
Dogs of all sizes are allowed for an additional pet fee of $10 per night per room. 2 dogs may be allowed.

Holiday Inn Express
5579 Spectrum Dr
Frederick, MD
301-695-2881 (877-270-6405)
Dogs of all sizes are allowed for an additional pet fee of $10 per night per room. Multiple dogs may be allowed.

Mainstay Suites
7310 Executive Way
Frederick, MD
301-668-4600
Dogs are allowed for an additional fee of $10 per night per pet. Multiple dogs may be allowed.

Residence Inn by Marriott
5230 Westview Drive
Frederick, MD
301-360-0010
Dogs of all sizes are allowed. There is a $75 one time fee and a pet

policy to sign at check in. They request you kennel your pet if you leave it in the room. Multiple dogs may be allowed.

Travelodge
200 E Walser Drive
Frederick, MD
301-663-0500
Dogs of all sizes are allowed. There is a $25 refundable deposit and a pet policy to sign at check in. Multiple dogs may be allowed.

Yough Valley Motel
138 Walnut St
Friendsville, MD
301-746-5700
Dogs of all sizes are allowed. There is a $10 per dog per night additional pet fee. 2 dogs may be allowed.

The Savage River Lodge
1600 Mount Aetna Rd
Frostburg, MD
301-689-3200
savageriverlodge.com/dogs.htm
This extremely pet friendly lodge has a special page on its website for visitors with pets. While there you may be greeted by Bodhi, the Lodge Dog. Visitors stay in individual non-smoking cabins. There is a $25 per night per pet fee. You must make advanced reservations with a pet. The lodge is about 30 minutes from Deep Creek Lake. 2 dogs may be allowed.

Comfort Inn at Shady Grove
16216 Frederick Road
Gaithersburg, MD
301-330-0023 (877-424-6423)
Dogs are allowed for an additional fee of $15 per night per pet. Multiple dogs may be allowed.

Motel 6 - Washington, DC - Gaithersburg
497 Quince Orchard Road
Gaithersburg, MD
301-977-3311 (800-466-8356)
One well-behaved family pet per room. Guest must notify front desk upon arrival. Guest is liable for any damages. In consideration of all guests, pets must never be left unattended in the guest rooms.

Residence Inn by Marriott
9721 Washington Blvd
Gaithersburg, MD
301-590-3003
Dogs of all sizes are allowed. There is a $75 one time fee and a pet policy to sign at check in. Multiple dogs may be allowed.

TownePlace Suites Gaithersburg
212 Perry Parkway
Gaithersburg, MD
301-590-2300
Dogs of all sizes are allowed. There is a $75 one time pet fee per visit and a $5 per night additional pet fee. 2 dogs may be allowed.

Days Inn Glen Burnie
6600 Ritchie Hwy
Glen Burnie, MD
410-761-8300 (800-329-7466)
Dogs of all sizes are allowed. There is a $20 per night pet fee per pet. 2 dogs may be allowed.

Comfort Inn
2541 Chestnut Ridge Road
Grantsville, MD
301-895-5993 (877-424-6423)
Dogs are allowed for an additional fee of $10 per night per pet. 2 dogs may be allowed.

Best Western Kent Narrows Inn
3101 Main Street
Grasonville, MD
410-827-6767 (800-780-7234)
Dogs are allowed for an additional fee of $10 per night per pet. Multiple dogs may be allowed.

Residence Inn by Marriott
6320 Golden Triangle Drive
Greenbelt, MD
301-982-1600
Dogs of all sizes are allowed. There is a $75 one time fee and a pet policy to sign at check in. Multiple dogs may be allowed.

Econo Lodge
18221 Mason Dixon Rd
Hagerstown, MD
301-791-5500
There is a $3 per day pet fee.

Motel 6 - Hagerstown
11321 Massey Boulevard
Hagerstown, MD
301-582-4445 (800-466-8356)
One well-behaved family pet per room. Guest must notify front desk upon arrival. Guest is liable for any damages. In consideration of all guests, pets must never be left unattended in the guest rooms.

Quality Inn
1101 Dual H
Hagerstown, MD
301-733-2700 (877-424-6423)
Dogs are allowed for an additional fee of $10 per night per pet. 2 dogs may be allowed.

Sleep Inn and Suites
18216 Colonel H K Douglas Drive
Hagerstown, MD
301-766-9449 (877-424-6423)
Dogs are allowed for an additional fee of $10 per night per pet. Multiple dogs may be allowed.

Super 8 Halfway/Hagerstown Area
16805 Blake Rd
Hagerstown, MD
301-582-1992 (800-800-8000)
Dogs of all sizes are allowed. There is a $15 returnable deposit required per room. There is a $11.10 one time per pet fee per visit. Only non-smoking rooms are used for pets. Reservations are recommended due to limited rooms for pets. 2 dogs may be allowed.

Super 8 Hancock
118 Limestone Rd
Hancock, MD
301-678-6101 (800-800-8000)
Dogs of all sizes are allowed. There is a $10 one time per pet fee per visit. Smoking and non-smoking rooms are available for pet rooms. 2 dogs may be allowed.

Red Roof Inn - Washington, DC - BW Parkway
7306 Parkway Drive South
Hanover, MD
410-712-4070 (800-RED-ROOF)
One well-behaved family pet per room. Guest must notify front desk upon arrival. Guest is liable for any damages. In consideration of all guests, pets must never be left unattended in the guest rooms.

Residence Inn by Marriott
7035 Arundel Mills Circle
Hanover, MD
410-799-7332
Dogs of all sizes are allowed but they must be able to fit into a kennel when out of room. There is a $75 one time fee and a pet policy to sign at check in.

Super 8 Havre de Grace
929 Pulaski Hwy
Havre De Grace, MD
410-939-1880 (800-800-8000)
Dogs of all sizes are allowed. There is a $10 per night pet fee per pet. Reservations are recommended due to limited rooms for pets. Smoking and non-smoking rooms are available for pet rooms. 2 dogs may be allowed.

Red Roof Inn - Washington, DC

Columbia - Jessup
8000 Washington Boulevard
Jessup, MD
410-796-0380 (800-RED-ROOF)
One well-behaved family pet per room. Guest must notify front desk upon arrival. Guest is liable for any damages. In consideration of all guests, pets must never be left unattended in the guest rooms.

Red Roof Inn - Washington, DC - Lanham
9050 Lanham Severn Road
Lanham, MD
301-731-8830 (800-RED-ROOF)
One well-behaved family pet per room. Guest must notify front desk upon arrival. Guest is liable for any damages. In consideration of all guests, pets must never be left unattended in the guest rooms.

Motel 6 - Washington, DC NE - Laurel
3510 Old Annapolis Road
Laurel, MD
301-497-1544 (800-466-8356)
One well-behaved family pet per room. Guest must notify front desk upon arrival. Guest is liable for any damages. In consideration of all guests, pets must never be left unattended in the guest rooms.

Red Roof Inn - Washington, DC - Laurel
12525 Laurel Bowie Road
Laurel, MD
301-498-8811 (800-RED-ROOF)
One well-behaved family pet per room. Guest must notify front desk upon arrival. Guest is liable for any damages. In consideration of all guests, pets must never be left unattended in the guest rooms.

Days Inn Lexington Park
21847 Three Notch Road
Lexington Park, MD
240-725-0100 (800-329-7466)
daysinn.com/DaysInn/control/home
Dogs of all sizes are allowed for an additional $8 per night per pet. Dogs must be leashed and cleaned up after. Multiple dogs may be allowed.

Candlewood Suites Baltimore-Linthicum
1247 Winterson Rd.
Linthicum, MD
410-850-9214 (877-270-6405)
Dogs of all sizes are allowed for an additional one time fee of $75 per pet. 2 dogs may be allowed.

Holiday Inn
890 Elkridge Landing Road
Linthicum, MD
410-859-8400 (877-270-6405)
Dogs of all sizes are allowed for an additional one time pet fee of $50 per room, and they must be crated when left alone in the room. Multiple dogs may be allowed.

Residence Inn by Marriott
1160 Winterson Road
Linthicum, MD
410-691-0255
Dogs of all sizes are allowed. There is a $75 one time fee and a pet policy to sign at check in. Multiple dogs may be allowed.

Staybridge Suites Baltimore Bwi Airport
1301 Winterson Road
Linthicum, MD
410-850-5666 (877-270-6405)
Dogs up to 50 pounds are allowed for an additional one time fee of $100 per pet. Multiple dogs may be allowed.

Comfort Suites BWI Airport
815 Elkridge Landing Road
Linthicum Heights, MD
410-691-1000 (877-424-6423)
Dogs are allowed for an additional one time pet fee of $25 per room. Multiple dogs may be allowed.

Homestead Hotel - BWI
939 International Drive
Linthicum Heights, MD
410-691-2500
All studio suite rooms offer a fully equipped kitchen. There is a $75 one time per stay pet fee.

Homewood Suites Hotel BWI
1181 Winterson Rd
Linthicum Heights, MD
410-684-6100
There is a $200.00 one time pet fee.

Motel 6 - Baltimore - BWI Airport
5179 Raynor Avenue
Linthicum Heights, MD
410-636-9070 (800-466-8356)
One well-behaved family pet per room. Guest must notify front desk upon arrival. Guest is liable for any damages. In consideration of all guests, pets must never be left unattended in the guest rooms.

Red Roof Inn - Washington, DC - BWI Airport
827 Elkridge Landing Road
Linthicum Heights, MD
410-850-7600 (800-RED-ROOF)

One well-behaved family pet per room. Guest must notify front desk upon arrival. Guest is liable for any damages. In consideration of all guests, pets must never be left unattended in the guest rooms.

Deep Creek Lake Resort Vacation Rentals
23789 Garrett Highway, Suite 3
McHenry, MD
301-387-5832 (800-336-7303)
deepcreekresort.com/
Every season here brings its own beauty, pleasures, and recreational pursuits, and this agency offers a variety of property options and amenities in the Deep Creek Lake area. Dogs of all sizes are allowed for an additional $65 per pet per stay. Dogs must be well trained, and under owner's control/care at all times. 2 dogs may be allowed.

WISP Resort & Conference Center
296 Marsh Hill Road
McHenry, MD
301-387-4911 (800-462-9477)
wispresort.com
Dogs up to 50 pounds are allowed in this resort lodge right at WISP ski resort. There is a $50 per stay additional pet fee. The entire property is non-smoking.

Alpine Village Inn
19638 Garrett Highway
Oakland, MD
301-387-5534 (800-745-1174)
alpinevillageinn.com
Dogs of all sizes are allowed in a few pet rooms. There is a $20 per night per pet additional pet fee. 2 dogs may be allowed.

Swallow Falls Inn
1691 Swallow Falls Rd
Oakland, MD
301-387-9348

Clarion Resort Fontainebleau Hotel
10100 Coastal H
Ocean City, MD
410-524-3535 (877-424-6423)
Dogs are allowed for an additional fee of $38.15 per night per pet. 2 dogs may be allowed.

Serene Hotel and Suites
12004 Coastal H
Ocean City, MD
410-250-4000
Dogs of all sizes are allowed. There is a pet policy to sign at check in and there are no additional pet fees. Multiple dogs may be allowed.

Combsberry
4837 Evergreen Road
Oxford, MD
410-226-5353
combsberry.net/
Sitting lakeside at the end of a private dirt road is this beautiful historic brick mansion surrounded by magnolias, willows, and formal gardens. Dogs of all sizes are allowed for no additional fee. Dogs must be well behaved, leashed, and cleaned up after at all times. 2 dogs may be allowed.

Days Inn Pocomoke
1540 Ocean Hwy on US 13
Pocomoke, MD
410-957-3000 (800-329-7466)
Dogs of all sizes are allowed. There is a $10 per night pet fee per pet. 2 dogs may be allowed.

Quality Inn
825 Ocean H
Pocomoke, MD
410-957-1300 (877-424-6423)
Dogs are allowed for no additional pet fee. 2 dogs may be allowed.

Waterloo Country Inn
28822 Mt. Vernon Road
Princess Anne, MD
410-651-0883
Dogs of all sizes are allowed. There are no additional pet fees. They request you keep large dogs off the beds and furniture, and there is only 1 pet friendly room available. 2 dogs may be allowed.

Huntingfield Manor Bed & Breakfast
4928 Eastern Neck Rd
Rock Hall, MD
410-639-7779
travelassist.com/reg/md104s.html
This B&B is located on a 70 acre working farm. Pets are allowed in the cottage which is not designated as smoking or non-smoking. There are no additional pet fees.

Best Western Washington Gateway Hotel
1251 W Montgomery Ave
Rockville, MD
301-424-4940 (800-780-7234)
Dogs are allowed for an additional fee of $10 per night per pet. Pit Bulls are not allowed. Multiple dogs may be allowed.

Red Roof Inn - Washington, DC - Rockville
16001 Shady Grove Road
Rockville, MD
301-987-0965 (800-RED-ROOF)

One well-behaved family pet per room. Guest must notify front desk upon arrival. Guest is liable for any damages. In consideration of all guests, pets must never be left unattended in the guest rooms.

Woodfin Suite Hotel
1380 Piccard Drive
Rockville, MD
301-590-9880
All well-behaved dogs are welcome. Every room is a suite with either a wet bar or full kitchen. Hotel amenities includes a pool, free video movies and a complimentary hot breakfast buffet. There is a $5 per day pet fee per pet. If you are staying for one month, the pet fee is $50 for the month.

Best Western Salisbury Plaza
1735 N Salisbury Blvd
Salisbury, MD
410-546-1300 (800-780-7234)
Dogs are allowed for an additional fee of $10 per night per pet. Multiple dogs may be allowed.

Comfort Inn
2701 N Salisbury Blvd
Salisbury, MD
410-543-4666 (877-424-6423)
Dogs are allowed for no additional pet fee. Multiple dogs may be allowed.

River House Inn Bed and Breakfast
201 E Market St
Snow Hill, MD
410-632-2722
riverhouseinn.com/
This B&B is a National Register Victorian home located on the Pocomoke River on Maryland's Eastern Shore.

Five Gables Inn and Spa
209 North Talbot Street
St Michaels, MD
410-745-0100 (877-466-0100)
fivegables.com/
This inn offers 19th century ambiance, an indoor pool and spa, numerous amenities, and there is also an upscale pet boutique among the shops. One dog up to 75 pounds is allowed for an additional $35 one time fee. Dogs must be leashed or crated and cleaned up after.

The Inn at Perry Cabin
308 Watkins Lane
St Michaels, MD
410-745-2200 (866-278-9601)
Rich in colonial history, this grand manor house resort now features

numerous amenities, a horizon-edged swimming pool, a spa, docking facilities, and a lot more. Dogs up to 75 pounds are allowed with advance notification for an additional fee of $75 per pet per stay. Dogs must be well mannered, leashed, and cleaned up after. 2 dogs may be allowed.

The Tilghman Island Inn
21384 Coopertown Road
Tilghman Island, MD
401-886-2141 (800-866-2141)
In addition to providing a scenic and magical setting, this waterside inn hosts several special events through the season, and also provides a venue for special occasions. Dogs are allowed for an additional $15 per night per pet in the 1st floor rooms. Dogs must be well behaved, leashed, and cleaned up after. 2 dogs may be allowed.

Red Roof Inn - Baltimore North - Timonium
111 West Timonium Road
Timonium, MD
410-666-0380 (800-RED-ROOF)
One well-behaved family pet per room. Guest must notify front desk upon arrival. Guest is liable for any damages. In consideration of all guests, pets must never be left unattended in the guest rooms.

Holiday Inn
1100 Cromwell Bridge Rd
Towson, MD
410-823-4410 (877-270-6405)
Dogs of all sizes are allowed for an additional one time pet fee of $40. 2 dogs may be allowed.

Days Inn Waldorf
11370 Days Court
Waldorf, MD
301-932-9200 (800-329-7466)
Dogs of all sizes are allowed. There is a $15 per night pet fee per pet. 2 dogs may be allowed.

Hampton Inn
3750 Crain H
Waldorf, MD
302-632-9600
Dogs of all sizes are allowed. There are no addional pet fees. Multiple dogs may be allowed.

Red Roof Inn - Hagerstown - Williamsport
310 East Potomac Street
Williamsport, MD
301-582-3500 (800-RED-ROOF)
One well-behaved family pet per

room. Guest must notify front desk upon arrival. Guest is liable for any damages. In consideration of all guests, pets must never be left unattended in the guest rooms.

Massachusetts Listings

Comfort Suites
4 Riverside Drive
Andover, MA
978-475-6000 (877-424-6423)
Well behaved dogs are allowed for an additional one time pet fee of $75 per room. Multiple dogs may be allowed.

La Quinta Inn & Suites Andover
131 River Road
Andover, MA
978-685-6200 (800-531-5900)
Dogs of all sizes are allowed. There are no additional pet fees. There is a pet waiver to sign at check in. Dogs must be leashed and cleaned up after. Multiple dogs may be allowed.

Residence Inn by Marriott
500 Minuteman Road
Andover, MA
978-683-0382
Dogs of all sizes are allowed. There is a $75 one time fee per pet and a pet policy to sign at check in. Multiple dogs may be allowed.

Staybridge Suites
4 Tech Drive
Andover, MA
978-686-2000 (877-270-6405)
Dogs of all sizes are allowed for an additional one time pet fee per room. Multiple dogs may be allowed.

Comfort Inn
426 Southbridge Street
Auburn, MA
508-832-8300 (877-424-6423)
Dogs are allowed for an additional one time pet fee of $20 per room. 2 dogs may be allowed.

La Quinta Inn Auburn/Worcester
446 Southbridge Street
Auburn, MA
508-832-7000 (800-531-5900)
Dogs of all sizes are allowed. There are no additional fees. There is a pet waiver to sign at check in. Dogs may not be left unattended, except

for short periods. Dogs must be leashed and cleaned up after. Multiple dogs may be allowed.

Best Western Roundhouse Suites
891 Massachusetts Avenue
Boston, MA
617-989-1000 (800-780-7234)
Dogs are allowed for an additional fee of $20 (plus tax) per night per pet. 2 dogs may be allowed.

Boston Harbor Hotel
70 Rowes Wharf
Boston, MA
617-439-7000
bhh.com/
There are no additional pet fees. Pet owners must sign a pet waiver.

Comfort Inn
900 Morrissey Blvd
Boston, MA
617-287-9200 (877-424-6423)
One dog is allowed for no additional fee. Dogs must be crated when left alone in the room.

Doubletree
400 Soldiers Field Road
Boston, MA
617-783-0090
Dogs of all sizes are allowed. There is a $250 refundable deposit per room. You must use the service elevators when you are with your dog. Multiple dogs may be allowed.

Hilton
85 Terminal Road
Boston, MA
617-568-6700
Dogs are allowed for no additional pet fee. 2 dogs may be allowed.

Hyatt Regency Boston
One Ave de Lafayette
Boston, MA
617-451-2600
Pet owners must sign a pet waiver. You need to specifically request a non-smoking pet room if you want one. Dogs need to stay in the first through fourth floors only. Pets may not be left alone in the rooms. The hotel can recommend pet sitters if needed.

Nine Zero Hotel
90 Tremont Street
Boston, MA
617-772-5800 (866-906-9090)
This boutique hotel located in downtown Boston, has all the amenities for the business and leisure traveler, and they are located across the street from Boston

Common, a pet-friendly 50 acre public park. Dogs of all sizes are welcome for no additional pet fee. They offer a pet bed, bowls, and a special treat for all their canine guests. Dogs may only be left alone in the room if assured they will be quiet, well behaved, and the "Dog in Room" sign is put on the door. Dogs must be leashed and cleaned up after at all times. Multiple dogs may be allowed.

Onyx Hotel
155 Portland Street
Boston, MA
617-557-9955 (866-660-6699)
onyxhotel.com
This Kimpton boutique hotel allows dogs of all sizes. There are no additional pet fees. Pet sitting is available for $20 per hour.

Residence Inn by Marriott
34-44 Charles River Avenue
Boston, MA
617-242-5554
Dogs of all sizes are allowed. There is a $75 one time fee per pet and a pet policy to sign at check in. Multiple dogs may be allowed.

Seaport Hotel
1 Seaport Ln
Boston, MA
617-385-4000
seaporthotel.com/
Dogs up to 50 pounds allowed.

Sheraton Boston Hotel
39 Dalton St.
Boston, MA
617-236-2000 (888-625-5144)
Dogs up to 50 pounds are allowed for no additional pet fee. Dogs may not be left alone in the room.

Taj Boston
15 Arlington Street
Boston, MA
617-536-5700 (800-223-6800)
This landmark luxury hotel is only a short walk from the financial and theater districts, and sits along side Boston's grand public garden. Dogs of all sizes are allowed for an additional one time pet fee of $125 per room. Dogs may not be left alone in the room, and they must be leashed and cleaned up after at all times. 2 dogs may be allowed.

The Eliot Suite Hotel
370 Commonwealth Ave
Boston, MA
617-267-1607
There are no additional pet fees.

Pets may not be left alone in the rooms.

The Ritz-Carlton, Boston Common
10 Avery Street
Boston, MA
617-574-7100 (800-241-3333)
This hotel of contemporary luxury and design with 193 guestrooms, offers dramatic city views, in-house gourmet dining, and is conveniently located between the financial and theater districts. Dogs of all sizes are welcome for an additional $125 one time fee per room, and there is a pet policy to sign at check in. Dogs may not be left alone in the room, and they must be leashed and cleaned up after at all times. 2 dogs may be allowed.

Holiday Inn
242 Adams Place
Boxborough, MA
978-263-8701 (877-270-6405)
Dogs up to 75 pounds are allowed for an additional one time pet fee of $75 per room. 2 dogs may be allowed.

Candlewood Suites
235 Wood Rd
Braintree, MA
781-849-7450 (877-270-6405)
Dogs of all sizes are allowed for an additional pet fee per room of $75 for 1 to 7 days, and $150 for 8 days or more. 2 dogs may be allowed.

Hampton Inn
215 Wood Road
Braintree, MA
781-380-3300
Dogs of all sizes are allowed. There are no additional pet fees. Multiple dogs may be allowed.

Holiday Inn Express
190 Wood Rd
Braintree, MA
781-848-1260 (877-270-6405)
Dogs up to 50 pounds are allowed for an additional one time fee of $10 per pet. 2 dogs may be allowed.

Motel 6 - Boston South - Braintree
125 Union Street
Braintree, MA
781-848-7890 (800-466-8356)
One well-behaved family pet per room. Guest must notify front desk upon arrival. Guest is liable for any damages. In consideration of all guests, pets must never be left unattended in the guest rooms.

Sheraton Braintree Hotel

37 Forbes Rd.
Braintree, MA
781-848-0600 (888-625-5144)
Dogs up to 60 pounds are allowed for no additional pet fee. Dogs may not be left alone in the room.

Greylin House
2311 Main St
Brewster, MA
508-896-0004 (800-233-6662)
capecodtravel.com/greylin/
1 room, non-smoking for pets. Dog must be able to get along with the owners 2 dogs.

Residence Inn by Marriott
124 Liberty Street
Brockton, MA
508-583-3600
Dogs of all sizes are allowed. There is a $75 one time fee and a pet policy to sign at check in. Multiple dogs may be allowed.

Holiday Inn Boston - Brookline
1200 Beacon St.
Brookline, MA
617-277-1200 (877-270-6405)
basshotels.com/holiday-inn
Dogs of all sizes are allowed for an additional pet fee of $15 per night per room. Multiple dogs may be allowed.

Staybridge Suites
11 Old Concord Rd
Burlington, MA
781-221-2233 (877-270-6405)
Dogs up to 50 pounds are allowed for an additional fee of $12 per night per pet to a maximum fee of $150. 2 dogs may be allowed.

Bay Motor Inn
223 Main St
Buzzards Bay, MA
508-759-3989
capecodtravel.com/baymotorinn/
There is a $10 per day pet fee. The motel has no designated smoking or non-smoking rooms. Pets must be attended at all times.

Best Western Hotel Tria
220 Alewife Brook Pkwy
Cambridge, MA
617-491-8000 (800-780-7234)
Dogs are allowed for an additional fee of $25 per night per pet. 2 dogs may be allowed.

Hotel Marlowe
25 Edwin H. Land Blvd.
Cambridge, MA
617-868-8000
Dogs of all kinds and sizes are

welcome at this pet-friendly and family-friendly hotel. The luxury boutique hotel offers both rooms and suites. Hotel amenities include a fitness room and 24 hour room service. There are no pet fees, just sign a pet waiver.

Residence Inn by Marriott
6 Cambridge Center
Cambridge, MA
617-349-0700
Dogs of all sizes are allowed. There is a $150 one time fee and a pet policy to sign at check in. They ask you make arrangements for housekeeping. Multiple dogs may be allowed.

Sheraton Commander Hotel
16 Garden St.
Cambridge, MA
617-547-4800 (888-625-5144)
Dogs up to 75 pounds are allowed for no additional pet fee. Dogs may not be left alone in the room.

The Charles Hotel in Harvard Square
1 Bennett St
Cambridge, MA
617-864-1200
boston4less.com/harvardsq.html
There is a $50 one time pet fee. Pets may not be left alone in the rooms, and pet owners must sign a pet agreement.

Centerville Corners Inn
1338 Craigville Beach Rd
Centerville, MA
508-775-7223
There is a $10 per day pet fee.

Motel 6 - Springfield - Chicopee
36 Johnny Cake Hollow Rd.
Chicopee, MA
413-592-5141 (800-466-8356)
One well-behaved family pet per room. Guest must notify front desk upon arrival. Guest is liable for any damages. In consideration of all guests, pets must never be left unattended in the guest rooms.

Park Inn
450 Memorial Drive
Chicopee, MA
413-739-7311
Dogs of all sizes are allowed. There is a $35 additional pet fee for the first night and $5 for each additional night.

Quality Inn
463 Memorial Drive
Chicopee, MA
413-592-6171 (877-424-6423)

Dogs are allowed for an additional one time pet fee of $15 per room. Dogs may not be left alone in the room for more than an hour unless crated. Multiple dogs may be allowed.

Best Western Historic Concord
740 Elm St
Concord, MA
978-369-6100 (800-780-7234)
Dogs are allowed for an additional fee of $10 per night per pet. Multiple dogs may be allowed.

Motel 6 - Boston - Danvers
65 Newbury Street/US Route 1 North
Danvers, MA
978-774-8045 (800-466-8356)
One well-behaved family pet per room. Guest must notify front desk upon arrival. Guest is liable for any damages. In consideration of all guests, pets must never be left unattended in the guest rooms.

Residence Inn by Marriott
51 Newbury Street
Danvers, MA
978-777-7171
Dogs of all sizes are allowed. There is a $75 one time fee and a pet policy to sign at check in. Multiple dogs may be allowed.

TownePlace Suites Boston North Shore/Danvers
238 Andover Street
Danvers, MA
978-777-6222
Dogs of all sizes are allowed. There is a $75 one time pet fee per visit. 2 dogs may be allowed.

Residence Inn by Marriott
259 Elm Street
Dedham, MA
781-407-0999
Dogs of all sizes are allowed. There is a $75 one time fee and a pet policy to sign at check in. Multiple dogs may be allowed.

Colonial Inn
38 North Water Street
Edgartown, MA
508-627-4711
colonialinnmvy.com/
This family friendly inn offers two pet-friendly suites for travelers with dogs. You can enjoy the daily complimentary continental breakfast outside in the Garden Courtyard with your pooch. There is a $30 per day pet fee. The entire inn is non-smoking.

Martha's Vineyard Vacation Homes
Call to Arrange.
Edgartown, MA
203-374-8624
vineyardvacationhomes.com/
Some of the vacation homes are pet-friendly. There is a $100 weekly pet fee, and a $150 security deposit for pet damage or additional cleaning.

Shiverick Inn
5 Pease Point Way
Edgartown, MA
508-627-3797
shiverickinn.com/
Pets up to about 75 pounds are allowed in the three bedroom suite which is located just off the library. Dogs are not allowed in the indoor common areas, just inside your room and outside. There is a $50 pet deposit. Pets cannot be left alone in the room. The entire inn is non-smoking.

Holiday Inn Express
110 Middle St.
Fairhaven, MA
508-997-1281 (877-270-6405)
Dogs of all sizes are allowed for an additional one time fee of $10 per pet; there can be 1 large dog or 2 small to medium dogs per room. 2 dogs may be allowed.

Foley Real Estate
703 Main Street/H28
Falmouth, MA
508-548-3415
This rental company offers several pet friendly vacation houses in the Falmouth area and pet policy and/or fees may vary per rental. Aggressive breeds are not allowed, and dogs must be under owner's control/care at all times.

Best Western Royal Plaza Hotel & Conf. Center
150 Royal Plaza Drive
Fitchburg, MA
978-342-7100 (800-780-7234)
Pets allowed

Residence Inn by Marriott
250 Foxborough Blvd
Foxborough, MA
508-698-2800
Dogs of all sizes are allowed. There is a $75 one time fee and a pet policy to sign at check in. Multiple dogs may be allowed.

Motel 6 - Boston West - Framingham
1668 Worcester Road
Framingham, MA

508-620-0500 (800-466-8356)
One well-behaved family pet per room. Guest must notify front desk upon arrival. Guest is liable for any damages. In consideration of all guests, pets must never be left unattended in the guest rooms.

Red Roof Inn - Boston Framingham
650 Cochituate Road
Framingham, MA
508-872-4499 (800-RED-ROOF)
One well-behaved family pet per room. Guest must notify front desk upon arrival. Guest is liable for any damages. In consideration of all guests, pets must never be left unattended in the guest rooms.

Residence Inn by Marriott
400 Staples Drive
Framingham, MA
508-370-0001
Dogs of all sizes are allowed. There is a $75 one time fee and a pet policy to sign at check in. Multiple dogs may be allowed.

Sheraton Framingham Hotel
1657 Worcester Rd.
Framingham, MA
508-879-7200 (888-625-5144)
Dogs up to 80 pounds are allowed for no additional pet fee. Dogs may not be left alone in the room.

Residence Inn by Marriott
4 Forge Parkway
Franklin, MA
508-541-8188
Dogs of all sizes are allowed. There is a $75 one time fee and a pet policy to sign at check in. Multiple dogs may be allowed.

Super 8 Gardner
22 N Pearson Blvd
Gardner, MA
978-630-2888 (800-800-8000)
Dogs up to 60 pounds are allowed. There is a $10 per night pet fee per pet. Reservations are recommended due to limited rooms for pets. Smoking and non-smoking rooms are available for pet rooms. 2 dogs may be allowed.

Cape Ann Motor Inn
33 Rockport Road
Gloucester, MA
978-281-2900
Well behaved and quiet dogs of all sizes are allowed. There are no additional pet fees. Multiple dogs may be allowed.

Quality Inn

237 Russell Street/H 9
Hadley, MA
413-584-9816 (877-424-6423)
Well behaved dogs are allowed for an additional one time fee of $25 per pet. 2 dogs may be allowed.

Best Western Merrimack Valley
401 Lowell Avenue
Haverhill, MA
978-373-1511 (800-780-7234)
Dogs up to 70 pounds are allowed for an additional pet fee of $20 per night per room. 2 dogs may be allowed.

Cape Cod Harbor House Inn
119 Ocean St
Hyannis, MA
508-771-1880
This inn has 19 non-smoking mini-suites located near the center of Hyannis. Pets are welcome, please mention your pet when making reservations.

Comfort Inn - Hyannis/Cape Cod
1470 Route 132
Hyannis, MA
508-771-4804 (877-424-6423)
comfortinn-hyannis.com
This hotel allows pets in a number of pet-friendly rooms for an additional $5 per night.

Simmons Homestead Inn
288 Scudder Ave.
Hyannis Port, MA
800-637-1649
SimmonsHomesteadInn.com
The B & B is at an 1800 Sea Captain's estate in Hyannis Port in the center of Cape Cod. 14 rooms in two buildings. Full breakfasts, wine hour(s), free bikes, beach stuff, billiards and a bunch more. A chance to see the collection of over 50 classic red sports cars behind the Inn at Toad Hall is probably worth the trip by itself.

Hampton Inn
224 Winthrop Ave
Lawrence, MA
978-975-4050
Dogs of all sizes are allowed. There is a $15 per night pet fee and a pet policy to sign at check in. Dogs are not allowed to be left alone in the room. Multiple dogs may be allowed.

Sally's Place
160 Orchard Street
Lee, MA
413-243-1982
This one bedroom apartment sleeps

up to four people and is only a few minutes from the lake. Dogs of all sizes are welcome for no additional fee, but they must be very friendly with children. Dogs must be well mannered, leashed, and cleaned up after at all times. 2 dogs may be allowed.

Birchwood Inn-Fireflies and Firesides
7 Hubbard Street
Lenox, MA
413-637-2600 (800-524-1646)
birchwood-inn.com
Located on the National Register of Historic Places, this 1767 mansion offers a colonial setting, and is located only a short distance to Lenox Village. There is a service dog on site and they ask that other pets do not disturb him while he is "working". Dogs of all sizes are welcome for an additional fee of $25 per night per pet and a pet policy to sign at check in. Dogs must be quiet, well trained, leashed and cleaned up after at all times, and crated when left alone in the room. Dogs are not allowed on the bed or any of the furnishings, and they must be walked off the property. 2 dogs may be allowed.

Cranwell Resort, Spa & Golf Club
55 Lee Road
Lenox, MA
413-637-1364 (800-272-6935)
cranwell.com/
This sprawling hilltop mansion is a premier year round resort that sits on 380 groomed acres and is home to the Golf Digest School, an 18 hole championship golf course, and a glass enclosed indoor heated pool. Dogs up to 35 pounds are allowed for an additional one time fee of $100 per pet. Dogs must be leashed, cleaned up after, and crated when in the room alone. 2 dogs may be allowed.

Seven Hills Inn
40 Plunkett Street
Lenox, MA
413-637-0060 (800-869-6518)
sevenhillsinn.com
The Seven Hills Inn offers pet-friendly accommodations in the Terrace House. Thanks to one of our readers who writes: "They are on 27 beautifully groomed acres with lots of room for pets to roam." There is a $40 per visit pet fee.

Walker House
64 Walker Street
Lenox, MA
413-637-1271 (800-235-3098)

walkerhouse.com/
A classic in American Federal architecture, this 1804 house features 8 rooms all theme decorated of favored composers, and they also have a cinema house where plays, films, and other notable events are shown on a large 12 foot screen. Dogs of all sizes are welcome for an additional pet fee of $10 per day. Dogs must be quiet, leashed, cleaned up after at all times, and cat-friendly. Dogs may only be left alone in the room if assured they will be well behaved. 2 dogs may be allowed.

Motel 6 - Leominster
48 Commercial Street
Leominster, MA
978-537-8161 (800-466-8356)
One well-behaved family pet per room. Guest must notify front desk upon arrival. Guest is liable for any damages. In consideration of all guests, pets must never be left unattended in the guest rooms.

Quality Inn and Suites
440 Bedford Street
Lexington, MA
781-861-0850 (877-424-6423)
Dogs are allowed for an additional one time fee of $25 per pet. 2 dogs may be allowed.

Holiday Inn Mansfield-Foxboro Area
31 Hampshire Street
Mansfield, MA
508-339-2200 (877-270-6405)
Dogs up to 50 pounds are allowed for an additional one time fee of $10 per pet. Multiple dogs may be allowed.

Red Roof Inn - Mansfield/Foxboro
60 Forbes Boulevard
Mansfield, MA
508-339-2323 (800-RED-ROOF)
One well-behaved family pet per room. Guest must notify front desk upon arrival. Guest is liable for any damages. In consideration of all guests, pets must never be left unattended in the guest rooms.

Holiday Inn Express
50 Fortune Blvd
Milford, MA
508-634-1054 (877-270-6405)
Dogs of all sizes are allowed for an additional one time fee of $25 per pet. Multiple dogs may be allowed.

La Quinta Inn Milford
24 Beaver Street
Milford, MA

508-478-8243 (800-531-5900)
Dogs of all sizes are allowed. There are no additional pet fees. Dogs must be leashed and cleaned up after, and they are not allowed in the breakfast area. Multiple dogs may be allowed.

Brass Lantern Inn
11 North Water Street
Nantucket, MA
508-228-4064
brasslanternnantucket.com/
Dogs up to about 65 pounds are allowed. Call to inquire if you have a larger dog. There is a $30 per day pet fee. All rooms are non-smoking.

Quidnuck Vacation Rental
Call to Arrange.
Nantucket, MA
202-663-8439
ifb.com/quidnuck/
One dog is allowed at this vacation rental home. They ask that you do not bring a puppy and to never leave your dog alone in the house. There is a $75 one time per stay pet fee which will be used towards spraying the house for fleas. Ask for Jack when calling.

Safe Harbor Guest House
2 Harbor View Way
Nantucket, MA
508-228-3222
beesknees.net/safeharbor/
Dogs are allowed at this guest house. All rooms have private bathrooms. If your dog will be on the bed, please bring a sheet with you to place over the bedspread. There is no pet fee, they just request that you give the housekeeper a tip for extra cleaning, if necessary.

The Cottages at the Boat Basin
(Woof Cottages)
New Whale Street P.O. Box 1139
Nantucket, MA
508-325-1499 (866-838-9253)
thecottagesnantucket.com
Dogs and cats are welcome in "The Woof Cottages." These cottages are one and two bedroom cottages which include special pet amenities like a welcome basket of pet treats and play toys, a pet bed, food and water bowls, and a Nantucket bandana. When you make a reservation, let them know what size your pet is, so they can have the appropriate size pet bed and bowls in the room. All cottages are non-smoking. There is a $25 one time per stay pet fee.

The Grey Lady
P.O. Box 1292
Nantucket, MA
508-228-9552
nantucket.net/lodging/greylady/
Pets and children are welcome at this guest house. While there is no pet fee, they have certain pet rooms which cost more per night than a standard room. All rooms are non-smoking. There may be a two or three night minimum stay during the summer. They also offer weekly cottage rentals at the Boat House.

Woof Hotel at Harbor House Village
South Beach Street
Nantucket, MA
508-228-1500 (866-325-9300)
harborhousevillage.com
This 12 room dog centric and friendly hotel has a fenced in yard for dogs to play, a pet concierge, welcome basket for canine visitors and a "Yappie Hour" on Fridays in the summer.

Crowne Plaza
1360 Worcester Road
Natick, MA
508-653-8800 (877-270-6405)
Dogs up to 50 pounds are allowed for no additional fee. 2 dogs may be allowed.

Sheraton Needham Hotel
100 Cabot St.
Needham, MA
781-444-1110 (888-625-5144)
Dogs of all sizes are allowed. There are no additional pet fees. Dogs are not allowed to be left alone in the room.

Captain Haskell's Octagon House
347 Union Street
New Bedford, MA
508-999-3933
Dogs of all sizes are allowed. There is a pet policy to sign at check in and there are no additional pet fees. They also provide you with a map of dog friendly places in the local area. Multiple dogs may be allowed.

The Porches Inn
231 River Street
North Adams, MA
413-664-0400
porches.com/
This inn features get-away packages, a nice long porch with rockers, and a year-round outdoor lap pool with heated deck. Dogs of all sizes are allowed for an additional $50 one time pet fee per room. One large dog or 2 small to medium dogs are allowed per room. Dogs must be

well mannered, leashed and cleaned up after at all times.

Comfort Inn
171 Faunce Corner Road
North Dartmouth, MA
508-996-0800 (877-424-6423)
Dogs are allowed for an additional one time pet fee of $50 per room. 2 dogs may be allowed.

Residence Inn by Marriott
181 Faunce Corner Road
North Dartmouth, MA
508-984-5858
Dogs of all sizes are allowed. There is a $75 one time fee and a pet policy to sign at check in. Multiple dogs may be allowed.

Outer Reach Resort
535 H 6
North Truro, MA
508-487-9500 (800-942-5388)
outerreachresort.com
Sitting on 12 acres of the highest bluff on the Lower Cape affords great views of the ocean and Pilgrim Lake, and in addition to a pool and gaming courts, there are great trails to walk with your pet down to the beach. They open for the season in mid-May. Dogs of all sizes are welcome for an additional $15 per night per pet. Dogs must be leashed and cleaned up after. 2 dogs may be allowed.

Martha's Vineyard Surfside Hotel
7 Oak Bluffs Avenue
Oak Bluffs, MA
508-693-2500 (800-537-3007)
mvsurfside.com
Overlooking Nantucket Sound, the Surfside offers a premier location in Oak Bluffs, with Oak Bluffs Harbor and the ocean in your backyard and shopping, fine restaurants and historic sites in your front y ard. A year round hotel with 39 rooms and suites just footsteps from the Oak Bluffs Ferry Dock, Inkwell Beach and the historic Flying Horses Carousel. They have no weight restrictions on dogs and offer a "doggie package" of treats and pet scooper. There is an additional $10 pet charge which may be refunded on checkout.

Holiday Inn Hotel & Suites Boston-Peabody
Us 1 North & Us 128 North
Peabody, MA
978-535-4600 (877-270-6405)
Dogs of all sizes are allowed for an additional one time fee of $25 per pet, and they may not be left alone in the room. Multiple dogs may be

allowed.

BayShore on the Water
493 Commercial Street
Provincetown, MA
508-487-9133
bayshorechandler.com
This five house complex has been converted to studios, one bedroom and two bedroom units. There are a few non-smoking units and the rest are not designated as smoking or non-smoking. There is a $15 per day pet fee for 1 dog, or a $20 per day pet fee for 2 dogs.

Cape Inn Resorts
698 Commercial Street
Provincetown, MA
508-487-1711 (800-422-4224)
capeinn.com
Cape Inn is located at the east end of Provincetown about one mile from the town center. Pets of all sizes are welcome, but may not be left alone in the rooms.

Four Gables Cottages
15 Race Road
Provincetown, MA
508-487-2427 (866-487-2427)
fourgables.com
These Provincetown cottages and apartments welcome your pets to visit with you. Properties have decks and porches.

Keep Inn
698 Commercial St
Provincetown, MA
508-487-1711
There are no additional pet fees. Pets must be attended at all times.

The Sandpiper Beach House
165 Commercial Street
Provincetown, MA
508-487-1928 (800-354-8628)
sandpiperbeachhouse.com
There is a $25 per visit pet fee.

White Sands Motel
1001 Commercial St.
Provincetown, MA
508-487-0244
provincetownlodging.com
This beachfront hotel in Provincetown allows pets in select rooms. Pets require approval at the time of reservation and there is a $20 per night pet fee. The hotel is within two miles of the Cape Cod National Seashore.

White Wind Inn
174 Commercial St
Provincetown, MA

508-487-1526

Days Inn Taunton
164 New State Hwy
Raynham, MA
508-824-8647 (800-329-7466)
Dogs of all sizes are allowed. There is a $10 per night pet fee per pet. 2 dogs may be allowed.

Comfort Inn and Suites Logan International Airport
85 American Legion H
Revere, MA
781-485-3600 (877-424-6423)
Dogs are allowed for an additional fee of $10 per night per pet. 2 dogs may be allowed.

Best Western Rockland
909 Hingham Street
Rockland, MA
781-871-5660 (800-780-7234)
Dogs are allowed for an additional pet fee of $25 per night per room. Dogs may not be left alone in the room Multiple dogs may be allowed.

Sandy Bay Motor Inn
173 Main St
Rockport, MA
978-546-7155
There is a $10 per day pet charge. The hotel has two non-smoking rooms in their pet building.

Hawthorne Hotel
18 Washington Square
Salem, MA
978-744-4080 (800-729-7829)
hawthornehotel.com/
Keeping in character with its New England charm, this historic hotel has tastefully appointed the rooms with 18th style reproduction furniture, they are within walking distance of several other attractions, and they are home to a restaurant specializing in fine seasonal cuisine and a full-service lounge. Dogs of all sizes are welcome for an additional fee of $10 per night per pet plus a $100 refundable deposit. Dogs must be leashed, cleaned up after, and a contact number left at the desk if they are in the room alone. 2 dogs may be allowed.

Stephen Daniels House
1 Daniels Street
Salem, MA
978-744-5709
This 300 year old house, furnished with antiques, offers canopy beds and fireplaces in every room, and a quaint English garden. Dogs of all sizes are welcome for no additional

fee. Dogs must be quiet, well behaved, leashed, and cleaned up after. 2 dogs may be allowed.

Sandwich Lodge and Resort
54 Route 6A
Sandwich, MA
508-888-2275
There is a $10.00 per night pet fee per pet. Pets are allowed in standard rooms only.

The Earl of Sandwich Motor Manor
378 Rt 6A
Sandwich, MA
508-888-1415
There are no additional pet fees.

Red Roof Inn - Boston Saugus
920 Broadway
Saugus, MA
781-941-1400 (800-RED-ROOF)
One well-behaved family pet per room. Guest must notify front desk upon arrival. Guest is liable for any damages. In consideration of all guests, pets must never be left unattended in the guest rooms.

Motel 6 - Providence - Seekonk
821 Fall River Avenue
Seekonk, MA
508-336-7800 (800-466-8356)
One well-behaved family pet per room. Guest must notify front desk upon arrival. Guest is liable for any damages. In consideration of all guests, pets must never be left unattended in the guest rooms.

Birch Hill Bed and Breakfast
254 S Undermountain Road/H 41
Sheffield, MA
413-229-2143 (800-359-3969)
birchhillbb.com/
This grand 1780 bed and breakfast filled with period antique furnishings, sits on 20 acres at the foot of Mt Everett, and offer a good variety of activities and recreation. Dogs of all sizes are allowed for no additional fee. Dogs may not be left alone in the room at any time; they are not allowed on the bed or furniture, and they must be walked away from the lawn, flowers, and pool areas. Dogs must be leashed and cleaned up after at all times. 2 dogs may be allowed.

Staveleigh House
59 Main Street
Sheffield, MA
413-229-2129 (800-980-2129)
staveleigh.com/
This stately 1817 colonial home provides comfort and a convenient location to several attractions and activities. One dog of any size is welcome for a one time pet fee of $20. Dogs must be well mannered, leashed, and cleaned up after at all times.

Quality Inn
1878 Wilbur Avenue
Somerset, MA
508-678-4545 (877-424-6423)
Dogs are allowed for no additional fee; there may be 1 average sized dog or 2 small dogs per room. 2 dogs may be allowed.

La Quinta Inn & Suites Boston Somerville
23 Cummings Street
Somerville, MA
617-625-5300 (800-531-5900)
One dog of any size is allowed. There are no additional pet fees. Dogs must be leashed, cleaned up after, and crated if left alone in the room.

Red Roof Inn - South Deerfield
9 Greenfield Road
South Deerfield, MA
413-665-7161 (800-RED-ROOF)
One well-behaved family pet per room. Guest must notify front desk upon arrival. Guest is liable for any damages. In consideration of all guests, pets must never be left unattended in the guest rooms.

Quality Inn
1314 H 28
South Yarmouth, MA
508-394-4000 (877-424-6423)
Dogs are allowed for an additional fee of $15 per night per pet. Multiple dogs may be allowed.

Red Roof Inn - Boston Southborough
367 Turnpike Road
Southborough, MA
508-481-3904 (800-RED-ROOF)
One well-behaved family pet per room. Guest must notify front desk upon arrival. Guest is liable for any damages. In consideration of all guests, pets must never be left unattended in the guest rooms.

Holiday Inn
711 Dwight St
Springfield, MA
413-781-0900 (877-270-6405)
Dogs of all sizes are allowed for an additional one time pet fee of $35 per room. Multiple dogs may be allowed.

Sheraton Springfield Monarch Place Hotel
One Monarch Place
Springfield, MA
413-781-1010 (888-625-5144)
One dog of any size is allowed for an additional one time pet fee of $50 per room. Dogs may not be left alone in the room.

The Red Lion Inn
30 Main Street
Stockbridge, MA
413-298-5545
redlioninn.com/home.html
The surroundings and décor of this historic inn offer visitors a look into the past, but they have also provided many modern niceties, including an outdoor heated pool and hot tub surrounded by a heated stone patio. Dogs up to 80 pounds are allowed for an additional fee of $40 per night per pet, and they must be declared at the time of reservations. Pooches also get a special treat upon arrival. Dogs must be quiet, well trained, leashed, cleaned up after, and crated when left alone in the room. 2 dogs may be allowed.

Comfort Inn and Suites Colonial
215 Charlton Road
Sturbridge, MA
508-347-3306 (877-424-6423)
Dogs are allowed for an additional fee of $15 per night per pet. Multiple dogs may be allowed.

Days Inn Sturbridge
66-68 Haynes St
Sturbridge, MA
508-347-3391 (800-329-7466)
Dogs of all sizes are allowed. There is a $7 per night pet fee per pet. 2 dogs may be allowed.

Publick House Historic Inn
On the Common, Route 131
Sturbridge, MA
508-347-3313 (800-PUBLICK)
publickhouse.com/
There is a $5 per day additional pet fee.

Sturbridge Host Hotel
366 Main Street
Sturbridge, MA
508-347-7393
Dogs of all sizes are allowed. There is a $15 fee for the first night; if more than one night, it is a $25 one time fee per room. There is a pet policy to sign at check in. Multiple dogs may be allowed.

Super 8 Sturbridge

358 Main Street
Sturbridge, MA
508-347-9000 (800-800-8000)
Dogs of all sizes are allowed. There is a $10 per night pet fee per pet. Smoking and non-smoking rooms are available for pet rooms. Multiple dogs may be allowed.

Clarion Carriage House Inn
738 Boston Post Road
Sudbury, MA
978-443-2223 (877-424-6423)
Dogs are allowed for an additional fee of $10 per night per pet. There is a pet agreement to sign at check in. 2 dogs may be allowed.

Holiday Inn
4 Highwood Drive
Tewksbury, MA
978-640-9000 (877-270-6405)
Dogs of all sizes are allowed for an additional one time pet fee of $50 per room. 2 dogs may be allowed.

Motel 6 - Tewksbury
95 Main Street
Tewksbury, MA
978-851-8677 (800-466-8356)
One well-behaved family pet per room. Guest must notify front desk upon arrival. Guest is liable for any damages. In consideration of all guests, pets must never be left unattended in the guest rooms.

Residence Inn by Marriott
1775 Andover Street
Tewksbury, MA
978-640-1003
Dogs of all sizes are allowed, however there can only be 2 small or 1 large dog per room. There is $75 one time fee and a pet policy to sign at check in.

TownePlace Suites Boston
Tewksbury/Andover
20 International Place
Tewksbury, MA
978-863-9800
Dogs of all sizes are allowed. There is a $75 one time pet fee per visit. 2 dogs may be allowed.

Martha's Vineyard Rental Houses
Call to Arrange.
Vineyard Haven, MA
508-693-6222
Select from a variety of pet-friendly rental homes. Pet fees may vary per property.

Sheraton Colonial Hotel & Golf Club
Boston North
One Audubon Rd.

Wakefield, MA
781-245-9300 (888-625-5144)
Dogs up to 80 pounds are allowed. There are no additional pet fees. Dogs are not allowed to be left alone in the room.

Holiday Inn Express
385 Winter St
Waltham, MA
781-890-2800 (877-270-6405)
Dogs of all sizes are allowed for an additional one time pet fee of $50 per room. 2 dogs may be allowed.

Homestead Village
52 Fourth Ave
Waltham, MA
781-890-1333
$75 one time fee. This is a long term stay hotel.

The Westin-Waltham Boston
70 Third Ave.
Waltham, MA
781-290-5600 (888-625-5144)
Dogs up to 50 pounds are allowed for no additional pet fee. Dogs may not be left alone in the room.

Candlewood Suites West
Springfield
572 Riverdale St.
West Springfield, MA
413-739-1122 (877-270-6405)
Dogs of all sizes are allowed for an additional pet fee per room of $25 per night. 2 dogs may be allowed.

Hampton Inn
1011 Riverdale Street
West Springfield, MA
413-732-1300
Dogs of all sizes are allowed. There is a $75 one time fee and a pet policy to sign at check in. Multiple dogs may be allowed.

Quality Inn
1150 Riverdale Street
West Springfield, MA
413-739-7261 (877-424-6423)
Dogs are allowed for an additional one time fee of $35 per pet for large dogs; the fee is $25 for small dogs. 2 dogs may be allowed.

Red Roof Inn - West Springfield
1254 Riverdale Street
West Springfield, MA
413-731-1010 (800-RED-ROOF)
One well-behaved family pet per room. Guest must notify front desk upon arrival. Guest is liable for any damages. In consideration of all guests, pets must never be left unattended in the guest rooms.

Residence Inn by Marriott
64 Border Way
West Springfield, MA
413-732-9543
Dogs of all sizes are allowed. There is a $75 one time fee and a pet policy to sign at check in. Multiple dogs may be allowed.

Comfort Inn
399 Turnpike Road
Westborough, MA
508-366-0202 (877-424-6423)
Dogs are allowed for an additional fee of $10 per night per pet. Multiple dogs may be allowed.

Residence Inn by Marriott
25 Connector Road
Westborough, MA
508-366-7700
Dogs up to 100 pounds are allowed. There is a $75 one time fee and a pet policy to sign at check in. 2 dogs may be allowed.

Residence Inn by Marriott
7 LAN Drive
Westford, MA
978-392-1407
Dogs of all sizes are allowed. There is a $75 one time fee and a pet policy to sign at check in. Multiple dogs may be allowed.

Cozy Corner Motel
284 Sand Springs Rd
Williamstown, MA
413-458-8006
There is a $10 per day additional pet fee.

The Inn at Crystal Cove
600 Shirley Street
Winthrop, MA
617-846-9217
inncrystalcove.com
Great view and wonderful dog-friendly people. The inn is located on Boston Harbor. The inn is a comfortable, colonial-style hotel located in a residential neighborhood of Winthrop, just minutes from downtown Boston. Their swimming pool and Jacuzzi make comfortable lodging at a reasonable rate.

Best Western New Englander
1 Rainin Road
Woburn, MA
781-935-8160 (800-780-7234)
Dogs are allowed for an additional fee of $10 per night per pet or $25 per pet for 3 days. 2 dogs may be allowed.

Holiday Inn Select Boston-Woburn
15 Middlesex Canal Park Road
Woburn, MA
781-935-8760 (877-270-6405)
Dogs of all sizes are allowed for an additional one time pet fee of $50 per room. 2 dogs may be allowed.

Red Roof Inn - Boston Woburn
19 Commerce Way
Woburn, MA
781-935-7110 (800-RED-ROOF)
One well-behaved family pet per room. Guest must notify front desk upon arrival. Guest is liable for any damages. In consideration of all guests, pets must never be left unattended in the guest rooms.

Residence Inn by Marriott
300 Presidential Way
Woburn, MA
781-376-4000
Dogs of all sizes are allowed. There is a $75 one time fee and a pet policy to sign at check in. Multiple dogs may be allowed.

Crowne Plaza
10 Lincoln Square
Worcester, MA
508-791-1600 (877-270-6405)
A dog up to 50 pounds is allowed for an additional pet fee of $25 per night, and pets must be crated when left alone in the room.

Colonial House
Old Kings Hwy
Yarmouth Port, MA
508-362-4348 (800-999-3416)
colonialhousecapecod.com/
There is a $5.00 per day pet charge.

Michigan Listings

Linda's Lighthouse Inn
5965 Pointe Tremble Road/H 29
Algonac, MI
810-794-2992
lindasbnb.com/
Rich in history from its prohibition days, this waterside inn on the St Clair River offers guests boat docking, a 300 foot dock, great views, and any help needed for special occasions, finding points of interest, or sightseeing. Dogs of all sizes are allowed for an additional fee of $15 per night per pet with prior arrangements. Dogs must be well behaved, leashed, and cleaned up after. When the weather permits, owners may dine with their pet on the

balcony overlooking the river. 2 dogs may be allowed.

Castle in the Country
340 H 40S
Allegan, MI
269-673-8054 (888-673-8054)
castleinthecountry.com/
A popular romantic haven, this inn and spa sits in a beautiful pastoral and wooded setting, and offers all the amenities for special occasions or a much needed getaway. One dog is allowed per room for an additional $20 per stay. Dogs must be quiet, well behaved, leashed, and cleaned up after.

Petticoat Inn
2454 W Monroe Road/H 46
Alma, MI
989-681-5728
This inn allows pets for no additional pet fee. Dogs may not be left unattended at any time, and they must be leashed and cleaned up after. Aggressive dogs are not allowed. 2 dogs may be allowed.

Days Inn Alpena
1496 M-32 West
Alpena, MI
989-356-6118 (800-329-7466)
Dogs of all sizes are allowed. There is a $10 per night pet fee per pet. 2 dogs may be allowed.

Fletcher Motel
1001 US 23N
Alpena, MI
989-354-4191 (800-334-5920)
Dogs allowed in all rooms except the luxury rooms.

Holiday Inn
1000 US 23 N.
Alpena, MI
989-356-2151 (877-270-6405)
Dogs of all sizes are allowed for no additional fee. Dogs may not be left alone in the room at any time. Multiple dogs may be allowed.

Best Western Executive Plaza
2900 Jackson Road
Ann Arbor, MI
734-665-4444 (800-780-7234)
Dogs are allowed for an additional one time pet fee of $25 per room. Multiple dogs may be allowed.

Candlewood Suites
701 Waymarket Way
Ann Arbor, MI
734-663-2818 (877-270-6405)
One dog of any size is allowed for an additional pet fee of $75 for 1 to

7 nights; the fee is $150 for 8 or more nights.

Hampton Inn
2300 Green Road
Ann Arbor, MI
734-996-4444
Dogs of all sizes are allowed. There is a $25 one time fee per room. Multiple dogs may be allowed.

Motel 6 - Ann Arbor
3764 S State St
Ann Arbor, MI
734-665-9900 (800-466-8356)
One well-behaved family pet per room. Guest must notify front desk upon arrival. Guest is liable for any damages. In consideration of all guests, pets must never be left unattended in the guest rooms.

Red Roof Inn - Ann Arbor - University North
3621 Plymouth Road
Ann Arbor, MI
734-996-5800 (800-RED-ROOF)
One well-behaved family pet per room. Guest must notify front desk upon arrival. Guest is liable for any damages. In consideration of all guests, pets must never be left unattended in the guest rooms.

Residence Inn by Marriott
800 Victors Way
Ann Arbor, MI
734-996-5666
Dogs of all sizes are allowed. There is a $15 per day per room fee up to a maximum total of $200 for studio and 1 and 2 bedroom suites, and $20 per day per room up to a maximum of $200 for Penthouse suites. They also have a pet policy to sign at check in. Multiple dogs may be allowed.

Candlewood Suites
1650 Opdyke Rd
Auburn Hills, MI
248-373-3342 (877-270-6405)
Dogs of all sizes are allowed for an additional pet fee of $75 per room. 2 dogs may be allowed.

Motel 6 - Detroit North - Auburn Hills
1471 Opdyke Rd
Auburn Hills, MI
248-373-8440 (800-466-8356)
One well-behaved family pet per room. Guest must notify front desk upon arrival. Guest is liable for any damages. In consideration of all guests, pets must never be left unattended in the guest rooms.

Staybridge Suites

2050 Featherstone Rd
Auburn Hills, MI
248-322-4600 (877-270-6405)
Dogs of all sizes are allowed for an additional pet fee of $75 per room. 2 dogs may be allowed.

Super 8 Baraga
790 Michigan Ave
Baraga, MI
906-353-6680 (800-800-8000)
Dogs of all sizes are allowed. There is a $5 per night pet fee per pet. Dogs are not allowed to be left alone in the room. Smoking and non-smoking rooms are available for pet rooms. 2 dogs may be allowed.

Days Inn Battle Creek
4786 Beckley Rd
Battle Creek, MI
269-979-3561 (800-329-7466)
Dogs of all sizes are allowed. There is a $10 per night pet fee per pet. 2 dogs may be allowed.

Motel 6 - Battle Creek
4775 Beckley Road
Battle Creek, MI
269-979-1141 (800-466-8356)
One well-behaved family pet per room. Guest must notify front desk upon arrival. Guest is liable for any damages. In consideration of all guests, pets must never be left unattended in the guest rooms.

Super 8 Battle Creek
5395 Beckley Rd
Battle Creek, MI
269-979-1828 (800-800-8000)
Dogs of all sizes are allowed. There is a $10 per night pet fee per pet. Smoking and non-smoking rooms are available for pet rooms. 2 dogs may be allowed.

Americinn of Bay City
3915 Three Mile Rd
Bay City, MI
989-671-0071
There are no additional pet fees.

Applesauce Inn
7296 H 88S
Bellaire, MI
231-533-6448
applesauceinn.com/
This wonderfully restored 100 year old country home is now a great getaway with numerous amenities, and it offers a good central location to many other sites of interest and recreation. There is one pet friendly room, and dogs of all sizes are allowed for an additional fee of $15 per night which is donated to Boxer

rescue. Dogs may not be left alone in the room or unsupervised at any time, they are not allowed on beds or furniture, and request guests bring their pet's bedding. Dogs must be housebroken, quiet, well mannered, sociable with other pets and people, leashed, and cleaned up after at all times. Dogs must be healthy and have all their shots. 2 dogs may be allowed.

Comfort Inn
45945 I 94 Service Drive
Belleville, MI
734-697-8556 (877-424-6423)
Dogs are allowed for an additional fee of $10 per night per pet. Multiple dogs may be allowed.

Red Roof Inn - Detroit Metro Airport - Belleville
45501 N Expy Service Drive
Belleville, MI
734-697-2244 (800-RED-ROOF)
One well-behaved family pet per room. Guest must notify front desk upon arrival. Guest is liable for any damages. In consideration of all guests, pets must never be left unattended in the guest rooms.

Days Inn Benton Harbor
2699 Michigan Rte 139
Benton Harbor, MI
269-925-7021 (800-329-7466)
Dogs of all sizes are allowed. There is a $5 per night pet fee per pet under 20 pounds and $10 per pet over 20 pounds. 2 dogs may be allowed.

Motel 6 - Benton Harbor
2063 Pipestone Rd
Benton Harbor, MI
269-925-5100 (800-466-8356)
One well-behaved family pet per room. Guest must notify front desk upon arrival. Guest is liable for any damages. In consideration of all guests, pets must never be left unattended in the guest rooms.

Red Roof Inn - Benton Harbor - St. Joseph
1630 Mall Drive
Benton Harbor, MI
269-927-2484 (800-RED-ROOF)
One well-behaved family pet per room. Guest must notify front desk upon arrival. Guest is liable for any damages. In consideration of all guests, pets must never be left unattended in the guest rooms.

Super 8 Benton Harbor
1950 E Napier Ave

Benton Harbor, MI
269-926-1371 (800-800-8000)
Dogs of all sizes are allowed. There is a $10 one time per pet fee per visit. Smoking and non-smoking rooms are available for pet rooms. 2 dogs may be allowed.

Bluffs View Motel
707 W Lead Street
Bessemer, MI
906-667-0311
Dogs only are allowed, and in all sizes. There is a $5 per night per pet additional fee. 2 dogs may be allowed.

Holiday Inn
1005 Perry Ave
Big Rapids, MI
231-796-4400 (877-270-6405)
Dogs of all sizes are allowed for an additional fee of $15 per night per pet. Multiple dogs may be allowed.

Quality Inn and Suites
1705 S State Street
Big Rapids, MI
231-592-5150 (877-424-6423)
Dogs are allowed for an additional fee of $6 per night per pet. Multiple dogs may be allowed.

Best Western of Birch Run/Frankenmuth
9087 Birch Run Rd
Birch Run, MI
989-624-9395 (800-780-7234)
Dogs up to 75 pounds are allowed for an additional one time pet fee of $25 per room. 2 dogs may be allowed.

Holiday Inn Express Detroit-Birmingham
35270 Woodward Ave.
Birmingham, MI
248-642-6200 (877-270-6405)
Dogs of all sizes are allowed for an additional pet fee of $50 per night per room. 2 dogs may be allowed.

Insel Haus
HCR 1, Box 157
Bois Blanc Island, MI
231-634-7393 (888-634-7393)
inselhausbandb.com/
A world class retreat, visitors arrive here by ferry, plane, or helicopter, and are welcomed to a home rich in colors and history, warm with antiques, bright with stained glass, and offering wonderful views of the Straits of Mackinac. One dog is allowed for an additional fee of $20 per night. Dogs must be quiet, well behaved, leashed, and cleaned up

after. Dogs may not be left unattended at any time, and they must be friendly to other pets and people; there is an older dog on site.

Dewey Lake Manor
11811 Laird Road
Brooklyn, MI
517-467-7122
deweylakemanor.com/
There 18 acres to explore at this lakeside inn. Outdoor amenities include grills, picnic tables, gaming areas, and use of the paddleboat and canoe. Dogs of all sizes are allowed for an additional $10 per night per pet; there can be 1 large dog or 2 small dogs per room. They request that owners bring their pets bedding. Dogs are not allowed in the dining area, but guests are welcome to dine on the veranda with their pet. Dogs must be well mannered, leashed, and cleaned up after.

Super 8 Brooklyn
155 Wamplers Lake Road
Brooklyn, MI
517-592-0888 (800-800-8000)
Dogs of all sizes are allowed. There is a $5 per night pet fee per pet. Dogs are not allowed to be left alone in the room. Smoking and non-smoking rooms are available for pet rooms. 2 dogs may be allowed.

Econo Lodge
2501 Sunnyside Dr
Cadillac, MI
231-775-6700
There is a $10 per day pet fee for the first three days of a stay.

McGuires Resort
7880 Mackinaw Trail
Cadillac, MI
231-775-9947
mcguiresresort.com
This resort is open year round. They have on-site restaurants, gift shop, swimming pool, golf, cross-country skiing and more. All well-behaved dogs are allowed for an extra $15 per night pet fee. During the winter dogs are allowed on their cross-country ski trails. Pets must be leashed at the resort and on the trails.

Days Inn Detroit/Canton
40500 Michigan Ave
Canton, MI
734-721-5200 (800-329-7466)
Dogs of all sizes are allowed. There are no additional pet fees. Pet must be kept in kennel when left alone. 2 dogs may be allowed.

La Quinta Inn Detroit/Canton
41211 Ford Road
Canton, MI
734-981-1808 (800-531-5900)
One large dog or up to 3 small to medium dogs are allowed. There are no additional pet fees unless the stay is over 7 days; then there is a $25 refundable deposit required. The front desk must be informed at check in of any pets so to inform housekeeping, and they must be leashed and cleaned up after.

Motel 6 - Detroit West - Canton
41216 Ford Rd
Canton Township, MI
734-981-5000 (800-466-8356)
One well-behaved family pet per room. Guest must notify front desk upon arrival. Guest is liable for any damages. In consideration of all guests, pets must never be left unattended in the guest rooms.

Lodge of Charlevoix
120 Michigan Ave
Charlevoix, MI
231-547-6565
There is a $10 per day pet fee.

Points North Inn
101 Michigan Ave
Charlevoix, MI
231-547-0055 (800-968-5433)
There is a $5 per day pet fee.

Super 8 Charlotte
828 E Shepherd St
Charlotte, MI
517-543-8288 (800-800-8000)
Dogs of all sizes are allowed. There are no additional pet fees. Smoking and non-smoking rooms are available for pet rooms. 2 dogs may be allowed.

Chelsea CenterTourist Home
120 S Streeet
Chelsea, MI
734-475-7397
Dogs of all sizes are allowed. There are no additional pet fees and dogs must be crated when guests are out of the room. There are only 4 pet friendly rooms. There are some breed restrictions. 2 dogs may be allowed.

Comfort Inn
1645 Commerce Park Drive
Chelsea, MI
734-433-8000 (877-424-6423)
Dogs up to 50 pounds are allowed for an additional pet fee of $15 per night per room. 2 dogs may be allowed.

Waterloo Gardens
7600 Werkener Road
Chelsea, MI
734-433-1612 (877-433 -1612)
waterloogardensbb.com/
A master spa, solarium, lush greenery, gardens, recreation, and much more are offered guests at this lovely inn. One dog is allowed per room for no additional fee. Dogs may not be left alone in the room at any time, and they must be leashed and cleaned up after at all times. Dogs must be friendly towards both other animals and people as there are 2 Golden Retrievers who live on site.

Red Roof Inn - Coldwater
348 South Willowbrook Road
Coldwater, MI
517-279-1199 (800-RED-ROOF)
One well-behaved family pet per room. Guest must notify front desk upon arrival. Guest is liable for any damages. In consideration of all guests, pets must never be left unattended in the guest rooms.

Super 8 Coldwater
600 Orleans Blvd
Coldwater, MI
517-278-8633 (800-800-8000)
Dogs of all sizes are allowed. There are no additional pet fees. Smoking and non-smoking rooms are available for pet rooms. 2 dogs may be allowed.

Red Roof Inn - Detroit - Dearborn
24130 Michigan Ave
Dearborn, MI
313-278-9732 (800-RED-ROOF)
One well-behaved family pet per room. Guest must notify front desk upon arrival. Guest is liable for any damages. In consideration of all guests, pets must never be left unattended in the guest rooms.

Ritz-Carlton
300 Town Center Drive
Dearborn, MI
313-441-2000
There is a $150 one time pet fee.

TownePlace Suites Detroit Dearborn
6141 Mercury Drive
Dearborn, MI
313-271-0200
Dogs of all sizes are allowed. There is a $75 one time pet fee per visit. 2 dogs may be allowed.

Holiday Inn Express Hotel & Suites Detroit-Downtown
1020 Washington Blvd

Michigan Listings - Please always call ahead to make sure an establishment is still dog-friendly.

Detroit, MI
313-887-7000 (877-270-6405)
Dogs of all sizes are allowed for an additional one time fee of $25 per pet. Multiple dogs may be allowed.

Drummond Island Resort & Conference Center
33494 S Maxton Road
Drummond Island, MI
906-493-1000 (800-999-6343)
drummondisland.com/
Resting on the shores of the US's largest freshwater island on 2000 lush acres filled with wildlife, this resort has all the amenities for business, relaxation, or recreation?including an 18-hole golf course and an ORV park. Dogs are allowed for an additional fee of $50 per pet per stay. Dogs must be well behaved, leashed, and cleaned up after. 2 dogs may be allowed.

H & H Resort
33185 S Water Street
Drummond Island, MI
800-543-4743
This beautiful oceanside park offers cabins and camping options. Dogs are allowed at either for no additional fee. They also have watercraft rentals that dogs are allowed on. Dogs must be well behaved, leashed, and cleaned up after. 2 dogs may be allowed.

Residence Inn by Marriott
1600 Grand River Avenue
East Lansing, MI
517-332-7711
Dogs of all sizes are allowed. There is a $75 one time fee for up to 2 pets and an additional $75 one time fee if there are more than 2. There is also a pet policy to sign at check in. Multiple dogs may be allowed.

TownePlace Suites East Lansin
2855 Hannah Blvd
East Lansing, MI
517-203-1000
Dogs of all sizes are allowed. There is a $75 one time pet fee per visit. 2 dogs may be allowed.

Candlewood Suites
37555 Hills Tech Drive
Farmington Hills, MI
248-324-0540 (877-270-6405)
Dogs up to 80 pounds are allowed for an additional one time pet fee of $75 per room for 1 to 6 days; the fee is $150 for 7 or more days. 2 dogs may be allowed.

Motel 6 - Detroit NW - Farmington

Hills
38300 Grand River Ave
Farmington Hills, MI
248-471-0590 (800-466-8356)
One well-behaved family pet per room. Guest must notify front desk upon arrival. Guest is liable for any damages. In consideration of all guests, pets must never be left unattended in the guest rooms.

Red Roof Inn - Detroit - Farmington Hills
24300 Sinacola Ct NE
Farmington Hills, MI
248-478-8640 (800-RED-ROOF)
One well-behaved family pet per room. Guest must notify front desk upon arrival. Guest is liable for any damages. In consideration of all guests, pets must never be left unattended in the guest rooms.

Glenn Country Inn
1286 64th Street
Fennville, MI
888-237-3009
glenncountryinn.com/
A quiet country inn located on 10 scenic farmland acres, this retreat features brightly colored gardens, walking trails, lush lawns, and special getaway packages. Dogs of all sizes are allowed for an additional $20 per pet per stay. Your pooch is welcomed with a plush doggy bed, yummy treats, a food bowl, and water dispenser. There is also a large, fenced area for a safe off-lead area. Dogs may not be left alone in the room at any time, and they are not allowed on the bed or furnishings. Dogs must be under owner's control, leashed, and cleaned up after. Dogs must be friendly and get along well with other animals and people. The dining room is pet friendly, and your pet may join you there for any of the meals. 2 dogs may be allowed.

Holiday Inn Express Hotel and Suites
17800 Silver Parkway
Fenton, MI
810-714-7171 (877-270-6405)
Dogs up to 50 pounds are allowed for no additional fee. 2 dogs may be allowed.

Days Inn Flint
2207 W Bristol Rd
Flint, MI
810-239-4681 (800-329-7466)
Dogs of all sizes are allowed. There is a $15 per night pet fee per pet. 2 dogs may be allowed.

Holiday Inn Express
1150 Longway Blvd
Flint, MI
810-238-7744 (877-270-6405)
Dogs of all sizes are allowed for an additional fee of $25 per night per pet. 2 dogs may be allowed.

Howard Johnson Express Inn
G-3277 Miller Road
Flint, MI
810-733-5910 (800-446-4656)
Dogs of all sizes are welcome. There is a $10 per day pet fee.

Motel 6 - Flint
2324 Austin Pkwy
Flint, MI
810-767-7100 (800-466-8356)
One well-behaved family pet per room. Guest must notify front desk upon arrival. Guest is liable for any damages. In consideration of all guests, pets must never be left unattended in the guest rooms.

Red Roof Inn - Flint
G-3219 Miller Rd
Flint, MI
810-733-1660 (800-RED-ROOF)
One well-behaved family pet per room. Guest must notify front desk upon arrival. Guest is liable for any damages. In consideration of all guests, pets must never be left unattended in the guest rooms.

Residence Inn by Marriott
2202 W Hill Road
Flint, MI
810-424-7000
Dogs of all sizes are allowed. There is a $75 one time fee and a pet policy to sign at check in. Multiple dogs may be allowed.

Drury Inn & Suites
260 South Main
Frankenmuth, MI
989-652-2800 (800-378-7946)
Dogs of all sizes are permitted. Pets are not allowed in the breakfast area of the hotel. Pets are not to be left unattended, and each guest must assume liability for damage of property or other guest complaints. There is a limit of one pet per room.

Valentine's Bay Lodge
8191 H 183
Garden, MI
906-644-5012
uprentalhome.com/
Warmly inviting, this mountain lodge style getaway is located on the scenic Garden Peninsula with beautiful lakefront views, lush

greenery, and tree-lined paths. Dogs of all sizes are allowed for no additional fee. Dogs may not be left unattended; they must be quiet, well behaved, leashed, and cleaned up after at all times. 2 dogs may be allowed.

Best Western Alpine Lodge
833 West Main St
Gaylord, MI
989-732-2431 (800-780-7234)
Dogs are allowed for no additional pet fee. Dogs may not be left alone in the room. 2 dogs may be allowed.

Quality Inn
137 West Street
Gaylord, MI
989-732-7541 (877-424-6423)
Dogs are allowed for an additional fee of $10 per night per pet. Multiple dogs may be allowed.

Red Roof Inn - Gaylord
510 S Wisconsin Ave
Gaylord, MI
989-731-6331 (800-RED-ROOF)
One well-behaved family pet per room. Guest must notify front desk upon arrival. Guest is liable for any damages. In consideration of all guests, pets must never be left unattended in the guest rooms.

Norway Pines Motel
7111 US 2, 41 and M-35
Gladstone, MI
906-786-5119
baydenoc.com/norway/
There are no additional pet fees.

Grand Haven
Grand Haven, MI
616-638-1262
There are a couple of pet friendly properties offered by this agency. Dogs of all sizes are allowed for an additional pet fee of $25 per stay per house plus a $100 refundable deposit. Dogs must be housetrained, well behaved, leashed, and cleaned up after at all times. 2 dogs may be allowed.

Best Western Hospitality Hotel & Suites
5500 28th Street SE
Grand Rapids, MI
616-949-8400 (800-780-7234)
Dogs up to 50 pounds are allowed for an additional fee of $10 per night per pet. Dogs may not be left alone in the room. Multiple dogs may be allowed.

Comfort Inn

4155 28th Street
Grand Rapids, MI
616-957-2080 (877-424-6423)
Dogs are allowed for an additional pet fee of $5 per night per room. There is a pet agreement to sign at check in, and dogs may not be left alone in the room. 2 dogs may be allowed.

Days Inn Grand Rapids Dwtn
310 Pearl St NW
Grand Rapids, MI
616-235-7611 (800-329-7466)
Dogs of all sizes are allowed. There is a $10 per night pet fee per pet. 2 dogs may be allowed.

Hampton Inn
4981 28th Street SE
Grand Rapids, MI
616-956-9304
Dogs of all sizes are allowed. There is a pet policy to sign at check in and there are no additional pet fees. Dogs are not allowed in food areas and they must be kenneled if you are out of the room. Multiple dogs may be allowed.

Homewood Suites
3920 Stahl Dr SE
Grand Rapids, MI
616-285-7100
There is an $80 one time pet fee and a $5 per day pet fee.

Howard Johnson Plaza Hotel
255 28th St. SW
Grand Rapids, MI
616-241-6444 (800-446-4656)
Dogs of all sizes are welcome. There is a $10 one time pet fee.

La Quinta Inn & Suites Grand Rapids
5500 28th Street
Grand Rapids, MI
616-949-8400 (800-531-5900)
Dogs of all sizes are allowed. There is a $10 per night per pet additional fee. Dogs may not be left unattended, and they must be leashed and cleaned up after. Multiple dogs may be allowed.

Motel 6 - Grand Rapids East - Airport
3524 28th St SE
Grand Rapids, MI
616-957-3511 (800-466-8356)
One well-behaved family pet per room. Guest must notify front desk upon arrival. Guest is liable for any damages. In consideration of all guests, pets must never be left unattended in the guest rooms.

Radisson Hotel Grand Rapids North
270 Ann Street NW
Grand Rapids, MI
616-363-9001
Dogs of all sizes are allowed. There is a $20 additional pet fee.

Red Roof Inn - Grand Rapids
5131 East 28th Street
Grand Rapids, MI
616-942-0800 (800-RED-ROOF)
One well-behaved family pet per room. Guest must notify front desk upon arrival. Guest is liable for any damages. In consideration of all guests, pets must never be left unattended in the guest rooms.

Residence Inn by Marriott
2701 E Beltline SE
Grand Rapids, MI
616-957-8111
Dogs of all sizes are allowed. There is a $75 one time fee and a pet policy to sign at check in. Multiple dogs may be allowed.

Residence Inn by Marriott
3451 Rivertown Point Court SW
Grandville, MI
616-538-1100
Dogs of all sizes are allowed. There is a $75 one time fee and a pet policy to sign at check in. Multiple dogs may be allowed.

Super 8 Grayling
5828 NA Miles Parkway
Grayling, MI
989-348-8888 (800-800-8000)
Dogs of all sizes are allowed. There is a $7350 per night pet fee per pet. Smoking and non-smoking rooms are available for pet rooms. 2 dogs may be allowed.

Best Western Copper Crown Motel
235 Hancock Ave
Hancock, MI
906-482-6111 (800-780-7234)
Dogs are allowed for an additional pet fee of $10 (plus tax) per night per room. 2 dogs may be allowed.

Best Western Holland Inn & Suites
2888 W Shore Drive
Holland, MI
616-994-0400 (800-780-7234)
Quiet dogs are allowed for an additional one time pet fee of $50 per room. Multiple dogs may be allowed.

Residence Inn by Marriott
631 Southpoint Ridge Road
Holland, MI
616-393-6900

Dogs of all sizes are allowed. There is a $75 one time fee and a pet policy to sign at check in. 2 dogs may be allowed.

Best Western Franklin Square Inn
820 Shelden Avenue
Houghton, MI
906-487-1700 (800-780-7234)
Dogs up to 50 pounds are allowed for an additional pet fee of $10 per night per room. Multiple dogs may be allowed.

Holiday Inn Express
200 Cloverleaf Lane
Houghton Lake, MI
989-422-7829 (877-270-6405)
Quiet dogs of all sizes are allowed for an additional one time fee of $25 for 1or 2 pets; a 3rd pet is an additional $25. Multiple dogs may be allowed.

Super 8 Houghton Lake
9580 W Lake City Rd
Houghton Lake, MI
989-422-3119 (800-800-8000)
Dogs of all sizes are allowed. There is a $5 per night pet fee per pet. Dogs are not allowed to be left alone in the room. Smoking and non-smoking rooms are available for pet rooms. 2 dogs may be allowed.

Days Inn Imlay
6692 Newark Rd
Imlay City, MI
810-724-8005 (800-329-7466)
Dogs of all sizes are allowed. There is a $8 per night pet fee per pet. 2 dogs may be allowed.

Super 8 Imlay City
6951 Newark Rd
Imlay City, MI
810-724-8700 (800-800-8000)
Dogs of all sizes are allowed. There is a $10 one time per pet fee per visit. Smoking and non-smoking rooms are available for pet rooms. 2 dogs may be allowed.

Days Inn Iron Mountain
W 8176 S US 2
Iron Mountain, MI
906-774-2181 (800-329-7466)
Dogs of all sizes are allowed. There is a $10 per night pet fee per pet. 2 dogs may be allowed.

Super 8 Ironwood
160 E Cloverland Dr
Ironwood, MI
906-932-3395 (800-800-8000)
Dogs of all sizes are allowed. There is a $10 per night pet fee per pet.

Smoking and non-smoking rooms are available for pet rooms. 2 dogs may be allowed.

Holiday Inn
2000 Holiday Inn Dr
Jackson, MI
517-783-2681 (877-270-6405)
Dogs up to 50 pounds are allowed for an additional pet fee per room of $15 for the 1st night and $5 for each night after. 2 dogs may be allowed.

Motel 6 - Jackson
830 Royal Dr
Jackson, MI
517-789-7186 (800-466-8356)
One well-behaved family pet per room. Guest must notify front desk upon arrival. Guest is liable for any damages. In consideration of all guests, pets must never be left unattended in the guest rooms.

Super 8 Jackson
2001 Shirley Dr
Jackson, MI
517-788-8780 (800-800-8000)
Dogs of all sizes are allowed. There is a $10 per night pet fee per pet. Dogs are not allowed to be left alone in the room. Smoking and non-smoking rooms are available for pet rooms. 2 dogs may be allowed.

Best Western Hospitality Inn
3640 E Cork Street
Kalamazoo, MI
269-381-1900 (800-780-7234)
Dogs are allowed for an additional fee of $15 per night per pet. Multiple dogs may be allowed.

Comfort Inn Airport
3820 Sprinkle Road
Kalamazoo, MI
269-381-7000 (877-424-6423)
Dogs are allowed for an additional one time pet fee of $15 per room. Multiple dogs may be allowed.

Holiday Inn Kalamazoo-W (W Michigan Univ)
2747 S. 11th St
Kalamazoo, MI
269-375-6000 (877-270-6405)
Dogs up to 50 pounds are allowed for an additional one time pet fee of $25 per room. 2 dogs may be allowed.

Knights Inn
1211 S Westernedge Ave
Kalamazoo, MI
269-381-5000

There is a $25 per stay pet fee.

Motel 6 - Kalamazoo
3704 Vanrick Drive
Kalamazoo, MI
269-344-9255 (800-466-8356)
One well-behaved family pet per room. Guest must notify front desk upon arrival. Guest is liable for any damages. In consideration of all guests, pets must never be left unattended in the guest rooms.

Red Roof Inn - Kalamazoo East
3701 East Cork Street
Kalamazoo, MI
269-382-6350 (800-RED-ROOF)
One well-behaved family pet per room. Guest must notify front desk upon arrival. Guest is liable for any damages. In consideration of all guests, pets must never be left unattended in the guest rooms.

Red Roof Inn - Kalamazoo West - University
5425 W Michigan Ave
Kalamazoo, MI
269-375-7400 (800-RED-ROOF)
One well-behaved family pet per room. Guest must notify front desk upon arrival. Guest is liable for any damages. In consideration of all guests, pets must never be left unattended in the guest rooms.

Residence Inn by Marriott
1500 E Kilgore
Kalamazoo, MI
269-349-0855
Dogs of all sizes are allowed. There is a $75 one time fee and a pet policy to sign at check in. Multiple dogs may be allowed.

Super 8 Kalamazoo
618 Maple Hill Dr
Kalamazoo, MI
269-345-0146 (800-800-8000)
Dogs of all sizes are allowed. There is a $10 per night pet fee per pet. Smoking and non-smoking rooms are available for pet rooms. 2 dogs may be allowed.

Staybridge Suites
3000 Lake Eastbrook Blvd SE
Kentwood, MI
616-464-3200 (877-270-6405)
Dogs of all sizes are allowed for an additional one time pet fee of $75 per room. Multiple dogs may be allowed.

Best Western Palace Inn
2755 S Lapeer Road
Lake Orion, MI
248-391-2755 (800-780-7234)

Dogs are allowed for an additional one time pet fee of $25 per room. Multiple dogs may be allowed.

The White Rabbit Inn
14634 Red Arrow H
Lakeside, MI
269-469-4620 (800-967-2224)
whiterabbitinn.com/
Popular as a relaxing, romantic getaway, this lovely inn is also only a short distance from a variety of other attractions and recreation. Dogs of all sizes are allowed in 2 of their cabins for no additional pet fee as long as there is advance notice that a dog will be coming. Dogs must be quiet, well mannered, leashed, cleaned up after at all times, and friendly towards people and other animals as there are 4 other resident dogs. Owners are responsible for any pet damage, so they suggest kenneling pets if they will be in the room alone, and they may only be left for very short periods. Multiple dogs may be allowed.

Best Western Midway Hotel
7711 W Saginaw Highway
Lansing, MI
517-627-8471 (800-780-7234)
One dog up to 50 pounds is allowed for no additional pet fee.

Candlewood Suites
3545 Forest Road
Lansing, MI
517-351-8181 (877-270-6405)
Dogs up to 80 pounds are allowed for an additional one time pet fee of $75 per room. Multiple dogs may be allowed.

Hampton Inn
525 N Canal Road
Lansing, MI
517-627-8381
Dogs of all sizes are allowed. There are no additional pet fees. Multiple dogs may be allowed.

Holiday Inn Lansing-West-Conference Ctr
7501 W Saginaw Hwy
Lansing, MI
517-627-3211 (877-270-6405)
Dogs of all sizes are allowed for no additional fee. Multiple dogs may be allowed.

Motel 6 - Lansing
7326 W Saginaw Hwy
Lansing, MI
517-321-1444 (800-466-8356)
One well-behaved family pet per room. Guest must notify front desk

upon arrival. Guest is liable for any damages. In consideration of all guests, pets must never be left unattended in the guest rooms.

Quality Suites
901 Delta Commerce Drive
Lansing, MI
517-886-0600
Dogs are allowed for an additional one time pet fee of $25 per room. Multiple dogs may be allowed.

Red Roof Inn - Lansing East - University
3615 Dunckel Rd
Lansing, MI
517-332-2575 (800-RED-ROOF)
One well-behaved family pet per room. Guest must notify front desk upon arrival. Guest is liable for any damages. In consideration of all guests, pets must never be left unattended in the guest rooms.

Red Roof Inn - Lansing West
7412 W Saginaw Hwy
Lansing, MI
517-321-7246 (800-RED-ROOF)
One well-behaved family pet per room. Guest must notify front desk upon arrival. Guest is liable for any damages. In consideration of all guests, pets must never be left unattended in the guest rooms.

Residence Inn by Marriott
922 Delta Commerce Drive
Lansing, MI
517-886-5030
Dogs of all sizes are allowed. There is a $75 one time fee and a pet policy to sign at check in. Multiple dogs may be allowed.

Sheraton Lansing Hotel
925 South Creyts Road
Lansing, MI
517-323-7100 (888-625-5144)
Dogs up to 80 pounds are allowed for no additional pet fee. Dogs may not be left alone in the room.

Residence Inn by Marriott
17250 Fox Drive
Livonia, MI
734-462-4201
Dogs of all sizes are allowed. There is a $75 one time fee and a pet policy to sign at check in. Multiple dogs may be allowed.

TownePlace Suites Detroit Livonia
17450 Fox Drive
Livonia, MI
734-542-7400
Dogs of all sizes are allowed. There

is a $75 one time pet fee per visit. 2 dogs may be allowed.

Candlelight Inn
709 E Ludington Avenue/H 10
Ludington, MI
231-845-8074 (877-997-0099)
candleliteinnludington.com/
Relaxation, romantic ambiance, historic surroundings, colorful gardens, special events and packages, and a variety of special amenities greet guests at this inn. Dogs of all sizes are allowed for an additional $10 per night per pet. Your pup is greeted with their own plush bed, food/water dishes, treats, a blanket to cover over the bed or furniture, and a doggie towel for occasional muddy paws. Dogs may not be left alone in the room except during breakfast, and they are not allowed in the dining room or other areas of the house. Dogs must be leashed and cleaned up after at all times; plastic bags are available.

Holiday Inn Express
5323 W. US 10
Ludington, MI
231-845-7004 (877-270-6405)
Dogs of all sizes are allowed for an additional fee of $10 per night per pet. 2 dogs may be allowed.

Nader's Lake Shore Motor Lodge
612 N Lakeshore Dr
Ludington, MI
231-843-8757 (800-968-0109)
Pets are allowed in the main lodge building and the poolside rooms. They are not allowed in the Suite Building. The hotel is closed during the winter months. Pets must be leashed and attended at all times.

Great Turtle Lodge
P.O. Box 519
Mackinac Island, MI
906-847-6237
greatturtlelodge.com
This accommodation offers a variety of room sizes including suites with full kitchens and living rooms. Each room has a private entrance. One and two bedroom apartments are also available. They are located around the corner from the Grand Hotel and within walking distance of West Bluff. Rooms range in price from $59 to $459. Prices are subject to change. When you call they will ask what price range you are interested in and then will find the right room for you. They are open year round. There is usually a two to three night minimum stay depending on the season. While they ask what

type of dog you have, well-behaved dogs of all kinds are welcome. Pets are not allowed on the beds, furniture, pillows or comforters. There is a $20 per stay or per day pet fee depending on the room and length of stay. To get there from the ferry, you can walk or take a horse taxi.

Mission Point Resort
One Lakeshore Drive
Mackinac Island, MI
906-847-3312
missionpoint.com
Amenities at this resort include an outdoor heated pool, sauna and steam rooms, movie theater, hair salon, lawn bowling, croquet, horseshoes, hot tubs, room service and full service health club. Well-behaved leashed dogs are allowed. Pets are not allowed in the main building but are welcome in the rooms at the adjacent wing. There is a $50 per stay pet fee. Reservations can be made at 1-800-833-7711. Once you reach the ferry docks on the island, your luggage will be tagged and sent directly to the Mission Point Resort. You will receive one claim ticket per bag and you can get your luggage at the hotel's bell stand. You can walk or take the horse taxi to the hotel.

Sunset Condominiums
Call to arrange.
Mackinac Island, MI
800-473-6960
Dogs are welcome in certain rooms and condos. All accommodations offer great views of the island and are non-smoking. The patio room costs about $145 per night with a $25 per stay pet fee. The one bedroom condo suite is like a studio and has a kitchen and living area. Rates are about $185 per night with a $50 per stay pet fee. If you need more space, an extra bedroom can be added to the one bedroom condo for a total of $295 per night with a $75 per stay pet fee. Rates are subject to change. Well-behaved leashed dogs of all sizes are welcome. They just ask that if you leave your dog alone in the room that he or she be in a crate that you provide. To get there from the ferry, you can take a horse taxi to the condos.

Holiday Inn Express Mackinaw City
364 Louvigney
Mackinaw City, MI
231-436-7100 (877-270-6405)
Dogs of all sizes are allowed for no

additional fee. Multiple dogs may be allowed.

Ramada Inn
450 S Nicolet
Mackinaw City, MI
231-436-5535
Well behaved dogs of all sizes are allowed. There is a $50 per night per room additional pet fee. Dogs are not allowed to be left alone in the room. Multiple dogs may be allowed.

Motel 6 - Detroit NE - Madison Heights
32700 Barrington Rd
Madison Heights, MI
248-583-0500 (800-466-8356)
One well-behaved family pet per room. Guest must notify front desk upon arrival. Guest is liable for any damages. In consideration of all guests, pets must never be left unattended in the guest rooms.

Red Roof Inn - Detroit - Madison Heights
32511 Concord Dr
Madison Heights, MI
248-583-4700 (800-RED-ROOF)
One well-behaved family pet per room. Guest must notify front desk upon arrival. Guest is liable for any damages. In consideration of all guests, pets must never be left unattended in the guest rooms.

Residence Inn by Marriott
32650 Stephenson Highway
Madison Heights, MI
248-583-4322
Dogs of all sizes are allowed. There is a $75 one time fee per pet and a pet policy to sign at check in. Multiple dogs may be allowed.

Comfort Inn
617 E Lakeshore Drive/H 2
Manistique, MI
906-341-6981 (877-424-6423)
Dogs are allowed for an additional fee of $10 per night per pet. Dogs may not be left alone in the room at any time. Multiple dogs may be allowed.

Mendon Country Inn
440 E Main Street/H 60
Mendon, MI
269-496-8132 (800-304-3366)
mendoncountryinn.com/
This retreat offers a long and colorful history from its 1843 beginnings, 14 lush acres with trails, a putting green, gardens, an island, canoes/kayaks for guests to

use during their stay, and numerous other amenities. Dogs of all sizes are welcome for no additional fee. Dogs may not be left alone in the room at any time, and they must be quiet, well mannered, leashed, and cleaned up after. 2 dogs may be allowed.

Econo Lodge on the Bay
2516 10th St
Menominee, MI
906-863-4431
There is a $25 per day additional pet fee per pet. The hotel provides pet beds, treats and water and food bowls for pets. Up to 2 pets are allowed per room. 2 dogs may be allowed.

Fairview Inn
2200 W Wackerly St
Midland, MI
517-631-0070 (800-422-2744)
fairviewinnmidland.com/
There is a $25 refundable deposit for pets.

Sleep Inn
2100 W Wackerly Street
Midland, MI
989-837-1010 (877-424-6423)
Dogs are allowed for an additional fee of $10 per night per pet. Multiple dogs may be allowed.

Best Western Prestige Inn
1900 Welcome Way
Monroe, MI
734-289-2330 (800-780-7234)
Dogs are allowed for an additional fee per pet of $10 for a 1 to 3 days stay. Multiple dogs may be allowed.

Comfort Inn
6500 E Albain Road
Monroe, MI
734-384-1500 (877-424-6423)
Dogs are allowed for an additional pet fee of $10 per night per room. 2 dogs may be allowed.

Comfort Inn
1 North River Road
Mount Clemens, MI
586-465-2185 (877-424-6423)
Dogs are allowed for an additional fee of $10 per night per pet. 2 dogs may be allowed.

Comfort Inn and Suites University Park
2424 S Mission Street
Mount Pleasant, MI
989-772-4000 (877-424-6423)
Dogs are allowed for an additional one time pet fee of $15 per room.

Multiple dogs may be allowed.

Holiday Inn Express Munising-Lakeview
E8990 M-28
Munising, MI
906-387-4800 (877-270-6405)
Dogs of all sizes are allowed for an additional fee of $10 per night per pet. Multiple dogs may be allowed.

Super 8 Muskegon
3380 Hoyt St
Muskegon, MI
231-733-0088 (800-800-8000)
Dogs of all sizes are allowed. There is a $15 per night pet fee per pet. Smoking and non-smoking rooms are available for pet rooms. 2 dogs may be allowed.

Holiday Inn Express Hotel & Suites New Buffalo
11500 Holiday Drive
New Buffalo, MI
269-469-1400 (877-270-6405)
Dogs of all sizes are allowed for an additional fee of $25 per pet for each 1 to 3 days stay. 2 dogs may be allowed.

New Buffalo Inn and Spa
231 E Buffalo Street/H 12
New Buffalo, MI
269-469-1000
newbuffaloinn.com/
This scenic retreat also offers a Women's Wellness Spa. Dogs of all sizes are allowed for an additional fee of $25 per night per pet in some of their cottages. Dogs are not allowed on the bed or furniture, and they ask that pets prone to being on them be placed in a crate when they are alone in the room. Dogs must be well mannered, leashed, and cleaned up after. 2 dogs may be allowed.

The Rainbow Lodge
9706 County Road 423
Newberry, MI
906-658-3357
The Rainbow Lodge also offers watercraft rentals, and it sits at the entrance of Big Two Hearted River overlooking Lake Superior; the river is considered one of the 10 best trout streams in the US. Dogs are allowed at the lodge and on the watercraft rentals for no additional fee. Dogs must be quiet, well behaved, leashed, and cleaned up after at all times. 2 dogs may be allowed.

Residence Inn by Marriott
27477 Cabaret Drive
Novi, MI

248-735-7400
Dogs of all sizes are allowed. There is a $100 one time fee and a pet policy to sign at check in. If you have more than one pet, please call the hotel before booking. Multiple dogs may be allowed.

Sheraton Detroit Novi
21111 Haggerty Road
Novi, MI
248-349-4000 (888-625-5144)
Dogs up to 80 pounds are allowed. There are no additional pet fees. Dogs are not allowed to be left alone in the room.

TownePlace Suites Detroit Novi
42600 Eleven Mile Road
Novi, MI
248-305-5533
Dogs of all sizes are allowed. There is a $75 one time pet fee per visit. 2 dogs may be allowed.

Comfort Inn and Suites
153 Ampey Road
Paw Paw, MI
269-655-0303 (877-424-6423)
Dogs up to 50 pounds are allowed for no additional pet fee. Multiple dogs may be allowed.

Holiday Inn Express
1600 Highway 31 North
Pellston, MI
231-539-7000 (877-270-6405)
Dogs of all sizes are allowed for an additional one time pet fee of $20 per room. Multiple dogs may be allowed.

Comfort Inn
1314 H 31N
Petoskey, MI
213-347-3220 (877-424-6423)
Dogs are allowed for no additional pet fee. Multiple dogs may be allowed.

Days Inn Petoskey
1420 US 131 South
Petoskey, MI
231-348-3900 (800-329-7466)
Dogs of all sizes are allowed. There is a $10 per night pet fee per pet. 2 dogs may be allowed.

Comfort Inn
622 Allegan Street
Plainwell, MI
269-685-9891 (877-424-6423)
Dogs are allowed for an additional fee of $10 per night per pet. 2 dogs may be allowed.

Red Roof Inn - Detroit - Plymouth

39700 Ann Arbor Rd
Plymouth, MI
734-459-3300 (800-RED-ROOF)
One well-behaved family pet per room. Guest must notify front desk upon arrival. Guest is liable for any damages. In consideration of all guests, pets must never be left unattended in the guest rooms.

Residence Inn by Marriott
3333 Centerpoint Parkway
Pontiac, MI
248-858-8664
Dogs of all sizes are allowed. There is a $75 one time fee and a pet policy to sign at check in. Multiple dogs may be allowed.

Hampton Inn
1655 Yeager Street
Port Huron, MI
810-966-9000
Dogs of all sizes are allowed. There is a $25 per stay per room pet fee. Multiple dogs may be allowed.

East Bay Lakefront Lodge
125 Twelfth Street
Prudenville, MI
989-366-5910
eastbaylodge.com/
Nestled among the pines along the shores of Houghton Lake, this 1925 lodge has all the charm of a mountain retreat with a wide variety of land and water recreational opportunities. Dogs of all sizes are allowed for no additional fee. Dogs must be friendly, well groomed, leashed, and cleaned up after. 2 dogs may be allowed.

Red Roof Inn - Detroit - Rochester Hills
2580 Crooks Rd
Rochester Hills, MI
248-853-6400 (800-RED-ROOF)
One well-behaved family pet per room. Guest must notify front desk upon arrival. Guest is liable for any damages. In consideration of all guests, pets must never be left unattended in the guest rooms.

Baymont Inn & Suites Detroit/Romulus Airport
9000 Wickham Road
Romulus, MI
734-722-6000 (800-531-5900)
A dog of any size is allowed. There are no additional pet fees with a credit card on file. Dogs must be leashed and cleaned up after.

Clarion Hotel Detroit Metro Airport
8600 Merriman Road

Romulus, MI
734-728-7900 (877-424-6423)
Dogs are allowed for an additional
fee of $10 per night per pet. 2 dogs
may be allowed.

Detroit Metro Airport Marriott
30559 Flynn Drive
Romulus, MI
734-729-7555 (800-228-9290)
One dog of any size is allowed.
There is a $75 one time additional
pet fee. Your dog must be leashed,
cleaned up after, and crated when
left alone in the room.

Days Inn Roseville
32851 Gratiot
Roseville, MI
586-293-3033 (800-329-7466)
Dogs of all sizes are allowed. There
is a $15 per night pet fee per pet. 2
dogs may be allowed.

Red Roof Inn - Detroit - Roseville
31800 Little Mack Ave
Roseville, MI
586-296-0310 (800-RED-ROOF)
One well-behaved family pet per
room. Guest must notify front desk
upon arrival. Guest is liable for any
damages. In consideration of all
guests, pets must never be left
unattended in the guest rooms.

Best Western Georgian Inn
31327 Gratiot Avenue
Roseville (Detroit), MI
586-294-0400 (800-780-7234)
Dogs are allowed for an additional
fee of $8 per night per pet. Multiple
dogs may be allowed.

Best Western Saginaw
1408 S Outer Drive
Saginaw, MI
989-755-0461 (800-780-7234)
Dogs are allowed for an additional
one time pet fee of $25 per room.
Multiple dogs may be allowed.

Hampton Inn
2222 Tittabawassee Road
Saginaw, MI
989-792-7666
Dogs of all sizes are allowed. There
is a $100 refundable deposit and a
pet policy to sign at check in. Multiple
dogs may be allowed.

Howard Johnson Plaza Hotel
400 Johnson Street
Saginaw, MI
989-753-6608 (800-446-4656)
Well-behaved dogs of all sizes are
allowed. There is a $20 refundable
pet deposit.

Knights Inn - Saginaw South
1415 S Outer Dr
Saginaw, MI
989-754-9200
There is a $10 one time pet fee.

Motel 6 - Saginaw - Frankenmuth
966 South Outer Drive
Saginaw, MI
989-754-8414 (800-466-8356)
One well-behaved family pet per
room. Guest must notify front desk
upon arrival. Guest is liable for any
damages. In consideration of all
guests, pets must never be left
unattended in the guest rooms.

Quality Inn
913 Boulevard Drive
Saint Ignace, MI
906-643-9700 (877-424-6423)
Dogs are allowed for an additional
fee of $10 per night per pet. Multiple
dogs may be allowed.

Park House Inn
888 Holland Street
Saugatuck, MI
269-857-4535 (866-321-4535)
parkhouseinn.com/
Flowers, greenery, trees, and 2
levels of wrap around porches to
view it all, are only a couple of the
favorites at this popular, historic
1857 inn. In addition to full
breakfasts and concierge services,
they offer spa and fireplace suites.
Dogs are allowed in the Rose
Garden Cottage (with hot tub) for an
additional $20 per night per pet with
advance reservations. Dogs must
be well behaved, leashed, and
cleaned up after at all times. 2 dogs
may be allowed.

Best Value Inn
3411 I-75 Business Spur
Sault Ste Marie, MI
906-635-9190
Dogs are allowed at this inn for an
additional $5 per night per pet.
Dogs must be quiet, leashed, and
cleaned up after at all times. 2 dogs
may be allowed.

Holiday Inn Express
1171 Riverview Way
Sault Ste Marie, MI
906-632-3999 (877-270-6405)
Dogs of all sizes are allowed for an
additional one time pet fee of $15
per room. 2 dogs may be allowed.

Best Western Sault Ste. Marie
4281 I-75 Business Spur
Sault Ste. Marie, MI

906-632-2170 (800-780-7234)
Dogs are allowed for an additional
one time pet fee of $20 per room. 2
dogs may be allowed.

Comfort Inn
4404 I 75 Business Spur
Sault Ste. Marie, MI
906-635-1118 (877-424-6423)
Quiet dogs are allowed for an
additional fee of $10 per night per
pet. Multiple dogs may be allowed.

Quality Inn and Suites Conference
Center
3290 I 75 Business Spur
Sault Ste. Marie, MI
906-635-6918 (877-424-6423)
Dogs are allowed for an additional
fee of $10 to $20 per night per pet,
depending on the size of the pet. 2
dogs may be allowed.

Super 8 Sault Sainte Marie
3826 I-75 Business Spur
Sault Ste. Marie, MI
903-632-8882 (800-800-8000)
Dogs of all sizes are allowed. There
are no additional pet fees. Dogs are
not allowed to be left alone in the
room. Smoking and non-smoking
rooms are available for pet rooms. 2
dogs may be allowed.

Candlewood Suites
1 Corporate Drive
Southfield, MI
248-945-0010 (877-270-6405)
Dogs up to 80 pounds are allowed
for an additional one time pet fee of
$75 per room for 1 to 6 days; the fee
is $150 for 7 or more days. 2 dogs
may be allowed.

Red Roof Inn - Detroit - Southfield
27660 Northwestern Hwy
Southfield, MI
248-353-7200 (800-RED-ROOF)
One well-behaved family pet per
room. Guest must notify front desk
upon arrival. Guest is liable for any
damages. In consideration of all
guests, pets must never be left
unattended in the guest rooms.

Residence Inn by Marriott
26700 Central Park Blvd
Southfield, MI
248-352-8900
Well behaved dogs of all sizes are
allowed. There is a $75 one time fee
and a pet policy to sign at check in.
Multiple dogs may be allowed.

The Westin
1500 Town Center
Southfield, MI

248-728-6536 (888-625-5144)
This hotel offers luxury accommodations, fine dining, a long list of amenities, and a convenient location to all the attractions the city has to offer. Dogs up to 40 pounds are allowed for no addition fee unless extra pet cleaning of the room is needed; there is a pet waiver to sign at check in. They also offer pet amenities including their own bed and dishes. Dogs must be well behaved, leashed, and cleaned up after at all times. 2 dogs may be allowed.

La Quinta Inn Detroit/Southgate
12888 Reeck Road
Southgate, MI
734-374-3000 (800-531-5900)
Dogs of all sizes are allowed. There are no additional fees. There is a pet waiver to sign at check in. Dogs must be well behaved, and a cell number needs to be left with the front office when the pet is in the room alone. Dogs must be leashed and cleaned up after. Multiple dogs may be allowed.

Holiday Inn
940 W Savidge Street
Spring Lake, MI
616-846-1000 (877-270-6405)
Dogs of all sizes are allowed for an additional fee of $10 per night per pet. 2 dogs may be allowed.

Hotel Dupont
913 Boulevard Dr
St Ignace, MI
906-643-9700
There is a $10 per day pet fee.

TownePlace Suites Detroit Sterling Heights
14800 Lakeside Circle
Sterling Heights, MI
586-566-0900
Dogs of all sizes are allowed. There is a $75 one time pet fee per visit. 2 dogs may be allowed.

Hampton Inn
5050 Red Arrow H
Stevensville, MI
269-429-2700
Dogs of all sizes are allowed. There are no additional pet fees. Multiple dogs may be allowed.

Tawas Motel - Resort
1124 W. Lake Street
Tawas City, MI
989-362-3822
Motel amenities include individual heating and cooling, free local calls,

free continental breakfast, Jacuzzi, heated outdoor pool and a picnic area with grills. Well-behaved dogs are welcome. There are no pet fees.

Red Roof Inn - Detroit - Taylor
21230 Eureka Rd
Taylor, MI
734-374-1150 (800-RED-ROOF)
One well-behaved family pet per room. Guest must notify front desk upon arrival. Guest is liable for any damages. In consideration of all guests, pets must never be left unattended in the guest rooms.

Crystal Mountain Resort
12500 Crystal Mountain Drive
Thompsonville, MI
800-968-7686
crystalmountain.com/lodging/
This resort offers a variety of accommodations and recreational pursuits both in the surrounding area and at the resort, including an adventure water park. They are also home to the Michigan Legacy Art Park, an expression of human and nature through major works of art on a 1.6 mile trail through hilly, wooded terrain. One large dog or 2 small to medium dogs are allowed per room for an additional fee of $50 for the 1st night and $10 each night after per pet. Dogs must be well behaved, leashed, and cleaned up after; they are not allowed in other resort buildings or on the cross-country ski trails in winter.

Best Western Four Seasons
305 Munson Ave
Traverse City, MI
231-946-8424 (800-780-7234)
Dogs are allowed for an additional pet fee of $10 per night per room. 2 dogs may be allowed.

Days Inn Traverse
420 Munson Ave
Traverse City, MI
231-941-0208 (800-329-7466)
Dogs of all sizes are allowed. There is a $10 per night pet fee per pet. 2 dogs may be allowed.

Holiday Inn
615 E. Front Street
Traverse City, MI
231-947-3700 (877-270-6405)
Dogs of all sizes are allowed for an additional fee of $10 per night per pet. Multiple dogs may be allowed.

Motel 6 - Traverse City
1582 US-31 North

Traverse City, MI
231-938-3002 (800-466-8356)
One well-behaved family pet per room. Guest must notify front desk upon arrival. Guest is liable for any damages. In consideration of all guests, pets must never be left unattended in the guest rooms.

Quality Inn by the Bay
1492 H 31N
Traverse City, MI
231-929-4423 (877-424-6423)
Dogs are allowed for an additional pet fee of $10 per night per room. Dogs may not be left alone in the room. Multiple dogs may be allowed.

Candlewood Suites
2550 Troy Center Drive
Troy, MI
248-269-6600 (877-270-6405)
Dogs of all sizes are allowed for an additional one time pet fee per room of $75 for 1 to 6 nights; the fee is $150 for 7 or more nights. 2 dogs may be allowed.

Drury Inn
575 W. Big Beaver Road
Troy, MI
248-528-3330 (800-378-7946)
Dogs of all sizes are permitted. Pets are not allowed in the breakfast area of the hotel. Pets are not to be left unattended, and each guest must assume liability for damage of property or other guest complaints. There is a limit of one pet per room.

Holiday Inn
2537 Rochester Court
Troy, MI
248-689-7500 (877-270-6405)
Dogs of all sizes are allowed for an additional one time fee of $30 per pet. 2 dogs may be allowed.

Red Roof Inn - Detroit - Troy
2350 Rochester Ct
Troy, MI
248-689-4391 (800-RED-ROOF)
One well-behaved family pet per room. Guest must notify front desk upon arrival. Guest is liable for any damages. In consideration of all guests, pets must never be left unattended in the guest rooms.

Staybridge Suites Detroit-Utica
46155 Utica Park Blvd
Utica, MI
586-323-0101 (877-270-6405)
Dogs up to 100 pounds are allowed for an additional one time pet fee of $75 per room. 2 dogs may be allowed.

Motel 6 - Grand Rapids North - Walker
777 3 Mile Rd
Walker, MI
616-784-9375 (800-466-8356)
One well-behaved family pet per room. Guest must notify front desk upon arrival. Guest is liable for any damages. In consideration of all guests, pets must never be left unattended in the guest rooms.

Candlewood Suites
7010 Convention Blvd
Warren, MI
586-978-1261 (877-270-6405)
Dogs up to 70 pounds are allowed for an additional one time pet fee of $75 per room for 1 to 7 days; the fee is $150 for 8 or more days. 2 dogs may be allowed.

La Quinta Inn Detroit/Warren Tech Center
30900 Van Dyke Avenue
Warren, MI
586-574-0550 (800-531-5900)
A dog of any size is allowed. There are no additional pet fees. Dogs may not be left unattended, and they must be leashed and cleaned up after.

Motel 6 - Detroit East - Warren
8300 Chicago Rd
Warren, MI
586-826-9300 (800-466-8356)
One well-behaved family pet per room. Guest must notify front desk upon arrival. Guest is liable for any damages. In consideration of all guests, pets must never be left unattended in the guest rooms.

Quality Inn and Suites
32035 Van Dyke
Warren, MI
586-264-0100 (877-424-6423)
Dogs are allowed for an additional fee of $10 per night per pet. 2 dogs may be allowed.

Red Roof Inn - Detroit - Warren
26300 Dequindre Road
Warren, MI
586-573-4300 (800-RED-ROOF)
One well-behaved family pet per room. Guest must notify front desk upon arrival. Guest is liable for any damages. In consideration of all guests, pets must never be left unattended in the guest rooms.

Residence Inn by Marriott
30120 Civic Center North
Warren, MI
586-558-8050

Dogs of all sizes are allowed. There is a $75 one time fee and a pet policy to sign at check in Multiple dogs may be allowed.

The Wren's Nest
7405 W Maple Street
West Bloomfield, MI
248-624-6874
thewrensnestbb.com/
An historic Greek Revival home dating back to the 1840's offers guests a country like setting with nature trails, plenty of bird and wildlife viewing, lush greenery, wild flowers everywhere, and of special interest is the Goatea Room, a special gathering place offering unique and rare teas from around the world. Dogs of all sizes are allowed for no additional pet fee. Dogs must be quiet, well behaved, leashed, and cleaned up after. 2 dogs may be allowed.

Super 8 West Branch
2596 Austin Way
West Branch, MI
989-345-8488 (800-800-8000)
Dogs of all sizes are allowed. There are no additional pet fees. Dogs are not allowed to be left alone in the room. Smoking and non-smoking rooms are available for pet rooms. 2 dogs may be allowed.

Best Western of Munising
M-28 E
Wetmore, MI
906-387-4864 (800-780-7234)
Dogs are allowed for an additional fee of $5 per night per pet. Multiple dogs may be allowed.

The Knollwood Motel
5777 H 31N
Williamsburg, MI
231-938-2040
knollwoodmotel.com/
Open from May 1st through October 31st, this small resort motel offers 180 feet of sandy beach, picnic and barbecue areas, paddle boats, a vine covered gazebo, and more. One dog is allowed per room (two dogs are allowed if they are under 5 pounds) for an additional fee of $9 per night per pet and there is advance notice. Dogs may not be left alone in the room at any time, and they must be leashed and cleaned up after at all times.

Super 8 Wyoming/Grand Rapids Area
727 44th St SW
Wyoming, MI
616-530-8588 (800-800-8000)

Dogs of all sizes are allowed. There is a $10 per night pet fee per pet. Smoking and non-smoking rooms are available for pet rooms. 2 dogs may be allowed.

Minnesota Listings

Days Inn Albert Lea
2301 East Main St
Albert Lea, MN
507-373-8291 (800-329-7466)
Dogs of all sizes are allowed. There is a $8 per night pet fee per pet. Reservations are recommended due to limited rooms for pets. 2 dogs may be allowed.

Super 8 Albert Lea
2019 E Main St
Albert Lea, MN
507-377-0591 (800-800-8000)
Dogs of all sizes are allowed. There is a $10 one time pet fee per visit. Smoking and non-smoking rooms are available for pet rooms. 2 dogs may be allowed.

Holiday Inn
5637 State Hwy 29 S.
Alexandria, MN
320-763-6577 (877-270-6405)
Dogs of all sizes are allowed for no additional fee. 2 dogs may be allowed.

Super 8 Appleton
900 N Musterman
Appleton, MN
320-289-2500 (800-800-8000)
Dogs of all sizes are allowed. There is a $5 per night pet fee per pet. Smoking and non-smoking rooms are available for pet rooms. 2 dogs may be allowed.

Timber Bay Lodge and Houseboats
Babbitt, MN
218-827-3682 (800-846-6821)
timberbay.com/
There is a $14 additional pet fee per day for a cabin or a houseboat. The cabins and houseboats are not designated as smoking or non-smoking.

Country Inns & Suites by Carlson
15058 Dellwood Drive
Baxter, MN
218-828-2161
Dogs of all sizes are allowed. There are no additional pet fees. Pets may not be left alone in the room.

Super 8 Becker
13804 1st Street
Becker, MN
763-262-8880 (800-800-8000)
Dogs of all sizes are allowed. There are no additional pet fees. Dogs are not allowed to be left alone in the room. Smoking and non-smoking rooms are available for pet rooms. 2 dogs may be allowed.

Best Western Bemidji Inn
2420 Paul Bunyon Dr NW
Bemidji, MN
218-751-0390 (800-780-7234)
Dogs are allowed for an additional one time fee of $10 per pet. 2 dogs may be allowed.

La Quinta Inn Minneapolis Airport/Bloomington
7815 Nicollet Avenue South
Bloomington, MN
952-881-7311 (800-531-5900)
Dogs of all sizes are allowed. There are no additional pet fees. Dogs must be quiet, well behaved, and leashed. Multiple dogs may be allowed.

Residence Inn by Marriott
7850 Bloomington Avenue S
Bloomington, MN
952-876-0900
Dogs of all sizes are allowed. There is a $50 one time fee and a pet policy to sign at check in. Multiple dogs may be allowed.

Staybridge Suites
5150 American Blvd West
Bloomington, MN
952-831-7900 (877-270-6405)
Dogs up to 150 pounds are allowed for an additional one time pet fee of $150 per room. 2 dogs may be allowed.

Super 8 Blue Earth
1420 Giant Dr
Blue Earth, MN
507-526-7376 (800-800-8000)
Dogs of all sizes are allowed. There is a $10 one time pet fee per visit. Reservations are recommended due to limited rooms for pets. Smoking and non-smoking rooms are available for pet rooms. 2 dogs may be allowed.

Motel 6 - Minneapolis-Brooklyn Center
2741 Freeway Boulevard
Brooklyn Center, MN
763-560-9789 (800-466-8356)
One well-behaved family pet per

room. Guest must notify front desk upon arrival. Guest is liable for any damages. In consideration of all guests, pets must never be left unattended in the guest rooms.

Holiday Inn Burnsville
14201 Nicollet Avenue South
Burnsville, MN
952-435-2100 (877-270-6405)
Located just south of the twin cities in Burnsville the Holiday Inn Burnsville serves as a pet-friendly gateway to the Minneapolis - St Paul area. The hotel is situated near I-35E, I-35W and Highway 77. Dogs up to 50 pounds are allowed. There is a $50 one time additional pet fee.

Red Roof Inn - Minneapolis Burnsville
12920 Aldrich Avenue South
Burnsville, MN
952-890-1420 (800-RED-ROOF)
One well-behaved family pet per room. Guest must notify front desk upon arrival. Guest is liable for any damages. In consideration of all guests, pets must never be left unattended in the guest rooms.

Super 8 Motel - Burnsville
1101 Burnsville Parkway
Burnsville, MN
952-894-3400 (800-800-8000)
innworks.com/burnsville
There is a $10 per stay additional pet fee. Up to three dogs are permitted in each room. The hotel allows a free 8 minute long distance call each night and offers a free continental breakfast. There is a pool and a laundry. I-35W, Exit 2 (Burnsville Pkwy). West on Burnsville Pkwy 1 block.

Best Western Chaska River Inn and Suites
Hwy 41 and 1st St
Chaska, MN
952-448-7877 (800-780-7234)
Dogs are allowed for a $70 refundable pet deposit per room. Multiple dogs may be allowed.

Super 8 Detroit Lakes
400 Morrow Ave
Detroit Lakes, MN
218-847-1651 (800-800-8000)
Dogs up to 80 pounds are allowed. There is a $10 one time per pet fee per visit. Smoking and non-smoking rooms are available for pet rooms. 2 dogs may be allowed.

Days Inn Duluth
909 Cottonwood Ave
Duluth, MN
218-727-3110 (800-329-7466)
Dogs of all sizes are allowed. There are no additional pet fees. 2 dogs may be allowed.

Motel 6 - Duluth
200 South 27th Avenue West
Duluth, MN
218-723-1123 (800-466-8356)
One well-behaved family pet per room. Guest must notify front desk upon arrival. Guest is liable for any damages. In consideration of all guests, pets must never be left unattended in the guest rooms.

Residence Inn by Marriott
3040 Eagandale Place
Eagan, MN
651-688-0363
Dogs of all sizes are allowed, however there can only be 1 large dog or 2 medium dogs per room, and there is a pet policy to sign at check in. 2 dogs may be allowed.

Staybridge Suites
4675 Rahncliff Road
Eagan, MN
651-994-7810 (877-270-6405)
Dogs of all sizes are allowed for an additional one time pet fee of $150 per room. Multiple dogs may be allowed.

TownePlace Suites Minneapolis-St Paul Airport/Eagan
3615 Crestridge Drive
Eagan, MN
651-994-4600
Dogs of all sizes are allowed. There is a $75 one time pet fee per visit. 2 dogs may be allowed.

Residence Inn by Marriott
7780 Flying Cloud Drive
Eden Prairie, MN
952-829-0033
Dogs of all sizes are allowed. There is a $75 one time fee and a pet policy to sign at check in. Multiple dogs may be allowed.

TownePlace Suites Minneapolis Eden Prairie
11588 Leona Rd
Eden Prairie, MN
952-942-6001
Dogs of all sizes are allowed. There is a $75 one time pet fee per visit. 2 dogs may be allowed.

Paddle Inn
1314 E Sheridan Street

Ely, MN
218-365-6036
Dogs up to 100 pounds are allowed. There is a $5 per night per pet fee and a pet policy to sign at check in. 2 dogs may be allowed.

Westgate
110 N 2nd Ave W
Ely, MN
218-365-4513
spacestar.net/users/westgate/
There is a $10 one time pet fee.

Holiday Inn
I 90 At Hwy 15
Fairmont, MN
507-238-4771 (877-270-6405)
Dogs of all sizes are allowed for no additional fee. Multiple dogs may be allowed.

Days Inn Faribault
1920 Cardinal Lane
Faribault, MN
507-334-6835 (800-329-7466)
Dogs of all sizes are allowed. There is a $10 one time per pet fee per visit. 2 dogs may be allowed.

Aspen Lodge
310 East U.S. Hwy. 61
Grand Marais, MN
218-387-2500 (800-247-6020)
Pets are allowed in the motel section. There are no additional pet fees.

Best Western Superior Inn and Suites
Hwy 61 East
Grand Marais, MN
218-387-2240 (800-780-7234)
Well behaved dogs are allowed for an additional pet fee of $10 per night per room. Dogs may not be left alone in the room Multiple dogs may be allowed.

Clearwater Lodge
774 Clearwater Rd
Grand Marais, MN
218-388-2254 (800-527-0554)
canoebwca.com/
There is a $60 per week pet fee. Dogs are allowed in cabins only, not in the main lodge.

Gunflint Lodge
143 South Gunflint Lake
Grand Marais, MN
218-388-2294
gunflint.com
This lodge allows well-behaved dogs of all sizes in their cabins. There is a $15 per day pet fee. They offer non-smoking cabins. Once a year, the lodge has a Dog Lovers Weekend which includes a special off-leash area, an agility course, dog treats and a special dinner for your dog delivered to your cabin. During the winter, they also have a 2 mile groomed cross-country ski trail for dogs. Pets need to be leashed.

Country Inns & Suites by Carlson
2601 S Highway 169
Grand Rapids, MN
218-327-4960
Dogs of all sizes are allowed. There are no additional pet fees.

Super 8 Grand Rapids
1702 S Pokegama Ave
Grand Rapids, MN
218-327-1108 (800-800-8000)
Dogs up to 80 pounds are allowed. There is a $25 returnable deposit required per room. Smoking and non-smoking rooms are available for pet rooms. 2 dogs may be allowed.

Super 8 Hibbing
1411 E 40th Street
Hibbing, MN
218-263-8982 (800-800-8000)
Dogs of all sizes are allowed. There are no additional pet fees. Reservations are recommended due to limited rooms for pets. Smoking and non-smoking rooms are available for pet rooms. 2 dogs may be allowed.

Days Inn Hinckley
104 Grindstone Court
Hinckley, MN
320-384-7751 (800-329-7466)
Dogs of all sizes are allowed. There is a $10.55 per night pet fee per pet. 2 dogs may be allowed.

Best Western Victorian Inn
1000 Highway 7 W
Hutchinson, MN
320-587-6030 (800-780-7234)
Dogs are allowed for an additional one time fee of $10 per pet. Dogs must be crated when left alone in the room. Multiple dogs may be allowed.

Super 8 International Falls
2326 Hwy 53 Frontage Rd
International Falls, MN
218-283-8811 (800-800-8000)
Dogs of all sizes are allowed. There is a $10 one time per pet fee per visit for non-smoking rooms. There are no additional pet fees for smoking rooms. 2 dogs may be allowed.

Motel 6 - Minneapolis South - Lakeville
11274 210th Street
Lakeville, MN
952-469-1900 (800-466-8356)
One well-behaved family pet per room. Guest must notify front desk upon arrival. Guest is liable for any damages. In consideration of all guests, pets must never be left unattended in the guest rooms.

Kah-Nee-Tah Gallery and Cottages
4210 W H 61
Lusten, MN
800-216-2585
Dogs of all sizes are allowed. There are no additional pet fees. Multiple dogs may be allowed.

Super 8 Luverne
I-90 and Hwy 75
Luverne, MN
507-283-9541 (800-800-8000)
Dogs of all sizes are allowed. There is a $5 per night pet fee per pet. Smoking and non-smoking rooms are available for pet rooms. 2 dogs may be allowed.

Comfort Inn
131 Apache Place
Mankato, MN
507-388-5107 (877-424-6423)
Dogs are allowed for an additional fee of $10 per night per pet. Multiple dogs may be allowed.

Holiday Inn
101 E. Main Street
Mankato, MN
507-345-1234 (877-270-6405)
Dogs of all sizes are allowed for no additional fee. Multiple dogs may be allowed.

Staybridge Suites
7821 Elm Creek Blvd
Maple Grove, MN
763-494-8856 (877-270-6405)
Dogs up to 60 pounds are allowed for an additional one time fee of $150 per pet. 2 dogs may be allowed.

Best Western Marshall Inn
1500 E College Dr Jct19/23
Marshall, MN
507-532-3221 (800-780-7234)
Dogs are allowed for an additional fee of $10 per night per pet. 2 dogs may be allowed.

Comfort Inn
1511 E College Drive/H 19
Marshall, MN
507-532-3070 (877-424-6423)

Dogs up to 50 pounds are allowed for an additional fee of $10 per night per pet. 2 dogs may be allowed.

Super 8 Milaca
215 10th Ave SE
Milaca, MN
320-983-2660 (800-800-8000)
Dogs of all sizes are allowed. There is a $5 per night pet fee per pet. Smoking and non-smoking rooms are available for pet rooms. 2 dogs may be allowed.

Doubletree
1500 Park Place Blvd
Minneapolis, MN
952-542-8600
Dogs up to 50 pounds are allowed. There is a $50 refundable deposit and a pet policy to sign at check in. Multiple dogs may be allowed.

Millennium Hotel
1313 Nicollet Mall
Minneapolis, MN
612-332-6000
Dogs of all sizes are allowed. There is a $10 per night per room additional pet fee. Multiple dogs may be allowed.

Minneapolis Marriott City Center
30 S Seventh Street
Minneapolis, MN
612-349-4000 (800-228-9290)
One dog of any size is allowed. There is a $75 one time additional pet fee. Your dog must be leashed, cleaned up after, crated or removed for housekeeping, and the Do Not Disturb sign put on the door if they are in the room alone.

Residence Inn by Marriott
45 S 8th Street
Minneapolis, MN
612-677-1000
Dogs of all sizes are allowed. There is a $75 one time fee and a pet policy to sign at check in. 2 dogs may be allowed.

Residence Inn by Marriott
425 S 2nd Street
Minneapolis, MN
612-340-1300
Dogs of all sizes are allowed. There is a $75 one time fee and a pet policy to sign at check in. Multiple dogs may be allowed.

Sheraton Bloomington Hotel,
Minneapolis South
7800 Normandale Blvd.
Minneapolis, MN
952-835-7800 (888-625-5144)

Dogs of all sizes are allowed for no additional pet fee with a credit card on file; there is a pet agreement to sign at check in. Dogs may not be left alone in the room.

Sheraton Minneapolis Midtown
Hotel
2901 Chicago Ave. South
Minneapolis, MN
612-821-7600 (888-625-5144)
Dogs of all sizes are allowed. There are no additional pet fees. Dogs are not allowed to be left alone in the room.

TownePlace Suites Minneapolis
Dwtn
525 N 2nd Street
Minneapolis, MN
612-340-1000
Dogs up to 75 pounds are allowed. There is a $75 one time pet fee per visit. 2 dogs may be allowed.

Minneapolis Marriott
5801 Opus Parkway
Minnetonka, MN
952-935-5500 (888-887-1681)
One dog up to 50 pounds is allowed. There are no additional pet fees. Dogs must be leashed, cleaned up after, and crated when left alone in the room.

Best Western Chelsea Inn & Suites
89 Chelsea Road
Monticello, MN
763-271-8880 (800-780-7234)
Dogs are allowed for an additional pet fee of $10 per night per room. 2 dogs may be allowed.

Super 8 New Ulm
1901 S Broadway
New Ulm, MN
507-359-2400 (800-800-8000)
Dogs of all sizes are allowed. There is a $10 per night pet fee per pet. Smoking and non-smoking rooms are available for pet rooms. 2 dogs may be allowed.

Days Inn Nisswa
24186 Smiley Rd
Nisswa, MN
218-963-3500 (800-329-7466)
Dogs of all sizes are allowed. There is a $10 per night pet fee per pet. 2 dogs may be allowed.

Best Western Kelly Inn
2705 N Annapolis Lane
Plymouth, MN
763-553-1600 (800-780-7234)
Dogs are allowed for no additional pet fee. There is a pet agreement to

sign at check in, and dogs may not be left alone in the room. Multiple dogs may be allowed.

Red Roof Inn - Minneapolis Plymouth
2600 Annapolis Lane North
Plymouth, MN
763-553-1751 (800-RED-ROOF)
One well-behaved family pet per room. Guest must notify front desk upon arrival. Guest is liable for any damages. In consideration of all guests, pets must never be left unattended in the guest rooms.

Days Inn Red Wing
955 7th St
Red Wing, MN
651-388-3568 (800-329-7466)
Dogs of all sizes are allowed. There is a $7 per night pet fee per pet. 2 dogs may be allowed.

Super 8 Red Wing
232 Withers Harbor Dr
Red Wing, MN
651-388-0491 (800-800-8000)
Dogs of all sizes are allowed. There is a $6 per night pet fee per pet. Smoking and non-smoking rooms are available for pet rooms. 2 dogs may be allowed.

Candlewood Suites
351 West 77th St
Richfield, MN
612-869-7704 (877-270-6405)
Dogs of all sizes are allowed for an additional pet fee of $75 per room for 1 to 6 nights; the fee is $150 for 7 or more nights. 2 dogs may be allowed.

Motel 6 - Minneapolis Airport-Mall Of Ame
7640 Cedar Avenue South
Richfield, MN
612-861-4491 (800-466-8356)
One well-behaved family pet per room. Guest must notify front desk upon arrival. Guest is liable for any damages. In consideration of all guests, pets must never be left unattended in the guest rooms.

Holiday Inn
1630 S. Broadway
Rochester, MN
507-288-1844 (877-270-6405)
Dogs of all sizes are allowed for an additional pet fee of $15 per night per room. Multiple dogs may be allowed.

Motel 6 - Rochester
2107 West Frontage Road
Rochester, MN
507-282-6625 (800-466-8356)

One well-behaved family pet per room. Guest must notify front desk upon arrival. Guest is liable for any damages. In consideration of all guests, pets must never be left unattended in the guest rooms.

Quality Inn and Suites
1620 1st Avenue
Rochester, MN
507-282-8091 (877-424-6423)
Dogs are allowed for an additional fee of $5 per night per pet. 2 dogs may be allowed.

Radisson Plaza Hotel Rochester
150 South Broadway
Rochester, MN
507-281-8000
Dogs of all sizes are allowed. There are no additional pet fees. Dogs are allowed in the rooms on the third floor where there are both smoking and non-smoking rooms.

Rochester Marriott May Clinic Area
101 SW First Avenue
Rochester, MN
507-280-6000 (800-228-9290)
Dogs of all sizes are allowed. There is a $40 one time additional pet fee per room. Dogs must be leashed, cleaned up after, and the Pet In Room sign put on the door if they are in the room alone. 2 dogs may be allowed.

Staybridge Suites
1211 Second St SW
Rochester, MN
507-289-6600 (877-270-6405)
Dogs of all sizes are allowed for an additional one time pet fee of $75 per room. 2 dogs may be allowed.

Residence Inn by Marriott
2985 Centre Pointe Drive
Roseville, MN
651-636-0680
Dogs of all sizes are allowed. There is a $75 one time fee per pet and a pet policy to sign at check in. Multiple dogs may be allowed.

Best Western Americanna Inn & Conference Center
520 Highway 10 S
Saint Cloud, MN
320-252-8700 (800-780-7234)
Quiet dogs are allowed for an additional one time pet fee of $10 per room. Multiple dogs may be allowed.

Comfort Inn
4040 Second Street S
Saint Cloud, MN
320-251-1500 (877-424-6423)

Dogs are allowed for an additional one time pet fee of $10 per room. Multiple dogs may be allowed.

Best Western Bandana Square
1010 Bandana Boulevard W
Saint Pauk, MN
651-647-1637 (800-780-7234)
Dogs up to 50 pounds are allowed for an additional one time fee of $10 per pet. Multiple dogs may be allowed.

Best Western Kelly Inn (Saint Cloud)
100 4th Ave South
St Cloud, MN
320-253-0606 (800-780-7234)
Quiet dogs are allowed for no additional pet fee. Multiple dogs may be allowed.

Holiday Inn Express
4322 Clearwater Rd
St Cloud, MN
320-240-8000 (877-270-6405)
Dogs of all sizes are allowed for no additional fee. Multiple dogs may be allowed.

Holiday Inn Hotel & Suites
75 S. 37th Avenue
St Cloud, MN
320-253-9000 (877-270-6405)
Dogs of all sizes are allowed for no additional fee. Multiple dogs may be allowed.

Super 8 St Cloud
50 Park Ave South
St Cloud, MN
320-253-5530 (800-800-8000)
Dogs of all sizes are allowed. There is a $10 one time per pet fee per visit. Smoking and non-smoking rooms are available for pet rooms. 2 dogs may be allowed.

Super 8 St James
1210 Heckman Ct
St James, MN
507-375-4708 (800-800-8000)
Dogs of all sizes are allowed. There is a $10 per night pet fee per pet. Smoking and non-smoking rooms are available for pet rooms. 2 dogs may be allowed.

Best Western Kelly Inn (Saint Paul)
161 St Anthony Ave
St Paul, MN
651-227-8711 (800-780-7234)
Dogs are allowed for no additional pet fee. Multiple dogs may be allowed.

Stillwater Inn

1750 W Frontage Rd
Stillwater, MN
651-430-1300 (800-647-4039)
Dogs are allowed for an additional fee of $10 per night per pet. Multiple dogs may be allowed.

Super 8 Stillwater/St Paul Area
2190 W Frontage Rd
Stillwater, MN
651-430-3990 (800-800-8000)
Dogs of all sizes are allowed. There are no additional pet fees. Dogs are not allowed to be left alone in the room. Smoking and non-smoking rooms are available for pet rooms. 2 dogs may be allowed.

The Springs Country Inn
361 Government St
Taylors Falls, MN
651-465-6565
There is a $7 per day pet fee. Dogs are allowed on the first 2 floors.

Motel 6 - St Cloud - I-94 Waite Park
815 1st Street South
Waite Park, MN
320-253-7070 (800-466-8356)
One well-behaved family pet per room. Guest must notify front desk upon arrival. Guest is liable for any damages. In consideration of all guests, pets must never be left unattended in the guest rooms.

Best Western White Bear Country Inn
4940 State Hwy 61
White Bear Lake, MN
651-429-5393 (800-780-7234)
Dogs are allowed for an additional fee of $10 per night per pet. 2 dogs may be allowed.

Holiday Inn
2100 East Highway 12
Willmar, MN
320-235-6060 (877-270-6405)
Dogs of all sizes are allowed for no additional fee. Multiple dogs may be allowed.

Super 8 Willmar
2655 S 1st St
Willmart, MN
320-235-4444 (800-800-8000)
Dogs of all sizes are allowed. There is a $10 one time per pet fee per visit. Smoking and non-smoking rooms are available for pet rooms. 2 dogs may be allowed.

Quality Inn
956 Mankato Avenue
Winona, MN
507-454-4390 (877-424-6423)

Dogs are allowed for an additional one time fee of $10 per pet. Dogs must be crated or removed for housekeeping. Multiple dogs may be allowed.

Red Roof Inn - Woodbury - St Paul
1806 Wooddale Drive
Woodbury, MN
651-738-7160 (800-RED-ROOF)
One well-behaved family pet per room. Guest must notify front desk upon arrival. Guest is liable for any damages. In consideration of all guests, pets must never be left unattended in the guest rooms.

Days Inn Worthington
207 Oxford St
Worthington, MN
507-376-6155 (800-329-7466)
Dogs of all sizes are allowed. There is a $6 per night pet fee per pet. 2 dogs may be allowed.

Mississippi Listings

Best Western Aberdeen Inn
801 E Commerce
Aberdeen, MS
662-369-4343 (800-780-7234)
Dogs are allowed for a $50 refundable deposit plus an additional fee of $10 per night per pet. 2 dogs may be allowed.

Comfort Inn
290 Power Drive
Batesville, MS
662-563-1188 (877-424-6423)
Well behaved dogs are allowed for an additional fee of $5 per night per pet. Multiple dogs may be allowed.

Biloxi Beachfront Hotel
2400 Beach Blvd
Biloxi, MS
228-388-3551
There is a $25 one time pet fee. There is a $100 refundable pet deposit.

Breakers Inn
2506 Beach Blvd
Biloxi, MS
228-388-6320 (800-624-5031)
biloxibreakersinn.com/
There is a $30 one time pet fee. There are no designated smoking or non-smoking rooms.

Motel 6 - Biloxi
2476 Beach Boulevard

Biloxi, MS
228-388-5130 (800-466-8356)
One well-behaved family pet per room. Guest must notify front desk upon arrival. Guest is liable for any damages. In consideration of all guests, pets must never be left unattended in the guest rooms.

Best Western College Inn
805 N 2nd Street
Booneville, MS
662-728-2244 (800-780-7234)
Dogs are allowed for a $30 refundable deposit per pet. Multiple dogs may be allowed.

Red Roof Inn - Jackson - Brandon
280 Old Highway 80
Brandon, MS
601-824-3839 (800-RED-ROOF)
One well-behaved family pet per room. Guest must notify front desk upon arrival. Guest is liable for any damages. In consideration of all guests, pets must never be left unattended in the guest rooms.

Super 8 Brookhaven
344 Dunn Ratcliff Rd NW
Brookhaven, MS
601-833-8580 (800-800-8000)
Dogs of all sizes are allowed. There is a $10 one time per pet fee per visit. Smoking and non-smoking rooms are available for pet rooms. 2 dogs may be allowed.

Best Western Canton Inn
137 Soldier Colony Rd
Canton, MS
601-859-8600 (800-780-7234)
Dogs are allowed for an additional fee of $10 per night per pet. Multiple dogs may be allowed.

Comfort Inn
145 Soldier Colony Road
Canton, MS
601-859-7575 (877-424-6423)
Dogs are allowed for an additional fee of $25 per night per pet. Multiple dogs may be allowed.

Best Western Executive Inn
710 S State Street
Clarksdale, MS
662-627-9292 (800-780-7234)
Dogs are allowed for an additional one time fee of $7 per pet. Multiple dogs may be allowed.

Motel 6 - Columbus
1203 Highway 45 North
Columbus, MS
662-327-4450 (800-466-8356)
One well-behaved family pet per

room. Guest must notify front desk upon arrival. Guest is liable for any damages. In consideration of all guests, pets must never be left unattended in the guest rooms.

Comfort Inn
2101 H 72W
Corinth, MS
662-287-4421 (877-424-6423)
Dogs are allowed for no additional pet fee with a credit card on file; there is a $25 refundable deposit if paying cash. Multiple dogs may be allowed.

Super 8 Durant
31201 Hwy 12
Durant, MS
662-653-3881 (800-800-8000)
Dogs of all sizes are allowed. There are no additional pet fees. Reservations are recommended due to limited rooms for pets. Smoking and non-smoking rooms are available for pet rooms. 2 dogs may be allowed.

Apple Tree Inn
I-20 at Highway 35, PO Box 402
Forest, MS
601-469-2640

Best Western Regency Inn & Conference Center
2428 Highway 82 E
Greenville, MS
662-334-6900 (800-780-7234)
Dogs are allowed for an additional one time fee of $25 per pet. Multiple dogs may be allowed.

Knights Inn
1632 Sunset Dr
Grenada, MS
662-226-8888
Dogs of all sizes are allowed. There is a $10 per night pet fee per pet. 2 dogs may be allowed.

Best Western Seaway Inn
9475 US Hwy 49 and I-10
Gulfport, MS
228-864-0050 (800-780-7234)
Dogs up to 50 pounds are allowed for an additional fee of $10 per night per pet. 2 dogs may be allowed.

Holiday Inn
9415 Hwy 49
Gulfport, MS
228-868-8200 (877-270-6405)
Dogs of all sizes are allowed for an additional one time fee of $35 per pet. Dogs may not be left alone in the room. Multiple dogs may be allowed.

Motel 6 - Gulfport
9355 US Highway 49
Gulfport, MS
228-863-1890 (800-466-8356)
One well-behaved family pet per room. Guest must notify front desk upon arrival. Guest is liable for any damages. In consideration of all guests, pets must never be left unattended in the guest rooms.

Howard Johnson Express Inn
6553 Hwy 49 North
Hattiesburg, MS
601-268-1410 (800-446-4656)
Dogs of all sizes are welcome. There is a $10 per day pet fee.

Motel 6 - Hattiesburg-Univ of Southern MS
6508 US Highway 49
Hattiesburg, MS
601-544-6096 (800-466-8356)
One well-behaved family pet per room. Guest must notify front desk upon arrival. Guest is liable for any damages. In consideration of all guests, pets must never be left unattended in the guest rooms.

Motel 6 - Memphis - Horn Lake
701 Southwest Drive
Horn Lake, MS
662-349-4439 (800-466-8356)
One well-behaved family pet per room. Guest must notify front desk upon arrival. Guest is liable for any damages. In consideration of all guests, pets must never be left unattended in the guest rooms.

South Drury Inn & Suites
735 Goodman Road West
Horn Lake, MS
662-349-6622 (800-378-7946)
Dogs of all sizes are permitted. Pets are not allowed in the breakfast area of the hotel. Pets are not to be left unattended, and each guest must assume liability for damage of property or other guest complaints. There is a limit of one pet per room.

Clarion Hotel and Suites
5075 I 55N
Jackson, MS
601-366-9411 (877-424-6423)
Dogs are allowed for an additional one time fee of $25 per pet. 2 dogs may be allowed.

Edison Walthall Hotel
225 E Capitol St
Jackson, MS
601-948-6161 (800-932-6161)
There is a $10 per day pet fee.

La Quinta Inn Jackson North
616 Briarwood Drive
Jackson, MS
601-957-1741 (800-531-5900)
Dogs of all sizes are allowed. There are no additional pet fees. Dogs must be leashed and cleaned up after. Multiple dogs may be allowed.

Leland Inn
150 Angle St
Jackson, MS
601-373-6110
There are no additional pet fees.

Motel 6 - Jackson
6145 I-55 North
Jackson, MS
601-956-8848 (800-466-8356)
One well-behaved family pet per room. Guest must notify front desk upon arrival. Guest is liable for any damages. In consideration of all guests, pets must never be left unattended in the guest rooms.

Red Roof Inn - Jackson - Fairgrounds
700 Larson Street
Jackson, MS
601-969-5006 (800-RED-ROOF)
One well-behaved family pet per room. Guest must notify front desk upon arrival. Guest is liable for any damages. In consideration of all guests, pets must never be left unattended in the guest rooms.

Residence Inn by Marriott
881 E River Place
Jackson, MS
601-355-3599
Dogs of all sizes are allowed. There is a $75 one time fee and a pet policy to sign at check in. Multiple dogs may be allowed.

Sleep Inn
2620 H 80W
Jackson, MS
601-354-3900 (877-424-6423)
Dogs are allowed for an additional one time fee of $10 per pet. Multiple dogs may be allowed.

Studio 6 - Jackson
5925 I-55 North
Jackson, MS
601-956-9988 (800-466-8356)
One well-behaved family pet per room. Guest must notify front desk upon arrival. Guest is liable for any damages. In consideration of all guests, pets must never be left unattended in the guest rooms.

Super 8 Kosciusko
718 Veterans Memorial Drive
Kosciusko, MS
662-289-7880 (800-800-8000)
Dogs of all sizes are allowed. There is a $20 returnable deposit required per room. Smoking and non-smoking rooms are available for pet rooms. 2 dogs may be allowed.

Best Western Red Hills Inn
201 Hwy 15 North
Louisville, MS
662-773-9090 (800-780-7234)
Dogs are allowed for no additional pet fee. Multiple dogs may be allowed.

Holiday Inn Express Hotel & Suites Lucedale
1287 Beaver Dam Road
Lucedale, MS
601-947-2099 (877-270-6405)
Dogs of all sizes are allowed for an additional one time fee of $30 per pet. Multiple dogs may be allowed.

Best Western Oak Tree Inn
12710 Highway 45 (& 14 Bypass)
Macon, MS
662-726-4334 (800-780-7234)
Dogs are allowed for an additional one time fee of $20 per pet. 2 dogs may be allowed.

Super 8 McComb
100 Commerce St
McComb, MS
601-684-7654 (800-800-8000)
Dogs of all sizes are allowed. There is a $15 one time per pet fee per visit. Smoking and non-smoking rooms are available for pet rooms. 2 dogs may be allowed.

Days Inn Meridian
145 US Hwy 80 East
Meridian, MS
601-483-3812 (800-329-7466)
Dogs of all sizes are allowed. There is a $5 per night pet fee per pet. 2 dogs may be allowed.

Holiday Inn
111 US Hwy 11 & 80
Meridian, MS
601-485-5101 (877-270-6405)
Dogs of all sizes are allowed for a one time pet fee of $25 per room. 2 dogs may be allowed.

La Quinta Inn Meridan
1400 Roebuck Drive
Meridian, MS
601-693-2300 (800-531-5900)
Dogs of all sizes are allowed. There are no additional fees. There is a pet

waiver to sign at check in, and a credit card must be on file in case of damages. Dogs may not be left unattended, and they must be leashed and cleaned up after. Multiple dogs may be allowed.

Motel 6 - Meridian
2309 South Frontage Road
Meridian, MS
601-482-1182 (800-466-8356)
One well-behaved family pet per room. Guest must notify front desk upon arrival. Guest is liable for any damages. In consideration of all guests, pets must never be left unattended in the guest rooms.

Quality Inn
1401 Roebuck Drive
Meridian, MS
601-693-4521 (877-424-6423)
Dogs are allowed for no additional pet fee. Multiple dogs may be allowed.

La Quinta Inn Moss Point
6292 Highway 63
Moss Point, MS
228-474-4488 (800-531-5900)
Dogs of all sizes are allowed. There are no additional pet fees. Dogs must be leashed, cleaned up after, and the Do Not Disturb sign put on the door if there is a pet in the room alone. Multiple dogs may be allowed.

Quality Inn
6800 H 63
Moss Point, MS
228-475-2477 (877-424-6423)
Dogs are allowed for an additional fee of $10 per night per pet. 2 dogs may be allowed.

Holiday Inn Express Hotel and Suites
300 Highway 30 West
New Albany, MS
662-534-8870 (877-270-6405)
Dogs of all sizes are allowed for an additional one time pet fee of $30 per room. Multiple dogs may be allowed.

Days Inn Biloxi
7305 Washington Ave
Ocean Springs, MS
228-872-8255 (800-329-7466)
Dogs of all sizes are allowed. There is a $10.70 per night pet fee per pet. Reservations are recommended due to limited rooms for pets. 2 dogs may be allowed.

Comfort Inn
7049 Enterprise Drive
Olive Branch, MS
662-895-0456 (877-424-6423)

Dogs are allowed for an additional pet fee of $12 (plus tax) per night per room. 2 dogs may be allowed.

Days Inn Oxford
1101 Frontage Road
Oxford, MS
662-234-9500 (800-329-7466)
Dogs of all sizes are allowed. There is a $15 one time per pet fee per visit. 2 dogs may be allowed.

Super 8 Oxford
2201 Jackson Ave West
Oxford, MS
662-234-7013 (800-800-8000)
Dogs of all sizes are allowed. There is a $15 one time per pet fee per visit. Smoking and non-smoking rooms are available for pet rooms. 2 dogs may be allowed.

La Quinta Inn & Suites Jackson Airport
501 S. Pearson Rd
Pearl, MS
601-664-0065 (800-531-5900)
Dogs of all sizes are allowed. There are no additional pet fees. Dogs must be leashed and cleaned up after. Dogs may not be left unattended unless they will be quiet and well behaved. Multiple dogs may be allowed.

Motel 6 - Jackson Airport- Pearl
216 North Pearson Road
Pearl, MS
601-936-9988 (800-466-8356)
One well-behaved family pet per room. Guest must notify front desk upon arrival. Guest is liable for any damages. In consideration of all guests, pets must never be left unattended in the guest rooms.

Drury Inn & Suites
610 E. County Line Road
Ridgeland, MS
601-956-6100 (800-378-7946)
Dogs of all sizes are permitted. Pets are not allowed in the breakfast area of the hotel. Pets are not to be left unattended, and each guest must assume liability for damage of property or other guest complaints. There is a limit of one pet per room.

Red Roof Inn - Jackson North - Ridgeland
810 Adcock Street
Ridgeland, MS
601-956-7707 (800-RED-ROOF)
One well-behaved family pet per room. Guest must notify front desk upon arrival. Guest is liable for any damages. In consideration of all

guests, pets must never be left unattended in the guest rooms.

Staybridge Suites Jackson
801 Ridgewood Road
Ridgeland, MS
601-206-9190 (877-270-6405)
Dogs up to 50 pounds are allowed for an additional one time pet fee of $75 per room. 2 dogs may be allowed.

Motel 6 - Senatobia
501 East Main Street
Senatobia, MS
662-562-5241 (800-466-8356)
One well-behaved family pet per room. Guest must notify front desk upon arrival. Guest is liable for any damages. In consideration of all guests, pets must never be left unattended in the guest rooms.

Comfort Suites
801 Russell Street
Starkville, MS
662-324-9595 (877-424-6423)
A dog up to 50 pounds is allowed for no additional pet fee.

Holiday Inn Express Hotel & Suites Starkville
110 Hwy 12 West
Starkville, MS
662-324-0076 (877-270-6405)
Dogs of all sizes are allowed for an additional one time pet fee of $50 per room. Multiple dogs may be allowed.

Executive Inn
1011 N Gloster St
Tupelo, MS
601-841-2222
There is a $15 one time pet fee.

Red Roof Inn - Tupelo
1500 McCullough Boulevard
Tupelo, MS
662-844-1904 (800-RED-ROOF)
One well-behaved family pet per room. Guest must notify front desk upon arrival. Guest is liable for any damages. In consideration of all guests, pets must never be left unattended in the guest rooms.

Battlefield Inn
4137 I-20 Frontage Rd
Vicksburg, MS
601-638-5811 (800-359-9363)
battlefieldinn.org/
There is a $5 per day pet fee.

Duff Green Mansion
1114 First East St
Vicksburg, MS
601-638-6662 (800-992-0037)

innbook.com/duff.html
There are no designated smoking or non-smoking rooms.

La Quinta Inn Vicksburg
4216 Washington Street
Vicksburg, MS
601-638-5750 (800-531-5900)
Dogs up to 70 pounds are allowed. There are no additional pet fees. Dogs must be leashed and cleaned up after, and they are not allowed in the lobby. Multiple dogs may be allowed.

Motel 6 - Vicksburg
4127 North Frontage Road
Vicksburg, MS
601-638-5077 (800-466-8356)
One well-behaved family pet per room. Guest must notify front desk upon arrival. Guest is liable for any damages. In consideration of all guests, pets must never be left unattended in the guest rooms.

Quality Inn and Suites
3332 Clay Street
Vicksburg, MS
601-636-0804 (877-424-6423)
Dogs up to 60 pounds are allowed for an additional one time pet fee of $15 per room. Dogs may not be left alone in the room. Multiple dogs may be allowed.

The Corners Bed and Breakfast Inn
601 Klien St
Vicksburg, MS
601-636-7421
thecorners.com/
There are no additional pet fees.

Missouri Listings

Cottages on Stouts Creek
H 72
Arcadia, MO
573-546-4036
missouricottages.com/
Located along Stouts Creek in the scenic Arcadia Valley, this resort offers a variety of amenities in addition to a convenient location to numerous local activities and recreation. Dogs are allowed for an additional fee of $15 per night per pet. 2 dogs may be allowed.

St Louis - Arnold Drury Inn
1201 Drury Lane
Arnold, MO
636-296-9600 (800-378-7946)
Dogs of all sizes are permitted. Pets

are not allowed in the breakfast area of the hotel. Pets are not to be left unattended, and each guest must assume liability for damage of property or other guest complaints. There is a limit of one pet per room.

Days Inn Kansas City/Blue Springs
3120 NW Jefferson
Blue Springs, MO
816-224-1122 (800-329-7466)
Dogs up to 70 pounds are allowed. There is a $5 per night pet fee per pet. 2 dogs may be allowed.

Hampton Inn
900 NW South Outer Road
Blue Springs, MO
816-220-3844
Dogs of all sizes are allowed. There are no additional pet fees, but a credit card needs to be on file. Multiple dogs may be allowed.

Motel 6 - Kansas City East - Blue Springs
901 Northwest Jefferson Street
Blue Springs, MO
816-228-9133 (800-466-8356)
One well-behaved family pet per room. Guest must notify front desk upon arrival. Guest is liable for any damages. In consideration of all guests, pets must never be left unattended in the guest rooms.

Comfort Inn
2427 Midamerican Industrial Drive
Boonville, MO
660-882-5317 (877-424-6423)
Dogs are allowed for an additional fee of $10 per night per pet. Multiple dogs may be allowed.

Branson Inn
448 MO 248
Branson, MO
417-334-5121 (800-334-5121)
There is a $5 per day pet fee. Pets must be out of the room for maid service.

Days Inn Branson
3524 Keeter St
Branson, MO
417-334-5544 (800-329-7466)
Dogs of all sizes are allowed. There is a $10 per night pet fee per pet. 2 dogs may be allowed.

Emory Creek Victorian Bed & Breakfast and Gift shop
143 Arizona Drive
Branson, MO
417-334-3805 (800-362-7404)
emorycreekbnb.com/
In addition to offering an elegant

Victorian setting, their special pet friendly room (The Dogwood Room) has a private porch with swing and a beautiful view over the gardens. Dogs are allowed for an additional pet fee per pet of $25 for 1 to 3 days, and $20 for the next 4 to 6 days. 2 dogs may be allowed.

Holiday Inn Express Hotel & Suites
Branson 76 Central
1970 W Hwy 76
Branson, MO
417-336-1100 (877-270-6405)
Dogs of all sizes are allowed for an additional one time pet fee of $25 per room. 2 dogs may be allowed.

Howard Johnson Hotel
3027-A West Hwy 76
Branson, MO
417-336-5151 (800-446-4656)
Dogs of all sizes are welcome. There is a $10 per day pet fee.

La Quinta Inn Branson Music City Centre
1835 W Highway 76
Branson, MO
417-332-1575 (800-531-5900)
Dogs of all sizes are allowed. There are no additional pet fees. Dogs must be leashed, cleaned up after, and be crated or attended to for housekeeping. Multiple dogs may be allowed.

Motel 6 - Branson
2651 Shepherd of the Hills Expressway
Branson, MO
417-336-6088 (800-466-8356)
One well-behaved family pet per room. Guest must notify front desk upon arrival. Guest is liable for any damages. In consideration of all guests, pets must never be left unattended in the guest rooms.

Red Roof Inn - Branson
220 South Wildwood Drive
Branson, MO
417-335-4500 (800-RED-ROOF)
One well-behaved family pet per room. Guest must notify front desk upon arrival. Guest is liable for any damages. In consideration of all guests, pets must never be left unattended in the guest rooms.

Residence Inn by Marriott
280 Wildwood Drive S
Branson, MO
417-336-4077
Dogs of all sizes are allowed. There is a $75 one time fee and a pet policy to sign at check in. Multiple

dogs may be allowed.

Settle Inn
3050 Green Mt Dr
Branson, MO
417-335-4700 (800-677-6906)
bransonsettleinn.com/home.htm
There is a $10 per day pet fee. Pets
are not allowed in theme rooms.

Motel 6 - St Louis - Bridgeton
3655 Pennridge Drive
Bridgeton, MO
314-291-6100 (800-466-8356)
One well-behaved family pet per
room. Guest must notify front desk
upon arrival. Guest is liable for any
damages. In consideration of all
guests, pets must never be left
unattended in the guest rooms.

Red Roof Inn - St Louis Bridgeton
3470 Hollenberg Drive
Bridgeton, MO
314-291-3350 (800-RED-ROOF)
One well-behaved family pet per
room. Guest must notify front desk
upon arrival. Guest is liable for any
damages. In consideration of all
guests, pets must never be left
unattended in the guest rooms.

Days Inn Butler
100 S Fran Ave
Butler, MO
660-679-4544 (800-329-7466)
Dogs of all sizes are allowed. There
is a $5 per night pet fee per pet. 2
dogs may be allowed.

Super 8 Butler
1114 W Ft Scott
Butler, MO
660-679-6183 (800-800-8000)
Dogs of all sizes are allowed. There
is a $5 per night pet fee per pet.
Smoking and non-smoking rooms
are available for pet rooms. 2 dogs
may be allowed.

Best Western Acorn Inn
I-35 and US 36
Cameron, MO
816-632-2187 (800-780-7234)
Dogs are allowed for no additional
pet fee. Multiple dogs may be
allowed.

Comfort Inn
1803 Comfort Lane
Cameron, MO
816-632-5655 (877-424-6423)
Dogs are allowed for no additional
pet fee. 2 dogs may be allowed.

Cape Girardeau Drury Lodge
104 S. Vantage Drive

Cape Girardeau, MO
573-334-7151 (800-378-7946)
Dogs of all sizes are permitted. Pets
are not allowed in the breakfast
area of the hotel. Pets are not to be
left unattended, and each guest
must assume liability for damage of
property or other guest complaints.
There is a limit of one pet per room.

Cape Girardeau Drury Suites
3303 Campster Drive
Cape Girardeau, MO
573-339-9500 (800-378-7946)
Dogs of all sizes are permitted. Pets
are not allowed in the breakfast
area of the hotel. Pets are not to be
left unattended, and each guest
must assume liability for damage of
property or other guest complaints.
There is a limit of one pet per room.

Cape Girardeau Pear Tree Inn
3248 William Street
Cape Girardeau, MO
573-334-3000 (800-378-7946)
Dogs of all sizes are permitted. Pets
are not allowed in the breakfast
area of the hotel. Pets are not to be
left unattended. There is a limit of
one pet per room.

Hampton Inn
103 Cape West Parkway
Cape Girardeau, MO
573-651-3000
Well behaved dogs of all sizes are
allowed. There are no additional pet
fees. Dogs are not allowed to be left
alone in the room unless they are
put in a kennel. Multiple dogs may
be allowed.

Best Western Precious Moments
Hotel
2701 Hazel Street
Carthage, MO
417-359-5900 (800-780-7234)
Dogs up to 50 pounds are allowed
for an additional pet fee of $10 per
night per room. Multiple dogs may
be allowed.

Super 8 Carthage
416 W Fir Road
Carthage, MO
417-359-9000 (800-800-8000)
Dogs of all sizes are allowed. There
is a $5 per night pet fee per pet.
Smoking and non-smoking rooms
are available for pet rooms. 2 dogs
may be allowed.

Comfort Inn
102 Drake Street
Charleston, MO
573-683-4200 (877-424-6423)

Dogs up to 50 pounds are allowed
for an additional pet fee of $15 per
night per room. 2 dogs may be
allowed.

Residence Inn by Marriott
15431 Conway Road
Chesterfield, MO
636-537-1444
Dogs of all sizes are allowed. There
is a $75 one time fee and a pet
policy to sign a check in. Multiple
dogs may be allowed.

Best Western Chillicothe Inn
1020 S Washington
Chillicothe, MO
660-646-0572 (800-780-7234)
Dogs are allowed for an additional
one time fee of $10 per pet. Multiple
dogs may be allowed.

Crowne Plaza Hotel St. Louis -
Clayton
7750 Carondelet Ave
Clayton, MO
314-726-5400 (877-270-6405)
Dogs of all sizes are allowed for no
additional fee. Dogs may not be left
alone in the room at any time.
Multiple dogs may be allowed.

Best Value Inn
201 W Rives Rd
Clinton, MO
660-885-6901
Dogs of all sizes are allowed. There
is a $10 per night pet fee per pet. 2
dogs may be allowed.

Baymont Inn & Suites Columbia
2500 I-70 Drive S.W.
Columbia, MO
573-445-1899 (800-531-5900)
Dogs of all sizes are allowed. There
are no additional pet fees. Dogs
must be leashed, cleaned up after,
and be crated or removed for
housekeeping Multiple dogs may be
allowed.

Candlewood Suites Columbia
3100 Wingate Court
Columbia, MO
573-817-0525 (877-270-6405)
Dogs of all sizes are allowed for an
additional one time pet fee of $75 per
room. Multiple dogs may be allowed.

Columbia Drury Inn
1000 Knipp Street
Columbia, MO
573-445-1800 (800-378-7946)
Dogs of all sizes are permitted. Pets
are not allowed in the breakfast area
of the hotel. Pets are not to be left
unattended, and each guest must

assume liability for damage of property or other guest complaints. There is a limit of one pet per room.

Days Inn Columbia
1900 I-70 Dr SW
Columbia, MO
573-445-8511 (800-329-7466)
Dogs of all sizes are allowed. There is a $10 one time per pet fee per visit. 2 dogs may be allowed.

Holiday Inn Express
801 Keene St
Columbia, MO
573-449-4422 (877-270-6405)
Dogs of all sizes are allowed for an additional one time pet fee of $25 per room. 2 dogs may be allowed.

Holiday Inn Select
2200 I-70 Dr. SW
Columbia, MO
573-445-8531 (877-270-6405)
Dogs of all sizes are allowed for an additional one time fee of $10 per pet. Multiple dogs may be allowed.

La Quinta Inn Columbia
901 Conley Road
Columbia, MO
573-443-4141 (800-531-5900)
Dogs of all sizes are allowed. There are no additional pet fees. Dogs must be leashed, cleaned up after, and crated if left alone in the room. Multiple dogs may be allowed.

Motel 6 - Columbia
1800 I-70 Drive Southwest
Columbia, MO
573-445-8433 (800-466-8356)
One well-behaved family pet per room. Guest must notify front desk upon arrival. Guest is liable for any damages. In consideration of all guests, pets must never be left unattended in the guest rooms.

Motel 6 - Columbia
3402 I - 70 Drive Southeast
Columbia, MO
573-815-0123 (800-466-8356)
One well-behaved family pet per room. Guest must notify front desk upon arrival. Guest is liable for any damages. In consideration of all guests, pets must never be left unattended in the guest rooms.

Quality Inn
1612 N Providence Road
Columbia, MO
573-449-2491 (877-424-6423)
Dogs are allowed for an additional pet fee of $10 per night per room. Multiple dogs may be allowed.

Red Roof Inn - Columbia, MO
201 East Texas Avenue
Columbia, MO
573-442-0145 (800-RED-ROOF)
One well-behaved family pet per room. Guest must notify front desk upon arrival. Guest is liable for any damages. In consideration of all guests, pets must never be left unattended in the guest rooms.

Travelodge
900 Vandover Dr
Columbia, MO
573-449-1065
There is a $5 per day pet fee.

Days Inn Concordia
301 NW 3rd St
Concordia, MO
660-463-7987 (800-329-7466)
Dogs of all sizes are allowed. There is a $5 per night pet fee per pet. 2 dogs may be allowed.

St Louis - Creve Coeur Drury Inn & Suites
11980 Olive Blvd
Creve Coeur, MO
314-989-1100 (800-378-7946)
Dogs of all sizes are permitted. Pets are not allowed in the breakfast area of the hotel. Pets are not to be left unattended, and each guest must assume liability for damage of property or other guest complaints. There is a limit of one pet per room.

Best Western Cuba Inn
246 Highway P
Cuba, MO
573-885-7707 (800-780-7234)
Dogs are allowed for an additional one time fee of $10 per pet. 2 dogs may be allowed.

Rock Eddy Bluff Farm
10245 Maries Road 511
Dixon, MO
573-759-6081 (800-335-5921)
rockeddy.com/
This vacation getaway is located along the Gasconade River among 150 acres of scenic Ozark forest in a country setting complete with farm animals. Dogs are allowed for no additional fee. Dogs are not allowed on the furniture or beds, and they must be crated when left alone in the units. 2 dogs may be allowed.

Candlewood Suites
3250 Rider Trail South
Earth City, MO
314-770-2744 (877-270-6405)
Dogs up to 80 pounds are allowed

for an additional one time pet fee of $75 per room for 1 to 6 nights; the fee is $150 for 7 or more nights. 2 dogs may be allowed.

Residence Inn by Marriott
3290 Rider Trail South
Earth City, MO
314-209-0995
Dogs of all sizes are allowed. There is a $75 one time fee and a pet policy to sign at check in. Multiple dogs may be allowed.

Holiday Inn at Six Flags
P. O. Box 999, 4901 Six Flags Road
Eureka, MO
636-938-6661 (877-270-6405)
stlouissixflags.holiday-inn.com
Dogs of all sizes are allowed for an additional pet fee of $25 per night per room. Multiple dogs may be allowed.

Motel 6 - St Louis Fenton-Southwest
1860 Bowles Avenue
Fenton, MO
636-349-1800 (800-466-8356)
One well-behaved family pet per room. Guest must notify front desk upon arrival. Guest is liable for any damages. In consideration of all guests, pets must never be left unattended in the guest rooms.

St Louis - Fenton Drury Inn & Suites
1088 South Highway Drive
Fenton, MO
636-343-7822 (800-378-7946)
Dogs of all sizes are permitted. Pets are not allowed in the breakfast area of the hotel. Pets are not to be left unattended, and each guest must assume liability for damage of property or other guest complaints. There is a limit of one pet per room.

St Louis - Fenton Pear Tree Inn
1100 S. Highway Drive
Fenton, MO
636-343-8820 (800-378-7946)
Dogs of all sizes are permitted. Pets are not allowed in the breakfast area of the hotel. Pets are not to be left unattended, and each guest must assume liability for damage of property or other guest complaints. There is a limit of one pet per room.

TownePlace Suites St Louis Fenton
1662 Fenton Business Park Court
Fenton, MO
636-305-7000
Dogs of all sizes are allowed. There is a $75 one time pet fee per visit. 2 dogs may be allowed.

Red Roof Inn - St Louis Florissant
307 Dunn Road
Florissant, MO
314-831-7900 (800-RED-ROOF)
One well-behaved family pet per room. Guest must notify front desk upon arrival. Guest is liable for any damages. In consideration of all guests, pets must never be left unattended in the guest rooms.

Best Western West 70 Inn
12 Hwy W
Foristell, MO
636-673-2900 (800-780-7234)
Dogs are allowed for an additional one time fee of $15 per pet. Multiple dogs may be allowed.

Holiday Inn Express
2205 Cardinal Drive
Fulton, MO
573-642-2600 (877-270-6405)
Dogs of all sizes are allowed for an additional fee of $10 per night per pet, and they ask that pets are declared at the time of reservations. Multiple dogs may be allowed.

Loganberry Inn
310 West Seventh Street
Fulton, MO
573-642-9229 (888-866-6661)
loganberryinn.com
Just 5 minutes from I-70, The Loganberry Inn has welcomed guests from throughout the world, including such luminaries as Margaret Thatcher and her Scotland Yard detectives. This grand 1899 Victorian home in historic Fulton features pampered elegance including stained glass windows, marble fireplaces and a pet-friendly room. The Loganberry Inn is strolling distance to the quaint downtown area of Fulton. Well-behaved pets are welcome in the Garden Room which has direct access to the fenced in yard.

Hayti Drury Inn & Suites
1317 Hwy 84
Hayti, MO
573-359-2702 (800-378-7946)
Dogs of all sizes are permitted. Pets are not allowed in the breakfast area of the hotel. Pets are not to be left unattended, and each guest must assume liability for damage of property or other guest complaints. There is a limit of one pet per room.

La Quinta Inn St. Louis Airport
5781 Campus Court
Hazelwood, MO
314-731-3881 (800-531-5900)
Dogs of all sizes are allowed. There

are no additional pet fees. Dogs must be leashed and cleaned up after. Dogs may not be left in the room for long periods, and they must be quiet and well behaved. 2 dogs may be allowed.

La Quinta Inn St. Louis/Hazelwood
318 Taylor Road
Hazelwood, MO
314-731-4200 (800-531-5900)
Dogs of all sizes are allowed. There are no additional pet fees. Dogs may not be left unattended, and they must be well behaved, leashed, and cleaned up after. Multiple dogs may be allowed.

Super 8 Higginsville
I 70 & Highway 13
Higginsville, MO
660-584-7781 (800-800-8000)
Dogs of all sizes are allowed. There is a $10 returnable deposit required per room. There is a $5 per night pet fee per pet. Smoking and non-smoking rooms are available for pet rooms. 2 dogs may be allowed.

Best Western Truman Inn
4048 S Lynn Court
Independence, MO
816-254-0100 (800-780-7234)
Dogs are allowed for an additional fee of $8 per night per pet. Multiple dogs may be allowed.

Quality Inn East
4200 S Noland Road
Independence, MO
816-373-8856 (877-424-6423)
Dogs up to 80 pounds are allowed for an additional one time pet fee of $10 per room. 2 dogs may be allowed.

Red Roof Inn - Kansas City Independence
13712 East 42nd Terrace
Independence, MO
816-373-2800 (800-RED-ROOF)
One well-behaved family pet per room. Guest must notify front desk upon arrival. Guest is liable for any damages. In consideration of all guests, pets must never be left unattended in the guest rooms.

Residence Inn by Marriott
3700 S Arrowhead Avenue
Independence, MO
816-795-6466
Dogs of all sizes are allowed. There is a $75 one time fee and a pet policy to sign at check in. Multiple dogs may be allowed.

Jackson Drury Inn & Suites
225 Drury Lane
Jackson, MO
573-243-9200 (800-378-7946)
Dogs of all sizes are permitted. Pets are not allowed in the breakfast area of the hotel. Pets are not to be left unattended, and each guest must assume liability for damage of property or other guest complaints. There is a limit of one pet per room.

Candlewood Suites Jefferson City
3514 Amazonas Drive
Jefferson City, MO
573-634-8822 (877-270-6405)
Dogs of all sizes are allowed for an additional pet fee per room of $25 for 1 or 2 nights; $50 for 3 to 6 nights; $75 for 1 to 14 nights; $100 for 15 to 29 nights, and $150 for 30 or more days. Multiple dogs may be allowed.

Motel 6 - Jefferson City
1624 Jefferson Street
Jefferson City, MO
573-634-4220 (800-466-8356)
One well-behaved family pet per room. Guest must notify front desk upon arrival. Guest is liable for any damages. In consideration of all guests, pets must never be left unattended in the guest rooms.

Super 8 Jefferson City
1710 Jefferson St
Jefferson City, MO
573-636-5456 (800-800-8000)
Dogs of all sizes are allowed. There is a $5 per night fee per pet. Smoking and non-smoking rooms are available for pet rooms. 2 dogs may be allowed.

Best Western Oasis Inn and Suites
3508 S Rangeline
Joplin, MO
417-781-6776 (800-780-7234)
Dogs are allowed for an additional fee of $10 per night for 2 pets; a 3rd pet is an additional $10 per night. There may only be one large dog per room. Multiple dogs may be allowed.

Candlewood Suites Joplin
3512 South Rangeline
Joplin, MO
417-623-9595 (877-270-6405)
Dogs of all sizes are allowed for an additional one time pet fee per room of $50 for pets under 50 pounds; the fee is $75 for dogs over 50 pounds. 2 dogs may be allowed.

Holiday Inn
3615 Range Line Rd
Joplin, MO

417-782-1000 (877-270-6405)
Dogs of all sizes are allowed for no additional fee with a credit card on file; there is a one time pet fee of $25 per room if paying by cash. Multiple dogs may be allowed.

Joplin Drury Inn & Suites
3601 Range Line Road
Joplin, MO
417-781-8000 (800-378-7946)
Dogs of all sizes are permitted. Pets are not allowed in the breakfast area of the hotel. Pets are not to be left unattended, and each guest must assume liability for damage of property or other guest complaints. There is a limit of one pet per room.

Motel 6 - Joplin
3031 South Range Line Road
Joplin, MO
417-781-6400 (800-466-8356)
One well-behaved family pet per room. Guest must notify front desk upon arrival. Guest is liable for any damages. In consideration of all guests, pets must never be left unattended in the guest rooms.

Sleep Inn
I 44 & H 43S
Joplin, MO
417-782-1212 (877-424-6423)
Dogs are allowed for an additional one time pet fee of $15 per room. Multiple dogs may be allowed.

Super 8 Joplin
2830 E 36th St
Joplin, MO
417-782-8765 (800-800-8000)
Dogs of all sizes are allowed. There is a $10 per night pet fee per pet. Smoking and non-smoking rooms are available for pet rooms. 2 dogs may be allowed.

Best Western Seville Plaza Hotel
4309 Main St
Kansas City, MO
816-561-9600 (800-780-7234)
Dogs up to 50 pounds are allowed for an additional one time fee of $30 per pet; the fee is $50 for dogs over 50 pounds. 2 dogs may be allowed.

Chase Suite Hotel
9900 NW Prairie View Road
Kansas City, MO
816-891-9009
This all suite hotel allows dogs for an additional pet fee of $20 per night per room. Multiple dogs may be allowed.

Hampton Inn

1051 N Cambridge
Kansas City, MO
816-483-7900
Dogs up to 50 pounds are allowed. There is a $10 per pet per stay fee. Multiple dogs may be allowed.

Holiday Inn
4011 Blue Ridge Cutoff
Kansas City, MO
816-353-5300 (877-270-6405)
Dogs of all sizes are allowed for an additional one time fee of $25 per pet. 2 dogs may be allowed.

Holiday Inn At The Plaza
One East 45th Street
Kansas City, MO
816-753-7400 (877-270-6405)
Dogs of all sizes are allowed for an additional pet fee of $25 per room with a $25 refundable deposit. Multiple dogs may be allowed.

Holiday Inn Express
801 Westport Road
Kansas City, MO
816-931-1000 (877-270-6405)
Dogs of all sizes are allowed for an additional one time pet fee of $25 per room Multiple dogs may be allowed.

Holiday Inn Kansas City Airport
11728 N. Ambassador Drive
Kansas City, MO
816-801-8400 (877-270-6405)
Dogs of all sizes are allowed for an additional one time pet fee of $30 per room. Multiple dogs may be allowed.

Holiday Inn Kansas City-Ne-I-435 North
7333 Parvin Road
Kansas City, MO
816-455-1060 (877-270-6405)
Dogs of all sizes are allowed for an additional fee of $20 per night per pet. Multiple dogs may be allowed.

Intercontinental Kansas City At The Plaza
401 Ward Parkway
Kansas City, MO
816-756-1500
Dogs up to 60 pounds are allowed for an additional fee of $25 per night per pet. 2 dogs may be allowed.

Kansas City - Stadium Drury Inn & Suites
3830 Blue Ridge Cutoff
Kansas City, MO
816-923-3000 (800-378-7946)
Dogs of all sizes are permitted. Pets are not allowed in the breakfast

area of the hotel. Pets are not to be left unattended, and each guest must assume liability for damage of property or other guest complaints. There is a limit of one pet per room.

La Quinta Inn Kansas City
1051 North Cambridge
Kansas City, MO
816-483-7900 (800-531-5900)
A dog of any size is allowed. There are no additional pet fees. Dogs may only be left unattended if they are housebroken, they will be quiet and well behaved, and a contact number is left at the front desk. Dogs must be leashed and cleaned up after.

Motel 6 - Kansas City North - Airport
8230 Northwest Prairie View Road
Kansas City, MO
816-741-6400 (800-466-8356)
One well-behaved family pet per room. Guest must notify front desk upon arrival. Guest is liable for any damages. In consideration of all guests, pets must never be left unattended in the guest rooms.

Motel 6 - Kansas City Southeast
6400 East 87th Street
Kansas City, MO
816-333-4468 (800-466-8356)
One well-behaved family pet per room. Guest must notify front desk upon arrival. Guest is liable for any damages. In consideration of all guests, pets must never be left unattended in the guest rooms.

Red Roof Inn - Kansas City North
3636 NE Randolph Road
Kansas City, MO
816-452-8585 (800-RED-ROOF)
One well-behaved family pet per room. Guest must notify front desk upon arrival. Guest is liable for any damages. In consideration of all guests, pets must never be left unattended in the guest rooms.

Residence Inn by Marriott
4601 Broadway
Kansas City, MO
816-753-0033
Dogs of all sizes are allowed. There is a $75 one time fee and a pet policy to sign at check in. Multiple dogs may be allowed.

Sheraton Suites Country Club Plaza
770 West 47th St.
Kansas City, MO
816-931-4400 (888-625-5144)
Dogs up to 60 pounds are allowed. Dogs are not allowed to be left alone in the room.

Sleep Inn Airport
7611 NW 97th Terrace
Kansas City, MO
816-891-0111 (877-424-6423)
Dogs are allowed for an additional one time pet fee of $20 per room. Multiple dogs may be allowed.

Su Casa B&B
9004 E. 92nd Street
Kansas City, MO
816-916-3444
sucasabb.com
Visit this dog-friendly ranch home with southwestern decor, situated on a five-acre lot at the outskirts of the city, but still only a 15 minute drive to Kansas City attractions. Pets must be approved in advance. There is room for dogs to run. Rates for dogs are $10 per night. Horses are $25 per night.

Super 8 Kansas City/NW/Airport
6900 NW 83 Terrace
Kansas City, MO
816-587-0808 (800-800-8000)
Dogs of all sizes are allowed. There is a $10 per night pet fee per pet. Smoking and non-smoking rooms are available for pet rooms. 2 dogs may be allowed.

Super 8 Kingdom City
3370 Gold Ave
Kingdom City, MO
573-642-2888 (800-800-8000)
Dogs of all sizes are allowed. There is a $5 per night pet fee per pet. Smoking and non-smoking rooms are available for pet rooms. 2 dogs may be allowed.

Budget Host Village Inn
1304 S Baltimore
Kirksville, MO
660-665-3722
There is a $5 per day pet fee.

Best Western Wyota Inn
Hwy I-44@ exit 130
Lebanon, MO
417-532-6171 (800-780-7234)
Dogs are allowed for an additional fee of $15 per night per pet. Multiple dogs may be allowed.

Holiday Inn Express Hotel & Suites Lebanon
1955 W. Elm
Lebanon, MO
417-532-1111 (877-270-6405)
Dogs of all sizes are allowed for an additional one time pet fee of $25 per room. Multiple dogs may be allowed.

Super 8 Liberty/NE Kansas City Area
115 N Stewart Rd
Liberty, MO
816-781-9400 (800-800-8000)
Dogs of all sizes are allowed. There is a $10 per night pet fee per pet. Smoking and non-smoking rooms are available for pet rooms. 2 dogs may be allowed.

Americas Best Value Inn
28933 Sunset Dr
Macon, MO
660-385-2125 (800-901-2125)
Dogs of all sizes are allowed. There is a $20 returnable deposit required per room. Pet must be kept in kennel when left alone. Smoking and non-smoking rooms are available for pets. Multiple dogs may be allowed.

Super 8 Macon
203 E Briggs
Macon, MO
660-385-5788 (800-800-8000)
Dogs of all sizes are allowed. There is a $10 per night pet fee per pet. Smoking and non-smoking rooms are available for pet rooms. 2 dogs may be allowed.

Super 8 Marshall
1355 W College St
Marshall, MO
660-886-3359 (800-800-8000)
Dogs of all sizes are allowed. There is a $15 per night pet fee per pet. Smoking and non-smoking rooms are available for pet rooms. 2 dogs may be allowed.

Super 8 Marston/New Madrid Area
I-55 at Hwy EE
Marston, MO
573-643-9888 (800-800-8000)
Dogs of all sizes are allowed. There is a $25 returnable deposit required per room. Smoking and non-smoking rooms are available for pet rooms. 2 dogs may be allowed.

Westport Drury Inn & Suites
12220 Dorsett Road
Maryland Heights, MO
314-576-9966 (800-378-7946)
Dogs of all sizes are permitted. Pets are not allowed in the breakfast area of the hotel. Pets are not to be left unattended, and each guest must assume liability for damage of property or other guest complaints. There is a limit of one pet per room.

Super 8 Maryville
Highway 71 S

Maryville, MO
660-582-8088 (800-800-8000)
Dogs of all sizes are allowed. There are no additional pet fees. Smoking and non-smoking rooms are available for pet rooms. 2 dogs may be allowed.

Super 8 Moberly
300 Hwy 24 E
Moberly, MO
660-263-8862 (800-800-8000)
Dogs of all sizes are allowed. There is a $10 one time per pet fee per visit. Smoking and non-smoking rooms are available for pet rooms. 2 dogs may be allowed.

La Quinta Inn Kansas City North
2214 Taney
N. Kansas City, MO
816-221-1200 (800-531-5900)
Dogs of all sizes are allowed. There are no additional pet fees. Dogs may not be left unattended, and they need to be removed or crated for housekeeping. Dogs must be leashed and cleaned up after. Multiple dogs may be allowed.

Super 8 Neosho
3085 Gardner/Edgewood Drive
Neosho, MO
417-455-1888 (800-800-8000)
Dogs of all sizes are allowed. There is a $10 per night fee per pet. Smoking and non-smoking rooms are available for pet rooms. 2 dogs may be allowed.

Days Inn New Florence
403 Booneslick Rd
New Florence, MO
573-835-7777 (800-329-7466)
Dogs up to 70 pounds are allowed. There is a $20 returnable deposit required per room. There is a $5 per night pet fee per pet. 2 dogs may be allowed.

Super 8 New Florence
202 Clark Dr
New Florence, MO
573-835-8888 (800-800-8000)
Dogs up to 40 pounds are allowed. There is a $5 per night pet fee per pet for one bed room and $10 for two beds. Smoking and non-smoking rooms are available for pet rooms. 2 dogs may be allowed.

Days Inn Motel - North Kansas City
2232 Taney Street
North Kansas City, MO
816-421-6000 (800-329-7466)
innworks.com/northkansascity
There is a $10 per stay additional pet

fee. Up to three dogs are permitted in each room. The hotel allows a free 8 minute long distance call each night and offers a free continental breakfast. There is a pool and a laundry. From I-35/I-29, take Hwy 210/Armour Road exit, East to Taney Street, then Left/North to motel.

Comfort Inn and Suites
100 Comfort Inn Court
O'Fallon, MO
636-696-8000 (877-424-6423)
Quiet dogs are allowed for an additional one time pet fee of $10 per room. Multiple dogs may be allowed.

Staybridge Suites
O'Fallon/Chesterfield
11 55 Technology Drive
OFallon, MO
636-300-0999 (877-270-6405)
Dogs of all sizes are allowed for an additional one time pet fee of $100 per room. 2 dogs may be allowed.

Days Inn Kansas City/Oak Grove
101 N Locust
Oak Grove, MO
816-690-8700 (800-329-7466)
Dogs up to 60 pounds are allowed. There is a $10 per night pet fee per pet. 2 dogs may be allowed.

Comfort Inn
1900 W Evangel Street
Ozark, MO
417-485-6686 (877-424-6423)
Dogs are allowed for an additional fee of $10 per night per pet. 2 dogs may be allowed.

Quality Inn near Six Flags St. Louis
1400 W Osage Street
Pacific, MO
636-257-8400 (877-424-6423)
Dogs up to 50 pounds are allowed for an additional fee of $15 per night per pet. 2 dogs may be allowed.

Best Western Prairie View Inn and Suites
2512 NW Prairie View Rd
Platte City, MO
816-858-0200 (800-780-7234)
Well behaved dogs are allowed for an additional one time pet fee of $25 per room. Multiple dogs may be allowed.

Poplar Bluff Drury Inn
2220 Westwood Blvd North
Poplar Bluff, MO
573-686-2451 (800-378-7946)
Dogs of all sizes are permitted. Pets are not allowed in the breakfast area of the hotel. Pets are not to be left

unattended, and each guest must assume liability for damage of property or other guest complaints. There is a limit of one pet per room.

Poplar Bluff Pear Tree Inn
2218 N. Westwood Blvd
Poplar Bluff, MO
573-785-7100 (800-378-7946)
Dogs of all sizes are permitted. Pets are not allowed in the breakfast area of the hotel. Pets are not to be left unattended, and each guest must assume liability for damage of property or other guest complaints. There is a limit of one pet per room.

Super 8 Riverside/Kansas City Area
800 NW Argosy Parkway
Riverside, MO
816-505-2888 (800-800-8000)
Dogs of all sizes are allowed. There are no additional pet fees. Only non-smoking rooms are used for pets. 2 dogs may be allowed.

Super 8 Rockport
1301 Hwy 136 West
Rock Port, MO
660-744-5357 (800-800-8000)
Dogs of all sizes are allowed. There is a $10 per night pet fee per pet. Smoking and non-smoking rooms are available for pet rooms. 2 dogs may be allowed.

Best Western Coachlight
1403 Martin Spring Dr
Rolla, MO
573-341-2511 (800-780-7234)
Dogs up to 30 pounds are allowed for an additional fee of $10 per night per pet; the fee is $20 per pet for dogs over 30 pounds. 2 dogs may be allowed.

Days Inn Rolla
1207 Kings Hwy
Rolla, MO
573-341-3700 (800-329-7466)
Dogs of all sizes are allowed. There are no additional pet fees. 2 dogs may be allowed.

Comfort Suites
1400 S Fifth Street
Saint Charles, MO
636-949-0694 (877-424-6423)
Dogs are allowed for no additional pet fee. There is a pet agreement to sign at check in . Multiple dogs may be allowed.

Best Western Classic Inn
4502 SE US Highway 169
Saint Joseph, MO
816-232-2345 (800-780-7234)

Dogs are allowed for a $50 refundable deposit per pet. Multiple dogs may be allowed.

Best Western Kirkwood Inn
1200 S Kirkwood Road
Saint Louis, MO
314-821-3950 (800-780-7234)
Dogs are allowed for an additional fee of $10 per night per pet. Multiple dogs may be allowed.

Best Western St. Louis Inn
6224 Heimos Industrial Park Drive
Saint Louis, MO
314-416-7639 (800-780-7234)
Dogs are allowed for an additional fee of $10 per night per pet. Dogs must be declared at the time of reservations at all times. Multiple dogs may be allowed.

Best Western Montis Inn
14086 Highway Z
Saint Robert, MO
573-336-4299 (800-780-7234)
Dogs are allowed for an additional fee of $10 per night per pet. Multiple dogs may be allowed.

Best Western State Fair Inn
3120 S 65 Hwy
Sedalia, MO
660-826-6100 (800-780-7234)
Dogs are allowed for no additional pet fee. Dogs must be declared at the time of reservations. Multiple dogs may be allowed.

Super 8 Sedalia
3402 W Broadway
Sedalia, MO
660-827-5890 (800-800-8000)
Dogs of all sizes are allowed. There is a $25 one time pet fee per visit. Smoking and non-smoking rooms are available for pet rooms. 2 dogs may be allowed.

Super 8 Seymour
1000 E Clinton
Seymour, MO
417-935-9888 (800-800-8000)
Dogs of all sizes are allowed. There is a $5 per night pet fee per pet. Reservations are recommended due to limited rooms for pets. Smoking and non-smoking rooms are available for pet rooms. 2 dogs may be allowed.

Green Cocoon
On Farm Road 2212
Shell Knob, MO
417-858-8800
Dogs of all sizes are allowed. There is a $10 per night per pet fee and a

pet policy to sign at check in. Multiple dogs may be allowed.

Days Inn Sikeston
1330 South Main St
Sikeston, MO
573-471-3930 (800-329-7466)
Dogs of all sizes are allowed. There is a $5 per night pet fee per pet. 2 dogs may be allowed.

Sikeston Drury Inn
2602 East Malone
Sikeston, MO
573-471-4100 (800-378-7946)
Dogs of all sizes are permitted. Pets are not allowed in the breakfast area of the hotel. Pets are not to be left unattended, and each guest must assume liability for damage of property or other guest complaints. There is a limit of one pet per room.

Sikeston Pear Tree Inn
2602 Rear East Malone
Sikeston, MO
573-471-8660 (800-378-7946)
Dogs of all sizes are permitted. Pets are not allowed in the breakfast area of the hotel. Pets are not to be left unattended, and each guest must assume liability for damage of property or other guest complaints. There is a limit of one pet per room.

Super 8 Sikeston/Miner Area
2609 E Malone
Sikeston, MO
573-471-7944 (800-800-8000)
Dogs of all sizes are allowed. There is a $10 per night pet fee per pet. Smoking and non-smoking rooms are available for pet rooms. 2 dogs may be allowed.

Super 8 Smithville Lake
112 Cuttings Dr
Smithville, MO
816-532-3088 (800-800-8000)
Dogs of all sizes are allowed. There is a $4 per night pet fee per pet. Smoking and non-smoking rooms are available for pet rooms. 2 dogs may be allowed.

Best Western Coach House Inn
2535 N Glenstone
Springfield, MO
417-862-0701 (800-780-7234)
Dogs are allowed for an additional one time fee of $10 per pet. Multiple dogs may be allowed.

Clarion Hotel
3333 S Glenstone Avenue
Springfield, MO
417-883-6550 (877-424-6423)

Dogs are allowed for an additional fee of $25 per night per pet. Multiple dogs may be allowed.

Days Inn Springfield South
621 W Sunshine
Springfield, MO
417-862-0153 (800-329-7466)
Dogs of all sizes are allowed. There is a $15 per night pet fee per pet. 2 dogs may be allowed.

La Quinta Inn Springfield
1610 East Evergreen
Springfield, MO
417-520-8800 (800-531-5900)
One average sized dog or 2 small dogs are allowed. There are no additional pet fees. Dogs must be leashed and cleaned up after.

La Quinta Inn Springfield South
2535 S. Campbell
Springfield, MO
417-890-6060 (800-531-5900)
Dogs are allowed, but they can not have a combined weight of over 100 pounds. There are not additional pet fees. Dogs may not be left unattended, and they must be leashed, and cleaned up after.

Motel 6 - Springfield
3114 North Kentwood Avenue
Springfield, MO
417-833-0880 (800-466-8356)
One well-behaved family pet per room. Guest must notify front desk upon arrival. Guest is liable for any damages. In consideration of all guests, pets must never be left unattended in the guest rooms.

Red Roof Inn - Springfield,MO
2655 North Glenstone Avenue
Springfield, MO
417-831-2100 (800-RED-ROOF)
One well-behaved family pet per room. Guest must notify front desk upon arrival. Guest is liable for any damages. In consideration of all guests, pets must never be left unattended in the guest rooms.

Residence Inn by Marriott
1303 E Kingsley Street
Springfield, MO
417-890-0020
Dogs of all sizes are allowed. There is a $75 one time fee and a pet policy to sign at check in. Multiple dogs may be allowed.

Springfield Drury Inn & Suites
2715 N. Glenstone Avenue
Springfield, MO
417-863-8400 (800-378-7946)

Dogs of all sizes are permitted. Pets are not allowed in the breakfast area of the hotel. Pets are not to be left unattended, and each guest must assume liability for damage of property or other guest complaints. There is a limit of one pet per room.

University Plaza Hotel
333 John Q. Hammons Parkway
Springfield, MO
417-864-7333
Dogs of all sizes are allowed. There is a $10 per night per room fee and a pet policy to sign at check in. Multiple dogs may be allowed.

Boone's Lick Trail Inn
1000 S Main Street
St Charles, MO
636-947-7000 (888-940-0002)
booneslick.com/
Located along the Missouri River, this 1840's Federal style inn offers guests an experience of colonial life with a touch of luxury. One dog is allowed for a $75 deposit; $35 is non-refundable. Dogs may not be left alone in the room at any time, and they are not allowed in the sitting room.

Motel 6 - St Louis - St Charles
3800 Harry S Truman Boulevard
St Charles, MO
636-925-2020 (800-466-8356)
One well-behaved family pet per room. Guest must notify front desk upon arrival. Guest is liable for any damages. In consideration of all guests, pets must never be left unattended in the guest rooms.

Red Roof Inn - St Louis- St Charles
2010 Zumbehl Road
St Charles, MO
636-947-7770 (800-RED-ROOF)
One well-behaved family pet per room. Guest must notify front desk upon arrival. Guest is liable for any damages. In consideration of all guests, pets must never be left unattended in the guest rooms.

TownePlace Suites St Louis/ St Charles
1800 Zumbehl Road
St Charles, MO
636-949-6800
Dogs of all sizes are allowed. There is a $75 one time pet fee per visit. 2 dogs may be allowed.

Super 8 St Clair
1010 S Outer Rd
St Clair, MO
636-629-8080 (800-800-8000)

Dogs of all sizes are allowed. There is a $10 per night pet fee per pet. Smoking and non-smoking rooms are available for pet rooms. 2 dogs may be allowed.

Holiday Inn
102 South Third St
St Joseph, MO
816-279-8000 (877-270-6405)
Dogs of all sizes are allowed for an additional pet fee of $15 per night per room. 2 dogs may be allowed.

Motel 6 - St Joseph
4021 Frederick Boulevard
St Joseph, MO
816-232-2311 (800-466-8356)
One well-behaved family pet per room. Guest must notify front desk upon arrival. Guest is liable for any damages. In consideration of all guests, pets must never be left unattended in the guest rooms.

St Joseph Riverfront Inn
102 S. 3rd Street
St Joseph, MO
816-279-8000
There is no additional pet fee. Dogs up to 60 pounds are allowed.

St. Joseph Drury Inn
4213 Frederick Blvd
St Joseph, MO
816-364-4700 (800-378-7946)
Dogs of all sizes are permitted. Pets are not allowed in the breakfast area of the hotel. Pets are not to be left unattended, and each guest must assume liability for damage of property or other guest complaints. There is a limit of one pet per room.

Clayton on the Park
8025 Bonhomme Avenue
St Louis, MO
314-290-1500 (800-323-7500)
claytononthepark.com/
All-inclusive for the business or leisure traveler, this impressive 23 story high-rise sits on 16 lush acres of recreational opportunities making it a worthy destination for a day or a year. Dogs are allowed for no additional pet fee with advance reservations. Upon arrival a pet place mat will be waiting with water, food, treats, and toys. There is a pet agreement to sign at check in. 2 dogs may be allowed.

Days Inn St Louis
3660 S Lindbergh
St Louis, MO
314-965-9733 (800-329-7466)
Dogs up to 70 pounds are allowed.

There is a $40 returnable deposit required per room. 2 dogs may be allowed.

Hampton Inn
2211 Market Street
St Louis, MO
314-241-3200
Dogs up to 50 pounds are allowed. There are no additional pet fees. 2 dogs may be allowed.

Hampton Inn
10820 Peartree Lane
St Louis, MO
314-429-2000
Dogs of all sizes are allowed. There are no additional pet fees. Multiple dogs may be allowed.

Hampton Inn
9 Lambert Drury Place
St Louis, MO
636-529-9020
Dogs of all sizes are allowed. There are no additional pet fees. Multiple dogs may be allowed.

Holiday Inn
5915 Wilson Avenue
St Louis, MO
314-645-0700 (877-270-6405)
Dogs of all sizes are allowed for an additional one time pet fee of $25 per room, plus a $75 refundable deposit. 2 dogs may be allowed.

Holiday Inn
10709 Watson Rd
St Louis, MO
314-821-6600 (877-270-6405)
Dogs of all sizes are allowed for an additional one time fee of $25 per pet. Dogs may not be left alone in the room alone. 2 dogs may be allowed.

Holiday Inn
4234 Butler Hill Rd
St Louis, MO
314-894-0700 (877-270-6405)
Dogs of all sizes are allowed for no additional fee with a credit card on file and a $50 refundable deposit. Multiple dogs may be allowed.

Motel 6 - St Louis - Airport
4576 Woodson Road
St Louis, MO
314-427-1313 (800-466-8356)
One well-behaved family pet per room. Guest must notify front desk upon arrival. Guest is liable for any damages. In consideration of all guests, pets must never be left unattended in the guest rooms.

Motel 6 - St Louis North
1405 Dunn Road
St Louis, MO
314-869-9400 (800-466-8356)
One well-behaved family pet per room. Guest must notify front desk upon arrival. Guest is liable for any damages. In consideration of all guests, pets must never be left unattended in the guest rooms.

Motel 6 - St Louis South
6500 South Lindbergh Boulevard
St Louis, MO
314-892-3664 (800-466-8356)
One well-behaved family pet per room. Guest must notify front desk upon arrival. Guest is liable for any damages. In consideration of all guests, pets must never be left unattended in the guest rooms.

Red Roof Inn - St Louis Hampton
5823 Wilson Avenue
St Louis, MO
314-645-0101 (800-RED-ROOF)
One well-behaved family pet per room. Guest must notify front desk upon arrival. Guest is liable for any damages. In consideration of all guests, pets must never be left unattended in the guest rooms.

Red Roof Inn - St Louis Westport
11837 Lackland Road
St Louis, MO
314-991-4900 (800-RED-ROOF)
One well-behaved family pet per room. Guest must notify front desk upon arrival. Guest is liable for any damages. In consideration of all guests, pets must never be left unattended in the guest rooms.

Residence Inn by Marriott
1881 Craigshire Drive
St Louis, MO
314-469-0060
Dogs of all sizes are allowed. There is a $75 one time fee and a pet policy to sign at check in. Multiple dogs may be allowed.

Sheraton Clayton Plaza Hotel St. Louis
7730 Bonhomme Ave.
St Louis, MO
314-863-0400 (888-625-5144)
Dogs up to 75 pounds are allowed for no additional pet fee; there is a pet agreement to sign at check in. Dogs may not be left alone in the room.

Sheraton St. Louis City Center Hotel & Suites
400 South 14th St.

St Louis, MO
314-231-5007 (888-625-5144)
Dogs up to 90 pounds are allowed for no additional pet fee. Dogs may not be left alone in the room.

Sheraton Westport Chalet Hotel St. Louis
191 Westport Plaza
St Louis, MO
314-878-1500 (888-625-5144)
Dogs of all sizes are allowed. There are no additional pet fees. Dogs are not allowed to be left alone in the room.

St Louis - Airport Drury Inn
10490 Natural Bridge Road
St Louis, MO
314-423-7700 (800-378-7946)
Dogs of all sizes are permitted. Pets are not allowed in the breakfast area of the hotel. Pets are not to be left unattended, and each guest must assume liability for damage of property or other guest complaints. There is a limit of one pet per room.

St Louis - Convention Center Drury Inn & Suites
711 North Broadway
St Louis, MO
314-231-8100 (800-378-7946)
Dogs of all sizes are permitted. Pets are not allowed in the breakfast area of the hotel. Pets are not to be left unattended, and each guest must assume liability for damage of property or other guest complaints. There is a limit of one pet per room.

St Louis - Drury Plaza Hotel
Fourth & Market Streets
St Louis, MO
314-231-3003 (800-378-7946)
Dogs of all sizes are permitted. Pets are not allowed in the breakfast area of the hotel. Pets are not to be left unattended, and each guest must assume liability for damage of property or other guest complaints. There is a limit of one pet per room.

St Louis - Union Station Drury Inn
201 South 20th Street
St Louis, MO
314-231-3900 (800-378-7946)
Dogs of all sizes are permitted. Pets are not allowed in the breakfast area of the hotel. Pets are not to be left unattended, and each guest must assume liability for damage of property or other guest complaints. There is a limit of one pet per room.

St Louis Marriott West
660 Maryville Centre Drive

St Louis, MO
816-421-6800 (800-228-929)
Dogs of all sizes are allowed. There is a $75 one time additional fee per room. Dogs must be leashed, cleaned up after, and the Do Not Disturb sign put on the door if they are in the room alone. 2 dogs may be allowed.

Staybridge Suites
1855 Craigshire Rd
St Louis, MO
314-878-1555 (877-270-6405)
Dogs up to 80 pounds are allowed for an additional one time fee of $100 per pet. 2 dogs may be allowed.

Holiday Inn Select
4221 S. Outer Rd
St Peters, MO
636-928-1500 (877-270-6405)
Dogs of all sizes are allowed for an additional $100 pet deposit per room. Dogs may not be left alone in the room. 2 dogs may be allowed.

St Louis - St. Peters Drury Inn
170 Westfield Drive
St Peters, MO
636-397-9700 (800-378-7946)
Dogs of all sizes are permitted. Pets are not allowed in the breakfast area of the hotel. Pets are not to be left unattended, and each guest must assume liability for damage of property or other guest complaints. There is a limit of one pet per room.

Candlewood Suites
140 Carmel Valley Way
St Robert, MO
573-451-2500 (877-270-6405)
Dogs up to 70 pounds are allowed for an additional pet fee of $20 per night per room. 2 dogs may be allowed.

Motel 6 - St Robert
545 Highway Z
St Robert, MO
573-336-3610 (800-466-8356)
One well-behaved family pet per room. Guest must notify front desk upon arrival. Guest is liable for any damages. In consideration of all guests, pets must never be left unattended in the guest rooms.

Red Roof Inn - St Robert
129 St Robert Avenue
St Robert, MO
573-336-2510 (800-RED-ROOF)
One well-behaved family pet per room. Guest must notify front desk upon arrival. Guest is liable for any

damages. In consideration of all guests, pets must never be left unattended in the guest rooms.

Super 8 Sullivan
601 N Service Rd
Sullivan, MO
573-468-8076 (800-800-8000)
Dogs of all sizes are allowed. There is a $10 per night pet fee per pet. Smoking and non-smoking rooms are available for pet rooms. 2 dogs may be allowed.

Super 8 Sweet Springs
208 West Old 40 Highway
Sweet Springs, MO
660-335-4888 (800-800-8000)
Dogs of all sizes are allowed. There is a $5 per night pet fee per pet. Smoking and non-smoking rooms are available for pet rooms. 2 dogs may be allowed.

Days Inn Warrensburg
204 East Cleveland
Warrensburg, MO
660-429-2400 (800-329-7466)
Dogs of all sizes are allowed. There is a $5 per night pet fee per pet. 2 dogs may be allowed.

Holiday Inn Express Warrenton
1008 North Hwy 47 And I-70
Warrenton, MO
636-456-2220 (877-270-6405)
Dogs of all sizes are allowed for an additional fee of $10 per night per pet. Multiple dogs may be allowed.

Holiday Inn
900 Corporate Parkway
Wentzville, MO
636-327-7001 (877-270-6405)
Dogs up to 50 pounds are allowed for no additional fee. 2 dogs may be allowed.

Best Western Grand Villa
220 Jan Howard Expwy
West Plains, MO
417-257-2711 (800-780-7234)
Dogs are allowed for an additional fee of $10 (plus tax) per night per pet. Multiple dogs may be allowed.

Super 8 West Plains
1210 Porter Wagoner Blvd
West Plains, MO
417-256-8088 (800-800-8000)
Dogs of all sizes are allowed. There are no additional pet fees. Dogs are not allowed to be left alone in the room. Smoking and non-smoking rooms are available for pet rooms. 2 dogs may be allowed.

Montana Listings

River's Edge Resort
22 S Frontage Road
Alberton, MT
406-722-3375
Dogs of all sizes are allowed. There is a $25 refundable pet deposit per room. Dogs may not be left unattended outside, and they must be leashed and cleaned up after. There is also a camping area on site that allows dogs at no additional fee. 2 dogs may be allowed.

Holiday Inn Express
6261 Jackrabbit Lane
Belgrade, MT
406-388-0800 (877-270-6405)
Dogs of all sizes are allowed for no additional fee unless there is excessive pet clean-up. Multiple dogs may be allowed.

La Quinta Inn & Suites Belgrade
6445 Jackrabbit Lane
Belgrade, MT
406-388-2222 (800-531-5900)
Dogs of all sizes are allowed. There are no additional pet fees. Dogs may not be left unattended, and they must be leashed and cleaned up after. Multiple dogs may be allowed.

Super 8 Big Timber
I-90 and Hwy 10 W
Big Timber, MT
406-932-8888 (800-800-8000)
Dogs of all sizes are allowed. There is a $20 one time per pet fee per visit. Reservations are recommended due to limited rooms for pets. Smoking and non-smoking rooms are available for pet rooms. 2 dogs may be allowed.

O'Duachain Country Inn Bed and Breakfast
675 Ferndale Dr
Bigfork, MT
406-837-6851 (800-837-7460)
ohwy.com/mt/d/duachain.htm
There is a $25 one time pet fee. The owner has a dog and a peacock, so your dog needs to be okay with them.

Timbers Motel
8540 Hwy. 35 South
Bigfork, MT
406-837-6200 (800-821-4546)
montanaweb.com/timbers/
There is a $5 per day pet fee.

Best Western Clock Tower Inn
2511 1st Avenue N
Billings, MT
406-259-5511 (800-780-7234)
Dogs are allowed for an additional fee of $10 per night per pet. Multiple dogs may be allowed.

Best Western Kelly Inn & Suites
4915 Southgate Drive
Billings, MT
406-256-9400 (800-780-7234)
Dogs are allowed for no additional pet fee. There is a pet agreement to sign at check in, and dogs may not be left alone in the room. Multiple dogs may be allowed.

Comfort Inn
2030 Overland Avenue
Billings, MT
406-652-5200 (877-424-6423)
Dogs are allowed for an additional one time pet fee of $15 per room. Multiple dogs may be allowed.

Days Inn Billings
843 Parkway Lane
Billings, MT
406-252-4007 (800-329-7466)
Dogs of all sizes are allowed. There is a $5 per night pet fee per pet. 2 dogs may be allowed.

Hilltop Inn
1116 N 28th St
Billings, MT
406-245-5000 (800-878-9282)
There is a $5 per day pet fee.

Holiday Inn The Grand Montana-Billings
5500 Midland Rd
Billings, MT
406-248-7701 (877-270-6405)
Dogs of all sizes are allowed for an additional one time pet fee of $25 per room. 2 dogs may be allowed.

Howard Johnson Express Inn
1001 S 27th St.
Billings, MT
406-248-4656 (800-446-4656)
Dogs of all sizes are welcome. There are no additional pet fees.

Motel 6 - Billings
5400 Midland Road
Billings, MT
406-252-0093 (800-466-8356)
One well-behaved family pet per room. Guest must notify front desk upon arrival. Guest is liable for any damages. In consideration of all guests, pets must never be left unattended in the guest rooms.

Red Roof Inn - Billings
5353 Midland Road
Billings, MT
406-248-7551 (800-RED-ROOF)
One well-behaved family pet per room. Guest must notify front desk upon arrival. Guest is liable for any damages. In consideration of all guests, pets must never be left unattended in the guest rooms.

War Bonnet Inn
2612 Belknap Avenue
Billings, MT
406-248-7761
Dogs of all sizes are allowed. There is a $10 refundable pet deposit per room. Multiple dogs may be allowed.

Best Western GranTree Inn
1325 N 7th Ave
Bozeman, MT
406-587-5261 (800-780-7234)
Dogs are allowed for no additional pet fee. 2 dogs may be allowed.

Comfort Inn
1370 N 7th Avenue
Bozeman, MT
406-587-2322 (877-424-6423)
Dogs are allowed for an additional fee of $10 per night per pet. Multiple dogs may be allowed.

Days Inn Bozeman
1321 N 7th Ave
Bozeman, MT
406-587-5251 (800-329-7466)
Dogs of all sizes are allowed. There is a $5 per night pet fee per pet. 2 dogs may be allowed.

Holiday Inn
5 Baxtor Lane
Bozeman, MT
406-587-4561 (877-270-6405)
Dogs of all sizes are allowed for no additional fee with a credit card on file; there is a $50 refundable deposit if paying in cash. 2 dogs may be allowed.

Super 8 Bozeman
800 Wheat Dr
Bozeman, MT
406-586-1521 (800-800-8000)
Dogs of all sizes are allowed. There is a $5 per night pet fee per pet. Reservations are recommended due to limited rooms for pets. Smoking and non-smoking rooms are available for pet rooms. 2 dogs may be allowed.

Western Heritage Inn
1200 E Main St
Bozeman, MT

406-586-8534
There is a $5 per day pet charge.

Best Western Butte Plaza Inn
2900 Harrison Ave
Butte, MT
406-494-3500 (800-780-7234)
Dogs are allowed for a $50
refundable pet deposit per room. 2
dogs may be allowed.

Comfort Inn
2777 Harrison Avenue
Butte, MT
406-494-8850 (877-424-6423)
Dogs are allowed for an additional
fee of $5 per night per pet. Multiple
dogs may be allowed.

Motel 6 - Butte
122005 Nissler Road
Butte, MT
406-782-5678 (800-466-8356)
One well-behaved family pet per
room. Guest must notify front desk
upon arrival. Guest is liable for any
damages. In consideration of all
guests, pets must never be left
unattended in the guest rooms.

Super 8 Butte
2929 Harrison Ave
Butte, MT
460-494-6000 (800-800-8000)
Dogs of all sizes are allowed. There
is a $50 returnable deposit required
per room. There is a $5 per night pet
fee per pet. Smoking and non-
smoking rooms are available for pet
rooms. 2 dogs may be allowed.

Super 8 Columbus
602 8th Ave
Columbus, MT
406-322-4101 (800-800-8000)
Dogs of all sizes are allowed. There
is a $5 per night pet fee per pet.
Smoking and non-smoking rooms
are available for pet rooms. 2 dogs
may be allowed.

Super 8 Conrad
215 N Main St
Conrad, MT
406-278-7676 (800-800-8000)
Dogs of all sizes are allowed. There
is a $5 per night pet fee per pet.
Smoking and non-smoking rooms
are available for pet rooms. 2 dogs
may be allowed.

Super 8 Deer Lodge
1150 North Main
Deer Lodge, MT
406-846-2370 (800-800-8000)
Dogs of all sizes are allowed. There
is a $10 per night pet fee per pet.

Reservations are recommended
due to limited rooms for pets.
Smoking and non-smoking rooms
are available for pet rooms. 2 dogs
may be allowed.

Best Western Paradise Inn
650 N Montana St
Dillon, MT
406-683-4214 (800-780-7234)
Dogs are allowed for an additional
fee of $10 per night. Multiple dogs
may be allowed.

Comfort Inn
450 N Interchange
Dillon, MT
406-683-6831 (877-424-6423)
Dogs are allowed for an additional
fee of $10 per night per pet. A credit
card must be on file, and dogs may
not be left alone in the room.
Multiple dogs may be allowed.

Super 8 Dillon
550 N Montana St
Dillon, MT
406-683-4288 (800-800-8000)
Dogs of all sizes are allowed. There
is a $5 per night pet fee per pet.
Smoking and non-smoking rooms
are available for pet rooms. 2 dogs
may be allowed.

Best Western Sundowner Inn
1018 Front St
Forsyth, MT
406-346-2115 (800-780-7234)
Dogs are allowed for an additional
fee of $10 per night per pet. Multiple
dogs may be allowed.

Best Western Mammoth Hot
Springs
Hwy 89
Gardiner, MT
406-848-7311 (800-780-7234)
Dogs are allowed for an additional
pet fee of $5 per night per room.
Dogs may not be left alone in the
room. Multiple dogs may be
allowed.

Super 8 Gardiner/Yellowstone Park
Area
US Highway 89
Gardiner, MT
406-848-7401 (800-800-8000)
Dogs of all sizes are allowed. There
is a $5 per night pet fee per pet.
Dogs are not allowed to be left
alone in the room. Only non-
smoking rooms are used for pets. 2
dogs may be allowed.

Cottonwood Inn
45 1st Avenue NE

Glasgow, MT
800-321-8213
Dogs of all sizes are allowed. There
are no additional pet fees. Dogs may
not be left unattended, and they must
be well behaved, leashed, and
cleaned up after. There is also an RV
park on site that allows dogs. 2 dogs
may be allowed.

Days Inn Glendive
2000 N Merrill Ave
Glendive, MT
406-365-6011 (800-329-7466)
Dogs of all sizes are allowed. There
are no additional pet fees. 2 dogs
may be allowed.

Super 8 Glendive
1904 N Merrill Ave
Glendive, MT
406-365-5671 (800-800-8000)
Dogs of all sizes are allowed. There
is a $5 per night pet fee per pet.
Smoking and non-smoking rooms
are available for pet rooms. 2 dogs
may be allowed.

Best Western Heritage Inn
1700 Fox Farm Road
Great Falls, MT
406-761-1900 (800-780-7234)
Dogs are allowed for no additional
pet fee. Multiple dogs may be
allowed.

Comfort Inn
1120 9th St S
Great Falls, MT
406-454-2727 (877-424-6423)
Dogs are allowed for an additional
one time fee of $10 per pet. Multiple
dogs may be allowed.

Days Inn Great Falls
101 14th Ave NW
Great Falls, MT
406-727-6565 (800-329-7466)
Dogs of all sizes are allowed. There
is a $5 per night pet fee per pet.
Reservations are recommended due
to limited rooms for pets. 2 dogs may
be allowed.

Hampton Inn
2301 14th Street SW
Great Falls, MT
406-453-2675
Dogs of all sizes are allowed. There
is a $20 per stay per room additional
pet fee. Multiple dogs may be
allowed.

Holiday Inn
400 10th Ave S.
Great Falls, MT
406-727-7200 (877-270-6405)

Dogs of all sizes are allowed for an additional fee of $10 per night per pet. Multiple dogs may be allowed.

La Quinta Inn & Suites Great Falls
600 River Drive South
Great Falls, MT
406-761-2600 (800-531-5900)
Dogs of all sizes are allowed. There are no additional pet fees. There is a pet waiver to sign at check in. Dogs may not be left unattended, and they must be leashed and cleaned up after. Multiple dogs may be allowed.

Motel 6 - Great Falls
2 Treasures State Drive
Great Falls, MT
406-453-1602 (800-466-8356)
One well-behaved family pet per room. Guest must notify front desk upon arrival. Guest is liable for any damages. In consideration of all guests, pets must never be left unattended in the guest rooms.

Super 8 Great Falls
1214 13th Street South
Great Falls, MT
406-727-7600 (800-800-8000)
Dogs of all sizes are allowed. There is a $3 per night pet fee per pet. Smoking and non-smoking rooms are available for pet rooms. Multiple dogs may be allowed.

Townhouse Inn
1411 10th Avenue South
Great Falls, MT
406-761-4600
There is a $5 per day pet charge.

Townhouse Inn
601 1st Street West
Havre, MT
406-265-6711
There is a $5 per day pet charge.

Barrister Bed and Breakfast
416 North Ewing
Helena, MT
406-443-7330 (800-823-1148)

Best Western Helena Great Northern Hotel
835 Great Northern Boulevard
Helena, MT
406-457-5500 (800-780-7234)
Dogs are allowed for an additional fee of $15 per night per pet. Multiple dogs may be allowed.

Comfort Inn
750 Fee Street
Helena, MT
406-443-1000 (877-424-6423)
Dogs are allowed for an additional

one time pet fee of $10 per room. Multiple dogs may be allowed.

Days Inn Helena
2001 Prospect Ave
Helena, MT
406-442-3280 (800-329-7466)
Dogs of all sizes are allowed. There is a $10 per three night pet fee per pet. 2 dogs may be allowed.

Hampton Inn
3000 Highway 12E
Helena, MT
406-443-5800
Dogs of all sizes are allowed. There is a $20 per stay per room additional pet fee. Multiple dogs may be allowed.

Motel 6 - Helena
800 North Oregon Street
Helena, MT
406-442-9990 (800-466-8356)
One well-behaved family pet per room. Guest must notify front desk upon arrival. Guest is liable for any damages. In consideration of all guests, pets must never be left unattended in the guest rooms.

Red Lion
2301 Colonial Drive
Helena, MT
406-443-2100
Dogs of all sizes are allowed. There is a $20 one time fee per stay and a pet policy to sign at check in. Multiple dogs may be allowed.

Shilo Inn
2020 Prospect Avenue
Helena, MT
406-442-0320 (800-222-2244)
shiloinn.com/Montana/helena.html
There is a $10 per day pet charge.

Super 8 Helena
2200 11th Ave
Helena, MT
406-443-2450 (800-800-8000)
Dogs of all sizes are allowed. There is a $10 one time per pet fee per visit. Smoking and non-smoking rooms are available for pet rooms. 2 dogs may be allowed.

Cavanaugh's
20 N Main St
Kalispell, MT
406-752-6660
There is a $15 one time pet fee.

Kalispell Grand Hotel
100 Main St
Kalispell, MT
406-755-8100

There are no additional pet fees.

La Quinta Inn & Suites Kalispell
255 Montclair Dr
Kalispell, MT
406-257-5255 (800-531-5900)
Dogs of all sizes are allowed. There are no additional pet fees. Dogs must be well behaved, leashed, and cleaned up after. Multiple dogs may be allowed.

Motel 6 - Kalispell
1540 US 93 South
Kalispell, MT
406-752-6355 (800-466-8356)
One well-behaved family pet per room. Guest must notify front desk upon arrival. Guest is liable for any damages. In consideration of all guests, pets must never be left unattended in the guest rooms.

Red Lion
1330 H 2 W
Kalispell, MT
406-755-6700
Dogs of all sizes are allowed. For pet fees there is a $10 additional fee per stay for smoking rooms and a $15 additional fee per stay for non-smoking rooms. Multiple dogs may be allowed.

Red Lion
North 20 Main
Kalispell, MT
406-751-5050
Dogs of all sizes are allowed. There is a $20 one time fee per pet. Multiple dogs may be allowed.

Super 8 Kalispell/Glacier Intl Arpt Area
1341 First Ave East
Kalispell, MT
406-755-1888 (800-800-8000)
Dogs of all sizes are allowed. There is a $10 one time per pet fee per visit. Smoking and non-smoking rooms are available for pet rooms. 2 dogs may be allowed.

Best Western Yellowstone Crossing
205 SE 4th Street
Laurel, MT
406-628-6888 (800-780-7234)
Dogs are allowed for an additional fee of $10 per night per pet. Multiple dogs may be allowed.

Pelican Motel & RV Park
11360 S Frontage
Laurel, MT
406-628-4324
Dogs of all sizes are allowed. There is a $10 one time fee for 1 or 2 dogs,

and a $20 one time fee for up to 3 dogs. Dogs may not be left unattended in the motel room, and they must be leashed and cleaned up after. Multiple dogs may be allowed.

Super 8 Libby
Hwy 2 West
Libby, MT
406-293-2771 (800-800-8000)
Dogs of all sizes are allowed. There is a $10 one time per pet fee per visit. Smoking and non-smoking rooms are available for pet rooms. 2 dogs may be allowed.

The Caboose Motel
714 W 9th Street
Libby, MT
406-293-6201
Dogs of all sizes are allowed. There is a pet policy to sign at check in and there are no additional pet fees. Dogs of all sizes are allowed. There are no additional pet fees. Multiple dogs may be allowed.

Best Western Yellowstone Inn
1515 West Park St
Livingston, MT
406-222-6110 (800-780-7234)
Dogs are allowed for an additional fee of $10 per night per pet. Multiple dogs may be allowed.

Days Inn Missoula South/Blue Mountain
11225 Hwy 93 S
Lolo, MT
406-273-2121 (800-329-7466)
Dogs of all sizes are allowed. There is a $10 per night pet fee per pet. 2 dogs may be allowed.

Best Western War Bonnet Inn
1015 S Haynes
Miles City, MT
406-234-4560 (800-780-7234)
Quiet dogs are allowed for an additional fee of $5 per night per pet. Dogs may only be left in the room for short periods. Multiple dogs may be allowed.

Budget Inn
1006 S. Haynes Ave.
Miles City, MT
406-232-3550 (800-329-7466)
There is a $5 per day pet charge.

Motel 6 - Miles City
1314 South Haynes Avenue
Miles City, MT
406-232-7040 (800-466-8356)
One well-behaved family pet per room. Guest must notify front desk

upon arrival. Guest is liable for any damages. In consideration of all guests, pets must never be left unattended in the guest rooms.

Best Western Grant Creek Inn
5280 Grant Creek Rd
Missoula, MT
406-543-0700 (800-780-7234)
Dogs are allowed for an additional pet fee of $10 per night per room. Multiple dogs may be allowed.

Comfort Inn
4545 N Reserve Street
Missoula, MT
406-542-0888 (877-424-6423)
Dogs are allowed for an additional fee of $15 per night per pet. Multiple dogs may be allowed.

Days Inn Airport
8600 Truck Stop Rd
Missoula, MT
406-721-9776 (800-329-7466)
Dogs of all sizes are allowed. There is a $5 per night pet fee per pet. 2 dogs may be allowed.

Doubletree
100 Madison
Missoula, MT
406-728-3100
Dogs of all sizes are allowed. There is a $20 per room per stay pet fee. Multiple dogs may be allowed.

Hampton Inn
4805 N Reserve Street
Missoula, MT
406-549-1800
Dogs of all sizes are allowed. There is a $10 per stay per room additional pet fee. Multiple dogs may be allowed.

Motel 6 - Missoula
3035 Expo Parkway
Missoula, MT
406-549-6665 (800-466-8356)
One well-behaved family pet per room. Guest must notify front desk upon arrival. Guest is liable for any damages. In consideration of all guests, pets must never be left unattended in the guest rooms.

Quality Inn and Conference Center
3803 Brooks Street
Missoula, MT
406-251-2665 (877-424-6423)
Dogs are allowed for an additional fee of $10 per night per pet. 2 dogs may be allowed.

Red Lion
700 W Broadway

Missoula, MT
406-728-3300
Dogs of all sizes are allowed. There is a $10 per night pet fee and a pet policy to sign at check in. Multiple dogs may be allowed.

Best Western KwaTaqNuk Resort
303 US Highway 93 E
Polson, MT
406-883-3636 (800-780-7234)
Dogs are allowed for an additional one time pet fee of $25 per room. Multiple dogs may be allowed.

Super 8 Polson/Flathead Lake Area
21 S Shore Rte
Polson, MT
406-883-6266 (800-800-8000)
Dogs of all sizes are allowed. There are no additional pet fees. Dogs are not allowed to be left alone in the room. Smoking and non-smoking rooms are available for pet rooms. 2 dogs may be allowed.

Star Lake Forest Rentals
14450 Bowers Drive
Ramsey, MT
866-888-8265
Dogs of all sizes are allowed. There is a pet policy to sign at check in and there are no additional pet fees. This is a monthly rental only. Multiple dogs may be allowed.

Best Western LuPine Inn
702 S Hauser
Red Lodge, MT
406-446-1321 (800-780-7234)
Dogs are allowed for no additional pet fee. Multiple dogs may be allowed.

Comfort Inn
612 N Broadway
Red Lodge, MT
406-446-4469 (877-424-6423)
Dogs are allowed for no additional pet fee. 2 dogs may be allowed.

Super 8 Red Lodge
1223 S Broadway
Red Lodge, MT
406-446-2288 (800-800-8000)
Dogs of all sizes are allowed. There is a $5 per night pet fee per pet. Smoking and non-smoking rooms are available for pet rooms. 2 dogs may be allowed.

Comfort Inn
455 McKinley
Shelby, MT
406-434-2212 (877-424-6423)
Dogs are allowed for an additional one time pet fee of $5 per room.

Multiple dogs may be allowed.

Super 8 St Regis
Old Highway 10
St Regis, MT
406-649-2422 (800-800-8000)
Dogs of all sizes are allowed. There is a $20 returnable deposit required per room. Smoking and non-smoking rooms are available for pet rooms. 2 dogs may be allowed.

Best Western Weston Inn
103 Gibbon St
West Yellowstone, MT
406-646-7373 (800-780-7234)
Dogs are allowed for an additional fee of $10 per night per pet. 2 dogs may be allowed.

Holiday Inn Sunspree Resort West Yellowstone
315 Yellowstone Avenue
West Yellowstone, MT
406-646-7365 (877-270-6405)
Dogs of all sizes are allowed for an additional one time fee of $50 per pet. 2 dogs may be allowed.

Pioneer Motel
515 Madison Avenue
West Yellowstone, MT
406-646-9705
Well behaved dogs up to 60 pounds are allowed. There are no additional pet fees. Dogs are not allowed on the beds, must be leashed on the property, and are not allowed to be left alone in the room. 2 dogs may be allowed.

Hibernation Station
212 Grey Wolf Avenue
West Yellowstonw, MT
406-646-4200
Dogs of all sizes are allowed in the cabins. There is a $10 per night per pet fee and a pet policy to sign at check in. Multiple dogs may be allowed.

All Seasons Inn
Highway 89 South
White Sulphur Springs, MT
406-547-8888 (800-800-8000)
Dogs of all sizes are allowed. There is a $6 per night pet fee per pet. Smoking and non-smoking rooms are available for pet rooms. 2 dogs may be allowed.

Best Western Rocky Mountain Lodg
6510 Hwy 93 S
Whitefish, MT
406-862-2569 (800-780-7234)
One dog is allowed for an additional one time pet fee of $15; two dogs is

$20. 2 dogs may be allowed.

Holiday Inn Express
6390 US Hwy 93 South
Whitefish, MT
406-862-4020 (877-270-6405)
Dogs of all sizes are allowed for an additional fee of $15 per night per pet. 2 dogs may be allowed.

Super 8 Whitefish/Glacier Park Area
800 Spokane Ave
Whitefish, MT
406-862-8255 (800-800-8000)
Dogs of all sizes are allowed. There is a $5 per night pet fee per pet. Reservations are recommended due to limited rooms for pets. Smoking and non-smoking rooms are available for pet rooms. 2 dogs may be allowed.

Fish Creek House
5913 Mt H 41
Whitehall, MT
406-287-2191
Well behaved dogs of all sizes are allowed. There is a $10 per stay per pet fee and a pet policy to sign at check in. 2 dogs may be allowed.

The Islander Inn
39 Orchard Lane
Woods Bay, MT
406-837-5472
Dogs of all sizes are allowed. There are no additional pet fees. Multiple dogs may be allowed.

Nebraska Listings

Holiday Inn Express Hotel & Suites
N. Hwy 77
Beatrice, NE
402-228-7000 (877-270-6405)
Dogs of all sizes are allowed for no additional fee. 2 dogs may be allowed.

Days Inn Omaha/Bellevue
1811 Hillcrest Dr
Bellevue, NE
402-292-3800 (800-329-7466)
Dogs of all sizes are allowed. There is a $10 per night pet fee per pet. Only non-smoking rooms are used for pets. 2 dogs may be allowed.

Super 8 Central City
1701 31st Street
Central City, NE
308-946-5055 (800-800-8000)

Dogs of all sizes are allowed. There is a $5.33 per night pet fee per pet. Smoking and non-smoking rooms are available for pet rooms. 2 dogs may be allowed.

Best Western West Hills Inn
1100 W 10th
Chadron, NE
308-432-3305 (800-780-7234)
Dogs are allowed for an additional one time pet fee of $15 per room. Multiple dogs may be allowed.

Motel 6 - Chadron
755 Microtel Drive
Chadron, NE
308-432-3000 (800-466-8356)
One well-behaved family pet per room. Guest must notify front desk upon arrival. Guest is liable for any damages. In consideration of all guests, pets must never be left unattended in the guest rooms.

Super 8 Chadron
840 W Hwy 20
Chadron, NE
308-432-4471 (800-800-8000)
Dogs of all sizes are allowed. There are no additional pet fees. Smoking and non-smoking rooms are available for pet rooms. 2 dogs may be allowed.

Days Inn Columbus
371 33rd Ave
Columbus, NE
402-564-2527 (800-329-7466)
Dogs of all sizes are allowed. There is a $10 one time per pet fee per visit. 2 dogs may be allowed.

Super 8 Crete
1880 W 12th Street
Crete, NE
402-826-3600 (800-800-8000)
Dogs of all sizes are allowed. There is a $5 per night pet fee per pet. Smoking and non-smoking rooms are available for pet rooms. 2 dogs may be allowed.

Super 8 Gothenburg
401 Platte River Dr
Gothenburg, NE
308-537-2684 (800-800-8000)
Dogs of all sizes are allowed. There are no additional pet fees. Reservations are recommended due to limited rooms for pets. Smoking and non-smoking rooms are available for pet rooms. 2 dogs may be allowed.

Days Inn Grand Island
2620 N Diers Ave

Grand Island, NE
308-384-8624 (800-329-7466)
Dogs of all sizes are allowed. There is a $7.50 per night pet fee per pet. 2 dogs may be allowed.

Holiday Inn
I-80 & Hwy 281
Grand Island, NE
308-384-7770 (877-270-6405)
Dogs of all sizes are allowed for an additional one time pet fee of $15 per room. 2 dogs may be allowed.

Howard Johnson Hotel
3333 Ramada Road
Grand Island, NE
308-384-5150 (800-446-4656)
Dogs of all sizes are welcome. There is a $10 one time pet fee.

Best Western North Shore Lodge
203 W 33rd Street
Hastings, NE
402-461-4076 (800-780-7234)
Dogs are allowed for an additional pet fee of $10 per night per room. 2 dogs may be allowed.

Super 8 Holdrege
420 Broadway
Holdrege, NE
308-995-2793 (800-800-8000)
Dogs up to 60 pounds are allowed. There is a $10 per night pet fee per pet. Dogs are not allowed to be left alone in the room. Smoking and non-smoking rooms are available for pet rooms. 2 dogs may be allowed.

Best Western Inn of Kearney
1010 3rd Ave
Kearney, NE
308-237-5185 (800-780-7234)
Dogs are allowed for an additional pet fee per room of $10 for each 1 to 7 days stay. Multiple dogs may be allowed.

Motel 6 - Kearney
101 Talmadge Road
Kearney, NE
308-338-0705 (800-466-8356)
One well-behaved family pet per room. Guest must notify front desk upon arrival. Guest is liable for any damages. In consideration of all guests, pets must never be left unattended in the guest rooms.

Super 8 Motel - Kearney
15 W. 8th Street
Kearney, NE
308-234-5513 (800-800-8000)
innworks.com/kearney
There is a $10 per stay additional pet fee. Up to three dogs are permitted

in each room. The hotel allows a free 8 minute long distance call each night and offers a free continental breakfast. There is a pool and a laundry. I-80, Exit 272, N 1/2 mile to W. 8th St. Turn Right.

Days Inn Kimball
611 E 3rd St
Kimball, NE
308-235-4671 (800-329-7466)
Dogs of all sizes are allowed. There is a $10 per night pet fee per pet. 2 dogs may be allowed.

Budget Host Minute Man Motel
801 Plum Creek Pkwy
Lexington, NE
308-324-5544
There is a $5 per day pet fee. Usually pets are in smoking rooms, but they will make exceptions.

Holiday Inn Express & Suites
2605 Plum Creek Pkwy
Lexington, NE
308-324-9900 (877-270-6405)
Dogs of all sizes are allowed for an additional pet fee of $10 per night per room. Multiple dogs may be allowed.

Candlewood Suites Lincoln
4100 Pioneer Woods Drive
Lincoln, NE
402-420-0330 (877-270-6405)
Dogs up to 80 pounds are allowed for an additional fee per pet of $75 for 1 to 7 days and $150 per pet for 8 or more days. 2 dogs may be allowed.

Comfort Suites
4231 Industrial Avenue
Lincoln, NE
402-476-8080 (877-424-6423)
Dogs are allowed for an additional fee of $10 per night per pet. Multiple dogs may be allowed.

Country Inns & Suites by Carlson
5353 N. 27th
Lincoln, NE
402-476-5353
Dogs of all sizes are allowed. There is a $10 per day additional pet fee. There is complimentary high-speed Internet.

Days Inn Lincoln
1140 Calvert St
Lincoln, NE
402-423-7111 (800-329-7466)
Dogs of all sizes are allowed. There is a $10 per night pet fee per pet. 2 dogs may be allowed.

Holiday Inn Express
1133 Belmont Ave
Lincoln, NE
402-435-0200 (877-270-6405)
Dogs of all sizes are allowed for no additional fee. Multiple dogs may be allowed.

Holiday Inn Express Hotel & Suites Lincoln South
8801 Amber Hill Court
Lincoln, NE
402-423-1176 (877-270-6405)
Dogs of all sizes are allowed for an additional fee of $25 per night per pet. Multiple dogs may be allowed.

Motel 6 - Lincoln Airport
3001 NW 12th Street
Lincoln, NE
402-475-3211 (800-466-8356)
One well-behaved family pet per room. Guest must notify front desk upon arrival. Guest is liable for any damages. In consideration of all guests, pets must never be left unattended in the guest rooms.

Staybridge Suites
2701 Fletcher Avenue
Lincoln, NE
402-438-7829 (877-270-6405)
Dogs of all sizes are allowed for an additional pet fee per room of $25 for 1 to 6 nights; 7 to 29 nights is $50, and 30 or more nights is $75. 2 dogs may be allowed.

Super 8 Lincoln/West "0"
2635 W O Street
Lincoln, NE
402-476-8887 (800-800-8000)
Dogs of all sizes are allowed. There is a $10 per night pet fee per pet. Smoking and non-smoking rooms are available for pet rooms. 2 dogs may be allowed.

Holiday Inn Express Mccook (Us 6/34 & Hwy 83)
1 Holiday Bison Drive
Mccook, NE
308-345-4505 (877-270-6405)
Dogs of all sizes are allowed for no additional fee. Dogs may not be left alone in the room. Multiple dogs may be allowed.

Pioneer Village Motel
224 E H 6
Minden, NE
800-445-4447
Dogs of all sizes are allowed. There is a $10.95 per night per room additional pet fee. Dogs may not be left unattended, and they must be leashed and cleaned up after. There

is only 1 non-smoking pet friendly room available, the rest are smoking rooms. Dogs are not allowed in the museum or in any of the outer pioneer village buildings. 2 dogs may be allowed.

Ramada Limited
4433 N 27th Street
N Lincoln, NE
402-476-2222
Dogs of all sizes are allowed. There is a $5 per night per room additional pet fee. If it is one small pet it is a one time fee of $5. Multiple dogs may be allowed.

Super 8 Norfolk
1223 Omaha Ave
Norfolk, NE
402-379-2220 (800-800-8000)
Dogs of all sizes are allowed. There is a $10 per night pet fee per pet. Smoking and non-smoking rooms are available for pet rooms. 2 dogs may be allowed.

Holiday Inn Express Hotel and Suites
300 Holiday Frontage Rd
North Platte, NE
308-532-9500 (877-270-6405)
Dogs of all sizes are allowed for an additional one time pet fee of $20 per room. Multiple dogs may be allowed.

Howard Johnson Express Inn
1209 S. Dewey Street
North Platte, NE
308-532-0130 (800-446-4656)
Well-behaved dogs of all sizes are allowed. There is a $10 per day additional pet fee.

La Quinta Inn & Suites North Platte
2600 Eagles Wings Place
North Platte, NE
308-534-0700 (800-531-5900)
Dogs of all sizes are allowed. There are no additional pet fees. There is a pet waiver to sign at check in. Dogs may not be left unattended, and they must be leashed and cleaned up after. Multiple dogs may be allowed.

Motel 6 - North Platte
1520 South Jeffers Street
North Platte, NE
308-534-6200 (800-466-8356)
One well-behaved family pet per room. Guest must notify front desk upon arrival. Guest is liable for any damages. In consideration of all guests, pets must never be left unattended in the guest rooms.

Quality Inn and Suites
2102 S Jeffers

North Platte, NE
308-532-9090 (877-424-6423)
Dogs are allowed for an additional one time fee of $10 per pet. Multiple dogs may be allowed.

Stanford Motel
1400 E 4th Street
North Platte, NE
308-532-9380 (800-743-4934)
There is a $3 per day pet fee. Puppies are not allowed but dogs are permitted.

Super 8 North Platte
220 Eugene Ave
North Platte, NE
308-532-4224 (800-800-8000)
Dogs of all sizes are allowed. There is a $10 per night fee per pet. Smoking and non-smoking rooms are available for pet rooms. 2 dogs may be allowed.

Best Western Stagecoach Inn
201 Stagecoach Trail
Ogallala, NE
308-284-3656 (800-780-7234)
Dogs are allowed for an additional fee of $7 per night per pet. Multiple dogs may be allowed.

Days Inn Ogallala
601 Stagecoach Trail
Ogallala, NE
308-284-6365 (800-329-7466)
Dogs of all sizes are allowed. There is a $6 per night pet fee per pet. 2 dogs may be allowed.

Holiday Inn Express
501 Stage Coach Drive
Ogallala, NE
308-284-2266 (877-270-6405)
Dogs of all sizes are allowed for an additional fee of $7 per night per pet. Multiple dogs may be allowed.

Super 8 Ogallala
500 East A Street South
Ogallala, NE
308-284-2076 (800-800-8000)
Dogs of all sizes are allowed. There is a $10 returnable deposit required per room. Reservations are recommended due to limited rooms for pets. Smoking and non-smoking rooms are available for pet rooms. 2 dogs may be allowed.

Best Western Kelly Inn
4706 S 108th Street
Omaha, NE
402-339-7400 (800-780-7234)
Dogs are allowed for no additional pet fee. Multiple dogs may be allowed.

Best Western Seville Plaza Hotel
3001 Chicago Street
Omaha, NE
402-345-2222 (800-780-7234)
Dogs are allowed for an additional one time pet fee of $40 for 2 dogs; a 3rd dog is an additional $40. Multiple dogs may be allowed.

Candlewood Suites
360 S 108th Ave
Omaha, NE
402-758-2848 (877-270-6405)
Dogs of all sizes are allowed for an additional one time fee of $75 per pet for 1 to 6 days; the fee is $150 per pet for 7 or more days. Multiple dogs may be allowed.

Clarion Hotel West
4888 S 118th Street
Omaha, NE
402-895-1000 (877-424-6423)
Dogs up to 50 pounds are allowed for an additional one time fee of $10 per pet. 2 dogs may be allowed.

Comfort Inn
9595 S 145th Street
Omaha, NE
402-896-6300 (877-424-6423)
Dogs are allowed for an additional one time fee of $10 per pet. Multiple dogs may be allowed.

Crowne Plaza
655 N. 108th Ave
Omaha, NE
402-496-0850 (877-270-6405)
Dogs up to 75 pounds are allowed for an additional one time fee of $25 per pet plus a $100 refundable deposit per pet. 2 dogs may be allowed.

Doubletree
7270 Cedar Street
Omaha, NE
402-397-5141
Dogs of all sizes are allowed. There is a $50 one time pet fee per room. Multiple dogs may be allowed.

Holiday Inn Express Hotel & Suites Omaha West
17677 Wright St
Omaha, NE
402-333-5566 (877-270-6405)
Dogs of all sizes are allowed for an additional one time pet fee of $25 per room. Multiple dogs may be allowed.

La Quinta Inn Omaha
3330 North 104th Ave.
Omaha, NE
402-493-1900 (800-531-5900)

Dogs of all sizes are allowed. There are no additional pet fees. There is a pet waiver to sign at check in. Dogs may not be left unattended, and they must be leashed and cleaned up after. Multiple dogs may be allowed.

La Quinta Inn Omaha Southwest
10760 M Street
Omaha, NE
402-592-5200 (800-531-5900)
Dogs of all sizes are allowed. There are no additional pet fees. Pets may not be left unattended, and they must be leashed and cleaned up after. Multiple dogs may be allowed.

Motel 6 - Omaha
10708 M Street
Omaha, NE
402-331-3161 (800-466-8356)
One well-behaved family pet per room. Guest must notify front desk upon arrival. Guest is liable for any damages. In consideration of all guests, pets must never be left unattended in the guest rooms.

Residence Inn by Marriott
6990 Dodge Street
Omaha, NE
402-553-8898
Dogs of all sizes are allowed. There is a $75 one time fee and a pet policy to sign a check in. Multiple dogs may be allowed.

Super 8 Omaha/AK-SAR-BEN Area
7111 Spring St
Omaha, NE
402-390-0700 (800-800-8000)
Dogs of all sizes are allowed. There is a $10 per night pet fee per pet. Smoking and non-smoking rooms are available for pet rooms. 2 dogs may be allowed.

Holiday Inn Express
1020 East Douglas St
Oneill, NE
402-336-4500 (877-270-6405)
Dogs of all sizes are allowed for an additional pet fee of $10 per night per room. Multiple dogs may be allowed.

Days Inn Paxton
851 Paxton Elsie Rd
Paxton, NE
308-239-4510 (800-329-7466)
Dogs of all sizes are allowed. There is a $10 per night pet fee per pet. Only non-smoking rooms are used for pets. 2 dogs may be allowed.

Point of Rocks Motel
8175 H 30

Potter, NE
308-879-4400
Dogs of all sizes are allowed. There are no additional pet fees. Dogs must be quiet, leashed, and cleaned up after. There is also a campground and RV park on site that allows dogs at no additional fee. Multiple dogs may be allowed.

Comfort Inn
1902 21st Avenue
Scottsbluff, NE
308-632-7510 (877-424-6423)
Dogs are allowed for no additional pet fee. 2 dogs may be allowed.

Days Inn Scottsbluff
1901 21st Ave
Scottsbluff, NE
308-635-3111 (800-329-7466)
Dogs of all sizes are allowed. There is a $5 per night pet fee per pet. 2 dogs may be allowed.

Lamplighter American Inn
606 E 27th St
Scottsbluff, NE
308-632-7108
There is a $6 per day additional pet fee.

Holiday Inn
664 Chase Blvd
Sidney, NE
308-254-2000 (877-270-6405)
Dogs of all sizes are allowed for an additional pet fee of $20 per room. Multiple dogs may be allowed.

Motel 6 - Sidney
3032 Silverberg Drive
Sidney, NE
308-254-5463 (800-466-8356)
One well-behaved family pet per room. Guest must notify front desk upon arrival. Guest is liable for any damages. In consideration of all guests, pets must never be left unattended in the guest rooms.

Sleep Inn and Suites
130 N 30th Road
Syracuse, NE
402-269-2700 (877-424-6423)
Dogs are allowed for an additional one time fee of $10 per pet. Multiple dogs may be allowed.

Super 8 West Point
1211 N Lincoln
West Point, NE
402-372-3998 (800-800-8000)
Dogs of all sizes are allowed. There is a $25 returnable deposit required per room. Smoking and non-smoking rooms are available for pet

rooms. 2 dogs may be allowed.

Wood River Motel
11774 S H 11
Wood River, NE
308-583-2256
Dogs of all sizes are allowed. There is a $5 per night per pet additional fee. Dogs may not be left unattended outside, and they must be leashed and cleaned up after. 2 dogs may be allowed.

Holiday Inn York-I-80
4619 South Lincoln Ave
York, NE
402-362-6661 (877-270-6405)
Dogs of all sizes are allowed for an additional one time pet fee of $25 per room. Multiple dogs may be allowed.

Super 8 York
4112 S Lincoln Ave
York, NE
402-362-3388 (800-800-8000)
Dogs of all sizes are allowed. There is a $10 one time per pet fee per visit. Smoking and non-smoking rooms are available for pet rooms. 2 dogs may be allowed.

Nevada Listings

Comfort Inn
521 E Front Street
Battle Mountain, NV
775-635-5880 (877-424-6423)
Dogs are allowed for an additional one time fee of $10 per pet. Multiple dogs may be allowed.

Super 8 Battle Mountain
825 Super 8 Lane
Battle Mountain, NV
775-635-8808 (800-800-8000)
Dogs of all sizes are allowed. There are only four non-smoking pet rooms available and there is a $10 per night additional pet fee. 2 dogs may be allowed.

Motel 6 - Beatty - Death Valley
550 US Route 95 North
Beatty, NV
775-553-9090 (800-466-8356)
One well-behaved family pet per room. Guest must notify front desk upon arrival. Guest is liable for any damages. In consideration of all guests, pets must never be left unattended in the guest rooms.

Best Western Lighthouse Inn and

Resort
110 Ville Dr
Boulder City, NV
702-293-6444 (800-780-7234)
Dogs are allowed for an additional
fee of $10 per night per pet. Multiple
dogs may be allowed.

Boulder Inn and Suites
704 Nevada Highway
Boulder City, NV
702-294-8888
Dogs of all sizes are allowed. There
is a $10 per night pet fee per pet.
Smoking and non-smoking rooms
are available for pet rooms. 2 dogs
may be allowed.

Comfort Inn Central
1018 Fir Street
Carlin, NV
775-754-6110 (877-424-6423)
Dogs are allowed for an additional
one time fee of $10 per pet. Dogs
may not be left alone in the room.
Multiple dogs may be allowed.

Best Value Motel
2731 S Carson St
Carson City, NV
775-882-2007
There is a $30 refundable pet
deposit.

Days Inn Carson City
3103 N Carson St
Carson City, NV
775-883-3343 (800-329-7466)
Dogs of all sizes are allowed. There
is a $10 per night pet fee per pet. 2
dogs may be allowed.

Holiday Inn Express Hotel & Suites
4055 North Carson Street
Carson City, NV
775-283-4055 (877-270-6405)
Dogs of all sizes are allowed for an
additional pet fee of $20 per room.
Multiple dogs may be allowed.

Motel 6 - Carson City
2749 South Carson Street
Carson City, NV
775-885-7710 (800-466-8356)
One well-behaved family pet per
room. Guest must notify front desk
upon arrival. Guest is liable for any
damages. In consideration of all
guests, pets must never be left
unattended in the guest rooms.

Best Western Gold Country Motor
Inn
2050 Idaho St
Elko, NV
775-738-8421 (800-780-7234)
Dogs are allowed for an additional

one time pet fee of $15 per room. 2
dogs may be allowed.

High Desert Inn
3015 Idaho Street
Elko, NV
775-738-8425
There is a $15 one time pet charge.

Motel 6 - Elko
3021 Idaho Street
Elko, NV
775-738-4337 (800-466-8356)
One well-behaved family pet per
room. Guest must notify front desk
upon arrival. Guest is liable for any
damages. In consideration of all
guests, pets must never be left
unattended in the guest rooms.

Shilo Inn
2401 Mountain City Highway
Elko, NV
775-738-5522 (800-222-2244)
shiloinn.com/Nevada/elko.html
There is a $10 per day pet charge.

Super 8 Elko
1755 Idaho St
Elko, NV
775-738-8488 (800-800-8000)
Dogs of all sizes are allowed. There
is a $10 per night pet fee per pet.
Smoking and non-smoking rooms
are available for pet rooms. 2 dogs
may be allowed.

Best Western Park Vue
930 Aultman
Ely, NV
775-289-4497 (800-780-7234)
Dogs are allowed for an additional
one time fee of $10 per pet. Multiple
dogs may be allowed.

Jailhouse Motel
211 5th Street
Ely, NV
775-289-3033
Dogs of all sizes are allowed. There
is a $10 per stay per room
additional pet fee. Multiple dogs
may be allowed.

Motel 6 - Ely
770 Avenue O
Ely, NV
775-289-6671 (800-466-8356)
One well-behaved family pet per
room. Guest must notify front desk
upon arrival. Guest is liable for any
damages. In consideration of all
guests, pets must never be left
unattended in the guest rooms.

Best Western Eureka Inn
251 N Main Street

Eureka, NV
775-237-5247 (800-780-7234)
Dogs are allowed for an additional
pet fee of $10 per night for 1 dog; the
fee is $25 per night for 2 or more
dogs. Multiple dogs may be allowed.

Comfort Inn
1830 W Williams Avenue
Fallon, NV
775-423-5554 (877-424-6423)
Dogs are allowed for an additional
one time fee of $10 per pet. There
may be 2 medium to large or 3 very
small dogs per room. Multiple dogs
may be allowed.

Motel 6 - Fallon
1705 South Taylor Street
Fallon, NV
775-423-2277 (800-466-8356)
One well-behaved family pet per
room. Guest must notify front desk
upon arrival. Guest is liable for any
damages. In consideration of all
guests, pets must never be left
unattended in the guest rooms.

Super 8 Fallon
855 W Williams Ave
Fallon, NV
775-423-6031 (800-800-8000)
Dogs of all sizes are allowed. There
is a $5 per night pet fee per pet.
Smoking and non-smoking rooms
are available for pet rooms. Multiple
dogs may be allowed.

Best Western Fernley Inn
1405 E Newlands Dr
Fernley, NV
775-575-6776 (800-780-7234)
Dogs are allowed for an additional
pet fee of $10 per night per room.
Multiple dogs may be allowed.

Best Western Topaz Lake Inn
3410 Sandy Bowers Avenue
Gardnerville (lake Topaz), NV
775-266-4661 (800-780-7234)
Dogs up to 50 pounds are allowed
for an additional fee of $12 per night
per pet. 2 dogs may be allowed.

Soldier Meadows Guest Ranch and
Lodge
Soldier Meadows Rd
Gerlach, NV
530-233-4881
soldiermeadows.com/
Dating back to 1865 when it was
known as Camp McGarry, this
historic cattle ranch lies in the Black
Rock Desert about three hours north
of Reno. Soldier Meadows is a family
owned working cattle ranch with over
500,000 acres of public and private

land to enjoy. It is one of the largest and remotest guest ranches in the nation. There are no phones, faxes, or computers here. Horseback riders can work with the cowboys, take trail rides to track wild mustangs and other wildlife, or ride out to the natural hot springs for a soak. Or you may chose to go mule deer hunting, fishing, hiking, mountain biking or 4-wheeling. The lodge offers 10 guest rooms, and one suite with a private bathroom and kitchenette. The main lodge has a common living room with a large fireplace. Pets are not allowed in the kitchen area. There is a $20 one time pet charge.

Loews Lake Las Vegas Resort
101 Montelago Boulevard
Henderson, NV
702-567-6000
This upscale resort on the shores of Lake Mead offers all the luxuries. All well-behaved dogs of any size are welcome. This upscale hotel resort offers their "Loews Loves Pets" program which includes special pet treats, local dog walking routes, and a list of nearby pet-friendly places to visit. The hotel is about 30 minutes from the Las Vegas Strip. There is a $25 one time additional pet fee. To get to the hotel take I-215 east until it ends into Lake Mead Blvd and proceed 7 miles on Lake Mead Blvd. The hotel will be on the left and you can follow the signs.

Best Western Main Street Inn
1000 North Main St
Las Vegas, NV
702-382-3455 (800-780-7234)
Dogs are allowed for an additional fee of $15 per night per pet. Multiple dogs may be allowed.

Best Western Parkview Inn
921 Las Vegas Blvd North
Las Vegas, NV
702-385-1213 (800-780-7234)
Dogs up to 50 pounds are allowed for a $100 refundable deposit plus an additional fee of $8 (plus tax) per night per pet, and a credit card must be on file. Dogs may not be left alone in the room. 2 dogs may be allowed.

Candlewood Suites
4034 South Paradise Road
Las Vegas, NV
702-836-3660 (877-270-6405)
One dog of any size is allowed for an additional pet fee per room of $75 for 1 to 6 nights; the fee is $150 for 7 or more nights.

Homestead Las Vegas

3045 S Maryland Parkway
Las Vegas, NV
702-369-1414
One dog of any size is allowed. There is a $25 per night pet fee up to 3 nights for a maximum total of $75 per room.

La Quinta Inn & Suites Las Vegas Summerlin Tech
7101 Cascade Valley Ct.
Las Vegas, NV
702-360-1200 (800-531-5900)
Dogs of all sizes are allowed. There are no additional pet fees. Dogs may not be left unattended, and they must be leashed and cleaned up after. Dogs are not allowed in the lounge, pool area, or the courtyard. Multiple dogs may be allowed.

La Quinta Inn & Suites Las Vegas West Lakes
9570 West Sahara
Las Vegas, NV
702-243-0356 (800-531-5900)
Dogs of all sizes are allowed. There are no additional pet fees. Dogs may not be left unattended, and they must be leashed and cleaned up after. 2 dogs may be allowed.

La Quinta Inn Las Vegas Nellis
4288 N Nellis Blvd.
Las Vegas, NV
702-632-0229 (800-531-5900)
Dogs of all sizes are allowed. There are no additional pet fees. Dogs must be crated if left alone in the room, and they must be leashed and cleaned up after. Multiple dogs may be allowed.

Motel 6 - Las Vegas - Boulder Highway
4125 Boulder Highway
Las Vegas, NV
702-457-8051 (800-466-8356)
One well-behaved family pet per room. Guest must notify front desk upon arrival. Guest is liable for any damages. In consideration of all guests, pets must never be left unattended in the guest rooms.

Motel 6 - Las Vegas - I-15
5085 South Industrial Road
Las Vegas, NV
702-739-6747 (800-466-8356)
One well-behaved family pet per room. Guest must notify front desk upon arrival. Guest is liable for any damages. In consideration of all guests, pets must never be left unattended in the guest rooms.

Motel 6 - Las Vegas - Tropicana
195 E Tropicana Avenue
Las Vegas, NV
702-798-0728 (800-466-8356)
One well-behaved family pet per room. Guest must notify front desk upon arrival. Guest is liable for any damages. In consideration of all guests, pets must never be left unattended in the guest rooms.

Residence Inn by Marriott
3225 Paradise Road
Las Vegas, NV
702-796-9300
Dogs up to 60 pounds are allowed. There is a $75 one time fee and a pet policy to sign at check in. Multiple dogs may be allowed.

Residence Inn by Marriott
370 Hughes Center Drive
Las Vegas, NV
702-650-0040
Dogs of all sizes are allowed. There is a $75 one time fee and a pet policy to sign at check in. Multiple dogs may be allowed.

Rodeway Inn & Suites
167 E. Tropicana Ave
Las Vegas, NV
702-795-3311
There is a $100 refundable pet deposit.

Pioneer Hotel and Gambling Hall
2200 S. Casino Drive
Laughlin, NV
702-298-2442 (800-634-3469)
This hotel allows dogs of all sizes. However, there are only ten pet rooms and these are all smoking rooms. There is a $100 refundable pet deposit required. We normally do not include smoking room only pet rooms but since the selection of pet friendly lodging in Laughlin is so limited we have listed this one.

Best Western Mesquite Inn
390 N Sandhill Boulevard
Mesquite, NV
702-346-7444 (800-780-7234)
Dogs up to 50 pounds are allowed for an additional fee of $15 per night per pet. 2 dogs may be allowed.

Virgin River Hotel and Casino
100 Pionner Blvd
Mesquite, NV
800-346-7721
Up to three dogs of all sizes are allowed at this hotel. There is a refundable pet deposit of $25 per room. Dogs must be leashed and cleaned up after, and they may not

be left unattended in the rooms unless crated. Multiple dogs may be allowed.

Best Western Minden
1795 Ironwood Dr
Minden, NV
775-782-7766 (800-780-7234)
Dogs are allowed for an additional fee of $12 per night per pet. 2 dogs may be allowed.

Mount Charleston Lodge and Cabins
HCR 38 Box 325
Mount Charleston, NV
800-955-1314
mtcharlestonlodge.com/
The lodge sits at over 7,700 feet above sea level and about 35 miles from the Las Vegas Strip. There are several dog-friendly trails nearby for hikers. Dogs are welcome for an additional $10 per day pet charge.

Comfort Inn North
910 E Cheyenne Road
North Las Vegas, NV
702-399-1500 (877-424-6423)
Dogs are allowed for an additional one time fee of $10 per pet. There may be 1 large or 2 small to medium dogs per room. 2 dogs may be allowed.

Best Western The North Shore Inn at Lake Mead
520 N Moapa Valley Blvd
Overton, NV
702-397-6000 (800-780-7234)
Dogs are allowed for an additional pet fee of $10 per night per room. Multiple dogs may be allowed.

Best Western Pahrump Station
1101 S Highway 160
Pahrump, NV
775-727-5100 (800-780-7234)
Dogs are allowed for an additional fee of $8 per night per pet. Multiple dogs may be allowed.

Atlantis Casino Resort Spa
3800 S Virigina Street
Reno, NV
775-825-4700 (800-723-6500)
Dogs of all sizes are allowed in the Motor Lodge section of this casino hotel. There is a $25 one time fee per pet. Dogs must be kept on leash and cleaned up after. Please place the Do Not Disturb sign on the door if there is a pet alone in the room. Multiple dogs may be allowed.

Best Western Airport Plaza Hotel
1981 Terminal Way
Reno, NV

775-348-6370 (800-780-7234)
Dogs are allowed for a $50 refundable pet deposit per room. 2 dogs may be allowed.

Days Inn Reno
701 E 7th
Reno, NV
775-786-4070 (800-329-7466)
Dogs of all sizes are allowed. There is a $10 per night pet fee per pet. 2 dogs may be allowed.

Holiday Inn Downtown
1000 E. 6th St.
Reno, NV
775-786-5151 (877-270-6405)
basshotels.com/holiday-inn
Dogs of all sizes are allowed for an additional pet fee of $20 (plus tax) per night per room. 2 dogs may be allowed.

La Quinta Inn Reno
4001 Market
Reno, NV
775-348-6100 (800-531-5900)
Dogs of all sizes are allowed. There are no additional pet fees. Dogs must be leashed, cleaned up after, and crated or removed for housekeeping. Multiple dogs may be allowed.

Motel 6 - Reno - Livestock Events Center
866 North Wells Avenue
Reno, NV
775-786-9852 (800-466-8356)
One well-behaved family pet per room. Guest must notify front desk upon arrival. Guest is liable for any damages. In consideration of all guests, pets must never be left unattended in the guest rooms.

Motel 6 - Reno - Virginia Plumb
1901 South Virginia Street
Reno, NV
775-827-0255 (800-466-8356)
One well-behaved family pet per room. Guest must notify front desk upon arrival. Guest is liable for any damages. In consideration of all guests, pets must never be left unattended in the guest rooms.

Motel 6 - Reno West
1400 Stardust Street
Reno, NV
775-747-7390 (800-466-8356)
One well-behaved family pet per room. Guest must notify front desk upon arrival. Guest is liable for any damages. In consideration of all guests, pets must never be left unattended in the guest rooms.

Quality Inn South
1885 S Virginia Street
Reno, NV
775-329-1001 (877-424-6423)
Dogs are allowed for an additional pet fee of $10 per night per room. Dogs must be crated when left alone in the room. 2 dogs may be allowed.

Residence Inn by Marriott
9845 Gateway Drive
Reno, NV
775-853-8800
Dogs up to 75 pounds are allowed, and up to 2 pets may be in the studios; up to 4 in the 1 and 2 bedroom suites. There is a $100 one time fee and a pet policy to sign at check in.

Rodeway Inn
2050 Market Street
Reno, NV
775-786-2500 (800-578-7878)
rodewayinn.com
This hotel (previously Travelodge) is about a mile from the Reno gambling strip. Amenities include a complimentary continental breakfast, heated outdoor pool, kitchenettes in some rooms, and wheelchair accessible rooms. There is a $10 per day pet charge.

Super 8 Reno/Meadowwood Courtyard
5851 S Virginia St
Reno, NV
775-829-4600 (800-800-8000)
Dogs of all sizes are allowed. There is a $10 per night pet fee per pet. Smoking and non-smoking rooms are available for pet rooms. 2 dogs may be allowed.

Truckee River Lodge
501 W. 1st Street
Reno, NV
775-786-8888 (800-635-8950)
truckee-river-lodge.com/
There is a $10 per day pet fee. All rooms in the hotel are non-smoking. There is a park across the street.

Vagabond Inn
3131 S. Virginia St.
Reno, NV
775-825-7134 (800-522-1555)
vagabondinn.com
This motel is located less than a couple miles from the downtown casinos and the Convention Center. Amenities include a swimming pool, 24 hour cable television, air conditioning, and more. There is a $10 per day pet fee.

Motel 6 - Reno Airport - Sparks
2405 Victorian Avenue
Sparks, NV
775-358-1080 (800-466-8356)
One well-behaved family pet per
room. Guest must notify front desk
upon arrival. Guest is liable for any
damages. In consideration of all
guests, pets must never be left
unattended in the guest rooms.

Best Western Hi-Desert Inn
320 Main St
Tonopah, NV
775-482-3511 (800-780-7234)
Dogs are allowed for no additional
pet fee. Multiple dogs may be
allowed.

Motel 6 - Wells
Old Highway 40 & US 93
Wells, NV
775-752-2116 (800-466-8356)
One well-behaved family pet per
room. Guest must notify front desk
upon arrival. Guest is liable for any
damages. In consideration of all
guests, pets must never be left
unattended in the guest rooms.

Super 8 Wells
930 6th Street
Wells, NV
775-752-3384 (800-800-8000)
Dogs of all sizes are allowed. There
is a $5 per night pet fee per pet.
Smoking and non-smoking rooms
are available for pet rooms. 2 dogs
may be allowed.

Super 8 Wendover
1325 Wendover Blvd
Wendover, NV
775-664-2888 (800-800-8000)
Dogs up to 100 pounds are allowed.
There is a $7.50 per night pet fee per
pet. Dogs are not allowed to be left
alone in the room. Smoking and non-
smoking rooms are available for pet
rooms. 2 dogs may be allowed.

Best Western Gold Country Inn
921 W Winnemucca Blvd
Winnemucca, NV
775-623-6999 (800-780-7234)
Dogs are allowed for an additional
one time pet fee of $10 per room.
Multiple dogs may be allowed.

Best Western Holiday Motel
670 W Winnemucca Boulevard
Winnemucca, NV
775-623-3684 (800-780-7234)
Dogs are allowed for no additional
pet fee. Multiple dogs may be
allowed.

Days Inn Winnemucca
511 W Winnemucca Blvd
Winnemucca, NV
775-623-3661 (800-329-7466)
Dogs of all sizes are allowed. There
is a $10 one time per pet over 25
pounds fee per visit. 2 dogs may be
allowed.

Holiday Inn Express
1987 W. Winnemucca Blvd
Winnemucca, NV
775-625-3100 (877-270-6405)
Dogs of all sizes are allowed for an
additional one time fee of $20 per
pet. Multiple dogs may be allowed.

Motel 6 - Winnemucca
1600 West Winnemucca Boulevard
Winnemucca, NV
775-623-1180 (800-466-8356)
One well-behaved family pet per
room. Guest must notify front desk
upon arrival. Guest is liable for any
damages. In consideration of all
guests, pets must never be left
unattended in the guest rooms.

Red Lion
741 W Winnemucca
Winnemucca, NV
775-623-2565
Dogs of all sizes are allowed. There
is no fee with a credit card on file
and there is a pet policy to sign at
check in. Dogs are not allowed to
be left alone in the room. Multiple
dogs may be allowed.

Santa Fe Motel
1620 W. Winnemucca Blvd
Winnemucca, NV
775-623-1119
There are no additional pet fees.

New Hampshire Listings

The Glynn House Inn
59 Highland Street
Ashland, NH
603-968-3775 (866-686-4362)
glynnhouse.com
Pets are allowed in four of the
deluxe suites. These have direct
access from the room to the
gardens. There is a $30 pet fee per
visit per dog. There is a $250 fully
refundable damage deposit and
pets may not be left alone in the
room.

Quality Inn Manchester Airport
121 S River Road/H3
Bedford, NH
603-622-3766 (877-424-6423)
Quiet dogs are allowed for an
additional pet fee of $25 per room for
each 1 to 7 days. 2 dogs may be
allowed.

Highland Inn
634 Francestown Rd
Bennington, NH
603-588-2777
There is a $10 one time pet fee.

Mountain Lake Inn
2871 Route 114
Bradford, NH
603-938-2136 (800-662-6005)
mountainlakeinn.com/
This 1760 dwelling sits on 168 acres
along the shores of Lake
Massasecum and offers 9 guest
rooms with private baths, walking
trails, and a private beach equipped
with a canoe and rowboat. Dogs of
all sizes are welcome for an
additional $25 one time pet fee per
room. Dogs must be well behaved,
leashed (at times), and cleaned up
after. Dogs must be friendly and very
well mannered with children and the
other pets in residence. 2 dogs may
be allowed.

Bretton Arms Country Inn
Route 302
Bretton Woods, NH
603-278-3000 (800-258-0330)
This inn is located less than a five
minute walk from the Mount
Washington Hotel. Well-behaved
dogs of any size are allowed for an
extra $30 per dog per day pet fee, up
to two dogs per room. During the
winter the Nordic center at the Mount
Washington Hotel allows dogs on a
special 8km cross-country ski trail.
Dogs need to be leashed on the
property and on the trail.

Lazy Dog Inn
201 White Mountain H/H 16
Chocorua Village, NH
603-323-8350 (888-323-8350)
lazydoginn.com/
This 160 year old New England
farmhouse really is a dog friendly
place (even the rooms have doggie
themed names), and there are plenty
of picturesque walking trails close by
too. Included in the rates is a fenced
in "Doggie Play Area" with agility
equipment and a climate controlled
Doggie Lodge providing doggie
daycare. They also offer a
bottomless treat jar for their canine
guests and a like jar of cookies for

their owners. Dogs must be at least 12 weeks old, and there are no additional pet fees for one dog. There may be an additional fee of $25 per night per pet for 2 pets or more depending on length of stay. Dogs must be friendly and well mannered with humans and the other pets in residence. Dogs must be leashed and cleaned up after. Multiple dogs may be allowed.

Claremont Motor Lodge
Beauregard St, near SR 103
Claremont, NH
603-542-2540
There are no additional pet fees.

Northern Comfort Motel
RR 1, Box 520
Colebrook, NH
603-237-4440
There is a $5.00 per day pet charge.

Comfort Inn
71 Hall Street
Concord, NH
603-226-4100 (877-424-6423)
Dogs are allowed for an additional one time fee of $15 per pet. Dogs may not be left alone in the room. 2 dogs may be allowed.

Foothills Farm
P. O. Box 1368
Conway, NH
207-935-3799
foothillsfarmbedandbreakfast.com
This restored 1820 farmhouse and guest cottage sits on 50 acres of fields, forests, and streams, has close proximity to several other recreational activities and tax free shopping, and much of the food served here comes straight from their on-site organic garden. Dogs of all sizes are allowed for an additional $15 per night per pet. Dogs are usually preferred in the 2-bedroom cottage, but sometimes there may be availability in the main house. Dogs must be leashed and cleaned up after, and crated when left alone in the room. 2 dogs may be allowed.

Tanglewood Motel and Cottages
1681 H 16
Conway, NH
603-447-5932 (866-TANGLEWOOD (826-4539))
tanglewoodmotel.com/
This family recreational destination sits alongside a beautiful mountain stream and offers guests a variety of activity areas, 2 central picnic spots with barbecues, and plenty of hiking trails are close by. Dogs are welcome in the cottages for an

additional fee of $10 per night per pet. Dogs must be friendly, well mannered, and leashed and cleaned up after at all times. 2 dogs may be allowed.

Days Inn Dwtn Dover
481 Central Ave
Dover, NH
603-742-0400 (800-329-7466)
Dogs of all sizes are allowed. There is a $50 returnable deposit required per room. 2 dogs may be allowed.

Hickory Pond Inn & Golf Course
1 Stagecoach Rd
Durham, NH
603-659-2227
There are several designated pet rooms. All rooms are non-smoking. There is a $10 one time pet fee.

The Inn at Crotched Mountain
534 Mountain Road
Francestown, NH
603-588-6840
This 180 year-old colonial house on 65 acres, once a stop for the Underground Railroad, has an amazing view of the Piscataugoug Valley, several hiking or winter skiing trails, food and flower gardens, an 18 hole golf course, an outdoor pool, and more. Dogs of all sizes are welcome for an additional $5 per night per pet. Dogs must be leashed, cleaned up after, and crated when left alone in the room. This inn closes for the first 3 weeks each April. Multiple dogs may be allowed.

Best Western White Mountain Resort
87 Wallace Hill Road
Franconia, NH
603-823-7422 (800-780-7234)
Dogs are allowed for an additional fee of $15 per night per pet. 2 dogs may be allowed.

Franconia Notch Vacations
Call or email to Arrange.
Franconia, NH
800-247-5536
franconiares.com/
Vacation rentals in Franconia and the surrounding White Mountains. Some dog-friendly rentals are available.

Horse & Hound
205 Wells Rd
Franconia, NH
603-823-5501 (800-450-5501)
There are no designated smoking or non-smoking rooms. There is an

$8.50 per day additional pet fee.

Lovetts Inn by Lafayette Brook
SR 18
Franconia, NH
603-823-7761
There are two pet rooms, both non-smoking. There is a $10 one time additional pet fee.

Westwind Vacation Cottages
1614 Profile Road
Franconia, NH
603-823-5532
Dogs of all sizes are allowed. There is a pet policy to sign at check in and there are no additional pet fees. Multiple dogs may be allowed.

Temperance Tavern
Old Providence Rd
Gilmanton, NH
603-267-7349
Owners have a dog and welcome well-trained potty trained dogs only. There is a $5 per day additional pet fee.

Town & Country Motor Inn
US 2
Gorham, NH
603-466-3315
townandcountryinn.com/map.html

Chieftain Motor Inn
84 Lyme Road
Hanover, NH
603-643-2550
chieftaininn.com/
Nestled along the banks of the Connecticut River, this scenic inn also offers an outdoor heated pool, complimentary canoes, barbecue areas, a gazebo, and a variety of land and water recreation. Dogs of all sizes are allowed for an additional fee of $35 per night per pet. Dogs must be quiet, well behaved, leashed, and cleaned up after. Dogs may only be left alone in the room if the owner is confident in their behavior. 2 dogs may be allowed.

Yankee Trail Motel
US 3
Holderness, NH
603-968-3535 (800-972-1492)
There are no additional pet fees.

Swiss Chalets Village Inn
Old Route 16A
Intervale, NH
603-356-2232 (800-831-2727)
swisschaletsvillage.com
Swiss Chalets Village Inn offers comfortable lodgings, some with fireplace Jacuzzi suites, plenty of

indoor and outdoor activities, and a bit of Swiss charm right in the midst of New Hampshire's White Mountains. Pets are welcome.

Dana Place Inn
SR 16
Jackson, NH
603-383-6822 (800-537-9276)
danaplace.com/
There are no additional pet fees.

The Village House
PO Box 359 Rt 16A
Jackson, NH
603-383-6666 (800-972-8343)
yellowsnowdoggear.com/
This bed and breakfast's rooms are located in a 100 year old barn behind the main house that houses the Yellow Snow Dog Gear collar and lead business. Rooms have kitchenettes, balconies, Jacuzzi tubs, and are decorated in the style of a B&B. There are 15 guest rooms and 13 have private baths. They welcome all well-behaved dogs and there are no size restrictions. Rates range from $65-140 depending on the season. There is a $10 per day pet fee.

Applebrook
110 Meadows Road/H 115A
Jefferson, NH
603-586-7713 (800-545-6504)
applebrook.com/
This large Victorian farmhouse is only about a minutes drive away from Santa's Village, which is also open year round. Dogs of all sizes are allowed for a one time additional pet fee of $25 per pet of which 50% is donated to the local humane society. Dogs may only be left alone in the room for short periods and they must be crated. Dogs must be under owner's control/care at all times, and please clean up after your pet. 2 dogs may be allowed.

Best Western Sovereign Hotel
401 Winchester ST
Keene, NH
603-357-3038 (800-780-7234)
Dogs are allowed for an additional one time pet fee of $25 per room. 2 dogs may be allowed.

Holiday Inn Express Keene
175 Key Rd.
Keene, NH
603-352-7616 (877-270-6405)
keenehi.com
Dogs are allowed in this family style pet-friendly hotel in historic Keene.

Super 8 Keene
3 Ashbrook Rd
Keene, NH
603-352-9780 (800-800-8000)
Dogs of all sizes are allowed. There is a $20 one time pet fee per visit. Smoking and non-smoking rooms are available for pet rooms. 2 dogs may be allowed.

The Lake Opechee Inn and Spa
62 Doris Ray Court
Laconia, NH
603-524-0111 (877-300-5253)
opecheeinn.com/
This peaceful retreat, on the shores of Lake Opechee, is an historic renovated mill building offering 34 luxury rooms, a steak and seafood restaurant, a conference center, and a full service spa. Dogs of all sizes are allowed for an additional fee of $20 per night per pet. Dogs must be quiet, leashed and cleaned up after, and crated when left alone in the room. 2 dogs may be allowed.

Residence Inn by Marriott
32 Centerra Parkway
Lebanon, NH
603-643-4511
Dogs of all sizes are allowed. There is a $75 one time fee and a pet policy to sign at check in. Multiple dogs may be allowed.

Comfort Inn and Suites
21 Railroad Street
Lincoln, NH
603-745-6700 (877-424-6423)
Dogs are allowed for an additional fee of $15 per night per pet. 2 dogs may be allowed.

The Beal House Inn
2 W Main Street
Littleton, NH
603-444-2661 (888-616-BEAL (2325))
bealhouseinn.com/
Offering fine dining, lodging, and a full bar specializing in martinis (over 250), this inn holds special events throughout the year, and they are central to numerous year round activities and recreation. Dogs of all sizes are welcome for an additional $25 to $35 per night per pet depending on the room/suite, and there may be a $150 refundable deposit. One of the suites has a fenced private yard. Dogs must be leashed, cleaned up after, and they must be crated when left alone in the room. 2 dogs may be allowed.

Red Roof Inn - Loudon

519 SR 106 South
Loudon, NH
603-225-8399 (800-RED-ROOF)
One well-behaved family pet per room. Guest must notify front desk upon arrival. Guest is liable for any damages. In consideration of all guests, pets must never be left unattended in the guest rooms.

Dowds County Inn
On the Common, Box 58
Lyme, NH
603-795-4712 (800-482-4712)
dowdscountryinn.com/
This country inn sits on 6 landscaped acres to explore with a natural duck pond, flower gardens, a water fountain, and historic stonework and buildings. Dogs of all sizes are welcome for an additional $10 per night per pet with a credit card on file. Dogs must be well behaved, leashed, and cleaned up after. 2 dogs may be allowed.

Loch Lyme Lodge
70 Orford Road
Lyme, NH
603-795-2141
Dog of all sizes are allowed. There are no additional pet fees, however you must have up to date vaccination information on your dog(s). 2 dogs may be allowed.

Comfort Inn
298 Queen City Avenue
Manchester, NH
603-668-2600 (877-424-6423)
Dogs are allowed for an additional fee of $25 per night per pet. Multiple dogs may be allowed.

Econo Lodge
75 W Hancock St
Manchester, NH
603-624-0111
There is a $100 refundable deposit and a $10 per day pet fee.

Holiday Inn Express Hotel and Suites
1298 South Porter St
Manchester, NH
603-669-6800 (877-270-6405)
Dogs of all sizes are allowed for a $50 refundable pet deposit per room. Multiple dogs may be allowed.

Ramada Hotel Manchester
700 Elm Street
Manchester, NH
603-625-1000
Dogs of all sizes are allowed. There is a $25 one time additional pet fee. Dogs may not be left alone in the rooms unless they are crated.

TownePlace Suites Manchester Airport
686 Huse Road
Manchester, NH
603-641-2288
Dogs of all sizes are allowed. There is a $75 one time pet fee per visit. . 2 dogs may be allowed.

Days Inn Merrimack
242 Daniel Webster Hwy
Merrimack, NH
603-429-4600 (800-329-7466)
Dogs of all sizes are allowed. There is a $10 per night pet fee per small pet and $25 per large pet. 2 dogs may be allowed.

Residence Inn by Marriott
246 Daniel Webster Highway
Merrimack, NH
603-424-8100
Dogs of all sizes are allowed. There is a $75 one time fee and a pet policy to sign at check in. 2 dogs may be allowed.

Best Western Sunapee Lake Lodge
1403 Route 103
Mount Sunapee, NH
603-763-2010 (800-780-7234)
Dogs are allowed for an additional pet fee of $10 per night per room. 2 dogs may be allowed.

Holiday Inn
9 Northeastern Blvd
Nashua, NH
603-888-1551 (877-270-6405)
Dogs of all sizes are allowed for an additional one time pet fee of $25 per room. 2 dogs may be allowed.

Motel 6 - Nashua
2 Progress Avenue
Nashua, NH
603-889-4151 (800-466-8356)
One well-behaved family pet per room. Guest must notify front desk upon arrival. Guest is liable for any damages. In consideration of all guests, pets must never be left unattended in the guest rooms.

Red Roof Inn - Nashua
77 Spitbrook Road
Nashua, NH
603-888-1893 (800-RED-ROOF)
One well-behaved family pet per room. Guest must notify front desk upon arrival. Guest is liable for any damages. In consideration of all guests, pets must never be left unattended in the guest rooms.

Sunapee Harbor Cottages (Lake

Station Realty
1066 H 103
Newbury, NH
603-763-3033 (800-639-9960)
cottagesrus.com/
This multi-listing company has about a dozen of their vacation rentals in the Lake Sunapee area that allow pets and the prices and policies vary per rental. Dogs must be under owner's control/care at all times, and they may not be left unattended in the rentals.

Adventure Suites
3440 White Mountain H/H16
North Conway, NH
603-356-9744 (800-N.CONWAY (606-6929))
adventuresuites.com/
This inn with various themed rooms offers 16 suites with a variety of adventures from a tree house setting to a unique 2 story cave dwelling, from the penthouse to the jungle, and more, and each suite has a Jacuzzi. Dogs of all sizes are welcome for an additional $10 per night per pet, and when you reserve ahead of time there is a special treat waiting in the room for them. Dogs must be at least 1 year old, quiet, and very well behaved as there are other animals on site. Dogs must be leashed and cleaned up after at all times, and dog depots are provided. Dogs may not be left alone in the room at any time. 2 dogs may be allowed.

Best Western Red Jacket Mountain View Resort & Conf. Ctr.
Route 16
North Conway, NH
603-356-5411 (800-780-7234)
Dogs are allowed for an additional fee of $25 per night per pet. 2 dogs may be allowed.

Spruce Moose Lodge and Cottages
207 Seavey Street
North Conway, NH
603-356-6239 (800-600-6239)
sprucemooselodge.com/
This inn, located in the scenic Mount Washington Valley, offers both lodge and cottage accommodations and they are only a short 5 minute walk to the village. Dogs of all sizes are welcome in the cottages and in one of the lodge rooms (breakfast is not included for cottage stays) for an additional pet fee of $10 per night per pet and there may be a $100 cash refundable security deposit required. Dogs must be quiet, well behaved, leashed, and cleaned up

after. Dogs may not be left alone in the lodge guest room at any time, but they may be left for a short time in the cottages if the owner is confident in the pet's behavior. 2 dogs may be allowed.

The Glen
77 The Glen Rd
Pittsburg, NH
603-538-6500
Pets are allowed in the cottages only. There are no pet fees. There are no designated smoking or non-smoking cottages.

The Common Man Inn
231 Main Street
Plymouth, NH
603-536-2200 (866-THE.C.MAN (843-2626))
thecmaninn.com/
This inn is also home to the Foster's Boiler Room Lounge offering a pub-style menu and unique creations, a full service spa with many amenities including a heated waterfall Jacuzzi, and a great location to several other attractions in the area. Dogs of all sizes are welcome for no additional pet fee. Your pooch is greeted with a personalized treat with food bowls, and pet friendly rooms also provide cushy pet beds. Dogs must be leashed, cleaned up after, and crated if left alone in the room. They also provide a designated pet walking area, and a separate pet entrance. 2 dogs may be allowed.

Meadowbrook Inn
Portsmouth Traffic Circle
Portsmouth, NH
603-436-2700 (800-370-2727)
meadowbrookinn.com/
This inn offers a convenient location for exploring the seacoast and taking advantage of the tax-free shopping. Dogs of all sizes are allowed for an additional $10 per night per pet. Dogs must be leashed, cleaned up after, and they may only be left alone in the room if they will be quiet and well behaved. Dobermans and Rottweilers are not allowed. 2 dogs may be allowed.

Motel 6 - Portsmouth
3 Gosling Road
Portsmouth, NH
603-334-6606 (800-466-8356)
One well-behaved family pet per room. Guest must notify front desk upon arrival. Guest is liable for any damages. In consideration of all guests, pets must never be left unattended in the guest rooms.

Sheraton Portsmouth Harborside
Hotel
250 Market St.
Portsmouth, NH
603-431-2300 (888-625-5144)
Dogs up to 80 pounds are allowed.
There are no additional pet fees.
Dogs are not allowed to be left alone
in the room.

Anchorage Inn
80 Main St
Rochester, NH
603-332-3350
There is a $10 per day additional pet
fee.

Holiday Inn
1 Keewaydin Drive
Salem, NH
603-893-5511 (877-270-6405)
Dogs of all sizes are allowed for an
additional fee per room of $25 (plus
tax) for 1 to 3 nights; 4 to 14 nights is
$50 (plus tax). 2 dogs may be
allowed.

Red Roof Inn - Salem, NH
15 Red Roof Lane
Salem, NH
603-898-6422 (800-RED-ROOF)
One well-behaved family pet per
room. Guest must notify front desk
upon arrival. Guest is liable for any
damages. In consideration of all
guests, pets must never be left
unattended in the guest rooms.

The Hilltop Inn
9 Norton Lane
Sugar Hill, NH
603-823-5695 (800-770-5695)
hilltopinn.com/
This 1895 traditional country inn sits
on 50 acres in the White Mountains
with an impressive array of relaxing
and recreational pursuits. There are
20 acres of un-groomed cross-
country skiing here and your pooch
is welcome to join you on them. They
also have a large fenced in yard for
pets to run free. Dogs of all sizes are
welcome for an additional pet fee of
$10 per night per room. They ask
that you clean up after your pet if
they do their business on the lawns,
but it's not necessary in the fields.
Dogs must be well behaved and
friendly towards the other pets in
residence. Dogs only need to be on
lead around the house or when felt
necessary by the owner, and they
may only be left alone in the room if
they will be quiet and the front desk
is informed. 2 dogs may be allowed.

Tamworth Inn
Tamworth Village

Tamworth, NH
603-323-7721 (800-642-7352)
tamworth.com/
Offering 16 rooms and suites all
with a private bath, this simple but
elegant lodge offers a full country
breakfast, an authentic New
England Pub, and they are central
to various other activities and
recreation. Dogs of all sizes are
allowed for an additional $15 per
night per pet on a space available
basis. Dogs must be quiet and well
mannered, and they are welcome
throughout the inn and grounds, just
not in the dining room or breakfast
areas. Dogs must be leashed and
cleaned up after, and they may only
be left alone in the room if they are
crated and the owners are on the
property. 2 dogs may be allowed.

The Inn at East Hill Farm
460 Monadnock Street
Troy, NH
603-588-6495 (800-242-6495)
east-hill-farm.com/
Whether it is a winter family farm
day, a special Caribbean
night/dinner, or a special getaway,
this inn offers year round events for
just about any and every occasion,
and there also have indoor/outdoor
pools, a winter indoor skating rink,
paddle or row boating, and cross-
country ski trails. Dogs of all sizes
are allowed for an additional $10
per night per pet. Dogs must be
quiet and well behaved, and they
are not allowed in the dining or
public rooms. Dogs must be
leashed and cleaned up after at all
times. 2 dogs may be allowed.

Johnson Motel and Cottages
364 H 3
Twin Mountain, NH
888-244-5561 (888-244-5561)
johnsonsmotel.com/
Located in the White Mountains
where there is year round activities,
this motel also include a picnic,
playground, and campfire area, in
addition to a nature trail leading to a
pond frequented by numerous birds
and wildlife. They also have direct
trail access for skiers and
snowmobilers. Dogs of all sizes are
allowed for an additional fee of $10
per night per pet, and special treats
are provided for their four-legged
guests. Aggressive dogs are not
allowed, and barkers must stay with
their owners at all times. They must
be friendly to humans and to the
other 2 dogs on site. Dogs must be
well behaved, leashed, and cleaned
up after. Dogs may only be left

alone in the room if the owner is
confident in the pet's behavior. 2
dogs may be allowed.

Victorian Cottage
#30 Veterans Ave
Weirs Beach, NH
603-279-4583
mailto:captstus@verizon.net
Remodeled antique home located at
Weirs Beach, NH. Spectacular view
of Lake Winnipesaukee and
surrounding mountains from the
house and porch. 3 bedrooms/sleeps
6. Pets are welcome to join you.

Chesterfield Inn
HCR 10 Box 59
West Chesterfield, NH
603-256-3211
chesterfieldinn.com/
There are no additional pet fees.

Airport Economy Inn
45 Airport Rd
West Lebanon, NH
603-298-8888
There is a $10 per day pet fee.

Fireside Inn and Suites
25 Airport Road
West Lebanon, NH
877-258-5900 (877-258-5900)
afiresideinn.com/
This inn, nestled in the beauty of the
River Valley amid numerous
educational, cultural, and
recreational opportunities, features a
garden court atrium, an indoor
heated pool and hot tub, and a full
breakfast buffet. Dogs must be well
behaved, leashed, and cleaned up
after. Dogs may not be left alone in
the room, and they must be under
owner's control/care at all times. 2
dogs may be allowed.

All Seasons Motel
36 Smith St
Woodsville, NH
603-747-2157 (800-660-0644)
quikpage.com/A/allseamotel/
There is a $6 per day pet fee. Dogs
must not be left alone in the rooms.

New Jersey Listings

Sheraton Atlantic City Convention
Center Hotel
Two Miss America Parkway
Atlantic City, NJ
609-344-3535 (888-625-5144)
Dogs up to 80 pounds are allowed.
There are no additional pet fees.

Dogs are not allowed to be left alone in the room.

Avon Manor Inn
109 Sylvania Avenue
Avon-by-the-Sea, NJ
732-776-7770
avonmanor.com
Complete remodeled and updated, this inn features indoor or outdoor dining, many extras around the property, is only 2 miles from Spring Lake, and sits only 1 block from the beach and boardwalk. Dogs of all sizes are allowed in the cottages for no additional fee. Dogs must be quiet, well behaved, leashed, cleaned up after, and may be left alone in the room only if the owner is confident in the dogs behavior. 2 dogs may be allowed.

Inn at Somerset Hills
80 Allen Road
Basking Ridge, NJ
908-580-1300 (800-688-0700)
shh.com
Located only 30 minutes from an international airport with plenty of recreational opportunities available, this inn is convenient for the business or leisure traveler. Dogs of all sizes are allowed for an additional pet fee of $25 per night per room. Dogs must be leashed, cleaned up after, and crated when left alone in the room. Multiple dogs may be allowed.

Engleside Inn
30 Engleside Avenue
Beach Haven, NJ
609-492-1251 (800-762-2214)
This is a nice place to go with your pet in the off season. They are right on the beach, have 3 in-house restaurants, and are only minutes from many attractions, activities, and recreation. Dogs of all sizes are allowed from September 10th to May 4th only (their off-season) for an additional fee of $10 per night per pet. Dogs must be leashed, cleaned up after, and they may only be left alone in the room for short periods if they will be quiet, comfortable, and well behaved. Multiple dogs may be allowed.

The Sea Shell Motel, Restaurant & Beach Club
10 S. Atlantic Ave.
Beach Haven, NJ
609-492-4611
seashellclub.com/
This premier ocean front retreat offers 2 eateries, a pool, and live entertainment as they are home to 2 party hotspots; the Beach Club and Tiki Bar. This resort opens about the 1st of April and dogs are allowed up until June 21st, and then they are not allowed again until after Labor Day. Dogs of all sizes are allowed for an additional fee of $10 per night per pet. Dogs must be leashed and cleaned up after. Multiple dogs may be allowed.

Howard Johnson Express Inn
832 North Black Horse Pike
Blackwood, NJ
856-228-4040 (800-446-4656)
Dogs of all sizes are welcome. There is a $10 per day pet fee.

Somerset Hills Hotel
200 Liberty Corner Road
Bridgewater, NJ
908-647-6700 (800-688-0700)
shh.com
This premier boutique hotel is reminiscent of the hotels of Europe, and they feature indoor and outdoor dining areas, room service, an outdoor pool, live entertainment on the weekends, and much more. Dogs of all sizes are allowed for an additional fee of $25 per night per pet. Dogs may not be left unattended in the room at any time, and they must be leashed and cleaned up after. 2 dogs may be allowed.

Billmae Cottage
1015 Washington Street
Cape May, NJ
609-898-8558
billmae.com
Billmae Cottage offers 1 and 2 bedroom suites each with a living room, bath, and kitchen. They have occasional "Yappie Hours" on the porch. Well behaved dogs of all sizes are welcome.

Holiday Inn Express Hotel and Suites
506 Pennsville-Auburn Rd
Carneys Point, NJ
856-351-9222 (877-270-6405)
Dogs of all sizes are allowed for no additional fee with a credit card on file. Multiple dogs may be allowed.

Clarion Hotel and Conference Center
H 70 and I 295
Cherry Hill, NJ
856-428-2300 (877-424-6423)
Dogs up to 50 pounds are allowed for an additional one time fee of $50 per pet. 2 dogs may be allowed.

Holiday Inn
Route 70 and Sayer Avenue
Cherry Hill, NJ
856-663-5300 (877-270-6405)
Dogs of all sizes are allowed for an additional $75 refundable pet deposit per room. 2 dogs may be allowed.

Residence Inn by Marriott
1821 Old Cuthbert Road
Cherry Hill, NJ
856-429-6111
Dogs of all sizes are allowed. There is a $75 one time fee and a pet policy to sign at check in. Multiple dogs may be allowed.

Wellesley Inn Clifton
265 Route 3 East
Clifton, NJ
973-778-6500 (800-531-5900)
Dogs of all sizes are allowed. There is a $10 per night per pet additional fee. Dogs may not be left unattended, and they must be leashed and cleaned up after. Multiple dogs may be allowed.

Staybridge Suites
1272 South River Road
Cranbury, NJ
609-409-7181 (877-270-6405)
Dogs of all sizes are allowed for an additional one time fee of $75 per pet. Multiple dogs may be allowed.

Residence Inn by Marriott
1154 Hurffville Road
Deptford, NJ
856-686-9188
Dogs of all sizes are allowed. There is a $75 one time fee and a pet policy to sign at check in. Multiple dogs may be allowed.

Motel 6 - East Brunswick
244 Route 18
East Brunswick, NJ
732-390-4545 (800-466-8356)
One well-behaved family pet per room. Guest must notify front desk upon arrival. Guest is liable for any damages. In consideration of all guests, pets must never be left unattended in the guest rooms.

Studio 6 - East Brunswick
246 Rt 18
East Brunswick, NJ
732-238-3330 (800-466-8356)
One well-behaved family pet per room. Guest must notify front desk upon arrival. Guest is liable for any damages. In consideration of all guests, pets must never be left unattended in the guest rooms.

Ramada Inn
130 H 10 W
East Hanover, NJ
973-386-5622
Dogs of all sizes are allowed. There is a pet policy to sign at check in and there are no additional pet fees. Multiple dogs may be allowed.

Sheraton Meadowlands Hotel & Conference Center
2 Meadowlands Plaza
East Rutherford, NJ
201-896-0500 (888-625-5144)
Dogs up to 50 pounds are allowed. There is a $50 one time additional pet fee. Dogs are not allowed to be left alone in the room.

Staybridge Suites Eatontown-Tinton Falls
4 Industrial Way East
Eatontown, NJ
732-380-9300 (877-270-6405)
Dogs of all sizes are allowed for an additional pet fee per room of $100 for 1 to 14 nights; the fee is $150 for 15 to 29 nights. 2 dogs may be allowed.

Red Roof Inn - Edison
860 New Durham Road
Edison, NJ
732-248-9300 (800-RED-ROOF)
One well-behaved family pet per room. Guest must notify front desk upon arrival. Guest is liable for any damages. In consideration of all guests, pets must never be left unattended in the guest rooms.

Sheraton Edison Hotel Raritan Center
125 Raritan Center Parkway
Edison, NJ
732-225-8300 (888-625-5144)
Dogs up to 50 pounds are allowed. There are no additional pet fees but there is a $50 refundable deposit. Dogs are not allowed to be left alone in the room.

Hilton
1170 Spring Street
Elizabeth, NJ
908-351-3900
Dogs are allowed for no additional pet fee. Multiple dogs may be allowed.

Residence Inn by Marriott
83 Glimcher Realty Way
Elizabeth, NJ
908-352-4300
Dogs of all sizes are allowed. There is a $75 one time fee and a pet policy to sign at check in. Multiple

dogs may be allowed.

Radisson Hotel Englewood
401 South Van Brunt Street
Englewood, NJ
201-871-2020
Dogs of all sizes are allowed. There is a $50 one time additional pet fee. Dogs may not be left alone in the rooms unless they are in a crate.

The Widow McCrea House
53 Kingwood Avenue
Frenchtown, NJ
908-996-4999
widowmccrea.com/
This attractive 1878 Italian Victorian Inn is only a 2 minute walk from all the town has to offer and the Delaware River, and they offer a cottage with an oversized Jacuzzi and a fireplace for guests with pets. Dogs of all sizes are allowed for an additional fee of $35 per night per pet with a credit card on file, and there is a pet agreement to sign at check in. Dogs must be well behaved, leashed, cleaned up after, and crated when left alone in the room. 2 dogs may be allowed.

Holiday Inn Hazlet
2870 Highway 35
Hazlet, NJ
732-888-2000 (877-270-6405)
Dogs of all sizes are allowed for an additional one time pet fee of $25 per room. 2 dogs may be allowed.

The Inn at Millrace Pond
313 Johnsonburg Road/H 519N
Hope, NJ
908-459-4884 (800-746-6467)
innatmillracepond.com/
Historic buildings, individually decorated rooms in period reproductions, and an active restaurant and tavern highlight this retreat. They offer a couple of pet-friendly rooms, and dogs of all sizes are allowed for no additional pet fee. Dogs must be leashed, cleaned up after, and they are not allowed on the beds. They request dogs be crated when left alone in the room unless the owner is confident the pet will be quiet and well mannered. 2 dogs may be allowed.

Sheraton Woodbridge Place Hotel
515 US Highway 1S
Iselin, NJ
732-634-3600 (888-625-5144)
Dogs up to 50 pounds are allowed. There are no additional pet fees. Dogs are not allowed to be left alone in the room.

Candlewood Suites Jersey City
21 Second Street
Jersey City, NJ
201-659-2500 (877-270-6405)
One dog of any size is allowed for an additional pet fee of $75 for 1 to 6 nights, and $150 for 7 nights or more.

Howard Johnson Inn
2995 Rt. 1 South
Lawrenceville, NJ
609-896-1100 (800-446-4656)
Dogs of all sizes are welcome. There is a $10 per day pet fee.

Red Roof Inn - Princeton
3203 Brunswick Pike
Lawrenceville, NJ
609-896-3388 (800-RED-ROOF)
One well-behaved family pet per room. Guest must notify front desk upon arrival. Guest is liable for any damages. In consideration of all guests, pets must never be left unattended in the guest rooms.

Days Inn Lake Hopatcong
1691 Route 46
Ledgewood, NJ
973-347-5100 (800-329-7466)
Dogs of all sizes are allowed. There are no additional pet fees. 2 dogs may be allowed.

Ocean Place Resort and Spa
One Ocean Blvd
Long Branch, NJ
732-571-4000 (800-411-6493)
oceanplaceresort.com/
This premier ocean front resort sits amid lush greenery and white sandy beaches, and serves as a great home base for a wide variety of activities and recreation. Dogs of all sizes are allowed for an additional one time fee of $150 per pet. Dogs must be well mannered, leashed, and cleaned up after. 2 dogs may be allowed.

Sheraton Mahwah Hotel
1 International Blvd., Route 17 North
Mahwah, NJ
201-529-1660 (888-625-5144)
Dogs of all sizes are allowed. There are no additional pet fees. Dogs are not allowed to be left alone in the room.

Motel 6 - Philadelphia - Mt Laurel
2798 Route 73 North
Maple Shade, NJ
856-235-3550 (800-466-8356)
One well-behaved family pet per room. Guest must notify front desk

upon arrival. Guest is liable for any damages. In consideration of all guests, pets must never be left unattended in the guest rooms.

Comfort Inn Middletown
750 Route 35 S
Middletown, NJ
732-671-3400 (877-424-6423)
Dogs are allowed for an additional pet fee of $25 per night per room. Multiple dogs may be allowed.

Best Western Millville
1701 N 2nd Street
Millville, NJ
856-327-3300 (800-780-7234)
Dogs are allowed for an additional fee of $10 per night per pet. 2 dogs may be allowed.

Red Roof Inn - Princeton North
208 New Road
Monmouth Jct, NJ
732-821-8800 (800-RED-ROOF)
One well-behaved family pet per room. Guest must notify front desk upon arrival. Guest is liable for any damages. In consideration of all guests, pets must never be left unattended in the guest rooms.

Candlewood Suites
100 Candlewood Drive
Morris Plains, NJ
973-984-9960 (877-270-6405)
One dog up to 75 pounds is allowed for an additional pet fee of $75 for 1 to 6 nights, and $150 for 7 nights or more.

Best Western Burlington Inn
2020 Rt 541, RD 1
Mount Holly, NJ
609-261-3800 (800-780-7234)
Dogs are allowed for an additional fee of $5 per night per pet. Multiple dogs may be allowed.

Candlewood Suites
4000 Crawford Place
Mount Laurel, NJ
856-642-7567 (877-270-6405)
Dogs up to 80 pounds are allowed for an additional one time fee of $75 per pet. 2 dogs may be allowed.

Radisson Hotel Mount Laurel
915 Route 73
Mount Laurel, NJ
856-234-7300
Dogs of all sizes are allowed. There is a $50 one time additional pet fee.

Red Roof Inn - Mt. Laurel
603 Fellowship Road
Mount Laurel, NJ

856-234-5589 (800-RED-ROOF)
One well-behaved family pet per room. Guest must notify front desk upon arrival. Guest is liable for any damages. In consideration of all guests, pets must never be left unattended in the guest rooms.

Staybridge Suites Philadelphia-Mt. Laurel
4115 Church Road
Mount Laurel, NJ
856-722-1900 (877-270-6405)
Dogs up to 60 pounds are allowed for an additional one time fee of $75 per pet. Dogs may not be left alone in the room. 2 dogs may be allowed.

TownePlace Suites Mt Laurel
450 Century Parkway
Mount Laurel, NJ
856-778-8221
Dogs of all sizes are allowed. There is a $75 one time pet fee per visit. 2 dogs may be allowed.

Days Inn Neptune
3310 Hwy 33 East
Neptune, NJ
732-643-8888 (800-329-7466)
Dogs of all sizes are allowed. There is a $10 per night pet fee per pet. 2 dogs may be allowed.

Sheraton Newark Airport Hotel
128 Frontage Road
Newark, NJ
973-690-5500 (888-625-5144)
Dogs up to 65 pounds are allowed. There are no additional pet fees. Dogs are not allowed to be left alone in the room.

Marquis de Lafayette Hotel
501 Beach Avenue
North Cape May, NJ
609-884-3500 (800-257-0432)
marquiscapemay.com/
This beach front inn affords wonderful ocean views and breezes and the inn is central to a wide variety of recreational pursuits, shops, eateries, and nightlife. Dogs of all sizes are allowed for an additional fee of $20 per night per pet, plus a $100 cash deposit (credit card not applicable), refundable upon inspection of the room. Dogs must be leashed and cleaned up after. Multiple dogs may be allowed.

Surf 16 Motel
1600 Surf Avenue
North Wildwood, NJ
609-522-1010

members.aol.com/surf16motl/
This motel near the beach is open during the summer only. Dogs of all sizes are accepted. They are open from May 1st through mid-October. Dogs are allowed on the beach before May 15 and after September 15. The hotel has a fenced in dog run. There is a $10 per day pet charge.

La Quinta Inn Paramus
393 North State Route 17
Paramus, NJ
201-265-4200 (800-531-5900)
Dogs of all sizes are allowed. There are no additional pet fees. There is a pet waiver to sign at check in. Dogs must be leashed, cleaned up after, and crated when left alone in the room. Multiple dogs may be allowed.

Red Roof Inn - Parsippany N.Y.C.
855 U.S. 46
Parsippany, NJ
973-334-3737 (800-RED-ROOF)
One well-behaved family pet per room. Guest must notify front desk upon arrival. Guest is liable for any damages. In consideration of all guests, pets must never be left unattended in the guest rooms.

Residence Inn by Marriott
3 Gatehall Drive
Parsippany, NJ
973-984-3313
Dogs of all sizes are allowed. There is a $75 one time fee and a pet policy to sign at check in. Multiple dogs may be allowed.

Sheraton Parsippany Hotel
199 Smith Road
Parsippany, NJ
973-515-2000 (888-625-5144)
Dogs up to 80 pounds are allowed. There are no additional pet fees. Dogs are not allowed to be left alone in the room.

Staybridge Suites Parsippany
61 Interpace Pkwy
Parsippany, NJ
973-334-2907 (877-270-6405)
Dogs up to 70 pounds are allowed for an additional fee of $150 per pet. 2 dogs may be allowed.

Wellesley Inn & Suites Carneys Point
517 S. Pennsville-Auburn Road
Penns Grove, NJ
856-299-3800 (800-531-5900)
Dogs of all sizes are allowed. There is a $10 per night per pet additional fee. Dogs may not be left unattended, and they must be

leashed and cleaned up after. Multiple dogs may be allowed.

Embassy Suites Hotel Piscataway - Somerset
121Centennial Avenue
Piscataway, NJ
732-980-0500
Dogs up to 50 pounds are allowed. There are no additional pet fees. Dogs are not allowed to be left alone in the room.

Motel 6 - Piscataway
1012 Stelton Road
Piscataway, NJ
732-981-9200 (800-466-8356)
One well-behaved family pet per room. Guest must notify front desk upon arrival. Guest is liable for any damages. In consideration of all guests, pets must never be left unattended in the guest rooms.

The Pillars of Plainfield
922 Central Avenue
Plainfield, NJ
908-753-0922 (888 PILLARS (745-5277))
pillars2.com/
This beautifully restored Victorian mansion is surrounded by lush greenery, gardens, and comfort, and they are central to numerous other activities, places of interest, and recreation. Dogs up to 50 pounds are allowed for no additional pet fee. Dogs are allowed on the 2nd floor only, they must be leashed and cleaned up after, and they must be crated when left alone in the room. 2 dogs may be allowed.

Clarion Hotel Palmer Inn
3499 Route 1 S
Princeton, NJ
609-452-2500 (877-424-6423)
Dogs are allowed for an additional pet fee of $20 per night per room. There may be 1 dog up to 50 pounds or 2 dogs up to 20 pounds each per room. 2 dogs may be allowed.

Residence Inn by Marriott
4225 US Route 1
Princeton, NJ
732-329-9600
Dogs of all sizes are allowed. There is a $100 one time fee and a pet policy to sign at check in. 2 dogs may be allowed.

Best Western The Inn at Ramsey
1315 Route 17 South
Ramsey, NJ
201-327-6700 (800-780-7234)
Dogs are allowed for an additional

fee of $10 per night per pet. 2 dogs may be allowed.

Best Western The Inn at Rockaway
14 Green Pond Rd
Rockaway, NJ
973-625-1200 (800-780-7234)
Dogs are allowed for an additional fee of $25 per night per pet. 2 dogs may be allowed.

Residence Inn by Marriott
7 Boroline Road
Saddle River, NJ
201-934-4144
Dogs of all sizes are allowed. There is a $75 one time fee and a pet policy to sign at check in. Multiple dogs may be allowed.

Holiday Inn Harmon Meadow
Secaucus
300 Plaza Dr
Secaucus, NJ
201-348-2000 (877-270-6405)
Dogs of all sizes are allowed for an additional one time pet fee of $50 per room. Dogs may not be left alone in the room. Multiple dogs may be allowed.

Red Roof Inn - Secaucus
Meadowlands N.Y.C.
15 Meadowlands Parkway
Secaucus, NJ
201-319-1000 (800-RED-ROOF)
One well-behaved family pet per room. Guest must notify front desk upon arrival. Guest is liable for any damages. In consideration of all guests, pets must never be left unattended in the guest rooms.

Residence Inn by Marriott
900 Mays Landing Road
Somers Point, NJ
609-927-6400
Dogs of all sizes are allowed. There is a $75 one time fee and a pet policy to sign at check in. Multiple dogs may be allowed.

Candlewood Suites Somerset
41 Worlds Fair Drive
Somerset, NJ
732-748-1400 (877-270-6405)
Dogs of all sizes are allowed for an additional one time fee of $75 per pet. Multiple dogs may be allowed.

Holiday Inn
195 Davidson Ave
Somerset, NJ
732-356-1700 (877-270-6405)
Dogs of all sizes are allowed for an additional fee of $15 per night per pet. Multiple dogs may be allowed.

Qualilty Inn
1850 Easton Avenue
Somerset, NJ
732-469-5050
One dog is allowed for an additional pet fee of $20 per night.

Residence Inn by Marriott
37 Worlds Fair Drive
Somerset, NJ
732-627-0881
Dogs of all sizes are allowed. There is a $75 one time fee and a pet policy to sign at check in. Multiple dogs may be allowed.

Staybridge Suites
260 Davidson Ave
Somerset, NJ
732-356-8000 (877-270-6405)
A dog up to 50 pounds is allowed for an additional one time pet fee of $150.

Holiday Inn
304 Rt 22 W
Springfield, NJ
973-376-9400 (877-270-6405)
Dogs are allowed for no additional fee. Dogs may not be left alone in the room. 2 dogs may be allowed.

Woolverton Inn
6 Woolverton Road
Stockton, NJ
609-397-0802 (888-264-6648)
woolvertoninn.com/
Set on 300 lush, scenic acres of rolling hills and woodlands, this 1792 stone manor luxury inn offers guests indoor or outdoor garden dining, and a favorite pastime here is a walk to the Delaware River to catch the amazing sunsets over the water. Dogs of all sizes are allowed in the Garden Cottage for no additional pet fee. Dogs must be housebroken, quiet, leashed, and cleaned up after. Dogs may only be left alone in the room if owners are confident in their behavior. 2 dogs may be allowed.

Red Roof Inn - Tinton Falls
11 Centre Plaza
Tinton Falls, NJ
732-389-4646 (800-RED-ROOF)
One well-behaved family pet per room. Guest must notify front desk upon arrival. Guest is liable for any damages. In consideration of all guests, pets must never be left unattended in the guest rooms.

Residence Inn by Marriott
90 Park Road
Tinton Falls, NJ

732-389-8100
Dogs of all sizes are allowed. There is a $75 one time fee and a pet policy to sign at check in. Multiple dogs may be allowed.

Sheraton Suites on the Hudson
500 Harbor Blvd.
Weehawken, NJ
201-617-5600 (888-625-5144)
Dogs of all sizes are allowed. There is a $75 one time pet fee per visit.

The Highland House
131 N Broadway
West Cape May, NJ
609-898-1198
Dogs of all sizes are allowed. There are no additional pet fees. 2 dogs may be allowed.

Residence Inn by Marriott
107 Prospect Avenue
West Orange, NJ
973-669-4700
Dogs of all sizes are allowed. There is a $75 one time cleaning fee plus $15 per night per pet and a pet policy to sign at check in. Multiple dogs may be allowed.

New Mexico Listings

Best Western Desert Aire Hotel
1021 S White Sands Blvd
Alamogordo, NM
505-437-2110 (800-780-7234)
Dogs are allowed for an additional fee of $10 per night per pet for the 1st night; each night after is an additional $5 per pet, and a credit card must be on file. 2 dogs may be allowed.

Motel 6 - Alamogordo
251 Panorama Boulevard
Alamogordo, NM
505-434-5970 (800-466-8356)
One well-behaved family pet per room. Guest must notify front desk upon arrival. Guest is liable for any damages. In consideration of all guests, pets must never be left unattended in the guest rooms.

Best Western InnSuites Hotel and Suites
2400 Yale Blvd SE
Albuquerque, NM
505-242-7022 (800-780-7234)
Dogs are allowed for an additional one time pet fee of $50 per room.

Multiple dogs may be allowed.

Brittania and WE Mauger Estate
701 Roma Ave NW
Albuquerque, NM
505-242-8755 (800-719-9189)
bbonline.com/nm/mauger/
This bed and breakfast has one pet room. This room has a doggie door which leads to an enclosed lawn area for your dog. There is a $30 one time additional pet fee.

Candlewood Suites
3025 Menaul Blvd
Albuquerque, NM
505-888-3424 (877-270-6405)
Dogs up to 80 pounds are allowed for an additional pet fee per room of $75 for 1 to 7 nights; the fee is $150 for 8 nights or more. 2 dogs may be allowed.

Casita Chamisa
850 Chamisal Road NW
Albuquerque, NM
505-897-4644
This unique bed and breakfast features an inviting Southwestern decor. Other amenities include an indoor heated swimming pool, a country style continental breakfast, and flower gardens and orchards to stroll through. There are also paths that lead to and along the river. Dogs of all sizes are allowed for no additional fee. Dogs may not be left alone in the room, and they must be leashed and cleaned up after at all times. 2 dogs may be allowed.

Comfort Inn East
13031 Central Avenue
Albuquerque, NM
505-294-1800 (877-424-6423)
Dogs are allowed for an additional pet fee of $7 per night per room. Multiple dogs may be allowed.

Comfort Inn and Suites North
5811 Signal Avenue NE
Albuquerque, NM
505-822-1090 (877-424-6423)
Dogs are allowed for an additional fee of $15 per night per pet. 2 dogs may be allowed.

Days Inn Albuquerque East
13317 Central Ave NE
Albuquerque, NM
505-294-3297 (800-329-7466)
Dogs of all sizes are allowed. There is a $5 per night pet fee per pet. Reservations are recommended due to limited rooms for pets. 2 dogs may be allowed.

Days Inn Albuquerque Northeast
10321 Hotel Ave NE
Albuquerque, NM
505-275-3297 (800-329-7466)
Dogs of all sizes are allowed. There is a $5 per night pet fee per pet. 2 dogs may be allowed.

Days Inn Albuquerque West
6031 Liff Rd NW
Albuquerque, NM
505-836-3297 (800-329-7466)
Dogs of all sizes are allowed. There is a $5 per night pet fee per pet under 40 pounds and $10 per pet over 40 pounds. 2 dogs may be allowed.

Econo Lodge
13211 Central Ave NE
Albuquerque, NM
505-292-7600
There is a $10 per day pet fee.

Hampton Inn
5101 Ellison NE
Albuquerque, NM
505-344-1555
Dogs of all sizes are allowed. There are no additional pet fees. Multiple dogs may be allowed.

Holiday Inn Express
6100 Iliff Rd
Albuquerque, NM
505-836-8600 (877-270-6405)
Dogs of all sizes are allowed for an additional fee of $10 per night per pet. Multiple dogs may be allowed.

Holiday Inn Express
10330 Hotel Ave NE
Albuquerque, NM
505-275-8900 (877-270-6405)
Dogs of all sizes are allowed for an additional one time fee of $25 per pet. Multiple dogs may be allowed.

Howard Johnson Express Inn
7630 Pan American Freeway NE
Albuquerque, NM
505-828-1600 (800-446-4656)
Dogs of all sizes are welcome. There is a $5 per day pet fee.

Howard Johnson Hotel
15 Hotel Circle NE
Albuquerque, NM
505-296-4852 (800-446-4656)
Dogs of all sizes are welcome. There is a $20 one time pet fee.

La Quinta Inn & Suites Albuquerque-Midtown
2011 Menaul Blvd NE
Albuquerque, NM
505-761-5600 (800-531-5900)

252

Dogs of all sizes are allowed. There are no additional pet fees. Dogs may only be left alone in the room if they will be quiet and well behaved, and if behavior is questionable, they must be crated. Dogs must be leashed, cleaned up after, and they are not allowed in the back patio area. Multiple dogs may be allowed.

La Quinta Inn Albuquerque Airport
2116 Yale Blvd. S.E.
Albuquerque, NM
505-243-5500 (800-531-5900)
Dogs of all sizes are allowed. There are no additional pet fees. Dogs must be leashed and cleaned up after. Multiple dogs may be allowed.

La Quinta Inn Albuquerque I-40 East
2424 San Mateo Blvd. N.E.
Albuquerque, NM
505-884-3591 (800-531-5900)
Dogs of all sizes are allowed. There are no additional pet fees. Dogs must be quiet, well behaved, leashed, and cleaned up after. Multiple dogs may be allowed.

La Quinta Inn Albuquerque North
5241 San Antonio Dr. N.E.
Albuquerque, NM
505-821-9000 (800-531-5900)
Dogs of all sizes are allowed. There are no additional pet fees. Dogs must be quiet, well behaved, leashed and cleaned up after. A contact number must be left with the front desk is there is a pet alone in the room, and arrangements need to be made with housekeeping if staying more than one day. Multiple dogs may be allowed.

La Quinta Inn Albuquerque Northwest
7439 Pan American Freeway N.E.
Albuquerque, NM
505-345-7500 (800-531-5900)
Dogs of all sizes are allowed. There are no additional pet fees. There is a pet waiver to sign at check in. Dogs must be crated if left alone in the room, and they must be leashed and cleaned up after. 2 dogs may be allowed.

Motel 6 - Albuquerque - Carlisle
3400 Prospect Avenue Northeast
Albuquerque, NM
505-883-8813 (800-466-8356)
One well-behaved family pet per room. Guest must notify front desk upon arrival. Guest is liable for any damages. In consideration of all guests, pets must never be left unattended in the guest rooms.

Motel 6 - Albuquerque - Midtown
1701 University Boulevard Northeast
Albuquerque, NM
505-843-9228 (800-466-8356)
One well-behaved family pet per room. Guest must notify front desk upon arrival. Guest is liable for any damages. In consideration of all guests, pets must never be left unattended in the guest rooms.

Motel 6 - Albuquerque East
13141 Central Avenue Northeast
Albuquerque, NM
505-294-4600 (800-466-8356)
One well-behaved family pet per room. Guest must notify front desk upon arrival. Guest is liable for any damages. In consideration of all guests, pets must never be left unattended in the guest rooms.

Motel 6 - Albuquerque South - Airport
1000 Avenida Cesar Chavez Southeast
Albuquerque, NM
505-243-8017 (800-466-8356)
One well-behaved family pet per room. Guest must notify front desk upon arrival. Guest is liable for any damages. In consideration of all guests, pets must never be left unattended in the guest rooms.

Motel 6 - Albuquerque West - Coors Road
5701 Iliff Road Northwest
Albuquerque, NM
505-831-8888 (800-466-8356)
One well-behaved family pet per room. Guest must notify front desk upon arrival. Guest is liable for any damages. In consideration of all guests, pets must never be left unattended in the guest rooms.

Plaza Inn
900 Medical Arts Ave NE
Albuquerque, NM
505-243-5693 (800-237-1307)
There is a $25 one time pet fee.

Quality Inn and Suites
411 McKnight Avenue NW
Albuquerque, NM
505-242-5228 (877-424-6423)
Dogs are allowed for an additional pet fee of $10 per night per room. Multiple dogs may be allowed.

Quality Suites
5251 San Antonio Blvd NE
Albuquerque, NM
505-797-0850

Dogs are allowed for an additional fee of $6 per night per pet. 2 dogs may be allowed.

Radisson Hotel Conference Center Albuquerque
2500 Carlisle Blvd Northeast
Albuquerque, NM
505-888-3311
Dogs of all sizes are allowed. There is a $25 one time pet fee.

Red Roof Inn - Albuquerque - Coors Road
6015 Iliff Road Northwest
Albuquerque, NM
505-831-3400 (800-RED-ROOF)
One well-behaved family pet per room. Guest must notify front desk upon arrival. Guest is liable for any damages. In consideration of all guests, pets must never be left unattended in the guest rooms.

Red Roof Inn - Albuquerque Midtown
1635 Candelaria Boulevard Northeast
Albuquerque, NM
505-344-5311 (800-RED-ROOF)
One well-behaved family pet per room. Guest must notify front desk upon arrival. Guest is liable for any damages. In consideration of all guests, pets must never be left unattended in the guest rooms.

Residence Inn by Marriott
3300 Prospect Avenue NE
Albuquerque, NM
505-881-2661
Dogs of all sizes are allowed. There is a $75 one time fee and a pet policy to sign at check in. Multiple dogs may be allowed.

Sheraton Albuquerque
2600 Louisiana Blvd. NE
Albuquerque, NM
505-881-0000 (888-625-5144)
Dogs up to 80 pounds are allowed for no additional pet fee with a credit card on file; there is a pet agreement to sign at check in. Dogs may not be left alone in the room.

Staybridge Suites Albuquerque North
5817 Signal Avenue Ne & Alameda
Albuquerque, NM
505-266-7829 (877-270-6405)
Dogs up to 50 pounds are allowed for an additional fee of $10 per night per pet, or $75 for a week or more. 2 dogs may be allowed.

Studio 6 - ALBUQUERQUE NORTH
4441 Osuna Road NE
Albuquerque, NM

505-344-7744 (800-466-8356)
One well-behaved family pet per room. Guest must notify front desk upon arrival. Guest is liable for any damages. In consideration of all guests, pets must never be left unattended in the guest rooms.

Super 8 Albuquerque/East
450 Paisano St NE
Albuquerque, NM
505-271-4807 (800-800-8000)
Dogs of all sizes are allowed. There is a $5 per night pet fee per pet. Smoking and non-smoking rooms are available for pet rooms. 2 dogs may be allowed.

Super 8 Albuquerque/Midtown
2500 University Blvd NE
Albuquerque, NM
505-888-4884 (800-800-8000)
Dogs of all sizes are allowed. There is a $5 per night pet fee per pet. Smoking and non-smoking rooms are available for pet rooms. 2 dogs may be allowed.

Super 8 Albuquerque/West
6030 Iliff NW
Albuquerque, NM
505-836-5560 (800-800-8000)
Dogs of all sizes are allowed. There is a $5 per night pet fee per pet. Smoking and non-smoking rooms are available for pet rooms. 2 dogs may be allowed.

TownePlace Suites Albuquerque Airport
2400 Centre Avenue SE
Albuquerque, NM
505-232-5800
Dogs of all sizes are allowed. There is a $75 one time pet fee per visit. 2 dogs may be allowed.

Travelodge
13139 Central Ave NE
Albuquerque, NM
505-292-4878
There is a $5.00 per day pet fee.

Angel Fire Resort
10 Miller Lane
Angel Fire, NM
505-377-6401 (800-633-7463)
This resort offers spacious rooms, an indoor pool, and a variety of other amenities. Dogs are welcome to stay in the hotel section of the resort, but not in the condominiums. There is a $25 one time additional fee per pet. Dogs must be well behaved, leashed and cleaned up after at all times. With a summit of 10,677 feet (base-8,600 feet), this is an active full

service ski area during their winter season, but there are a variety of recreational activities to do in the summer as well with plenty of great hiking trails. Dogs are allowed to hike the trails, with the exception of the ski trails during the winter season. 2 dogs may be allowed.

Days Inn Albuquerque Bernalillo
107 N Camino Del Pueblo Ave
Bernalillo, NM
505-771-7000 (800-329-7466)
Dogs of all sizes are allowed. There is a $30 returnable deposit required per room. 2 dogs may be allowed.

Super 8 Bernalillo
265 Hwy 44 E
Bernalillo, NM
505-867-0766 (800-800-8000)
Dogs of all sizes are allowed. There is a $10 returnable deposit required per room. Smoking and non-smoking rooms are available for pet rooms. 2 dogs may be allowed.

Best Western Stevens Inn
1829 S Canal Street
Carlsbad, NM
505-887-2851 (800-780-7234)
Dogs are allowed for an additional fee of $20 per night per pet. Multiple dogs may be allowed.

Days Inn Carlsbad
3910 National Parks Hwy
Carlsbad, NM
505-887-7800 (800-329-7466)
Dogs of all sizes are allowed. There is a $10 per night pet fee per pet. 2 dogs may be allowed.

Motel 6 - Carlsbad
3824 National Parks Highway
Carlsbad, NM
505-885-0011 (800-466-8356)
One well-behaved family pet per room. Guest must notify front desk upon arrival. Guest is liable for any damages. In consideration of all guests, pets must never be left unattended in the guest rooms.

Super 8 Carlsbad
3817 National Parks Hwy
Carlsbad, NM
505-887-8888 (800-800-8000)
Dogs of all sizes are allowed. There is a $10 per night pet fee per pet. Smoking and non-smoking rooms are available for pet rooms. 2 dogs may be allowed.

Hacienda Dona Andrea de Santa Fe
78 Vista del Oro

Cerrillos, NM
505-424-8995
hdasantafe.com
This is a large hotel on 64 acres in the mountains overlooking Santa Fe. Well behaved dogs are welcome. The hotel has a resident terrier named Daisy. There are hiking trails in the area for you to hike with your dog.

High Feather Ranch
29 High Feather Ranch Road
Cerrillos, NM
505-424-1333 (800-757-4410)
This award-winning, 65 acre B&B offers plenty of privacy, and luxury guest rooms amid the rustic backdrop of incredible views of thousands of acres of high mountain desert. Just off the Turquoise Trail National Scenic Byway, there are also miles of hiking and wildflower trails on the ranch, and they also host Astronomy Adventure Star parties. Some of the amenities include a bountiful gourmet breakfast, private patios, in-room fireplaces, whirlpool baths, and more. Dogs of all sizes are welcome. There is a $20 per night per pet additional fee. Dogs may only be left alone in the room for short periods if they are crated, and they must be well behaved, quiet, leashed, and cleaned up after. Dogs are not allowed on the beds or the food areas. 2 dogs may be allowed.

Best Western Kokopelli Lodge
702 S 1st
Clayton, NM
505-374-2589 (800-780-7234)
Dogs are allowed for an additional fee of $5 per night per pet. Multiple dogs may be allowed.

Super 8 Clayton
1425 Hwy 87
Clayton, NM
505-374-8127 (800-800-8000)
Dogs of all sizes are allowed. There is a $7 per night pet fee per pet. Smoking and non-smoking rooms are available for pet rooms. 2 dogs may be allowed.

The Lodge Resort
#1 Corona Place
Cloudcroft, NM
505-682-2566 (800-395-6343)
thelodgeresort.com/
Weathered by a cultured and intriguing past, this elegant mountain lodge is surrounded by over 200,000 acres of national forest, and offer plush accommodations, gourmet dining, and luxurious grounds.

Amenities/features include a heated pool, sauna, outdoor hot tub, lawn games, a traditional Scottish 9-hole golf course, and a variety of scenic hiking trails. There is one unit set aside in the bed and breakfast section that is separate from the main lodge where dogs are allowed. There is a $25 (plus tax) one time additional pet fee. Dogs are allowed on the trails and around the grounds; they must be leashed and cleaned up after at all times.

Howard Johnson Express Inn
2920 Mabry Drive
Clovis, NM
505-769-1953 (800-446-4656)
Dogs up to 50 pounds are allowed. There is a $10 per day pet fee.

La Quinta Inn & Suites Clovis
4521 N. Prince St.
Clovis, NM
505-763-8777 (800-531-5900)
Dogs of all sizes are allowed. There are no additional pet fees. Dogs must be leashed and cleaned up after. Dogs may not be left unattended unless they will be quiet and well behaved, and it is for a short period. Multiple dogs may be allowed.

Holiday Inn
Exit 85 I-10
Deming, NM
505-546-2661 (877-270-6405)
Dogs of all sizes are allowed for no additional pet fee. Multiple dogs may be allowed.

La Quinta Inn & Suites Deming
4300 E Pine St
Deming, NM
505-546-0600 (800-531-5900)
Dogs of all sizes are allowed. There are no additional pet fees. Dogs must be leashed and cleaned up after. Multiple dogs may be allowed.

Motel 6 - Deming
I-10 & Motel Drive
Deming, NM
505-546-2623 (800-466-8356)
One well-behaved family pet per room. Guest must notify front desk upon arrival. Guest is liable for any damages. In consideration of all guests, pets must never be left unattended in the guest rooms.

Best Western Jicarilla Inn and Casino
233 Jicarilla Blvd/US Hwy 64
Dulce, NM
505-759-3663 (800-780-7234)

Dogs are allowed for an additional fee of $10 per night per pet. Multiple dogs may be allowed.

Comfort Inn
604-B S Riverside Drive
Espanola, NM
505-753-2419 (877-424-6423)
Dogs are allowed for an additional fee of $10 per night per pet. Multiple dogs may be allowed.

Days Inn Espanola
807 S Riverside Dr
Espanola, NM
505-747-1242 (800-329-7466)
Dogs of all sizes are allowed. There is a $5 per night pet fee per pet. 2 dogs may be allowed.

Super 8 Espanola
811 S Riversidw
Espanola, NM
505-753-5374 (800-800-8000)
Dogs of all sizes are allowed. There are no additional pet fees. Smoking and non-smoking rooms are available for pet rooms. 2 dogs may be allowed.

Comfort Inn
555 Scott Avenue
Farmington, NM
505-325-2626 (877-424-6423)
Dogs are allowed for an additional fee of $10 per night per pet. Multiple dogs may be allowed.

Days Inn Farmington
1901 E Broadway
Farmington, NM
505-325-3700 (800-329-7466)
Dogs of all sizes are allowed. There is a $50 returnable deposit required per room. There is a $15 per night pet fee per pet. 2 dogs may be allowed.

Holiday Inn Express
2110 Bloomfield Blvd
Farmington, NM
505-325-2545 (877-270-6405)
Dogs of all sizes are allowed for an additional one time pet fee of $25 per room. Multiple dogs may be allowed.

La Quinta Inn Farmington
675 Scott Ave.
Farmington, NM
505-327-4706 (800-531-5900)
Dogs of all sizes are allowed. There are no additional pet fees. Dogs must be leashed and cleaned up after. Multiple dogs may be allowed.

Motel 6 - Farmington

1600 Bloomfield Boulevard
Farmington, NM
505-326-4501 (800-466-8356)
One well-behaved family pet per room. Guest must notify front desk upon arrival. Guest is liable for any damages. In consideration of all guests, pets must never be left unattended in the guest rooms.

Best Western Inn and Suites at Gallup
3009 W Highway 66
Gallup, NM
505-722-2221 (800-780-7234)
Dogs are allowed for an additional one time fee of $10 per pet. Multiple dogs may be allowed.

Best Western Royal Holiday Motel
1903 W Historic Highway 66
Gallup, NM
505-722-4900 (800-780-7234)
Dogs are allowed for an additional fee of $7 per night per pet. Multiple dogs may be allowed.

Comfort Inn
3208 W H 66
Gallup, NM
505-722-0982 (877-424-6423)
Dogs are allowed for an additional fee of $10 per night per pet. 2 dogs may be allowed.

Days Inn Gallup East
1603 W Hwy 66
Gallup, NM
505-863-3891 (800-329-7466)
Dogs up to 100 pounds are allowed. There is a $10 one time per pet fee per visit. 2 dogs may be allowed.

Days Inn Gallup West
3201 W Hwy 66
Gallup, NM
505-863-6889 (800-329-7466)
Dogs of all sizes are allowed. There is a $10 one time per pet fee per visit. Reservations are recommended due to limited rooms for pets. 2 dogs may be allowed.

Motel 6 - Gallup
3306 West US 66
Gallup, NM
505-863-4492 (800-466-8356)
One well-behaved family pet per room. Guest must notify front desk upon arrival. Guest is liable for any damages. In consideration of all guests, pets must never be left unattended in the guest rooms.

Red Roof Inn - Gallup
3304 West Highway 66
Gallup, NM

255

505-722-7765 (800-RED-ROOF)
One well-behaved family pet per room. Guest must notify front desk upon arrival. Guest is liable for any damages. In consideration of all guests, pets must never be left unattended in the guest rooms.

Super 8 Gallup
1715 W Hwy 66
Gallup, NM
505-722-5300 (800-800-8000)
Dogs of all sizes are allowed. There is a $5 per night pet fee per pet. Smoking and non-smoking rooms are available for pet rooms. 2 dogs may be allowed.

Comfort Inn
1551 E Santa Fe Avenue
Grants, NM
505-287-8700 (877-424-6423)
Dogs are allowed for an additional one time pet fee of $10 per room. Multiple dogs may be allowed.

Days Inn Grant
1504 E Santa Fe Ave
Grants, NM
505-287-8883 (800-329-7466)
Dogs of all sizes are allowed. There is a $10 per night pet fee per pet. 2 dogs may be allowed.

Holiday Inn Express
1496 E Santa Fe Ave
Grants, NM
505-285-4676 (877-270-6405)
Dogs of all sizes are allowed for an additional fee of $20 per night per pet. Multiple dogs may be allowed.

Motel 6 - Grants
1505 East Santa Fe Avenue
Grants, NM
505-285-4607 (800-466-8356)
One well-behaved family pet per room. Guest must notify front desk upon arrival. Guest is liable for any damages. In consideration of all guests, pets must never be left unattended in the guest rooms.

Super 8 Grants
1604 E Santa Fe Ave
Grants, NM
505-287-8811 (800-800-8000)
Dogs of all sizes are allowed. There is a $50 returnable deposit required per room. There is a $10 one time per pet fee per visit. Reservations are recommended due to limited rooms for pets. Smoking and non-smoking rooms are available for pet rooms. 2 dogs may be allowed.

Best Western Executive Inn

309 N Marland
Hobbs, NM
505-397-7171 (800-780-7234)
Dogs are allowed for an additional fee of $10 per night per pet. Multiple dogs may be allowed.

Days Inn Hobbs
211 N Marland
Hobbs, NM
505-397-6541 (800-329-7466)
Dogs of all sizes are allowed. There is a $10 per night pet fee per pet. Reservations are recommended due to limited rooms for pets. 2 dogs may be allowed.

Howard Johnson Inn
501 N Marland Blvd.
Hobbs, NM
505-397-3251 (800-446-4656)
Dogs up to 50 pounds are allowed. There is a $20 refundable pet deposit.

Laughing Lizard Inn and Cafe
17526 H 4
Jemez Springs, NM
505-829-3108
This Inn is uniquely decorated in Southwestern decor, and offers spectacular views of the surrounding mesas. Some of the amenities include hand-painted sleeping rooms with comfortable beds, a sitting area, private baths, and a cafe with outdoor dining so that your canine companion may join you. Dogs of all sizes are allowed for no additional fee. Dogs may not be left alone in the room at any time, and they must be leashed and cleaned up after at all times. 2 dogs may be allowed.

Best Western Mesilla Valley Inn
901 Avenida de Mesilla
Las Cruces, NM
505-524-8603 (800-780-7234)
Dogs are allowed for an additional fee of $20 per night per pet. Multiple dogs may be allowed.

Comfort Suites
2101 S Triviz
Las Cruces, NM
505-522-1300 (877-424-6423)
Dogs are allowed for an additional one time fee of $15 per pet, and there is a pet agreement to sign at check in. 2 dogs may be allowed.

Hampton Inn
755 Avenida de Mesilla
Las Cruces, NM
505-536-8311
Well behaved dogs of all sizes are

allowed. There are no additional pet fees. 2 dogs may be allowed.

Holiday Inn Express
2200 South Valley Drive
Las Cruces, NM
505-527-9947 (877-270-6405)
Dogs of all sizes are allowed for no additional pet fee. Multiple dogs may be allowed.

La Quinta Inn Las Cruces
790 Avenida de Mesilla
Las Cruces, NM
505-524-0331 (800-531-5900)
Dogs of all sizes are allowed. There are no additional pet fees. Dogs must be leashed and cleaned up after. Dogs may not be left unattended at any time. Multiple dogs may be allowed.

La Quinta Inn Las Cruces Organ Mountain
1500 Hickory Drive
Las Cruces, NM
505-523-0100 (800-531-5900)
Dogs of all sizes are allowed. There are no additional pet fees. Dogs must have current shot records, not be left alone in the room, and be leashed at all times. Multiple dogs may be allowed.

Motel 6 - Las Cruces
235 La Posada Lane
Las Cruces, NM
505-525-1010 (800-466-8356)
One well-behaved family pet per room. Guest must notify front desk upon arrival. Guest is liable for any damages. In consideration of all guests, pets must never be left unattended in the guest rooms.

Motel 6 - Las Cruces - Telshor
2120 Summit Court
Las Cruces, NM
505-525-2055 (800-466-8356)
One well-behaved family pet per room. Guest must notify front desk upon arrival. Guest is liable for any damages. In consideration of all guests, pets must never be left unattended in the guest rooms.

Sleep Inn
2121 S Triviz
Las Cruces, NM
505-522-1700 (877-424-6423)
Dogs are allowed for an additional one time pet fee of $15 per room. 2 dogs may be allowed.

Teakwood Inn and Suites
2600 S Valley Drive
Las Cruces, NM

505-526-4441
This inn features 130 spacious rooms, complimentary breakfasts, and an indoor pool. Dogs of all sizes are allowed for an additional $10 per night per pet. Dogs must be quiet, leashed, and cleaned up after at all times. Multiple dogs may be allowed.

The Coachlight Inn and RV Park
301 S Motel Blvd
Las Cruces, NM
505-526-3301
Dogs of all sizes are allowed. There is an additional $5 per night per pet fee for small dogs, and a $10 per night per pet fee for medium to large dogs. Dogs may not be left unattended outside, and they must be leashed and cleaned up after. There is an RV only park also on site that allows dogs for no additional fee. 2 dogs may be allowed.

TownePlace Suites Las Cruces
2143 Telshor Court
Las Cruces, NM
505-532-6500
Dogs of all sizes are allowed. There is a $75 one time pet fee per visit. 2 dogs may be allowed.

Plaza Hotel
230 Plaza
Las Vegas, NM
505-425-3591 (800-328-1882)
plazahotel-nm.com/amenities.htm
Although built in 1882, this hotel has been beautifully restored and offers all the 21st century amenities one would expect. It is listed on the National Register of Historic Places, and its elegance and amenities make it a premiere place for both business and vacation travelers. Amenities include a complimentary hot breakfast each morning, room service, a saloon with entertainment, a guest computer, meeting facilities, and more. Dogs of all sizes are allowed. There is a $10 per night per pet additional fee. Dogs must be crated when left alone in the room and they must be leashed and cleaned up after at all times. 2 dogs may be allowed.

Holiday Inn Express
1408 South Main
Lordsburg, NM
505-542-3666 (877-270-6405)
Dogs of all sizes are allowed for an additional fee of $25 per night per pet. 2 dogs may be allowed.

Best Western Hilltop House Hotel
400 Trinity Drive at Central
Los Alamos, NM

505-662-2441 (800-780-7234)
One dog up to 60 pounds is allowed for an additional one time pet fee of $25.

Days Inn Los Lunas
1919 Main St SW
Los Lunas, NM
505-865-5995 (800-329-7466)
Dogs of all sizes are allowed. There is a $10 one time per pet fee per visit. 2 dogs may be allowed.

Comfort Inn
119 Route 66 E
Moriarty, NM
505-832-6666 (877-424-6423)
Dogs are allowed for no additional pet fee. Multiple dogs may be allowed.

Days Inn Moriarty
1809 W Route 66
Moriarty, NM
505-832-4451 (800-329-7466)
Dogs of all sizes are allowed. There is a $5 per night pet fee per pet. 2 dogs may be allowed.

Super 8 Moriarty
1611 Old Route 66
Moriarty, NM
505-832-6730 (800-800-8000)
Dogs of all sizes are allowed. There is a $20 returnable deposit required per room. Reservations are recommended due to limited rooms for pets. Smoking and non-smoking rooms are available for pet rooms. 2 dogs may be allowed.

Holiday Inn Express Hotel & Suites Raton
101 Card Avenue
Raton, NM
505-445-1500 (877-270-6405)
Dogs of all sizes are allowed for an additional fee of $10 per night per pet. Multiple dogs may be allowed.

Motel 6 - Raton
1600 Cedar Street
Raton, NM
505-445-2777 (800-466-8356)
One well-behaved family pet per room. Guest must notify front desk upon arrival. Guest is liable for any damages. In consideration of all guests, pets must never be left unattended in the guest rooms.

Best Western Rivers Edge
301 W River St
Red River, NM
505-754-1766 (800-780-7234)
Dogs are allowed for an additional fee of $10 per night per pet. Multiple

dogs may be allowed.

Black Bear Inn
517 Main Street/H 38
Red River, NM
505-754-2262
This family owned motel sits in a scenic little valley at over 8,500 feet altitude, and is very close to a variety of recreational pursuits, restaurants, and shops. Dogs of all sizes are allowed for no additional pet fee with a credit card on file. There is only one or two dogs allowed per room depending on the size of the dog and the room. Dogs must be leashed, cleaned up after, and crated when left alone in the room.

Terrace Towers Lodge
712 West Main Street
Red River, NM
800-695-6343
terracetowers-lodge.com
The rooms at this lodge overlook the town of Red River and the Red River Ski Area. The lodge offers 16 two bedroom suites with a living/dining/kitchen area. Amenities include cable TV, hot tub, picnic and playground areas, guest laundry and Internet. There is a small pet fee and a limit of 2 pets per unit. There is no size or weight limit for dogs. Pets need to be leashed while on the property.

Days Inn Albuquerque/Rio Rancho
4200 Crestview Dr
Rio Rancho, NM
505-892-8800 (800-329-7466)
Dogs of all sizes are allowed. There is a $10 one time per pet fee per visit. 2 dogs may be allowed.

Best Western El Rancho Palacio
2205 E Main St
Roswell, NM
505-622-2721 (800-780-7234)
Dogs are allowed for no additional pet fee. Multiple dogs may be allowed.

Comfort Inn
3595 N Main Street
Roswell, NM
505-623-4567 (877-424-6423)
Dogs are allowed for no additional pet fee. 2 dogs may be allowed.

Cozy Cowboy Cottage Rentals
804 W 4th Street
Roswell, NM
505-624-3258
The number and size of pets depends on the size and type of unit rented. There is a $250 refundable

deposit per stay per unit and a pet policy to sign at check in.

Days Inn Roswell
1310 N Main St
Roswell, NM
505-623-4021 (800-329-7466)
Dogs of all sizes are allowed. There are no additional pet fees. 2 dogs may be allowed.

Frontier Motel
3010 N Main St
Roswell, NM
505-622-1400 (800-678-1401)
There are no additional pet fees.

Holiday Inn Express Roswell
2300 North Main Street
Roswell, NM
505-627-9900 (877-270-6405)
A dog up to 50 pounds is allowed for no additional fee.

La Quinta Inn & Suites Roswell
200 East 19th Street
Roswell, NM
505-622-8000 (800-531-5900)
Dogs of all sizes are allowed. There are no additional pet fees. There is a pet waiver to sign at check in. Dogs may not be left unattended, and they must be leashed at all times and cleaned up after. Dogs must be crated or removed for housekeeping. Multiple dogs may be allowed.

Motel 6 - Roswell
3307 North Main Street
Roswell, NM
505-625-6666 (800-466-8356)
One well-behaved family pet per room. Guest must notify front desk upon arrival. Guest is liable for any damages. In consideration of all guests, pets must never be left unattended in the guest rooms.

Apache Village Cabins
311 Mechem Drive
Ruidoso, NM
505-257-2435
Well behaved dogs of all sizes are allowed. There is a $15 per stay per room additional fee. There must also be a credit card on file. 2 dogs may be allowed.

Hawthorne Suites Conference and Golf Resort
107 Sierra Blanca Drive
Ruidoso, NM
505-258-5500 (888-323-5216)
ruidosohawthorn.com/
This resort offers world class accommodations and services, and some of the amenities include the

city's largest pool and Jacuzzi (enclosed in a 2-story atrium), private balconies, fireplaces, a 24 hour convenience store, a full service bar, and a complimentary full hot American breakfast. Dogs of all sizes are welcome for no additional fee or deposit; there is a pet policy to sign at check in. Dogs may not be left alone in the room at any time, and they must be leashed and cleaned up after at all times. Multiple dogs may be allowed.

Motel 6 - Ruidoso
412 US 70 West
Ruidoso, NM
505-630-1166 (800-466-8356)
One well-behaved family pet per room. Guest must notify front desk upon arrival. Guest is liable for any damages. In consideration of all guests, pets must never be left unattended in the guest rooms.

Quailty Inn
307 H 70W
Ruidoso, NM
505-378-4051
Dogs under 20 pounds are allowed for an additional fee of $10 per night per pet; the fee is $25 per night per pet for dogs over 20 pounds. Multiple dogs may be allowed.

Swiss Chalet Inn
1451 Meecham Drive
Ruidoso, NM
505-258-3333 (800-47-SWISS (477-9477))
sciruidoso.com/
This inn sits atop the Alto Crest nestled among towering Ponderosa Pines, and in addition to luxury and stunning views, amenities also include a complimentary continental breakfast, an indoor pool, hot tub, and easy access to several recreational activities. Dogs of all sizes are allowed for a $25 one time additional fee per pet. Dogs must be well mannered, and leashed and cleaned up after at all times. Multiple dogs may be allowed.

Whispering Pines Cabins
422 Main Road
Ruidoso, NM
505-257-4311
Well behaved dogs of all sizes are allowed. There is a $10 one time fee per pet additional fee. Dogs are not allowed to be left alone in the room. Multiple dogs may be allowed.

Best Western Pine Springs Inn
1420 Hwy 70

Ruidoso Downs, NM
505-378-8100 (800-780-7234)
Dogs are allowed for no additional pet fee. Multiple dogs may be allowed.

Alexander's Inn
529 East Palace Avenue
Santa Fe, NM
505-986-1431 (888-321-5123)
This intimate inn offers their visitors privacy and a host of amenities, some of which include a welcome basket full of goodies, a lavish continental breakfast, an afternoon wine and cheese reception, luxurious authentic Southwestern decor, kiva-style fireplaces, full kitchens and patios, and a guest membership at a full-service health club. Dogs of all sizes are allowed for an additional pet fee of $20 per pet per stay, and there is a pet policy to sign at check in. They even keep a supply of doggie biscuits to treat their canine visitors. Dogs must be crated if left alone in the room, be well behaved, and leashed and cleaned up after at all times. 2 dogs may be allowed.

Comfort Inn
4312 Cerrillos Road
Santa Fe, NM
505-474-7330 (877-424-6423)
Dogs are allowed for an additional fee of $5 per night per pet. Dogs may not be left alone in the room. Multiple dogs may be allowed.

El Dorado Hotel & Spa
309 West San Francisco
Santa Fe, NM
505-988-4455 (800-955-4455)
eldoradohotel.com
This pet-friendly hotel and spa is located close to the historic plaza. There is a $50 one time additional pet fee. Pets are not allowed in the restaurant or retail outlets. Pet sitting is available with advanced notice.

El Paradero Bed and Breakfast Inn
220 W. Manhattan Ave
Santa Fe, NM
505-988-1177 (866-558-0918)
elparadero.com
This B&B is located just a few minute walk from the Plaza and the Railyard District. Dogs of all sizes are allowed. There is a $20 nightly fee for dogs.

Hacienda Nicholas
320 Marcy C
Santa Fe, NM
505-992-8385 (888-284-3170)
Behind extra thick adobe walls, this intimate, authentic hacienda offers all

the amenities of a luxury hotel. It also features a beautiful, lush garden courtyard with an outdoor kiva fireplace and an afternoon wine and cheese reception. Organic and vegetarian food is available. Dogs of all sizes are allowed for an additional pet fee of $20 per pet per stay, and a pet policy to sign at check in. They even keep a supply of doggie biscuits for their canine visitors. Dogs must be crated if left alone in the room, and they must be well behaved, and leashed and cleaned up after at all times. 2 dogs may be allowed.

Hampton Inn
3625 Cerrillos Road
Santa Fe, NM
505-474-3900
Dogs of all sizes are allowed. There is a pet policy to sign at check in and there are no additional pet fees. Dogs are not allowed to be left alone in the room. Multiple dogs may be allowed.

Hilton
100 Sandoval Street
Santa Fe, NM
505-988-2811
Dogs up to 60 pounds are allowed for an additional one time pet fee of $50 per room. 2 dogs may be allowed.

Holiday Inn Express Santa Fe Cerrillos
3450 Cerrillos Road
Santa Fe, NM
505-474-7570 (877-270-6405)
Dogs of all sizes are allowed for no additional pet fee. Multiple dogs may be allowed.

Holiday Inn Santa Fe
4048 Cerrillos Road
Santa Fe, NM
505-473-4646 (877-270-6405)
Dogs of all sizes are allowed for an additional one time fee of $25 per pet. Multiple dogs may be allowed.

Hotel Santa Fe
1501 Paseo De Peralta
Santa Fe, NM
505-982-1200
Dogs of all sizes are allowed. There is a $20 per night per pet additional fee. Multiple dogs may be allowed.

Inn of the Anasazi
113 Washington Ave
Santa Fe, NM
505-988-3030 (800-688-8100)
slh.com/pages/a/aziusaba.html

There is a $20 one time pet fee.

Inn of the Five Graces
150 E. DeVargas Street
Santa Fe, NM
505-992-0957
This unique hotel features an intricate blending of the Orient and the Old West creating a warm and interesting luxurious background, for which they are the recipient of several accolades and awards. They offer a continental breakfast, and a number of amenities and services. The Gate House restaurant on site features a Tapas menu, and offer courtyard seating amid mature trees; dogs are allowed there also. Dogs of all sizes are allowed. There is a $50 per night per room additional pet fee. Dogs may not be left alone in the room, and they must be well behaved, leashed, and cleaned up after. 2 dogs may be allowed.

Inn on the Alameda
303 E Alameda
Santa Fe, NM
505-984-2121 (888-984-2121)
Peaceful, garden adobe courtyards and their 71 suites will immerse visitors in luxurious authentic Southwestern decor. They offer a continental breakfast, an afternoon wine and cheese reception, outdoor whirlpools, fireplaces/patios/balconies, and a great location for exploring the area. Dogs of all sizes are allowed for an additional fee of $20 per night per pet. Dogs may not be left alone in the rooms, and they must be leashed and cleaned up after at all times. 2 dogs may be allowed.

La Quinta Inn Santa Fe
4298 Cerrillos Rd.
Santa Fe, NM
505-471-1142 (800-531-5900)
Dogs of all sizes are allowed. There are no additional pet fees. Dogs may not be left unattended, and they must be leashed and cleaned up after. Multiple dogs may be allowed.

Motel 6 - Santa Fe
3007 Cerrillos Road
Santa Fe, NM
505-473-1380 (800-466-8356)
One well-behaved family pet per room. Guest must notify front desk upon arrival. Guest is liable for any damages. In consideration of all guests, pets must never be left unattended in the guest rooms.

Pecos Trail Inn
2239 Old Pecos Trail
Santa Fe, NM
505-982-1943
Dogs of all sizes are allowed. There are no additional pet fees. Multiple dogs may be allowed.

Quality Inn
3011 Cerrillos Road
Santa Fe, NM
505-471-1211 (877-424-6423)
Dogs are allowed for an additional fee of $10 per night per pet. Multiple dogs may be allowed.

Red Roof Inn - Santa Fe - Cerrillos Road
3695 Cerrillos Road
Santa Fe, NM
505-471-4140 (800-RED-ROOF)
One well-behaved family pet per room. Guest must notify front desk upon arrival. Guest is liable for any damages. In consideration of all guests, pets must never be left unattended in the guest rooms.

Residence Inn by Marriott
1698 Galisteo Street
Santa Fe, NM
505-988-7300
Dogs of all sizes are allowed. There is a $75 one time fee and a pet policy to sign at check in. 2 dogs may be allowed.

Santa Fe Sage Inn
725 Cerrillos
Santa Fe, NM
505-982-5952 (866-433-0335)
This Inn offers comfortable Southwestern themed rooms, an extended continental breakfast, a swimming pool, many other amenities, and a great central location to several shopping opportunities and various attractions. Dogs of all sizes are allowed. There is a $25 per pet per stay additional fee. Dogs must be leashed and cleaned up after at all times. Multiple dogs may be allowed.

Sunrise Springs Inn and Retreat
242 Los Pinos Road
Santa Fe, NM
505-471-3600
Dogs of all sizes are allowed. There is a $25 per night per pet fee and a pet policy to sign at check in. Dogs must be crated when left in the room. 2 dogs may be allowed.

Ten Thousand Waves Japanese Spa and Resort
3451 Hyde Park Road

Santa Fe, NM
505-992-5003
tenthousandwaves.com
Ten Thousand Waves is a Japanese style spa in the mountains above Santa Fe with outdoor and indoor hot tubs, facials, spa services, and many types of massage. There are 13 guest houses, most with fireplaces and either enclosed courtyards or decks. Some have full kitchens and/or separate bedrooms. The resort is about ten minutes from downtown. Pets are $20 per night for one or more.

Best Western Adobe Inn
1501 E Will Rogers Dr
Santa Rosa, NM
505-472-3446 (800-780-7234)
Dogs are allowed for no additional pet fee. Multiple dogs may be allowed.

Best Western Santa Rosa Inn
3022 Historic Route 66
Santa Rosa, NM
505-472-5877 (800-780-7234)
Dogs are allowed for an additional pet fee of $10 per night per room. 2 dogs may be allowed.

Comfort Inn
3343 Historic Route 66
Santa Rosa, NM
505-472-5570 (877-424-6423)
Dogs 30 pounds and under are allowed for an additional fee of $15 per night per pet; the fee is $20 per night per pet for dogs from 31 to 80 pounds. 2 dogs may be allowed.

Days Inn Santa Rosa
1830 Will Rogers Dr
Santa Rosa, NM
505-472-5985 (800-329-7466)
Dogs of all sizes are allowed. There is a $5 per night pet fee per pet. 2 dogs may be allowed.

Holiday Inn Express Santa Rosa
3202 Historic Route 66
Santa Rosa, NM
505-472-5411 (877-270-6405)
Dogs of all sizes are allowed for an additional pet fee of $25 per night per room. Multiple dogs may be allowed.

La Quinta Inn Santa Rosa
1701 Will Rogers Dr.
Santa Rosa, NM
505-472-4800 (800-531-5900)
Dogs of all sizes are allowed. There are no additional pet fees as long as pets are reported at the time of registration. Dogs may not be left

unattended, and they must be leashed and cleaned up after. Multiple dogs may be allowed.

Motel 6 - Santa Rosa
3400 Will Rogers Drive
Santa Rosa, NM
505-472-3045 (800-466-8356)
One well-behaved family pet per room. Guest must notify front desk upon arrival. Guest is liable for any damages. In consideration of all guests, pets must never be left unattended in the guest rooms.

Econo Lodge
1120 H 180
Silver City, NM
505-534-1111 (877-424-6423)
econolodgesilvercity.com/
This lodge offers 59 deluxe rooms and 3 suites and features well kept grounds, an atrium with comfortable benches and a fountain in the middle, a hot tub, and a great indoor heated pool area. Some of the other amenities include a conference room, many in-room perks, and a free continental breakfast. Dogs of all sizes are allowed for an additional pet fee of $7 (plus tax) per night per room, and there is a pet policy to sign at check in. Dogs may not be left alone in the room, they must be leashed and cleaned up after at all times, and crated or removed for housekeeping.

Holiday Inn Express
1103 Superior St
Silver City, NM
505-538-2525 (877-270-6405)
Dogs of all sizes are allowed for no additional pet fee with a credit card on file, and the must be declared at the time of reservations. Multiple dogs may be allowed.

Best Western Socorro Hotel & Suites
1100 N California Street
Socorro, NM
505-838-0556 (800-780-7234)
Dogs are allowed for an additional fee of $10 per night per pet. Multiple dogs may be allowed.

Motel 6 - Socorro
807 South US 85
Socorro, NM
505-835-4300 (800-466-8356)
One well-behaved family pet per room. Guest must notify front desk upon arrival. Guest is liable for any damages. In consideration of all guests, pets must never be left unattended in the guest rooms.

Adobe and Pines Inn
4107 H 68
Taos, NM
505-751-0947 (800-723-8267)
adobepines.com
This luxurious, romantic hideaway is a 170+ year old adobe hacienda that has been preserved with original architecture and transformed into lush grounds with an inviting Southwestern decor. Amenities include full gourmet breakfasts, a brook with an old stone bridge, acres of country gardens, private patios, an outdoor fire ring, spa services, and more. Dogs of all sizes are welcome. There is a $20 one time additional fee per pet. Dogs may also be walked in the large yard next door, and if your dog is under good voice control, they may be off lead in that area. On the property, dogs must be leashed and cleaned up after at all times. Dogs must be crated when left alone in the room. Multiple dogs may be allowed.

Alpine Village Suites
PO Box 917
Taos, NM
505-776-8540 (800-576-2666)
alpine-suites.com
Located in Taos Ski Valley, this hotel offers a completely non-smoking environment. All 24 Suites and Studios have mini-kitchens, and most have private balconies with views. Many of the suites have fireplaces, and all suites have TV/VCR's, full baths and telephones. They are located steps from the lifts, restaurants, nightlife, and shopping. The Alpine Village complex houses two full service ski shops, a restaurant and bar. They welcome kids of all ages and the family pet. There is a $10 per day pet charge.

American Artist Gallery House
132 Frontier Lane
Taos, NM
505-758-4446 (800-532-2041)
This B&B offers southwest hospitality in a secluded, romantic setting, and they feature luxury accommodations, gourmet breakfasts, and a stunning view of Taos Mountain. Some of the amenities include Jacuzzi suites, kiva fireplaces, private bath, an outdoor hot tub, and a guest computer. Dogs of all sizes are allowed. There is a $25 additional fee per pet for the first 1 or 2 days, and then an additional $10 per pet per day thereafter. Dogs may not be left alone in the room at any time, and they must be well mannered,

leashed, and cleaned up after at all times. Dogs are not allowed on the beds or furnishings, or in the common or breakfast areas. Shots must be current. Dogs are allowed on the trails surrounding the B&B. 2 dogs may be allowed.

Artist's Casita
between Taos and Ski Valley
Taos, NM
505-758-8091
ann-cole.com/rental.html
This charming one-bedroom casita on the Valdez Rim Road is available for rental. Dogs are welcomed at no additional fee. The rental is about twenty minutes from skiing and from downtown Taos.

Casa Europa
840 Upper Ranchitos Road (HC68, Box 3F)
Taos, NM
505-758-9798 (888-758-9798)
casaeuropanm.com/
This spacious 18th century, pueblo-style estate features a warm inviting Southwestern decor with enclosed garden courtyards and water fountains. Amenities include a full gourmet breakfast, afternoon snacks, an outdoor Jacuzzi and sauna, rooms with fireplaces/private baths/whirlpool tubs, and they are close to many hiking opportunities. Dogs of all sizes are allowed in the apartment suite. There is a $25 per night per pet additional fee. They ask that if you leave your pet in the room, that they are either crated or put in the Jacuzzi room. Dogs must be leashed and cleaned up after. 2 dogs may be allowed.

El Monte Sagrado Living Resort and Spa
317 Kit Carson Road
Taos, NM
505-758-3502 (800-828-TAOS (8267))
This retreat, with several accolades to their name, specializes in luxury accommodations with an emphasis on environmental and ecological harmony. On site are a Biolarium, lush gardens, a spa, and a decor that reflects an array of global influences inspired by Native American culture. World class cuisine is featured on site, and although dogs are not allowed in dining areas, they have an in-suite dining menu available. Dogs of all sizes are allowed. There is a $150 one time fee per stay for one dog, and an additional $75 one time fee per stay for a 2nd dog. Dogs must be quiet, well behaved,

leashed, and cleaned up after at all times. 2 dogs may be allowed.

La Dona Luz Inn
114 Kit Carson Road
Taos, NM
505-758-4874 (800-758-9187)
ladonaluz.com/
Thanks to one of our readers for recommending this dog-friendly bed and breakfast. A large dog is welcome to stay here if they are well-behaved and if the dog owner agrees to pay for room damages caused by their dog. There is a $10 per night pet fee. This historic B&B offers 5 rooms (up a narrow spiral stairway), all with private baths. Room rates are approximately $75 to $150 per night. This B&B has been recommended by both The New York Times and USA Today Weekend.

Quality Inn
1043 Paseo Del Pueblo Spur
Taos, NM
505-758-2200 (877-424-6423)
Dogs are allowed for an additional fee of $7 per night per pet. 2 dogs may be allowed.

San Geronimo Lodge
1101 Witt Road
Taos, NM
505-751-3776 (800-894-4119)
sangeronimolodge.com/
This lodge offers a great location to several activities/recreational pursuits, great dining, and old historic charm with all the comforts and conveniences of modern day accommodations. Amenities include a seasonal pool, home-cooked meals (special diets-no problem), an outside hot tub, and complete concierge service. Dogs of all sizes are welcome; however pet rooms are limited so be sure to phone ahead. There is a $10 refundable deposit per pet. There is a large field, and a trail from the lodge that leads to the river for some great walking areas for your canine companion. Dogs must be well behaved and social with other animals, as there are other friendly animals in residence too. Dogs must be leashed and cleaned up after. 2 dogs may be allowed.

Best Western Hot Springs Inn
2270 N Date St
Truth or Consequences, NM
505-894-6665 (800-780-7234)
Dogs are allowed for no additional pet fee. Multiple dogs may be allowed.

Comfort Inn and Suites
2205 N Dale Street
Truth or Consequences, NM
505-894-1660 (877-424-6423)
Dogs are allowed for no additional pet fee. 2 dogs may be allowed.

Marshall Hot Springs
311 Marr Street
Truth or Consequences, NM
505-894-9286
marshallhotsprings.com/
Hot springs feed spring-fed pools at this dog-friendly hotel. Dogs of all sizes are allowed. There is a fee of $5 per dog per stay. All dogs receive dog biscuits and sheets for dogs that sleep on the bed. Multiple dogs may be allowed.

Super 8 Truth or Consequences
2151 N Date St
Truth or Consequences, NM
505-894-7888 (800-800-8000)
Dogs of all sizes are allowed. There are no additional pet fees. Smoking and non-smoking rooms are available for pet rooms. 2 dogs may be allowed.

Best Western Discovery Inn
200 East Estrella Ave
Tucumcari, NM
505-461-4884 (800-780-7234)
Dogs are allowed for an additional fee of $5 per night per pet. Multiple dogs may be allowed.

Comfort Inn
2800 E Tucumcari Blvd
Tucumcari, NM
505-461-4094 (877-424-6423)
Dogs are allowed for an additional one time fee of $12 per pet. Multiple dogs may be allowed.

Days Inn Tucumcari
2623 S First St
Tucumcari, NM
505-461-3158 (800-329-7466)
Dogs of all sizes are allowed. There is a $5 per night pet fee per pet. 2 dogs may be allowed.

Howard Johnson Express Inn
3604 E. Rt. 66 Blvd.
Tucumcari, NM
505-461-2747 (800-446-4656)
Dogs of all sizes are welcome. There is a $6 per day pet fee.

Motel 6 - Tucumcari
2900 East Tucumcari Boulevard
Tucumcari, NM
505-461-4791 (800-466-8356)
One well-behaved family pet per

room. Guest must notify front desk upon arrival. Guest is liable for any damages. In consideration of all guests, pets must never be left unattended in the guest rooms.

Whites City Resort
17 Carlsbad Cavern H
White's City, NM
505-785-2291 (800-CAVERNS(228-3767))
Dogs of all sizes are allowed. There is a $10 per night per pet additional fee for the Walnut Inn. Dogs must be quiet, well behaved, leashed, and cleaned up after. There is also a campground on site that allows dogs at no additional fee. Multiple dogs may be allowed.

New York Listings

Best Western Sovereign Hotel - Albany
1228 Western Avenue
Albany, NY
518-489-2981 (800-780-7234)
Dogs are allowed with advance reservations for an additional fee of $15 per night per pet. Dogs may not be left alone in the room. Multiple dogs may be allowed.

Comfort Inn and Suites
1606 Central Avenue
Albany, NY
518-869-5327 (877-424-6423)
Dogs are allowed for an additional pet fee of $15 per night per room. 2 dogs may be allowed.

Cresthill Suites Hotel
1415 Washington Avenue
Albany, NY
518-454-0007 (888-723-1655)
cresthillsuites.com
In addition to offering a great starting location to many other local attractions, this hotel also has an outdoor courtyard pool with a patio and barbecues, and lots of extras. Dogs of all sizes are allowed for an additional $75 one time fee per pet. They request that dogs be removed or crated for housekeeping. Dogs must be leashed, cleaned up after, and may only be left alone in the room if they will be quiet and well behaved. Multiple dogs may be allowed.

Holiday Inn Albany On Wolf Road
205 Wolf Rd.
Albany, NY

518-458-7250 (877-270-6405)
Dogs of all sizes are allowed for an additional pet fee per room of $35 (plus tax) for 1 to 3 nights; the fee is $100 for 4 or more nights. 2 dogs may be allowed.

Motel 6 - ALBANY, NY
100 Watervliet Avenue
Albany, NY
518-438-7447 (800-466-8356)
One well-behaved family pet per room. Guest must notify front desk upon arrival. Guest is liable for any damages. In consideration of all guests, pets must never be left unattended in the guest rooms.

Red Roof Inn - Albany
188 Wolf Road
Albany, NY
518-459-1971 (800-RED-ROOF)
One well-behaved family pet per room. Guest must notify front desk upon arrival. Guest is liable for any damages. In consideration of all guests, pets must never be left unattended in the guest rooms.

TownePlace Suites Albany SUNY
1379 Washington Avenue
Albany, NY
518-435-1900
Dogs of all sizes are allowed. There is a $75 one time pet fee per visit. 2 dogs may be allowed.

Gansett Green Manor
273 Main Street
Amagansett, NY
631-267-3133
Well behaved dogs of all sizes are allowed. There can be up to 3 small dogs or 2 big dogs per room. The fee is $20 for the 1st 4 days then $5 for each day thereafter per pet. Dogs must be healthy and free of tics and fleas.

Comfort Inn University
1 Flint Road
Amherst, NY
716-688-0811 (877-424-6423)
Dogs are allowed for an additional fee of $20 per night per pet. 2 dogs may be allowed.

Lord Amherst
5000 Main St
Amherst, NY
716-839-2200 (800-544-2200)
There are no additional pet fees.

Motel 6 - Buffalo - Amherst
4400 Maple Road
Amherst, NY
716-834-2231 (800-466-8356)

One well-behaved family pet per room. Guest must notify front desk upon arrival. Guest is liable for any damages. In consideration of all guests, pets must never be left unattended in the guest rooms.

Red Roof Inn - Buffalo Amherst
42 Flint Road
Amherst, NY
716-689-7474 (800-RED-ROOF)
One well-behaved family pet per room. Guest must notify front desk upon arrival. Guest is liable for any damages. In consideration of all guests, pets must never be left unattended in the guest rooms.

Quality Inn Binghamton West
7666 Route 434
Apalachin, NY
607-625-4441 (877-424-6423)
Dogs are allowed for an additional fee of $10 per night per pet. Multiple dogs may be allowed.

Wellesley Inn Armonk
94 Business Park Drive
Armonk, NY
914-273-9090 (800-531-5900)
Dogs of all sizes are allowed. There are no additional pet fees. Dogs may only be left alone in the room if they will be quiet and well behaved, and they must be leashed and cleaned up after. 2 dogs may be allowed.

Days Inn Auburn
37 William Street
Auburn, NY
315-252-7567 (800-329-7466)
Dogs of all sizes are allowed. There is a $5 per night pet fee per pet. 2 dogs may be allowed.

Super 8 Auburn/Finger Lakes Area
19 McMaster St
Auburn, NY
315-253-8886 (800-800-8000)
Dogs of all sizes are allowed. There is a $10 per night pet fee per pet. Smoking and non-smoking rooms are available for pet rooms. 2 dogs may be allowed.

Caboose Motel
8620 State Route 415
Avoca, NY
607-566-2216
Large dogs are allowed in the cabooses. There are no additional pet fees.

Comfort Inn
4371 Federal Drive
Batavia, NY
585-344-9999 (877-424-6423)

Dogs are allowed for an additional one time fee of $10 per pet. Multiple dogs may be allowed.

Days Inn Batavia
200 Oak St
Batavia, NY
585-343-6000 (800-329-7466)
Dogs of all sizes are allowed. There is a $10 per night pet fee per pet. 2 dogs may be allowed.

Quality Inn and Suites
8200 Park Road
Batavia, NY
585-344-7000 (877-424-6423)
Dogs are allowed for an additional fee of $10 per night per pet. Multiple dogs may be allowed.

Days Inn Bath
330 W Morris St
Bath, NY
607-776-7644 (800-329-7466)
Dogs of all sizes are allowed. There are no additional pet fees. 2 dogs may be allowed.

Clarion Collection: The Grand Royal Hotel
80 State Street
Binghamton, NY
607-722-0000 (877-424-6423)
Dogs are allowed for an additional fee of $10 per night per pet. 2 dogs may be allowed.

Motel 6 - Binghamton
1012 Front Street
Binghamton, NY
607-771-0400 (800-466-8356)
One well-behaved family pet per room. Guest must notify front desk upon arrival. Guest is liable for any damages. In consideration of all guests, pets must never be left unattended in the guest rooms.

Quality Inn and Suites
1156 Front Street
Binghamton, NY
607-722-5353 (877-424-6423)
Dogs are allowed for an additional one time pet fee of $15 per room. Multiple dogs may be allowed.

Super 8 Binghamton/Front Street
650 Old Front St
Binghamton, NY
607-773-8111 (800-800-8000)
Dogs of all sizes are allowed. There is a $35 returnable deposit required per room. Reservations are recommended due to limited rooms for pets. Smoking and non-smoking rooms are available for pet rooms. 2 dogs may be allowed.

Clarion Hotel
S-3950 McKinley Parkway
Blasdell, NY
716-648-5700 (877-424-6423)
One dog is allowed for an additional pet fee of $10 per night.

Red Roof Inn - Buffalo Airport
146 Maple Drive
Bowmansville, NY
716-633-1100 (800-RED-ROOF)
One well-behaved family pet per room. Guest must notify front desk upon arrival. Guest is liable for any damages. In consideration of all guests, pets must never be left unattended in the guest rooms.

Holiday Inn Express
4908 South Lake Rd
Brockport, NY
585-395-1000 (877-270-6405)
Dogs of all sizes are allowed for an additional one time fee of $15 per pet. Multiple dogs may be allowed.

Holiday Inn Express New York-Brooklyn
625 Union St.
Brooklyn, NY
718-797-1133 (877-270-6405)
Dogs of all sizes are allowed for an additional one time fee of $50 per pet. 2 dogs may be allowed.

Holiday Inn
620 Delaware Avenue
Buffalo, NY
716-886-2121 (877-270-6405)
Dogs of all sizes are allowed for an additional one time pet fee of $30 per room; dogs must be crated when alone in the room. Multiple dogs may be allowed.

Residence Inn by Marriott
107 Anderson Road
Buffalo, NY
716-892-5410
Dogs of all sizes are allowed. There is a $75 one time fee and a pet policy to sign at check in. 2 dogs may be allowed.

Cedar Terrace Resort
665 Main Street
Cairo, NY
518-622-9313
Nestled in the scenic Northern Catskill Mountains, this picturesque resort offers a relaxing atmosphere in addition to well-manicured grounds and gardens, great views, and comfortable rooms. Some of their features include gaming courts, a 9-hole miniature golf

course, a multi-use sports field with bleachers, big swings, a pool, table tennis, catering for groups, and wonderful wooded hiking paths. Dogs of all sizes are allowed. There is a $10 per night per pet additional fee. Dogs may not be left alone in the room at any time, and they must be leashed and cleaned up after. Multiple dogs may be allowed.

Blue Harbor House
67 Elm Street
Camden, NY
207-236-3196 (800-248-3196)
blueharborhouse.com/
This 1810 harbor house features a nice blending of old and new worlds, and is about a 4 minute walk to the harbor and a quaint coastal village. They offer one suite for guests with pets, complete with a whirlpool tub and it's own outside entrance. One dog of any size is allowed for an additional fee of $25 per night. Dogs must be leashed and cleaned up after.

The Inn at The Shaker Mill Farm
40 Cherry Lane
Canaan, NY
518-794-9345
shakermillfarminn.com/
This converted 1824 Shaker mill, complete with a brook and waterfall, features 20 uniquely different rooms with private baths, and woodland trails to explore. Dogs of all sizes are allowed for no additional fee. Dogs must be very well behaved, quiet, leashed, and cleaned up after. Multiple dogs may be allowed.

Econo Lodge
170 Eastern Blvd
Canandaigua, NY
716-394-9000 (800-797-1222)
There are no additional pet fees.

Inn On The Lake
777 S. Main St
Canandaigua, NY
716-394-7800 (800-228-2801)
theinnonthelake.com
There is a $25 per day additional pet fee.

Days Inn Syracuse/Canastota
377 N Petersboro St
Canastota, NY
315-697-3309 (800-329-7466)
Dogs of all sizes are allowed. There are no additional pet fees. 2 dogs may be allowed.

Quality Inn and Conference Center
704 H 23

Catskill, NY
518-943-5800 (877-424-6423)
Dogs are allowed for an additional fee of $20 (plus tax) per night per pet. 2 dogs may be allowed.

Mountain View Log Home
Hunter Mountain
Catskills, NY
212-381-2375
This fully-loaded, ready to enjoy tri-level log cabin sits on 10 elevated hilly, wooded acres and offers a sauna, a pool/gaming room, many extras-including great views of Hunter Mountain, and they are just minutes from an abundance of activities and recreation. Dogs of all sizes are welcome for no additional pet fee. They ask that dogs are kept off the furniture and the bedroom. Dogs must be leashed and cleaned up after. 2 dogs may be allowed.

Lincklaen House
79 Albany St
Cazenovia, NY
315-655-3461
cazenovia.com/lincklaen/
A landmark since 1836, this hotel was built as a luxurious stopover for colonial travelers. All rooms are non-smoking. There are no additional pet fees.

Holiday Inn Buffalo-Intl Airport
4600 Genesee Street
Cheektowaga, NY
716-634-6969 (877-270-6405)
Dogs of all sizes are allowed for an additional one time pet fee of $25 per room. Multiple dogs may be allowed.

Holiday Inn Express Hotel and Suites
131 Buell Avenue
Cheektowaga, NY
716-631-8700 (877-270-6405)
One dog of any size is allowed for an additional one time pet fee of $30.

Asa Ransom House
10529 Main Street
Clarence, NY
716-759-2315
Dog only are allowed and of all sizes. There is a $100 refundable deposit and a pet policy to sign at check in. 2 dogs may be allowed.

Best Western Inn of Cobleskill
121 Burgin Dr
Cobleskill, NY
518-234-4321 (800-780-7234)
Dogs are allowed for an additional pet fee of $15 per night per room. Multiple dogs may be allowed.

Super 8 Cobleskill/Howe Caverns
955 E Main St
Cobleskill, NY
518-234-4888 (800-800-8000)
Dogs of all sizes are allowed. There is a $10 one time per pet fee per visit. Reservations are recommended due to limited rooms for pets. Smoking and non-smoking rooms are available for pet rooms. 2 dogs may be allowed.

Staybridge Suites
201 Townley Avenue
Corning, NY
607-936-7800 (877-270-6405)
Dogs up to 60 pounds are allowed for an additional one time pet fee of $75 per room. Multiple dogs may be allowed.

Stiles Motel
9239 Victory Highway
Corning, NY
607-962-5221
There is a $3 per day pet charge.

Holiday Inn Cortland
2 River Street
Cortland, NY
607-756-4431 (877-270-6405)
Dogs up to 50 pounds are allowed for an additional fee of $15 per night per pet. Multiple dogs may be allowed.

Quality Inn
188 Clinton Avenue
Cortland, NY
607-756-5622 (877-424-6423)
Dogs are allowed for an additional one time pet fee of $20 per room. Multiple dogs may be allowed.

Days Inn Danville
1 Commerce Dr
Dansville, NY
585-335-6023 (800-329-7466)
Dogs of all sizes are allowed. There are no additional pet fees. 2 dogs may be allowed.

Best Western Dunkirk and Fredonia
3912 Vineyard Dr
Dunkirk, NY
716-366-7100 (800-780-7234)
Dogs are allowed for an additional pet fee per pet of $10 for the 1st night and $5 for each additional night. Multiple dogs may be allowed.

Comfort Inn
3925 Vineyard Drive
Dunkirk, NY
716-672-4450 (877-424-6423)
Dogs up to 50 pounds are allowed

for an additional fee of $10 per night per pet. 2 dogs may be allowed.

Bend In the Road Guest House
58 Spring Close H
East Hampton, NY
631-324-4592
bendintheroadguesthouse.com/
With a convenient location to the beaches, eateries, and shops, this inn (that also functions as a pottery studio) sits on 22 acres of farmland featuring a driving range for golfers, a private jogging path great for running the pooch, a large lawn area, and a secluded garden with a large swimming pool. Dogs of all sizes are welcome for no additional pet fee. Dogs may not be left alone in the room at any time, and they must be leashed and cleaned up after in common areas. Multiple dogs may be allowed.

The Bassett House Inn
128 Montauk H
East Hampton, NY
631-324-6127
bassetthouseinn.com/
This spacious, country 1830's inn offers 12 individually adorned guest rooms, garden-style grounds, a central location to the village, walking trails, and beaches. Dogs of all sizes are welcome (with prior notice) for an additional $15 per night per pet. Dogs must be well behaved, and leashed and cleaned up after. They may only be left alone in the room for a short time if they will be quiet and the owner is confident in their behavior. 2 dogs may be allowed.

The Mill House Inn
31 N Main Street
East Hampton, NY
631-324-9766
millhouseinn.com
This inn has been recently renovated to allow guests to have a true Long Island lodging experience with great ocean views, gas fireplaces, whirlpool baths, private decks, and the dog friendly suites have heated stone floors. Dogs of all sizes are allowed for an additional $50 per night per pet. Dogs may only be left alone in the suite if they will be quiet and owners are confident in their behavior. Dogs must be under owner's care/control at all times, and please clean up after your pet. Multiple dogs may be allowed.

Holiday Inn
6555 Old Collamer Rd South
East Syracuse, NY
315-437-2761 (877-270-6405)

Two dogs up to 50 pounds, or 1 dog 50 pounds or over, are allowed per room for a one time pet fee of $25 per room. 2 dogs may be allowed.

Motel 6 - Syracuse
6577 Baptist Way
East Syracuse, NY
315-433-1300 (800-466-8356)
One well-behaved family pet per room. Guest must notify front desk upon arrival. Guest is liable for any damages. In consideration of all guests, pets must never be left unattended in the guest rooms.

The Jefferson Inn
3 Jefferson Street
Ellicottville, NY
716-699-5869 (800-577-8451)
thejeffersoninn.com/
A central location to numerous recreational activities, a wide wraparound porch, relaxed ambiance, and a village park a short distance away make this a nice destination for pets and their owners. Dogs of all sizes are allowed in the efficiency units for an additional fee of $10 per night per pet. Dogs must be leashed and cleaned up after, and they may only be left alone in the room if assured they will be quiet, relaxed, and well mannered. Multiple dogs may be allowed.

Residence Inn by Marriott
14 Schuyler Blvd
Fishkill, NY
854-896-5210
Dogs of all sizes are allowed. There is a $75 one time fee and a pet policy to sign at check in. 2 dogs may be allowed.

River Run
882 Main Street
Fleischmanns, NY
845-254-4884
riverrunbedandbreakfast.com/
This large custom built Victorian house sits elevated on 10 acres, features a fun "Retro Suite" (50/60's era), is just a short walk to the village park and a stream, and is central to an array of activities and recreational pursuits. Dogs over a year old of all sizes are welcome during the spring, summer, and fall seasons only, and they must be declared at the time of reservations. Dogs must be friendly, quiet, well behaved, flea free, clean, and current on all vaccinations. There is a $10 per night per pet additional fee, and they ask that you register before bringing in your pet. Feeding mats are provided, but please bring their own food, bedding,

comfort toys, etc. They have poop-n-scoop bags, and ask that dogs be cleaned up after and leashed at all times. Dogs may not be left alone in the room, except while in the inn, and then they must be crated. Multiple dogs may be allowed.

Sheraton La Guardia East Hotel
135-20 39th Ave.
Flushing, NY
718-460-6666 (888-625-5144)
Dogs up to 60 pounds are allowed. There are no additional pet fees. Dogs are not allowed to be left alone in the room.

Inn at Lake Joseph
400 Saint Joseph Road
Forestburgh, NY
845-791-9506
lakejoseph.com
The inn is a romantic 135-year-old Victorian Country Estate on a 250-acre private lake, surrounded by thousands of acres of hardwood forest and wildlife preserve. The Inn provides a variety of summer and winter recreational facilities including the use of their nearby full service health and fitness club. Breakfast is served on the screened-in Veranda allowing you to enjoy the sounds and feel of the lush green forest. When glassed in during winter, you can experience the beauty of a surrounding snowscape. Dogs are welcomed in their Carriage House and Cottage. The inn is located in Forestburgh at Lake Joseph.

Brookside Manor
3728 Route 83
Fredonia, NY
716-672-7721 (800-929-7599)
bbonline.com/ny/brookside/
Built in 1875 with over 6,000 square feet of living space, this Victorian manor sits on 5.5 partially wooded acres with its own spring-fed brook, manicured lawns and gardens, and there is beauty and activities here year round. Dogs of all sizes are welcome for no additional fee with advance registration; when doing so on line they request that you make note in the "special needs" comments that pets will be coming. Dogs must be well mannered, leashed, and cleaned up after. Multiple dogs may be allowed.

Motel 6 - Geneva
485 Hamilton Street
Geneva, NY
315-789-4050 (800-466-8356)
One well-behaved family pet per

room. Guest must notify front desk upon arrival. Guest is liable for any damages. In consideration of all guests, pets must never be left unattended in the guest rooms.

Ramada Geneva Lakefront
41 Lakefront Drive
Geneva, NY
315-789-0400
ramada.com/Ramada/control/home
This lakefront hotel offers a long list of amenities and services. Dogs of all sizes are allowed for an additional fee of $10 per night per pet. Dog may not be left alone in the room at any time, and they must be leashed and cleaned up after. Dogs are not allowed in common areas; they may come through the lobby to the elevators and in the corridors going to the room. 2 dogs may be allowed.

Chateau Motor Lodge
1810 Grand Island Blvd
Grand Island, NY
716-773-2868
There is an $9 per day pet fee.

Holiday Inn
100 Whitehaven Rd
Grand Island, NY
716-773-1111 (877-270-6405)
Dogs of all sizes are allowed for an additional one time pet fee of $25 per room. Multiple dogs may be allowed.

The Trout House Village Resort
9117 Lakeshore Drive
Hague, NY
518-543-6088 (800-368-6088)
trouthouse.com/
This resort, on the shores of Lake George, offers beautiful views of the lake and surrounding Adirondack Mountains, and provides a wide array of activities and recreation, a 9-hole putting green, and rentals for bikes and watercraft. Although dogs are not allowed during the summer months between June 15th and September 15th, the beauty and activities here are year round. One dog is allowed per unit for an additional pet fee of $25 per night. Dogs are not allowed on the bed or the furniture, they must be leashed and cleaned up after, and they may not be left alone in the room. Dogs must be quiet and well mannered.

Comfort Inn and Suites
3615 Commerce Place
Hamburg, NY
716-648-2922 (877-424-6423)
Dogs are allowed for an additional fee of $10 per night per pet. Multiple dogs may be allowed.

Holiday Inn
5440 Camp Road (NY 75)
Hamburg, NY
716-649-0500 (877-270-6405)
Dogs of all sizes are allowed for an additional fee of $15 per night per pet. Multiple dogs may be allowed.

Red Roof Inn - Buffalo Hamburg
5370 Camp Road
Hamburg, NY
716-648-7222 (800-RED-ROOF)
One well-behaved family pet per room. Guest must notify front desk upon arrival. Guest is liable for any damages. In consideration of all guests, pets must never be left unattended in the guest rooms.

Bowen's by the Bays
177 West Montauk Highway
Hampton Bays, NY
631-728-1158 (800-533-3139)
gobowens.com
This lovely resort, located in the heart of the Hamptons, is very pet friendly. It offers individually decorated guest rooms and guest cottages, swimming pool, tennis court, small pond with waterfall and beautiful gardens. Pets are welcome in the guest cottages. Pet fees are $15 per pet/per day and guests are required to abide by the posted pet regulations, i.e. pets must be on leash, owners must clean up after pet, etc. Bowen's is situated on four landscaped acres, and is close to restaurants, shopping, and the North Fork, as well as the charming towns of the Hamptons.

Residence Inn by Marriott
850 Veterans Memorial Highway
Hauppauge, NY
631-724-4188
Dogs of all sizes are allowed. There is a $75 one time fee and a pet policy to sign at check in. Multiple dogs may be allowed.

Sheraton Long Island
110 Motor Parkway
Hauppauge, NY
631-231-1100 (888-625-5144)
Dogs up to 80 pounds are allowed. There are no additional pet fees. Dogs are not allowed to be left alone in the room.

Red Roof Inn - Rochester Henrietta
4820 West Henrietta Road
Henrietta, NY
585-359-1100 (800-RED-ROOF)
One well-behaved family pet per room. Guest must notify front desk

upon arrival. Guest is liable for any damages. In consideration of all guests, pets must never be left unattended in the guest rooms.

Herkimer Motel
100 Marginal Rd
Herkimer, NY
315-866-0490
There are no additional pet fees. Dogs must not be left alone in the rooms.

Residence Inn by Marriott
25 Middle Avenue
Holtsville, NY
631-475-9500
Dogs of all sizes are allowed. There is a $75 one time fee and a pet policy to sign at check in. 2 dogs may be allowed.

Days Inn Hornell
Route 36 & Webb Xing
Hornell, NY
607-324-6222 (800-329-7466)
Dogs of all sizes are allowed. There is a $10 per night pet fee per pet. 2 dogs may be allowed.

Best Western Marshall Manor
3527 Watkins Rd
Horseheads, NY
607-739-3891 (800-780-7234)
Dogs are allowed for an additional fee of $10 per night for 1 pet, and $5 for each additional pet. 2 dogs may be allowed.

Motel 6 - Elmira - Horseheads
4133 Route 17
Horseheads, NY
607-739-2525 (800-466-8356)
One well-behaved family pet per room. Guest must notify front desk upon arrival. Guest is liable for any damages. In consideration of all guests, pets must never be left unattended in the guest rooms.

Hunter Inn
7344 Main Street
Hunter, NY
518-263-3777 (800-270-3992)
hunterinn.com/
In addition to having beautiful vistas of the Catskill Mountains and hundreds of hiking trails, this inn offers a cocktail lounge, a family game room, and an outdoor hot tub. Dogs of all sizes are allowed during the months of May through October only; there is an additional $20 per night per pet fee plus a $50 refundable deposit. Dogs must be well behaved, leashed, and cleaned up after. 2 dogs may be allowed.

Clarion University Hotel and Conference Center
1 Sheraton Drive
Ithaca, NY
607-257-2000 (877-424-6423)
Dogs are allowed for an additional one time pet fee of $20 per room. 2 dogs may be allowed.

Comfort Inn
356 Elmira Road
Ithaca, NY
607-272-0100 (877-424-6423)
Dogs of all sizes are allowed. There is a $25 per stay per room fee and a pet policy to sign at check in. 2 dogs may be allowed.

Econo Lodge
Cayuga Mall
Ithaca, NY
607-257-1400
There is a $10 per day pet charge.

Hampton Inn
337 Elmira Road
Ithaca, NY
607-277-5500
Dogs up to 60 pounds are allowed. There is a pet policy to sign at check in and there are no addition pet fees. 2 dogs may be allowed.

Holiday Inn
222 South Cayuga Street
Ithaca, NY
607-272-1000 (877-270-6405)
Dogs of all sizes are allowed for an additional one time pet fee of $15 per room. Dogs may not be left alone in the room at any time. Multiple dogs may be allowed.

Log Country Inn
South Danby and La Rue Roads
Ithaca, NY
607-589-4771 (800-274-4771)
logtv.com/inn/hispeed.html
Sitting at the edge of a vast state forest in a scenic country setting on 100 wooded acres, this spacious log home features custom made country furniture and rooms with "around the world" themes (there are even "themed" hiking trails), and they are close to wide variety of activities, recreation, and the Ithaca Falls. Dogs of all sizes are welcome for no additional pet fee. Dogs must be well behaved, leashed, and cleaned up after. Puppies must always be crated when left alone in the room, and if the owner's are confident in their dogs behavior (must be quiet), older dogs do not have to be crated. 2 dogs may be allowed.

The William Henry Miller Inn
303 N Aurora Street
Ithaca, NY
607-256-4553 (877-25-MILLER (256-4553))
millerinn.com/
Originally built in 1880 by Cornell University's 1st student of architecture, the house is rich in detail with stained glass windows and woodwork, and it is located near the Ithaca Commons area that is abundant with eateries, shops, theaters, and recreation. There is 1 pet friendly suite in the Carriage House, and dogs of all sizes are welcome for no additional pet fee. They will provide water and food dishes, but they ask that you bring your own pets bedding. Dogs must be leashed, cleaned up after, and they may not be left alone in the room at any time. 2 dogs may be allowed.

Best Western Downtown Jamestown
200 W 3rd Street
Jamestown, NY
716-484-8400 (800-780-7234)
Dogs are allowed for an additional one time fee of $25 per pet. Multiple dogs may be allowed.

Comfort Inn
2800 N Main Street
Jamestown, NY
716-664-5920 (877-424-6423)
Dogs are allowed for an additional one time fee of $15 per pet. Multiple dogs may be allowed.

Red Roof Inn - Jamestown-Falconer
1980 East Main Street
Jamestown, NY
716-665-3670 (800-RED-ROOF)
One well-behaved family pet per room. Guest must notify front desk upon arrival. Guest is liable for any damages. In consideration of all guests, pets must never be left unattended in the guest rooms.

Fourpeaks
Stonehouse Road
Jay, NY
518-524-6726
4peaks.com/home.htm
Fourpeaks sits secluded in a hidden valley at the end of a dirt road, and they offer a variety of accommodations, year round land and water recreation, numerous hiking trails (4 with major destinations), and cabins with full kitchens. The resident pooch here welcomes all friendly canine guests to play, go hiking, running,

swimming, or just kick back at this scenic 700-acre wilderness playground of private forest land, and if they are under voice control and well behaved-no leashes are required. There are no additional pet fees. Dogs must be under owner's control/care at all times. Multiple dogs may be allowed.

Jay Lodge
13112 NY State H 9N
Jay, NY
518-946-7467
Dogs of all sizes are allowed. There are no additional pet fees, and dogs must be on a leash when out. Dogs are not allowed to be left alone in the room. Multiple dogs may be allowed.

La Quinta Inn Johnson City
581 Harry L. Drive
Johnson City, NY
607-770-9333 (800-531-5900)
A dog of any size is allowed. There are no additional pet fees. There is a pet waiver to sign at check in. Dogs are not allowed to be left alone in the rooms, but if you have to go for a short time, a contact number must be left with the front desk.

Red Roof Inn - Binghamton
590 Fairview Street
Johnson City, NY
607-729-8940 (800-RED-ROOF)
One well-behaved family pet per room. Guest must notify front desk upon arrival. Guest is liable for any damages. In consideration of all guests, pets must never be left unattended in the guest rooms.

Holiday Inn
308 N. Comrie Ave
Johnstown, NY
518-762-4686 (877-270-6405)
Dogs of all sizes are allowed for no additional fee. 2 dogs may be allowed.

Trails End Inn
62 Trails End Way
Keene Valley, NY
518-576-9860 (800-281-9860)
trailsendinn.com/
Secluded, but easily accessible, this 1902 mountain lodge offers a large front yard and porches, a barbecue and picnic area, whirlpool tubs, and it is in a great location for numerous year round recreational pursuits. Dogs of all sizes are allowed for an additional $20 per night per pet, and owners are responsible for any pet-incurred damages. There can be 1

large dog or 2 small dogs per room, and please keep them off the furniture and beds. Dogs may only be left alone in the room if assured they will be quiet and they must be crated. Dogs are not allowed in the common areas like the front porch or through the interior halls of the inn; use outer doors or stairs. Outside the inn dogs can be off lead if they are under good voice control, and "doggy towels" are provided for muddy paws. Dogs must be picked up after at all times.

Super 8 Kenmore/Buffalo/Niagara Falls Area
1288 Sheridan Drive
Kenmore, NY
716-876-4020 (800-800-8000)
Dogs of all sizes are allowed. There are no additional pet fees. Pet must be kept in kennel when left alone and not for long periods of time. Smoking and non-smoking rooms are available for pet rooms. 2 dogs may be allowed.

Villa Rosa B&B Inn
121 Highland Street
Kings Park, NY
631-724-4872
thevillarosainn.com/
Built in 1920, this bed and breakfast inn is surrounded by spacious landscaped grounds. Some of the inn's rooms have private baths. This dog-friendly inn offers a fenced dog park area. Guests are welcome to bring their well-behaved dog, but pets must be leashed when in shared areas. There is a $20 per day pet charge. Weekly and monthly rates are available. They also have parking for larger vehicles like motorhomes and trailers.

Holiday Inn
503 Washington Ave
Kingston, NY
845-338-0400 (877-270-6405)
Dogs of all sizes are allowed for an additional fee of $10 per night per pet. Multiple dogs may be allowed.

Lake George Gardens Motel
2107 H 9N
Lake George, NY
518-668-2232
Dogs of all sizes are allowed. There is a $25 refundable deposit per stay and there is a 2 night minimum stay. There are weekly rates available. Dogs may not be left unattended for very long at a time and must be on a leash when out. Multiple dogs may be allowed.

Luzerne Court
508 Lake Ave
Lake Luzerne, NY
518-696-2734
saratoga.org/luzernecourt/
There are no additional pet fees.
Dogs must not be left alone in the rooms.

Art Devline's Olympic
350 Main St
Lake Placid, NY
518-523-3700
artdevlins.com/
There are no additional pet fees.

Comfort Inn
2125 Saranac Avenue/H 86
Lake Placid, NY
518-523-9555 (877-424-6423)
Dogs are allowed for no additional pet fee. Dogs may not be left alone in the room. Multiple dogs may be allowed.

Crowne Plaza Resort & Golf Club
101 Olympic Drive
Lake Placid, NY
518-523-2556 (877-270-6405)
Dogs of all sizes are allowed for an additional fee of $10 per night per pet. Dogs may not be left alone in the room at any time. Multiple dogs may be allowed.

Edge of the Lake Motel
56 Saranac Ave
Lake Placid, NY
518-523-9430
There is a $10.00 per night charge per dog. Dogs are permitted up to 75 pounds. There are no designated smoking or non-smoking rooms.

Fourpeaks - Adirondack Camps & Guest Barns
Stonehouse Road
Lake Placid, NY
518-946-7313 (800-373-8445)
4peaks.com
Looking for a vacation with your dog? Fourpeaks - Adirondack Camps & Guest Barns is an outdoor adventure resort in the dog-friendly High Peaks. 700 acres. Dog-friendly hiking/skiing trails. River swimming.

Hilton
One Mirror Lake Drive
Lake Placid, NY
518-523-4411
Dogs are allowed for an additional one time fee of $25 per pet, and there is a pet agreement to sign at check in. Dogs must be declared at the time of registration, and they may only be left alone in the room for

short periods. 2 dogs may be allowed.

Lake Placid Lodge
Whiteface Inn Rd.
Lake Placid, NY
518-523-2700
lakeplacidlodge.com
There is a $50 one time pet fee. Pets are allowed in the cabins.

Century House Inn
997 New Loudon Road
Latham, NY
518-785-0931
centuryhouse.inter.net/
There is a $15 one time pet fee.

Holiday Inn Express
946 New Loudon Road US 9
Latham, NY
518-783-6161 (877-270-6405)
Dogs of all sizes are allowed for an additional fee of $20 per night per pet. Multiple dogs may be allowed.

Microtel
7 Rensselaer Ave
Latham, NY
518-782-9161
There are no additional pet fees.

Quality Inn
611 Troy-Schenectady RoadH 7
Latham, NY
518-785-5891 (877-424-6423)
Dogs are allowed for an additional one time pet fee of $35 per room. 2 dogs may be allowed.

Residence Inn by Marriott
1 Residence Inn Drive
Latham, NY
518-783-0600
Dogs of all sizes are allowed. There is a $75 one time fee and a pet policy to sign at check in. Multiple dogs may be allowed.

The Century House Hotel
997 New Loudon Road
Latham, NY
518-785-0931 (888-674-6873)
thecenturyhouse.com/
In additional to a complimentary country-style breakfast buffet, this hotel also offers a full service restaurant and bar, an outdoor pool and tennis courts, and an historic nature trail to walk your four legged companion. Dogs of all sizes are allowed for an additional fee of $15 per night per pet. Dogs may only be left alone in the room if they will be quiet, well behaved, and a contact number is left with the front desk. Dogs must be leashed and cleaned

up after. Multiple dogs may be allowed.

Best Western Little Falls Motor Inn
20 Albany St
Little Falls, NY
315-823-4954 (800-780-7234)
Dogs are allowed for a $10 refundable pet deposit per room, and a credit card must be on file. Multiple dogs may be allowed.

BN on 7th North
400 7th North St
Liverpool, NY
315-451-1511
Dogs of all sizes are allowed. There is a $10 per night pet fee per pet. 2 dogs may be allowed.

Knights Inn
430 Electronics Pkwy
Liverpool, NY
315-453-6330 (800-843-5644)
There is a $8 per day pet charge.

The Guest House
408 Debruce Road
Livingston Manor, NY
845-439-4000
Dogs of all sizes are allowed. There is a $10 per night per room additional pet fee. 2 dogs may be allowed.

Comfort Inn
551 S Transit Road
Lockport, NY
716-434-4411 (877-424-6423)
Dogs up to 50 pounds are allowed for an additional fee of $10 per night per pet. 2 dogs may be allowed.

Holiday Inn Lockport
515 South Transit Rd
Lockport, NY
716-434-6151 (877-270-6405)
Dogs of all sizes are allowed for an additional pet fee of $10 per night per room, and there is a pet agreement to sign at check in. 2 dogs may be allowed.

Howard Johnson Hotel
551 Rt. 211 East
Middletown, NY
845-342-5822 (800-446-4656)
Dogs of all sizes are welcome. There are no additional pet fees.

Buttermilk Inn and Spa
220 North Road
Milton, NY
845-795-1310 (877-7-INN-SPA (877-746-6772))
buttermilkfallsinn.com/
This inn, set on 70 acres of meticulously landscaped acres

(affording exceptional hiking), offers lush garden and river views, an extended breakfast buffet, and a number of amenities/services for business or leisure travelers and special events. Dogs of all sizes are allowed in the carriage house only for an additional one time pet fee of $25 plus a $190 refundable deposit. Pets are not allowed in the main house. Dogs must be leashed and cleaned up after, and they may only be left alone for short time periods. 2 dogs may be allowed.

Hither House Cottages
10 Lincoln Road
Montauk, NY
631-668-2714
hitherhouse.com/
This well-kept, scenic retreat offers various sized cottages, is only a mile from the ocean, and they are just minutes from numerous activities, recreation, and eateries. From Memorial Day to October 1st dogs are not allowed on the beaches between the hours of 10 am and 6 pm, but off season pooches are welcome to run off lead if they are under voice control. Dogs of all sizes are allowed for an additional fee of $15 per night, and there is a pet policy to sign at check in. Dogs are welcome in the garden and on the lawn, but it is requested that they be walked off the premises to do their business. They are not allowed on the furniture and with tiled floors they suggest bringing the pets bedding. Dogs must be well behaved, leashed, cleaned up after, and they may be left alone in the cottage only if they will be quiet and the owner is confident in their behavior. 2 dogs may be allowed.

Super 8 Montgomery/Maybrook Area
207 Montgomery Rd
Montgomery, NY
845-457-3143 (800-800-8000)
Dogs of all sizes are allowed. There is a $10 one time per pet fee per visit. Reservations are recommended due to limited rooms for pets. Smoking and non-smoking rooms are available for pet rooms. 2 dogs may be allowed.

Glen Highland Farm
217 Pegg Road
Morris, NY
607-263-5415
glenhighlandfarm.com/
This "Canine County Getaway" sits on 175 picturesque acres complete with ponds, a stream, trails, open meadows and forests, and dogs may explore anywhere on the farm off leash. The farm is home to several dogs but it is also a Border Collie rescue sanctuary that functions as a training/recovery and placement center, and their complete obstacle course is also available to guests and their dogs. There are several mini-activity camps/programs available to help strengthen the bond between dogs and their companions such as "Canine Discovery" to learn about how smart your dog really is, the "Inner Dog" camp for a greater understanding of your dog, or there is even a trainer on staff available to work one on one with guests. The getaway lodging for guests and their canine companions include cottages, cabins, rentable RVs, a few RV spaces, and a camping shelter that has all the amenities on hand for meal prep plus private showers and flush toilets are only a few feet away. There are no additional pet fees. Dogs may not be left alone, they just have to be friendly and have a great time. Multiple dogs may be allowed.

Holiday Inn
1 Holiday Inn Dr
Mount Kisco, NY
914-241-2600 (877-270-6405)
Dogs of all sizes are allowed for an additional one time pet fee of $49 per room. 2 dogs may be allowed.

Emerson Resort and Spa
5340 H 28
Mount Tremper, NY
845-688-2828 (877-688-2828)
emersonplace.com/
Lovingly restored, sitting among tall pines and manicured grounds alongside a stream with Mt. Tremper in the background, this resort has become a premier vacation destination for a variety of reasons. A visitor favorite is the 64 foot silo they have turned into the world's largest Kaleidoscope. Dogs are allowed for an additional fee of $25 per night per pet, and advance notification. Dogs may not be left alone in the room, and they need to be removed for housekeeping. Dogs must be quiet, well behaved, under owner's control, leashed, and cleaned up after at all times. Dogs are not allowed in the pool or food areas, or the General Store. 2 dogs may be allowed.

Doubletree
6701 Buckley Road
N Syracuse, NY
315-457-4000 (800-572-1602)
Dogs up to 60 pounds are allowed. There are no additional pet fees. 2 dogs may be allowed.

Candlewood Suites
20 Overlook Blvd
Nanuet, NY
845-371-4445 (877-270-6405)
Dogs up to 70 pounds is allowed for an additional one time pet fee of $75 per room. 2 dogs may be allowed.

Days Inn Nanuet
367 Rte 59
Nanuet, NY
845-623-4567 (800-329-7466)
Dogs of all sizes are allowed. There is a $10 per night pet fee per pet. 2 dogs may be allowed.

The Vagabond Inn
3300 Sliter Road
Naples, NY
585-554-6271
thevagabondinn.com/
Secluded on a mountain, this 7000 square foot inn offers great views, but they are also home to an American craft gallery, a seasonal outdoor pool, a Japanese garden, lush lawns and grounds, and many other pluses. They offer 2 pet friendly rooms, and dogs of all sizes are welcome for no additional pet fee. Dogs must be well trained, friendly, leashed, and cleaned up after. They may only be left alone in the room for a short time if they will be quiet and owners are confident in their behavior. 2 dogs may be allowed.

LeFevre House
14 Southside Avenue
New Paltz, NY
845-255-4747
lefevrehouse.com/
In addition to offering a spa, and tailor-made services and dining requests for one or many, this 1870's Victorian home also features an International art gallery (many items for sale), and gives access to a variety of scenic trails. Dogs of all sizes are allowed for an additional $75 one time pet fee per pet, and there is a pet waiver to sign at check in. Dogs are not allowed on the furniture and they must be crated when left alone in the room. Dogs must be leashed and cleaned up after at all times. 2 dogs may be allowed.

Residence Inn by Marriott
35 Le Count Place
New Rochelle, NY
914-636-7888

Dogs of all sizes are allowed. There is a $75 one time fee and a pet policy to sign at check in. Multiple dogs may be allowed.

70 Park Avenue Hotel
70 Park Ave
New York, NY
212-973-2400 (877-707-2752)
70parkave.com
This Kimpton boutique hotel is located at Park Avenue and 38th Street. Dogs of all sizes are allowed. There are no additional pet fees.

Embassy Suites Hotel New York
102 North End Avenue
New York, NY
212-945-0100
Dogs of all sizes are allowed. There is a $75 one time pet fee per visit. Dogs are not allowed to be left alone in the room.

Hotel Wales
1295 Madison Avenue
New York, NY
212-876-6000 (866-WALES-HOTEL)
waleshotel.com
This recently renovated Upper East Side hotel close to Central Park offers 88 guestrooms, including 42 suites. There is a $75 per stay pet fee and dogs up to 100 pounds are allowed.

Le Parker Meridien New York
118 West 57th St.
New York, NY
212-245-5000
Dogs of all sizes are allowed. There are no additional pet fees. Dogs are not allowed to be left alone in the room.

Novotel - New York
226 West 52nd Street
New York, NY
212-315-0100
Novotel Hotels welcome a maximum of 2 animals (cats and dogs) per room and never require a fee. Each guest checking in with a pet will be given a Royal Canine/Novotel Pet Welcome Kit.

Regency Hotel
540 Park Avenue
New York, NY
212-759-4100
All well-behaved dogs of any size are welcome. This upscale hotel offers their "Loews Loves Pets" program which includes special pet treats, local dog walking routes, and a list of nearby pet-friendly places to visit. There are no pet fees.

Renaissance New York Hotel
714 7th Avenue
New York, NY
212-765-7676
renaissancehotel.com/NYCRT/
They allow dogs up to about 70 pounds. This hotel is located in Times Square. It is located at the intersection of Broadway and Seventh Avenue. Amenities include room service, an in-room refreshment center, and an exercise/weight room. The hotel lobby is located on the third floor. There is a $65 one time charge for pets.

Ritz-Carlton Central Park
50 Central Park S
New York, NY
212-308-9100
Dogs up to 100 pounds are allowed. There are no additional pet fees. 2 dogs may be allowed.

Sofitel Hotel
45 West 44th Street
New York, NY
212-354-8844
tribecagrand.com
This French hotel overlooks 5th Ave. Amenities include a fitness room. There are no additional pet fees.

Soho Grand Hotel
310 West Broadway
New York, NY
212-965-3000
sohogrand.com/
This hotel is VERY pet-friendly and there are no size restrictions at all for dogs. They are owned by the Hartz Mountain Company which manufactures the 2 in 1 pet products. The hotel is located in the artistic heart of New York's cultural capital SoHo (South of Houston Street), and within an easy walking distance to the surrounding neighborhoods of Tribeca, Greenwich Village, Little Italy and Chinatown. The hotel is also just steps from Wall Street, and only minutes from Midtown Manhattan. Amenities include 24 room service and a fitness center. One of our readers has this to say about the hotel: "This is the most incredibly dog friendly hotel. Bellboys carry dog treats, there is a dog room service menu, doggie day care is provided. It's also one of New York's super chic hotels." There are no pet fees.

Swissotel NY -The Drake

440 Park Avenue
New York, NY
212-421-0900
swissotel.com/brochure/nyc/
Located in Midtown Manhattan, The Drake is just a couple of blocks from several dog-friendly stores and only 5 blocks from Central Park. Amenities include 24 hour room service and a fitness center/spa. No extra pet charge, just sign a pet waiver. Dogs up to about eighty pounds are allowed.

The Muse
130 West 46th Street
New York, NY
212-485-2400 (877-NYC-MUSE)
themusehotel.com
There are no additional pet fees at this pet-friendly Kimpton boutique hotel. They offer a pampered pooch package for an additional fee. 2 dogs may be allowed.

The Regency Hotel
540 Park Avenue
New York, NY
212-759-4100
Dogs of all sizes are allowed. There is a pet policy to sign at check in and there are no additional pet fees. If you leave your pet in the room you must leave a cell number. Multiple dogs may be allowed.

Tribeca Grand Hotel
2 Avenue of the Americas
New York, NY
212-519-6600
tribecagrand.com
This dog-friendly hotel is located just 2 blocks from it's sister hotel, the dog-friendly Soho Grand Hotel. This hotel is located within walking distance of Little Italy, Chinatown, Greenwich Village, and many department stores. Room rates begin at $399 and up. There are no pet fees.

Trump International Hotel & Tower
1 Central Park West
New York, NY
888-448-7867
trumpintl.com/
This luxury hotel allows small dogs only up to 15 pounds are allowed. There is a $250 per visit pet fee.

W New York - Union Square
201 Park Avenue South
New York, NY
212-253-9119
Dogs up to 50 pounds are allowed. There is a $100 one time pet fee per visit and a $25 per night additional pet fee. Dogs are not allowed to be

left alone in the room.

Holiday Inn Express New York City
Fifth Avenue
15 West 45th Street
New York City, NY
212-302-9088 (877-270-6405)
One dog of any size is allowed for no
additional fee; there is a pet
agreement to sign at check in.

Holiday Inn Express Nyc Manhattan
Chelsea Area
232 West 29th Street
New York City, NY
212-695-7200 (877-270-6405)
Quiet dogs of all sizes are allowed
for an additional one time fee of $25
per pet. Multiple dogs may be
allowed.

Quality Inn Finger Lakes Region
125 N Main Street
Newark, NY
315-331-9500 (877-424-6423)
Dogs are allowed for no additional
pet fee with a credit card on file;
there is a $25 refundable deposit if
paying cash. Multiple dogs may be
allowed.

Super 8 Newburgh
1287 Route 300
Newburgh, NY
845-564-5700 (800-800-8000)
Dogs of all sizes are allowed. There
is a $10 per night pet fee per pet.
Smoking and non-smoking rooms
are available for pet rooms. 2 dogs
may be allowed.

Howard Johnson Hotel
454 Main St.
Niagara Falls, NY
716-285-5261 (800-446-4656)
Dogs of all sizes are welcome. There
is a $10 per day pet fee. Dogs are
allowed in all rooms.

Quality Hotel and Suites
240 Rainbow Blvd
Niagara Falls, NY
716-282-1212
Dogs are allowed for an additional
fee of $20 per night per pet. 2 dogs
may be allowed.

Best Western Summit Inn
9500 Niagara Falls Boulevard
Niagara Falls, NY
716-297-5050 (800-780-7234)
Dogs are allowed for an additional
fee of $8 per night per pet. Multiple
dogs may be allowed.

Super 8 Norwich
6067 St Route 12

Norwich, NY
607-336-8880 (800-800-8000)
Dogs of all sizes are allowed. There
are no additional pet fees. Smoking
and non-smoking rooms are
available for pet rooms. 2 dogs may
be allowed.

Quality Inn
6765 H 37
Ogdensburg, NY
315-393-4550 (877-424-6423)
Dogs are allowed for an additional
fee of $10 per night per pet. 2 dogs
may be allowed.

Holiday Inn
5206 State Highway 23
Oneonta, NY
607-433-2250 (877-270-6405)
Dogs up to 60 pounds are allowed
for an additional one time pet fee of
$25 (plus tax) per room. 2 dogs
may be allowed.

Super 8 Oneonta
4973 State Hwy 23 Southside
Oneonta, NY
607-432-9505 (800-800-8000)
Dogs of all sizes are allowed. There
are no additional pet fees. Dogs are
not allowed to be left alone in the
room. Smoking and non-smoking
rooms are available for pet rooms. 2
dogs may be allowed.

Holiday Inn Orangeburg-
Rockland/Bergen Co
329 Route 303
Orangeburg, NY
845-359-7000 (877-270-6405)
Dogs up to 70 pounds are allowed
for no additional fee. 2 dogs may be
allowed.

Tillinghast Manor
7246 S Main Street
Ovid, NY
716-869-3584
This historical 1873 Victorian home
is located in the heart of the Finger
Lakes area, and offers a central
location to several other activities
and recreational pursuits. Dogs of
all sizes are welcome for no
additional pet fee. Dogs must be
quiet, well mannered, leashed, and
cleaned up after. Dogs may only be
left alone in the room if the owner is
confident in their behavior. 2 dogs
may be allowed.

Best Western Lodge on the Green
3171 Canada Rd
Painted Post, NY
607-962-2456 (800-780-7234)
Dogs are allowed for no additional

pet fee. Multiple dogs may be
allowed.

Rufus Tanner House
60 Sagetown Road
Pine City, NY
607-732-0213 (800-360-9259)
rufustanner.com/
Built in 1864 in Greek revival style
and renovated for privacy and
relaxation, this 2.5 acre farmhouse
features a garden hideaway, large
porches and decks, an outdoor hot
tub, and is only minutes from several
other activities, eateries, and plenty
of recreation. Dogs of all sizes are
allowed for no additional pet fees.
Dogs must be leashed, cleaned up
after, and crated when left alone in
the room. 2 dogs may be allowed.

Residence Inn by Marriott
9 Gerhard Road
Plainview, NY
516-433-6200
Dogs of all sizes are allowed. There
is a $75 one time fee per pet and a
pet policy to sign at check in. 2 dogs
may be allowed.

Best Western The Inn at Smithfield
446 Route 3
Plattsburgh, NY
518-561-7750 (800-780-7234)
Dogs are allowed for an additional
one time pet fee of $10 per room.
Multiple dogs may be allowed.

La Quinta Inn Plattsburgh
16 Plaza Boulevard
Plattsburgh, NY
518-562-4000 (800-531-5900)
Dogs of all sizes are allowed. There
are no additional fees. There is a pet
waiver to sign at check in. Dogs must
be attended or removed for
housekeeping. Dogs must be
leashed and cleaned up after.
Multiple dogs may be allowed.

Super 8 Plattsburgh
7129 Route 9 North
Plattsburgh, NY
518-562-8888 (800-800-8000)
Dogs of all sizes are allowed. There
is a $10 per night pet fee per pet.
Reservations are recommended due
to limited rooms for pets. Smoking
and non-smoking rooms are
available for pet rooms. 2 dogs may
be allowed.

Best Western Inn & Conference
Center
2170 South Road
Poughkeepsie, NY
845-462-4600 (800-780-7234)

Dogs are allowed for no additional pet fee with a credit card on file. There is a $50 refundable deposit if paying cash. Dogs may not be left alone in the room. Multiple dogs may be allowed.

Residence Inn by Marriott
2525 South Road
Poughkeepsie, NY
845-463-4343
Dogs of all sizes are welcome. There is a $75 one time fee and a pet policy to sign at check in. Multiple dogs may be allowed.

Super 8 Queensbury/Glen Falls Area
191 Corinth Rd
Queensbury, NY
518-761-9780 (800-800-8000)
Dogs up to 50 pounds are allowed. There is a $30 pet fee per pet for the first night and $10 per night pet fee per pet. Reservations are required with notification about the pet. 2 dogs may be allowed.

WhistleWood Farm
52 Pells Road
Rhinebeck, NY
845-876-6838
whistlewood.com/
Guests can explore the wooded trails and wildflower gardens, sit out on large decks enjoying the views, take in the afternoon desert fare, and more at this retreat. Housebroken dogs of all sizes are allowed for an additional pet fee of $20 per night per pet. Dogs must be quiet, well behaved, leashed and cleaned up after, and crated when left alone in the room. 2 dogs may be allowed.

Holiday Inn Express Hotel & Suites East End
1707 Old Country Rd.
Riverhead, NY
631-548-1000 (877-270-6405)
Dogs up to 60 pounds are allowed for an additional one time fee of $50 per pet. 2 dogs may be allowed.

Clarion Hotel Riverside
120 Main Street E
Rochester, NY
585-546-6400 (877-424-6423)
Dogs are allowed for a $50 refundable pet deposit. 2 dogs may be allowed.

Comfort Inn West
1501 W Ridge Road
Rochester, NY
585-621-5700 (877-424-6423)
Dogs are allowed for an additional pet fee of $10 per night per room.

Multiple dogs may be allowed.

Comfort Suites
2085 Hylan Drive
Rochester, NY
585-334-6620 (877-424-6423)
Dogs up to 50 pounds are allowed for an additional one time pet fee of $75 per room. 2 dogs may be allowed.

Hampton Inn
500 Center Place Drive
Rochester, NY
585-663-6070
Dogs of all sizes are allowed, however there can only be 1 large or 2 medium/small pets per room. There is a pet policy to sign at check in, and there are no additional pet fees.

Holiday Inn Express
2200 Goodman St N
Rochester, NY
585-342-0430 (877-270-6405)
Dogs of all sizes are allowed for an additional one time pet fee of $75 per room 2 dogs may be allowed.

Residence Inn by Marriott
1300 Jefferson Road
Rochester, NY
585-272-8850
Dogs of all sizes are allowed. There is a $75 one time fee and a pet policy to sign at check in. Multiple dogs may be allowed.

Residence Inn by Marriott
500 Paddy Creek Circle
Rochester, NY
585-865-2090
Dogs of all sizes are welcome. There is a $75 one time fee and a pet policy to sign at check in. 2 dogs may be allowed.

Best Western Mill River Manor
173 Sunrise Highway
Rockville Centre, NY
516-678-1300 (800-780-7234)
Dogs are allowed for an additional fee of $15 per night per pet. Multiple dogs may be allowed.

Holiday Inn Express Hotel and Suites
779 Broad Street
Salamanca, NY
716-945-7600 (877-270-6405)
Dogs up to 50 pounds are allowed for an additional one time pet fee of $25 per room. There can be 1 medium/large dog or 2 small dogs per room. 2 dogs may be allowed.

Lake Flower Inn
15 Lake Flower Ave
Saranac Lake, NY
518-891-2310
Management requests that dogs are not left alone in the rooms and that guests clean up after their pets. Dogs are not allowed on the beds.

Lake Side
27 Lake Flower Ave
Saranac Lake, NY
518-891-4333
There are a limited number of pets allowed in the hotel at a time. There are no additional pet fees.

Best Western Park Inn
3291 S Broadway
Saratoga Springs, NY
518-584-2350 (800-780-7234)
Dogs under 50 pounds are allowed for an additional fee of $15 per night per pet; the fee is $20 for dogs over 50 pounds. Multiple dogs may be allowed.

Holiday Inn
232 Broadway Rt 9
Saratoga Springs, NY
518-584-4550 (877-270-6405)
Dogs of all sizes are allowed for no additional fee. A contact number must be left with the front desk if a pet is left alone in the room. Multiple dogs may be allowed.

Super 8 Saratoga Springs
17 Old Gick Rd
Saratoga Springs, NY
518-587-6244 (800-800-8000)
Dogs of all sizes are allowed. There are no additional pet fees. Smoking and non-smoking rooms are available for pet rooms. 2 dogs may be allowed.

Union Gables
55 Union Avenue
Saratoga Springs, NY
518-584-1558 (800-398-1558)
uniongables.com/
This stately Queen Anne-style 100 year old plus residence complete with a large lawn area and big verandas, sits central to several attractions, recreation, eateries and shops. Dogs of all sizes are allowed for a $25 one time additional pet fee per room. Dogs must be quiet, well behaved, leashed, and cleaned up after. Multiple dogs may be allowed.

Fire Island Real Estate Fire Island Pines
P. O. Box 219
Sayville, NY

631-597-7575
pinesharbor.com/
This realty offers vacation homes in the Fire Island Pines area (a premiere gay community), and about 90% of the rentals allow dogs. Special conditions for the pets or deposits and fees, and the location of the rental in question are disclosed at the time of reservations. Dogs must be housetrained, well mannered, leashed, and cleaned up after. 2 dogs may be allowed.

Days Inn Albany/Schenectady
167 Nott Terrace
Schenectady, NY
518-370-3297 (800-329-7466)
Dogs of all sizes are allowed. There is a $10 per night pet fee per pet. 2 dogs may be allowed.

Super 8 Schenectady/Albany Area
3083 Carman Rd
Schenectady, NY
518-355-2190 (800-800-8000)
Dogs of all sizes are allowed. There is a $10 per night pet fee per pet. Reservations are recommended due to limited rooms for pets. Smoking and non-smoking rooms are available for pet rooms. 2 dogs may be allowed.

Holiday Inn Express Hotel and Suites
160 Holiday Way
Schoharie, NY
518-295-6088 (877-270-6405)
One dog of any size is allowed for an additional pet fee of $17 per night per room.

Blue Ridge Motel
Route 9
Schroon Lake, NY
518-532-7521

Starry Night Cabins
37 Fowler Avenue
Schroon Lake, NY
518-532-7907
Dogs of all sizes are allowed. There is a $5 per night per pet fee for a short haired dog, and there is a $10 per night per pet fee for long haired dogs. Dogs are not allowed to be left alone in the room. Multiple dogs may be allowed.

Microtel Inn
1966 Routes 5 an 20
Seneca Falls, NY
318-539-8438 (888-771-7171)
senecafallsmicrotelinn.com/
This inn provides clean comfortable lodging and a central location to several attractions and activities in the Finger Lakes areas. Dogs up to 80 pounds are allowed for an additional pet fee of $15 per night per room. Dogs must be quiet, well mannered, leashed, and cleaned up after at all times. Dogs may only be left alone in the room for a short time, and a contact number must be left with the front desk. Multiple dogs may be allowed.

Super 8 Sidney
4 Mang Drive
Sidney, NY
607-563-8880 (800-800-8000)
Dogs of all sizes are allowed. There is a $10 per night pet fee per pet. Smoking and non-smoking rooms are available for pet rooms. 2 dogs may be allowed.

Bird's Nest
1601 E Genesee St
Skaneateles, NY
315-685-5641
There is a $150.00 refundable pet deposit.

Skaneateles Suites
4114 W Genesee Street
Skaneateles, NY
315-685-7568
Dogs of all sizes are allowed. There is a $35 one time fee per pet and a pet policy to sign at check in. Multiple dogs may be allowed.

The Atlantic
1655 County Road 39
Southampton, NY
631-283-6100
hrhresorts.com/atlantic.htm
This boutique motel sits on 5 groomed acres 3 miles from the ocean, is a premier vacation, special occasion, and event destination, and they offer a variety of land and water recreation on site. Dogs up to 40 pounds are allowed for an additional fee of $40 per night per pet; larger dogs may be allowed at an increased fee. Pets must have current vaccinations for rabies, distemper, and bordetella, and owners must provide documentation if needed. Dogs must be leashed and cleaned up after at all times, and plastic bags are available at the front desk if needed. Please walk your pets on the acres surrounding the property. Dogs may not be left alone in the room at any time. 2 dogs may be allowed.

The Bentley
161 Hill Station Road
Southampton, NY
631-283-6100
hrhresorts.com/bentley.htm
This retreat offers 39 large suites (750 sq. ft.), groomed grounds, an outdoor pool, can accommodate special events, and is only 3 miles from the ocean. Dogs up to 40 pounds are allowed for an additional fee of $40 per night per pet; larger dogs may be allowed at an increased fee. Pets must have current vaccinations for rabies, distemper, and bordetella, and be able to provide documentation if needed. Dogs must be leashed and cleaned up after at all times, and plastic bags are available at the front desk if needed. Please walk your pets on the acres surrounding the property. Dogs may not be left alone in the room at any time. 2 dogs may be allowed.

Mountain House
150 Berkshire Way
Stephentown, NY
800-497-0176
berkshirebb.com/
A spring-fed pond, 50 rolling acres of meadows and woods, walking trails, and a spacious house on the hill with great views of all, make this a popular retreat. Dogs of all sizes are welcome for no additional fees. Dogs must be friendly with other dogs and well mannered. Dogs must be under owner's control and cleaned up after at all times. 2 dogs may be allowed.

Inn at Stone Ridge
Route 209
Stone Ridge, NY
845-687-0736
innatstoneridge.com/
Whether it's by the entire inn as a guest house or by individual rooms, this 18th century Dutch Colonial mansion has a lot to offer, including 150 acres of well manicured lawns and gardens, unspoiled woods, and an apple orchard. Dogs of all sizes are welcome for no additional pet fee. Dogs must be friendly, well trained, leashed and cleaned up after. Dogs may not be left alone unless owners are confident in their behavior. Multiple dogs may be allowed.

Holiday Inn Suffern
#3 Executive Blvd
Suffern, NY
845-357-4800 (877-270-6405)
A dog up to 50 pounds is allowed for an additional one time pet fee of $50. 2 dogs may be allowed.

Wellesley Inn Suffern
17 North Airmont Road

Suffern, NY
845-368-1900 (800-531-5900)
Dogs of all sizes are allowed. There is a $10 one time additional pet fee per room. Dogs may only be left alone in the room if they will be quiet and well behaved. Dogs must be leashed and cleaned up after. Multiple dogs may be allowed.

Candlewood Suites
6550 Baptist Way
Syracuse, NY
315-432-1684 (877-270-6405)
Dogs of all sizes are allowed for an additional one time fee of $25 per pet. Multiple dogs may be allowed.

Candlewood Suites
5414 South Bay Road
Syracuse, NY
315-454-8999 (877-270-6405)
Dogs up to 75 pounds are allowed for an additional one time pet fee of $25 per room. 2 dogs may be allowed.

Comfort Inn
6491 Thompson Road
Syracuse, NY
315-437-0222 (877-424-6423)
Dogs up to 50 pounds are allowed for an additional one time pet fee of $30 per room. Multiple dogs may be allowed.

Comfort Inn Fairgrounds
7010 Interstate Island Road
Syracuse, NY
315-453-0045 (877-424-6423)
Dogs are allowed for an additional one time pet fee of $20 per room. Multiple dogs may be allowed.

Holiday Inn
100 Farrell Rd
Syracuse, NY
315-457-8700 (877-270-6405)
Dogs of all sizes are allowed for an additional one time pet fee of $25 per room. Multiple dogs may be allowed.

Red Roof Inn - Syracuse
6614 North Thompson Road
Syracuse, NY
315-437-3309 (800-RED-ROOF)
One well-behaved family pet per room. Guest must notify front desk upon arrival. Guest is liable for any damages. In consideration of all guests, pets must never be left unattended in the guest rooms.

Residence Inn by Marriott
6420 Yorktown Circle
Syracuse, NY
315-432-4488

Dogs of all sizes are allowed. There is a $75 one time fee and a pet policy to sign at check in. Multiple dogs may be allowed.

Sheraton Syracuse University Hotel & Conference Center
801 University Ave.
Syracuse, NY
315-475-3000 (888-625-5144)
Dogs up to 80 pounds are allowed. There are no additional pet fees. Dogs are not allowed to be left alone in the room.

Circle Court
440 Montcalm St
Ticonderoga, NY
518-585-7660

Microtel
1 Hospitality Centre Way
Tonawanda, NY
716-693-8100 (800-227-6346)
There is a $10 per day additional pet fee.

The Wawbeek on Upper Saranac Lake
553 Hawk Ridge
Tupper Lake, NY
518-359-2656 (800-953-2656)
wawbeek.com/
This mountain inn sits on 40 scenic acres along the shores of the Upper Saranac Lake giving guests a true Adirondack experience and great views, hiking and cross-country opportunities, use of their boats, and Lake Placid's Olympic Village is only a short distance away. Dogs of all sizes are allowed for an additional fee of $25 per night per pet. Dogs must be leashed, cleaned up after, and may be crated when left alone in the room if they will be quiet and comfortable. Multiple dogs may be allowed.

Best Western Gateway Adirondack Inn
175 N Genesee St
Utica, NY
315-732-4121 (800-780-7234)
Dogs are allowed for an additional one time fee of $25 per pet. Multiple dogs may be allowed.

Motel 6 - Utica
150 N Genesee Street
Utica, NY
315-797-8743 (800-466-8356)
One well-behaved family pet per room. Guest must notify front desk upon arrival. Guest is liable for any damages. In consideration of all guests, pets must never be left

unattended in the guest rooms.

Red Roof Inn - Utica
20 Weaver Street
Utica, NY
315-724-7128 (800-RED-ROOF)
One well-behaved family pet per room. Guest must notify front desk upon arrival. Guest is liable for any damages. In consideration of all guests, pets must never be left unattended in the guest rooms.

Super 8 Utica
309 N Genesee St
Utica, NY
315-797-0964 (800-800-8000)
Dogs of all sizes are allowed. There is a $5 per night pet fee per pet. Smoking and non-smoking rooms are available for pet rooms. 2 dogs may be allowed.

Residence Inn by Marriott
4610 Vestal Parkway E
Vestal, NY
607-770-8500
Dogs of all sizes are allowed. There is a $75 one time fee and a pet policy to sign at check in. Multiple dogs may be allowed.

Holiday Inn
4105 Vestal Parkway
Vestal Parkway, NY
607-729-6371 (877-270-6405)
Quiet dogs of all sizes are allowed for an additional one time pet fee of $25 per room. 2 dogs may be allowed.

Hampton Inn
7637 New York St Route 96
Victor, NY
585-924-4400
Dogs of all sizes are allowed. There are no additional pet fees. Dogs are not allowed to be left alone in the room except for short periods. Multiple dogs may be allowed.

Audrey's Farmhouse
2188 Brunswyck Road
Wallkill, NY
845-895-3440 (800-501-3872)
audreysfarmhouse.com/
Sweeping manicured lawns, stately trees, an outdoor pool, Jacuzzi, and sundeck, a central location to an array of other activities, and known to be very doggy friendly, make this 1740's country inn an attractive destination for both owners and their dogs. Pets also like the many hiking trails in the area. Dogs of all sizes are allowed for no additional pet fee. Dogs must be well mannered,

leashed, and cleaned up after. Multiple dogs may be allowed.

Daggett Lake Campsites & Cabins
660 Glen Athol Rd
Warrensburg, NY
518-623-2198
daggettlake.com
Well behaved, leashed pets are welcome in the RV Park and the cabins. There is no additional charge for pets in the campground and a $50 cleaning fee for cabins. Proof of rabies shots are required in the campground and fleas control in the cabins. This campground is home of the "DOG BEACH" where dogs can go off leash if they are under voice control. There are 400 acres with hiking and mountain biking trails, canoe, kayak, and rowboat rentals, and a sandy swim beach for people.

MeadowLark Farm
180 Union Corners Road
Warwick, NY
845-651-4286
meadowlarkfarm.com/
Every season gets its full due at this scenic 1800's English style farm house and there is also a variety of local year round activities and recreational opportunities available. Dogs of all sizes are allowed for an additional fee of $10 per night per pet, but they must be friendly towards other animals as well as humans as there are other pets that live on site. Dogs may not be left alone in the room, and they must be house trained, leashed, and cleaned up after. 2 dogs may be allowed.

Holiday Inn
2468 Nys Rt 414 Mound Road
Waterloo, NY
315-539-5011 (877-270-6405)
Dogs of all sizes are allowed for an additional fee of $10 per night per pet. Multiple dogs may be allowed.

Best Western Carriage House Inn and Conf Cntr
300 Washington St
Watertown, NY
315-782-8000 (800-780-7234)
Dogs are allowed for an additional fee of $15 per night per pet. 2 dogs may be allowed.

Best Western New Baltimore Inn
12600 Route 9 W
West Coxsackie, NY
518-731-8100 (800-780-7234)
Dogs are allowed for an additional fee of $10 per night per pet. Multiple dogs may be allowed.

Red Roof Inn - Long Island
699 Dibblee Drive
Westbury, NY
516-794-2555 (800-RED-ROOF)
One well-behaved family pet per room. Guest must notify front desk upon arrival. Guest is liable for any damages. In consideration of all guests, pets must never be left unattended in the guest rooms.

Residence Inn by Marriott
5 Barker Avenue
White Plains, NY
914-761-7700
Dogs of all sizes are allowed. There is a $75 one time fee and a pet policy to sign at check in. Multiple dogs may be allowed.

Summerfield Suites
101 Corporate Park Drive
White Plains, NY
914-251-9700
Dogs of all sizes are allowed. There is a $150 one time fee per room and a pet policy to sign at check in. Multiple dogs may be allowed.

Willkommen Hof
5367 H 86
Whiteface, NY
518-946-SNOW (7669) (800-541-9119)
willkommenhof.com/
This comfort-minded mountain inn features an outdoor spa and indoor sauna, and its location allows for numerable outdoor year round activities. Dogs of all sizes are allowed for an additional $10 per night per pet plus a $50 refundable security deposit. They must be kenneled when left in the room alone, or they may be put in the inn's outdoor run; kennels can be provided if needed. Dogs are not allowed on the beds or furniture. Dogs must be friendly, well behaved, leashed, and cleaned up after at all times. 2 dogs may be allowed.

Residence Inn by Marriott
100 Maple Road
Williamsville, NY
716-623-6622
Dogs of all sizes are allowed. There is a $75 one time fee and a pet policy to sign at check in. Multiple dogs may be allowed.

Hungry Trout
(on Route 86)
Wilmington, NY
518-946-2217 (800-766-9137)

hungrytrout.com/
Additional $5 per day charge for a pet.

Point Lookout Mountain Inn
7604 H 23
Windham, NY
518-734-3381
pointlookoutinn.com/
This mountain inn is known for quality lodging, dining (inside or out), as a "special occasion" place, and as the inn with the spectacular 5 state view. There is also a wide variety of activities and recreation available here. They have 2 pet friendly rooms available, and dogs must have their own bedding. Dogs may only be left alone in the room if guests are in-house, such as in the lounge or restaurant; dogs must go with owners when they leave the property. There is an additional $25 pet fee per night. Dogs must be well mannered, leashed, and cleaned up after.

Fall Foliage Ski Vacation Rental
Call to Arrange
Woodstock, NY
845-246-6666
waterfallrental.com
This vacation rental is pet-friendly and sleeps 2 to 6 people. There are two bedrooms with separate bathrooms. The house is available for weekends, weeks or monthly.

North Carolina Listings

Motel 6 - Pinehurst - Aberdeen
1408 North Sandhills Boulevard
Aberdeen, NC
910-944-5633 (800-466-8356)
One well-behaved family pet per room. Guest must notify front desk upon arrival. Guest is liable for any damages. In consideration of all guests, pets must never be left unattended in the guest rooms.

Best Western Executive Inn
Albemarle, NC
704-983-6990 (800-780-7234)
Dogs under 40 pounds are allowed for an additional one time fee of $40 per pet; the fee is $100 for dogs over 40 pounds. Multiple dogs may be allowed.

Comfort Inn Asheville Airport
15 Rockwell Road

Arden, NC
828-687-9199 (877-424-6423)
Dogs up to 50 pounds are allowed for an additional pet fee of $15 per night per room. 2 dogs may be allowed.

Asheville Cabins Cottages & More
Call to Arrange
Asheville, NC
828-255-0704
accandm.com
There are five year-round cabins situated on between 1/2 and 25 acres with outdoor hot tubs. Pets are welcome at all cabins with a refundable deposit. Some of the cabins are supplied with dog biscuits.

Asheville Connections
Call to Arrange
Asheville, NC
828-274-6978
ashevilleconnections.com
Many of these cabins, homes and lodges in the mountains have hot tubs and privacy. Many of these cabins allow your dog. There is a fee of $75 per dog if it weighs under 40 pounds. and a $125 fee if it is over 40 pounds. Dogs are not allowed on furniture or beds and must be on a flea program. Dog may not be left alone in the properties.

Best Western of Asheville Biltmore East
501 Tunnel Road
Asheville, NC
828-298-5562 (800-780-7234)
Dogs are allowed for an additional fee of $10 per night per pet. Multiple dogs may be allowed.

Carolina Mornings/Asheville Cabins
Call to Arrange
Asheville, NC
800-770-9055
asheville-cabins.com
This vacation rental company centered in Asheville offers cabins in town and out in the country. They manage over 95 vacation properties that are pet-friendly.

Comfort Suites Biltmore Square Mall
890 Brevard Road
Asheville, NC
828-665-4000 (877-424-6423)
Dogs are allowed for an additional pet fee of $20 per night per room. Multiple dogs may be allowed.

Days Inn Asheville Biltmore East
1435 Tunnel Road
Asheville, NC
828-298-4000 (800-329-7466)
Dogs of all sizes are allowed. There is a $15 per first night pet fee per pet and $5 for each additional night. 2 dogs may be allowed.

Days Inn Asheville Mall
201 Tunnel Rd
Asheville, NC
828-252-4000 (800-329-7466)
Dogs up to 60 pounds are allowed. There is a $15 per first night pet fee per pet and $5 for each additional nights. 2 dogs may be allowed.

Days Inn Asheville Patton Ave
120 Patton Ave
Asheville, NC
828-254-9661 (800-329-7466)
Dogs of all sizes are allowed. There is a $15 per first night pet fee per pet and $5 for each additional night. 2 dogs may be allowed.

Engadine Cabins
2630 Smoky Park Highway
Asheville, NC
828-665-8325 (800-665-8868)
engadinecabins.com
The Cabins At Engadine are situated on a hilltop overlooking the Inn. The cabins are only 20 minutes from one of the best known ski resorts in North Carolina, Cataloochee Ski Resort. Also nearby are whitewater rafting, tubing, horse back riding, and hot air ballooning. The cabins are 15 minutes to downtown Asheville. Both Cabins offer privacy and are self-contained with bedroom, kitchen, living area, bathroom with Hot Tub, and porches with a panoramic view of the Blue Ridge Mountains. The Reese Cabin is a single-bedroom unit and the Alex Andrea is a two-bedroom unit. Children and Pets of any size are welcome. The cabins are both non-smoking.

Holiday Inn - Blue Ridge Parkway
1450 Tunnel Rd
Asheville, NC
828-298-5611 (877-270-6405)
ashevilleholidayinn.com
The Holiday Inn is nestled in the Blue Ridge Mountains and near the area's most popular attractions. There are mountain views and a heated outdoor pool. They have a number of pet friendly rooms for a pet fee of $20 per night. They provide pet walking areas and complimentary treats for dogs.

Holiday Inn Sunspree Resorts
One Holiday Inn Drive
Asheville, NC
828-254-3211 (877-270-6405)
Dogs of all sizes are allowed for an additional one time pet fee of $20 per room. Multiple dogs may be allowed.

Hummingbird Pond
Call to Arrange
Asheville, NC
828-712-3504
hummingbirdpond.com
This dog-friendly vacation rental in the mountains is fifteen minutes from downtown Asheville. It has five bedrooms and 3 baths. There is also a private pond and high speed Internet.

Log Cabin Motor Court
330 Weaverville Highway
Asheville, NC
828-645-6546 (800-295-3392)
cabinlodging.com
There are 18 one or two bedroom log cabins available. There is a $15 per night additional pet fee. Dogs must be crated if left alone in the cabin. Up to 2 dogs are allowed in each cabin.

Motel 6 - Asheville
1415 Tunnel Road
Asheville, NC
828-299-3040 (800-466-8356)
One well-behaved family pet per room. Guest must notify front desk upon arrival. Guest is liable for any damages. In consideration of all guests, pets must never be left unattended in the guest rooms.

Red Roof Inn - Asheville West
16 Crowell Road
Asheville, NC
828-667-9803 (800-RED-ROOF)
One well-behaved family pet per room. Guest must notify front desk upon arrival. Guest is liable for any damages. In consideration of all guests, pets must never be left unattended in the guest rooms.

Residence Inn by Marriott
701 Biltmore Avenue
Asheville, NC
828-281-3361
Dogs of all sizes are allowed. There is a $75 one time fee and a pet policy to sign at check in. Multiple dogs may be allowed.

Sleep Inn West
1918 Old Haywood Road
Asheville, NC
828-670-7600 (877-424-6423)
Dogs are allowed for an additional pet fee of $25 per night per room. 2 dogs may be allowed.

Super 8 Asheville/Biltmore Square Area
9 Wedgefield Rd
Asheville, NC
828-670-8800 (800-800-8000)
Dogs of all sizes are allowed. There is a $15 per night pet fee per pet. Smoking and non-smoking rooms are available for pet rooms. 2 dogs may be allowed.

Super 8 Asheville/East
1329 Tunnel Rd
Asheville, NC
828-298-7952 (800-800-8000)
Dogs of all sizes are allowed. There is a $15 one time per pet fee per visit. Smoking and non-smoking rooms are available for pet rooms. 2 dogs may be allowed.

Atlantis Lodge
123 Salter Path Road
Atlantic Beach, NC
252-726-5168 (800-682-7057)
atlantislodge.com
The Atlantis has 42 units on the ocean, most with efficiency kitchens, dining, living and sleeping areas. All have patios or decks facing the surf. Use of beach chairs, lounges and umbrellas is complimentary. The outdoor pool is not the normal concrete hole, but an environment created within the woods. Great for reading, lounging or floating. They accept dogs for a minimal fee, no matter the size as long as they are well behaved. 2 dogs may be allowed.

Best Western Mountain Lodge at Banner Elk
1615 Tynecastle Highway - Highway 184
Banner Elk, NC
828-898-4571 (800-780-7234)
bestwesternbannerelk.com
The Best Western is located in the "Heart of the High Country" in a mountain setting. The hotel offers a full service restaurant and lounge, conference facilities, picnic areas, guest laundry, game room, and a large outdoor heated pool that is open year round. They have dog treats and a large dog walking area.

Howard Johnson Inn
7568 NC 48
Battleboro, NC
252-977-9595 (800-446-4656)
Dogs of all sizes are welcome. There is a $5 per day pet fee.

Carteret Country Home
299 H 101
Beaufort, NC

252-728-4611
One large dog or 2 small dogs are allowed per room. There is a $15 per night per pet additional fee.

Tea House on Goose Bay
862 Crow Hill Rd.
Beaufort, NC
252-728-7806
teahouseongoosebay.com
This vacation rental cabin allows dogs for a $50 one time additional pet fee.

Days Inn Benson
202 N Honeycutt St
Benson, NC
919-894-2031 (800-329-7466)
Dogs of all sizes are allowed. There is a $7 per night pet fee per pet. 2 dogs may be allowed.

Days Inn Biscoe
531 East Main St
Biscoe, NC
910-428-2525 (800-329-7466)
Dogs of all sizes are allowed. There is a $5 per night pet fee per pet. 2 dogs may be allowed.

Super 8 Black Mountain
101 Flat Creek Rd
Black Mountain, NC
828-669-8076 (800-800-8000)
Dogs of all sizes are allowed. There is a $5 per night pet fee per pet. Smoking and non-smoking rooms are available for pet rooms. 2 dogs may be allowed.

Holiday Inn Express Hotel and Suites
1570 Asheville Hwy
Brevard, NC
828-862-8900 (877-270-6405)
Dogs of all sizes are allowed for an additional one time pet fee of $50 per room. Multiple dogs may be allowed.

Mountain Vista Log Cabins
300 Fernwood Drive
Bryson City, NC
828-508-4391 (888-508-4838)
Dogs of all sizes are allowed. There is a $45 one time additional pet fee per cabin. Multiple dogs may be allowed.

Days Inn Burlington
978 Plantation Dr
Burlington, NC
336-227-3681 (800-329-7466)
Dogs of all sizes are allowed. There is a $10 per night pet fee per pet. 2 dogs may be allowed.

La Quinta Inn Burlington
2444 Maple Ave.
Burlington, NC
336-229-5203 (800-531-5900)
Dogs of all sizes are allowed. There are no additional pet fees. Dogs must be leashed, cleaned up after, and crated or removed for housekeeping. Multiple dogs may be allowed.

Motel 6 - Burlington
2155 Hanford Road
Burlington, NC
336-226-1325 (800-466-8356)
One well-behaved family pet per room. Guest must notify front desk upon arrival. Guest is liable for any damages. In consideration of all guests, pets must never be left unattended in the guest rooms.

Red Roof Inn - Burlington, NC
2133 West Hanford Road
Burlington, NC
336-227-1270 (800-RED-ROOF)
One well-behaved family pet per room. Guest must notify front desk upon arrival. Guest is liable for any damages. In consideration of all guests, pets must never be left unattended in the guest rooms.

Blue Ridge Motel
204 West Blvd
Burnsville, NC
828-682-9100
Dogs of all sizes are allowed. There is a $5 per day per room or $25 per week additional pet fee. Multiple dogs may be allowed.

Mounain View Motel
H 19E
Burnsville, NC
828-682-2115
Dogs of all sizes are allowed. There is a $5 per night per pet fee for small dogs and a $10 per night per pet fee for large dogs. 2 dogs may be allowed.

Apple Blossom Cottage
46 Drawspring Road
Candler, NC
828-255-0704
Dogs of all sizes are allowed. There is a $100 refundable pet deposit and pets must be flea protected. Multiple dogs may be allowed.

Days Inn Asheville West
2551 Smoky Park Hwy
Candler, NC
828-667-9321 (800-329-7466)
Dogs of all sizes are allowed. There is a $5 per night pet fee per pet. 2

dogs may be allowed.

Suzanne's Farm and Gardens
31 Toms Road
Candler, NC
828-670-5248
Well behaved dogs of all sizes are
allowed. There are no additional pet
fees. Dogs are not allowed on the
beds. Multiple dogs may be allowed.

United Beach Vacations
1001 North Lake Park Blvd.
Carolina Beach, NC
800-334-5806
pleasureislandholiday.com
This vacation rental company has
many pet-friendly vacation rentals in
the Carolina Beach area. Rentals
range in size from 2 to 5 bedrooms.

Best Western Cary Inn & Extended
Stay
1722 Walnut Street
Cary, NC
919-481-1200 (800-780-7234)
Dogs are allowed for an additional
one time fee of $125 per pet. 2 dogs
may be allowed.

Comfort Suites
350 Ashville Avenue
Cary, NC
919-852-4318 (877-424-6423)
Dogs up to 20 pounds are allowed
for an additional one time pet fee of
$50 per room; the fee is $75 for dogs
over 20 pounds, and a 2nd pet (any
size) is an additional one time fee of
$25. 2 dogs may be allowed.

La Quinta Inn & Suites Raleigh Cary
191 Crescent Commons
Cary, NC
919-851-2850 (800-531-5900)
Dogs of all sizes are allowed. There
are no additional pet fees. Dogs
must be leashed, cleaned up after,
and crated when left alone in the
room. Multiple dogs may be allowed.

Red Roof Inn - Raleigh Southwest -
Cary
1800 Walnut Street
Cary, NC
919-469-3400 (800-RED-ROOF)
One well-behaved family pet per
room. Guest must notify front desk
upon arrival. Guest is liable for any
damages. In consideration of all
guests, pets must never be left
unattended in the guest rooms.

Residence Inn by Marriott
2900 Regency Parkway
Cary, NC
919-467-4080

Dogs of all sizes are allowed. There
is a $75 one time fee and a pet
policy to sign at check in. 2 dogs
may be allowed.

TownePlace Suites Raleigh
Cary/Weston Pkwy
120 Sage Commons Way
Cary, NC
919-678-0005
Dogs of all sizes are allowed. There
is a $75 one time pet fee per visit. 2
dogs may be allowed.

Holiday Inn
1301 N Fordham Blvd
Chapel Hill, NC
919-929-2171 (877-270-6405)
Dogs of all sizes are allowed for an
additional one time pet fee of $35
per room. 2 dogs may be allowed.

Candlewood Suites
5840 Westpark Drive
Charlotte, NC
704-529-7500 (877-270-6405)
Dogs up to 60 pounds are allowed
for an additional one time fee of $75
per pet. 2 dogs may be allowed.

Candlewood Suites
8812 University East Drive
Charlotte, NC
704-598-9863 (877-270-6405)
Dogs of all sizes are allowed for an
additional one time fee of $75 per
pet. 2 dogs may be allowed.

Comfort Inn Executive Park
5822 Westpark Drive
Charlotte, NC
704-525-2626 (877-424-6423)
Dogs are allowed for an additional
one time fee of $25 per pet. Multiple
dogs may be allowed.

Comfort Inn UNCC
5111 Equipment Drive
Charlotte, NC
704-598-0007 (877-424-6423)
Well groomed dogs are allowed for
an additional fee of $20 (plus tax)
per night per pet. 2 dogs may be
allowed.

Comfort Suites
7735 University City Blvd
Charlotte, NC
704-547-0049 (877-424-6423)
Dogs are allowed for an additional
one time pet fee of $25 per room.
Multiple dogs may be allowed.

Crowne Plaza Hotel Crowne Plaza
Charlotte
201 South Mcdowell St.
Charlotte, NC

704-372-7550 (877-270-6405)
Dogs of all sizes are allowed for an
additional one time pet fee of $50 per
room. Multiple dogs may be allowed.

Days Inn Charlotte Central
601 N Tryon
Charlotte, NC
704-333-4733 (800-329-7466)
Dogs of all sizes are allowed. There
is a $10 per night pet fee per pet.
Reservations are recommended due
to limited rooms for pets. 2 dogs may
be allowed.

Days Inn Charlotte North
1408 W Sugar Creek Rd
Charlotte, NC
704-597-8110 (800-329-7466)
Dogs of all sizes are allowed. There
is a $5.38 per night pet fee per pet. 2
dogs may be allowed.

Drury Inn & Suites
415 West W.T. Harris Blvd.
Charlotte, NC
704-593-0700 (800-378-7946)
Dogs of all sizes are permitted. Pets
are not allowed in the breakfast area
of the hotel. Pets are not to be left
unattended, and each guest must
assume liability for damage of
property or other guest complaints.
There is a limit of one pet per room.

Holiday Inn
321 W Woodlawn Road
Charlotte, NC
704-523-1400 (877-270-6405)
Dogs of all sizes are allowed for an
additional one time pet fee of $35 per
room. Multiple dogs may be allowed.

La Quinta Inn & Suites Charlotte
Airport South
4900 S. Tryon Street
Charlotte, NC
704-523-5599 (800-531-5900)
Dogs of all sizes are allowed. There
are no additional pet fees. Dogs
must be leashed and cleaned up
after. Dogs may not be left
unattended unless they will be quiet,
well behaved, and a contact number
left with the front desk. Multiple dogs
may be allowed.

La Quinta Inn Charlotte Airport
3100 Queen City Drive
Charlotte, NC
704-393-5306 (800-531-5900)
Dogs of all sizes are allowed. There
are no additional pet fees. Dogs
must be leashed, cleaned up after,
and the Do Not Disturb sign left on
the door if there is a pet alone in the
room. Multiple dogs may be allowed.

Motel 6 - Charlotte Coliseum
131 Red Roof Drive
Charlotte, NC
704-529-1020 (800-466-8356)
One well-behaved family pet per room. Guest must notify front desk upon arrival. Guest is liable for any damages. In consideration of all guests, pets must never be left unattended in the guest rooms.

Motel 6 - Charlotte East University
5116 North I-85
Charlotte, NC
704-596-8222 (800-466-8356)
One well-behaved family pet per room. Guest must notify front desk upon arrival. Guest is liable for any damages. In consideration of all guests, pets must never be left unattended in the guest rooms.

Quality Inn
440 Griffith Road
Charlotte, NC
704-525-0747 (877-424-6423)
Dogs are allowed for an additional one time pet fee of $35 per room. 2 dogs may be allowed.

Red Roof Inn - Charlotte - Huntersville
13830 Statesville Road
Charlotte, NC
704-875-7880 (800-RED-ROOF)
One well-behaved family pet per room. Guest must notify front desk upon arrival. Guest is liable for any damages. In consideration of all guests, pets must never be left unattended in the guest rooms.

Red Roof Inn - Charlotte Airport (West)
3300 Queen City Drive
Charlotte, NC
704-392-2316 (800-RED-ROOF)
One well-behaved family pet per room. Guest must notify front desk upon arrival. Guest is liable for any damages. In consideration of all guests, pets must never be left unattended in the guest rooms.

Residence Inn by Marriott
5115 Piper Station Drive
Charlotte, NC
704-319-3900
One dog up to 85 pounds is allowed. There is a $75 one time fee and a pet policy to sign at check in. Per city ordinance, no Rottweilers or Pit Bulls are allowed.

Residence Inn by Marriott
6030 J.A. Jones Drive

Charlotte, NC
704-554-7001
Dogs of all sizes are allowed. There is a $75 one time fee and a pet policy to sign at check in. Multiple dogs may be allowed.

Residence Inn by Marriott
8503 N Tryon Street
Charlotte, NC
704-547-1122
Dogs of all sizes are allowed. There is a $75 one time fee and a pet policy to sign at check in. Multiple dogs may be allowed.

Residence Inn by Marriott
404 S Mint Street
Charlotte, NC
704-340-4000
Dogs of all sizes are allowed. There is a $75 one time fee and a pet policy to sign at check in. Multiple dogs may be allowed.

Sheraton Charlotte Airport Hotel
3315 Scott Futkell Dr.
Charlotte, NC
704-392-1200 (888-625-5144)
Dogs of all sizes are allowed. There are no additional pet fees.

Staybridge Suites
15735 John J Delaney Drive
Charlotte, NC
704-248-5000 (877-270-6405)
Dogs of all sizes are allowed for an additional one time pet fee per room of $100 for 1 or 2 nights; 3 or more nights is $200. Multiple dogs may be allowed.

Staybridge Suites
7924 Forest Pine Drive
Charlotte, NC
704-527-6767 (877-270-6405)
Dogs of all sizes are allowed for an additional one time pet fee of $100 per room. Multiple dogs may be allowed.

Studio 6 - Charlotte Airport
3420 Queen City Drive
Charlotte, NC
704-394-4993 (800-466-8356)
One well-behaved family pet per room. Guest must notify front desk upon arrival. Guest is liable for any damages. In consideration of all guests, pets must never be left unattended in the guest rooms.

Summerfield Suites
4920 S Tryon Street
Charlotte, NC
704-525-2600
Dogs of all sizes are allowed. There

is a $75 one time per room additional pet fee. Pet rooms are located on the first floor. 2 dogs may be allowed.

Super 8 Charlotte/Sunset Road
4930 Sunset Road
Charlotte, NC
704-598-7710 (800-800-8000)
Dogs of all sizes are allowed. There is a $10 per night pet fee per pet. Smoking and non-smoking rooms are available for pet rooms. 2 dogs may be allowed.

The Westin Charlotte
601 South College St.
Charlotte, NC
704-375-2600 (888-625-5144)
Dogs up to 50 pounds are allowed for no additional pet fee. A contact number must be left with the front desk if a pet is in the room alone.

TownePlace Suites Charlotte Arrowood
7805 Forest Point Blvd
Charlotte, NC
704-227-2000
Dogs of all sizes are allowed. There is a $75 one time pet fee per visit. 2 dogs may be allowed.

TownePlace Suites Charlotte University Research Park
8710 Research Drive
Charlotte, NC
704-548-0388
Dogs of all sizes are allowed. There is a $75 one time pet fee per visit. 2 dogs may be allowed.

Days Inn Concord
5125 Davidson Hwy
Concord, NC
704-786-9121 (800-329-7466)
Dogs of all sizes are allowed. There is a $10 per night pet fee per pet. 2 dogs may be allowed.

Super 8 Concord
1601 US 29 North
Concord, NC
704-786-5181 (800-800-8000)
Dogs of all sizes are allowed. There is a $1 per pound fee per pet. Smoking and non-smoking rooms are available for pet rooms. 2 dogs may be allowed.

Twiddy & Company Realtors
Call to Arrange
Corolla, NC
252-457-1100 (866-457-1190)
twiddy.com
Over 150 pet-friendly homes are available for rent in Corolla and Duck on the North Carolina Outer Banks.

There are no additional pet fees.

Paramount Destinations
Call to Arrange
Corolla and Duck, NC
866-753-3045
paramountdestinations.com
This vacation home rental
management company has many
dog-friendly rentals in the Corolla
and Duck areas. A $100 or more
non-refundable pet fee is charged.
Other pets beside dogs require
special homeowner approval. 2 dogs
may be allowed.

Outer Banks Blue Realty
Call to Arrange
Duck, NC
888-623-2583
outerbanksblue.com
This realtor has a large number of
pet-friendly vacation rentals in the
North Carolina Outer Banks areas of
Duck, Kill Devil Hills, Nags Head and
Corolla. Call them for more
information.

www.weloveobx.com
Beach Vacation Rental Homes
Duck, NC
252-261-7911
weloveobx.com
Three vacation rentals, with 4 to 6
bedrooms each, are located near the
beach. Dogs are welcome to join you
in these rentals.

The Ramada Inn
1011 E Cumberland Street
Dunn, NC
910-892-8010
Dogs of all sizes are allowed. There
is a $15 per night per pet additional
fee and they state this amount is
flexible depending on how long and
type of dog. Multiple dogs may be
allowed.

Best Western Skyland Inn
5400 US Hwy 70 West
Durham, NC
919-383-2508 (800-780-7234)
Dogs are allowed for an additional
fee of $10 per night per pet. Multiple
dogs may be allowed.

Candlewood Suites
1818 E Highway 54
Durham, NC
919-484-9922 (877-270-6405)
One dog of any size is allowed for an
additional pet fee of $75 for 1 to 14
days, and 15 or more days is $125.

Comfort Inn University
3508 Moriah Road

Durham, NC
919-490-4949 (877-424-6423)
Dogs up to 60 pounds are allowed
for no additional pet fee unless a
pet amenity kit is requested for $49
per pet. Multiple dogs may be
allowed.

Holiday Inn Express Durham
2516 Guess Road
Durham, NC
919-313-3244 (877-270-6405)
Dogs up to 50 pounds are allowed
for an additional fee of $10 per night
per pet. Multiple dogs may be
allowed.

Holiday Inn Express Hotel & Suites
Research Triangle Park
4912 South Miami Blvd
Durham, NC
919-474-9800 (877-270-6405)
Dogs up to 50 pounds are allowed
for an additional fee of $25 per night
per pet. 2 dogs may be allowed.

La Quinta Inn & Suites Durham
Chapel Hill
4414 Durham Chapel Hill Blvd.
Durham, NC
919-401-9660 (800-531-5900)
Dogs of all sizes are allowed. There
are no additional pet fees. Dogs
must be leashed and cleaned up
after. Dogs may not be left
unattended, and they are not
allowed in the lobby or the pool
area. Multiple dogs may be allowed.

Red Roof Inn - Chapel Hill
5623 Durham-Chapel Hill Boulevard
Durham, NC
919-489-9421 (800-RED-ROOF)
One well-behaved family pet per
room. Guest must notify front desk
upon arrival. Guest is liable for any
damages. In consideration of all
guests, pets must never be left
unattended in the guest rooms.

Red Roof Inn - Durham - Duke
University Medical Center
1915 North Pointe Drive
Durham, NC
919-471-9882 (800-RED-ROOF)
One well-behaved family pet per
room. Guest must notify front desk
upon arrival. Guest is liable for any
damages. In consideration of all
guests, pets must never be left
unattended in the guest rooms.

Red Roof Inn - Durham Triangle
Park
4405 APEX Highway 55 East
Durham, NC
919-361-1950 (800-RED-ROOF)

One well-behaved family pet per
room. Guest must notify front desk
upon arrival. Guest is liable for any
damages. In consideration of all
guests, pets must never be left
unattended in the guest rooms.

Residence Inn by Marriott
201 Residence Inn Blvd
Durham, NC
919-361-1266
Dogs of all sizes are welcome. There
is a $75 one time fee and a pet
policy to sign at check in. Multiple
dogs may be allowed.

Sleep Inn
5208 New Page Road
Durham, NC
919-993-3393 (877-424-6423)
A dog up to 60 pounds is allowed for
no additional pet fee.

Super 8 Durham/University Area
2337 Guess Rd
Durham, NC
919-286-7746 (800-800-8000)
Dogs of all sizes are allowed. There
is a $6 per night pet fee per pet.
Smoking and non-smoking rooms
are available for pet rooms. 2 dogs
may be allowed.

Days Inn Elizabeth City
308 South Hughes Blvd
Elizabeth City, NC
252-335-4316 (800-329-7466)
Dogs of all sizes are allowed. There
is a $10 per night pet fee per pet. 2
dogs may be allowed.

Quality Inn
522 S Hughes Blvd
Elizabeth City, NC
252-338-3951 (877-424-6423)
Dogs are allowed for an additional
one time pet fee of $25 per room for
the first night, and $10 for each
additional night. Multiple dogs may
be allowed.

Crystal Coast Vacation Rentals!
Call To Arrange
Emerald Isle, NC
888-258-9287
bluewatergmac.com
Many of these vacation home rentals
on the Crystal Coast are pet-friendly.
Contact them for more information or
the make reservations.

Best Western Fayetteville-Ft Bragg
2910 Sigman St
Fayetteville, NC
910-485-0520 (800-780-7234)
Dogs are allowed for an additional
fee of $15 per pet for each 1 to 3

nights stay. Multiple dogs may be allowed.

Comfort Inn
1957 Cedar Creek Road
Fayetteville, NC
910-323-8333 (877-424-6423)
Dogs are allowed for an additional fee of $10 per night per pet. Multiple dogs may be allowed.

Comfort Inn Cross Creek
1922 Skibo Road
Fayetteville, NC
910-867-1777 (877-424-6423)
Dogs up to 50 pounds are allowed for an additional one time pet fee of $49 per room. 2 dogs may be allowed.

Days Inn Fayetteville East of Ft Bragg
333 Person St
Fayetteville, NC
910-483-0431 (800-329-7466)
Dogs of all sizes are allowed. There is a $15 per night pet fee per pet. 2 dogs may be allowed.

Holiday Inn
1944 Cedar Creek Rd
Fayetteville, NC
910-323-1600 (877-270-6405)
Dogs of all sizes are allowed for an additional one time pet fee of $25 per room. Multiple dogs may be allowed.

Motel 6 - Fayetteville
2076 Cedar Creek Road
Fayetteville, NC
910-485-8122 (800-466-8356)
One well-behaved family pet per room. Guest must notify front desk upon arrival. Guest is liable for any damages. In consideration of all guests, pets must never be left unattended in the guest rooms.

Red Roof Inn - Fayetteville, NC
1569 Jim Johnson Road
Fayetteville, NC
910-321-1460 (800-RED-ROOF)
One well-behaved family pet per room. Guest must notify front desk upon arrival. Guest is liable for any damages. In consideration of all guests, pets must never be left unattended in the guest rooms.

Days Inn Asheville Airport
183 Underwood Rd
Fletcher, NC
828-684-2281 (800-329-7466)
Dogs of all sizes are allowed. There is a $25 one time per pet fee per visit. 2 dogs may be allowed.

Holiday Inn
550 Airport Road
Fletcher, NC
828-684-1213 (877-270-6405)
Dogs of all sizes are allowed for an additional one time pet fee of $50 per room. Multiple dogs may be allowed.

Days Inn Franklin
1320 East Main St
Franklin, NC
828-524-6491 (800-329-7466)
Dogs of all sizes are allowed. There is a $15 per three nights pet fee per pet. 2 dogs may be allowed.

Carambola Inn Bed and Breakfast
7155 Sunset Lake Rd
Fuquay Varina, NC
919-552-3091
This B&B has a small fenced in area and trails to walk dog. It is located about 12 miles south of Raleigh.

Sleep Inn
105 Commerce Parkway
Garner, NC
919-772-7771 (877-424-6423)
Dogs are allowed for an additional one time fee of $25 per pet. 2 dogs may be allowed.

Holiday Inn Express Gastonia
1911 Broadcast Drive
Gastonia, NC
704-884-3300 (877-270-6405)
Dogs of all sizes are allowed for an additional fee of $10 per night per pet. Dogs may not be left alone in the room at any time. Multiple dogs may be allowed.

Motel 6 - Gastonia
1721 Broadcast Street
Gastonia, NC
704-868-4900 (800-466-8356)
One well-behaved family pet per room. Guest must notify front desk upon arrival. Guest is liable for any damages. In consideration of all guests, pets must never be left unattended in the guest rooms.

Mountain View Lodge & Cabins
Blue Ridge Parkway Mile Post 256
Glendale Springs, NC
336-982-2233 (800-903-6811)
mtnviewlodge.com
Vacation with your pet at this retreat on the Blue Ridge Parkway in the northern mountains of North Carolina. Trails, grassy lawn for romping, nearby pond for swimming. 1-2 bedroom cabins with kitchenettes, full bathrooms and

porches. There is no size limit for dogs.

Best Western Goldsboro Inn
801 Hwy 70 Bypass E
Goldsboro, NC
919-735-7911 (800-780-7234)
Dogs are allowed for an additional pet fee of $10 per night per room. Multiple dogs may be allowed.

Days Inn Goldsboro
2000 Wayne Memorial Dr
Goldsboro, NC
919-734-9471 (800-329-7466)
Dogs of all sizes are allowed. There is a $5 per night pet fee per pet. 2 dogs may be allowed.

Holiday Inn Express
909 N Spence Ave
Goldsboro, NC
919-751-1999 (877-270-6405)
Dogs of all sizes are allowed for an additional one time pet fee of $20 per room. 2 dogs may be allowed.

Candlewood Suites
7623 Thorndike Rd
Greensboro, NC
336-454-0078 (877-270-6405)
Dogs of all sizes are allowed for an additional one time fee of $75 per pet. 2 dogs may be allowed.

Clarion Hotel Greensboro Airport
415 Swing Road
Greensboro, NC
336-299-7650 (877-424-6423)
Dogs are allowed for an additional one time pet fee of $50 per room. 2 dogs may be allowed.

Days Inn Greensboro Airport
501 S Regional Rd
Greensboro, NC
336-668-0476 (800-329-7466)
Dogs of all sizes are allowed. There is a $25 one time per pet fee per visit. 2 dogs may be allowed.

Drury Inn & Suites
3220 High Point Road
Greensboro, NC
336-856-9696 (800-378-7946)
Dogs of all sizes are permitted. Pets are not allowed in the breakfast area of the hotel. Pets are not to be left unattended, and each guest must assume liability for damage of property or other guest complaints. There is a limit of one pet per room.

La Quinta Inn & Suites Greensboro
1201 Lanada Road
Greensboro, NC
336-316-0100 (800-531-5900)

Dogs of all sizes are allowed. There are no additional pet fees. Dogs may not be left unattended, and they must be leashed and cleaned up after. Multiple dogs may be allowed.

Motel 6 - Greensboro Airport
605 South Regional Road
Greensboro, NC
336-668-2085 (800-466-8356)
One well-behaved family pet per room. Guest must notify front desk upon arrival. Guest is liable for any damages. In consideration of all guests, pets must never be left unattended in the guest rooms.

Motel 6 - Greensboro South
831 Greenhaven Drive
Greensboro, NC
336-854-0993 (800-466-8356)
One well-behaved family pet per room. Guest must notify front desk upon arrival. Guest is liable for any damages. In consideration of all guests, pets must never be left unattended in the guest rooms.

Red Roof Inn - Greensboro Airport
615 Regional Road South
Greensboro, NC
336-271-2636 (800-RED-ROOF)
One well-behaved family pet per room. Guest must notify front desk upon arrival. Guest is liable for any damages. In consideration of all guests, pets must never be left unattended in the guest rooms.

Red Roof Inn - Greensboro Coliseum
2101 West Meadowview Road
Greensboro, NC
336-852-6560 (800-RED-ROOF)
One well-behaved family pet per room. Guest must notify front desk upon arrival. Guest is liable for any damages. In consideration of all guests, pets must never be left unattended in the guest rooms.

Residence Inn by Marriott
2000 Veasley Street
Greensboro, NC
336-294-8600
Dogs of all sizes are allowed. There is a $75 one time fee and a pet policy to sign at check in. Multiple dogs may be allowed.

Motel 6 - Greenville
301 Southeast Greenville Boulevard
Greenville, NC
252-756-2792 (800-466-8356)
One well-behaved family pet per room. Guest must notify front desk upon arrival. Guest is liable for any damages. In consideration of all

guests, pets must never be left unattended in the guest rooms.

Comfort Inn
206 Mitchell Drive
Hendersonville, NC
828-693-8800 (877-424-6423)
Dogs are allowed for an additional pet fee of $10 per night per room. Multiple dogs may be allowed.

Red Roof Inn - Hendersonville, NC
240 Mitchelle Drive
Hendersonville, NC
828-697-1223 (800-RED-ROOF)
One well-behaved family pet per room. Guest must notify front desk upon arrival. Guest is liable for any damages. In consideration of all guests, pets must never be left unattended in the guest rooms.

Holiday Inn Express
2250 Highway 70 SE
Hickory, NC
828-328-2081 (877-270-6405)
Dogs up to 70 pounds are allowed for an additional one time pet fee of $35 per room. 2 dogs may be allowed.

Red Roof Inn - Hickory
1184 Lenoir Rhyne Boulevard
Hickory, NC
828-323-1500 (800-RED-ROOF)
One well-behaved family pet per room. Guest must notify front desk upon arrival. Guest is liable for any damages. In consideration of all guests, pets must never be left unattended in the guest rooms.

Radisson Hotel High Point
135 South Main Street
High Point, NC
336-889-8888
Dogs of all sizes are allowed. There is a $50 one time additional pet fee.

Hampton Inn
474 Western Blvd
Jacksonville, NC
910-347-6500
Dogs of all sizes are allowed. There are no additional pet fees. Kennel dog for housekeeping. Multiple dogs may be allowed.

Super 8 Motel - Jacksonville
2149 N. Marine Blvd.
Jacksonville, NC
910-455-6888 (800-800-8000)
innworks.com/jacksonville
There is a $10 per stay additional pet fee. Up to three dogs are permitted in each room. The hotel allows a free 8 minute long distance

call each night and offers a free continental breakfast. There is a pool and a laundry. US Hwy 17, 1/2 mile North of Western Blvd.

Comfort Inn
1633 Winston Road
Jonesville, NC
336-835-9400 (877-424-6423)
Dogs are allowed for an additional fee of $10 per night per pet. 2 dogs may be allowed.

Holiday Inn Express
I-77 and US 67 Exit 82
Jonesville, NC
336-835-6000 (877-270-6405)
Dogs of all sizes are allowed for an additional fee of $10 per night per pet. 2 dogs may be allowed.

MainStay Suites
3200 Cloverleaf Parkway
Kannapolis, NC
704-788-2140
Dogs are allowed for an additional one time pet fee of $35 per room. Multiple dogs may be allowed.

Days Inn Kenly
1139 Johnston Pkwy
Kenly, NC
919-284-3400 (800-329-7466)
Dogs of all sizes are allowed. There is a $10 per night pet fee per pet. 2 dogs may be allowed.

Joe Lamb Jr. & Associates
5101 N. Croatan Hwy
Kitty Hawk, NC
252-261-4444 (800-552-6257)
joelambjr.com
This company manages over 75 pet friendly vacation homes ranging in size from 3 to 7 bedrooms.

Hampton Inn
115 Hampton Circle
Laurinburg, NC
910-277-1516
Dogs up to 50 pounds are allowed. There is a pet policy to sign at check in and there are no additional pet fees. There are only 2 non-smoking pet rooms available, and dogs are not allowed in the lobby between 6 & 10 AM. 2 dogs may be allowed.

Days Inn Lenoir
206 Blowing Rock Blvd
Lenoir, NC
828-754-0731 (800-329-7466)
Dogs of all sizes are allowed. There is a $5 per night pet fee per pet. 2 dogs may be allowed.

Days Inn Lincolnton

614 Clark Drive
Lincolnton, NC
704-735-8271 (800-329-7466)
Dogs of all sizes are allowed. There is a $10 per night pet fee per pet. 2 dogs may be allowed.

Best Western Inn at Lumberton
201 Jackson Ct
Lumberton, NC
910-618-9799 (800-780-7234)
Dogs are allowed for an additional fee of $10 per night per pet. Multiple dogs may be allowed.

Days Inn Lumberton Outlet Mall
3030 N Roberts Ave
Lumberton, NC
910-738-6401 (800-329-7466)
Dogs of all sizes are allowed. There is a $10 per night pet fee per pet. 2 dogs may be allowed.

Motel 6 - Lumberton
2361 Lackey Road
Lumberton, NC
910-738-2410 (800-466-8356)
One well-behaved family pet per room. Guest must notify front desk upon arrival. Guest is liable for any damages. In consideration of all guests, pets must never be left unattended in the guest rooms.

Quality Inn and Suites
3608 Kahn Drive
Lumberton, NC
910-738-8261 (877-424-6423)
Dogs are allowed for an additional pet fee of $25 per night per room. Multiple dogs may be allowed.

Super 8 Lumberton
150 Jackson Court
Lumberton, NC
910-671-4444 (800-800-8000)
Dogs of all sizes are allowed. There is a $5 per night pet fee per pet. Smoking and non-smoking rooms are available for pet rooms. 2 dogs may be allowed.

Maggie Mountain
60 Twin Hickory
Maggie Valley, NC
828-926-4258
Dogs of all sizes are allowed. There is a $10 per night fee for one pet and $5 per night for each additional pet. Multiple dogs may be allowed.

Super 8 Marion
4281 Hwy 221 South
Marion, NC
828-659-7940 (800-800-8000)
Dogs of all sizes are allowed. There is a $20 one time per pet fee per

visit. Smoking and non-smoking rooms are available for pet rooms. 2 dogs may be allowed.

Country Inns & Suites by Carlson
2001 Mount Harmony Church Rd
Matthews, NC
704-846-8000
Dogs of all sizes are allowed. There is a $5 per day additional pet fee.

Quality Inn
1500 Yadkinville Road
Mocksville, NC
336-751-7310 (877-424-6423)
Dogs up to 70 pounds are allowed for an additional one time pet fee of $25 per room. 2 dogs may be allowed.

Holiday Inn Express Monroe
608 E. West Roosevelt Blvd
Monroe, NC
704-289-1555 (877-270-6405)
Dogs of all sizes are allowed for an additional fee of $10 per night per pet. 2 dogs may be allowed.

Motel 6 - Monroe
350 Venus Street
Monroe, NC
704-289-9111 (800-466-8356)
One well-behaved family pet per room. Guest must notify front desk upon arrival. Guest is liable for any damages. In consideration of all guests, pets must never be left unattended in the guest rooms.

Holiday Inn Express Hotel and Suites
5063 Executive Dr
Morehead City, NC
252-247-5001 (877-270-6405)
Dogs of all sizes are allowed for an additional one time pet fee of $25 (plus tax) per room. 2 dogs may be allowed.

Comfort Inn and Suites
1273 Burkmount Avenue
Morganton, NC
828-430-4000 (877-424-6423)
Dogs are allowed for an additional one time fee of $25 per pet. Multiple dogs may be allowed.

Holiday Inn
2400 South Sterling St
Morganton, NC
828-437-0171 (877-270-6405)
Dogs of all sizes are allowed for an additional one time pet fee of $25 per room. Multiple dogs may be allowed.

Residence Inn by Marriott

2020 Hospitality Court
Morrisville, NC
919-467-8689
Dogs of all sizes are allowed. There is a $75 one time fee and a pet policy to sign at check in. 2 dogs may be allowed.

Staybridge Suites
1012 Airport Blvd
Morrisville, NC
919-468-0180 (877-270-6405)
Dogs of all sizes are allowed for an additional one time pet fee of $150 per room. Multiple dogs may be allowed.

Quality Inn (formally-Comfort Inn)
2136 Rockford Street
Mount Airy, NC
336-789-2000 (877-424-6423)
Dogs are allowed for an additional one time pet fee of $25 per room. 2 dogs may be allowed.

Best Western of Murphy
1522 Andrews Rd
Murphy, NC
828-837-3060 (800-780-7234)
Dogs up to 20 pounds are allowed for an additional fee per night per pet of $10; $15 for dogs 21 to 39 pounds, and $20 for dogs from 40 to 60 pounds. Multiple dogs may be allowed.

Smoky Mountain Hideaway
Mary King Mountain
Murphy, NC
727-864-0526
Dogs of all sizes are allowed. There is a $100 refundable pet deposit per room. Multiple dogs may be allowed.

Comfort Inn South Oceanfront
8031 Old Oregon Inlet Road
Nags Head, NC
252-441-6315 (877-424-6423)
Dogs are allowed for an additional fee of $10 per night per pet. 2 dogs may be allowed.

Village Realty
5301 South Croatan Highway
Nags Head, NC
800-548-9688
villagerealtyobx.com
Many of the homes represented by Village Realty will allow pets for a $75 non-refundable pet cleaning fee. Up to two well-behaved pets are allowed.

Broad Creek Guest Quarters Resort
6229 Harbourside Dr. (Fairfield Harbour)
New Bern, NC

252-474-5329
This B&B welcomes your dog or cat and offers complimentary pet sitting. There is a $20 per night pet fee and dogs of all sizes are welcome.

Sheraton New Bern Hotel & Marina
100 Middle Street
New Bern, NC
252-638-3585 (888-625-5144)
Dogs of all sizes are allowed. There are no additional pet fees. Pets are limited to rooms on the 1st floor only. Dogs are not allowed to be left alone in the room.

Idyll-by-the-Sea Two
134 Ocean View Lane
North Topsail Beach, NC
603-524-4000
This large vacation rental has 8 bedrooms and can sleep up to 18 people. It is almost 6000 square feet in size. Well behaved dogs of all sizes are welcome. You may contact the owners to make reservations at relax@idyll-by-the-sea.com or at 603-524-4000 or 240-238-4050 during business hours (ET).

Oak Island Accommodations, Inc
8901 East Oak Island Drive
Oak Island, NC
910-278-6011 (800-243-8132)
rentalsatthebeach.com
This rental agency offers over 600+ resort rentals from Oceanfront to Sound-side. Pets allowed in designated homes. Dogs 60 pounds and under allowed with a non-refundable $100 + tax pet fee for Cleaning and Extermination.

Weddens Way, Too
231 Legra Rd
Piney Creek, NC
336-372-2985
sparta-nc.com/weddensway/
Fully furnished cabin overlooking the New River. Sleeps up to 7, rate for two is $80 plus tax per night. Pets are welcome for a $50 fee for the entire stay. Fish, canoe or enjoy the view.

Days Inn Raeford
115 Fayetteville Rd/115 US 401 Byp
Raeford, NC
910-904-1050 (800-329-7466)
Dogs of all sizes are allowed. There is a $7 per night pet fee per pet. Reservations are recommended due to limited rooms for pets. 2 dogs may be allowed.

Best Western Raleigh North
2715 Capital Boulevard

Raleigh, NC
919-872-5000 (800-780-7234)
Dogs up to 80 pounds are allowed for an additional pet fee of $50 per night per room; a 3rd dog would be another $25 per night. Multiple dogs may be allowed.

Candlewood Suites
1020 Buck Jones Road
Raleigh, NC
919-468-4222 (877-270-6405)
Dogs up to 80 pounds are allowed for an additional pet fee of $12 per night per room. Multiple dogs may be allowed.

Candlewood Suites
4433 Lead Mine Road
Raleigh, NC
919-789-4840 (877-270-6405)
Dogs up to 40 pounds are allowed. There is a $75 one time pet fee per visit. Only non-smoking rooms are used for pets.

Holiday Inn
2805 Highwoods Blvd
Raleigh, NC
919-872-3500 (877-270-6405)
Dogs of all sizes are allowed for an additional one time pet fee of $35 per room. Multiple dogs may be allowed.

Holiday Inn
4100 Glenwood Ave
Raleigh, NC
919-782-8600 (877-270-6405)
A dog up to 50 pounds is allowed for an additional one time fee of $50.

La Quinta Inn Raleigh
1001 Aerial Center Parkway
Raleigh, NC
919-481-3600 (800-531-5900)
Dogs of all sizes are allowed. There are no additional pet fees. Dogs must be well behaved, leashed, and cleaned up after. Multiple dogs may be allowed.

Motel 6 - Raleigh Northwest
3921 Arrow Drive
Raleigh, NC
919-782-7071 (800-466-8356)
One well-behaved family pet per room. Guest must notify front desk upon arrival. Guest is liable for any damages. In consideration of all guests, pets must never be left unattended in the guest rooms.

Motel 6 - Raleigh Southwest - Cary
1401 Buck Jones Road
Raleigh, NC

919-467-6171 (800-466-8356)
One well-behaved family pet per room. Guest must notify front desk upon arrival. Guest is liable for any damages. In consideration of all guests, pets must never be left unattended in the guest rooms.

Quality Suites
4400 Capital Blvd
Raleigh, NC
919-876-2211
Dogs up to 50 pounds are allowed. The fee for 2 pets is $25 for the 1st night and $10 for each night after; 3 dogs would be $35 for the 1st night and $20 for each additional night. Multiple dogs may be allowed.

Red Roof Inn - Raleigh Downtown NCSU
1813 South Saunders Street
Raleigh, NC
919-833-6005 (800-RED-ROOF)
One well-behaved family pet per room. Guest must notify front desk upon arrival. Guest is liable for any damages. In consideration of all guests, pets must never be left unattended in the guest rooms.

Red Roof Inn - Raleigh East (New Bern Avenue)
3520 Maitland Drive
Raleigh, NC
919-231-0200 (800-RED-ROOF)
One well-behaved family pet per room. Guest must notify front desk upon arrival. Guest is liable for any damages. In consideration of all guests, pets must never be left unattended in the guest rooms.

Residence Inn by Marriott
1000 Navaho Drive
Raleigh, NC
919-878-6100
Dogs of all sizes are allowed. There is a $100 one time fee and a pet policy to sign at check in. Multiple dogs may be allowed.

Residence Inn by Marriott
2200 Summit Park Lane
Raleigh, NC
919-279-3000
Dogs of all sizes are allowed. There is a $75 one time fee and a pet policy to sign at check in. Multiple dogs may be allowed.

Motel 6 - Roanoke Rapids
1911 Julian Alsbrook Highway
Roanoke Rapids, NC
252-537-5252 (800-466-8356)
One well-behaved family pet per room. Guest must notify front desk

upon arrival. Guest is liable for any damages. In consideration of all guests, pets must never be left unattended in the guest rooms.

Best Western Inn I-95/Gold Rock
7095 Rte 4
Rocky Mount, NC
252-985-1450 (800-780-7234)
Dogs are allowed for an additional fee of $20 per night per pet. Multiple dogs may be allowed.

Best Western Rocky Mount Inn
1921 N Wesleyan Boulevard
Rocky Mount, NC
252-442-8101 (800-780-7234)
Dogs are allowed for an additional fee of $20 per night per pet. Multiple dogs may be allowed.

Comfort Inn
200 Gateway Blvd
Rocky Mount, NC
252-937-7765 (877-424-6423)
Dogs are allowed for an additional one time pet fee of $25 per room. 2 dogs may be allowed.

Comfort Inn North
7048 H 4
Rocky Mount, NC
252-972-9426 (877-424-6423)
Dogs are allowed for an additional fee of $10 per night per pet. 2 dogs may be allowed.

Red Roof Inn - Rocky Mount
1370 North Wesleyan Boulevard
Rocky Mount, NC
252-984-0907 (800-RED-ROOF)
One well-behaved family pet per room. Guest must notify front desk upon arrival. Guest is liable for any damages. In consideration of all guests, pets must never be left unattended in the guest rooms.

Residence Inn by Marriott
230 Gateway Blvd
Rocky Mount, NC
252-451-5600
Dogs of all sizes are allowed. There is a $75 one time fee and a pet policy to sign at check in. Multiple dogs may be allowed.

Super 8 Rocky Mount/Mosley Court Area
307 Mosley Court
Rocky Mount, NC
252-977-2858 (800-800-8000)
Dogs of all sizes are allowed. There is a $5 per night pet fee per pet. Smoking and non-smoking rooms are available for pet rooms. 2 dogs may be allowed.

Days Inn Rowland
14723 US Hwy 301
Rowland, NC
910-422-3366 (800-329-7466)
Dogs of all sizes are allowed. There are no additional pet fees. 2 dogs may be allowed.

Hampton Inn
1001 Klumac Road
Salisbury, NC
704-637-8000
Dogs of all sizes are allowed. There are no additional pet fees. Dogs are not allowed to be left alone in the room. Multiple dogs may be allowed.

Holiday Inn
530 Jake Alexander Blvd South
Salisbury, NC
704-637-3100 (877-270-6405)
Dogs up to 25 pounds are allowed for an additional one time fee of $15 per pet. 2 dogs may be allowed.

Spring Pond Cabin
640 E US Hwy 176
Saluda, NC
828-749-9824
saluda.com/springpond
This cozy cabin in the woods is available for rent to you and your pets. There is a covered porch with fenced in area as well as a half mile hiking loop on the property which is wooded and has two spring fed ponds. The cabin is fully equipped and sleeps five. They ask that you bring your own linens if your dog sleeps on the bed.

Fire Mountain Inn
On H 106
Scaley Mountain, NC
828-526-4446 (800-775-4446)
One dog up to 80 pounds is allowed, however they may accept 2 dogs if they are small. This place takes dogs only and they must be over a year old and well house trained. There is a $25 per night per pet fee plus a $150 refundable deposit and a pet policy to sign at check in. Dogs are allowed in the cabins only.

Super 8 Motel
735 Industrial Park Drive
Smithfield, NC
919-989-8988 (800-800-8000)
Dogs of all sizes are allowed. There is a $6 per night per pet additional fee. Dogs must be leashed, cleaned up after, and a contact number left with the front desk if they are in the

room alone. 2 dogs may be allowed.

Hampton Inn
1675 H 1S
Southern Pines, NC
910-692-9266
Dogs of all sizes are allowed. There is a $10 per night additional pet fee. Multiple dogs may be allowed.

Residence Inn by Marriott
105 Bruce Wood Road
Southern Pines, NC
910-693-3400
Dogs of all sizes are allowed. There is a $50 one time fee and a pet policy to sign at check in. Multiple dogs may be allowed.

Holiday Inn Express Hotel and Suites
103 Brook Lane
Spring Lake, NC
910-436-1900 (877-270-6405)
Dogs of all sizes are allowed; 1 dogs is a $65 one time additional fee; a 2nd dog would be an additional one time fee of $15. 2 dogs may be allowed.

Best Western Statesville Inn
1121 Morland Dr
Statesville, NC
704-881-0111 (800-780-7234)
Dogs are allowed for an additional pet fee of $15 per night per room. Multiple dogs may be allowed.

Motel 6 - Statesville
1137 Morland Drive
Statesville, NC
704-871-1115 (800-466-8356)
One well-behaved family pet per room. Guest must notify front desk upon arrival. Guest is liable for any damages. In consideration of all guests, pets must never be left unattended in the guest rooms.

Red Roof Inn - Statesville
1508 East Broad Street
Statesville, NC
704-878-2051 (800-RED-ROOF)
One well-behaved family pet per room. Guest must notify front desk upon arrival. Guest is liable for any damages. In consideration of all guests, pets must never be left unattended in the guest rooms.

Super 8 Statesville
1125 Greenland Dr
Statesville, NC
704-878-9888 (800-800-8000)
Dogs of all sizes are allowed. There is a $6 per night pet fee per pet. Smoking and non-smoking rooms are available for pet rooms. 2 dogs

may be allowed.

Sunset Properties
419 S. Sunset Blvd
Sunset Beach, NC
910-579-9900 (888-339-2670)
sunsetbeachnc.com
Some of these vacation rentals on Sunset Beach are pet-friendly. Those that are pet-friendly require a $150 non-refundable one time pet fee.

Valle Crucis Log Cabin Rentals
P.O. Box 554
Valle Crucis, NC
828-963-7774
This company has many properties and one large dog or 2 small dogs are allowed. There is a $50 one time fee per pet additional fee. They ask you bring a blanket to cover the bed or furniture if your pet is inclined to get on them.

Days Inn Fayetteville North
3945 Goldsboro Hwy
Wade, NC
910-323-1255 (800-329-7466)
Dogs of all sizes are allowed. There is a $6 per night pet fee per pet. 2 dogs may be allowed.

Days Inn Weldon
1611 Roanoke Rapids Rd
Weldon, NC
252-536-4867 (800-329-7466)
Dogs of all sizes are allowed. There is a $6 per night pet fee per pet. 2 dogs may be allowed.

Carolina Mountain Resort
8 N Jefferson Avenue
West Jefferson, NC
336-246-3010
Dogs of all sizes are allowed. There is a $50 one time fee and a pet policy to sign at check in. Multiple dogs may be allowed.

Dog House Resort
134 John H. Pierce Sr. Lane
West Jefferson, NC
336-977-3482
dog-house-resort.com
Dog House Resort is a Bed & Breakfast for people vacationing with their dogs on three acres overlooking the Blue Ridge Mountains. Dogs of all sizes are welcome. There is a fenced-in dog park and pet-sitting is available.

Holiday Inn
US 17-64 Box 711
Williamston, NC
252-792-3184 (877-270-6405)
Dogs up to 50 pounds are allowed

for no additional fee. 2 dogs may be allowed.

Camellia Cottage Bed and Breakfast
118 S. 4th Street
Wilmington, NC
910-763-9171
camelliacottage.net/
Well-behaved dogs are welcome in the Crane Suite at this bed and breakfast inn. The pet-friendly room is located next to the front door, on the first floor. There are no pet fees.

Days Inn Wilmington
5040 Market St
Wilmington, NC
910-799-6300 (800-329-7466)
Dogs of all sizes are allowed. There is a $15 per night pet fee per pet. Pet must be kept in kennel when left alone. 2 dogs may be allowed.

Motel 6 - Wilmington
2828 Market Street
Wilmington, NC
910-762-0120 (800-466-8356)
One well-behaved family pet per room. Guest must notify front desk upon arrival. Guest is liable for any damages. In consideration of all guests, pets must never be left unattended in the guest rooms.

Residence Inn by Marriott
1200 Culbreth Drive
Wilmington, NC
910-256-0098
Dogs of all sizes are allowed. There is a $75 one time fee and a pet policy to sign at check in. Multiple dogs may be allowed.

Waterway Lodge
7246 Wrightsville Avenue
Wilmington, NC
910-256-3771 (800-677-3771)
waterwaylodge.com
The Waterway Lodge offers standard motel rooms as well as one bedroom condo units with full kitchens. It is located on the Intercoastal Waterway, and a short walk to numerous shops, restaurants, marinas and the beach.

Best Western La Sammana
817-A Ward Blvd
Wilson, NC
252-237-8700 (800-780-7234)
Dogs are allowed for an additional fee of $10 per night per pet. Multiple dogs may be allowed.

Holiday Inn Express Hotel and Suites

2308 Montgomery Dr
Wilson, NC
252-246-1588 (877-270-6405)
Dogs up to 65 pounds are allowed for an additional one time fee of $20 per pet. Dogs may not be left alone in the room at any time. 2 dogs may be allowed.

Days Inn Winston - Salem Convention Cntr
3330 Silas Creek Pkwy
Winston - Salem, NC
336-760-4770 (800-329-7466)
Dogs of all sizes are allowed. There is a $10 per night pet fee per pet. 2 dogs may be allowed.

Motel 6 - Winston - Salem
3810 Patterson Avenue
Winston - Salem, NC
336-661-1588 (800-466-8356)
One well-behaved family pet per room. Guest must notify front desk upon arrival. Guest is liable for any damages. In consideration of all guests, pets must never be left unattended in the guest rooms.

BW Salem Inn & Suites
127 S Cherry Street
Winston-Salem, NC
336-725-8561
Dogs are allowed for an additional one time pet fee of $25 per room. Multiple dogs may be allowed.

La Quinta Inn & Suites Winston-Salem
2020 Griffith Road
Winston-Salem, NC
336-765-8777 (800-531-5900)
Dogs of all sizes are allowed. There are no additional pet fees. Dogs must be leashed, cleaned up after, and a contact number left with the front desk if there is a pet in the room alone. Multiple dogs may be allowed.

Residence Inn by Marriott
7835 North Point Blvd
Winston-Salem, NC
336-759-0777
Dogs up to 75 pounds are allowed. There is a $75 one time fee and a pet policy to sign at check in. 2 dogs may be allowed.

Days Inn Yanceyville
1858 NC Hwy 86 North
Yanceyville, NC
336-694-9494 (800-329-7466)
Dogs of all sizes are allowed. There is a $10 per night pet fee per pet. 2 dogs may be allowed.

North Dakota Listings

Comfort Inn
1030 E Interstate Avenue
Bismarck, ND
701-223-1911 (877-424-6423)
Dogs are allowed for no additional pet fee. Multiple dogs may be allowed.

Comfort Suites
929 Gateway Avenue
Bismarck, ND
701-223-4009 (877-424-6423)
Dogs are allowed for no additional pet fee. Multiple dogs may be allowed.

Days Inn Bismarck
1300 E Capitol Ave
Bismarck, ND
701-223-9151 (800-329-7466)
Dogs of all sizes are allowed. There is a $5 per night pet fee per pet. 2 dogs may be allowed.

Motel 6 - Bismarck
2433 State Street
Bismarck, ND
701-255-6878 (800-466-8356)
One well-behaved family pet per room. Guest must notify front desk upon arrival. Guest is liable for any damages. In consideration of all guests, pets must never be left unattended in the guest rooms.

Radisson Hotel Bismarck
605 East Broadway Avenue
Bismarck, ND
701-255-6000
Dogs of all sizes are allowed. There are no additional pet fees. Dogs may not be left alone in the rooms.

Super 8 Bismarck
1124 E Capitol Ave
Bismarck, ND
701-255-1314 (800-800-8000)
Dogs of all sizes are allowed. There is a $10 per night pet fee per pet. Smoking and non-smoking rooms are available for pet rooms. 2 dogs may be allowed.

Governor's RV Park and Campground
2050 Governor's Drive
Casselton, ND
701-347-4524
Dogs of all sizes are allowed. There is a $9 per night per pet additional fee. Dogs may be crated when out of the room if they will be quiet and comfortable. Dogs must be leashed and cleaned up after. There is also a campground on site where dogs are allowed at no additional fee. 2 dogs may be allowed.

Woodland Resort
1012 Woodland Drive
Devil's Lake, ND
701-662-5996
Dogs of all sizes are allowed. There is a $10 per night per pet, or $50 per week per pet, additional fee for the lodge, motel, or cabins. There are no additional pet fees for the campground on site. Dogs may not be left unattended, and they must be leashed and cleaned up after. Multiple dogs may be allowed.

Days Inn Devils Lake
1109 Highway 20 S
Devils Lake, ND
701-662-5381 (800-329-7466)
Dogs of all sizes are allowed. There is a $7 per night pet fee per pet. 2 dogs may be allowed.

Quality Inn and Suites
71 Museum Drive
Dickinson, ND
701-225-9510 (877-424-6423)
Dogs are allowed for an additional fee of $10 per night per pet. Multiple dogs may be allowed.

Comfort Inn
493 Elk Drive
Dickinson, ND
701-264-7300 (877-424-6423)
Dogs are allowed for an additional fee of $10 per night per pet. Multiple dogs may be allowed.

Holiday Inn Express Hotel and Suites
103 14th Street West
Dickinson, ND
701-456-8000 (877-270-6405)
Dogs of all sizes are allowed for an additional pet fee per room of $10 for each 1 to 7 day period. 2 dogs may be allowed.

Super 8 Dickinson
637 12th St West
Dickinson, ND
701-227-1215 (800-800-8000)
Dogs of all sizes are allowed. There is a $5 per night pet fee per pet. Smoking and non-smoking rooms are available for pet rooms. 2 dogs may be allowed.

Best Western Kelly Inn

3800 Main Ave
Fargo, ND
701-282-2143 (800-780-7234)
Dogs are allowed for no additional pet fee. Multiple dogs may be allowed.

Candlewood Suites Fargo-N. Dakota State Univ.
1831 Ndsu Research Dr.
Fargo, ND
701-235-8200 (877-270-6405)
Dogs of all sizes are allowed for an additional one time pet fee of $75 per room. Multiple dogs may be allowed.

Comfort Suites
1415 35th Street S
Fargo, ND
701-237-5911 (877-424-6423)
Dogs are allowed for an additional pet fee of $10 per night per room. Dogs are to be crated when left alone in the room and a contact number must be left with the front desk. Multiple dogs may be allowed.

Holiday Inn
3803 13th Ave S.
Fargo, ND
701-282-2700 (877-270-6405)
Dogs of all sizes are allowed for an additional one time pet fee of $10 per room. Multiple dogs may be allowed.

Holiday Inn Express
1040 40th Street South
Fargo, ND
701-282-2000 (877-270-6405)
Dogs of all sizes are allowed for an additional one time fee of $10 per pet. Multiple dogs may be allowed.

MainStay Suites
1901 44th Street SW
Fargo, ND
701-277-4627
Dogs are allowed for no additional pet fee in a smoking room; there is an additional one time pet fee of $50 per room for a non-smoking room. Multiple dogs may be allowed.

Motel 6 - Fargo
1202 36th Street South
Fargo, ND
701-232-9251 (800-466-8356)
One well-behaved family pet per room. Guest must notify front desk upon arrival. Guest is liable for any damages. In consideration of all guests, pets must never be left unattended in the guest rooms.

Sleep Inn
1921 44th Street SW
Fargo, ND

701-281-8240 (877-424-6423)
Dogs are allowed for no additional pet fee in a smoking room; there is an additional one time pet fee of $25 per room for a non-smoking room. Multiple dogs may be allowed.

Super 8 Grafton
948 W 12th Street
Grafton, ND
701-352-0888 (800-800-8000)
Dogs of all sizes are allowed. There is a $5 per night pet fee per pet. Smoking and non-smoking rooms are available for pet rooms. 2 dogs may be allowed.

Econo Lodge
900 N 43rd St
Grand Forks, ND
701-746-6666
There is a $5 per day additional pet fee.

Comfort Inn
811 20th St. SW
Jamestown, ND
701-252-7125 (877-424-6423)
Dogs are allowed for no additional pet fee. Multiple dogs may be allowed.

Quality Inn and Suites
507 25th Street SW
Jamestown, ND
701-252-3611
Dogs are allowed for an additional one time pet fee of $10 per room. Multiple dogs may be allowed.

Super 8 Jamestown
I-94 and Hwy 281
Jamestown, ND
701-252-4715 (800-800-8000)
Dogs of all sizes are allowed. There is a $10 per night pet fee per pet. Smoking and non-smoking rooms are available for pet rooms. 2 dogs may be allowed.

Best Western Seven Seas Inn and Conf Cntr
2611 Old Red Trail
Mandan, ND
701-663-7401 (800-780-7234)
Dogs are allowed for an additional pet fee of $10 per night per room. There may be 1 dog to a maximum weight of 50 pounds, or 2 small dogs totaling no more than 50 pounds are allowed per room. 2 dogs may be allowed.

Americinn Motel and Suites
75 E River Rd
Medora, ND
701-623-4800

There is a $20 one time pet fee.

Comfort Inn
1515 22nd Avenue SW
Minot, ND
701-852-2201 (877-424-6423)
Dogs are allowed for an additional one time pet fee of $10 per room. Multiple dogs may be allowed.

Days Inn Minot
2100 4th St SW
Minot, ND
701-852-3646 (800-329-7466)
Dogs of all sizes are allowed. There are no additional pet fees. 2 dogs may be allowed.

Select Inn
225 22nd Ave NW
Minot, ND
701-852-3411
There is a $25 refundable pet deposit and a $5 per day pet fee.

Super 8 Minot
1315 N Broadway
Minot, ND
701-852-1817 (800-800-8000)
Dogs of all sizes are allowed. There is a $10 per night pet fee per pet. Reservations are recommended due to limited rooms for pets. Smoking and non-smoking rooms are available for pet rooms. 2 dogs may be allowed.

Four Bears Lodge
SR 23W
New Town, ND
701-627-4018
There is a $50 one time pet fee.

Spirit Lake Casino and Resort
7889 H 57
St Michael, ND
701-766-4747
Dogs of all sizes are allowed. There is a $25 per stay per pet additional fee. Dogs may not be left unattended, and they must be leashed and cleaned up after. Multiple dogs may be allowed.

Super 8 West Fargo/Main Ave
825 East Main Ave
West Fargo, ND
701-478-7378 (800-800-8000)
Dogs of all sizes are allowed. There is a $5 per night pet fee per pet. Smoking and non-smoking rooms are available for pet rooms. 2 dogs may be allowed.

Super 8 Williston
2324 2nd Ave West
Williston, ND

701-572-8371 (800-800-8000)
Dogs up to 80 pounds are allowed. There is a $5 per night pet fee per pet. Smoking and non-smoking rooms are available for pet rooms. 2 dogs may be allowed.

Ohio Listings

Days Inn Akron South
3237 S Arlington Rd
Akron, OH
330-644-1204 (800-329-7466)
Dogs up to 60 pounds are allowed. There is a $5 per night pet fee per pet. 2 dogs may be allowed.

Motel 6 - Akron North
99 Rothrock Road
Akron, OH
330-666-0566 (800-466-8356)
One well-behaved family pet per room. Guest must notify front desk upon arrival. Guest is liable for any damages. In consideration of all guests, pets must never be left unattended in the guest rooms.

Red Roof Inn - Akron South
2939 South Arlington Road
Akron, OH
330-644-7748 (800-RED-ROOF)
One well-behaved family pet per room. Guest must notify front desk upon arrival. Guest is liable for any damages. In consideration of all guests, pets must never be left unattended in the guest rooms.

Residence Inn by Marriott
120 Montrose West Avenue
Akron, OH
330-666-4811
Dogs of all sizes are allowed. There is a $75 one time fee for the studios and a $150 one time fee for the Penthouse. There is also a pet policy to sign at check in. Multiple dogs may be allowed.

Comfort Inn
2500 W State Street
Alliance, OH
330-821-5555 (877-424-6423)
Dogs are allowed for an additional pet fee of $10 per night per room. Multiple dogs may be allowed.

Motel 6 - Cleveland-Lorain/Amherst
704 North Leavitt Road
Amherst, OH
440-988-3266 (800-466-8356)
One well-behaved family pet per room. Guest must notify front desk

upon arrival. Guest is liable for any damages. In consideration of all guests, pets must never be left unattended in the guest rooms.

Days Inn Ashland
County Rd 1575
Ashland, OH
419-289-0101 (800-329-7466)
Dogs of all sizes are allowed. There are no additional pet fees. 2 dogs may be allowed.

Red Lion
400 Industry Street
Astoria, OH
503-325-5786
Dogs of all sizes are allowed. There is a $10 per night per room additional pet fee. Multiple dogs may be allowed.

Days Inn Athens
330 Columbus Rd
Athens, OH
740-592-4000 (800-329-7466)
Dogs up to 60 pounds are allowed. There is a $5 per night pet fee per pet. Dogs are not allowed to be left alone in the room. 2 dogs may be allowed.

Comfort Inn
1860 Austinburg Road
Austinburg, OH
440-275-2711 (877-424-6423)
Dogs are allowed for an additional fee of $15 per night per pet. 2 dogs may be allowed.

Comfort Inn and Suites
5425 Clarkins Drive
Austintown, OH
330-792-9740 (877-424-6423)
Quiet dogs are allowed for an additional pet fee of $10 (plus tax) per night per room. Multiple dogs may be allowed.

Motel 6 - Austintown
5431 Seventy Six Drive
Austintown, OH
330-793-9305 (800-466-8356)
One well-behaved family pet per room. Guest must notify front desk upon arrival. Guest is liable for any damages. In consideration of all guests, pets must never be left unattended in the guest rooms.

Hilton
3663 Park East Drive
Beachwood, OH
216-464-5950
Dogs up to 75 pounds are allowed for an additional one time pet fee of $50 per room. 2 dogs may be

allowed.

Holiday Inn
3750 Orange Place
Beachwood, OH
216-831-3300 (877-270-6405)
Dogs up to 50 pounds are allowed for an additional one time fee of $20 per pet. 2 dogs may be allowed.

Residence Inn by Marriott
3628 Park East Drive
Beachwood, OH
216-831-3030
Dogs of all sizes are allowed. There is a $75 one time fee and a pet policy to sign at check in. Multiple dogs may be allowed.

Residence Inn by Marriott
2779 Fairfield Commons
Beavercreek, OH
937-427-3914
Dogs of all sizes are allowed. There is a $75 one time fee and a pet policy to sign at check in. Multiple dogs may be allowed.

Red Roof Inn - Cleveland - Bedford Heights
24801 Rockside Road
Bedford Heights, OH
440-439-2500 (800-RED-ROOF)
One well-behaved family pet per room. Guest must notify front desk upon arrival. Guest is liable for any damages. In consideration of all guests, pets must never be left unattended in the guest rooms.

Comfort Inn
260 Northview
Bellefontaine, OH
937-599-5555 (877-424-6423)
Dogs are allowed for an additional fee of $15 per night per pet. Multiple dogs may be allowed.

Days Inn Bellville
880 St Rt 97
Bellville, OH
419-886-3800 (800-329-7466)
Dogs of all sizes are allowed. There is a $5 per night pet fee per pet. 2 dogs may be allowed.

Candlewood Suites
10665 Techwoods Circle
Blue Ash, OH
513-733-0100 (877-270-6405)
Dogs of all sizes are allowed for an additional one time fee of $75 per pet. 2 dogs may be allowed.

Red Roof Inn - Cincinnati Northeast - Blue Ash
5900 Pfeiffer Road

Blue Ash, OH
513-793-8811 (800-RED-ROOF)
One well-behaved family pet per room. Guest must notify front desk upon arrival. Guest is liable for any damages. In consideration of all guests, pets must never be left unattended in the guest rooms.

Residence Inn by Marriott
11401 Reed Hartman Highway
Blue Ash, OH
513-530-5060
Dogs of all sizes are allowed. There is a $75 one time fee and a pet policy to sign at check in. They also ask that you make arrangements for housekeeping. 2 dogs may be allowed.

TownePlace Suites Cincinnati Blue Ash
4650 Cornell Road
Blue Ash, OH
513-469-8222
Dogs of all sizes are allowed. There is a $75 one time pet fee per visit. 2 dogs may be allowed.

Days Inn Youngstown South
8392 Market St
Boardman, OH
330-758-2371 (800-329-7466)
Dogs of all sizes are allowed. There is a $5 per night pet fee per pet. 2 dogs may be allowed.

Microtel
7393 South Avenue
Boardman, OH
330-758-1816
There is a $20 one time per stay pet fee.

Days Inn Bowling Green
1550 E Wooster
Bowling Green, OH
419-352-5211 (800-329-7466)
Dogs of all sizes are allowed. There is a $10 per night pet fee per pet. 2 dogs may be allowed.

Quality Inn and Suites
1630 E Wooster Street
Bowling Green, OH
419-352-2521 (877-424-6423)
Dogs are allowed for an additional fee of $10 per night per pet. Multiple dogs may be allowed.

Days Inn Dayton/Brookville
100 Parkview Dr
Brookville, OH
937-833-4003 (800-329-7466)
Dogs of all sizes are allowed. There is a $10 per night pet fee per pet. 2 dogs may be allowed.

Sleep Inn
1435 S Carpenter Road
Brunswick, OH
330-273-1112 (877-424-6423)
Dogs are allowed for an additional fee of $10 per night per pet for dogs up to 25 pounds; the fee is $15 per night per pet for dogs over 25 pounds. Multiple dogs may be allowed.

Super 8 Buckeye Lake
I-70 and SR 79
Buckeye Lake, OH
740-929-1015 (800-800-8000)
Dogs of all sizes are allowed. There are no additional pet fees. Dogs are not allowed to be left alone in the room. Smoking and non-smoking rooms are available for pet rooms. 2 dogs may be allowed.

Best Western Cambridge
1945 Southgate Parkway
Cambridge, OH
740-439-3581 (800-780-7234)
Dogs are allowed for an additional fee of $10 per night per pet. Multiple dogs may be allowed.

Comfort Inn
2327 Southgate Parkway
Cambridge, OH
740-435-3200 (877-424-6423)
Dogs are allowed for an additional one time fee of $10 per pet. Multiple dogs may be allowed.

Days Inn Cambridge
2328 Southgate Pkwy
Cambridge, OH
740-432-5691 (800-329-7466)
Dogs of all sizes are allowed. There are no additional pet fees. 2 dogs may be allowed.

Holiday Inn
2248 Southgate Pkwy
Cambridge, OH
740-432-7313 (877-270-6405)
Dogs of all sizes are allowed for no additional pet fee. Multiple dogs may be allowed.

Courtyard by Marriott
4375 Metro Circle NW
Canton, OH
330-494-6494
Dogs of all sizes are allowed for an additional one time pet fee of $49 per room.

Residence Inn by Marriott
5280 Broadmoor Circle NW
Canton, OH
330-493-0004

Dogs of all sizes are allowed. There is a $75 one time fee and a pet policy to sign at check in. Multiple dogs may be allowed.

Super 8 Canton/North
3950 Convenience Circle NW
Canton, OH
330-492-5030 (800-800-8000)
Dogs of all sizes are allowed. There is a $5 per night pet fee per pet. Smoking and non-smoking rooms are available for pet rooms. 2 dogs may be allowed.

County Line Cabins
Call to Arrange
Carbondale, OH
740-385-1358
hockinghills.com/countyline/
Rent a cabin or a large country home in the Hocking Hills area. Both are furnished and offer a fully equipped kitchen, gas fireplace, ceiling fans, central air and heat, hot tub on the deck, catch and release pond and fire ring. Linens and towels are provided. Depending on a weekday or weekend stay (two night min. required on weekends), rates are $130 to $140 per night. There is a $15 fee for each additional person after two special allowances for children. Children under 2 years old stay free. Well-behaved pets are welcome. There is a $10 fee per pet per day and pets need to be leashed when outside your cabin. Cabins are non-smoking but you can smoke outside. Hunters are also welcome.

Best Western Adena Inn
1250 N. Bridge Street
Chillicothe, OH
740-775-7000 (800-780-7234)
Dogs are allowed for an additional pet fee of $10 per night per room. Multiple dogs may be allowed.

Comfort Inn
20 N Plaza Blvd
Chillicothe, OH
740-775-3500 (877-424-6423)
Quiet, well behaved dogs are allowed for no additional pet fee. Multiple dogs may be allowed.

Days Inn Chillicothe
1250 N Bridge St
Chillicothe, OH
740-775-7000 (800-329-7466)
Dogs up to 60 pounds are allowed. There is a $10 per night pet fee per pet. 2 dogs may be allowed.

Best Western Hotel Clermont

4004 Williams Dr
Cincinnati, OH
513-528-7702 (800-780-7234)
Dogs up to 15 pounds are allowed for an additional one time fee of $10 per pet; the fee is $20 for dogs over 15 pounds. Multiple dogs may be allowed.

Days Inn Cincinnati East
4056 Mt Carmel Tobasco Rd
Cincinnati, OH
513-528-3800 (800-329-7466)
Dogs of all sizes are allowed. There is a $10 per night pet fee per pet. 2 dogs may be allowed.

Days Inn Cincinnati/Sharonville
11775 Lebanon Rd
Cincinnati, OH
513-554-1400 (800-329-7466)
Dogs of all sizes are allowed. There is a $10 per night pet fee per pet. 2 dogs may be allowed.

Holiday Inn
4501 Eastgate Blvd
Cincinnati, OH
513-752-4400 (877-270-6405)
Dogs of all sizes are allowed for no additional pet fee. 2 dogs may be allowed.

Howard Johnson Inn
5410 Ridge Ave.
Cincinnati, OH
513-631-8500 (800-446-4656)
Dogs of all sizes are welcome. There are no additional pet fees.

Howard Johnson Inn
400 Glensprings Drive
Cincinnati, OH
513-825-3129 (800-446-4656)
Dogs of all sizes are welcome. There is a $20 refundable pet deposit.

La Quinta Inn & Suites Cincinnati Sharonville
11029 Dowlin Drive
Cincinnati, OH
513-771-0300 (800-531-5900)
Dogs of all sizes are allowed. There are no additional pet fees. Dogs may not be left unattended, and they must be quiet, well behaved, leashed, and cleaned up after. Multiple dogs may be allowed.

Motel 6 - Cincinnati - Beechmont
3960 Nine Mile Rd
Cincinnati, OH
513-752-2262 (800-466-8356)
One well-behaved family pet per room. Guest must notify front desk upon arrival. Guest is liable for any damages. In consideration of all

guests, pets must never be left unattended in the guest rooms.

Motel 6 - Cincinnati Central - Norwood
5300 Kennedy Avenue
Cincinnati, OH
513-531-6589 (800-466-8356)
One well-behaved family pet per room. Guest must notify front desk upon arrival. Guest is liable for any damages. In consideration of all guests, pets must never be left unattended in the guest rooms.

Red Roof Inn - Cincinnati East - Beechmont
4035 Mount Carmel-Tobasco Road
Cincinnati, OH
513-528-2741 (800-RED-ROOF)
One well-behaved family pet per room. Guest must notify front desk upon arrival. Guest is liable for any damages. In consideration of all guests, pets must never be left unattended in the guest rooms.

Residence Inn by Marriott
11689 Chester Road
Cincinnati, OH
513-771-2525
Dogs of all sizes are allowed. There is a $75 one time fee and a pet policy to sign at check in. Multiple dogs may be allowed.

Sheraton Cincinnati North Hotel
11320 Chester Road
Cincinnati, OH
513-771-2080 (888-625-5144)
Dogs of all sizes are allowed. There are no additional pet fees. Dogs are not allowed to be left alone in the room.

TownePlace Suites Cincinnati NE
9369 Waterstone Blvd
Cincinnati, OH
513-774-0610
Dogs of all sizes are allowed. There is a $75 one time pet fee per visit. 2 dogs may be allowed.

Holiday Inn Express Hotel & Suites Circleville
23911 Us Rt 23 South
Circleville, OH
740-420-7711 (877-270-6405)
Dogs up to 50 pounds are allowed for an additional one time pet fee of $50 per room. 2 dogs may be allowed.

Cleveland Airport Marriott
4277 W 150th Street
Cleveland, OH
216-252-5333 (800-228-9290)

Dogs of all sizes are allowed. There is a $50 one time additional pet fee per room. Dogs may not be left alone in the room, and they must be leashed and cleaned up after. 2 dogs may be allowed.

Edgewater Estates
9803 Lake Avenue
Cleveland, OH
216-961-1764
Well behaved, friendly dogs are allowed. There is a $25 one time fee per room and there must be a credit card on file. They are across the street from a park and dog beach. Multiple dogs may be allowed.

La Quinta Inn Cleveland Airport
4222 W. 150 Street
Cleveland, OH
216-251-8500 (800-531-5900)
Dogs of all sizes are allowed. There are no additional fees. Dogs may not be left unattended, except for short periods, and a cell number must be left with the front desk. Dogs must be leashed, and removed or crated for housekeeping. Multiple dogs may be allowed.

Residence Inn by Marriott
527 Prospect Avenue
Cleveland, OH
216-443-9043
Dogs of all sizes are allowed. There is a $75 one time fee and a pet policy to sign at check in. Multiple dogs may be allowed.

Residence Inn by Marriott
30100 Clemens Road
Cleveland, OH
440-892-2254
Dogs of all sizes are allowed. There is a $75 one time fee and a pet policy to sign at check in. Multiple dogs may be allowed.

Sheraton Cleveland Airport Hotel
5300 Riverside Drive
Cleveland, OH
216-267-1500 (888-625-5144)
Dogs up to 50 pounds are allowed for a $250 refundable pet deposit. Dogs may not be left alone in the room.

Red Roof Inn - Clyde
1363 West McPherson Highway
Clyde, OH
419-547-6660 (800-RED-ROOF)
One well-behaved family pet per room. Guest must notify front desk upon arrival. Guest is liable for any

damages. In consideration of all guests, pets must never be left unattended in the guest rooms.

Best Western Columbus North
888 E Dublin-Granville Road
Columbus, OH
614-888-8230 (800-780-7234)
Dogs up to 50 pounds are allowed for a $50 refundable pet deposit per room. Multiple dogs may be allowed.

Candlewood Suites Polaris
8515 Lyra Drive
Columbus, OH
614-436-6600 (877-270-6405)
Dogs of all sizes are allowed for an additional one time pet fee of $75 per room. Multiple dogs may be allowed.

Comfort Suites
4270 Sawyer Road
Columbus, OH
614-237-5847 (877-424-6423)
Dogs are allowed for an additional one time pet fee of $25 per room. Multiple dogs may be allowed.

Days Inn Columbus North
1212 E Dublin Granville Rd
Columbus, OH
614-885-9696 (800-329-7466)
Dogs of all sizes are allowed. There is a $10 per night pet fee per pet. 2 dogs may be allowed.

Days Inn Columbus/Esposition Center
1700 Clara St
Columbus, OH
614-299-4300 (800-329-7466)
Dogs of all sizes are allowed. There is a $10 per night pet fee per pet. 2 dogs may be allowed.

Doubletree
50 S Front Street
Columbus, OH
614-228-4600
Dogs up to 50 pounds are allowed. There is a $50 one time pet fee per room. 2 dogs may be allowed.

Holiday Inn
328 W. Lane Ave
Columbus, OH
614-294-4848 (877-270-6405)
Quiet dogs of all sizes are allowed for no additional pet fee. A contact number must be left with the front desk it a pet is alone in the room. 2 dogs may be allowed.

Holiday Inn-Worthington
175 Hutchinson Ave
Columbus, OH
614-885-3334 (877-270-6405)

Dogs of all sizes are allowed for an additional one time pet fee of $50 per room. 2 dogs may be allowed.

Knight's Inn
1559 W Broad St
Columbus, OH
614-275-0388
Dogs of all sizes are allowed. There is a $10 per night pet fee per pet. 2 dogs may be allowed.

Knights Inn
4320 Groves Road
Columbus, OH
614-864-0600
There is a $35 refundable pet deposit.

Motel 6 - Columbus - OSU
750 Morse Rd
Columbus, OH
614-846-8520 (800-466-8356)
One well-behaved family pet per room. Guest must notify front desk upon arrival. Guest is liable for any damages. In consideration of all guests, pets must never be left unattended in the guest rooms.

Motel 6 - Columbus - Worthington
7474 N High St
Columbus, OH
614-431-2525 (800-466-8356)
One well-behaved family pet per room. Guest must notify front desk upon arrival. Guest is liable for any damages. In consideration of all guests, pets must never be left unattended in the guest rooms.

Motel 6 - Columbus East
5910 Scarborough Blvd
Columbus, OH
614-755-2250 (800-466-8356)
One well-behaved family pet per room. Guest must notify front desk upon arrival. Guest is liable for any damages. In consideration of all guests, pets must never be left unattended in the guest rooms.

Motel 6 - Columbus North
1289 E. Dublin-Granville Rd
Columbus, OH
614-846-9860 (800-466-8356)
One well-behaved family pet per room. Guest must notify front desk upon arrival. Guest is liable for any damages. In consideration of all guests, pets must never be left unattended in the guest rooms.

Motel 6 - Columbus West
5500 Renner Rd
Columbus, OH
614-870-0993 (800-466-8356)

One well-behaved family pet per room. Guest must notify front desk upon arrival. Guest is liable for any damages. In consideration of all guests, pets must never be left unattended in the guest rooms.

Quality Inn and Suites North
1001 Schrock Road
Columbus, OH
614-431-0208 (877-424-6423)
Dogs are allowed for an additional one time pet fee of $25 per room. Multiple dogs may be allowed.

Red Roof Inn - Columbus - Ohio State University
441 Ackerman Road
Columbus, OH
614-267-9941 (800-RED-ROOF)
One well-behaved family pet per room. Guest must notify front desk upon arrival. Guest is liable for any damages. In consideration of all guests, pets must never be left unattended in the guest rooms.

Red Roof Inn - Columbus Downtown & Convention Center
111 East Nationwide Boulevard
Columbus, OH
614-224-6539 (800-RED-ROOF)
One well-behaved family pet per room. Guest must notify front desk upon arrival. Guest is liable for any damages. In consideration of all guests, pets must never be left unattended in the guest rooms.

Red Roof Inn - Columbus North - Worthington
7480 North High Street
Columbus, OH
614-846-3001 (800-RED-ROOF)
One well-behaved family pet per room. Guest must notify front desk upon arrival. Guest is liable for any damages. In consideration of all guests, pets must never be left unattended in the guest rooms.

Red Roof Inn - Columbus West
5001 Renner Road
Columbus, OH
614-878-9245 (800-RED-ROOF)
One well-behaved family pet per room. Guest must notify front desk upon arrival. Guest is liable for any damages. In consideration of all guests, pets must never be left unattended in the guest rooms.

Residence Inn by Marriott
3999 Easton Loop W
Columbus, OH
614-414-1000
Dogs of all sizes are allowed. There

is a $75 one time fee and a pet policy to sign at check in. Multiple dogs may be allowed.

Residence Inn by Marriott
6191 Zumstein Drive
Columbus, OH
614-431-1819
Dogs of all sizes are allowed. There is a $75 one time fee for the studios and a $100 one time fee for the Penthouse and a pet policy to sign at check in. Multiple dogs may be allowed.

Residence Inn by Marriott
2084 S Hamilton Road
Columbus, OH
614-864-8844
Dogs of all sizes are allowed. There is a $75 one time fee and a pet policy to sign at check in. Multiple dogs may be allowed.

Residence Inn by Marriott
7300 Huntington Park Drive
Columbus, OH
614-885-0799
One large dog or two small dogs (maximum 2)are allowed per room. There is a $125 one time fee and a pet policy to sign at check in.

Sheraton Suites Columbus
201 Hutchinson Avenue
Columbus, OH
614-436-0004 (888-625-5144)
Dogs up to 80 pounds are allowed. There are no additional pet fees. Dogs are not allowed to be left alone in the room.

Super 8 Columbus/University/Dwtn
3232 Olentangy River Road
Columbus, OH
614-261-7141 (800-800-8000)
Dogs of all sizes are allowed. There is a $5 per night pet fee per pet. Smoking and non-smoking rooms are available for pet rooms. 2 dogs may be allowed.

TownePlace Suites Columbus Airport Gahanna
695 Taylor Road
Columbus, OH
614-861-1400
Dogs of all sizes are allowed. There is a $75 one time pet fee per visit. 2 dogs may be allowed.

TownePlace Suites Columbus Worthington
7272 Huntington Park Drive
Columbus, OH
614-885-1557
Dogs of all sizes are allowed. There

is a $75 one time pet fee per visit. 2 dogs may be allowed.

University Plaza Hotel and Conference Center
3110 Olentangy River Road
Columbus, OH
614-267-7461
There is a $20 refundable pet deposit.

Days Inn Conneaut
600 Days Blvd
Conneaut, OH
440-593-6000 (800-329-7466)
Dogs up to 100 pounds are allowed. There is a $10 per night pet fee per pet. 2 dogs may be allowed.

Roscoe Hillside Cabins
46971 County Road 495
Coshocton, OH
866-582-8146
These three cabin rentals are located on the outskirts of Historic Roscoe Village. Cabin rates are about $150 per night. Well-behaved pets are allowed. There is a $250 refundable pet deposit if paying with a check and no deposit required if paying with a credit card.

Sheraton Suites Akron/Cuyahoga Falls
1989 Front Street
Cuyahoga Falls, OH
330-929-3000 (888-625-5144)
Dogs up to 50 pounds are allowed. There are no additional pet fees. Dogs are not allowed to be left alone in the room.

Dayton Marriott
1414 S Patterson Blvd
Dayton, OH
937-223-1000 (800-228-9290)
Dogs of all sizes are allowed. There is a $50 one time additional pet fee for a 1 to 3 nights stay, and a $75 one time fee for 4 or more nights. Dogs must be healthy, well behaved, leashed, and cleaned up after. Dogs must be attended to or removed for housekeeping, and the Do Not Disturb sign put on the door if they are in the room alone. 2 dogs may be allowed.

Holiday Inn Hotel and Suites
2455 Dryden Road
Dayton, OH
937-294-1471 (877-270-6405)
Dogs of all sizes are allowed for an additional one time fee of $10 per pet. Multiple dogs may be allowed.

Howard Johnson Express Inn

7575 Poe Avenue
Dayton, OH
937-454-0550 (800-446-4656)
Dogs of all sizes are welcome. There is a $20 per day pet fee.

Motel 6 - Dayton North
7130 Miller Ln
Dayton, OH
937-898-3606 (800-466-8356)
One well-behaved family pet per room. Guest must notify front desk upon arrival. Guest is liable for any damages. In consideration of all guests, pets must never be left unattended in the guest rooms.

Red Roof Inn - Dayton - Englewood
9325 North Main Street
Dayton, OH
937-836-8339 (800-RED-ROOF)
One well-behaved family pet per room. Guest must notify front desk upon arrival. Guest is liable for any damages. In consideration of all guests, pets must never be left unattended in the guest rooms.

Red Roof Inn - Dayton North
7370 Miller Lane
Dayton, OH
937-898-1054 (800-RED-ROOF)
One well-behaved family pet per room. Guest must notify front desk upon arrival. Guest is liable for any damages. In consideration of all guests, pets must never be left unattended in the guest rooms.

Residence Inn by Marriott
7070 Poe Avenue
Dayton, OH
937-898-7764
Dogs of all sizes are allowed. There is a $75 one time fee and a pet policy to sign at check in. Multiple dogs may be allowed.

La Quinta Inn Columbus/Dublin
6145 Parkcenter Circle
Dublin, OH
614-792-8300 (800-531-5900)
Dogs of all sizes are allowed. There are no additional pet fees, but a credit card must be on file. Dogs may only be left alone in the room if they will be quiet, well behaved, and the Do Not Disturb sign is put on the door. Dogs must be leashed, cleaned up after, and they are not allowed in the breakfast area. Multiple dogs may be allowed.

Northwest Drury Inn & Suites
6170 Parkcenter Circle
Dublin, OH
614-798-8802 (800-378-7946)

Dogs of all sizes are permitted. Pets are not allowed in the breakfast area of the hotel. Pets are not to be left unattended, and each guest must assume liability for damage of property or other guest complaints. There is a limit of one pet per room.

Quality Inn and Suites
3950 Tuller Road
Dublin, OH
614-764-0770 (877-424-6423)
Dogs are allowed for an additional one time fee of $25 per pet. 2 dogs may be allowed.

Red Roof Inn - Columbus - Dublin
5125 Post Road
Dublin, OH
614-764-3993 (800-RED-ROOF)
One well-behaved family pet per room. Guest must notify front desk upon arrival. Guest is liable for any damages. In consideration of all guests, pets must never be left unattended in the guest rooms.

Residence Inn by Marriott
435 Metro Place S
Dublin, OH
614-791-0403
Dogs up to 100 pounds are allowed. There is a $100 one time fee and a pet policy to sign at check in. They also request you make arrangements with housekeeping. Multiple dogs may be allowed.

Staybridge Suites Columbus-Dublin
6095 Emerald Parkway
Dublin, OH
614-734-9882 (877-270-6405)
Dogs of all sizes are allowed for an additional one time pet fee of $100 per room. Multiple dogs may be allowed.

Woodfin Suite Hotel
4130 Tuller Road
Dublin, OH
614-766-7762
All well-behaved dogs are welcome. Every room is a suite with a full kitchen. Hotel amenities include a pool, exercise facility, complimentary video movies and a complimentary hot breakfast buffet. There is a $50 one time per stay pet charge.

Comfort Inn
739 Leona Street
Elyria, OH
440-324-7676 (877-424-6423)
Quiet dogs are allowed for an additional fee of $10 per night per pet. Multiple dogs may be allowed.

Holiday Inn
1825 Lorain Blvd
Elyria, OH
440-324-5411 (877-270-6405)
Quiet dogs of all sizes are allowed
for no additional pet fee. Multiple
dogs may be allowed.

Motel 6 - Dayton Airport - Englewood
1212 S Main St
Englewood, OH
937-832-3770 (800-466-8356)
One well-behaved family pet per
room. Guest must notify front desk
upon arrival. Guest is liable for any
damages. In consideration of all
guests, pets must never be left
unattended in the guest rooms.

Super 8 Englewood
15 Rockridge Rd
Englewood, OH
937-832-3350 (800-800-8000)
Dogs of all sizes are allowed. There
is a $10 per night pet fee per pet.
Smoking and non-smoking rooms
are available for pet rooms. 2 dogs
may be allowed.

Holiday Inn Dayton/Fairborn 1-675
2800 Presidential Dr
Fairborn, OH
937-426-7800 (877-270-6405)
Dogs up to 75 pounds are allowed
for an additional one time pet fee of
$75 per room. 2 dogs may be
allowed.

Homewood Suites-Fairborn
2750 Presidential Drive
Fairborn, OH
937-429-0600 (800-225-5466)
There is a $100 one time pet charge.

Red Roof Inn - Dayton East -
Fairborn
2580 Colonel Glenn Highway
Fairborn, OH
937-426-6116 (800-RED-ROOF)
One well-behaved family pet per
room. Guest must notify front desk
upon arrival. Guest is liable for any
damages. In consideration of all
guests, pets must never be left
unattended in the guest rooms.

Knights Inn
22115 Brookpark Road
Fairview Park, OH
440-734-4500
There are no pet fees.

Quality Inn
1020 Interstate Court
Findlay, OH
419-423-4303 (877-424-6423)
Dogs are allowed for an additional

fee of $15 per night per pet. Multiple
dogs may be allowed.

Red Roof Inn - Findlay, OH
1951 Broad Avenue
Findlay, OH
419-424-0466 (800-RED-ROOF)
One well-behaved family pet per
room. Guest must notify front desk
upon arrival. Guest is liable for any
damages. In consideration of all
guests, pets must never be left
unattended in the guest rooms.

Super 8 Findlay
1600 Fox St
Findlay, OH
419-422-8863 (800-800-8000)
Dogs of all sizes are allowed. There
is a $5.34 per night pet fee per pet.
Smoking and non-smoking rooms
are available for pet rooms. 2 dogs
may be allowed.

TownePlace Suites Findlay
2501 Tiffin Avenue
Findlay, OH
419-425-9545
Dogs of all sizes are allowed. There
is a $50 one time pet fee per visit. .
2 dogs may be allowed.

Best Western Fostoria Inn & Suites
1690 N Countyline Street
Fostoria, OH
419-436-3600 (800-780-7234)
One dog up to 80 pounds is allowed
for an additional pet fee of $10 per
night; aggressive breed dogs are
not allowed. Dogs must be crated
when left alone in the room, and
they may not be left alone for more
than 3 hours or at night.

Country Club Inn and Suites
737 Independence Rd
Fostoria, OH
419-435-6511
Dogs of all sizes are allowed. There
are no additional pet fees. 2 dogs
may be allowed.

Best Western Regency Inn
6475 Culbertson Road
Franklin, OH
513-424-3551 (800-780-7234)
Dogs are allowed for an additional
pet fee per room of $10 for 1 night
and $20 for 2 or more nights. 2
dogs may be allowed.

Quality Inn
2000 William C Goode Blvd
Franklin, OH
937-743-8881 (877-424-6423)
Dogs are allowed for an additional
fee of $10 per night per pet. Multiple

dogs may be allowed.

Comfort Inn and Suites
840 Sean Drive
Fremont, OH
419-355-9300 (877-424-6423)
Dogs are allowed for an additional
one time fee of $25 per pet. Multiple
dogs may be allowed.

Holiday Inn
3422 Port Clinton Road
Fremont, OH
419-334-2682 (877-270-6405)
Dogs of all sizes are allowed for an
additional one time pet fee of $20 per
room. Multiple dogs may be allowed.

Candlewood Suites
590 Taylor Rd
Gahanna, OH
614-863-4033 (877-270-6405)
Dogs of all sizes are allowed for an
additional per pet fee of $75 for 1 to
6 nights, and $150 for 7 nights or
more. Multiple dogs may be allowed.

Holiday Inn
577 State Rt 7 N
Gallipolis, OH
740-446-0090 (877-270-6405)
Dogs of all sizes are allowed for no
additional fee. Dogs may not be left
alone in the room. Multiple dogs may
be allowed.

Holiday Inn
1620 Motor Inn Drive
Girard, OH
330-759-0606 (877-270-6405)
Dogs of all sizes are allowed for an
additional one time fee of $50 per
pet. Multiple dogs may be allowed.

La Quinta Inn Grove City
3962 Jackpot Rd
Grove City, OH
614-539-6200 (800-531-5900)
Dogs of all sizes are allowed. There
is a $25 refundable pet deposit if
paying by cash. There is a pet policy
to sign at check in. Dogs may not be
left unattended, and they must be
leashed and cleaned up after. They
are not allowed in the food or pool
areas. Multiple dogs may be allowed.

Motel 6 - Columbus South
1900 Stringtown Road
Grove City, OH
614-875-8543 (800-466-8356)
One well-behaved family pet per
room. Guest must notify front desk
upon arrival. Guest is liable for any
damages. In consideration of all
guests, pets must never be left
unattended in the guest rooms.

Quality Inn
733 Hebron Road
Heath, OH
740-522-1165 (877-424-6423)
Dogs are allowed for an additional fee of $20 per night per pet. Multiple dogs may be allowed.

Red Roof Inn - Columbus - Hebron
10668 Lancaster Road Southwest
Hebron, OH
740-467-7663 (800-RED-ROOF)
One well-behaved family pet per room. Guest must notify front desk upon arrival. Guest is liable for any damages. In consideration of all guests, pets must never be left unattended in the guest rooms.

Motel 6 - Columbus - Hilliard
3950 Parkway Ln
Hilliard, OH
614-771-1500 (800-466-8356)
One well-behaved family pet per room. Guest must notify front desk upon arrival. Guest is liable for any damages. In consideration of all guests, pets must never be left unattended in the guest rooms.

Lily Ponds Bed and Breakfast
6720 Wakefield Rd
Hiram, OH
330-569-7502
lilypondsbedandbreakfast.com
This B&B allows dogs but not cats. Dogs have their own dishes, sheets, towels, toys and treats.

Holiday Inn Express Hotel and Suites
13399 State Hwy 15
Holiday City, OH
419-485-0008 (877-270-6405)
Dogs of all sizes are allowed for an additional fee of $10 per night per pet. Multiple dogs may be allowed.

Red Roof Inn - Toledo - Holland
1214 Corporate Drive
Holland, OH
419-866-5512 (800-RED-ROOF)
One well-behaved family pet per room. Guest must notify front desk upon arrival. Guest is liable for any damages. In consideration of all guests, pets must never be left unattended in the guest rooms.

Residence Inn by Marriott
6101 Trust Drive
Holland, OH
419-867-9555
Dogs of all sizes are allowed. There is a $75 one time fee and a pet policy to sign at check in. Multiple dogs may be allowed.

Holiday Inn Express Hotel and Suites
5612 Merily Way
Huber Heights, OH
937-235-2000 (877-270-6405)
Dogs of all sizes are allowed for an additional one time fee of $25 per room. Multiple dogs may be allowed.

Red Roof Inn - Cleveland - Independence
6020 Quarry Lane
Independence, OH
216-447-0030 (800-RED-ROOF)
One well-behaved family pet per room. Guest must notify front desk upon arrival. Guest is liable for any damages. In consideration of all guests, pets must never be left unattended in the guest rooms.

Sheraton Independence Hotel
5300 Rockside Road
Independence, OH
216-524-0700 (888-625-5144)
Dogs up to 70 pounds are allowed. There are no additional pet fees. Dogs are not allowed to be left alone in the room.

Comfort Inn
605 E Main Street
Jackson, OH
740-286-7581 (877-424-6423)
Dogs up to 60 pounds are allowed for an additional one time pet fee of $20 per room. 2 dogs may be allowed.

Red Roof Inn - Jackson, OH
1000 Acy Avenue
Jackson, OH
740-288-1200 (800-RED-ROOF)
One well-behaved family pet per room. Guest must notify front desk upon arrival. Guest is liable for any damages. In consideration of all guests, pets must never be left unattended in the guest rooms.

Super 8 Kent/Akron Area
4380 Edson Rd
Kent, OH
330-678-8817 (800-800-8000)
Dogs of all sizes are allowed. There is a $5.56 per night pet fee per pet. Smoking and non-smoking rooms are available for pet rooms. 2 dogs may be allowed.

Hanna's Cottage in the Woods
Call to Arrange.
Killbuck, OH
330-377-5208
valkyrie.net/~kak/

This cottage rental is surrounded by trees and has two bedrooms, two bathrooms, full kitchen, living room and porch. The cottage is handicap accessible. Well-behaved leashed pets are welcome. No smoking or alcohol is allowed. The cabin costs about $90 per night per couple and an extra $20 per night for a child or dog. There are trails located on the property or you can visit the nearby Mohican State Park which allows leashed dogs on their 13 miles of trails. Call ahead to make a reservation.

Days Inn Cleveland/Lakewood
12019 Lake Ave
Lakewood, OH
216-226-4800 (800-329-7466)
Dogs of all sizes are allowed. There is a $100 returnable deposit required per room. 2 dogs may be allowed.

Holiday Inn Express
1861 Riverway Drive
Lancaster, OH
740-654-4445 (877-270-6405)
Dogs of all sizes are allowed for an additional pet fee of $25 for 1 to 3 days and $10 for each day thereafter per room. There may be 1 large or 2 small dogs per room. 2 dogs may be allowed.

Knights Inn
1327 River Valley Blvd
Lancaster, OH
740-687-4823
There are no pet fees.

Days Inn Lima
1250 Neubrecht Rd
Lima, OH
419-227-6515 (800-329-7466)
Dogs of all sizes are allowed. There is a $10 per night pet fee per pet. 2 dogs may be allowed.

Holiday Inn
1920 Roschman Ave
Lima, OH
419-222-0004 (877-270-6405)
Dogs of all sizes are allowed for no additional pet fee. 2 dogs may be allowed.

Motel 6 - Lima
1800 Harding Hwy
Lima, OH
419-228-0456 (800-466-8356)
One well-behaved family pet per room. Guest must notify front desk upon arrival. Guest is liable for any damages. In consideration of all guests, pets must never be left unattended in the guest rooms.

Acorn Acres
14805 Berry Road
Logan, OH
740-380-1074
Acorn Acres is located on 37 acres of trees and natural vegetation with cleared trails and a stocked pond. They offer two rental cabins and one rental cottage. All rentals units are furnished and offer air conditioning, heating, kitchenettes, bathrooms, towels and linens. Pets are allowed with prior management approval. They need to be leashed and cleaned up after. There is a $25 fee per pet per stay. Cabin rates range from about $135 to $155 per night. Prices are subject to change. The office is open from 9am to 9pm. Call ahead to make a reservation. Please do not call after 9pm.

Four Seasons Cabin Rentals
14435 Nickel Plate Road
Logan, OH
800-242-8453
fourseasonscabinrental.com/
These two cabin rentals are family owned and operated and located on 55 acres along with the owner's house. Both rental cabins are about 200 feet apart with trees in between them. Each cabin comes with a living room, two bedrooms, fully equipped kitchen, heating and air conditioning, linens, bath towels, hot tub, wood burning fireplace, picnic area, deck, fire ring. There are hiking trails located on the property. Rates are about $85 to $165 depending on season and weekday/weekend. Rates are for two adults and two children. Each additional adult or child is $15 extra, up to a total of four adults per cabin. Quiet well-behaved pets are welcome. Pets need to be leashed when outside the cabin and cleaned up after. There is a $10 per day pet fee. The cabins are located one exit south of the exit for Old Man's Cave, Conkles Hollow and Lake Logan. Call for details about reservations and payment.

Bullfrog Cabin Rentals
Call to arrange.
Loudonville, OH
800-368-2791
bullfrogmountain.com/
These two cabins rentals are located in the Amish Country. They are furnished and have fully equipped kitchens, bedrooms, bathrooms, heating, ceiling fans and sleep up to 6 people. Cabin rates range from about $100 to $150 per night depending on the cabin and the day

of the week. There is no charge for children 10 and under. Well-behaved pets are allowed and there is a $10 fee per pet per night.

Motel 6 - Cleveland East-Macedonia
311 E. Highland Rd
Macedonia, OH
330-468-1670 (800-466-8356)
One well-behaved family pet per room. Guest must notify front desk upon arrival. Guest is liable for any damages. In consideration of all guests, pets must never be left unattended in the guest rooms.

Comfort Inn North
500 N Trimble Road
Mansfield, OH
419-529-1000 (877-424-6423)
Dogs are allowed for no additional pet fee. Multiple dogs may be allowed.

La Quinta Inn Mansfield
120 Stander Avenue
Mansfield, OH
419-774-0005 (800-531-5900)
Dogs of all sizes are allowed. There are no additional fees. Dogs may not be left unattended, and they must be leashed and cleaned up after. Multiple dogs may be allowed.

Majestic Motel
8629 Northshore Blvd
Marblehead, OH
419-798-4921
Dogs of all sizes are allowed. There are no additional pet fees. Multiple dogs may be allowed.

Best Western Marietta
279 Muskingum Dr
Marietta, OH
740-374-7211 (800-780-7234)
Dogs are allowed for no additional pet fee. 2 dogs may be allowed.

Comfort Inn
700 Pike Street
Marietta, OH
740-374-8190 (877-424-6423)
Dogs are allowed for an additional fee of $10 per night per pet. Multiple dogs may be allowed.

Super 8 Marietta
46 Acme St
Marietta, OH
740-374-8888 (800-800-8000)
Dogs of all sizes are allowed. There is a $5 per night pet fee per pet. Dogs are not allowed to be left alone in the room. Smoking and non-smoking rooms are available

for pet rooms. 2 dogs may be allowed.

Comfort Inn
256 Jamesway
Marion, OH
740-389-5552 (877-424-6423)
Dogs are allowed for an additional fee of $10 per night per pet. Multiple dogs may be allowed.

Motel Inn
10220 US 42
Marysville, OH
614-873-4100 (800-800-8000)
Dogs of all sizes are allowed. There is a $5 per night pet fee per pet. Smoking and non-smoking rooms are available for pet rooms. 2 dogs may be allowed.

Days Inn Cincinnati/Near Kings Island
9735 Mason-Montgomery Rd
Mason, OH
513-398-3297 (800-329-7466)
Dogs of all sizes are allowed. There is a $10 per night pet fee per pet. 2 dogs may be allowed.

Red Roof Inn - Cincinnati Northeast - Mason-Kings Island
9847 Bardes Road
Mason, OH
513-398-3633 (800-RED-ROOF)
One well-behaved family pet per room. Guest must notify front desk upon arrival. Guest is liable for any damages. In consideration of all guests, pets must never be left unattended in the guest rooms.

Comfort Inn West
1426 S Reynolds Road
Maumee, OH
419-893-2800 (877-424-6423)
Dogs are allowed for an additional fee of $10 per night per pet. Multiple dogs may be allowed.

Days Inn Toledo/Maumee
1704 Tollgate Dr
Maumee, OH
419-897-6900 (800-329-7466)
Dogs of all sizes are allowed. There is a $10 per night pet fee per pet. 2 dogs may be allowed.

Red Roof Inn - Toledo - Maumee
1570 Reynolds Road
Maumee, OH
419-893-0292 (800-RED-ROOF)
One well-behaved family pet per room. Guest must notify front desk upon arrival. Guest is liable for any damages. In consideration of all guests, pets must never be left

unattended in the guest rooms.

Staybridge Suites Cleveland East
Mayfield Hts.
6103 Landerhaven Dr
Mayfield Heights, OH
440-442-9200 (877-270-6405)
Dogs of all sizes are allowed for an
additional one time fee of $50 per
pet. Multiple dogs may be allowed.

Holiday Inn Express Medina
2850 Medina Road
Medina, OH
330-723-4994 (877-270-6405)
Dogs up to 50 pounds are allowed
for an additional fee of $10 per night
per pet. Multiple dogs may be
allowed.

Motel 6 - Cleveland - Medina
3122 Eastpointe Drive
Medina, OH
330-723-3322 (800-466-8356)
One well-behaved family pet per
room. Guest must notify front desk
upon arrival. Guest is liable for any
damages. In consideration of all
guests, pets must never be left
unattended in the guest rooms.

Red Roof Inn - Cleveland - Medina
5021 Eastpointe Drive
Medina, OH
330-725-1395 (800-RED-ROOF)
One well-behaved family pet per
room. Guest must notify front desk
upon arrival. Guest is liable for any
damages. In consideration of all
guests, pets must never be left
unattended in the guest rooms.

Super 8 Medina/Akron Area
5161 Montville Dr
Medina, OH
330-723-8118 (800-800-8000)
Dogs of all sizes are allowed. There
is a $20 per night pet fee per pet.
Smoking and non-smoking rooms
are available for pet rooms. 2 dogs
may be allowed.

Best Western Lawnfield Inn & Suites
8434 Mentor Avenue
Mentor, OH
440-205-7378 (800-780-7234)
Dogs are allowed for an additional
one time fee of $20 per pet. There is
a pet agreement to sign at check in,
and there must be a credit card on
file. Multiple dogs may be allowed.

Motel 6 - Cleveland Northeast -
Mentor
8370 Broadmoor Rd
Mentor, OH
440-953-8835 (800-466-8356)

One well-behaved family pet per
room. Guest must notify front desk
upon arrival. Guest is liable for any
damages. In consideration of all
guests, pets must never be left
unattended in the guest rooms.

Residence Inn by Marriott
5660 Emerald Court
Mentor, OH
440-392-0800
Dogs of all sizes are allowed. There
is a $75 one time fee and a pet
policy to sign at check in. Multiple
dogs may be allowed.

Studio 6 - Cleveland - Mentor
7677 Reynolds Road
Mentor, OH
440-946-0749 (800-466-8356)
All well-behaved dog are allowed.
There is a $10 per day pet fee up to
a maximum of $50 per visit.

Super 8 Mentor/Cleveland Area
7325 Palisades Parkway
Mentor, OH
440-951-8558 (800-800-8000)
Dogs of all sizes are allowed. There
is a $10 per night pet fee per pet.
Smoking and non-smoking rooms
are available for pet rooms. 2 dogs
may be allowed.

Doubletree
300 Prestige Place
Miamisburg, OH
937-436-2400
Dogs of all sizes are allowed. There
is a $50 one time fee per room and
dogs are not allowed to be left
alone in the room. Multiple dogs
may be allowed.

Holiday Inn
31 Prestige Plaza Dr
Miamisburg, OH
937-434-8030 (877-270-6405)
Dogs of all sizes are allowed for an
additional one time pet fee of $30
per room. Multiple dogs may be
allowed.

Red Roof Inn - Dayton South -
Miamisburg
222 Byers Road
Miamisburg, OH
937-866-0705 (800-RED-ROOF)
One well-behaved family pet per
room. Guest must notify front desk
upon arrival. Guest is liable for any
damages. In consideration of all
guests, pets must never be left
unattended in the guest rooms.

Residence Inn by Marriott
155 Prestige Place

Miamisburg, OH
937-434-7881
Dogs of all sizes are allowed. There
is a $75 one time fee and a pet
policy to sign at check in. Multiple
dogs may be allowed.

Studio 6 - Dayton - Miamisburg
8101 Springboro Pike
Miamisburg, OH
937-434-8750 (800-466-8356)
One well-behaved family pet per
room. Guest must notify front desk
upon arrival. Guest is liable for any
damages. In consideration of all
guests, pets must never be left
unattended in the guest rooms.

Johnston's Lakefront Cottages
1555 Diest Road
Middle Bass Island, OH
419-285-2314
ohiocottages.com
These rental cottages offer a view of
the water and a large treed yard. The
cottages are not designated as
smoking or non-smoking. Well-
behaved dogs of all sizes are
allowed for a $50 refundable pet fee
but need to be leashed and picked
up after. To get to the cottages, you
will need to take the dog-friendly
Miller Ferry Boat Line. The ferry
requires reservations if you plan on
bringing your car. To make a
reservation, call the ferry service at
1-800-500-2421 to make
reservations.

Comfort Inn Cleveland Airport
17550 Rosbough Drive
Middleburg Heights, OH
440-234-3131 (877-424-6423)
Dogs up to 150 pounds are allowed
for an additional one time pet fee of
$35 per room. 2 dogs may be
allowed.

Motel 6 - Cleveland - Middleburg
Heights
7219 Engle Road
Middleburg Heights, OH
440-234-0990 (800-466-8356)
One well-behaved family pet per
room. Guest must notify front desk
upon arrival. Guest is liable for any
damages. In consideration of all
guests, pets must never be left
unattended in the guest rooms.

Red Roof Inn - Cleveland -
Middleburg Heights
17555 Bagley Road
Middleburg Heights, OH
440-243-2441 (800-RED-ROOF)
One well-behaved family pet per
room. Guest must notify front desk
upon arrival. Guest is liable for any

damages. In consideration of all guests, pets must never be left unattended in the guest rooms.

TownePlace Suites Cleveland Airport
7325 Engle Road
Middleburg Heights, OH
440-816-9300
Dogs of all sizes are allowed. There is a $75 one time pet fee per visit. 2 dogs may be allowed.

Manchester Inn
1027 Manchester Avenue
Middletown, OH
513-422-5481
Dogs of all sizes are allowed. There is a $25 refundable deposit per room. Multiple dogs may be allowed.

Motel 6 - Sandusky - Milan
11406 US 250 North
Milan, OH
419-499-8001 (800-466-8356)
One well-behaved family pet per room. Guest must notify front desk upon arrival. Guest is liable for any damages. In consideration of all guests, pets must never be left unattended in the guest rooms.

Red Roof Inn - Milan
11303 US 250 North
Milan, OH
419-499-4347 (800-RED-ROOF)
One well-behaved family pet per room. Guest must notify front desk upon arrival. Guest is liable for any damages. In consideration of all guests, pets must never be left unattended in the guest rooms.

Super 8 Moraine/Dayton Area
2450 Dryden Rd
Moraine, OH
937-298-0380 (800-800-8000)
Dogs of all sizes are allowed. There is a $10 per night pet fee per pet. Smoking and non-smoking rooms are available for pet rooms. 2 dogs may be allowed.

Comfort Inn
150 Howard Street
Mount Vernon, OH
740-392-6886 (877-424-6423)
Dogs are allowed for an additional fee of $10 per night per pet. Multiple dogs may be allowed.

Best Western Napoleon Inn & Suites
1290 Independence Drive
Napoleon, OH
419-599-0850 (800-780-7234)
Dogs are allowed for an additional pet fee of $12 per night per room. 2 dogs may be allowed.

Hampton Inn
1299 W High Avenue
New Philadelphia, OH
330-339-7000
One dog up to 50 pounds is allowed. There are no additional pet fees.

Motel 6 - New Philadelphia
181 Bluebell Dr SW
New Philadelphia, OH
330-339-6446 (800-466-8356)
One well-behaved family pet per room. Guest must notify front desk upon arrival. Guest is liable for any damages. In consideration of all guests, pets must never be left unattended in the guest rooms.

Schoenbrunn Inn
1186 West High Avenue
New Philadelphia, OH
330-339-4334
There is a $10 one time per stay pet fee.

Super 8 New Philadelphia
131 1/2 Bluebell Drive SW
New Philadelphia, OH
330-339-6500 (800-800-8000)
Dogs of all sizes are allowed. There is a $10 per night pet fee per pet. Smoking and non-smoking rooms are available for pet rooms. 2 dogs may be allowed.

Hampton Inn
200 Morris Crossing
Newcomerstown, OH
740-498-9800
Well behaved dogs of all sizes are allowed. There are no additional pet fees, and they request you kennel or remove your dog for housekeeping. Multiple dogs may be allowed.

Super 8 Newcomerstown
299 Adena Dr
Newcomerstown, OH
740-498-4116 (800-800-8000)
Dogs of all sizes are allowed. There is a $5 per night pet fee per pet. Smoking and non-smoking rooms are available for pet rooms. 2 dogs may be allowed.

Motel 6 - Canton
6880 Sunset Strip Ave NW
North Canton, OH
330-494-7611 (800-466-8356)
One well-behaved family pet per room. Guest must notify front desk upon arrival. Guest is liable for any damages. In consideration of all guests, pets must never be left

unattended in the guest rooms.

Red Roof Inn - Canton
5353 Inn Circle Court Northwest
North Canton, OH
330-499-1970 (800-RED-ROOF)
One well-behaved family pet per room. Guest must notify front desk upon arrival. Guest is liable for any damages. In consideration of all guests, pets must never be left unattended in the guest rooms.

Oberlin Inn
7 N Main Street
Oberlin, OH
440-775-1111
Dogs of all sizes are allowed. There are no additional pet fees. Multiple dogs may be allowed.

Radisson Hotel Cleveland Airport
25070 Country Club Blvd
Olmsted, OH
440-734-5060
Dogs up to 100 pounds are allowed. There is a $50 one time additional pet fee.

Days Inn Toledo/Perrysburg
10667 Fremont Pike
Perrysburg, OH
419-874-8771 (800-329-7466)
Dogs of all sizes are allowed. There is a $5 per night pet fee per pet. 2 dogs may be allowed.

Howard Johnson Inn
I-280 & Hanley Road
Perrysburg, OH
419-837-5245 (800-446-4656)
Dogs of all sizes are welcome. There is a $10 per day pet fee.

La Quinta Inn Toledo/Perrysburg
1154 Professional Drive
Perrysburg, OH
419-872-0000 (800-531-5900)
Dogs of all sizes are allowed. There are no additional pet fees. Dogs may not be left unattended in the rooms except for a short time, and they must be leashed and cleaned up after. Multiple dogs may be allowed.

Comfort Inn
987 E Ash Street
Piqua, OH
937-778-8100 (877-424-6423)
Dogs are allowed for an additional fee of $25 per night per pet. Multiple dogs may be allowed.

La Quinta Inn Piqua
950 East Ash Street
Piqua, OH
937-615-0140 (800-531-5900)

Dogs of all sizes are allowed. There are no additional pet fees. Dogs may not be left unattended, and they must be leashed and cleaned up after. Dogs are not allowed in food or pool areas, and are not to be brought in the front lobby entrance. Multiple dogs may be allowed.

Red Roof Inn - Boardman
1051 Tiffany South
Poland, OH
330-758-1999 (800-RED-ROOF)
One well-behaved family pet per room. Guest must notify front desk upon arrival. Guest is liable for any damages. In consideration of all guests, pets must never be left unattended in the guest rooms.

Residence Inn by Marriott
7396 Tiffany S
Poland, OH
330-726-1747
Dogs of all sizes are allowed. There is a $75 one time fee and a pet policy to sign at check in. Multiple dogs may be allowed.

Country Hearth Inn
1815 E. Perry Road
Port Clinton, OH
419-732-2111
Amenities include complimentary breakfast, waterfront outdoor pool, picnic area, boat parking, complimentary fresh baked cookies, guest laundry, vending room and non-smoking rooms. Well-behaved dogs of all sizes are welcome. There is no pet fee. From State Route 2, exit to 163 West.

Holiday Village Resort
3247 N.E. Catawba Road
Port Clinton, OH
419-797-4732
holidayvillageresort.com
All rooms are not designated as smoking or non-smoking rooms. Pets are allowed and there is no pet fee.

Lakeland Motel
121 East Perry Street
Port Clinton, OH
419-734-2101
lakelandmotel.com/
This motel is located on the water and just 1.5 blocks to the ferry which goes to Put-in-Bay. The motel offers non-smoking rooms. Well-behaved dogs of all sizes are welcome. There is no pet fee.

Days Inn Portsmouth
3762 US Hwy 23 North
Portsmouth, OH

740-354-2851 (800-329-7466)
Dogs of all sizes are allowed. There is a $10 per night pet fee per pet. 2 dogs may be allowed.

Bormans Cottages
Located on Monument Bay
Put-in-Bay, OH
419-285-3223
1awsm.com/BormansCottages.htm
These rental cottages are located on Monument Bay and a ten minute walk to downtown Put-in-Bay or a five minute walk to Perry Monument. All cottages accommodate up to six people, have lake access, a boat ramp, fully equipped kitchens, TVs, ceiling fans, grills and picnic tables. Pets are allowed and there is a $25 one time per stay pet fee. None of the cottages are designated as smoking or non-smoking. Make a reservation early as the cottages usually tend to get booked quickly.

East Point Cottages
611 Massie Lane
Put-in-Bay, OH
419-285-2204
Each of the seven cottage rentals offer color TV with cable, kitchenettes and air conditioning. The cottages are not designated smoking or non-smoking. Well-behaved dogs are allowed with a $20 one time per stay fee. Please clean up after your pet.

Red Roof Inn - Columbus East - Reynoldsburg
2449 Brice Road
Reynoldsburg, OH
614-864-3683 (800-RED-ROOF)
One well-behaved family pet per room. Guest must notify front desk upon arrival. Guest is liable for any damages. In consideration of all guests, pets must never be left unattended in the guest rooms.

Howard Johnson Inn
5171 Breckville Road
Richfield, OH
330-659-6116 (800-446-4656)
Well-behaved dogs of all sizes are allowed. There is a $5 per day additional pet fee.

Quality Inn
4742 Brecksvillle Road/H 21
Richfield, OH
330-659-6151 (877-424-6423)
Dogs are allowed for an additional one time pet fee of $25 per room. 2 dogs may be allowed.

Deer Run Manors
23095 Buena Vista Road
Rockbridge, OH
740-380-2369
Choose from the "A" Frame rental or the Manor House rental. Both rentals are two story two bedroom furnished homes with full kitchens, ceiling fans, hot tubs. Each rental sleeps up to 6 people. Rates range from about $100 to $135 per night. Rates are based on double occupancy. There is a $25 per night fee per extra person. Rates are subject to change. Pets and children are welcome. There is a $25 pet fee. Call ahead to make a reservation.

La Quinta Inn Sandusky
3304 Milan Rd
Sandusky, OH
419-626-6766 (800-531-5900)
Dogs of all sizes are allowed. There are no additional pet fees. There is a pet policy to sign at check in. Dogs may not be left unattended, and they must be leashed and cleaned up after. Multiple dogs may be allowed.

Motel 6 - Cincinnati - Sharonville
2000 E Kemper Rd
Sharonville, OH
513-772-5944 (800-466-8356)
One well-behaved family pet per room. Guest must notify front desk upon arrival. Guest is liable for any damages. In consideration of all guests, pets must never be left unattended in the guest rooms.

Motel 6 - Cincinnati North
3850 Hauck Rd
Sharonville, OH
513-563-1123 (800-466-8356)
One well-behaved family pet per room. Guest must notify front desk upon arrival. Guest is liable for any damages. In consideration of all guests, pets must never be left unattended in the guest rooms.

Red Roof Inn - Cincinnati - Sharonville
2301 Sharon Road
Sharonville, OH
513-771-5552 (800-RED-ROOF)
One well-behaved family pet per room. Guest must notify front desk upon arrival. Guest is liable for any damages. In consideration of all guests, pets must never be left unattended in the guest rooms.

Comfort Inn
1959 W Michigan Avenue
Sidney, OH
937-492-3001 (877-424-6423)
Small dogs are allowed for an

additional one time pet fee of $25 per room; the fee is $25 per pet for large dogs. 2 dogs may be allowed.

Days Inn Sidney
420 Folkerth Ave
Sidney, OH
937-492-1104 (800-329-7466)
Dogs of all sizes are allowed. There is a $5 per night pet fee per pet. 2 dogs may be allowed.

Holiday Inn Sidney
400 Folkerth Avenue
Sidney, OH
937-492-1131 (877-270-6405)
Dogs up to 80 pounds are allowed for an additional one time pet fee of $50 per room. 2 dogs may be allowed.

Chestnut Grove Cabins
23101 Chestnut Grove Rd
South Bloomingville, OH
740-332-7122
chestnutgrovecabins.com/
Rent a log home in the Hocking Hills area. The homes have two bedrooms, fully equipped kitchens, a hot tub, air conditioning, heating, a back porch and are wheelchair accessible. The homes are smoke free but smoking is permitted outside. Rates are about $139 to $169 per night per couple. Additional guests are $10 per person. Children 12 and under stay for free. Pets are allowed and there is a $25 one time pet fee. Pets need to be leashed when outside the rental unit and please clean up after your pet. Reservation require a 50% deposit and the balance is due upon arrival. Cancellations must be made 7 days prior to arrival for a refund of your deposit. They accept credit cards.

Getaway Cabins in the Hocking Hills
26366 Chapel Ridge Road
South Bloomingville, OH
740-385-3734
Cabins and cottages nestled in the Hocking Hills of southeastern Ohio. Each features fireplace and hot tub, and accommodates 2-6 guests. Located close to hiking, state parks, canoeing, horseback riding, gift & antique hops, hunting, and fishing. Pets are welcome in designated cabins. The pet fee is $30/pet per stay. Up to three pets allowed.

Top O' The Caves Cabin Rentals
26780 Chapel Ridge Road
South Bloomingville, OH
800-967-2434
topothecaves.com/
This 60 acre resort offers cabins

rentals as well as RV and tent sites. They are surrounded by dog-friendly state parks (dogs on leash) which you can walk to from your accommodation. The rustic cabins have two beds, a refrigerator, gas stove, picnic table inside and outside, heating, and ceiling fan. Cabin rates are about $50 to $75 per night. The resort also has two resort cabins, Hickory and Acorn, which have their own bathrooms (towels and linens provided), heating, air conditioning and full kitchens. They rent for about $100 or more per night. And there is one large vacation rental home which runs about $275 to $335 per night. Resort amenities include two modern shower houses with hot water, a large swimming pool, kids playground, mini golf, large game arcade, gift shop, laundry facilities and Sunday worship services. Pets are welcome and there are no pet fees. Please keep your dog leashed and clean up after them. Rental rates are subject to change. Please call ahead to check pricing or to make a reservation. The resort is located on Chapel Ridge Road, near Highway 374.

La Quinta Inn Cincinnati North
12150 Springfield Pike
Springdale, OH
513-671-2300 (800-531-5900)
Dogs of all sizes are allowed. There are no additional fees. There is a pet waiver to sign at check in. Dogs may not be left unattended, except for short periods, and a cell number must be left with the front desk. Dogs must be leashed, and removed or crated for housekeeping. Multiple dogs may be allowed.

Holiday Inn - Springfield South
383 East Leffel Lane
Springfield, OH
937-323-8631 (877-270-6405)
Dogs of all sizes are allowed for no additional pet fee; there is a pet agreement to sign at check in. Multiple dogs may be allowed.

Knights Inn
2207 West Main Street
Springfield, OH
937-325-8721
There is a $10 per day pet fee. The hotel is located at I-70 and Highway 68 North, at exit 52B.

Red Roof Inn - Springfield, OH
155 West Leffel Lane
Springfield, OH

937-325-5356 (800-RED-ROOF)
One well-behaved family pet per room. Guest must notify front desk upon arrival. Guest is liable for any damages. In consideration of all guests, pets must never be left unattended in the guest rooms.

Red Roof Inn - St Clairsville
68301 Red Roof Lane
St Clairsville, OH
740-695-4057 (800-RED-ROOF)
One well-behaved family pet per room. Guest must notify front desk upon arrival. Guest is liable for any damages. In consideration of all guests, pets must never be left unattended in the guest rooms.

Super 8 St Clairsville OH/Wheeling WV Area
68400 Matthews Dr
St Clairsville, OH
740-695-1994 (800-800-8000)
Dogs of all sizes are allowed. There is a $5 per night pet fee per pet. Smoking and non-smoking rooms are available for pet rooms. 2 dogs may be allowed.

Holiday Inn Steubenville
1401 University Blvd
Steubenville, OH
740-282-0901 (877-270-6405)
Dogs up to 50 pounds are allowed for an additional pet fee of $25 per night per room. 2 dogs may be allowed.

TownePlace Suites Cleveland Streetsboro
795 Mondial Parkway
Streetsboro, OH
330-422-1855
Dogs of all sizes are allowed. There is a $75 one time pet fee per visit. 2 dogs may be allowed.

Days Inn Cleveland Airport
9029 Pearl Rd
Strongsville, OH
440-234-3575 (800-329-7466)
Dogs of all sizes are allowed. There is a $10 per night pet fee per pet. 2 dogs may be allowed.

Motel 6 - Cleveland - Strongsville
15385 Royalton Road
Strongsville, OH
440-238-0170 (800-466-8356)
One well-behaved family pet per room. Guest must notify front desk upon arrival. Guest is liable for any damages. In consideration of all guests, pets must never be left unattended in the guest rooms.

Hide-A-Way Cabin
29043 Hide A Way Hills Road
Sugar Grove, OH
740-746-9012
This cabin rental is on 1.5 wooded acres and is located in a private gated resort in Hocking County. The cabin has two bedrooms, one bathroom, wood burning fireplace, skylights, fully equipped kitchen and cable TV with VCR/DVD player. Linens and towels are provided. The cabin is non-smoking but there are smoking areas outside. Cabin rates range from $85 to $120 per night. Children 10 and under stay for free when accompanied by an adult. Prices are subject to change. Pets are allowed but must be leashed when outside the cabin and cannot be left unattended in the cabin. The cabin is located about 45 minutes south of Columbus.

Days Inn Columbus/Sunbury
7323 State Rt 37 E
Sunbury, OH
740-362-6159 (800-329-7466)
Dogs of all sizes are allowed. There is a $10 per night pet fee per pet. 2 dogs may be allowed.

Hampton Inn
7329 State Route 37E
Sunbury, OH
740-363-4700
One dog up to 50 pounds is allowed. There is a $20 per night pet fee and a pet policy to sign at check in.

Super 8 Swanton/Toledo Airport
10753 Airport Highway
Swanton, OH
419-865-2002 (800-800-8000)
Dogs of all sizes are allowed. There is a $10 one time per pet fee per visit. Dogs are not allowed to be left alone in the room. Smoking and non-smoking rooms are available for pet rooms. 2 dogs may be allowed.

Holiday Inn Express Tiffin
78 Shaffer Park Drive
Tiffin, OH
419-443-5100 (877-270-6405)
Dogs of all sizes are allowed for an additional one time pet fee of $20 per room. Multiple dogs may be allowed.

Quality Inn
1927 S H 53
Tiffin, OH
419-447-6313 (877-424-6423)
Dogs are allowed for an additional fee of $15 (plus tax) per night per pet. Multiple dogs may be allowed.

Motel 6 - Toledo
5335 Heatherdowns Boulevard
Toledo, OH
419-865-2308 (800-466-8356)
One well-behaved family pet per room. Guest must notify front desk upon arrival. Guest is liable for any damages. In consideration of all guests, pets must never be left unattended in the guest rooms.

Radisson Hotel
101 North Summit Street
Toledo, OH
419-241-3000
Well-behaved dogs of all sizes are allowed. There are no pet fees. Dog owners must sign a pet waiver.

Red Roof Inn - Toledo - University
3530 Executive Parkway
Toledo, OH
419-536-0118 (800-RED-ROOF)
One well-behaved family pet per room. Guest must notify front desk upon arrival. Guest is liable for any damages. In consideration of all guests, pets must never be left unattended in the guest rooms.

Super 8 Toledo/Perrysburg Area
3491 Latcha Rd
Toledo, OH
419-837-6409 (800-800-8000)
Dogs of all sizes are allowed. There is a $10 per night pet fee per pet. Smoking and non-smoking rooms are available for pet rooms. 2 dogs may be allowed.

Econo Lodge
1210 Brukner Drive
Troy, OH
937-335-0013
There is a $5 per day pet fee.

Holiday Inn Express Hotel and Suites
60 Troy Town Drive
Troy, OH
937-332-1700 (877-270-6405)
Dogs of all sizes are allowed for an additional one time pet fee of $25 per room. Multiple dogs may be allowed.

Knights Inn
30 Troy Town Drive
Troy, OH
937-339-1515
There is a $10 one time per stay pet fee.

Residence Inn by Marriott
87 Troy Town Drive
Troy, OH
937-440-9303

Dogs of all sizes are allowed. There is a $75 one time fee and a pet policy to sign at check in. Multiple dogs may be allowed.

Comfort Suites
2716 Creekside Drive
Twinsburg, OH
330-963-5909 (877-424-6423)
Small dogs are allowed for an additional one time pet fee of $15 per room; the fee is $15 per pet for large dogs. 2 dogs may be allowed.

Best Western Country Inn
111 McCauley Dr
Uhrichsville, OH
740-922-0774 (800-780-7234)
Dogs are allowed for an additional fee of $5 per night per pet. 2 dogs may be allowed.

Super 8 Vandalia/Dayton Intl Airport
550 E National Rd
Vandalia, OH
937-898-7636 (800-800-8000)
Dogs of all sizes are allowed. There are no additional pet fees. Smoking and non-smoking rooms are available for pet rooms. 2 dogs may be allowed.

Days Inn Lima Area
1659 Bellefontaine St
Wapakoneta, OH
419-738-2184 (800-329-7466)
Dogs of all sizes are allowed. There is a $5 per night pet fee per pet. 2 dogs may be allowed.

Super 8 Wapakoneta
1011 Lunar Dr
Wapakoneta, OH
419-738-8810 (800-800-8000)
Dogs of all sizes are allowed. There is a $10 one time per pet fee per visit. Smoking and non-smoking rooms are available for pet rooms. 2 dogs may be allowed.

Comfort Inn
136 N Park Avenue
Warren, OH
330-393-1200 (877-424-6423)
Dogs are allowed for an additional fee of $10 per night per pet. 2 dogs may be allowed.

Best Western Del Mar
8319 SH 108
Wauseon, OH
419-335-1565 (800-780-7234)
Dogs are allowed for an additional one time pet fee of $15 per room. Multiple dogs may be allowed.

Staybridge Suites Cincinnati North

(West Chester)
8955 Lakota Drive West
West Chester, OH
513-874-1900 (877-270-6405)
One dog of any size is allowed for no additional pet fee.

Holiday Inn Cleveland-West
(Westlake)
1100 Crocker Rd
Westlake, OH
440-871-6000 (877-270-6405)
Dogs of all sizes are allowed for an additional one time pet fee of $25 per room. Multiple dogs may be allowed.

Red Roof Inn - Cleveland - Westlake
29595 Clemens Road
Westlake, OH
440-892-7920 (800-RED-ROOF)
One well-behaved family pet per room. Guest must notify front desk upon arrival. Guest is liable for any damages. In consideration of all guests, pets must never be left unattended in the guest rooms.

TownePlace Suites Cleveland
Westlake
25052 Sperry Drive
Westlake, OH
440-892-4275
Dogs of all sizes are allowed. There is a $75 one time pet fee per visit. 2 dogs may be allowed.

Holiday Inn
28600 Ridgehills Dr
Wickliffe, OH
440-585-0600 (877-270-6405)
Dogs up to 50 pounds are allowed for a $100 refundable pet deposit. 2 dogs may be allowed.

Red Roof Inn - Cleveland East
4166 SR 306
Willoughby, OH
440-946-9872 (800-RED-ROOF)
One well-behaved family pet per room. Guest must notify front desk upon arrival. Guest is liable for any damages. In consideration of all guests, pets must never be left unattended in the guest rooms.

Holiday Inn Express
155 Holiday Drive
Wilmington, OH
937-382-5858 (877-270-6405)
Dogs up to 50 pounds are allowed for an additional one time pet fee of $20 per room. 2 dogs may be allowed.

Holiday Inn Wilmington
123 Gano Road
Wilmington, OH

937-283-3200 (877-270-6405)
Dogs of all sizes are allowed for no additional fee with a credit card on file; there is a $200 refundable deposit if paying by cash. 2 dogs may be allowed.

Super 8 Wooster
969 Timken Rd
Wooster, OH
330-264-6211 (800-800-8000)
Dogs of all sizes are allowed. There is a $4 per night pet fee per pet. Smoking and non-smoking rooms are available for pet rooms. 2 dogs may be allowed.

Microtel Inn
7500 Vantage Drive
Worthington, OH
614-436-0556
There is a $10 per day pet fee.

Best Western Meander Inn
870 North Canfield-Niles Rd
Youngstown, OH
330-544-2378 (800-780-7234)
Dogs are allowed for an additional fee of $10.65 per night per pet. Multiple dogs may be allowed.

Super 8 Youngstown/Airport
4250 Belmont Ave
Youngstown, OH
330-759-0040 (800-800-8000)
Dogs of all sizes are allowed. There is a $10 one time per pet fee per visit. Smoking and non-smoking rooms are available for pet rooms. 2 dogs may be allowed.

Best Western B. R. Guest
4929 East Pike
Zanesville, OH
740-453-6300 (800-780-7234)
Dogs are allowed for an additional fee of $10 per night per pet. Multiple dogs may be allowed.

Econo Lodge
135 N 7th St
Zanesville, OH
740-452-4511
Dogs up to 50 pounds are allowed for an additional one time pet fee of $10 per room. 2 dogs may be allowed.

Holiday Inn
4645 East Pike
Zanesville, OH
740-453-0771 (877-270-6405)
Dogs of all sizes are allowed for an additional one time pet fee of $20 per room. 2 dogs may be allowed.

Red Roof Inn - Zanesville

4929 East Pike
Zanesville, OH
740-453-6300 (800-RED-ROOF)
One well-behaved family pet per room. Guest must notify front desk upon arrival. Guest is liable for any damages. In consideration of all guests, pets must never be left unattended in the guest rooms.

Super 8 Zanesville
2440 National Rd
Zanesville, OH
740-455-3124 (800-800-8000)
Dogs of all sizes are allowed. There is a $10 per night pet fee per pet. Smoking and non-smoking rooms are available for pet rooms. 2 dogs may be allowed.

Oklahoma Listings

Best Western Altus
2804 N Main St
Altus, OK
580-482-9300 (800-780-7234)
Dogs are allowed for no additional pet fee. Multiple dogs may be allowed.

Best Western Ardmore Inn
6 Holiday Dr
Ardmore, OK
580-223-7525 (800-780-7234)
Dogs are allowed for no additional pet fee. Multiple dogs may be allowed.

Comfort Inn
2700 W Broadway
Ardmore, OK
580-226-1250 (877-424-6423)
Dogs are allowed for an additional one time pet fee of $10 per room. Multiple dogs may be allowed.

Days Inn Ardmore
2614 West Broadway
Ardmore, OK
580-226-1761 (800-329-7466)
Dogs of all sizes are allowed. There is a $15 one time per pet fee per visit. 2 dogs may be allowed.

Guest Inn
2519 W H 142
Ardmore, OK
580-223-1234
Dogs of all sizes are allowed. There are no additional pet fees. Multiple dogs may be allowed.

Holiday Inn

2705 Holiday Drive
Ardmore, OK
580-223-7130 (877-270-6405)
Dogs of all sizes are allowed for an additional one time fee of $20 per pet. Multiple dogs may be allowed.

La Quinta Inn Ardmore
2432 Veterans Blvd
Ardmore, OK
580-223-7976 (800-531-5900)
Dogs of all sizes are allowed. There are no additional pet fees. There is a pet waiver to sign at check in. Dogs must be leashed and cleaned up after. Dogs must be crated when left alone in the room, and the Do Not Disturb sign hung on the door. Arrangements must be made with housekeeping if stay is longer than one day. Multiple dogs may be allowed.

Motel 6 - Ardmore
120 Holiday Drive
Ardmore, OK
580-226-7666 (800-466-8356)
One well-behaved family pet per room. Guest must notify front desk upon arrival. Guest is liable for any damages. In consideration of all guests, pets must never be left unattended in the guest rooms.

Best Western Atoka Inn
2101 S Mississippi
Atoka, OK
580-889-7381 (800-780-7234)
Dogs are allowed for an additional pet fee of $10 per night per room. Multiple dogs may be allowed.

Best Western Weston Inn
222 SE Washington Blvd
Bartlesville, OK
918-335-7755 (800-780-7234)
Dogs are allowed for no additional pet fee with a credit card on file; there is a $25 refundable deposit if paying cash. Multiple dogs may be allowed.

Super 8 Bartlesville
211 SE Washington Blvd
Bartlesville, OK
918-335-1122 (800-800-8000)
Dogs of all sizes are allowed. There are no additional pet fees. Pet must be kept in kennel when left alone. Smoking and non-smoking rooms are available for pet rooms. 2 dogs may be allowed.

Lake Eufaula Inn
HC60 Box 1835
Checotah, OK
918-473-2376

Dogs of all sizes are allowed. The 1st pet is free and for each additional pet the fee is $5 per stay. Multiple dogs may be allowed.

Best Western Inn of Chickasha
2101 S 4th St
Chickasha, OK
405-224-4890 (800-780-7234)
Dogs are allowed for an additional fee of $10 per night per pet. 2 dogs may be allowed.

Holiday Inn Express Hotel and Suites
2610 South 4th Street
Chickasha, OK
405-224-8883 (877-270-6405)
Dogs of all sizes are allowed for an additional one time fee of $25 per pet. 2 dogs may be allowed.

Best Western Will Rogers Inn
940 S Lynn Riggs Blvd
Claremore, OK
918-341-4410 (800-780-7234)
Dogs are allowed for no additional pet fee. Multiple dogs may be allowed.

Days Inn Claremore
1720 S Lynn Riggs
Claremore, OK
918-343-3297 (800-329-7466)
Dogs of all sizes are allowed. There is a $10 per night pet fee per pet. 2 dogs may be allowed.

Super 8 Claremore
1100 E Will Rogers Blvd
Claremore, OK
918-341-2323 (800-800-8000)
Dogs of all sizes are allowed. There is a $5 per night pet fee per pet. Reservations are recommended due to limited rooms for pets. Smoking and non-smoking rooms are available for pet rooms. 2 dogs may be allowed.

Trade Winds Courtyard Inn
2128 Gary Blvd
Clinton, OK
580-323-2610
Dogs are allowed for an additional fee of $10 per night per pet. The fee may be slightly lower when staying multiple days. 2 dogs may be allowed.

La Quinta Inn Oklahoma City Del City
5501 Tinker Diagonal
Del City, OK
405-672-0067 (800-531-5900)
Dogs of all sizes are allowed. There are no additional pet fees. Dogs

must be leashed and cleaned up after. Dogs must be crated or removed for housekeeping. Multiple dogs may be allowed.

Best Western Hensley's
2701 S Country Club Rd
El Reno, OK
405-262-6490 (800-780-7234)
Dogs are allowed for a $25 refundable deposit plus an additional fee of $5 per night per pet. Multiple dogs may be allowed.

Comfort Inn
1707 SW 27th Street
El Reno, OK
405-262-3050 (877-424-6423)
Well behaved dogs are allowed for an additional one time pet fee of $15 per room. Multiple dogs may be allowed.

Days Inn El Reno
2700 S Country Club Rd
El Reno, OK
405-262-8720 (800-329-7466)
Dogs of all sizes are allowed. There is a $10 one time per pet fee per visit. 2 dogs may be allowed.

Motel 6 - El Reno
1506 Domino Drive
El Reno, OK
405-262-6060 (800-466-8356)
One well-behaved family pet per room. Guest must notify front desk upon arrival. Guest is liable for any damages. In consideration of all guests, pets must never be left unattended in the guest rooms.

Days Inn Elk City
2500 S Main St
Elk City, OK
580-225-0305 (800-329-7466)
Dogs up to 70 pounds are allowed. There is a $5 per night pet fee per pet. 2 dogs may be allowed.

Holiday Inn
101 Meadow Ridge
Elk City, OK
580-225-6637 (877-270-6405)
Dogs of all sizes are allowed for an additional one time pet fee of $20 per room. 2 dogs may be allowed.

Motel 6 - Elk City
2604 East Highway 66
Elk City, OK
580-225-2541 (800-466-8356)
One well-behaved family pet per room. Guest must notify front desk upon arrival. Guest is liable for any damages. In consideration of all guests, pets must never be left

unattended in the guest rooms.

Best Western Inn of Enid
2818 South Van Buren On Hwy 81
Enid, OK
580-242-7110 (800-780-7234)
Dogs are allowed for an additional
fee of $7 per night per pet.

Days Inn Enid
2901 S Van Buren
Enid, OK
580-237-6000 (800-329-7466)
Dogs of all sizes are allowed. There
is a $10 per night pet fee per pet. 2
dogs may be allowed.

Motel 6 - Enid
2523 Mercer Drive
Enid, OK
580-237-3090 (800-466-8356)
One well-behaved family pet per
room. Guest must notify front desk
upon arrival. Guest is liable for any
damages. In consideration of all
guests, pets must never be left
unattended in the guest rooms.

Days Inn Erick
Ih 40 & Highway 30
Erick, OK
580-526-3315 (800-329-7466)
Dogs of all sizes are allowed. There
is a $5 per night pet fee per pet.
Reservations are recommended due
to limited rooms for pets. 2 dogs may
be allowed.

Best Western Glenpool/Tulsa
14831 S Casper, Hwy 75 S
Glenpool, OK
918-322-5201 (800-780-7234)
Dogs are allowed for an additional
fee per pet of $20 for each 1 to 3
days. Multiple dogs may be allowed.

Best Western TimberRidge Inn
120 E 18th St
Grove, OK
918-786-6900 (800-780-7234)
Dogs are allowed for an additional
fee of $10 per night per pet. Multiple
dogs may be allowed.

Ambassador Inn
1909 N Highway 64
Guymon, OK
580-338-5555
There are no additional pet fees.

Townsman Inn
212 NE Hwy 54
Guymon, OK
580-338-6556 (800-245-0335)
Dogs are allowed for no additional
pet fee for nightly stays. Dogs are
not allowed for weekly renters.

Multiple dogs may be allowed.

Gateway Inn
Hwy 75 and Trudgeon St
Henryetta, OK
918-652-4448
There is a $25 refundable deposit.

Super 8 Henryetta
Rte 1 Box 98
Henryetta, OK
918-652-2533 (800-800-8000)
Dogs of all sizes are allowed. There
are no additional pet fees. Smoking
and non-smoking rooms are
available for pet rooms. 2 dogs may
be allowed.

Comfort Suites
400 SE Lincoln Blvd
Idabel, OK
580-286-9393 (877-424-6423)
Dogs up to 50 pounds are allowed
for an additional fee per pet of $15
for each 1 to 3 nights. Multiple dogs
may be allowed.

Quality Inn
H 70 W
Idabel, OK
580-286-6501 (877-424-6423)
Dogs are allowed for an additional
one time fee of $10 per pet. Multiple
dogs may be allowed.

**Best Western Lawton Hotel &
Convention Center**
1125 E Gore Boulevard
Lawton, OK
580-353-0200 (800-780-7234)
Dogs are allowed for an additional
one time fee of $40 per pet Multiple
dogs may be allowed.

Days Inn Lawton
3110 Cache Rd
Lawton, OK
580-353-3104 (800-329-7466)
Dogs of all sizes are allowed. There
is a $7 per night pet fee per pet. 2
dogs may be allowed.

Motel 6 - Lawton
202 SE Lee Boulevard
Lawton, OK
580-248-8848 (800-466-8356)
One well-behaved family pet per
room. Guest must notify front desk
upon arrival. Guest is liable for any
damages. In consideration of all
guests, pets must never be left
unattended in the guest rooms.

Red Lion
3134 NW Cache Road
Lawton, OK
580-353-1682

Dogs up to 60 pounds are allowed.
There is a $25 one time fee per stay
and a pet policy to sign at check in. 2
dogs may be allowed.

Super 8 Lawton
2202 NW Hwy 277
Lawton, OK
580-353-0310 (800-800-8000)
Dogs of all sizes are allowed. There
is a $6 per night pet fee per pet.
Reservations are recommended due
to limited rooms for pets. Smoking
and non-smoking rooms are
available for pet rooms. 2 dogs may
be allowed.

Best Western Inn of McAlester
1215 George Nigh Expressway
McAlester, OK
918-426-0115 (800-780-7234)
Dogs are allowed for an additional
one time fee of $25 per pet Multiple
dogs may be allowed.

Best Western Inn of Miami
2225 E Steve Owens Blvd
Miami, OK
918-542-6681 (800-780-7234)
Dogs are allowed for no additional
pet fee. Multiple dogs may be
allowed.

**Motel 6 - Oklahoma City East-
Midwest City**
6166 Tinker Diagonal
Midwest City, OK
405-737-6676 (800-466-8356)
One well-behaved family pet per
room. Guest must notify front desk
upon arrival. Guest is liable for any
damages. In consideration of all
guests, pets must never be left
unattended in the guest rooms.

**Sheraton Midwest City Hotel at the
Reed Conference Center**
5750 Will Rogers Road.
Midwest City, OK
405-455-1800 (888-625-5144)
Dogs up to 60 pounds are allowed.
There is a $25 per night pet fee per
pet. There are no additional pet fees.
Dogs are not allowed to be left alone
in the room.

**Candlewood Suites Oklahoma City-
Moore**
1701 North Moore Ave.
Moore, OK
405-735-5151 (877-270-6405)
Dogs up to 60 pounds are allowed
for an additional one time fee of $25
per pet. 2 dogs may be allowed.

Days Inn Muskogee
900 S 32nd St

Muskogee, OK
918-683-3911 (800-329-7466)
Dogs of all sizes are allowed. There is a $5 per night pet fee per small pet and $10 per large pet. 2 dogs may be allowed.

La Quinta Inn & Suites Muskogee
3031 Military Boulevard
Muskogee, OK
918-687-9000 (800-531-5900)
Dogs of all sizes are allowed. There are no additional pet fees. Dogs must be leashed and cleaned up after. There is only one dog room available at this hotel. Multiple dogs may be allowed.

Motel 6 - Muskogee
903 South 32nd Street
Muskogee, OK
918-683-8369 (800-466-8356)
One well-behaved family pet per room. Guest must notify front desk upon arrival. Guest is liable for any damages. In consideration of all guests, pets must never be left unattended in the guest rooms.

Holiday Inn
1000 North Interstate Dr
Norman, OK
405-364-2882 (877-270-6405)
Dogs of all sizes are allowed for an additional one time pet fee of $20 per room. 2 dogs may be allowed.

Quality Inn
100 SW 26th Drive
Norman, OK
405-364-5554 (877-424-6423)
Quiet dogs are allowed for an additional fee of $5 per night per pet. Multiple dogs may be allowed.

Residence Inn by Marriott
2681 Jefferson Street
Norman, OK
405-366-0900
Dogs of all sizes are allowed. There is a $75 one time fee and a pet policy to sign at check in. Multiple dogs may be allowed.

Baymont Inn Oklahoma City South
8315 South I-35
Oklahoma City, OK
405-631-8661 (800-531-5900)
Dogs of all sizes are allowed. There are no additional pet fees. Dogs must be leashed, cleaned up after, and they must be crated or removed for housekeeping. Multiple dogs may be allowed.

Best Western Memorial Inn & Suites
1301 W Memorial Road

Oklahoma City, OK
405-286-5199 (800-780-7234)
Dogs are allowed for an additional fee of $10 per night per pet. Multiple dogs may be allowed.

Candlewood Suites Oklahoma City
4400 River Park Drive
Oklahoma City, OK
405-680-8770 (877-270-6405)
Dogs of all sizes are allowed for an additional one time pet fee of $75 per room. Multiple dogs may be allowed.

Clarion Hotel Airport
737 S Meridian Avenue
Oklahoma City, OK
405-942-8511 (877-424-6423)
Dogs are allowed for no additional pet fee. Multiple dogs may be allowed.

Comfort Inn North
4625 NE 120th Steet
Oklahoma City, OK
405-478-7282 (877-424-6423)
Dogs up to 10 pounds are allowed for an additional fee of $10 per night per pet; 11 to 40 pounds is $20 per night per pet, and over 40 pounds is $25 to $30 per night per pet. 2 dogs may be allowed.

Days Inn Oklahoma City North
12013 I-35 North Service Rd
Oklahoma City, OK
405-478-2554 (800-329-7466)
Dogs of all sizes are allowed. There is a $5 per night pet fee per pet. 2 dogs may be allowed.

Days Inn Oklahoma City South
2616 S I-35
Oklahoma City, OK
405-677-0521 (800-329-7466)
Dogs of all sizes are allowed. There is a $10 per night pet fee per pet. 2 dogs may be allowed.

Days Inn Oklahoma City West
504 S Meridian
Oklahoma City, OK
405-942-8294 (800-329-7466)
Dogs of all sizes are allowed. There is a $10 per night pet fee per pet. 2 dogs may be allowed.

Embassy Suites Hotel Oklahoma City-Will Rogers Airport
1815 S. Meridian
Oklahoma City, OK
405-682-6000
Dogs up to 75 pounds are allowed. There is a $35 one time pet fee per visit. Dogs are not allowed to be left alone in the room.

Four Points Sheraton Oklahoma City Airport
6300 East Terminal Dr.
Oklahoma City, OK
405-681-3500 (888-625-5144)
Dogs of all sizes are allowed. There is a $30 one time pet fee per visit. Dogs are not allowed to be left alone in the room.

Howard Johnson Express Inn
400 South Meridian
Oklahoma City, OK
405-943-9841 (800-446-4656)
Dogs of all sizes are welcome. There is a $6 per day pet fee.

La Quinta Inn & Suites Oklahoma City NW Expwy
4829 Northwest Expressway
Oklahoma City, OK
405-773-5575 (800-531-5900)
Dogs of all sizes are allowed. There are no additional pet fees. Dogs must be leashed, cleaned up after, and they must be crated or removed for housekeeping. Dogs are not allowed to go through the lobby during breakfast hours. Multiple dogs may be allowed.

La Quinta Inn & Suites Oklahoma City North
3003 W. Memorial Rd
Oklahoma City, OK
405-755-7000 (800-531-5900)
Dogs of all sizes are allowed. There are no additional pet fees if one of the pet friendly rooms are available. If there is not one available, then there is a $50 one time additional pet fee per room. Dogs may not be left unattended, and they must be leashed and cleaned up after. 2 dogs may be allowed.

La Quinta Inn Oklahoma City Airport
800 S. Meridian Avenue
Oklahoma City, OK
405-942-0040 (800-531-5900)
Dogs of all sizes are allowed. There are no additional pet fees. Dogs must be leashed and cleaned up after. Multiple dogs may be allowed.

Motel 6 - Oklahoma City - Airport
820 South Meridian Avenue
Oklahoma City, OK
405-946-6662 (800-466-8356)
One well-behaved family pet per room. Guest must notify front desk upon arrival. Guest is liable for any damages. In consideration of all guests, pets must never be left unattended in the guest rooms.

Motel 6 - Oklahoma City N-Frontier City
12121 North I-35 Service Road
Oklahoma City, OK
405-478-4030 (800-466-8356)
One well-behaved family pet per room. Guest must notify front desk upon arrival. Guest is liable for any damages. In consideration of all guests, pets must never be left unattended in the guest rooms.

Motel 6 - Oklahoma City West - Fairgrounds
4200 West I-40 Service Road
Oklahoma City, OK
405-947-6550 (800-466-8356)
One well-behaved family pet per room. Guest must notify front desk upon arrival. Guest is liable for any damages. In consideration of all guests, pets must never be left unattended in the guest rooms.

Quality Inn North
1200 N I35 Service Road
Oklahoma City, OK
405-478-0400 (877-424-6423)
Dogs are allowed for an additional fee of $10 per night per pet. Multiple dogs may be allowed.

Residence Inn by Marriott
1111E I240 Service Road
Oklahoma City, OK
405-634-9696
Dogs of all sizes are allowed. There is a $75 one time fee and a pet policy to sign at check in. Multiple dogs may be allowed.

Residence Inn by Marriott
4361 W Reno Avenue
Oklahoma City, OK
405-942-4500
Dogs of all sizes are allowed. There is a $75 one time fee and a pet policy to sign at check in. 2 dogs may be allowed.

Sheraton Oklahoma City Hotel
One North Broadway
Oklahoma City, OK
405-235-2780 (888-625-5144)
Dogs up to 50 pounds are allowed for no additional pet fee. Dogs may not be left alone in the room.

Studio 6 - Oklahoma City - Midwest City
5801 Tinker Diagonal
Oklahoma City, OK
405-737-8851 (800-466-8356)
One well-behaved family pet per room. Guest must notify front desk upon arrival. Guest is liable for any damages. In consideration of all guests, pets must never be left unattended in the guest rooms.

Super 8 OKC/Frontier City Area
11935 North I-35 Service Road
Oklahoma City, OK
405-478-8288 (800-800-8000)
Dogs of all sizes are allowed. There is a $10 per night pet fee per pet. Smoking and non-smoking rooms are available for pet rooms. 2 dogs may be allowed.

Super 8 Perry
2608 Fir St
Perry, OK
580-336-1600 (800-800-8000)
Dogs of all sizes are allowed. There is a $5 per night pet fee per pet. Smoking and non-smoking rooms are available for pet rooms. Reservations are recommended due to limited rooms for pets. 2 dogs may be allowed.

Days Inn Pryor
6800 S Mill
Pryor, OK
918-825-7600 (800-329-7466)
Dogs of all sizes are allowed. There is a $5 per night pet fee per pet. 2 dogs may be allowed.

Days Inn Roland
207 Cherokee Blvd
Roland, OK
918-427-1000 (800-329-7466)
Dogs up to 80 pounds are allowed. There is a $10 per night pet fee per pet. 2 dogs may be allowed.

Days Inn Sallisaw
1700 West Cherokee St
Sallisaw, OK
918-775-4406 (800-329-7466)
Dogs of all sizes are allowed. There is a $7 per night pet fee per pet. 2 dogs may be allowed.

Motel 6 - Sallisaw
1300 East Cherokee Avenue
Sallisaw, OK
918-775-6000 (800-466-8356)
One well-behaved family pet per room. Guest must notify front desk upon arrival. Guest is liable for any damages. In consideration of all guests, pets must never be left unattended in the guest rooms.

Super 8 Sallisaw
924 S Kerr
Sallisaw, OK
918-775-8900 (800-800-8000)
Dogs of all sizes are allowed. There is a $5.45 per night pet fee per pet. Smoking and non-smoking rooms are available for pet rooms. 2 dogs may be allowed.

Days Inn Tulsa/Sand Springs
1110 Charles Page Blvd
Sand Springs, OK
918-245-0283 (800-329-7466)
Dogs of all sizes are allowed. There is a $10 one time pet fee per visit. Multiple dogs may be allowed.

Motel 6 - Shawnee
4981 North Harrison Street
Shawnee, OK
405-275-5310 (800-466-8356)
One well-behaved family pet per room. Guest must notify front desk upon arrival. Guest is liable for any damages. In consideration of all guests, pets must never be left unattended in the guest rooms.

Best Western Stillwater
600 E McElroy
Stillwater, OK
405-377-7010 (800-780-7234)
Quiet dogs are allowed for no additional pet fee. Multiple dogs may be allowed.

Holiday Inn
2515 West 6th Avenue
Stillwater, OK
405-372-0800 (877-270-6405)
Dogs of all sizes are allowed for no additional pet fee. 2 dogs may be allowed.

Motel 6 - Stillwater
5122 West 6th Avenue
Stillwater, OK
405-624-0433 (800-466-8356)
One well-behaved family pet per room. Guest must notify front desk upon arrival. Guest is liable for any damages. In consideration of all guests, pets must never be left unattended in the guest rooms.

Best Western Stroud Motor Lodge
1200 N Eighth Ave
Stroud, OK
918-968-9515 (800-780-7234)
Dogs are allowed for an additional fee of $5 per night per pet. Multiple dogs may be allowed.

Baymont Inn & Suites Tulsa
4530 E. Skelly Drive
Tulsa, OK
918-488-8777 (800-531-5900)
Dogs of all sizes are allowed. There are no additional pet fees. Dogs must be leashed, cleaned up after, and crated or removed for housekeeping. Multiple dogs may be allowed.

Best Value Inn
8201 E Skelly Dr
Tulsa, OK
918-665-6800
Dogs of all sizes are allowed. There is a $8 per night pet fee per pet. 2 dogs may be allowed.

Best Western - Airport
222 N Garnett Road
Tulsa, OK
918-438-0780 (800-780-7234)
Dogs are allowed for an additional one time pet fee of $25 per room. Multiple dogs may be allowed.

Cambridge Suites
8181 E 41st St
Tulsa, OK
918-664-7241
guesthouse.net/tulsa.html
There is an $75 one time pet fee.

Candlewood Suites
10008 E 73rd Street South
Tulsa, OK
918-294-9000 (877-270-6405)
Dogs up to 150 pounds are allowed for an additional $75 for each 1 to 7 days. Dogs must be crated when left alone in the room. 2 dogs may be allowed.

Doubletree
616 W Seventh Street
Tulsa, OK
918-587-8000
Dogs of all sizes are allowed. There is a $50 one time pet fee. Multiple dogs may be allowed.

Doubletree
6110 S Yale Avenue
Tulsa, OK
918-495-1000
Two dogs up to 50 pounds are allowed. If the dog(s) are 25 pounds and under there is a one time fee of $25 per pet. If the dog(s) are over 25 pounds there is a one time fee of $50 per pet.

Embassy Suites Hotel Tulsa - I-44
3332 South 79th East Avenue
Tulsa, OK
918-622-4000
Dogs of all sizes are allowed. There is a $50 one time pet fee per visit. Dogs are not allowed to be left alone in the room.

Hilton
7902 South Lewis Avenue
Tulsa, OK
918-492-5000
Dogs are allowed for an additional one time pet fee of $50 per room. 2 dogs may be allowed.

Holiday Inn Select
5000 East Skelly Drive
Tulsa, OK
918-622-7000 (877-270-6405)
Dogs of all sizes are allowed for an additional one time pet fee of $25 per room. Multiple dogs may be allowed.

La Quinta Inn Tulsa Airport
35 N. Sheridan Rd.
Tulsa, OK
918-836-3931 (800-531-5900)
Dogs of all sizes are allowed. There is a $25 per pet per stay additional fee. Dogs may only be left in the room alone if they will be quiet and well behaved, and they must be leashed and cleaned up after. Multiple dogs may be allowed.

La Quinta Inn Tulsa South
12525 East 52nd Street South
Tulsa, OK
918-254-1626 (800-531-5900)
Dogs of all sizes are allowed. There are no additional pet fees. Dogs must be leashed, cleaned up after, and crated or removed for housekeeping. Multiple dogs may be allowed.

Motel 6 - Tulsa East
1011 South Garnett Road
Tulsa, OK
918-234-6200 (800-466-8356)
One well-behaved family pet per room. Guest must notify front desk upon arrival. Guest is liable for any damages. In consideration of all guests, pets must never be left unattended in the guest rooms.

Motel 6 - Tulsa West
5828 West Skelly Drive
Tulsa, OK
918-445-0223 (800-466-8356)
One well-behaved family pet per room. Guest must notify front desk upon arrival. Guest is liable for any damages. In consideration of all guests, pets must never be left unattended in the guest rooms.

Red Roof Inn - Tulsa, OK
4717 South Yale Avenue
Tulsa, OK
918-622-6776 (800-RED-ROOF)
One well-behaved family pet per room. Guest must notify front desk upon arrival. Guest is liable for any damages. In consideration of all guests, pets must never be left unattended in the guest rooms.

Residence Inn by Marriott
11025 E 73rd Street S
Tulsa, OK
918-250-4850
Dogs of all sizes are allowed. There is a $75 one time fee and a pet policy to sign at check in. Multiple dogs may be allowed.

Super 8 Tulsa/West
5811 S 49th West
Tulsa, OK
918-446-6000 (800-800-8000)
Dogs of all sizes are allowed. There are no additional pet fees. Smoking and non-smoking rooms are available for pet rooms. 2 dogs may be allowed.

Super 8 Big Cabin/Vinita Area
30954 S Hwy 69
Vinita, OK
918-783-5888 (800-800-8000)
Dogs of all sizes are allowed. There are no additional pet fees. Smoking and non-smoking rooms are available for pet rooms. 2 dogs may be allowed.

Days Inn Woodward
1212 NW Hwy 270
Woodward, OK
580-256-1546 (800-329-7466)
Dogs of all sizes are allowed. There is a $7 per night pet fee per pet. 2 dogs may be allowed.

Northwest Inn
Hwy. 270 and First St
Woodward, OK
580-256-7600 (800-727-7606)
There is a $10 one time pet fee.

Super 8 Woodward
4120 Williams Ave
Woodward, OK
580-254-2964 (800-800-8000)
Dogs of all sizes are allowed. There is a $10 per night pet fee per pet. Smoking and non-smoking rooms are available for pet rooms. 2 dogs may be allowed.

Wayfarer Inn
2901 Williams Ave
Woodward, OK
580-256-5553 (800-832-3273)

Best Western Inn and Suites-Yukon
11440 West I-40 Service Rd
Yukon, OK
405-265-2995 (800-780-7234)
Dogs are allowed for an additional fee of $6 per night per pet. Multiple dogs may be allowed.

Super 8 Yukon/West/OKC Area
321 N Mustang Rd
Yukon, OK
405-324-1000 (800-800-8000)
Dogs of all sizes are allowed. There is a $10 returnable deposit required per room for small pets and $15 for large pets. Smoking and non-smoking rooms are available for pet rooms. 2 dogs may be allowed.

Oregon Listings

Days Inn Albany
1100 Price Road SE
Albany, OR
541-928-5050 (800-329-7466)
Dogs of all sizes are allowed. There is a $10 per night pet fee per pet. 2 dogs may be allowed.

Holiday Inn Express Hotel and Suites
105 Opal court
Albany, OR
541-928-8820 (877-270-6405)
Dogs of all sizes are allowed for an additional one time pet fee of $30 per room. Multiple dogs may be allowed.

La Quinta Inn & Suites Albany
251 Airport Rd SE
Albany, OR
541-928-0921 (800-531-5900)
Dogs of all sizes are allowed. There are no additional pet fees. There is a pet waiver to sign at check in. Dogs must be leashed and cleaned up after. Multiple dogs may be allowed.

Motel 6 - Albany
2735 East Pacific Boulevard
Albany, OR
541-926-4233 (800-466-8356)
One well-behaved family pet per room. Guest must notify front desk upon arrival. Guest is liable for any damages. In consideration of all guests, pets must never be left unattended in the guest rooms.

Inn Arch Cape
79340 H 101
Arch Cape, OR
503-738-7373
Dogs of all sizes are allowed. There is a $15 per night per pet fee and a pet policy to sign at check in. 2 dogs may be allowed.

Best Western Bard's Inn
132 N Main St
Ashland, OR
541-482-0049 (800-780-7234)
Dogs are allowed with advance

registration for an additional fee of $15 per night per pet. Multiple dogs may be allowed.

Best Western Windsor Inn
2520 Ashland St
Ashland, OR
541-488-2330 (800-780-7234)
Dogs are allowed for an additional fee of $15 per night per pet. 2 dogs may be allowed.

La Quinta Inn & Suites Ashland
434 Valley View Rd
Ashland, OR
541-482-6932 (800-531-5900)
Dogs of all sizes are allowed. There are no additional pet fees. There is a pet waiver to sign at check in. Dogs may not be left unattended, and they must be leashed at all times, and cleaned up after. Multiple dogs may be allowed.

Super 8 Ashland
2350 Ashland St
Ashland, OR
541-482-8887 (800-800-8000)
Dogs of all sizes are allowed. There is a $10 per night pet fee per pet. Smoking and non-smoking rooms are available for pet rooms. 2 dogs may be allowed.

Windmill Inn and Suites
2525 Ashland Street
Ashland, OR
541-482-8310
Dogs of all sizes are allowed. There is a pet policy to sign at check in and there are no additional pet fees. Multiple dogs may be allowed.

Best Western Astoria Inn
555 Hamburg Ave
Astoria, OR
503-325-2205 (800-780-7234)
Dogs up to 55 pounds are allowed for an additional fee of $15 per night per pet. 2 dogs may be allowed.

Crest Motel
5366 Leif Erikson Drive
Astoria, OR
503-325-3141
Dogs of all sizes are allowed. There are no additional pet fees. Multiple dogs may be allowed.

Holiday Inn Express Hotel and Suites
204 West Marine Dr
Astoria, OR
888-898-6222 (877-270-6405)
Dogs of all sizes are allowed for an additional pet fee of $15 per night per room. Dogs may not be left

alone in the room. 2 dogs may be allowed.

Best Western Sunridge Inn
1 Sunridge Lane
Baker City, OR
541-523-6444 (800-780-7234)
Dogs are allowed with advance registration for an additional pet fee of $15 per night per room and a $50 refundable deposit. Multiple dogs may be allowed.

Best Western Inn at Face Rock
3225 Beach Loop Rd
Bandon, OR
541-347-9441 (800-780-7234)
One or two dogs are allowed for an additional one time pet fee of $15 per room; the fee is $30 for 3 or more. 2 dogs may be allowed.

Driftwood Motel
460 Hwy 101
Bandon, OR
541-347-9022
There is a $10 per day pet fee.

Sunset Motel
1755 Beach Loop Rd
Bandon, OR
541-347-2453 (800-842-2407)
sunsetmotel.com/
There is a $10 per day pet charge. All rooms are non-smoking.

Best Western Inn and Suites of Bend
721 NE 3rd St
Bend, OR
541-382-1515 (800-780-7234)
Dogs are allowed for an additional fee of $10 per night per pet. Multiple dogs may be allowed.

Entrada Lodge
19221 Century Dr
Bend, OR
541-382-4080
There is a $5 per day pet fee. Pets may not be left alone in the room.

Hampton Inn
15 NE Butler Market Road
Bend, OR
541-388-4114
Dogs of all sizes are allowed. There is a $10 per night per pet fee. There are only 2 non-smoking pet rooms available. Multiple dogs may be allowed.

La Quinta Inn Bend
61200 S Highway 97
Bend, OR
541-388-2227 (800-531-5900)
Dogs of all sizes are allowed. There are no additional pet fees. There is a

pet waiver to sign at check in. Dogs must be leashed and cleaned up after. They prefer that dogs are not left unattended in the room, but if you must be out for a short time, they must be crated. Multiple dogs may be allowed.

Motel 6 - Bend
201 Northeast 3rd Street
Bend, OR
541-382-8282 (800-466-8356)
One well-behaved family pet per room. Guest must notify front desk upon arrival. Guest is liable for any damages. In consideration of all guests, pets must never be left unattended in the guest rooms.

Quality Inn
20600 Grandview Drive
Bend, OR
541-318-0848 (877-424-6423)
Dogs up to 100 pounds are allowed for an additional fee of $10 per night per pet. 2 dogs may be allowed.

Red Lion
1415 NE Third Street
Bend, OR
541-382-7011
Dogs of all sizes are allowed. There is a pet policy to sign at check in and there are no additional fees. Multiple dogs may be allowed.

Red Lion
849 NE Third Street
Bend, OR
541-382-8384
Dogs of all sizes are allowed. There is a pet policy to sign at check in and there are no additional fees. Multiple dogs may be allowed.

Sleep Inn
600 N E Bellvue
Bend, OR
541-330-0050 (877-424-6423)
One dog is allowed for an additional one time $10 fee.

Super 8 Bend
1275 S Hwy 97
Bend, OR
541-388-6888 (800-800-8000)
Dogs of all sizes are allowed. There is a $25 returnable deposit required per room. There is a $10 one time per pet fee per visit. Smoking and non-smoking rooms are available for pet rooms. 2 dogs may be allowed.

The Riverhouse Resort
3075 N Hwy 97
Bend, OR
541-389-3111

You need to sign a pet policy.

Westward Ho Motel
904 SE Third Street
Bend, OR
541-382-2111
Dogs only are allowed and of all sizes. There are no additional pet fees. 2 dogs may be allowed.

Whaleshead Beach Resort
19921 Whaleshead Road
Brookings, OR
541-469-7446 (800-943-4325)
whalesheadresort.com/
This enchanting resort features individually decorated cottages with ocean, creek, or forest settings, and there is access to the beautiful Whaleshead Beach via a 700 foot tunnel or a short drive by car (dogs are allowed on the beach under voice control or a 6 foot leash). Some of the amenities include ocean view dining and lounge, TV/VCRs, coffee makers, barbecues, and hot tubs. Dogs of all sizes are allowed for an additional fee of $10 per night per pet. Two cabins will allow 2 pets; the others will only accept 1 pet per room. Dogs must be leashed and cleaned up after, and may only be left alone in the room if they will be quiet and well behaved. There is also an RV area on site and dogs are welcome there for no additional fees or number of dog restrictions.

Days Inn Burns
577 W Monroe
Burns, OR
541-573-2047 (800-329-7466)
Dogs of all sizes are allowed. There is a $5 per night pet fee per pet. Reservations are recommended due to limited rooms for pets. Only non-smoking rooms are used for pets.

Silver Spur Motel
789 N Broadway Avenue
Burns, OR
541-573-2077
This motel features a breakfast buffet, HBO/cable TV and refrigerators/microwaves in all rooms. Dogs of all sizes are allowed for an additional fee of $5 per night per pet for 2 dogs, and an additional $5 more per night if there are more than 2. Dogs must be well behaved, leashed, cleaned up after, and crated when left alone in the room. Multiple dogs may be allowed.

Hallmark Inns
1400 S Hemlock

Cannon Beach, OR
503-436-1566
Dogs of all sizes are allowed. There is a $12 per night per pet additional fee. 2 dogs may be allowed.

McBee Cottages
888 South Hemlock
Cannon Beach, OR
503-436-1396 (800-238-4107)
mcbeecottages.com
Dogs of all sizes are allowed in these cottages near the beach. There is a $25 per day additional pet fee.

Surfsand Resort
148 W. Gower
Cannon Beach, OR
503-436-2274 (1-800-547-6100)
surfsand.com/
This resort offers views of Haystack Rock and the Pacific Ocean from oceanfront and ocean-view rooms. The Surfsand is a nice vacation spot for families and couples. The hotel caters to four-legged family members and they host an annual "For Fun" Dog Show. The resort is entirely non-smoking and it is located near a dog-friendly restaurant called The Local Scoop. There is a $12 per day pet fee.

The Haystack Resort
3361 S. Hemlock
Cannon Beach, OR
503-436-1577 (1-800-499-2220)
haystackresort.com/
Every room and suite at the Haystack Resort offers complete ocean views. Your pet is always welcome. They are located near a dog-friendly restaurant called "The Local Scoop. There is a $10 per day additional pet fee.

The Inn at Cannon Beach
3215 S. Hemlock
Cannon Beach, OR
503-436-9085 (800-321-6304)
There is a $10 per day pet fee. A maximum of two pets per room is allowed.

Best Western Columbia River Inn
735 Wanapa St
Cascade Locks, OR
541-374-8777 (800-780-7234)
Dogs are allowed for an additional fee of $10 per night per pet. Multiple dogs may be allowed.

Junction Inn
406 Redwood Hwy
Cave Junction, OR
541-592-3106
There is a $5 per day additional pet

fee. They normally put dogs in smoking rooms, but will make exceptions.

Motel 6 - Coos Bay
1445 Bayshore Drive
Coos Bay, OR
541-267-7171 (800-466-8356)
One well-behaved family pet per room. Guest must notify front desk upon arrival. Guest is liable for any damages. In consideration of all guests, pets must never be left unattended in the guest rooms.

Red Lion
1313 N Bayshore Drive
Coos Bay, OR
541-267-4141
Dogs of all sizes are allowed. There is no fee if a credit card is on file; if cash, it is a $40 refundable deposit. Multiple dogs may be allowed.

Best Western Grand Manor Inn
925 NW Garfield Avenue
Corvallis, OR
541-758-8571 (800-780-7234)
Dogs are allowed for an additional fee of $10 per night per pet. 2 dogs may be allowed.

Holiday Inn Express
781 NE Second Street
Corvallis, OR
541-752-0800 (877-270-6405)
Dogs of all sizes are allowed for an additional pet fee of $15 per night per room. Multiple dogs may be allowed.

Motel 6 - Corvallis
935 Northwest Garfield Avenue
Corvallis, OR
541-758-9125 (800-466-8356)
One well-behaved family pet per room. Guest must notify front desk upon arrival. Guest is liable for any damages. In consideration of all guests, pets must never be left unattended in the guest rooms.

Super 8 Corvallis
407 NW 2nd Street
Corvallis, OR
541-758-8088 (800-800-8000)
Dogs of all sizes are allowed. There is a $25 returnable deposit required per room. Smoking and non-smoking rooms are available for pet rooms. 2 dogs may be allowed.

Comfort Inn
845 Gateway Blvd
Cottage Grove, OR
541-942-9747 (877-424-6423)
Dogs are allowed for an additional

fee of $10 per night per pet. 2 dogs may be allowed.

Holiday Inn Express
1601 Gateway Blvd
Cottage Grove, OR
541-942-1000 (877-270-6405)
Dogs of all sizes are allowed for an additional fee of $10 per night per pet. Multiple dogs may be allowed.

Best Western Creswell Inn
345 E Oregon Ave
Creswell, OR
541-895-3341 (800-780-7234)
Dogs are allowed for an additional one time pet fee of $10 per room. Multiple dogs may be allowed.

Trollers Lodge
355 SW H 101
Depoe Bay, OR
541-765-2287
Dogs of all sizes are allowed. There is an $8 per night per pet additional fee. 2 dogs may be allowed.

Diamond Lake Resort
350 Resort Drive
Diamond Lake, OR
541-793-3333
diamondlake.net
This resort is located on the eastern shore of Diamond Lake. Recreation in the summer includes hiking in the nearby dog-friendly national forest, fishing and water sports. Winter recreation activities include dog-friendly cross-country skiing. Pets are allowed in the cabins and motel rooms, including non-smoking rooms. Well-behaved dogs of all sizes are welcome. There is a $5 per day pet fee. Pets cannot be left alone in the rooms or cabins.

Ponderosa Motel
102 E Greenwood
Enterprise, OR
541-426-3186
Dogs up to 100 pounds are allowed. There is a $10 per night per pet additional fee. Dogs are not allowed to be left alone in the room. Multiple dogs may be allowed.

Best Western New Oregon Motel
1655 Franklin Blvd
Eugene, OR
541-683-3669 (800-780-7234)
Dogs are allowed for a $30 refundable pet deposit per room. Multiple dogs may be allowed.

Days Inn Eugene
1859 Franklin Blvd
Eugene, OR

541-342-6383 (800-329-7466)
Dogs of all sizes are allowed. There are no additional pet fees. Reservations are recommended due to limited rooms for pets. 2 dogs may be allowed.

Hilton
66 E 6th Avenue
Eugene, OR
541-342-2000
2 dogs may be allowed.

La Quinta Inn & Suites Eugene
155 Day Island Rd
Eugene, OR
541-344-8335 (800-531-5900)
Dogs of all sizes are allowed. There are no additional pet fees, but there must be a credit card on file. Dogs may not be left unattended, and they must be leashed and cleaned up after. Multiple dogs may be allowed.

Motel 6 - Eugene South - Springfield
3690 Glenwood Drive
Eugene, OR
541-687-2395 (800-466-8356)
One well-behaved family pet per room. Guest must notify front desk upon arrival. Guest is liable for any damages. In consideration of all guests, pets must never be left unattended in the guest rooms.

Red Lion
205 Coburg Road
Eugene, OR
541-342-5201
Dogs of all sizes are allowed. There is a pet policy to sign at check in and there is a $20 per night pet fee per pet. Multiple dogs may be allowed.

Residence Inn by Marriott
25 Club Road
Eugene, OR
541-342-7171
Dogs of all sizes are allowed. There is a $75 one time fee and a pet policy to sign at check in. Multiple dogs may be allowed.

Valley River Inn
1000 Valley River Way
Eugene, OR
541-687-0123
Dogs of all sizes are allowed and pet rooms are located on the 1st floor. There are no additional pet fees and dogs are not allowed to be left alone in the room. Multiple dogs may be allowed.

Best Western Pier Point Inn
85625 Highway 101
Florence, OR

541-997-7191 (800-780-7234)
Dogs are allowed for an additional fee of $10 per night per pet. Multiple dogs may be allowed.

Ocean Breeze Motel
85165 H 101S
Florence, OR
541-997-2642
Dogs of all sizes are accepted on an individual basis, but no cats. There is an $8 per night per pet fee plus a $50 refundable deposit, and a credit card must be on file. Dogs are not allowed to be left alone in the room, and they ask you cover the furniture. Multiple dogs may be allowed.

Whales Watch Vacation Rentals
88572 2nd Ave
Florence, OR
541-999-1493 (800-760-1866)
whaleswatch.com
Whales Watch Vacation Rentals homes are located on Heceta Beach. Enjoy your time at the coast with all the comforts of home. Some of the vacation homes allow dogs - when you reserve a house you need to request a dog-friendly home. There may be additional pet fees. Cats are not permitted at any of the houses. There is a two night minimum rental and you can call to make reservations at their toll-free number 800-760-1866.

Best Western University Inn & Suites
3933 Pacific Avenue
Forest grove, OR
503-992-8888 (800-780-7234)
Dogs up to 50 pounds are allowed for an additional fee of $15 per night per pet. Known aggressive breeds are not allowed. 2 dogs may be allowed.

Comfort Inn
502 Garibaldi Avenue
Garibaldi, OR
503-322-3338 (877-424-6423)
Dogs up to 50 pounds are allowed for an additional fee of $20 per night per pet. 2 dogs may be allowed.

Gearhart Ocean Inn
67 N Cottage Avenue
Gearhart, OR
503-738-7373
Dogs of all sizes are allowed. There is a $15 per night per pet fee and a pet policy to sign at check in. 2 dogs may be allowed.

Econo Lodge
29171 Eltensburg Ave
Gold Beach, OR

541-247-6606
There is a $5 one time pet fee.

Jot's Resort
94360 Wedderburn Loop
Gold Beach, OR
541-247-6676 (800-FOR-JOTS)
jotsresort.com/
There is a $10 per day pet fee. Pets are allowed in the deluxe rooms overlooking the river.

Best Western Grants Pass Inn
111 NE Agness Ave
Grants Pass, OR
541-476-1117 (800-780-7234)
Dogs are allowed for an additional fee of $10 per night per pet. Multiple dogs may be allowed.

Best Western Inn at the Rogue
8959 Rogue River Highway
Grants Pass, OR
541-582-2200 (800-780-7234)
Dogs under 20 pounds are allowed for an additional fee of $10 per night per pet; the fee is $20 per night per pet for dogs over 20 pounds. 2 dogs may be allowed.

Comfort Inn
1889 NE 6th Street
Grants Pass, OR
541-479-8301 (877-424-6423)
Dogs are allowed for an additional fee of $10 per pet for each 1 to 7 days. Multiple dogs may be allowed.

Grants Pass Vacation Rental . com
Call to Arrange
Grants Pass, OR
541-660-5673
GrantsPassVacationRental.com
Grants Pass Vacation Rental is centrally located in Grants Pass. This 3 bedroom, 2 bath home offers a fenced yard for your dog or kids, wireless Internet and a Nautilus work out system.

Holiday Inn Express
105 NE Agness Ave
Grants Pass, OR
541-471-6144 (877-270-6405)
Dogs of all sizes are allowed for an additional fee of $10 per night per pet. Multiple dogs may be allowed.

La Quinta Inn & Suites Grants Pass
243 NE Morgan Lane
Grants Pass, OR
541-472-1808 (800-531-5900)
Dogs of all sizes are allowed. There are no additional pet fees. Dogs must be leashed and cleaned up after. Dogs may only left for short periods, and only then if they will be

quiet and well behaved. If they disturb other quests when you are away, they add a $25 fee. Multiple dogs may be allowed.

Motel 6 - Grants Pass
1800 NE 7th Street
Grants Pass, OR
541-474-1331 (800-466-8356)
One well-behaved family pet per room. Guest must notify front desk upon arrival. Guest is liable for any damages. In consideration of all guests, pets must never be left unattended in the guest rooms.

Redwood Motel
815 NE 6th Street
Grants Pass, OR
541-476-0878
redwoodmotel.com
Dogs of all sizes are allowed for a $10 additional pet fee. There are limited pet rooms so you need to tell the hotel about your pet when making reservations.

Super 8 Grants Pass
1949 NE 7th St
Grants Pass, OR
541-474-0888 (800-800-8000)
Dogs of all sizes are allowed. There is a $25 returnable deposit required per room. Smoking and non-smoking rooms are available for pet rooms. 2 dogs may be allowed.

Quality Inn and Suites
2323 NE 181st Avenue
Gresham, OR
503-492-4000 (877-424-6423)
Dogs are allowed for an additional one time fee of $20 per pet. 2 dogs may be allowed.

Super 8 Gresham/Portland Area
121 NE 181st Ave
Gresham, OR
503-661-5100 (800-800-8000)
Dogs of all sizes are allowed. There is a $10 per night pet fee per pet. Smoking and non-smoking rooms are available for pet rooms. 2 dogs may be allowed.

Best Western Beachfront Inn
16008 Boat Basin Rd
Harbor, OR
541-469-7779 (800-780-7234)
Dogs are allowed for an additional fee of $10 per night per pet. Multiple dogs may be allowed.

Red Lion
3500 NE Cornell Road
Hillsboro, OR
503-648-3500

Dogs of all sizes are allowed. There is a $10 per night per room fee up to a maximum charge of $50 and a pet policy to sign at check in. Multiple dogs may be allowed.

Residence Inn by Marriott
18855 NW Tanasbourne Drive
Hillsboro, OR
503-531-3200
Dogs of all sizes are allowed. There is a $10 per night fee and a pet policy to sign at check in. Multiple dogs may be allowed.

TownePlace Suites Portland Hillsboro
6550 NE Brighton St
Hillsboro, OR
503-268-6000
Dogs of all sizes are allowed. There is a $10 per night pet fee per pet. 2 dogs may be allowed.

Best Western Rory & Ryan Inns
534 Highway 20 N
Hines, OR
541-573-5050 (800-780-7234)
Dogs are allowed for an additional pet fee of $15 per night per room. 2 dogs may be allowed.

Comfort Inn
504 N H 20
Hines, OR
541-573-3370 (877-424-6423)
Dogs are allowed for an additional fee of $10 per night per pet. There may be 1 large or 2 small dogs per room. 2 dogs may be allowed.

Best Western Hood River Inn
1108 E Marina Way
Hood River, OR
541-386-2200 (800-780-7234)
Dogs are allowed for an additional fee of $12 per night per pet. Multiple dogs may be allowed.

Columbia Gorge Hotel
4000 Westcliff Dr
Hood River, OR
541-386-5566 (800-345-1921)
columbiagorgehotel.com/
Dogs of all sizes are allowed. There is a $25 pet charge.

Pheasant Valley's Bed & Breakfast and Winery
3890 Acree Drive
Hood River, OR
541-387-3040 (877-386-BEDS (2337))
This Bed and Breakfast offers a two bedroom cottage that is complete with a kitchen, living and dining area, bath, private covered deck, and a

campfire. They feature a full sized breakfast, and a great view of Mt Hood. They offer summer/winter rates for monthly, weekly, or nightly. Dogs of all sizes are allowed for no additional fee. Dogs may not be left unattended at any time, and they must be leashed and properly cleaned up after. If your pet is used to being on the furniture or bed, they request the furnishings be covered with a clean mat or blanket. Set in this picturesque setting is also an award-winning winery, and a certified organic pear and apple orchard Dogs are not allowed in the main B&B. 2 dogs may be allowed.

Mountain View Motel and RV Park
83450 Joseph H
Joseph, OR
541-432-2982
Dogs of all sizes are allowed. There are no additional pet fees. There are some breed restrictions. Multiple dogs may be allowed.

Best Western Klamath Inn
4061 South Sixth St
Klamath Falls, OR
541-882-1200 (800-780-7234)
Dogs are allowed for an additional fee of $10 per night per pet. Multiple dogs may be allowed.

Cimarron Motor Inn
3060 S Sixth St
Klamath Falls, OR
541-882-4601
There is a $5 one time fee for pets.

CrystalWood Lodge
38625 Westside Road
Klamath Falls, OR
541-381-2322
Located in the Southern Oregon Cascades, this lodge welcomes all well-behaved dogs. There is no pet fee.

Motel 6 - Klamath Falls
5136 South 6th Street
Klamath Falls, OR
541-884-2110 (800-466-8356)
One well-behaved family pet per room. Guest must notify front desk upon arrival. Guest is liable for any damages. In consideration of all guests, pets must never be left unattended in the guest rooms.

Quality Inn
100 Main Street
Klamath Falls, OR
541-882-4666 (877-424-6423)
Dogs are allowed for an additional fee of $10 per night per pet. Multiple

dogs may be allowed.

Shilo Suites Hotel
2500 Almond St
Klamath Falls, OR
541-885-7980
There is a $10 per day pet fee.

Super 8 Klamath Falls
3805 Hwy 97N
Klamath Falls, OR
541-884-8880 (800-800-8000)
Dogs of all sizes are allowed. There is a $25 returnable deposit required per room. Smoking and non-smoking rooms are available for pet rooms. 2 dogs may be allowed.

Crowne Plaza
14811 Kruse Oaks Dr
Lake Oswego, OR
503-624-8400 (877-270-6405)
Quiet dogs of all sizes are allowed for an additional pet fee of $20 per night per room, and dogs must be crated when left alone in the room. 2 dogs may be allowed.

Residence Inn by Marriott
15200 SW Bangy Road
Lake Oswego, OR
503-684-2603
Dogs of all sizes are allowed. There is a $75 one time fee and a pet policy to sign at check in. Multiple dogs may be allowed.

Chinook Winds Casino Resort Hotel
1501 NW 40th Place
Lincoln City, OR
541-996-5825 (877-4BEACH1 (423-2241))
This hotel offers ocean front property located right next to the casino. They offer an indoor heated swimming pool, sauna, spa, a full service restaurant and lounge with live entertainment on weekends, and a complimentary shuttle to the casino. Dogs of all sizes are allowed for an additional fee of $15 per night per pet. Dogs may not be left unattended, and they must be leashed and cleaned up after. Dogs are allowed in the front lobby and around most of the grounds. There are also special dog walk areas. Dogs are not allowed in the casino, the pool, or in food service areas. Multiple dogs may be allowed.

Ester Lee Motel
3803 SW H 101
Lincoln City, OR
541-996-3606
Dogs of all sizes are allowed in the cottages but not the motel. There is a

312

$7 per night per pet fee and a pet policy to sign at check in. 2 dogs may be allowed.

Motel 6 - Lincoln City
3517 N Highway 101
Lincoln City, OR
541-996-9900 (800-466-8356)
One well-behaved family pet per room. Guest must notify front desk upon arrival. Guest is liable for any damages. In consideration of all guests, pets must never be left unattended in the guest rooms.

Best Western Rama Inn
12 SW 4th St
Madras, OR
541-475-6141 (800-780-7234)
One dog under 25 pounds is $10 per night; the fee is $20 per night for dogs over 25 pounds.

Red Lion
2535 NE Cumulus Avenue
McMinnville, OR
503-472-1500
Dogs of all sizes are allowed. There is a $10 per night per pet fee and a pet policy to sign at check in. Multiple dogs may be allowed.

Best Western Horizon Inn
1154 E Barnett Road
Medford, OR
541-779-5085 (800-780-7234)
Dogs are allowed for an additional fee of $20 per night per pet. Multiple dogs may be allowed.

Candlewood Suites Medford
3548 Heathrow Way
Medford, OR
541-772-2800 (877-270-6405)
Dogs of all sizes are allowed for an additional one time pet fee of $50 per room. 2 dogs may be allowed.

Motel 6 - Medford North
2400 Biddle Road
Medford, OR
541-779-0550 (800-466-8356)
One well-behaved pet is welcome. There are no additional pet fees. Pets may not be left unattended in the room.

Motel 6 - Medford South
950 Alba Drive
Medford, OR
541-773-4290 (800-466-8356)
One well-behaved family pet per room. Guest must notify front desk upon arrival. Guest is liable for any damages. In consideration of all guests, pets must never be left unattended in the guest rooms.

Red Lion
200 N Riverside Avenue
Medford, OR
541-779-5811
Dogs of all sizes are allowed. There are no additional pet fees. Multiple dogs may be allowed.

Reston Hotel
2300 Crater Lake Hwy
Medford, OR
541-779-3141
restonhotel.com/
There is a $20 one time pet fee.

Windmill Inn
1950 Biddle Road
Medford, OR
541-779-0050
Dogs of all sizes are allowed. There are no additional pet fees. Multiple dogs may be allowed.

Sweet Virginia's Bed and Breakfast
407 6th Street
Metolius, OR
541-546-3031
The house was built in 1915 at a time when Metolius, Oregon was a booming railroad town. The city is smaller now. Three guest rooms are available. Well-behaved dogs are welcome and the owners have two dogs on the property. They have two large fenced yards. Dog beds and other supplies are available.

Cooper Spur Mountain Resort
10755 Cooper Spur Rd
Mount Hood, OR
541-352-6692
cooperspur.com
There are designated pet rooms. There is a $20 one time per stay additional pet fee. Multiple dogs may be allowed.

Terimore Lodging by the Sea
5105 Crab Avenue
Netarts Bay, OR
503-842-4623 (800-635-1821)
oregoncoast.com/terimore/
Located off the beaten path, and in one of the most beautiful areas along the coast, this inn offers ocean views, TV with HBO/ESPN, and some of the units have kitchens and fireplaces. Dogs of all sizes are allowed for an additional fee of $7 per night for one dog and $10 per night for two dogs. Dogs may only be left for a short time if they will be quiet, well behaved, and a contact number is left with the front desk. Dogs must be leashed and cleaned up after at all times. 2 dogs may be

allowed.

Best Western Agate Beach Inn
3019 N Coast Highway
Newport, OR
541-265-9411 (800-780-7234)
Dogs are allowed for an additional one time fee of $20 per pet. 2 dogs may be allowed.

Hallmark Resort
744 SW Elizabeth St
Newport, OR
541-265-2600
ohwy.com/or/h/hallresn.htm
There is a $5 per day pet fee, Dogs are allowed on the first floor only.

La Quinta Inn & Suites Newport
45 SE 32nd Street
Newport, OR
541-867-7727 (800-531-5900)
Dogs of all sizes are allowed. There are no additional pet fees. Dogs may not be left unattended, and they must be well behaved, leashed and cleaned up after. 2 dogs may be allowed.

Shilo Oceãnfront Resort
536 SW Elizabeth St
Newport, OR
541-265-7701
There is a $10 per day pet fee.

Best Western Oakridge Inn
47433 Hwy 58
Oakridge, OR
541-782-2212 (800-780-7234)
Dogs are allowed for an additional fee of $10 per night per pet. 2 dogs may be allowed.

Holiday Inn
1249 Topadera Ave
Ontario, OR
541-889-8621 (877-270-6405)
Dogs of all sizes are for an additional one time pet fee of $10 per room for 1 or 2 dogs; a 3rd dog is an additional $10. Multiple dogs may be allowed.

Motel 6 - Ontario
275 NE 12th Street
Ontario, OR
541-889-6617 (800-466-8356)
One well-behaved family pet per room. Guest must notify front desk upon arrival. Guest is liable for any damages. In consideration of all guests, pets must never be left unattended in the guest rooms.

Holiday Inn Express
600 SE Nye Ave
Pendleton, OR

541-966-6520 (877-270-6405)
Dogs of all sizes are allowed for an additional one time pet fee of $10 per room. Multiple dogs may be allowed.

Motel 6 - Pendleton
325 Southeast Nye Avenue
Pendleton, OR
541-276-3160 (800-466-8356)
One well-behaved family pet per room. Guest must notify front desk upon arrival. Guest is liable for any damages. In consideration of all guests, pets must never be left unattended in the guest rooms.

Red Lion
304 SE Nye Avenue
Pendleton, OR
541-276-6111
Dogs of all sizes are allowed. There is a $20 refundable deposit if paying with cash and no fee with a credit card on file. There is a pet policy to sign at check in. Multiple dogs may be allowed.

Best Western Inn at the Meadows
1215 N Hayden Meadows Drive
Portland, OR
503-286-9600 (800-780-7234)
Dogs are allowed for an additional pet fee of $20 per night per room. 2 dogs may be allowed.

Days Inn Portland North
9930 N Whitaker Road
Portland, OR
503-289-1800 (800-329-7466)
Dogs of all sizes are allowed. There is a $15 one time per pet fee per visit. 2 dogs may be allowed.

Four Points by Sheraton Portland Downtown
50 Southwest Morrison
Portland, OR
503-221-0711 (888-625-5144)
Dogs up to 50 pounds are allowed for no additional pet fee. Dogs may not be left alone in the room.

Hilton
921 SW Sixth Avenue
Portland, OR
503-226-1611
Dogs up to 50 pounds are allowed for an additional one time pet fee of $25 per room. 2 dogs may be allowed.

Holiday Inn Portland-Airport (I-205)
8439 Ne Columbia Blvd.
Portland, OR
503-256-5000 (877-270-6405)
Dogs of all sizes are allowed for an additional one time pet fee of $25 per

room. 2 dogs may be allowed.

Hotel Lucia
400 SW Broadway
Portland, OR
503-228-7221
There is a $35 non-refundable one time pet fee.

Hotel Monaco Portland
506 S.W. Washington
Portland, OR
503-222-0001
monaco-portland.com
Well-behaved dogs of all sizes are welcome at this pet-friendly hotel. The luxury boutique hotel offers both rooms and suites. Hotel amenities include complimentary evening wine service, and a 24 hour on-site fitness room. There are no pet fees, just sign a pet liability form.

Hotel Vintage Plaza
422 SW Broadway
Portland, OR
503-228-1212
vintageplaza.com/
Well-behaved dogs of all sizes are welcome at this pet-friendly hotel. The luxury boutique hotel offers both rooms and suites. Hotel amenities include complimentary evening wine service, complimentary high-speed Internet access in all guest rooms, 24 hour room service and an on-site fitness room. There are no pet fees, just sign a pet liability form.

La Quinta Inn & Suites Portland Airport
11207 NE Holman St.
Portland, OR
503-382-3820 (800-531-5900)
Dogs of all sizes are allowed. There are no additional pet fees, but a credit card must be on file. Dogs must be quiet, leashed, cleaned up after, and crated if left alone in the room. Dogs are not allowed in the pool or breakfast areas. Multiple dogs may be allowed.

La Quinta Inn & Suites Portland Northwest
4319 NW Yeon
Portland, OR
503-497-9044 (800-531-5900)
Dogs of all sizes are allowed. There are no additional pet fees. Dogs must be leashed, cleaned up after, and the Do Not Disturb sign on the door if there is a pet alone in the room. Multiple dogs may be allowed.

La Quinta Inn Portland Convention Center
431 NE Multnomah
Portland, OR
503-233-7933 (800-531-5900)
Dogs of all sizes are allowed. There are no additional pet fees. Dogs must be leashed and cleaned up after. Dogs must be crated if left alone in the room. Multiple dogs may be allowed.

Mallory Hotel
729 SW 15th
Portland, OR
503-223-6311 (800-228-8657)
malloryhotel.com/
There is a $10 one time fee for pets.

Motel 6 - Portland Central
3104-06 Se Powell Boulevard
Portland, OR
503-238-0600 (800-466-8356)
One well-behaved family pet per room. Guest must notify front desk upon arrival. Guest is liable for any damages. In consideration of all guests, pets must never be left unattended in the guest rooms.

Motel 6 - Portland Mall - 205
9225 Southeast Stark Street
Portland, OR
503-255-0808 (800-466-8356)
One well-behaved family pet per room. Guest must notify front desk upon arrival. Guest is liable for any damages. In consideration of all guests, pets must never be left unattended in the guest rooms.

Motel 6 - Portland North
1125 North Schmeer Road
Portland, OR
503-247-3700 (800-466-8356)
One well-behaved family pet per room. Guest must notify front desk upon arrival. Guest is liable for any damages. In consideration of all guests, pets must never be left unattended in the guest rooms.

Red Lion
5019 NE 102nd Street
Portland, OR
503-252-6397
Dogs of all sizes are allowed. There is a $15 per stay per room fee for 2 pets any size. There is an additional $15 per stay if more than 2. There is a pet policy to sign at check in.

Residence Inn by Marriott
1710 NE Multnomah Street
Portland, OR
503-288-1400

Dogs of all sizes are allowed. There is a $50 one time fee and a pet policy to sign at check in. 2 dogs may be allowed.

Residence Inn by Marriott
2115 SW River Parkway
Portland, OR
503-552-9500
Well behaved dogs of all sizes are allowed. There is a $10 per night per pet fee and a pet policy to sign at check in. Multiple dogs may be allowed.

Sheraton Airport Hotel
8235 Northeast Airport Way
Portland, OR
503-281-2500 (888-625-5144)
Dogs of all sizes are allowed for an additional one time pet fee of $25 per room. Dogs may not be left alone in the room.

Sleep Inn East
2261 NE 181 Avenue
Portland, OR
503-618-8400 (877-424-6423)
Dogs are allowed for an additional fee of $15 per night per pet. 2 dogs may be allowed.

Staybridge Suites
11936 NE Glenn Widing Drive
Portland, OR
503-262-8888 (877-270-6405)
Dogs up to 50 pounds are allowed for a $100 one time fee plus an additional pet fee of $25 per night per room. 2 dogs may be allowed.

Super 8 Portland/Airport
11011 NE Holman
Portland, OR
503-257-8988 (800-800-8000)
Dogs of all sizes are allowed. There is a $25 returnable deposit required per room. Smoking and non-smoking rooms are available for pet rooms. 2 dogs may be allowed.

The Benson Hotel
309 SW Broadway
Portland, OR
503-228-2000
Dogs up to 75 pounds are allowed. There is a $75 one time additional pet fee per room. 2 dogs may be allowed.

The Heathman Hotel
1001 SW Broadway at Salmon
Portland, OR
503-241-4100
Dogs of all sizes are allowed. There is a pet policy to sign at check in and there are no additional pet fees.

Multiple dogs may be allowed.

The Mark Spencer Hotel
409 SW 11th Avenue
Portland, OR
503-224-3293
Dogs of all sizes are allowed. There is a $10 per night per pet additional fee. Multiple dogs may be allowed.

The Westin Portland
750 Southwest Alder St.
Portland, OR
503-294-9000 (888-625-5144)
Dogs up to 50 pounds are allowed for no additional pet fee. Dogs may not be left alone in the room.

Best Western Prineville Inn
1475 NE Third St
Prineville, OR
541-447-8080 (800-780-7234)
Dogs are allowed for an additional pet fee of $15 per night per room. 2 dogs may be allowed.

Motel 6 - Redmond
2247 South US Route 97
Redmond, OR
541-923-2100 (800-466-8356)
One well-behaved family pet per room. Guest must notify front desk upon arrival. Guest is liable for any damages. In consideration of all guests, pets must never be left unattended in the guest rooms.

Super 8 Redmond
3629 SW 21st Place
Redmond, OR
541-548-8881 (800-800-8000)
Dogs of all sizes are allowed. There is a $10 one time per pet fee per visit. Smoking and non-smoking rooms are available for pet rooms. 2 dogs may be allowed.

Best Western Salbasgeon Inn and Suites of Reedsport
1400 Hwy Ave US 101
Reedsport, OR
541-271-4831 (800-780-7234)
Dogs are allowed for an additional fee of $10 per night per pet. Multiple dogs may be allowed.

Economy Inn
1593 Highway Ave 101
Reedsport, OR
541-271-3671
There is a $5 per day pet fee.

Loon Lake Lodge and RV Resort
9011 Loon Lake Road
Reedsport, OR
541-599-2244
Well behaved and friendly dogs of

all sizes are allowed. There are no additional pet fees. Multiple dogs may be allowed.

Best Western Rice Hill
621 John Long Road
Rice Hill, OR
541-849-3335 (800-780-7234)
Dogs are allowed for an additional pet fee of $10 per night per room. Multiple dogs may be allowed.

Ocean Locomotion
19130 Alder
Rockaway, OR
503-355-2093
Dogs only are allowed and of all sizes. You can have up to 3 dogs if they are under 50 pounds and up to 2 dogs if they are over 50 pounds. There is a $5 per night per pet fee and a pet policy to sign at check in.

Holiday Inn Express
375 Harvard Blvd
Roseburg, OR
541-673-7517 (877-270-6405)
Dogs of all sizes are allowed for an additional pet fee of $10 per night per room. Multiple dogs may be allowed.

Motel 6 - Roseburg
3100 Northwest Aviation
Roseburg, OR
541-464-8000 (800-466-8356)
One well-behaved family pet per room. Guest must notify front desk upon arrival. Guest is liable for any damages. In consideration of all guests, pets must never be left unattended in the guest rooms.

Quality Inn Central
427 NW Garden Valley Blvd
Roseburg, OR
541-673-5561 (877-424-6423)
Dogs are allowed for a $50 refundable deposit plus an additional pet fee of $10 per night per room. Multiple dogs may be allowed.

Sleep Inn and Suites
2855 NW Edenbower Blvd
Roseburg, OR
541-464-8338 (877-424-6423)
Dogs are allowed for an additional one time pet fee of $10 per room. Multiple dogs may be allowed.

Super 8 Roseburg
3200 NW Aviation Dr
Roseburg, OR
541-672-8880 (800-800-8000)
Dogs of all sizes are allowed. There is a $25 returnable deposit required per room. Smoking and non-smoking

rooms are available for pet rooms. 2 dogs may be allowed.

Windmill Inn
1450 NW Mulholland Drive
Roseburg, OR
541-673-0901
Dogs of all sizes are allowed. There is a pet policy to sign at check in and there are no additional pet fees. Multiple dogs may be allowed.

Best Western Black Bear Inn
1600 Motor Court NE
Salem, OR
503-581-1559 (800-780-7234)
Dogs are allowed for an additional pet fee of $10 per night per room. Multiple dogs may be allowed.

Best Western Pacific Highway Inn
4646 Portland Rd NE
Salem, OR
503-390-3200 (800-780-7234)
Dogs are allowed for an additional pet fee per room of $20 for 1 to 2 days; $40 for 3 to 5 days, and $60 for 6 days or more. 2 dogs may be allowed.

Motel 6 - Salem
1401 Hawthorne Avennue Northeast
Salem, OR
503-371-8024 (800-466-8356)
One well-behaved family pet per room. Guest must notify front desk upon arrival. Guest is liable for any damages. In consideration of all guests, pets must never be left unattended in the guest rooms.

Phoenix Inn - Salem South
4370 Commercial St SE
Salem, OR
503-588-9220 (800-445-4498)
There is a $10 per day pet charge.

Red Lion
3301 Market Street
Salem, OR
503-370-7888
Dogs of all sizes are allowed. There is a $10 per night per pet additional fee.

Residence Inn by Marriott
640 Hawthorne Avenue SE
Salem, OR
503-585-6500
Dogs of all sizes are allowed. There is a $75 one time fee and a pet policy to sign at check in. 2 dogs may be allowed.

Super 8 Salem
1288 Hawthorne NE
Salem, OR

503-370-8888 (800-800-8000)
Dogs of all sizes are allowed. There is a $25 returnable deposit required per room. There is a $10 one time per pet fee per visit. Reservations are recommended due to limited rooms for pets. Smoking and non-smoking rooms are available for pet rooms. 2 dogs may be allowed.

Best Western Sandy Inn
37465 Hwy 26
Sandy, OR
503-668-7100 (800-780-7234)
Dogs are allowed for an additional fee of $10 per night per pet. Multiple dogs may be allowed.

Best Western Ocean View Resort
414 N Prom
Seaside, OR
503-738-3334 (800-780-7234)
Dogs are allowed for an additional fee of $20 per night per pet. Multiple dogs may be allowed.

Motel 6 - Seaside
2369 South Roosevelt Drive
Seaside, OR
503-738-6269 (800-466-8356)
One well-behaved family pet per room. Guest must notify front desk upon arrival. Guest is liable for any damages. In consideration of all guests, pets must never be left unattended in the guest rooms.

Seaside Convention Center Inn
441 Second Ave
Seaside, OR
503-738-9581 (800-699-5070)
seasideccinn.com/
There is a $10.00 per day pet charge.

Best Western Ponderosa Lodge
500 Hwy 20 West
Sisters, OR
541-549-1234 (800-780-7234)
Dogs are allowed for an additional fee of $10 per night per pet. 2 dogs may be allowed.

Motel 6 - Eugene North - Springfield
3752 International Court
Springfield, OR
541-741-1105 (800-466-8356)
One well-behaved family pet per room. Guest must notify front desk upon arrival. Guest is liable for any damages. In consideration of all guests, pets must never be left unattended in the guest rooms.

Quality Inn and Suites
3550 Gateway Street
Springfield, OR

541-726-9266 (877-424-6423)
Dogs are allowed for an additional fee of $5 per night per pet. Multiple dogs may be allowed.

Best Western Grand Manor Inn
971 Kruse Way
Springfield (Eugene), OR
541-726-4769 (800-780-7234)
Dogs are allowed for an additional fee of $10 per night per pet. Multiple dogs may be allowed.

Best Western Oak Meadows Inn
585 S Columbia River Hwy
St Helens, OR
503-397-3000 (800-780-7234)
Dogs are allowed for an additional one time pet fee of $10 per room. 2 dogs may be allowed.

Sunray Vacation Rentals
Call to Arrange
Sunriver, OR
541-593-3225 (800-531-1130)
sunrayinc.com
These vacation properties allow pets for a $25 fee per pet. Some homes have limits on the size and quantity of pets so be sure and check when making reservations.

Sunset Realty
56805 Ventura Lane
Sunriver, OR
541-593-5018 (800-541-1756)
sunriverlodging.com/
This realty company offers dozens of pet friendly, fully-furnished vacation homes and condos in the Sunriver resort area of Oregon. They feature many different amenities such as private hot tubs, pool/foos tables, barbecues, fireplaces with supplies, phones in all units, cable TV, and completely equipped kitchens. Dogs are allowed for an additional fee of $10 per night per pet, or $15 per night if there is more than one pet. Dogs must be well mannered, leashed, and cleaned up after. Multiple dogs may be allowed.

Comfort Inn Columbia Gorge
351 Lone Pine Drive
The Dalles, OR
541-298-2800 (877-424-6423)
Dogs are allowed for an additional one time pet fee of $10 per room. Multiple dogs may be allowed.

Motel 6 - The Dalles
2500 West 6th Street
The Dalles, OR
541-296-1191 (800-466-8356)
One well-behaved family pet per room. Guest must notify front desk

upon arrival. Guest is liable for any damages. In consideration of all guests, pets must never be left unattended in the guest rooms.

Best Western Northwind Inn and Suites
16105 SW Pacific Hwy
Tigard, OR
503-431-2100 (800-780-7234)
Dogs under 20 pounds are allowed for an additional fee of $10 per night per pet; the fee is $20 per night per pet for dogs over 20 pounds. Multiple dogs may be allowed.

Embassy Suites Hotel Portland - Washington Square
9000 S.W. Washington Square Road
Tigard, OR
503-644-4000
Dogs of all sizes are allowed. There is a $25 one time pet fee per visit and an additional $10 per night per pet fee. Dogs are not allowed to be left alone in the room.

Motel 6 - Portland S- Lake Oswego -Tigard
17950 Southwest McEwan Road
Tigard, OR
503-620-2066 (800-466-8356)
One well-behaved family pet per room. Guest must notify front desk upon arrival. Guest is liable for any damages. In consideration of all guests, pets must never be left unattended in the guest rooms.

Red Roof Inn - Portland Tigard - Lake Oswego
17959 Southwest McEwan Road
Tigard, OR
503-684-0760 (800-RED-ROOF)
One well-behaved dog up to about 80 pounds is allowed. There are no additional pet fees.

Comfort Inn and Suites
477 NW Phoenix Drive
Troutdale, OR
503-669-6500 (877-424-6423)
Dogs are allowed for an additional fee of $10 per night per pet. Multiple dogs may be allowed.

Holiday Inn Express
1000 NW Graham Road
Troutdale, OR
503-492-2900 (877-270-6405)
Dogs of all sizes are allowed for an additional pet fee per room of $10 for the 1st night and $5 for each additional night. Multiple dogs may be allowed.

Motel 6 - Portland East - Troutdale

1610 Nw Frontage Road
Troutdale, OR
503-665-2254 (800-466-8356)
One well-behaved family pet per room. Guest must notify front desk upon arrival. Guest is liable for any damages. In consideration of all guests, pets must never be left unattended in the guest rooms.

Comfort Inn and Suites
7640 SW Warm Springs Street
Tualatin, OR
503-612-9952 (877-424-6423)
Dogs are allowed for an additional fee of $15 per night per pet. 2 dogs may be allowed.

Shilo Inn
1609 E Harbor Drive
Warrenton, OR
503-861-2181 (800-222-2244)
There is a $10 per day pet fee.

Comfort Inn
8855 SW Citizen Drive
Wilsonville, OR
503-682-9000 (877-424-6423)
Dogs are allowed for an additional pet fee of $15 per night per room. Multiple dogs may be allowed.

Holiday Inn Select
25425 SW 95th Ave
Wilsonville, OR
503-682-2211 (877-270-6405)
Dogs of all sizes are allowed for an additional pet fee of $15 per night per room. Multiple dogs may be allowed.

La Quinta Inn Wilsonville
8815 SW Sun Place
Wilsonville, OR
503-682-3184 (800-531-5900)
Dogs of all sizes are allowed. There are no additional pet fees. Dogs must be leashed, cleaned up after, and crated for housekeeping. Multiple dogs may be allowed.

Super 8 Wilsonville/Portland Area
25438 SW Parkway Ave
Wilsonville, OR
503-682-2088 (800-800-8000)
Dogs of all sizes are allowed. There is a $25 returnable deposit required per room. Smoking and non-smoking rooms are available for pet rooms. 2 dogs may be allowed.

La Quinta Inn & Suites Woodburn
120 Arney Rd NE
Woodburn, OR
503-982-1727 (800-531-5900)
Dogs of all sizes are allowed. There are no additional pet fees. Dogs

must be leashed and cleaned up after. Dogs may only be left alone in the room if they will be quiet and well behaved, and they must be crated. Multiple dogs may be allowed.

Super 8 Woodburn
821 Evergreen Rd
Woodburn, OR
503-981-8881 (800-800-8000)
Dogs of all sizes are allowed. There is a $50 returnable deposit required per room. There is a $10 one time per pet fee per visit. Smoking and non-smoking rooms are available for pet rooms. 2 dogs may be allowed.

Adobe Resort
1555 US 101
Yachats, OR
541-547-3141
adoberesort.com/
There is a $10 per day pet charge.

See Vue Hotel
95590 H 101
Yachats, OR
541-547-3227
Dogs of all sizes are allowed. There is an $8 per night per pet additional fee. 2 dogs may be allowed.

Shamrock Lodgettes
US 101
Yachats, OR
541-547-3312 (800-845-5028)
beachesbeaches.com/shamrock.html
Pets are allowed in cabins only. There is an additional $30 per day charge. All units are non-smoking and have fireplaces.

The Fireside Inn
Hwy 101
Yachats, OR
800-336-3573 (800-336-3573)
overleaflodge.com/fireside/
There is a $9 per day per pet charge. Dogs cannot be left unattended in the room. All rooms are non-smoking.

Pennsylvania Listings

Adamstown Inn
62 W Main Street
Adamstown, PA
717-484-0800 (800-594-4808)
adamstown.com/
Located in a premier antiques and recreational destination, and only 10 minutes from an outlet shopping

mecca, this garden inn offers 1 Victorian and 2 English style pet friendly cottages. Dogs of all sizes are allowed for an additional one time pet fee of $50. Dogs must be well behaved, housebroken, and leashed and cleaned up after. Dogs may not be left alone in the cottage at any time. 2 dogs may be allowed.

Black Forest Inn
500 Lancaster Ave
Adamstown, PA
717-484-4801
There is a $10 per day additional pet fee.

The Barnyard Inn
2145 Old Lancaster Pike
Adamstown, PA
717-484-1111 (888-738-6624)
barnyardinn.com/
Although quite an elegant inn, there really is a barnyard of farm animals and llamas here at this 150 year old restored German schoolhouse that sits on 2½ wooded acres in the heart of a busy antique shopping area, and close to the Pennsylvania Dutch attractions. Dogs of all sizes are allowed in the Carriage House and the Chicken Coop (a cute new addition) for an additional one time pet fee of $20 per room. Dogs must be friendly to humans and the other animals on site, leashed, and cleaned up after. 2 dogs may be allowed.

The Boxwood
1320 Diamond Street
Akron, PA
717-859-3466 (800-238-3466)
theboxwoodinn.net/
Surrounded by wooded and well kept grounds, this renovated colonial stone farmhouse sits on over 3 acres, and is a graceful setting for the casual or business traveler, and for special events. Dogs of all sizes are allowed in the carriage house for an additional one time pet fee of $15 (not neutered is $15 per night per pet). Dogs must be well behaved, leashed, and cleaned up after. 2 dogs may be allowed.

Red Rose Inn
243 Meckesville Road
Albrightsville, PA
570-722-3526
theredroseinn.com/
Secluded, yet central to numerous recreational activities, this B&B sits surrounded by flourishing greenery, tall trees, and some beautiful walking paths. One dog is allowed for no additional pet fee. Dogs must be

quiet, leased or crated, and cleaned up after.

Allenwood Motel
1058 Hausman Rd
Allentown, PA
610-395-3707
There is a $15 per day pet fee.

Comfort Inn
7625 Imperial Way
Allentown, PA
610-391-0344 (877-424-6423)
Dogs are allowed for an additional one time fee of $25 per pet. Multiple dogs may be allowed.

Crowne Plaza Hotel Allentown
904 West Hamilton St
Allentown, PA
610-433-2221 (877-270-6405)
Dogs of all sizes are allowed for an additional one time fee of $30 per pet. Multiple dogs may be allowed.

Days Inn Allentown Conference Cntr
1151 Bulldog Drive
Allentown, PA
610-395-3731 (800-329-7466)
Dogs of all sizes are allowed. There is a $15 per night pet fee per pet. Pet must be kept in kennel when left alone. 2 dogs may be allowed.

Four Points Sheraton Hotel & Suites Allentown Jetport
3400 Airport Road, Road #4
Allentown, PA
610-266-1000 (888-625-5144)
Dogs of all sizes are allowed. There is a $49 per stay additional pet fee per pet. This includes a pet care kit with a bed, treats and toys. Pets are restricted to 1st floor rooms only. Dogs are not allowed to be left alone in the room.

Holiday Inn
7736 Adrienne Drive
Allentown, PA
610-391-1000 (877-270-6405)
Dogs of all sizes are allowed for an additional one time fee of $49 per pet. Multiple dogs may be allowed.

Red Roof Inn - Allentown Bethlehem
1846 Catasauqua Road
Allentown, PA
610-264-5404 (800-RED-ROOF)
One well-behaved family pet per room. Guest must notify front desk upon arrival. Guest is liable for any damages. In consideration of all guests, pets must never be left unattended in the guest rooms.

Sleep Inn
327 Star Road
Allentown, PA
610-395-6603 (877-424-6423)
Dogs are allowed for an additional fee of $15 per night per pet. 2 dogs may be allowed.

Staybridge Suites
1787 A. Airport Road
Allentown, PA
610-443-5000 (877-270-6405)
Dogs of all sizes are allowed for an additional one time pet fee per room of $50 for 1 to 14 days, and $100 for 15 days or more. 2 dogs may be allowed.

Staybridge Suites Allentown West
327c Star Road
Allentown, PA
610-841-5100 (877-270-6405)
Dogs of all sizes are allowed for an additional one time pet fee of $100 per room. 2 dogs may be allowed.

Super 8 Allentown
1715 Plaza Lane
Allentown, PA
610-435-7880 (800-800-8000)
Dogs up to 80 pounds are allowed. There is a $10 per night pet fee per pet. Smoking and non-smoking rooms are available for pet rooms. 2 dogs may be allowed.

Econo Lodge
2906 Pleasant Valley Blvd/H 220
Altoona, PA
814-944-3555 (877-424-6423)
Central to a wealth of historic sites and recreation, this inn also has an oriental restaurant on site. Dogs are allowed for no additional fee. Dogs must be quiet, well behaved, leashed, and cleaned up after. Multiple dogs may be allowed.

Motel 6 - Altoona
1500 Sterling Street
Altoona, PA
814-946-7601 (800-466-8356)
One well-behaved family pet per room. Guest must notify front desk upon arrival. Guest is liable for any damages. In consideration of all guests, pets must never be left unattended in the guest rooms.

Ramada Inn
1 Sheraton Drive
Altoona, PA
814-946-1631 (800-311-5192)
ramada.com/Ramada/control/home
Dogs of all sizes are allowed for an additional $20 one time cleaning fee

per room. Dogs must be well behaved, leashed, and cleaned up after at all times. Multiple dogs may be allowed.

Super 8 Altoona
3535 Fairway Dr
Altoona, PA
814-942-5350 (800-800-8000)
Dogs of all sizes are allowed. There is a $6 per night pet fee per pet. Smoking and non-smoking rooms are available for pet rooms. 2 dogs may be allowed.

Comfort Inn
137 Gibb Road
Barkeyville, PA
814-786-7901 (877-424-6423)
Dogs are allowed for an additional fee of $10 per night per pet. Multiple dogs may be allowed.

Holiday Inn
7195 Eastwood Rd
Beaver Falls, PA
724-846-3700 (877-270-6405)
Dogs of all sizes are allowed for an additional one time pet fee of $35 per room. 2 dogs may be allowed.

Best Western Bedford Inn
4517 Business 220 Exit 146 PA Tpk
Bedford, PA
814-623-9006 (800-780-7234)
Dogs are allowed for an additional pet fee of $10 per night per room. Multiple dogs may be allowed.

Quality Inn Bedford
4407 BH 220
Bedford, PA
814-623-5188 (877-424-6423)
Dogs up to 50 pounds are allowed for an additional fee of $15 per night per pet. Multiple dogs may be allowed.

Super 8 Bedford
4498 Business 220
Bedford, PA
814-623-5880 (800-800-8000)
Dogs of all sizes are allowed. There is a $5 per night pet fee per pet. Smoking and non-smoking rooms are available for pet rooms. 2 dogs may be allowed.

Holiday Inn
3499 Street Rd
Bensalem, PA
215-638-1500 (877-270-6405)
Dogs up to 50 pounds are allowed for an additional one time pet fee of $30 per room. 2 dogs may be allowed.

Residence Inn by Marriott
600 W Swedesford Road
Berwyn, PA
610-640-0330
Dogs of all sizes are allowed. There is a $150 one time fee and a pet policy to sign at check in. 2 dogs may be allowed.

Best Western Lehigh Valley Hotel & Conference Center
300 Gateway Drive
Bethlehem, PA
610-866-5800 (800-780-7234)
Dogs are allowed for an additional fee of $10 per night per pet. Multiple dogs may be allowed.

Comfort Inn
H 22 and H 191
Bethlehem, PA
610-865-6300 (877-424-6423)
Dogs are allowed for an additional fee of $10 (plus tax) per night per pet. 2 dogs may be allowed.

Residence Inn by Marriott
2180 Motel Drive
Bethlehem, PA
610-317-2662
Dogs of all sizes are allowed. There is a $100 one time cleaning fee plus $6 per night and a pet policy to sign at check in. Multiple dogs may be allowed.

Best Western Inn at Blakeslee-Pocono
Route 115
Blakeslee, PA
570-646-6000 (800-780-7234)
Dogs are allowed for a $50 refundable deposit. Multiple dogs may be allowed.

Best Western Bradford Inn
100 Davis St
Bradford, PA
814-362-4501 (800-780-7234)
Dogs are allowed for an additional fee of $10 per night per pet. Multiple dogs may be allowed.

Comfort Inn
76 Elm Street
Bradford, PA
814-368-6772 (877-424-6423)
Dogs are allowed for an additional fee of $10 per night per pet. 2 dogs may be allowed.

Best Western Plaza Motor Lodge
16407 Lincoln Highway
Breezewood, PA
814-735-4352 (800-780-7234)
Dogs are allowed for an additional fee of $10 per night per pet. Multiple dogs may be allowed.

Penn-Aire Motel
16359 Lincoln Way
Breezewood, PA
814-735-4351
Dogs of all sizes are allowed. There are no additional pet fees. Multiple dogs may be allowed.

Days Inn Brookville
230 Allegheny Blvd
Brookville, PA
814-849-8001 (800-329-7466)
Dogs of all sizes are allowed. There is a $10 per night pet fee per pet. Reservations are recommended due to limited rooms for pets. 2 dogs may be allowed.

Holiday Inn Express
235 Allegheny Blvd
Brookville, PA
814-849-8381 (877-270-6405)
Dogs of all sizes are allowed for an additional one time fee of $15 per pet. Multiple dogs may be allowed.

Comfort Inn
1 Comfort Lane
Butler, PA
724-287-7177 (877-424-6423)
Dogs are allowed for an additional fee of $20 per night per pet. 2 dogs may be allowed.

Days inn Butler
139 Pittsburgh Rd
Butler, PA
724-287-6761 (800-DAYS-INN)
Dogs of all sizes are allowed. There is a $30 per night pet fee per pet. 2 dogs may be allowed.

The Merry Inn
H 390
Canadensis, PA
570-595-2011 (800-858-4182)
themerryinn.com/
Nestled amongst lush greenery and towering trees, this mountain inn offers an outdoor hot tub on an upper deck facing the woods, and they sit central to a host of other activities and year round recreational pursuits. Dogs of all sizes are allowed for a one time additional pet fee of $22 per room. Dogs must be quiet, leashed, cleaned up after, and they may be left alone in the room only if the owner is confident in the pet's behavior. 2 dogs may be allowed.

Comfort Suites
10 S Hanover Street
Carlisle, PA
717-960-1000 (877-424-6423)

Dogs are allowed for an additional fee of $10 per night per pet. Multiple dogs may be allowed.

Days Inn Carlisle
101 Alexander Spring Rd
Carlisle, PA
717-258-4147 (800-329-7466)
Dogs of all sizes are allowed. There is a $6 per night pet fee per pet. There is a $10 fee per night for smoking rooms. 2 dogs may be allowed.

Hampton Inn
1164 Harrisburg Pike
Carlisle, PA
717-240-0200
Well behaved dogs of all sizes are allowed. There are no additional pet fees, and a cell number needs to be left with the front desk if your pet is left in the room. 2 dogs may be allowed.

Holiday Inn
1450 Harrisburg Pike
Carlisle, PA
717-245-2400 (877-270-6405)
Dogs of all sizes are allowed for an additional fee of $10 per night per pet. Multiple dogs may be allowed.

Motel 6 - Harrisburg - Carlisle
1153 Harrisburg Pike
Carlisle, PA
717-249-7622 (800-466-8356)
One well-behaved family pet per room. Guest must notify front desk upon arrival. Guest is liable for any damages. In consideration of all guests, pets must never be left unattended in the guest rooms.

Pheasant Field
150 Hickorytown Road
Carlisle, PA
717-258-0717 (877-258-0717)
pheasantfield.com/
Pastoral fields, wooded and nature walks, a labyrinth, gardens, and a pond are all compliment to this 200 year old restored brick farmhouse, and they are also in an area famous for collector car shows. Dogs of all sizes are welcome in the Pet-sylvania Room for an additional pet fee of $10 per night per room. Dogs must be well behaved, leashed, cleaned up after, and crated when left alone in the room. Arrangements need to be made for housekeeping, and if the owner is confident in their pets behavior and housekeeping is done, pets may be in the room without being crated, just inform the front desk they are there. Multiple dogs may be allowed.

Quality Inn
1255 Harrisburg Pike
Carlisle, PA
717-243-6000 (877-424-6423)
Dogs are allowed for an additional fee of $10 per night per pet. Multiple dogs may be allowed.

Super 8 Carlisle/South
100 Alexander Spring Rd
Carlisle, PA
717-245-9898 (800-800-8000)
Dogs of all sizes are allowed. There is a $6 per night pet fee per pet. Smoking and non-smoking rooms are available for pet rooms. 2 dogs may be allowed.

The Pennsbury Inn
883 Baltimore Pike/H1
Chadds Ford, PA
610-388-1435
pennsburyinn.com/
Rich in colonial heritage and country charm, and listed on the National Register of Historic Places, this inn, surrounded by lush greenery and award winning gardens, serves also for a good starting point to several other activities and historic sites. Dogs of all sizes are allowed for an additional fee of $15 to $20 per pet, depending on size/hair. Dogs must be quiet, very well mannered, leashed and cleaned up after, and crated when left alone in the room. 2 dogs may be allowed.

Best Western Chambersburg
211 Walker Rd
Chambersburg, PA
717-262-4994 (800-780-7234)
Dogs are allowed for an additional fee of $9 per night per pet. 2 dogs may be allowed.

Comfort Inn
3301 Black Gap Road
Chambersburg, PA
717-263-6655 (877-424-6423)
Dogs are allowed for an additional fee of $10 per night per pet. 2 dogs may be allowed.

Days Inn Chambersburg
30 Falling Spring Rd
Chambersburg, PA
717-263-1288 (800-329-7466)
Dogs of all sizes are allowed. There is a $10.90 per night pet fee per pet. 2 dogs may be allowed.

Hamanassett B&B and Carriage House
Indian Springs Drive

Chester Heights, PA
610-459-3000 (877-836-8212)
hamanassett.com
Blending old world charm and elegance with modern-day comforts, this 1856 English country-style home and estate offers guests exceptional dining, landscaped grounds complete with forested areas, green pastures, and koi ponds, and a convenient location to several other local attractions. Dogs of all sizes are welcome for an additional fee of $25 per night per pet. One dog is allowed per room in the house area, and up to 3 dogs are allowed in the carriage house, which also has a yard. Dogs must be well mannered, leashed, and cleaned up after at all times.

Holiday Inn
I-80 Rt 68
Clarion, PA
814-226-8850 (877-270-6405)
Dogs of all sizes are allowed for an additional pet fee of $10 per night per room. 2 dogs may be allowed.

Quality Inn and Suites
24 United Drive
Clarion, PA
814-226-8682 (877-424-6423)
Dogs are allowed for no additional pet fee. Multiple dogs may be allowed.

Super 8 Clarion
135 Hotel Road
Clarion, PA
814-226-4550 (800-800-8000)
Dogs of all sizes are allowed. There are no additional pet fees. Smoking and non-smoking rooms are available for pet rooms. 2 dogs may be allowed.

Comfort Inn
811 Northern Blvd
Clarks Summit, PA
570-586-9100 (877-424-6423)
Dogs are allowed for an additional pet fee of $10 per night per room. Multiple dogs may be allowed.

Comfort Inn
1821 Industrial Park Road
Clearfield, PA
814-768-6400 (877-424-6423)
Dogs are allowed for an additional pet fee of $15 per night per room. Multiple dogs may be allowed.

Days Inn Clearfield
14451 Clearfield Shawville Hwy
Clearfield, PA
814-765-5381 (800-329-7466)
Dogs of all sizes are allowed. There

is a $10 per night pet fee per pet. 2 dogs may be allowed.

Super 8 Clearfield
14597 Clearfield/Shawville Hwy
Clearfield, PA
814-768-7580 (800-800-8000)
Dogs of all sizes are allowed. There is a $5 per night pet fee per pet. Smoking and non-smoking rooms are available for pet rooms. 2 dogs may be allowed.

Victorian Loft
216 S Front Street
Clearfield, PA
814-765-4805 (800-798-0456)
victorianloft.com/
This beautiful 1894 Victorian home sits along the river just a short walk from the town and a variety of activities, eateries, and recreation. Dogs of all sizes are allowed for an additional pet fee of $10 per night for one dog, and if there are 2 dogs, the second dog is an additional $5 per night. Dogs may not be left alone in the room at any time, and they must be leashed and cleaned up after. 2 dogs may be allowed.

Residence Inn by Marriott
191 Washington Street
Conshohocken, PA
610-828-8800
Dogs of all sizes are allowed. There is a $75 one time fee and a pet policy to sign at check in. They also request a cell number if you leave your pet in the room. Multiple dogs may be allowed.

Crowne Plaza Hotel Pittsburgh-Intl Airport
1160 Thorn Run Road
Coraopolis, PA
412-262-2400 (877-270-6405)
Dogs of all sizes are allowed for no additional pet fee; there is a pet agreement to sign at check in. Multiple dogs may be allowed.

Motel 6 - Pittsburgh Airport
1170 Thorn Run Road
Coraopolis, PA
412-269-0990 (800-466-8356)
One well-behaved family pet per room. Guest must notify front desk upon arrival. Guest is liable for any damages. In consideration of all guests, pets must never be left unattended in the guest rooms.

Pittsburgh Airport Marriott
777 Aten Road
Coraopolis, PA
412-788-8800 (800-328-9297)

Dogs of all sizes are allowed. There is a $50 one time additional pet fee per pet. Dogs must be leashed, cleaned up after, and the Pet in Room sign put on the door when they are in the room alone. 2 dogs may be allowed.

Holiday Inn Express
20003 Rt 19
Cranberry Township, PA
724-772-1000 (877-270-6405)
Dogs of all sizes are allowed for an additional fee of $10 per night per room. 2 dogs may be allowed.

Red Roof Inn - Pittsburgh North
Cranberry TWP
20009 U.S.19 & Marguerite Road
Cranberry Township, PA
724-776-5670 (800-RED-ROOF)
One well-behaved family pet per room. Guest must notify front desk upon arrival. Guest is liable for any damages. In consideration of all guests, pets must never be left unattended in the guest rooms.

Residence Inn by Marriott
1308 Freedom Road
Cranberry Township, PA
724-779-1000
Dogs of all sizes are allowed. There is a $75 one time fee and a pet policy to sign at check in. Multiple dogs may be allowed.

Quality Inn & Suites
15 Valley West Road
Danville, PA
570-275-5100 (877-424-6423)
Dogs up to 50 pounds are allowed for an additional one time fee of $25 per pet. 2 dogs may be allowed.

Red Roof Inn - Danville
300 Red Roof Road
Danville, PA
570-275-7600 (800-RED-ROOF)
One well-behaved family pet per room. Guest must notify front desk upon arrival. Guest is liable for any damages. In consideration of all guests, pets must never be left unattended in the guest rooms.

Super 8 Delmont
180 Sheffield Dr
Delmont, PA
724-468-4888 (800-800-8000)
Dogs of all sizes are allowed. There is a $5 per night pet fee per pet. Dogs are not allowed to be left alone in the room. Smoking and non-smoking rooms are available for pet rooms. 2 dogs may be allowed.

Comfort Inn
2017 N Reading Road
Denver, PA
717-336-4649 (877-424-6423)
Dogs up to 50 pounds are allowed for an additional one time pet fee of $20 per room. 2 dogs may be allowed.

Holiday Inn
1 Denver Road
Denver, PA
717-336-7541 (877-270-6405)
Dogs of all sizes are allowed for an additional fee of $10 per night per pet. 2 dogs may be allowed.

Residence Inn by Marriott
947 Viewmont Drive
Dickson City, PA
570-343-5121
Dogs of all sizes are allowed. There is a $75 one time fee and a pet policy to sign at check in. Multiple dogs may be allowed.

Best Western Inn & Conference Center
82 N Park Place
DuBois, PA
814-371-6200 (800-780-7234)
Dogs are allowed for an additional fee of $10 per night per pet. 2 dogs may be allowed.

Days Inn Scranton/Dunmore
1226 O'Neill Hwy
Dunmore, PA
570-348-6101 (800-329-7466)
Dogs of all sizes are allowed. There is a $5 per night pet fee per pet. 2 dogs may be allowed.

Holiday Inn
200 Tigue St
Dunmore, PA
570-343-4771 (877-270-6405)
Dogs of all sizes are allowed for an additional fee of $10 per night per pet. Multiple dogs may be allowed.

Sleep Inn and Suites
102 Monahan Avenue
Dunmore, PA
570-961-1116 (877-424-6423)
Dogs are allowed for an additional fee of $10 per night per pet. Multiple dogs may be allowed.

Super 8 Dunmore/Scranton Area
1027 Oneill Hwy
Dunmore, PA
570-346-8782 (800-800-8000)
Dogs of all sizes are allowed. There is a $10 per night pet fee per pet. Smoking and non-smoking rooms

are available for pet rooms. 2 dogs may be allowed.

Budget Inn and Suites
340 Greentree Drive
East Stroudsburg, PA
570-424-5451 (888-233-8144)
poconobudgetinn.com/
Dogs of all sizes are allowed for no additional pet fees. A credit card must be on file and there is a pet waiver to sign at check in. Dogs must be quiet, leashed or crated, cleaned up after, and crated when left alone in the room. Multiple dogs may be allowed.

Comfort Inn
H 22 at 25th Street
Easton, PA
610-253-0546 (877-424-6423)
Dogs up to 65 pounds are allowed for an additional fee of $20 per night per pet. Multiple dogs may be allowed.

The Lafayette Inn
525 W Monroe Street
Easton, PA
610-253-4500 (800-509-6990)
lafayetteinn.com
This inn has a big wrap around porch, is surrounded by trees and gardens with a fountain, and serves as a great home base to a variety of activities, recreation, and historical sites. Dogs of all sizes are allowed for an additional fee of $20 per night per pet; they provide treats, mat, a towel, and clean-up bags. Dogs must be leashed and cleaned up after at all times, and crated when left alone in the room. 2 dogs may be allowed.

Comfort Inn
111 Cook Road
Ebensburg, PA
814-472-6100 (877-424-6423)
Dogs are allowed for an additional fee of $15 (plus tax) per night per pet with a credit card on file. There is an extra refundable deposit of $25 if paying by cash. Multiple dogs may be allowed.

Best Western Erie Inn and Suites
7820 Perry Highway
Erie, PA
814-864-1812 (800-780-7234)
Dogs are allowed for an additional one time fee of $10 per pet. Dogs must be quiet and well behaved. Multiple dogs may be allowed.

Country Inns & Suites by Carlson
8040 Oliver Road
Erie, PA

814-864-5810
Dogs up to 75 pounds are allowed. There is a $25 one time additional pet fee.

Days Inn Erie
7415 Schultz Rd
Erie, PA
814-868-8521 (800-329-7466)
Dogs of all sizes are allowed. There is a $5 per night pet fee per pet. 2 dogs may be allowed.

Motel 6 - Erie
7875 Peach Street
Erie, PA
814-864-4811 (800-466-8356)
One well-behaved family pet per room. Guest must notify front desk upon arrival. Guest is liable for any damages. In consideration of all guests, pets must never be left unattended in the guest rooms.

Red Roof Inn - Erie
7865 Perry Highway
Erie, PA
814-868-5246 (800-RED-ROOF)
One well-behaved family pet per room. Guest must notify front desk upon arrival. Guest is liable for any damages. In consideration of all guests, pets must never be left unattended in the guest rooms.

Residence Inn by Marriott
8061 Peach Street
Erie, PA
814-864-2500
Dogs of all sizes are allowed. There is a $75 one time fee and a pet policy to sign at check in. Multiple dogs may be allowed.

Super 8 Erie/I-90
8040 Perry Hwy
Erie, PA
814-864-9200 (800-800-8000)
Dogs of all sizes are allowed. There is a $5 per night pet fee per pet. Smoking and non-smoking rooms are available for pet rooms. 2 dogs may be allowed.

Golden Pheasant Inn
763 River Road/H 32S
Erwinna, PA
610-294-9595 (800-830-4474)
goldenpheasant.com/
This inn, sitting along the Delaware Canal, specializes in French cuisine, and in the spring they offer cooking classes. There is a gated cottage suite with a porch overlooking the canal for guests with pets, and dogs up to 55 pounds are allowed for an

additional pet fee of $25 per night per pet. Dogs must be well mannered, leashed, and cleaned up after. 2 dogs may be allowed.

Holiday Inn
45 Industrial hwy
Essington, PA
610-521-2400 (877-270-6405)
Dogs of all sizes are allowed for an additional one time pet fee of $50 per room. 2 dogs may be allowed.

Motel 6 - Philadelphia Airport - Essington
43 Industrial Highway
Essington, PA
610-521-6650 (800-466-8356)
One well-behaved family pet per room. Guest must notify front desk upon arrival. Guest is liable for any damages. In consideration of all guests, pets must never be left unattended in the guest rooms.

Red Roof Inn - Philadelphia Airport
49 Industrial Highway
Essington, PA
610-521-5090 (800-RED-ROOF)
One well-behaved family pet per room. Guest must notify front desk upon arrival. Guest is liable for any damages. In consideration of all guests, pets must never be left unattended in the guest rooms.

Hampton Inn
4 N Pottstown Pike
Exton, PA
610-363-5555
Dogs of all sizes are allowed. There are no additional pet fees. Multiple dogs may be allowed.

Residence Inn by Marriott
10 N Pottstown Pike
Exton, PA
610-594-9705
Well behaved dogs of all sizes are allowed. There is a $75 one time fee and a pet policy to sign at check in. Multiple dogs may be allowed.

Super 8 Franklin
847 Allegheny Blvd
Franklin, PA
814-432-2101 (800-800-8000)
Dogs of all sizes are allowed. There is a $10 per night pet fee per pet. Dogs are not allowed to be left alone in the room. Smoking and non-smoking rooms are available for pet rooms. 2 dogs may be allowed.

Sheraton Great Valley Hotel
707 East Lancaster Ave, Route 202 & 30

Frazer, PA
610-524-5500 (888-625-5144)
Dogs up to 85 pounds are allowed.
There are no additional pet fees.
Dogs are not allowed to be left alone
in the room

America Best Inn
301 Steinwehr Avenue
Gettysburg, PA
717-334-1188
Friendly dogs of all sizes are
allowed. They say they perfer to take
only 2 dogs per room, but if well
behaved, will take up to 4 dogs.
There are no additional pet fees.

Comfort Inn
871 York Road
Gettysburg, PA
717-337-2400 (877-424-6423)
Dogs are allowed for an additional
fee of $10 per night per pet. Multiple
dogs may be allowed.

Gettysburg Travelodge
64 Steinwehr Ave
Gettysburg, PA
717-334-9281
There are no pet fees.

Holiday Inn
516 Baltimore St
Gettysburg, PA
717-334-6211 (877-270-6405)
Dogs of all sizes are allowed for an
additional one time pet fee of $10 per
room. Multiple dogs may be allowed.

Comfort Inn North
5137 H 8
Gibsonia, PA
724-444-8700 (877-424-6423)
Dogs up to 50 pounds are allowed
for an additional fee of $10 per night
per pet. Multiple dogs may be
allowed.

Sweetwater Inn
50 Sweetwater Road
Glen Mills, PA
610-459-4711 (800-SWEETWATER
(793-3892))
sweetwaterfarmbb.com/
This wooded 50 acre estate of lush
greenery has some great hiking
trails, features a golf green, Jacuzzi
and pool, indoor and outdoor dining
(when weather permits), a large patio
and porch, and also serves as a
good starting point to explore the
attractions of Brandywine Valley.
Dogs of all sizes are allowed in the
cottages only for an additional fee of
$35 per night per pet. Dogs must be
well mannered, leashed, and cleaned
up after. Multiple dogs may be

allowed.

Motel 6 - Gordonville
2959 Lincoln Hwy East
Gordonville, PA
717-687-3880 (800-466-8356)
One well-behaved family pet per
room. Guest must notify front desk
upon arrival. Guest is liable for any
damages. In consideration of all
guests, pets must never be left
unattended in the guest rooms.

Holiday Inn
Hershey Exit 28 I-81
Grantville, PA
717-469-0661 (877-270-6405)
Dogs of all sizes are allowed for no
additional fee with a credit card on
file; there is a $70 refundable
deposit if paying by cash. After 1-1-
08 there may be an additional daily
fee. 2 dogs may be allowed.

Comfort Inn
50 Pine Drive
Greencastle, PA
717-597-8164 (877-424-6423)
Dogs are allowed for an additional
fee of $10 per night per pet. Multiple
dogs may be allowed.

Four Points by Sheraton
Greensburg
100 Sheraton Dr., Route 30 East
Greensburg, PA
724-836-6060 (888-625-5144)
Dogs of all sizes are allowed. There
is a $10 per stay pet fee per pet.
Dogs are not allowed to be left
alone in the room.

Old Arbor Rose
114 W Main Street
Grove City, PA
724-458-6425 (877 596-6767)
oldarborrosebnb.com/
This 1912 rambling house offers a
hint of the sea in the décor, a full
gourmet breakfast, a hot tub on a
private deck, and they are central to
a wide variety of activities,
recreation, shops, and eateries.
Dogs of all sizes are allowed for an
additional fee of $10 per night per
pet. Dogs must be well behaved,
leashed, and cleaned up after.
Multiple dogs may be allowed.

Howard Johnson Inn
1080 Carlisle Street
Hanover, PA
717-646-1000 (800-446-4656)
Well-behaved dogs of all sizes are
allowed. There is a $10 per day
additional pet fee.

Best Western Capital Plaza
150 Nationwide Drive
Harrisburg, PA
717-545-9089 (800-780-7234)
Dogs are allowed for no additional
pet fee. Multiple dogs may be
allowed.

Best Western Harrisburg/Hershey
Hotel & Suites
300 N Mountain Road
Harrisburg, PA
717-652-7180 (800-780-7234)
Dogs are allowed in the standard
rooms for an additional pet fee of
$10 per night per room; the fee is
$25 for suites. Multiple dogs may be
allowed.

Comfort Inn
7744 Linglestown Road
Harrisburg, PA
717-540-8400 (877-424-6423)
Dogs are allowed for an additional
fee of $10 per night per pet in the
winter months (November to
February), and $25 per night per pet
during the other months. 2 dogs may
be allowed.

Comfort Inn East
4021 Union Deposit Road
Harrisburg, PA
717-561-8100 (877-424-6423)
Dogs are allowed for an additional
fee of $10 per night per pet. Multiple
dogs may be allowed.

Comfort Inn Riverfront
525 S Front Street
Harrisburg, PA
717-233-1611 (877-424-6423)
Dogs up to 50 pounds are allowed
for an additional fee of $25 per night
per pet. Multiple dogs may be
allowed.

Crowne Plaza Hotel Harrisburg-
Hershey
23 S Second St
Harrisburg, PA
717-234-5021 (877-270-6405)
Dogs up to 50 pounds are allowed
for an additional one time pet fee of
$50 per room. 2 dogs may be
allowed.

Daystop Harrisburg
7848 Linglestown Rd
Harrisburg, PA
717-652-9578 (800-329-7466)
Dogs of all sizes are allowed. There
is a $6 per night pet fee per pet. 2
dogs may be allowed.

Holiday Inn
4751 Lindle Rd

Harrisburg, PA
717-939-7841 (877-270-6405)
Dogs up to 50 pounds are allowed
for a $75 refundable deposit. 2 dogs
may be allowed.

Holiday Inn Express Hotel and Suites
5680 Allentown Blvd
Harrisburg, PA
717-657-2200 (877-270-6405)
Dogs of all sizes are allowed for an
additional fee of $25 per night per
pet. There may be no more than 5
beings per room. Multiple dogs may
be allowed.

Howard Johnson
7930 Linglestown Rd.
Harrisburg, PA
717-540-9100 (800-446-4656)
Well-behaved dogs of all sizes are
allowed. There is a $10 per day
additional pet fee.

La Quinta Inn Harrisburg
Airport/Hershey
990 Eisenhower Boulevard
Harrisburg, PA
717-939-8000 (800-531-5900)
Dogs of all sizes are allowed. There
are no additional fees. Dogs must be
leashed and cleaned up after. Dogs
must be crated if left unattended in
the room, and removed or crated for
housekeeping. Multiple dogs may be
allowed.

Red Roof Inn - Harrisburg North
400 Corporate Circle
Harrisburg, PA
717-657-1445 (800-RED-ROOF)
One well-behaved family pet per
room. Guest must notify front desk
upon arrival. Guest is liable for any
damages. In consideration of all
guests, pets must never be left
unattended in the guest rooms.

Red Roof Inn - Harrisburg South
950 Eisenhower Boulevard
Harrisburg, PA
717-939-1331 (800-RED-ROOF)
One well-behaved family pet per
room. Guest must notify front desk
upon arrival. Guest is liable for any
damages. In consideration of all
guests, pets must never be left
unattended in the guest rooms.

Residence Inn by Marriott
4480 Lewis Road
Harrisburg, PA
717-561-1900
Dogs up to 80 pounds are allowed.
There is a $100 one time fee and a
pet policy to sign at check in. 2 dogs
may be allowed.

Super 8 Harrisville/Barkeyville Area
1010 Dholu Road
Harrisville, PA
814-786-8375 (800-800-8000)
Dogs of all sizes are allowed. There
is a $5 per night pet fee per pet.
Smoking and non-smoking rooms
are available for pet rooms. 2 dogs
may be allowed.

Falls Port Inn
330 Main Ave
Hawley, PA
570-226-2600
Large dogs are allowed in the larger
rooms. There is a $20 one time pet
fee.

Best Western Genetti Lodge
Route 309, RR2
Hazleton, PA
570-454-2494 (800-780-7234)
Dogs are allowed for an additional
fee of $10 per night per pet. Multiple
dogs may be allowed.

Hazleton Motor Inn
615 E Broad Street
Hazleton, PA
570-459-1451
hazletonmotorinn.com/
This motor inn sits central to a
variety of activities and recreational
opportunities. Dogs of all sizes are
allowed for an additional fee of $5
per night per pet. Dogs must be
leashed, cleaned up after, and they
may only be left for a short time in
the room if they will be quiet and
well behaved. Guests with one dog
may request a non-smoking room;
guests with two or more dogs are
placed in a smoking room. Multiple
dogs may be allowed.

Best Western Inn Hershey
Route 422 & Sipe Avenue
Hershey, PA
717-533-5665 (800-780-7234)
Dogs are allowed for an additional
one time pet fee of $25 per room.
Multiple dogs may be allowed.

Barley Sheaf Farm
5281 York Road/H 202/263
Holicong, PA
215-794-5104
barleysheaf.com/
Set in the heart of a cultural and
historic region, this 100+ acre luxury
estate contains woodlands,
pastures, gardens, 2 ponds,
picturesque walking paths, a junior
Olympic swimming pool, and more.
One dog of any size is allowed in
the "Beggar on Horseback" room

for an additional fee of $50 per night
with advanced reservations, and
there is a pet policy to sign at check
in. Dogs must be well behaved,
leashed and cleaned up after at all
times, and crated when left alone in
the room.

Candlewood Suites
250 Business Center Drive
Horsham, PA
215-328-9119 (877-270-6405)
Dogs of all sizes are allowed for an
additional one time fee of $75 per
pet. 2 dogs may be allowed.

Days Inn Philadelphia/Horsham
245 Easton Rd
Horsham, PA
215-674-2500 (800-329-7466)
Dogs of all sizes are allowed. There
is a $10 per night pet fee per pet. 2
dogs may be allowed.

Residence Inn by Marriott
3 Walnut Grove Drive
Horsham, PA
215-443-7330
Dogs of all sizes are allowed. There
is a $150 one time fee plus $6 per
night per room and a pet policy to
sign at check in. Multiple dogs may
be allowed.

TownePlace Suites Philadelphia
Horsham
198 Precision Drive
Horsham, PA
215-323-9900
Dogs up to 75 pounds are allowed.
There is a $75 one time pet fee per
visit. 2 dogs may be allowed.

Comfort Inn at the Park
1200 Mae Street
Hummelstown, PA
717-566-2050 (877-424-6423)
Dogs of all sizes are allowed. There
is a $35 one time fee per room and a
pet policy to sign at check in. Multiple
dogs may be allowed.

Best Western University Inn
1545 Wayne Ave
Indiana, PA
724-349-9620 (800-780-7234)
Dogs are allowed for an additional
fee of $10 per night per pet. Dogs
may not be left alone in the room.
Multiple dogs may be allowed.

Comfort Inn and Suites
455 Theatre Drive
Johnstown, PA
814-266-3678 (877-424-6423)
Dogs are allowed for an additional
fee of $15 per night per pet. Multiple

dogs may be allowed.

Holiday Inn
250 Market St
Johnstown, PA
814-535-7777 (877-270-6405)
Dogs of all sizes are allowed for an additional one time pet fee of $10 per room 2 dogs may be allowed.

Holiday Inn Express
1440 Scalp Ave
Johnstown, PA
814-266-8789 (877-270-6405)
Dogs of all sizes are allowed for an additional one time fee of $25 per pet. Dogs may not be left alone in the room. Multiple dogs may be allowed.

Sleep Inn
453 Theatre Drive
Johnstown, PA
814-262-9292 (877-424-6423)
Dogs are allowed for an additional fee of $15 per night per pet. Multiple dogs may be allowed.

Super 8 Johnstown
627 Soloman Run Rd
Johnstown, PA
814-535-5600 (800-800-8000)
Dogs of all sizes are allowed. There are no additional pet fees. Smoking and non-smoking rooms are available for pet rooms. 2 dogs may be allowed.

Days Inn Lebanon
3 Everest Lane
Jonestown, PA
717-865-4064 (800-329-7466)
Dogs of all sizes are allowed. There is a $10 per night pet fee per pet. 2 dogs may be allowed.

Motel 6 - Philadelphia - King of Prussia
815 West Dekalb Pike
King of Prussia, PA
610-265-7200 (800-466-8356)
One well-behaved family pet per room. Guest must notify front desk upon arrival. Guest is liable for any damages. In consideration of all guests, pets must never be left unattended in the guest rooms.

Comfort Inn
13 Hilltop Plaza
Kittanning, PA
724-543-5200 (877-424-6423)
Well behaved dogs up to 30 pounds are allowed for an additional one time fee of $15 per pet. 2 dogs may be allowed.

Quality Inn Royle
405 Butler Road
Kittanning, PA
724-543-1159 (877-424-6423)
Dogs are allowed for an additional fee of $5 per night per pet. 2 dogs may be allowed.

Comfort Inn
117 Twin Rocks Road
Lake Ariel, PA
570-689-4148 (877-424-6423)
Dogs are allowed for an additional fee of $15 per night per pet. Dogs may not be left alone in the room. Multiple dogs may be allowed.

Comfort Inn
31 Comfort Inn Lane
Lamar, PA
570-726-4901 (877-424-6423)
Dogs are allowed for an additional pet fee of $10 per night per room. Multiple dogs may be allowed.

Super 8 Lancaster
2129 Lincoln Hwy East
Lancaster, PA
717-393-8888 (800-800-8000)
Dogs of all sizes are allowed. There is a $10 per night pet fee per pet. Smoking and non-smoking rooms are available for pet rooms. 2 dogs may be allowed.

Travel Lodge
2101 Columbia Avenue
Lancaster, PA
717-397-4201
Dogs of all sizes are allowed. There is a $10 per night per pet additional fee. Multiple dogs may be allowed.

Red Roof Inn - Philadelphia Oxford Valley
3100 Cabot Boulevard West
Langhorne, PA
215-750-6200 (800-RED-ROOF)
One well-behaved family pet per room. Guest must notify front desk upon arrival. Guest is liable for any damages. In consideration of all guests, pets must never be left unattended in the guest rooms.

Sheraton Bucks County Hotel
400 Oxford Valley Road.
Langhorne, PA
215-547-4100 (888-625-5144)
Dogs up to 70 pounds are allowed. There are no additional pet fees. Dogs are not allowed to be left alone in the room.

Quality Inn Lebanon Valley
625 Quentin Road
Lebanon, PA

717-273-6771 (877-424-6423)
Dogs are allowed for an additional fee of $10 per night per pet. Multiple dogs may be allowed.

The Berry Patch
115 Moore Road
Lebanon, PA
717-865-7219
berrypatchbnb.com
Set amid lush lawns and towering trees on 20 acres, this newly built log home features large verandas with a view, the Strawberry Rose Garden, is close to hiking/biking trails, and are central to many other activities and attractions. Dogs of all sizes are allowed for an additional fee of $10 per night per pet. Dogs must be well behaved, leashed and cleaned up after, and crated when left alone in the room. 2 dogs may be allowed.

General Sutter Inn
14 E Main St
Lititz, PA
717-626-2115
generalsutterinn.com
Dogs up to 75 pounds are permitted.

Best Western Lake Haven
101 East Walnut St
Lock Haven, PA
570-748-3297 (800-780-7234)
Dogs are allowed for an additional fee of $10 per night per pet. Multiple dogs may be allowed.

Homewood Suites
12 E Swedesford Rd
Malvern, PA
610-296-3500
For those people who are staying 1 - 6 nights there is a $25 non-refundable pet fee. The one-time fee is $50 for 7 - 29 nights and the fee is $100 for 30 or more nights.

Staybridge Suites
20 Morehall Road
Malvern, PA
610-296-4343 (877-270-6405)
Dogs of all sizes are allowed for an additional fee of $10 per night per pet. Dogs must be crated when left alone in the room. Multiple dogs may be allowed.

Comfort Inn
300 Gateway Drive
Mansfield, PA
570-662-3000 (877-424-6423)
Dogs are allowed for an additional fee of $10 per night per pet. Dogs must be crated when left alone in the room. Multiple dogs may be allowed.

B. F. Hiestand House
722 E Market Street
Marietta, PA
717-426-8415 (877-560-8415)
bfhiestandhouse.com/
This Queen Anne style 1887 Victorian treasure sits along Susquehanna River and offers a convenient location to numerous attractions, recreational pursuits, shops, and eateries. Dogs of all sizes are allowed for an additional fee of $10 per night per pet. Dogs must be leashed at all times when out of guests' room, cleaned up after, and they may be left crated in the room alone for short time periods only. There are other pets on site. Multiple dogs may be allowed.

Comfort Inn Cranberry Twp.
924 Sheraton Drive
Mars, PA
724-772-2700 (877-424-6423)
Dogs up to 100 pounds are allowed for an additional one time fee of $10 per pet. 2 dogs may be allowed.

Motel 6 - Pittsburgh - Cranberry
19025 Perry Highway
Mars, PA
724-776-4333 (800-466-8356)
One well-behaved family pet per room. Guest must notify front desk upon arrival. Guest is liable for any damages. In consideration of all guests, pets must never be left unattended in the guest rooms.

Days Inn Meadville
18360 Conneaut Lake Rd
Meadville, PA
814-337-4264 (800-329-7466)
Dogs of all sizes are allowed. There is a $10 per night pet fee per pet. 2 dogs may be allowed.

Motel 6 - Meadville
11237 Shaw Avenue
Meadville, PA
814-724-6366 (800-466-8356)
One well-behaved family pet per room. Guest must notify front desk upon arrival. Guest is liable for any damages. In consideration of all guests, pets must never be left unattended in the guest rooms.

Comfort Inn Capital City
1012 Wesley Drive
Mechanicsburg, PA
717-766-3700 (877-424-6423)
Dogs are allowed for an additional fee of $25 per night per pet. 2 dogs may be allowed.

Howard Johnson Inn

835 Perry Hwy.
Mercer, PA
724-748-3030 (800-446-4656)
Dogs of all sizes are allowed. There are no additional pet fees.

Days Inn Harrisburg East
800 South Eisenhower Blvd
Middletown, PA
717-939-4147 (800-329-7466)
Dogs of all sizes are allowed. There is a $10 per night pet fee per pet. 2 dogs may be allowed.

Super 8 Mifflinville
450 WEST 3RD STREET
Mifflinville, PA
570-759-6778 (800-800-8000)
Dogs of all sizes are allowed. There is a $10 one time per pet fee per visit. Smoking and non-smoking rooms are available for pet rooms.

Holiday Inn
I-80 & US 150 N
Milesburg, PA
814-355-7521 (877-270-6405)
Dogs of all sizes are allowed for no additional pet fee. Multiple dogs may be allowed.

The New Muir House
102 H 2001
Milford, PA
570-722-3526
muirhouse.com/
This inn and restaurant allows dogs at the inn for no additional pet fee, and they are also welcome to sit with their owner's at the outside dining tables. Dogs must be quiet, under owner's control, leashed or crated, and cleaned up after at all times. 2 dogs may be allowed.

Holiday Inn Express Hotel and Suites
105 Stone Quarry Rd
Monaca, PA
724-728-5121 (877-270-6405)
Dogs of all sizes are allowed for an additional fee of $10 per night per pet. 2 dogs may be allowed.

Days Inn Pittsburgh/Monroeville
2727 Mosside Blvd
Monroeville, PA
412-856-1610 (800-329-7466)
Dogs of all sizes are allowed. There is a $25 per night pet fee per pet. 2 dogs may be allowed.

Red Roof Inn - Pittsburgh East - Monroeville
2729 Mosside Boulevard
Monroeville, PA
412-856-4738 (800-RED-ROOF)

One well-behaved family pet per room. Guest must notify front desk upon arrival. Guest is liable for any damages. In consideration of all guests, pets must never be left unattended in the guest rooms.

Holiday Inn - Airport
8256 University Blvd.
Moon Township, PA
412-262-3600 (877-270-6405)
Dogs of all sizes are allowed for an additional one time pet fee of $50 per room. Multiple dogs may be allowed.

La Quinta Inn Pittsburgh Airport
8507 University Boulevard
Moon Township, PA
412-269-0400 (800-531-5900)
Dogs of all sizes are allowed. There are no additional pet fees. Dogs must be quiet, well behaved, leashed and cleaned up after. Multiple dogs may be allowed.

Holiday Inn
6170 Morgantown Rd
Morgantown, PA
610-286-3000 (877-270-6405)
Dogs of all sizes are allowed for an additional fee of $20 per night per pet. Multiple dogs may be allowed.

The Olde Square Inn
127 E Main Street
Mount Joy, PA
717-653-4525 (800-742-3533)
oldesquareinn.com/
Located near the heart of Amish country, and numerous other attractions/activities, and year round recreation, this lovely inn, surrounded by lawns and gardens, offers a full breakfast buffet with indoor or outdoor dining, and a seasonal outdoor pool. Dogs of all sizes are welcome for an additional one time pet fee of $10 per room, and are asked to come in and meet the innkeeper; there are also other dogs on site. Dogs must be leashed at all times when out of the room and be cleaned up after inside and out. Please use a mat under the pet's food and water, and a cover for the bed and/or furniture if the pet is on them. Dogs must be crated when left alone in the room and they suggest leaving on the radio or TV and having a comfort item for the pup. 2 dogs may be allowed.

MainStay Suites
314 Primrose Lane
Mountville, PA
717-285-2500
Dogs are allowed for an additional fee of $10 per night per pet. Multiple

Pennsylvania Listings - Please always call ahead to make sure an establishment is still dog-friendly.

dogs may be allowed.

Comfort Inn
330 Commerce Park
New Columbia, PA
570-568-8000 (877-424-6423)
Dogs are allowed for no additional pet fee; there is a pet agreement to sign at check in. Multiple dogs may be allowed.

Holiday Inn Express
160 Commerce Park Drive
New Columbia, PA
570-568-1100 (877-270-6405)
Dogs of all sizes are allowed for an additional one time pet fee of $25 per room. 2 dogs may be allowed.

Days Inn Harrisburg South
353 Lewisburg Rd
New Cumberland, PA
717-774-4156 (800-329-7466)
Dogs of all sizes are allowed. There is a $15 per night pet fee per pet. 2 dogs may be allowed.

Motel 6 - Harrisburg
200 Commerce Drive
New Cumberland, PA
717-774-8910 (800-466-8356)
One well-behaved family pet per room. Guest must notify front desk upon arrival. Guest is liable for any damages. In consideration of all guests, pets must never be left unattended in the guest rooms.

The Hollander Motel
320 E Main St
New Holland, PA
717-354-4377
There is a $5.00 per day pet charge.

1833 Umpleby House
111 W Bridge Street
New Hope, PA
215-862-3936
1833umplebyhouse.com/index.htm
Sitting on 2 park-like acres, this 1833 Classic Revival manor house is on the National Registry of Historic Places, is only minutes from the village center and the Delaware River, and registered guests are welcome at the inn's private mountainpool and tennis club. One well traveled and well behaved dog is allowed per room for an additional $20 per night. Dogs must be flee and tic free, have their own bedding, and they may not be left alone in the room. Dogs must be quiet, well mannered, leashed, and cleaned up after at all times.

Wedgwood Inn

111 W Bridge Street
New Hope, PA
215-862-2570
wedgwoodinn.com/index.htm
This historic 1870 Wedgwood-blue Victorian home features 2 acres of lush lawns and gardens, home baked goodies available all day, and is only a short walk to the eclectic, vibrant village of New Hope, and to the walking bridge to New Jersey. Dogs of all sizes are allowed for an additional fee of $20 per night per pet. Dogs may be left alone only for short periods and only if they will be quiet, well behaved, and a contact number is left with the front desk. Dogs must be leashed and cleaned up after at all times. 2 dogs may be allowed.

Clarion Hotel
300 Tarentum Bridge Road
New Kensington, PA
724-335-9171 (877-424-6423)
Dogs are allowed for no additional pet fee. There is a pet agreement to sign at check in, and dogs may not be left alone in the room. Multiple dogs may be allowed.

Howard Johnson Inn
112 W. Byers Ave.
New Stanton, PA
724-925-3511 (800-446-4656)
Well-behaved dogs of all sizes are allowed. There is a $7 per day additional pet fee.

Quality Inn
110 N Main
New Stanton, PA
724-925-6755 (877-424-6423)
Dogs are allowed for an additional fee of $10 per night per pet. Multiple dogs may be allowed.

Residence Inn by Marriott
1110 Bethlehem Pike
North Wales, PA
267-468-0111
Dogs of all sizes are allowed. There is a $75 one time fee and a pet policy to sign at check in. Multiple dogs may be allowed.

Residence Inn by Marriott
3896 Bigelow Blvd
Oakland, PA
412-621-2200
Dogs of all sizes are allowed. There is a fee of $10 per night per room up to 30 days. If the stay is 30 days or more then it is a $100 one time fee. There is also a pet policy to sign at check in. Multiple dogs may be allowed.

Arlington Hotel
1 Seneca St
Oil City, PA
814-677-1221
There is a $10 per day additional pet fee.

Our Farm Under the Mimosa Tree
1487 Blue School Road
Perkasie, PA
215-249-9420
mimosatreebnb.com/
This scenic 20 acre, 200 year old farmhouse surrounded by mimosa trees, has numerous farm animals, peacocks, 2 ponds, a Japanese garden complete with a koi pond, hiking trails, and many places for picnicking and exploring. Dogs of all sizes are allowed for no additional pet fee. Puppies are not allowed, and dogs must be friendly toward humans and the farm animals. Dogs must be well behaved, leashed, cleaned up after, and they are not allowed on the furnishings. 2 dogs may be allowed.

Four Points by Sheraton at Philadelphia Airport
4010 A Island Ave.
Philadelphia, PA
215-492-0400 (888-625-5144)
Dogs up to 80 pounds are allowed. There are no additional pet fees. Dogs are not allowed to be left alone in the room.

Loews Philadelphia Hotel
1200 Market Street
Philadelphia, PA
215-627-1200
All well-behaved dogs of any size are welcome. This upscale hotel offers their "Loews Loves Pets" program which includes special pet treats, local dog walking routes, and a list of nearby pet-friendly places to visit. There are no pet fees.

Residence Inn by Marriott
One East Penn Square
Philadelphia, PA
215-557-0005
Dogs of all sizes are allowed. There is a $150 one time fee and a pet policy to sign at check in. Multiple dogs may be allowed.

Sheraton Philadelphia City Center Hotel
17th & Race St.
Philadelphia, PA
215-448-2000 (888-625-5144)
Dogs up to 50 pounds are allowed. There are no additional pet fees.

327

Dogs are not allowed to be left alone in the room.

Sheraton Society Hill Hotel
One Dock Street
Philadelphia, PA
215-238-6000 (888-625-5144)
Dogs up to 75 pounds are allowed. There are no additional pet fees. Dogs are not allowed to be left alone in the room.

Sheraton Suite Philadelphia
4101 B Island Ave.
Philadelphia, PA
215-365-6600 (888-625-5144)
Dogs up to 80 pounds are allowed. There are no additional pet fees. Dogs are not allowed to be left alone in the room.

Sheraton University City Hotel
36th and Chestnut Streets
Philadelphia, PA
215-387-8000 (888-625-5144)
Dogs up to 80 pounds are allowed. There are no additional pet fees. Dogs are not allowed to be left alone in the room.

The Conwell Inn
1331 W Berks Street
Philadelphia, PA
215-235-6200 (888-379-9737)
conwellinn.com/
This historic, landmark hotel is located in the middle of Temple University, and is close to downtown and numerous sites of interest. Dogs of all sizes are allowed for an additional fee of $20 per night per room. Dogs must be quiet, leashed, cleaned up after, and crated if left alone in the room. 2 dogs may be allowed.

The Rittenhouse
210 W Rittenhouse Square
Philadelphia, PA
215-546-9000
rittenhousehotel.com/
There are no additional pet fees.

Comfort Inn
H 443 and I 81
Pine Grove, PA
570-345-8031 (877-424-6423)
Dogs are allowed for an additional pet fee of $10 per night per room. Multiple dogs may be allowed.

Candlewood Suites
100 Chauvet Drive
Pittsburgh, PA
412-787-7770 (877-270-6405)
A dog up to 80 pounds is allowed for an additional fee of $75 for 1 to 6

days; the fee is $150 for 7 or more days.

Comfort Inn Conference Center
699 Rodi Road
Pittsburgh, PA
412-244-1600 (877-424-6423)
Quiet dogs are allowed for an additional fee of $10 per night per pet. Multiple dogs may be allowed.

Comfort Inn and Suites
2898 Banksville Road
Pittsburgh, PA
412-343-3000 (877-424-6423)
Dogs are allowed for a $100 refundable deposit plus an additional fee of $15 per night per pet. Multiple dogs may be allowed.

Days Inn Pittsburgh/Harmarville
6 Landings Drive
Pittsburgh, PA
412-828-5400 (800-329-7466)
Dogs of all sizes are allowed. There is a $10 one time per pet fee per visit. 2 dogs may be allowed.

Embassy Suites Hotel Pittsburgh - International Airport
550 Cherrington Parkway
Pittsburgh, PA
412-269-9070
Dogs of all sizes are allowed. There is a $50 one time pet fee per visit. Dogs are not allowed to be left alone in the room.

Hampton Inn
555 Trumbull Drive
Pittsburgh, PA
412-922-0100
Dogs of all sizes are allowed. There is a pet policy to sign at check in and there are no additional pet fees. They request you kennel your pet for housekeeping and dogs are not allowed in food areas. Multiple dogs may be allowed.

Holiday Inn
401 Holiday Dr
Pittsburgh, PA
412-922-8100 (877-270-6405)
Dogs of all sizes are allowed for no additional pet fee. Multiple dogs may be allowed.

Holiday Inn Express Hotel & Suites
Pittsburgh Airport
5311 Campbells Run Road
Pittsburgh, PA
412-788-8400 (877-270-6405)
Dogs of all sizes are allowed for an additional one time pet fee of $15 per room. 2 dogs may be allowed.

Holiday Inn Hotel and Suites
180 Gamma Dr
Pittsburgh, PA
412-963-0600 (877-270-6405)
A dog up to 50 pounds is allowed for no additional fee with a credit card on file; a $50 refundable deposit is required if paying by cash.

MainStay Suites
1000 Park Lane Drive
Pittsburgh, PA
412-490-7343
Dogs up to 50 pounds are allowed for a fee per pet of $25 for 1 to 4 nights; $50 for 5 to 10 nights; $75 for 11 to 28 nights, and $100 for 29+ nights. 2 dogs may be allowed.

Morning Glory Inn
2119 Sarah Street
Pittsburgh, PA
412-431-1707
morningglorybedandbreakfast.com
A perfect blend of sophistication and casual comfort, this 1862 Italian style Victorian brick inn features lush greenery, a beautiful garden patio, and they are central to a host of other activities and an active nightlife. Dogs of all sizes are allowed in one suite for no additional fee. Dogs must be well mannered, they are not allowed on the furnishings, and they must be leashed and cleaned up after. Multiple dogs may be allowed.

Motel 6 - Pittsburgh - Crafton
211 Beecham Drive
Pittsburgh, PA
412-922-9400 (800-466-8356)
One well-behaved family pet per room. Guest must notify front desk upon arrival. Guest is liable for any damages. In consideration of all guests, pets must never be left unattended in the guest rooms.

Radisson Hotel Pittsburgh Green Tree
101 Radisson Drive
Pittsburgh, PA
412-922-8400
Dogs of all sizes are allowed. There are no additional pet fees. Pet owners need to sign a pet waiver.

Red Roof Inn - Pittsburgh South Airport
6404 Steubenville Pike
Pittsburgh, PA
412-787-7870 (800-RED-ROOF)
One well-behaved family pet per room. Guest must notify front desk upon arrival. Guest is liable for any damages. In consideration of all guests, pets must never be left

unattended in the guest rooms.

Residence Inn by Marriott
1500 Park Lane Drive
Pittsburgh, PA
412-787-3300
Dogs of all sizes are allowed. There is a $75 one time fee and a pet policy to sign at check in. Multiple dogs may be allowed.

Super 8 Pittsburgh/Monroeville Area
1807 RT 286
Pittsburgh, PA
724-733-8008 (800-800-8000)
Dogs of all sizes are allowed. There is a $5 per night pet fee per pet. Smoking and non-smoking rooms are available for pet rooms. 2 dogs may be allowed.

Comfort Inn
99 Robinson Street
Pottstown, PA
610-326-5000 (877-424-6423)
Dogs are allowed for an additional pet fee of $10 per night per room. Multiple dogs may be allowed.

Days Inn Pottstown
29 High St
Pottstown, PA
610-970-1101 (800-329-7466)
Dogs of all sizes are allowed. There is a $10 per night pet fee per pet. 2 dogs may be allowed.

Motel 6 - Pottstown
78 Robinson Street
Pottstown, PA
610-819-1288 (800-466-8356)
One well-behaved family pet per room. Guest must notify front desk upon arrival. Guest is liable for any damages. In consideration of all guests, pets must never be left unattended in the guest rooms.

Hampton Inn
1915 John Fries H
Quakertown, PA
215-536-7779
A dog up to 50 pounds is allowed. There is a $10 per night additional pet fee.

Jackson House
6 E Main Street
Railroad, PA
717-227-2022 (877-782-4672)
jacksonhousebandb.com/
This scenic inn features terraced gardens offering great views from the top, a relaxing waterfall, and they are the only state inn to sit right on the multi-use Heritage Rail Trail, a 21 mile trail that also connects to the 20

mile long Northern Central Rail Trail. They offer 1 pet friendly room with a private entrance, and there is an additional one time fee of $20 per pet. Dogs are not allowed in the common areas of the house, and they must be crated when left alone in the room. Dogs must be well behaved, leashed, and cleaned up after at all times. 2 dogs may be allowed.

Sheraton Reading Hotel
1741 Papermill Road
Reading, PA
610-376-3811 (888-625-5144)
Dogs of all sizes are allowed. There is a $10 per night pet fee per pet. Dogs are not allowed to be left alone in the room.

Comfort Inn
195 Comfort Lane
Saint Marys, PA
814-834-2030 (877-424-6423)
Dogs are allowed for an additional fee of $15 (plus tax) per night per pet. Multiple dogs may be allowed.

Best Western Grand Victorian Inn
255 Spring Street
Sayre, PA
570-888-7711 (800-780-7234)
Dogs are allowed for an additional fee of $10 per night per pet. Dogs must be quiet and well mannered. Multiple dogs may be allowed.

Clarion Hotel
300 Meadow Avenue
Scranton, PA
570-344-9811 (877-424-6423)
Dogs are allowed for an additional pet fee of $25 per night per room. 2 dogs may be allowed.

Days Inn Scranton
1946 Scranton-Carbondale hwy
Scranton, PA
570-383-9979 (800-329-7466)
Dogs of all sizes are allowed. There is a $5 per night pet fee per small pet or $20 per large pet. 2 dogs may be allowed.

Howard Johnson Express Inn
320 Franklin Ave.
Scranton, PA
570-346-7061 (800-446-4656)
Dogs of all sizes are welcome. There is a $10 per day pet fee.

Hampton Inn
3 Stettler Avenue
Selinsgrove, PA
570-743-2223
Well behaved dogs of all sizes are

allowed. There is a $25 per pet per stay fee. Multiple dogs may be allowed.

Comfort Inn
710 H 11/15
Sellinsgrove, PA
570-374-8880 (877-424-6423)
Quiet dogs are allowed for an additional one time fee of $10 per pet. Dogs must be crated when left alone in the room. 2 dogs may be allowed.

Quality Inn and Suites
2 Susquehanna Trail
Shamokin Dam, PA
570-743-1111 (877-424-6423)
Dogs of all sizes are allowed. There is a $10 per night per pet additional fee. 2 dogs may be allowed.

Whispering Winds Campground
277 Tollgate Road
Sheffield, PA
814-968-4377
WhisperingWindsPA.com
This family campground has full camping facilities, a laundry, playground and a pool. Pets are welcome with no additional fee. They must be kept on a leash or in a crate or a pen and under control. There is a pet walk area.

Best Western Shippensburg Hotel
125 Walnut Bottom Road
Shippensburg, PA
717-532-5200 (800-780-7234)
Dogs are allowed for an additional fee of $10 per night per pet. Multiple dogs may be allowed.

Best Western Executive Inn of Somerset
165 Waterworks Rd
Somerset, PA
814-445-3996 (800-780-7234)
Dogs are allowed for an additional fee of $7 per night per pet. Multiple dogs may be allowed.

Days Inn Somerset
220 Waterworks Rd
Somerset, PA
814-445-9200 (800-329-7466)
Dogs of all sizes are allowed. There is a $6 per night pet fee per pet. 2 dogs may be allowed.

Holiday Inn
202 Harmon St
Somerset, PA
814-445-9611 (877-270-6405)
Dogs of all sizes are allowed for an additional one time pet fee of $35 per room. 2 dogs may be allowed.

Knights Inn
585 Ramada Rd
Somerset, PA
814-445-8933 (800-843-5644)
There are no additional pet fees.

Quality Inn
215 Ramada Road
Somerset, PA
814-443-4646 (877-424-6423)
Dogs are allowed for an additional
fee of $10 per night per pet. 2 dogs
may be allowed.

Super 8 Somerset
125 Lewis Dr
Somerset, PA
814-445-8788 (800-800-8000)
Dogs of all sizes are allowed. There
is a $7 per night pet fee per pet.
Smoking and non-smoking rooms
are available for pet rooms. 2 dogs
may be allowed.

The Inn at Starlight Lake
2890 Starlight Lake Road
Starlight, PA
570-798-2519 (800-248-2519)
innatstarlightlake.com/
Set among lush greenery on the
lakefront, this family getaway
features a game room, sunroom,
restaurant and bar, and they are
central to a wide variety of land and
water year round recreation. Dogs of
all sizes are allowed in the cottages
only for no additional pet fee. Dogs
must be at least one year old, they
are not allowed in the main house,
and they may not be left unattended
in the room for more than 2 hours.
Dogs must be leashed and cleaned
up after at all times. 2 dogs may be
allowed.

Comfort Suites
132 Village Drive
State College, PA
814-235-1900 (877-424-6423)
Dogs are allowed for a $50
refundable deposit plus an additional
fee of $20 per night per pet. 2 dogs
may be allowed.

Days Inn Penn State
240 S Pugh St
State College, PA
814-238-8454 (800-329-7466)
Dogs of all sizes are allowed. There
is a $10 per night pet fee per pet. 2
dogs may be allowed.

Motel 6 - STATE COLLEGE - PENN
STATE UNIVERSITY
1274 North Atherton Street
State College, PA

814-234-1600 (800-466-8356)
One well-behaved family pet per
room. Guest must notify front desk
upon arrival. Guest is liable for any
damages. In consideration of all
guests, pets must never be left
unattended in the guest rooms.

Residence Inn by Marriott
1555 University Drive
State College, PA
814-285-6960
Dogs of all sizes are allowed. There
is a $175 one time fee and a pet
policy to sign at check in. Multiple
dogs may be allowed.

River View Inn
103 Chestnut Street
Sunbury, PA
570-286-4800 (866-592-4800)
riverview-inn.com/
This 1870's elegant Victorian inn
sits along the Susquehanna River
and across from the Merle Phillips
Park, and is updated with all the
modern comforts. They have one
pet friendly room and one dog of
any size is allowed for an additional
pet fee of $25 per night. Dogs must
be very quiet and well behaved,
leashed and cleaned up after inside
and out, and shots up to date. Dogs
may not be left alone in the room.

Radisson Hotel Philadelphia NE
2400 Old Lincoln Highway
Trevose, PA
215-638-8300 (800-333-3333)
Pets must stay on the first floor.
Dogs up to 75 pounds are allowed.
People with Pets must book the
'pet-friendly rate' when making
reservations.

Red Roof Inn - Philadelphia
Trevose
3100 Lincoln Highway
Trevose, PA
215-244-9422 (800-RED-ROOF)
One well-behaved family pet per
room. Guest must notify front desk
upon arrival. Guest is liable for any
damages. In consideration of all
guests, pets must never be left
unattended in the guest rooms.

Days Inn Breezewood
9648 Old 126
Warfordsburg, PA
814-735-3860 (800-329-7466)
Dogs of all sizes are allowed. There
is a $10 per night pet fee per pet. 2
dogs may be allowed.

Motel 6 - Washington, PA
1283 Motel 6 Drive

Washington, PA
724-223-8040 (800-466-8356)
One well-behaved family pet per
room. Guest must notify front desk
upon arrival. Guest is liable for any
damages. In consideration of all
guests, pets must never be left
unattended in the guest rooms.

Red Roof Inn - Washington
1399 West Chestnut Street
Washington, PA
724-228-5750 (800-RED-ROOF)
One well-behaved family pet per
room. Guest must notify front desk
upon arrival. Guest is liable for any
damages. In consideration of all
guests, pets must never be left
unattended in the guest rooms.

Indian Rock Inn
155 Keen Lake
Waymart, PA
610-982-9600
Well behaved dogs up to 75 pounds
are allowed. There is a $15 one time
additional pet fee per room. 2 dogs
may be allowed.

Keen Lake Camping and Cottage
Resort
155 Keen Lake
Waymart, PA
570-488-5522
Dogs of all sizes are allowed. There
is a $50 one time pet fee for cottages
and there is no additional pet fee for
the camp sites. Dogs are not to be
left alone at any time. 2 dogs may be
allowed.

Kaltenbachs Inn
743 Stoney Fork Road
Wellsboro, PA
570-724-4954 (800-722-4954)
kaltenbachsinn.com/
This sprawling country inn is on a 72
acre ranch with farm animals, plenty
of wildlife, views, pastures and
forests, picnicking areas with
barbecues, and they are also only a
short biking/driving distance from the
newly opened 62 mile Pine Creek
Rail Trail. Dogs of all sizes are
allowed for an additional fee of $5
per night per pet. Dogs must be very
well behaved, quiet, leashed,
cleaned up after, and crated when
left alone in the room. 2 dogs may be
allowed.

Comfort Inn
58 H 93
West Hazleton, PA
570-455-9300 (877-424-6423)
Dogs are allowed for an additional
fee of $10 per night per pet. Multiple
dogs may be allowed.

Holiday Inn Express Hotel and Suites
3122 Lebanon Church Rd
West Mifflin, PA
412-469-1900 (877-270-6405)
Dogs of all sizes are allowed for an additional fee of $10 per night per pet. Multiple dogs may be allowed.

Best Western Genetti Hotel & Conference Center
77 E Market Street
Wilkes-Barre, PA
570-823-6152 (800-780-7234)
Dogs are allowed for an additional pet fee of $10 per night per room. Multiple dogs may be allowed.

Holiday Inn
880 Kidder St, Rt 115 & 309
Wilkes-Barre, PA
570-824-8901 (877-270-6405)
Dogs of all sizes are allowed for an additional one time pet fee of $15 per room. Multiple dogs may be allowed.

Red Roof Inn - Wilkes-Barre
1035 Highway 315
Wilkes-Barre, PA
570-829-6422 (800-RED-ROOF)
One well-behaved family pet per room. Guest must notify front desk upon arrival. Guest is liable for any damages. In consideration of all guests, pets must never be left unattended in the guest rooms.

Best Western Williamsport Inn
1840 E 3rd Street
Williamsport, PA
570-326-1981 (800-780-7234)
Dogs are allowed for an additional one time pet fee of $15 per room. 2 dogs may be allowed.

Candlewood Suites Williamsport
1836 East Third St.
Williamsport, PA
570-601-9100 (877-270-6405)
Dogs of all sizes are allowed for additional one time fees ranging from $35 to $150 per room, depending on the length of stay and size of dog. 2 dogs may be allowed.

Quality Inn & Conference Center
234 H 15
Williamsport, PA
570-323-9801 (877-424-6423)
One dog is allowed for an additional one time pet fee of $25.

Comfort Inn
RR 6 Box 6167A
Wysox, PA
570-265-5691 (877-424-6423)
Dogs are allowed for an additional

one time pet fee of $15 (plus tax) per room, and there is a pet agreement to sign at check in. 2 dogs may be allowed.

Holiday Inn
2000 Loucks Rd
York, PA
717-846-9500 (877-270-6405)
Dogs of all sizes are allowed for an additional fee of $10 per night per room. Multiple dogs may be allowed.

Motel 6 - York
125 Arsenal Road
York, PA
717-846-6260 (800-466-8356)
One well-behaved family pet per room. Guest must notify front desk upon arrival. Guest is liable for any damages. In consideration of all guests, pets must never be left unattended in the guest rooms.

Quality Inn and Suites
2600 E Market Street
York, PA
717-755-1966 (877-424-6423)
Dogs are allowed for an additional fee of $10 per night per pet. There may be 1 large or 2 small dogs per room. 2 dogs may be allowed.

Red Roof Inn - York
323 Arsenal Road
York, PA
717-843-8181 (800-RED-ROOF)
One well-behaved family pet per room. Guest must notify front desk upon arrival. Guest is liable for any damages. In consideration of all guests, pets must never be left unattended in the guest rooms.

Rhode Island Listings

The Blue Dory Inn
Dodge Street
Block Island, RI
401-466-2254 (800-992-7290)
blockislandinns.com/
This historic 1862 mansion sits at the head of Crescent Beach only a mile from the Atlantic Ocean on 5 rolling acres, and every afternoon guests can meet in the parlor for wine, hors d'oevres and their specialty-Blue Dory cookies. Dogs of all sizes are welcome for an additional $25 one time fee per pet. Dogs must be leashed and cleaned

up after. 2 dogs may be allowed.

The Island Home
Beach Avenue
Block Island, RI
401-466-5944
One large dog up to about 50 pounds or 2 dogs at about 10 pounds each are allowed. There is a pet policy to sign at check in and there are no additional pet fees.

Vacation Rentals by Owner
Calico Hill
Block Island, RI
401-497-0631
vrbo.com/90721
Set upon rolling hills with views of the harbor and the town only a few minutes away, this 1871 farmhouse offers all the modern amenities, and a great starting point for a wide variety of activities, and land and water recreation. Dogs of all sizes are allowed for no additional pet fees. Dogs must be house trained, well behaved, and leashed and cleaned up after at all times inside and outside. Multiple dogs may be allowed.

Howard Johnson Inn
351 West Main Rd.
Middletown, RI
401-849-2000 (800-446-4656)
Dogs of all sizes are welcome. There is a $10 per day pet fee. Pets may not be left unattended in the room.

Almy Cottage
141 Coggeshall Ave
Newport, RI
401-864-0686
This vacation cottage is close to many of the attractions that draw people here such as Mansion Row on Bellevue Avenue or the exhilarating Cliff Walk, and it is only a short walk to a small private beach. Dogs of all sizes are welcome for no additional pet fee. They are allowed in the garden cottage only, and they must be leashed and cleaned up after at all times. Dogs may only be left alone in the cottage if they are comfortable being alone and will be quiet and well behaved. Multiple dogs may be allowed.

Chestnut Inn
99 3rd Street
Newport, RI
401-847-6949
members.aol.com/chstnut99/
This year round family or couples destination feature 2 oversized Victorian bedrooms, a continental breakfast, and a great location to

several other attractions and recreational pursuits. Dog of all sizes are allowed for no additional fee. There can only be one dog if only 1 room is rented; however, up to 2 dogs are allowed if both rooms are taken. Dogs must be well mannered, leashed, and cleaned up after.

Dun Rovin
7 Florence Ave.
Newport, RI
401-846-2294
3 bedroom 2 bath house in the southern part of Newport. All pets are welcome. The home is near the Ocean Drive, Gooseberry Beach, Bellevue Ave. mansions,Ft. Adams, New York yacht club and Salve Regina University. All linens, dishes etc. are provided as well as cable TV, DVD, garden patio, W/D,local phone. There is a separate apt. on the premise which is occupied from time to time. There is no smoking allowed.

Hotel Viking
One Bellview Avenue
Newport, RI
401-847-3300 (800-556-7126)
hotelviking.com/viking_home.aspx
Although a small boutique hotel of former days and registered with Historic Hotels of America, this wonderfully updated spa hotel has numerous amenities and services for the business or leisure traveler, a convenient location to a number of sites of interest, fine dining, and more. Dogs of all sizes are allowed for an additional fee of $75 per pet per stay. Complimentary organic doggy biscuits await their canine guests, and Canine room service is only a call away. Dogs must be quiet, well behaved, leashed, cleaned up after, and crated when left alone in the room. 2 dogs may be allowed.

Motel 6 - Newport
249 JT Connell Highway
Newport, RI
401-848-0600 (800-466-8356)
One well-behaved family pet per room. Guest must notify front desk upon arrival. Guest is liable for any damages. In consideration of all guests, pets must never be left unattended in the guest rooms.

Murray House
1 Murray Place
Newport, RI
401-846-3337
murrayhouse.com/
Located in the famed Newport Mansion District, this guest house

features a nice beach a short walk away, private entrance to each of the rooms, a gourmet breakfast brought to your room or served on your private patio area, an in-ground pool and hot-tub, and flower gardens. Dogs of all sizes are allowed for an additional fee of $10 per night per pet for small dogs and $35 per night per pet for medium-large to large dogs. There can be 1 large dog or 2 small to medium dogs per room. Dogs must be leashed and cleaned up after at all times.

The Beech Tree Inn
34 Rhode Island Avenue
Newport, RI
401-847-9794 (800-748-6565)
beechtreeinn.com/
This modernized 1880's Victorian home features bright, spacious rooms, a garden, and rooftop decks. Dogs of all sizes are welcome for an additional fee of $25 per night per pet. There can be 1 large dog or 2 small to medium dogs per room. Dogs may only be left alone in the room if they are comfortable being alone and will be quiet and well behaved. Dogs must be leashed, cleaned up after, and crated with a contact number left at the front desk if they are in the room alone. 2 dogs may be allowed.

The Poplar House
19 Poplar Avenue
Newport, RI
401-846-0976
Well behaved, clean, friendly dogs of all sizes are allowed. There is a $10 per night per room additional pet fee. Dogs are not allowed to be left alone in the room. Multiple dogs may be allowed.

Providence Marriott Downtown
One Orms Street
Providence, RI
401-272-2400 (800-228-9290)
One dog up to 50 pounds is allowed. There is a $50 one time additional pet fee. Dogs may not be left alone in the room, and they must be leashed and cleaned up after.

The Cady House
127 Power Street
Providence, RI
401-273-5398
cadyhouse.com/
Built in 1838, the Cady house offers rooms individually decorated with period antiques and items from around the world, a garden patio

where guests can dine in good weather, and a convenient location to an array of local activities, universities, shops, and eateries. Dogs of all sizes are welcome for no additional pet fee. Dogs are allowed in the garden apartment only, and they must be well behaved and friendly towards the other pets in residence. Dogs must be leashed and cleaned up after, and they may only be left alone in the room if they will be calm and comfortable. 2 dogs may be allowed.

The Kings' Rose
1747 Mooresfield Road
South Kingston, RI
401-783-5222
This colonial style home, listed on the National Register of Historic Places, features 16 guest rooms, over 2 acres of gardens, and a convenient location to several other attractions and activities. Dogs of all sizes are welcome for no additional pet fees. Dogs must be leashed, cleaned up after, and crated when left alone in the room. 2 dogs may be allowed.

Crowne Plaza
801 Greenwich Ave
Warwick, RI
401-732-6000 (877-270-6405)
Dogs of all sizes are allowed for no additional fee; dogs must be crated when left alone in the room. Multiple dogs may be allowed.

Hampton Inn
2100 Post Road
Warwick, RI
401-739-8888
Dogs of all sizes are allowed. There are no additional pet fees. Multiple dogs may be allowed.

Holiday Inn Express & Suites
901 Jefferson Blvd
Warwick, RI
401-736-5000 (877-270-6405)
Dogs of all sizes are allowed for a $50 refundable pet deposit per room. Multiple dogs may be allowed.

Motel 6 - Providence - Warwick
20 Jefferson Boulevard
Warwick, RI
401-467-9800 (800-466-8356)
One well-behaved family pet per room. Guest must notify front desk upon arrival. Guest is liable for any damages. In consideration of all guests, pets must never be left unattended in the guest rooms.

Residence Inn by Marriott
500 Kilvert Street
Warwick, RI
401-737-7100
Dogs of all sizes are allowed, however only two pets can be in the studio or double rooms, and up to three pets in the Penthouse suite. There is also a pet policy to sign at check in.

Sheraton Providence Airport Hotel
1850 Post Road
Warwick, RI
401-738-4000 (888-625-5144)
Dogs up to 80 pounds are allowed for no additional pet fee. Dogs may not be left alone in the room.

South Carolina Listings

Holiday Inn Express
155 Colony Pkwy - Whiskey Rd
Aiken, SC
803-648-0999 (877-270-6405)
Dogs of all sizes are allowed for an additional one time pet fee of $45 per room. Multiple dogs may be allowed.

Howard Johnson Express Inn
1936 Whiskey Road South
Aiken, SC
803-649-5000 (800-446-4656)
Dogs of all sizes are welcome. There is a $11.10 per day pet fee.

Quality Inn
110 E Frontage Road
Aiken, SC
803-502-0900 (877-424-6423)
Dogs are allowed for an additional one time pet fee of $15 per room. 2 dogs may be allowed.

Quality Inn and Suites
3608 Richland Avenue W
Aiken, SC
803-641-1100 (877-424-6423)
Dogs are allowed for an additional fee of $10 per night per pet. Multiple dogs may be allowed.

Country Inns & Suites by Carlson
116 Interstate Blvd
Anderson, SC
864-622-2200
Dogs of all sizes are allowed. There is a $15 one time additional pet fee.

Days Inn Anderson
1007 Smith Mill Rd
Anderson, SC

864-375-0375 (800-329-7466)
Dogs of all sizes are allowed. There is a $10 per night pet fee per pet. 2 dogs may be allowed.

La Quinta Inn Anderson
3430 Clemson Blvd.
Anderson, SC
864-225-3721 (800-531-5900)
Dogs of all sizes are allowed. There are no additional pet fees. Dogs may not be left unattended, and they must be leashed and cleaned up after. Dogs may not be left unattended, unless they will be quiet and well behaved. Multiple dogs may be allowed.

MainStay Suites
151 Civic Center Blvd
Anderson, SC
864-226-1112
Dogs are allowed for an additional one time pet fee of $35 per room. 2 dogs may be allowed.

Super 8 Anderson/Clemson Area
3302 Cinema Ave
Anderson, SC
864-225-8384 (800-800-8000)
Dogs of all sizes are allowed. There is a $25 one time per pet fee per visit. Smoking and non-smoking rooms are available for pet rooms. 2 dogs may be allowed.

Howard Johnson Express Inn
3651 Trask Parkway, US Hwy 21
Beaufort, SC
843-524-6020 (800-446-4656)
Dogs of all sizes are welcome. There is a $25 one time pet fee.

Best Western Charleston Downtown
250 Spring Street
Charleston, SC
843-722-4000 (800-780-7234)
CharlestonBestWestern.com
Dogs of all sizes are allowed at this downtown Charleston hotel. There is a $25.00 nightly pet fee per pet. 2 dogs may be allowed.

Charleston Cottage
Call to Arrange
Charleston, SC
207-342-5444
landworkswaterfront.com
Located on the corner of East Bay and Tradd, this vacation rental is one block from the waterfront park and diagonally across the street from the dog park. Restaurants, historic spots of interest, fine shopping, galleries and the Battery are all within walking distance.

Indigo Inn
Maiden Lane
Charleston, SC
843-577-5900 (800-845-7639)
aesir.com/IndigoInn/Welcome.html
There is a $20 per day pet fee.

La Quinta Inn Charleston Riverview
11 Ashley Pointe Drive
Charleston, SC
843-556-5200 (800-531-5900)
Dogs of all sizes are allowed. There are no additional pet fees. Dogs must be declared at the time of check in, and there is a pet waiver to sign. Dogs must be leashed, cleaned up after, and the Do Not Disturb sign put on the door if there is a pet in the room alone. Multiple dogs may be allowed.

Motel 6 - Charleston South
2058 Savannah Highway
Charleston, SC
843-556-5144 (800-466-8356)
One well-behaved family pet per room. Guest must notify front desk upon arrival. Guest is liable for any damages. In consideration of all guests, pets must never be left unattended in the guest rooms.

Quality Suites Convention Center
5225 N Arco Lane
Charleston, SC
843-747-7300
Dogs up to 50 pounds are allowed for an additional one time fee of $49 per pet. 2 dogs may be allowed.

Residence Inn by Marriott
90 Ripley Point Drive
Charleston, SC
843-571-7979
Dogs of all sizes are allowed. There is a $75 one time fee and a pet policy to sign at check in. Multiple dogs may be allowed.

Days Inn Cheraw
820 Market St
Cheraw, SC
843-537-5554 (800-329-7466)
Dogs of all sizes are allowed. There is a $5 per night pet fee per pet. 2 dogs may be allowed.

Comfort Inn
105 Trade Street
Clinton, SC
864-833-5558 (877-424-6423)
Quiet dogs are allowed for no additional pet fee. Multiple dogs may be allowed.

Carolinian Hotel

7510 Two Notch Rd, I-20 & US-1
Columbia, SC
803-736-3000
There is a $25 one time pet fee. Pets must be leashed when they are not in your room.

Days Inn Columbia
133 Plumbers Rd
Columbia, SC
803-754-4408 (800-329-7466)
Dogs of all sizes are allowed. There is a $8 per night pet fee per pet. 2 dogs may be allowed.

La Quinta Inn Columbia NE/Fort Jackson
1538 Horseshoe Drive
Columbia, SC
803-736-6400 (800-531-5900)
Dogs of all sizes are allowed. There are no additional pet fees. Dogs must be crated if left alone in the room. Dogs are not allowed in the breakfast area, and they must be leashed and cleaned up after. Multiple dogs may be allowed.

Motel 6 - Columbia East
7541 Nates Road
Columbia, SC
803-736-3900 (800-466-8356)
One well-behaved family pet per room. Guest must notify front desk upon arrival. Guest is liable for any damages. In consideration of all guests, pets must never be left unattended in the guest rooms.

Motel 6 - Columbia West
1776 Burning Tree Road
Columbia, SC
803-798-9210 (800-466-8356)
One well-behaved family pet per room. Guest must notify front desk upon arrival. Guest is liable for any damages. In consideration of all guests, pets must never be left unattended in the guest rooms.

Red Roof Inn - Columbia East, SC
7580 Two Notch Road
Columbia, SC
803-736-0850 (800-RED-ROOF)
One well-behaved family pet per room. Guest must notify front desk upon arrival. Guest is liable for any damages. In consideration of all guests, pets must never be left unattended in the guest rooms.

Red Roof Inn - Columbia West, SC
10 Berryhill Road
Columbia, SC
803-798-9220 (800-RED-ROOF)
One well-behaved family pet per room. Guest must notify front desk

upon arrival. Guest is liable for any damages. In consideration of all guests, pets must never be left unattended in the guest rooms.

Residence Inn by Marriott
150 Stoneridge Drive
Columbia, SC
803-779-7000
Well behaved dogs of all sizes are allowed. There is a $50 one time fee on the first night. Starting the second night is a $10 per night fee, and there will be a pet policy to sign at check in. Multiple dogs may be allowed.

TownePlace Suites Columbia
350 Columbiana Drive
Columbia, SC
803-781-9391
Dogs of all sizes are allowed. There is a $75 one time pet fee per visit. Multiple dogs may be allowed.

Best Value Inn
904 Redford Blvd
Dillon, SC
843-774-5111
There is a $12 per day additional pet fee.

Deluxe Inn
818 Radford Blvd
Dillon, SC
843-774-6041
Dogs of all sizes are allowed. There is a $8 per night pet fee per small pet and $12 for large pet. 2 dogs may be allowed.

Super 8 Dillon
1203 Radford Blvd
Dillon, SC
843-774-4161 (800-800-8000)
Dogs of all sizes are allowed. There is a $5 per night pet fee per small pet or $10 per large pet. Smoking and non-smoking rooms are available for pet rooms. 2 dogs may be allowed.

Days Inn Spartanburg Airport
1386 E Main St
Duncan, SC
864-433-1122 (800-329-7466)
Dogs of all sizes are allowed. There is a $25 one time per pet fee per visit. 2 dogs may be allowed.

Holiday Inn Express Hotel & Suites Greenville-Spartanburg(Duncan)
Hwy 290 & I-85
Duncan, SC
864-486-9191 (877-270-6405)
Dogs of all sizes are allowed for an additional one time pet fee of $35

per room 2 dogs may be allowed.

Days Inn Easley
121 Days Inn Drive
Easley, SC
864-859-9902 (800-329-7466)
Dogs of all sizes are allowed. There is a $10 per night pet fee per pet. 2 dogs may be allowed.

Atwood Vacations
Call To Arrange
Edisto Island, SC
843-869-2151 (866-713-5214)
atwoodvacations.com
Located 45 miles south of Charleston, this vacation rental management company has many pet friendly rentals.

Comfort Inn
1916 W Lucas Street
Florence, SC
843-665-4558 (877-424-6423)
Dogs are allowed for an additional fee of $10 per night per pet. Multiple dogs may be allowed.

Days Inn Florence North/I-95
2111 W Lucas St
Florence, SC
843-665-4444 (800-329-7466)
Dogs of all sizes are allowed. There are no additional pet fees. 2 dogs may be allowed.

Days Inn Florence South/I-95
3783 W Palmetto St
Florence, SC
843-665-8550 (800-329-7466)
Dogs of all sizes are allowed. There is a $10 per night pet fee per pet. 2 dogs may be allowed.

Econo Lodge
1811 W Lucas St
Florence, SC
843-665-8558
There is a $6 per day additional pet fee.

Holiday Inn Hotel & Suites Florence Sc @ I-95 & Us Hwy 52
1819 Lucas St
Florence, SC
843-665-4555 (877-270-6405)
Dogs of all sizes are allowed for an additional one time pet fee of $25 per room. Multiple dogs may be allowed.

Motel 6 - Florence
1834 West Lucas Street
Florence, SC
843-667-6100 (800-466-8356)
One well-behaved family pet per room. Guest must notify front desk upon arrival. Guest is liable for any

damages. In consideration of all guests, pets must never be left unattended in the guest rooms.

Red Roof Inn - Florence, SC
2690 David McLeod Boulevard
Florence, SC
843-678-9000 (800-RED-ROOF)
One well-behaved family pet per room. Guest must notify front desk upon arrival. Guest is liable for any damages. In consideration of all guests, pets must never be left unattended in the guest rooms.

Thunderbird Motor Inn
2004 W Lucas St
Florence, SC
843-669-1611
There are no additional pet fees.

Young's Plantation Inn
US 76 and I-95
Florence, SC
843-669-4171
There is a $4 per day pet fee.

Motel 6 - Charlotte Carowinds
255 Carowinds Bouelvard
Fort Mill, SC
803-548-9656 (800-466-8356)
One well-behaved family pet per room. Guest must notify front desk upon arrival. Guest is liable for any damages. In consideration of all guests, pets must never be left unattended in the guest rooms.

Peach Tree Inn
136 Peachoid Rd
Gaffney, SC
864-489-7172
Dogs of all sizes are allowed. There are no additional pet fees. 2 dogs may be allowed.

Quality Inn
143 Corona Drive
Gaffney, SC
864-487-4200 (877-424-6423)
Dogs are allowed for an additional pet fee of $10 per night per room. Multiple dogs may be allowed.

Red Roof Inn - Gaffney
132 New Painter Road
Gaffney, SC
864-206-0200 (800-RED-ROOF)
One well-behaved family pet per room. Guest must notify front desk upon arrival. Guest is liable for any damages. In consideration of all guests, pets must never be left unattended in the guest rooms.

Days Inn Charleston/Goose Creek
1430 Redbank Rd

Goose Creek, SC
843-797-6000 (800-329-7466)
Dogs of all sizes are allowed. There is a $10 per night pet fee per pet. Reservations are recommended due to limited rooms for pets. 2 dogs may be allowed.

Quality Inn
103 Red Bank Road
Goose Creek, SC
843-572-9500 (877-424-6423)
Dogs are allowed for an additional one time pet fee of $25 per room. 2 dogs may be allowed.

Best Western Greenville Airport Inn
5009 Pelham Road
Greenville, SC
864-297-5353 (800-780-7234)
Dogs are allowed for an additional pet fee of $10 per night per room. Multiple dogs may be allowed.

Comfort Inn Executive Center
540 N Pleasantburg Drive
Greenville, SC
864-271-0060 (877-424-6423)
Dogs are allowed for an additional one time pet fee of $15 per room. Multiple dogs may be allowed.

Comfort Inn Executive Center
540 N Pleasantburg Drive
Greenville, SC
864-963-2777 (877-424-6423)
Dogs of all sizes are allowed. There is a $15 one time additional pet fee per room. Multiple dogs may be allowed.

Crowne Plaza
851 Congaree Rd
Greenville, SC
864-297-6300 (877-270-6405)
Dogs of all sizes are allowed for an additional fee of $50 per pet. 2 dogs may be allowed.

Days Inn Greenville Conference Cntr
2756 Laurens Rd
Greenville, SC
864-288-6900 (800-329-7466)
Dogs of all sizes are allowed. There is a $10 per night pet fee per pet. 2 dogs may be allowed.

Greenville Airport Inn
5009 Pelham Rd
Greenville, SC
864-297-5353
There is a $10 per day pet fee.

Holiday Inn
4295 Augusta Rd, I-85 Exit 46A
Greenville, SC

864-277-8921 (877-270-6405)
Dogs of all sizes are allowed for an additional one time pet fee of $30 per room. Multiple dogs may be allowed.

La Quinta Inn & Suites Greenville Haywood
65 W. Orchard Park Drive
Greenville, SC
864-233-8018 (800-531-5900)
Dogs of all sizes are allowed. There are no additional pet fees. Dogs must be leashed and cleaned up after. Multiple dogs may be allowed.

La Quinta Inn Greenville Woodruff Rd
31 Old Country Rd.
Greenville, SC
864-297-3500 (800-531-5900)
Dogs of all sizes are allowed. There are no additional pet fees. Dogs may not be left unattended, and they must be leashed and cleaned up after. Multiple dogs may be allowed.

MainStay Suites Pelham Road
2671 Dry Pocket Road
Greenville, SC
864-987-5566
Dogs are allowed for an additional fee of $10 per night per pet. Multiple dogs may be allowed.

Motel 6 - Greenville
224 Bruce Road
Greenville, SC
864-277-8630 (800-466-8356)
One well-behaved family pet per room. Guest must notify front desk upon arrival. Guest is liable for any damages. In consideration of all guests, pets must never be left unattended in the guest rooms.

Quality Inn and Suites
1314 Pleasantburg Drive
Greenville, SC
864-770-3737 (877-424-6423)
Dogs are allowed for an additional one time pet fee of $25 per room. 2 dogs may be allowed.

Red Roof Inn - Greenville, SC
2801 Laurens Road
Greenville, SC
864-297-4458 (800-RED-ROOF)
One well-behaved family pet per room. Guest must notify front desk upon arrival. Guest is liable for any damages. In consideration of all guests, pets must never be left unattended in the guest rooms.

Residence Inn by Marriott
120 Milestone Way
Greenville, SC

864-627-0001
Dogs of all sizes are allowed. There is a $75 one time fee and a pet policy to sign at check in. Multiple dogs may be allowed.

Sleep Inn Palmetto Expo Center
231 N Pleasantburg Drive
Greenville, SC
864-240-2006 (877-424-6423)
Dogs are allowed for an additional one time pet fee of $20 per room. Multiple dogs may be allowed.

Staybridge Suites
Greenville/Spartanburg
31 Market Point Drive
Greenville, SC
864-288-4448 (877-270-6405)
Dogs of all sizes are allowed for an additional pet fee of $50 for 1 to 7 days; $75 for 8 to 13 days; $100 for 14 to 30 days, and a $150 fee for 31 or more days. Multiple dogs may be allowed.

TownePlace Suites Greenville
Haywood Mall
75 Mall Connector Rd
Greenville, SC
864-675-1670
Dogs of all sizes are allowed. There is a $100 one time pet fee per visit. 2 dogs may be allowed.

Comfort Inn
3755 Grandview Drive
Greenville/Simpsonville, SC
864-963-2777 (877-424-6423)
Dogs of all sizes are allowed. There is a $7 per night per pet additional fee. Multiple dogs may be allowed.

Holiday Inn Express Hotel and Suites
2681 Dry Pocket Road
Greer, SC
864-213-9331 (877-270-6405)
Dogs of all sizes are allowed for an additional one time pet fee of $20 per room. 2 dogs may be allowed.

South of the Border
3346 H 301N
Hamer, SC
843-774-2411
Dogs of all sizes are allowed, but there can only be six beings to a room including the pets. There are no additional pet fees. Dogs may not be left unattended unless they will be quiet and well behaved. Dogs must be leashed and cleaned up after. There is also a campground on site that allows dogs at no extra fee. Multiple dogs may be allowed.

Comfort Inn

Box 544
Hardeeville, SC
843-784-2188 (877-424-6423)
Dogs are allowed for an additional fee of $10 per night per pet. Multiple dogs may be allowed.

Days Inn Hardeeville
US Highway 17 & I 95
Hardeeville, SC
843-784-2281 (800-329-7466)
Dogs of all sizes are allowed. There is a $7 per night pet fee per pet. 2 dogs may be allowed.

Quality Inn and Suites
19000 Whyte Hardee Blvd
Hardeeville, SC
843-784-7060
Dogs are allowed for an additional fee of $10 per night per pet. Multiple dogs may be allowed.

Sleep Inn
I 95 & H 17
Hardeeville, SC
843-784-7181 (877-424-6423)
Dogs are allowed for an additional fee of $20 per night per pet.

Hilton Head Rentals & Golf
Hilton Head, SC
843-785-8687 (800-445-8664)
hiltonheadvacation.com
Hilton Head Rentals features one, two, and three bedroom pet-friendly vacation homes, villas, and condos. Some of the properties include fenced in yards and all rentals are near the beach, dog walks, and parks. There are no additional pet fees.

Beachwalk Hotel & Condominiums
40 Waterside Drive
Hilton Head Island, SC
843-842-8888 (888-843-4136)
hiltonheadbeachwalkhotel.com
This hotel on Hilton Head Island near the beach allows up to 2 dogs. There is a $40 non-refundable one time pet fee.

Daufuskie Island Resort & Breathe Spa
421 Squire Pope Road
Hilton Head Island, SC
800-648-6778
daufuskieislandresort.com
Daufuskie Island is a family friendly island golf and spa resort located a short ferry boat cruise from Hilton Head Island. They have a "Deluxe Doggie package" for your best friends for $35 per night per dog. They provide a Canine goodie bag at check - in, which includes doggie

treats, chew toy, doggie pick-up bags, a Daufuskie Island Resort & Breathe Spa dog tag with phone number and a "Dog Guest in residence" door hanger!. Awaiting your friend in the room is a doggie bed, extra towels, food and water bowl with bottled water. The resort has two 18 hole championship golf courses.

Motel 6 - Hilton Head
830 William Hilton Parkway
Hilton Head Island, SC
843-785-2700 (800-466-8356)
They allow small and medium sized dogs but will accept a large well-behaved, trained dog. There are no additional pet fees.

Red Roof Inn - Hilton Head Island
5 Regency Parkway
Hilton Head Island, SC
843-686-6808 (800-RED-ROOF)
One well-behaved family pet per room. Guest must notify front desk upon arrival. Guest is liable for any damages. In consideration of all guests, pets must never be left unattended in the guest rooms.

Days Inn Lake City
170 S Ron McNair Blvd
Lake City, SC
843-394-3269 (800-329-7466)
Dogs of all sizes are allowed. There is a $10 per night pet fee per pet. 2 dogs may be allowed.

The Red Horse Inn
310 N Campbell Road
Landrum, SC
864-895-4968
Dogs up to 75 pounds are allowed in their 1 pet friendly cottage. There is a $25 one time fee per pet and a pet policy to sign at check in. A credit card must be on file. No ex-large or drooler dogs are allowed. 2 dogs may be allowed.

Quality Inn & Suites
328 W Main Street
Lexington, SC
803-359-3099 (877-424-6423)
Dogs totaling no more than 60 pounds are allowed for an additional fee of $50 per night per pet. 2 dogs may be allowed.

Sunrise Inn
529 Hwy 601
Lugoff, SC
803-438-6990
Dogs of all sizes are allowed. There is a $6 per night pet fee per pet. 2 dogs may be allowed.

Best Western Palmetto Inn
2825 Paxville Hwy
Manning, SC
803-473-4021 (800-780-7234)
Dogs under 20 pounds are allowed
for an additional pet fee of $5 per
night per pet; the fee is $10 per night
per pet for dogs over 20 pounds. 2
dogs may be allowed.

Comfort Inn
3031 Paxville H
Manning, SC
803-473-7550 (877-424-6423)
Dogs are allowed for an additional
one time pet fee of $9 per room 2
dogs may be allowed.

Days Inn Charleston Patriots Point
261 Johnnie Dodds Blvd
Mount Pleasant, SC
843-881-1800 (800-329-7466)
Dogs of all sizes are allowed. There
is a $10 per night pet fee per pet. 2
dogs may be allowed.

MainStay Suites
400 McGrath Darby Blvd.
Mount Pleasant, SC
843-881-1722
This is a 71 suite hotel with a
designated dog walk area and treats
from the staff in the lobby . A $10
fee per day is charged plus any
damages will be repaired and
charged at cost to the guest.

Masters Inn
300 Wingo Way
Mount Pleasant, SC
843-884-2814
There is a $5 per day pet fee.

Red Roof Inn - Charleston - Mt
Pleasant, SC
301 Johnnie Dodds Boulevard
Mount Pleasant, SC
843-884-1411 (800-RED-ROOF)
One well-behaved family pet per
room. Guest must notify front desk
upon arrival. Guest is liable for any
damages. In consideration of all
guests, pets must never be left
unattended in the guest rooms.

Residence Inn by Marriott
Isle of Palms Connector
Mount Pleasant, SC
843-881-1599
Dogs of all sizes are allowed. There
is a $75 one time fee and a pet
policy to sign at check in. 2 dogs
may be allowed.

Booe Realty

7728 N. Kings Hwy
Myrtle Beach, SC
800-845-0647
booerealty.com
Serving the Myrtle Beach and
Grand Strand area for more than 31
years, Booe Realty offers many
properties (condos and houses) that
are pet friendly.

La Quinta Inn & Suites Myrtle
Beach
1561 21st Avenue North
Myrtle Beach, SC
843-916-8801 (800-531-5900)
Dogs of all sizes are allowed. There
are no additional pet fees. Dogs
must be quiet, well behaved,
leashed and cleaned up after. Dogs
may not be left alone in the room for
long periods. Multiple dogs may be
allowed.

Mariner Motel
7003 N Ocean Blvd
Myrtle Beach, SC
843-449-5281
Dogs only are allowed and of all
sizes. There is a $9 per night per
pet additional fee. Multiple dogs
may be allowed.

Red Roof Inn - Myrtle Beach
2801 South Kings Highway
Myrtle Beach, SC
843-626-4444 (800-RED-ROOF)
One well-behaved family pet per
room. Guest must notify front desk
upon arrival. Guest is liable for any
damages. In consideration of all
guests, pets must never be left
unattended in the guest rooms.

Staybridge Suites
3163 Outlet Blvd
Myrtle Beach, SC
843-903-4000 (877-270-6405)
Dogs up to 50 pounds are allowed
for an additional fee of $20 per night
per room to a maximum fee of
$100. 2 dogs may be allowed.

The Palm House - Dog Friendly
Vacation Rental
P O Box 51165
Myrtle Beach, SC
843-236-6623
This dog-friendly vacation rental
home offers a fenced in yard and a
central location.

The Sea Mist Resort
1200 S Ocean Blvd
Myrtle Beach, SC
843-448-1551
seamist.com/
There is a $50 pet fee per stay (per

week).

Days Inn Newberry
50 Thomas Griffin Rd
Newberry, SC
803-276-2294 (800-329-7466)
Dogs up to 75 pounds are allowed.
There is a $10 per night pet fee per
pet. Reservations are recommended
due to limited rooms for pets. 2 dogs
may be allowed.

Candlewood Suites I-26 @
Northwoods Mall
2177 Northwoods Blvd
North Charleston, SC
843-797-3535 (877-270-6405)
Dogs of all sizes are allowed, but
there may only be 1 large or 2 dogs
per room. There is an additional pet
fee of $12 per night for up to 11
nights; 12 nights and over is a
maximum fee of $150. 2 dogs may
be allowed.

Motel 6 - Charleston North
2551 Ashley Phosphate Road
North Charleston, SC
843-572-6590 (800-466-8356)
One well-behaved family pet per
room. Guest must notify front desk
upon arrival. Guest is liable for any
damages. In consideration of all
guests, pets must never be left
unattended in the guest rooms.

Quality Inn
7415 Northside Drive
North Charleston, SC
843-572-6677 (877-424-6423)
Dogs up to 65 pounds are allowed
for an additional one time fee of $15
per pet. 2 dogs may be allowed.

Red Roof Inn - Charleston North, SC
7480 Northwoods Boulevard
North Charleston, SC
843-572-9100 (800-RED-ROOF)
One well-behaved family pet per
room. Guest must notify front desk
upon arrival. Guest is liable for any
damages. In consideration of all
guests, pets must never be left
unattended in the guest rooms.

Residence Inn by Marriott
7645 Northwoods Blvd
North Charleston, SC
843-572-5757
Dogs up to 60 pounds are allowed.
There is a $75 one time fee and a
pet policy to sign at check in. 2 dogs
may be allowed.

Sheraton Hotel North Charleston
Convention Center
4770 Goer Dr.

North Charleston, SC
843-747-1900 (888-625-5144)
Dogs of all sizes are allowed for an additional one time pet fee of $40 per room. Dogs may not be left alone in the room. 2 dogs may be allowed.

Red Roof Inn - North Myrtle Beach
1601 US 17 N
North Myrtle Beach, SC
843-280-4555 (800-RED-ROOF)
One well-behaved family pet per room. Guest must notify front desk upon arrival. Guest is liable for any damages. In consideration of all guests, pets must never be left unattended in the guest rooms.

Retreat Myrtle Beach
500 Main Street
North Myrtle Beach, SC
843-280-3015 (800-645-3618)
retreatmyrtlebeach.com
Vacation rentals for all groups and travelers with pets! Properties range from ocean front luxury condos to rustic family beach bungalows. All rentals are equipped to provide the comforts of home and meet basic resort rental standards. Pet fees range from $50 to $100 for the stay.

Days Inn Orangeburg Industrail Park
Rte 2 Box 215
Orangeburg, SC
803-534-0500 (800-329-7466)
Dogs of all sizes are allowed. There is a $7 per night pet fee per pet. Reservations are recommended due to limited rooms for pets. 2 dogs may be allowed.

Days Inn Orangeburg North
3691 St Mathews Rd
Orangeburg, SC
803-531-2590 (800-329-7466)
Dogs of all sizes are allowed. There is a $10 per night pet fee per pet. 2 dogs may be allowed.

Quality Inn and Suites
1415 John C Calhoun Drive
Orangeburg, SC
803-531-4600 (877-424-6423)
Dogs are allowed for an additional one time fee of $10 per pet. 2 dogs may be allowed.

Super 8 Orangeburg
610 John C Calhoun Dr
Orangeburg, SC
803-531-1921 (800-800-8000)
Dogs of all sizes are allowed. There is a $5 per night pet fee per pet. Smoking and non-smoking rooms are available for pet rooms. 2 dogs may be allowed.

Best Western Hammock Inn
7903 Ocean Hwy
Pawleys Island, SC
843-237-4261 (800-780-7234)
Dogs are allowed for an additional one time fee of $10 per pet. Multiple dogs may be allowed.

Super 8 Richburg/Chester Area
3085 Lancaster Hwy
Richburg, SC
803-789-7888 (800-800-8000)
Dogs of all sizes are allowed. There is a $5 per night pet fee per pet. Smoking and non-smoking rooms are available for pet rooms. 2 dogs may be allowed.

Comfort Inn
200 James F Taylor Blvd
Ridgeland, SC
843-726-2121 (877-424-6423)
Dogs are allowed for an additional one time pet fee of $10 per room. Multiple dogs may be allowed.

Days Inn Ridgeland
516 East Main Street
Ridgeland, SC
843-726-5553 (800-329-7466)
Dogs of all sizes are allowed. There is a $7 per night pet fee per pet. 2 dogs may be allowed.

Quality Inn and Suites
2625 Cherry Road
Rock Hill, SC
803-329-3121 (877-424-6423)
Dogs are allowed for an additional fee of $10 per night per pet. Multiple dogs may be allowed.

Comfort Inn
139 Motel Drive
Saint George, SC
843-563-4180 (877-424-6423)
Dogs are allowed for an additional fee of $10 per night per pet. Multiple dogs may be allowed.

Quality Inn
6014 W Jim Bilton Blvd
Saint George, SC
843-563-4581 (877-424-6423)
Dogs are allowed for an additional one time pet fee of $10 per night per room. Multiple dogs may be allowed.

Days Inn Santee
9074 Old Hwy 6
Santee, SC
803-854-2175 (800-329-7466)
Dogs of all sizes are allowed. There is a $6 per night pet fee per pet. 2 dogs may be allowed.

Howard Johnson Express Inn
I-95 Ex 102, Rd 400
Santee, SC
803-478-7676 (800-446-4656)
There is an additional $10 per day pet fee.

Days Inn Greenville/Simpsonville
45 Ray East Talley Court
Simpsonville, SC
864-963-7701 (800-329-7466)
Dogs of all sizes are allowed. There is a $10 per night pet fee per pet. 2 dogs may be allowed.

Motel 6 - Greenville - Simpsonville
3706 Grandview Drive
Simpsonville, SC
864-962-8484 (800-466-8356)
One well-behaved family pet per room. Guest must notify front desk upon arrival. Guest is liable for any damages. In consideration of all guests, pets must never be left unattended in the guest rooms.

Campus Place/Extended Stay
1050 Charisma Drive
Spartanburg, SC
864-699-1088
Dogs of all sizes are allowed. There is a $20 one time per small pet fee per visit and $25 for large pet. 2 dogs may be allowed.

Days Inn Spartanburg
115 Rogers Commerce Blvd
Spartanburg, SC
864-814-0560 (800-329-7466)
Dogs of all sizes are allowed. There is a $10 per night pet fee per pet. Dogs are not allowed to be left alone in the room. Reservations are recommended due to limited rooms for pets. Only non-smoking rooms are used for pets. 2 dogs may be allowed.

Motel 6 - Spartanburg
105 Jones Road
Spartanburg, SC
864-573-6383 (800-466-8356)
One well-behaved family pet per room. Guest must notify front desk upon arrival. Guest is liable for any damages. In consideration of all guests, pets must never be left unattended in the guest rooms.

Days Inn St George
128 Interstate Dr
St George, SC
843-563-4027 (800-329-7466)
Dogs of all sizes are allowed. There is a $5 per night pet fee per pet. 2 dogs may be allowed.

Super 8 St George
114 Winningham Road
St George, SC
843-563-5551 (800-800-8000)
Dogs of all sizes are allowed. There is a $5 per night pet fee per pet. Smoking and non-smoking rooms are available for pet rooms. 2 dogs may be allowed.

Comfort Inn
1005 Jockey Court
Summerville, SC
843-851-2333 (877-424-6423)
Large dogs are allowed for an additional one time fee of $35 per pet, and small dogs for $25 per pet. Multiple dogs may be allowed.

Holiday Inn Express
120 Holiday Inn Drive, I-26 Exit 199A
Summerville, SC
843-875-3300 (877-270-6405)
Quiet dogs of all sizes are allowed for no additional pet fee. Multiple dogs may be allowed.

Holiday Inn Oceanfront @ Surfside Beach
1601 N Ocean Blvd
Surfside Beach, SC
843-238-5601 (877-270-6405)
Dogs of all sizes are allowed for an additional one time pet fee of $125 per room. Multiple dogs may be allowed.

Sleep Inn
110 Hawkins Road
Travelers Rest, SC
864-834-7040 (877-424-6423)
Quiet dogs are allowed for an additional pet fee of $15 per night per room. Multiple dogs may be allowed.

Days Inn Turbeville
378 Mydher Beach Hwy
Turbeville, SC
843-659-8060 (800-329-7466)
Dogs of all sizes are allowed. There are no additional pet fees. 2 dogs may be allowed.

Best Western Walterboro
1428 Sniders Highway
Walterboro, SC
843-538-3600 (800-780-7234)
Dogs are allowed for an additional fee of $15 per night per pet. Multiple dogs may be allowed.

Econo Lodge
1145 Sniders Hwy
Walterboro, SC
843-538-3830

There are no additional pet fees.

Howard Johnson Express Inn
1120 Sniders Hwy.
Walterboro, SC
843-538-5473 (800-446-4656)
Dogs of all sizes are welcome. There is a $8 per day pet fee.

Rice Planters Inn
I-95 and SR 63
Walterboro, SC
843-538-8964
There is a $5 per day additional pet fee.

Super 8 Walterboro
1972 Bells Hwy
Walterboro, SC
843-538-5383 (800-800-8000)
Dogs of all sizes are allowed. There is a $5 per night pet fee per pet. Reservations are recommended due to limited rooms for pets. Smoking and non-smoking rooms are available for pet rooms. 2 dogs may be allowed.

Days Inn Winnsboro
1894 US Hwy 321 Bypass
Winnsboro, SC
803-635-1447 (800-329-7466)
Dogs up to 60 pounds are allowed. There is a $7.50 per night pet fee per pet. 2 dogs may be allowed.

Days Inn Point South/Yemassee
3196 Point South Dr
Yemassee, SC
843-726-8156 (800-329-7466)
Dogs of all sizes are allowed. There is a $10 per night pet fee per pet. 2 dogs may be allowed.

Holiday Inn Express
40 Frampton Drive
Yemassee, SC
843-726-9400 (877-270-6405)
Dogs of all sizes are allowed for an additional one time fee of $20 per pet. Multiple dogs may be allowed.

Super 8 Yemassee
409 Yemassee Hwy
Yemassee, SC
843-589-2177 (800-800-8000)
Dogs of all sizes are allowed. There is a $3 per night pet fee per pet. Smoking and non-smoking rooms are available for pet rooms. 2 dogs may be allowed.

Days Inn York
1568 Alexander Love Hwy
York, SC
803-684-2525 (800-329-7466)
Dogs of all sizes are allowed. There

is a $5 per night pet fee per pet. 2 dogs may be allowed.

South Dakota Listings

Comfort Inn
2923 6th Avenue SE
Aberdeen, SD
605-226-0097 (877-424-6423)
Dogs are allowed for a $35 refundable pet deposit per room. Multiple dogs may be allowed.

Holiday Inn Express Hotel and Suites
3310 7th Ave SE
Aberdeen, SD
605-725-4000 (877-270-6405)
Dogs of all sizes are allowed for an additional one time pet fee of $20 per room. Multiple dogs may be allowed.

Super 8 Aberdeen/East
2405 SE 6th Ave
Aberdeen, SD
605-229-5005 (800-800-8000)
Dogs of all sizes are allowed. There is a $6 per night pet fee per pet. Smoking and non-smoking rooms are available for pet rooms. 2 dogs may be allowed.

Super 8 Aberdeen/North
770 NW Hwy 281
Aberdeen, SD
605-226-2288 (800-800-8000)
Dogs of all sizes are allowed. There is a $6 per night pet fee per pet. Smoking and non-smoking rooms are available for pet rooms. 2 dogs may be allowed.

Super 8 Aberdeen/West
714 S Hwy 281
Aberdeen, SD
605-225-1711 (800-800-8000)
Dogs of all sizes are allowed. There is a $6 per night pet fee per pet. Smoking and non-smoking rooms are available for pet rooms. 2 dogs may be allowed.

White House Inn
500 6th Avenue SW
Aberdeen, SD
605-225-5000
There is a $5 per day pet charge during hunting season. There is no pet charge during the rest of the year.

Motel 6 - Belle Fourche
1815 5th Avenue

Belle Fourche, SD
605-892-6663 (800-466-8356)
One well-behaved family pet per room. Guest must notify front desk upon arrival. Guest is liable for any damages. In consideration of all guests, pets must never be left unattended in the guest rooms.

Super 8 Beresford
1410 W Cedar
Beresford, SD
605-763-2001 (800-800-8000)
Dogs of all sizes are allowed. There is a $10 one time per pet fee per visit. Smoking and non-smoking rooms are available for pet rooms. 2 dogs may be allowed.

Holiday Inn Express Hotel and Suites
3020 Lefevre Drive
Brookings, SD
605-692-9060 (877-270-6405)
Dogs of all sizes are allowed for an additional fee of $10 per night per pet. Multiple dogs may be allowed.

Super 8 Chamberlain
S Main St
Chamberlain, SD
605-734-6548 (800-800-8000)
Dogs of all sizes are allowed. There is a $10.80 one time per pet fee per visit. Smoking and non-smoking rooms are available for pet rooms. 2 dogs may be allowed.

Days Inn Chamberlain
Exit 260 I 90
Chamberlain/Oacoma, SD
605-734-4100 (800-329-7466)
Dogs of all sizes are allowed. There is a $5 per night pet fee per pet. Only non-smoking rooms are used for pets. 2 dogs may be allowed.

Legion Lake Resort in Custer State Park
Highway 16a
Custer, SD
605-255-4521
Dogs are allowed in the cabins at the Blue Bell Lodge. There is a $5 per day pet charge.

State Game Lodge in Custer State Park
Highway 16
Custer, SD
605-255-4541
Dogs are allowed in the cabins only. There is a $5 per day pet charge. This lodge was known as the Summer White House after hosting Presidents Coolidge and Eisenhower. It is open from mid-May through mid-October. All cabins are non-smoking.

Super 8 Faulkton
700 Main St
Faulkton, SD
605-598-4567 (800-800-8000)
Dogs of all sizes are allowed. There is a $10 one time per pet fee per visit. Smoking and non-smoking rooms are available for pet rooms. 2 dogs may be allowed.

Super 8 Gettysburg
719 E Hwy 212
Gettysburg, SD
605-765-2373 (800-800-8000)
Dogs of all sizes are allowed. There is a $10.80 per night pet fee per pet. Smoking and non-smoking rooms are available for pet rooms. 2 dogs may be allowed.

Best Western Golden Spike Inn & Suites
106 Main Street
Hill City, SD
605-574-2577 (800-780-7234)
Dogs are allowed for an additional pet fee of $10 per night per room. 2 dogs may be allowed.

Best Western Sundowner Inn
737 S 6th Street
Hot Springs, SD
605-745-7378 (800-780-7234)
Dogs are allowed for no additional pet fee. Multiple dogs may be allowed.

Super 8 Hot Springs
800 Mammoth St
Hot Springs, SD
605-745-3888 (800-800-8000)
Dogs of all sizes are allowed. There is a $10.80 one time per pet fee per visit. Smoking and non-smoking rooms are available for pet rooms. 2 dogs may be allowed.

Best Western of Huron
2000 Dakota South
Huron, SD
605-352-2000 (800-780-7234)
Dogs are allowed for no additional pet fee. Multiple dogs may be allowed.

Dakota Plains Inn
Highway 14E
Huron, SD
605-352-1400
There is a $20 refundable pet deposit.

Super 8 Huron
2189 Dakota Ave South
Huron, SD

605-352-0740 (800-800-8000)
Dogs of all sizes are allowed. There is a $5 per night pet fee per pet. Smoking and non-smoking rooms are available for pet rooms. 2 dogs may be allowed.

Best Western Four Presidents Lodge
24075 Highway 16A
Keystone, SD
605-666-4472 (800-780-7234)
Dogs up to 100 pounds are allowed for an additional fee of $10 per night per pet. 2 dogs may be allowed.

Super 8 Madison
Jct Hwy 34 and 81
Madison, SD
605-256-6931 (800-800-8000)
Dogs of all sizes are allowed. There is a $5 per night pet fee per pet. Smoking and non-smoking rooms are available for pet rooms. 2 dogs may be allowed.

Best Western Motor Inn
1001 S Burr St
Mitchell, SD
605-996-5536 (800-780-7234)
Dogs are allowed for no additional pet fee with a credit card on file. Multiple dogs may be allowed.

Holiday Inn
1525 W. Havens Ave
Mitchell, SD
605-996-6501 (877-270-6405)
Dogs of all sizes are allowed for an additional one time fee of $10 per pet. Multiple dogs may be allowed.

Kelly Inns
1010 Cabella Drive
Mitchell, SD
605-995-0500
Dogs of all sizes are allowed. There is a pet policy to sign at check in and there are no additional pet fees. Multiple dogs may be allowed.

Motel 6 - Mitchell
1309 South Ohlman Street
Mitchell, SD
605-996-0530 (800-466-8356)
One well-behaved family pet per room. Guest must notify front desk upon arrival. Guest is liable for any damages. In consideration of all guests, pets must never be left unattended in the guest rooms.

Siesta Motel
1210 West Havens
Mitchell, SD
605-996-5544 (800-424-0537)
siestamotel.com/
There are no additional pet fees.

Best Western Graham's
301 W 5th
Murdo, SD
605-669-2441 (800-780-7234)
Dogs are allowed for no additional pet fee. Dogs may not be left alone in the room. Multiple dogs may be allowed.

Comfort Inn
1311 River Drive
North Sioux City, SD
605-232-3366 (877-424-6423)
Dogs are allowed for an additional fee of $10 per night per pet. Multiple dogs may be allowed.

Comfort Inn
203 E H 16
Oacoma, SD
605-734-4222 (877-424-6423)
Dogs are allowed for an additional fee of $10 per night per pet. Multiple dogs may be allowed.

Holiday Inn Express
100 W Hwy 16
Oacoma, SD
605-734-5593 (877-270-6405)
Dogs of all sizes are allowed for an additional fee of $10 per night per pet. Dogs may not be left alone in the room at any time. 2 dogs may be allowed.

Best Western Ramkota Hotel
920 W Sioux Ave
Pierre, SD
605-224-6877 (800-780-7234)
Dogs are allowed for no additional pet fee. Multiple dogs may be allowed.

Capitol Inn & Suites
815 Wells Avenue
Pierre, SD
605-224-6387
There are no additional pet fees.

Comfort Inn
410 W Sioux Avenue/H 14
Pierre, SD
605-224-0377 (877-424-6423)
Quiet dogs are allowed for an additional one time pet fee of $10 per night per room. Multiple dogs may be allowed.

Days Inn Pierre
520 W Sioux Blvd
Pierre, SD
605-224-0411 (800-329-7466)
Dogs of all sizes are allowed. There is a $5 per night pet fee per pet. 2 dogs may be allowed.

Super 8 Pierre
320 W Sioux
Pierre, SD
605-224-1617 (800-800-8000)
Dogs of all sizes are allowed. There is a $5 per night pet fee per pet. Smoking and non-smoking rooms are available for pet rooms. 2 dogs may be allowed.

Super 8 Plankinton
801 S Main
Plankinton, SD
605-942-7722 (800-800-8000)
Dogs of all sizes are allowed. There is a $8 per night pet fee per pet. Smoking and non-smoking rooms are available for pet rooms. 2 dogs may be allowed.

Best Western Ramkota Hotel
2111 N LaCrosse Street
Rapid City, SD
605-343-8550 (800-780-7234)
Dogs are allowed for no additional pet fee. Multiple dogs may be allowed.

Holiday Inn
505 North Fifth St
Rapid City, SD
605-348-4000 (877-270-6405)
Dogs of all sizes are allowed for an additional one time pet fee of $15 per room. Multiple dogs may be allowed.

Holiday Inn Express Hotel and Suites
645 East Disk Drive
Rapid City, SD
605-355-9090 (877-270-6405)
Dogs of all sizes are allowed for an additional pet fee of $10 per night per room. 2 dogs may be allowed.

Motel 6 - Rapid City
620 East Latrobe Street
Rapid City, SD
605-343-3687 (800-466-8356)
One well-behaved family pet per room. Guest must notify front desk upon arrival. Guest is liable for any damages. In consideration of all guests, pets must never be left unattended in the guest rooms.

Red Roof Inn - Rapid City - Mount Rushmore
620 Howard Street
Rapid City, SD
605-343-5434 (800-RED-ROOF)
One well-behaved family pet per room. Guest must notify front desk upon arrival. Guest is liable for any damages. In consideration of all guests, pets must never be left unattended in the guest rooms.

Super 8 Rapid City/Rushmore Area
2520 Tower Rd
Rapid City, SD
605-342-4911 (800-800-8000)
Dogs of all sizes are allowed. There is a $5 per night pet fee per pet. Smoking and non-smoking rooms are available for pet rooms. 2 dogs may be allowed.

Best Western Empire Towers
4100 W Shirley Place
Sioux Falls, SD
605-361-3118 (800-780-7234)
Well behaved dogs up to 50 pounds are allowed for an additional pet fee of $15 per night per room. Dogs may not be left alone in the room. 2 dogs may be allowed.

Best Western Ramkota Hotel
3200 W Maple St
Sioux Falls, SD
605-336-0650 (800-780-7234)
Dogs are allowed for no additional pet fee. Multiple dogs may be allowed.

Comfort Inn North
5100 N Cliff Avenue
Sioux Falls, SD
605-331-4490 (877-424-6423)
Dogs are allowed for an additional one time pet fee of $10 per room. 2 dogs may be allowed.

Comfort Inn South
3216 S Carolyn Avenue
Sioux Falls, SD
605-361-2822 (877-424-6423)
Dogs are allowed for an additional fee of $10 per night per pet. Multiple dogs may be allowed.

Comfort Suites
3208 S Carolyn Avenue
Sioux Falls, SD
605-362-9711 (877-424-6423)
Dogs are allowed for an additional pet fee of $10 per night per room. Dogs may not be left alone in the room. Multiple dogs may be allowed.

Days Inn Sioux Falls Airport
5001 N Cliff Ave
Sioux Falls, SD
605-331-5959 (800-329-7466)
Dogs of all sizes are allowed. There is a $7.63 per night pet fee per pet. 2 dogs may be allowed.

Kelly Inn
3101 W. Russell Street
Sioux Falls, SD
605-338-6242

kellyinns.com/locations.html
There is no extra charge for pets, just sign a pet damage waiver.

Motel 6 - Sioux Falls
3009 West Russell Street
Sioux Falls, SD
605-336-7800 (800-466-8356)
One well-behaved family pet per room. Guest must notify front desk upon arrival. Guest is liable for any damages. In consideration of all guests, pets must never be left unattended in the guest rooms.

Quality Inn and Suites
5410 N Granite Lane
Sioux Falls, SD
605-336-1900 (877-424-6423)
Dogs are allowed for an additional pet fee of $10 per night per room. Multiple dogs may be allowed.

Red Roof Inn - Sioux Falls
3500 Gateway Boulevard
Sioux Falls, SD
605-361-1864 (800-RED-ROOF)
One well-behaved family pet per room. Guest must notify front desk upon arrival. Guest is liable for any damages. In consideration of all guests, pets must never be left unattended in the guest rooms.

Residence Inn by Marriott
4509 W Empire Place
Sioux Falls, SD
605-361-2202
Dogs of all sizes are allowed, however there may only be 2 large or 3 medium to small dogs per room. There is a $75 one time fee and a pet policy to sign at check in.

Staybridge Suites Sioux Falls
2505 S. Carolyn Ave.
Sioux Falls, SD
605-361-2298 (877-270-6405)
Quiet dogs of all sizes are allowed for an additional pet fee per room of $25 for the 1st night, and $15 for each additional night. Multiple dogs may be allowed.

TownePlace Suites Sioux Falls
4545 W Homefield Drive
Sioux Falls, SD
605-361-2626
Dogs of all sizes are allowed. There is a $75 one time pet fee per visit. 2 dogs may be allowed.

Best Western Black Hills Lodge
540 E Jackson Blvd
Spearfish, SD
605-642-7795 (800-780-7234)
Dogs are allowed for an additional

fee of $5 per night per pet. Multiple dogs may be allowed.

Days Inn Spearfish
240 Ryan Rd
Spearfish, SD
605-642-7101 (800-329-7466)
Dogs of all sizes are allowed. There is a $10 per night pet fee per pet. Reservations are recommended due to limited rooms for pets. 2 dogs may be allowed.

Holiday Inn
I-90 & Exit 14, PO Box 399
Spearfish, SD
605-642-4683 (877-270-6405)
Dogs of all sizes are allowed for an additional one time fee of $25 per pet. Multiple dogs may be allowed.

Howard Johnson Express Inn
323 S. 27th St.
Spearfish, SD
605-642-8105 (800-446-4656)
Dogs of all sizes are welcome. There is a $10 per day pet fee. Pets must be declared when making a reservation.

Super 8 Spearfish
440 Heritage Drive
Spearfish, SD
605-642-4721 (800-800-8000)
Dogs of all sizes are allowed. There is a $5 per night pet fee per pet. Smoking and non-smoking rooms are available for pet rooms. 2 dogs may be allowed.

Comfort Inn
701 W Cherry Street/H 50
Vermillion, SD
605-624-8333 (877-424-6423)
Dogs are allowed for an additional fee of $10 per night per pet. Multiple dogs may be allowed.

Best Western Plains Motel
712 Glenn St
Wall, SD
605-279-2145 (800-780-7234)
Dogs are allowed for an additional fee of $10 per night per pet. 2 dogs may be allowed.

Days Inn Wall
10 Ave
Wall, SD
605-279-2000 (800-329-7466)
Dogs of all sizes are allowed. There is a $10 per night pet fee per pet. 2 dogs may be allowed.

Motel 6 - Wall
211 10th Street
Wall, SD

605-279-2133 (800-466-8356)
One well-behaved family pet per room. Guest must notify front desk upon arrival. Guest is liable for any damages. In consideration of all guests, pets must never be left unattended in the guest rooms.

Best Western Ramkota Hotel of Watertown
1901 9th Ave SW
Watertown, SD
605-886-8011 (800-780-7234)
Dogs are allowed for no additional pet fee. 2 dogs may be allowed.

Comfort Inn
800 35th Street Circle
Watertown, SD
605-886-3010 (877-424-6423)
Dogs are allowed for an additional one time pet fee of $15 per room. Multiple dogs may be allowed.

Days Inn Watertown
2900 9th Ave SE
Watertown, SD
605-886-3500 (800-329-7466)
Dogs of all sizes are allowed. There is a $10 per night pet fee per pet. 2 dogs may be allowed.

Tennessee Listings

Days Inn Nashville/Bell Road
501 Collins Park Dr
Antioch, TN
615-731-7800 (800-329-7466)
Dogs of all sizes are allowed. There is a $10 per night pet fee per pet. 2 dogs may be allowed.

Holiday Inn
201 Crossings Place
Antioch, TN
615-731-2361 (877-270-6405)
Quiet dogs of all sizes are allowed for no additional pet fee. Multiple dogs may be allowed.

Days Inn Athens
2541 Decatur Pike
Athens, TN
423-745-5800 (800-329-7466)
Dogs of all sizes are allowed. There is a $5 per night pet fee per pet. 2 dogs may be allowed.

Motel 6 - Athens
2002 Whitaker Road
Athens, TN
423-745-4441 (800-466-8356)
One well-behaved family pet per

room. Guest must notify front desk upon arrival. Guest is liable for any damages. In consideration of all guests, pets must never be left unattended in the guest rooms.

Motel 6 - Brownsville - Bells
9740 US 70 East
Bells, TN
731-772-9500 (800-466-8356)
One well-behaved family pet per room. Guest must notify front desk upon arrival. Guest is liable for any damages. In consideration of all guests, pets must never be left unattended in the guest rooms.

Candlewood Suites
5129 Virginia Way
Brentwood, TN
615-309-0600 (877-270-6405)
Dogs up to 80 pounds are allowed for an additional pet fee per room of $75 for 1 to 6 nights; the fee is $150 for 7 nights or more. 2 dogs may be allowed.

Red Roof Inn - Nashville Brentwood
8097 Moores Lane
Brentwood, TN
615-309-8860 (800-RED-ROOF)
One well-behaved family pet per room. Guest must notify front desk upon arrival. Guest is liable for any damages. In consideration of all guests, pets must never be left unattended in the guest rooms.

Residence Inn by Marriott
Maryland Farms 206 Ward Circle
Brentwood, TN
615-371-0100
Dogs of all sizes are allowed. There is a $75 one time fee and a pet policy to sign at check in. Multiple dogs may be allowed.

Sleep Inn
1611 Galleria Blvd
Brentwood, TN
615-376-2122 (877-424-6423)
Dogs are allowed for an additional pet fee of $10 per night per room. Multiple dogs may be allowed.

Days inn Bristol
3281 W State St
Bristol, TN
423-968-9119 (800-DAYS-INN)
Dogs of all sizes are allowed. There is a $7 per night pet fee per pet. Reservations are recommended due to limited rooms for pets. Multiple dogs may be allowed.

O'Bannon Signature Hotel
120 Sunny Hill Cave

Brownsville, TN
731-772-4030
Dogs of all sizes are allowed. There are no additional pet fees. Smoking and non-smoking rooms are available for pets. 2 dogs may be allowed.

Paris Landing State Park Inn
16055 H 79N
Buchanan, TN
731-642-4311 (800-250-8614)
Located in the Paris Landing State Park, there is a variety of activities and land and water recreation available. Dogs of all sizes are allowed at $10 per night per pet additional fee. Dogs may not be left unattended, and they must be leashed and cleaned up after. There is also a tent and RV camping area on site where dogs are allowed at no additional fee. Multiple dogs may be allowed.

Best Western Executive Inn
50 Speedway Ln
Bulls Gap, TN
423-235-9111 (800-780-7234)
Dogs are allowed for an additional pet fee of $15 per night per room. 2 dogs may be allowed.

Super 8 Bulls Gap/Greenville Area
90 Speedway Lane
Bulls Gap, TN
423-235-4112 (800-800-8000)
Dogs up to 60 pounds are allowed. There is a $10 one time per pet fee per visit. Smoking and non-smoking rooms are available for pet rooms. 2 dogs may be allowed.

Montgomery Bell Resort and Conference Center
1020 Jackson Hill Road
Burns, TN
615-797-3101
This resort is located in the Montgomery Bell State Park, and a variety of land and water recreation is available. Dogs of all sizes are allowed for an additional $10 per night per pet. There is also a camping area on site that allows dogs at no additional fee. Dogs may not be left unattended, and they must be leashed at all times, and cleaned up after. Dogs are not allowed in the lake or other park buildings, but they are allowed on the trails.

Iron Mountain Inn
138 Moreland Drive
Butler, TN
423-768-2446
Dogs of all sizes are allowed. There

is a $100 refundable pet deposit per stay. Dogs are not allowed to be left unattended. Multiple dogs may be allowed.

Lakeside Cottage
1035 Piercetown Road
Butler, TN
423-768-2446
Dogs of all sizes are allowed. There is a $100 refundable pet deposit per stay. Dogs are not allowed to be left unattended. Multiple dogs may be allowed.

Relax Inn (former Days Inn)
30 Old Route One
Camden, TN
731-584-3111 (800-DAYS-INN)
Dogs of all sizes are allowed. There is a $5 per night pet fee per pet. 2 dogs may be allowed.

Super 8 Caryville/Cove Lake
200 John Mcghee Blvd
Caryville, TN
423-562-8476 (800-800-8000)
Dogs of all sizes are allowed. There is a $5.71 per night pet fee per pet. Smoking and non-smoking rooms are available for pet rooms. 2 dogs may be allowed.

Cedar Hill Resort
2371 Cedar Hill Road
Celina, TN
931-243-3201
Dogs of all sizes are allowed. There is a $25 per day per pet fee for the houseboat or $125 for the week per pet. The cabins are $20 per night per pet or $100 for the week per pet. Multiple dogs may be allowed.

Days Inn Centerville
634 David St
Centerville, TN
931-729-5600 (800-329-7466)
Dogs of all sizes are allowed. There is a $5 per night pet fee per pet. 2 dogs may be allowed.

Best Western Royal Inn
3644 Cummings Highway
Chattanooga, TN
423-821-6840 (800-780-7234)
Dogs are allowed for an additional fee of $10 per night per pet. 2 dogs may be allowed.

Comfort Inn Hixson
4833 Hixson Pike
Chattanooga, TN
423-877-8388 (877-424-6423)
Dogs are allowed for an additional pet fee of $10 (plus tax) per night per room. 2 dogs may be allowed.

Days Inn Chattanooga Downtown
101 E 20th St
Chattanooga, TN
423-267-9761 (800-329-7466)
Dogs of all sizes are allowed. There is a $10 per night pet fee per pet. 2 dogs may be allowed.

Holiday Inn Chattanooga-Choo Choo
1400 Market St
Chattanooga, TN
423-266-5000 (877-270-6405)
Dogs of all sizes are allowed for an additional one time pet fee of $25 per room. Multiple dogs may be allowed.

Howard Johnson Plaza Hotel
6700 Ringgold Rd.
Chattanooga, TN
423-892-8100 (800-446-4656)
Dogs of all sizes are allowed. There is a $15 one time additional pet fee.

La Quinta Inn Chattanooga
7017 Shallowford Rd.
Chattanooga, TN
423-855-0011 (800-531-5900)
Dogs of all sizes are allowed. There are no additional pet fees. Dogs must be quiet, well behaved, leashed and cleaned up after. Dogs may not be left alone in the room for long periods. Multiple dogs may be allowed.

Motel 6 - Chattanooga Downtown
2440 Williams Street
Chattanooga, TN
423-265-7300 (800-466-8356)
One well-behaved family pet per room. Guest must notify front desk upon arrival. Guest is liable for any damages. In consideration of all guests, pets must never be left unattended in the guest rooms.

Motel 6 - Chattanooga East
7707 Lee Highway
Chattanooga, TN
423-892-7707 (800-466-8356)
One well-behaved family pet per room. Guest must notify front desk upon arrival. Guest is liable for any damages. In consideration of all guests, pets must never be left unattended in the guest rooms.

Quality Inn & Suites
3109 Parker Lane
Chattanooga, TN
423-821-1499 (877-424-6423)
Dogs are allowed for an additional fee of $15 per night per pet. Multiple dogs may be allowed.

Red Roof Inn - Chattanooga Airport

7014 Shallowford Road
Chattanooga, TN
423-899-0143 (800-RED-ROOF)
One well-behaved family pet per room. Guest must notify front desk upon arrival. Guest is liable for any damages. In consideration of all guests, pets must never be left unattended in the guest rooms.

Residence Inn by Marriott
215 Chestnut Street
Chattanooga, TN
423-266-0600
Dogs of all sizes are allowed. There is a $75 one time fee and a pet policy to sign at check in. Multiple dogs may be allowed.

Sheraton Read House Hotel at Chattanooga
827 Broad St.
Chattanooga, TN
423-266-4121 (888-625-5144)
Dogs of all sizes are allowed for an additional one time pet fee of $50 per room. Dogs may not be left alone in the room.

Staybridge Suites
1300 Carter Street
Chattanooga, TN
423-267-0900 (877-270-6405)
Dogs of all sizes are allowed for an additional pet fee per room of $25 for 1 to 3 days; 4 nights or more is $75. Multiple dogs may be allowed.

Super 8 Chattanooga/Lookout Mtn Area
20 Birmingham Rd
Chattanooga, TN
423-821-8880 (800-800-8000)
Dogs of all sizes are allowed. There is a $20 one time per pet fee per visit. Reservations are recommended due to limited rooms for pets. Smoking and non-smoking rooms are available for pet rooms. 2 dogs may be allowed.

Candlewood Suites Clarksville
3050 Clay Lewis Road
Clarksville, TN
931-906-0900 (877-270-6405)
Dogs of all sizes are allowed for an additional one time fee per pet of $75 for 1 to 5 nights; 6 or more nights is $150 per pet. Multiple dogs may be allowed.

Days Inn Clarksville
1100 Highway 76
Clarksville, TN
931-358-3194 (800-329-7466)
Dogs of all sizes are allowed. There is a $6 per night pet fee per pet. 2

dogs may be allowed.

Motel 6 - Clarksville
254 Holiday Road
Clarksville, TN
931-552-2663 (800-466-8356)
One well-behaved family pet per room. Guest must notify front desk upon arrival. Guest is liable for any damages. In consideration of all guests, pets must never be left unattended in the guest rooms.

Quality Inn South
1112 H 76
Clarksville, TN
931-358-2020 (877-424-6423)
Dogs are allowed for an additional fee of $10 per night per pet. Multiple dogs may be allowed.

Red Roof Inn - Clarksville
197 Holiday Drive
Clarksville, TN
931-905-1555 (800-RED-ROOF)
One well-behaved family pet per room. Guest must notify front desk upon arrival. Guest is liable for any damages. In consideration of all guests, pets must never be left unattended in the guest rooms.

Days Inn Cleveland
2550 Georgetown Rd
Cleveland, TN
423-476-2112 (800-329-7466)
Dogs of all sizes are allowed. There is a $10 per night pet fee per pet. 2 dogs may be allowed.

Quality Inn & Suites
153 James Asbury Drive
Cleveland, TN
423-478-5265 (877-424-6423)
Dogs under 25 pounds are allowed for an additional fee of $10 per night per pet, and the fee is $15 per night per pet for dogs 25 to 50 pounds. 2 dogs may be allowed.

Days Inn Columbia
1504 Nashville Hwy
Columbia, TN
931-381-3297 (800-329-7466)
Dogs of all sizes are allowed. There is a $10 per night pet fee per pet. 2 dogs may be allowed.

Alpine Lodge & Suites
2021 E. Spring St.
Cookeville, TN
931-526-3333 (800-213-2016)
tndirectory.com/alpinelodge/
They have had Great Danes stay here before. As long as the dog is well-behaved, size does not matter. There is a $5 per day pet charge.

Best Western Thunderbird Motel
900 South Jefferson Ave
Cookeville, TN
931-526-7115 (800-780-7234)
Dogs are allowed for an additional
fee of $10 per night per pet. Multiple
dogs may be allowed.

Hampton Inn
1025 Interstate Drive
Cookeville, TN
931-520-1117
Dogs of all sizes are allowed. There
are no additional pet fees. Multiple
dogs may be allowed.

Quality Suites
8166 Varnavas Drive
Cordova, TN
901-386-4600
Dogs up to 50 pounds are allowed
for no additional pet fee. 2 dogs may
be allowed.

Comfort Inn
901 H 51N
Covington, TN
901-475-0380 (877-424-6423)
A dog is allowed for an additional pet
fee of $10 per night.

Days Inn Crossville
305 Executive Dr
Crossville, TN
931-484-9691 (800-329-7466)
Dogs of all sizes are allowed. There
is a $10 per night pet fee per pet. 2
dogs may be allowed.

Comfort Inn
620 Green Valley Drive
Dandridge, TN
865-397-2090 (877-424-6423)
Dogs are allowed for an additional
fee of $10 per night per pet. Multiple
dogs may be allowed.

Holiday Inn Express
119 Sharon Drive
Dandridge, TN
865-397-1910 (877-270-6405)
Dogs of all sizes are allowed. There
is a one time fee of $25 for dogs up
to 50, and a $50 one time pet fee for
dogs over 50 pounds. 2 dogs may be
allowed.

Scottish Inn (former Days Inn)
3914 Rhea County Hwy
Dayton, TN
423-775-9718 (800-DAYS-INN)
Dogs of all sizes are allowed. There
is a $3 per night pet fee per pet. 2
dogs may be allowed.

Best Western Executive Inn of

Dickson
2338 Hwy 46 South
Dickson, TN
615-446-0541 (800-780-7234)
Dogs are allowed for an additional
fee of $5 per night per pet. Multiple
dogs may be allowed.

Comfort Inn
1025 E Christi Drive
Dickson, TN
615-441-5252 (877-424-6423)
Dogs up to 75 pounds are allowed
for an additional fee of $10 per night
per pet. 2 dogs may be allowed.

Days Inn Dickson
2415 Hwy 46 South
Dickson, TN
615-446-7561 (800-329-7466)
Dogs of all sizes are allowed. There
is a $20 returnable deposit required
per room. 2 dogs may be allowed.

Holiday Inn
2420 Hwy 46 S.
Dickson, TN
615-446-9081 (877-270-6405)
Dogs of all sizes are allowed for an
additional one time pet fee of $10
per room. Multiple dogs may be
allowed.

Motel 6 - Dickson
2325 SR 46
Dickson, TN
615-446-2423 (800-466-8356)
One well-behaved family pet per
room. Guest must notify front desk
upon arrival. Guest is liable for any
damages. In consideration of all
guests, pets must never be left
unattended in the guest rooms.

Super 8 Dickson
150 Suzanne Dr
Dickson, TN
615-446-1923 (800-800-8000)
Dogs of all sizes are allowed. There
is a $10 per night pet fee per pet.
Smoking and non-smoking rooms
are available for pet rooms. 2 dogs
may be allowed.

Hampton Inn
2750 Mall Loop Road
Dryersburg, TN
731-285-4778
Well behaved dogs of all sizes are
allowed. There are no additional pet
fees. Dogs are not allowed to be left
alone in the room. Multiple dogs
may be allowed.

Best Western Dyersburg Inn
770 US Highway 51 Bypass W
Dyersburg, TN

731-285-8601 (800-780-7234)
Dogs are allowed for an additional
fee of $10 (plus tax) per night per
pet. Multiple dogs may be allowed.

Traveller's Inn (former Days Inn)
505 W Elk Ave
Elizabethton, TN
423-543-3344 (800-DAYS-INN)
Dogs of all sizes are allowed. There
is a $15 one time pet fee per visit. 2
dogs may be allowed.

Sleep Inn Tennessee Overhill
600 N Tennessee Avenue/H 411
Etowah, TN
423-263-4343 (877-424-6423)
Dogs up to 50 pounds are allowed
for an additional fee of $10 (plus tax)
per night per pet; $15 per night per
pet for dogs 51 to 100 pounds, and
$25 per night per pet for dogs over
100 pounds. There may only be 2
dogs per room if they are over 50
pounds. Multiple dogs may be
allowed.

Days Inn Fayetteville/Lynchburg
1653 Huntsville Hwy
Fayetteville, TN
931-433-6121 (800-329-7466)
Dogs of all sizes are allowed. There
is a $5 per night pet fee per pet. 2
dogs may be allowed.

Best Western Franklin Inn
1308 Murfreesboro Rd
Franklin, TN
615-790-0570 (800-780-7234)
Dogs are allowed for an additional
one time fee of $10 per pet. Multiple
dogs may be allowed.

Days Inn Nashville/Franklin
4217 S Carothers Rd
Franklin, TN
615-790-1140 (800-329-7466)
Dogs of all sizes are allowed. There
is a $10 per night pet fee per pet. 2
dogs may be allowed.

Ramada Inn and Suites
6210 Hospitality Drive
Franklin, TN
615-791-4004
Dogs of all sizes are allowed. There
is a $15 per night per pet additional
fee. Multiple dogs may be allowed.

Greenbrier Valley Resorts
Gatlinburg, TN
865-436-2015 (800-546-1144)
welovegatlinburg.com
Many of these 1 to 12 bedroom log
cabins and chalets are pet friendly.
There is a $10 per night per pet fee
as well as a $100 refundable pet

security deposit. Most of the homes are in the Village of Cobbly Nob, with golf, tennis and swimming pools.

Holiday Inn Sunspree Resort
520 Historic Nature Trail
Gatlinburg, TN
865-436-9201 (877-270-6405)
basshotels.com/holiday-inn
Dogs of all sizes are allowed for an additional one time fee of $15 per pet. 2 dogs may be allowed.

The Treehouse
Call to Arrange
Gatlinburg, TN
865-777-0469 (877-780-3160)
This vacation rental is just a few minutes from Pigeon Forge and Gatlinburg. There is a one time $50 pet fee. Dogs of all sizes are allowed.

Comfort Inn and Suites
7787 Wolf River Blvd
Germantown, TN
901-757-7800 (877-424-6423)
Dogs are allowed for no additional pet fee. Multiple dogs may be allowed.

Residence Inn by Marriott
9314 Poplar Pike
Germantown, TN
901-752-0900
Dogs of all sizes are allowed. There is a $75 one time fee and a pet policy to sign at check in. Multiple dogs may be allowed.

Best Western Fairwinds Inn
100 Northcreek Blvd
Goodlettsville, TN
615-851-1067 (800-780-7234)
Dogs are allowed for an additional fee of $10 per night per pet. Multiple dogs may be allowed.

Motel 6 - Nashville - Goodlettsville
323 Cartwright Street
Goodlettsville, TN
615-859-9674 (800-466-8356)
One well-behaved family pet per room. Guest must notify front desk upon arrival. Guest is liable for any damages. In consideration of all guests, pets must never be left unattended in the guest rooms.

Quality Inn
925 Conference Drive
Goodlettsville, TN
615-859-5400 (877-424-6423)
Dogs are allowed for an additional fee of $10 per night per pet. 2 dogs may be allowed.

Red Roof Inn - Nashville North
110 Northgate Drive
Goodlettsville, TN
615-859-2537 (800-RED-ROOF)
One well-behaved family pet per room. Guest must notify front desk upon arrival. Guest is liable for any damages. In consideration of all guests, pets must never be left unattended in the guest rooms.

Comfort Inn
1790 E Andrew Johnson H
Greeneville, TN
423-639-4185 (877-424-6423)
Dogs of all sizes are allowed. There is a $10 per night per room fee and a pet policy to sign at check in. 2 dogs may be allowed.

Super 8 Harriman
1867 South Roane St
Harriman, TN
865-882-6600 (800-800-8000)
Dogs of all sizes are allowed. There is a $10 per night pet fee per small pet and $15 per large pet. Smoking and non-smoking rooms are available for pet rooms. 2 dogs may be allowed.

Days Inn Holladay
13845 Hwy 641 North
Holladay, TN
731-847-2278 (800-329-7466)
Dogs of all sizes are allowed. There is a $20 returnable deposit required per room. 2 dogs may be allowed.

Best Western Huntingdon
11790 Lexington St
Huntingdon, TN
731-986-2281 (800-780-7234)
Dogs are allowed for no additional pet fee. 2 dogs may be allowed.

Best Western of Hurricane Mills
15542 Hwy 13 South
Hurricane Mills, TN
931-296-4251 (800-780-7234)
Dogs under 20 pounds are allowed for an additional fee of $10 per night per pet; the fee is $12 for dogs 20 to 50 pounds, and $20 for dogs over 50 pounds. Multiple dogs may be allowed.

Days Inn Hurricane Mills
15415 Hwy 13 South
Hurricane Mills, TN
931-296-7647 (800-329-7466)
Dogs of all sizes are allowed. There is a $5 per night pet fee per pet. 2 dogs may be allowed.

Super 8 Hurricane Mills/Buffalo Area

15470 Hwy 13 South
Hurricane Mills, TN
931-296-2432 (800-800-8000)
Dogs of all sizes are allowed. There is a $5 per night pet fee per pet. Smoking and non-smoking rooms are available for pet rooms. 2 dogs may be allowed.

Days Inn Jackson/N Hollywood
2239 N Hollywood Dr
Jackson, TN
731-668-4840 (800-329-7466)
Dogs of all sizes are allowed. There is a $5 per night pet fee per pet. 2 dogs may be allowed.

Garden Plaza Hotel
1770 Hwy 45
Jackson, TN
731-664-6900
There is a $5 per day additional pet fee.

La Quinta Inn Jackson
2370 N. Highland
Jackson, TN
731-664-1800 (800-531-5900)
Dogs of all sizes are allowed. There are no additional fees. Dogs may not be left unattended, and they must be leashed and cleaned up after. Multiple dogs may be allowed.

Motel 6 - Jackson
1940 US 45 Bypass
Jackson, TN
731-661-0919 (800-466-8356)
One well-behaved family pet per room. Guest must notify front desk upon arrival. Guest is liable for any damages. In consideration of all guests, pets must never be left unattended in the guest rooms.

Super 8 Jackson
2295 N Highland
Jackson, TN
731-668-1145 (800-800-8000)
Dogs of all sizes are allowed. There is a $6 per night pet fee per pet. Smoking and non-smoking rooms are available for pet rooms. 2 dogs may be allowed.

Holiday Plaza
I-75 Exit 160
Jellico, TN
423-784-7241
Dogs are allowed for an additional fee of $5 per night per pet. 2 dogs may be allowed.

Days Inn Nashville/Joelton
201 Gifford Place
Joelton, TN
615-876-3261 (800-329-7466)

Dogs of all sizes are allowed. There are no additional pet fees. 2 dogs may be allowed.

Comfort Inn
1900 S Roan Street
Johnson City, TN
423-928-9600 (877-424-6423)
Dogs are allowed for an additional fee of $15 per night per pet. Multiple dogs may be allowed.

Holiday Inn
101 West Springbrook Drive
Johnson City, TN
423-282-4611 (877-270-6405)
Dogs of all sizes are allowed for an additional one time fee of $25 per pet. Multiple dogs may be allowed.

Red Roof Inn - Johnson City
210 Broyles Drive
Johnson City, TN
423-282-3040 (800-RED-ROOF)
One well-behaved family pet per room. Guest must notify front desk upon arrival. Guest is liable for any damages. In consideration of all guests, pets must never be left unattended in the guest rooms.

Sleep Inn and Suites
2020 Franklin Terrace Court
Johnson City, TN
423-915-0081 (877-424-6423)
Dogs are allowed for an additional pet fee of $10 per night per room. 2 dogs may be allowed.

Days Inn Kimball
130 Main St
Kimball, TN
423-837-7933 (800-329-7466)
Dogs of all sizes are allowed. There is a $8 per night pet fee per pet. 2 dogs may be allowed.

Comfort Inn
100 Indian Center Court
Kingsport, TN
423-378-4418 (877-424-6423)
Dogs are allowed for an additional fee of $12 per night per pet. Multiple dogs may be allowed.

La Quinta Inn Kingsport Tri-Cities Airport
10150 Airport Parkway
Kingsport, TN
423-323-0500 (800-531-5900)
Dogs of all sizes are allowed. There are no additional pet fees. Dogs may not be left unattended, and they must be leashed and cleaned up after. Multiple dogs may be allowed.

Sleep Inn

200 Hospitality Place
Kingsport, TN
423-279-1811 (877-424-6423)
Dogs of all sizes are allowed. There are no additional pet fees. Multiple dogs may be allowed.

Comfort Inn
905 N Kentucky Street
Kingston, TN
865-376-4965 (877-424-6423)
Dogs are allowed for an additional fee of $10 per night per pet. Multiple dogs may be allowed.

Days Inn Knoxville/Kingston
495 Gallaher Rd
Kingston, TN
865-376-2069 (800-329-7466)
Dogs of all sizes are allowed. There is a $10 per night pet fee per pet. 2 dogs may be allowed.

Best Western Harpeth Inn
116 Luyben Hills Rd
Kingston Springs, TN
615-952-3961 (800-780-7234)
Dogs are allowed for an additional fee of $10 per night per pet. Multiple dogs may be allowed.

Best Western Knoxville Suites
5317 Pratt Road
Knoxville, TN
865-687-9922 (800-780-7234)
Dogs are allowed for an additional fee of $10 per night per pet. Multiple dogs may be allowed.

Best Western West of Knoxville
500 Lovell Rd
Knoxville, TN
865-675-7666 (800-780-7234)
Dogs are allowed for an additional fee of $10 per night per pet. Multiple dogs may be allowed.

Candlewood Suites
10206 Parkside Dr
Knoxville, TN
865-777-0400 (877-270-6405)
Dogs of all sizes are allowed for an additional one time pet fee of $75 per room for 1 to 7days; 8 days or more is $150 per room. 2 dogs may be allowed.

Crowne Plaza Knoxville
401 West Summit Hill Drive
Knoxville, TN
865-522-2600 (877-270-6405)
Dogs up to 50 pounds are allowed for an additional one time fee of $25 per pet. 2 dogs may be allowed.

Days Inn Knoxville West
326 Lovell Rd

Knoxville, TN
865-966-5801 (800-329-7466)
Dogs of all sizes are allowed. There is a $10 per night pet fee per pet. 2 dogs may be allowed.

Holiday Inn
1315 Kirby Road
Knoxville, TN
865-584-3911 (877-270-6405)
Dogs of all sizes are allowed for an additional one time pet fee of $75 per room. Multiple dogs may be allowed.

Holiday Inn Express Knoxville-Strawberry Plains
730 Rufus Graham Road
Knoxville, TN
865-525-5100 (877-270-6405)
Dogs of all sizes are allowed for an additional one time fee of $15 per night per pet. 2 dogs may be allowed.

Holiday Inn Select
304 N Cedar Bluff Road
Knoxville, TN
865-693-1011 (877-270-6405)
Dogs of all sizes are allowed for an additional one time pet fee of $50 per room. Multiple dogs may be allowed.

Howard Johnson Plaza Hotel
7621 Kinston Pike
Knoxville, TN
865-693-8111 (800-446-4656)
Well-behaved dogs of all sizes are allowed. There is a $15 one time additional pet fee.

La Quinta Inn Knoxville West
258 North Peters Road
Knoxville, TN
865-690-9777 (800-531-5900)
Dogs of all sizes are allowed. There are no additional pet fees. Dogs must be leashed and cleaned up after. Dogs may not be left unattended unless they will be quiet, well behaved, and a contact number left at the front desk. Multiple dogs may be allowed.

Motel 6 - Knoxville
1550 Cracker Barrell Lane
Knoxville, TN
865-633-6646 (800-466-8356)
One well-behaved family pet per room. Guest must notify front desk upon arrival. Guest is liable for any damages. In consideration of all guests, pets must never be left unattended in the guest rooms.

Motel 6 - Knoxville North
5640 Merchants Center Boulevard.
Knoxville, TN

865-689-7100 (800-466-8356)
One well-behaved family pet per room. Guest must notify front desk upon arrival. Guest is liable for any damages. In consideration of all guests, pets must never be left unattended in the guest rooms.

Motel 6 - Knoxville West
402 Lovell Road
Knoxville, TN
865-675-7200 (800-466-8356)
One well-behaved family pet per room. Guest must notify front desk upon arrival. Guest is liable for any damages. In consideration of all guests, pets must never be left unattended in the guest rooms.

Quality Inn
6712 Central Avenue Pike
Knoxville, TN
865-689-6600 (877-424-6423)
Dogs up to 50 pounds are allowed for an additional fee of $10 per night per pet. 2 dogs may be allowed.

Red Roof Inn - Knoxville West
209 Advantage Place
Knoxville, TN
865-691-1664 (800-RED-ROOF)
One well-behaved family pet per room. Guest must notify front desk upon arrival. Guest is liable for any damages. In consideration of all guests, pets must never be left unattended in the guest rooms.

Residence Inn by Marriott
Langley Place at North Peters Road
Knoxville, TN
865-539-5339
Pets of all sizes are allowed. There is a $75 one time fee and a pet policy to sign at check in. Multiple dogs may be allowed.

Super 8 Knoxville/Downtown/West
6200 Papermill Rd
Knoxville, TN
865-584-8511 (800-800-8000)
Dogs of all sizes are allowed. There are no additional pet fees. Smoking and non-smoking rooms are available for pet rooms.

Super 8 Knoxville/West
11748 Snyder Rd
Knoxville, TN
865-675-5566 (800-800-8000)
Dogs of all sizes are allowed. There is a $6 per night pet fee per pet. Smoking and non-smoking rooms are available for pet rooms. 2 dogs may be allowed.

TownePlace Suites Knoxville Cedar

Bluff
205 Langley Place
Knoxville, TN
865-693-5216
Dogs of all sizes are allowed. There is a $75 one time pet fee per visit. 2 dogs may be allowed.

Comfort Inn Interstate
155 Dumplin Valley Road
Kodak, TN
865-933-1719 (877-424-6423)
Dogs up to 60 pounds are allowed for an additional fee of $10 per night per pet. Multiple dogs may be allowed.

Holiday Inn Express & Suites
2863 Winfield Dunn Parkway
Kodak, TN
865-933-9448 (877-270-6405)
Dogs up to 80 pounds are allowed for an additional pet fee of $10 per night per room. 2 dogs may be allowed.

Motel 6 - Kodak
184 East Dumplin Valley Road
Kodak, TN
865-933-8141 (800-466-8356)
One well-behaved family pet per room. Guest must notify front desk upon arrival. Guest is liable for any damages. In consideration of all guests, pets must never be left unattended in the guest rooms.

Days Inn Knoxville/Lake City
221 Colonial Lane
Lake City, TN
865-426-2816 (800-329-7466)
Dogs of all sizes are allowed. There is a $10 per night pet fee per pet. 2 dogs may be allowed.

Days Inn Memphis East
9822 Huff N Puff Rd
Lakeland, TN
901-388-7120 (800-329-7466)
Dogs of all sizes are allowed. There is a $10 per night pet fee per pet. 2 dogs may be allowed.

Best Western Villa Inn
2126 N Locust Ave
Lawrenceburg, TN
931-762-4448 (800-780-7234)
Dogs are allowed for an additional fee of $10 per night per pet. Multiple dogs may be allowed.

Comfort Inn
829 S Cumberland Street/H 231
Lebanon, TN
615-444-1001 (877-424-6423)
Dogs are allowed for an additional fee of $10 per night per pet. Multiple

dogs may be allowed.

Days Inn Knoxville/Lenoir City
1110 Hwy 321 North
Lenoir City, TN
865-986-2011 (800-329-7466)
Dogs of all sizes are allowed. There is a $10 per night pet fee per pet. 2 dogs may be allowed.

Super 8 Loudon
12452 Hwy 72 North
Loudon, TN
865-458-5669 (800-800-8000)
Dogs of all sizes are allowed. There are no additional pet fees. Smoking and non-smoking rooms are available for pet rooms. 2 dogs may be allowed.

Country Inns & Suites by Carlson
126 Expressway Dr
Manchester, TN
931-728-7551
Dogs of all sizes are allowed. There are no additional pet fees.

Super 8 Manchester
2430 Hillsboro Blvd
Manchester, TN
931-728-9720 (800-800-8000)
Dogs of all sizes are allowed. There is a $5 per night pet fee per pet. Reservations are recommended due to limited rooms for pets. Smoking and non-smoking rooms are available for pet rooms. 2 dogs may be allowed.

Days Inn Martin/Union City
800 University St
Martin, TN
731-587-9577 (800-329-7466)
Dogs of all sizes are allowed. There is a $10 per night pet fee per pet. 2 dogs may be allowed.

Baymont Inn & Suites Memphis East
6020 Shelby Oaks Drive
Memphis, TN
901-377-2233 (800-531-5900)
Dogs of all sizes are allowed. There are no additional pet fees. Dogs must be leashed, cleaned up after, and crated when left alone in the room. Multiple dogs may be allowed.

Best Western Travelers Inn
5024 Hwy 78
Memphis, TN
901-363-8430 (800-780-7234)
Dogs are allowed for an additional fee of $15 per night per pet, and a credit card must be on file. 2 dogs may be allowed.

Clarion Hotel Airport/Graceland Area

1471 E Brooks Road
Memphis, TN
901-332-3500 (877-424-6423)
Dogs are allowed for an additional
one time fee of $25 per pet. 2 dogs
may be allowed.

Days inn Memphis Near Graceland
3839 Elvis Presley Blvd
Memphis, TN
901-346-5500 (800-DAYS-INN)
Dogs of all sizes are allowed. There
is a $10 per night pet fee per pet. 2
dogs may be allowed.

East Drury Inn & Suites
1556 Sycamore View
Memphis, TN
901-373-8200 (800-378-7946)
Dogs of all sizes are permitted. Pets
are not allowed in the breakfast area
of the hotel. Pets are not to be left
unattended, and each guest must
assume liability for damage of
property or other guest complaints.
There is a limit of one pet per room.

La Quinta Inn & Suites Memphis
Primacy Parkway
1236 Primacy Parkway
Memphis, TN
901-374-0330 (800-531-5900)
Dogs of all sizes are allowed. There
are no additional pet fees. Dogs may
not be left unattended, and they must
be leashed and cleaned up after.
Multiple dogs may be allowed.

Motel 6 - Memphis
4000 US 78
Memphis, TN
901-365-7999 (800-466-8356)
One well-behaved family pet per
room. Guest must notify front desk
upon arrival. Guest is liable for any
damages. In consideration of all
guests, pets must never be left
unattended in the guest rooms.

Motel 6 - Memphis Downtown
210 South Pauline Street
Memphis, TN
901-528-0650 (800-466-8356)
One well-behaved family pet per
room. Guest must notify front desk
upon arrival. Guest is liable for any
damages. In consideration of all
guests, pets must never be left
unattended in the guest rooms.

Motel 6 - Memphis East
1321 Sycamore View Road
Memphis, TN
901-382-8572 (800-466-8356)
One well-behaved family pet per
room. Guest must notify front desk
upon arrival. Guest is liable for any

damages. In consideration of all
guests, pets must never be left
unattended in the guest rooms.

Motel 6 - Memphis Graceland-
Airport South
1117 East Brooks Road
Memphis, TN
901-346-0992 (800-466-8356)
One well-behaved family pet per
room. Guest must notify front desk
upon arrival. Guest is liable for any
damages. In consideration of all
guests, pets must never be left
unattended in the guest rooms.

Quality Inn Airport/Graceland
1581 Brooks Road
Memphis, TN
901-345-3344 (877-424-6423)
Dogs are allowed for an additional
fee of $10 per night per pet. Multiple
dogs may be allowed.

Red Roof Inn - Memphis Downtown
42 South Camilla Street
Memphis, TN
901-526-1050 (800-RED-ROOF)
One well-behaved family pet per
room. Guest must notify front desk
upon arrival. Guest is liable for any
damages. In consideration of all
guests, pets must never be left
unattended in the guest rooms.

Red Roof Inn - Memphis East
6055 Shelby Oaks Drive
Memphis, TN
901-388-6111 (800-RED-ROOF)
One well-behaved family pet per
room. Guest must notify front desk
upon arrival. Guest is liable for any
damages. In consideration of all
guests, pets must never be left
unattended in the guest rooms.

Residence Inn by Marriott
110 Monroe at Main
Memphis, TN
901-578-3700
Dogs up to 65 pounds are allowed.
There is a $75 one time fee and a
pet policy to sign at check in. 2
dogs may be allowed.

Residence Inn by Marriott
6141 Old Poplar Pike
Memphis, TN
901-685-9595
Dogs of all sizes are allowed. There
is a $75 one time fee and a pet
policy to sign at check in. Multiple
dogs may be allowed.

Sleep Inn
2855 Old Austin Peay H
Memphis, TN

901-312-7777 (877-424-6423)
Dogs are allowed for an additional
$15 one time pet fee per room. 2
dogs may be allowed.

Studio 6 - Memphis
4300 American Way
Memphis, TN
901-366-9333 (800-466-8356)
One well-behaved family pet per
room. Guest must notify front desk
upon arrival. Guest is liable for any
damages. In consideration of all
guests, pets must never be left
unattended in the guest rooms.

Super 8 Memphis/Downtown
340 W Illinois St
Memphis, TN
901-948-9005 (800-800-8000)
Dogs of all sizes are allowed. There
is a $5 per night pet fee per pet.
Smoking and non-smoking rooms
are available for pet rooms. 2 dogs
may be allowed.

Super 8 Memphis/East/Macon Cove
Area
6015 Macon Cove Rd
Memphis, TN
901-373-4888 (800-800-8000)
Dogs of all sizes are allowed. There
is a $10 per night pet fee per pet.
Smoking and non-smoking rooms
are available for pet rooms. 2 dogs
may be allowed.

Best Western Smokehouse Lodge
850 W Main Street
Monteagle, TN
931-924-2268 (800-780-7234)
Dogs are allowed for an additional
one time fee of $10 per pet. Multiple
dogs may be allowed.

Days Inn Monteagle
742 Dixie Lee Ave
Monteagle, TN
931-924-2900 (800-329-7466)
Dogs of all sizes are allowed. There
is a $8 per night pet fee per pet. 2
dogs may be allowed.

Comfort Suites
3660 W Andrew Johnson H
Morristown, TN
423-585-4000 (877-424-6423)
Dogs are allowed for an additional
fee of $10 per night per pet. Multiple
dogs may be allowed.

Motel 6 - Morristown
5984 West Andrew Johnson
Highway
Morristown, TN
423-586-4666 (800-466-8356)
One well-behaved family pet per

room. Guest must notify front desk upon arrival. Guest is liable for any damages. In consideration of all guests, pets must never be left unattended in the guest rooms.

Super 8 Morristown/South
5400 S Davey Crockett Parkway
Morristown, TN
423-318-8888 (800-800-8000)
Dogs of all sizes are allowed. There is a $9 per night pet fee per pet. Smoking and non-smoking rooms are available for pet rooms. 2 dogs may be allowed.

Quality Inn and Suites
1000 Hershel Drive
Mount Juliet, TN
615-773-3600 (877-424-6423)
Dogs are allowed for an additional one time pet fee per pet of $25 per pet. Multiple dogs may be allowed.

Best Western Chaffin Inn
168 Chaffin Place
Murfreesboro, TN
615-895-3818 (800-780-7234)
Dogs are allowed for an additional fee of $15 per night per pet. Dogs may not be left alone in the room. 2 dogs may be allowed.

Doubletree
1850 Old Fort Parkway
Murfreesboro, TN
615-895-5555
Dogs up to 75 pounds are allowed. There is a $25 per pet per stay additional pet fee. Multiple dogs may be allowed.

Hampton Inn Murfreesboro
2230 Armory Drive
Murfreesboro, TN
615-896-1172 (800-hampton)
hamptoninnmurfreesboro.com
Dogs of all sizes are allowed in the pet rooms. Some of the pet rooms are non-smoking. There is a $10 per day additional pet fee.

Holiday Inn
2227 Old Fort Pkwy
Murfreesboro, TN
615-896-2420 (877-270-6405)
Dogs of all sizes are allowed for an additional pet fee of $15 per night per room. Multiple dogs may be allowed.

Motel 6 - Murfreesboro
114 Chaffin Place
Murfreesboro, TN
615-890-8524 (800-466-8356)
One well-behaved family pet per room. Guest must notify front desk

upon arrival. Guest is liable for any damages. In consideration of all guests, pets must never be left unattended in the guest rooms.

Red Roof Inn - Murfreesboro
2282 Armory Drive
Murfreesboro, TN
615-893-0104 (800-RED-ROOF)
One well-behaved family pet per room. Guest must notify front desk upon arrival. Guest is liable for any damages. In consideration of all guests, pets must never be left unattended in the guest rooms.

Best Western Music Row
1407 Division St
Nashville, TN
615-242-1631 (800-780-7234)
Dogs are allowed for an additional fee of $10 per night per pet. Multiple dogs may be allowed.

Comfort Inn
1501 Demonbreun Street
Nashville, TN
615-255-9977 (877-424-6423)
Dogs are allowed for an additional fee of $10 per night per pet. 2 dogs may be allowed.

Days Inn Nashville Downtown
1800 W End Ave
Nashville, TN
615-327-0922 (800-329-7466)
Dogs of all sizes are allowed. There is a $10 per night pet fee per pet. 2 dogs may be allowed.

Days Inn Nashville West
269 White Bridge Rd
Nashville, TN
615-356-9100 (800-329-7466)
Dogs of all sizes are allowed. There is a $10 per night pet fee per pet. 2 dogs may be allowed.

Drury Inn & Suites
555 Donelson Pike
Nashville, TN
615-902-0400 (800-378-7946)
Dogs of all sizes are permitted. Pets are not allowed in the breakfast area of the hotel. Pets are not to be left unattended, and each guest must assume liability for damage of property or other guest complaints. There is a limit of one pet per room.

La Quinta Inn Nashville Airport
2345 Atrium Way
Nashville, TN
615-885-3000 (800-531-5900)
Dogs of all sizes are allowed. There are no additional pet fees. Dogs may not be left unattended at any

time, and they must be leashed and cleaned up after. Multiple dogs may be allowed.

La Quinta Inn Nashville Airport
531 Donelson Pike
Nashville, TN
615-885-3100 (800-531-5900)
Dogs of all sizes are allowed. There are no additional pet fees. Dogs may only be left unattended in the room if they will be quiet and well behaved. Dogs must be leashed and cleaned up after. Multiple dogs may be allowed.

La Quinta Inn Nashville South
4311 Sidco Drive
Nashville, TN
615-834-6900 (800-531-5900)
Dogs of all sizes are allowed. There are no additional pet fees. Dogs must be leashed and cleaned up after. Multiple dogs may be allowed.

Loews Vanderbilt Hotel
2100 West End Ave
Nashville, TN
615-320-1700
All well-behaved dogs of any size are welcome. This upscale hotel offers their "Loews Loves Pets" program which includes special pet treats, local dog walking routes, and a list of nearby pet-friendly places to visit. There are no pet fees.

Motel 6 - Nashville Airport
420 Metroplex Drive
Nashville, TN
615-833-8887 (800-466-8356)
One well-behaved family pet per room. Guest must notify front desk upon arrival. Guest is liable for any damages. In consideration of all guests, pets must never be left unattended in the guest rooms.

Motel 6 - Nashville North
311 West Trinity Lane
Nashville, TN
615-227-9696 (800-466-8356)
One well-behaved family pet per room. Guest must notify front desk upon arrival. Guest is liable for any damages. In consideration of all guests, pets must never be left unattended in the guest rooms.

Motel 6 - Nashville South
95 Wallace Road
Nashville, TN
615-333-9933 (800-466-8356)
One well-behaved family pet per room. Guest must notify front desk upon arrival. Guest is liable for any damages. In consideration of all

guests, pets must never be left unattended in the guest rooms.

Pear Tree Inn
343 Harding Place
Nashville, TN
615-834-4242 (800-378-7946)
Dogs of all sizes are permitted. Pets are not allowed in the breakfast area of the hotel. Pets are not to be left unattended, and each guest must assume liability for damage of property or other guest complaints. There is a limit of one pet per room.

Quality Inn
981 Murfreesboro Road
Nashville, TN
615-367-9150 (877-424-6423)
Dogs are allowed for an additional fee of $10 per night per pet. Multiple dogs may be allowed.

Red Roof Inn - Nashville - Opryland Area
2460 Music Valley Drive
Nashville, TN
615-889-0090 (800-RED-ROOF)
One well-behaved family pet per room. Guest must notify front desk upon arrival. Guest is liable for any damages. In consideration of all guests, pets must never be left unattended in the guest rooms.

Red Roof Inn - Nashville Airport
510 Claridge Drive
Nashville, TN
615-872-0735 (800-RED-ROOF)
One well-behaved family pet per room. Guest must notify front desk upon arrival. Guest is liable for any damages. In consideration of all guests, pets must never be left unattended in the guest rooms.

Red Roof Inn - Nashville South
4271 Sidco Drive
Nashville, TN
615-832-0093 (800-RED-ROOF)
One well-behaved family pet per room. Guest must notify front desk upon arrival. Guest is liable for any damages. In consideration of all guests, pets must never be left unattended in the guest rooms.

Residence Inn by Marriott
2300 Elm Hill Pike
Nashville, TN
615-889-8600
Dogs of all sizes are allowed. There is a $75 one time fee and a pet policy to sign at check in. Multiple dogs may be allowed.

Sheraton Music City Hotel

777 McGavock Pike
Nashville, TN
615-885-2200 (888-625-5144)
Dogs up to 50 pounds are allowed. Dogs are not allowed to be left alone in the room.

Sheraton Nashville Downtown Hotel
623 Union St.
Nashville, TN
615-259-2000 (888-625-5144)
Dogs of all sizes are allowed for no additional pet fee; there is a pet agreement to sign at check in. Dogs may not be left alone in the room.

Sleep Inn
3200 Dickerson Pike
Nashville, TN
615-227-8686 (877-424-6423)
Dogs are allowed for an additional fee of $10 per night per pet. Multiple dogs may be allowed.

South Drury Inn
341 Harding Place
Nashville, TN
615-834-7170 (800-378-7946)
Dogs of all sizes are permitted. Pets are not allowed in the breakfast area of the hotel. Pets are not to be left unattended, and each guest must assume liability for damage of property or other guest complaints. There is a limit of one pet per room.

Super 8 Nashville/West
6924 Charlotte Pike
Nashville, TN
615-356-6005 (800-800-8000)
Dogs up to 100 pounds are allowed. There is a $10 per night pet fee per pet. Smoking and non-smoking rooms are available for pet rooms. 2 dogs may be allowed.

Comfort Inn
1149 Smokey Mountain Lane
Newport, TN
423-623-5355 (877-424-6423)
Dogs are allowed for an additional fee of $10 per night per pet. Multiple dogs may be allowed.

Holiday Inn
1010 Cosby Hwy
Newport, TN
423-623-8622 (877-270-6405)
Dogs of all sizes are allowed for an additional one time fee of $25 per pet. Multiple dogs may be allowed.

Motel 6 - Newport
255 Heritage Boulevard
Newport, TN
423-623-1850 (800-466-8356)
One well-behaved family pet per

room. Guest must notify front desk upon arrival. Guest is liable for any damages. In consideration of all guests, pets must never be left unattended in the guest rooms.

Days Inn Knoxville/Oak Ridge
206 S Illinois
Oak Ridge, TN
865-483-5615 (800-329-7466)
Dogs of all sizes are allowed. There is a $5 per night pet fee per pet. 2 dogs may be allowed.

Doubletree
215 S Illinois Avenue
Oak Ridge, TN
865-481-2468
Dogs of all sizes are allowed. There is a $25 one time pet fee per room. Multiple dogs may be allowed.

Staybridge Suites Knoxville Oak Ridge
420 South Illinois Avenue
Oak Ridge, TN
800-238-8000 (877-270-6405)
Dogs up to 50 pounds are allowed for an additional one time pet fee of $100 per room. 2 dogs may be allowed.

Super 8 Oak Ridge
1590 Oak Ridge Turnpike
Oak Ridge, TN
865-483-1200 (800-800-8000)
Dogs of all sizes are allowed. There is a $5 per night pet fee per pet. Smoking and non-smoking rooms are available for pet rooms. 2 dogs may be allowed.

Days Inn Oakland
6805 Hwy 64
Oakland, TN
901-465-5630 (800-329-7466)
Dogs of all sizes are allowed. There is a $10 per night pet fee per pet. 2 dogs may be allowed.

Great Outdoor Rentals
1191 Wears Valley Rd
Pigeon Forge, TN
865-429-7878 (800-720-6978)
greatoutdoorrentals.com
The vacation rentals offer a number of pet-friendly properties in the Pigeon Forge and Gatlinburg areas. There is a $50 non-refundable pet fee for one dog, and an $80 non-refundable pet fee for two dogs.

Hampton Inn & Suites Pigeon Forge
2025 Parkway
Pigeon Forge, TN
865-428-1600 (800-310-8082)
hamptoninnpigeonforge.com

Sept 18/09

This pet-friendly hotel offers pet treats at check-in and a pet walking area. They have a fitness center, heated outdoor pool and hot breakfast included with your room. There is a $20 per night additional pet fee.

Heartlander Country Resort
2385 Parkway (US 441)
Pigeon Forge, TN
865-453-4106
There is a $20 one time pet charge.

Holiday Inn
3230 Parkway
Pigeon Forge, TN
865-428-2700 (877-270-6405)
Dogs up to 25 pounds are allowed for an additional one time fee of $15 per pet. 2 dogs may be allowed.

Jewel of the Smokies
Dogwood Farms
Pigeon Forge, TN
865-777-0469 (877-806-5002)
tncabin.com
This 3 bedroom pet-friendly cabin offers views of the mountains and close proximity to Pigeon Forge. This is a non-smoking cabin.

River Stone Resort
212 Dollywood Lane
Pigeon Forge, TN
865-908-0660 (866-908-0660)
RiverStoneResort.com
Some of these one to four bedroom condos are pet friendly. They offer dog runs and pet packages.

Sunset Cottage Rentals and Realty
3603 S River Road
Pigeon Forge, TN
865-429-8478
Dogs of all sizes are allowed in two of their cottages. There is a $100 refundable deposit per pet plus a $25 one time fee per room and a pet policy to sign at check in. Multiple dogs may be allowed.

Fall Creek Falls Inn
2536 Lakeside Drive
Pikeville, TN
423-881-5298 (800-250-8610)
This inn is located in the Fall Creek Falls State Park and sparkling streams, gorges, cascading waterfalls, a variety of scenic trails, ecosystems, and abundant recreation are part of the package. Dogs of all sizes are allowed for an additional $10 (plus tax) per night per pet. Dogs must be crated when out of the room. There is also a camping area on site where dogs are allowed

at no additional fee. Dogs must be leashed and cleaned up after. Dogs are not allowed on the Overnight Trail, but they are allowed on the other trails in the park. Multiple dogs may be allowed.

Comfort Inn
323 E Emory Road
Powell, TN
865-938-5500 (877-424-6423)
Dogs are allowed for an additional fee of $10 per night per pet. Multiple dogs may be allowed.

Comfort Inn River Suites
860 Winfield Dunn Parkway
Sevierville, TN
865-428-5519 (877-424-6423)
Dogs are allowed for an additional fee of $10 per night per pet. Multiple dogs may be allowed.

Hidden Springs Resort Rentals
1576 Nucum Hollow Road
Sevierville, TN
865-774-2136 (888-477-8366)
hiddenspringsresort.com
These log cabins with full kitchens and outdoor hot tubs, allow pets with a $100 cash deposit that will be returned within 10 days if no damage or extra cleaning has occurred.

Best Western Celebration Inn & Suites
724 Madison Street
Shelbyville, TN
931-684-2378 (800-780-7234)
Dogs are allowed for an additional pet fee of $15 per night per room. Multiple dogs may be allowed.

Days Inn Nashville/Smyrna
1300 Plaza Dr
Smyrna, TN
915-355-6161 (800-329-7466)
Dogs of all sizes are allowed. There is a $10 per night pet fee per pet. 2 dogs may be allowed.

Best Western Sweetwater
1421 Murray's Chapel Rd
Sweetwater, TN
423-337-3541 (800-780-7234)
Dogs are allowed for an additional one time pet fee of $15 per room. Multiple dogs may be allowed.

Comfort Inn
731 S Main Street
Sweetwater, TN
423-337-6646 (877-424-6423)
Dogs up to 50 pounds are allowed for an additional fee of $10 per night per pet; the fee is $15 per night per

pet for dogs over 50 pounds. 2 dogs may be allowed.

Days Inn Sweetwater
229 Hwy 68
Sweetwater, TN
423-337-4200 (800-329-7466)
Dogs of all sizes are allowed. There is a $10 per night pet fee per pet. 2 dogs may be allowed.

Quality Inn and Suites
1116 H 68
Sweetwater, TN
423-337-4900 (877-424-6423)
Dogs up to 15 pounds are allowed for an additional one time pet fee of $10 per room; $15 for dogs 16 to 35 pounds, and $20 for dogs over 35 pounds. Multiple dogs may be allowed.

Comfort Inn
340 Hester Drive
White Horse, TN
615-672-8850 (877-424-6423)
Dogs are allowed for an additional pet fee of $5 to $7 per night per pet. 2 dogs may be allowed.

Days Inn White Pine
3670 Roy Messer Hwy
White Pine, TN
865-674-2573 (800-329-7466)
Dogs of all sizes are allowed. There is a $6 per night pet fee per pet. 2 dogs may be allowed.

Super 8 Whiteville
2040 Hwy 64
Whiteville, TN
731-254-8884 (800-800-8000)
Dogs of all sizes are allowed. There is a $10 per night pet fee per pet. Smoking and non-smoking rooms are available for pet rooms. 2 dogs may be allowed.

Best Western Crossroads Inn
21045 Hwy 22 North
Wildersville, TN
731-968-2532 (800-780-7234)
Dogs are allowed for an additional fee of $10 per night per pet. 2 dogs may be allowed.

Texas Listings

Best Western Mall South
3950 Ridgemont Drive
Abilene, TX
325-695-1262 (800-780-7234)
Dogs are allowed for an additional

fee of $30 per night per pet. Multiple dogs may be allowed.

Civic Plaza Hotel
505 Pine St
Abilene, TX
800-588-0222
There is a one time pet fee of $10.

Comfort Inn
1758 E I 20
Abilene, TX
325-676-0203 (877-424-6423)
Dogs are allowed for an additional one time fee of $25 per pet. Multiple dogs may be allowed.

Comfort Suites
3165 S Danville Drive
Abilene, TX
325-795-8500 (877-424-6423)
Dogs are allowed for an additional fee of $30 per night per pet. 2 dogs may be allowed.

Days Inn Abilene
1702 I-20 E
Abilene, TX
325-672-6433 (800-329-7466)
Dogs of all sizes are allowed. There is a $10 one time per pet fee per visit. 2 dogs may be allowed.

La Quinta Inn Abilene
3501 West Lake Road
Abilene, TX
325-676-1676 (800-531-5900)
Dogs of all sizes are allowed. There are no additional pet fees. Although there is no set allotment for dogs, their preference is for no more than 2 large dogs or 3 small dogs per room. Dogs must be removed for housekeeping. Dogs may not be left unattended, and they must be leashed and cleaned up after.

Motel 6 - Abilene
4951 West Stamford Street
Abilene, TX
325-672-8462 (800-466-8356)
One well-behaved family pet per room. Guest must notify front desk upon arrival. Guest is liable for any damages. In consideration of all guests, pets must never be left unattended in the guest rooms.

Whitten Inn
1625 State Route 351
Abilene, TX
915-673-5271
There are no additional pet fees.

Motel 6 - Dallas - Addison
4325 Beltline Road
Addison, TX

972-386-4577 (800-466-8356)
All well-behaved, trained dogs are welcome. There are no additional pet fees.

Super 8 Addison/Dallas North Area
4150 Beltway Dr
Addison, TX
972-233-2525 (800-800-8000)
Dogs of all sizes are allowed. There is a $10 one time per pet fee per visit. Smoking and non-smoking rooms are available for pet rooms. 2 dogs may be allowed.

Big Texan Steak Ranch Motel
7701 E I 40
Amarillo, TX
800-657-7177
bigtexan.com/
This 1800's themed motel offers a convenient location to food, fun, and a variety of attractions. Dogs are allowed for an additional fee of $10 per night per pet. Multiple dogs may be allowed.

Days Inn Amarillo
8601 Canyon Dr
Amarillo, TX
806-468-7100 (800-329-7466)
Dogs of all sizes are allowed. There is a $10 per night pet fee per pet. 2 dogs may be allowed.

Days Inn Amarillo East
1701 I-40 E
Amarillo, TX
806-379-6255 (800-329-7466)
Dogs of all sizes are allowed. There is a $10 per night pet fee per pet. Reservations are recommended due to limited rooms for pets. 2 dogs may be allowed.

Hampton Inn
1700 I 40E
Amarillo, TX
806-372-1425
Well behaved dogs of all sizes are allowed. There are no additional pet fees. Multiple dogs may be allowed.

Holiday Inn
1911 I-40 East
Amarillo, TX
806-372-8741 (877-270-6405)
Dogs of all sizes are allowed for an additional one time pet fee of $25 per room. Multiple dogs may be allowed.

Kiva Motel
2501 Interstate Highway 40 East
Amarillo, TX
806-379-6555 (800-272-6232)
There is a $25 one time pet fee.

La Quinta Inn Amarillo East/Airport Area
1708 I-40 East
Amarillo, TX
806-373-7486 (800-531-5900)
Dogs of all sizes are allowed. There are no additional pet fees. Dogs must be leashed, cleaned up after, and crated for housekeeping. Multiple dogs may be allowed.

Motel 6 - Amarillo Central
2032 Paramount Boulevard
Amarillo, TX
806-355-6554 (800-466-8356)
One well-behaved family pet per room. Guest must notify front desk upon arrival. Guest is liable for any damages. In consideration of all guests, pets must never be left unattended in the guest rooms.

Motel 6 - Amarillo East
3930 I-40 East
Amarillo, TX
806-374-6444 (800-466-8356)
One well-behaved family pet per room. Guest must notify front desk upon arrival. Guest is liable for any damages. In consideration of all guests, pets must never be left unattended in the guest rooms.

Motel 6 - Amarillo West
6030 I-40 West
Amarillo, TX
806-359-7651 (800-466-8356)
One well-behaved family pet per room. Guest must notify front desk upon arrival. Guest is liable for any damages. In consideration of all guests, pets must never be left unattended in the guest rooms.

Red Roof Inn - Amarillo - Airport
4301 I-40 East
Amarillo, TX
806-373-3045 (800-RED-ROOF)
One well-behaved family pet per room. Guest must notify front desk upon arrival. Guest is liable for any damages. In consideration of all guests, pets must never be left unattended in the guest rooms.

Residence Inn by Marriott
6700 I 40 W
Amarillo, TX
806-354-2978
Dogs of all sizes are allowed. There is a $75 one time fee and a pet policy to sign at check in. Multiple dogs may be allowed.

Best Western Angleton Inn
1809 N Velasco

Angleton, TX
979-849-5822 (800-780-7234)
Dogs are allowed for an additional
one time fee of $25 per pet. 2 dogs
may be allowed.

Best Western Cooper Inn & Suites
4024 Melear Drive
Arlington, TX
817-784-9490 (800-780-7234)
Dogs up to 10 pounds are allowed
for an additional fee of $5 per night
per pet; the fee is $10 for dogs over
10 pounds. Multiple dogs may be
allowed.

Candlewood Suites
2221 Brookhollow Plaza Dr
Arlington, TX
817-649-3336 (877-270-6405)
Dogs up to 80 pounds are allowed
for an additional one time fee per pet
of $75 for 1 to 6 nights; the fee is
$150 for 7 nights or more. Multiple
dogs may be allowed.

Days Inn Dallas/Ballpark at Arlington
910 N Collins
Arlington, TX
817-261-8444 (800-329-7466)
Dogs of all sizes are allowed. There
is a $10 per night pet fee per pet. 2
dogs may be allowed.

Hawthorn Suites Hotel
2401 Brookhollow Plaza Drive
Arlington, TX
817-640-1188
There is a $50 one time pet charge.

Howard Johnson Express Inn
2001 Copland Road
Arlington, TX
817-461-1122 (800-446-4656)
Well-behaved dogs of all sizes are
allowed. There is a $10 per day
additional pet fee.

La Quinta Inn & Suites Dallas
Arlington North
825 North Watson Rd.
Arlington, TX
817-640-4142 (800-531-5900)
Dogs of all sizes are allowed. There
are no additional pet fees. Dogs
must be leashed and cleaned up
after. You must inform of the pet(s)
at the time of reservations, and make
arrangements for housekeeping.
Place the Do Not Disturb sign on the
door if the pet is unattended. Multiple
dogs may be allowed.

La Quinta Inn & Suites Dallas
Arlington South
4001 Scot's Legacy Dr.
Arlington, TX

817-467-7756 (800-531-5900)
Dogs of all sizes are allowed. There
are no additional pet fees. Dogs
must be quiet, well behaved,
leashed and cleaned up after.
Multiple dogs may be allowed.

Motel 6 - Dallas - Arlington
2626 East Randol Mill Road
Arlington, TX
817-649-0147 (800-466-8356)
One well-behaved family pet per
room. Guest must notify front desk
upon arrival. Guest is liable for any
damages. In consideration of all
guests, pets must never be left
unattended in the guest rooms.

Residence Inn by Marriott
1050 Brookhollow Plaza Drive
Arlington, TX
817-649-7300
Dogs of all sizes are allowed. There
is a $75 one time fee and a pet
policy to sign at check in. Multiple
dogs may be allowed.

Sleep Inn Maingate Six Flags
750 Six Flags Drive
Arlington, TX
817-649-1010 (877-424-6423)
Dogs are allowed for an additional
fee of $10.80 per night per pet. 2
dogs may be allowed.

Studio 6 - Dallas - South Arlington
1980 West Pleasant Ridge Road
Arlington, TX
817-465-8500 (800-466-8356)
One well-behaved family pet per
room. Guest must notify front desk
upon arrival. Guest is liable for any
damages. In consideration of all
guests, pets must never be left
unattended in the guest rooms.

TownePlace Suites Arlington
1709 E Lamar Blvd
Arlington, TX
817-861-8728
Dogs of all sizes are allowed. There
is a $75 one time pet fee per visit. 2
dogs may be allowed.

Best Western Inn on the Hill
2050 State Highway 31 E
Athens, TX
903-675-9214 (800-780-7234)
Dogs are allowed for a $50
refundable deposit plus an
additional pet fee of $10 per night
per room. 2 dogs may be allowed.

Austin Folk House
506 W 22nd Street
Austin, TX
512-472-6700

Dogs of all sizes are allowed. There
are no additional pet fees, but a
credit card needs to be on file. They
can not take dogs that shed or bark
alot. Multiple dogs may be allowed.

Brava House
1108 Blanco Street
Austin, TX
512-478-5034
bravahouse.com/
This beautiful 1880's Victorian home
offers guests a peaceful warm
setting and a great location to
numerous local eateries, shops,
activities, and recreation. Dogs are
allowed for an additional pet fee of
$30 per night per room for small
dogs, and per pet for large dogs. 2
dogs may be allowed.

Candlewood Suites Austin
Arboretum-Northwest
9701 Stonelake Blvd.
Austin, TX
512-338-1611 (877-270-6405)
One dog is allowed for an additional
pet fee of $75 for 1 to 6 nights, and
$150 for 7 nights or more.

Candlewood Suites Austin-South
4320 Interstate 35 Service S
Austin, TX
512-444-8882 (877-270-6405)
Dogs up to 80 pounds are allowed
for an additional one time fee per pet
of $75 for 1 to 6 nights; the fee is
$150 for 7 nights or more. 2 dogs
may be allowed.

Comfort Suites Austin Airport
7501 E Ben White Blvd
Austin, TX
512-386-6000 (877-424-6423)
Dogs are allowed for an additional
one time pet fee of $30 per room.
Multiple dogs may be allowed.

Days Inn Austin Dwtn
3105 N IH-35
Austin, TX
512-478-1631 (800-329-7466)
Dogs of all sizes are allowed. There
are no additional pet fees. 2 dogs
may be allowed.

Days Inn Austin North Central
820 E Anderson Lane
Austin, TX
512-835-4311 (800-329-7466)
Dogs of all sizes are allowed. There
is a $50 one time pet fee per visit. 2
dogs may be allowed.

Embassy Suites Hotel Austin - North
5901 North IH-35
Austin, TX

512-454-8004
Dogs up to 50 pounds are allowed. There is a $25 one time pet fee per visit. Dogs are not allowed to be left alone in the room.

Hampton Inn
3908 W Braker Lane
Austin, TX
512-349-9898
Dogs of all sizes are allowed. There is a $75 one time cleaning fee and a pet policy to sign at check in. Multiple dogs may be allowed.

Hawthorn Suites-Austin South
4020 IH 35 South
Austin, TX
512-440-7722
There is a $50 one time pet charge and a $5 per day additional pet fee.

Holiday Inn-Northwest Plaza
8901 Business Park Drive
Austin, TX
512-343-0888 (877-270-6405)
Dogs up to 50 pounds are allowed for an additional one time pet fee of $25 per room. Multiple dogs may be allowed.

La Quinta Inn & Suites Austin Airport
7625 E. Ben White Blvd.
Austin, TX
512-386-6800 (800-531-5900)
Dogs of all sizes are allowed. There are no additional pet fees. Dogs must be quiet, leashed, and cleaned up after. Multiple dogs may be allowed.

La Quinta Inn & Suites Round Rock South
150 Parker Drive
Austin, TX
512-246-2800 (800-531-5900)
Dogs of all sizes are allowed. There are no additional pet fees. Dogs must be leashed, cleaned up after, and a contact number left with the front desk if there is a pet alone in the room. Multiple dogs may be allowed.

La Quinta Inn Austin Capitol
300 E. 11th St.
Austin, TX
512-476-1166 (800-531-5900)
Dogs of all sizes are allowed. There are no additional pet fees. Dogs may only be left in the room if they will be quiet and well behaved, and leashed and cleaned up after. Multiple dogs may be allowed.

La Quinta Inn Austin Highland Mall
5812 I-35 North

Austin, TX
512-459-4381 (800-531-5900)
Dogs of all sizes are allowed. There are no additional pet fees. Dogs must be leashed and cleaned up after, and arrangements need to be made with housekeeping if the stay is longer than one day. Multiple dogs may be allowed.

La Quinta Inn Austin I-35 S. Ben White
4200 I-35 South
Austin, TX
512-443-1774 (800-531-5900)
Dogs of all sizes are allowed. There are no additional pet fees. Place the "Do Not Disturb" sign on the door if your pet is in the room alone. Please leash and clean up after your pet. Multiple dogs may be allowed.

Lost Parrot Cabins Resort
15116 Storm Drive
Austin, TX
512-266-8916
austincabinrentals.com/
Located on 8 wooded acres near Lake Travis, this intimate resort offers colorful themed accommodations for a truly unique visit. Dogs are allowed (with prior approval) for an additional fee of $15 to $30 per night per pet. There is a pet agreement to sign at check in. Multiple dogs may be allowed.

Motel 6 - Austin Central - North
8010 I-35 North
Austin, TX
512-837-9890 (800-466-8356)
One well-behaved family pet per room. Guest must notify front desk upon arrival. Guest is liable for any damages. In consideration of all guests, pets must never be left unattended in the guest rooms.

Motel 6 - Austin Central-South/Univ. of TX
5330 North Interregional Highway
Austin, TX
512-467-9111 (800-466-8356)
One well-behaved family pet per room. Guest must notify front desk upon arrival. Guest is liable for any damages. In consideration of all guests, pets must never be left unattended in the guest rooms.

Motel 6 - Austin North
9420 I-35 North
Austin, TX
512-339-6161 (800-466-8356)
One well-behaved family pet per room. Guest must notify front desk upon arrival. Guest is liable for any

damages. In consideration of all guests, pets must never be left unattended in the guest rooms.

Motel 6 - Austin South - Airport
2707 Interregional Highway South
Austin, TX
512-444-5882 (800-466-8356)
One well-behaved family pet per room. Guest must notify front desk upon arrival. Guest is liable for any damages. In consideration of all guests, pets must never be left unattended in the guest rooms.

Red Lion
6121 N. I 35 at H 20
Austin, TX
512-323-5466
Dogs of all sizes are allowed and must be kept on a leash at all times when out of the room. There is a $25 one time pet fee per room. Multiple dogs may be allowed.

Red Roof Inn - Austin North
8210 N. Interregional Highway 35
Austin, TX
512-835-2200 (800-RED-ROOF)
One well-behaved family pet per room. Guest must notify front desk upon arrival. Guest is liable for any damages. In consideration of all guests, pets must never be left unattended in the guest rooms.

Red Roof Inn - Austin South
4701 South I-35
Austin, TX
512-448-0091 (800-RED-ROOF)
One well-behaved family pet per room. Guest must notify front desk upon arrival. Guest is liable for any damages. In consideration of all guests, pets must never be left unattended in the guest rooms.

Residence Inn by Marriott
12401 N Larmar Blvd
Austin, TX
512-977-0544
Dogs of all sizes are allowed. There is a $75 one time fee and a pet policy to sign at check in. Multiple dogs may be allowed.

Staybridge Suites - Northwest
10201 Stonelake Blvd
Austin, TX
512-349-0888 (877-270-6405)
There is a $50 one time pet fee. Dogs up to 80 pounds are allowed.

Studio 6 - Austin Midtown
6603 North I-35
Austin, TX
512-458-5453 (800-466-8356)

One well-behaved family pet per room. Guest must notify front desk upon arrival. Guest is liable for any damages. In consideration of all guests, pets must never be left unattended in the guest rooms.

Studio 6 - Austin Northwest
11901 Pavilion Boulevard
Austin, TX
512-258-3556 (800-466-8356)
One well-behaved family pet per room. Guest must notify front desk upon arrival. Guest is liable for any damages. In consideration of all guests, pets must never be left unattended in the guest rooms.

Super 8 Austin North
8128 N Interstate 35
Austin, TX
512-339-1300 (800-800-8000)
Dogs of all sizes are allowed. There are no additional pet fees. Pet must be kept in kennel when left alone. Smoking and non-smoking rooms are available for pet rooms. 2 dogs may be allowed.

TownePlace Suites Austin Northwest
10024 Capital of Texas Hwy North
Austin, TX
512-231-9360
Dogs of all sizes are allowed. There is a $75 one time pet fee per visit. . 2 dogs may be allowed.

Pecan Street Inn
1010 Pecan Street
Bastrop, TX
512-321-3315
Dogs of all sizes are allowed, however they may not stay in the rooms. There is a large laundry room where they can be crated for the night. There are no additional pet fees. Multiple dogs may be allowed.

La Quinta Inn Baytown
5215 I-10 East
Baytown, TX
281-421-7300 (800-531-5900)
Dogs of all sizes are allowed. There are no additional pet fees. Dogs may only be left in the room alone if they will be quiet and well behaved, and they must be leashed and cleaned up after. Multiple dogs may be allowed.

Motel 6 - Houston East - Baytown
8911 SR 146
Baytown, TX
281-576-5777 (800-466-8356)
One well-behaved family pet per room. Guest must notify front desk upon arrival. Guest is liable for any

damages. In consideration of all guests, pets must never be left unattended in the guest rooms.

Best Western Jefferson Inn
1610 IH-10 S
Beaumont, TX
409-842-0037 (800-780-7234)
Dogs are allowed for no additional pet fee. 2 dogs may be allowed.

Candlewood Suites Beaumont
5355 Clearwater Court
Beaumont, TX
409-842-9000 (877-270-6405)
Dogs of all sizes are allowed for an additional one time pet fee per room of $75 for 1 to 7 nights, and $150 for 8 nights or more. Multiple dogs may be allowed.

Holiday Inn
2095 N 11th Street at I-10
Beaumont, TX
409-892-2222 (877-270-6405)
Dogs up to 80 pounds are allowed for an additional one time pet fee of $25 per room. 2 dogs may be allowed.

Holiday Inn
3950 I-10 S at Walden Rd
Beaumont, TX
409-842-5995 (877-270-6405)
Dogs of all sizes are allowed for an additional pet fee of $25 per night per room. Multiple dogs may be allowed.

La Quinta Inn Beaumont Midtown
220 I-10 North
Beaumont, TX
409-838-9991 (800-531-5900)
Dogs of all sizes are allowed. There are no additional pet fees. There needs to be a credit card on file for damages, and dogs must be leashed and cleaned up after. Multiple dogs may be allowed.

Motel 6 - Beaumont
1155 I-10 South
Beaumont, TX
409-835-5913 (800-466-8356)
One well-behaved family pet per room. Guest must notify front desk upon arrival. Guest is liable for any damages. In consideration of all guests, pets must never be left unattended in the guest rooms.

Super 8 Beaumont/I-10 East
2850 I-10 East
Beaumont, TX
409-899-3040 (800-800-8000)
Dogs of all sizes are allowed. There is a $11.50 one time per pet fee per

visit. Smoking and non-smoking rooms are available for pet rooms. 2 dogs may be allowed.

Holiday Inn
3005 West Airport Freeway
Bedford, TX
817-267-3181 (877-270-6405)
Dogs of all sizes are allowed. There is a $25 per night pet fee per pet. Smoking and non-smoking rooms are available for pet rooms.

TownePlace Suites Fort Worth Bedford
2301 Plaza Parkway
Bedford, TX
817-283-3725
Dogs of all sizes are allowed. There is a $75 one time pet fee per visit. 2 dogs may be allowed.

Days Inn Beeville
400 South US 181 Bypass
Beeville, TX
361-358-4000 (800-329-7466)
Dogs of all sizes are allowed. There is a $5 per night pet fee per pet. 2 dogs may be allowed.

Motel 6 - Waco - Bellmead
1509 Hogan Lane
Bellmead, TX
254-799-4957 (800-466-8356)
One well-behaved family pet per room. Guest must notify front desk upon arrival. Guest is liable for any damages. In consideration of all guests, pets must never be left unattended in the guest rooms.

Motel 6 - Ft Worth - Benbrook
8601 Benbrook Boulevard
Benbrook, TX
817-249-8885 (800-466-8356)
One well-behaved family pet per room. Guest must notify front desk upon arrival. Guest is liable for any damages. In consideration of all guests, pets must never be left unattended in the guest rooms.

Motel 6 - Big Spring
600 West I-20
Big Spring, TX
432-267-1695 (800-466-8356)
One well-behaved family pet per room. Guest must notify front desk upon arrival. Guest is liable for any damages. In consideration of all guests, pets must never be left unattended in the guest rooms.

Super 8 Big Spring
700 West I-20
Big Spring, TX
432-267-1601 (800-800-8000)

Dogs of all sizes are allowed. There is a $6 per night pet fee per pet. Smoking and non-smoking rooms are available for pet rooms. 2 dogs may be allowed.

Best Western Texas Country Inn
35150 I-10 West, Hwy 46
Boerne, TX
830-249-9791 (800-780-7234)
Dogs are allowed for an additional one time pet fee of $20 per room. Multiple dogs may be allowed.

Days Inn Brady
2108 S Bridge St
Brady, TX
325-597-0789 (800-329-7466)
Dogs of all sizes are allowed. There are no additional pet fees. 2 dogs may be allowed.

America's Best Value Inn (former Days Inn)
201 Hwy 290 Loop East
Brenham, TX
979-830-1110 (800-DAYS-INN)
Dogs of all sizes are allowed. There is a $7 per night pet fee per pet. 2 dogs may be allowed.

Best Western Caprock Inn
321 Lubbock Inn
Brownfield, TX
806-637-9471 (800-780-7234)
Dogs are allowed for an additional one time fee of $10 per pet. Multiple dogs may be allowed.

Motel 6 - Brownsville
2255 North Expressway
Brownsville, TX
956-546-4699 (800-466-8356)
One well-behaved family pet per room. Guest must notify front desk upon arrival. Guest is liable for any damages. In consideration of all guests, pets must never be left unattended in the guest rooms.

Red Roof Inn - Brownsville
2377 North Expressway 83
Brownsville, TX
956-504-2300 (800-RED-ROOF)
One well-behaved family pet per room. Guest must notify front desk upon arrival. Guest is liable for any damages. In consideration of all guests, pets must never be left unattended in the guest rooms.

Residence Inn by Marriott
3975 N Expressway 83
Brownsville, TX
956-350-8100
Dogs of all sizes are allowed. There is a $75 one time fee and a pet

policy to sign at check in. Multiple dogs may be allowed.

Staybridge Suites Brownsville
2900 Pablo Kisel Blvd
Brownsville, TX
956-504-9500 (877-270-6405)
Dogs up to 75 pounds are allowed for an additional one time pet fee of $75 per room. 2 dogs may be allowed.

Best Value Brownwood Inn
410 E Commerce St
Brownwood, TX
325-646-3511 (877-646-3513)
Dogs are allowed for an additional fee of $10 per night per pet. Multiple dogs may be allowed.

Days Inn Brownwood
515 E Commerce
Brownwood, TX
325-646-2551 (800-329-7466)
Dogs of all sizes are allowed. There is a $15 one time per pet fee per visit. 2 dogs may be allowed.

Days Inn Fort Worth/Burleson
329 S Burleson Blvd
Burleson, TX
817-447-1111 (800-329-7466)
Dogs of all sizes are allowed. There is a $10 per night pet fee per pet. 2 dogs may be allowed.

Best Western Post Oak Inn
908 Buchanan Drive
Burnet, TX
512-756-4747 (800-780-7234)
Dogs are allowed for an additional fee of $10 per night per pet. Multiple dogs may be allowed.

Best Western Canton Inn
2251 N Trade Days Blvd
Canton, TX
903-567-6591 (800-780-7234)
Dogs up to 50 pounds are allowed for an additional fee of $5 per night per pet. 2 dogs may be allowed.

Best Western Palo Duro Canyon Inn & Suites
2801 4th Avenue
Canyon, TX
806-655-1818 (800-780-7234)
Dogs are allowed for an additional pet fee of $25 per night per room. 2 dogs may be allowed.

Holiday Inn Express Hotel & Suites
2901 4th Ave
Canyon, TX
806-655-4445 (877-270-6405)
Dogs of all sizes are allowed for an additional one time pet fee of $25

per room. Multiple dogs may be allowed.

The Mermaids Cove & Sculpture Ranch Cabins and Lodge
Hwy 386 & Eagle Rock Rd
Canyon Lake, TX
830-885-4297
themermaidcove.com
Have your pet join you in an area known for its outdoor adventure. Mermaids Cove offers cabin rentals and a 5 acre sculpture ranch.

Red Roof Inn - Dallas - Carrollton
1720 South Broadway Street
Carrollton, TX
972-245-1700 (800-RED-ROOF)
One well-behaved family pet per room. Guest must notify front desk upon arrival. Guest is liable for any damages. In consideration of all guests, pets must never be left unattended in the guest rooms.

Comfort Inn
300 E Whitestone Blvd
Cedar Park, TX
512-259-1810 (877-424-6423)
Dogs are allowed for an additional fee of $10 per night per pet. Dogs may not be left alone in the room. 2 dogs may be allowed.

Best Western Houston East
15919 I-10 East
Channelview, TX
281-452-1000 (800-780-7234)
One dog is allowed for an additional pet fee of $20 per night; a 2nd dog is an additional $10 per night. 2 dogs may be allowed.

Best Western Childress
1801 Ave F NW
Childress, TX
940-937-6353 (800-780-7234)
Dogs under 10 pounds are allowed for an additional one time fee of $10 per pet; $15 for dogs 10 to 20 pounds, and $20 for dogs over 20 pounds.. 2 dogs may be allowed.

Comfort Inn
1804 Avenue F NW
Childress, TX
940-937-6363 (877-424-6423)
Dogs are allowed for an additional fee of $10 per night per pet. Multiple dogs may be allowed.

Super 8 Childress
411 Ave FNE
Childress, TX
940-937-8825 (800-800-8000)
Dogs of all sizes are allowed. There is a $10 per night pet fee per pet.

Smoking and non-smoking rooms are available for pet rooms. 2 dogs may be allowed.

Best Western Red River Inn
902 W 2nd Street
Clarendon, TX
806-874-0160 (800-780-7234)
Dogs up to 50 pounds are allowed for an additional fee of $10 per night per pet. 2 dogs may be allowed.

La Quinta Inn Clute/Lake Jackson
1126 S. Hwy. 332 West
Clute, TX
979-265-7461 (800-531-5900)
Dogs of all sizes are allowed. There are no additional pet fees. Dogs must be leashed and cleaned up after. Multiple dogs may be allowed.

MainStay Suites
1003 W H 332
Clute, TX
979-388-9300
Dogs are allowed for an additional one time pet fee of $300 per room. 2 dogs may be allowed.

Motel 6 - Freeport - Clute
1000 SR 332
Clute, TX
979-265-4764 (800-466-8356)
One well-behaved family pet per room. Guest must notify front desk upon arrival. Guest is liable for all damages. In consideration of all guests, pets must never be left unattended in the guest rooms.

Howard Johnson Express Inn
3702 State Highway 6 South
College Station, TX
979-693-6810 (800-446-4656)
Well-behaved dogs of all sizes are allowed. There is a $5 per day additional pet fee.

La Quinta Inn College Station
607 Texas Avenue
College Station, TX
979-696-7777 (800-531-5900)
A dog of any size is allowed. There are no additional pet fees. Dogs may not be left unattended, and they must be leashed and cleaned up after.

Motel 6 - College Station - Bryan
2327 Texas Avenue South
College Station, TX
979-696-3379 (800-466-8356)
One well-behaved family pet per room. Guest must notify front desk upon arrival. Guest is liable for any damages. In consideration of all guests, pets must never be left unattended in the guest rooms.

TownePlace Suites Bryan College Station
1300 University Drive East
College Station, TX
979-260-8500
Dogs of all sizes are allowed. There is a $75 one time pet fee per visit. 2 dogs may be allowed.

Holiday Inn Express Hotel & Suites
4321 I-10
Columbus, TX
979-733-9300 (877-270-6405)
Dogs of all sizes are allowed for an additional one time fee of $25 per pet. Multiple dogs may be allowed.

Holiday Inn Express Hotel and Suites
2207 Culver Street
Commerce, TX
903-886-4777 (877-270-6405)
Dogs up to 50 pounds are allowed for an additional fee of $25 per night per pet. 2 dogs may be allowed.

La Quinta Inn & Suites Conroe
4006 Sprayberry Lane
Conroe, TX
936-228-0790 (800-531-5900)
Dogs of all sizes are allowed. There are no additional pet fees. There is a pet policy to sign at check in. Dogs must be quiet, well behaved, leashed and cleaned up after. Multiple dogs may be allowed.

Motel 6 - Conroe
820 I-45 South
Conroe, TX
936-760-4003 (800-466-8356)
One well-behaved family pet per room. Guest must notify front desk upon arrival. Guest is liable for any damages. In consideration of all guests, pets must never be left unattended in the guest rooms.

Bayfront Inn
601 North Shoreline Blvd.
Corpus Christi, TX
361-883-7271
There is a $20 pet fee for every 3 days of a stay.

Best Western Garden Inn
11217 IH-37
Corpus Christi, TX
361-241-6675 (800-780-7234)
Dogs are allowed for an additional fee of $15 per night per pet. Multiple dogs may be allowed.

Comfort Inn and Suites
3838 H 77
Corpus Christi, TX

361-241-6363 (877-424-6423)
Dogs are allowed for an additional pet fee of $20 per night per room. 2 dogs may be allowed.

Days Inn Corpus Christi
2838 SPID
Corpus Christi, TX
361-854-0005 (800-329-7466)
Dogs of all sizes are allowed. There is a $30 one time per pet fee per visit. 2 dogs may be allowed.

Holiday Inn
1102 S. Shoreline Blvd
Corpus Christi, TX
361-883-5731 (877-270-6405)
Dogs of all sizes are allowed for an additional one time pet fee of $20 per room. Multiple dogs may be allowed.

Holiday Inn - Padre Island Drive
5549 Leopard St.
Corpus Christi, TX
361-289-5100 (877-270-6405)
basshotels.com/holiday-inn
Dogs of all sizes are allowed for an additional one time fee of $25 per pet. Multiple dogs may be allowed.

La Quinta Inn Corpus Christi North
5155 I-37 North
Corpus Christi, TX
361-888-5721 (800-531-5900)
Dogs of all sizes are allowed. There are no additional pet fees. Dogs must be leashed and cleaned up after. Multiple dogs may be allowed.

Motel 6 - Corpus Christi East - N. Padre
8202 South Padre Island Drive
Corpus Christi, TX
361-991-8858 (800-466-8356)
All well-behaved dogs are welcome. There are no additional pet fees.

Motel 6 - Corpus Christi Northwest
845 Lantana Street
Corpus Christi, TX
361-289-9397 (800-466-8356)
One well-behaved family pet per room. Guest must notify front desk upon arrival. Guest is liable for any damages. In consideration of all guests, pets must never be left unattended in the guest rooms.

Quality Inn and Suites
3202 Surfside Blvd
Corpus Christi, TX
361-883-7456 (877-424-6423)
Dogs are allowed for an additional pet fee of $20 per night per room. 2 dogs may be allowed.

Red Roof Inn - Corpus Christi -

Airport
6301 Interstate 37
Corpus Christi, TX
361-289-6925 (800-RED-ROOF)
One well-behaved family pet per room. Guest must notify front desk upon arrival. Guest is liable for any damages. In consideration of all guests, pets must never be left unattended in the guest rooms.

Red Roof Inn - Corpus Christi South
6805 South Padre Island Drive
Corpus Christi, TX
361-992-9222 (800-RED-ROOF)
One well-behaved family pet per room. Guest must notify front desk upon arrival. Guest is liable for any damages. In consideration of all guests, pets must never be left unattended in the guest rooms.

Residence Inn by Marriott
5229 Blanche Moore Drive
Corpus Christi, TX
361-985-1113
Dogs of all sizes are allowed. There is a $75 one time fee per pet and a pet policy to sign at check in. Multiple dogs may be allowed.

Surfside Condo Apartments
15005 Windward Drive
Corpus Christi, TX
361-949-8128 (800-548-4585)
surfsidecondos.com/
Dogs up to 50 pounds are allowed. There is a $15 per day pet charge and a $200 refundable pet deposit.

Best Western Nursanickel Motel
102 Scott St
Dalhart, TX
806-244-5637 (800-780-7234)
Dogs up to 50 pounds are allowed for an additional fee of $5 per night per pet. Multiple dogs may be allowed.

Best Western Executive Inn
12670 E Northwest Highway
Dallas, TX
972-613-5000 (800-780-7234)
Dogs are allowed for an additional fee of $10 per night per pet. Multiple dogs may be allowed.

Candlewood Suites
12525 Greenville Avenue
Dallas, TX
972-669-9606 (877-270-6405)
One dog is allowed for an additional pet fee of $75 for 1 to 6 nights, and $150 for 7 nights or more.

Candlewood Suites
7930 North Stemmons Freeway

Dallas, TX
214-631-3333 (877-270-6405)
Dogs of all sizes are allowed for an additional one time fee of $75 per pet. 2 dogs may be allowed.

Comfort Inn by the Galleria
14975 Landmark Blvd
Dallas, TX
972-701-0881 (877-424-6423)
Dogs are allowed for an additional pet fee of $10 per night per room. 2 dogs may be allowed.

Crowne Plaza Suites
7800 Alpha Rd
Dallas, TX
972-233-7600 (877-270-6405)
Dogs of all sizes are allowed for a $100 refundable deposit plus an additional one time pet fee of $25 per room. 2 dogs may be allowed.

Dallas Marriott Suites Market Center
2493 N Stemmons Freeway
Dallas, TX
214-905-0050 (800-228-9290)
One dog of any size is allowed. There is a $50 one time additional pet fee. Dogs must be leashed, cleaned up after, and a contact number left with the front desk if they are in the room alone.

Embassy Suites Hotel Dallas - Market Center
2727 Stemmons Freeway
Dallas, TX
214-630-5332
Dogs of all sizes are allowed. If you have a larger dog please call the hotel directly to get approval for your dog. There is a $25 per night pet fee per pet. Dogs are not allowed to be left alone in the room.

Harvey Hotel
7815 LBJ Freeway
Dallas, TX
972-960-7000
There is a $125 deposit for pets and $100 is refundable.

Hawthorn Suites
7900 Brookriver Dr
Dallas, TX
214-688-1010
There is a $50 one time pet fee. Dogs must be less than 75 pounds.

Hota Zaza
2332 Leonard Street
Dallas, TX
214-468-8399 (800-597-8399)
hotelzaza.com/dallas
This luxury boutique hotel is located

in the city's entertainment/arts and business district offering a wide variety of activities and recreational opportunities. Their restaurant Dragonfly has outside seating, weather permitting, where your pet may dine with you. Dogs up to 50 pounds are allowed for an additional fee of $50 per pet for the 1st night and $25 for each additional night. 2 dogs may be allowed.

Hotel Lumen
6101 Hillcrest Ave
Dallas, TX
214-219-2400 (800-908-1140)
hotellumen.com
This Kimpton boutique hotel allows dogs of all sizes. There are no additional pet fees.

Hotel Palomar Dallas
5300 E Mockingbird Lane
Dallas, TX
214-520-7969 (888-253-9030)
hotelpalomar-dallas.com/
With sophisticated modern architecture and a rich color scheme, this luxury boutique hotel offers 198 guestrooms and upscale suites. Some of the highlights include 2 great restaurants (Central 214-with an exhibition kitchen and Trader Vic?s), plenty of meeting space, an Exhale Spa, a pool, 24 hour room service and business center, and a hosted evening wine reception. Dogs of all sizes are allowed for no additional fee unless you purchase their Pet Package which includes a big comfy bed, treats, water and bowl, and a one-hour yoga-massage combo. Dogs must be quiet, leashed, and cleaned up after. Multiple dogs may be allowed.

La Quinta Inn & Suites Dallas Addison-Galleria
14925 Landmark Blvd.
Dallas, TX
972-404-0004 (800-531-5900)
Dogs of all sizes are allowed. There are no additional pet fees. Dogs may not be left unattended unless they will be quiet and well behaved. Dogs must be leashed and cleaned up after. Multiple dogs may be allowed.

La Quinta Inn & Suites Dallas North Central
10001 N. Central Expressway
Dallas, TX
214-361-8200 (800-531-5900)
Dogs of all sizes are allowed. There are no additional pet fees. Dogs must be leashed and cleaned up after. Dogs may not be left unattended unless they will be quiet,

well behaved, and a contact number is left with the front desk. Dogs are not allowed in the pool area. Multiple dogs may be allowed.

La Quinta Inn Dallas Cityplace
4440 North Central Expressway
Dallas, TX
214-821-4220 (800-531-5900)
Dogs of all sizes are allowed. There are no additional pet fees. Dogs must be leashed, cleaned up after, and removed for housekeeping. Multiple dogs may be allowed.

La Quinta Inn Dallas East (I-30)
8303 East R. L. Thornton Freeway
Dallas, TX
214-324-3731 (800-531-5900)
Dogs of all sizes are allowed. There are no additional pet fees. Dogs must be leashed, cleaned up after, and the front desk informed if there is a pet in the room alone. Multiple dogs may be allowed.

Motel 6 - Dallas - Forest Lane
2660 Forest Lane
Dallas, TX
972-484-9111 (800-466-8356)
One well-behaved family pet per room. Guest must notify front desk upon arrival. Guest is liable for any damages. In consideration of all guests, pets must never be left unattended in the guest rooms.

Motel 6 - Dallas - Josey Lane
2753 Forest Lane
Dallas, TX
972-620-2828 (800-466-8356)
One well-behaved family pet per room. Guest must notify front desk upon arrival. Guest is liable for any damages. In consideration of all guests, pets must never be left unattended in the guest rooms.

Motel 6 - Dallas East
8108 East RL Thornton Freeway
Dallas, TX
214-388-8741 (800-466-8356)
One well-behaved family pet per room. Guest must notify front desk upon arrival. Guest is liable for any damages. In consideration of all guests, pets must never be left unattended in the guest rooms.

Motel 6 - Dallas Northeast
10921 Estate Lane
Dallas, TX
214-340-2299 (800-466-8356)
One well-behaved family pet per room. Guest must notify front desk upon arrival. Guest is liable for any damages. In consideration of all

guests, pets must never be left unattended in the guest rooms.

Motel 6 - Dallas Northwest
10335 Gardner Road
Dallas, TX
972-506-8100 (800-466-8356)
One well-behaved family pet per room. Guest must notify front desk upon arrival. Guest is liable for any damages. In consideration of all guests, pets must never be left unattended in the guest rooms.

Motel 6 - Dallas Southwest
4220 Independence Drive
Dallas, TX
972-296-3331 (800-466-8356)
One well-behaved family pet per room. Guest must notify front desk upon arrival. Guest is liable for any damages. In consideration of all guests, pets must never be left unattended in the guest rooms.

Quality Inn and Suites
2421 Walnut Hill Lane
Dallas, TX
972-484-3330 (877-424-6423)
Dogs are allowed for an additional one time pet fee of $25 per room. Multiple dogs may be allowed.

Red Roof Inn - Dallas - Market Center
1550 Empire Central Drive
Dallas, TX
214-638-5151 (800-RED-ROOF)
One well-behaved family pet per room. Guest must notify front desk upon arrival. Guest is liable for any damages. In consideration of all guests, pets must never be left unattended in the guest rooms.

Renaissance Hotel
2222 Stemmons Freeway
Dallas, TX
214-631-2222
Dogs of all sizes are allowed. There is a $75 one time fee per pet and a pet policy to sign at check in. Multiple dogs may be allowed.

Residence Inn by Marriott
14975 Quorum Drive
Dallas, TX
972-866-9933
Dogs of all sizes are allowed. There is a $75 one time fee and a pet policy to sign at check in. Multiple dogs may be allowed.

Residence Inn by Marriott
10333 N Central Expressway
Dallas, TX
214-750-8220

Dogs of all sizes are allowed. There is a $75 one time fee per pet and a pet policy to sign at check in. Multiple dogs may be allowed.

Residence Inn by Marriott
6950 N Stemmons Freeway
Dallas, TX
214-631-2472
Dogs of all sizes are allowed. There is a $75 one time fee and a pet policy to sign at check in. Multiple dogs may be allowed.

Residence Inn by Marriott
7642 LBJ Freeway
Dallas, TX
972-503-1333
Dogs of all sizes are allowed. There is a $75 one time fee and a pet policy to sign at check in. Multiple dogs may be allowed.

Sheraton Suites Market Center
2102 Stemmons Freeway
Dallas, TX
214-747-3000 (888-625-5144)
Dogs up to 80 pounds are allowed for no additional pet fee. Dogs may not be left alone in the room.

Staybridge Suites
7880 Alpha Rd
Dallas, TX
972-391-0000 (877-270-6405)
Dogs of all sizes are allowed for an additional one time pet fee per room of $125 for 1 to 6 nights, and $175 for 7 nights or more. 2 dogs may be allowed.

Studio 6 - Dallas Northeast
9801 Adleta Court
Dallas, TX
214-342-5400 (800-466-8356)
One well-behaved family pet per room. Guest must notify front desk upon arrival. Guest is liable for any damages. In consideration of all guests, pets must never be left unattended in the guest rooms.

Studio 6 - Dallas Northwest
2395 Stemmons Trail
Dallas, TX
214-904-1400 (800-466-8356)
One well-behaved family pet per room. Guest must notify front desk upon arrival. Guest is liable for any damages. In consideration of all guests, pets must never be left unattended in the guest rooms.

The Mansion on Turtle Creek
2821 Turtle Creek Blvd
Dallas, TX
214-559-2100

mansiononturtlecreek.com/
There is a $200 one time pet fee.

Red Roof Inn - Dallas - DeSoto
1401 North Beckley Avenue
DeSoto, TX
972-224-7100 (800-RED-ROOF)
One well-behaved family pet per
room. Guest must notify front desk
upon arrival. Guest is liable for any
damages. In consideration of all
guests, pets must never be left
unattended in the guest rooms.

Best Western Decatur Inn
1801 S Hwy 287
Decatur, TX
940-627-5982 (800-780-7234)
Dogs are allowed for an additional
fee of $15 per night per pet. 2 dogs
may be allowed.

Days Inn Decatur
1900 S Trinity Street
Decatur, TX
940-627-2463 (800-329-7466)
Dogs of all sizes are allowed. There
is a $10 per night pet fee per pet. 2
dogs may be allowed.

Best Western Deer Park Inn & Suites
1401 Center Street
Deer Park, TX
281-476-1900 (800-780-7234)
Dogs are allowed for an additional
fee of $10 per night per pet. 2 dogs
may be allowed.

Best Western Inn of Del Rio
810 Ave F
Del Rio, TX
830-775-7511 (800-780-7234)
Dogs are allowed for an additional
fee of $10 per night per pet. 2 dogs
may be allowed.

Comfort Inn and Suites
3616 Veterans Blvd
Del Rio, TX
830-775-2933 (877-424-6423)
Dogs are allowed for an additional
fee of $10 per night per pet. Multiple
dogs may be allowed.

La Quinta Inn Del Rio
2005 Veterans Blvd.
Del Rio, TX
830-775-7591 (800-531-5900)
Dogs of all sizes are allowed. There
are no additional pet fees. Dogs
must be leashed and cleaned up
after. A contact number must be left
with the front desk if there is a pet
unattended in the room. Multiple
dogs may be allowed.

Motel 6 - Del Rio

2115 Veterans Boulevard
Del Rio, TX
830-774-2115 (800-466-8356)
One well-behaved family pet per
room. Guest must notify front desk
upon arrival. Guest is liable for any
damages. In consideration of all
guests, pets must never be left
unattended in the guest rooms.

Motel 6 - Denison
615 North Highway 75
Denison, TX
903-465-4446 (800-466-8356)
One well-behaved family pet per
room. Guest must notify front desk
upon arrival. Guest is liable for any
damages. In consideration of all
guests, pets must never be left
unattended in the guest rooms.

Holiday Inn Express
801 Hwy 75
Denison-Lake Texoma, TX
903-464-0340 (877-270-6405)
Dogs up to 50 pounds are allowed
for an additional one time fee of $25
per pet. 2 dogs may be allowed.

La Quinta Inn Denton
700 Ft. Worth Dr.
Denton, TX
940-387-5840 (800-531-5900)
Dogs of all sizes are allowed. There
are no additional pet fees. Dogs
must be leashed and cleaned up
after. Multiple dogs may be allowed.

Motel 6 - Denton
4125 I-35 North
Denton, TX
940-566-4798 (800-466-8356)
One well-behaved family pet per
room. Guest must notify front desk
upon arrival. Guest is liable for any
damages. In consideration of all
guests, pets must never be left
unattended in the guest rooms.

Quality Inn and Suites
1500 Dallas Drive
Denton, TX
940-387-3511 (877-424-6423)
Dogs are allowed for an additional
one time fee of $20 per pet. Multiple
dogs may be allowed.

Radisson Hotel Denton
2211 I-35 East North
Denton, TX
940-565-8499
Dogs of all sizes are allowed. There
are no additional pet fees.

Best Western Diboll Inn
910 North Temple Dr
Diboll, TX

936-829-2055 (800-780-7234)
One dog is allowed for an additional
pet fee of $7 per night.

Best Western Windsor Inn
1701 S Dumas Avenue
Dumas, TX
806-935-9644 (800-780-7234)
Dogs are allowed for a $20
refundable deposit plus an additional
fee of $10 per night per pet. 2 dogs
may be allowed.

Holiday Inn Express
1525 South Dumas Ave
Dumas, TX
806-935-4000 (877-270-6405)
Dogs of all sizes are allowed for an
additional one time pet fee of $15 per
room. Multiple dogs may be allowed.

Motel 6 - Dallas - Duncanville
202 Jellison Boulevard
Duncanville, TX
972-296-0345 (800-466-8356)
One well-behaved family pet per
room. Guest must notify front desk
upon arrival. Guest is liable for any
damages. In consideration of all
guests, pets must never be left
unattended in the guest rooms.

Holiday Inn Express Hotel and Suites
2007 Veterans Blvd
Eagle Pass, TX
830-757-3050 (877-270-6405)
One dog up to 10 pounds is allowed
for no additional pet fee.

La Quinta Inn Eagle Pass
2525 E. Main St.
Eagle Pass, TX
830-773-7000 (800-531-5900)
Dogs of all sizes are allowed. There
are no additional pet fees. Dogs
must be well behaved, leashed, and
cleaned up after. Multiple dogs may
be allowed.

Super 8 Eastland
3900 I-20 East
Eastland, TX
254-629-3336 (800-800-8000)
Dogs of all sizes are allowed. There
is a $5 per night pet fee per small pet
and $10 per large pet. Smoking and
non-smoking rooms are available for
pet rooms. 2 dogs may be allowed.

Best Western Edinburg Inn and
Suites
2708 S Business Hwy 281 (Closner
Blvd)
Edinburg, TX
956-318-0442 (800-780-7234)
Dogs are allowed for an additional
fee of $10 per night per pet. 2 dogs

may be allowed.

Camino Real Hotel
101 S El Paso St
El Paso, TX
915-534-3000
caminoreal.com/elpaso/
There are no additional pet fees.

Chase Suite Hotel by Woodfin
6791 Montana Ave
El Paso, TX
915-772-8000
All well-behaved dogs are welcome.
Every room is a suite with a full
kitchen. Hotel amenities include a
complimentary breakfast buffet.
There is a $5 per day pet fee.

Hilton
2027 Airway Blvd
El Paso, TX
915-778-4241
Dogs are allowed for a $150
refundable pet deposit per room.
There may be 1 large or 2 small dogs
per room.

La Quinta Inn El Paso Airport
6140 Gateway East
El Paso, TX
915-778-9321 (800-531-5900)
Dogs of all sizes are allowed. There
are no additional pet fees. Dogs
must be leashed and cleaned up
after. The front desk must be
informed when a pet is in the room
alone, and they are not allowed to be
left for long periods. 2 dogs may be
allowed.

La Quinta Inn El Paso Bartlett
7620 North Mesa
El Paso, TX
915-585-2999 (800-531-5900)
Dogs of all sizes are allowed. There
are no additional pet fees. Dogs
must be kept leashed. Multiple dogs
may be allowed.

La Quinta Inn El Paso Cielo Vista
9125 Gateway West
El Paso, TX
915-593-8400 (800-531-5900)
Dogs of all sizes are allowed. There
are no additional pet fees. Dogs
must be leashed and cleaned up
after. The Do Not Disturb sign must
be placed on the door if there is a pet
unattended in the room. Multiple
dogs may be allowed.

La Quinta Inn El Paso East
7944 Gateway East
El Paso, TX
915-591-3300 (800-531-5900)
Dogs of all sizes are allowed. There

are no additional pet fees. Dogs
must be leashed and cleaned up
after. Multiple dogs may be allowed.

La Quinta Inn El Paso Lomaland
11033 Gateway Blvd. West
El Paso, TX
915-591-2244 (800-531-5900)
Dogs of all sizes are allowed. There
are no additional pet fees. Dogs
must be leashed, cleaned up after,
and crated or removed for
housekeeping. Multiple dogs may
be allowed.

La Quinta Inn El Paso West
7550 Remcon Circle
El Paso, TX
915-833-2522 (800-531-5900)
Dogs of all sizes are allowed. There
are no additional pet fees. Dogs
may not be left unattended, and
they must be leashed and cleaned
up after. 2 dogs may be allowed.

Motel 6 - El Paso Central
4800 Gateway Boulevard East
El Paso, TX
915-533-7521 (800-466-8356)
One well-behaved family pet per
room. Guest must notify front desk
upon arrival. Guest is liable for any
damages. In consideration of all
guests, pets must never be left
unattended in the guest rooms.

Motel 6 - El Paso East
1330 Lomaland Drive
El Paso, TX
915-592-6386 (800-466-8356)
One well-behaved family pet per
room. Guest must notify front desk
upon arrival. Guest is liable for any
damages. In consideration of all
guests, pets must never be left
unattended in the guest rooms.

Red Roof Inn - El Paso East
11400 Chito Samaniego Drive
El Paso, TX
915-599-8877 (800-RED-ROOF)
One well-behaved family pet per
room. Guest must notify front desk
upon arrival. Guest is liable for any
damages. In consideration of all
guests, pets must never be left
unattended in the guest rooms.

Red Roof Inn - El Paso West
7530 Remcon Circle
El Paso, TX
915-587-9977 (800-RED-ROOF)
One well-behaved family pet per
room. Guest must notify front desk
upon arrival. Guest is liable for any
damages. In consideration of all
guests, pets must never be left

unattended in the guest rooms.

Sleep Inn
953 Sunland Park Drive
El Paso, TX
915-585-7577 (877-424-6423)
Dogs are allowed for an additional
one time fee of $20 per pet. 2 dogs
may be allowed.

Studio 6 - El Paso East
11049 Gateway Boulevard West
El Paso, TX
915-594-8533 (800-466-8356)
One well-behaved family pet per
room. Guest must notify front desk
upon arrival. Guest is liable for any
damages. In consideration of all
guests, pets must never be left
unattended in the guest rooms.

Days Inn Dallas/Euless
13954 Trinity Blvd
Euless, TX
817-399-9500 (800-329-7466)
Dogs of all sizes are allowed. There
is a $10 per night pet fee per pet. 2
dogs may be allowed.

La Quinta Inn Dallas DFW Airport
West-Euless
1001 W. Airport Freeway
Euless, TX
817-540-0233 (800-531-5900)
Dogs of all sizes are allowed. There
are no additional pet fees. There is a
pet waiver to sign at check in. Dogs
may only be left in the room alone if
they will be quiet and well behaved,
and they must be leashed, cleaned
up after, and crated or removed for
housekeeping. Multiple dogs may be
allowed.

Motel 6 - Dallas - Euless
110 West Airport Freeway
Euless, TX
817-545-0141 (800-466-8356)
One well-behaved family pet per
room. Guest must notify front desk
upon arrival. Guest is liable for any
damages. In consideration of all
guests, pets must never be left
unattended in the guest rooms.

Comfort Inn
14040 Stemmons Road
Farmers Branch, TX
972-406-3030 (877-424-6423)
Dogs are allowed for an additional
fee of $15 per night per pet. Multiple
dogs may be allowed.

La Quinta Inn Dallas Northwest-
Farmers Branch
13235 Stemmons Frwy.
Farmers Branch, TX

972-620-7333 (800-531-5900)
Dogs of all sizes are allowed. There are no additional pet fees. Dogs must be leashed, cleaned up after, and crated if left alone in the room. Multiple dogs may be allowed.

Best Western Floresville Inn
1720 10th St
Floresville, TX
830-393-0443 (800-780-7234)
Dogs are allowed for an additional fee of $10 per night per pet. Multiple dogs may be allowed.

Hotel Limpia
P.O. Box 1341
Fort Davis, TX
800-662-5517 (800-662-5517)
hotellimpia.com/
This restored 1912 historic hotel charges an additional $10 per day pet charge.

Motel 6 - Ft Stockton
3001 West Dickinson Boulevard
Fort Stockton, TX
432-336-9737 (800-466-8356)
One well-behaved family pet per room. Guest must notify front desk upon arrival. Guest is liable for any damages. In consideration of all guests, pets must never be left unattended in the guest rooms.

Candlewood Suites
5201 Endicott Avenue
Fort Worth, TX
817-838-8229 (877-270-6405)
Dogs up to 50 pounds are allowed for an additional one time fee per pet of $75 for 1 to 6 nights, and $150 for 7 nights or more. 2 dogs may be allowed.

Days Inn Fort Worth
1551 S University Dr
Fort Worth, TX
817-336-9823 (800-329-7466)
Dogs of all sizes are allowed. There is a $10 per night pet fee per pet. 2 dogs may be allowed.

Green Oaks Hotel
6901 West Freeway
Fort Worth, TX
817-738-7311 (800-433-2174)
greenoakshotel.com
The Green Oaks hotel is located on the suburban west side of Fort Worth's business district and 5 minutes from downtown. Pets are welcome for a $25.00 one time pet fee.

La Quinta Inn & Suites Fort Worth Southwest

4900 Bryant Irvin Rd.
Fort Worth, TX
817-370-2700 (800-531-5900)
Dogs of all sizes are allowed. There are no additional pet fees. Dogs must be well behaved, leashed, and cleaned up after. A contact number must be left with the front desk if there is a pet alone in the room. Multiple dogs may be allowed.

Motel 6 - Ft Worth East
1236 Oakland Boulevard
Fort Worth, TX
817-834-7361 (800-466-8356)
One well-behaved family pet per room. Guest must notify front desk upon arrival. Guest is liable for any damages. In consideration of all guests, pets must never be left unattended in the guest rooms.

Motel 6 - Ft Worth North
3271 I-35W
Fort Worth, TX
817-625-4359 (800-466-8356)
One well-behaved family pet per room. Guest must notify front desk upon arrival. Guest is liable for any damages. In consideration of all guests, pets must never be left unattended in the guest rooms.

Motel 6 - Ft Worth South
6600 South Freeway
Fort Worth, TX
817-293-8595 (800-466-8356)
One well-behaved family pet per room. Guest must notify front desk upon arrival. Guest is liable for any damages. In consideration of all guests, pets must never be left unattended in the guest rooms.

Motel 6 - Ft Worth West
8701 I-30 West
Fort Worth, TX
817-244-9740 (800-466-8356)
One well-behaved family pet per room. Guest must notify front desk upon arrival. Guest is liable for any damages. In consideration of all guests, pets must never be left unattended in the guest rooms.

Residence Inn by Marriott
5801 Sandshell
Fort Worth, TX
817-439-1300
Dogs of all sizes are allowed. There is a $75 one time fee and a pet policy to sign at check in. Multiple dogs may be allowed.

Residence Inn by Marriott
1701 S University Drive
Fort Worth, TX

817-870-1011
Dogs of all sizes are allowed. There is a $75 one time fee and a pet policy to sign at check in. Multiple dogs may be allowed.

The Texas White House Bed and Breakfast
1417 Eighth Avenue
Fort Worth, TX
817-923-3597 (800-279-6491)
texaswhitehouse.com/
In addition to providing spacious accommodations and various amenities, they also provide a great starting point for exploring the numerous local attractions and activities. Dogs are allowed for no additional pet fee; they must be crated when left alone in the room. 2 dogs may be allowed.

TownePlace Suites Fort Worth Southwest
4200 International Plaza
Fort Worth, TX
817-732-2224
Dogs of all sizes are allowed. There is a $75 one time pet fee per visit. 2 dogs may be allowed.

Barons CreekSide
316 Goehmann Lane
Fredericksburg, TX
830-990-4048
baronscreekside.com/
Termed as rustic and romantic, this retreat offers a wonderful country ambiance, 26 wooded acres with ponds and a creek, and a close location to the town's attractions. Dogs are allowed for an additional fee of $30 per night per pet, and the fee may be reduced for longer stays. Multiple dogs may be allowed.

Quality Inn
908 S Adams Street
Fredericksburg, TX
830-997-9811 (877-424-6423)
Dogs are allowed for an additional fee of $20 per night per pet. Multiple dogs may be allowed.

Best Western Inn by the Bay
3902 N Hwy 35
Fulton, TX
361-729-8351 (800-780-7234)
Dogs are allowed for an additional fee of $10 per night per pet. Multiple dogs may be allowed.

La Quinta Inn Galveston
1402 Seawall Blvd.
Galveston, TX
409-763-1224 (800-531-5900)
Dogs of all sizes are allowed. There

are no additional pet fees. Dogs must be leashed and cleaned up after. Dogs must be crated when left unattended in the room or the Do Not Disturb sign placed on the door. Multiple dogs may be allowed.

Motel 6 - Galveston
7404 Avenue J
Galveston, TX
409-740-3794 (800-466-8356)
One well-behaved family pet per room. Guest must notify front desk upon arrival. Guest is liable for any damages. In consideration of all guests, pets must never be left unattended in the guest rooms.

Sand 'N Sea Pirates Beach Vacation Rentals
13706 FM 3005
Galveston, TX
800-880-2554
They offer several pet-friendly vacation home rentals.

The Reef Resort
8502 Seawall Blvd.
Galveston, TX
409-740-0492
The weight limit for dogs is usually 25 pounds, but they can allow a larger dog if he or she is well-behaved. There is a $20 per day pet fee and a $150 refundable pet deposit. There are no designated smoking or non-smoking rooms.

Best Western Lakeview Inn
1635 East I-30 at Chaha Rd
Garland, TX
972-303-1601 (800-780-7234)
Dogs up to 20 pounds are allowed for an additional fee of $5 per night per pet; the fee is $10 for dogs over 20 pounds. Multiple dogs may be allowed.

Days Inn Dallas/Garland
6222 Broadway Blvd
Garland, TX
972-226-7621 (800-329-7466)
Dogs of all sizes are allowed. There is a $10 per night pet fee per pet. 2 dogs may be allowed.

La Quinta Inn Dallas Garland
12721 I-635
Garland, TX
972-271-7581 (800-531-5900)
Dogs of all sizes are allowed. There are no additional pet fees. Dogs must be leashed, cleaned up after, and crated or removed for housekeeping. Multiple dogs may be allowed.

Motel 6 - Dallas - Garland
436 West I-30
Garland, TX
972-226-7140 (800-466-8356)
One well-behaved family pet per room. Guest must notify front desk upon arrival. Guest is liable for any damages. In consideration of all guests, pets must never be left unattended in the guest rooms.

Best Western Chateau Ville Motor Inn
2501 E Main St
Gatesville, TX
254-865-2281 (800-780-7234)
Dogs are allowed for no additional pet fee. Extra large dogs are not allowed. 2 dogs may be allowed.

Best Western George West Executive Inn
208 N Nueces Hwy 281 N
George West, TX
361-449-3300 (800-780-7234)
Dogs are allowed for an additional one time fee of $25 per pet. Multiple dogs may be allowed.

La Quinta Inn Georgetown
333 North I-35
Georgetown, TX
512-869-2541 (800-531-5900)
Dogs of all sizes are allowed. There are no additional pet fees, but a credit card must be on file. Dogs must be leashed, cleaned up after, and removed from the room for housekeeping. Multiple dogs may be allowed.

Country Woods Inn
420 Grand Avenue
Glen Rose, TX
817-279-3002
countrywoodsinn.com/
From the barnyard, to the swimming hole, to the scenic wildlife trails, farm and wildlife, and numerous activities, there is something for everyone at this 40 acre family vacation getaway. Dogs are allowed for an additional one time pet fee of $25 per room. 2 dogs may be allowed.

Best Western Granbury Inn & Suites
1517 Plaza Drive
Granbury, TX
817-573-4239 (800-780-7234)
Dogs are allowed for an additional pet fee of $25 per night per room. Multiple dogs may be allowed.

Comfort Inn
1201 Plaza Drive

Granbury, TX
817-573-2611 (877-424-6423)
Dogs are allowed for an additional fee of $15 per night per pet. Multiple dogs may be allowed.

La Quinta Inn Dallas Grand Prairie
1410 N.W. 19th St.
Grand Prairie, TX
972-641-3021 (800-531-5900)
Dogs of all sizes are allowed. There are no additional pet fees. Dogs may not be left unattended for long periods, and they must be leashed and cleaned up after. Multiple dogs may be allowed.

Motel 6 - Dallas - Grand Prairie
406 Palace Parkway
Grand Prairie, TX
972-642-9424 (800-466-8356)
One well-behaved family pet per room. Guest must notify front desk upon arrival. Guest is liable for any damages. In consideration of all guests, pets must never be left unattended in the guest rooms.

Super 8 Grapevine/DFW Arpt/NW
250 E State Hwy 114
Grapevine, TX
817-329-7222 (800-800-8000)
Dogs of all sizes are allowed. There is a $10 per night pet fee per pet. Smoking and non-smoking rooms are available for pet rooms. 2 dogs may be allowed.

Holiday Inn Express Hotel and Suites
2901 Mustang Crossing
Greenville, TX
903-454-8680 (877-270-6405)
Dogs of all sizes are allowed for a $100 refundable deposit. 2 dogs may be allowed.

La Quinta Inn & Suites Greenville
3001 Mustang Crossing
Greenville, TX
903-454-3700 (800-531-5900)
Dogs of all sizes are allowed. There are no additional pet fees. There is a pet waiver to sign at check in. Dogs must be leashed, cleaned up after, and crated or removed for housekeeping. Multiple dogs may be allowed.

Motel 6 - Greenville
5109 I-30
Greenville, TX
903-455-0515 (800-466-8356)
One well-behaved family pet per room. Guest must notify front desk upon arrival. Guest is liable for any damages. In consideration of all guests, pets must never be left

unattended in the guest rooms.

Super 8 Greenville
5010 Hwy 69 South
Greenville, TX
903-454-3736 (800-800-8000)
Dogs of all sizes are allowed. There is a $7.50 per night pet fee per pet under 10 pounds. There is a $10 per night pet fee per pet between 10-20 pounds. There is a $15 per night pet fee per pet between 20-25 pounds. There is a $25 per night pet fee per pet over 25 pounds. Smoking and non-smoking rooms are available for pet rooms. 2 dogs may be allowed.

Best Western Executive Inn
207 US Highway 77 S
Hallettsville, TX
361-798-9200 (800-780-7234)
Dogs are allowed for an additional fee of $10 per night per pet. The fee may be reduced for multiple days. 2 dogs may be allowed.

Country Inns & Suites by Carlson
3825 S. Expressway 83
Harlingen, TX
956-428-0043
Dogs up to 75 pounds are allowed. There is a $25 one time additional pet fee.

La Quinta Inn Harlingen
1002 S. Expwy. 83
Harlingen, TX
956-428-6888 (800-531-5900)
Dogs of all sizes are allowed; just inform them at check in that you have a pet. There are no additional pet fees. Dogs must be leashed, cleaned up after, and crated for housekeeping. Multiple dogs may be allowed.

Motel 6 - Harlingen
205 North Expressway 77
Harlingen, TX
956-423-9292 (800-466-8356)
One well-behaved family pet per room. Guest must notify front desk upon arrival. Guest is liable for any damages. In consideration of all guests, pets must never be left unattended in the guest rooms.

Best Western Red Carpet Inn
830 W 1st St
Hereford, TX
806-364-0540 (800-780-7234)
Dogs are allowed for no additional pet fee. Dogs may not be left alone in the room at any time, and they must be removed for housekeeping. 2 dogs may be allowed.

Holiday Inn Express
1400 West First St
Hereford, TX
806-364-3322 (877-270-6405)
Dogs of all sizes are allowed for an additional fee of $20 per night per pet. Multiple dogs may be allowed.

Best Western Hillsboro Inn
307 I-35 W Service Rd
Hillsboro, TX
254-582-8465 (800-780-7234)
Dogs are allowed for an additional pet fee of $10 per night per room. 2 dogs may be allowed.

Motel 6 - Hillsboro
1506 Hillview Drive
Hillsboro, TX
254-580-9000 (800-466-8356)
One well-behaved family pet per room. Guest must notify front desk upon arrival. Guest is liable for any damages. In consideration of all guests, pets must never be left unattended in the guest rooms.

Horseshoe Bay Resort Marriott Hotel
200 Hi Circle North
Horseshoe Bay, TX
830-598-8600 (800-228-9290)
Dogs of all sizes are allowed. There is a $100 one time fee per pet, and they they are allowed in the 1 and 2 bedroom condos only. After reservations are made at the 800 number, the hotel must also be called and informed that there will be pets so they can make sure you get an accommodating room. Dogs must be leashed, cleaned up after, and the Do Not Disturb sign put on the door and the front desk informed if they are in the room alone. 2 dogs may be allowed.

Baymont Inn Houston Hobby Airport
9902 Gulf Frwy.
Houston, TX
713-941-0900 (800-531-5900)
Dogs of all sizes are allowed. There are no additional pet fees. Dogs must be leashed and cleaned up after. The Do Not Disturb sign needs to be left on the door if there is a pet alone in the room. Multiple dogs may be allowed.

Candlewood Suites
4900 Loop Central Drive
Houston, TX
713-839-9411 (877-270-6405)
Dogs up to 80 pounds are allowed for an additional one time pet fee per room of $75 for 1 to 6 nights, and $150 for 7 or more nights. 2 dogs may be allowed.

Candlewood Suites
2737 Bay Area Blvd
Houston, TX
281-461-3060 (877-270-6405)
Dogs of all sizes are allowed for an additional one time pet fee per room of $75 for 1 to 6 nights, and $150 for 7 nights or more. Multiple dogs may be allowed.

Candlewood Suites
10503 Town and Country Way
Houston, TX
713-464-2677 (877-270-6405)
Dogs up to 80 pounds are allowed for an additional one time fee per pet of $75 for 1 to 6 nights, and $150 for 7 or more nights. 2 dogs may be allowed.

Comfort Inn Galleria/Westchase
9041 Westheimer Road
Houston, TX
713-783-1400 (877-424-6423)
Dogs are allowed for an additional one time fee of $25 per pet. Dogs must be flea free. 2 dogs may be allowed.

Comfort Suites
6221 Richmond Avenue
Houston, TX
713-787-0004 (877-424-6423)
Dogs are allowed for an additional one time fee of $50 per pet. Multiple dogs may be allowed.

Doubletree
5353 Westheimer Road
Houston, TX
713-961-9000
Dogs of all sizes are allowed. There is a $25 one time fee per stay plus a one time $25 per room fee. There is a pet policy to sign at check in. Multiple dogs may be allowed.

Hilton
1600 Lamar
Houston, TX
713-739-8000
Dogs are allowed for an additional one time fee of $25 per pet. 2 dogs may be allowed.

Holiday Inn Express Hotel and Suites
1330 N Same Houston Pkwy East
Houston, TX
281-372-1000 (877-270-6405)
Dogs up to 50 pounds are allowed for an additional one time pet fee of $75 per room. 2 dogs may be allowed.

Holiday Inn Houston-Astrodome @ Reliant Pk

8111 Kirby Dr.
Houston, TX
713-790-1900 (877-270-6405)
Dogs of all sizes are allowed for no additional pet fee. Multiple dogs may be allowed.

Holiday Inn Select
2712 Southwest Freeway
Houston, TX
713-523-8448 (877-270-6405)
Dogs of all sizes are allowed for an additional one time fee of $50 per pet. Multiple dogs may be allowed.

Hotel Derek
2525 W Loop S
Houston, TX
713-961-3000
Dogs of all sizes are allowed. There is a $50 one time fee per pet. Multiple dogs may be allowed.

Houston - Near the Galleria Drury Inn & Suites
1615 West Loop South
Houston, TX
713-963-0700 (800-378-7946)
Dogs of all sizes are permitted. Pets are not allowed in the breakfast area of the hotel. Pets are not to be left unattended, and each guest must assume liability for damage of property or other guest complaints. There is a limit of one pet per room.

Houston - West Drury Inn & Suites
1000 North Highway 6
Houston, TX
281-558-7007 (800-378-7946)
Dogs of all sizes are permitted. Pets are not allowed in the breakfast area of the hotel. Pets are not to be left unattended, and each guest must assume liability for damage of property or other guest complaints. There is a limit of one pet per room.

Houston Hobby Airport Marriott
9100 Gulf Freeway
Houston, TX
713-943-7979 (800-228-9290)
Dogs up to 50 pounds are allowed. There is a $50 one time additional pet fee per pet. Dogs must be leashed, cleaned up after, and the Do Not Disturb sign put on the door if they are in the room alone. 2 dogs may be allowed.

Houston Marriott Medical Center
6580 Fannin Street
Houston, TX
713-796-0080 (800-228-9290)
Dogs up to 50 pounds are allowed. There is a $50 one time additional pet fee per room. Dogs must be

leashed, cleaned up after, and the Pet in Room sign put on the door if they are in the room alone. 2 dogs may be allowed.

Howard Johnson Express Inn
9604 S Main St.
Houston, TX
713-666-1411 (800-446-4656)
Dogs of all sizes are welcome. There is a $35 one time pet fee.

La Quinta Inn & Suites Houston Bush Intl Airport
15510 JFK Blvd.
Houston, TX
281-219-2000 (800-531-5900)
One dog of any size is allowed. There are no additional pet fees. Dogs must be leashed and cleaned up after. Dogs are not allowed to go through the lobby.

La Quinta Inn & Suites Houston Park 10
15225 Katy Freeway
Houston, TX
281-646-9200 (800-531-5900)
Dogs of all sizes are allowed. There are no additional pet fees. Dogs must be leashed, cleaned up after, and crated or removed for housekeeping. Multiple dogs may be allowed.

La Quinta Inn & Suites Willowbrook
18828 HWY 249
Houston, TX
281-897-8868 (800-531-5900)
Dogs of all sizes are allowed. There is a $25 one time fee per pet. Dogs must be leashed, cleaned up after, and crated when left alone in the room. Multiple dogs may be allowed.

La Quinta Inn Houston Brookhollow
11002 Northwest Freeway
Houston, TX
713-688-2581 (800-531-5900)
Dogs of all sizes are allowed. There are no additional pet fees. Dogs must be leashed, cleaned up after, and attended to or removed for housekeeping. Dogs are not allowed in the lobby. Multiple dogs may be allowed.

La Quinta Inn Houston Cy Fair
13290 FM 1960 West
Houston, TX
281-469-4018 (800-531-5900)
Dogs of all sizes are allowed. There are no additional pet fees. Dogs must be leashed and cleaned up after. Dogs must be crated or removed for housekeeping, or place

the Do Not Disturb sign on the door. Multiple dogs may be allowed.

La Quinta Inn Houston East
11999 East Freeway
Houston, TX
713-453-5425 (800-531-5900)
Dogs of all sizes are allowed. There are no additional pet fees. Dogs must be quiet, well behaved, leashed and cleaned up after. Multiple dogs may be allowed.

La Quinta Inn Houston Greenway Plaza
4015 Southwest Freeway
Houston, TX
713-623-4750 (800-531-5900)
Dogs of all sizes are allowed. There are no additional pet fees. Dogs must be leashed, cleaned up after, and attended to for housekeeping. Multiple dogs may be allowed.

La Quinta Inn Houston I-45 North
17111 North Frwy.
Houston, TX
281-444-7500 (800-531-5900)
Dogs of all sizes are allowed. There are no additional pet fees. Dogs must be leashed and cleaned up after. Multiple dogs may be allowed.

La Quinta Inn Houston Northwest
11130 N.W. Freeway
Houston, TX
713-680-8282 (800-531-5900)
Two large dogs or 3 small dogs are allowed. There are no additional pet fees. Dogs may not be left unattended, and they must be leashed and cleaned up after.

La Quinta Inn Houston Reliant/Medical Center
9911 Buffalo Speedway
Houston, TX
713-668-8082 (800-531-5900)
Dogs of all sizes are allowed. There are no additional pet fees. Dogs must be leashed and cleaned up after. The Do Not Disturb sign needs to be left on the door if there is a pet alone in the room. Multiple dogs may be allowed.

La Quinta Inn Houston Southwest
6790 Southwest Freeway
Houston, TX
713-784-3838 (800-531-5900)
There are no additional pet fees. Dogs may not be left unattended, and they must be leashed and cleaned up after.

Lovett Inn
501 Lovett Blvd
Houston, TX
713-522-5224 (800-779-5224)
lovettinn.com/main.php
Sitting on a tree lined street near the Montrose Museum District, this beautiful colonial styled 1923 home offers a convenient location to a number of local eateries, shops, attractions, and recreation. Dogs are allowed for an additional one time pet fee of $25 per room. 2 dogs may be allowed.

Motel 6 - Houston - Hobby Airport
8800 Airport Boulevard
Houston, TX
713-941-0990 (800-466-8356)
One well-behaved family pet per room. Guest must notify front desk upon arrival. Guest is liable for any damages. In consideration of all guests, pets must never be left unattended in the guest rooms.

Motel 6 - Houston - Jersey Village
16884 Northwest Freeway
Houston, TX
713-937-7056 (800-466-8356)
One well-behaved family pet per room. Guest must notify front desk upon arrival. Guest is liable for any damages. In consideration of all guests, pets must never be left unattended in the guest rooms.

Motel 6 - Houston - Westchase
2900 West Sam Houston Parkway South
Houston, TX
713-334-9188 (800-466-8356)
One well-behaved family pet per room. Guest must notify front desk upon arrival. Guest is liable for any damages. In consideration of all guests, pets must never be left unattended in the guest rooms.

Motel 6 - Houston Northwest
5555 West 34th Street
Houston, TX
713-682-8588 (800-466-8356)
One well-behaved family pet per room. Guest must notify front desk upon arrival. Guest is liable for any damages. In consideration of all guests, pets must never be left unattended in the guest rooms.

Motel 6 - Houston Six Flags-Astrodome
3223 South Loop West
Houston, TX
713-664-6425 (800-466-8356)
One well-behaved family pet per room. Guest must notify front desk upon arrival. Guest is liable for any

damages. In consideration of all guests, pets must never be left unattended in the guest rooms.

Motel 6 - Houston Southwest
9638 Plainfield Road
Houston, TX
713-778-0008 (800-466-8356)
One well-behaved family pet per room. Guest must notify front desk upon arrival. Guest is liable for any damages. In consideration of all guests, pets must never be left unattended in the guest rooms.

Motel 6 - Houston West - Katy
14833 Katy Freeway
Houston, TX
281-497-5000 (800-466-8356)
One well-behaved family pet per room. Guest must notify front desk upon arrival. Guest is liable for any damages. In consideration of all guests, pets must never be left unattended in the guest rooms.

Red Roof Inn - Houston - Hobby Airport
9005 Airport Boulevard
Houston, TX
713-943-3300 (800-RED-ROOF)
One well-behaved family pet per room. Guest must notify front desk upon arrival. Guest is liable for any damages. In consideration of all guests, pets must never be left unattended in the guest rooms.

Red Roof Inn - Houston - Westchase
2960 West Sam Houston Parkway South
Houston, TX
713-785-9909 (800-RED-ROOF)
One well-behaved family pet per room. Guest must notify front desk upon arrival. Guest is liable for any damages. In consideration of all guests, pets must never be left unattended in the guest rooms.

Red Roof Inn - Houston Northwest
12929 Northwest Freeway
Houston, TX
713-939-0800 (800-RED-ROOF)
One well-behaved family pet per room. Guest must notify front desk upon arrival. Guest is liable for any damages. In consideration of all guests, pets must never be left unattended in the guest rooms.

Red Roof Inn - Houston West
15701 Park Ten Place
Houston, TX
281-579-7200 (800-RED-ROOF)
One well-behaved family pet per

room. Guest must notify front desk upon arrival. Guest is liable for any damages. In consideration of all guests, pets must never be left unattended in the guest rooms.

Residence Inn by Marriott
525 Bay Area Blvd
Houston, TX
281-486-2424
Well behaved dogs of all sizes are allowed. There is a $75 one time fee and a pet policy to sign at check in. 2 dogs may be allowed.

Residence Inn by Marriott
65 N Sam Houston Parkway W
Houston, TX
281-820-4563
Dogs of all sizes are allowed. There is a $75 one time fee and a pet policy to sign at check in. Multiple dogs may be allowed.

Residence Inn by Marriott
7311 W Greens Road
Houston, TX
832-237-2002
Dogs of all sizes are allowed. There is a $75 one time fee and a pet policy to sign at check in. Multiple dogs may be allowed.

Residence Inn by Marriott
9965 Westheimer at Elmside
Houston, TX
713-974-5454
Dogs up to 75 pounds are allowed. There is a $75 one time fee and a pet policy to sign at check in. 2 dogs may be allowed.

Robin's Nest
4104 Greeley Street
Houston, TX
713-528 5821 (800-622-8343)
therobin.com/
Located near the city's Museum District with numerous activities, eateries, and educational institutions nearby, this guest house offers 8 rooms, lush gardens, dinner mysteries, and it also happens to sit in a good dog walking neighborhood. Well behaved dogs are allowed for an additional one time fee of $30 per pet. Dogs are not allowed on the furniture or bed, and they must be crated when left alone in the room. Dogs must be well groomed, have current vaccinations, and be sociable with other pets and people. 2 dogs may be allowed.

Sheraton Houston Brookhollow Hotel
3000 Northloop West Freeway
Houston, TX

Texas Listings - Please always call ahead to make sure an establishment is still dog-friendly.

713-688-0100 (888-625-5144)
Dogs up to 50 pounds are allowed
for no additional pet fee. Dogs may
not be left alone in the room.

Sheraton Suites Houston Near The
Galleria
2400 West Loop South
Houston, TX
713-586-2444 (888-625-5144)
Dogs up to 80 pounds are allowed
for no additional pet fee. Dogs may
not be left alone in the room.

Staybridge Suites
5190 Hidalgo
Houston, TX
713-355-8888 (877-270-6405)
Dogs of all sizes are allowed for an
additional one time pet fee of $75 per
room. Multiple dogs may be allowed.

Staybridge Suites Houston
Willowbrook
10750 N. Gessner Road
Houston, TX
281-807-3700 (877-270-6405)
Dogs of all sizes are allowed for an
additional one time fee of $75 per
pet; dogs must be crated when left
alone in the room. Multiple dogs may
be allowed.

Studio 6 - Houston - Hobby
12700 Featherwood Drive
Houston, TX
281-929-5400 (800-466-8356)
One well-behaved family pet per
room. Guest must notify front desk
upon arrival. Guest is liable for any
damages. In consideration of all
guests, pets must never be left
unattended in the guest rooms.

Studio 6 - Houston - Spring
220 Bammel Westfield Road
Houston, TX
281-580-2221 (800-466-8356)
One well-behaved family pet per
room. Guest must notify front desk
upon arrival. Guest is liable for any
damages. In consideration of all
guests, pets must never be left
unattended in the guest rooms.

Studio 6 - Houston - Westchase
3030 W. Sam Houston Parkway
South
Houston, TX
713-785-8550 (800-466-8356)
One well-behaved family pet per
room. Guest must notify front desk
upon arrival. Guest is liable for any
damages. In consideration of all
guests, pets must never be left
unattended in the guest rooms.

Studio 6 - Houston Northwest
14255 Northwest Freeway
Houston, TX
713-895-2900 (800-466-8356)
One well-behaved family pet per
room. Guest must notify front desk
upon arrival. Guest is liable for any
damages. In consideration of all
guests, pets must never be left
unattended in the guest rooms.

Studio 6 - Houston West
1255 North Highway 6
Houston, TX
281-579-6959 (800-466-8356)
One well-behaved family pet per
room. Guest must notify front desk
upon arrival. Guest is liable for any
damages. In consideration of all
guests, pets must never be left
unattended in the guest rooms.

The Lovett Inn
501 Lovett Blvd
Houston, TX
713-522-5224
lovettinn.com/
There is one pet room in this bed
and breakfast.

TownePlace Suites Houston
Central/Northwest Freeway
12820 NW Freeway
Houston, TX
713-690-4035
Dogs of all sizes are allowed. There
is a $75 one time pet fee per visit. 2
dogs may be allowed.

TownePlace Suites Houston Clear
Lake
1050 Bay Area Blvd
Houston, TX
281-286-2132
Dogs of all sizes are allowed. There
is a $75 one time pet fee per visit. 2
dogs may be allowed.

TownePlace Suites Houston
Northwest
11040 Louetta Road
Houston, TX
281-374-6767
Dogs of all sizes are allowed. There
is a $75 one time pet fee per visit. 2
dogs may be allowed.

TownePlace Suites Houston West
15155 Katy Freeway
Houston, TX
281-646-0058
Dogs of all sizes are allowed. There
is a $75 one time pet fee per visit. 2
dogs may be allowed.

Motel 6 - Houston - Humble
15319 Eastex Freeway

Humble, TX
281-441-7887 (800-466-8356)
One well-behaved family pet per
room. Guest must notify front desk
upon arrival. Guest is liable for any
damages. In consideration of all
guests, pets must never be left
unattended in the guest rooms.

Holiday Inn Express
201 West Hill Park Circle
Huntsville, TX
936-293-8800 (877-270-6405)
Dogs of all sizes are allowed for an
additional one time fee of $20 per
pet. Dogs must be crated when left
alone in the room. Multiple dogs may
be allowed.

Motel 6 - Huntsville
122 I-45
Huntsville, TX
936-291-6927 (800-466-8356)
One well-behaved family pet per
room. Guest must notify front desk
upon arrival. Guest is liable for any
damages. In consideration of all
guests, pets must never be left
unattended in the guest rooms.

Hampton Inn
1600 Hurst Town Center Drive
Hurst, TX
817-503-7777
Dogs of all sizes are allowed. There
is a $50 per pet per stay fee. Multiple
dogs may be allowed.

Best Western Naval Station Inn
2025 State hwy 361
Ingleside, TX
361-776-2767 (800-780-7234)
Dogs are allowed for an additional
fee of $10 per night per pet for large
dogs, and the fee is per room for
small dogs. 2 dogs may be allowed.

Clarion Hotel South DFW Airport
4440 W Airport Freeway
Irving, TX
972-399-1010 (877-424-6423)
Dogs are allowed for an additional
one time fee of $25 per pet. Multiple
dogs may be allowed.

Dallas - Ft. Worth Airport Drury Inn &
Suites
4210 W. Airport Freeway
Irving, TX
972-986-1200 (800-378-7946)
Dogs of all sizes are permitted. Pets
are not allowed in the breakfast area
of the hotel. Pets are not to be left
unattended, and each guest must
assume liability for damage of
property or other guest complaints.
There is a limit of one pet per room.

Hampton Inn
4340 W Airport Freeway
Irving, TX
972-986-3606
Dogs of all sizes are allowed. There are no additional pet fees. Dogs are not allowed to be left alone in the room. Multiple dogs may be allowed.

La Quinta Inn & Suites D/FW Airport South
4105 West Airport Freeway
Irving, TX
972-252-6546 (800-531-5900)
Dogs of all sizes are allowed. There are no additional pet fees. Dogs must be leashed, cleaned up after, and crated or removed for housekeeping. Multiple dogs may be allowed.

La Quinta Inn & Suites Dallas D/FW Airport North
4850 West John Carpenter Frwy
Irving, TX
972-915-4022 (800-531-5900)
Dogs of all sizes are allowed. There are no additional pet fees. Dogs must be quiet, leashed, and cleaned up after. Multiple dogs may be allowed.

Motel 6 - Dallas - DFW Airport North
7800 Heathrow Drive
Irving, TX
972-915-3993 (800-466-8356)
One well-behaved family pet per room. Guest must notify front desk upon arrival. Guest is liable for any damages. In consideration of all guests, pets must never be left unattended in the guest rooms.

Motel 6 - Dallas - DFW Airport South
2611 West Airport Freeway
Irving, TX
972-570-7500 (800-466-8356)
One well-behaved family pet per room. Guest must notify front desk upon arrival. Guest is liable for any damages. In consideration of all guests, pets must never be left unattended in the guest rooms.

Motel 6 - Dallas - Irving
510 South Loop 12
Irving, TX
972-438-4227 (800-466-8356)
One well-behaved family pet per room. Guest must notify front desk upon arrival. Guest is liable for any damages. In consideration of all guests, pets must never be left unattended in the guest rooms.

Red Roof Inn - Dallas - DFW Airport

North
8150 Esters Boulevard
Irving, TX
972-929-0020 (800-RED-ROOF)
One well-behaved family pet per room. Guest must notify front desk upon arrival. Guest is liable for any damages. In consideration of all guests, pets must never be left unattended in the guest rooms.

Residence Inn by Marriott
950 W Walnut Hill Lane
Irving, TX
972-580-7773
Dogs of all sizes are allowed. There is a $75 one time fee per pet and a pet policy to sign at check in. Multiple dogs may be allowed.

Staybridge Suites
1201 Executive Circle
Irving, TX
972-465-9400 (877-270-6405)
Dogs of all sizes are allowed for an additional one time pet fee of $75 per room. 2 dogs may be allowed.

TownePlace Suites Dallas Las Colinas
900 W Walnut Hill Lane
Irving, TX
972-550-7796
Dogs of all sizes are allowed. There is a $75 one time pet fee per visit. 2 dogs may be allowed.

Best Western Executive Inn
1659 S Jackson Street
Jacksonville, TX
903-586-0007 (800-780-7234)
Dogs are allowed for an additional pet fee of $20 per night per room. 2 dogs may be allowed.

Holiday Inn Express
1848 South Jackson
Jacksonville, TX
903-589-8500 (877-270-6405)
Dogs of all sizes are allowed for an additional fee of $15 per night per pet. Multiple dogs may be allowed.

The Exotic Resort Zoo
235 Zoo Trail
Johnson City, TX
830-868-4357
zooexotics.com/
This truly unique family vacation destination allows guest to experience the natural surroundings of wild animals; a tram (dogs allowed) takes guests through the 137 acres of woods and waterways that is home to more than 500 animals and about 80 species. Very well behaved dogs are allowed for

an additional fee of $10 per night per pet. Dogs must be comfortable/friendly toward other animals, and they are not allowed at the petting zoo. Dogs are to be leashed and picked up after at all times. 2 dogs may be allowed.

Days Inn Junction
111 S Martinex St
Junction, TX
325-446-3730 (800-329-7466)
Dogs of all sizes are allowed. There is a $4 per night pet fee per pet. Reservations are recommended due to limited rooms for pets. 2 dogs may be allowed.

Holiday Inn Express
22105 Katy Freeway
Katy, TX
281-395-4800 (877-270-6405)
Dogs of all sizes are allowed for an additional one time fee of $50 per pet. Multiple dogs may be allowed.

Super 8 Katy
22157 Katy Freeway
Katy, TX
281-395-5757 (800-800-8000)
Dogs of all sizes are allowed. There is a $15 per night pet fee per pet. Smoking and non-smoking rooms are available for pet rooms. 2 dogs may be allowed.

La Quinta Inn & Suites Kerrville
1940 Sidney Baker Street
Kerrville, TX
830-896-9200 (800-531-5900)
Dogs of all sizes are allowed. There are no additional pet fees. Dogs may not be left unattended, and they must be leashed and cleaned up after. 2 dogs may be allowed.

Motel 6 - Kerrville
1810 Sidney Baker Street
Kerrville, TX
830-257-1500 (800-466-8356)
One well-behaved family pet per room. Guest must notify front desk upon arrival. Guest is liable for any damages. In consideration of all guests, pets must never be left unattended in the guest rooms.

Days Inn Kilgore
3505 Hwy 259 N
Kilgore, TX
903-983-2975 (800-329-7466)
Dogs of all sizes are allowed. There is a $10 per night pet fee per pet. 2 dogs may be allowed.

Candlewood Suites Killeen
2300 Florence Rd.

Killeen, TX
254-501-3990 (877-270-6405)
Dogs of all sizes are allowed for an additional one time pet fee per room of $75 for 1 to 6 nights, and $150 for 7 nights or more. Multiple dogs may be allowed.

La Quinta Inn Killeen
1112 S. Fort Hood St.
Killeen, TX
254-526-8331 (800-531-5900)
Dogs of all sizes are allowed. There are no additional pet fees. Dogs must be leashed, cleaned up after, and crated when in the room unattended. Arrangements need to be made for housekeeping if the stay is more than 1 day. Multiple dogs may be allowed.

Motel 6 - Kingsville
101 North US 77
Kingsville, TX
361-592-5106 (800-466-8356)
One well-behaved family pet per room. Guest must notify front desk upon arrival. Guest is liable for any damages. In consideration of all guests, pets must never be left unattended in the guest rooms.

La Quinta Inn & Suites Kingwood
22790 US 59
Kingwood, TX
281-359-6611 (800-531-5900)
Dogs of all sizes are allowed. There are no additional pet fees. There is a pet waiver to sign at check in. Dogs must be leashed, cleaned up after, and crated or removed for housekeeping. Multiple dogs may be allowed.

Best Western La Grange Inn & Suites
600 E State Highway 71 Bypass
La Grange, TX
979-968-6800 (800-780-7234)
Dogs are allowed for an additional pet fee of $15 per night per room. Multiple dogs may be allowed.

La Quinta Inn Houston La Porte
1105 Hwy. 146 South
La Porte, TX
281-470-0760 (800-531-5900)
Dogs of all sizes are allowed. There are no additional pet fees, but there must be a credit card on file. Dogs must be leashed and cleaned up after. 2 dogs may be allowed.

Family Gardens Inn
5830 San Bernardo
Laredo, TX
956-723-5300 (800-292-4053)

They have onsite kennels available if you need to leave your room during the day and can't bring your pup with you. There is a $50 refundable pet deposit. You have to provide your own locks for the kennels.

La Quinta Inn & Suites Laredo
7220 Bob Bullock Loop
Laredo, TX
956-724-7222 (800-531-5900)
Dogs of all sizes are allowed. There is a $50 refundable pet deposit if paying for the room with cash; there is no deposit required with a credit card on file. Dogs must be leashed and cleaned up after, and if your room needs to be serviced, they ask that you remove your pet. Multiple dogs may be allowed.

La Quinta Inn Laredo
3610 Santa Ursula
Laredo, TX
956-722-0511 (800-531-5900)
Dogs of all sizes are allowed. There are no additional pet fees. Dogs must be leashed, cleaned up after, and removed for housekeeping. Multiple dogs may be allowed.

Motel 6 - Laredo North
5920 San Bernardo Avenue
Laredo, TX
956-722-8133 (800-466-8356)
One well-behaved family pet per room. Guest must notify front desk upon arrival. Guest is liable for any damages. In consideration of all guests, pets must never be left unattended in the guest rooms.

Motel 6 - Laredo South
5310 San Bernardo Avenue
Laredo, TX
956-725-8187 (800-466-8356)
One well-behaved family pet per room. Guest must notify front desk upon arrival. Guest is liable for any damages. In consideration of all guests, pets must never be left unattended in the guest rooms.

Red Roof Inn - Laredo
1006 West Calton Road
Laredo, TX
956-712-0733 (800-RED-ROOF)
One well-behaved family pet per room. Guest must notify front desk upon arrival. Guest is liable for any damages. In consideration of all guests, pets must never be left unattended in the guest rooms.

Staybridge Suites Laredo
7010 Bob Bullock Loop

Laredo, TX
956-722-0444 (877-270-6405)
Dogs of all sizes are allowed for an additional one time pet fee of $150 per room. 2 dogs may be allowed.

Comfort Suites
755A Vista Ridge Mall Drive
Lewisville, TX
972-315-6464 (877-424-6423)
Dogs are allowed for an additional pet fee of $10 per night per room. Multiple dogs may be allowed.

Country Inns & Suites by Carlson
755 B Vista Ridge Mall Drive
Lewisville, TX
972-315-6565
Dogs of all sizes are allowed. There is a $50 per stay additional pet fee.

Days Inn Dallas/Lewisville
200 N Stemmons Frwy
Lewisville, TX
972-434-1000 (800-329-7466)
Dogs of all sizes are allowed. There is a $5 per night pet fee per small pet or $7 per large pet. 2 dogs may be allowed.

La Quinta Inn Dallas Lewisville
1657 S. Stemmons Freeway
Lewisville, TX
972-221-7525 (800-531-5900)
Dogs of all sizes are allowed. There are no additional pet fees. Dogs must be well behaved, leashed, and cleaned up after. Multiple dogs may be allowed.

Motel 6 - Dallas - Lewisville
1705 Lakepointe Drive
Lewisville, TX
972-436-5008 (800-466-8356)
One well-behaved family pet per room. Guest must notify front desk upon arrival. Guest is liable for any damages. In consideration of all guests, pets must never be left unattended in the guest rooms.

Days Inn Tyler/Lindale
13307 CR 472 East
Lindale, TX
903-882-7800 (800-329-7466)
Dogs of all sizes are allowed. There is a $10 per night pet fee per pet. 2 dogs may be allowed.

La Quinta Inn Longview
502 S. Access Rd.
Longview, TX
903-757-3663 (800-531-5900)
Dogs of all sizes are allowed. There are no additional pet fees. Dogs must be leashed and cleaned up after. Multiple dogs may be allowed.

Motel 6 - Longview
110 South Access Road
Longview, TX
903-758-5256 (800-466-8356)
One well-behaved family pet per
room. Guest must notify front desk
upon arrival. Guest is liable for any
damages. In consideration of all
guests, pets must never be left
unattended in the guest rooms.

Hyatt Regency Lost Pines Resort
and Spa
575 Hyatt Lost Pines Road
Lost Pines, TX
512-308-1234 (800-633-7313)
There are many activities and
amenities available for the business
or vacationing guest on this 700 acre
full-service hotel resort including a
comprehensive business center, a
championship golf course, and live
entertainment on weekends. Dogs of
all sizes are welcome for an
additional one time pet fee of $100
per room. Dogs may only be left
alone in the room if owners are
confident their pet will be quiet and
well behaved, and they may either be
crated or put into the bathroom.
Dogs must be leashed or crated, and
cleaned up after at all times. 2 dogs
may be allowed.

Best Western Lubbock Windsor Inn
5410 Interstate 27
Lubbock, TX
806-762-8400 (800-780-7234)
Dogs are allowed for an additional
fee of $10 per night per pet. Multiple
dogs may be allowed.

Days Inn Lubbock Downtown
2401 4th St
Lubbock, TX
806-747-7111 (800-329-7466)
Dogs of all sizes are allowed. There
are no additional pet fees. 2 dogs
may be allowed.

La Quinta Inn Lubbock Civic Center
601 Avenue Q
Lubbock, TX
806-763-9441 (800-531-5900)
Dogs of all sizes are allowed. There
is a $25 per room additional pet fee.
Dogs must be leashed and cleaned
up after. Multiple dogs may be
allowed.

La Quinta Inn Lubbock West/Medical
Center
4115 Brownfield Hwy.
Lubbock, TX
806-792-0065 (800-531-5900)
Dogs of all sizes are allowed. There

are no additional pet fees. Dogs
may not be left unattended, and
they must be leashed and cleaned
up after. 2 dogs may be allowed.

Motel 6 - Lubbock
909 66th Street
Lubbock, TX
806-745-5541 (800-466-8356)
One well-behaved family pet per
room. Guest must notify front desk
upon arrival. Guest is liable for any
damages. In consideration of all
guests, pets must never be left
unattended in the guest rooms.

TownePlace Suites Lubbock
5310 West Loop 289
Lubbock, TX
806-799-6226
Dogs of all sizes are allowed. There
is a $75 one time pet fee per visit. .
2 dogs may be allowed.

Days Inn Lufkin
2130 S First
Lufkin, TX
936-639-3301 (800-329-7466)
Dogs up to 60 pounds are allowed.
There is a $25 one time per pet fee
per visit. 2 dogs may be allowed.

Holiday Inn
4306 S. 1st Street
Lufkin, TX
936-639-3333 (877-270-6405)
There is a $10 one time additional
pet fee.

Motel 6 - Lufkin
1110 South Timberland Drive
Lufkin, TX
936-637-7850 (800-466-8356)
One well-behaved family pet per
room. Guest must notify front desk
upon arrival. Guest is liable for any
damages. In consideration of all
guests, pets must never be left
unattended in the guest rooms.

Days Inn Lytle
19525 McDonald St
Lytle, TX
830-772-4777 (800-329-7466)
Dogs of all sizes are allowed. There
is a $10 one time per pet fee per
visit. 2 dogs may be allowed.

Quality Inn and Suites
11301 H 290 E
Manor, TX
512-272-9373 (877-424-6423)
Dogs are allowed for an additional
fee of $10 per night per pet. Dogs
must be crated or removed for
housekeeping. Multiple dogs may
be allowed.

Best Western Executive Inn
5201 East End Blvd South
Marshall, TX
903-935-0707 (800-780-7234)
Dogs up to 20 pounds are allowed
for an additional fee of $10 per night
per pet; 21 to 40 pounds is $15, and
over 40 pounds is $20. 2 dogs may
be allowed.

Days Inn Marshall
100 I-20 West
Marshall, TX
903-927-1718 (800-329-7466)
Dogs of all sizes are allowed. There
is a $7 per night pet fee per pet. 2
dogs may be allowed.

La Quinta Inn Marshall
5301 E End Blvd S
Marshall, TX
903-927-0009 (800-531-5900)
Dogs of all sizes are allowed. There
are no additional pet fees. There is a
pet waiver to sign at check in. Dogs
must be leashed, cleaned up after,
and crated or removed for
housekeeping. Multiple dogs may be
allowed.

Motel 6 - Marshall
300 I-20 East
Marshall, TX
903-935-4393 (800-466-8356)
One well-behaved family pet per
room. Guest must notify front desk
upon arrival. Guest is liable for any
damages. In consideration of all
guests, pets must never be left
unattended in the guest rooms.

Drury Inn
612 W. Expressway 83
McAllen, TX
956-687-5100 (800-378-7946)
Dogs of all sizes are permitted. Pets
are not allowed in the breakfast area
of the hotel. Pets are not to be left
unattended, and each guest must
assume liability for damage of
property or other guest complaints.
There is a limit of one pet per room.

La Quinta Inn McAllen
1100 South 10th St.
McAllen, TX
956-687-1101 (800-531-5900)
Two large dogs or 3 small dogs are
allowed. There are not additional pet
fees. There is a pet waiver to sign at
check in. Dogs must be well
behaved, leashed, cleaned up after,
and crated or removed for
housekeeping.

Motel 6 - McAllen

700 West Expressway 83
McAllen, TX
956-687-3700 (800-466-8356)
One well-behaved family pet per
room. Guest must notify front desk
upon arrival. Guest is liable for any
damages. In consideration of all
guests, pets must never be left
unattended in the guest rooms.

Posada Ana Inn
620 W. Expressway 83
McAllen, TX
956-631-6700 (800-378-7946)
Dogs of all sizes are permitted. Pets
are not allowed in the breakfast area
of the hotel. Pets are not to be left
unattended, and each guest must
assume liability for damage of
property or other guest complaints.
There is a limit of one pet per room.

Residence Inn by Marriott
220 W Expressway 83
McAllen, TX
956-994-8626
Dogs of all sizes are allowed. There
is a $75 one time fee and a pet
policy to sign at check in. Multiple
dogs may be allowed.

Studio 6 - McAllen
700 Savannah Avenue
McAllen, TX
956-668-7829 (800-466-8356)
One well-behaved family pet per
room. Guest must notify front desk
upon arrival. Guest is liable for any
damages. In consideration of all
guests, pets must never be left
unattended in the guest rooms.

Days Inn McKinney
2104 N Central Expressway
McKinney, TX
972-548-8888 (800-329-7466)
Dogs of all sizes are allowed. There
is a $5 per night pet fee per pet. 2
dogs may be allowed.

Holiday Inn
1300 North Central Expressway
McKinney, TX
972-542-9471 (877-270-6405)
Dogs up to 75 pounds are allowed
for an additional one time pet fee of
$25 per room. 2 dogs may be
allowed.

Motel 6 - McKinney
2125 White Avenue
McKinney, TX
972-542-8600 (800-466-8356)
One well-behaved family pet per
room. Guest must notify front desk
upon arrival. Guest is liable for any
damages. In consideration of all

guests, pets must never be left
unattended in the guest rooms.

Super 8 McKinney/Plano Area
910 N Central Expressway
McKinney, TX
972-548-8880 (800-800-8000)
Dogs of all sizes are allowed. There
is a $10 per night pet fee per pet.
Smoking and non-smoking rooms
are available for pet rooms. 2 dogs
may be allowed.

La Quinta Inn & Suites
Dallas/Mesquite
118 East US Highway 80
Mesquite, TX
972-216-7460 (800-531-5900)
Dogs of all sizes are allowed. There
are no additional pet fees. Dogs
may only be left alone in the room if
they will be quiet. Dogs must be
leashed and cleaned up after.
Multiple dogs may be allowed.

Super 8 Mesquite/Dallas Area
121 Grand Junction
Mesquite, TX
972-289-5481 (800-800-8000)
Dogs of all sizes are allowed. There
are no additional pet fees. Smoking
and non-smoking rooms are
available for pet rooms. 2 dogs may
be allowed.

Hilton
117 West Wall Street
Midland, TX
432-683-6131
Dogs are allowed for an additional
one time pet fee of $25 per room.
Multiple dogs may be allowed.

La Quinta Inn Midland
4130 West Wall Street
Midland, TX
432-697-9900 (800-531-5900)
Dogs of all sizes are allowed. There
are no additional pet fees. Dogs
must be well behaved, leashed, and
cleaned up after. The front desk
needs to be informed when there is
a pet alone in the room, and the Do
Not Disturb sign placed on the door.
Multiple dogs may be allowed.

Best Western Club House Inn &
Suites
4410 Highway 180 E
Mineral Wells, TX
940-325-2270 (800-780-7234)
Quiet dogs are allowed for an
additional one time pet fee of $10
per room 2 dogs may be allowed.

Best Western Mt Pleasant Inn &
Suites

102 E Burton Road
Mount Pleasant, TX
903-572-5051 (800-780-7234)
Quiet, well behaved dogs are
allowed for an additional fee of $10
per night per pet. Dogs may only be
left alone in the room for very short
times. 2 dogs may be allowed.

Holiday Inn Express Hotel and Suites
1306 Greenhill Road
Mount Pleasant, TX
903-577-3800 (877-270-6405)
Dogs of all sizes are allowed for no
additional pet fee. 2 dogs may be
allowed.

Super 8 Mt Vernon
401 West I-30 at Hwy 37
Mount Vernon, TX
903-588-2882 (800-800-8000)
Dogs of all sizes are allowed. There
is a $5 per night pet fee per pet.
Smoking and non-smoking rooms
are available for pet rooms. 2 dogs
may be allowed.

La Quinta Inn Nacogdoches
3215 South St.
Nacogdoches, TX
936-560-5453 (800-531-5900)
Dogs of all sizes are allowed. There
are no additional pet fees. Dogs
must be leashed and cleaned up
after. A contact number must be left
with the front desk if there is a pet
left unattended in the room. Multiple
dogs may be allowed.

Candlewood Suites Nederland
2125 Hwy 69
Nederland, TX
409-729-9543 (877-270-6405)
Dogs of all sizes are allowed for an
additional one time pet fee of $75 for
each 1 to 6 days. Multiple dogs may
be allowed.

Best Western Inn of New Boston
1024 North Center
New Boston, TX
903-628-6999 (800-780-7234)
Dogs are allowed for an additional
fee of $15 per night per pet. Multiple
dogs may be allowed.

Best Western Inn and Suites
1493 IH-35 North
New Braunfels, TX
830-625-7337 (800-780-7234)
Dogs are allowed for an additional
fee of $10 per night per pet. Extra
large dogs can not be
accommodated. 2 dogs may be
allowed.

Holiday Inn

1051 I-35 E.
New Braunfels, TX
830-625-8017 (877-270-6405)
Dogs of all sizes are allowed for an additional one time fee of $25 per pet. Multiple dogs may be allowed.

La Quinta Inn & Suites New Braunfels
365 Hwy 46 South
New Braunfels, TX
830-627-3333 (800-531-5900)
Dogs of all sizes are allowed. There are no additional pet fees. There is a pet waiver to sign at check in. Dogs must be leashed and cleaned up after. 2 dogs may be allowed.

Motel 6 - New Braunfels
1275 North I-35
New Braunfels, TX
830-626-0600 (800-466-8356)
One well-behaved family pet per room. Guest must notify front desk upon arrival. Guest is liable for any damages. In consideration of all guests, pets must never be left unattended in the guest rooms.

Quality Inn and Suites
1533 IH 35N
New Braunfels, TX
830-643-9300 (877-424-6423)
Dogs are allowed for a $50 refundable deposit (if paying by cash) plus an additional one time pet fee of $25 per room. 2 dogs may be allowed.

Red Roof Inn - New Braunfels
815 I-35 South
New Braunfels, TX
830-626-7000 (800-RED-ROOF)
One well-behaved family pet per room. Guest must notify front desk upon arrival. Guest is liable for any damages. In consideration of all guests, pets must never be left unattended in the guest rooms.

Super 8 New Braunfels
510 Hwy 46 South
New Braunfels, TX
830-629-1155 (800-800-8000)
Dogs of all sizes are allowed. There is a $10 per night pet fee per pet. Smoking and non-smoking rooms are available for pet rooms.

Motel 6 - Ft Worth - North Richland Hills
7804 Bedford Euless Road
North Richland Hills, TX
817-485-3000 (800-466-8356)
One well-behaved family pet per room. Guest must notify front desk upon arrival. Guest is liable for any

damages. In consideration of all guests, pets must never be left unattended in the guest rooms.

Studio 6 - Ft Worth - North Richland Hills
7450 NE Loop 820
North Richland Hills, TX
817-788-6000 (800-466-8356)
One well-behaved family pet per room. Guest must notify front desk upon arrival. Guest is liable for any damages. In consideration of all guests, pets must never be left unattended in the guest rooms.

Days Inn Odem
Hwy 77 South
Odem, TX
361-368-2166 (800-329-7466)
Dogs of all sizes are allowed. There are no additional pet fees. 2 dogs may be allowed.

Best Western Garden Oasis
110 West Interstate 2
Odessa, TX
432-337-3006 (800-780-7234)
Dogs are allowed for no additional pet fee. There must be a credit card on file, and dogs may not be left alone in the room. Multiple dogs may be allowed.

La Quinta Inn Odessa
5001 E. Bus. I-20
Odessa, TX
432-333-2820 (800-531-5900)
Dogs of all sizes are allowed. There are no additional pet fees. Dogs may not be left unattended, and they must be leashed and cleaned up after. 2 dogs may be allowed.

Motel 6 - Odessa
200 East I-20 Service Road
Odessa, TX
432-333-4025 (800-466-8356)
One well-behaved family pet per room. Guest must notify front desk upon arrival. Guest is liable for any damages. In consideration of all guests, pets must never be left unattended in the guest rooms.

Quality Inn and Suites
3001 E Business Loop 20
Odessa, TX
432-333-3931 (877-424-6423)
Dogs are allowed for an additional one time pet fee of $25 per room. 2 dogs may be allowed.

Motel 6 - Orange
4407 27th Street
Orange, TX
409-883-4891 (800-466-8356)

One well-behaved family pet per room. Guest must notify front desk upon arrival. Guest is liable for any damages. In consideration of all guests, pets must never be left unattended in the guest rooms.

Super 8 Ozona
I-10 and Taylor Box Road
Ozona, TX
325-392-2611 (800-800-8000)
Dogs of all sizes are allowed. There are no additional pet fees. Reservations are recommended due to limited rooms for pets. Smoking and non-smoking rooms are available for pet rooms. 2 dogs may be allowed.

Best Western Palestine Inn
1601 W Palestine Ave
Palestine, TX
903-723-4655 (800-780-7234)
Dogs are allowed for an additional fee of $10 per night per pet. Multiple dogs may be allowed.

Quality Inn and Suites
1101 E Palestine Avenue
Palestine, TX
903-723-7300 (877-424-6423)
Dogs up to 50 pounds are allowed for an additional one time pet fee of $10 per room. Multiple dogs may be allowed.

Best Western Inn of Paris
3755 North East Loop 286
Paris, TX
903-785-5566 (800-780-7234)
Dogs under 40 pounds are allowed for an additional fee of $10 per night per pet; the fee is $20 for dogs over 40 pounds. 2 dogs may be allowed.

Holiday Inn
3560 NE Loop 286
Paris, TX
903-785-5545 (877-270-6405)
Dogs up to 50 pounds are allowed for an additional pet fee of $20 per night per room. Dogs must be crated when left alone in the room. 2 dogs may be allowed.

Cielito Guest Ranch Bed and Breakfast Cabins
1308 Clemons Switch Road
Pattison, TX
281-375-6469 (888-375-6469)
cielitoranch.com/
For a truly "back to the farm" experience, this working farm guest ranch offers 177 park-like acres, all the farm animals, miles of trails, and a variety of land and water recreational opportunities. Dogs are

allowed for an additional fee of $15 per night per pet. There are kennels available when needed, and they also offer well behaved dogs extended accommodations where they have free range on the ranch (except at night) for when their owners must be away for longer periods. 2 dogs may be allowed.

Best Western Pearland Inn
1855 N Main Street (Hwy 35)
Pearland, TX
281-997-2000 (800-780-7234)
Dogs are allowed for an additional fee of $20 per night per pet. 2 dogs may be allowed.

Motel 6 - Pecos
3002 South Cedar Street
Pecos, TX
432-445-9034 (800-466-8356)
One well-behaved family pet per room. Guest must notify front desk upon arrival. Guest is liable for any damages. In consideration of all guests, pets must never be left unattended in the guest rooms.

Best Western Perryton Inn
3505 S Main Street
Perryton, TX
806-434-2850 (800-780-7234)
Dogs are allowed for an additional fee of $10 per night per pet. Multiple dogs may be allowed.

La Quinta Inn & Suites Rio Grande Valley
4603 North Cage
Pharr, TX
956-787-2900 (800-531-5900)
Dogs of all sizes are allowed. There are no additional pet fees. There is a pet waiver to sign at check in. Dogs must be leashed and cleaned up after. Multiple dogs may be allowed.

Motel 6 - Pharr
4701 North Cage Boulevard
Pharr, TX
956-781-7202 (800-466-8356)
One well-behaved family pet per room. Guest must notify front desk upon arrival. Guest is liable for any damages. In consideration of all guests, pets must never be left unattended in the guest rooms.

Best Western Conestoga
600 North I-27
Plainview, TX
806-293-9454 (800-780-7234)
Dogs are allowed for an additional fee of $15 per night per pet. Multiple dogs may be allowed.

Days Inn Plainview
3600 Olton Rd
Plainview, TX
806-293-2561 (800-329-7466)
Dogs of all sizes are allowed. There is a $6 per night pet fee per pet. 2 dogs may be allowed.

Holiday Inn Express Hotel and Suites
4213 W 13th Street
Plainview, TX
806-296-9900 (877-270-6405)
Dogs of all sizes are allowed for an additional pet fee of $20 per night per room. Multiple dogs may be allowed.

Best Western Park Suites Hotel
640 E Park Boulevard
Plano, TX
972-578-2243 (800-780-7234)
Dogs are allowed for an additional one time fee of $25 per pet. 2 dogs may be allowed.

Candlewood Suites
4701 Legacy Drive
Plano, TX
972-618-5446 (877-270-6405)
Dogs up to 75 pounds are allowed for an additional one time pet fee of $75 per room. 2 dogs may be allowed.

Hampton Inn
4901 Old Shepard Place
Plano, TX
972-519-1000
Dogs of all sizes are allowed. There are no additional pet fees. Multiple dogs may be allowed.

Holiday Inn Express Hotel and Suites
700 Central Parkway East
Plano, TX
972-881-1881 (877-270-6405)
Dogs of all sizes are allowed for an additional one time pet fee of $50 per room. 2 dogs may be allowed.

La Quinta Inn & Suites Dallas Plano West
4800 West Plano Pkwy.
Plano, TX
972-599-0700 (800-531-5900)
Dogs of all sizes are allowed. There are no additional pet fees. Dogs must be leashed and cleaned up after. 2 dogs may be allowed.

La Quinta Inn Dallas Plano East
1820 North Central Expwy.
Plano, TX
972-423-1300 (800-531-5900)
Dogs of all sizes are allowed. There

are no additional pet fees. Dogs must be leashed, cleaned up after, and crated or removed for housekeeping. Multiple dogs may be allowed.

Motel 6 - Dallas - Plano NE
2550 North Central Expressway
Plano, TX
972-578-1626 (800-466-8356)
One well-behaved family pet per room. Guest must notify front desk upon arrival. Guest is liable for any damages. In consideration of all guests, pets must never be left unattended in the guest rooms.

Red Roof Inn - Dallas - Plano
301 Ruisseau Drive
Plano, TX
972-881-8191 (800-RED-ROOF)
One well-behaved family pet per room. Guest must notify front desk upon arrival. Guest is liable for any damages. In consideration of all guests, pets must never be left unattended in the guest rooms.

Residence Inn by Marriott
5001 Whitestone Lane
Plano, TX
972-473-6761
Dogs of all sizes are allowed. There is a $75 one time fee and a pet policy to sign at check in. Multiple dogs may be allowed.

Staybridge Suites N Dallas Plano
301 Silverglen Road
Plano, TX
972-612-8180 (877-270-6405)
Dogs of all sizes are allowed for an additional one time pet fee of $125 per room. 2 dogs may be allowed.

TownePlace Suites Dallas Plano
5005 Whitestone Lane
Plano, TX
972-943-8200
Dogs of all sizes are allowed. There is a $75 one time pet fee per visit. 2 dogs may be allowed.

Studio 6 - Port Arthur
3000 Jimmy Johnson Boulevard
Port Arthur, TX
409-729-6611 (800-466-8356)
One well-behaved family pet per room. Guest must notify front desk upon arrival. Guest is liable for any damages. In consideration of all guests, pets must never be left unattended in the guest rooms.

MD Resort Bed and Breakfast Country Inn
601 Old Base Road

Rhome, TX
817-489-5150 (866-489-5150)
mdresort.com/
A real Texas guest ranch, they offer
many modern amenities, an outdoor
pool and spa, and a number of fun
activities. Dogs are allowed for an
additional one time fee of $50 per
pet. 2 dogs may be allowed.

Residence Inn by Marriott
1040 Waterwood Drive
Richardson, TX
972-669-5888
Dogs of all sizes are allowed. There
is a $75 one time fee and a pet
policy to sign at check in. Multiple
dogs may be allowed.

Executive Inn (former Days Inn)
320 Hwy 77 South
Robstown, TX
361-387-9416 (800-DAYS-INN)
Dogs of all sizes are allowed. There
is a $5 per night pet fee per pet. 2
dogs may be allowed.

Days Inn Rockport
1212 Laurel
Rockport, TX
361-729-6379 (800-329-7466)
Dogs of all sizes are allowed. There
is a $15 per night pet fee per pet. 2
dogs may be allowed.

La Quinta Inn & Suites Rockwall
689 East Interstate 30
Rockwall, TX
972-771-1685 (800-531-5900)
Dogs of all sizes are allowed. There
are no additional pet fees. There is a
pet waiver to sign at check in. Dogs
must be leashed and cleaned up
after. Multiple dogs may be allowed.

Holiday Inn Express Hotel & Suites
27927 S.W. Freeway
Rosenberg, TX
281-342-7888 (877-270-6405)
Dogs of all sizes are allowed for an
additional fee of $20 per night per
pet. Multiple dogs may be allowed.

Candlewood Suites
521 South IH-35
Round Rock, TX
512-828-0899 (877-270-6405)
Dogs of all sizes are allowed for an
additional one time fee per pet of $75
for 1 to 7 nights, and $150 for 8
nights or more. Multiple dogs may be
allowed.

Days Inn Round Rock/North Austin
1802 South IH-35
Round Rock, TX
512-246-0055 (800-329-7466)

Dogs of all sizes are allowed. There
is a $15 per night pet fee per pet. 2
dogs may be allowed.

La Quinta Inn Austin Round Rock
2004 North I-35
Round Rock, TX
512-255-6666 (800-531-5900)
Dogs of all sizes are allowed. There
are no additional pet fees. Dogs
may not be left unattended, and
they must be leashed and cleaned
up after. Multiple dogs may be
allowed.

Red Roof Inn - Austin - Round Rock
1990 North I-35
Round Rock, TX
512-310-1111 (800-RED-ROOF)
One well-behaved family pet per
room. Guest must notify front desk
upon arrival. Guest is liable for any
damages. In consideration of all
guests, pets must never be left
unattended in the guest rooms.

Holiday Inn Express Hotel & Suites
Salado
1991 N. Stagecoach Road
Salado, TX
254-947-4004 (877-270-6405)
Dogs of all sizes are allowed for an
additional one time pet fee of $50
per room. Dogs must be crated
when left alone in the room. 2 dogs
may be allowed.

Best Western San Angelo
3017 W Loop 306
San Angelo, TX
325-223-1273 (800-780-7234)
Dogs are allowed for an additional
pet fee of $25 per night per room.
Multiple dogs may be allowed.

Comfort Inn
2502 Loop 306
San Angelo, TX
325-944-2578 (877-424-6423)
Dogs are allowed for no additional
pet fee. Multiple dogs may be
allowed.

Days Inn San Angelo
4613 S Jackson
San Angelo, TX
325-658-6594 (800-329-7466)
Dogs of all sizes are allowed. There
are no additional pet fees. 2 dogs
may be allowed.

La Quinta Inn and Conference
Center San Angelo
2307 Loop 306
San Angelo, TX
325-949-0515 (800-531-5900)
Dogs of all sizes are allowed. There

are no additional pet fees. Dogs
must be leashed, cleaned up after,
and crated or attended to for
housekeeping. Multiple dogs may be
allowed.

Motel 6 - San Angelo
311 North Bryant Boulevard
San Angelo, TX
325-658-8061 (800-466-8356)
One well-behaved family pet per
room. Guest must notify front desk
upon arrival. Guest is liable for any
damages. In consideration of all
guests, pets must never be left
unattended in the guest rooms.

Best Western Posada Ana Inn -
Medical Center
9411 Wurzbach Road
San Antonio, TX
210-691-9550 (800-780-7234)
Dogs up to 75 pounds are allowed
for no additional pet fee. There is a
pet agreement to sign at check in;
aggressive breed dogs are not
allowed: dogs may not be left alone
in the room, and they must be
removed for housekeeping. 2 dogs
may be allowed.

Brackenridge House
230 Madison
San Antonio, TX
210-271-3442 (800-221-1412)
brackenridgehouse.com/
Located in the King William historic
district, this inn offers the ambience
of yesteryear with the amenities of
modern day, and a convenient
location to numerous local attractions
and activities. Dogs are allowed for
no additional pet fee. 2 dogs may be
allowed.

Candlewood Suites
9350 IH 10 West
San Antonio, TX
210-615-0550 (877-270-6405)
Dogs of all sizes are allowed for an
additional one time pet fee per room
of $75 for 1 to 6 nights, and $150 for
7 nights or more. Multiple dogs may
be allowed.

Comfort Inn
4403 I 10E
San Antonio, TX
210-333-9430 (877-424-6423)
Dogs are allowed for no additional
pet fee. Multiple dogs may be
allowed.

Crowne Plaza
111 Pecan Street East
San Antonio, TX
210-354-2800 (877-270-6405)

Dogs up to 50 pounds are allowed for an additional one time pet fee of $50 per room. 2 dogs may be allowed.

Days Inn San Antonio Downtown
1500 I-35 South
San Antonio, TX
210-271-3334 (800-329-7466)
Dogs of all sizes are allowed. There is a $25 one time per pet fee per visit. 2 dogs may be allowed.

Days Inn San Antonio East of Dwtn
4039 E Houston St
San Antonio, TX
210-333-9100 (800-329-7466)
Dogs of all sizes are allowed. There is a $10 per night pet fee per pet. 2 dogs may be allowed.

Days Inn San Antonio NE or Dwtn
3443 I-35 North
San Antonio, TX
210-225-4040 (800-329-7466)
Dogs of all sizes are allowed. There is a $6 one time pet fee per visit for pets under 10 pounds and $25 per pet over 10 pounds. 2 dogs may be allowed.

Hampton Inn
8818 Jones Maltsberger
San Antonio, TX
210-366-1800
Dogs that weigh 50 pounds total together are welcome. There are no additional pet fees. You must leave a cell or contact number if you leave your pet in the room unattended.

Hampton Inn Six Flags
11010 IH 10W
San Antonio, TX
210-561-9058
Dogs of all sizes are allowed. There is a $10 per night per pet fee. Multiple dogs may be allowed.

Holiday Inn
318 W. Durango Blvd
San Antonio, TX
210-225-3211 (877-270-6405)
There is a $125 refundable pet deposit and a $25 one time pet fee. Dogs up to 50 pounds are allowed.

Holiday Inn Express San Antonio-Airport
91 Ne Loop 410
San Antonio, TX
210-308-6700 (877-270-6405)
Dogs of all sizes are allowed for no additional pet fee. Multiple dogs may be allowed.

Holiday Inn Select

77 NE Loop 410
San Antonio, TX
210-349-9900 (877-270-6405)
Dogs of all sizes are allowed for a $100 refundable deposit plus an additional one time pet fee of $25 per room. Multiple dogs may be allowed.

Howard Johnson Express Inn
13279 IH-10 West
San Antonio, TX
210-558-7152 (800-446-4656)

Howard Johnson Express Inn
2755 IH-35N
San Antonio, TX
210-229-9220 (800-446-4656)
Dogs of all sizes are welcome. There is a $20 one time pet fee.

La Quinta Inn & Suites San Antonio Airport
850 Halm Blvd
San Antonio, TX
210-342-3738 (800-531-5900)
Dogs of all sizes are allowed. There are no additional pet fees. Dogs must be leashed, cleaned up after, the front desk informed if a pet is in the room alone, and the Do Not Disturb sign placed on the door. Multiple dogs may be allowed.

La Quinta Inn & Suites San Antonio Downtown
100 W Durango Blvd
San Antonio, TX
210-212-5400 (800-531-5900)
Dogs of all sizes are allowed. There are no additional pet fees. Dogs may only be left unattended in the rooms for a short time, and they must be quiet, well behaved, leashed, and cleaned up after. Multiple dogs may be allowed.

La Quinta Inn San Antonio I-10 East
6075 I-10 East
San Antonio, TX
210-661-4545 (800-531-5900)
Dogs of all sizes are allowed. There are no additional pet fees. There is a pet waiver to sign at check in. Dogs must be leashed and cleaned up after. 2 dogs may be allowed.

La Quinta Inn San Antonio I-35 N at Rittiman Rd
6410 I-35 North
San Antonio, TX
210-653-6619 (800-531-5900)
One dog of any size is allowed. There are no additional pet fees. Dogs must be leashed, cleaned up after, and arrangements made for housekeeping.

La Quinta Inn San Antonio I-35 N at Toepperwein
12822 I-35 North
San Antonio, TX
210-657-5500 (800-531-5900)
Dogs of all sizes are allowed. There are no additional pet fees. Dogs must be leashed, cleaned up after, and crated or removed for housekeeping. Multiple dogs may be allowed.

La Quinta Inn San Antonio Lackland
6511 Military Drive West
San Antonio, TX
210-674-3200 (800-531-5900)
Dogs of all sizes are allowed. There are no additional pet fees. Dogs must be leashed, cleaned up after, and arrangements made for. Multiple dogs may be allowed.

La Quinta Inn San Antonio Market Square
900 Dolorosa St.
San Antonio, TX
210-271-0001 (800-531-5900)
Dogs of all sizes are allowed. There are no additional pet fees. Dogs must be leashed and cleaned up after. Multiple dogs may be allowed.

La Quinta Inn San Antonio Sea World/Ingram Park
7134 N.W. Loop 410
San Antonio, TX
210-680-8883 (800-531-5900)
Dogs of all sizes are allowed. There are no additional pet fees. Dogs must be leashed, cleaned up after, and arrangements made for housekeeping. Multiple dogs may be allowed.

La Quinta Inn San Antonio South Park
7202 South Pan Am Expwy.
San Antonio, TX
210-922-2111 (800-531-5900)
Dogs of all sizes are allowed. There are no additional pet fees. Dogs must be leashed, cleaned up after, and the Do Not Disturb sign left on the door if a pet is in the room alone. Multiple dogs may be allowed.

La Quinta Inn San Antonio Vance Jackson
5922 I-10 West
San Antonio, TX
210-734-7931 (800-531-5900)
Dogs of all sizes are allowed. There are no additional pet fees. Dogs must be leashed, cleaned up after, and crated or removed for housekeeping. Multiple dogs may be

allowed.

La Quinta Inn San Antonio Wurzbach
9542 I-10 West
San Antonio, TX
210-593-0338 (800-531-5900)
Dogs of all sizes are allowed. There are no additional pet fees. Dogs must be leashed, cleaned up after, and a contact number left with the front desk if there is a pet alone in the room. Multiple dogs may be allowed.

Marriott Plaza San Antonio
555 S Alamo Street
San Antonio, TX
210-229-1000 (800-228-9290)
Dogs up to 50 pounds are allowed. There is a $25 one time additional fee per pet. Dogs must be leashed, cleaned up after, attended to or removed for housekeeping, and the Do Not Disturb sign put on the door if they are in the room alone. 2 dogs may be allowed.

Motel 6 - San Antonio - Alamo Dome South
748 Hot Wells Boulevard
San Antonio, TX
210-533-6667 (800-466-8356)
One well-behaved family pet per room. Guest must notify front desk upon arrival. Guest is liable for any damages. In consideration of all guests, pets must never be left unattended in the guest rooms.

Motel 6 - San Antonio - Fiesta
16500 I-10 West
San Antonio, TX
210-697-0731 (800-466-8356)
One well-behaved family pet per room. Guest must notify front desk upon arrival. Guest is liable for any damages. In consideration of all guests, pets must never be left unattended in the guest rooms.

Motel 6 - San Antonio - Ft Sam Houston
5522 North Pan Am Expressway
San Antonio, TX
210-661-8791 (800-466-8356)
One well-behaved family pet per room. Guest must notify front desk upon arrival. Guest is liable for any damages. In consideration of all guests, pets must never be left unattended in the guest rooms.

Motel 6 - San Antonio Downtown - Riverwalk
211 North Pecos Street
San Antonio, TX
210-225-1111 (800-466-8356)

One well-behaved family pet per room. Guest must notify front desk upon arrival. Guest is liable for any damages. In consideration of all guests, pets must never be left unattended in the guest rooms.

Motel 6 - San Antonio East
138 North WW White Road
San Antonio, TX
210-333-1850 (800-466-8356)
One well-behaved family pet per room. Guest must notify front desk upon arrival. Guest is liable for any damages. In consideration of all guests, pets must never be left unattended in the guest rooms.

Motel 6 - San Antonio NW-Medical Center
9400 Wurzbach Road
San Antonio, TX
210-593-0013 (800-466-8356)
One well-behaved family pet per room. Guest must notify front desk upon arrival. Guest is liable for any damages. In consideration of all guests, pets must never be left unattended in the guest rooms.

Motel 6 - San Antonio North
9503 I-35 North
San Antonio, TX
210-650-4419 (800-466-8356)
One well-behaved family pet per room. Guest must notify front desk upon arrival. Guest is liable for any damages. In consideration of all guests, pets must never be left unattended in the guest rooms.

Motel 6 - San Antonio Northeast
4621 East Rittiman Road
San Antonio, TX
210-653-8088 (800-466-8356)
One well-behaved family pet per room. Guest must notify front desk upon arrival. Guest is liable for any damages. In consideration of all guests, pets must never be left unattended in the guest rooms.

Motel 6 - San Antonio South
7950 South Pan Am Expressway
San Antonio, TX
210-928-2866 (800-466-8356)
One well-behaved family pet per room. Guest must notify front desk upon arrival. Guest is liable for any damages. In consideration of all guests, pets must never be left unattended in the guest rooms.

Motel 6 - San Antonio West - SeaWorld
2185 SW Loop 410
San Antonio, TX

210-673-9020 (800-466-8356)
One well-behaved family pet per room. Guest must notify front desk upon arrival. Guest is liable for any damages. In consideration of all guests, pets must never be left unattended in the guest rooms.

Red Roof Inn - San Antonio - Airport
333 Wolfe Road
San Antonio, TX
210-340-4055 (800-RED-ROOF)
One well-behaved family pet per room. Guest must notify front desk upon arrival. Guest is liable for any damages. In consideration of all guests, pets must never be left unattended in the guest rooms.

Red Roof Inn - San Antonio - Lackland Southwest
6861 Highway 90 West
San Antonio, TX
210-675-4120 (800-RED-ROOF)
One well-behaved family pet per room. Guest must notify front desk upon arrival. Guest is liable for any damages. In consideration of all guests, pets must never be left unattended in the guest rooms.

Red Roof Inn - San Antonio Downtown
1011 East Houston Street
San Antonio, TX
210-229-9973 (800-RED-ROOF)
One well-behaved family pet per room. Guest must notify front desk upon arrival. Guest is liable for any damages. In consideration of all guests, pets must never be left unattended in the guest rooms.

Red Roof Inn - San Antonio West - SeaWorld
6880 NW Loop 410
San Antonio, TX
210-509-3434 (800-RED-ROOF)
One well-behaved family pet per room. Guest must notify front desk upon arrival. Guest is liable for any damages. In consideration of all guests, pets must never be left unattended in the guest rooms.

Residence Inn by Marriott
1014 NE Loop 410
San Antonio, TX
210-805-8118
Dogs of all sizes are allowed. There is a $75 one time fee and a pet policy to sign at check in. 2 dogs may be allowed.

Residence Inn by Marriott
425 Bonham Street
San Antonio, TX

210-212-5555
Dogs of all sizes are allowed. There is a $100 one time fee and a pet policy to sign at check in. Multiple dogs may be allowed.

Residence Inn by Marriott
628 S Santa Rosa Blvd
San Antonio, TX
210-231-6000
Dogs of all sizes are allowed. There is a $75 one time fee and a pet policy to sign at check in. 2 dogs may be allowed.

San Antonio Marriott Rivercenter
101 Bowie Street
San Antonio, TX
210-223-1000 (800-648-4462)
Dogs up to 50 pounds are allowed. There is a $25 one time additional fee per pet. Dogs must be quiet, well behaved, leashed, cleaned up after, and the Do Not Disturb sign put on the door and a contact number left with the front desk if they are in the room alone. 2 dogs may be allowed.

San Antonio Marriott Riverwalk
711 E Riverwalk
San Antonio, TX
210-224-4555 (800-228-9290)
Dogs up to 50 pounds are allowed. There is a $25 one time additional fee per pet. Dogs may not be left alone in the room, and they must be leashed and cleaned up after. 2 dogs may be allowed.

Sheraton Gunter Hotel San Antonio
205 East Houston St.
San Antonio, TX
210-227-3241 (888-625-5144)
Dogs up to 80 pounds are allowed. Dogs are not allowed to be left alone in the room.

Staybridge Suites
4320 Spectrum One Rd
San Antonio, TX
210-558-9009 (877-270-6405)
Dogs up to 50 pounds are allowed for an additional pet fee of $75 per room. Multiple dogs may be allowed.

Studio 6 - San Antonio - Medical Center
7719 Louis Pasteur Court
San Antonio, TX
210-349-3100 (800-466-8356)
One well-behaved family pet per room. Guest must notify front desk upon arrival. Guest is liable for any damages. In consideration of all guests, pets must never be left unattended in the guest rooms.

Studio 6 - San Antonio - Six Flags
11802 I-10 West
San Antonio, TX
210-691-0121 (800-466-8356)
One well-behaved family pet per room. Guest must notify front desk upon arrival. Guest is liable for any damages. In consideration of all guests, pets must never be left unattended in the guest rooms.

Super 8 Antonio/Airport
11355 San Pedro Ave
San Antonio, TX
210-342-8488 (800-800-8000)
Dogs of all sizes are allowed. There is a $10 per night pet fee per pet. Smoking and non-smoking rooms are available for pet rooms. 2 dogs may be allowed.

Crystal River Inn
326 West Hopkins
San Marcos, TX
512-396-3739 (888 396-3739)
crystalriverinn.com/
In addition to the beautiful gardens and wooded areas, the handcrafted foods and ambiance of this 1883 Victorian inn, they also provide a variety of fun activities and special events year round. Dogs are allowed for an additional pet fee of $50 per room. Dogs must be crated when left alone in the room. 2 dogs may be allowed.

La Quinta Inn San Marcos
1619 I-35 North
San Marcos, TX
512-392-8800 (800-531-5900)
Dogs of all sizes are allowed. There are no additional pet fees. Dogs may not be left unattended for long periods, and they must be leashed and cleaned up after. The Do Not Disturb sign must be on the door if a pet is in the room alone, and arrangements need to be made with housekeeping is the stay is longer than 1 day. Multiple dogs may be allowed.

Motel 6 - San Marcos
1321 North I-35
San Marcos, TX
512-396-8705 (800-466-8356)
One well-behaved family pet per room. Guest must notify front desk upon arrival. Guest is liable for any damages. In consideration of all guests, pets must never be left unattended in the guest rooms.

Red Roof Inn - San Marcos
817 IH 35 North
San Marcos, TX
512-754-8899 (800-RED-ROOF)

One well-behaved family pet per room. Guest must notify front desk upon arrival. Guest is liable for any damages. In consideration of all guests, pets must never be left unattended in the guest rooms.

La Quinta Inn & Suites Houston-NASA/Seabrook
3636 Nasa Road 1
Seabrook, TX
281-326-7300 (800-531-5900)
Dogs up to 60 pounds are allowed. There are no additional pet fees. Dogs must be leashed, cleaned up after, and a contact number left with the front desk if a pet is alone in the room. Multiple dogs may be allowed.

Best Western Inn of Sealy
2107 Highway 36 S
Sealy, TX
979-885-3707 (800-780-7234)
Dogs are allowed for an additional pet fee per pet of $20 for each 1 to 5 days. 2 dogs may be allowed.

Best Western Shamrock Inn & Suites
1802 N Main Street
Shamrock, TX
806-256-1001 (800-780-7234)
Dogs are allowed for an additional fee of $10 per night per pet. Multiple dogs may be allowed.

Days Inn Sherman
1831 Texoma Pkwy
Sherman, TX
903-982-0433 (800-329-7466)
Dogs of all sizes are allowed. There is a $5 per night pet fee per pet. 2 dogs may be allowed.

Motel 6 - Sinton
8154 US 77
Sinton, TX
361-364-1853 (800-466-8356)
One well-behaved family pet per room. Guest must notify front desk upon arrival. Guest is liable for any damages. In consideration of all guests, pets must never be left unattended in the guest rooms.

Katy House
201 Ramona Street
Smithville, TX
512-237-4262 (800-843-5289)
katyhouse.com/
Rich in turn-of-the-century charm, this inn also provides a convenient location to numerous local activities, recreation, and historical sites. Dogs are allowed for no additional fee with advance registration as long as there is no additional clean-up required for the pet. 2 dogs may be allowed.

Comfort Inn
311 N H 277
Sonora, TX
325-387-5800 (877-424-6423)
Dogs are allowed for an additional one time pet fee of $10 per room. Multiple dogs may be allowed.

Days Inn Sonora
1312 N Service Road
Sonora, TX
325-387-3516 (800-329-7466)
Dogs of all sizes are allowed. There is a $4 per night pet fee per pet. 2 dogs may be allowed.

Affordable Beach House Vacation Rentals
PO Box 3061
South Padre Island, TX
956-761-8750
They offer pet-friendly condos and vacation home rentals.

Best Western Fiesta Isles Hotel
5701 Padre Blvd
South Padre Island, TX
956-761-4913 (800-780-7234)
Dogs are allowed for an additional one time fee of $25 per pet. Multiple dogs may be allowed.

DCH Condo Rentals
111 E Hybiscus
South Padre Island, TX
956-459-7499
Well behaved dogs up to about 60 pounds are allowed. There is a $20 one time fee by the week, and a $50 one time fee by the month, plus a $50 refundable deposit. There are some breed restrictions. Multiple dogs may be allowed.

Days Inn South Padre Island
3913 Padre Blvd
South Padre Island, TX
956-761-7831 (800-329-7466)
Dogs of all sizes are allowed. There is a $25 one time per pet fee per visit. Pets are not allowed during summer months (Memorial Day through Labor Day). 2 dogs may be allowed.

Econo Lodge
3813 Padre Blvd.
South Padre Island, TX
956-761-8500
There is a $25 per day pet charge.

Island Inn
5100 Gulf Blvd.
South Padre Island, TX
956-761-7677
There is a $10 per day pet fee.

La Quinta Inn & Suites South Padre Beach Resort
7000 Padre Blvd
South Padre Island, TX
956-772-7000 (800-531-5900)
Dogs of all sizes are allowed. There are no additional pet fees. There is a pet waiver to sign at check in. Dogs must be leashed and cleaned up after, and a contact number left with the front desk if there is a pet alone in the room. Multiple dogs may be allowed.

Motel 6 - South Padre Island
4013 Padre Boulevard
South Padre Island, TX
956-761-7911 (800-466-8356)
One well-behaved family pet per room. Guest must notify front desk upon arrival. Guest is liable for any damages. In consideration of all guests, pets must never be left unattended in the guest rooms.

Motel 6 - Houston North - Spring
19606 Cypresswood Court
Spring, TX
281-350-6400 (800-466-8356)
One well-behaved family pet per room. Guest must notify front desk upon arrival. Guest is liable for any damages. In consideration of all guests, pets must never be left unattended in the guest rooms.

La Quinta Inn Houston Stafford/Sugarland
12727 Southwest Freeway
Stafford, TX
281-240-2300 (800-531-5900)
Dogs of all sizes are allowed. There are no additional pet fees. Dogs must be leashed, cleaned up after, and crated or removed for housekeeping. Multiple dogs may be allowed.

Studio 6 - Houston - Sugarland
12827 Southwest Freeway
Stafford, TX
281-240-6900 (800-466-8356)
One well-behaved family pet per room. Guest must notify front desk upon arrival. Guest is liable for any damages. In consideration of all guests, pets must never be left unattended in the guest rooms.

Best Western Cross Timbers
1625 South Loop
Stephenville, TX
254-968-2114 (800-780-7234)
Dogs are allowed for an additional pet fee of $10 per night per room. 2 dogs may be allowed.

Days Inn Stephenville
701 SE Loop
Stephenville, TX
254-968-3392 (800-329-7466)
Dogs of all sizes are allowed. There are no additional pet fees. 2 dogs may be allowed.

Holiday Inn
2865 W. Washington
Stephenville, TX
254-968-5256 (877-270-6405)
Dogs of all sizes are allowed for a $150 refundable pet deposit per room. Multiple dogs may be allowed.

Easter Egg Valley Motel
H 170 1/2 mile W of H 118
Study Butte, TX
432-371-2254
This motel is at the gateway to the Big Bend National Park. Dogs of all sizes are allowed with a one time fee of $10 per room. Dogs may not be left alone uncrated in the room. Multiple dogs may be allowed.

Comfort Suites
1521 Industrial Drive E
Sulphur Springs, TX
903-438-0918 (877-424-6423)
Dogs are allowed for an additional pet fee of $5 per night per room. 2 dogs may be allowed.

Motel 6 - Sweetwater
510 NW Georgia Avenue
Sweetwater, TX
325-235-4387 (800-466-8356)
One well-behaved family pet per room. Guest must notify front desk upon arrival. Guest is liable for any damages. In consideration of all guests, pets must never be left unattended in the guest rooms.

Howard Johnson Express Inn
1912 S. 31st St
Temple, TX
254-778-5521 (800-446-4656)
Well-behaved dogs of all sizes are allowed. There is a $10 per day additional pet fee.

La Quinta Inn Temple
1604 W. Barton Ave.
Temple, TX
254-771-2980 (800-531-5900)
Dogs of all sizes are allowed. There are no additional pet fees. Dogs must be leashed, cleaned up after, and attended to or removed for housekeeping. Multiple dogs may be allowed.

Motel 6 - Temple

1100 North General Bruce Drive
Temple, TX
254-778-0272 (800-466-8356)
One well-behaved family pet per
room. Guest must notify front desk
upon arrival. Guest is liable for any
damages. In consideration of all
guests, pets must never be left
unattended in the guest rooms.

Motel 6 - Terrell
101 Mira Place
Terrell, TX
972-563-0300 (800-466-8356)
One well-behaved family pet per
room. Guest must notify front desk
upon arrival. Guest is liable for any
damages. In consideration of all
guests, pets must never be left
unattended in the guest rooms.

Budget Hotel
400 W 53rd St
Texarkana, TX
903-793-6565 (800-262-0048)
There is no fee for 1 small dog; there
is a $20 one time pet fee per room
for 2 dogs, or a large or shedding
dog. 2 dogs may be allowed.

Holiday Inn Express
5401 North State Line Ave
Texarkana, TX
903-792-3366 (877-270-6405)
Dogs of all sizes are allowed for an
additional one time pet fee of $25 per
room. 2 dogs may be allowed.

La Quinta Inn Texarkana
5201 State Line Ave.
Texarkana, TX
903-794-1900 (800-531-5900)
Dogs of all sizes are allowed. There
are no additional pet fees. Dogs may
not be left unattended, and they must
be leashed and cleaned up after.
Multiple dogs may be allowed.

Motel 6 - Texarkana
1924 Hampton Road
Texarkana, TX
903-793-1413 (800-466-8356)
One well-behaved family pet per
room. Guest must notify front desk
upon arrival. Guest is liable for any
damages. In consideration of all
guests, pets must never be left
unattended in the guest rooms.

Comfort Suites
4796 Memorial Drive
The Colony, TX
972-668-5555 (877-424-6423)
Dogs up to 50 pounds are allowed
for an additional one time fee of $25
per pet. 2 dogs may be allowed.

Holiday Inn Express Hotel & Suites
The Woodlands
24888 Ih 45 N
The Woodlands, TX
281-681-8088 (877-270-6405)
Dogs of all sizes are allowed for an
additional one time fee of $25 pet .
2 dogs may be allowed.

Houston - The Woodlands Drury Inn
& Suites
28099 I-45 North
The Woodlands, TX
281-362-7222 (800-378-7946)
Dogs of all sizes are permitted. Pets
are not allowed in the breakfast
area of the hotel. Pets are not to be
left unattended, and each guest
must assume liability for damage of
property or other guest complaints.
There is a limit of one pet per room.

La Quinta Inn & Suites Woodlands
South
24868 I-45 North
The Woodlands, TX
281-681-9188 (800-531-5900)
Dogs of all sizes are allowed. There
are no additional pet fees. Dogs
must be leashed and cleaned up
after. Dogs are not allowed in the
dining area at any time. Multiple
dogs may be allowed.

La Quinta Inn The Woodlands North
28673 I-45 North
The Woodlands, TX
281-367-7722 (800-531-5900)
Dogs up to 100 pounds are allowed.
There are no additional pet fees.
Dogs must be friendly, leashed,
cleaned up after, and crated or
removed for housekeeping. 2 dogs
may be allowed.

Residence Inn by Marriott
1040 Lake Front Circle
The Woodlands, TX
281-292-3252
Dogs of all sizes are allowed. There
is a $75 one time fee and a pet
policy to sign at check in. Multiple
dogs may be allowed.

Residence Inn by Marriott
9333 Six Pines
The Woodlands, TX
281-419-1542
Dogs of all sizes are allowed. There
is a $75 one time fee and a pet
policy to sign at check in. Multiple
dogs may be allowed.

La Quinta Inn & Suites Tomball
14000 Medical Complex Drive
Tomball, TX
281-516-0400 (800-531-5900)

Dogs of all sizes are allowed. There
are no additional pet fees. There is a
pet waiver to sign at check in, and
there must be a credit card on file.
Dogs must be leashed and cleaned
up after. 2 dogs may be allowed.

Candlewood Suites
315 E Rieck Rd
Tyler, TX
903-509-4131 (877-270-6405)
Dogs of all sizes are allowed for an
additional one time pet fee of $75 per
room. Multiple dogs may be allowed.

Days Inn Tyler/Northeast
12732 Hwy 155 N
Tyler, TX
903-877-9227 (800-329-7466)
Dogs of all sizes are allowed. There
is a $10 per night pet fee per pet. 2
dogs may be allowed.

Holiday Inn Select
5701 South Broadway
Tyler, TX
903-561-5800 (877-270-6405)
One dog of any size is allowed for an
additional one time pet fee of $50.

Motel 6 - Tyler
3236 Gentry Parkway
Tyler, TX
903-595-6691 (800-466-8356)
One well-behaved family pet per
room. Guest must notify front desk
upon arrival. Guest is liable for any
damages. In consideration of all
guests, pets must never be left
unattended in the guest rooms.

Residence Inn by Marriott
3303 Troup Highway
Tyler, TX
903-595-5188
Dogs of all sizes are allowed. There
is a $75 one time fee and a pet
policy to sign at check in. Multiple
dogs may be allowed.

Holiday Inn
920 E. Main
Uvalde, TX
830-278-4511 (877-270-6405)
Dogs of all sizes is allowed for no
additional pet fee. Multiple dogs may
be allowed.

Best Western Inn of Van Horn
1705 W Broadway
Van Horn, TX
432-283-2410 (800-780-7234)
Dogs up to 50 pounds are allowed
for an additional fee of $12 per night
per pet. Multiple dogs may be
allowed.

Days Inn Van Horn
600 E Broadway
Van Horn, TX
432-283-1007 (800-329-7466)
Dogs of all sizes are allowed. There is a $8 per night pet fee per pet. 2 dogs may be allowed.

Motel 6 - Van Horn
1805 West Broadway
Van Horn, TX
432-283-2992 (800-466-8356)
One well-behaved family pet per room. Guest must notify front desk upon arrival. Guest is liable for any damages. In consideration of all guests, pets must never be left unattended in the guest rooms.

Best Western Country Inn
1800 West Vega Blvd
Vega, TX
806-267-2131 (800-780-7234)
Dogs are allowed for an additional fee of $10 per night per pet. Multiple dogs may be allowed.

Comfort Inn
1005 S Main Street
Vega, TX
806-267-0126 (877-424-6423)
Dogs are allowed for an additional pet fee of $10 per night per room. The fee may be slightly higher for large dogs. 2 dogs may be allowed.

Best Western Village Inn
1615 Expressway
Vernon, TX
940-552-5417 (800-780-7234)
Dogs are allowed for an additional one time fee of $10 per pet. Multiple dogs may be allowed.

Days Inn Vernon
3110 Frontage Rd
Vernon, TX
940-552-9982 (800-329-7466)
Dogs of all sizes are allowed. There is a $25 per night pet fee per pet. 2 dogs may be allowed.

Best Western Victoria Inn & Suites
8106 NE Zac Lentz Pkwy
Victoria, TX
361-485-2300 (800-780-7234)
Dogs up to 50 pounds are allowed for an additional fee of $10 per night per pet. 2 dogs may be allowed.

Comfort Inn
1906 Houston H
Victoria, TX
361-574-9393 (877-424-6423)
Dogs are allowed for a $35 refundable deposit plus an additional pet fee of $10 per night per room.

Multiple dogs may be allowed.

La Quinta Inn Victoria
7603 N. Navarro
Victoria, TX
361-572-3585 (800-531-5900)
Dogs of all sizes are allowed. There are no additional pet fees. Dogs may not be left unattended, and they must be leashed and cleaned up after. Multiple dogs may be allowed.

Motel 6 - Victoria
3716 Houston Highway
Victoria, TX
361-573-1273 (800-466-8356)
One well-behaved family pet per room. Guest must notify front desk upon arrival. Guest is liable for any damages. In consideration of all guests, pets must never be left unattended in the guest rooms.

La Quinta Inn Vidor
165 East Courtland Street
Vidor, TX
409-783-2600 (800-531-5900)
Dogs of all sizes are allowed. There are no additional pet fees. Dogs may not be left unattended for long periods and not at all during the night. Dogs must be leashed and cleaned up after. Multiple dogs may be allowed.

Best Western Waco Mall
6624 Hwy 84 West
Waco, TX
254-776-3194 (800-780-7234)
Dogs up to around knee high are allowed for an additional one time fee of $10 per pet. 2 dogs may be allowed.

La Quinta Inn Waco University
1110 S. 9th St.
Waco, TX
254-752-9741 (800-531-5900)
Dogs of all sizes are allowed. There are no additional pet fees. Dogs must be leashed, cleaned up after, and crated or removed for housekeeping. Multiple dogs may be allowed.

Motel 6 - Waco South
3120 Jack Kultgen Freeway
Waco, TX
254-662-4622 (800-466-8356)
One well-behaved family pet per room. Guest must notify front desk upon arrival. Guest is liable for any damages. In consideration of all guests, pets must never be left unattended in the guest rooms.

Residence Inn by Marriott
501 S University Parks Drive
Waco, TX
254-714-1386
Dogs of all sizes are allowed. There is a $150 one time fee and a pet policy to sign at check in. Multiple dogs may be allowed.

Super 8 Waco
1320 S Jack Kultgen Fwy
Waco, TX
254-754-1023 (800-800-8000)
Dogs of all sizes are allowed. There is a $10 per night pet fee per pet under 45 pounds. and $15 per pet over 45 pounds. Smoking and non-smoking rooms are available for pet rooms. 2 dogs may be allowed.

Best Western Santa Fe Inn
1927 Santa Fe Dr
Weatherford, TX
817-594-7401 (800-780-7234)
Dogs up to 10 pounds are allowed for an additional fee of $5 per night per pet; the fee is $10 for dogs over 10 pounds. 2 dogs may be allowed.

Days Inn Weatherford
1106 W Park Ave
Weatherford, TX
817-594-3816 (800-329-7466)
Dogs of all sizes are allowed. There is a $10 per night pet fee per pet. 2 dogs may be allowed.

Holiday Inn Express Hotel and Suites
2500 Hwy 51 South
Weatherford, TX
817-599-3700 (877-270-6405)
Dogs of all sizes are allowed for an additional fee of $10 per night per pet. Multiple dogs may be allowed.

La Quinta Inn & Suites Weatherford
1915 Wall Street (c/o Adams St.)
Weatherford, TX
817-594-4481 (800-531-5900)
Dogs of all sizes are allowed. There are no additional pet fees. Dogs may not be left unattended, and they must be quiet, leashed, and cleaned up after. Multiple dogs may be allowed.

Motel 6 - Weatherford
150 Alford Drive
Weatherford, TX
817-594-1740 (800-466-8356)
One well-behaved family pet per room. Guest must notify front desk upon arrival. Guest is liable for any damages. In consideration of all guests, pets must never be left unattended in the guest rooms.

La Quinta Inn & Suites Webster -

Clearlake
520 West Bay Area Boulevard
Webster, TX
281-554-5290 (800-531-5900)
Dogs of all sizes are allowed. There are no additional pet fees. Dogs may not be left unattended, and they must be leashed and cleaned up after. Multiple dogs may be allowed.

Motel 6 - Houston - NASA
1001 West NASA Road 1
Webster, TX
281-332-4581 (800-466-8356)
One well-behaved family pet per room. Guest must notify front desk upon arrival. Guest is liable for any damages. In consideration of all guests, pets must never be left unattended in the guest rooms.

Best Western Palm Aire Motor Inn and Suites
415 S International Blvd
Weslaco, TX
956-969-2411 (800-780-7234)
Dogs are allowed for no additional pet fee. 2 dogs may be allowed.

La Quinta Inn Fort Worth West/Medical Center
7888 I-30 West
White Settlement, TX
817-246-5511 (800-531-5900)
Dogs of all sizes are allowed. There are no additional pet fees. Dogs must be leashed, cleaned up after, and crated or removed for housekeeping. Multiple dogs may be allowed.

Best Western Wichita Falls Inn
1032 Central Fwy
Wichita, TX
940-766-6881 (800-780-7234)
Dogs are allowed for an additional fee of $10 per night per pet. Multiple dogs may be allowed.

Best Western Northtown Inn
1317 Kenley Avenue
Wichita Falls, TX
940-766-3300 (800-780-7234)
Dogs are allowed for an additional one time fee of $10 per pet. Multiple dogs may be allowed.

Holiday Inn Wichita Falls (At The Falls)
100 Central Freeway
Wichita Falls, TX
940-761-6000 (877-270-6405)
Dogs of all sizes are allowed for an additional one time pet fee of $25 per room. Multiple dogs may be allowed.

La Quinta Inn Wichita Falls Airport

Area
1128 Central Frwy. North
Wichita Falls, TX
940-322-6971 (800-531-5900)
Dogs of all sizes are allowed. There are no additional pet fees. Dogs must be quiet, well behaved, leashed, and crated when left alone in the room. Multiple dogs may be allowed.

Motel 6 - Wichita Falls
1812 Maurine Street
Wichita Falls, TX
940-322-8817 (800-466-8356)
One well-behaved family pet per room. Guest must notify front desk upon arrival. Guest is liable for any damages. In consideration of all guests, pets must never be left unattended in the guest rooms.

Studio 6 - Winnie
134 Spur 5
Winnie, TX
409-296-3611 (800-466-8356)
One well-behaved family pet per room. Guest must notify front desk upon arrival. Guest is liable for any damages. In consideration of all guests, pets must never be left unattended in the guest rooms.

Best Western Inn By the Lake
Rt 1, Box 252
Zapata, TX
956-765-8403 (800-780-7234)
Dogs are allowed for no additional pet fee. Extra large dogs can not be accommodated. 2 dogs may be allowed.

Utah Listings

Best Western Butch Cassidy Inn
161 South Main
Beaver, UT
435-438-2438 (800-780-7234)
Dogs are allowed for an additional fee of $5 per night per pet. Multiple dogs may be allowed.

Best Western Paradise Inn
1451 North 300 West
Beaver, UT
435-438-2455 (800-780-7234)
Dogs are allowed for an additional pet fee of $9 per night per room. Multiple dogs may be allowed.

Quality Inn
781 West 1800 S
Beaver, UT
435-438-5426 (877-424-6423)

Dogs up to 50 pounds are allowed for no additional pet fee. 2 dogs may be allowed.

Four Corners Inn
131 E Center St
Blanding, UT
435-678-3257
moabutah.com/fourcornersinn/
There are no additional pet fees. Dogs are not allowed on the beds.

Howard Johnson Inn
1167 S Main St.
Brigham City, UT
435-723-8511 (800-446-4656)
Dogs of all sizes are welcome. There are no additional pet fees.

Best Western Ruby's Inn
Utah Hwy 63
Bryce, UT
435-834-5341 (800-780-7234)
Dogs are allowed for an additional one time pet fee of $10 per room. Multiple dogs may be allowed.

Days Inn Cedar City
1204 South Main
Cedar City, UT
435-867-8877 (800-329-7466)
Dogs of all sizes are allowed. There is a $10 per night pet fee per pet. 2 dogs may be allowed.

Holiday Inn Express Hotel and Suites
1555 S Old Highway 91
Cedar City, UT
435-865-7799 (877-270-6405)
Dogs up to 100 pounds are allowed for an additional pet fee of $10 per night per room. Multiple dogs may be allowed.

Motel 6 - Cedar City
1620 West 200 North
Cedar City, UT
435-586-9200 (800-466-8356)
One well-behaved family pet per room. Guest must notify front desk upon arrival. Guest is liable for any damages. In consideration of all guests, pets must never be left unattended in the guest rooms.

Super 8 Cedar City
145 N 1550 West
Cedar City, UT
735-586-8880 (800-800-8000)
Dogs of all sizes are allowed. There is a $9 per night pet fee per pet. Smoking and non-smoking rooms are available for pet rooms. 2 dogs may be allowed.

Traveller's Inn
572 N Main St

Clearfield, UT
801-825-8000
Dogs of all sizes are allowed. There is a $10 per night pet fee per pet. Smoking and non-smoking rooms are available for pet rooms. 2 dogs may be allowed.

Best Western Holiday Hills
210 South 200 West
Coalville, UT
435-336-4444 (800-780-7234)
Dogs are allowed for an additional pet fee of $15 per night for 1 dog, and $5 for each additional dog per night. Multiple dogs may be allowed.

Best Western Motor Inn
527 East Topaz Blvd
Delta, UT
435-864-3882 (800-780-7234)
Dogs are allowed for an additional one time fee of $25 per pet. Multiple dogs may be allowed.

Best Western Paradise Inn and Resort
905 N Main
Filimore, UT
435-743-6895 (800-780-7234)
Dogs are allowed for no additional pet fee. Dogs must be declared at the time of reservations. 2 dogs may be allowed.

Holiday Inn Express
965 East Main Street
Green River, UT
435-564-4439 (877-270-6405)
Dogs of all sizes are allowed for an additional fee of $10 per night per pet. Multiple dogs may be allowed.

Motel 6 - Green River
946 East Main Street
Green River, UT
435-564-3436 (800-466-8356)
One well-behaved family pet per room. Guest must notify front desk upon arrival. Guest is liable for any damages. In consideration of all guests, pets must never be left unattended in the guest rooms.

Super 8 Green River
1248 E Main
Green River, UT
435-564-8888 (800-800-8000)
Dogs of all sizes are allowed. There is a $5 per night pet fee per pet. Reservations are recommended due to limited rooms for pets. Smoking and non-smoking rooms are available for pet rooms. 2 dogs may be allowed.

Motel 6 - Hurricane

650 West State Street
Hurricane, UT
435-635-4010 (800-466-8356)
One well-behaved family pet per room. Guest must notify front desk upon arrival. Guest is liable for any damages. In consideration of all guests, pets must never be left unattended in the guest rooms.

Best Western Red Hills
125 W Center
Kanab, UT
435-644-2675 (800-780-7234)
Dogs are allowed for an additional one time pet fee of $10 per room. 2 dogs may be allowed.

Holiday Inn Express
815 E. Hwy 89
Kanab, UT
435-644-8888 (877-270-6405)
Dogs up to 100 pounds are allowed for an additional pet fee of $10 per night per room. Multiple dogs may be allowed.

Parry Lodge
89 East Center Street
Kanab, UT
435-644-2601 (800-748-4104)
infowest.com/parry/
There are 3 non-smoking pet rooms. There is a $5 per day pet fee.

Shilo Inn
296 West 100 North
Kanab, UT
435-644-2562 (800-222-2244)
shiloinns.com/Utah/kanab.html
There is a $10 one time pet fee.

Super 8 Kanab
70 South 200 West
Kanab, UT
435-644-5500 (800-800-8000)
Dogs of all sizes are allowed. There is a $10 per night pet fee per pet. Smoking and non-smoking rooms are available for pet rooms. 2 dogs may be allowed.

Comfort Inn
877 N 400 W
Layton, UT
801-544-5577 (877-424-6423)
Dogs are allowed for a $20 refundable deposit. Multiple dogs may be allowed.

Hampton Inn
1702 N Woodland Park Drive
Layton, UT
801-775-8800
Dogs of all sizes are allowed. There are no additional pet fees. There is

a pet policy to sign at check in and they only have a few non-smoking rooms available. Dogs are not allowed to be left alone in the room. Multiple dogs may be allowed.

Holiday Inn Express
1695 Woodland Park Dr
Layton, UT
801-773-3773 (877-270-6405)
Dogs of all sizes are allowed for an additional one time pet fee of $50. 2 dogs may be allowed.

La Quinta Inn Salt Lake City Layton
1965 North 1200 W.
Layton, UT
801-776-6700 (800-531-5900)
Dogs of all sizes are allowed. There are no additional pet fees. Dogs must be quiet, well behaved, leashed, and cleaned up after. Multiple dogs may be allowed.

TownePlace Suites Salt Lake City/Layton
1743 Woodland Park Drive
Layton, UT
801-779-2422
Dogs of all sizes are allowed. There is a $75 one time pet fee per visit. 2 dogs may be allowed.

Best Western Timpanogos Inn
195 South 850 East
Lehi, UT
801-768-1400 (800-780-7234)
Dogs are allowed for an additional one time pet fee of $10 per room. Multiple dogs may be allowed.

Motel 6 - Salt Lake City South - Lehi
210 South 1200 East
Lehi, UT
801-768-2668 (800-466-8356)
One well-behaved family pet per room. Guest must notify front desk upon arrival. Guest is liable for any damages. In consideration of all guests, pets must never be left unattended in the guest rooms.

Best Western Weston Inn
250 N Main Street
Logan, UT
435-752-5700 (800-780-7234)
Dogs are allowed for an additional pet fee of $10 per night per room. 2 dogs may be allowed.

Motel 6 - Salt Lake City South - Midvale
7263 South Catalpa Road
Midvale, UT
801-561-0058 (800-466-8356)
One well-behaved family pet per room. Guest must notify front desk

upon arrival. Guest is liable for any damages. In consideration of all guests, pets must never be left unattended in the guest rooms.

Best Western Executive Inn
280 W 7200 S
Midvale (Salt Lake City), UT
801-566-4141 (800-780-7234)
Dogs up to 50 pounds are allowed for an additional fee of $15 per night per pet. 2 dogs may be allowed.

Apache Hotel
166 S 400 East
Moab, UT
435-259-5727 (800-228-6882)
moab-utah.com/apachemotel/
There is a 1 dog limit per room. There are no additional pet fees.

Bowen Motel
169 N Main St
Moab, UT
435-259-7132
moab-utah.com/bowen/motel.html
There is a $5 per day pet fee.

Comfort Suites
800 S Main S treet
Moab, UT
435-259-5252 (877-424-6423)
Dogs are allowed for no additional pet fee. Multiple dogs may be allowed.

La Quinta Inn Moab
815 S. Main St.
Moab, UT
435-259-8700 (800-531-5900)
Dogs of all sizes are allowed. There are no additional pet fees. There is a pet waiver to sign at check in. Dogs must be leashed, cleaned up after, and crated if left alone in the room. Dogs are not allowed in the food areas, and they must be walked at the designated pet walk area. Multiple dogs may be allowed.

Moab Valley Inn
711 S Main St
Moab, UT
435-259-4419 (800-831-6622)
moabvalleyinn.com/
There is a $10 per day per room additional pet fee.

Motel 6 - Moab
1089 North Main Street
Moab, UT
435-259-6686 (800-466-8356)
One well-behaved family pet per room. Guest must notify front desk upon arrival. Guest is liable for any damages. In consideration of all guests, pets must never be left

unattended in the guest rooms.

River Canyon Lodge
71 W 200 N
Moab, UT
435-259-8838
Dogs of all sizes are allowed. There is a $10 one time fee per pet for pets under 10 pounds. There is a $15 one time fee per pet for pets 15 to 20 pounds, and a $20 one time fee per pet for pets over 21 pounds. There is a pet policy to sign at check in. Multiple dogs may be allowed.

Sleep Inn
1051 S Main Street
Moab, UT
435-259-4655 (877-424-6423)
Dogs are allowed for a $50 refundable deposit. Multiple dogs may be allowed.

The Gonzo Inn
100 W 200 S
Moab, UT
435-259-2515
Dogs of all sizes are allowed. There is a $25 per night per room fee and a pet policy to sign at check in. Multiple dogs may be allowed.

Best Western Wayside Motor Inn
197 E Central
Monticello, UT
435-587-2261 (800-780-7234)
Dogs are allowed for an additional fee of $10 per night per pet. Multiple dogs may be allowed.

Goulding's Lodge
1000 Main Street
Monument Valley, UT
435-727-3231
gouldings.com/
Well-behaved leashed dogs of all sizes are welcome. There is a $50 refundable pet deposit. The rooms offer views of Monument Valley. The lodge is located north of the Arizona and Utah border, adjacent to the Navajo Tribal Park in Monument Valley. Thanks to one of our readers for recommending this lodging.

Studio 6 - Salt Lake City - Fort Union
975 East 6600 South
Murray, UT
801-685-2102 (800-466-8356)
One well-behaved family pet per room. Guest must notify front desk upon arrival. Guest is liable for any damages. In consideration of all guests, pets must never be left

unattended in the guest rooms.

Motel 6 - Nephi
2195 South Main Street
Nephi, UT
435-623-0666 (800-466-8356)
One well-behaved family pet per room. Guest must notify front desk upon arrival. Guest is liable for any damages. In consideration of all guests, pets must never be left unattended in the guest rooms.

Best Western CottonTree Inn
1030 N 400 E
North Sallt Lake City, UT
801-292-7666 (800-780-7234)
Dogs are allowed for no additional pet fee. Multiple dogs may be allowed.

Best Western Country Inn
1335 W 12th St
Ogden, UT
801-394-9474 (800-780-7234)
Dogs are allowed for no additional pet fee. Multiple dogs may be allowed.

Comfort Suites
2250 S 1200 W
Ogden, UT
801-621-2545 (877-424-6423)
Dogs are allowed for no additional pet fee with a credit card on file; there is a $150 refundable deposit if paying cash. Multiple dogs may be allowed.

Holiday Inn Express Hotel & Suites
2245 S. 1200 West
Ogden, UT
801-392-5000 (877-270-6405)
Dogs of all sizes is allowed for no additional pet fee. Multiple dogs may be allowed.

Motel 6 - Ogden
1455 Washington Boulevard
Ogden, UT
801-627-4560 (800-466-8356)
One well-behaved family pet per room. Guest must notify front desk upon arrival. Guest is liable for any damages. In consideration of all guests, pets must never be left unattended in the guest rooms.

Red Roof Inn - OGDEN - RIVERDALE
1500 West Riverdale Road
Ogden, UT
801-627-2880 (800-RED-ROOF)
One well-behaved family pet per room. Guest must notify front desk upon arrival. Guest is liable for any damages. In consideration of all

guests, pets must never be left unattended in the guest rooms.

Super 8 Ogden
1508 W 2100 South
Ogden, UT
801-731-7100 (800-800-8000)
Dogs of all sizes are allowed. There is a $25 returnable deposit required per room. Smoking and non-smoking rooms are available for pet rooms.

La Quinta Inn & Suites Orem
University Parkway
521 W. University Parkway
Orem, UT
801-226-0440 (800-531-5900)
Dogs of all sizes are allowed. There are no additional pet fees. Dogs must be quiet, leashed, and cleaned up after. Multiple dogs may be allowed.

La Quinta Inn Orem/Provo North
1100 West 780 North
Orem, UT
801-235-9555 (800-531-5900)
Dogs of all sizes are allowed. There are no additional pet fees. Dogs may not be left unattended, and they must be quiet, well behaved, leashed and cleaned up after. Multiple dogs may be allowed.

Bryce Junction Inn
3090 E Highway 12 & Jct 89
Panguitch, UT
435-676-8886
This hotel is open from March 15 to Nov 15. There are no additional pet fees.

Bryce Way Motel
429 N Main St
Panguitch, UT
435-676-2400
brycemotel.com
Pets are allowed for a $5 per night additional pet fee.

Marianna Inn Motel
699 N Main St
Panguitch, UT
435-676-8844
mariannainn.com
Dogs of all sizes are allowed for a $5 per night additional pet fee. The hotel is about 20 miles from Bryce.

Best Western Landmark Inn
6560 N Landmark Dr
Park City, UT
435-649-7300 (800-780-7234)
Dogs are allowed for an additional fee of $10 per night per pet. Multiple dogs may be allowed.

Holiday Inn Express Hotel & Suites
1501 West Ute Blvd
Park City, UT
435-658-1600 (877-270-6405)
Dogs of all sizes are allowed for an additional pet fee of $20 per night per room. 2 dogs may be allowed.

The Gables Hotel
1335 Lowell Avenue, PO Box 905
Park City, UT
435-655-3315 (800-443-1045)
thegablespc.com
Pets receive a Pet Gift basket upon arrival. The Gables Hotel features 20 one bedroom condominiums and one or two bedroom penthouse suites each with a queen or king bed in the master bedroom, fully equipped kitchen, living area with a queen sofa sleeper, dining area, fireplace, balcony and bathroom with an oversized jetted tub. Property amenities include an outdoor Jacuzzi, sauna and laundry facilities. Rates start at $85.00 per night. There is a $20 per night additional pet fee. There is a $100 refundable pet deposit upon arrival.

Days Inn Parowan
625 W 200 South
Parowan, UT
435-477-3326 (800-329-7466)
Dogs of all sizes are allowed. There is a $10 per night pet fee per pet. Reservations are recommended due to limited rooms for pets. 2 dogs may be allowed.

Comfort Inn
830 N Main Street
Payson, UT
801-465-4861 (877-424-6423)
Dogs are allowed for no additional pet fee. Multiple dogs may be allowed.

National 9
641 W. Price River Drive
Price, UT
435-637-7000
There is a $5 per day pet fee.

Days Inn Provo
1675 N 200 West
Provo, UT
801-375-8600 (800-329-7466)
Dogs of all sizes are allowed. There is a $5 per night pet fee per pet. 2 dogs may be allowed.

Hampton Inn
1511 S 40 East
Provo, UT
801-377-6396
Dogs of all sizes are allowed. There

is a $20 one time cleaning fee and a pet policy to sign at check in. Multiple dogs may be allowed.

Sleep Inn
1505 South 40 East
Provo, UT
801-377-6597 (877-424-6423)
Dogs up to 50 pounds are allowed for an additional fee of $10 per night per pet. Multiple dogs may be allowed.

Apple Tree Inn
145 South Main
Richfield, UT
435-896-5481
Dogs are allowed for an additional pet fee of $6 per night per room. Multiple dogs may be allowed.

Days Inn Richfield
333 N Main St
Richfield, UT
435-896-6476 (800-329-7466)
Dogs of all sizes are allowed. There is a $10 per night pet fee per pet. 2 dogs may be allowed.

Frontier Motel
75 S 200 E
Roosevelt, UT
435-722-2201
There are no additional pet fees.

Super 8 Salina/Scenic Hills Area
1500 South 80 East
Salina, UT
435-529-7483 (800-800-8000)
Dogs of all sizes are allowed. There is a $10 per night pet fee per pet. Smoking and non-smoking rooms are available for pet rooms. 2 dogs may be allowed.

Candlewood Suites
2170 W. North Temple
Salt Lake City, UT
801-359-7500 (877-270-6405)
Dogs up to 50 pounds are allowed for an additional one time pet fee of $75 per room. 2 dogs may be allowed.

Candlewood Suites
6990 South Park Centre Drive
Salt Lake City, UT
801-567-0111 (877-270-6405)
One dog is allowed for an additional pet fee of $75 per room.

Comfort Inn
200 N Admiral Bird Road
Salt Lake City, UT
801-537-7444 (877-424-6423)
Dogs of all sizes are allowed. There is a $20 one time additional fee per

pet.

Days Inn Salt Lake City Airport
1900 West North Temple St
Salt Lake City, UT
801-539-8538 (800-329-7466)
Dogs of all sizes are allowed. There
are no additional pet fees.
Reservations are recommended due
to limited rooms for pets. 2 dogs may
be allowed.

Days Inn Salt Lake City Central
315 West 3300 South
Salt Lake City, UT
801-486-8780 (800-329-7466)
Dogs of all sizes are allowed. There
are no additional pet fees. 2 dogs
may be allowed.

Hilton
5151 Wiley Post Way
Salt Lake City, UT
801-539-1515
Dogs are allowed for an additional
one time pet fee of $25 per room.
Multiple dogs may be allowed.

Hilton
255 S West Temple
Salt Lake City, UT
801-328-2000
Dogs are allowed for an additional
one time fee of $15 per pet. 2 dogs
may be allowed.

Holiday Inn
999 South Main Street
Salt Lake City, UT
801-359-8600 (877-270-6405)
Dogs up to 45 pounds are allowed.
There is a $35 one time per pet fee
per visit. Only non-smoking rooms
are used for pets.

Holiday Inn Express Hotel & Suites
Salt Lake City-Airport East
200 North 2100 West
Salt Lake City, UT
801-741-1500 (877-270-6405)
Dogs of all sizes are allowed for an
additional one time pet fee of $15 per
room. Multiple dogs may be allowed.

Holiday Inn Express Salt Lake City
4465 Century Drive
Salt Lake City, UT
801-268-2533 (877-270-6405)
Dogs of all sizes are allowed for an
additional one time pet fee per room
of $25 for 1 dog; a 2nd dog is an
additional $15 fee. Dogs may not be
left alone in the room. 2 dogs may be
allowed.

Hotel Monaco Salt Lake City
15 West 200 South

Salt Lake City, UT
801-595-0000
monaco-saltlakecity.com/
Well-behaved dogs of all sizes are
welcome at this pet-friendly hotel.
The luxury boutique hotel offers
both rooms and suites. Hotel
amenities include complimentary
evening wine service, 24 hour room
service and a 24 hour on-site
fitness room. There are no pet fees,
just sign a pet liability form.

La Quinta Inn & Suites Salt Lake
City Airport
4905 W. Wiley Post Way
Salt Lake City, UT
801-366-4444 (800-531-5900)
Dogs of all sizes are allowed. There
are no additional pet fees. Dogs
must be leashed, cleaned up after,
and crated when left alone in the
room. Multiple dogs may be
allowed.

Motel 6 - Salt Lake City Downtown
176 W 600th S Street
Salt Lake City, UT
801-531-1252 (800-466-8356)
One well-behaved family pet per
room. Guest must notify front desk
upon arrival. Guest is liable for any
damages. In consideration of all
guests, pets must never be left
unattended in the guest rooms.

Motel 6 - Salt Lake City West -
Airport
1990 West North Temple Street
Salt Lake City, UT
801-364-1053 (800-466-8356)
One well-behaved family pet per
room. Guest must notify front desk
upon arrival. Guest is liable for any
damages. In consideration of all
guests, pets must never be left
unattended in the guest rooms.

Red Lion
161 W 600 S
Salt Lake City, UT
801-521-7373
Well behaved dogs of all sizes are
allowed. There is a $50 refundable
deposit. Multiple dogs may be
allowed.

Residence Inn by Marriott
4883 W Douglas Corrigan Way
Salt Lake City, UT
801-532-4101
Dogs of all sizes are allowed. There
is a $75 one time fee and a pet
policy to sign at check in. They also
request you make arrangements for
housekeeping. 2 dogs may be
allowed.

Residence Inn by Marriott
285 W Broadway (300S)
Salt Lake City, UT
801-355-3300
Dogs of all sizes are allowed. There
is a $75 one time fee and a pet
policy to sign at check in. Multiple
dogs may be allowed.

Residence Inn by Marriott
6425 S 3000 East
Salt Lake City, UT
801-453-0430
Well behaved dogs of all sizes are
allowed. There is a $75 one time fee
and a pet policy to sign at check in. 2
dogs may be allowed.

Salt Lake City Centre Travelodge
524 S West Temple
Salt Lake City, UT
801-531-7100
There is a $10 per day pet fee.

Sheraton City Centre Hotel, Salt
Lake City
150 West 500 South
Salt Lake City, UT
801-401-2000 (888-625-5144)
Dogs up to 80 pounds are allowed.
There are no additional pet fees.
Dogs are not allowed to be left alone
in the room.

Comfort Inn
8955 S 255 West
Sandy, UT
801-255-4919 (877-424-6423)
Dogs are allowed for an additional
fee of $10 per night per pet. Multiple
dogs may be allowed.

Residence Inn by Marriott
270 W 10000S
Sandy, UT
801-561-5005
Dogs of all sizes are allowed. There
is a $75 one time fee and a pet
policy to sign at check in. Multiple
dogs may be allowed.

Super 8 Scipio
230 West 400 North
Scipio, UT
435-758-9188 (800-800-8000)
Dogs of all sizes are allowed except
puppies. There is a $10 per night pet
fee per pet. Reservations are
recommended due to limited rooms
for pets. Smoking and non-smoking
rooms are available for pet rooms. 2
dogs may be allowed.

Sleep Inn
10676 S 300 W
South Jordan, UT

801-572-2020 (877-424-6423)
Quiet dogs are allowed for an additional fee of $10 per night per pet. Dogs may not be left alone in the room. Multiple dogs may be allowed.

Super 8 South Jordan/Sandy/SLC Area
10722 South 300 West
South Jordan, UT
801-553-8888 (800-800-8000)
Dogs of all sizes are allowed. There is a $10 per night pet fee per pet. Dogs are not allowed to be left alone in the room. Smoking and non-smoking rooms are available for pet rooms. 2 dogs may be allowed.

Driftwood Lodge
1515 Zion Park Blvd
Springdale, UT
435-772-3262 (888-801-8811)
driftwoodlodge.net/index.html
There is a $10 one time pet fee.

El Rio Lodge
995 Zion Park Blvd
Springdale, UT
435-772-3205 (888-772-3205)
elriolodge.com/
This small 10 room motel is located in the Zion canyon with 360 degree views of the fascinating landscape of deep canyons, soaring cliffs, and geological surprises. (The Pa-rus Trail is the only trail that dogs are allowed on in the park.) They offer affordable prices, and clean, comfortable rooms with a great location to eateries and other attractions. Dogs of all sizes are allowed for an additional pet fee of $15 per night per room. Dogs may not be left alone in the room at any time, and they must be leashed and cleaned up after. 2 dogs may be allowed.

Best Western Cotton Tree Inn of Springville
1455 N 1750 West
Springville, UT
801-489-3641 (800-780-7234)
Dogs are allowed for an additional fee of $10 per night per pet. Dogs must be crated overnight. 2 dogs may be allowed.

Motel 6 - St. George
205 N 1000 E Street
St George, UT
435-628-7979 (800-466-8356)
One well-behaved family pet per room. Guest must notify front desk upon arrival. Guest is liable for any damages. In consideration of all guests, pets must never be left

unattended in the guest rooms.

Holiday Inn Express Hotel & Suites Tooele
1531 North Main
Tooele, UT
435-833-0500 (877-270-6405)
Dogs of all sizes are allowed for an additional pet fee of $15 per night per room. 2 dogs may be allowed.

Days Inn Torrey
675 E Hwy 24
Torrey, UT
435-425-3111 (800-329-7466)
Dogs of all sizes are allowed. There is a $10 per night pet fee per pet. Only non-smoking rooms are used for pets. 2 dogs may be allowed.

Super 8 Torrey/Capitol Reef Area
600 East Hwy 24
Torrey, UT
435-425-3688 (800-800-8000)
Dogs of all sizes are allowed. There are no additional pet fees. Reservations are recommended due to limited rooms for pets. Only non-smoking rooms are used for pets. 2 dogs may be allowed.

Motel 6 - Vernal
1092 West Highway 40
Vernal, UT
435-789-0666 (800-466-8356)
One well-behaved family pet per room. Guest must notify front desk upon arrival. Guest is liable for any damages. In consideration of all guests, pets must never be left unattended in the guest rooms.

Sage Motel
54 W Main St
Vernal, UT
435-789-1442
There is a $5 one time pet fee.

Holiday Inn Express Hotel & Suites Washington
2450 N Town Center Drive
Washington, UT
435-986-1313 (877-270-6405)
Dogs up to 150 pounds are allowed for an additional one time pet fee of $35 per room. 2 dogs may be allowed.

Motel 6 - Wendover
561 East Wendover Boulevard
Wendover, UT
435-665-2267 (800-466-8356)
One well-behaved family pet per room. Guest must notify front desk upon arrival. Guest is liable for any damages. In consideration of all guests, pets must never be left

unattended in the guest rooms.

Baymont Inn & Suites Salt Lake City/West Valley
2229 W. City Center Court
West Valley City, UT
801-886-1300 (800-531-5900)
Dogs of all sizes are allowed. There are no additional pet fees. Dogs must be quiet, well behaved, leashed and cleaned up after, and the Do Not Disturb sign put on the door if there is a pet in the room alone. Multiple dogs may be allowed.

Hampton Inn
2393 S 800 West
Woods Cross, UT
801-296-1211
Dogs of all sizes are allowed. There are no additional pet fees. Multiple dogs may be allowed.

Motel 6 - Salt Lake City Nrth-Woods Cross
2433 South 800 West
Woods Cross, UT
801-298-0289 (800-466-8356)
One well-behaved family pet per room. Guest must notify front desk upon arrival. Guest is liable for any damages. In consideration of all guests, pets must never be left unattended in the guest rooms.

Vermont Listings

Whitford House Inn
912 Grandey Road
Addison, VT
802-758-2704 (800-746-2704)
whitfordhouseinn.com/rooms.html
This restored 1790's New England inn, sitting amid rich farm land on 37 acres of beautifully kept grounds, offers bicycles and canoes for guests, a bottomless cookie jar, and a path that leads to a wildlife preserve. One gentle dog of any size is allowed in the guest house only. The dog must be very friendly and well behaved towards other animals as there are sheep, a cat, and dogs on site. Dogs may not be left alone at any time, and they must be leashed and cleaned up after.

Inn at Maplemont
2742 H 5S
Barnet, VT
802-633-4880
Dogs of all sizes are allowed. There is a pet policy to sign at check in and there are no additional pet fees.

Multiple dogs may be allowed.

Everyday Inn
593 Rockingham Road
Bellows Falls, VT
802-463-4536
everydayinn.com/
Although they are central to many other activities, recreation, and ski areas, each season brings its own beauty to this inn that sits on 7 acres of lawns and woods along the Connecticut River. Dogs of all sizes are allowed for an additional fee of $10 (plus tax) per night per pet. Dogs must be well behaved, leashed, and cleaned up after. 2 dogs may be allowed.

Knotty Pine Motel
130 Northside Drive
Bennington, VT
802-442-5487
Dogs of all sizes are allowed. There are no additional pet fees. Dogs may not be left unattended at any time and they are not allowed on the bed and furniture. Multiple dogs may be allowed.

South Gate Motel
US 7S
Bennington, VT
802-447-7525
There is a $6 per day pet fee.

The Vermonter Motor Lodge
2968 West Road
Bennington, VT
802-442-2529
thevermontermotorlodge.com
This motor lodge offers on or two bed rooms. There is a $10 per night additional pet fee per pet.

Greenhurst Inn
88 North Road
Bethel, VT
802-234-9474 (800-510-2553)
This Queen Anne Victorian mansion sits just a short distance from the White River and several other local attractions. Dogs of all sizes are welcome for no additional pet fee. Dogs must be well behaved, leashed and cleaned up after and friendly towards the other pets in residence. Dogs may not be left alone in the room at any time. Multiple dogs may be allowed.

The Black Bear Inn
4010 Bolton Access Road
Bolton Valley, VT
802-434-2126 (800-395-6335)
blackbearinn.travel/
There are miles and miles of trails to explore and enjoy at this retreat sitting on 6000 private acres, as well as tennis courts, an outdoor heated pool, a gift shop, a bar, and dinning for breakfast and dinner. They have a couple of standard rooms that are pet friendly, and there is an additional fee of $20 per night per pet. Dogs must be quiet, well mannered, and leashed and cleaned up after at all times. This inn also features the "Bone and Biscuit Inn"; a seasonal kennel with 3 private indoor/outdoor combination runs for an additional fee of $10 per day per pet. 2 dogs may be allowed.

Lilac Inn
53 Parks Street
Brandon, VT
802-247-5463 (800-221-0720)
lilacinn.com/
Whether a vacation getaway or to host your own special celebration, this beautifully restored 1900 mansion has all the amenities, 2 acres of perennial gardens, and a full service English Tavern. Dogs of all sizes are allowed for an additional one time pet fee of $30 per room. Dogs must be well behaved, leashed and cleaned up after at all times, and crated when left alone in the room. 2 dogs may be allowed.

Forty Putney Road
192 Putney Road/H 5
Brattleboro, VT
802-254-6268 (800-941-2413)
fortyputneyroad.com/
This graceful French provincial estate overlooks a wildlife sanctuary and the West River, features individually decorated rooms, beautiful lawns and gardens, and they allow for indoor or outdoor (weather permitting) wining and dining. They are open seasonally. Dogs of all sizes are allowed for an additional fee of $15 per night per pet. Dogs must be friendly towards other animals as there is an older dog on site. Dogs must be leashed and cleaned up after at all times, and may only be left alone in the room if owners are confident the dog will be quiet, well behaved, and a contact number is left at the front desk. 2 dogs may be allowed.

Motel 6 - Brattleboro
1254 Putney Road
Brattleboro, VT
802-254-6007 (800-466-8356)
One well-behaved family pet per room. Guest must notify front desk upon arrival. Guest is liable for any damages. In consideration of all guests, pets must never be left unattended in the guest rooms.

The Pond House Inn
PO Box #234-423 Shattuck Hill Road
Brownsville, VT
802-484-0011
pondhouseinn.com
Nestled in the mountains just south of Woodstock, this inn features a stone walled herb garden and patio, a spring-fed pond with a jumping board for the pooch, and being close to 3 major ski resorts, there are plenty of year round recreational opportunities. Sociable, friendly dogs of all sizes are allowed for an additional fee of $10 per night per pet. There can be 1 large or 2 small dogs per room, and they are to be leashed in and around the house and around other guests. Dogs are not allowed on the furniture or in the dining areas, and they must be cleaned up after at all times. They also allow horses.

Sheraton Burlington Hotel & Conference Center
870 Williston Road
Burlington, VT
802-865-6600 (888-625-5144)
Dogs of all sizes are allowed. There are no additional pet fees. Dogs are not allowed to be left alone in the room.

Mountian Top Inn and Resort
196 Mountain Top Road
Chittenden, VT
802-483-2311 (800.445.2100)
mountaintopinn.com/
This year round resort sits on 350 acres above a beautiful mountain lake and a vast national forest. Dogs of all sizes are allowed in the cabins and chalets for an additional pet fee of $25 per night per pet plus a $200 security deposit. They are not allowed in the lodge area. Your pooch will feel pampered here with a doggy bed, food and water bowls, and a treat upon arrival. Dogs must be leashed, cleaned up after, and crated when left alone in the room. Pet sitters are available with a 3 day advance notice. Pets are allowed on select cross country ski trails and on all the hiking trails. Multiple dogs may be allowed.

Hampton Inn
42 Lower Mountain View Drive
Colchester, VT
802-655-6177
Dogs of all sizes are allowed. There

are no additional pet fees. Dogs are not allowed to be left alone in the room. Multiple dogs may be allowed.

Motel 6 - Burlington - Colchester
74 South Park Drive
Colchester, VT
802-654-6860 (800-466-8356)
One well-behaved family pet per room. Guest must notify front desk upon arrival. Guest is liable for any damages. In consideration of all guests, pets must never be left unattended in the guest rooms.

Craftsburg Outdoor Center
535 Lost Nation Road
Craftsbury Common, VT
802-586-7767
craftsbury.com
This 320 acre four season resort is located beside a secluded lake. They allow dogs in a couple of their non-smoking cabins. There is a $50 one time pet fee. Well-behaved dogs of all sizes are welcome and there is limit of 2 pets per cabin. Summer activities include hiking and mountain biking. Winter activities include dog-friendly cross-country skiing on 7 kilometers of groomed trails.

Inn on the Common
1162 N Craftsbury Road
Craftsbury Common, VT
802-586-9619
Dogs of all sizes are allowed. There is a $25 per night per pet fee and a pet policy to sign at check in. 2 dogs may be allowed.

Inn at Mountain View Farm
3383 Darling Hill Road
East Burke, VT
802-626-9924 (800-572-4509)
innmtnview.com/
This 440-acre historic farm estate presents visitors with breathtaking views, pastoral settings, and they are home to the Mountain View Farm Animal Sanctuary on the same property, and miles and miles of multi-use, all season trails nationally known as the Kingdom Trails. Dogs of all sizes are allowed for an additional fee of $25 per night per pet. Dogs must be quiet, well mannered, leashed, cleaned up after, and crated when left alone in the room. 2 dogs may be allowed.

The Inn at Essex
94 Poker Hill Road
Essex, VT
802-878-1100 (800-727-4295)
VTCulinaryResort.com
A luxury hotel featuring the acclaimed New England Culinary

Institute. There is a $25 per night pet fee. There is a $300 fully refundable pet-damage deposit required.

Inn at Buckhollow Farm
2150 Buckhollow Farm
Fairfax, VT
802-849-2400
Dogs of all sizes are allowed. There is a $10 one time fee per room for one night, and a $15 one time fee per room for 2 or more nights. Shots for pets must be up to date. Multiple dogs may be allowed.

Silver Maple Lodge
520H 5 S
Fairlee, VT
802-333-4326 (800-666-1946)
silvermaplelodge.com/
In addition to being the states oldest continually running inn, they are also central to an array of year round local attractions and activities. Dogs of all sizes are welcome for no additional fee in the cottages but not in the lodge. Dogs must be very well behaved, under owner's control at all times, and leashed and cleaned up after. 2 dogs may be allowed.

Blueberry Hill Inn
1307 Goshen Ripton Road
Goshen, VT
802-247-6735 (800-448-0707)
blueberryhillinn.com/
This early 1800's mountain inn offers traditional country ambiance, a spring fed swimming pond, gardens, gourmet dining for both breakfast and dinner (included in the rates), and plenty of skiing and hiking trails. They offer 1 pet friendly cottage and dogs of all sizes are allowed for no additional pet fee. Dogs are allowed on all the trails year round except the groomed ski trails in winter, and they are not allowed inside the inn. Dogs must be leashed and cleaned up after at all times. 2 dogs may be allowed.

The Cascades Lodge
Killington Village, 58 Old Mill Rd
Killington, VT
802-422-3731 (800-345-0113)
cascadeslodge.com/contact/
This mountain ski resort offers 45 guest rooms, an indoor pool, eateries and a lounge, and year round recreation. Dogs of all sizes are allowed for an additional pet fee of $50 per night per pet with advance notice only and a credit card on file. Dogs must be current

on all vaccinations, and be flee and tic free. Dogs must be leashed and cleaned up after at all times; there are waste bags in the room and more at the front desk if needed. Dogs may not be left alone in the room at any time. 2 dogs may be allowed.

The Cortina Inn and Resort
Route 4
Killington, VT
800-451-6108 (800-451-6108)
cortinainn.com
This inn caters to pets. They have pet treats on arrival and make your pet feel welcome. There is a $10 per day additional pet fee.

The Paw House
1376 Clarendon Avenue
Killington, VT
802-438-2738 (866-PAW-HOUSE)
pawhouseinn.com
The Paw House Inn is a B&B that caters exclusively to dog owners and their pets. Dog care is available on site. Before staying here with your dog you will be required to submit an application in advance.

Wise Vacations
P. O. Box 231
Killington, VT
802-422-3139 (800-639-4680)
wisevacations.com/
This vacation rental company offers pet friendly accommodations in the Killington area; there are 3 tri-level homes listed-Telefon Trail, The Meadows, and Dream Maker. The pet policy may vary some as well as the fee and number of pets allowed, but there would be no higher than a $250 one time pet fee. Dogs must be well behaved, cleaned up after inside and out, and depending on the location of the property, dogs may not have to be leashed if they are under voice control.

Best Western Ludlow Colonial -
Ludlow, VT
93 Main Street
Ludlow, VT
802-228-8188 (800-780-7234)
bestwesternludlow.com
This pet-friendly hotel is located in the heart of the Green Mountains.

The Combs Family Inn
953 E Lake Road
Ludlow, VT
802-228-8799 (802-822-8799)
combsfamilyinn.com/
Located in the state's lush lake and mountain region on 50 acres of meadows and woods, this inn offers

all the comforts of a cozy home, and a great location to numerous year round local activities and events. Dogs of all sizes are welcome for no additional pet fee. Dogs must be quiet, well behaved, leashed, and cleaned up after. 2 dogs may be allowed.

Red Clover Inn
7 Woodward Road
Mendon, VT
802-775-2290 (800-752-0571)
redcloverinn.com/
This scenic 1840's farmhouse estate is located on 13 country acres, offers a warm and cozy atmosphere, an intimate pub, a restaurant, and it also serves as a great starting point for a wide variety of year round activities and recreation. Dogs of all sizes are allowed in certain rooms in the Carriage House for an additional fee of $20 per night per pet. Dogs must be leashed and cleaned up after at all times, and crated when left alone in the room. Dogs are not allowed in the main inn building. 2 dogs may be allowed.

Fairhill
724 E Munger Street
Middlebury, VT
802-388-3044
midvermont.com/fairhill/
This nicely restored 1825 farmhouse is surrounded by lush lawns and gardens, and offers a great view of the mountains and valley below. Up to 2 dogs of all sizes are allowed and there is no additional pet fee; however, when they have a full house only 1 dog is allowed per room. Dogs may not be left alone in the room at any time, and they must be leashed and cleaned up after.

Middlebury Inn
14 Courthouse Square
Middlebury, VT
802-388-4961
middleburyinn.com
Dogs are allowed and will be given a treat on check-in. There are nearby dog-friendly trails to walk your dog on.

Phineas Swann Inn
195 Main Street
Montgomery Center, VT
802-326-4306
phineasswann.com/
In an area bustling with activity and recreational opportunities, this Victorian home offers guests year round lodging, antique laden and doggie accessorized surroundings, beautiful grounds, and fresh baked goodies available all day. It is evident that there is a love of dogs here as the owner has been collecting just about everything "Dog" for over 30 years; there are hundreds of dog figurines from the 1880's to the 1950's, advertising items, tins, furniture, and signs. Some of the collection is at the inn and most of the rest is at their antique store a short distance away. Since most items are for sale, they say "just ask", and your well mannered pooch is welcome inside the antique store as well. There are no addition pet fees. Dogs must be under owner's care/control at all times. Multiple dogs may be allowed.

The Mount Tabor Inn
217 Troll Hill Road
Mount Tabor, VT
802-293-5907
Well behaved and housebroken dogs of all sizes are allowed. There is a $10 per night per room fee and a pet policy to sign at check in. They also request you feed your dog in the bathroom as the floor is easier to clean. Multiple dogs may be allowed.

Four Colulms Inn
21 West Street
Newfane, VT
802-365-7713 (800-787-6633)
fourcolumnsinn.com/
This Federal style inn sits on a 150 acre private mountain with wooded nature trails, manicured lawns, a fine dining restaurant that is open for diner, and they are central to numerous activities and recreation. Dogs of all sizes are allowed for an additional fee of $35 per night per pet. There may be up to 2 small to medium or 1 large dog per room. Dogs must be leashed and cleaned up after at all times.

Lady Pearl's Inn and Lodging
1724 E Main Street
Newport, VT
802-334-6748
Dogs of all sizes are allowed in the motel or cabins, but not the inn. There are no additional pet fees, but a credit card must be on file. Multiple dogs may be allowed.

Quality Inn at Quechee Gorge
5817 Woodstock Road
Quechee, VT
802-295-7600 (877-424-6423)
Dogs are allowed for an additional one time pet fee of $10 per room. Multiple dogs may be allowed.

The Parker House Inn and Restaurant
1792 Main Street
Quechee, VT
802-295-6077
theparkerhouseinn.com
This B&B allows pets with the prior permission of management. They reserve the right to limit the size of a dog to sixty pounds, but may allow larger dogs. There is horse and other large animal boarding at the owners nearby farm. There is a $30 pet fee per night, per pet.

Bailey's Mills Bed and Breakfast
1347 Baileys Mills Road
Reading, VT
802-484-7809 (800-639-3437)
baileysmills.com
This B&B on 48 acres with trails welcomes dogs "up to the size of a golden retriever". Dogs should not be left alone in the rooms.

Holiday Inn
476 US Route 7 South
Rutland, VT
802-775-1911 (877-270-6405)
Dogs of all sizes are allowed for an additional fee of $25 per night per pet. Multiple dogs may be allowed.

Red Roof Inn - Rutland - Killington
401 US Route 7 South
Rutland, VT
802-775-4303 (800-RED-ROOF)
One well-behaved family pet per room. Guest must notify front desk upon arrival. Guest is liable for any damages. In consideration of all guests, pets must never be left unattended in the guest rooms.

Holiday Inn
1068 Williston Rd
S. Burlington, VT
802-863-6363 (877-270-6405)
Dogs of all sizes are allowed for an additional one time pet fee of $20. 2 dogs may be allowed.

North Cove Cottages
1958 Lake Dunmore Road
Salisbury, VT
802-352-4236 (711-802-352-9064 (line for deaf))
Quiet, friendly, and well behaved dogs of all sizes are allowed. There is an $18 one time pet fee per room. The owner requests the dogs be walked off grounds and that you bring extra linens to cover the furniture or beds if your pet is used to being on them. She asks to be contacted ahead of time so she

knows, and can ok, the number and type of animal. There is also a 2 night minimum stay. 2 dogs may be allowed.

Best Western Windjammer Inn & Conference Center
1076 Williston Road
South Burlington, VT
802-863-1125 (800-780-7234)
Dogs are allowed for an additional fee of $10 per night per pet. Multiple dogs may be allowed.

Paradise Bay
50 Light House Road
South Hero, VT
802-372-5393
This scenic inn sits by the lake, and dogs of all sizes are welcome for no additional pet fees. They request that if your pooch goes swimming to make sure they are dried off before entering the rooms. Dogs must be friendly to humans and other animals, and be quiet and well behaved. Dogs must be leashed and cleaned up after. 2 dogs may be allowed.

Kedron Valley Inn
10467 South Road
South Woodstock, VT
802-457-1473 (800-836-1193)
kedronvalleyinn.com/
This 175 year old guest house is still offering guests a variety of services and modern amenities with plenty to explore, like the spring-fed pond with 2 white sandy beaches or the many trails, and although every season brings its own beauty and activities here, it is especially convenient for a variety of winter recreation. Dogs of all sizes are allowed in the Lodge or Tavern buildings for an additional one time fee of $15 per pet. Dogs must be leashed, cleaned up after, and they may only be left alone in the room if owners are confident that the dog will be quiet and well behaved. Dogs are not allowed in the main house. Multiple dogs may be allowed.

Holiday Inn Express Springfield
818 Charlestown Road
Springfield, VT
802-885-4516 (877-270-6405)
A quiet dog is allowed for an additional pet fee of $25 (plus tax) per night.

Aime's Motel
RR 1, Box 332
St Johnsbury, VT
802-748-3194

Fairbanks Inn
401 Western Avenue
St Johnsbury, VT
802-748-5666
stjay.com
There is a $5 per day pet fee.

Andersen Lodge - An Austrian Inn
3430 Mountain Road
Stowe, VT
802-253-7336
The lodge is open from May 30 to October 25 each year. There are no additional pet fees.

Commodores Inn
823 South Main St
Stowe, VT
802-253-7131
There are no additional pet fees.

LJ's Lodge
2526 Waterbury Rd
Stowe, VT
802-253-7768 (800-989-7768)
ljslodge.com
Dogs are allowed in this lodge with mountain views of the Vermont mountains. There is a fenced in dog play area. There is a one time $5 pet fee and there are dog beds and bowls for your room.

Stowe Motel and Snowdrift
2043 Mountain Road
Stowe, VT
802-253-7629 (800-829-7629)
stowemotel.com/
This scenic mountain resort sits on 16 meticulously landscaped grounds with great mountain views, an alpine stream, year round activities and recreation, a central location to a variety shops and restaurants, and it is near the award-winning Stowe Recreation Path. Dogs of all sizes are allowed for an additional fee of $10 per night per pet. Dogs must be leashed, cleaned up after, and crated if left alone in the room. 2 dogs may be allowed.

Ten Acres Lodge
14 Barrows Rd
Stowe, VT
802-253-7638
tenacres.newnetwork.com/
Dogs are welcome in the cottages. There are no additional pet fees.

The Mountain Road Resort
1007 Mountain Rd
Stowe, VT
802-253-4566
There is a $15 one time pet fee.

Maximum of 1 pet per room.

The Riverside Inn
1965 Mountain Road
Stowe, VT
802-253-4217 (800-966-4217)
rivinn.com
This early 1800's converted farmhouse gives visitors a comfy stay while offering a great location to several activities, shops, and eateries, and they are also backed right up to the river and Stowe's well-known recreation path. Dogs of all sizes are allowed for an additional fee of $5 per night per pet. Dogs must be quiet, well behaved, leashed, and cleaned up after. Dogs may only be left alone in the room if the owner is confident in the pet's behavior. 2 dogs may be allowed.

Topnotch at Stowe Resort and Spa
4000 Mountain Road
Stowe, VT
802-253-8585 (800-451-8686)
topnotchresort.com
This 120-acre resort is nestled into a Vermont mountainside. There are no additional pet fees.

Basin Harbor Club
4800 Basin Harbor Road
Vergennes, VT
802-475-2311 (800-622-4000)
Lush and sitting on the shores of beautiful Lake Champlain, this 700+ acre resort offers a complete vacation experience with a variety of accommodations, land and water recreation for all age levels, miles of hiking trails, various eateries, splendid gardens, a golf course, and much more. Dogs of all sizes are allowed in the cottages only for an additional fee of $10 per night per pet; they are not allowed in any of the 4 guesthouses. Dogs must be leashed and cleaned up after at all times, and they are not allowed in the pool or waterfront areas. Multiple dogs may be allowed.

Grunberg Haus
94 Pine Street/3 miles S of Waterbury on H 100
Waterbury, VT
802-244-7726
Dogs of all sizes are allowed in the cabins. There can be one large dog or 2 small dogs per cabin. There is a $5 per night per room additional pet fee. They are open from May to late October.

Snow Goose Inn
259 H 100, Box 366
West Dover, VT

802-464-3984
Dogs of all sizes are allowed. There is a $25 per night per pet additional fee. Dogs must be leashed while on site. There are only 2 pet friendly rooms. 2 dogs may be allowed.

Comfort Inn
56 Ralph Lehman Drive
White River Junction, VT
802-295-3051 (877-424-6423)
Dogs are allowed for no additional pet fee. Dogs may not be left alone in the room. 2 dogs may be allowed.

Super 8 White River Junction
Route 5 S
White River Junction, VT
802-295-7577 (800-800-8000)
Dogs of all sizes are allowed. There are no additional pet fees. Dogs are not allowed to be left alone in the room. Smoking and non-smoking rooms are available for pet rooms. 2 dogs may be allowed.

Residence Inn by Marriott
35 Hurricane Lane
Williston, VT
802-878-2001
Dogs of all sizes are allowed. There is a $75 one time fee and a pet policy to sign at check in. Multiple dogs may be allowed.

TownePlace Suites Burlington Williston
66 Zephyr Road
Williston, VT
802-872-5900
Dogs of all sizes are allowed. There is a $75 one time pet fee per visit. 2 dogs may be allowed.

Virginia Listings

Days Inn Abingdon
887 Empire Drive
Abingdon, VA
276-628-7131 (800-329-7466)
Dogs of all sizes are allowed. There is a $8 per night pet fee per pet. 2 dogs may be allowed.

Holiday Inn Express Abingdon
940 E. Main St
Abingdon, VA
276-676-2829 (877-270-6405)
Dogs up to 50 pounds are allowed for an additional one time pet fee of $25 per room. 2 dogs may be allowed.

Super 8 Abingdon
298 Town Centre Dr
Abingdon, VA
276-676-3329 (800-800-8000)
Dogs of all sizes are allowed. There are no additional pet fees. Smoking and non-smoking rooms are available for pet rooms. 2 dogs may be allowed.

Holiday Inn Hotel and Suites
625 First Street
Alexandria, VA
703-548-6300 (877-270-6405)
Dogs of all sizes are allowed for an additional fee of $25 per night per pet. Multiple dogs may be allowed.

Morrison House Hotel
116 S Alfred St
Alexandria, VA
703-838-8000
morrisonhouse.com
This Kimpton boutique hotel allows dogs of all sizes. There are no additional pet fees.

Red Roof Inn - Washington, DC - Alexandria
5975 Richmond Highway
Alexandria, VA
703-960-5200 (800-RED-ROOF)
One well-behaved family pet per room. Guest must notify front desk upon arrival. Guest is liable for any damages. In consideration of all guests, pets must never be left unattended in the guest rooms.

Sheraton Suites Old Town Alexandria
801 North Saint Asaph St.
Alexandria, VA
703-836-4700 (888-625-5144)
Dogs up to 70 pounds are allowed. There are no additional pet fees. Dogs are not allowed to be left alone in the room.

Washington Suites
100 South Reynolds Street
Alexandria, VA
703-370-9600
washingtonsuitesalexandria.com/
Once an apartment building, this hotel offers the largest suites in the area from 500 to 1,600 square feet and is only 9 miles from Washington DC. Dogs of all sizes are allowed for an additional $20 per night per pet. Dogs must be quiet, leashed, and cleaned up after. Multiple dogs may be allowed.

Comfort Suites
1558 Main Street
Altavista, VA

434-369-4000 (877-424-6423)
Dogs are allowed for an additional fee of $6 per night per pet. Dogs may not be left alone in the room. 2 dogs may be allowed.

Quality Inn Courthouse Plaza
1200N Courthouse Road
Arlington, VA
703-524-4000 (877-424-6423)
Dogs of all sizes are allowed. There is a $35 fee for the first night then it is $10 per night per pet. Multiple dogs may be allowed.

Residence Inn by Marriott
550 Army Navy Drive
Arlington, VA
703-413-6630
Dogs of all sizes are allowed, however there can only be 1 large pet or 2 medium to small pets per room. There is a $200 one time cleaning fee plus $8 per night per pet and a pet policy to sign at check in.

Sheraton Crystal City Hotel
1800 Jefferson Davis Highway
Arlington, VA
703-486-1111 (888-625-5144)
Dogs of all sizes are allowed. There are no additional pet fees. Dogs are not allowed to be left alone in the room.

Days Inn Ashland
806 England St
Ashland, VA
804-798-4262 (800-329-7466)
Dogs of all sizes are allowed. There is a $10 per night pet fee per pet. 2 dogs may be allowed.

Quality Inn and Suites
810 England Street
Ashland, VA
804-798-4231 (877-424-6423)
Dogs are allowed for an additional fee of $15 per night per pet. 2 dogs may be allowed.

Days Inn Bedford
921 Blue Ridge Ave
Bedford, VA
540-586-8286 (800-329-7466)
Dogs of all sizes are allowed. There is a $10 per night pet fee per pet. 2 dogs may be allowed.

The Lost Dog
211 S Church Street
Berryville, VA
540-955-1181
Well behaved pets of all sizes are allowed. There is a town leash law to obey. There are no additional pet fees, but prior approval of your dogs

are required. Dogs are not allowed to be left alone in the room. There are 3 pet friendly rooms. 2 dogs may be allowed.

Clay Corner Inn B&B
401 Clay Street SW
Blacksburg, VA
540-953-2604
claycorner.com
There is a $15 per day pet fee.

Comfort Inn
3705 S Main Street
Blacksburg, VA
540-951-1500 (877-424-6423)
Dogs are allowed for no additional pet fee. There is a pet agreement to sign at check in and a contact number must be left with the front desk if there is a pet alone in the room. Multiple dogs may be allowed.

Motel 6 - Bristol
21561 Clear Creek Road
Bristol, VA
276-466-6060 (800-466-8356)
One well-behaved family pet per room. Guest must notify front desk upon arrival. Guest is liable for any damages. In consideration of all guests, pets must never be left unattended in the guest rooms.

Super 8 Bristol
2139 Lee Hwy
Bristol, VA
276-466-8800 (800-800-8000)
Dogs up to 60 pounds are allowed. There is a $10 one time per pet fee per visit. Smoking and non-smoking rooms are available for pet rooms. 2 dogs may be allowed.

Kiptopeke Inn
29106 Lankford hwy
Cape Charles, VA
757-331-1000
Dogs of all sizes are allowed. There is a $10 per night pet fee per pet. 2 dogs may be allowed.

Days Inn Carmel Church
24320 Rogers Clark Blvd
Carmel Church, VA
804-448-2011 (800-329-7466)
Dogs of all sizes are allowed. There is a $10 per night pet fee per pet. 2 dogs may be allowed.

TownePlace Suites Chantilly
14036 Thunderbolt Place
Chantilly, VA
703-709-0453
Dogs of all sizes are allowed. There is a $75 one time pet fee per visit. 2 dogs may be allowed.

Comfort Inn
1807 Emmet Street
Charlottesville, VA
434-293-6188 (877-424-6423)
Dogs are allowed for an additional fee of $10 per night per pet. Multiple dogs may be allowed.

Days Inn Charlottesville/University Area
1600 Emmet St
Charlottesville, VA
434-293-9111 (800-329-7466)
Dogs of all sizes are allowed. There is a $10 per night pet fee per pet. 2 dogs may be allowed.

Holiday Inn
1200 5th Street
Charlottesville, VA
434-977-5100 (877-270-6405)
Dogs of all sizes are allowed for an additional fee of $15 per night per pet. Multiple dogs may be allowed.

Quality Inn
1600 Emmet Street
Charlottesville, VA
434-971-3746 (877-424-6423)
Dogs are allowed for an additional fee of $10 per night per pet. Multiple dogs may be allowed.

Red Roof Inn - Charlottesville
1309 West Main Street
Charlottesville, VA
434-295-4333 (800-RED-ROOF)
One well-behaved family pet per room. Guest must notify front desk upon arrival. Guest is liable for any damages. In consideration of all guests, pets must never be left unattended in the guest rooms.

Residence Inn by Marriott
1111 Millmont Street
Charlottesville, VA
434-923-0300
Dogs of all sizes are allowed. There is a fee of $75 for 1 to 3 nights; 4 to 5 nights is $100, and continues up to a maximum total of $200 per stay. There is also a pet policy to sign at check in.

Sleep Inn and Suites Monticello
1185 5th Street SW
Charlottesville, VA
434-244-9969 (877-424-6423)
Dogs are allowed for an additional fee of $15 per night per pet. Multiple dogs may be allowed.

Red Roof Inn - Chesapeake
724 Woodlake Drive
Chesapeake, VA

757-523-0123 (800-RED-ROOF)
One well-behaved family pet per room. Guest must notify front desk upon arrival. Guest is liable for any damages. In consideration of all guests, pets must never be left unattended in the guest rooms.

TownePlace Suites Chesapeake
2000 Old Greenbrier Road
Chesapeake, VA
757-523-5004
Dogs of all sizes are allowed. There is a $75 one time pet fee per visit. 2 dogs may be allowed.

Days Inn Chester
2410 W Hundred Rd
Chester, VA
804-748-5871 (800-329-7466)
Dogs of all sizes are allowed. There is a $6 per night pet fee per pet. 2 dogs may be allowed.

Channel Bass Inn
6228 Church Street
Chincoteague, VA
757-336-6148 (800-249-0818)
channelbassinn.com/
This beautiful 1892, 6,800 square foot home sits surrounded by Japanese and perennial gardens with a pond, and provide a good central location for exploring the island; they also have complimentary bikes for guests. One dog of any size is welcome for an additional $10 per night, and they must be people and pet friendly as there are resident cats. Dogs must be well behaved, leashed, and cleaned up after.

Chincoteague Island
6378 Church Street
Chincoteague Island, VA
757-336-3100 (800-668-7836)
Offering a variety of property options and amenities in various locations around the island, this agency has more than 20 pet friendly vacation rentals available. Dogs of all sizes (depending on the rental) are allowed for an additional fee of $75 per pet per stay. Dogs must be housebroken, well behaved, leashed, and cleaned up after in and out of the unit. Dogs may not be left unattended, and they are not allowed in a "no pet" house. Dogs are not allowed anywhere on the refuge, even if they are in a car. 2 dogs may be allowed.

VIP Island Vacation Rentals
6353 Maddox Blvd
Chincoteague Island, VA
757-336-7288
This company offers several

properties with various amenities at a variety of sites on this small island that is accessed from the mainland by a 4 mile long bypass. Dogs of all sizes are allowed for an additional fee of $75 per pet per stay. Dogs must be well behaved, leashed, and cleaned up after. Multiple dogs may be allowed.

Days Inn Christiansburg
2635 Roanoke St
Christiansburg, VA
540-382-0261 (800-329-7466)
Dogs of all sizes are allowed. There is a $5 per night pet fee per small pet and $10 for large pet. 2 dogs may be allowed.

Howard Johnson Express Inn
100 Bristol Drive
Christiansburg, VA
540-381-0150 (800-446-4656)
Dogs of all sizes are welcome. There is a $7 per day pet fee for small pets and a $10 per day pet fee for a larger pet.

Quality Inn
50 Hampton Blvd
Christiansburg, VA
540-382-2055 (877-424-6423)
Dogs are allowed for an additional pet fee of $10 per night per room. Multiple dogs may be allowed.

Super 8 Christiansburg/Blacksburg Area
55 Laurel Street NE
Christiansburg, VA
540-382-5813 (800-800-8000)
Dogs of all sizes are allowed. There is a $20 one time per pet fee per visit. Smoking and non-smoking rooms are available for pet rooms. 2 dogs may be allowed.

Super 8 Christiansburg/East
2780 Roanoke St
Christiansburg, VA
540-382-7421 (800-800-8000)
Dogs of all sizes are allowed. There is a $10 per night pet fee per pet. Smoking and non-smoking rooms are available for pet rooms. 2 dogs may be allowed.

Needmoor Inn Bed and Breakfast
801 Virginia Avenue
Clarksville, VA
434-374-2866
kerrlake.com/needmoor
This Bed and Breakfast Inn is a Virginia landmark that has welcomed guests for over a century. This wonderfully restored farmhouse style B&B can be your destination for

recreation and relaxation, or your place of rest on a longer journey. The inn has an area for dogs to play, and many parks nearby. The owners have a dog that loves company. Room rates are approximately $75.

Quality Inn Dutch Inn
2360 Virginia Avenue
Collinsville, VA
276-647-3721 (877-424-6423)
Dogs are allowed for an additional fee of $10 per night per pet. Multiple dogs may be allowed.

Days Inn Petersburg/Walthall
2310 Indian Hill Rd
Colonial Heights, VA
804-520-1010 (800-329-7466)
Dogs of all sizes are allowed. There is a $6 per night pet fee per pet. 2 dogs may be allowed.

Best Value Inn
908 Valley Ridge Drive
Covington, VA
540-962-7600 (800-843-5644)
There is a $10 one time pet charge.

Best Western Mountain View
820 E Madison Street
Covington, VA
540-962-4951 (800-780-7234)
Dogs are allowed for an additional one time pet fee of $12 per room. Multiple dogs may be allowed.

Montfair Resort Farm
2500 Bezaleel Drive
Crozet, VA
434-823-5202
montfairresortfarm.com
These pet-friendly cottages and country retreat allows dogs. They are located just 15 miles from Charlottesville. There is a $24.00 additional one time pet fee for your first pet plus $5 for any additional pets. Montfair's rustic lodge is available for a variety of pet-friendly events such as weddings, retreats or reunions.

Comfort Inn
890 Willis Lane
Culpeper, VA
540-825-4900 (877-424-6423)
Dogs are allowed for an additional fee of $15 per night per pet. Multiple dogs may be allowed.

Comfort Inn and Suites
100 Tower Drive
Danville, VA
434-793-2000 (877-424-6423)
Dogs are allowed for an additional

pet fee of $10 per night per room. 2 dogs may be allowed.

Days Inn Danville
1390 Piney Forest Rd
Danville, VA
434-836-6745 (800-329-7466)
Dogs of all sizes are allowed. There is a $5 per night pet fee per pet. 2 dogs may be allowed.

Holiday Inn Express Danville
2121 Riverside Dr
Danville, VA
434-793-4000 (877-270-6405)
Dogs of all sizes are allowed for an additional fee of $10 per night per pet. Multiple dogs may be allowed.

Super 8 Danville
2385 Riverside Dr
Danville, VA
434-799-5845 (800-800-8000)
Dogs of all sizes are allowed. There is a $20 one time per pet fee per visit. Smoking and non-smoking rooms are available for pet rooms. 2 dogs may be allowed.

Best Western Kings Quarters
16102 Theme Park Way
Doswell, VA
804-876-3321 (800-780-7234)
Dogs are allowed for a $25 refundable deposit per room. Multiple dogs may be allowed.

Comfort Inn
4424 Cleburne Blvd
Dublin, VA
540-674-1100 (877-424-6423)
Dogs are allowed for an additional fee of $10 per night per pet. 2 dogs may be allowed.

Quarterpath Inn
620 York Street
East Williamsburg, VA
757-220-0960 (800-446-9222)
quarterpathinn.com/
This inn is located only a short walk to the historical restored town of Colonial Williamsburg. Dogs of all sizes are allowed for no additional fee. Dogs must be quiet, well behaved, leashed, cleaned up after at all times, and the Do Not Disturb sign put on the door when alone in the room. 2 dogs may be allowed.

Best Western Emporia
1100 West Atlantic ST
Emporia, VA
434-634-3200 (800-780-7234)
Dogs are allowed for an additional fee of $10 per night per pet. Multiple dogs may be allowed.

Comfort Inn
1411 Skippers Road
Emporia, VA
434-348-3282 (877-424-6423)
Dogs are allowed for an additional fee of $5 per night per pet. Multiple dogs may be allowed.

Hampton Inn
1207 W Atlantic Street
Emporia, VA
434-634-9200
Dogs of all sizes are allowed. There are no additional pet fees. Multiple dogs may be allowed.

Candlewood Suites
11400 Random Hills Road
Fairfax, VA
703-359-4490 (877-270-6405)
Dogs of all sizes are allowed for an additional one time pet fee of $75 per room. 2 dogs may be allowed.

Comfort Inn University Center
11180 Fairfax Blvd
Fairfax, VA
703-591-5900 (877-424-6423)
Dogs are allowed: 1 dog is an additional one time pet fee of $25 per room; a 2nd dog is an additional one time fee of $10. 2 dogs may be allowed.

Residence Inn by Marriott
12815 Fair Lakes Parkway
Fairfax, VA
703-266-4900
Dogs of all sizes are allowed. There is a $150 one time fee and a pet policy to sign at check in. Multiple dogs may be allowed.

Residence Inn by Marriott
8125 Gatehouse Road
Falls Church, VA
703-573-5200
Dogs of all sizes are allowed. There is a $150 one time fee and a pet policy to sign at check in. Multiple dogs may be allowed.

TownePlace Suites Falls Church
205 Hillwood Avenue
Falls Church, VA
703-237-6172
Dogs of all sizes are allowed. There is a $75 one time pet fee per visit. 2 dogs may be allowed.

Doe Run Lodging
Milepost 189 Blue Ridge Parkway
Fancy Gap, VA
276-398-4099 (866-398-4099)
doerunlodging.com/rentals/
Lush green hills against a backdrop

of wooded areas, spectacular valley views from the 3000 feet altitude, and a variety of rental options make this an attractive mountain getaway. Dogs of all sizes are allowed for an additional fee of $25 per pet per stay. Dogs must be housebroken, well mannered, leashed, and cleaned up after. 2 dogs may be allowed.

Grasssy Creek Cabooses
278 Caboose Lane
Fancy Gap, VA
276-398-1100
grassycreekcabooses.com/
Sitting on grassy knolls on 33 acres along Grassy Creek, these refurbished cabooses with modern amenities (including an inside Jacuzzi) make for a unique getaway. One dog is welcome; they must be quiet, of a friendly nature, and well mannered. Dogs must be leashed and cleaned up after, and they are not allowed on the furniture.

Miracle Farm Spa and Resort
179 Ida Rose Lane
Floyd, VA
540-789-2214
miraclefarmbnb.com/
In addition to providing guests as healthy an environment and cuisine as possible, this inn also helps to support a non-profit animal sanctuary for injured and abandoned animals. Vegetarian food (with meat substitutes) is the fare, there are several maintained hiking paths, and for guest wanting to learn about eco-friendly living?they are encouraged to observe operations or to participate. Dogs of all sizes are allowed for an additional fee of $25 per stay for one dog, and $10 per stay for each subsequent dog. Dogs must be under owner's control, leashed, and cleaned up after at all times. Pet sitting may be available if notified in advance. Multiple dogs may be allowed.

Days Inn Franklin
1660 Armory Dr
Franklin, VA
757-562-2225 (800-329-7466)
Dogs of all sizes are allowed. There is a $5 per night pet fee per pet. 2 dogs may be allowed.

Best Western Fredericksburg
2205 William St
Fredericksburg, VA
540-371-5050 (800-780-7234)
Dogs are allowed for an additional

fee of $10 per night per pet. Multiple dogs may be allowed.

Country Inn and Suites Fredericksburg South
5327 Jefferson Davis Highway
Fredericksburg, VA
540-898-1800 (800-456-4000)
countryinns.com/fredericksburgva
Dogs of all sizes are allowed for a pet fee of $20 per visit.

Days Inn Fredericksburg North
14 Simpson Rd
Fredericksburg, VA
540-373-5340 (800-329-7466)
Dogs of all sizes are allowed. There is a $5 per night pet fee per pet. 2 dogs may be allowed.

Days Inn Fredericksburg South
5316 Jefferson Davis Hwy
Fredericksburg, VA
540-898-6800 (800-329-7466)
Dogs of all sizes are allowed. There is a $5 per night pet fee per pet. 2 dogs may be allowed.

Holiday Inn
564 Warrenton Rd
Fredericksburg, VA
540-371-5550 (877-270-6405)
Dogs of all sizes is allowed for no additional pet fee. Multiple dogs may be allowed.

Motel 6 - Fredericksburg
401 Warrenton Road
Fredericksburg, VA
540-371-5443 (800-466-8356)
One well-behaved family pet per room. Guest must notify front desk upon arrival. Guest is liable for any damages. In consideration of all guests, pets must never be left unattended in the guest rooms.

Quality Inn
543 Warrenton Road
Fredericksburg, VA
540-373-0000 (877-424-6423)
Dogs are allowed for an additional fee of $10 per night per pet. Multiple dogs may be allowed.

TownePlace Suites Fredericksburg
4700 Market Street
Fredericksburg, VA
540-891-0775
Dogs of all sizes are allowed. There is a $75 one time pet fee per visit. 2 dogs may be allowed.

Bluemont Inn
1525 N. Shenandoah Ave.
Front Royal, VA
540-635-9447

They have several pet rooms. There are no additional pet fees.

Hot Tub Heaven
Off I 66 (address given with reservation)
Front Royal, VA
540-636-1522
Dogs only are allowed and of all sizes. There is a $20 1st night fee for up to 2 dogs, thereafter it is an additional $10 per dog per night. There is a pet policy to sign at check in and one of the rooms has a tall fenced in back yard. Multiple dogs may be allowed.

Quality Inn Skyline Drive
10 Commerce Avenue
Front Royal, VA
540-635-3161 (877-424-6423)
Dogs up to 50 pounds are allowed for an additional fee of $15 per night per pet. 2 dogs may be allowed.

Super 8 Front Royal
111 South St
Front Royal, VA
540-636-4888 (800-800-8000)
Dogs of all sizes are allowed. There is a $6 per night pet fee per pet. Smoking and non-smoking rooms are available for pet rooms. 2 dogs may be allowed.

Candlewood Suites
4120 Brookriver Drive
Glen Allen, VA
804-364-2000 (877-270-6405)
Dogs of all sizes are allowed for an additional one time fee of $75 per pet. Multiple dogs may be allowed.

TownePlace Suites Richmond
4231 Park Place Court
Glen Allen, VA
804-747-5253
Dogs of all sizes are allowed. There is a $75 one time pet fee per visit. 2 dogs may be allowed.

Arrow Inn
3361 Commander Shepard Boulevard
Hampton, VA
757-865-0300 (800-833-2520)
arrowinn.com/
This inn offers fully equipped efficiencies and kitchenettes, and a great central location to several other points of interest and recreational opportunities. Dogs are allowed for $5 per night per pet or $30 by the month. Dogs must be well mannered, leashed, and cleaned up after at all times. 2 dogs may be allowed.

Candlewood Suites
401 Butler Farm Road
Hampton, VA
757-766-8976 (877-270-6405)
Dogs up to 80 pounds are allowed for an additional one time pet fee per room of $75 for 1 to 6 nights; $150 for 7 or more nights, and there is a pet agreement to sign at check in. 2 dogs may be allowed.

Holiday Inn
1815 W. Mercury Blvd.
Hampton, VA
757-838-0200 (877-270-6405)
Dogs up to 80 pounds are allowed for an additional one time pet fee per room of $75 for 1 to 6 nights; $150 for 7 or more nights, and there is a pet agreement to sign at check in. 2 dogs may be allowed.

Red Roof Inn - Hampton, VA
1925 Coliseum Drive
Hampton, VA
757-838-1870 (800-RED-ROOF)
One well-behaved family pet per room. Guest must notify front desk upon arrival. Guest is liable for any damages. In consideration of all guests, pets must never be left unattended in the guest rooms.

Candlewood Suites Harrisonburg
1560 Country Club Road
Harrisonburg, VA
540-437-1400 (877-270-6405)
Dogs up to 50 pounds are allowed for an additional one time pet fee of $50 per room. Multiple dogs may be allowed.

Comfort Inn
1440 E Market Street
Harrisonburg, VA
540-433-6066 (877-424-6423)
Dogs are allowed for an additional fee of $10 per night per pet. Multiple dogs may be allowed.

Days Inn Harrisonburg
1131 Forest Hill Rd
Harrisonburg, VA
540-433-9353 (800-329-7466)
Dogs of all sizes are allowed. There is a $10 per night pet fee per pet. 2 dogs may be allowed.

Motel 6 - Harrisonburg
10 Linda Lane
Harrisonburg, VA
540-433-6939 (800-466-8356)
One well-behaved family pet per room. Guest must notify front desk upon arrival. Guest is liable for any damages. In consideration of all guests, pets must never be left

unattended in the guest rooms.

Super 8 Harrisonburg
3330 S Main
Harrisonburg, VA
540-433-8888 (800-800-8000)
Dogs of all sizes are allowed. There is a $10 per night pet fee per pet. Smoking and non-smoking rooms are available for pet rooms. 2 dogs may be allowed.

Candlewood Suites
13845 Sunrise Valley Drive
Herndon, VA
703-793-7100 (877-270-6405)
Dogs of all sizes are allowed for an additional one time fee per pet of $75 for 1 to 15 days, and $150 for 16 or more days. 2 dogs may be allowed.

Residence Inn by Marriott
315 Elden Street
Herndon, VA
703-435-0044
Dogs of all sizes are allowed. There is a $75 one time fee and a pet policy to sign at check in. Multiple dogs may be allowed.

Staybridge Suites - Dulles
13700 Coppermine Rd
Herndon, VA
703-713-6800 (877-270-6405)
Dogs up to 50 pounds are allowed for an additional one time pet fee of $150 for a 1 bedroom suite, and $250 for a 2 bedroom suite. Multiple dogs may be allowed.

Best Western Four Seasons South
57 Airport Road
Hillsville, VA
276-728-4136 (800-780-7234)
Dogs are allowed for an additional one time pet fee of $10 per room. Multiple dogs may be allowed.

Candlewood Suites
5113 Plaza Drive
Hopewell, VA
804-541-0200 (877-270-6405)
Dogs up to 80 pounds are allowed for an additional pet fee per room of $75 for 1 to 14 nights, and $150 for 15 or more nights. 2 dogs may be allowed.

Hope and Glory Inn
65 Tavern Road
Irvington, VA
804-438-6053 (800-497-8228)
Wooded areas, wide open fields, manicured lawns, and English gardens all add to the ambiance of this beautiful 1890's waterfront inn that sits central to a wide range of

land and water recreational opportunities. Dogs of all sizes are allowed in 2 of the cottages for an additional fee of $40 per night per pet. Dogs must be well groomed (no heavy shedders), well mannered, leashed and cleaned up after. Dogs are not allowed on the bed or any of the furniture. There is a great lawn across from the inn where dogs may want to take in a good run. 2 dogs may be allowed.

Days Inn Leesburg Dwtn
721 E Market St
Leesburg, VA
703-777-6622 (800-329-7466)
Dogs of all sizes are allowed. There is a $6 per night pet fee per pet. 2 dogs may be allowed.

1780 Stone House, rental #1350
218 S Main Street/H 11
Lexington, VA
540-463-2521
vrbo.com/1350
This 200 year old, restored stone home has 2 foot thick walls, guaranteeing quiet times after exploring the areas many sites of interests. Dogs of all sizes are allowed for no additional fee. Dogs must be well behaved, leashed, and cleaned up after inside and out. 2 dogs may be allowed.

Applewood Inn
242 Tarn Beck Lane
Lexington, VA
540-463-1962 (800-463-1902)
applewoodbb.com/
Although there are a variety of activities and sites of interest guests can explore here and in the vicinity, this place also makes a good "back to nature" getaway with plenty of wildlife, scenic views, nature trails, seasonal gardens, and a lot more. Dogs are allowed for an additional fee. One dog is $20 for the 1st night and each night after is $10 per night. A second dog is an additional $10 per night. Dogs must be well mannered, leashed, and cleaned up after.

Best Western Inn at Hunt Ridge
25 Willow Springs Rd
Lexington, VA
540-464-1500 (800-780-7234)
Dogs are allowed for an additional one time pet fee of $25 per room. Multiple dogs may be allowed.

Best Western Lexington Inn
850 N Lee Highway
Lexington, VA
540-458-3020 (800-780-7234)

Dogs are allowed for an additional one time pet fee of $25 per room. Multiple dogs may be allowed.

Days Inn Lexington
325 West Midland Trail
Lexington, VA
540-463-2143 (800-329-7466)
Dogs of all sizes are allowed. There is a $10 per night pet fee per pet. Reservations are recommended due to limited rooms for pets. 2 dogs may be allowed.

Howard Johnson Inn
2836 N. Lee Hwy.
Lexington, VA
540-463-9181 (800-446-4656)
Dogs of all sizes are welcome. There is a $5 per day pet fee.

Super 8 Lexington
1139 North Lee Hwy
Lexington, VA
540-463-7858 (800-800-8000)
Dogs of all sizes are allowed. There are no additional pet fees. Smoking and non-smoking rooms are available for pet rooms. 2 dogs may be allowed.

Fox Hill Bed & Breakfast & Cottage Suites
4383 Borden Grant Trail
Lexington/Fairfield, VA
540-377-9922 (800-369-8005)
foxhillbb.com
This 38 acre B&B in the Virginia countryside allows dogs of all sizes. There is a $12 per dog pet fee per night. Dogs may be left alone in the room if crated and if a cell phone number is left.

Comfort Inn Gunston Corner
8180 Silverbrook Road
Lorton, VA
703-643-3100 (877-424-6423)
Dogs are allowed for an additional one time pet fee of $25 per room. Multiple dogs may be allowed.

Inn at Meander Plantation
2333 N James Madison H
Lotus Dale, VA
540-672-4912 (800-385-4936)
meander.net/
This country inn offers visitors everything they need to have a fun, relaxing visit with gaming areas, trails through woods and fields with plenty of bird and wildlife, landscaped grounds and gardens, and good food. Dogs of all sizes are allowed for an additional fee of $25 per night per pet. Dogs must be leashed and cleaned up after at all

times. Please take pets to the back yard; scoopers are available. They request that the "dog sheet" they provide be used if pets are accustomed to being on the bed or furniture. Dogs are not allowed in the main house, and they may be only left alone in the room for short times and they must be crated. Dogs must be quiet, well behaved, and friendly to both people and other animals on site. 2 dogs may be allowed.

Ginger Hill
47 Holly Springs Drive
Louisa, VA
540-967-3260
Dogs of all sizes are allowed. There are no additional pet fees. Dogs are placed in a covered outdoor kennel with a dog house that are just outside of the guest rooms. Multiple dogs may be allowed.

Accokeek Farm
170 Kibler Drive
Luray, VA
540-743-2305
shentel.net/accokeek/
Nestled at the base of a mountain along the river, this inn offers guests lodging in an historic restored 19th century, 4 story bank barn, several recreation areas, canoes, and a great starting location for exploring several other sites of interest. Dogs of all sizes are allowed for an additional fee of $50 per pet per stay. Dogs must be well mannered, leashed, and cleaned up after at all times. 2 dogs may be allowed.

Adventures Await
Luray, VA
540-743-5766 (800-433-6077)
adventuresawait.com/
This company offers several properties with various amenities in the Shenandoah River valley and mountain region around Luray. Dogs of all sizes are allowed for no additional fee. Dogs must be well behaved, leashed, and cleaned up after at all times. 2 dogs may be allowed.

Allstar Lodging
21 Wallace Avenue
Luray, VA
540-843-0606 (866-780-STAR (7827))
allstarlodging.com/
This realty offers several vacation rentals with various amenities in and around Luray in the scenic Shenandoah Valley. Dogs are allowed in their cabins for an additional fee of $10 per night per

pet. Dogs must be under owner's control/care, leashed, and cleaned up after. 2 dogs may be allowed.

Days Inn Luray
138 Whispering Hill Rd
Luray, VA
540-743-4521 (800-329-7466)
Dogs of all sizes are allowed. There is a $10 per night pet fee per pet. 2 dogs may be allowed.

Holiday Inn Select
601 Main Street
Lynchburg, VA
434-528-2500 (877-270-6405)
Dogs of all sizes are allowed for an additional one time pet fee of $25 per room. 2 dogs may be allowed.

Quality Inn
3125 Albert Lankford Drive
Lynchburg, VA
434-847-9041 (877-424-6423)
Dogs are allowed for an additional one time pet fee of $25 per room. Multiple dogs may be allowed.

Best Western Battlefield Inn
10820 Balls Ford Road
Manassas, VA
703-361-8000 (800-780-7234)
Dogs are allowed for an additional fee of $10 per night per pet. Extra large dogs can not be accommodated. Multiple dogs may be allowed.

Red Roof Inn - Washington, DC - Manassas
10610 Automotive Drive
Manassas, VA
703-335-9333 (800-RED-ROOF)
One well-behaved family pet per room. Guest must notify front desk upon arrival. Guest is liable for any damages. In consideration of all guests, pets must never be left unattended in the guest rooms.

Best Western Martinsville
1755 Virginia Ave
Martinsville, VA
276-632-5611 (800-780-7234)
Dogs are allowed for an additional pet fee of $10 per night per room. 2 dogs may be allowed.

Holiday Inn Express
1895 Virginia Ave
Martinsville, VA
276-666-6835 (877-270-6405)
Dogs of all sizes are allowed for an additional one time pet fee of $25 per room. 2 dogs may be allowed.

Super 8 Ft Chiswell/Max Meadows

Area
194 Ft Chiswell Rd
Max Meadows, VA
276-637-4141 (800-800-8000)
Dogs of all sizes are allowed. There is a $10.50 per night pet fee per pet. Smoking and non-smoking rooms are available for pet rooms. 2 dogs may be allowed.

Best Western Tysons Westpark
8401 Westpark Drive
McLean, VA
703-734-2800 (800-780-7234)
Dogs are allowed for no additional pet fee. Multiple dogs may be allowed.

Staybridge Suites
6845 Old Dominion Dr
McLean, VA
703-448-5400 (877-270-6405)
Dogs of all sizes are allowed for an additional one time pet fee of $75 per room. Multiple dogs may be allowed.

Super 8 Middletown/Winchester Area
2120 Reliance Rd
Middletown, VA
540-868-1800 (800-800-8000)
Dogs of all sizes are allowed. There is a $10 per night pet fee per pet. Smoking and non-smoking rooms are available for pet rooms. 2 dogs may be allowed.

Highland Inn
68 West Main Street/H 250
Monterey, VA
540-468-2143 (888-466-4682)
highland-inn.com/
Beautiful in any season, this 1904 3-story inn is a great starting point to a number of other activities, historic sites, and recreation. Dogs are allowed for an additional $20 per night per room. Dogs must be quiet, well behaved, leashed, and cleaned up after at all times. 2 dogs may be allowed.

The Widow Kip's Country Inn
355 Orchard Drive
Mount Jackson, VA
540-477-2400 (800-478-8714)
widowkips.com/
This 1830 restored Victorian homestead features 7 rural acres overlooking the Shenandoah River with 3½ acres of landscaped grounds and a fenced 5 acre field for plenty of safe pet exercise. Dogs of all sizes are allowed in the cottages for an additional fee of $15 per night per pet. Dogs must be well behaved, leashed (except in field)

and cleaned up after at all times. 2 dogs may be allowed.

Rugby Creek Cabins and Equestrian Resort
1228 Rugby Road
Mouth of Wilson, VA
276-579-4215
rugbycreek.com
Nestled high in the Blue Ridge Mountains, this 63 acre private farm is a place you can vacation with both your horse and your pooch (or just your pooch). Dogs of all sizes are allowed in the Overlook Cabin with prior approval for an additional fee of $10 per night per pet, and they provide doggy beds, bowls, toys, and a fenced yard for their canine guests. Dogs must be leashed and cleaned up after. 2 dogs may be allowed.

1926 Caboose Vacation Rental
218 S Main Street/H 11
Natural Bridge, VA
540-463-2521
guestcaboose.com/
This interesting 1926 Caboose vacation getaway is one of two of their rentals that allow pets. Dogs of all sizes are allowed for no additional fee. Dogs must be well trained, leashed, and cleaned up after inside and outside of the units.

Natural Bridge Hotel
15 Appledore Lane
Natural Bridge, VA
540-291-2121 (800-533-1410)
naturalbridgeva.com/hotel.html
This unique getaway has been serving travelers since the late 1700's, and there are a variety of attractions here in addition to the accommodations such as the Natural Bridge and the Drama of Creation seasonal, nightly shows, a styrofoam replica of Stonehenge, and much more. Dogs are allowed in the cottages for no additional pet fee. Dogs must be leashed and cleaned up after at all times. Dogs are not allowed in buildings, the museums, or the caverns; they are allowed on the trails and at Natural Bridge Park. 2 dogs may be allowed.

Garden and Sea Inn
4188 Nelson Road
New Church, VA
800-824-0672
gardenandseainn.com/
With an emphasis on privacy and relaxation, this historic 1804 inn sits on 4 gorgeous landscaped acres with gardens, ponds, a seasonal pool, and they also offer gourmet dining and a convenient location to

several other activities. Dogs of all sizes are allowed for no additional fee. Dogs must be quiet, leashed, and cleaned up after at all times. 2 dogs may be allowed.

Days Inn New Market
9360 George Collins Pkwy
New Market, VA
540-740-4100 (800-329-7466)
Dogs of all sizes are allowed. There is a $5 per night pet fee per pet. 2 dogs may be allowed.

Quality Inn Shenandoah Valley
162 W Old Cross Road
New Market, VA
540-740-3141 (877-424-6423)
Dogs are allowed for an additional one time pet fee of $10.50 per room. 2 dogs may be allowed.

Comfort Inn
12330 Jefferson Avenue
Newport News, VA
757-249-0200 (877-424-6423)
Dogs are allowed for an additional fee of $50 per night per pet. Multiple dogs may be allowed.

Days Inn Newport News
14747 Warwick Blvd
Newport News, VA
757-874-0201 (800-329-7466)
Dogs of all sizes are allowed. There is a $10 per night pet fee per pet. 2 dogs may be allowed.

Days Inn Newport News/Oyster Point
11829 Fishing Pt Dr
Newport News, VA
757-873-6700 (800-329-7466)
Dogs of all sizes are allowed. There is a $15 per night pet fee per pet. 2 dogs may be allowed.

Motel 6 - Newport News
797 J Clyde Morris Boulevard
Newport News, VA
757-595-6336 (800-466-8356)
One well-behaved family pet per room. Guest must notify front desk upon arrival. Guest is liable for any damages. In consideration of all guests, pets must never be left unattended in the guest rooms.

Days Inn Norfolk Marina/Beachfront
1631 Bayville St
Norfolk, VA
757-583-4521 (800-329-7466)
Dogs of all sizes are allowed. There is a $15 per night pet fee per pet. Reservations are recommended due to limited rooms for pets. 2 dogs may be allowed.

Econo Lodge
9601 4th View St
Norfolk, VA
757-480-9611
There is a $5 per day pet fee.

Motel 6 - Norfolk
853 North Military Highway
Norfolk, VA
757-461-2380 (800-466-8356)
One well-behaved family pet per room. Guest must notify front desk upon arrival. Guest is liable for any damages. In consideration of all guests, pets must never be left unattended in the guest rooms.

Page House Inn
323 Fairfax Avenue
Norfolk, VA
757-625-5033 (800-599-7659)
pagehouseinn.com/
This stately historic mansion gives guests a glimpse of past luxury, as well as a good central location to a variety of recreation, shopping, and dining. Dogs of all sizes are allowed for an additional fee of $25 per night per pet. Dogs must be quiet, well behaved, leashed, and cleaned up after. Dogs must be crated if left alone for more than a few minutes and a cell number left at the front desk. 2 dogs may be allowed.

Quality Suites Lake Wright
6280 Northampton Blvd
Norfolk, VA
757-461-6251
Dogs are allowed for an additional one time fee of $25 per pet for the standard rooms; the fee is $35 per pet for suites. Multiple dogs may be allowed.

Residence Inn by Marriott
1590 N Military Highway
Norfolk, VA
757-333-3000
Dogs of all sizes are allowed. There is a $75 one time fee and a pet policy to sign at check in. Multiple dogs may be allowed.

Sheraton Norfolk Waterside Hotel
777 Waterside Drive
Norfolk, VA
757-622-6664 (888-625-5144)
Dogs up to 60 pounds are allowed. There are no additional pet fees. Dogs are not allowed to be left alone in the room.

Sleep Inn Lake Wright
6280 Northampton Blvd
Norfolk, VA
757-461-1133 (877-424-6423)

Dogs are allowed for an additional one time fee of $25 per pet for the standard rooms; the fee is $35 per pet for suites. Multiple dogs may be allowed.

Holladay House
155 W Main Street
Orange, VA
540-672-4893 (800-358-4422)
holladayhousebandb.com/
Historically significant, this 1830's home features a rich Federal architecture, an extensive civil war and classical novel library, a variety of refreshments throughout the day, and close proximity to a number of area attractions and activities. Dogs are allowed in the Garden or Ivy rooms for an additional fee of $25 per night per pet. Dogs must be quiet, well mannered, leashed, and cleaned up after at all times. Multiple dogs may be allowed.

Days Inn Petersburg/Fort Lee South
12208 S Crater Rd
Petersburg, VA
804-733-4400 (800-329-7466)
Dogs up to 60 pounds are allowed. There is a $10 per night pet fee per pet. 2 dogs may be allowed.

Quality Inn
11974 S Crater Road
Petersburg, VA
804-732-2900 (877-424-6423)
Dogs are allowed for an additional fee of $5 per night per pet. Multiple dogs may be allowed.

Holiday Inn
8 Crawford Pkwy
Portsmouth, VA
757-393-2573 (877-270-6405)
Dogs of all sizes are allowed for an additional pet fee of $10 per night per pet. Multiple dogs may be allowed.

Holiday Inn Express Hotel & Suites
Claypool Hill (Richlands Area)
180 Clay Dr.
Pounding Mill, VA
276-596-9880 (877-270-6405)
Dogs up to 60 pounds are allowed for an additional fee of $25 per night per pet. 2 dogs may be allowed.

Days Inn Pulaski
3063 Old Rt 100 Rd
Pulaski, VA
540-980-2230 (800-329-7466)
Dogs of all sizes are allowed. There is a $10 per night pet fee per pet. 2 dogs may be allowed.

Best Western Radford Inn
1501 Tyler Avenue
Radford, VA
540-639-3000 (800-780-7234)
Dogs are allowed for an additional
fee of $10 per night per pet. Multiple
dogs may be allowed.

Super 8 Radford
1600 Tyler Ave
Radford, VA
540-731-9355 (800-800-8000)
Dogs of all sizes are allowed. There
is a $15.75 one time per pet fee per
visit. Smoking and non-smoking
rooms are available for pet rooms. 2
dogs may be allowed.

Days Inn Raphine
584 Oakland Cr
Raphine, VA
540-377-2604 (800-329-7466)
Dogs of all sizes are allowed. There
is a $5 per night pet fee per pet. 2
dogs may be allowed.

Fleeton Fields
2783 Fleeton Road
Reedville, VA
804-453-7016 (800-497-8215)
fleetonfields.com/
Set in a gorgeous park-like setting
with garden benches, manicured
lawns, a tidal pond, and herb and
flower gardens, this beautiful colonial
style, Victorian inspired retreat also
offers guests complimentary
bicycles, kayaks, and canoes. Dogs
of all sizes are allowed for no
additional fee. Dogs must be well
behaved, leashed, and cleaned up
after at all times. 2 dogs may be
allowed.

Sheraton Reston Hotel
11810 Sunrise Valley Dr.
Reston, VA
703-620-9000 (888-625-5144)
Dogs up to 80 pounds are allowed.
Dogs are not allowed to be left alone
in the room.

Candlewood Suites
4301 Commerce Road
Richmond, VA
804-271-0016 (877-270-6405)
Dogs up to 80 pounds are allowed
for an additional one time fee of $50
per pet. Multiple dogs may be
allowed.

Days Inn Richmond
6910 Midlothian Turnpike
Richmond, VA
804-745-7100 (800-329-7466)
Dogs of all sizes are allowed. There
is a $20 one time per pet fee per

visit. 2 dogs may be allowed.

Jefferson Hotel
101 West Franklin Street
Richmond, VA
804-788-8000
Noted for its outstanding public
spaces and accommodations, this
hotel is centrally located in the
downtown historic district. Dogs of
all sizes are allowed for an
additional $40 per night per pet.
Dogs may not be left alone in the
room, and they must be leashed
and cleaned up after at all times.
There is a dog sitting and/or walking
service for an additional fee of
$7.50 per hour. 2 dogs may be
allowed.

Motel 6 - Richmond Chippenham
100 Greshamwood Place
Richmond, VA
804-745-0600 (800-466-8356)
One well-behaved family pet per
room. Guest must notify front desk
upon arrival. Guest is liable for any
damages. In consideration of all
guests, pets must never be left
unattended in the guest rooms.

Quality Inn West End
8008 W Broad Street
Richmond, VA
804-346-0000 (877-424-6423)
One dog is allowed for an additional
one time pet fee of $35.

Red Roof Inn - Richmond South,
VA
4350 Commerce Road
Richmond, VA
804-271-7240 (800-RED-ROOF)
One well-behaved family pet per
room. Guest must notify front desk
upon arrival. Guest is liable for any
damages. In consideration of all
guests, pets must never be left
unattended in the guest rooms.

Residence Inn by Marriott
3940 Westerre Parkway
Richmond, VA
804-762-9852
Dogs of all sizes are allowed. There
is a $75 one time fee and a pet
policy to sign at check in. Multiple
dogs may be allowed.

Residence Inn by Marriott
2121Dickens Road
Richmond, VA
804-285-8200
Dogs of all sizes are allowed. There
is a $75 one time fee and a pet
policy to sign at check in. Multiple
dogs may be allowed.

Sheraton Park South Hotel
9901 Midlothian Turnpike
Richmond, VA
804-323-1144 (888-625-5144)
Dogs up to 80 pounds are allowed.
There are no additional pet fees.
Dogs are not allowed to be left alone
in the room.

Sheraton Richmond West Hotel
6624 West Broad St.
Richmond, VA
804-285-2000 (888-625-5144)
Dogs up to 50 pounds are allowed.
There are no additional pet fees.
Dogs are not allowed to be left alone
in the room.

Super 8 Richmond/Midlothian Tnpk
8260 Midlothian Turnpike
Richmond, VA
804-320-2823 (800-800-8000)
Dogs of all sizes are allowed. There
is a $25 per night pet fee per pet.
Smoking and non-smoking rooms
are available for pet rooms. 2 dogs
may be allowed.

Best Western Inn at Valley View
5050 Valley View Boulevard NW
Roanoke, VA
540-362-2400 (800-780-7234)
Dogs are allowed for an additional
one time pet fee of $20 per room.
Multiple dogs may be allowed.

Comfort Inn Airport
5070 Valley View Road
Roanoke, VA
540-527-2020 (877-424-6423)
Dogs are allowed for an additional
one time fee of $25 per pet. Multiple
dogs may be allowed.

Days Inn Roanoke Airport
8118 Plantation Rd
Roanoke, VA
540-366-0341 (800-329-7466)
Dogs of all sizes are allowed. There
is a $15 one time per pet fee per
visit. 2 dogs may be allowed.

Days Inn Roanoke Civic Center/Dwtn
535 Orange AVe
Roanoke, VA
540-342-4551 (800-329-7466)
Dogs of all sizes are allowed. There
is a $5 per night pet fee per small pet
and $10 for large pet. 2 dogs may be
allowed.

Motel 6 - Roanoke
3695 Thirlane Road
Roanoke, VA
540-563-0229 (800-466-8356)
One well-behaved family pet per

room. Guest must notify front desk upon arrival. Guest is liable for any damages. In consideration of all guests, pets must never be left unattended in the guest rooms.

Quality Inn Roanoke Airport
6626 Thirlane Road
Roanoke, VA
540-366-8861 (877-424-6423)
Dogs are allowed for an additional one time fee of $15 per pet. Multiple dogs may be allowed.

Super 8 Roanoke
6616 Thirlane Rd
Roanoke, VA
540-563-8888 (800-800-8000)
Dogs of all sizes are allowed. There is a $10 returnable deposit required per room. Smoking and non-smoking rooms are available for pet rooms. 2 dogs may be allowed.

Comfort Inn Smith Mt Lake
1730 N Main Street
Rocky Mount, VA
540-489-4000 (877-424-6423)
Dogs are allowed for an additional one time pet fee of $25 per room. Multiple dogs may be allowed.

Holiday Inn Express Hotel & Suites Rocky Mount/Smith Mtn Lake
395 Old Franklin Trnpk.
Rocky Mount, VA
540-489-5001 (877-270-6405)
Dogs of all sizes are allowed for an additional one time pet fee of $25 per room. 2 dogs may be allowed.

Howard Johnson Express Inn
23786 Rogers Clark Blvd.
Ruther Glen, VA
804-448-2499 (800-446-4656)
Dogs of all sizes are welcome. There is a $5 per day pet fee. Please place a Do Not Disturb Sign on the door so that housekeepers do not open the door while the pet is in the room.

Red Roof Inn - Ruther Glen - Carmel Church
23500 Welcome Way Drive
Ruther Glen, VA
804-448-2828 (800-RED-ROOF)
One well-behaved family pet per room. Guest must notify front desk upon arrival. Guest is liable for any damages. In consideration of all guests, pets must never be left unattended in the guest rooms.

Days Inn Richmond Airport
5500 Williamsburg Rd
Sandston, VA
804-222-2041 (800-329-7466)

Dogs of all sizes are allowed. There is no charge for small pet and a $20 fee per large pet per night. 2 dogs may be allowed.

Motel 6 - Richmond Airport
5704 Williamsburg Road (US Route 60)
Sandston, VA
804-222-7600 (800-466-8356)
One well-behaved family pet per room. Guest must notify front desk upon arrival. Guest is liable for any damages. In consideration of all guests, pets must never be left unattended in the guest rooms.

Holiday Inn Express
1074 Bill Tuck Highway
South Boston, VA
434-575-4000 (877-270-6405)
Dogs of all sizes are allowed for an additional fee of $20 per night per pet. 2 dogs may be allowed.

Quality Inn
2001 Seymour Drive
South Boston, VA
434-572-4311 (877-424-6423)
Dogs of all sizes are allowed. There is a $10 per night per room additional pet fee. Multiple dogs may be allowed.

Comfort Inn
918 E Atlantic Street
South Hill, VA
434-447-2600 (877-424-6423)
Dogs are allowed for an additional fee of $10 per night per pet. 2 dogs may be allowed.

Hopkins Ordinary
47 Main Street
Sperryville, VA
540-987-3383
hopkinsordinary.com/
Listed on the National Register of Historic Places and built around 1820 as a roadside inn and tavern, it once served the needs of the "ordinary" traveler, and now provides visitors extra-ordinary accommodations and fare, and close proximity to a number of area attractions and activities. Dogs are allowed in the garden cottage for an additional fee of $25 per night per pet (adjustable for multiple days). Dogs must be friendly (other animals on site), well mannered, leashed or crated when out of the cottage, and cleaned up after at all times. 2 dogs may be allowed.

Comfort Inn
6560 Loisdale Court

Springfield, VA
703-922-9000 (877-424-6423)
Dogs up to 50 pounds are allowed for no additional pet fee. Dogs must be crated when left alone in the room and a contact number left with the front desk. 2 dogs may be allowed.

Hampton Inn
6550 Loisdale Court
Springfield, VA
703-924-9444
Well behaved dogs of all sizes are allowed. There are no additional pet fees. Multiple dogs may be allowed.

Red Roof Inn - Washington, DC Southwest - Springfield
6868 Springfield Boulevard
Springfield, VA
703-644-5311 (800-RED-ROOF)
One well-behaved family pet per room. Guest must notify front desk upon arrival. Guest is liable for any damages. In consideration of all guests, pets must never be left unattended in the guest rooms.

TownePlace Suites Springfield
6245 Brandon Avenue
Springfield, VA
703-569-8060
Dogs of all sizes are allowed. There is a $75 one time pet fee per visit. 2 dogs may be allowed.

Holiday Inn Express
28 Greenspring Drive
Stafford, VA
540-657-5566 (877-270-6405)
Dogs of all sizes are allowed: Dogs 15 pounds or under is an additional $10 per night; the fee is 20 per night for dogs over 15 pounds. 2 dogs may be allowed.

Best Western Staunton Inn
92 Rowe Rd
Staunton, VA
540-885-1112 (800-780-7234)
Dogs are allowed for no additional pet fee. Multiple dogs may be allowed.

Comfort Inn
1302 Richmond Avenue
Staunton, VA
540-886-5000 (877-424-6423)
Dogs up to 50 pounds are allowed for an additional fee of $10 per night per pet. 2 dogs may be allowed.

Days Inn Staunton
273 D Bells Lane
Staunton, VA
540-248-0888 (800-329-7466)
Dogs of all sizes are allowed. There

is a $10 per night pet fee per pet. 2 dogs may be allowed.

Days Inn Staunton/Blue Ridge Mountains
372 White Hill Rd
Staunton, VA
540-337-3031 (800-329-7466)
Dogs of all sizes are allowed. There is a $8 per night pet fee per pet. 2 dogs may be allowed.

Holiday Inn
152 Fairway Lane
Staunton, VA
540-248-6020 (877-270-6405)
Dogs of all sizes are allowed: Non-priority guests pay an additional one time pet fee per room of $15 for 1 pet and $5 for a 2nd pet; priority club members pay a $10 one time fee and $5 for a 2nd pet. 2 dogs may be allowed.

Quality Inn
96 Baker Lane
Staunton, VA
540-248-5111 (877-424-6423)
Dogs are allowed for an additional fee of $10 per night per pet. Multiple dogs may be allowed.

Sleep Inn
222 Jefferson H
Staunton, VA
540-887-6500 (877-424-6423)
Dogs are allowed for no additional pet fee. Dogs may not be left alone in the room. 2 dogs may be allowed.

Super 8 Staunton
1015 Richmond Rd
Staunton, VA
540-886-2888 (800-800-8000)
Dogs of all sizes are allowed. There is a $10 per night pet fee per pet. Smoking and non-smoking rooms are available for pet rooms. 2 dogs may be allowed.

Twelfth Night Inn
402 E Beverly
Staunton, VA
540-885-1733
Dogs of all sizes are allowed. There is a $15 per night fee for one pet and it is $20 per night for two. 2 dogs may be allowed.

Comfort Inn
167 Town Run Lane
Stephens City, VA
540-869-6500 (877-424-6423)
Dogs are allowed for an additional pet fee of $15 per night per room. 2 dogs may be allowed.

Candlewood Suites
45520 East Severn Way
Sterling, VA
703-674-2288 (877-270-6405)
Dogs of all sizes are allowed for an additional one time pet fee of $75 per room. 2 dogs may be allowed.

Hampton Inn
46331 McClellan Way
Sterling, VA
703-450-9595
Well behaved dogs of all sizes are allowed. There is an additional $25 per room for the 1st night, and each night thereafter the fee is $10 per room. There is a pet policy to sign at check in. Multiple dogs may be allowed.

Hampton Inn
45440 Holiday Drive
Sterling, VA
703-471-8300
Dogs of all sizes are allowed. There is a $25 per pet per stay fee and a pet policy to sign at check in. Multiple dogs may be allowed.

Holiday Inn Washington-Dulles Intl Airport
1000 Sully Rd
Sterling, VA
703-471-7411 (877-270-6405)
Dogs up to 50 pounds are allowed for an additional one time pet fee of $50 per room. 2 dogs may be allowed.

TownePlace Suites Sterling
21123 Whitfield Place
Sterling, VA
703-421-1090
Dogs of all sizes are allowed. There is a $75 one time pet fee per visit. 2 dogs may be allowed.

TownePlace Suites Washington Dulles Airport
22744 Holiday Park Dr
Sterling, VA
703-707-2017
Dogs of all sizes are allowed. There is a $75 one time pet fee per visit. 2 dogs may be allowed.

Hampton Inn
10476 Blue Star H
Stony Creek, VA
434-246-5500
Dogs up to 50 pounds are allowed. There is a $10 one time cleaning fee. 2 dogs may be allowed.

Sleep Inn
11019 Blue Star H
Stony Creek, VA

434-246-5100 (877-424-6423)
Dogs up to 60 pounds are allowed for an additional fee of $15 per pet for the 1st night, and $10 per pet for each additional night. 2 dogs may be allowed.

Days Inn Suffolk
1526 Holland Road
Suffolk, VA
757-539-5111 (800-329-7466)
Dogs of all sizes are allowed. There is a $7 per night pet fee per pet. 2 dogs may be allowed.

Days Inn Tappahannock Dwtn
1414 Tappahannock Blvd
Tappahannock, VA
804-443-9200 (800-329-7466)
Dogs of all sizes are allowed. There is a $10 per night pet fee per pet. 2 dogs may be allowed.

Quality Inn
6409 Danbell Lane
Thornburg, VA
540-582-1097 (877-424-6423)
Dogs are allowed for an additional fee of $10 per night per pet. Multiple dogs may be allowed.

Comfort Inn
2545 Lee H
Troutville, VA
540-992-5600 (877-424-6423)
Dogs are allowed for an additional one time pet fee of $20 per room. Multiple dogs may be allowed.

Red Roof Inn - Roanoke - Troutville
3231 Lee Highway South
Troutville, VA
540-992-5055 (800-RED-ROOF)
One well-behaved family pet per room. Guest must notify front desk upon arrival. Guest is liable for any damages. In consideration of all guests, pets must never be left unattended in the guest rooms.

Homestead Tyson's Corner
8201 Old Courthouse Road
Vienna, VA
703-356-6300
Dogs of all sizes are allowed. There is a $75 one time fee per pet. Multiple dogs may be allowed.

Residence Inn by Marriott
8616 Westwood Center Drive
Vienna, VA
703-893-0120
One dog of any size is allowed. There is a $75 one time fee and a pet policy to sign at check in.

Residence Inn by Marriott

8400 Old Courthouse Road
Vienna, VA
703-917-0800
Dogs of all sizes are allowed. There is a $75 one time fee and a pet policy to sign at check in. Multiple dogs may be allowed.

Candlewood Suites Virginia Beach/Norfolk
4437 Bonney Road
Virginia Beach, VA
757-213-1500 (877-270-6405)
Dogs of all sizes are allowed for an additional pet fee per room of $75 for 1 to 6 nights, and $150 for 7 nights or more. 2 dogs may be allowed.

Days Inn Virginia Beach Oceanfront
3107 Atlantic Ave
Virginia Beach, VA
757-428-7233 (800-329-7466)
Dogs of all sizes are allowed. There is a $25 per night pet fee per pet. 2 dogs may be allowed.

Doubletree
1900 Pavilion Drive
Virginia Beach, VA
757-422-8900
Two dogs with no more than a combined weight of 90 pounds are allowed. There is a $25 per week per room fee and a pet policy to sign at check in. 2 dogs may be allowed.

Holiday Inn Hotel & Suites Va Beach-Surfside (26Th St)
2607 Atlantic Ave
Virginia Beach, VA
757-491-6900 (877-270-6405)
Dogs of all sizes are allowed for an additional one time pet fee of $40 per room. Multiple dogs may be allowed.

La Quinta Inn Norfolk Virginia Beach
192 Newtown Rd.
Virginia Beach, VA
757-497-6620 (800-531-5900)
Dogs of all sizes are allowed. There are no additional pet fees. Dogs must be leashed, cleaned up after, and crated if left unattended in the room. Multiple dogs may be allowed.

Red Roof Inn - Virginia Beach
196 Ballard Court
Virginia Beach, VA
757-490-0225 (800-RED-ROOF)
One well-behaved family pet per room. Guest must notify front desk upon arrival. Guest is liable for any damages. In consideration of all guests, pets must never be left unattended in the guest rooms.

Red Roof Inn - Virginia Beach -

Norfolk Airport
5745 Northampton Boulevard
Virginia Beach, VA
757-460-3414 (800-RED-ROOF)
One well-behaved family pet per room. Guest must notify front desk upon arrival. Guest is liable for any damages. In consideration of all guests, pets must never be left unattended in the guest rooms.

Sandbridge Realty
581 Sandbridge Road
Virginia Beach, VA
757-426-6262 (800-933-4800)
sandbridge.com/
This realty offers a variety of vacation rentals with various amenities in the Sandbridge Beach area. Dogs of all sizes are allowed in the house rentals (not the condos) for an additional fee of $115 per pet per stay. Dogs must be licensed, and leashed and cleaned up after at all times. Dogs are not allowed on the beach, the boardwalk, or the grassy area west of the boardwalk between Rudee Inlet and 42nd Street from the Friday before Memorial Day to Labor Day unless they are in an escape-proof container. 2 dogs may be allowed.

Sheraton Oceanfront Hotel
3501 Atlantic Ave.
Virginia Beach, VA
757-425-9000 (888-625-5144)
Dogs up to 60 pounds are allowed. Pets are restricted to first and third floor rooms only. Dogs are not allowed to be left alone in the room.

TownePlace Suites Virginia Beach
5757 Cleveland St
Virginia Beach, VA
757-490-9367
Dogs up to 75 pounds are allowed. There is a $75 one time pet fee per visit. 2 dogs may be allowed.

Comfort Inn
7379 Comfort Inn Drive
Warrenton, VA
540-349-8900 (877-424-6423)
Dogs are allowed for an additional fee of $10 per night per pet. Multiple dogs may be allowed.

Hampton Inn
501 Blackwell Road
Warrenton, VA
540-349-4200
Dogs of all sizes are allowed. There are no additional pet fees. Multiple dogs may be allowed.

Howard Johnson Inn
6 Broadview Ave.
Warrenton, VA
540-347-4141 (800-446-4656)
Dogs up to 85 pounds are allowed. There is a $10 per day pet fee.

Days Inn Waynesboro
2060 Rosser Ave
Waynesboro, VA
540-943-1101 (800-329-7466)
Dogs of all sizes are allowed. There is a $10 per night pet fee per pet. 2 dogs may be allowed.

Quality Inn
640 W Broad Street
Waynesboro, VA
540-942-1171 (877-424-6423)
Dogs are allowed for an additional pet fee of $10 per night per room. Multiple dogs may be allowed.

Super 8 Waynesboro
2045 Rosser Ave
Waynesboro, VA
540-943-3888 (800-800-8000)
Dogs of all sizes are allowed. There is a $5 per night pet fee per pet. Smoking and non-smoking rooms are available for pet rooms. 2 dogs may be allowed.

Days Inn Williamsburg/Colonial Dwtn
902 Richmond Rd
Williamsburg, VA
757-229-5060 (800-329-7466)
Dogs of all sizes are allowed. There is a $10 per night pet fee per small pet and $15 per large pet. 2 dogs may be allowed.

Four Points by Sheraton
Williamsburg Historic District
351 York St.
Williamsburg, VA
757-229-4100 (888-625-5144)
Dogs of all sizes are allowed. There is a $25 per night pet fee per pet. After 3 nights the nightly fee per pet is higher. Dogs are not allowed to be left alone in the room.

Motel 6 - Williamsburg
3030 Richmond Road
Williamsburg, VA
757-565-3433 (800-466-8356)
One well-behaved family pet per room. Guest must notify front desk upon arrival. Guest is liable for any damages. In consideration of all guests, pets must never be left unattended in the guest rooms.

Red Roof Inn - Williamsburg
824 Capitol Landing Rd
Williamsburg, VA

757-259-1948 (800-RED-ROOF)
One well-behaved family pet per room. Guest must notify front desk upon arrival. Guest is liable for any damages. In consideration of all guests, pets must never be left unattended in the guest rooms.

Residence Inn by Marriott
1648 Richmond Road
Williamsburg, VA
757-941-2000
Dogs of all sizes are allowed. There is a $75 one time fee and a pet policy to sign at check in. Multiple dogs may be allowed.

Woodlands Cascades Motel
105 Visitor Center Drive
Williamsburg, VA
757-229-1000
This contemporary Motor Inn, surrounded by landscaped grounds, is adjacent to Colonial Williamsburg and an abundance of activities. Dogs up to a combined weight of 60 pounds are allowed for no additional fee. Dogs must be well behaved, leashed, and cleaned up after. 2 dogs may be allowed.

Best Value Inn
2649 Valley Avenue
Winchester, VA
540-662-2521 (888-315-2378)
This inn offers a number of amenities plus 4 meticulously landscaped acres to explore with your pooch. Dogs are allowed for an additional fee of $5 per pet per night. Dogs must be quiet, well behaved, leashed, and cleaned up after. 2 dogs may be allowed.

Best Western Lee-Jackson Motor Inn
711 Millwood Ave
Winchester, VA
540-662-4154 (800-780-7234)
Dogs are allowed for an additional fee of $5 per night per pet. Multiple dogs may be allowed.

Candlewood Suites Winchester
1135 Millwood Pike
Winchester, VA
540-667-8323 (877-270-6405)
Dogs up to 80 pounds are allowed for an additional fee of $12 per night per pet. 2 dogs may be allowed.

Days Inn Winchester
2951 Valley Ave
Winchester, VA
540-667-1200 (800-329-7466)
Dogs of all sizes are allowed. There is a $5 per night pet fee per pet. 2 dogs may be allowed.

Holiday Inn
1017 Millwood Pike
Winchester, VA
540-667-3300 (877-270-6405)
Dogs up to 60 pounds are allowed for no additional pet fee. 2 dogs may be allowed.

Red Roof Inn - Winchester
991 Millwood Pike
Winchester, VA
540-667-5000 (800-RED-ROOF)
One well-behaved family pet per room. Guest must notify front desk upon arrival. Guest is liable for any damages. In consideration of all guests, pets must never be left unattended in the guest rooms.

Super 8 Winchester
1077 Millwood Pike
Winchester, VA
540-665-4450 (800-800-8000)
Dogs of all sizes are allowed. There is a $7 per night pet fee per pet. Smoking and non-smoking rooms are available for pet rooms. 2 dogs may be allowed.

Quality Inn
1109 Hormer Road
Woodbridge, VA
703-494-0300 (877-424-6423)
Dogs are allowed for an additional fee of $20 (plus tax) per night per pet. Multiple dogs may be allowed.

Residence Inn by Marriott
14301 Crossing Place
Woodbridge, VA
703-490-4020
Dogs of all sizes are allowed. There is a $75 one time fee and a pet policy to sign at check in. Multiple dogs may be allowed.

Comfort Inn
1011 Motel Drive
Woodstock, VA
540-459-7600 (877-424-6423)
Dogs are allowed for an additional fee of $10 per night per pet. 2 dogs may be allowed.

Best Western Wytheville Inn
355 Nye Rd
Wytheville, VA
276-228-7300 (800-780-7234)
Dogs are allowed for an additional pet fee of $6.66 per night per room. Multiple dogs may be allowed.

Comfort Inn
2594 East Lee H
Wytheville, VA
276-637-4281 (877-424-6423)

Dogs are allowed for an additional fee of $10 per night per pet. Multiple dogs may be allowed.

Days Inn Wytheville
150 Malin Dr
Wytheville, VA
276-228-5500 (800-329-7466)
Dogs of all sizes are allowed. There is a $5 per night pet fee per pet. 2 dogs may be allowed.

Motel 6 - Wytheville
220 Lithia Road
Wytheville, VA
276-228-7988 (800-466-8356)
One well-behaved family pet per room. Guest must notify front desk upon arrival. Guest is liable for any damages. In consideration of all guests, pets must never be left unattended in the guest rooms.

Super 8 Wytheville
130 Nye Circle
Wytheville, VA
276-228-6620 (800-800-8000)
Dogs of all sizes are allowed. There is a $10 one time per pet fee per visit. Smoking and non-smoking rooms are available for pet rooms. 2 dogs may be allowed.

Candlewood Suites
329 Commonwealth Drive
Yorktown, VA
757-952-1120 (877-270-6405)
Dogs up to 80 pounds are allowed for an additional one time fee of $75 per pet per. Multiple dogs may be allowed.

Marl Inn
220 Church Street
Yorktown, VA
757-898-3859 (800-799-6207)
marlinnbandb.com/
This colonial styled inn sits only a short distance from a number of activities, the river, historical sites, and an eclectic array of eateries and shops. Dogs of all sizes are allowed for no additional fee. Dogs must be housebroken, well behaved, leashed, cleaned up after, and friendly to the other pets on site. 2 dogs may be allowed.

TownePlace Suites Newport News/Yorktown
200 Cybernetics Way
Yorktown, VA
757-874-8884
Dogs of all sizes are allowed. There is a $75 one time pet fee per visit. 2 dogs may be allowed.

Washington Listings

America's Best Value
521 W Wishkah
Aberdeen, WA
360-532-5210
Dogs of all sizes are allowed. There is a $10 per night pet fee. 2 dogs may be allowed.

Anacortes Inn
3006 Commercial Ave
Anacortes, WA
360-293-3153
ohwy.com/wa/a/anactinn.htm
There is a $10 per night pet fee.

Fidalgo Country Inn
7645 St Route 20
Anacortes, WA
360-293-3494
There is a $20 per day pet charge. There are 2 pet rooms.

Best Western Bainbridge Island Suites
350 NE High School Road
Bainbridge Island, WA
206-855-9666 (800-780-7234)
Well behaved dogs are allowed for an additional one time pet fee of $50 per room 2 dogs may be allowed.

Residence Inn by Marriott
14455 NE 29th Place
Bellevue, WA
425-882-1222
Dogs of all sizes are allowed. There is a $75 one time fee and a pet policy to sign at check in. Multiple dogs may be allowed.

Sheraton Bellevue Seattle East Hotel
100 112th Avenue SE
Bellevue, WA
425-455-3330 (888-625-5144)
Dogs of all sizes are allowed. There are no additional pet fees. Dogs are not allowed to be left alone in the room.

Aloha Motel
315 N Samish Way
Bellingham, WA
360-733-4900
One dog of any size is allowed. There is an additional $5 per night pet fee.

Best Western Heritage Inn
151 E McLeod Road
Bellingham, WA

360-647-1912 (800-780-7234)
Dogs are allowed for an additional fee of $20 per night per pet. 2 dogs may be allowed.

Days Inn Bellingham
125 E Kellogg Rd
Bellingham, WA
360-671-6200 (800-329-7466)
Dogs of all sizes are allowed. There is a $7 per night pet fee per pet. 2 dogs may be allowed.

Holiday Inn Express
4160 Guide Meridian
Bellingham, WA
360-671-4800 (877-270-6405)
Dogs of all sizes are allowed for an additional one time pet fee of $15 per room. Multiple dogs may be allowed.

Motel 6 - Bellingham
3701 Byron Street
Bellingham, WA
360-671-4494 (800-466-8356)
One well-behaved family pet per room. Guest must notify front desk upon arrival. Guest is liable for any damages. In consideration of all guests, pets must never be left unattended in the guest rooms.

Quality Inn Baron Suites
100 E Kellogg Road
Bellingham, WA
360-647-8000 (877-424-6423)
Dogs are allowed for an additional one time pet fee of $25 per room. Multiple dogs may be allowed.

Madrona West Home Vacations
Many accomodations-address given with reservations
Birch Bay, WA
360-738-32233
Well behaved adult dogs over a year old, and of all sizes are allowed. There is a pet policy to sign at check in and there are no additional pet fees. 2 dogs may be allowed.

Super 8 Bremerton
5068 Kitsap Way
Bremerton, WA
360-377-8881 (800-800-8000)
Dogs of all sizes are allowed. There is a $15 returnable deposit required per room. There is a $10 one time pet fee per visit. Smoking and non-smoking rooms are available for pet rooms. 2 dogs may be allowed.

Motel 6 - Centralia
1310 Belmont Avenue
Centralia, WA

360-330-2057 (800-466-8356)
One well-behaved family pet per room. Guest must notify front desk upon arrival. Guest is liable for any damages. In consideration of all guests, pets must never be left unattended in the guest rooms.

Motel 6 - Clarkston
222 Bridge Street
Clarkston, WA
509-758-1631 (800-466-8356)
One well-behaved family pet per room. Guest must notify front desk upon arrival. Guest is liable for any damages. In consideration of all guests, pets must never be left unattended in the guest rooms.

Best Western Wheatland Inn
701 N Main Street
Colfax, WA
509-397-0397 (800-780-7234)
Dogs are allowed for an additional fee of $10 per night per pet. 2 dogs may be allowed.

Iron Springs Ocean Beach Resort
P. O. Box 207
Copalis Beach, WA
360-276-4230
ironspringsresort.com
Iron Springs is a 100 acre resort on the Washington Coast located halfway between Copalis and Pacific Beach. They offer individual cottages with fireplaces and great ocean views. The cottages are nestled among the rugged spruce trees on a low lying bluff overlooking the Pacific Ocean. They are located near miles of sandy beaches. There is a $15.00 per day charge for pets. There are no designated smoking or non-smoking cabins. They are located 130 miles from Seattle and 160 miles from Portland. Multiple dogs may be allowed.

Best Western Lincoln Inn & Suites
211 W Umptanum Road
Ellensburg, WA
509-925-4244 (800-780-7234)
Dogs are allowed for an additional pet fee of $25 per night per room. 2 dogs may be allowed.

Comfort Inn
1722 Canyon Road
Ellensburg, WA
509-925-7037 (877-424-6423)
Dogs are allowed for an additional pet fee of $10 per night per room. Multiple dogs may be allowed.

Super 8 Ellensburg
1500 Canyon Rd

Ellensburg, WA
509-962-6888 (800-800-8000)
Dogs of all sizes are allowed. There
is a $10 one time per pet fee per
visit. Smoking and non-smoking
rooms are available for pet rooms. 2
dogs may be allowed.

Days Inn Seattle/ Everett
1602 SE Everett Mall Way
Everett, WA
425-355-1570 (800-329-7466)
Dogs of all sizes are allowed. There
is a $10 one time per pet fee per
visit. 2 dogs may be allowed.

Holiday Inn Downtown-Everett
3105 Pine St
Everett, WA
425-339-2000 (877-270-6405)
Dogs of all sizes are allowed for an
additional one time pet fee of $40 per
room. Multiple dogs may be allowed.

Motel 6 - Everett North
10006 Evergreen Way
Everett, WA
425-347-2060 (800-466-8356)
One well-behaved family pet per
room. Guest must notify front desk
upon arrival. Guest is liable for any
damages. In consideration of all
guests, pets must never be left
unattended in the guest rooms.

Motel 6 - Everett South
224 128th Street Southwest
Everett, WA
425-353-8120 (800-466-8356)
One well-behaved family pet per
room. Guest must notify front desk
upon arrival. Guest is liable for any
damages. In consideration of all
guests, pets must never be left
unattended in the guest rooms.

Comfort Inn
31622 Pacific H S
Federal Way, WA
253-529-0101 (877-424-6423)
A dog up to 50 pounds is allowed for
an additional one time $20 pet fee.

Super 8 Federal WAy
1688 S 348th St
Federal Way, WA
253-838-8808 (800-800-8000)
Dogs of all sizes are allowed. There
is a $10 per night pet fee per pet.
Smoking and non-smoking rooms are
available for pet rooms. 2 dogs
may be allowed.

Super 8 Ferndale/Bellingham Area
5788 Barrett Ave
Ferndale, WA
360-384-8881 (800-800-8000)

Dogs of all sizes are allowed. There
is a $10 one time per pet fee per
visit. Smoking and non-smoking
rooms are available for pet rooms. 2
dogs may be allowed.

Motel 6 - Tacoma - Fife
5201 20th Street East
Fife, WA
253-922-1270 (800-466-8356)
One well-behaved family pet per
room. Guest must notify front desk
upon arrival. Guest is liable for any
damages. In consideration of all
guests, pets must never be left
unattended in the guest rooms.

Quality Inn
5601 Pacific H E
Fife, WA
253-926-2301 (877-424-6423)
Dogs are allowed for an additional
one time pet fee of $15 per room.
The fee for large dogs is $15 for the
1st night and $10 for each
additional night per room. 2 dogs
may be allowed.

Kalaloch Ocean Lodge
157151 Hwy. 101
Forks, WA
360-962-2271
kalaloch.com
Perched on a bluff, overlooking the
Pacific Ocean, sits the Kalaloch
Lodge located in Olympic National
Park. The Olympic National Forest
is also located nearby. Dogs are not
allowed in the lodge, but they are
welcome in the cabins. This resort
offers over 40 cabins and half of
them have ocean views. There are
no designated smoking or non-
smoking cabins. Thanks to one of
our readers who writes "This is a
great place where you can rent
cabins situated on a bluff
overlooking the Pacific Ocean.
Great for watching storms pound
the beaches and walking wide sand
beaches at low tide. Near rain forest
with wooded hikes and lakes
throughout. Not all units allow dogs,
but you can still get a good view."
There is a $12.50 per day pet fee.
Multiple dogs may be allowed.

Blair House Bed and Breakfast
345 Blair Street
Friday Harbor, WA
360-378-5907 (800-899-3030)
friday-harbor.net/blair/
Blair House is located in Friday
Harbor, Washington on San Juan
Island, just five short blocks from
the ferry landing. The two acre
grounds are wooded and
landscaped. The Blair House

Cottage is 800 square feet of private
living where you, your children and
your pets are welcome. You will need
to take a car ferry to the island.

The Inn at Friday Harbor
Friday Harbor, WA
360-378-4000 (800-752-5752)
theinns.com/
There is a $50.00 one time pet fee.
You need to take a car ferry to the
island.

Best Western Wesley Inn of Gig
Harbor
6575 Kimball
Gig Harbor, WA
253-858-9690 (800-780-7234)
Dogs are allowed for an additional
fee of $10 per night per pet. Multiple
dogs may be allowed.

Mt. Baker Lodging
7463 Mt. Baker Highway
Glacier, WA
360-599-2453 (1-800-709-7669)
mtbakerlodging.com/
Private vacation rental homes
located at the gateway to Mt. Baker.
There are a wide variety of rental
homes to choose, from honeymoon
getaways and family cabins, to
accommodations for group retreats
and family reunions. All properties
are privately owned, unique and
completely self-contained.

Motel 6 - Seattle East - Issaquah
1885 15th Place NW
Issaquah, WA
425-392-8405 (800-466-8356)
One well-behaved family pet per
room. Guest must notify front desk
upon arrival. Guest is liable for any
damages. In consideration of all
guests, pets must never be left
unattended in the guest rooms.

Motel 6 - Kelso - Mt St Helens
106 Minor Road
Kelso, WA
360-425-3229 (800-466-8356)
One well-behaved family pet per
room. Guest must notify front desk
upon arrival. Guest is liable for any
damages. In consideration of all
guests, pets must never be left
unattended in the guest rooms.

Red Lion
510 Kelso Drive
Kelso, WA
360-636-4400
Dogs of all sizes are allowed. There
is a $25 one time fee per stay and a
pet policy to sign at check in. Multiple
dogs may be allowed.

Super 8 Kelso/Longview Area
250 Kelso Dr
Kelso, WA
360-423-8880 (800-800-8000)
Dogs of all sizes are allowed. There is a $10 one time per pet fee per visit. Smoking and non-smoking rooms are available for pet rooms. 2 dogs may be allowed.

Best Western Kennewick
4001 W 27th Avenue
Kennewick, WA
509-586-1332 (800-780-7234)
Dogs are allowed for an additional one time pet fee of $10 per room. Multiple dogs may be allowed.

Comfort Inn
7801 W Quinault Avenue
Kennewick, WA
509-783-8396 (877-424-6423)
Dogs are allowed for an additional fee of $10 per night per pet. 2 dogs may be allowed.

La Quinta Inn & Suites Kennewick
4220 W 27th Place
Kennewick, WA
509-736-3326 (800-531-5900)
Dogs of all sizes are allowed. There are no additional pet fees. Dogs may not be left unattended at any time, and they must be leashed and cleaned up after. 2 dogs may be allowed.

Red Lion
1101 N Columbia Center Blvd
Kennewick, WA
509-738-0611
Dogs of all sizes are allowed. There is a pet policy to sign at check in and no additional fees. Multiple dogs may be allowed.

Super 8 Kennewick/Tri-Cities Area
626 N Columbia Center Blvd
Kennewick, WA
509-736-6888 (800-800-8000)
Dogs of all sizes are allowed. There is a $10 per night pet fee per pet. Smoking and non-smoking rooms are available for pet rooms. 2 dogs may be allowed.

Comfort Inn
22311 84th Avenue S
Kent, WA
253-872-2211 (877-424-6423)
Dogs up to 35 pounds are allowed for an additional fee of $10 per night per pet; the fee is $20 per night per pet for dogs over 35 pounds. 2 dogs may be allowed.

Howard Johnson Inn
1233 North Central
Kent, WA
253-852-7224 (800-446-4656)
Well-behaved dogs up to 80 pounds are allowed. There is a $15 one time additional pet fee.

TownePlace Suites Seattle Southcenter
18123 72nd Avenue South
Kent, WA
253-796-6000
Dogs of all sizes are allowed. There is a $10 per night pet fee per pet or $150 per stay. 2 dogs may be allowed.

La Quinta Inn Seattle Bellevue Kirkland
10530 NE Northup Way
Kirkland, WA
425-828-6585 (800-531-5900)
Dogs of all sizes are allowed. There are no additional pet fees. Dogs must be leashed, cleaned up after, and the Do Not Disturb sign put on the door if there is a dog alone in the room. Multiple dogs may be allowed.

Motel 6 - Seattle North - Kirkland
12010 120th Place Northeast
Kirkland, WA
425-821-5618 (800-466-8356)
One well-behaved family pet per room. Guest must notify front desk upon arrival. Guest is liable for any damages. In consideration of all guests, pets must never be left unattended in the guest rooms.

Quality Inn and Suites
120 College Street SE
Lacey, WA
360-493-1991 (877-424-6423)
Dogs are allowed for an additional fee of $15 per night per pet. Multiple dogs may be allowed.

Super 8 Lacey/Olympia Area
112 College St SE
Lacey, WA
360-459-8888 (800-800-8000)
Dogs of all sizes are allowed. There is a $10 per night pet fee per pet. Smoking and non-smoking rooms are available for pet rooms. 2 dogs may be allowed.

Quality Inn and Suites
185 H 2
Leavenworth, WA
509-548-7992 (877-424-6423)
Dogs are allowed for an additional fee of $15 per night per pet. 2 dogs may be allowed.

Super 8 Long Beach
500 Ocean Beach Blvd
Long Beach, WA
360-642-8988 (800-800-8000)
Dogs of all sizes are allowed. There is a $5.39 per night pet fee per pet. Smoking and non-smoking rooms are available for pet rooms. 2 dogs may be allowed.

Island Vacation Rentals
1695 Seacrest Drive
Lummi Island, WA
360-758-7064
Well behaved adult dogs over a year old, and of all sizes are allowed. There is a pet policy to sign at check in and there are no additional fees. 2 dogs may be allowed.

La Quinta Inn Lynnwood
4300 Alderwood Mall Blvd
Lynnwood, WA
425-775-7447 (800-531-5900)
Dogs of all sizes are allowed, and 2 dogs per room are preferred, but 3 dogs are ok if they are small dogs. There are no additional pet fees. Dogs may not be left unattended, and they must be leashed and cleaned up after. Dogs are not allowed in any of the food areas.

Residence Inn by Marriott
18200 Alderwood Mall Parkway
Lynnwood, WA
425-771-1100
Two dogs are allowed per room, however they will not accept extra large dogs, and they must be well behaved. There is a $15 per night per room fee to a maximum total of $75 per stay and a pet policy to sign at check in.

Gull Wing Inn
Across the street from the Pacific Ocean
Moclips, WA
360-276-0014
gullwinginn.com
This small inn has three suites with kitchen and is directly across the street from the ocean. There is a $10 a night dog fee and rooms are about $60 to $85 per night.

Hi-Tide Ocean Beach Resort
4890 Railroad Avenue
Moclips, WA
360-276-4142 (800-MOCLIPS (WA Only))
hitideresort.com
This pet-friendly resort located right on the beach allows dogs to visit with you. There is a $12 to $15 pet fee

per night depending on the season. Dogs must be leashed while on the property.

Ocean Crest Resort
4651 SR 109
Moclips, WA
360-276-4465
ohwy.com/wa/o/ocecrere.htm
There is a $15 per day pet fee. Pets are allowed in some of the units. All rooms are non-smoking.

Best Western Baron Inn
19233 Highway 2
Monroe, WA
360-794-3111 (800-780-7234)
Dogs are allowed for an additional fee of $15 per night per pet. Multiple dogs may be allowed.

Best Western Lakeside Inn
3000 Marina Dr
Moses Lake, WA
509-765-9211 (800-780-7234)
Dogs are allowed for an additional one time pet fee of $20 per room. Multiple dogs may be allowed.

Motel 6 - Moses Lake
2822 West Driggs Drive
Moses Lake, WA
509-766-0250 (800-466-8356)
One well-behaved family pet per room. Guest must notify front desk upon arrival. Guest is liable for any damages. In consideration of all guests, pets must never be left unattended in the guest rooms.

Best Western College Way Inn
300 W College Way
Mount Vernon, WA
360-424-4287 (800-780-7234)
Dogs are allowed for an additional fee of $20 per night per pet. Multiple dogs may be allowed.

Days Inn Mt Vernon
2009 Riverside Dr
Mount Vernon, WA
360-424-4141 (800-329-7466)
Dogs of all sizes are allowed. There is a $10 per night pet fee per pet. 2 dogs may be allowed.

Quality Inn
1910 Freeway Drive
Mount Vernon, WA
360-428-7020 (877-424-6423)
Dogs are allowed for an additional fee of $10 per night per pet. Multiple dogs may be allowed.

Studio 6 - SEATTLE - MOUNTLAKE TERRACE
6017 244th Street SW

Mountlake Terrace, WA
425-771-3139 (800-466-8356)
One well-behaved family pet per room. Guest must notify front desk upon arrival. Guest is liable for any damages. In consideration of all guests, pets must never be left unattended in the guest rooms.

TownePlace Suites Seattle North/Mukilteo
8521 Mukilteo Speedway
Mukilteo, WA
425-551-5900
Dogs up to 75 pounds are allowed. There is a $10 per night pet fee per pet. . 2 dogs may be allowed.

Charles Nelson Guest House
26205 Sandridge Road
Ocean Park, WA
360-665-3016 (888-862-9756)
charlesnelsonbandb.com
This B&B is within walking distance of the Pacific Ocean and features a view of Willapa Bay. There is a large field nearby for dog walking. There is a $25 one time pet fee.

Coastal Cottages of Ocean Park
1511 264th Place
Ocean Park, WA
360-665-4658 (800-200-0424)
The cottages are located in a quiet setting and have full kitchens and fireplaces. There is a $5 per day pet charge. There are no designated smoking or non-smoking rooms.

The Polynesian Condominium Resort
615 Ocean Shores Blvd
Ocean Shores, WA
360-289-3361
There is a $15 per day fee for pets. Pets are allowed on the ground floor only.

West Coast Inn
2300 Evergreen Park Drive
Olympia, WA
360-943-4000
There is a $45.00 one time pet fee.

Best Western Lincoln Inn
1020 East Cedar St.
Othello, WA
509-488-5671 (800-780-7234)
Dogs are allowed for an additional one time fee of $15 per pet. Multiple dogs may be allowed.

Pacific Beach Inn
12 First Street S
Pacific Beach, WA
360-276-4433
pbinn.com/main_page.htm

Offering 12 intimate rooms, most with a full ocean view, this great get-a-way sits on the edge of one of the most majestic beaches in the world. Dogs of all sizes are allowed for an additional fee of $10 per night per pet. Dogs may not be left alone in the room at any time, and they must be leashed and cleaned up after. 2 dogs may be allowed.

Sand Dollar Inn & Cottages
56 Central Avenue
Pacific Beach, WA
360-276-4525
sanddollarinn.net
This inn and cottages has one and two bedroom pet friendly units. Some of the units have kitchens. Some have fenced yards or a dog kennel. There is a $10 per night pet fee.

Sandpiper Ocean Beach Resort
4159 State Route 109
Pacific Beach, WA
360-276-4580
Thanks to one of our readers who writes "A great place on the Washington Coast with miles of sand beach to run." There is a $13 per day pet fee. All rooms are non-smoking. Multiple dogs may be allowed.

Red Lion
2525 N 20th Avenue
Pasco, WA
509-547-0701
Dogs of all sizes are allowed. There are no additional pet fees, and dogs are not allowed to be left alone in the room. Multiple dogs may be allowed.

Sleep Inn
9930 Bedford Street
Pasco, WA
509-545-9554 (877-424-6423)
Dogs are allowed for an additional pet fee of $10 per night per room. Multiple dogs may be allowed.

Quality Inn Uptown
101 E 2nd Street
Port Angeles, WA
360-457-9434
Well mannered dogs are allowed for an additional fee of $10 per night per pet. Multiple dogs may be allowed.

Red Lion
221 N Lincoln
Port Angeles, WA
360-452-9215
Dogs of all sizes are allowed. There is a pet policy to sign at check in and there are no additional fees. Multiple dogs may be allowed.

Super 8 Port Angeles
2104 E 1st Street
Port Angeles, WA
360-452-8401 (800-800-8000)
Dogs of all sizes are allowed. There is a $10 one time per pet fee per visit. Smoking and non-smoking rooms are available for pet rooms. 2 dogs may be allowed.

Days Inn Port Orchard
220 Bravo Terrace
Port Orchard, WA
360-895-7818 (800-329-7466)
Dogs of all sizes are allowed. There is a $10 per night pet fee per pet. 2 dogs may be allowed.

Holiday Inn Express
19801 7th Avenue NE
Poulsbo, WA
360-697-4400 (877-270-6405)
Dogs of all sizes are allowed for an additional pet fee of $15 per night per room for dogs 20 pounds or under, and a fee of $30 per night for dogs over 20 pounds. 2 dogs may be allowed.

Holiday Inn Express
1190 SE Bishop Blvd
Pullman, WA
509-334-4437 (877-270-6405)
Dogs of all sizes are allowed for no additional pet fee. Multiple dogs may be allowed.

Quality Inn Paradise Creek
SE 1400 Bishop Blvd
Pullman, WA
509-332-0500 (877-424-6423)
Quiet dogs are allowed for no additional pet fee. If a designated pet room is not available, a regular room may be assigned for a pet for an additional one time pet fee of $30 per room. Multiple dogs may be allowed.

Best Western Park Plaza
620 South Hill Park Dr
Puyallup, WA
253-848-1500 (800-780-7234)
Dogs are allowed for an additional one time pet fee of $25 per room, and there is a pet agreement to sign at check in. Multiple dogs may be allowed.

Holiday Inn Express & Suites
812 South Hill Park Drive
Puyallup, WA
253-848-4900 (877-270-6405)
Dogs of all sizes are allowed for an additional one time pet fee of $25 (plus tax) per room. 2 dogs may be allowed.

Residence Inn by Marriott
7575 164th Avenue NE
Redmond, WA
425-497-9226
Dogs of all sizes are allowed. There is a $75 one time fee and a pet policy to sign at check in. Multiple dogs may be allowed.

Days Inn Richland
615 Jadwin Ave
Richland, WA
509-943-4611 (800-329-7466)
Dogs of all sizes are allowed. There is a $10 per night pet fee per pet. 2 dogs may be allowed.

Holiday Inn Express Hotel and Suites
1970 Center Parkway
Richland, WA
509-737-8000 (877-270-6405)
Quiet dogs of all sizes are allowed for an additional fee of $10 per night per pet. Dogs must be crated when left alone in the room. Multiple dogs may be allowed.

Motel 6 - Richland - Kennewick
1751 Fowler Street
Richland, WA
509-783-1250 (800-466-8356)
One well-behaved family pet per room. Guest must notify front desk upon arrival. Guest is liable for any damages. In consideration of all guests, pets must never be left unattended in the guest rooms.

Royal Hotel
1515 George Washington Way
Richland, WA
509-946-4121
There is a $25 one time pet fee.

Best Western Bronco Inn
105 Galbreath Way
Ritzville, WA
509-659-5000 (800-780-7234)
Dogs are allowed for an additional pet fee of $10 per night per room. Multiple dogs may be allowed.

La Quinta Inn Ritzville
1513 Smitty's Blvd.
Ritzville, WA
509-659-1007 (800-531-5900)
Dogs of all sizes are allowed. There are no additional pet fees. Dogs must be quiet, well behaved, leashed and cleaned up after. Dogs must be walked at the designated pet walk area, and they are not allowed in the lobby during breakfast hours. 2 dogs may be allowed.

Alexis Hotel
1007 First Avenue
Seattle, WA
206-624-4844
alexishotel.com/
Well-behaved dogs up to 200 pounds are welcome at this pet-friendly hotel. The luxury boutique hotel offers both rooms and suites. Hotel amenities include complimentary evening wine service, 24 hour room service and an on-site fitness room. This hotel is located near the historic Pioneer Square and Pike's Place Market. There are no pet fees, just sign a pet liability form.

Clarion Hotel Seattle Airport
3000 S 176th Street
Seattle, WA
206-242-0200 (877-424-6423)
Well mannered dogs are allowed for an additional one time pet fee of $20 (plus tax) per room. 2 dogs may be allowed.

Crowne Plaza Downtown
1113 Sixth Avenue
Seattle, WA
206-464-1980 (877-270-6405)
basshotels.com/holiday-inn
Dogs of all sizes are allowed for an additional one time pet fee of $50 per room. There may be 1 large or 2 small to medium dogs per room. 2 dogs may be allowed.

Doubletree
18740 International Blvd
Seattle, WA
206-246-8600
Dogs of all sizes are allowed. There are no additional pet fees and pet rooms are located on the 1st floor. Multiple dogs may be allowed.

Holiday Inn Express Hotel & Suites
19621 International Blvd
Seattle, WA
206-824-3200 (877-270-6405)
Dogs up to 50 pounds are allowed for a $75 refundable deposit, plus an additional one time pet fee of $50 per room. 2 dogs may be allowed.

Hotel Monaco Seattle
1101 4th Avenue
Seattle, WA
206-621-1770
monaco-seattle.com/
Well-behaved dogs of all sizes are welcome at this pet-friendly hotel. The luxury boutique hotel offers both rooms and suites. Hotel amenities include complimentary evening wine service, complimentary high speed Internet access in all guest rooms, 24 hour room service and a 24 hour

on-site fitness room. There are no pet fees, just sign a pet liability form.

Hotel Nexus
2140 N Northgate Way
Seattle, WA
206-365-0700 (800-435-0754)
hotelnexusseattle.com
Pets are welcome at this hotel with easy access to downtown Seattle and the University District. There is a $35 per stay additional pet fee.

Hotel Vintage Park
1100 Fifth Avenue
Seattle, WA
206-624-8000
hotelvintagepark.com/
Well-behaved dogs of all sizes are welcome at this pet-friendly hotel. The luxury boutique hotel offers both rooms and suites. Hotel amenities include complimentary evening wine service, complimentary high speed Internet access, and 24 hour room service. There are no pet fees, just sign a pet liability form.

La Quinta Inn & Suites Seattle Downtown
2224 8th Avenue
Seattle, WA
206-624-6820 (800-531-5900)
Dogs of all sizes are allowed. There are no additional pet fees. Dogs may not be left unattended, and they must be leashed and cleaned up after. Multiple dogs may be allowed.

La Quinta Inn Seattle Sea-Tac
2824 S. 188th St.
Seattle, WA
206-241-5211 (800-531-5900)
Dogs of all sizes are allowed. There are no additional pet fees. Dogs must be leashed, cleaned up after, and attended to or removed for housekeeping. Multiple dogs may be allowed.

Motel 6 - Seattle Sea - Tac Airport South
18900 47th Avenue South
Seattle, WA
206-241-1648 (800-466-8356)
One well-behaved dog up to about 75 pounds is allowed. There are no additional pet fees.

Motel 6 - Seattle Airport
16500 Pacific Highway South
Seattle, WA
206-246-4101 (800-466-8356)
One well-behaved family pet per room. Guest must notify front desk upon arrival. Guest is liable for any damages. In consideration of all

guests, pets must never be left unattended in the guest rooms.

Motel 6 - Seattle South
20651 Military Road
Seattle, WA
206-824-9902 (800-466-8356)
One well-behaved family pet per room. Guest must notify front desk upon arrival. Guest is liable for any damages. In consideration of all guests, pets must never be left unattended in the guest rooms.

Pensione Nichols Bed and Breakfast
1923 1st Avenue
Seattle, WA
206-441-7125 (800-440-7125)
seattle-bed-breakfast.com
Thanks to one of our readers who writes: "A charming and very dog-friendly place to stay in downtown Seattle." Large dogs are allowed to stay here if they are well-behaved. This B&B also requires that you do not leave your dog in the room alone. The Pensione Nichols is the only bed-and-breakfast located in the retail and entertainment core of downtown Seattle. Housed in a remodeled, turn-of-the-century building in the historic Smith Block, Pensione Nichols overlooks the Pike Place Market. This B&B has 10 guest rooms and suites (the suites have private bathrooms). Rates are approximately $75 (guest rooms) to $175 (suites). During the summer, there is a 2 night minimum.

Red Lion
18220 International Blvd
Seattle, WA
206-246-5535
Dogs of all sizes are allowed. There is a $10 per night per room additional pet fee. Multiple dogs may be allowed.

Red Lion
11244 Pacific Highway S
Seattle, WA
206-762-0300
Dogs of all sizes are allowed. There is a $35 deposit, $15 of which is refundable per pet, and a pet policy to sign at check in. 2 dogs may be allowed.

Red Roof Inn - SEATTLE - AIRPORT
16838 International Boulevard
Seattle, WA
206-248-0901 (800-RED-ROOF)
One well-behaved family pet per room. Guest must notify front desk

upon arrival. Guest is liable for any damages. In consideration of all guests, pets must never be left unattended in the guest rooms.

Residence Inn by Marriott
800 Fairview Avenue North
Seattle, WA
206-624-6000
Well behaved dogs of all sizes are allowed. There is a $10 per night per pet fee and a pet policy to sign at check in. Multiple dogs may be allowed.

Residence Inn by Marriott
16201 W Valley Highway
Seattle, WA
425-226-5500
Dogs of all sizes are allowed. There is a $75 one time fee and a pet policy to sign at check in. 2 dogs may be allowed.

Seattle Pacific Hotel
325 Aurora Avenue N
Seattle, WA
206-441-0400 (888-451-0400)
seattlepacifichotel.com/
Located just minutes from some of Seattle's most impressive sites; this hotel offers 59 nicely-appointed rooms with many in-room amenities, a free continental breakfast, and a seasonal outdoor pool and Jacuzzi. Dogs of all sizes are allowed. There is a $15 per night per pet additional fee for dogs under 15 pounds, and a $25 per night per pet additional fee for dogs over 15 pounds. Dogs must be leashed, cleaned up after, and crated or removed for housekeeping. 2 dogs may be allowed.

Sheraton Seattle Hotel
1400 6th Ave.
Seattle, WA
206-621-9000 (888-625-5144)
Dogs up to 50 pounds are allowed for no additional pet fee. Dogs may not be left alone in the room.

Super 8 Seattle/Sea-Tac Intl Arpt
3100 S 192nd
Seattle, WA
206-433-8188 (800-800-8000)
Dogs of all sizes are allowed. There is a $25 returnable deposit required per room. Smoking and non-smoking rooms are available for pet rooms. 2 dogs may be allowed.

University Inn
4140 Roosevelt Way NE
Seattle, WA
206-632-5055
Dogs only are allowed and up to 80

pounds. There is a $20 per night per room fee and a pet policy to sign at check in. Dogs are not to be left unattended. 2 dogs may be allowed.

Vagabond Inn by the Space Needle
325 Aurora Ave N
Seattle, WA
206-441-0400
This motel is located just several blocks from the Space Needle, the waterfront and Washington St. Convention Center. The motel has a heated swimming pool and Jacuzzi, 24 hour cable television and more. There is a $10 per day pet charge

W Seattle
1112 4th Avenue
Seattle, WA
206-264-6000
Dogs of all sizes are allowed for a $100 refundable deposit plus an additional pet fee of $25 per night per room. Dogs may not be left alone in the room; pet sitting services are available.

Quality Inn and Suites
142 River Road
Sequim, WA
360-683-2800
Dogs are allowed for an additional fee of $10 per night per pet. 2 dogs may be allowed.

Sunset Marine Resort
40 Buzzard Ridge Road
Sequim, WA
360-681-4166
Dogs of most sizes are allowed; no extra large dogs. There is a $15 per night per pet fee and a pet policy to sign at check in. 2 dogs may be allowed.

Super 8 Shelton
2943 Northview Circle
Shelton, WA
360-426-1654 (800-800-8000)
Dogs of all sizes are allowed. There is a $15 per night pet fee per pet under 20 pounds or $25 per pet over 20 pounds. Smoking and non-smoking rooms are available for pet rooms. 2 dogs may be allowed.

Red Lion
3073 NW Bucklin Hill Road
Silverdale, WA
360-698-1000
Dogs of all sizes are allowed. There is a $20 per night per room fee and a pet policy to sign at check in. Multiple dogs may be allowed.

Pacific Beach Inn

12 First Street
South Pacific Beach, WA
360-276-4433
Dogs of all sizes are allowed. There is a $10 per night per pet additional fee. 2 dogs may be allowed.

Best Western Pheasant Hill
12415 E Mission Avenue
Spokane, WA
509-926-7432 (800-780-7234)
Dogs are allowed for an additional pet fee of $15 per night per room. Multiple dogs may be allowed.

Cavanaughs River Inn
N 700 Division St
Spokane, WA
509-326-5577
There are no additional pet fees.

Comfort Inn North
7111 N Division Street/H 395
Spokane, WA
509-467-7111 (877-424-6423)
Dogs are allowed for an additional fee of $7 (plus tax) per night per pet. 2 dogs may be allowed.

Doubletree
322 N Spokane Falls Court
Spokane, WA
509-455-9600
Dogs of all sizes are allowed. There is a $25 per room per stay additional pet fee. 2 dogs may be allowed.

Holiday Inn
1616 South Windsor Dr
Spokane, WA
509-838-1170 (877-270-6405)
Dogs up to 50 pounds are allowed for a $50 refundable pet deposit per room. 2 dogs may be allowed.

Holiday Inn Express
9220 E Mission
Spokane, WA
509-927-7100 (877-270-6405)
Dogs of all sizes are allowed for no additional pet fee. There is a pet agreement to sign at check in and dogs may not be left alone in the room. Multiple dogs may be allowed.

Howard Johnson Inn
South 211 Division St.
Spokane, WA
509-838-6630 (800-446-4656)
Dogs of all sizes are welcome. There is a $10 per day pet fee.

La Quinta Inn & Suites Spokane
3808 N Sullivan Rd
Spokane, WA

509-893-0955 (800-531-5900)
Dogs of all sizes are allowed. There are no additional pet fees. Dogs must be leashed, cleaned up after, and crated when left alone in the room. Multiple dogs may be allowed.

Motel 6 - Spokane East
1919 North Hutchinson Road
Spokane, WA
509-926-5399 (800-466-8356)
One well-behaved family pet per room. Guest must notify front desk upon arrival. Guest is liable for any damages. In consideration of all guests, pets must never be left unattended in the guest rooms.

Motel 6 - Spokane West-Airport
1508 South Rustle Street
Spokane, WA
509-459-6120 (800-466-8356)
One well-behaved family pet per room. Guest must notify front desk upon arrival. Guest is liable for any damages. In consideration of all guests, pets must never be left unattended in the guest rooms.

Red Lion
303 W North River Drive
Spokane, WA
509-326-8000
Dogs of all sizes are allowed. There is a $10 per stay fee, and there must be a credit card on file. There is a pet policy to sign at check in. 2 dogs may be allowed.

Red Lion
700 N Division
Spokane, WA
509-326-5577
Dogs of all sizes are allowed. There is a pet policy to sign at check in and there are no additional fees. Multiple dogs may be allowed.

Red Lion
515 W Sprague Avenue
Spokane, WA
509-838-2711
Dogs of all sizes are allowed. There is a $100 refundable deposit per room and a pet policy to sign at check in. Multiple dogs may be allowed.

Rodeway Inn
901 W 1st Sreet
Spokane, WA
509-399-2056
Dogs of all sizes are allowed. There are no additional pet fees. Dogs are not allowed to be left alone in the room. Multiple dogs may be allowed.

Super 8 Spokane/Airport/West
W 11102 Westbow Blvd
Spokane, WA
509-838-8800 (800-800-8000)
Dogs of all sizes are allowed. There
is a $15 one time per pet fee per
visit. Smoking and non-smoking
rooms are available for pet rooms. 2
dogs may be allowed.

The Davenport Hotel
10 S Post Street
Spokane, WA
509-455-8888 (800-899-1482)
thedavenporthotel.com/#
This hotel offers a long, rich history
and feature 1, 2, and 3 bedroom
luxury guest rooms and suites with
many in-room amenities, world class
dining including a Champagne
Sunday Brunch, indoor pool and
Jacuzzi, and they even offer an
historic walking tour. They are also
home to the popular Peacock Room
Lounge that showcases a giant
stained-glass peacock ceiling, and
provides great nightlife
entertainment. Dogs of all sizes are
allowed for no additional fee. Dogs
may only be left alone in the room if
they will be quiet and well behaved,
and they must be leashed and
cleaned up after at all times. Multiple
dogs may be allowed.

Comfort Inn Valley
905 N Sullivan Road
Spokane Valley, WA
509-924-3838 (877-424-6423)
Dogs up to 50 pounds are allowed
for an additional fee of $10 per night
per pet. 2 dogs may be allowed.

Doubletree
1100 N Sullivan Road
Spokane Valley, WA
509-924-9000
Dogs of all sizes are allowed. There
is a $50 refundable deposit per pet
and a pet policy to sign at check in.
Dogs are not allowed to be left alone
except for short periods while having
meals at the hotel. Multiple dogs may
be allowed.

Super 8 Spokane Valley
2020 North Argonne Rd
Spokane Valley, WA
509-928-4888 (800-800-8000)
Dogs of all sizes are allowed. There
is a $15 one time per pet fee per
visit. Smoking and non-smoking
rooms are available for pet rooms. 2
dogs may be allowed.

Best Western Grapevine Inn
1849 Quail Ln
Sunnyside, WA

509-839-6070 (800-780-7234)
One dog up to 50 pounds (or about
knee high) is allowed for an
additional pet fee of $20 per night.

Days Inn Tacoma Mall
6802 Tacoma Mall Blvd
Tacoma, WA
253-475-5900 (800-329-7466)
Dogs of all sizes are allowed. There
is a $30 one time per pet fee per
visit. Only non-smoking rooms are
used for pets. 2 dogs may be
allowed.

La Quinta Inn & Suites Seattle
Tacoma
1425 E. 27th St.
Tacoma, WA
253-383-0146 (800-531-5900)
Dogs of all sizes are allowed. There
are no additional pet fees. Dogs
must be quiet, well behaved,
leashed and cleaned up after. 2
dogs may be allowed.

Motel 6 - Tacoma South
1811 South 76th Street
Tacoma, WA
253-473-7100 (800-466-8356)
One well-behaved family pet per
room. Guest must notify front desk
upon arrival. Guest is liable for any
damages. In consideration of all
guests, pets must never be left
unattended in the guest rooms.

Sheraton Tacoma Hotel
1320 Broadway Plaza
Tacoma, WA
253-572-3200 (888-625-5144)
Dogs of all sizes are allowed. There
are no additional pet fees. Dogs are
not allowed to be left alone in the
room.

Best Western Toppenish Inn
515 S Elm Street
Toppenish, WA
509-865-7444 (800-780-7234)
Dogs are allowed for an additional
fee of $10 per night per pet. Multiple
dogs may be allowed.

Comfort Inn
1620 74th Avenue SW
Tumwater, WA
360-352-0691 (877-424-6423)
Dogs are allowed for an additional
fee of $10 per night per pet. Multiple
dogs may be allowed.

Motel 6 - Tumwater - Olympia
400 West Lee Street
Tumwater, WA
360-754-7320 (800-466-8356)
One well-behaved family pet per

room. Guest must notify front desk
upon arrival. Guest is liable for any
damages. In consideration of all
guests, pets must never be left
unattended in the guest rooms.

Super 8 Union Gap/Yakima Area
2605 Rucklin Rd
Union Gap, WA
509-248-8880 (800-800-8000)
Dogs of all sizes are allowed. There
is a $25 returnable deposit required
per room. Smoking and non-smoking
rooms are available for pet rooms. 2
dogs may be allowed.

Comfort Inn
13207 NE 20th Avenue
Vancouver, WA
360-574-6000 (877-424-6423)
Dogs are allowed for an additional
fee of $15 per night per pet. Multiple
dogs may be allowed.

Hilton
301 W 6th Street
Vancouver, WA
360-993-4500
Dogs up to 50 pounds are allowed
for an additional one time pet fee of
$35 per room. 2 dogs may be
allowed.

Quality Inn and Suites
7001 NE H 99
Vancouver, WA
360-696-0516 (877-424-6423)
Dogs are allowed for an additional
pet fee of $10 (plus tax) per night per
room. Multiple dogs may be allowed.

Red Lion
100 Columbia Street
Vancouver, WA
360-694-8341
Dogs of all sizes are allowed. There
is an additional $25 per pet per stay
fee. Multiple dogs may be allowed.

Red Lion
1500 NE 134th Street
Vancouver, WA
360-566-1100
Dogs of all sizes are allowed. There
is a $25 per stay per room fee and a
pet policy to sign at check in. Multiple
dogs may be allowed.

Residence Inn by Marriott
8005 NE Parkway Drive
Vancouver, WA
360-253-4800
Dogs of all sizes are allowed. There
is a $75 one time fee and a pet
policy to sign at check in. Multiple
dogs may be allowed.

Staybridge Suites
7301 NE 41st St
Vancouver, WA
360-891-8282 (877-270-6405)
Dogs up to a combined total of 75 pounds is allowed for an additional one time pet fee of $75 per room. 2 dogs may be allowed.

Best Western Walla Walla Suites Inn
7 E Oak Street
Walla Walla, WA
509-525-4700 (800-780-7234)
Dogs are allowed for an additional fee of $10 per night per pet. Multiple dogs may be allowed.

Holiday Inn Express
1433 W Pine Street
Walla Walla, WA
509-525-6200 (877-270-6405)
Dogs of all sizes are allowed for an additional fee of $20 per night per pet. Multiple dogs may be allowed.

La Quinta Inn Walla Walla
520 North 2nd Avenue
Walla Walla, WA
509-525-2522 (800-531-5900)
Dogs of all sizes are allowed. There are no additional pet fees. Dogs must be leashed and cleaned up after. The Do Not Disturb sign must be put on the door and the front desk informed if there is a dog alone in the room. Multiple dogs may be allowed.

Super 8 Walla Walla
2315 Eastgate St N
Walla Walla, WA
509-525-8800 (800-800-8000)
Dogs of all sizes are allowed. There is a $25 returnable deposit required per room. There is a $10 one time per pet fee per visit. Smoking and non-smoking rooms are available for pet rooms. 2 dogs may be allowed.

Holiday Inn Express
1921 N. Wenatchee Ave
Wenatchee, WA
509-663-6355 (877-270-6405)
Dogs of all sizes are allowed for no additional pet fee; there is a pet agreement to sign at check in. Multiple dogs may be allowed.

La Quinta Inn & Suites Wenatchee
1905 N Wenatchee Ave
Wenatchee, WA
509-664-6565 (800-531-5900)
Dogs of all sizes are allowed. There are no additional pet fees. Dogs may not be left unattended, and they must be leashed and cleaned up after. 2 dogs may be allowed.

Red Lion
1225 N Wenatchee Avenue
Wenatchee, WA
509-663-0711
Dogs of all sizes are allowed. There is a pet policy to sign at check in and there are no additional fees. Multiple dogs may be allowed.

Inn of the White Salmon
172 W Jewett
White Salmon, WA
509-493-2335 (800-972-5226)
gorge.net/lodging/iws/
There is a $10 per day pet fee. All rooms are non-smoking.

The Winthrop Inn
960 H 20
Winthrop, WA
509-996-2217
One well behaved dog up to 70 pounds is allowed. There is a $7 per night additional pet fee. They request you bring your dog's sleeping mat and that you keep them leashed while on the grounds. There is a beach on the river close by where the dogs can run unleashed.

Cedars Inn
1500 Atlantic Avenue
Woodland, WA
360-225-6548 (800-444-9667)
Frequently referred to as Woodland's Best, this Inn has parking that will accommodate RVs and 18-wheelers, and they offer 60 spacious, nicely-appointed rooms with many in-room amenities, and a deluxe complimentary breakfast. Dogs of all sizes are allowed for an additional one time fee of $10 per pet. There may be a discount available for guests there for the dog shows. Dogs may not be left alone in the room at any time, and they must be leashed and cleaned up after. Multiple dogs may be allowed.

Best Western Ahtanum Inn
2408 Rudkin Rd
Yakima, WA
509-248-9700 (800-780-7234)
One dog up to 50 pounds is allowed for an additional pet fee of $10 per night.

Best Western Lincoln Inn
1614 N 1st Street
Yakima, WA
509-453-8898 (800-780-7234)
Dogs are allowed for an additional pet fee of $20 per night per room. Multiple dogs may be allowed.

Clarion Hotel and Conference Center
1507 N First Street
Yakima, WA
509-248-7850 (877-424-6423)
Dogs are allowed for an additional fee of $10 per night per pet. Multiple dogs may be allowed.

Holiday Inn Express Yakima
1001 East A Street
Yakima, WA
509-249-1000 (877-270-6405)
Dogs up to 70 pounds are allowed for an additional fee of $10 per night per pet. 2 dogs may be allowed.

Motel 6 - Yakima
1104 North 1st Street
Yakima, WA
509-454-0080 (800-466-8356)
One well-behaved family pet per room. Guest must notify front desk upon arrival. Guest is liable for any damages. In consideration of all guests, pets must never be left unattended in the guest rooms.

Quality Inn
12 E Valley Mall Blvd
Yakima, WA
509-248-6924 (877-424-6423)
Dogs up to 50 pounds are allowed for an additional fee of $10 per night per pet. 2 dogs may be allowed.

Red Lion
607 E Yakima Avenue
Yakima, WA
509-248-5900
Dogs of all sizes are allowed. There is a $5 per night per pet fee and a pet policy to sign at check in.

Red Lion
9 N 9th Street
Yakima, WA
509-452-6511
Dogs of all sizes are allowed. There is a $5 per night per pet fee and a pet policy to sign at check in. Multiple dogs may be allowed.

Comfort Inn
911 Vintage Valley Parkway
Zillah, WA
509-829-3399 (877-424-6423)
Dogs are allowed for an additional fee of $10 per night per pet. Multiple dogs may be allowed.

West Virginia Listings

Comfort Inn
249 Mall Road
Barboursville, WV
304-733-2122 (877-424-6423)
Dogs are allowed for an additional one time pet fee of $20 per room. Multiple dogs may be allowed.

Best Western Four Seasons Inn
1939 Harper Road
Beckley, WV
304-252-0671 (800-780-7234)
Dogs are allowed for an additional fee of $5.60 per night per pet. Multiple dogs may be allowed.

Comfort Inn
1909 Harper Road
Beckley, WV
304-255-2161 (877-424-6423)
Dogs are allowed for no additional pet fee. Multiple dogs may be allowed.

Super 8 Beckley
2014 Harper Rd
Beckley, WV
304-253-0802 (800-800-8000)
Dogs up to 70 pounds are allowed. There is a $10 one time per pet fee per visit. Smoking and non-smoking rooms are available for pet rooms. 2 dogs may be allowed.

Berkeley Springs Motel
468 Wilkes Street
Berkeley Springs, WV
304-258-1776
berkeleyspringsmotel.net/
Dogs are allowed for no additional pet fee. 2 dogs may be allowed.

Hannah's House
867 Libby's Ridge Road
Berkeley Springs, WV
304-258-1718 (800-526-0807)
This antique farm home offers seclusion and convenience to a number of local activities and recreation. Well behaved dogs are allowed for an additional fee of $25 per pet for weekends, and $50 per pet by the week. Dogs are not allowed on the furniture, and they must be crated when left alone in the room. Multiple dogs may be allowed.

Sleepy Creek Tree Farm
37 Shades Lane
Berkeley Springs, WV

304-258-4324 (866-275-8303)
maggiedot.com/sleepycreektree/
Located on 8 scenic acres of a Christmas tree farm, this is a nature lover's get-a-way. One dog is allowed for no additional pet fee. Dogs must be able to climb stairs (or be carried); they must be friendly to cats and other dogs, and they may not be left unattended at any time.

Sunset Mountain Farm
Stickey Kline Road
Berkeley Springs, WV
304-258-4239
sunsetmountainfarm.com/
Great views, 40 private acres, convenience to a number of local activities and recreation, and more are offered at this get-away. Dogs are allowed for an additional one time fee of $25 per pet. Dogs must be well behaved, quiet, and the furniture/beds must be covered if pets are used to being on furnishings. 2 dogs may be allowed.

Econo Lodge
3400 Cumberland Rd.
Bluefield, WV
304-327-8171
There is a $10 per day pet charge.

Holiday Inn
US 460
Bluefield, WV
304-325-6170 (877-270-6405)
Dogs of all sizes are allowed for an additional fee of $10 per night per pet. Multiple dogs may be allowed.

Holiday Inn
100 Lodgeville Rd
Bridgeport, WV
304-842-5411 (877-270-6405)
One dog of any size is allowed for an additional pet fee of $5 per night.

Knights Inn
1235 West Main Street
Bridgeport, WV
304-842-7115 (800-843-5644)
There are no additional pet fees.

Sleep Inn
115 Tolley Road
Bridgeport, WV
304-842-1919 (877-424-6423)
Dogs are allowed for no additional pet fee. Multiple dogs may be allowed.

Super 8 Bridgeport/Clarksburg Area
168 Barnett Run Rd
Bridgeport, WV
304-842-7381 (800-800-8000)

Dogs of all sizes are allowed. There are no additional pet fees. Smoking and non-smoking rooms are available for pet rooms. 2 dogs may be allowed.

Centennial Motel
22 N Locust St
Buckhannon, WV
304-472-4100
There are no additional pet fees.

North Fork Mountain Inn
Smoke Hole Road
Cabins, WV
304-257-1108
northforkmtninn.com/
Located in a lush mountain setting, this retreat is open year round offering the best of all the seasons. Dogs are allowed at the Hideaway Cabin here but not in the inn. There is a fee of $15 per night per pet. 2 dogs may be allowed.

A Room with A View
Black Bear Woods Resort-Northside
Cortland Rd
Canaan Valley, WV
301-767-6853
This is Unit 132 in the Black Bear Woods Resort. It is a single room suite without a kitchen with a view of Canaan Valley. There are two Queen beds and a large bathroom with a Jacuzzi. Well-behaved dogs are welcome for a $30 cleaning fee per stay.

Charleston Marriott Town Center
200 Lee Street E
Charleston, WV
304-345-6500 (800-228-9290)
Dogs of all sizes are allowed. There is a $75 one time additional pet fee per room. Dogs must be quiet, leashed, cleaned up after, and the Do Not Disturb sign put on the door and a contact number left with the front desk if they are in the room alone. Multiple dogs may be allowed.

Comfort Suites
107 Alex Lane
Charleston, WV
304-925-1171 (877-424-6423)
Dogs up to 50 pounds are allowed for an additional one time fee of $25 per pet. 2 dogs may be allowed.

Country Inns & Suites by Carlson
105 Alex Lane
Charleston, WV
304-925-4300
There are no room discounts if bringing a pet and there is a $5 per day pet fee per pet if you are

bringing more than one dog.

Motel 6 - Charleston East
6311 MacCorkle Ave SE
Charleston, WV
304-925-0471 (800-466-8356)
One well-behaved family pet per
room. Guest must notify front desk
upon arrival. Guest is liable for any
damages. In consideration of all
guests, pets must never be left
unattended in the guest rooms.

Residence Inn by Marriott
200 Hotel Circle Northgate Business
Park
Charleston, WV
304-345-4200
Dogs of all sizes are allowed. There
is a $100 one time cleaning fee plus
$5 per night per pet and a pet policy
to sign at check in. Multiple dogs
may be allowed.

Comfort Inn West
102 Racer Drive
Cross Lanes, WV
800-798-7886 (877-424-6423)
Dogs up to 100 pounds are allowed
for an additional pet fee of $15 per
night per room. Dogs are not allowed
in the lobby, and they may not be left
alone in the room. 2 dogs may be
allowed.

**Motel 6 - Charleston West-Cross
Lanes**
330 Goff Mountain Rd
Cross Lanes, WV
304-776-5911 (800-466-8356)
One well-behaved family pet per
room. Guest must notify front desk
upon arrival. Guest is liable for any
damages. In consideration of all
guests, pets must never be left
unattended in the guest rooms.

The Resort at Glade Springs
255 Resort Drive
Daniels, WV
866-562-8054 (800-634-5233)
gladesprings.com/
This resort offers year round
recreational activities with a
complete Leisure Center that offers a
10-lane bowling alley, an indoor
poor, a small movie theater, arcade,
gaming courts, and more. Dogs up to
50 pounds are welcome with
advance registration for a fee per pet
of $70 for the 1st night and $20 for
each additional night. Dogs may not
be left alone in the room at any time,
and the front desk will also provide
sanitary bags for pets. 2 dogs may
be allowed.

Cheat River Lodge
Route 1, Box 115
Elkins, WV
304-636-2301
cheatriverlodge.com/
Dogs are allowed in the lodge and
the cabins at this riverside getaway.
The fee is $10 per night per pet for
the lodge, and $20 per night per pet
for the cabins. Dogs may be left for
short periods if they are crated
when left alone in the room. 2 dogs
may be allowed.

Days Inn Elkins
1200 Harrison Ave
Elkins, WV
304-637-4667 (800-329-7466)
Dogs of all sizes are allowed. There
is a $5 per night pet fee per pet. 2
dogs may be allowed.

Econo Lodge
U.S. 33 East
Elkins, WV
304-636-5311 (800-553-2666)
There is a $5 per day pet charge.

Days Inn Fairmont
228 Middletown Road
Fairmont, WV
304-366-5995 (800-329-7466)
Dogs of all sizes are allowed. There
is a $10 per night pet fee per pet. 2
dogs may be allowed.

Red Roof Inn - Fairmont, WV
50 Middletown Road
Fairmont, WV
304-366-6800 (800-RED-ROOF)
One well-behaved family pet per
room. Guest must notify front desk
upon arrival. Guest is liable for any
damages. In consideration of all
guests, pets must never be left
unattended in the guest rooms.

Super 8 Fairmont
2208 Pleasant Valley Rd
Fairmont, WV
304-363-1488 (800-800-8000)
Dogs up to 60 pounds are allowed.
There are no additional pet fees.
Smoking and non-smoking rooms
are available for pet rooms. 2 dogs
may be allowed.

Holiday Inn Express North
1220 TJ Jackson Drive
Falling Waters, WV
304-274-6100 (877-270-6405)
Dogs of all sizes are allowed for an
additional fee of $10 per night per
pet. Dogs may not be left alone in
the room at any time. Multiple dogs
may be allowed.

Quality Inn New River Gorge
103 Elliotts Way
Fayetteville, WV
304-574-3443 (877-424-6423)
Dogs are allowed for an additional
fee of $5 per night per pet. Multiple
dogs may be allowed.

Econo Lodge
3325 US 60 E.
Huntington, WV
304-529-1331 (800-55-ECONO)
There is a $10 per day pet charge.

Red Roof Inn - Huntington, WV
5190 US Route 60 E
Huntington, WV
304-733-3737 (800-RED-ROOF)
One well-behaved family pet per
room. Guest must notify front desk
upon arrival. Guest is liable for any
damages. In consideration of all
guests, pets must never be left
unattended in the guest rooms.

Stone Lodge
5600 U.S. Route 60 East
Huntington, WV
304-736-3451
There are no additional pet fees.

**Red Roof Inn - Charleston West -
Hurricane, WV**
500 Putnam Village Drive
Hurricane, WV
304-757-6392 (800-RED-ROOF)
One well-behaved family pet per
room. Guest must notify front desk
upon arrival. Guest is liable for any
damages. In consideration of all
guests, pets must never be left
unattended in the guest rooms.

Super 8 Hurricane
419 Hurricane Creek Rd
Hurricane, WV
304-562-3346 (800-800-8000)
Dogs of all sizes are allowed. There
is a $10 per night pet fee per pet.
Smoking and non-smoking rooms
are available for pet rooms. 2 dogs
may be allowed.

**Red Roof Inn - Charleston -
Kanawha City, WV**
6305 MacCorkle Avenue SE
Kanawha City, WV
304-925-6953 (800-RED-ROOF)
One well-behaved family pet per
room. Guest must notify front desk
upon arrival. Guest is liable for any
damages. In consideration of all
guests, pets must never be left
unattended in the guest rooms.

Holiday Inn Express Hotel and Suites
101 George Costas Drive

Logan, WV
304-752-6495 (877-270-6405)
Dogs up to 30 pounds are allowed for an additional fee of $25 per night per pet. Dogs may not be left alone in the room. Multiple dogs may be allowed.

Old Clark Inn
302 Third Avenue
Marlington, WV
304-799-6377
Dogs of all sizes are allowed, however the number and size of pets is determined by the room that is rented. There is a $5 per day per pet fee and a pet policy to sign at check in. There is a day kennel with a 4 foot high fence that also has a dog house. This is for small dogs and there is a $5 per day fee for guests only to use.

Days Inn Martinsburg
209 Viking Way
Martinsburg, WV
304-263-1800 (800-329-7466)
Dogs of all sizes are allowed. There are no additional pet fees. 2 dogs may be allowed.

Holiday Inn
301 Foxcroft Avenue
Martinsburg, WV
304-267-5500 (877-270-6405)
Quiet dogs of all sizes are allowed for an additional one time pet fee of $15 per room. Multiple dogs may be allowed.

Knights Inn
1599 Edwin Miller Blvd
Martinsburg, WV
304-267-2211 (800-843-5644)
There is a $5 per day additional pet fee.

Alpine Lake
700 West Alpine Drive
Morgantown, WV
304-789-2481 (800-752-7179)
alpinelake.com/
In addition to its beautiful location and numerous amenities, this resort is also a year round recreational destination. Dogs are allowed for an additional $10 per night per pet. 2 dogs may be allowed.

Comfort Inn
225 Comfort Inn Drive
Morgantown, WV
304-296-9364 (877-424-6423)
Dogs are allowed for a $25 refundable pet deposit per room. Dogs are not allowed in the lobby, and they may not be left alone in the room. Multiple dogs may be allowed.

Econo Lodge Coliseum
3506 Monongahela Blvd.
Morgantown, WV
304-599-8181 (800-55-ECONO)
There are no additional pet fees.

Blennerhassett Hotel
Fourth and Market Streets
Parkersburg, WV
304-422-3131 (800-678-8946)
This 1889 hotel is listed on the National Register of Historic Hotels. There is a $50 one time pet charge.

Expressway Motor Inn
6333 Emerson Ave
Parkersburg, WV
304-485-1851
There is a $5 per day pet charge.

Motel 6 - Parkersburg
3604 1/2 East 7th Street
Parkersburg, WV
304-424-5100 (800-466-8356)
One well-behaved family pet per room. Guest must notify front desk upon arrival. Guest is liable for any damages. In consideration of all guests, pets must never be left unattended in the guest rooms.

Red Roof Inn - Parkersburg
3714 East 7th Street
Parkersburg, WV
304-485-1741 (800-RED-ROOF)
One well-behaved family pet per room. Guest must notify front desk upon arrival. Guest is liable for any damages. In consideration of all guests, pets must never be left unattended in the guest rooms.

Holiday Inn Express Princeton/I-77
805 Oakvale Rd.
Princeton, WV
304-425-8156 (877-270-6405)
Dogs up to 50 pounds are allowed for an additional fee of $20 per night per pet. 2 dogs may be allowed.

Sleep Inn and Suites
1015 Oakvale Road
Princeton, WV
304-431-2800 (877-424-6423)
Dogs are allowed for no additional pet fee. Multiple dogs may be allowed.

Best Western McCoys Inn & Conference Center
701 Main Street W
Ripley, WV
304-372-9122 (800-780-7234)
Dogs are allowed for no additional

pet fee. Dogs may not be left alone in the room. Multiple dogs may be allowed.

Holiday Inn Express
One Hospitality Drive
Ripley, WV
304-372-5000 (877-270-6405)
Dogs of all sizes are allowed for no additional pet fee. Multiple dogs may be allowed.

Morning Glory Inn
H 219
Snowshoe, WV
304-572-5000 (866-572-5700)
morninggloryinn.com/
Guests can relax and enjoy the views from their 90 foot front porch or explore a myriad of local activities and recreation from this retreat. One dog is allowed for no additional pet fee. Dogs must be quiet and well mannered.

Comfort Inn
Dallas Pike
Triadelphia, WV
304-547-0610 (877-424-6423)
Dogs are allowed for an additional fee of $10 per night per pet. Multiple dogs may be allowed.

Holiday Inn Express
I-70 Exit 11 Dallas Pike
Triadelphia, WV
304-547-1380 (877-270-6405)
Dogs of all sizes are allowed for an additional fee of $25 per night per pet. Multiple dogs may be allowed.

Holiday Inn
350 Three Springs Drive
Weirton, WV
304-723-5522 (877-270-6405)
Dogs of all sizes are allowed for an additional one time fee per room of $25 for dogs under 25 pounds, and $50 for dogs over 25 pounds. 2 dogs may be allowed.

Comfort Inn
2906 H 33E
Weston, WV
304-269-7000 (877-424-6423)
Dogs up to 50 pounds are allowed for an additional pet fee of $10 per night per room. Multiple dogs may be allowed.

Oglebay's Wilson Lodge
Route 88 North
Wheeling, WV
304-243-4000 (800-624-6988)
oglebay-resort.com/lodge.htm
Dogs are not allowed in the lodge, but are welcome in the cottages.

There are no designated smoking or non-smoking cottages. There are no additional pet fees.

Wisconsin Listings

Super 8 Adams
2188 Hwy 13
Adams, WI
608-339-6088 (800-800-8000)
Dogs of all sizes are allowed. There is a $4 per night pet fee per pet. Dogs are not allowed to be left alone in the room. Smoking and non-smoking rooms are available for pet rooms. 2 dogs may be allowed.

Best Western Midway Hotel
3033 W College Avenue
Appleton, WI
920-731-4141 (800-780-7234)
Dogs up to 50 pounds are allowed for an additional fee of $10 per night per pet. 2 dogs may be allowed.

Budgetel Inn Appleton
3920 W College Avenue
Appleton, WI
920-734-6070 (800-531-5900)
Dogs of all sizes are allowed. There are no additional pet fees, and there is a pet waiver to sign at check in. Dogs may not be left unattended, and they must be leashed and cleaned up after. 2 dogs may be allowed.

Candlewood Suites Appleton
4525 West College Avenue
Appleton, WI
920-739-8000 (877-270-6405)
Dogs up to 75 pounds are allowed for an additional one time pet fee of $75 per pet. Dogs must be current on vaccinations. 2 dogs may be allowed.

Comfort Suites Comfort Dome
3809 W Wisconsin Avenue
Appleton, WI
920-730-3800 (877-424-6423)
Dogs are allowed for no additional pet fee. Multiple dogs may be allowed.

La Quinta Inn & Suites Appleton
College Avenue
3730 W. College Avenue
Appleton, WI
920-734-7777 (800-531-5900)
Dogs of all sizes are allowed. There are no additional pet fees. Dogs must be leashed, cleaned up after, and crated if they are left in the room

alone. Dogs are not allowed in the common areas. Multiple dogs may be allowed.

Residence Inn by Marriott
310 Metro Drive
Appleton, WI
920-954-0570
Dogs of all sizes are allowed. There is a $75 one time fee and a pet policy to sign at check in. Multiple dogs may be allowed.

Americinn Motel and Suites
3009 Lakeshore Drive East
Ashland, WI
715-682-9950
There is a $6 per day pet charge.

Best Western Lake Superior Lodge
30600 US Highway 2
Ashland, WI
715-682-5235 (800-780-7234)
Dogs up to 50 pounds are allowed for an additional fee of $10 per night per pet. 2 dogs may be allowed.

Lake Aire Inn
101 E. Lake Shore Dr.
Ashland, WI
715-682-4551 (888-666-2088)
lakeaireinn.com/
There is a $10 one time pet fee.

Comfort Inn
2786 Milwaukee Road
Beloit, WI
608-362-2666 (877-424-6423)
Dogs are allowed for an additional fee of $10 per night per pet. Multiple dogs may be allowed.

Super 8 Motel - Beloit
3002 Milwaukee Road
Beloit, WI
608-365-8680 (800-800-8000)
innworks.com/beloit
There is a $10 per stay additional pet fee. Up to three dogs are permitted in each room. The hotel allows a free 8 minute long distance call each night and offers a free continental breakfast. There is a pool and a laundry. I-90, Exit 185A. Intersection of Hwy 81, I-43 & I-90.

Best Western Arrowhead Lodge and Suites
600 Oasis Rd
Black River, WI
715-284-9471 (800-780-7234)
Dogs are allowed for an additional fee of $10 per night per pet. Multiple dogs may be allowed.

Days Inn Black River Falls
919 Hwy 54

Black River Falls, WI
715-284-4333 (800-329-7466)
Dogs of all sizes are allowed. There is a $10 per night pet fee per pet. 2 dogs may be allowed.

La Quinta Inn Milwaukee West/Brookfield
20391 W. Bluemound Road
Brookfield, WI
262-782-9100 (800-531-5900)
Dogs of all sizes are allowed. There are no additional fees. Dogs may not be left unattended, but if they must be left in the room in case of emergency, they must be crated. 2 dogs may be allowed.

Motel 6 - Milwaukee West - Brookfield
20300 West Bluemound Road
Brookfield, WI
262-786-7337 (800-466-8356)
One well-behaved family pet per room. Guest must notify front desk upon arrival. Guest is liable for any damages. In consideration of all guests, pets must never be left unattended in the guest rooms.

Residence Inn by Marriott
950 S Pinehurst Court
Brookfield, WI
262-782-5990
Dogs of all sizes are allowed. There is a $175 one time fee and a pet policy to sign at check in. Multiple dogs may be allowed.

Sheraton Milwaukee Brookfield Hotel
375 South Moorland Road
Brookfield, WI
262-786-1100 (888-625-5144)
Dogs up to 80 pounds are allowed. Dogs are not allowed to be left alone in the room.

TownePlace Suites Milwaukee Brookfield
600 N Calhoun Rd
Brookfield, WI
262-784-8450
Dogs of all sizes are allowed. There is a $75 one time pet fee per visit. . 2 dogs may be allowed.

Best Western Midway Hotel
1005 S Moorland Road
Brookfield (Milwaukee), WI
262-786-9540 (800-780-7234)
Dogs totaling no more than 70 pounds are allowed for no additional fee with a credit card on file; there is a $50 refundable deposit if paying by cash. 2 dogs may be allowed.

Telemark Resort

4225 Telemark Road
Cable, WI
715-798-3999
Dogs of all sizes are allowed. There is a $35 per pet per stay additional fee. 2 dogs may be allowed.

Super 8 Chetek
115 2nd St
Chetek, WI
715-924-4888 (800-800-8000)
Dogs of all sizes are allowed. There is a $50 returnable deposit required per room. There is a $10 per night pet fee per pet. Smoking and non-smoking rooms are available for pet rooms. 2 dogs may be allowed.

Americinn Motel and Suites
11 West South Avenue
Chippewa Falls, WI
715-723-5711
No extra pet charge, just sign a pet waiver. They have 2 non-smoking pet rooms.

Indianhead Motel
501 Summit Avenue
Chippewa Falls, WI
715-723-9171 (888-315-BEST (2378))
bestvalueinn.com/Lodges/W152.htm
There is a $5 per day pet charge.

Clarion Collection Kress Inn
300 Grant Street
De Pere, WI
920-403-5100 (877-424-6423)
Well behaved dogs are allowed for an additional one time pet fee of $15 per room. Dogs must be declared at the time of reservation. 2 dogs may be allowed.

Holiday Inn Express
7184 Morrisonville Rd
DeForest, WI
608-846-8686 (877-270-6405)
Dogs of all sizes are allowed for an additional one time pet fee of $20 per room. 2 dogs may be allowed.

La Quinta Inn Milwaukee-Delafield
2801 Hillside Drive
Delafield, WI
262-646-8500 (800-531-5900)
Dogs of all sizes are allowed. There are no additional pet fees. There is a pet waiver to sign at check in. Dogs may not be left unattended, and they must be leashed and cleaned up after. Multiple dogs may be allowed.

Best Western Quiet House and Suites
1130 N Johns St
Dodgeville, WI

608-935-7739 (800-780-7234)
Dogs are allowed for an additional fee of $15 per night per pet. Multiple dogs may be allowed.

Best Western Trail Lodge Hotel & Suites
3340 Mondovi Road
Eau Claire, WI
715-838-9989 (800-780-7234)
Dogs are allowed for an additional pet fee of $20 per night per room. Multiple dogs may be allowed.

Comfort Inn
3117 Craig Road
Eau Claire, WI
715-833-9798 (877-424-6423)
Dogs are allowed for an additional fee of $10 per night per pet. Multiple dogs may be allowed.

Econo Lodge
4608 Royal Dr.
Eau Claire, WI
715-833-8818 (800-55-ECONO)
There is a $10 per night additional pet fee. The hotel is smoke free.

Quality Inn Conference Center
809 W Clairemont Avenue
Eau Claire, WI
715-834-6611 (877-424-6423)
Dogs are allowed for an additional pet fee of $10 per night per room. Multiple dogs may be allowed.

Comfort Inn
11102 Goede Road
Edgerton, WI
608-884-2118 (877-424-6423)
Dogs are allowed for an additional fee of $10 per night per pet. Multiple dogs may be allowed.

The Feathered Star
6202 H 42
Egg Harbor, WI
920-743-4066
Dogs of all sizes are allowed. There is an $8 per night per room additional pet fee. Multiple dogs may be allowed.

Days Inn Fond Du Lac
107 N Pioneer Road
Fond Du Lac, WI
920-923-6790 (800-329-7466)
Dogs of all sizes are allowed. There is a $6 per night pet fee per pet. 2 dogs may be allowed.

Holiday Inn Express Hotel and Suites
1680 Madison Avenue
Fort Atkinson, WI
920-563-3600 (877-270-6405)

Dogs of all sizes are allowed for no additional pet fee. Multiple dogs may be allowed.

Super 8 Germantown/Milwaukee Area
N 96 West 17490 County Q
Germantown, WI
262-255-0880 (800-800-8000)
Dogs of all sizes are allowed. There is a $5 per night pet fee per pet. Smoking and non-smoking rooms are available for pet rooms. 2 dogs may be allowed.

Harbor House Inn Bed and Breakfast
12666 SR 42
Gills Rock, WI
920-854-5196
door-county-inn.com/
This B&B has private beach access, outdoor grills and park-like grounds. You and your pup can also stroll through the quaint fishing village of Gills Rock. They are open late April through September. There is a $20 per day pet fee per pet.

La Quinta Inn & Suites Milwaukee-Glendale
5423 N. Port Washington Road
Glendale, WI
414-962-6767 (800-531-5900)
Dogs of all sizes are allowed. There are no additional pet fees. Dogs must be leashed, cleaned up after, and crated or removed for housekeeping. Multiple dogs may be allowed.

La Quinta Inn Milwaukee Northeast/Glendale
5110 N. Port Washington Road
Glendale, WI
414-964-8484 (800-531-5900)
Dogs up to 60 pounds are allowed. There are no additional pet fees. Dogs may not be left unattended, and they must be leashed at all times. 2 dogs may be allowed.

Residence Inn by Marriott
7175 N Port Washington Road
Glendale, WI
414-352-0070
Dogs of all sizes are allowed. There is a $75 one time fee and a pet policy to sign at check in. Multiple dogs may be allowed.

Americinn
2032 Velp Ave
Green Bay, WI
920-434-9790
inbsonline.com/americinn/
There is a $10 per day additional pet fee.

Candlewood Suites Green Bay
1125 East Mason Street
Green Bay, WI
920-430-7040 (877-270-6405)
Dogs of all sizes are allowed for an additional pet fee per room of $75 for 1 to 6 nights, and $150 for 7 nights or more. 2 dogs may be allowed.

Days Inn Green Bay City Centre
406 N Washington Way
Green Bay, WI
920-435-4484 (800-329-7466)
Dogs of all sizes are allowed. There is a $75 returnable deposit required per room. There is a $12 per night pet fee per pet. Two small dogs or one large dog are allowed in each room.

Motel 6 - Green Bay
1614 Shawano Avenue
Green Bay, WI
920-494-6730 (800-466-8356)
One well-behaved family pet per room. Guest must notify front desk upon arrival. Guest is liable for any damages. In consideration of all guests, pets must never be left unattended in the guest rooms.

Residence Inn by Marriott
335 W St. Joseph Street
Green Bay, WI
920-435-2222
Dogs of all sizes are allowed. There is a $75 one time fee and a pet policy to sign at check in. 2 dogs may be allowed.

Super 8 Hartford
1539 E Summer St
Hartford, WI
262-673-7431 (800-800-8000)
Dogs of all sizes are allowed. There is a $10 per night pet fee per pet. Smoking and non-smoking rooms are available for pet rooms. 2 dogs may be allowed.

Comfort Suites
15586 County Road B
Hayward, WI
715-634-0700 (877-424-6423)
Dogs are allowed for an additional pet fee of $12.50 per night per room. 2 dogs may be allowed.

Super 8 Hayward
10444 N St Hwy 27 South
Hayward, WI
715-634-2646 (800-800-8000)
Dogs of all sizes are allowed. There are no additional pet fees. Dogs are not allowed to be left alone in the room. Smoking and non-smoking

rooms are available for pet rooms. 2 dogs may be allowed.

Sleep Inn
1235 Water Avenue
Hillsboro, WI
608-489-3000 (877-424-6423)
Dogs are allowed for an additional pet fee of $10 per night per room. 2 dogs may be allowed.

Comfort Inn
811 Dominion Drive
Hudson, WI
715-386-6355 (877-424-6423)
Dogs are allowed for an additional fee of $5 per night per pet. 2 dogs may be allowed.

Best Western Janesville
3900 Milton Ave
Janesville, WI
608-756-4511 (800-780-7234)
Dogs up to 80 pounds are allowed for an additional fee of $15 per night per pet. 2 dogs may be allowed.

Microtel Inn
3121 Wellington Pl
Janesville, WI
608-752-3121
There is a $10 one time pet fee.

Motel 6 - Janesville
3907 Milton Avenue
Janesville, WI
608-756-1742 (800-466-8356)
One well-behaved family pet per room. Guest must notify front desk upon arrival. Guest is liable for any damages. In consideration of all guests, pets must never be left unattended in the guest rooms.

Select Inn
3520 Milton Ave
Janesville, WI
608-754-0251
There is a $25 refundable deposit and a $5.25 charge per day.

Days Inn Johnson Creek
W 4545 Linmar Lane
Johnson Creek, WI
920-699-8000 (800-329-7466)
Dogs of all sizes are allowed. There is a $5 per night pet fee per pet. 2 dogs may be allowed.

Days Inn La Crosse Conference Cntr
101 Sky Harbour Dr
La Crosse, WI
608-783-1000 (800-329-7466)
Dogs of all sizes are allowed. There is a $10 per night pet fee per pet. Reservations are recommended

due to limited rooms for pets. 2 dogs may be allowed.

Radisson Hotel La Crosse
200 Harborview Plaza
La Crosse, WI
608-784-6680
Dogs of all sizes are allowed. There are no additional pet fees.

Woods Manor
RR 1, Box 7
La Pointe, WI
715-747-3102
Dogs up to 75 pounds are allowed. There is a $25 one time additional fee per pet. There are some breed restrictions. 2 dogs may be allowed.

Eleven Gables Inn on Lake Geneva
493 Wrigley Drive
Lake Geneva, WI
262-248-8393
Dogs of all sizes are allowed. There are no additional pet fees. There are 3 pet friendly rooms. Multiple dogs may be allowed.

Best Western Countryside Inn
W 9250 Prospect Dr
Lodi, WI
608-592-1450 (800-780-7234)
Dogs are allowed for an additional pet fee of $10 per night per room. Multiple dogs may be allowed.

Clarion Suites Central
2110 Rimrock Road
Madison, WI
608-284-1234 (877-424-6423)
Dogs are allowed for an additional fee of $25 per night per pet. 2 dogs may be allowed.

Collins House Bed and Breakfast
704 E Gorham St
Madison, WI
608-255-4230
collinshouse.com/
This B&B is listed on the National Register of Historic Places as a classic example of Prairie School Architecture. Pets are not allowed on the furniture nor should they be left alone in a room. Pets must be leashed in all common areas. There are no additional pet fees.

Comfort Suites
1253 John Q. Hammons Drive
Madison, WI
608-836-3033
Dogs are allowed for no additional pet fee. Multiple dogs may be allowed.

Days Inn Madison/Monona

4402 E Broadway Service Rd
Madison, WI
608-223-1800 (800-329-7466)
Dogs of all sizes are allowed. There
is a $50 returnable deposit required
per room. There is a $10 per night
pet fee per pet. 2 dogs may be
allowed.

La Quinta Inn & Suites Madison
American Center
5217 E. Terrace Drive
Madison, WI
608-245-0123 (800-531-5900)
Dogs of all sizes are allowed. There
are no additional pet fees. Dogs
must be leashed, cleaned up after,
and crated or removed for
housekeeping. Dogs are not allowed
to come in through the front lobby
door, or to be in the lobby area
during breakfast hours. 2 dogs may
be allowed.

Motel 6 - Madison North
1754 Thierer Road
Madison, WI
608-241-8101 (800-466-8356)
One well-behaved family pet per
room. Guest must notify front desk
upon arrival. Guest is liable for any
damages. In consideration of all
guests, pets must never be left
unattended in the guest rooms.

Quality Inn and Suites
2969 Cahill Main
Madison, WI
608-274-7200 (877-424-6423)
Dogs are allowed for an additional
pet fee of $12.50 per night per room.
2 dogs may be allowed.

Red Roof Inn - Madison
4830 Hayes Road
Madison, WI
608-241-1787 (800-RED-ROOF)
One well-behaved family pet per
room. Guest must notify front desk
upon arrival. Guest is liable for any
damages. In consideration of all
guests, pets must never be left
unattended in the guest rooms.

Residence Inn by Marriott
4862 Hayes Road
Madison, WI
608-244-5047
Dogs of all sizes are allowed. There
is a $75 one time fee and a pet
policy to sign at check in. Multiple
dogs may be allowed.

Sheraton Madison Hotel
706 John Nolen Dr.
Madison, WI
608-251-2300 (888-625-5144)

Dogs up to 100 pounds are allowed
for an additional one time pet fee of
$25 per room.

Staybridge Suites Madison-East
3301 City View Dr.
Madison, WI
608-241-2300 (877-270-6405)
Dogs of all sizes are allowed for an
additional pet fee of $150 per room.
There can be 1 large or 2 small
dogs per room. 2 dogs may be
allowed.

Best Western Lakefront Hotel
101 Maritime Drive
Manitowoc, WI
920-682-7000 (800-780-7234)
Dogs are allowed for an additional
one time pet fee of $25 per room.
Multiple dogs may be allowed.

Comfort Inn
2200 S 44th Street
Manitowoc, WI
920-683-0220 (877-424-6423)
Dogs are allowed for an additional
one time pet fee of $25 per room.
Multiple dogs may be allowed.

Holiday Inn
4601 Calumet Ave
Manitowoc, WI
920-682-6000 (877-270-6405)
Dogs of all sizes are allowed for no
additional pet fee. 2 dogs may be
allowed.

Chalet Motel
1301 Marinette Ave
Marinette, WI
715-735-6687

Comfort Inn
114 E Upham Street
Marshfield, WI
715-387-8691 (877-424-6423)
Dogs are allowed for a $40
refundable pet deposit per room
plus an additional fee of $15 per
night per pet. Multiple dogs may be
allowed.

Holiday Inn Conference Ctr
Marshfield
750 South Central Avenue
Marshfield, WI
715-486-1500 (877-270-6405)
Dogs up to 60 pounds are allowed
for an additional one time pet fee of
$50 per room. 2 dogs may be
allowed.

Best Western Park Oasis Inn
W5641 State Road 82 E
Mauston, WI
608-847-6255 (800-780-7234)

Dogs are allowed for an additional
fee of $5 per night per pet. Multiple
dogs may be allowed.

Super 8 Mauston
1001A Hwy 82 East
Mauston, WI
608-847-2300 (800-800-8000)
Dogs of all sizes are allowed. There
is a $5 per night pet fee per pet.
Smoking and non-smoking rooms
are available for pet rooms.

Comfort Inn
1721 Plaza Drive
Menomonie, WI
715-233-1500 (877-424-6423)
Dogs are allowed for an additional
one time fee of $10 per pet. Multiple
dogs may be allowed.

Motel 6 - Menomonie
2100 Stout Street
Menomonie, WI
715-235-6901 (800-466-8356)
One well-behaved family pet per
room. Guest must notify front desk
upon arrival. Guest is liable for any
damages. In consideration of all
guests, pets must never be left
unattended in the guest rooms.

Best Western Quiet House and
Suites
10330 N Port Washington Rd
Mequon, WI
262-241-3677 (800-780-7234)
Dogs are allowed for an additional
fee of $15 per night per pet. 2 dogs
may be allowed.

Madison Marriott West
1313 John Q Hammons Drive
Middleton, WI
608-831-2000 (800-228-9290)
Dogs of all sizes are allowed. There
is a $50 one time additional pet fee
per room. Dogs must be leashed,
cleaned up after, and the Pet in
Room sign put on the door if they are
in the room alone. 2 dogs may be
allowed.

Residence Inn by Marriott
8400 Market Street
Middleton, WI
608-662-1100
Dogs of all sizes are welcome. There
is a $75 one time fee and a pet
policy to sign at check in. Multiple
dogs may be allowed.

Hotel Wisconsin
720 N Old World 3rd St
Milwaukee, WI
414-271-4900
Built in 1913, this is a vintage

Milwaukee hotel. There are no additional pet fees.

La Quinta Inn Milwaukee Northwest
5442 N. Lovers Lane Road
Milwaukee, WI
414-535-1300 (800-531-5900)
Dogs of all sizes are allowed. There are no additional pet fees. Dogs must be attended when housekeeping is present, and may not be left alone in the room unless they will be quiet and well behaved. Dogs must be leashed. Multiple dogs may be allowed.

Motel 6 - Milwaukee South - Airport
5037 South Howell Avenue
Milwaukee, WI
414-482-4414 (800-466-8356)
One well-behaved family pet per room. Guest must notify front desk upon arrival. Guest is liable for any damages. In consideration of all guests, pets must never be left unattended in the guest rooms.

Comfort Inn
8729 H 51N
Minocqua, WI
715-358-2588 (877-424-6423)
Dogs are allowed for an additional fee of $10 per night per pet. 2 dogs may be allowed.

Comfort Inn
1510 County H XX
Mosinee, WI
715-355-4449 (877-424-6423)
Dogs are allowed for an additional fee per room of $15 for the 1st night and $5 for each night after. 2 dogs may be allowed.

La Quinta Inn & Suites Milwaukee SW/New Berlin
15300 W. Rock Ridge Rd.
New Berlin, WI
262-717-0900 (800-531-5900)
Dogs of all sizes are allowed. There are no additional pet fees. Dogs must be leashed, cleaned up after, and the Do Not Disturb sign put on the door if there is a pet in the room alone. Multiple dogs may be allowed.

Super 8 New Richmond
1561 Dorset Ln
New Richmond, WI
715-246-7829 (800-800-8000)
Dogs of all sizes are allowed. There is a $15 one time per pet fee per visit. Dogs are not allowed to be left alone in the room. Smoking and non-smoking rooms are available for pet rooms. 2 dogs may be allowed.

Comfort Suites Milwaukee Airport
6362 S 13th Street
Oak Creek, WI
414-570-1111 (877-424-6423)
Dogs are allowed for an additional fee of $5 per night per pet. Multiple dogs may be allowed.

La Quinta Inn Milwaukee Airport/Oak Creek
7141 S. 13th Street
Oak Creek, WI
414-762-2266 (800-531-5900)
Dogs of all sizes are allowed. There are no additional fees. Dogs may not be left unattended, and they must be leashed and cleaned up after. Multiple dogs may be allowed.

MainStay Suites
1001 W College Avenue
Oak Creek, WI
414-571-8800
Dogs up to 80 pounds are allowed for an additional one time fee per pet of $25 for 1 to 11 days; $50 for 12 to 29 days, and $75 for 30 or more days. 2 dogs may be allowed.

Red Roof Inn - Milwaukee
6360 South 13th Street
Oak Creek, WI
414-764-3500 (800-RED-ROOF)
One well-behaved family pet per room. Guest must notify front desk upon arrival. Guest is liable for any damages. In consideration of all guests, pets must never be left unattended in the guest rooms.

Holiday Inn Express
9409 Hwy 16
Onalaska, WI
608-783-6555 (877-270-6405)
Dogs of all sizes are allowed for no additional pet fee. Multiple dogs may be allowed.

Holiday Inn Express & Suites
2251 Westowne Ave
Oshkosh, WI
920-303-1300 (877-270-6405)
Dogs of all sizes are allowed for no additional pet fee. 2 dogs may be allowed.

Howard Johnson Inn
1919 Omro Road
Oshkosh, WI
920-233-1200 (800-446-4656)
Dogs of all sizes are welcome. There are no additional pet fees.

La Quinta Inn Oskosh
1950 Omro Road
Oshkosh, WI
920-233-4190 (800-531-5900)

Dogs of all sizes are allowed. There are no additional pet fees. Dogs may not be left unattended, and they must be leashed and cleaned up after. Multiple dogs may be allowed.

Super 8 Oshkosh/Airport
1581 W Southpark Ave
Oshkosh, WI
920-426-2885 (800-800-8000)
Dogs of all sizes are allowed. There is a $5 per night pet fee per pet. Smoking and non-smoking rooms are available for pet rooms. 2 dogs may be allowed.

Super 8 Park Falls
1212 Hwy 13 South
Park Falls, WI
715-762-3383 (800-800-8000)
Dogs of all sizes are allowed. There are no additional pet fees. Smoking and non-smoking rooms are available for pet rooms. 2 dogs may be allowed.

Best Western Waukesha Grand
2840 N Grandview Blvd
Pewaukee, WI
262-524-9300 (800-780-7234)
Dogs are allowed for an additional one time pet fee of $10 per room. Dogs may not be left alone in the room at any time. 2 dogs may be allowed.

Super 8 Phillips
Hwy 13 Wouth
Phillips, WI
715-339-2898 (800-800-8000)
Dogs of all sizes are allowed. There are no additional pet fees. Smoking and non-smoking rooms are available for pet rooms. 2 dogs may be allowed.

Governer Dodge Hotel and Convention Center
300 Bus H 151
Platteville, WI
608-348-2301
Dogs of all sizes are allowed. There is a $10 per night per room additional pet fee. 2 dogs may be allowed.

Super 8 Platteville
100 Hwy 80/81 South
Platteville, WI
608-348-8800 (800-800-8000)
Dogs of all sizes are allowed. There is a $10 per night pet fee per pet. Smoking and non-smoking rooms are available for pet rooms. 2 dogs may be allowed.

Holiday Inn Express Hotel & Suites
Pleasant Prairie / Kenosha

7887 94th Avenue
Pleasant Prairie, WI
262-942-6000 (877-270-6405)
Dogs up to 80 pounds are allowed for an additional pet fee per room of $50 for 1 to 3 nights, and $100 for 4 or more nights. 2 dogs may be allowed.

Super 8 Pleasant Prairie/Kenosha Area
7601 118th Ave
Pleasant Prairie, WI
262-857-7963 (800-800-8000)
Dogs of all sizes are allowed. There is a $10 per night pet fee per pet. Smoking and non-smoking rooms are available for pet rooms. 2 dogs may be allowed.

Holiday Inn
135 East Grand Avenue
Port Washington, WI
262-284-9461 (877-270-6405)
Dogs of all sizes are allowed for a $25 one time pet fee per room. 2 dogs may be allowed.

Super 8 Portage
3000 New Pinery Rd
Portage, WI
608-742-8330 (800-800-8000)
Dogs of all sizes are allowed. There is a $10 per night pet fee per pet. Smoking and non-smoking rooms are available for pet rooms. 2 dogs may be allowed.

Days Inn Racine
3700 Northwestern Ave
Racine, WI
262-637-9311 (800-329-7466)
Dogs of all sizes are allowed. There are no additional pet fees. Pet must be kept in kennel when left alone. 2 dogs may be allowed.

Racine Marriott
7111 Washington Avenue
Racine, WI
262-886-6100 (800-228-9290)
Dogs up to 50 pounds are allowed. There is a $20 refundable pet deposit per room. Dogs must be leashed, cleaned up after, and a contact number left with the front desk if they are in the room alone. 2 dogs may be allowed.

Best Western Claridge Motor Inn
70 North Stevens St
Rhinelander, WI
715-362-7100 (800-780-7234)
Dogs are allowed for an additional fee of $10 per night per pet. 2 dogs may be allowed.

Comfort Hotel
1490 Lincoln Street
Rhinelander, WI
715-369-1100
Quiet dogs are allowed for an additional fee of $10 per night per pet. Dogs may not be left alone in the room. Multiple dogs may be allowed.

Holiday Acres Resort on Lake Thompson
4060 S Shore Road
Rhinelander, WI
715-369-1500
Dogs of all sizes are allowed. There is a $14.50 plus tax per night per pet additional pet fee. 2 dogs may be allowed.

Holiday Inn Express
668 W. Kemp Street
Rhinelander, WI
715-369-3600 (877-270-6405)
Quiet dogs of all sizes are allowed for an additional one time pet fee of $30 per room. Multiple dogs may be allowed.

Super 8 Rhinelander
667 W Kemp St
Rhinelander, WI
715-369-5880 (800-800-8000)
Dogs of all sizes are allowed. There is a $5 per night pet fee per pet. Smoking and non-smoking rooms are available for pet rooms. 2 dogs may be allowed.

Currier's Lakeview Lodge
2010 E. Sawyer Street
Rice Lake, WI
715-234-7474 (800-433-5253)
currierslakeview.com
Located on Rice Lake's scenic east side, Currier's Lakeview is the city's only all-season resort motel. The motel sits on a wooded 4-acre peninsula that is located between two beautiful bays. There are no additional pet fees.

Super 8 Rice Lake
2401 S Main
Rice Lake, WI
715-234-6956 (800-800-8000)
Dogs of all sizes are allowed. There is a $10 per night pet fee per pet. Smoking and non-smoking rooms are available for pet rooms. 2 dogs may be allowed.

Super 8 Richland Center
Hwy 14 East
Richland Center, WI
608-647-8988 (800-800-8000)
Dogs of all sizes are allowed. There

is a $50 returnable deposit required per room. Smoking and non-smoking rooms are available for pet rooms. 2 dogs may be allowed.

Comfort Suites at Royal Ridges
2 Westgate Drive
Ripon, WI
920-748-5500 (877-424-6423)
Dogs are allowed for an additional fee of $15 per night per pet.

Super 8 Shawano
211 Waukechon St
Shawano, WI
715-526-6688 (800-800-8000)
Dogs of all sizes are allowed. There is a $25 returnable deposit required per room. Smoking and non-smoking rooms are available for pet rooms. 2 dogs may be allowed.

La Quinta Inn Sheboygan
2932 Kohler Memorial Drive
Sheboygan, WI
920-457-2321 (800-531-5900)
Dogs of all sizes are allowed. There are no additional pet fees. Dogs may not be left unattended unless they will be quiet and well behaved. Dogs must be leashed and cleaned up after. Multiple dogs may be allowed.

Super 8 Motel - Sheboygan
3402 Wilgus Road
Sheboygan, WI
920-458-8080 (800-800-8000)
innworks.com/sheboygan
There is a $10 per stay additional pet fee. Up to three dogs are permitted in each room. The hotel allows a free 8 minute long distance call each night and offers a free continental breakfast. There is a pool and a laundry. I-43, Exit 126 onto WI 23 East to Taylor Dr; Left on Taylor Dr 1 block; Left on Wilgus 1 block.

Scandia Cottages
11062 Beach Road
Sister Bay, WI
920-854-2447
Dogs of all sizes are allowed. There are no additional pet fees. Multiple dogs may be allowed.

Country Inn by Carlson
737 Avon Rd
Sparta, WI
608-269-3110
There is a $5 per day pet fee.

Justin Trails Resort
7452 Kathryn Avenue
Sparta, WI
608-269-4522
justintrails.com

This bed and breakfast inn welcomes both pets and children in their cabins and cottage. The rooms are non-smoking. There is a $15 per day pet fee. Hiking trails and cross-country ski trails are located on the property. Dogs need to be leashed except when in the open field.

Americas Best Value Inn
247 N. Division Street
Stevens Point, WI
715-341-8888 (800-800-8000)
innworks.com/stevenspoint
There is a $10 per stay additional pet fee. Up to three dogs are permitted in each room. The hotel allows a free 8 minute long distance call each night and offers a free continental breakfast. There is a pool and a laundry. From US 10, Take Bus. 51 North. From US 51/39, Exit 161, South on Bus. 51, 1 block.

Holiday Inn Express Hotel & Suites
Stevens Point-Wisconsin Rapids
1100 Amber Avenue
Stevens Point, WI
715-344-0000 (877-270-6405)
Dogs of all sizes are allowed for an additional fee of $25 per night per pet. Multiple dogs may be allowed.

La Quinta Inn Stevens Point
4917 Main Street
Stevens Point, WI
715-344-1900 (800-531-5900)
Dogs of all sizes are allowed. There are no additional fees. Dogs may not be left unattended at any time, and they must be leashed and cleaned up after. Multiple dogs may be allowed.

Holiday Motel
29 N Second Ave
Sturgeon Bay, WI
920-743-5571
There is a $5 per day pet fee.

Snug Harbor Inn & Cottages
1627 Memorial Drive
Sturgeon Bay, WI
920-743-2337 (800-231-5767)
snugharborinn.com
The inn boasts 300 feet of park-like waterfront. Most suites, cottages and rooms have hot tubs and fireplaces. There is a 30 slip marina with boat and jet ski rental available. The inn is located 1 mile from downtown Sturgeon Bay. Dogs of all sizes are allowed. There is a $10 per day additional pet fee. Pets may not be left alone in the room.

Super 8 Sturgeon Bay

409 Green Bay Road
Sturgeon Bay, WI
920-743-9211 (800-800-8000)
Dogs of all sizes are allowed. There is a $5 per night pet fee per pet. Smoking and non-smoking rooms are available for pet rooms. 2 dogs may be allowed.

Days Inn Superior
110 Harborview Parkway
Superior, WI
715-392-4783 (800-329-7466)
Dogs of all sizes are allowed. There is a $10 per night pet fee per pet. 2 dogs may be allowed.

Americinn
750 Vandervort St
Tomah, WI
608-372-4100
There is a $50 refundable deposit for pets. There is one non-smoking pet room.

Comfort Inn
305 Wittig Road
Tomah, WI
608-372-6600 (877-424-6423)
Dogs are allowed for an additional one time pet fee of $10 per room. Dogs may not be left alone in the room. Multiple dogs may be allowed.

Cranberry Suites
319 Wittig Rd
Tomah, WI
608-374-2801
There is a $5 per day pet fee.

Econo Lodge
2005 N Superior Ave
Tomah, WI
608-372-9100
There is a $5 per day pet fee.

Holiday Inn
Junction I-94 and Hwy 21
Tomah, WI
608-372-3211 (877-270-6405)
Dogs of all sizes are allowed for no additional pet fee. Multiple dogs may be allowed.

Lark Inn
229 N Superior Ave
Tomah, WI
608-372-5981
larkinn.com/
This inn has been sheltering travelers since the early 1900s. It is a comfortable retreat with country quilts and antiques. Dogs are allowed in the larger hotel rooms and the log cabins. There is a $6

per day pet fee.

Super 8 Tomah
1008 E McCoy Blvd
Tomah, WI
608-372-3901 (800-800-8000)
Dogs of all sizes are allowed. There is a $10 one time per pet fee per visit. Smoking and non-smoking rooms are available for pet rooms. 2 dogs may be allowed.

Comfort Inn
4738 Comfort Drive
Tomahawk, WI
715-453-8900 (877-424-6423)
Dogs are allowed for an additional one time pet fee of $25 per room. Multiple dogs may be allowed.

Knights Inn - Milwaukee
9420 S 20th St
Value Inn, WI
414-761-3807
There is a $10 per day additional pet fee.

Super 8 Washburn
Harbor View Dr Box 626
Washburn, WI
715-373-5671 (800-800-8000)
Dogs of all sizes are allowed. There are no additional pet fees. Smoking and non-smoking rooms are available for pet rooms. 2 dogs may be allowed.

Viking Village Motel
Main Road at Detroit Harbor, P.O. Box 188.
Washington Island, WI
920-847-2551 (888-847-2144)
There are no designated smoking or non-smoking rooms. There are no additional pet fees. There is an extra charge if you do not pick up after your pet.

Flags Inn Motel
N627 H 26
Watertown, WI
920-261-9400
Well behaved dogs of all sizes are allowed. There is a $5 per night per pet additional fee. Multiple dogs may be allowed.

Super 8 Watertown
1730 S Church St
Watertown, WI
920-261-1188 (800-800-8000)
Dogs of all sizes are allowed. There is a $50 returnable deposit required per room. Dogs are not allowed to be left alone in the room. Smoking and non-smoking rooms are available for pet rooms. 2 dogs may be allowed.

Best Western Grand Seasons Hotel
110 Grand Seasons Drive
Waupaca, WI
715-258-9212 (800-780-7234)
Dogs are allowed for no additional pet fee. There is a pet agreement to sign at check in. Multiple dogs may be allowed.

Days Inn Wausau
4700 Rib Mountain Dr
Wausau, WI
715-355-5501 (800-329-7466)
Dogs of all sizes are allowed. There is a $10 per night pet fee per pet. 2 dogs may be allowed.

La Quinta Inn Wausau
1910 Stewart Avenue
Wausau, WI
715-842-0421 (800-531-5900)
Dogs of all sizes are allowed. There are no additional pet fees. Dogs may not be left unattended, and they must be leashed and cleaned up after. Multiple dogs may be allowed.

Stewart Inn
521 Grant Street
Wausau, WI
715-849-5858
stewartinn.com
The Stewart Inn is a small European Inn with modern amenities. Pets are welcome in three of the five guest rooms at no extra charge. Pet owners will need to sign a pet agreement.

Super 8 Wautoma
W7607 State Road 21 and 73
Wautoma, WI
920-787-4811 (800-800-8000)
Dogs of all sizes are allowed. There is a $25 returnable deposit required per room. Smoking and non-smoking rooms are available for pet rooms. 2 dogs may be allowed.

Howard Johnson Hotel
655 Frontage Rd. North
Wisconsin Dells, WI
608-254-8306 (800-446-4656)
Dogs of all sizes are welcome. There is a $10 per day pet fee. Pets may not be left unattended in the room.

Super 8 Motel - Wisconsin Rapids
3410 8th Street S.
Wisconsin Rapids, WI
715-423-8080 (800-800-8000)
innworks.com/wisconsinrapids
There is a $10 per stay additional pet fee. Up to three dogs are permitted in each room. The hotel allows a free 8 minute long distance call each

night and offers a free continental breakfast. There is a pool and a laundry. South Hwy 13 btwn Cook & Two Mile Ave.

Wyoming Listings

Best Western Crossroads Inn
75 N Bypass Road
Buffalo, WY
307-684-2256 (800-780-7234)
Dogs are allowed for an additional fee of $15 per night per pet. 2 dogs may be allowed.

Comfort Inn
65 H 16E
Buffalo, WY
307-684-9564 (877-424-6423)
Dogs are allowed for an additional fee of $10 per night per pet. 2 dogs may be allowed.

Motel 6 - Buffalo
100 Flat Iron Drive
Buffalo, WY
307-684-7000 (800-466-8356)
One well-behaved family pet per room. Guest must notify front desk upon arrival. Guest is liable for any damages. In consideration of all guests, pets must never be left unattended in the guest rooms.

Super 8 Buffalo
655 E Hart St
Buffalo, WY
307-684-2531 (800-800-8000)
Dogs of all sizes are allowed. There is a $5.25 per night pet fee per pet. Reservations are recommended due to limited rooms for pets. Smoking and non-smoking rooms are available for pet rooms. 2 dogs may be allowed.

Days Inn Casper
301 East E Street
Casper, WY
307-234-1159 (800-329-7466)
Dogs of all sizes are allowed. There are no additional pet fees. 2 dogs may be allowed.

Hampton Inn
400 West F Street
Casper, WY
307-235-6668
Dogs up to 50 pounds are allowed. There is a $25 plus tax one time cleaning fee. 2 dogs may be allowed.

Holiday Inn
300 West F Street
Casper, WY
307-235-2531 (877-270-6405)
Dogs of all sizes are allowed for no additional pet fee. Multiple dogs may be allowed.

Motel 6 - Casper
1150 Wilkins Circle
Casper, WY
307-234-3903 (800-466-8356)
One well-behaved family pet per room. Guest must notify front desk upon arrival. Guest is liable for any damages. In consideration of all guests, pets must never be left unattended in the guest rooms.

Quality Inn and Suites
821 N Poplar Street
Casper, WY
307-266-2400 (877-424-6423)
Dogs are allowed for an additional pet fee of $10 per night per room. Multiple dogs may be allowed.

Super Casper West
3838 Cy Ave
Casper, WY
307-266-3480 (800-800-8000)
Dogs of all sizes are allowed. There are no additional pet fees. Smoking and non-smoking rooms are available for pet rooms. 2 dogs may be allowed.

Best Western Hitching Post Inn Resort and Conf Cntr
1700 W Lincoln Way
Cheyenne, WY
307-638-3301 (800-780-7234)
Dogs under 50 pounds are allowed for an additional fee of $15 per night per pet; the fee is $50 per night per pet for dogs over 50 pounds. 2 dogs may be allowed.

Days Inn Cheyenne
2360 W Lincolnway
Cheyenne, WY
307-778-8877 (800-329-7466)
Dogs of all sizes are allowed. There is a $10 per night pet fee per pet. 2 dogs may be allowed.

Holiday Inn
204 W. Fox Farm Road
Cheyenne, WY
307-638-4466 (877-270-6405)
Dogs of all sizes are allowed for an additional one time pet fee of $25 per room. There can be 1 or 2 large or up to 3 small dogs per room. Multiple dogs may be allowed.

La Quinta Inn Cheyenne

2410 W. Lincolnway
Cheyenne, WY
307-632-7117 (800-531-5900)
Dogs of all sizes are allowed. There
are no additional pet fees. Dogs may
not be left unattended, and they must
be leashed and cleaned up after.
Multiple dogs may be allowed.

Lincoln Court
1720 W Lincolnway
Cheyenne, WY
307-638-3302
There are no additional pet fees.

Motel 6 - Cheyenne
1735 Westland Road
Cheyenne, WY
307-635-6806 (800-466-8356)
One well-behaved family pet per
room. Guest must notify front desk
upon arrival. Guest is liable for any
damages. In consideration of all
guests, pets must never be left
unattended in the guest rooms.

Windy Hills Guest House
393 Happy Jack Rd
Cheyenne, WY
307-632-6423
windyhillswyo.com/
There are no additional pet fees.

The Ranch at UCross
2673 US Hwy 14 East
Clearmont, WY
307-737-2281 (800-447-0194)
Secluded, inclusive resort.

Best Western Sunset Motor Inn
1601 8th ST
Cody, WY
307-587-4265 (800-780-7234)
Dogs are allowed for an additional
one time fee of $25 per pet. The fee
is $50 for extra large dogs. 2 dogs
may be allowed.

Kelly Inn of Cody
2513 Greybull Hwy
Cody, WY
307-527-5505
There are no additional pet fees.

Super 8 Cody
730 Yellowstone Rd
Cody, WY
307-527-6214 (800-800-8000)
Dogs of all sizes are allowed. There
are no additional pet fees. Smoking
and non-smoking rooms are
available for pet rooms. 2 dogs may
be allowed.

Best Western Douglas Inn and Conf
Cntr
1450 Riverbend Dr

Douglas, WY
307-358-9790 (800-780-7234)
Dogs are allowed for an additional
pet fee of $10 per night per room. 2
dogs may be allowed.

Holiday Inn Express Hotel and
Suites
900 West Yellowstone Highway
Douglas, WY
307-358-4500 (877-270-6405)
Dogs of all sizes are allowed for an
additional fee of $20 per night for
one dog; each additional dog is $10
per night. Multiple dogs may be
allowed.

Branding Iron Inn
401 W Ramshorn
Dubois, WY
307-455-2893
brandingironinn.com/
There is a $10 per day additional
pet fee.

Chinook Winds Mountain Lodge
640 S 1st St
Dubois, WY
307-455-2987
There is a $5 per day pet fee.

Pinnacle Buttes Lodge and
Campground
3577 US Hwy 26W
Dubois, WY
307-455-2506
There is a $50 refundable pet
deposit. There are no designated
smoking or non-smoking rooms.

Super 8 Dubois
1412 Warm Springs Dr
Dubois, WY
307-455-3694 (800-800-8000)
Dogs of all sizes are allowed. There
is a $5.30 per night pet fee per pet.
Smoking and non-smoking rooms
are available for pet rooms. 2 dogs
may be allowed.

Comfort Inn
1931 Harrison Drive
Evanston, WY
307-789-7799 (877-424-6423)
Dogs are allowed for an additional
one time pet fee of $10 per room.
Multiple dogs may be allowed.

Motel 6 - Evanston
261 Bear River Drive
Evanston, WY
307-789-0791 (800-466-8356)
One well-behaved family pet per
room. Guest must notify front desk
upon arrival. Guest is liable for any
damages. In consideration of all
guests, pets must never be left

unattended in the guest rooms.

Super 8 Evanston
70 Bear River Dr
Evanston, WY
307-789-7510 (800-800-8000)
Dogs of all sizes are allowed. There
is a $25 returnable deposit required
per room. Smoking and non-smoking
rooms are available for pet rooms. 2
dogs may be allowed.

Comfort Inn
480 Lathrop Road
Evansville, WY
307-235-3038 (877-424-6423)
Quiet dogs are allowed for no
additional pet fee. Multiple dogs may
be allowed.

Sleep Inn and Suites
6733 Bonanza Road
Evansville, WY
307-235-3100 (877-424-6423)
Dogs are allowed for an additional
fee of $10 per night per pet. Multiple
dogs may be allowed.

Super 8 Casper East
269 Miracle St
Evansville, WY
307-237-8100 (800-800-8000)
Dogs of all sizes are allowed. There
are no additional pet fees. Smoking
and non-smoking rooms are
available for pet rooms. 2 dogs may
be allowed.

Best Western Tower West Lodge
109 N US Highway 14-16
Gillette, WY
307-686-2210 (800-780-7234)
Dogs are allowed for an additional
pet fee of $10 per night per room.
Multiple dogs may be allowed.

Holiday Inn Express Hotel & Suites
1908 Cliff Davis Drive
Gillette, WY
307-686-9576 (877-270-6405)
Dogs of all sizes are allowed for no
additional pet fee. Multiple dogs may
be allowed.

Motel 6 - Gillette
2105 Rodgers Drive
Gillette, WY
307-686-8600 (800-466-8356)
One well-behaved family pet per
room. Guest must notify front desk
upon arrival. Guest is liable for any
damages. In consideration of all
guests, pets must never be left
unattended in the guest rooms.

Colter Bay Cabins
Jackson Lake

Grand Teton National Park, WY
800-628-9988
gtlc.com/
There are over 200 log cabins and a number of tent cabins. Pets are allowed and there are no additional pet fees.

Jackson Lake Lodge
Jackson Lake
Grand Teton National Park, WY
800-628-9988
gtlc.com/
Dogs are allowed in the classic rooms. There is a $10 per night additional pet fee.

Super 8 Green River
280 W Flaming Gorge
Green River, WY
307-875-9330 (800-800-8000)
Dogs of all sizes are allowed. There is a $5 per night pet fee per pet. Reservations are recommended due to limited rooms for pets. Smoking and non-smoking rooms are available for pet rooms. 2 dogs may be allowed.

Elk Country Inn
480 W Pearl Avenue
Jackson, WY
307-733-2364
Well behaved dogs of all sizes are allowed at the inn but not in the cabins. There are no additional pet fees. Dogs are not allowed to be left alone in the room. Multiple dogs may be allowed.

Flat Creek Inn
1935 N H 89/26
Jackson, WY
307-733-5276
Dogs of all sizes are allowed. There are no additional pet fees. Multiple dogs may be allowed.

Motel 6 - Jackson
600 South Highway 89
Jackson, WY
307-733-1620 (800-466-8356)
One well-behaved family pet per room. Guest must notify front desk upon arrival. Guest is liable for any damages. In consideration of all guests, pets must never be left unattended in the guest rooms.

Quality Inn and Suites 49'er
330 W Pearl Street
Jackson, WY
307-733-7550 (877-424-6423)
Dogs are allowed for no additional pet fee. Dogs may not be left alone in the room. Multiple dogs may be allowed.

Painted Buffalo Inn
400 West Broadway
Jackson Hole, WY
307-733-4340
paintedbuffalo.com/
There is a $10 one time pet fee.

Snow King Resort
400 E Snow King Ave
Jackson Hole, WY
307-733-5200 (800-522-5464)
There is a $100 pet deposit. $50 of this is refundable.

Howard Johnson Inn
1555 Snowy Range Road
Laramie, WY
307-742-8371 (800-446-4656)
Dogs of all sizes are welcome. There is a $10 per day pet fee.

Motel 6 - Laramie
621 Plaza Lane
Laramie, WY
307-742-2307 (800-466-8356)
One well-behaved family pet per room. Guest must notify front desk upon arrival. Guest is liable for any damages. In consideration of all guests, pets must never be left unattended in the guest rooms.

Super 8 Lovell
595 E Main
Lovell, WY
307-548-2725 (800-800-8000)
Dogs of all sizes are allowed. There are no additional pet fees. Smoking and non-smoking rooms are available for pet rooms. 2 dogs may be allowed.

Chico Hot Springs Resort
#1 Chico Road
Pray, MT
406-333-4933 (800-HOT-WADA)
chicohotsprings.com/
"We're pet-friendly, so bring your four-legged friends along." This resort has a lodge and cabins which sit on 150 acres. There are miles of hiking trails for you and your pup. They are located 30 miles from the north Yellowstone National Park entrance. There is a $10 per day pet fee.

Best Western Cotton Tree Inn
23rd at Spruce
Rawlins, WY
307-324-2737 (800-780-7234)
Dogs up to 100 pounds are allowed for an additional pet fee of $10 per night per room. Dogs must be crated when left alone in the room. Multiple dogs may be allowed.

Days inn Rawlins
2222 East Cedar St
Rawlins, WY
307-324-6615 (800-DAYS-INN)
Dogs of all sizes are allowed. There are no additional pet fees. Dogs are not allowed to be left alone in the room. 2 dogs may be allowed.

Holiday Inn Express Rawlins
201 Airport Road
Rawlins, WY
307-324-3760 (877-270-6405)
Dogs of all sizes are allowed for no additional pet fee. There can be up to 2 large dogs or 3 small dogs per room. Multiple dogs may be allowed.

Quality Inn
1801 E Cedar Street
Rawlins, WY
307-324-2783 (877-424-6423)
Dogs are allowed for an additional one time pet fee of $20 per room. Multiple dogs may be allowed.

Comfort Inn and Suites
2020 N Federal Blvd/H 26
Riverton, WY
307-856-8900 (877-424-6423)
Dogs are allowed for an additional pet fee of $15 per night per room. Multiple dogs may be allowed.

Days Inn Riverton
909 W Main St
Riverton, WY
307-856-9677 (800-329-7466)
Dogs of all sizes are allowed. There is a $10 per night pet fee per pet. 2 dogs may be allowed.

Holiday Inn
900 E. Sunset
Riverton, WY
307-856-8100 (877-270-6405)
Dogs of all sizes are allowed for a one time pet fee of $20 per room. 2 dogs may be allowed.

Sundowner Station
1616 N Federal Blvd
Riverton, WY
307-856-6503
There are no additional pet fees.

Super 8 Riverton
1040 N Federal Blvd
Riverton, WY
307-857-2400 (800-800-8000)
Dogs of all sizes are allowed. There is a $5.30 per night pet fee per pet. Smoking and non-smoking rooms are available for pet rooms. 2 dogs may be allowed.

Holiday Inn
1675 Sunset Drive
Rock Springs, WY
307-382-9200 (877-270-6405)
Dogs of all sizes are allowed for an additional one time pet fee of $10 per room. 2 dogs may be allowed.

La Quinta Inn-Rock Springs
2717 Dewar Drive
Rock Springs, WY
307-362-1770 (800-531-5900)
Dogs of all sizes are allowed. There are no additional pet fees. Dogs may not be left unattended at night, and they must be leashed, cleaned up after, and attended to or removed for housekeeping. Multiple dogs may be allowed.

Motel 6 - Rock Springs
2615 Commercial Way
Rock Springs, WY
307-362-1850 (800-466-8356)
One well-behaved family pet per room. Guest must notify front desk upon arrival. Guest is liable for any damages. In consideration of all guests, pets must never be left unattended in the guest rooms.

Guest House Motel
2007 N Main St
Sheridan, WY
307-674-7496
There is a $5 per day pet fee.

Holiday Inn
1809 Sugarland Dr
Sheridan, WY
307-672-8931 (877-270-6405)
Dogs of all sizes are allowed for no additional fee with a credit card on file. There is a $50 refundable pet deposit if paying cash. Multiple dogs may be allowed.

Motel 6 - Sheridan
911 Sibley Circle
Sheridan, WY
307-673-9500 (800-466-8356)
One well-behaved family pet per room. Guest must notify front desk upon arrival. Guest is liable for any damages. In consideration of all guests, pets must never be left unattended in the guest rooms.

Best Western Inn at Sundance
2719 E Cleveland
Sundance, WY
307-283-2800 (800-780-7234)
Dogs are allowed for an additional fee of $10 per night per pet. Multiple dogs may be allowed.

Holiday Inn

115 E Park St - Hot Springs St. Pk
Thermopolis, WY
307-864-3131 (877-270-6405)
Dogs of all sizes are allowed for an additional fee of $10 per night per pet. Multiple dogs may be allowed.

Green Creek Inn
2908 Yellowstone Hwy
Wapiti, WY
307-587-5004
There is a $5 per day pet fee.

Best Western Torchlite Motor Inn
1809 N 16th St
Wheatland, WY
307-322-4070 (800-780-7234)
Dogs are allowed for an additional fee of $5 (plus tax) per night per pet. Multiple dogs may be allowed.

Motel 6 - Wheatland
95 16th Street
Wheatland, WY
307-322-1800 (800-466-8356)
One well-behaved family pet per room. Guest must notify front desk upon arrival. Guest is liable for any damages. In consideration of all guests, pets must never be left unattended in the guest rooms.

Vimbo's Motel
203 16th St
Wheatland, WY
307-322-3842
There are no additional pet fees.

Canyon Western Cabins
Yellowstone National Park, WY
307-344-7311
travelyellowstone.com
Dogs are allowed in the Cabins only. There are no additional pet fees. The Cabins are open seasonally from about May to September each year.

Flagg Ranch Village
Hwy 89 Yellowstone South Entrance
Yellowstone National Park, WY
307-543-2861 (800-443-2311)
flaggranch.com/
Dogs are allowed in cabins. This is a seasonal hotel and is not open year round. There is a $5 per day additional pet fee.

Lake Lodge Cabins
Lake Lodge
Yellowstone National Park, WY
307-344-7311
travelyellowstone.com
Dogs are allowed in the Cabins only. There are no additional pet fees. The Cabins are open

seasonally from about May to September each year.

Lake Yellowstone Cabins
Lake Yellowstone
Yellowstone National Park, WY
307-344-7311
travelyellowstone.com
Dogs are allowed in the Cabins only. There are no additional pet fees. The Cabins are open seasonally from about May to September each year.

Mammoth Hot Springs Cabins
Mammoth Hot Springs
Yellowstone National Park, WY
307-344-7311
travelyellowstone.com
Dogs are allowed in the Cabins only. There are no additional pet fees. The Cabins are open seasonally from about May to September each year.

Old Faithful Lodge Cabins
Old Faithful
Yellowstone National Park, WY
307-344-7311
travelyellowstone.com
Dogs are allowed in the Cabins only. There are no additional pet fees. The Cabins are open seasonally from about May to September each year. These cabins are within easy walking distance of Old Faithful.

Pioneer Cabins

Yellowstone National Park, WY
307-344-7311
travelyellowstone.com
Dogs are allowed in the Cabins only. There are no additional pet fees. The Cabins are open seasonally from about May to September each year.

Canada

Alberta Listings

Super 8 Airdrie
815 East Lake Blvd
Airdrie, AB
403-948-4188 (800-800-8000)
Dogs of all sizes are allowed. There is a $10 one time per pet fee per visit. Smoking and non-smoking rooms are available for pet rooms. 2 dogs may be allowed.

Best Western Athabasca Inn
5211 41st Ave
Athabasca, AB
780-675-2294 (800-780-7234)
Dogs are allowed for an additional fee of $15 per night per pet. 2 dogs may be allowed.

Super 8 Athabasca
4820B Wood Heights Rd
Athabasca, AB
780-675-8888 (800-800-8000)
Dogs up to 60 pounds are allowed. There is a $10 per night pet fee per pet. Smoking and non-smoking rooms are available for pet rooms. 2 dogs may be allowed.

Best Western Siding 29 Lodge
453 Marten St
Banff, AB
403-762-5575 (800-780-7234)
Quiet dogs are allowed for no additional pet fee. Multiple dogs may be allowed.

Driftwood Inn
337 Banff Avenue
Banff, AB
403-762-4496
Dogs of all sizes are allowed. There is a $15 per night per pet additional fee. Multiple dogs may be allowed.

Fairmont Banff Springs
405 Spray Avenue
Banff, AB
403-762-2211 (800-257-7544)
fairmont.com/banffsprings/
Reminiscent of a Scottish baronial castle, this resort high in the Rocky Mountains offers unparalleled views and recreational opportunities. Dogs are allowed for an additional pet fee of $25 per night per room. Dogs may only be left alone in the room is they will be quiet, well behaved, and a contact number is left with the front desk. Dogs must be leashed and

cleaned up after at all times. Multiple dogs may be allowed.

Beaverlodge Motor Inn
116 6A St
Beaverlodge, AB
780-354-2291
beaverlodgemotorinn.com
Dogs of all sizes are allowed. There is a $10 per night per pet additional pet fee.

Westbrook Motel
404 8th Avenue
Brooks, AB
403-362-2929
One dog of any size is allowed. There are no additional pet fees. Dogs may not be left unattended, must be leashed, and cleaned up after. There is an RV park also on site that allows dogs.

Calgary Westways Guest House
216 - 25 Ave SW
Calgary, AB
403-229-1758 (866-846-7038)
westways.ab.ca
There is an $8 per day additional pet fee. Pets are welcome in this B&B as long as they are well-behaved and do not become a nuisance to other guests.

Coast Plaza Hotel at Calgary
1316 - 33rd Street N.E.
Calgary, AB
403-248-8888 (800-663-1144)
All Coast Hotels have on hand extra pet amenities if you forget something. For dogs, they have extra doggy dishes, sleeping cushions, nylon chew toys and dog food. If your dog needs one of these items, just ask the front desk. There is a $15 per day additional pet fee.

Days Inn Calgary South
3828 Macleod Trail SE
Calgary, AB
403-243-5531 (800-329-7466)
Dogs of all sizes are allowed. There is a $10 per night pet fee per pet. Reservations are recommended due to limited rooms for pets. 2 dogs may be allowed.

Holiday Inn - Macleod Trail South
4206 Macleod Trail S.
Calgary, AB
403-287-2700 (877-270-6405)
Dogs of all sizes are allowed for an additional one time pet fee of $20 per room. Multiple dogs may be allowed.

Holiday Inn Express

2227 Banff Trail NW
Calgary, AB
403-289-6600 (877-270-6405)
Dogs of all sizes are allowed for no additional pet fee. Multiple dogs may be allowed.

Holiday Inn Express Hotel and Suites
12025 Lake Fraser Drive SE
(Anderson and Macleod Trail)
Calgary, AB
403-225-3000 (877-270-6405)
Dogs of all sizes are allowed for an additional one time fee of $20 per pet. Multiple dogs may be allowed.

Howard Johnson Express Inn
5307 Macleod Trail South
Calgary, AB
403-258-1064 (800-446-4656)
There is a $10 per day additional pet fee. Dogs are allowed at the hotel, cats are not allowed.

Quality Inn Airport
4804 Edmonton Trail NE
Calgary, AB
403-276-3391 (877-424-6423)
Dogs are allowed for no additional pet fee. There is a pet agreement to sign at check in. 2 dogs may be allowed.

Sheraton Suites Calgary Eau Claire
255 Barclay Parade SW
Calgary, AB
403-266-7200 (888-625-5144)
Located in the heart of downtown, this hotel is central to numerous shopping and recreation areas. Dogs of all sizes are allowed for no additional pet fee. Dogs may not be left alone in the rooms, and they must be under owner's control/care at all times. 2 dogs may be allowed.

Super 8 Calgary/Airport
3030 Barlow Trail NE
Calgary, AB
403-291-9888 (800-800-8000)
Dogs of all sizes are allowed. There is a $10 per night pet fee per pet. Smoking and non-smoking rooms are available for pet rooms. 2 dogs may be allowed.

Super 8 Calgary/Motel Village Area
1904 Crowchild Trail NW
Calgary, AB
403-289-9211 (800-800-8000)
Dogs of all sizes are allowed. There is a $10 per night pet fee per pet. Smoking and non-smoking rooms are available for pet rooms. 2 dogs may be allowed.

The Westin Calgary

320 4th Avenue SW
Calgary, AB
403-266-1611 (888-625-5144)
This hotel sits along the city's pedestrian walkway that gives access to numerous eateries, shopping, and recreational activities. Dogs are allowed for no additional fee, and a Heavenly dog bed can be ready for your pooch if requested at the time of reservations. There is a pet waiver to sign at check in. Dogs must be leashed, cleaned up after, and crated when left alone in the room. 2 dogs may be allowed.

Westways Bed and Breakfast
216 - 25 Avenue SW
Calgary, AB
403-229-1758 (866-846-7038)
westways.ab.ca/
Located within walking distance to the city, this Victorian accented heritage home offers a number of "little extras" such as jetted tubs, gas fireplaces, private restrooms, and if desired guests can be picked up in a Rolls Royce. Dogs of all sizes are allowed for an additional fee of $8 per night per pet. Dogs must be well mannered, leashed, and cleaned up after at all times. 2 dogs may be allowed.

Residence Inn by Marriott
91 Three Sisters Drive
Canmore, AB
403-678-3400
Dogs of all sizes are allowed. There is a $75 one time fee and a pet policy to sign at check in. Multiple dogs may be allowed.

Lazy J Motel
5225 1st Street/H 2
Claresholm, AB
403-625-4949
Dogs of all sizes are allowed for an additional fee of $5 per night per pet. Dogs must be well behaved, leashed, and cleaned up after. 2 dogs may be allowed.

Coast Edmonton Hotel
10155-105th Street
Edmonton, AB
780-423-4811 (800-663-1144)
All Coast Hotels have on hand extra pet amenities if you forget something. For dogs, they have extra doggy dishes, sleeping cushions, nylon chew toys and dog food. If your dog needs one of these items, just ask the front desk. There is an extra person charge for dogs which is $10 Cdn. per day.

Comfort Inn West

17610 100th Avenue
Edmonton, AB
780-484-4415 (877-424-6423)
Dogs are allowed for an additional fee of $10 per night per pet. 2 dogs may be allowed.

Crowne Plaza
10111 Bellamy Hill
Edmonton, AB
780-428-6611 (877-270-6405)
Quiet dogs of all sizes are allowed for an additional one time fee of $15 per pet. 2 dogs may be allowed.

Holiday Inn
4235 Gateway Blvd
Edmonton, AB
780-438-1222 (877-270-6405)
Quiet dogs of all sizes are allowed for an additional fee of $10 per night per pet. Multiple dogs may be allowed.

Holiday Inn Express
10010 104th Street
Edmonton, AB
780-423-2450 (877-270-6405)
Dogs of all sizes are allowed for an additional one time fee of $25 per pet. Multiple dogs may be allowed.

Super 8 Edmonton/South/Hotel
3610 Gateway Blvd NW
Edmonton, AB
780-433-8688 (800-800-8000)
Dogs of all sizes are allowed. There is a $15 per night pet fee per pet. Smoking and non-smoking rooms are available for pet rooms. 2 dogs may be allowed.

The Fairmont Hotel MacDonald
10065 100th Street
Edmonton, AB
780-424-5181 (800-257-7544)
fairmont.com/macdonald/
This elegant 1915 hotel features 199 opulent guestrooms and suites (18) with state-of-the-art amenities, stunning views of the Saskatchewan River Valley, exquisite dining opportunities, a lounge, 24 hour room service, an indoor pool and spa, and wonderful gardens. Dogs of all sizes are welcome for an additional pet fee of $25 per night per room (a portion of which is donated to the SPCA). Dogs must be well mannered, leashed, and cleaned up after at all times. They must be crated when left alone in the room. Dogs are not allowed on the patio or in the gardens behind the hotel. They suggest dogs be walked at the park in front of the hotel. 2 dogs may be allowed.

The Westin Edmonton
10135 100th Street
Edmonton, AB
780-426-3636 (888-625-5144)
This hotel, connected to the Shaw Conference Center, is also central to numerous eateries, shopping, and recreational activities. Dogs are allowed for no additional fee, and a Heavenly dog bed can be ready for your pooch if requested at the time of reservations. There is a pet waiver to sign at check in. They prefer that dogs are not left unattended in the room, but if it is necessary for a short time, they must be crated. Dogs must be under owner's control/care, and leashed at all times.

D.J. Motel
416 Main Street
Fort MacLeod, AB
403-553-4011
djmotel.com
Dogs up to around medium sized are allowed. There are no additional pet fees and there are smoking and non-smoking rooms for pet owners.

Sunset Motel
104 Highway 3 West
Fort MacLeod, AB
403-553-4448
telusplanet.net/public/sunsetmo/
Dogs of all sizes are allowed. There is no additional pet fee.

Super 8 Fort McMurray
321 Sakitawaw Trail
Fort McMurray, AB
780-799-8450 (800-800-8000)
Dogs up to 60 pounds are allowed. There is a $10 per night pet fee per pet. Smoking and non-smoking rooms are available for pet rooms.

Foxwood Inn & Suites
210 Highway Avenue
Fox Creek, AB
780-622-2280 (877-723-9797)
foxwoodinnandsuites.com/
This modern inn and suite with high speed Internet access allows dogs of all sizes. There are no additional pet fees and pets can stay in non-smoking or smoking rooms.

Best Western Grande Prairie Hotel and Suites
10745 117th Ave
Grande Prairie, AB
780-402-2378 (800-780-7234)
Dogs are allowed for an additional pet fee of $25 per night per room. Multiple dogs may be allowed.

Holiday Inn Hotel and Suites
9816 107 Street
Grande Prairie, AB
780-402-6886 (877-270-6405)
Dogs of all sizes are allowed for an additional pet fee of $25 per night per room. Dogs may be left alone in the room for short periods only. 2 dogs may be allowed.

Stanford Inn
11401 100th Ave
Grande Prairie, AB
780-539-5678
grandeprairiestanfordhotel.com
Dogs of all sizes are allowed. There is a $6.50 per night pet fee.

Old Entrance Cabins
P.O. Box 6054
Hinton, AB
780-865-4760
Well behaved dogs of all sizes are allowed. There is a $7 per night per pet additional fee. Dogs are not allowed on beds, but you may bring your own cover for a chair. Multiple dogs may be allowed.

The Fairmont Jasper Park Lodge
Old Lodge Road
Jasper, AB
780-852-3301 (800-257-7544)
fairmont.com/jasper/
This resort provides visitors with a true Grand Canadian lodge encounter in addition to its unparalleled views and many recreational opportunities. Dogs of all sizes are welcome for an additional $50 per night per pet. Dogs may only be left alone in the room if they will be quiet and well behaved, and they must be leashed and cleaned up after at all times. Multiple dogs may be allowed.

Comfort Inn
3226 Fairway Plaza Road S
Lethbridge, AB
403-320-8874 (877-424-6423)
Dogs are allowed for an additional fee of $10 per night per pet. 2 dogs may be allowed.

Days Inn Lethbridge
100 3rd Avenue South
Lethbridge, AB
403-327-6000 (800-329-7466)
daysinnlethbridge.com
Dogs of all sizes are allowed. There is a $10 per night per pet additional pet fee.

Econo Lodge
1124 Mayor Magrath Drive South
Lethbridge, AB

403-328-5591
Dogs of all sizes are allowed. There is a $7 per night additional pet fee.

Holiday Inn Express & Suites
120 Stafford Drive
Lethbridge, AB
403-394-9292 (877-270-6405)
Dogs of all sizes are allowed for an additional one time fee of $45 per pet. Multiple dogs may be allowed.

Lethbridge Lodge Hotel and Conf Centre
320 Scenic Drive
Lethbridge, AB
403-328-1123 (800-661-1232)
lethbridgelodge.com/
This large and luxurious hotel is located in downtown Lehtbridge. Dogs of all sizes are allowed. There is a $10 per night additional pet fee.

Holiday Inn Express Hotel & Suites Medicine Hat Transcanada Hwy 1
9 Strachan Bay Se
Medicine Hat, AB
403-504-5151 (877-270-6405)
Dogs of all sizes are allowed for no additional pet fee. Multiple dogs may be allowed.

Howard Johnson Hotel
3216 13th Ave. SE
Medicine Hat, AB
403-526-7487 (800-446-4656)

Motel 6 - Medicine Hat
20 Strachan Court Southeast
Medicine Hat, AB
403-527-1749 (800-466-8356)
One well-behaved family pet per room. Guest must notify front desk upon arrival. Guest is liable for any damages. In consideration of all guests, pets must never be left unattended in the guest rooms.

Super 8 Medicine Hat
1280 Trans-Canada Way
Medicine Hat, AB
403-528-8888 (800-800-8000)
Dogs of all sizes are allowed. There is a $5 per night pet fee per pet. Pet must be kept in kennel when left alone. Smoking and non-smoking rooms are available for pet rooms. 2 dogs may be allowed.

Holiday Inn Express
1102 4th Street
Nisku, AB
780-955-1000 (877-270-6405)
Dogs of all sizes are allowed for an additional fee of $25 per night per pet. 2 dogs may be allowed.

Best Western Red Deer Inn and Suites
6839 66th Street
Red Deer, AB
403-346-3555 (800-780-7234)
Dogs of all sizes are allowed. There is a $10 per pet per night fee.

Comfort Inn and Suites
6846 66th Street
Red Deer, AB
403-348-0025 (877-424-6423)
Dogs up to 50 pounds are allowed for an additional one time fee of $20 per pet. 2 dogs may be allowed.

Deers Park Inn
37557 Hwy. 2
Red Deer, AB
403-343-8444 (800-424-9454)
Dogs of all sizes are allowed. There is a $10 per night additional pet fee.

Motel 6 Red Deer #5706
900-5001 19th Street
Red Deer, AB
403-340-1749
Dogs of all sizes are allowed. There are no additional pet fees.

Sandman Hotel Red Deer
2818 Gaetz Ave
Red Deer, AB
403-343-7400 (800-SAN-DMAN)
Dogs of all sizes are allowed. There are no additional pet fees. Dogs are allowed in smoking or non-smoking rooms.

Super 8 Slave Lake
101 14th Ave SW
Slave Lake, AB
780-805-3100 (800-800-8000)
Dogs of all sizes are allowed. There is a $10 per night pet fee per pet. Or there is a $25 one time per pet fee per visit. Smoking and non-smoking rooms are available for pet rooms. 2 dogs may be allowed.

High Rigg Retreat
#3-51119 RR 255
Spruce Grove, AB
780-470-0462
highriggretreat.com/
Although providing comfort in a beautiful country setting, this inn is only a mile from the city limits and a wide variety of activities. (They usually close for a few months during the hardest part of the winter.) Dogs are allowed for no additional fee, and they need to be declared at the time of booking. Dogs may not be left unattended in the room, and they must be under owner's control/care and cleaned up after at all times.

There is a full kennel/run and 5 acres of fenced property for pets to have some fun times too. 2 dogs may be allowed.

Super 8 Stettler
5720-44 Ave
Stettler, AB
403-742-3391 (800-800-8000)
Dogs of all sizes are allowed. There is a $10 per night pet fee per pet. Smoking and non-smoking rooms are available for pet rooms. 2 dogs may be allowed.

Best Western Strathmore Inn
550 Hwy 1
Strathmore, AB
403-934-5777 (800-780-7234)
Dogs are allowed for an additional one time pet fee of $10 per room. Multiple dogs may be allowed.

Hi Valley Motor Inn
4001 Hwy Street
Valleyview, AB
780-524-3324
Dogs of all sizes are allowed. There is a $5 per night additional pet fee. Dogs are allowed in smoking or non-smoking rooms.

Horizon Motel & Steakhouse
5204 Highway Street
Valleyview, AB
780-524-3904

Alaska Highway Motel
3511 Highway St
Whitecourt, AB
780-778-4156
Dogs of all sizes are allowed. There are no additional pet fees.

Super 8 Whitecourt
4121 Kepler St
Whitecourt, AB
780-778-8908 (800-800-8000)
Dogs of all sizes are allowed. There is a $20 one time per pet fee per visit. Smoking and non-smoking rooms are available for pet rooms. 2 dogs may be allowed.

British Columbia Listings

Best Western Bakerview Inn
1821 Sumas Way
Abbotsford, BC
604-859-1341 (800-780-7234)
Dogs are allowed for no additional pet fee with a credit card on file.

Multiple dogs may be allowed.

Coast Abbotsford Hotel & Suites
2020 Sumas Way
Abbotsford, BC
604-853-1880 (800-716-6199)
Dogs of all sizes are allowed. There is a $10 per night additional pet fee for small dogs, and a $25 per night pet fee for large dogs. Dogs must be crated and a phone number left at the desk if dogs are left alone in the room. 2 dogs may be allowed.

Comfort Inn
2073 Clearbrook Road
Abbotsford, BC
604-859-6211 (877-424-6423)
Dogs are allowed for an additional fee of $10 per night per pet. Multiple dogs may be allowed.

Super 8
1881 Sumas Way
Abbotsford, BC
604-853-1141 (800-800-8000)
super8.com
Dogs of all sizes are allowed. There is a $10 per night additional pet fee. Multiple dogs may be allowed.

Best Value Inn Desert Motel
1069 South Trans Canada Hwy
Cache Creek, BC
250-457-6226
This motel on the Trans-Canada Highway and the main western route to Alaska has three pet rooms available. Dogs of all sizes are allowed. There are no additional pet fees.

Robbie's Motel
1067 Todd
Cache Creek, BC
250-457-6221
Dogs of all sizes are allowed. There is a $10 additional pet fee for each pet per night.

Tumbleweed Motel
1221 Quartz
Cache Creek, BC
250-457-6522
Dogs of all sizes are allowed. There are no additional pet fees.

Best Western Austrian Chalet
462 S Island Hwy
Campbell River, BC
250-923-4231 (800-780-7234)
Dogs are allowed for an additional fee of $5 per night per pet. Multiple dogs may be allowed.

Coast Discovery Inn and Marina
975 Shoppers Row

Campbell River, BC
250-287-7155 (800-663-1144)
All Coast Hotels have on hand extra pet amenities if you forget something. For dogs, they have extra doggy dishes, sleeping cushions, nylon chew toys and dog food. If your dog needs one of these items, just ask the front desk. There is a $10 per day additional pet fee.

Quality Inn
1935 Columbia Avenue
Castlegar, BC
250-365-2177 (877-424-6423)
Dogs are allowed for an additional fee of $10 per night per pet. Multiple dogs may be allowed.

Super 8 Castlegar
651-18th Street
Castlegar, BC
250-365-2700 (800-800-8000)
Dogs of all sizes are allowed. There is a $10 per night pet fee per pet. Smoking and non-smoking rooms are available for pet rooms. 2 dogs may be allowed.

Chetwynd Court Motel
5104 N Access
Chetwynd, BC
250-788-2271
Dogs of all sizes are allowed. There are no additional pet fees.

Pine Cone Motor Inn
5224 53rd Ave
Chetwynd, BC
250-788-3311
Dogs of all sizes are allowed. There is $17 per night additional pet fee.

Stagecoach Inn
5413 S Access
Chetwynd, BC
250-788-9666
Dogs of all sizes are allowed. There is a $20 pet deposit. $10 of this deposit is refundable.

Best Western Rainbow Country Inn
43971 Industrail Way
Chilliwack, BC
604-795-3828 (800-780-7234)
Dogs are allowed for an additional fee of $10 per night per pet. Multiple dogs may be allowed.

Comfort Inn
45405 Luckabuck Way
Chilliwack, BC
604-858-0636 (877-424-6423)
Dogs are allowed for no additional pet fee. Multiple dogs may be allowed.

Ranch Park Rentals
Off H 1; locations with reservations
Chilliwack, BC
480-600-5114
Well behaved dogs of all sizes are allowed, and they must be friendly to other dogs as well. There is a $10 per night per pet fee and a pet policy to sign at check in. A credit card must also be on file. They don't want dogs on the bed unless under 10 pounds, and suggest to keep small dogs in at night. There is lots of room for the dogs to run here. Multiple dogs may be allowed.

Travelodge Chilliwack
45466 Yale Road
Chilliwack, BC
604-792-4240
travelodgechilliwack.com
Dogs of all sizes are allowed. There is a $10 per night per pet additional pet fee. Pets must be crated if left alone and they may only be left alone for a short period. 2 dogs may be allowed.

Best Western Coquitlam Inn Conv Centre
319 North Rd
Coquitlam, BC
604-931-9011 (800-780-7234)
Dogs are allowed for an additional fee of $20 per night per pet. 2 dogs may be allowed.

Coast Westerly Hotel
1590 Cliffe Avenue
Courtenay, BC
250-338-7741 (800-663-1144)
All Coast Hotels have on hand extra pet amenities if you forget something. For dogs, they have extra doggy dishes, sleeping cushions, nylon chew toys and dog food. If your dog needs one of these items, just ask the front desk. There is a $10 per day additional pet fee.

Airport Inn
800 120 Avenue
Dawson Creek, BC
250-782-9404
airportinn.ca
Well-behaved dogs of all sizes are allowed. There is a $10 per night additional pet fee.

Inn On The Creek
10600 8 Street
Dawson Creek, BC
250-782-8136
innonthecreek.bc.ca
Dogs of all sizes are allowed. There is a $50 refundable pet deposit. There is a $22.80 fee per dog.

Lodge Motor Inn
1317 Alaska Avenue
Dawson Creek, BC
250-782-4837
lodgemotorinn.com
Dogs of all sizes are allowed. There is a $6 per day additional pet fee. There are a number of pet rooms and all of the pet rooms are upstairs.

Ramada Limited Dawson Creek
1748 Alaska Avenue
Dawson Creek, BC
250-782-8595
Dogs of all sizes are allowed. There is a $10 per day additional pet fee.

Super 8 Dawson Creek
1440 Alaska Ave
Dawson Creek, BC
250-782-8899 (800-800-8000)
Dogs of all sizes are allowed. There is a $10 per night pet fee per pet. Reservations are recommended due to limited rooms for pets. Smoking and non-smoking rooms are available for pet rooms. 2 dogs may be allowed.

Best Western Cowichan Valley Inn
6474 Trans Canada Hwy
Duncan, BC
250-748-2722 (800-780-7234)
Dogs are allowed for an additional one time fee of $20 per pet. 2 dogs may be allowed.

Howard Johnson Inn
1510 George St.
Enderby, BC
250-838-6825 (800-446-4656)
Dogs of all sizes are welcome. There is a $5 per day pet fee.

Super 8 Fernie
2021 Hwy 3
Fernie, BC
250-423-6788 (800-800-8000)
Dogs of all sizes are allowed. There is a $10 per night pet fee per pet. Reservations are recommended due to limited rooms for pets. Smoking and non-smoking rooms are available for pet rooms. 2 dogs may be allowed.

Blue Bell Inn
4720 50 Ave
Fort Nelson, BC
250-774-6961
bluebellinn.ca
There is one non-smoking pet room and one dog is allowed. There are no additional pet fees.

Pioneer Motel
5207-50 Ave S
Fort Nelson, BC
250-774-5800
karo-ent.com/pioneer.htm
Dogs of all sizes are allowed. There is a $5 per night pet fee for large dogs. There is also a pet-friendly RV Park on the premises. 2 dogs may be allowed.

Ramada Limited
5035 - 51 Avenue West
Fort Nelson, BC
250-774-2844
Dogs of all sizes are allowed. There is a $10 per night additional pet fee. 2 dogs may be allowed.

Super 8 Fort Nelson
4003 50th Ave South
Fort Nelson, BC
250-233-5025 (800-800-8000)
Dogs of all sizes are allowed. There is a $25 per night pet fee per pet. Smoking and non-smoking rooms are available for pet rooms. 2 dogs may be allowed.

Lakeview Inn and Suites
10103 98 Avenue
Fort St John, BC
250-787-0779
lakeviewhotels.com
Dogs of all sizes are allowed. Ther e is a $10 per night per pet additional pet fee. 2 dogs may be allowed.

Quality Inn Northern Grand
9830 100th Avenue
Fort St John, BC
250-787-0521 (877-424-6423)
Small dogs are allowed for an additional fee of $15 per night per pet; large dogs are $20 per night per pet. 2 dogs may be allowed.

The Shepherd's Inn
Mile 72 Alaska Highway
Fort St John, BC
250-827-3676
karo-ent.com/shepherds.htm
One dog of any size is allowed. There is only one pet room.

Harrison Beach Hotel
160 Esplanade Avenue
Harrison Hot Springs, BC
604-796-1111 (866-338-8111)
harrisonbeachhotel.com
Dogs of all sizes are allowed. There is a $15 per pet per night additional pet fee. 2 dogs may be allowed.

Harrison Hot Springs Resort
100 Esplanade Avenue
Harrison Hot Springs, BC

604-796-2244 (866-638-5075)
harrisonresort.com
This resort and spa is located against the mountains at the south end of Harrison Lake. Dogs of all sizes are allowed. There is a $100 one time pet fee. Dogs must be crated if you are out of the room. 2 dogs may be allowed.

Inn Towne Motel
510 Trans-Canada Hwy
Hope, BC
604-869-7276
2 dogs may be allowed.

Maple Leaf Motor Inn
377 Old Hope Princeton Way
Hope, BC
604-869-7107
Dogs of all sizes are allowed. There is a $7 per night per pet additional pet fee. 2 dogs may be allowed.

Quality Inn
350 Old Hope Princeton Way
Hope, BC
604-869-9951 (877-424-6423)
Dogs are allowed for no additional pet fee. Dogs may not be left alone in the room. 2 dogs may be allowed.

Windsor Motel
778 3rd Avenue
Hope, BC
604-869-9944 (888-588-9944)
bcwindsormotel.com
Dogs of all sizes are allowed. There is a $5 per pet per night additional pet fee. 2 dogs may be allowed.

Houston Motor Inn
2940 H 16W
Houston, BC
250-845-7112 (800-994-8333)
This 56 room inn has a restaurant and coffee shop, and a full hook-up RV park on site that allows dogs for no additional fee. Dogs are allowed at the inn for an additional fee of $10 per night per pet. Dogs are not allowed on the bedding; they request owner's bring their pet's bedding. Dogs must be leashed and cleaned up after. 2 dogs may be allowed.

Best Western Invermere Inn
1310 7th Ave
Invermere, BC
250-342-9246 (800-780-7234)
Dogs are allowed for an additional fee of $15 (plus tax) per night per pet. Dogs may not be left alone in the room at any time. Multiple dogs may be allowed.

Accent Inn Kamloops

1325 Columbia Street W
Kamloops, BC
250-374-8877 (800-663-0298)
This inn offers a seasonal outdoor heated pool, whirlpool, and a sauna. Dogs of all sizes are welcome for an additional pet fee of $15 per night per room. Dogs may not be left alone in the room, and they must be leashed and cleaned up after at all times. 2 dogs may be allowed.

Coast Canadian Inn
339 St. Paul Street
Kamloops, BC
250-372-5201 (800-663-1144)
All Coast Hotels have on hand extra pet amenities if you forget something. For dogs, they have extra doggy dishes, sleeping cushions, nylon chew toys and dog food. If your dog needs one of these items, just ask the front desk. There is a $10 per day additional pet fee.

Days Inn Kamloops
1285 W Trans Can Hwy
Kamloops, BC
250-374-5911 (800-329-7466)
Dogs of all sizes are allowed. There is a $20 per night pet fee per pet. Only non-smoking rooms are used for pets. 2 dogs may be allowed.

Howard Johnson Inn
610 West Columbia Street
Kamloops, BC
250-374-1515 (800-446-4656)
Dogs of all sizes are welcome. There are no additional pet fees.

Super 8 Kamloops
1521 Hugh Allen Dr
Kamloops, BC
250-374-8688 (800-800-8000)
Dogs of all sizes are allowed. There is a $6 per night pet fee per pet. Smoking and non-smoking rooms are available for pet rooms. 2 dogs may be allowed.

Accent Inn Kelowna
1140 Harvey Avenue
Kelowna, BC
250-862-8888 (800-663-0298)
This inn offers a seasonal outdoor heated pool, whirlpool, and a sauna. Dogs of all sizes are welcome for an additional pet fee of $15 per night per room. Dogs must be leashed and cleaned up after at all times, and crated when left alone in the room. Multiple dogs may be allowed.

Coast Capri Hotel

1171 Harvey Avenue
Kelowna, BC
250-860-6060 (800-663-1144)
All Coast Hotels have on hand extra pet amenities if you forget something. For dogs, they have extra doggy dishes, sleeping cushions, nylon chew toys and dog food. If your dog needs one of these items, just ask the front desk. There is an extra person charge for dogs which is $20 -$25 Cdn. per day.

Comfort Inn Westside
1655 Westgate Road
Kelowna, BC
250-769-2355 (877-424-6423)
Dogs are allowed for an additional fee of $10 per night per pet. Multiple dogs may be allowed.

Residence Inn by Marriott
500 Stemwinder Drive
Kimberley, BC
250-427-5175
Up to two large dogs, or up to three small dogs per room are allowed. There is a $75 one time per pet fee and a pet policy to sign at check in. .

Holiday Inn Express Hotel and Suites
8750 204th St
Langley, BC
604-882-2000 (877-270-6405)
Dogs of all sizes are allowed for an additional pet fee of $10 per night per room. 2 dogs may be allowed.

Liard Hot Springs Lodge
Mile 497 Alaska H
Liard River, BC
250-776-7349
In addition to offering a full service restaurant, fuel station, gift shop, and campsites, this lodge is also located across from the Liard Hot Springs. Dogs are allowed for an additional fee of $50 per pet per stay. Dogs must be leashed and cleaned up after at all times. 2 dogs may be allowed.

The Counting Sheep Inn
8715 Eagle Road, R.R. #3
Mission, BC
604-820-5148
countingsheep.com/
They are 60 minutes from Vancouver and 45 minutes from Bellingham, Washington. This is an elegant Bed and Breakfast in the country and dogs are allowed in one of their rooms, the Carriage Suite. Check out their great season packages.

Northern Rockies Lodge
Mile 462 Alaska Highway

Muncho Lake, BC
250-776-3481 (800-663-5269)
northernrockieslodge.com
Dogs are allowed in the rooms and
the cabins. There is a $50 refundable
pet deposit and a $10 per pet per
night additional pet fee. 2 dogs may
be allowed.

Best Western Dorchester Hotel
70 Church St
Nanaimo, BC
250-754-6835 (800-780-7234)
Dogs are allowed for an additional
fee of $15 per night per pet. They are
not allowed in the suites. 2 dogs may
be allowed.

Best Western Northgate Inn
6450 Metral Dr
Nanaimo, BC
250-390-2222 (800-780-7234)
Dogs are allowed for an additional
pet fee per room of $20 for each 1 to
5 days. 2 dogs may be allowed.

Coast Bastion Inn
11 Bastion Street
Nanaimo, BC
250-753-6601 (800-663-1144)
All Coast Hotels have on hand extra
pet amenities if you forget
something. For dogs, they have extra
doggy dishes, sleeping cushions,
nylon chew toys and dog food. If your
dog needs one of these items, just
ask the front desk. There is a $10
per day additional pet fee.

Best Western Baker Street Inn and
Conv Centre
153 Baker St
Nelson, BC
250-352-3525 (800-780-7234)
Dogs are allowed for an additional
fee of $10 per night per pet. 2 dogs
may be allowed.

Holiday Inn Hotel and Suites
700 Old Lillooet Rd
North Vancouver, BC
604-985-3111 (877-270-6405)
One dog of any size is allowed for an
additional pet fee of $25 per night.

Quality Resort Bayside
240 Dogwood Street
Parksville, BC
250-248-8333
Dogs are allowed for an additional
fee of $15 per night per pet. Multiple
dogs may be allowed.

Buckinghorse River Lodge
Mile 175 Alaska Highway
Pinkmountain, BC
250-772-4999

buckinghorseriverlodge.com
Dogs of all sizes are allowed. There
is a $10 per night per pet additional
pet fee. Dogs are allowed in
smoking rooms only. 2 dogs may be
allowed.

Coast Hospitality Inn
3835 Redford Street
Port Alberni, BC
250-723-8111 (800-663-1144)
All Coast Hotels have on hand extra
pet amenities if you forget
something. For dogs, they have
extra doggy dishes, sleeping
cushions, nylon chew toys and dog
food. If your dog needs one of these
items, just ask the front desk. There
are no additional pet fees.

Powell River Town Centre Hotel
4660 Joyce Avenue
Powell River, BC
604-485-3000
There is a $10 per day per pet fee.

Best Western City Centre
910 Victoria Street
Prince George, BC
250-563-1267 (800-780-7234)
Dogs are allowed for an additional
pet fee of $25 per night per room. 2
dogs may be allowed.

Bon Voyage Motor Inn
4222 Highway 16 West
Prince George, BC
250-964-2333
Dogs of all sizes are allowed. There
is a $15 per night additional pet fee.

Coast Inn of the North
770 Brunswick Street
Prince George, BC
250-563-0121 (800-663-1144)
All Coast Hotels have on hand extra
pet amenities if you forget
something. For dogs, they have
extra doggy dishes, sleeping
cushions, nylon chew toys and dog
food. If your dog needs one of these
items, just ask the front desk. There
is a $10 per day additional pet fee.

Sandman Inn and Suites
1650 Central Street
Prince George, BC
250-563-8131
sandmanhotels.com
Dogs of all sizes are allowed. There
is a $10 per night additional pet fee.

Anchor Inn
1600 Park Avenue/H 16
Prince Rupert, BC
250-627-8522 (888-627-8522)
anchor-inn.com/

In addition to having a good central
location to all modes of travel, there
is also a trailed park behind the inn
that leads to the city and its many
attractions. Dogs off all sizes are
allowed for an additional fee of $10
per night per room. Dogs must be
leashed and cleaned up after. 2 dogs
may be allowed.

Coast Prince Rupert Hotel
118 6th Street
Prince Rupert, BC
250-624-6711 (800-663-1144)
All Coast Hotels have on hand extra
pet amenities if you forget
something. For dogs, they have extra
doggy dishes, sleeping cushions,
nylon chew toys and dog food. If your
dog needs one of these items, just
ask the front desk. There are no
additional pet fees.

Crest Hotel
222 1st Avenue West
Prince Rupert, BC
250-624-6771 (800-663-8150)
cresthotel.bc.ca/
Amenities for the business or leisure
traveler, this hotel offers great views,
a convenient location to other sites of
interest, a lounge, and a restaurant
that specializes in BC cuisine and
fresh seafood. Dogs are allowed for
an additional fee of $10 per night per
pet on the 1st floor only. Dogs must
be quiet, leashed, and cleaned up
after. 2 dogs may be allowed.

Pacific Inn
909 3rd Avenue W
Prince Rupert, BC
250-627-1711 (888-663-1999)
pacificinn.bc.ca/
Dogs of all sizes are allowed. There
is an additional fee of $10 per night
per pet for dogs up to 25 pounds,
and an additional fee of $20 per night
per pet for dogs over 25 pounds.
Dogs must be quiet, leashed, and
cleaned up after. 2 dogs may be
allowed.

Best Western Princeton
169 Hwy 3
Princeton, BC
250-295-3537 (800-780-7234)
Dogs are allowed for an additional
fee of $15 per night per pet. Multiple
dogs may be allowed.

Ramada Ltd
383 St Laurent Avenue
Quesnel, BC
250-992-5575
ramada.ca
Dogs of all sizes are allowed. There
is a $10 per night per pet additional

pet fee. 2 dogs may be allowed.

Super 8 Quesnel
2010 Valhalla Rd
Quesnel, BC
250-747-1111 (800-800-8000)
Dogs up to 60 pounds are allowed.
There is a $5 per night pet fee per
pet. Reservations are recommended
due to limited rooms for pets.
Smoking and non-smoking rooms
are available for pet rooms. 2 dogs
may be allowed.

Best Western Wayside Inn
190 Laforme Blvd
Revelstoke, BC
250-837-6161 (800-780-7234)
Dogs are allowed for no additional
pet fee. Dogs may not be left alone
in the room at any time. Multiple
dogs may be allowed.

The Coast Hillcrest Resort Hotel
2100 Oak Drive
Revelstoke, BC
250-837-3322
Dogs of all sizes are allowed. There
is a $15 per night per room additional
pet fee. Pet rooms are located on the
1st floor. Multiple dogs may be
allowed.

Accent Inn Vancouver-Airport
10551 St Edwards Drive
Richmond, BC
604-273-3311 (800-663-0298)
Located just minutes from the
Vancouver Airport and downtown,
this hotel is also home to an IHOP
restaurant. Dogs of all sizes are
welcome for an additional pet fee of
$15 per night per room, and they
must be pre-registered. Dogs must
be crated when left alone in the
room, and they must be leashed and
cleaned up after at all times. Multiple
dogs may be allowed.

Best Western Richmond Hotel and
Conv Centre
7551 Westminister Hwy
Richmond, BC
604-273-7878 (800-780-7234)
Dogs are allowed for an additional
fee of $15 per night per pet. 2 dogs
may be allowed.

Fairmont Vancouver Airport
3111 Gran McConachie Way
Richmond, BC
604-207-5200 (800-257-7544)
fairmont.com/vancouverairport/
This sound-proofed hotel offers a
backdrop of majestic mountains and
ocean views, and is located just
steps up from the airport terminals.

Dogs of all sizes are allowed for an
additional pet fee of $25 per night
per pet. Dogs must be well
mannered, leashed and cleaned up
after. Multiple dogs may be allowed.

Hampton Inn
5911 Minoru Blvd
Richmond, BC
604-273-6336
Dogs of all sizes are allowed. There
is a $25 per night per pet fee and a
pet policy to sign at check in. 2
dogs may be allowed.

Holiday Inn
10720 Combie Rd
Richmond, BC
604-821-1818 (877-270-6405)
Dogs of all sizes are allowed for an
additional fee of $15 per night per
pet. 2 dogs may be allowed.

La Quinta Inn Vancouver Airport
8640 Alexandra Road
Richmond, BC
604-276-2711 (800-531-5900)
Dogs of all sizes are allowed. There
are no additional pet fees. Dogs
must be leashed, cleaned up after,
and crated or removed for
housekeeping. The pet floor is on
the 5th floor, which is a smoking
floor; however, there are non-
smoking rooms on that floor.
Multiple dogs may be allowed.

River Rock Casino Resort
8811 River Road
Richmond, BC
604-247-8900 (866-748-3718)
riverrock.com
Featuring cascading waterfalls,
entertainment, table games and slot
machines, this Casino Resort is
located just outside Vancouver.
They allow up to two 90 pound dogs
in each suite. There is a $25 per
day per dog pet fee, up to a
maximum of $75 per stay. Dogs
must be crated or leashed if left
alone in the room.

Quality Inn Waddling Dog
2476 Mt Newton Cross Roads
Saanichton, BC
250-652-1146 (877-424-6423)
Dogs are allowed for an additional
fee of $10 per night per pet. Multiple
dogs may be allowed.

Super 8 Saanichton/Victoria Airport
2477 Mt Newton Cross Rd
Saanichton, BC
250-652-6888 (800-800-8000)
Dogs of all sizes are allowed. There
is a $10 per night pet fee per pet.

Smoking and non-smoking rooms
are available for pet rooms. 2 dogs
may be allowed.

Wintercott Country House
1950 Nicholas Rd.
Saanichton, BC
250-652-2117
wintercott.com
This bed and breakfast inn is located
about 15 minutes from Victoria. Well-
behaved dogs of all sizes are
welcome. There is no pet fee.

Best Western Villager West Motor
Inn
61-10th Street SW
Salmon Arm, BC
250-832-9793 (800-780-7234)
Dogs are allowed for an additional
fee of $15 per night per pet. Dogs
must be declared at the time of
registration. Multiple dogs may be
allowed.

Holiday Inn Express Hotel and Suites
1090-22nd St NE
Salmon Arm, BC
250-832-7711 (877-270-6405)
Dogs of all sizes are allowed for an
additional fee of $10 per night per
pet. Dogs must be declared at the
time of reservations, and dogs may
not be left alone in the room. 2 dogs
may be allowed.

Super 8 Salmon Arm
2901 10th Ave NE
Salmon Arm, BC
250-832-8812 (800-800-8000)
Dogs of all sizes are allowed. There
is a $10 per night per additional
pet fee. The entire hotel is non-
smoking. 2 dogs may be allowed.

Sundog
1409 Rauma Avenue
Sicamous, BC
250-833-9005
There are 2 pet friendly rooms and
they each have a fenced back yard.
Dogs of all sizes are allowed,
however there can only be 3 dogs to
a room if they are under 50 pounds,
and 2 dogs to a room if they are over
50 pounds. There is a $15 per night
per pet additional fee for the 1st
three nights then the rate for the pets
could be lower. $5 of the $15 is
donated to the local SPCA. The dogs
must be spayed or neutered and of
had a flea treatment within the past 2
months. Dogs are not allowed in the
Bed and Breakfast or the common
areas.

Best Western Emerald Isle Motor Inn

2306 Beacon Ave
Sidney, BC
250-656-4441 (800-780-7234)
Dogs are allowed for an additional fee of $15 per night per pet. Multiple dogs may be allowed.

Cedarwood Motel
9522 Lochside Dr
Sidney, BC
250-656-5551
cedrwood.com/
There is a $15 per day additional pet fee.

Victoria Airport Travelodge
2280 Beacon Ave
Sidney, BC
250-656-1176
There is a $10 per day additional pet fee.

Gordon's Beach Farm Stay B&B
4530 Otter Point Road
Sooke, BC
250-642-5291
gordonsbeachbandb.com
A well-behaved dog is allowed in one of their suite rooms that has marble flooring. There is a $10 one time per stay pet fee.

Ocean Wilderness Country Inn
109 W Coast Rd
Sooke, BC
250-646-2116
bestinns.net/canada/bc/ow.html
There is a $15 pet fee per visit.

Sooke Harbour House
1528 Whiffen Spit Rd
Sooke, BC
250-642-3421
There is a $30 per night pet fee.

King Edward Hotel and Motel
5th Avenue/P. O. Box 86
Stewwart, BC
250-636-2244 (800-663-3126)
kingedwardhotel.com/
This rest stop has an eatery, a pub, motel, a hotel, and they are only a short distance from the famed Grizzly Bear viewing station for spawning salmon at Fish Creek. Dogs of all sizes are allowed in the motel for no additional fee with a credit card on file; they are not allowed in the hotel. Dogs must be well behaved, leashed, and cleaned up after. 2 dogs may be allowed.

Super 8 Surrey/Sky Train Station Area
13893 Fraser Hwy
Surrey, BC
604-581-7122 (800-800-8000)

Dogs of all sizes are allowed. There is a $10 per night pet fee per pet. Smoking and non-smoking rooms are available for pet rooms. 2 dogs may be allowed.

Best Western Terrace Inn
4553 Greig Ave
Terrace, BC
250-635-0083 (800-780-7234)
Dogs are allowed for an additional fee of $10 per night per pet. 2 dogs may be allowed.

Toad River Lodge
Mile 422 Alaska H
Toad River, BC
250-232-5401
karo-ent.com/toadriv.htm
A lot can be accomplished at this stop with a motel and RV park that accepts pets, a restaurant and bakery, showers, laundry facilities, a dump station, fuels, and a 6,000+ hat collection adorning the lodge. Dogs are allowed in the motel for $5 per night per pet, and there is no additional fee in the camp area. Dogs are also allowed at the outer tables of the restaurant?weather permitting. Dogs must be well mannered, under owner's control, leashed, and cleaned up after at all times. Multiple dogs may be allowed.

Best Western Sands Hotel
1755 Davie Street
Vancouver, BC
604-682-1831 (800-780-7234)
rpbhotels.com
The Sands is situated in Downtown Vancouver near Stanley Park. The hotel offers 2 lounges, restaurant, room service, fitness room and a sauna. The pet fee is $10.00 per day. Pets receive a welcome doggy bag upon arrival.

Coast Plaza Suite Hotel at Stanley Park
1763 Comox Street
Vancouver, BC
604-688-7711 (800-663-1144)
All Coast Hotels have on hand extra pet amenities if you forget something. For dogs, they have extra doggy dishes, sleeping cushions, nylon chew toys and dog food. If your dog needs one of these items, just ask the front desk. There is a $20 per day additional pet fee.

Fairmont Hotel Vancouver
900 W Georgia Street
Vancouver, BC
604-684-3131 (800-257-7544)
fairmont.com/hotelvancouver/

This historic hotel sits amid the city?s cultural, entertainment, and business districts, and offers outstanding mountain and ocean views. Dogs are allowed for an additional fee of $25 per night per pet. Dogs may not be left alone in the room, and they must be leashed and cleaned up after. Multiple dogs may be allowed.

Fairmont Vancouver Waterfront Hotel
900 Canada Place Way
Vancouver, BC
604-691-1991 (800-257-7544)
fairmont.com/waterfront/
This hotel boosts a year round 50 foot outdoor heated pool, a convenient enclosed walkway to the Convention/Exhibition Center and the cruise ship terminal, and they are within walking distance to Stanley Park with it?s mile long seawall. Dogs are allowed for an additional pet fee of $25 per night per room. Dogs may not be left alone in the room at any time, and they must be leashed and cleaned up after. Multiple dogs may be allowed.

Four Seasons Hotel Vancouver
791 West Georgia St.
Vancouver, BC
604-689-9333
Dogs of all sizes are allowed. There are no additional pet fees. Dogs are not allowed to be left alone in the room.

Granville Island Hotel
1253 Johnston St
Vancouver, BC
604-683-7373
granvilleislandhotel.com/
This hotel has a restaurant on the premises called the Dockside Restaurant. You can dine there with your pet at the outdoor tables that are closest to the grass. The hotel charges a $25 per night pet fee per room.

Hampton Inn
6083 McKay Avenue
Vancouver, BC
604-438-1200
Dogs of all sizes are allowed. There is a $75 one time cleaning fee and a pet policy to sign at check in.

Holiday Inn
711 W Broadway at Heather
Vancouver, BC
604-879-0511 (877-270-6405)
Dogs of all sizes are allowed for an additional pet fee of $15 per night per room. 2 dogs may be allowed.

Holiday Inn Express
2889 East Hastings St
Vancouver, BC
604-254-1000 (877-270-6405)
Dogs of all sizes are allowed for an additional one time pet fee of $20 per room. 2 dogs may be allowed.

Hyatt Regency Vancouver
655 Burrard Street
Vancouver, BC
604-683-1234
The Hyatt Regency Vancouver offers stunning city views from many of the spacious rooms. The hotel offers a heated pool, health club and a central location to many of Vancouver's activities. Dogs of all sizes are welcome. There is a $50 one time additional pet fee.

Metropolitan Hotel
645 Howe Street
Vancouver, BC
604-687-1122
metropolitan.com/vanc/index.htm
There are no additional pet fees.

Pacific Palisades Hotel
1277 Robson Street
Vancouver, BC
604-688-0461
pacificpalisadeshotel.com/
Well-behaved dogs of all sizes are welcome at this hotel which offers both rooms and suites. Amenities include workout rooms, an indoor swimming pool, and 24 hour room service. There is a $25 one time per stay pet fee and $5 of this is sent to the SPCA.

Quality Hotel Downtown
1335 Howe Street
Vancouver, BC
604-682-0229
Dogs are allowed for an additional fee of $15 per night per pet. Multiple dogs may be allowed.

Residence Inn by Marriott
1234 Hornby Street
Vancouver, BC
604-688-1234
Dogs of all sizes are allowed. There is a $75 one time fee and a pet policy to sign at check in. Multiple dogs may be allowed.

Sheraton Vancouver Wall Centre
1088 Burrard Street
Vancouver, BC
604-331-1000 (888-625-5144)
This hotel offers numerous amenities for the business or leisure traveler, and there is a Sea Wall Walking Tour close by for some great scenery of

the Pacific Ocean. One dog up to 90 pounds is allowed for an additional one time pet fee of $60, and there is a pet waiver to sign at check in. Dogs must be under owner's control/care, leashed, crated when alone in the room, and removed or crated for housekeeping.

Sylvia Hotel
1154 Gilford St
Vancouver, BC
604-681-9321
sylviahotel.com/
There are no additional pet fees.

Vancouver Marriott Pinnacle Hotel
1128 West Hastings Street
Vancouver, BC
604-684-1128 (800-207-4150)
This four star hotel is located in downtown Vancouver. The pet-friendly hotel has convention facilities and an excellent restaurant.

Best Western Vernon Lodge and Conf Cntr
3914 32nd St
Vernon, BC
250-545-3385 (800-780-7234)
Dogs are allowed for an additional pet fee of $15 per night per room. 2 dogs may be allowed.

Holiday Inn Express Hotel & Suites Vernon
4716 34th Street
Vernon, BC
250-550-7777 (877-270-6405)
One dog of any size is allowed for an additional one time pet fee of $20.

Accent Inn Victoria
3233 Maple Street
Victoria, BC
250-475-7500 (800-663-0298)
In addition to many amenities and 118 rooms, there is also a family-style restaurant and a 40 person theater style meeting room at this hotel. Dogs of all sizes are allowed for an additional fee of $15 per night per pet. Dogs may not be left alone in the room, and they must be leashed and cleaned up after at all times. 2 dogs may be allowed.

Best Western Carlton Plaza Hotel
642 Johnson St
Victoria, BC
250-388-5513 (800-780-7234)
Dogs are allowed for an additional fee of $10 per night per pet. 2 dogs may be allowed.

Coast Harbourside Hotel and Marina
146 Kingston Street
Victoria, BC
250-360-1211 (800-663-1144)
coasthotels.com/hotels/vic.htm
All Coast Hotels have on hand extra pet amenities if you forget something. For dogs, they have extra doggy dishes, sleeping cushions, nylon chew toys and dog food. If your dog needs one of these items, just ask the front desk. There is a $20 per day additional pet fee.

Executive House Hotel
777 Douglas Street
Victoria, BC
250-388-5111 (800-663-7001)
executivehouse.com
Enjoy European ambience in a downtown Victoria hotel. The hotel is directly across from the Victoria Conference Centre, one block from the magnificent Inner Harbour, Royal BC Museum, National Geographic Theatre, shopping and attractions. Pets are welcome for $15 per night extra.

Harbour Towers Hotel
345 Quebec St
Victoria, BC
250-385-2405
harbourtowers.com/
There is a $15 per day additional pet fee.

Howard Johnson Hotel
310 Gorge Rd. East
Victoria, BC
250-382-2151 (800-446-4656)
Dogs up to 60 pounds are allowed. There is a refundable pet deposit required.

Howard Johnson Hotel
4670 Elk Lake Drive
Victoria, BC
250-704-4656 (800-446-4656)
Dogs of all sizes are welcome. There is a $15 per day pet fee.

Ocean Island Suites
143 Government Street
Victoria, BC
250-385-1788 (888-888-4180)
oisuites.com
This vacation rental is located in the historic James Bay neighborhood of Victoria. There are three pet-friendly apartments and the apartments feature a fenced in yard, high-speed Internet, and a 24 hour front desk. The house is located near dog-friendly parks and beaches. There is a $10 per night pet fee. Dogs of all

sizes are welcome.

Ryan's Bed and Breakfast
224 Superior St
Victoria, BC
250-389-0012
ryansbb.com/
There is a $10 per night pet fee.

Tally Ho Motor Inn
3020 Douglas St
Victoria, BC
250-386-6141
There are no additional pet fees.

Holiday Inn
2569 Dobbin Rd
Westbank, BC
250-768-8879 (877-270-6405)
Dogs of all sizes are allowed for an
additional fee of $10 per night per
pet. Dogs must be crated when left
alone in the room. 2 dogs may be
allowed.

Best Western Listel Whistler Hotel
4121 Village Green
Whistler, BC
604-932-1133 (800-780-7234)
Dogs are allowed for an additional
fee of $25 per night per pet. There
may be 1 large or 2 small dogs per
room. 2 dogs may be allowed.

Chateau Whistler Resort
4599 Chateau Blvd
Whistler, BC
604-938-8000
fairmonthotels.com
This is a 5 star resort. There is no
weight limit for dogs. There is a $25
per night additional pet fee. They
also provide your dog with a pet
amenity package. Multiple dogs may
be allowed.

Coast Whistler Hotel
4005 Whistler Way
Whistler, BC
604-932-2522 (800-663-5644)
All Coast Hotels have on hand extra
pet amenities if you forget
something. For dogs, they have extra
doggy dishes, sleeping cushions,
nylon chew toys and dog food. If your
dog needs one of these items, just
ask the front desk. There is a $25
one time pet fee.

Delta Whistler Village Suites
4308 Main Street
Whistler, BC
604-905-3987 (888-299-3987)
A year round recreational
destination, this all-suite hotel offers
a full range of amenities, great views,
a year round heated outdoor pool, a

Solarice Wellness Spa, and more.
Dogs of all sizes are allowed for an
additional fee of $35 per pet for
every 5 days. Dogs must be quiet,
leashed, and cleaned up after. 2
dogs may be allowed.

Four Seasons Resort
4591 Blackcomb Way
Whistler, BC
604-935-3400 (800-819-5053)
fourseasons.com/whistler/
Only a short distance from the ski
slopes of the Whistler Blackcomb
Mountains (the site of the 2010
Olympic Winter Games), this world
class resort offers a long list of
amenities and access to a wide
range of year round recreation.
Dogs of all sizes are allowed for no
additional pet fee. Dogs may not be
left alone in the room at any time,
and they must be leashed and
cleaned up after at all times. 2 dogs
may be allowed.

Hilton Whistler Resort and Spa
Hotel
4050 Whistler Way
Whistler, BC
604-932-1982 (800-515-4050)
hiltonwhistler.com
This resort and spa welcomes pets
with treats and a "Pooch case" of
toys and other items. Dogs of all
sizes are welcome.

Residence Inn by Marriott
4899 Painted Cliff Road
Whistler, BC
604-905-3400
Dogs of all sizes are allowed. There
is a $25 per night per room fee and
a pet policy to sign at check in.
Multiple dogs may be allowed.

Summit Lodge
4359 Main Street
Whistler, BC
604-932-2778
summitlodge.com/
Well-behaved dogs of all sizes are
welcome at this hotel. Amenities
include a year-round heated
outdoor pool and hot tub. There are
no additional pet fees.

Drummond Lodge
1405 Cariboo Highway South
Williams Lake, BC
250-392-5334
drummondlodge.com
Dogs of all sizes are allowed. There
is a $7 per night per pet additional
pet fee. Up to two small dogs or one
large dog may be allowed.

Sandman Inn and Suites Williams
Lake
664 Oliver Street
Williams Lake, BC
250-392-6557
sandmanhotels.com
Dogs of all sizes are allowed. There
is a $10 additional pet fee. Some of
the rooms have kitchenettes.

Springhouse Trails Ranch
3061 Dog Creek Road
Williams Lake, BC
250-392-4780
springhousetrails.com/
Pets are allowed in the cabins with
kitchenettes. Some of the units have
fireplaces. There is a $15 additional
nightly pet fee. This is a functioning
horse ranch and horseback rides are
offered on the premises. The
Springhouse Trails Ranch lodging
cabins are open from May through
September annually.

The Fraser Inn Hotel
285 Donald Road
Williams Lake, BC
250-398-7055 (888-311-8863 (in
US))
fraserinn.com/
This lakeside inn is only a couple of
minuets from downtown, has
amenities for the leisure or business
traveler, restaurants, and sits central
to a variety of interesting sites and
attractions. Dogs of all sizes are
allowed in first floor rooms for no
additional fee with advance notice at
the time of reservations. Dogs must
be well behaved, leashed, and
cleaned up after. Multiple dogs may
be allowed.

Manitoba Listings

Comfort Inn
925 Middleton Avenue
Brandon, MB
204-727-6232 (877-424-6423)
Dogs are allowed for an additional
fee of $5 per night per pet. Multiple
dogs may be allowed.

Victoria Inn
3550 Victoria Ave
Brandon, MB
204-725-1532
There is a $5 per day additional pet
fee. They have 2 non-smoking pet
rooms.

Victoria Inn North
160 Hwy 10A N

Flin Flon, MB
204-687-7555

Solmundson Gesta Hus B&B
Hwy 8 in Hecla
Hecla, MB
204-279-2088
heclatourism.nb.ca
Pets must be leashed when outside
the room. Please make sure that
your dog doesn't chase the ducks.

Super 8 Morris
400 Main South
Morris, MB
204-746-6879 (800-800-8000)
Dogs of all sizes are allowed. There
are no additional pet fees.
Reservations are recommended due
to limited rooms for pets. Smoking
and non-smoking rooms are
available for pet rooms. 2 dogs may
be allowed.

Days Inn Portage La Prairie
Hwy 1 and Yellowquill Trail
Portage La Prairie, MB
204-857-9791 (800-329-7466)
Dogs of all sizes are allowed. There
is a $8 per night pet fee per pet.
Reservations are recommended due
to limited rooms for pets. 2 dogs may
be allowed.

Super 8 Portage La Prairie
Hwy 1A West
Portage La Prairie, MB
204-857-8883 (800-800-8000)
Dogs of all sizes are allowed. There
are no additional pet fees. Smoking
and non-smoking rooms are
available for pet rooms. 2 dogs may
be allowed.

Super 8 The Pas
1717 Gordon Ave
The Pas, MB
204-623-1888 (800-800-8000)
Dogs of all sizes are allowed. There
are no additional pet fees. Dogs are
not allowed to be left alone in the
room. Smoking and non-smoking
rooms are available for pet rooms. 2
dogs may be allowed.

Country Inns & Suites by Carlson
730 King Edward Street
Winnipeg, MB
204-783-6900
Dogs of all sizes are allowed. There
are no additional pet fees. The hotel
has high speed Internet and a
Fitness Center.

Holiday Inn
1330 Pembina Hwy
Winnipeg, MB

204-452-4747 (877-270-6405)
Dogs of all sizes are allowed for no
additional pet fee. There is a pet
agreement to sign at check in. 2
dogs may be allowed.

Place Louis Riel All-Suite Hotel
190 Smith St
Winnipeg, MB
204-947-6961
There are no additional pet fees.
Pet owners must sign a pet release
form.

Quality Inn
635 Pembina H
Winnipeg, MB
204-453-8247 (877-424-6423)
Dogs are allowed for an additional
fee of $10 per night per pet. 2 dogs
may be allowed.

Radisson Hotel Winnipeg
Downtown
288 Portage Avenue
Winnipeg, MB
204-956-0410
Dogs of all sizes are allowed. There
are no additional pet fees.

Super 8 Winnipeg/East
1485 Niakwa Rd East
Winnipeg, MB
204-253-1935 (800-800-8000)
Dogs of all sizes are allowed. There
is a $100 returnable deposit
required per room. Pet must be kept
in kennel when left alone. Smoking
and non-smoking rooms are
available for pet rooms. 2 dogs may
be allowed.

The Fairmont Winnipeg
2 Lombard Place
Winnipeg, MB
204-957-1350 (800-257-7544)
fairmont.com/winnipeg/
Sitting amidst a vibrant
cosmopolitan city and one of the
world?s largest historical districts,
this hotel is perfectly located for the
leisure or business traveler. Dogs
are allowed for an additional pet fee
of $25 per night per room. Your pup
gets a special goody bag, and they
also provide clean up bags. Dogs
may not be left alone in the room at
any time, and they must be leashed
and cleaned up after. Multiple dogs
may be allowed.

New Brunswick Listings

Comfort Inn
1170 St. Peter Avenue
Bathurst, NB
506-547-8000 (877-424-6423)
Dogs are allowed for no additional
pet fee. Multiple dogs may be
allowed.

Comfort Inn
111 Val D'Amour Road
Campbellton, NB
506-753-4121 (877-424-6423)
Dogs are allowed for no additional
pet fee. 2 dogs may be allowed.

Howard Johnson Hotel
157 Water Street
Campbellton, NB
506-753-4133 (800-446-4656)
Dogs of all sizes are welcome. There
are no additional pet fees.

Comfort Inn
5 Bateman Avenue
Edmundston, NB
506-739-8361 (877-424-6423)
Dogs are allowed for no additional
pet fee. Multiple dogs may be
allowed.

Days Inn Edmundston
10 Rue Mathieu
Edmundston, NB
506-263-0000 (800-329-7466)
Dogs of all sizes are allowed. There
are no additional pet fees. 2 dogs
may be allowed.

Comfort Inn
797 Prospect Street
Fredericton, NB
506-453-0800 (877-424-6423)
Dogs are allowed for no additional
pet fee. Multiple dogs may be
allowed.

Crowne Plaza Hotel Fredericton-Lord
Beaverbrook
659 Queen Street
Fredericton, NB
506-455-3371 (877-270-6405)
Dogs of all sizes are allowed for an
additional pet fee of $15 per night
per room. Multiple dogs may be
allowed.

Holiday Inn
35 Mactaquac Rd
Fredericton, NB
506-363-5111 (877-270-6405)

Dogs of all sizes are allowed for no additional pet fee. Multiple dogs may be allowed.

Comfort Inn East
20 Maplewood Drive
Moncton, NB
506-859-6868 (877-424-6423)
Dogs are allowed for no additional pet fee. Multiple dogs may be allowed.

Country Inns & Suites by Carlson
2475 Mountain Road
Moncton, NB
506-852-7000
Dogs of all sizes are allowed. There is a $5 per day additional pet fee.

Holiday Inn Express Hotel & Suites
2515 Mountain Rd
Moncton, NB
506-384-1050 (877-270-6405)
Dogs of all sizes are allowed for no additional pet fee. Multiple dogs may be allowed.

Howard Johnson Plaza Hotel
1005 Main St.
Moncton, NB
506-854-6340 (800-446-4656)
Dogs of all sizes are welcome. There are no pet fees.

Double Barn Ranch
566 West Galloway Road
Rexton, NB
506-523-9217
doublebarnranch.com
These log cottages are located on 293 acres of ranch land. There is a CDN $10 per night pet fee. Dogs of all sizes are allowed.

Comfort Inn
1155 Fairville Blvd
Saint John, NB
506-674-1873 (877-424-6423)
Dogs are allowed for no additional pet fee. Multiple dogs may be allowed.

Hilton
One Market Square
Saint John, NB
506-693-8484
Well mannered dogs are allowed for no additional pet fee. Multiple dogs may be allowed.

Holiday Inn Express Hotel & Suites
Saint John Harbour Side
400 Main St. And Chesley Drive
Saint John, NB
506-642-2622 (877-270-6405)
Dogs of all sizes are allowed for no additional pet fee. Multiple dogs may

be allowed.

The Fairmont Algonquin
184 Adolphus Street
St Andrews by the Sea, NB
506-529-8823 (800-257-7544)
fairmont.com/frontenac/
There is a stunning seaside golf course and year round recreational activities offered at this resort. Dogs of all sizes are allowed for an additional pet fee of $25 (plus tax) per night per room. During the summer season they have been known to offer an amenity package for their canine guests. Dogs may not be left alone in the room at any time, and they must be leashed and cleaned up after. 2 dogs may be allowed.

Newfoundland Listings

Comfort Inn
41 Maple Valley Road
Corner Brook, NF
709-639-1980 (877-424-6423)
Dogs are allowed for no additional pet fee. Multiple dogs may be allowed.

Comfort Inn
112 Trans Canada H
Gander, NF
709-256-3535 (877-424-6423)
Dogs are allowed for no additional pet fee. Dogs may not be left alone in the room. Multiple dogs may be allowed.

The Valhalla Lodge
Address with reservation
L'Anse aux Meadows, NF
709-754-3105 (877-623-2018)
Dogs up to 75 pounds are allowed. There is one pet friendly cottage, and dogs are not allowed in the lodge. There is a $15 per night per pet additional fee. 2 dogs may be allowed.

Wild Berry Country Lodge
787 St Anthony
St Anthony, NF
709-454-2662 (866-454-2662)
Dogs of all sizes are allowed. There are no additional pet fees. Multiple dogs may be allowed.

Comfort Inn Airport
106 Airport Road
St John's, NF

709-753-3500 (877-424-6423)
Dogs are allowed for an additional one time pet fee of $35 (plus tax) per room. 2 dogs may be allowed.

Fairmont Newfoundland
115 Cavendish Square
St Johns, NF
709-726-4980 (800-257-7544)
fairmont.com/newfoundland/
Located in the heart of North America?s oldest city, this hotel also offers fantastic views of the harbor and this historic city. Dogs of all sizes are allowed for an additional pet fee of $25 per night per room. There can be one large dog over 30 pounds or 2 small dogs up to 30 pounds each per room. Dogs must be leashed, cleaned up after, and crated when left alone in the room.

Holiday Inn
180 Portugal Cove Rd
St Johns, NF
709-722-0506 (877-270-6405)
Dogs of all sizes are allowed for no additional pet fee. Multiple dogs may be allowed.

Holiday Inn
44 Queen Street
Stephenville, NF
709-643-6666 (877-270-6405)
Dogs of all sizes are allowed for no additional pet fee. Dogs may not be left alone in the room. Multiple dogs may be allowed.

Northwest Territories Listings

Fraser Tower Suite Hotel
5303 52nd St
Yellowknife, NT
867-873-8700
There is a $5 per day additional pet fee. Pets must be crated if left alone in the room.

Super 8 Yellowknife
308 Old Airport Road
Yellowknife, NT
867-669-8888 (800-800-8000)
Dogs of all sizes are allowed. There is a $25 one time per pet fee per visit. Only non-smoking rooms are used for pets. 2 dogs may be allowed.

Nova Scotia Listings

Comfort Inn
143 S Albion Street
Amherst, NS
902-667-0404 (877-424-6423)
Quiet dogs are allowed for no additional pet fee. Multiple dogs may be allowed.

Super 8 Amherst
40 Lord Amherst Drive
Amherst, NS
902-660-8888 (800-800-8000)
Dogs of all sizes are allowed. There is a $10 one time per pet fee per visit. Only non-smoking rooms are used for pets. 2 dogs may be allowed.

Comfort Inn
49 North Street
Bridgewater, NS
902-543-1498 (877-424-6423)
Well behaved dogs are allowed for no additional pet fee with a credit card on file. 2 dogs may be allowed.

Comfort Inn
456 Windmill Road
Dartmouth, NS
902-463-9900 (877-424-6423)
One dog is allowed for no additional pet fee and may not be left alone in the room.

Comfort Inn
456 Windmill Road
Dartmouth, NS
902-755-6450 (877-424-6423)
Dogs are allowed for no additional pet fee. Multiple dogs may be allowed.

Holiday Inn
101 Wyse Road
Dartmouth, NS
902-463-1100 (877-270-6405)
Dogs of all sizes are allowed for an additional one time pet fee of $25 per room. 2 dogs may be allowed.

Quality Inn
313 Prince Albert Road
Dartmouth, NS
902-469-5850 (877-424-6423)
Dogs are allowed for no additional pet fee. Multiple dogs may be allowed.

Holiday Inn Express
133 Kearney Lake Road

Halifax, NS
902-445-1100 (877-270-6405)
Dogs of all sizes are allowed for an additional one time pet fee of $25 per room. Multiple dogs may be allowed.

Holiday Inn Select
1980 Robie St
Halifax, NS
902-423-1161 (877-270-6405)
Dogs of all sizes are allowed for no additional pet fee. 2 dogs may be allowed.

Howard Johnson Hotel
20 St. Margaret's Bay Rd.
Halifax, NS
902-477-5611 (800-446-4656)
Dogs of all sizes are welcome. There are no pet fees.

Quality Inn and Suites
980 Parkland Drive
Halifax, NS
902-444-6700 (877-424-6423)
Dogs are allowed for no additional pet fee. Multiple dogs may be allowed.

Residence Inn by Marriott
1599 Grafton Street
Halifax, NS
902-422-0493
One dog up to 100 pounds is allowed. There is a $75 one time fee and a pet policy to sign at check in.

The Westin Nova Scotian
1181 Hollis Street
Halifax, NS
902-421-1000 (888-625-5144)
This hotel offers a prime location in the heart of the city a short distance from the harbor and numerous activities. Dogs up to 60 pounds are allowed for no additional pet fee; there is a pet waiver to sign at check in. Dogs must be leashed and cleaned up after. 2 dogs may be allowed.

Country Inns & Suites by Carlson
700 Westville Road
New Glasgow, NS
902-928-1333
Dogs of all sizes are allowed. There is a $5 per day additional pet fee. There is also a refundable pet deposit. Pets may not be left alone in the rooms and are not allowed in the breakfast area.

Caribou River Cottage Lodge
1308 Shore Road, RR# 3
Pictou, NS

902-485-6352
sunrise-trail.com/caribou/
There are no additional pet fees.

Comfort Inn
368 Kings Road
Sydney, NS
902-562-0200 (877-424-6423)
Quiet dogs are allowed for no additional pet fee. Multiple dogs may be allowed.

Days Inn Sydney
480 Kings Rd
Sydney, NS
902-539-6750 (800-329-7466)
Dogs of all sizes are allowed. There are no additional pet fees. 2 dogs may be allowed.

Quality Inn
560 Kings Road
Sydney, NS
902-539-8101 (877-424-6423)
Dogs are allowed for no additional pet fee. Multiple dogs may be allowed.

Comfort Inn
12 Meadow Drive
Truro, NS
902-893-0330 (877-424-6423)
Dogs are allowed for no additional pet fee. Multiple dogs may be allowed.

Howard Johnson Hotel
437 Prince St.
Truro, NS
902-895-1651 (800-446-4656)
Dogs of all sizes are welcome. There are no pet fees.

Best Western Mermaid
545 Main St
Yarmouth, NS
902-742-7821 (800-780-7234)
Dogs are allowed for no additional pet fee. Multiple dogs may be allowed.

Comfort Inn
96 Starrs Road
Yarmouth, NS
902-742-1119 (877-424-6423)
Dogs are allowed for no additional pet fee. Multiple dogs may be allowed.

Ontario Listings

In 2005, Ontario passed legislation banning Pit Bulls and "similar" dogs from the province. For more information on this see http://www.dogfriendly.com/server/newsletters/bslontario.shtml

Quality Inn
70 Madawaska Blvd
Arnprior, ON
613-623-7991 (877-424-6423)
Dogs are allowed for an additional fee of $10 per night per pet. Multiple dogs may be allowed.

Comfort Inn
75 Hart Drive
Barrie, ON
705-722-3600 (877-424-6423)
Dogs are allowed for no additional pet fee. Multiple dogs may be allowed.

Days Inn Barrie
60 Bryne Drive
Barrie, ON
705-733-8989 (800-329-7466)
Dogs of all sizes are allowed. There is a $10 per night pet fee per pet. 2 dogs may be allowed.

Holiday Inn
20 Fairview Rd
Barrie, ON
705-728-6191 (877-270-6405)
Dogs of all sizes are allowed for no additional pet fee. 2 dogs may be allowed.

Holiday Inn Express Hotel and Suites
506 Bryne Dr
Barrie, ON
705-725-1002 (877-270-6405)
Dogs of all sizes are allowed for an additional fee of $15 per pet for 1 to 3 days; the price begins to reduce after 4 days. 2 dogs may be allowed.

Comfort Inn
200 North Park Street
Belleville, ON
613-966-7703 (877-424-6423)
Dogs are allowed for no additional pet fee. Dogs may not be left alone in the room. 2 dogs may be allowed.

Sleep Inn
510 Muskoka Road
Bracebridge, ON
705-645-2519 (877-424-6423)
Dogs are allowed for no additional pet fee. Multiple dogs may be allowed.

Howard Johnson Express Inn
226 Queen St. East
Brampton, ON
905-451-6000 (800-446-4656)
Well-behaved dogs of all sizes are allowed. There is a $10 per day additional pet fee.

Motel 6 - Toronto - Brampton
160 Steelwell Road
Brampton, ON
905-451-3313 (800-466-8356)
One well-behaved family pet per room. Guest must notify front desk upon arrival. Guest is liable for any damages. In consideration of all guests, pets must never be left unattended in the guest rooms.

Days Inn Brantford
460 Fairview Dr
Brantford, ON
519-759-2700 (800-329-7466)
Dogs of all sizes are allowed. There is a $10 one time per pet fee per visit. 2 dogs may be allowed.

Comfort Inn
7777 Kent Blvd
Brockville, ON
613-345-0042 (877-424-6423)
Dogs are allowed for an additional fee of $5 per night per pet. Multiple dogs may be allowed.

Comfort Inn
3290 S Service Road
Burlington, ON
905-639-1700 (877-424-6423)
Dogs are allowed for no additional pet fee, and they must be crated when left alone in the room. 2 dogs may be allowed.

Motel 6 - Toronto West-Burlington/Hamilton
4345 N Service Rd
Burlington, ON
905-331-1955 (800-466-8356)
One well-behaved family pet per room. Guest must notify front desk upon arrival. Guest is liable for any damages. In consideration of all guests, pets must never be left unattended in the guest rooms.

Quality Suites Toronto Airport
262 Carlingview Drive
CN309, ON
416-674-8442
Dogs are allowed for no additional pet fee. Multiple dogs may be allowed.

Comfort Inn
1100 Richmond Street
Chatham, ON
519-352-5500 (877-424-6423)
Dogs are allowed for no additional pet fee. Multiple dogs may be allowed.

Best Western Cobourg Inn and Conv Centre
930 Burnham St
Cobourg, ON
905-372-2105 (800-780-7234)
Dogs are allowed for no additional pet fee. Dogs must be crated when left alone in the room. 2 dogs may be allowed.

Comfort Inn
121 Densmore Road
Cobourg, ON
905-372-7007 (877-424-6423)
Well behaved dogs are allowed for no additional pet fee; there is a pet agreement to sign at check in, and dogs must be removed for housekeeping. Multiple dogs may be allowed.

Comfort Inn
220 Holiday Inn Drive
Combridge, ON
519-658-1100 (877-424-6423)
Quiet dogs are allowed for no additional pet fee. Multiple dogs may be allowed.

Best Western Parkway Inn and Conf Centre
1515 Vincent Massey Dr
Cornwall, ON
613-932-0451 (800-780-7234)
Dogs are allowed for no additional pet fee. Dogs may not be left alone in the room at any time. Multiple dogs may be allowed.

Comfort Inn
1625 Vincent Massey Drive
Cornwall, ON
613-937-0111 (877-424-6423)
Well behaved dogs are allowed for no additional pet fee; there is a pet agreement to sign at check in, and dogs must be removed for housekeeping. Multiple dogs may be allowed.

Comfort Inn
522 Government Street
Dryden, ON
807-223-3893 (877-424-6423)
Well behaved dogs are allowed for no additional pet fee. Multiple dogs may be allowed.

Comfort Inn Clifton Hill
1 Hospitality Drive
Fort Erie, ON
905-871-8500 (877-424-6423)
Dogs are allowed for an additional pet fee of $10 per night per room. Multiple dogs may be allowed.

Holiday Inn

1485 Garrison Rd
Fort Erie, ON
905-871-8333 (877-270-6405)
Dogs up to 60 pounds are allowed
for an additional fee of $30 per night
per pet. 2 dogs may be allowed.

Super 8 Grimsby
11 Windward Drive
Grimsby, ON
905-309-8800 (800-800-8000)
Dogs of all sizes are allowed. There
is a $10 per night pet fee per pet.
Smoking and non-smoking rooms
are available for pet rooms. 2 dogs
may be allowed.

Comfort Inn
480 Silvercreek Parkway
Guelph, ON
519-763-1900 (877-424-6423)
Dogs are allowed for no additional
pet fee. Multiple dogs may be
allowed.

Holiday Inn
601 Scottsdale Dr
Guelph, ON
519-836-0231 (877-270-6405)
Dogs of all sizes are allowed for no
additional pet fee. Multiple dogs may
be allowed.

Sheraton Hamilton Hotel
116 King Street W
Hamilton, ON
905-529-8266 (888-625-5144)
Although situated in the heart of the
business district, there is plenty of
recreational activities to be found
close by. Dogs of all sizes are
allowed for no additional pet fee;
there is a pet waiver to sign at check
in. Dogs must be well mannered,
leashed, cleaned up after, and crated
when left alone in the room. Multiple
dogs may be allowed.

Staybridge Suites Hamilton-
Downtown
118 Market Street
Hamilton, ON
905-577-9000 (877-270-6405)
Dogs of all sizes are allowed for an
additional one time pet fee of $95 per
room. 2 dogs may be allowed.

Comfort Inn
86 King William Street
Huntsville, ON
705-789-1701 (877-424-6423)
Dogs are allowed for no additional
pet fee. 2 dogs may be allowed.

Comfort Inn West
222 Hearst Way
Kanata, ON

613-592-2200 (877-424-6423)
Dogs are allowed for no additional
pet fee. 2 dogs may be allowed.

Howard Johnson Inn
4022 Count Rd. 43 East
Kemptville, ON
613-258-5939 (800-446-4656)
Dogs of all sizes are welcome.
There is a $10 per day pet fee.

Comfort Inn
1230 H 17 E
Kenora, ON
807-468-8845 (877-424-6423)
Dogs are allowed for no additional
pet fee. Multiple dogs may be
allowed.

Days Inn Kenora
920 Hwy 17 E
Kenora, ON
807-468-2003 (800-329-7466)
Dogs of all sizes are allowed. There
are no additional pet fees. 2 dogs
may be allowed.

Comfort Inn
55 Warne Crescent
Kingston, ON
613-546-9500 (877-424-6423)
Dogs are allowed for no additional
pet fee. Multiple dogs may be
allowed.

Comfort Inn Midtown
1454 Princess Street
Kingston, ON
613-549-5550 (877-424-6423)
Dogs are allowed for no additional
pet fee. Dogs may not be left alone
in the room. Multiple dogs may be
allowed.

Holiday Inn
2 Princess St
Kingston, ON
613-549-8400 (877-270-6405)
Dogs of all sizes are allowed for an
additional pet fee of $20 per night
per room. Multiple dogs may be
allowed.

Howard Johnson Hotel
237 Ontario Street
Kingston, ON
613-549-6300 (800-446-4656)
Dogs of all sizes are welcome.
There is a $15 per day pet fee. Pets
are allowed on the first and second
floors only.

Howard Johnson Inn
50 Government Rd. East
Kirkland, ON
705-567-3241 (800-446-4656)
Dogs of all sizes are welcome.

There is a $5 one time pet fee.

Howard Johnson Hotel
1333 Weber St.
Kitchener, ON
519-893-1234 (800-446-4656)
Dogs of all sizes are welcome. There
is a $15 per day pet fee.

Comfort Inn
279 Erie Street S
Leamington, ON
519-326-9071 (877-424-6423)
Dogs are allowed for an additional
pet fee of $10 per night per room.
Multiple dogs may be allowed.

Comfort Inn
1156 Wellington Road
London, ON
519-685-9300 (877-424-6423)
Dogs are allowed for no additional
pet fee. 2 dogs may be allowed.

Days Inn London
1100 Wellington Rd S
London, ON
519-681-1240 (800-329-7466)
Dogs of all sizes are allowed. There
are no additional pet fees. 2 dogs
may be allowed.

Holiday Inn Hotel and Suites
864 Exter Rd
London, ON
519-680-0077 (877-270-6405)
Dogs of all sizes are allowed for an
additional one time pet fee of $20 per
room. Multiple dogs may be allowed.

Howard Johnson Hotel
1170 Wellington Road
London, ON
519-681-1550 (800-446-4656)
Well-behaved quiet dogs of all sizes
are allowed. There are no additional
pet fees.

Quality Suites
1120 Dearness Drive
London, ON
519-680-1024
Dogs are allowed for no additional
pet fee. Multiple dogs may be
allowed.

Residence Inn by Marriott
383 Colborne Street
London, ON
519-433-7222
Dogs of all sizes are allowed. There
is a $75 one time fee, and they
request you make arrangements for
housekeeping. Multiple dogs may be
allowed.

Comfort Inn

8330 Woodbine Avenue
Markham, ON
905-477-6077 (877-424-6423)
Dogs are allowed for an additional fee of $15 (plus tax) per night per pet. 2 dogs may be allowed.

Residence Inn by Marriott
55 Minthorn Blvd
Markham, ON
905-707-7933
Dogs of all sizes are allowed. There is a $75 one time fee per pet and a pet policy to sign at check in. Multiple dogs may be allowed.

Mohawk Motel
335 Sable Street
Massey, ON
705-865-2722
Dogs of all sizes are allowed. There is a $6 per night per room fee and a pet policy to sign at check in. Dogs are not allowed to be left alone in the room. 2 dogs may be allowed.

Comfort Inn
980 King Street
Midland, ON
705-526-2090 (877-424-6423)
Dogs are allowed for no additional pet fee. Multiple dogs may be allowed.

Four Points by Sheraton
Mississauga Meadowvale
2501 Argentia Road
Mississauga, ON
905-858-2424 (888-625-5144)
This hotel is located in the heart of the business district near several corporate headquarters, and yet it is still close to a variety of recreational activities. Dogs of all sizes are allowed for an additional fee of $20 per night per pet. Dogs must be leashed and cleaned up after. 2 dogs may be allowed.

Hilton
5875 Airport Road
Mississauga, ON
905-677-9900
One dog is allowed per room for no additional fee; there is a pet agreement to sign at check in. Dogs must be crated when left alone in the room.

Motel 6 - Toronto - Mississauga
2935 Argentia Road
Mississauga, ON
905-814-1664 (800-466-8356)
One well-behaved family pet per room. Guest must notify front desk upon arrival. Guest is liable for any damages. In consideration of all

guests, pets must never be left unattended in the guest rooms.

Residence Inn by Marriott
7005 Century Avenue
Mississauga, ON
905-567-2577
Dogs of all sizes are allowed. There is a $75 one time fee and a pet policy to sign at check in. Multiple dogs may be allowed.

Staybridge Suites Toronto
Mississauga
6791 Hurontario St.
Mississauga, ON
905-564-6892 (877-270-6405)
One dog of any size is allowed for an additional one time pet fee of $75.

Studio 6 - Toronto - Mississauga
60 Britannia Road East
Mississauga, ON
905-502-8897 (800-466-8356)
One well-behaved family pet per room. Guest must notify front desk upon arrival. Guest is liable for any damages. In consideration of all guests, pets must never be left unattended in the guest rooms.

Niagara Parkway Court Motel
3708 Main Street
Niagara Falls, ON
905-295-3331
goniagarafalls.com/npcm/
There is a $10 per day additional pet fee. The hotel only has one pet room so make your reservations early.

Sheraton Fallsview Hotel and
Conference Center
6755 Fallsview Blvd
Niagara Falls, ON
905-374-1077 (888-625-5144)
This 4-diamond hotel offers guests a 5-star view of the Niagara Falls and it is also central to numerous other nearby recreational pursuits. Dogs are allowed on the 3rd floor only for an additional $25 per night per pet, and there is a pet waiver to sign at check in. If there is more than 1 dog, they may not exceed a combined weight of more than 80 pounds. Dogs may not be left unattended in the room, and they must be leashed and cleaned up after at all times.

Sheraton on the Falls Hotel
5875 Falls Avenue
Niagara Falls, ON
905-374-4445 (888-625-5144)
Positioned directly across the street

from the Niagara Falls in the largest hotel and entertainment complex in North America, this hotel is also home to the largest state-of-the-art conference facility in Niagara. Dogs up to 80 pounds are allowed for no additional pet fee; there is a pet waiver to sign at check in. Dogs may not be left alone in the room, and they must be leashed and cleaned up after at all times. 2 dogs may be allowed.

For-Rest Villa
1418 East-West Line
Niagara on the Lake, ON
905-468-7659
Dogs of all sizes are allowed. There is a $20 fee per night per room for small dogs, and a $30 fee per night per room for medium to large dogs. Dogs with extra heavy fur can stay in an extra large dog house close by. There is a pet policy to sign at check in. 2 dogs may be allowed.

Best Western North Bay
700 Lakeshore Dr
North Bay, ON
705-474-5800 (800-780-7234)
Dogs are allowed for no additional pet fee. Multiple dogs may be allowed.

Clarion Resort Pinewood Park
201 Pinewood Park
North Bay, ON
705-472-0810 (877-424-6423)
Dogs are allowed for no additional pet fee; there is a pet agreement to sign at check in. Multiple dogs may be allowed.

Comfort Inn
676 Lakeshore Drive
North Bay, ON
705-494-9444 (877-424-6423)
Dogs are allowed for no additional pet fee. Dogs must be removed for housekeeping. Multiple dogs may be allowed.

Comfort Inn Airport
1200 O'Brien Street
North Bay, ON
705-476-5400 (877-424-6423)
Dogs are allowed for no additional pet fee. Multiple dogs may be allowed.

Super 8 North Bay
570 Lakeshore Drive
North Bay, ON
705-495-4551 (800-800-8000)
Dogs of all sizes are allowed. There are no additional pet fees. Smoking and non-smoking rooms are

available for pet rooms. 2 dogs may be allowed.

Comfort Inn Downsview
66 Norfinch Drive
North York, ON
416-736-4700 (877-424-6423)
Dogs are allowed for no additional pet fee. Multiple dogs may be allowed.

Holiday Inn Express
30 Norfinch Dr
North York, ON
416-665-3500 (877-270-6405)
Dogs of all sizes are allowed for no additional pet fee. Multiple dogs may be allowed.

Novotel - Toronto North York
3 Park Home Avenue
North York, ON
416-733-2929
Novotel Hotels welcome a maximum of 2 animals (cats and dogs) per room and never require a fee. Each guest checking in with a pet will be given a Royal Canine/Novotel Pet Welcome Kit.

Holiday Inn
590 Argus Road
Oakville, ON
905-842-5000 (877-270-6405)
Dogs of all sizes are allowed for an additional fee of $15 per night per room. 2 dogs may be allowed.

The Kings Inn
370 Lacie Street
Orilla, ON
705-325-2354 (800-530-7416)
Well behaved dogs that are quiet and clean, and of all sizes are allowed. There are no additional pet fees, but a credit card must be on file. Multiple dogs may be allowed.

Comfort Inn
75 Progress Drive
Orillia, ON
705-327-7744 (877-424-6423)
Dogs are allowed for an additional fee of $10 per night per pet. Multiple dogs may be allowed.

Comfort Inn
605 Bloor Street W
Oshawa, ON
905-434-5000 (877-424-6423)
Dogs are allowed for no additional pet fee. Multiple dogs may be allowed.

Holiday Inn
1011 Bloor St E.
Oshawa, ON

905-576-5101 (877-270-6405)
Dogs of all sizes are allowed for an additional pet fee of $15 per night per room. 2 dogs may be allowed.

Delta Ottawa Hotel and Suites
361 Queen Street
Ottawa, ON
613-238-6000
There is an additional $50 fee for a dog if you stay for 5 or more days.

Holiday Inn Hotel and Suites
111 Cooper St
Ottawa, ON
613-238-1331 (877-270-6405)
Dogs of all sizes are allowed for no additional pet fee. 2 dogs may be allowed.

Les Suites Hotel
130 Besserer St
Ottawa, ON
613-232-2000
les-suites.com/english/
There is a $25 one time pet fee.

Novotel - Ottawa
33 Nicholas Street
Ottawa, ON
613-230-3033
Novotel Hotels welcome a maximum of 2 animals (cats and dogs) per room and never require a fee. Each guest checking in with a pet will be given a Royal Canine/Novotel Pet Welcome Kit.

Quality Hotel Downtown
290 Rideau Street
Ottawa, ON
613-789-7511
One dog is allowed for a $25 refundable pet deposit per night.

Residence Inn by Marriott
161 Laurier Avenue West
Ottawa, ON
613-231-2020
Dogs of all sizes are allowed. There is a $150 one time fee and a pet policy to sign at check in. Multiple dogs may be allowed.

Sheraton Ottawa Hotel
150 Albert Street/H 42
Ottawa, ON
613-238-1500 (888-625-5144)
This hotel is central to numerous other activities and attractions, including the world's longest skating rink, a very busy Festival Plaza, and many recreational opportunities. Dogs of all sizes are allowed for no additional fee on the 3rd floor, and there is a pet waiver to sign at check in. Dogs must be well

behaved, leashed, and cleaned up after at all times. 2 dogs may be allowed.

Southway Inn
2431 Bank Street
Ottawa, ON
613-737-0811
southway.com/
There is a $15 pet fee for the first night and $5 each additional night.

The Westin Ottawa
11 Colonel By Drive
Ottawa, ON
613-560-7000 (888-625-5144)
At the heart of city, this hotel has much to offer the business or leisure traveler. Dogs up to 80 pounds are allowed for no additional fee, and a Heavenly dog bed can be ready for your pooch if requested at the time of reservations. There is a pet waiver to sign at check in. Dogs may not be left alone in the room, and they must be well mannered, leashed, and cleaned up after at all times. 2 dogs may be allowed.

Comfort Inn
955 9th Avenue E
Owne Sound, ON
519-371-5500 (877-424-6423)
Dogs are allowed for no additional pet fee. Multiple dogs may be allowed.

Best Western Georgian Inn
48 Joseph St
Parry Sound, ON
705-746-5837 (800-780-7234)
Dogs are allowed for no additional pet fee. Multiple dogs may be allowed.

Quality Inn and Conference Center
1 J.R. Drive
Parry Sound, ON
705-378-2461 (877-424-6423)
Dogs are allowed for an additional one time pet fee of $10 per room. Multiple dogs may be allowed.

Comfort Inn
959 Pembroke Street E
Pembroke, ON
613-735-1057 (877-424-6423)
Dogs are allowed for no additional pet fee. Multiple dogs may be allowed.

King Bethune Guest House and Spa
270 King Street
Peterborough, ON
705-743-4101 (800-574-3664)
kingbethunehouse.com
Full breakfast included. Located in

the the Kawartha Lakes Cottage country. There is a $10 charge per night for pets. Pets may not be left in the rooms.

Quality Inn
1074 Lansdowne Street
Petersborough, ON
705-748-6801 (877-424-6423)
Dogs are allowed for no additional pet fee. Multiple dogs may be allowed.

Comfort Inn
533 Kingston Road
Pickering, ON
905-831-6200 (877-424-6423)
Dogs are allowed for no additional pet fee. Dogs may not be left alone in the room. Multiple dogs may be allowed.

Comfort Inn
Easton's Service Center corner of H 401/28
Port Hope, ON
905-885-7000 (877-424-6423)
Dogs are allowed for no additional pet fee. Multiple dogs may be allowed.

Sheraton Parkway Toronto North Hotel and Suites
600 H 7 E
Richmond Hills, ON
905-881-2121 (888-625-5144)
In addition to being central to many outside attractions and activities, this hotel also offers onsite social programs. One dog is allowed per room for no additional fee; there is a pet waiver to sign at check in. Pet friendly rooms are limited. Dogs must be well behaved, leashed, and cleaned up after at all times.

Holiday Inn
1498 Venetian Blvd
Sarnia, ON
519-336-4130 (877-270-6405)
Dogs of all sizes are allowed for an additional pet fee of $25 per night per room. Multiple dogs may be allowed.

Holiday Inn
208 St Marys River Dr
Sault Ste Marie, ON
705-949-0611 (877-270-6405)
Dogs of all sizes are allowed for no additional pet fee. Multiple dogs may be allowed.

Super 8 Sault Ste Marie
184 Great Northern Road
Sault Ste Marie, ON
705-254-6441 (800-800-8000)

Dogs of all sizes are allowed. There is a $15 one time per pet fee per visit. Smoking and non-smoking rooms are available for pet rooms. 2 dogs may be allowed.

Algoma Cabins
1713 Queen Street East
Sault Ste. Marie, ON
705-256-8681
Dogs of all sizes are allowed. There are no additional pet fees. Multiple dogs may be allowed.

Comfort Inn
333 Great Northern Road
Sault Ste. Marie, ON
705-759-8000 (877-424-6423)
Dogs are allowed for an additional fee of $5 per night per pet. 2 dogs may be allowed.

Sleep Inn
727 Bay Street
Sault Ste. Marie, ON
705-253-7533 (877-424-6423)
Dogs are allowed for no additional pet fee. Multiple dogs may be allowed.

Best Western Little River Inn
203 Queensway West
Simcoe, ON
519-426-2125 (800-780-7234)
Dogs are allowed for no additional pet fee. Multiple dogs may be allowed.

Comfort Inn
85 The Queensway E
Simcoe, ON
519-426-2611 (877-424-6423)
Dogs are allowed for no additional pet fee. Dogs may not be left alone in the room. Multiple dogs may be allowed.

Comfort Inn
2 Dunlop Drive
St Catharines, ON
905-687-8890 (877-424-6423)
Dogs are allowed for no additional pet fee. Multiple dogs may be allowed.

Holiday Inn St Catharines
2 N Service Rd
St Catharines, ON
905-934-8000 (877-270-6405)
holidayinnstcath.com/
Dogs of all sizes are allowed for an additional pet fee of $15 per night per room. Multiple dogs may be allowed.

Quality Hotel Parkway Convention Centre

327 Ontario Street
St Catharines, ON
905-688-2324
Dogs are allowed for an additional one time pet fee of $10 per room. Multiple dogs may be allowed.

Comfort Inn
100 Centennial Avenue
St Thomas, ON
519-633-4082 (877-424-6423)
A dog is allowed for an additional one time pet fee of $20 per room.

Best Western Downtown Sudbury-Centre-Ville
151 Larch St
Sudbury, ON
705-673-7801 (800-780-7234)
Quiet dogs are allowed for an additional fee of $15 (plus tax) per night per pet. 2 dogs may be allowed.

Comfort Inn
2171 Regent Street S
Sudbury, ON
705-522-1101 (877-424-6423)
Dogs are allowed for no additional pet fee. Multiple dogs may be allowed.

Holiday Inn Sudbury
1696 Regent Street
Sudbury, ON
705-522-3000 (877-270-6405)
Dogs of all sizes are allowed for no additional pet fee. 2 dogs may be allowed.

Quality Inn and Conference Centre Downtown
390 Elgin Street S
Sudbury, ON
705-675-1273 (877-424-6423)
Dogs are allowed for no additional pet fee. Multiple dogs may be allowed.

Staybridge Suites
355 SOuth Park Rd
Thornhill, ON
905-771-9333 (877-270-6405)
Dogs up to 60 pounds are allowed for an additional one time fee of $75 per pet. 2 dogs may be allowed.

Four Points by Sheraton St. Catharines Niagara Suites
3530 Schmon Parkway
Thorold, ON
905-984-8484 (888-625-5144)
Located only minutes from Niagara Falls and all the unique recreational opportunities the area has to offer, this hotel is also close to several major corporate headquarters. Dogs

of all sizes are allowed an additional fee of $10 per night per pet in the standard rooms on the 1st or 2nd floor. Dogs must be quiet, leashed, cleaned up after, and crated when left alone in the room. 2 dogs may be allowed.

Best Western Crossroads Motor Inn
655 W Arthur St
Thunder Bay, ON
807-577-4241 (800-780-7234)
Dogs up to 50 pounds are allowed for an additional one time pet fee of $15 per room. 2 dogs may be allowed.

Comfort Inn
660 W Arthur Street (H 11/17)
Thunder Bay, ON
807-475-3155 (877-424-6423)
Dogs are allowed for no additional pet fee. 2 dogs may be allowed.

Super 8 Tillsonburg
92 Simcoe St
Tilsonburg, ON
519-842-7366 (800-800-8000)
Dogs of all sizes are allowed. There is a $10 per night pet fee per pet. Smoking and non-smoking rooms are available for pet rooms. 2 dogs may be allowed.

Days Inn Timmins Conference Cntr
14 Mountjoy Street South
Timmins, ON
705-267-6211 (800-329-7466)
Dogs of all sizes are allowed. There are no additional pet fees. Pet must be kept in kennel when left alone. 2 dogs may be allowed.

Beaches Bed and Breakfast Inn
174 Waverley Road
Toronto, ON
416-699-0818
members.tripod.com/beachesbb/
This B&B, located in The Beaches neighborhood, is just 1.5 blocks from the beach. Pets and children are welcome at this bed and breakfast. Most of the rooms offer private bathrooms. The owner has cats on the premises.

Delta Toronto Airport Hotel
801 Dixon Rd West
Toronto, ON
416-675-6100
There are no additional pet fees.

Fairmont Royal York
100 Front Street
Toronto, ON
416-368-2511 (800-257-7544)
fairmont.com/royalyork/

Dogs are allowed for an additional pet fee of $ 25 per night per room. Dogs may not be left alone in the room at any time, and they must be leashed and cleaned up after. 2 dogs may be allowed.

Four Seasons Hotel Toronto
21 Avenue Road
Toronto, ON
416-964-0411
Dogs of all sizes are allowed for no additional pet fee. Dogs may not be left alone in the room; pet sitting services are available.

Hilton
145 Richmond Street West
Toronto, ON
416-869-3456
Dogs up to 50 pounds are allowed for a $50 refundable pet deposit. Multiple dogs may be allowed.

Holiday Inn Express Toronto-Downtown
111 Lombard Street
Toronto, ON
416-367-5555 (877-270-6405)
One dog of any size is allowed for no additional pet fee. Dogs may not be left alone in the room.

Holiday Inn Toronto-Midtown
280 Bloor St. West
Toronto, ON
416-968-0010 (877-270-6405)
One dog of any size is allowed for an additional pet fee of $25 per night.

Holiday Inn on King (Downtown)
370 King Street West
Toronto, ON
416-599-4000 (877-270-6405)
hiok.com/
One dog up to 50 pounds is allowed for an additional one time pet fee of $35.

International Plaza Hotel and Conference Centre
655 Dixon Rd
Toronto, ON
416-244-1711
You must sign a pet waiver for your dog. There are no additional pet fees.

Novotel - Toronto Center
45 The Esplanade
Toronto, ON
416-367-8900
Novotel Hotels welcome a maximum of 2 animals (cats and dogs) per room and never require a fee. Each guest checking in with a

pet will be given a Royal Canine/Novotel Pet Welcome Kit.

Novotel - Toronto Mississauga
3670 Hurontario Street
Toronto, ON
905-896-1000
Novotel Hotels welcome a maximum of 2 animals (cats and dogs) per room and never require a fee. Each guest checking in with a pet will be given a Royal Canine/Novotel Pet Welcome Kit.

Sheraton Centre Toronto Hotel
123 Queen Street W
Toronto, ON
416-361-1000 (888-625-5144)
There is a pet policy to sign at check in. Dogs may not be left alone in the room, and they must be leashed and cleaned up after at all times. 2 dogs may be allowed.

Sheraton Gateway Hotel in Toronto International Airport
Terminal 3, Toronto AMF
Toronto, ON
905-672-7000 (888-625-5144)
Dogs of all sizes are allowed for no additional fee. Dogs may only be left for a short time, and they request that the front desk be informed when they are alone in the room. Dogs must be well behaved, leashed, and cleaned up after. 2 dogs may be allowed.

The Westin Bristol Place Toronto Airport
950 Dixon Road
Toronto, ON
819-778-6111 (888-625-5144)
Dogs up to 80 pounds are allowed for no additional fee, and there is a pet waiver to sign at check in. 2 dogs may be allowed.

Travelodge Hotel
925 Dixon Road
Toronto, ON
416-674-2222
There are no additional pet fees.

Comfort Inn
68 Monogram Place
Trenton, ON
613-965-6660 (877-424-6423)
Dogs are allowed for no additional pet fee. Multiple dogs may be allowed.

Holiday Inn
99 Glen Miller Rd
Trenton, ON
613-394-4855 (877-270-6405)
Dogs of all sizes are allowed for an

additional fee of $5 per night per pet. Multiple dogs may be allowed.

Super 8 Wallaceburg
76 McNaughton Ave
Wallaceburg, ON
519-627-0781 (800-800-8000)
Dogs of all sizes are allowed. There is a $10 per night pet fee per pet. Pet must be kept in kennel when left alone. Smoking and non-smoking rooms are available for pet rooms. 2 dogs may be allowed.

Comfort Inn
190 Webber Street N
Waterloo, ON
519-747-9400 (877-424-6423)
Dogs are allowed for no additional pet fee. Multiple dogs may be allowed.

Comfort Inn
870 Niagara Street
Welland, ON
905-732-4811 (877-424-6423)
Dogs are allowed for an additional pet fee of $10 per night per room. 2 dogs may be allowed.

Massey Motel
295 Sable Street
West Massey, ON
705-865-2500
Dogs of all sizes are allowed. There are no additional pet fees. Multiple dogs may be allowed.

Motel 6 - Toronto East - Whitby
165 Consumers Drive
Whitby, ON
905-665-8883 (800-466-8356)
One well-behaved family pet per room. Guest must notify front desk upon arrival. Guest is liable for any damages. In consideration of all guests, pets must never be left unattended in the guest rooms.

Quality Suites
1700 Champlain Avenue
Whitby, ON
905-432-8800
Dogs are allowed for no additional pet fee. Multiple dogs may be allowed.

Comfort Inn
2955 Dougall Avenue
Windsor, ON
519-966-7800 (877-424-6423)
Dogs up to 50 pounds are allowed for no additional pet fee. 2 dogs may be allowed.

Comfort Inn Ambassador Bridge
2765 Huron Church Road

Windsor, ON
519-972-1331 (877-424-6423)
Dogs are allowed for no additional pet fee with a credit card on file. Dogs may not be left alone in the room at any time. Multiple dogs may be allowed.

Hampton Inn
1840 Huron Church
Windsor, ON
519-972-0770
Dogs of all sizes are allowed. There is a pet policy to sign at check in and no additional pet fees. Multiple dogs may be allowed.

Hilton
277 Riverside Drive West
Windsor, ON
519-973-5555
Dogs up to 50 pounds are allowed for an additional one time pet fee of $50 per room. 2 dogs may be allowed.

Holiday Inn Select
1855 Huron Church Rd
Windsor, ON
519-966-1200 (877-270-6405)
Dogs of all sizes are allowed for no additional pet fee. Multiple dogs may be allowed.

Quality Suites Downtown
250 Dougall Avenue
Windsor, ON
519-977-9707
Dogs up to 50 pounds are allowed for a $50 one time pet fee per room. 2 dogs may be allowed.

Quality Hotel and Suites
580 Bruin Blvd
Woodstock, ON
519-537-5587
Dogs are allowed for no additional pet fee. 2 dogs may be allowed.

Prince Edward Island Listings

Comfort Inn East
240 Boul Sainte-Anne
Beauport, PE
418-666-1226 (877-424-6423)
Dogs are allowed for an additional one time pet fee of $15 per room. Multiple dogs may be allowed.

Comfort Inn
112 Trans Canada H

Charlottetown, PE
902-566-4424 (877-424-6423)
Dogs are allowed for no additional pet fee. Multiple dogs may be allowed.

Holiday Inn Express & Suites
Trans Canada Hwy #1
Charlottetown, PE
902-892-1201 (877-270-6405)
Dogs of all sizes are allowed for no additional pet fee. Multiple dogs may be allowed.

Clarion Collection Cavendish
Gateway Resort
Box 5506/ H 13
Mayfield, PE
902-963-2213 (877-424-6423)
Dogs are allowed for no additional pet fee. 2 dogs may be allowed.

Quality Inn Garden of the Gulf
618 Water Street
Summerside, PE
902-436-2295 (877-424-6423)
Dogs are allowed for an additional one time pet fee of $10 per room. Multiple dogs may be allowed.

Quebec Listings

Hotel Baie-Saint-Paul
911 boul Mgr Laval
Baie-St-Paul, PQ
418-435-3683

Hilton
12505 Cote De Liesse
Dorval, PQ
514-631-2411
Quiet dogs are allowed for an additional one time pet fee of $25 per room. 2 dogs may be allowed.

Comfort Inn
630 Boul La Gappe
Gatineau, PQ
819-243-6010 (877-424-6423)
Dogs are allowed for an additional one time pet fee of $25 per room. Multiple dogs may be allowed.

Four Points by Sheraton & Conference Centre Gatineau-Ottawa
35 Rue Laurier
Gatineau, PQ
819-778-6111 (888-625-5144)
This hotel sits central to numerous activities and recreational pursuits. Dogs of all sizes are allowed for no additional fee, and there is a pet waiver to sign at check in. Dogs are

not allowed in public areas, and they must be leashed, cleaned up after, and crated when left alone in the room. 2 dogs may be allowed.

Hotel du Lac Carling
2255 Route #327 Nord
Grenville-sur-la-Rouge, PQ
450-533-9211 (800-661-9211)
laccarling.com
Dogs of all sizes are allowed. There is a $25 pet fee per stay. Dogs must be left in a crate if you are out of the room. Up to 2 dogs are allowed per room.

Holiday Inn
2 Montcalm St
Hull, PQ
819-778-3880 (877-270-6405)
Dogs of all sizes are allowed for an additional one time pet fee of $35 per room. Multiple dogs may be allowed.

Fairmont Le Manoir Richelieu
181 rue Richelieu
La Malbaie, PQ
418-665-3703 (800-257-7544)
fairmont.com/richelieu/
This world class resort, stately nestled amid the sea and mountains, offers every amenity for the business or leisure traveler and a variety of recreational opportunities. Dogs are allowed for an additional fee of $25 per night per pet. Dogs may not be left alone in the room at any time, and they must be leashed and cleaned up after. Multiple dogs may be allowed.

Mont-Tremblant Cottage Rental
Call to Arrange
Labelle, PQ
514-923-5787
One dog of any size is allowed. The dog must be house-trained and well-behaved. There are no additional pet fees.

La Paysanne Motel
42 rue Queen
Lennoxville, PQ
819-569-5585
connect-quebec.com/la_paysanne/
There are no additional pet fees.

Gite du Carrefour
11 ave St-Laurent ouest
Louiseville, PQ
819-228-4932
There are no additional pet fees.

Le Grand Lodge Mont-Tremblant
2396 rue Labelle
Mont-Tremblant, PQ
819-425-2734 (800 567-6763)

legrandlodge.com/indexEng.html
This luxury hotel is located 5 minutes from the Tremblant ski resort. Dogs up to 40 pounds are allowed. There is a $25 per night additional pet fee. Dogs may not be left alone in the rooms and there are a limited number of pet rooms.

Auberge du vieux-port
97 rue de la Commune Est
Montreal, PQ
514-876-0081
aubergeduvieuxport.com
The Auberge du vieux-port is located across from the Old Port of Montreal in Old Montreal. Dogs of all sizes are allowed. There is a $7 per pet per night fee for small dogs and a $14 per pet per night pet fee for larger dogs. You need to leave a cell phone number if you are leaving a dog alone in the room. One dog is allowed in the rooms but up to two dogs may be allowed in the studio lofts. 2 dogs may be allowed.

Chateau Versailles
1659 Sherbrooke Street West
Montreal, PQ
514-933-8111 (888-933-8111)
This hotel is located in the downtown area. There is a $17.25 nightly pet fee per pet. Dogs must be leashed on the premises and may not be left alone in the room. 2 dogs may be allowed.

Delta Montreal
475 avenue Président-Kennedy
Montreal, PQ
514-286-1986
deltamontreal.com/en/delta.html
There is a 30.00 pet fee.

Four Points by Sheraton Montreal Centre-Ville
475 Sherbrooke Street West/H 138
Montreal, PQ
514-842-3961 (888-625-5144)
The prime location of this hotel gives visitors a good starting point for numerous activities and recreational opportunities. Dogs of all sizes are allowed for no additional fee. Dogs may not be left alone in the room, and they must be leashed and cleaned up after at all times. Multiple dogs may be allowed.

Holiday Inn
420 Sherbrooke St W.
Montreal, PQ
514-842-6111 (877-270-6405)
Dogs of all sizes are allowed for an additional one time pet fee of $35

per room. Multiple dogs may be allowed.

Holiday Inn - Airport
6500 Cote de Liesse
Montreal, PQ
514-739-3391 (877-270-6405)
Dogs of all sizes are allowed for an additional one time fee of $35 per pet. 2 dogs may be allowed.

Hotel Godin
10 Sherbrooke Ouest
Montreal, PQ
514-843-6000 (866-744-6346)
hotelgodin.com
This boutique hotel allows dogs of all sizes. There is a special doggy menu on the room service menu and they can provide a doggy bed if requested. There is a $50 one time additional pet fee.

Hotel Le Germain
2050, rue Mansfield
Montreal, PQ
514-849-2050 (877-333-2050)
hotelgermain.com
This boutique hotel is located in the downtown district of the city. Dogs of all sizes are allowed. There is a $30 per night additional pet fee. Dogs may only be left in the rooms for very short times. 2 dogs may be allowed.

Hotel Maritime Plaza
1155 rue Guy
Montreal, PQ
514-932-1411
hotelmaritime.com/
There is a $35 per night fee for the pet.

Hotel Travelodge Montreal Centre
50 boul Rene-Levesque ouest
Montreal, PQ
514-874-9090
There is a $20 per night pet fee.

Intercontinental Montreal
360 Saint Antoine Street Ouest
Montreal, PQ
514-987-9900
Dogs up to 45 pounds are allowed for an additional one time pet fee of $35 per room. 2 dogs may be allowed.

Le Saint-Sulpice
414 rue St-Sulpice
Montreal, PQ
514-288-1000 (877-SUL-PICE)
lesaintsulpice.com/
This Old Montreal boutique hotel allows dogs of any size. You need to declare pets at the time that you make reservations. There is a $30

one time pet fee. Multiple dogs may be allowed.

Loews Hotel Vogue
1425 Rue De La Montagne
Montreal, PQ
514-285-5555
All well-behaved dogs of any size are welcome. This upscale hotel offers their "Loews Loves Pets" program which includes special pet treats, local dog walking routes, and a list of nearby pet-friendly places to visit. There are no pet fees.

Novotel - Montreal Center
1180 Rue de la Montagne
Montreal, PQ
514-861-6000
Novotel Hotels welcome a maximum of 2 animals (cats and dogs) per room and never require a fee. Each guest checking in with a pet will be given a Royal Canine/Novotel Pet Welcome Kit.

Quality Hotel Dorval Aeroport
7700 Cote de Liesse
Montreal, PQ
514-731-7821
One dog is allowed for an additional one time pet fee of $25 per room.

Residence Inn by Marriott
2045 Peel Street
Montreal, PQ
514-982-6064
Dogs of all sizes are allowed, however there can only be one large or two medium to small dogs per room. There is a $250 one time fee plus tax and a pet policy to sign at check in.

Residence Inn by Marriott
2170 Lincoln Avenue
Montreal, PQ
514-935-9224
Dogs of all sizes are allowed. There is a $105 plus tax one time fee and a pet policy to sign at check in. 2 dogs may be allowed.

Ritz-Carlton Montreal
1228 Sherbrooke Street West
Montreal, PQ
514-842-4212 (800-363-0366)
ritzmontreal.com
The Ritz-Carlton is located in the Golden Square Mile area in downtown. Dogs of all sizes are allowed. There is a $150 one time additional pet fee. The Ritz-Carlton also offers in house pet-sitting for $15 per hour. 2 dogs may be allowed.

Sheraton Four Points
475 rue Sherbrooke ouest
Montreal, PQ
514-842-3961 (888-625-5144)
There are no additional pet fees.

Hotel Motel Manoir de Perce
212 Route 132
Perce, PQ
418-782-2022
There are no additional pet fees.

Clarion Hotel
3125 Hochelaga Blvd
Quebec, PQ
418-653-4901 (877-424-6423)
Dogs are allowed for no additional pet fee. 2 dogs may be allowed.

Days Inn Quebec West
3145 Avenue des Hotels
Quebec, PQ
418-653-9321 (800-329-7466)
Dogs of all sizes are allowed. There are no additional pet fees. 2 dogs may be allowed.

Delta Quebec Hotel
690 Boul Rene-Levesque E
Quebec, PQ
418-647-1717
The Delta Quebec Hotel is located in the heart of the walled city of Quebec. There is a $35 one time additional pet fee. One large dog is allowed. Two smaller dogs may be allowed. Dogs must be well-behaved and leashed at all times.

Fairmont Le Château Frontenac
1 rrue des Carrieres
Quebec, PQ
418-692-3861 (800-257-7544)
fairmont.com/frontenac/
This regal heritage hotel looks out over the St Lawrence River and historic old Quebec, a United Nations World Heritage Site. One dog of any size is welcome for an additional $25 per night. Dogs may not be left alone in the room at any time, and they must be leashed and cleaned up after.

Hilton
1100 Rene-Levesque East
Quebec, PQ
418-647-2411
Dogs are allowed for an additional one time pet of $25 per room. 2 dogs may be allowed.

Hotel Dominion 1912
126 St Pierre
Quebec, PQ
418-692-2224
hoteldominion.com

Dogs of any size are allowed at this boutique hotel in Quebec City. Many of the rooms have views of Old Quebec or the St Lawrence River. Up to two dogs are allowed. There is a $30 one time additional pet fee per dog. Dogs must be leashed at all times.

L'Hotel du Vieux Quebec
1190 rue St-Jean
Quebec, PQ
418-692-1850
hvq.com/
There are no additional pet fees.

Quality Suites
1600 Rue Bouvier
Quebec, PQ
418-622-4244
Dogs are allowed for an additional one time pet fee of $25 per room. Multiple dogs may be allowed.

Chalets-Village Mont-Sainte-Anne
Call to Arrange
Quebec City, PQ
418-826-3331 (800-461-2030)
chaletsvillage.ca
Pet-friendly country villas for rent at the base of Mnt-Sainte-Anne. Thirty minutes from downtown. There are houses for families and up to 9 bedrooms for that large group.

Loews Le Concorde Hotel
1225 Cours Du General De Montcalm
Quebec City, PQ
418-647-2222
All well-behaved dogs of any size are welcome. This upscale hotel offers their "Loews Loves Pets" program which includes room service for pets, special pet treats, local dog walking routes, and a list of nearby pet-friendly places to visit. There are no pet fees.

Comfort Inn
455 Boul St Germain Ouest
Rimouski, PQ
418-724-2500 (877-424-6423)
One dog is allowed for no additional pet fee.

Days Inn Riviere-du-Loup
182 rue Fraser
Riviere-du-Loup, PQ
418-862-6354 (800-329-7466)
Dogs of all sizes are allowed. There is a $10 per night pet fee per pet. 2 dogs may be allowed.

Comfort Inn
700 Rue Gadbois
St Jean-Sur-Richelieu, PQ

450-359-4466 (877-424-6423)
Dogs are allowed for no additional pet fee. Multiple dogs may be allowed.

Hotel du Jardin
1400 boul du Jardin
St-Felicien, PQ
418-679-8422
There are no additional pet fees.

Auberge du Faubourg
280 ave de Gaspe ouest
St-Jean-Port-Joli, PQ
418-598-6455
There are no additional pet fees.

Days Inn Ste-Helene-de-Bagot
410 Couture
Ste-Helene-de-Bagot, PQ
450-791-2580 (800-329-7466)
Dogs of all sizes are allowed. There is a $5.75 per night pet fee per pet. 2 dogs may be allowed.

Comfort Inn Airport
7320 Boul Wilfrid-Hamel
Ste. Foy, PQ
418-872-5038 (877-424-6423)
Dogs are allowed for an additional one time pet fee of $25 per room. Multiple dogs may be allowed.

Comfort Inn
123 Boul Frontenac Ouest/H 112
Thetford Mines, PQ
418-338-0171 (877-424-6423)
Small dogs are allowed for no additional pet fee. 2 dogs may be allowed.

Delta Trois-Rivieres
1620 rue Notre-Dame
Trois-Rivieres, PQ
819-376-1991
There are no additional pet fees.

Saskatchewan Listings

The Pilgrim Inn
510 College Dr (Hwy 1 W)
Caronport, SK
306-756-5002
There is a $10 per day pet fee. All rooms are non-smoking.

Best Western Westridge Motor Inn
Junction Hwy 7 and 21
Kindersley, SK
306-463-4687 (800-780-7234)
Dogs are allowed for no additional pet fee. Multiple dogs may be allowed.

Super 8 Kindersley
508 12th Ave East
Kindersley, SK
306-463-8218 (800-800-8000)
Dogs of all sizes are allowed. There is a $5 per night pet fee per small pet and $10 per large pet. Smoking and non-smoking rooms are available for pet rooms. 2 dogs may be allowed.

Comfort Inn and Suites
155 Thatcher Drive W
Moose Jaw, SK
306-692-2100 (877-424-6423)
Dogs are allowed for an additional pet fee of $15 per night per room. 2 dogs may be allowed.

Super 8 North Battleford
1006 Hwy 16
North Battleford, SK
306-446-8888 (800-800-8000)
Dogs of all sizes are allowed. There is a $10 per night pet fee per pet. Smoking and non-smoking rooms are available for pet rooms. 2 dogs may be allowed.

Comfort Inn
3863 2nd Avenue W
Prince Albert, SK
306-763-4466 (877-424-6423)
Dogs are allowed for no additional pet fee. 2 dogs may be allowed.

Comfort Inn
3221 E Eastgate Drive
Regina, SK
306-789-5522 (877-424-6423)
Dogs are allowed for an additional pet fee of $7.95 (plus tax) per night per room. Multiple dogs may be allowed.

Holiday Inn Express Hotel & Suites Regina
1907 11th Avenue
Regina, SK
306-569-4600 (877-270-6405)
Dogs of all sizes are allowed for an additional pet fee of $15 per night per room. Multiple dogs may be allowed.

Quality Hotel
1717 Victoria Avenue
Regina, SK
306-569-4656
Dogs are allowed for an additional pet fee of $7.95 (plus tax) per night per room. Dogs may not be left alone in the room. 2 dogs may be allowed.

Radisson Plaza Hotel
2125 Victoria Avenue
Regina, SK
306-522-7691
Dogs of all sizes are allowed. There is a $50 one time additional pet fee.

Country Inns & Suites by Carlson
617 Cynthia Street
Saskatoon, SK
306-934-3900
Dogs of all sizes are allowed. There is a $10 one time additional pet fee.

Holiday Inn Express
315 Idylwyld Dr N
Saskatoon, SK
306-384-8844 (877-270-6405)
Dogs of all sizes are allowed for an additional pet fee of $10 per night per room. Multiple dogs may be allowed.

Motel 6 - Saskatoon
231 Marquis Drive
Saskatoon, SK
306-665-6688 (800-466-8356)
One well-behaved family pet per room. Guest must notify front desk upon arrival. Guest is liable for any damages. In consideration of all guests, pets must never be left unattended in the guest rooms.

Radisson Saskatoon
405 20th Street East
Saskatoon, SK
306-665-3322
Dogs of all sizes are allowed. There is a $25 one time additional pet fee.

Sheraton Cavalier Saskatoon Hotel
612 Spadina Crescent
Saskatoon, SK
306-652-6770 (888-625-5144)
This contemporary, river-front hotel offers a water park and the city's only rooftop ballroom. Dogs of all sizes are allowed for no additional fee. Dogs may not be left alone in the room, and they must be quiet, well behaved, leashed, and cleaned up after. Multiple dogs may be allowed.

Super 8 Saskatoon
706 Circle Drive East
Saskatoon, SK
306-384-8989 (800-800-8000)
Dogs of all sizes are allowed. There is a $5 per night pet fee per pet. Dogs are not allowed to be left alone in the room. Smoking and non-smoking rooms are available for pet rooms. 2 dogs may be allowed.

Days Inn Swift Current
Mobile Rte 35, Hwy 1 East

Swift Current, SK
306-773-4643 (800-329-7466)
Dogs of all sizes are allowed. There is a $10 per night pet fee per pet. 2 dogs may be allowed.

Comfort Inn and Suites
22 Dracup Avenue
Yorkton, SK
306-783-0333 (877-424-6423)
Dogs are allowed for an additional fee of $5 per night per pet. Multiple dogs may be allowed.

Yukon Listings

1202 Motor Inn and RV Park
Mile 1202 Alaska H
Beaver Creek, YU
867-862-7600 (800-661-0540)
karo-ent.com/ahytwest.htm
Offering travelers year round motel lodging, this rest stop also has a restaurant and bakery, lounge, a gift shop, and fuel services. Dogs of all sizes are allowed for no additional fee. Dogs must be well behaved, leashed, and cleaned up after. There are also RV accommodations on site that accept pets. Two dogs are allowed at the motel and there is no set limit on dogs in one's RV.

Westmark Inn Beaver Creek
Mile 1202 Alaska Hwy
Beaver Creek, YU
867-862-7501 (800-544-0970)
westmarkhotels.com
Dogs of all sizes are allowed. There is a $15 per day additional pet fee. The hotel is open from May to September annually.

Spirit Lake Resort
MM 72.1 S Klondike H
Carcross, YU
866-739-8566
Dogs of all sizes are allowed. There is a $5 per night per pet additional fee. Dogs are not allowed on the bed, and must be leashed and cleaned up after. Dogs may not be left unattended. There is an RV park on site that also allows dogs. 2 dogs may be allowed.

Hotel Carmacks
On Free Gold Road
Carmacks, YU
867-863-5221
Dogs of all sizes are allowed. There are no additional pet fees. Dogs must be leashed and cleaned up after. The motel is also part of an RV

park where dogs are allowed. 2 dogs may be allowed.

Bonanza Gold Motel
715.2 N Klondike H
Dawson City, YU
867-993-6789
Dogs of all sizes are allowed. There is a $20 one time fee per pet, and dogs must be leashed and cleaned up after. There is a seasonal RV park on site that also allows dogs. 2 dogs may be allowed.

Downtown Hotel
1026 2nd Avenue
Dawson City, YU
867-993-5346
downtownhotel.ca/
Although it has the look of the Klondike era, this renovated hotel has all the modern amenities and some nice new features too. Dogs are allowed here from mid-September to mid-May for an additional pet fee of $10 per room per stay. Dogs must be well behaved, leashed, and cleaned up after; they are not allowed in the dining areas. 2 dogs may be allowed.

Klondike Kate's Cabins and Restaurant
3rd Avenue and King Street
Dawson City, YU
867-993-6527
klondikekates.ca/
Travelers stopping here will find clean, new log cabins centrally located to all of the town's major attractions, and a restaurant that specializes in Canadian and ethnic foods; they also have espresso coffees. They are open from Good Friday until mid-September, depending on weather. Dogs are allowed in the cabins for an additional fee of $20 per pet per stay. Dogs must be friendly, leashed, and cleaned up after. Dogs are not allowed at the restaurant. 2 dogs may be allowed.

Whitehouse Cabins
1626 Front Street/H 2
Dawson City, YU
867-993-5576
whitehousecabins.com/
Nestled among the trees just 2 blocks from the ferry landing, this riverfront camp area offers numerous amenities and modernized accommodations in historic Gold Rush era cabins. The park can also be reached by free passage on the George Black ferry on H 9 that operates 24/7 during the

summer months. Dogs of all sizes are allowed for an additional fee of $15 per night per pet. Dogs may not be left unattended in the rooms or on the premises at any time, and they must be leashed and cleaned up after; guest rooms keep a supply of clean-up bags. There is also a large outdoor area nearby for giving the pooch a good exercising. 2 dogs may be allowed.

Destruction Bay Lodge
Mile 1083 Alaska Hwy
Destruction Bay, YU
867-841-5332
Dogs of all sizes are allowed. There are no additional pet fees.

Talbot Arm Motel
Mile 1083 Alaska Hwy
Destruction Bay, YU
867-841-4461
Dogs of all sizes are allowed. There are no additional pet fees.

Eagle Plains Hotel
On the Dempster H
Eagle Plains, YU
867-993-2453
Dogs of all sizes are allowed. There are no additional pet fees. Dogs must be well behaved, quiet, and cleaned up after. Dogs may be off lead if friendly and under voice control. There is also a tent and RV park on site that allows dogs. Multiple dogs may be allowed.

Alcan Motor Inn
Box 5460
Haines Junction, YU
867-634-2371 (888-265-1018)
Dogs of all sizes are allowed. There is a $10.50 per night additional pet fee.

Kluane Park Inn
1635 Alaska Highway
Haines Junction, YU
867-634-2261
Dogs of all sizes are allowed. There is a $5 additional pet fee. There is a Chinese Restaurant on the premises.

Iron Creek Lodge
596 Alaska H
Iron Creek, YU
867-536-2266
Dogs of all sizes are allowed, but they perfer no extra large dogs at the lodge in the summer; winter is ok. There is a $5 per night per pet additional fee. Dogs must be leashed and cleaned up after. There is a tent and RV park on site that also allows dogs. 2 dogs may be allowed.

Kluane Wilderness Village Motel
1118 Alaska H
Kluane Wilderness Village, YU
867-841-4141
Dogs of all sizes are allowed. There is a $5 per night per pet additional fee. Dogs must be friendly, well behaved, leashed, and cleaned up after. 2 dogs may be allowed.

Stewart Valley Bedrock Motel
Lot 99 H 11
Mayo, YU
867-996-2290
Dogs of all sizes are allowed. There are no additional pet fees. Dogs may not be left unattended at any time, must be leashed, and cleaned up after. There is a tent and RV park on site that also allows dogs. 2 dogs may be allowed.

Continental Divide Lodge and RV Park
Mile 721 Alaska H
Swift River, YU
867-851-6451
karo-ent.com/akhwyyt.htm
Nestled between the Mackenzie and Yukon Rivers less than a mile from the divide, this motel offers a restaurant, a gift store, a pub, and a camp area with hook-ups. Dogs are allowed in the motel and the campground for no additional fee. Dogs must be well behaved, leashed, and cleaned up after. 2 dogs may be allowed.

Dawson Peaks Resort and RV Park
KM 1232 Alaska H
Teslin, YU
867-390-2244
One lightly furred dog of any size is allowed. There are no additional pet fees. Dogs must be leashed at all times and cleaned up after. Dogs are not allowed on the furniture. There is a connecting tent and RV park that do allow more than one dog per site.

Mukluk Annie's Salmon Bake and Motel
Mile 784 Alaska Hwy
Teslin, YU
867-390-2600
This restaurant and lodge offers meals of Salmon. Dogs of all sizes are allowed in the motel and there is a $10 per night additional pet fee. There is also free dry camping at the site.

Nisultin Trading Post Motel
Mile 804 Alaska Hwy
Teslin, YU

867-390-2521
Dogs of all sizes are allowed. There are no additional pet fees.

Yukon Motel
Mile 804 Alaska Hwy
Teslin, YU
867-390-2575
yukonmotel.com
Dogs of all sizes are allowed. There is a pet fee of $15 per room for some rooms in the hotel.

Belvedere Motor Hotel
Box 370
Watson Lake, YU
867-536-7712
watsonlakehotels.com/Belvedere/
Dogs of all sizes are allowed. There is a $15 per night additional pet fee.

Big Horn Hotel
Frank Trail just S of Alaska Hwy
Watson Lake, YU
867-536-2020
Dogs of all sizes are allowed. There are no additional pet fees. A credit card is necessary as a security deposit for pet damage.

Gateway Motor Inn
Box 370
Watson Lake, YU
867-536-7744
watsonlakehotels.com/Gateway/
Dogs of all sizes are allowed. There is a $20 per day additional pet fee.

Northern Beaver Post Lodge
KM 1003 Alaska H
Watson Lake, YU
867-536-2307
Dogs of all sizes are allowed. There is a $10 per night per room additional pet fee. Dogs must be leashed at all times and cleaned up after. 2 dogs may be allowed.

Racheria Lodge
MM 710 Alaska H
Watson Lake, YU
867-851-6456
Dogs of all sizes are allowed. There is a $10 per night per pet additional fee. Dogs may not be left unattended, must be leashed, and cleaned up after. 2 dogs may be allowed.

Airport Chalet
91634 Alaska Hwy
Whitehorse, YU
867-668-2166
Dogs of all sizes are allowed. There is a $10 one time additional pet fee.

Best Western Gold Rush Inn

411 Main St
Whitehorse, YU
867-668-4500 (800-780-7234)
Dogs are allowed for an additional one time fee of $25 per pet. Multiple dogs may be allowed.

Hi Country Inn
4051 4th Avenue
Whitehorse, YU
867-667-4471 (800-554-4471)
highcountryinn.yk.ca/
Offering numerous amenities for the business or leisure traveler, this hotel is also closest to the city's historic waterfront and offers some great views. Dogs of all sizes are allowed for an additional fee of $15 per night per pet on the ground floor. Dogs must be quiet, leashed, cleaned up after, and they are not allowed in the bar or restaurant area. 2 dogs may be allowed.

Inn on the River Wilderness Resort
PO Box 10420
Whitehorse, YU
867-660-5253
This wilderness resort offers a wide range of year round land, air, and water activities, and great views of the Northern Lights. They offer 2 pet friendly cabins where dogs are welcome for no additional fee. Dogs must be well behaved, leashed, and cleaned up after at all times. Dogs are not allowed on the plane or boat tours. 2 dogs may be allowed.

River View Hotel
102 Wood Street
Whitehorse, YU
867-667-7801
riverviewhotel.ca
Dogs of all sizes are allowed. There are no additional pet fees.

The Yukon Inn
4220 4th Avenue
Whitehorse, YU
867-667-2527 (800-661-0454)
yukoninn.com/index2.html
Dogs are allowed at the inn for an additional pet fee of $15.90 per room per stay. Dogs must be quiet, well behaved, leashed, and cleaned up after. Multiple dogs may be allowed.

Westmark Whitehorse Hotel
201 Wood Street
Whitehorse, YU
867-393-9700 (800-544-0970)
westmarkhotels.com
This hotel has a gift shop and a restaurant. Dogs of all sizes are allowed. There are no additional pet fees.